DICTIONARY

for

Artists,

Performers,

Managers

&

Entrepreneurs

(The Arts-Related Vocabulary of Columbia College Chicago)

Third Edition
(Previous editions entitled
Dictionary for Artists and Performers and Managers)

Compiled and edited by Chuck Suber

Associate Editor, Randall K. Albers

Senior Consultant, J. Dennis Rich

AEMMPubs

Arts, Entertainment & Media Management Publications,

a Project of the Arts, Entertainment & Media Management Department

of Columbia College Chicago

CCC $22.50
Other $24.95

Printing History:
DAPME third edition, September 2002
(Previous editions entitled *Dictionary for
Artists and Performers and Managers*)
DAPM second edition, September 1998
DAPM first edition, September 1997
DAPM beta version 2.5, February 1997
DAPM beta version 2.0, September 1996
DAPM bet version 1.5, February 1996
DAPM bet version 1.0, December 1995

Printed in the United States of America.

ISBN 0-929911-05-9

Visit the Arts, Entertainment & Media Management Department website
http://www.colum.edu/undergraduate/management/index.html

ARTS, ENTERTAINMENT & MEDIA MANAGEMENT PUBLICATIONS
Arts, Entertainment & Media Management Department (AEMMDept)
Columbia College Chicago
624 South Michigan Avenue • Chicago, IL 60605
Voice 312-344-7652 • Fax 312-344-8063
Email comments or questions to >AEMMPubs@aol.com<

CONTENTS

Preface

"Knowledge is of two kinds, We know a subject ourselves, or we know where we can find information on it." — Samuel Johnson (1709-1784), *Dictionary of the English Language* (1755).

"New information resides nowhere until it has been identified, objectified, assembled, and communicated." — William Shawn (1907-1992, Editor, *The New Yorker*), *NY Times,* 09/09/92, 15.

Welcome to DAPME. the third edition of the *Dictionary for Artists, Performers, Managers & Entrepreneurs* (The Arts-Related Vocabulary of Columbia College Chicago) published by Arts, Entertainment & Media Management Publications (AEMMPubs), a Project of the Arts, Entertainment & Media Management Department (AEMMDept), Columbia College Chicago (CCC).

Contributing Editors from ten CCC departments have reviewed or supplied more than 12,200 entries plus 15,600 indexed topical cross-references.

The previous two editions plus four beta versions, entitled *Dictionary for Artists and Performers and Managers* have been use-tested during the past seven school years by undergraduate and graduate students in the AEMMDept, English as a Second Language (ESL) program, and foreign students from 42 countries.

This hardcover edition is a required reference text for all students enrolled in AEMMDept classes. It is also used by certain classes in other CCC departments, and by Arts Administration/Arts Management programs in other colleges, and by Arts Administrators in Australia, England, Germany, and Russia.

Coming this Winter 2002:

DAPME/On-line created and produced in cooperation with the CCC/Interactive Multimedia Program, Wade Roberts, Director. This expanded version of DAPME/HardCopy will feature fully searchable database, graphics, and sound. It will be available by low-cost subscription free quarterly updates.

For more information visit >http://interactive.colum.edu/ dapme/<.

• • •

The intent of the DAPME is to assist its readers learn:

• Vocabulary used by professionals in the arts and in arts management to describe their work, their tools, their critical judgment, and their passion.

• Mutuality of the arts, i.e., how artists, performers, managers, and entrepreneurs relate to each other, to audiences, to the inner forces of aesthetics, criticism, and ethics; and to the outer forces of economics, politics, society, and technology.

Criteria For Entries

• Contributing editors – all of whom teach and work in one or more areas of the arts or arts management – recommend words and terms they expect aspiring and working professionals to know and to use in their own and related (for-profit and non-profit) fields of arts, entertainment, and media management.

[We professionals know by experience that you **cannot be in a profession without knowing the language of the profession.**]

• New words or definitions are added or altered when found by contributing editors or readers printed in a trade or professional journal or a mainstream newspaper or magazine. Cumulative Addenda are updated monthly on – and may be freely downloaded from – the AEMMDept web site >http://www.colum.edu/undergraduate/management/index.html<.

• • •

Contents

Contributing Editors and Consultants. Bio sketch of those who quite literally make the DAPME "The Arts-Related Vocabulary of Columbia College Chicago .".

Explanatory Notes details how the entries and cross-references are organized and formatted.

Abbreviations used in this edition.

The Arts & Business Dynamic© diagrams and text, on the following pages, illustrate and explain the core concept of the AEMMDept, and by extension, the core concept of this dictionary.

Main Text entries are organized A-Z and are classified by one or more of 37 topics.

Index to Topics. All entries in the Main Text are listed A-Z and classified by topic.

Citations references the 440+ direct quotations from within the entries.

AEMMPubs Catalog. Information about current and forthcoming hardcover and on-line publications from Arts, Entertainment & Media Management Publications.

Reader's Notes for suggested new or altered entries, assignments, or whatever.

• • •

Responsibility for the final choice of entries, definitions, quotations, and topical references lies with the senior editor. [His occasional comments are enclosed in brackets.]

This third edition is a continuation of a work-in-progress. The language of our profession speaks for a dynamically rich arts and entertainment environment that demands current attention.

The Dictionary will never be really "completed," not so long as artists and performers – abetted and exploited by managers, valued and devalued by critics, idolized and scorned by audiences – continue to amuse, appall, astonish, create, disturb, entertain, originate, outrage, shock, startle, and unsettle.

• • •

Appreciation and thanks are due many people for their willingness to share their expertise.

Contributing Editors and Consultants! Please see their bio sketches on the following pages.

The eighty-plus full- and part-time faculty and staff of the Arts, Entertainment & Media Management Department who make the Dictionary work successfully each semester for the AEMMDept's 1,000+ students.

Columbia College Administration: Warrick L. Carter, President; Steven Kapelke, Provost; Keith Cleveland, Acting Dean Of Graduate And Continuing Education; Michael DeSalle, Vice President/Finance; and Woodie T. White, Vice President/College Affairs.

Columbia College colleagues for their on-going support, particularly: Dennis Rich, Chair, AEMMDept; Randy Albers, Chair/Fiction Writing Dept.; Doreen Bartoni, Dean, School of Media Arts; Paula Epstein, Coordinator of Library Outreach; Joan Erdman, Anthropologist/Liberal Education Dept.; Fred Fine, Director, Public Affairs; Suzanne Flandreau, Librarian/Archivist, Center for Black Music Research; Mary Johnson, Director, Creative and Printing Services.

Alia Sweis, my multi-talented graduate assistant; and Eric Bailey, AEMMDept's web master, for his technical savvy and many a search and rescue mission.

And Helen Kenney for reasons both personal and professional.

Chuck Suber
Artist-in-Residence, CCC/AEMMDept
Chicago and New Orleans
September 2002

Contributing Editors and Consultants

J. Dennis Rich *Senior Consultant, Fnding* • (Ph.D., U. Wis.-Madison) Chair, CCC/AEMMDept • ExecDir. & Chair, Chicago Center for Arts Policy • Intl. consultant, researcher, lecturer, guest prof.: Internationales Zentrum für Kultur und Mangement (Salzburg), Fachhochschule Potsdam, Interstudio (St. Petersburg, Russia), and other venues. • jdrich@colum.edu

Randall K. Albers *Associate Editor* • *Aes&Creat, Crit& Eval, LitArts* • (Ph.D., U. of Chicago) • Chair, CCC/Fiction Writing Dept. • Writings: *Prairie Schooner, Chicago Review, Northfield Mag*azine, *Mendocino Review, Writing From Start to Finish, f Magazine*, and elsewhere. • ralbers@colum.edu

• • •

Norman Alexandroff *Consultant* • CCC/Director of Publications • Editor, *Gravity* magazine • voice 312/344-7416 • nalexandroff@colum.edu

Eric B. Bailey • *InfoMgt* • (B.A., Music Business, CCC) • Instructor, "InfoMgt" and Web consultant, CCC/AEMM • Bass Guitarist and Leader • FunkyBe@yahoo.com

Janell Baxter *Interactive MultiMedia* • (B.F.A, U. of Illinois-Chicago) • Artist-in-Residence, CCC/Interactive Multimedia Program • Classically trained visual artist, interactive designer • Oxbow Fellow, Art Institute Chicago • www.janellbaxter.net. • jbaxter@colum.edu

Steven I. Berlin *Ethcs&Phil* • (M.A., U. of Chicago; J.D., Northwestern U.) • Instructor, "Business Ethics," CCC/-AEMM • Deputy Dir., City of Chicago Board of Ethics. • princeton1@attbi.com

Johann S. Buis *Cult&Soc, MusArts* •(London U, Ball State U., U. of Cape Town, U. of South Africa, U. of the Western Cape) • "History of Black Music," Coordinator, Intl. Initiatives, CCC/Center for Black Music Research (CBMR) • Published author and intl. lecturer re ethnomusicology and music. • jbuis@CBMR.colum.edu

Keith Cleveland *Aes&Creat, Crit&Eval, Ethics* • (J.D., U. Chicago) • CCC/Acting Dean Of Graduate And Continuing Education • Guest lectr.: "Seminar: AEMM" • Lectr., Liberal Arts, U. Chicago: "Basic Program of Liberal Education for Adults." • kcleveland@colum.edu

Maury Collins *PerfA&C* • (M.B.A.-Industrial Relations & Personnel Admin., American U.) • "Decision Making: Performing Arts Mgt.," CCC/AEMMDept • Adjunct Prof., DePaul U. • former general mgr., Shubert Org. (Chgo) • partner, Collins Yamamoto Consulting • Trustee, Pension, Welfare & Annuity Funds, IATSE and ATPAM • maurycollins@compuserve

Rebecca Courington *InfoMgt* • (M.A., . Governors State U.) • CCC/Director of the Center for Instructional Technology • "Personal Productivity Tools" • Online Manuals: "Introduction to the Internet", "Using Excel", "Introduction to FileMaker Pro". • rcourington@colum.edu

Rose Economou *BcstJourn* • (Nieman Fellow, Harvard U.; Eagelton Fellow, Rutgers U.; B.A.-Political Science, U. of Illinois-Chicago) faculty, CCC/Journalism Dept.• 7-time Emmy winner • Author, *While America Sleeps* • Board, *In These Times* • reconomou @colum.edu

Paula Epstein *InfoMgt* • (M.A.L.S., Rosary C.) • Coordinator, CCC/Library Outreach and Reference Librarian • Resource material developer for Student Life programs •

Chair, American Library Association, ARTS Liaison Com.; Chair, North American Relations Com., ARLIS/NA • pepstein@colum.edu

Joan Erdman *Culture & Society* (Ph.D., Anthropology, U. Chicago). Lecturer, "Origins of Art," CCC/AEMMDept • Prof., Anthropology, CCC/Liberal Education Dept. • Research Associate with the Committee on Southern Asian Studies, U. Chicago. • jerdman@colum.edu

Dianne Erpenbach *Fashion / Retail Marketing* (M.A., National Louis U.) Coordinator, Fashion/Retail Management, CCC/AEMMDept • derpenbach@colum.edu

Carmelo Esterrich *Aes&Creat, Crit&Eval, Cult&Soc, Flm&Vid, MusArts* • (Ph.D., U. of Wisconsin-Madison).• Dir., Cultural Studies Program, prof., Spanish & Humanities. Research on Latin American cinema, music, and literature, CCC/Liberal Ed. Dept. • cesterrich@colum.edu

Monica Grayless *PerfA&C, Recording A&S* • (Cert., Community Law Program, John Marshall Law School; B.A.-History, Edgewood C.) • "Special Events," CCC/AEMMDept • Owner-Prod., Dress Rehearsals Ltd.; Service Dir., Musicians' Service Bureau • http://www.freeyellow.com/members/famefactory/

Clarke Greene *Eco&Fin, EntreP, Mgt* (B.S.-Labor Economics, Carleton C., U. Wis.-Madison,) Instructor, "Intro. to Management," "Small Business Challenges & Opportunities," CCC/AEMMDept. • Clarke Green/Creative Group, marketing and organizational consulting • cgreene@colum.edu

Andrew Hicks *iMedia* (B.A.) Instructor, CCC/Interactive Multimedia Program • Freelance multimedia designer. • ahicks@interactive.colum.edu

Phyllis A. Johnson *Human Resources & Labor Relations* • (M.B.A., Kellogg Graduate School, Northwestern U.) • Coordinator, Music Business concentration and AEMM Internship Program, CCC/AEMMDept Assistant Chair, CCC/Strategic Planning Com. • Treasurer, Past Pres., Music/Theatre Workshop. • pjohnson@colum.edu

Joseph A. Leonardi *IntelProp* • (J.D., John Marshall Law School; B.S.-Business Mgt. (Accounting, U. of Wisconsin-Parkside) • "Music Publishing," CCC/AEMMDept • Law Offices of Joseph A. Leonardi • leonardija@cs.com

Angelo Luciano *Eco&Fin, E&F-Acc* (M.S., DePaul U.) Coordinator: Accounting, Finance, and Media Mgt.,CCC/AEMMDept • Chair, CCC Budget& Priorities Com. • Board, shawchicago • aluciano@colum.edu

Jun Mhoon (B.A.,Music Performance) "Music Business," CCC/AEMMDept • Music/TV producer/entrepreneur •.*Formerly* Pres, I Am Records (10 gold/6 platinum albums) • jun@mhoonmedia.net

Michael Niederman *Flm&Video* • (MFA, Northwestern U.) • Chair, CCC/Television Department • Award winning Film/Video maker • Board of Governors, NATAS/Midwest Chapter • Writer/Creative Consultant, various corporations and organizations. • mneiderman@colum.edu

Jamie O'Reilly *PerfA&C* • (BFA, DePaul U. School of Music) •"Self-Mgt.," CCC/AEMM • Award-winning Artist/Consultant/Mgr./Performer • Pres , J. O'Reilly Productions; Bird Avenue Publishing. • Jamiejoan@aol.com

Sheldon Patinkin *PerfA&C, TheatArts* •Chair, CCC/ Theater Dept. • Artistic Consultant to The Second City and Steppenwolf Theatres • Author, *The Second City: Backstage at the World's Greatest Comedy Theater* • teacher, director. • spatinkin@colum.edu

Nora Kay Pelt *Dance* (BFA, Dance, U of Illinois/Champaign-Urbana) • Thesis status, M.A.-Performing Arts Management, CCC/AEMM • Artists and Community Services Program Representative, Illinois Arts Council.
• norakay@arts.state.il.us

Philippe Ravanas *SportsEnt* • (M.B.A., U. Wisconsin-Madison; M.B.A., Graduate Business School of Marseille, Fr.) • "Mktg. the Arts," "Intl. Arts Mgt." CCC/AEMMDept • Sr. Consult., Cendant Intercultural. *Formerly* V.P., Client Development Christie's, London; V.P., Corp. Communications, Euro Disney, Paris • pravanas@aol.com

Joseph S. Roberts *Arts EntreP* (Ph.D., U. of Chicago) • "Arts Entrepreneurship/Small Business Mgt.," CCC/AEMMDept.; Coleman Foundation Professor of Arts Entrepreneurship and Small Business • Pres., USA Inc. (Small & Medium Business Consulting Services Co.); designer, community entrepreneurship programs • jroberts@colum.edu

Wade Roberts *iMedia* • Dir., CCC/Interactive Multimedia Program; faculty, Television and Fiction Writing Depts. Wide experience in writing, film, video, photography, audio, and interactive media, mostly in documentary form.
• wroberts@colum.edu

Marlene Robin *Eco&Fin* • (M.A.-HRD/ Northeastern Ill. U.) • Accounting/Finance, CCC/AEMMDept • Employment & Training Program, Compliance, Career Centers & Outplacement Counselor, Employment & Employer Services (Mayor's Office Workforce Development & President's Office Employment Training); Tax Consultant Midwest Tax Clinic • marlenerobinietc@hotmail.com

John Schultz *LitArts*• Prof. Emeritus, CCC/Fiction Writing Dept. • Pres.: SGI, F Magazine.• Originator/developer, Story Workshop approach to the teaching of writing • Books/articles/stories: *The Chicago Conspiracy Trial, Evergreen Review, The Georgia Review, The Reader*, and elsewhere. •jschultz@colum.edu

Betty Shiflett *LitArts* (B.S., Texas Women's U.) *LitArts*• Prof. Emeritus, CCC/Fiction Writing Dept.; Principal, Story Workshop Master Teacher; CCC/Inaugural Fellow, Teaching Excellence • Stories/articles: *Life, Evergreen Review, College English, F Magazine, Emergence, The Private Arts, American Fiction,* and elsewhere.
• bshiflett@colum.edu

Bruce Sheridan *Flm&Vid* (BA Honors, U of Auckland, New Zealand) • Chair, CCC/Film; Video. Chair CCC/Chairs Council.• Drama and Documentary director/producer/writer • Winner, Best Drama, 2000 New Zealand TV Awards.
• bsheridan@colum.edu

Dolores Smith *Human Resources* • (M.A. Communications, Ohio U-Athens); "Human Resources," "Applied Marketing: MediaMgt," CCC/AEMM • Pres., D. J. Smith Enterprises: Organizational Development Consultants • djse@msn.com

Chuck Suber *Compiler/Editor* (B.Ed., LSU) • "Seminar: AEMM," "Decision Making: Music Business," "Ethics Sessions," Artist-in-Residence, Dir. of Publications, CCC/-AEMMDept • Pres., Charles Suber & Associates, Inc.
• chucksuber@aol.com

Alia Sweis *iMedia* • (B.A.-Graphic Design, Dominican U.) • Media Mgt. grad student, CCC/AEMMDept • 2001 Recipient, *Who's Who in American Colleges and Universities.*
• aliasweis@yahoo.com

Carol Yamamoto *Mgt, Mktg* • (M.B.A., UCLA) • Coordinator, Marketing and Visual Arts Mgt., CCC/AEMMDept • Founding board chair of Arts Bridge (business incubator for small and emerging Chicago arts orgs)• national arts consultant • cyamamoto@colum.edu

Contributing Editors
to previous editions

Paul Berger *EntreP*
Ron Bergin *Mktg*
Penelope Cagney *Fnding*
Dana Calderon *Mgt, PerfA&C, Rdio/TV*
Darlene Brooks *Music Therapy*
Malane Collins *VisA&C*
James Dauer *InfoMgt*
Elizabeth Dorsey *Fnding*
Fred Gardaphe *Crit&Eval, LitArts*
Don Gold *Journ*
Jane Ganet-Sigel *Dance/Movement Therapy*
Bernice Grohskopf *Genl, LitArts*
David Kaufman *Drama-Therapy*
Robert Kornfeld *PA-Theat*
Dawn Larsen *IntelProp, LegalAsp*
David P. Leonard *InfoMgt, IntelProp, Rdio&TV*
Ed Morris *Rdio/TV*
Gary Phillips *InfoMgt*
Cally Chance Rakita *Dance/Movement Therapy*
Beverly A. Reid *IntelProp, LglAsp*
Gina Richardson *Flm&Video*
Kate Suber *TheatArts*
John T. Turchon *Mktg, PerfA&C*
Kimo Williams *MusArts, RecA&S*
Michael N.J. Wright *Flm&Vid*

Student Contributors
to this or previous editions

Shanieka Brooks *RecA&S*
Jennifer Clark *Fashn, Flm&Vid*
Randall J. Clark *MusInstr*
Christopher Elmore *LegalAsp*
Shannon Jungkans *Fashn*
So-Young Kim *VisA&C*
Kila King *MusArts*
Keith R. Knox *Genl*
Thomas J. Lewy *Mgt, Mktg*
Gretchen A. Luther *Crit&Eval, Flm&Vid*
Cristian Macht *Mgt, MusArts*
Mike McGhee *LegalAsp*
LaTonya Morrison *Crit&Eval, LegalAsp, MusArts*
Michael O'Brien *ArtPerf, Crit&Eval, RecA&S*
Yadira Rivera *ArtPerf, Crit&Eval, RecA&S*
Matthew Sommers *Crit&Eval, InfoMgt, LitArts, VA-Prntng*
Timisha Waters *Mktg*
Angela White *IntelProp, LglAsp, Mktg*

DAPME

Explanatory Notes

KEY WORDS and SYMBOLS

<example>	Examples are enclosed in angle brackets, shown immediately after the definition to which it applies. <a *MusArts* **alto** <alto flute, alto saxophone>
entry	Any word or term in **boldface** type within an **entry** is itself listed elsewhere as an **entry**. <**A above middle C** *LegalAsp* Piano tuning instruction, the requirement for which can be a **rider** to an **engagement contract**. *Also see* **tech rider**.>
(how-to-say)	Pronunciation guide, where needed, shown within parens immediately after **entry**. <**a priori** (ay-pree-or-ee ...)>
(Foreign	language label) shown within parens immediately after **entry**. <(**à jour**, Fr.)>
Topic	Each **entry** is classified by one or more topics. See "Key to Index to Topics" (pp. 227-228) for complete list of 37 topics. <*ArtPerf*> Artist/Performer
...	An ellipse substitutes for non-essential words. <**actual malice** ... "The case ...">
»	See the following **entry** for definition. <**a** *MusArts* » **alto**>
aka	Also known as <**Coltrane, John** (*aka* "Trane")>
Also see	Also see the following related entry or entries. Shown at the end of the entry. <**A side** ... *Also see* **flip side**.>
Origin	Origin of entry word or term. Shown immediately after the definition to which it applies. <**Boston version** ... *Origin* For many years, Boston had the strictest censorship in the U.S.>
(Passé)	Entry as defined is no longer in common use; archaic. Shown immediately preceding the definition to which it applies. <**Boston version** *Crit&Eval, TheatArts* (Passé) Show purged of indecencies. ... >

MARKS

à	grave accent mark <**à jour**>
ç	cedilla accent mark <**alençon**>
é	acute accent mark <**bawdy** ... **risqué**.>
î	circumflex accent mark <**boîte**>
©	» **copyright**
®	» **register mark**
™	» **trademark**
Ω	**Entry** needs better definition. Shown at the end of the last line of the **entry**. <**ACDA** ... Ω > [Readers, please assist.]<

ENTRY ORDER

- **Entry** words or terms are shown in **boldface** type flush left of the text column. All **entries**, including abbreviations and compound words, are listed in strict alphabetical order.
- **Secondary variants**. Entries with two or more different spellings are shown in preferential order in accordance with AEMM usage.
<**A&R, a&r**>

- **Topical sequence**. When an **entry** is classified by two or more related *topics*, the *topics* are arranged A-Z. <**adaptation** *Flm&Vid, LitArts, PerfA&C*>
- **Definition sequence**. When an entry has more than one definition within a topic, the definitions are numbered and arranged (**1, 2, 3,** etc.) in accordance with AEMM usage. <**ad lib** ...>, <**aesthete** ...>

ABBREVIATIONS and ACRONYMS

- Abbreviations related to particular topics are entered in the Main Text. See page x for topic and general abbreviations.
- AEMM. Acronym for "Arts, Entertainment, and Media Management."
- Abbreviations and acronyms are listed as separate **entries**, and are also shown in parens immediately after the word or term they represent.
<**admin.** *Mgt* **administration**>
<**ABA** *LegalAsp* **American Bar Association**>
<**Actors' Equity Association** (AEA *or* Equity)>
- If an **acronym** is more commonly used than the term it represents, the definition is shown with the acronym.
<**ABA** *LegalAsp* **American Bar Association**>
- If a term is more commonly used than its **acronym**, the definition is shown with the term.
<**American Arbitration Association** (AAA)>
- Abbreviation of a musical term does not require a period.
<**b** *MusArts* » **bass**>
- "especially" and "usually" abbreviate to "esp." and "usu." except when beginning a sentence.
<**apparel** *Fashn* Clothing, esp. outer garments ...>
- "established" abbreviates to "est." when followed by a date. <**AFI** *Flm&Vid* **American Film Institute**. Independent, **nonprofit** est. 1967 ... >

PERSONS and PLACES

- DAPME only includes those persons referred to in one or more **entries**. Some persons with multiple references may have her or his own **entry**; others may have a brief bio sketch immediately after their names within an **entry**. All persons shown in Main Text are listed in the "Index of Topics" by last name first.
<**Algonquin Round Table** ... <Robert Benchley (1889-1945, humorist, act., crit.), **Dorothy Parker**, Edna Ferber (» *Showboat*), Robert Sherwood (1896-1955, Pulitzer-plywri.), Alexander Woolcott (1887-1943, drama crit., journ.)>
- Name **entries** contain, when known, professional and legal names, birth-death dates, occupations and examples of their work and awards. <**Allen, Woody** ...>
- Names are alphabetized by last name except when the name is part of a title.
<**Kennedy, John F.** ... >
<**John F. Kennedy Center** ...>
- Alternative names are separate entries as well as birth or professional names.
<**Mark Twain**> and <**Clemens, Samuel**>
<**Satchmo**> and <**Armstrong, Louis**>
- **Occupations** and their abbreviations are separate **entries**.
<**biographer** (biog.)> and <**biog.**>
<**bandleader** (bndldr.)> and <**bndldr.**>
- Gender order: "her" precedes "him"; "he" precedes "she."
<**actor manager** ... "An actor who has her or his own

company in which he or she is both …">

- Consider all persons as born in the United States unless otherwise indicated.
  <"Ger.-born" indicates the person was born in Germany but spent most of her or his career in the U.S.>
- Consider all organizations and places located in the U.S. unless otherwise indicated.
- *Collective Entries* is an assemblage of related entries: <Country Music Styles> <Guilds & Unions>

PUNCTUATION

- **<Angle brackets>** enclose examples of AEMM usage.
- **[Brackets]** enclose editor's comments.
- **Commas.** Serial commas are used throughout DAPME, except when written otherwise within a direct quotation, i.e., a comma is placed before the conjunction in a series of three or more words or phrases. [Thus we hold with Strunk & White's *The Elements of Style* rather than the *NY Times*.] **<art theatre** … design, presentation, and script.>
- **Dashes**
  em dash — width of an "m" Usually used before an author's name at the end of a quotation or statement.
  <accordion … — George Shearing>
  en dash – width of an "n" Used mainly to denote an abrupt change in thought in a sentence.
  <AFM … – approx. 130,000 members in the U.S. and Canada – instrumentalists … >
  short dash - (hyphen) Used to connect two or more related words. **<African-American>**
- **Ellipse** … used as a three-letter word, i.e., with a character space before and after the three periods.
- **Periods.** Generally used only to end a sentence that uses a verb or a verbal adjective.
- **Quotation marks.** "Double quotation marks" enclose direct quotations. Commas, periods, exclamation and question marks are placed inside quotation marks; semicolons, and colons outside.

Format and Style

- *Italics* indicate titles of a complete, free-standing work, such as: *ballets* (except for titles of movements), *books* (except titles of chapters or individual poems), law cases <*New York Times vs. Sullivan*>, *magazines* and *newspapers* (except titles of sections), *musical compositions* (except titles of movements), *paintings* and *sculptures*, *plays* (except titles of acts), *radio* and *television programs* (except titles of episodes), and *songs*, including individual *songs* in a collection.
- **Pronunciation** is provided phonetically for foreign words and certain words whose pronunciation changes with usage. *Ex.* lead (leed) as in "lead sheet"; leading (ledding) as in "space between lines of printed type."
- **Quotations.** Source of an indirect or direct quotation is cited immediately following the quotation. The complete citation is listed alphabetically by **entry** in "Citations," (pp. 274-280) In some **entries**, a quotation may serve as the definition.
- SMALL CAPS. Synonyms or variants of the **entry**. Shown at the end of the **entry** to which it applies.
  <à la carte news … AUTOMAT NEWS>
- The following elements are not used in this dictionary: antonyms, etymology, inflected forms, parts of speech, stylistic labels, subsense number, syllabication, and temporal labels. For these elements and the resources of a good standard dictionary, we recommend *Webster's New World College Dictionary, 4th ed.*

STYLE REFERENCES

- William Strunk Jr. and E. B. White, *The Elements of Style,* 4th ed. (NY: Macmillan, 2001).
- *The Associated Press Stylebook and Briefing on Media Law,* Norm Goldstein, ed. (Cambridge, Mass.: Perseus Publishing, 2000).
- *Webster's New World College Dictionary,* 4th ed. (Foster City, Ca.: IDG Books Worldwide, 2001). The Official Dictionary of the Associated Press.

PRODUCTION

- DAPME manuscript, except covers, produced on a Macintosh G4 (OS 9.2.2) computer using Nisus® Writer 6.5 word processing application.
- Font: New Century Schoolbook – plain, **bold**, *italic,* and SMALL CAPS – used throughout except in The Arts Dynamic© and The Business Dynamic© diagrams.
- Master copies printed by an Apple® LaserWriter Select 360 Printer (600 dpi).

Notice
Because of close-to-deadline mechanical problems, some punctuation in the Main Text may not conform to DAPME style

DAPME

Abbreviations

Abbreviations related to particular topics are in the Main Text

(Abbreviations of musical instruments and terms do not require a period.)

bari	baritone
bassn	bassoon
cl	clarinet
d, drm	drum(s)
fr-h	french horn
gtr	guitar
p, pno	piano
sax	saxophone
tb	trombone
tp	trumpet
tym	tympani

act.	actor, actress
ad, advert	advertisement
adj	adjective
AEMM	Arts, Entertainment & Media Management
agt.	agent
aka	also known as
anon.	anonymous
approx.	approximately
archt.	architect, architecture
Assn.	Association
Assn.	**Association**
assoc.	associate
asst.	assistant
Aus.	Austrian
auth.	author

b.	born
bibliog	bibliographer
Brit.	British

c/o	Care of
ca.	circa; about
Can.	Canada, Canada
CCC	Columbia College Chicago
celeb	celebrity
choreog.	choreographer
Co.	Company
comm.	commission
Com.	Committee
comp.	composer
contemp.	contemporary
Corp.	Corporation,
crit.	critic

d.	died
d.b.a.	doing business as
DAPME	*Dictionary for Artists, Performers, Managers & Entrepreneurs*
dept.	department
dir.	director
dncr.	dancer
dsgnr.	designer

e.g.	for example
ea.	each
ency.	encyclopedia
Eng.	England, English
engr.	engineer
ent.	entertainment
esp.	especially
est.	established (date)
Ex.	Example(s)

Fr.	France, French
freq.	frequently

Ger.	German, Germany
gov.	government

hist.	historian
Holly.	Hollywood

i.e.	that is (Id est)
ibid	Same reference as the one immediately preceding
ID	identification
id.	idem, same persons
inc.	including
ind.	independent, industry
Inst.	Institute
instr.	instrument
intl.	international

lib.	liberal

math.	mathematician
Mex.	Mexican, Mexico
mfd.	manufactured
mfg.	manufacture
mm	millimeter

neg.	negative
(n)	noun
no., nos.	number(s)
Nor.	Norway, Norwegian
NYC	New York City

obs.	obsolete
off.	office
org.	organization
orgs.	organizations

perf.	performer
phil.	philosophy
philos.	philosopher
pkg.	package
pl.	plural
pop, pop.	popular
prep	prepare
prob.	probably; problem
prod.	producer
pseud.	pseudonym
pub.	publisher, publication
publ.	publicity

"QAPME"	*"Quotations for Artists, Performers, Managers & Entrepreneurs"*

re	relate to; concerning
ref	reference
reg., reg	regulation
rep	reputation
rep, rep	representative

sch	school
schd	schedule
scrnwrtr	screenwriter
sig	signal
Span	Spanish
sub	substitute
syn.	syndicated

tba	to be advised, to be announced
tchr.	teacher
temp.	temporary
th.	theater

U.	University
unk.	unknown
USSR	United Soviet Socialist Republics (now Russia)
usu.	usually

(v)	verb

Topics assigned to Main Text entries

Aes&Creat	Aesthetics & Creativity
ArtPerf	Artist & Performer
BcstJourn	Broadcast Journalism
Crit&Eval	Criticism & Evaluation
Cult&Soc	Culture & Society
Dnce	Dance
E&F-Acc	Economics & Finance-accounting
Eco&Fin	Economics & Finance
Entrep	Entrepreneurship
Ethcs	Ethics & Philosophy
Fashn	Fashion/Retail Management
Flm&Vid	Film & Video
Fnding	Fund Raising
Genl	General Interest
HR&LR	Human Resources & Labor Relations
iMedia	Interactive MultiMedia
IntelProp	Intellectual Property
InfoMgt	Information Management
Journ	Journalism
Law&Pol	Law & Politics
LegAsp	Legal Aspects
LitArts	Literary Arts
Mgt	Management
Mktg	Marketing
MusArts	Musical Arts
MusInstr	Musical Instruments
PA-Variety	Performing Arts-Variety
PerfA&C	Performing Arts & Crafts
Rdio/TV	Radio & Television
RecA&S	Recording Arts & Sciences
Sci&Tech	Science & Technology
SportsEnt	Sports Entertainment
Th-MakeUp	Theatrical Makeup
TheatArts	Theater Arts
VA-Prntng	Visual Arts-printing
VisArts	Visual Arts

DAPME

THE ARTS DYNAMIC©

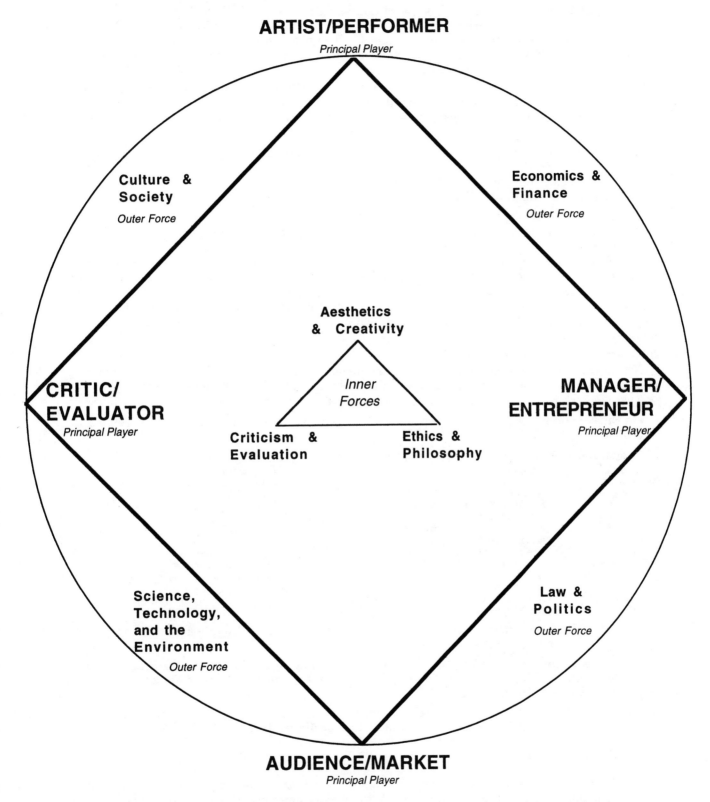

ARTIST/PERFORMER
Principal Player

Culture & Society
Outer Force

Economics & Finance
Outer Force

Aesthetics & Creativity

Inner Forces

CRITIC/ EVALUATOR
Principal Player

MANAGER/ ENTREPRENEUR
Principal Player

Criticism & Evaluation

Ethics & Philosophy

Science, Technology, and the Environment
Outer Force

Law & Politics
Outer Force

AUDIENCE/MARKET
Principal Player

All elements of The Arts Dynamic interrelate at varying times and places.

The Arts & Business Dynamic©

The Arts Dynamic© applies to five Areas of Concentration within the Arts, Entertainment & Media Management Department (AEMMDept) of Columbia College Chicago (CCC): Arts Entrepreneurship/Small Business Management (with emphasis on the arts), Media Management, Music Business, Performing Arts Management, and Visual Arts Management — in both for-profit and non-profit segments.

The Business Dynamic© is essentially similar to The Arts Dynamic© but applies particularly to the areas of Arts Entrepreneurship/Small Business Management (with emphasis on business), and Fashion/Retail Management — in both for-profit and non-profit segments.

The Arts Dynamic© diagrams the dynamic and synergistic relationships between and among the Principal Players and the Inner and Outer Forces which continuously influence the arts and artists and are continuously influenced by the arts and artists. These relationships are fluid — all elements interrelate at varying times and places.

- PRINCIPAL PLAYERS (clockwise from the top of the diagram)

    These creative people cannot be strictly defined. It is not unusual for working artists and performers to also be successful arts managers/entrepreneurs or critics/evaluators.

    » **Artist/Performer**. The unique individual who creates art, culture, entertainment — and employment for arts managers. These artists/performers include musicians, non-musical performers, visual artists, and writers. They are assisted and supported by professional artisans, craftspersons, and technicians.

    » **Arts Manager**. The essential person or organization that brings together the Artist/Performer and the Audience/Market for their mutual benefit. (Each AEMMDept class helps the aspiring arts manager/entrepreneur bring this about.)

    There are two categories of arts managers.

    (1) Those who represent the artist: personal manager, road (or tour) manager, lawyer, business manager, merchandising manager, music publisher, talent agent, public relations director

    (2) Those who represent the audience: producer, promoter, presenter, exhibitor, booker, distributor.

    » **Arts Entrepreneur**. A person who organizes, operates, and assumes the risk for an arts-related enterprise.

    ### Key Differences Between Managers and Entrepreneurs

Topic	Managers	Entrepreneurs
Mission	Follow a set mission	Set the mission
Policy	Execute policy	Determine policy
Goals	Provide resources to achieve predetermined goals	Determine and provide goals
Schedule	Maintain a regular schedule to achieve predetermined goals	On call 24/7.
Resources	Use provided resources	Provide resources
Leadership	Lead administration of enterprise	Lead entire enterprise
Ownership	Limited	Complete
Risk	Do not risk own money	Ownership *is* risk
Organization	Act as trustees to protect the organization	Assumes risk and takes chances
Rewards	Receive predetermined rewards	Unlimited

    » **Audience/Market** (sometimes referred to as the **Consumer**). The ultimate decision maker of the status and value of art, and the reputation and immortality of the artist.

    » **Critic/Evaluator**. Someone who has the paid job of evaluating the artist and the artist's work to the other Principal Players, and evaluating the effects of the Inner and Outer Forces on the other elements of The Arts Dynamic©.

- INNER FORCES underlie all art. They are, in brief:
    » Aesthetics & Creativity. Perception of beauty and its embodiment in art.
    » Criticism & Evaluation. Critical judgment and analysis.
    » Ethics & Philosophy. Principles and values.

- OUTER FORCES represent those conditions and institutions that influence the artist and the creation of art, the management and presentation of art, the makeup and deportment of audiences, and the environment in which criticism and evaluation is formed and communicated.
    » Culture & Society   » Law & Politics
    » Economics & Finance   » Science, Technology, and the Environment

    "Nothing in the arts is not affected by what happens in the world." — ISAAC STERN

The Business Dynamic© diagrams the dynamic and synergistic relationships between and among the Principal Forces and the Inner and Outer Forces which continuously influence business, and are continuously influenced by business.

- PRINCIPAL FORCES (clockwise from the top of the diagram)
  - » **Creator/Inventor**. The unique individual who creates or invents a product or service.
  - » **Manager**. The person or organization that brings together the Creator/Inventor and the Market for their mutual benefit.
  - » **Entrepreneur**. A person who organizes, operates, and assumes the risk for a business venture. (See The Arts Dynamic© for "Key Differences Between Managers and Entrepreneurs.")
  - » **Market**. The ultimate decision maker of what is acceptable, enduring, and valuable.
  - » **Evaluator**. Someone who has the paid job of evaluating the Creator/Inventor to the other Principal Players, and evaluating the effects of the Inner and Outer Forces on the other elements of The Business Dynamic©. Generic titles include: banks, contributors, investors, regulatory agencies.

- INNER FORCES underlie all business. They are, in brief:
  - » Design & Creativity. Measured by what is value-added.
  - » Analysis & Evaluation. Critical judgment and analysis.
  - » Ethics & Philosophy. Principles and values.

- OUTER FORCES represent those conditions and institutions that influence the societal role of business, the financing and marketing of business, the regulation of business, and the effect of human invention and the environment on business.
  - » Culture & Society
  - » Economics & Finance
  - » Law & Politics
  - » Science, Technology, and the Environment

• • •

Editor's Commentary

Artists vs. Business. Artistic talent and a talent for business are not mutually exclusive. Crossovers abound, especially in the performing arts. Successful, contemporary artists/arts managers include: Alvin Ailey, Kenneth Branagh, Ray Charles, Clint Eastwood, Quincy Jones, Madonna, Wynton Marsalis, Mike Nichols, Dolly Parton, Robert Redford, Barbra Streisand, Twyla Tharp, Scott Turrow, and Oprah Winfrey.

There is also crossover in the literary arts. Many authors earn income as critics, editors, and publishers.

Fine (visual) artists tend to shy away from "business." Compared to music and performing arts programs, few fine arts schools offer marketing or management courses, or even the concept of intellectual property.

Artists and performers can excel as arts managers and entrepreneurs. They know the vocabulary, they can deal with audience response, they can handle rejection. Learning the business skills is relatively easy.

For those artists who feel queasy about self-management, they should – for their professional survival – learn enough about business to connect to a capable arts manager.

The force of competition between individuals and businesses is an important motivating force in The Business Dynamic©. However, competition within The Arts Dynamic© is somewhat different. Artists and performers do compete for roles and recognition and money, but the unquenchable desire to fulfill their aesthetic vision and quest for immortality is stronger motivation.

Achieving success in the arts or in business depends largely on three factors:
- **focus** — the ability to concentrate on the objective.
- **critical judgment** — careful, exact evaluation coupled with well-reasoned resolution.
- **passion** — boundless enthusiasm and commitment.

Needs and Fears of Artists/Performers

What the artist/performer wants above all is to be loved. Applause, honors, money are welcomed, but to be cherished and loved even for the moment, that's Nirvana!

> "You're talking to someone who's spent a lifetime being loved — and there's nothing like it." — JUDY GARLAND

> "I work for love. ... I see myself as a bottomless pit, that I'll just never get enough love. Anything I have ever done has been for love.'" — CARLY SIMON

What the artist/performer fears the most – and must deal with always – is rejection: a likely result of every act of creativity, every audition, every interview, every performance, every showing.

> "I realize that every writer is necessarily a critic — that is, each sentence is a skeleton accompanied by enormous activity of rejection." — THORNTON WILDER.

> "I don't know anybody – anybody – who takes more rejection than an actor." — JANE ALEXANDER 2

"You must realize that as an actor, you will face rejection every day." — COLLEEN DEWHURST 1

"It is the tradition of the performer ... braving rejection every time he faces the public." — JOHN RUSSELL

Characteristics of a successful Artist/Performer

• **Ego**. Something inside that must be expressed.

• **Ambition**. Ruthless will to succeed.

• **Talent/Technique**. Talent is a combination of strong physical qualities such as breath and muscle control, good hearing and vision, coordination and stamina — all of which need professional-level technique to be marketable. A necessary characteristic for non-performing artists – composers, writers, visual artists – is the ability to focus on the task at hand.

> "Ego means what you're all about." — MARTINA NAVRATILOVA
>
> "Bigger ego, better architect." — PHILIP C. JOHNSON
>
> "In fact, in the end, [ego] was all that any so-called creative artist possessed." — JOHN MARQUAND 1
>
> "Ambition was not given to a man for nothing; it can be of service to mankind." — LAWRENCE OLIVIER 4

• But in order for the artist/performer to remain successful, he or she must have mental and physical discipline to avoid spinning out of control like Judy Garland, Billie Holiday, Janice Joplin, Jimi Hendrix, Jim Morrison, Elvis Presley, and too many others.

> "Judy Garland was quick-witted, tough, damaged and utterly self-obsessed. 'There wasn't a thing that that gal couldn't do — except take care of herself.'" — Bing Crosby » JUDY GARLAND

• Physical discipline. The performer's body must be able to function at maximum efficiency. A health regimen is a professional necessity.

• Mental discipline. How to deal with rejection and insecurity. This requires adherence to a physical discipline regimen, no chemical stimuli, and the capacity to grow up emotionally. Gain the maturity to see the sudden money, expensive toys, adulation, for what they are: kicks not fulfillment.

> "You collect Ferraris and then you've got to collect people to look after your Ferraris, and you've got to collect buildings to house the Ferraris. Life gets very complicated. And eventually, at least in my case, you think 'I don't need this stuff.' And suddenly life gets simpler." — DAVID GILMOUR

Characteristics of a successful Arts Manager

• Know your own aesthetic so you can appreciate that of the artist and the audience.

• If you represent the artist, you must know her or his aesthetic output in order to find an audience willing to buy the artist's product or service.

• If you represent the audience, you must know its aesthetic demands in order for you to find the artist(s) able to satisfy that demand.

• Never give the artist the impression that you are responsible for the artist's success. You must sublimate your ego to that of the artist. Her or his ego does not easily allow for sharing credit.

• Help the artist create a positive empathic response (positive relationship) with the audience by planning suitable: arrangements/orchestrations, backdrops, choreography, lighting, makeup, public relations, security, sound, and venues worthy of the performer's image and ability.

• Be ethical. It's not easy adhering to your personal sense of right or wrong, but in the long run, it's the best way to live the good life — and enjoy good business.

> "The business of managing the arts ... requires a special love and dedication that goes beyond mere competence in various job skills." — STEPHEN LANGLEY & JAMES ABRUZZO
>
> "A good agent is more than a 'ten-percenter.' The ideal agent not only has the respect of producers, directors, and, in today's business, the casting directors, but he also gives the actor a sense of stature and dignity." — COLLEEN DEWHURST 2
>
> "We can help, we can guide, we can kick ass once in a while, but the client is the guy, he has to have the creative ability." — CHARLIE JOFFE (Woody Allen's personal manager)
>
> "If the artist, having engaged a professional manager, cannot resolve to trust that manager, especially in out-of-house arrangements where the artist may not be able to monitor results as closely as desired, then the relationship will be a difficult one." — IVAN SYGODA

Characteristics of a successful Critic/Evaluator

• Know the historical and cultural background of whomever or whatever you are evaluating.

• Clearly differentiate between the discernible facts and your opinion or interpretation of the facts.

• No one is completely objective but do your best by acknowledging your own biases and conflicts of interest. Admit error.

> "There are three main qualifications for a musical critic, besides the general qualification of good sense and knowledge of the world. He must have a cultivated taste for music; he must be a skilled writer; and he must be a practiced critic." — GEORGE BERNARD SHAW 4

Characteristics of a responsible Audience

• Pay for the use of intellectual property. Artists deserve fair payment for their unique creativity and the pleasures derived from it. [Note. he arts manager's income is dependent on the artist's income.]

- Don't encourage "art" that preaches hate or violence. You and yours could be the next target.

- Don't deny free expression. If you don't agree with the artist's message, exercise your right to not buy it, or listen to it, or look at it. But don't interfere with the right of others to do as they wish.

> "Censors never feel that their own psyche or moral health is in jeopardy." — J.W. EHRLIGH

> "A curious phenomenon in censorship is the censors' personal immunity to the infectious book." — CHARLES REMBAR 4

> "It is not only the actors on stage who make this event happen – through their living presence, their actions, and their lives — but the people in the audience as well." — VACLAV HAVEL

> "You work for the sake of the work and hope there is an audience out there, but you can't try to create a body of work based on what you think the audience is going to like." — PAUL NEWMAN

> "To be a good listener means to pay attention, allow the music to stand on its own, and to be open to what is new." — KENYON C. ROSENBERG 2

> "The only verdict that counts is the public's." — HENRY PLEASANTS 7

The quotations in this section are excerpted from the Main Text of
"Quotations for Artists, Performers, Managers & Entrepreneurs," 4th rev. ed.
(Chicago: CCC/AEMMPubs, Sep 2002)

The Arts & Business Dynamic©: Copyright © 2002 by Charles Suber & Associates, Inc.

DAPME

THE BUSINESS DYNAMIC©

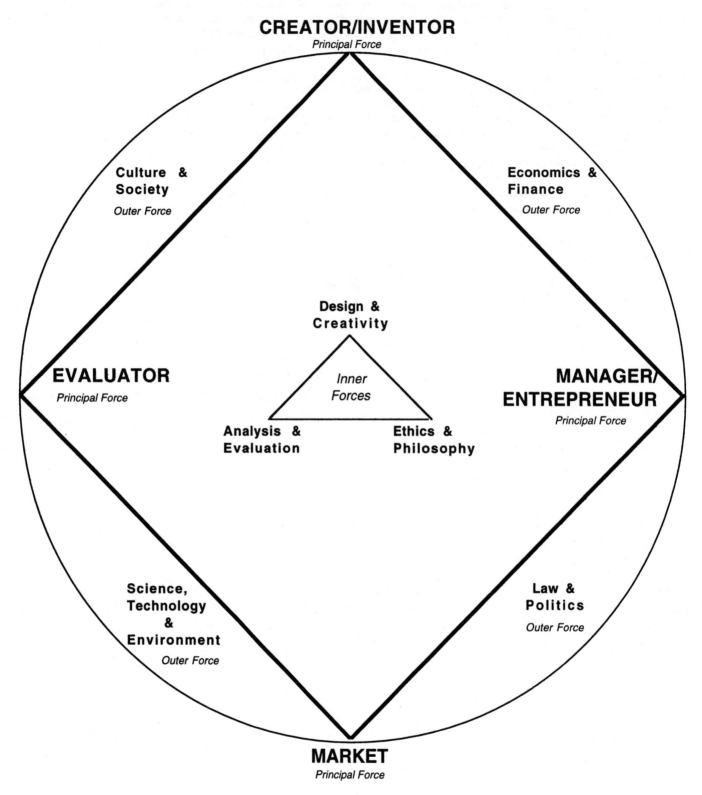

CREATOR/INVENTOR
Principal Force

**Culture &
Society**
Outer Force

**Economics &
Finance**
Outer Force

**Design &
Creativity**

*Inner
Forces*

EVALUATOR
Principal Force

**MANAGER/
ENTREPRENEUR**
Principal Force

**Analysis &
Evaluation**

**Ethics &
Philosophy**

**Science,
Technology
&
Environment**
Outer Force

**Law &
Politics**
Outer Force

MARKET
Principal Force

All elements of The Business Dynamic interrelate at varying times and places.

Main Text

- Main Text **entries** organized A-Z classified by one or more topics.

- Any word or term in **boldface** type within an **entry** is itself listed elsewhere as an **entry**.

- See "Index I to Topics" (p. 227) for a complete listing of the 37 topics assigned to Main Text **entries.**

- See "Explanatory Notes" (pp. viii-ix))for detailed format and style information.

Dictionary for Artists, Performers, Managers & Entrepreneurs

Ω   **Incomplete entry.**

(??)   **Missing data.**

- A -

2Market *InfoMgt, Mktg* Interactive personal shopping service combining **CD-ROM** with online services.

3/4 time *MusArts* » **three-quarter time**

5 minutes *PerfA&C* Announcement on backstage **PA** five minutes before **curtain**. *Also see* **fifteen minutes, half-hour, places.**

5/4 time *MusArts* Jazz-waltz time: five beats to the **measure**, every quarter-note gets one beat.

10% rule *LegAsp* Usually, the total percentage of material quoted from any one book should not exceed 10% of the total number of pages from the original book.

12-bar blues *MusArts* Most blues are played as a **12-bar** composition. Few are played as **16-bars**, the standard number for pop music. *Also see* **Blues.**

12-tone *MusArts* Relating to an **atonal arrangement** of the traditional 12 **chromatic** tones. *Also see* **serial music.**

15 minutes *PerfA&C* Announcement on backstage **PA** fifteen minutes before **curtain**. *Also see* **five minutes, half-hour, places.**

16-bar song *MusArts* Standard for pop music. *Also see* **twelve-bar blues.**

30 sheet *Mktg* Paper measuring 9'7" x 21'7" with pre-printed advertisements (usu. movies) that are mounted on panels 10'5" x 22'8"

33-1⁄3ʳᵈs *RecA&S* Usually 12-inch record disks played at 33-1/3 **rpm** introduced by Columbia Records in 1948. *Also see* **battle of the speeds.** *Also see* **battle of the speeds.**

44-minute pilot *Flm&Vid* Standard length of a one-hour TV show without ads.

78s *RecA&S* Phonograph disks recorded at 78 rpm. Preceded by **wax cylinders**, succeeded by 45s, LPs (33-1/3) rpm, and CDs. *Also see* **Music Playback Devices.**

88ᵗʰ episode *Flm&Vid* With 88 episodes available to sell, studios can very profitably **syndicate** the show to local stations and overseas, e.g., a successful comedy.

401k plans *EntreP* Retirement plans established to accept employee contributions via salary reductions. Employers may match a portion of the employee's contribution. The 401k is also a vehicle for distributing profit sharing contributions. » **Cash or Deferred Arrangement plan** (CODA)

501(c)(3) *Fnding* Section of the Internal Revenue code that defines nonprofit, charitable (as broadly defined), tax-exempt organizations; 501(c)(3) organizations are further defined as public charities, **private operating foundations**, and **private non-operating foundations**. *Also see* **operating foundation, private foundation, public charity.**

501(c)(3) *Fndng, LegAsp* Designation given by the IRS to charitable organizations entitling them to certain tax privileges.

503b *EntreP* » **tax sheltered annuity**

504 loan program *EntreP* SBA program that borrows money from large investors, then uses the proceeds to make small business loans.

555 *InfoMgt,PerfA&C* Three-numeral telephone code used as fictional dialog. *Origin* Code for information service: 555-1212.

1984 *Cult&Soc, LitArts* Satiric novel (1949) by **George Orwell** in which **totalitarian** state rule by **conformity** is enforced by **Big Brother**. *Also see* ***Brave New World, Fahrenheit 451.***

a *MusArts* alto

a *MusInstr* alto <flute, saxophone> *Also see* **Musical Instrument Families.**

A above middle C *LegAsp* Piano tuning instruction, the requirement for which can be a **rider** to an **engagement contract**. *Also see* **tech rider.**

A above middle C *MusArts* Specific **pitch** on the piano with a **frequency** of 440 **Hz**, i.e. 440 complete **cycles** or **sound waves** per second. Standard tuning for acoustic piano. *Also see* **concert pitch, international pitch, tuning fork.**

a capella (ah kapella, Ital.) *MusArts* Singing without accompaniment.

à jour (ah jour, Fr.) *Fashn* Openwork that makes the design in lace.

à la carte news (ah lah cart, Fr.) *InfoMgt, Journ* News delivered by electronic means for readers or viewers who have indicated a prior interest. AUTOMAT NEWS, CAFETERIA NEWS

a priori (ay-pree-or-ee, Latin) *Crit&Eval* Proceeding from a known or assumed cause to a necessarily related effect. DEDUCTIVE.

a programming language (APL) *InfoMgt* 1 Mathematically structured programming language, popular for problem-solving applications. 2 Performs the functions of an intelligent calculator. *Also see* **Programming Languages**

A side *RecA&S* Featured side of a **record disc** *Also see* **flip side.**

a tempo (ah tempo, Ital.) *MusArts* Instruction to return to the initial **tempo** after a deviation in tempo. *Also see* **Music Directions, time.**

A&R *also* **a&r** *RecA&S* **Artists and Repertoire, Artists and Repertory** Employee of a record company who has three principal responsibilities: (1) Scout new and established talent, (2) Find music suitable for company's talent roster, (3) Be the **liaison** among the company and the artist, and her or his **personal manager**, in all phases of production and career planning.

A-team *Flm&Vid* Description of the on camera actors or stuntpersons in a scene; regarded as a separate unit from the **stand-ins** who helped to set up the shot. FIRST-STRING *Also see* **B-team, second unit.**

a.m. Morning newspaper

A/C, a/c *Eco&Fin* account

A/PE&F-Acc **accounts payable**

A/RE&F-Acc **accounts receivable**

AAA *HR&LR* **American Arbitration Association**

AAAA *HR&LR* Association of Artist and Artistes organization founded in order to affiliate **Actor's Equity Association** with the **AFL-CIO.**

AAAA *Mktg* **American Association of Advertising Agencies** Est. 1917 in NYC, as the national trade organization representing the advertising agency business. Election to the AAAA is the highest professional recognition an agency can achieve.

AAAL *Genl* **American Academy of Arts and Letters** Members are U.S. artists, writers, and composers qualified by notable achievement in their field. Membership limited to 250. Honorary members are American choreographers, film-makers, photographers, and foreign artists, writers and composers. Promotes literature and the **fine arts** in the U.S.

AADA *TheatArts* » **American Academy of Dramatic Art**

AAEC *Journ, VisArts* **Association of American Editorial Cartoonists** Professional group of editorial cartoonists whose numbers are shrinking from the downsizing and downgrading of independent journalism. *Also see* **Golden Spike Award.**

AAFRC *Fnding* **American Association of Fund Raising Counsel** Members are fund-raising consulting firms that adhere to a specific code of ethics. The association publishes *Giving USA*, an annual compilation of data on philanthropic activity.

AAMD *VisArts* **American Association of Museum Directors** Members are art, history, and science museums, art associations and centers, historic houses and societies, preservation projects, planetariums, zoos, aquariums, botanical gardens, college and university museums, libraries, and special museums; trustees and professional employees of museums and others interested in the museum field. Has an accrediting system for museums. Maintains placement service for museum professionals.

AAR *LitArts* **Association of Authors Representatives** Members are literary and dramatic agents who market books, plays, and other literary and dramatic material.

AARC *RecA&S* **Alliance of Artists and Recording Companies** Est. 1992 by **RIAA** to distribute **Audio Home Recording Act** royalties to artists and record companies.

ABA *LegAsp* **American Bar Association** largest and most influential professional organization of lawyers

ABA *Law&Pol, LitArts* **American Booksellers Association** Works toward the establishment, improvement, and maintenance of favorable trade conditions. Long-time defendant of **First Amendment** rights. Sponsors **Banded Books Week**. *Also see* **Anti-Censorship Organizations**.

abatement *LegAsp* Act of eliminating or annulling.

Abbey Theater *TheatArts* Founded as the Irish National Theatre (in Dublin, 1902) by playwrights **William Butler Yeats** and **Lady Gregory**. *Also see* **Theaters & Theatres**.

Abbott, George (1887-1995) *ArtPerf, LitArts, Mgt, TheatArts* Legendary theatrical producer who wrote and directed many Broadway productions. *<Damn Yankees* (**Tony**: author, 1956), *Fiorello!* (**Tonys**: author and director; **Pulitzer**: author, 1959), **Kennedy Center** honoree (1982)>

ABC *Journ, Mktg, Rdio/TV* **Audit Bureau of Circulations** Nonprofit, cooperative, tripartite organization of advertisers, advertising agencies, and publishers that audits paid circulation figures of magazines, newspapers, and **CD-ROMs**. ABC also publishes advertising rates, marketing data, and mechanical specifications in separate monthly editions for Newspapers, Consumer Magazines, Business Magazines, Radio Stations, and Television Stations. *Also see* **rate card**, **space buyer**, **time buyer**.

ABC *Rdio/TV* **American Broadcasting Cos** Major radio and TV network bought by Disney in July 1995 from **Capital Cities, Inc**. *Origin* **Blue Network** of the **National Broadcasting Company** (NBC) *Also see* **network radio**.

ABC art *VisArts* » **minimalism**

ABC method *EntreP* System of classifying inventory by value.

Abe Olman Award *ArtPerf, MusArts* "Excellence in Music Publishing" by the **Songwriters Hall of Fame**. *Also see* **Awards & Prizes**, **NAPM**.

ABL *SportsEnt* American Basketball League, created to compete against the **NBA**. In December 1998, after its second season, the ABL declared bankruptcy and ceased operating.

abort *InfoMgt* To terminate execution of a program when an unrecoverable error or malfunction occurs.

above-the-fold *Journ* Top half of a folded newspaper page, favored position for a story or **byline**.

above-the-line costs *Eco&Fin, Flm&Vid* Costs that must, at least in part, be met regardless of whether or not a project actually goes into production <story rights, script, producer> For large ('Hollywood') productions a director and 'stars' will also be required to develop a project. *Also see* **below-the-line costs**.

aboveboard *Crit&Eval* Without deceit or trickery, straightforward in manner.

ABP *Journ* **American Business Press** Trade association of business magazines and relatively small consumer magazines.

abridge *LitArts* To reduce the length of a written text. CONDENSE

absolute deviation *EntreP* Difference between the actual amount and the forecasted amount is always expressed as a positive number.

absolute music *MusArts* Instrumental music that depends solely on its rhythmic, melodic, and **contrapuntal** structures.

absolute path *iMedia* Programming: complete instructions pointing to something (i.e., a directory, file, object, variable, etc.) Syntax varies by language.

absolute pitch *MusArts* Rare ability to identify or sing any **pitch** heard. PERFECT PITCH.

absorbent cotton *Perf-MkUp* Used for stuffing the cheeks to enlarge them and for building up the face, neck, or hands in combination with **spirit gum** or **latex**.

abstract *Aes&Creat* Having an intellectual and affective artistic content that depends solely on **intrinsic form** rather than on narrative content or pictorial representation.

abstract *Fnding* Brief summary of a grant proposal located in the beginning of the proposal.

abstract art *VisArts* Art works with little or no resemblance to objects in the real world, relying for their interest and emotional impact on form and color alone; also known as **nonobjective** art or **nonrepresentational** art. *Also see* **Paul Cézanne**, **Dadaism**.

abstract expressionism *VisArts* School of painting that flourished after World War II until the early 1960s, characterized by the view that art is **nonrepresentational** and chiefly improvisational. Abstract expressionism was the first art movement with joint European-American roots, reflecting the influence of European artists who had fled Hitler-dominated Europe. Abstract expressionists synthesized many sources from the history of modern painting: from **expressionism** and **fauvism** to **surrealism**. Only geometric art and Realist art played no part in this mixture of intensively retrospective and even spiritual elements, often painted on mural-sized canvases. <Willem de Kooning (1904-1997, Dutch-born pntr.), Robert Motherwell (1915-91, pntr., tchr., theoretician), Barnett Newman (1905-71, pntr.), Jackson Pollock (1912-56, pntr.), Mark Rothko (1903-70, Russ.-born pntr.)> *Also see* **action painting**, **American-style painting**, **Art Movements and Periods**, **informal**, **modern art**.

abstract improvisation *MusArts* Spontaneous improvisation » **free jazz** <Muhal Richard Abrams (1930-, arr-comp., pno., cl., educ.)> *Also see* **free jazz**.

abstract setting *PerfA&C, VisArts* Stage setting **stylized** rather than **representational**.

absurd *Crit&Eval* **1** Ridiculously incongruous or unreasonable; foolish. **2** "The condition or state in which human beings exist in a meaningless, irrational universe wherein people's lives have no purpose or meaning." *Also see* **theatre of the absurd**.

absurdism *Crit&Eval* Philosophy, often translated into art forms, holding that human beings exist in a meaningless, irrational universe and that any search for order by them will bring them into direct conflict with this universe.

ABT *Dnce* **American Ballet Theatre**

ACA *Mgt* **American Council for the Arts**. National membership association primarily involved in arts advocacy and a major publisher of books in the field.

academician *Crit&Eval* Member of an art, literary, or scientific academy or society.

Academy *Ethcs&Phil* **Plato's** school for advanced education.

academy *Genl* **1** Society of scholars, scientists, or artists. **2** Private secondary or college-preparatory school.

Academy Awards *Flm&Vid* » Annual **Oscar** awards by the **Academy of Motion Picture Arts and Sciences** (AMPAS) for achievement in movies. *Also see* **Awards & Prizes**.

academy leader *Flm&Vid* Standard film **leader** designed by **AMPAS**, attached to the beginning of each reel of film; contains **cue marks** to aid in projection.

Academy of American Poets *LitArts* Known for its annual Academy of American Poets Awards. *Also see* **Awards & Prizes**.

Academy of Country Music (ACM) *MusArts* » **ACM**

Academy of Motion Picture Arts and Sciences (AMPAS) *Flm&Vid* Est. 1927 for the advancement of the arts and sciences of motion pictures and to foster cooperation among the creative leadership of the motion picture industry to cultural education and technical progress. *Also see* **Academy Awards**.

ACC *Genl* **American Craft Council** National service association of individuals and institutions who work with crafts.

acc *MusInstr* **accordion**

accel *MusArts* **accelerando**

accelerando (accel) *MusArts* Gradually accelerate the time. *Also see* **Music Directions**.

Accelerated Cost Recover System (ACRS) *EntreP* U.S. depreciation schedule that covered items which were placed in use prior to January 1, 1987.

accelerated depreciation methods *E&F-Acc* Methods of calculating **depreciation** when costs are reckoned quicker in the earlier years of the **assets useful life**. <double declining method, sum of the year digits>

accelerator theory *EntreP* Theory of investment that says current investment spending depends positively on the expected future growth of real GDP.

accent *Fashn, VisArts* Distinctive feature or quality, such as a feature that accentuates or complements a decorative style.

accent *LitArts* Rhythmically significant stress in a line of verse.

accent *MusArts* Special stress given to a note within a phrase; mark representing this stress.

accent *TheatArts* Distinctive utterances produced in one language by a native speaker of another.

accent lighting *Flm&Vid, PerfA&C* Lighting that stresses certain areas to control viewer attention and support other parameters such as characterization and dramatic content. *Also see* **Stage Lighting**.

acceptance sampling *EntreP* Use of a random, representative portion of a sample to determine the acceptability of the whole.

access *InfoMgt* To retrieve data from primary memory or from a **peripheral** storage device such as a **floppy disk.**

access number *InfoMgt* Usually a local telephone number by which one's **modem** may access an **online** service.

access time *InfoMgt* Time lag between a request for information stored in a computer and its delivery.

accession *VisArts* Formal process to accept and record an item as a collection object. *Also see* **deaccession.**

accessory *MusInstr* Supplementary item for a musical instrument that contributes to a sound effect. <**mute** for a brass instrument>

acclamation *Crit&Eval* Oral vote of enthusiastic approval taken without formal ballot. <The motion passed by acclamation>

accolade *Crit&Eval* Expression of approval. PRAISE, AWARD

accompanist *ArtPerf, Dnce, MusArts* **1** One who accompanies instrumental or vocal soloist(s) **2** One who provides musical accompaniment for dance classes.

accompany (comp.) *MusArts* Provide rhythmic and **harmonic** background and support. *Also see* **comp, comping.**

according to the ink *Flm&Vid, TheatArts* Acting direction: keep to the script, do not **improvise.**

accordion (acc.) *MusInstr* Portable instrument with a small keyboard and metal reeds that sound when air is forced past them by pleated bellows operated by the player. SQUEEZE BOX **1** "A true gentlemen is someone who knows how to play the accordion but doesn't play it," — George Shearing (1919-, jazz pno) **2** "An instrument in harmony with the sentiments of an assassin." — Ambrose Bierce (1842-1914, n-fict., fict., wit) DIATONIC ACCORDION, PIANO ACCORDION *Also see* **Musical Instrument Families.**

accordionist *MusArts* **accordion** player

account (acct., A/C) *Eco&Fin* **1** Formal banking, brokerage, or business relationship which provides for regular services and transactions. <Investor usu. opens a brokerage account with her/his broker> **2** Precise list of financial transactions. **3** Money deposited for checking, savings, or brokerage use. **4** Customer having a business or credit relationship with a firm. <The customer asked for her or his account representative>

account executive (AE) *Mgt, Mktg* Advertising agency executive who is the **liaison** between the agency and the client.

account executive (AE) *Rdio/TV* Radio or TV sales rep who deals with a particular ad agency or advertiser.

account *Genl* **1** Worth, standing, or importance. <an advertiser of some account> **2** Profit or advantage. <He turned his copying skills to good account> **3** Narrative or record of events.

account return on investment technique *EntreP* Capital budgeting technique that evaluates a capital expenditure based on the average annual after-tax profits relative to the average book value of an investment.

accounting *E&F-Acc* System that measures business activities, processes that information into reports and **financial statements**, and communicates the findings to decision makers.

accounting cycle *E&F-Acc* Process by which accountants produce an entity's **financial statements** for a specific period.

accounting equation *E&F-Acc* **Assets = liabilities + equity.** Basis for the **balance sheet** and **double entry bookkeeping.**

accounting profit *EntreP* Is what a business has left from its revenues after paying all of its expenses. Is typically shown on the bottom of a business income statement.

accounting rate of return (ARR) *EntreP* In capital budgeting, it is the rate of return on an investment that is found by dividing the average annual income by the average cost.

accounting statements (financial statements) *EntreP* Reports of a company's financial performance and resources, including an income statement, a balance sheet, and a statement of cash flows.

accounts payable (A/P) *E&F-Acc* **General ledger** accounts that fall under the **liability** category and reflect the debts owed by the business to other **creditors.** Also reflects the current position of **long-term debt.**

accounts payable (trade credit) *EntreP* Outstanding credit payable to suppliers.

accounts receivable (A/R) *E&F-Acc* **General ledger** accounts that fall under the category of **current assets** reflect debts owed to the business by its customers from the sale of goods or services.

accounts receivable (A/R) *EntreP* Amount of credit extended to customers for services or products.

accounts receivable turnover *EntreP* Number of times accounts receivable sold rolls over during an accounting cycle.

accrue *E&F-Acc* Gain, an addition, or an increment. <Interest accruing in one's saving account is **compounded**>

accrual accounting *E&F-Acc* Revenues and expenses recognized in the period earned or incurred.

accrual method (accrual-basis accounting) *EntreP* Method of accounting that matches revenues when they are earned against the expenses associated with those revenues.

accrued expenses *E&F-Acc* Expenses incurred by the business but not yet paid, typically the current position of a **long-term debt.** <**Social Security Taxes Payable, Property Taxes Payable**>

accrued expenses *EntreP* Short-term liabilities that have been incurred but not paid.

accrued liabilities *EntreP* Obligations of company that are accumulated during the normal course of business and are paid after the books are closed.

accrued revenue *E&F-Acc* Revenue that has been earned but not yet received in cash.

acct. *Eco&Fin* **account.** A/C, A/C

accumulated depreciation *E&F-Acc* Used to accumulate the **depreciation** recognized to date, this is a **contra asset** account.

accumulated depreciation *EntreP* Total depreciation (wearing allowance) that an asset has on a balance sheet, from the asset's acquisition, until the asset is disposed of by the business.

ACDA *MusArts* **American Choral Directors Association** Ω

acerbic, acerb *Crit&Eval* Sour or bitter in taste, character, or tone of voice. *Also see* **H.L Mencken.**

acetone *Perf-MkUp* Clear liquid solvent for **collodion** and **spirit gum.**

ACFRE *Fnding* **Advanced Certified Fund Raising Executive.** Title awarded to those who have worked ten years in the field and pass a test by **NSFRE.**

acid rock *MusArts* Rock music characterized by extremely high **decibel** level with screeching guitar **riffs.** <Grateful Dead (» Bill Graham) *Also see* **Rock Music Styles.**

acid test *E&F-Acc* » **quick ratio**

acid-test ratio (quick ratio) *EntreP* Measure of a company's liquidity that excludes inventories.

ACLU *Law&Pol, LegAsp* **American Civil Liberties Union.** Est. 1920, NYC. National non-partisan organization "dedicated to protecting the principles embodied in the **Bill of Rights.**" *Also see* **Anti-Censorship Organizations.**

ACM *MusArts* **Academy of Country Music** Est. 1964 to promote and increase the market for **country music**; approx. 4,000 members.

acoustic coupler *InfoMgt* Device used in **telecommunications** that connects to a standard telephone handset and converts **digital** computer signals to continuous telephone signals and vice versa.

acoustic instrument *MusInstr* Musical instrument that uses the natural amplification of its materials, e.g., brass, reeds, strings, wood, to produce its sound, rather than electronic devices. <acoustic guitar, acoustic bass> Musicians usu. refer to an acoustic piano simply as a "piano." *Also see* **electronic instruments, Musical Instrument Families.**

acoustical recording *RecA&S* Obsolete method of recording by **megaphone**-like horns as introduced by **Thomas Edison.** Superseded by **electrical recording** via **microphones**, i.e., **transducers**, ca. 1924 *Also see* **Music Playback Devices.**

acoustician *Sci&Tech* Specialist in **acoustics.**

acoustics *PerfA&C, RecA&S* Qualities in the constructions and furnishing of an auditorium that affect the transmission and hearing of sound. *Also see* **ambiance, ambient sound, psychoacoustics.**

acoustics *Sci&Tech* Scientific study of sound and **sound waves.** *Also see* **psychoacoustics.**

ACPA *InfoMgt* **Association of Computer Programmers and Analysts.** International organization that offers its members opportunities to develop their professional skills via seminars, workshops, conferences, and publications.

acquisition *EntreP* Purchase of a new venture, usually made in order to add to an existing venture. First-time launch by acquisition is usually referred to as a **buyout**.

acquisitions editor *LitArts, MusArts* One who reviews submitted manuscripts on behalf of the book or music publisher. May also determine areas in which publisher's lists are weak, develop new titles, and recruit authors.

acrobats *PA-Variety* Typical opening act in **vaudeville**. [An opening act so all the special equipment could be put in place during the preceding movie. Second act was usu. a **song and dance team** that played front stage while the acrobatic gear was flown or removed to the wings.].

act *LitArts, TheatArts* Main division of a dramatic work in which a definite part of the action is completed.

act *PerfA&C* Perform as an actor. <act a part, sustain the part of a character in a dramatic work>

ACT *TheatArts* **American Conservatory Theatre** Ω

act curtain *PerfA&C* Curtain raised or drawn to reveal the stage during an act or scene. ACT DROP *Also see* **Stage Curtains**.

act of God clause *LegAsp* Clause in an **engagement** or **management contract** that exempts the parties from liability in the event of an unusual, extraordinary, or unforeseeable manifestation of the forces of nature beyond the powers of human intervention, such as a tornado or a bolt of lightning. *Also see* **Contracts**.

act out *PerfA&C* Perform as if in a play. <act out a song> DRAMATIZE

act utilitarian *Ethcs&Phil* » **utilitarianism**

act. *ArtPerf, Flm&Vid, Rdio/TV TheatArts* » **actor**

ACTA *ArtPerf, TheatArts* **Acting Coaches and Teachers Association**. Ω

acting *TheatArts* "The response to an assumption by doing something to somebody at a given place and time in order to bring about human behavior which can be seen and heard by an audience." — Uta Hagen (» **talent**)

acting areas *PerfA&C* Areas of the stage on which specific scenes, or parts of scenes, are played.

Acting Coaches and Teachers Association (ACTA) *ArtPerf, TheatArts* » **ACTA**

acting edition *LitArts, TheatArts* Published text of a play with alterations and information for stage production. ACTING TEXT, ACTING VERSION

acting property *TheatArts* **Property** used by an actor. PROPS

action *ArtPerf* **Deportment** of an actor

action *Ethcs&Phil* Thing done intentionally.

action *Flm&Vid* **1** That which is filmed or taped within camera range; activity of a certain scene. **2** Command called by a director or assistant director to begin performance and/or camera movement.

action *LitArts* Movement or development of the plot.

action *MusInstr* Mechanism in a musical instrument that transfers player's impulse to keys, strings, valves, etc.

action *TheatArts* **1** Complete sequence of dramatic events, with a beginning, middle, and end, that make up the **plot**. **2** Physical movement of an actor or actors on stage. *Also see* **intention**.

action *VisArts* Movement, process, or expression of artistic philosophy or sensitivity similar to a **happening**. <Ger. artist Joseph Beuys (1921-86)> *Also see* **performance art**.

action painting *VisArts* **1** Style of abstract painting that uses techniques such as the dribbling or splashing of paint to achieve a spontaneous effect. **2** Avant-garde movement of abstract paintings begun in NYC after WWII. Also called "**American-Type paintings**" <**Jackson Pollock** (» **abstract expressionism**)> For the action painting artists, the action itself is more important than the completed work. *Origin* Term originated by art critic Harold Rosenberg in 1952 GESTURE PAINTING

action plan *Mgt, PerfA&C* Individual or group strategy expressed in a written outline of goals, objectives, and tasks to be completed for a particular project.

active application program *InfoMgt* **Application** in current use.

Active Server Pages (ASP) *iMedia* Scripting environment for Microsoft Internet Information Server in which you can combine HTML, scripts and reusable ActiveX server components to create dynamic web pages.

active voice *BcstJourn, Journ* Verb form in which the thing or person responsible for the action precedes the verb. (Broadcast newswriters always try to use active voice.)

activity ratios *EntreP* Those ratios that indicate how efficiently a business is using its assets.

active program *InfoMgt, iMedia* Any program currently being executed in the computer.

active window *InfoMgt, iMedia* Foremost window displayed on the computer screen where the next action will take place.

activism *HR&LR* Theory or practice of assertive or militant action as a means of opposing or supporting a controversial issue. <mass demonstrations or strikes>

activity ratios *E&F-Acc* Indicate how rapidly the company is turning its assets into cash. *Also see* **fixed asset turnover, inventory turnover, receivables turnover, total asset turnover.**

actor (act.) *ArtPerf, Flm&Vid, Rdio/TV, TheatArts,*Performer presenting a dramatic characterization; traditionally male but increasingly used to refer to both genders. "In my heart of hearts I only know that I am far from sure when I am acting and when I am not or, should I more frankly put it, when I am lying and when I am not. For what is acting but lying, and what is good acting but convincing lying?" — **Laurence Olivier** *Also see* **actress.**

actor *Genl* participant

actor-manager *ArtPerf, Mgt* Actor who has her or his own company in which he or she is both producer and star. <Richard Burbage (1567?-1619, Eng. act.-mgr.), Sir Henry Irving (1838-1905, Brit. act.-mgr.), **Sir Laurence Olivier, William Shakespeare, Orson Welles**> *Also see* **Managers.**

actor's bible *Journ, TheatArts* Publication respected by actors as the gospel truth. <*Hollywood Reporter, Variety*>

actor-proof *TheatArts* Role or script practically certain to be effective even if badly acted.

Actors Studio *ArtPerf, TheatArts* New York school famous for its **process** approach to acting based on the **Stanislavski** method. Organized in 1947 by **Cheryl Crawford, Elia Kazan**, and Robert Lewis (*aka* Bobby Lewis, 1909-1997, stage act., dir., tchr.) *Also see* **Group Theater, Method.**

Actors' Equity Association (AEA, Equity) *ArtPerf, HR&LR, TheatArts* » **Equity**

actress (act.) *ArtPerf, BcstMedia, Flm&Vid, TheatArts* Female performer presenting a dramatic characterization. Usage is being replaced by **actor** as a genderless term, as opposed to the specific female attribution of 'actress'.

actual contract *LegAsp* Either an **express contract** or an **implied-in-fact contract**. *Also see* **Contracts**.

actual malice *Journ, LegAsp* "The case ("*New York Times v. Sullivan*") held essentially that criticism of public officials in the performance of their official function is for the most part (and in the absence of clear and convincing proof of 'actual malice,' in the new sense of 'knowledge of falsity' or '**reckless disregard**') constitutionally protected." — Renata Adler (1938-, social critic)

actuality *BcstJourn* Radio term for field recordings of interviews or events. Portions of actualities, often called **bites**, may be used in a newscast.

actuarial *Eco&Fin* Statistician who computes insurance risks and premiums.

ACUAA *Mgt, PerfA&C* **Association of College & University Arts Administrators**. Name changed to **Association of Performing Arts Presenters**. » **APAP**

ad *Mktg* **advertisement**

ad art *Mktg, VisArts* Creative art combined with title, credits, and copy for **print media** advertising.

ad hoc *Genl* **1** Formed for or concerned with one specific purpose. <an **ad hoc** fair employment committee> **2** Improvised and often impromptu.

ad lib *MusArts* **1** Improvise, improvisation. **2** Vary from written music. **3** Passage interpolated in a score.

ad lib *PerfA&C* **1** Improvise, improvisation. **2** Speak or perform spontaneously. **3** Remark or witticism supposedly not rehearsed or scripted. "Let those that play your clowns speak no more than is set down for them." — Hamlet "I carefully prepare my ad-libs." — Jack Benny (1894-1974, act., comic in Radio/TV, film/stage/vaudeville)

ad lib (*ad libitum*, Latin for "at pleasure") *TheatArts* Applies to lines supplied by the actor wherever they may be required, as in crowd scenes or to till in where there would otherwise be an undesirable pause,

ad libitum *MusArts,PerfA&C* » **ad-lib**

ad stacks *Journ, Mktg* Stacking newspaper ads one atop the other.

ADA *InfoMgt, iMedia* High level language used exclusively for all Dept. of Defense computer programs; named for **Ada Augusta Byron**. *Also see* **Difference Engine No. 1**.

ADAA *Mgt, VisArts* » **Art Dealers Association of America**

adagio *Dnce* **1** Any dance to slow music. **2** (Ballet) Section of a **pas de deux** in which the ballerina and her partner perform steps requiring lyricism and great skill in lifting, balancing, and turning. **3** Technique of partnering. **4** Generic term for a series of exercises designed to develop grace, sense of line, and balance.

adagio *MusArts* Play in a slow tempo, i.e., quarter note equals fifty beats per minute. *Also see* **Music Directions**.

adapt *iMedia* To change in response » **adaptation**

adaptation *Flm&Vid, LitArts, TheatArts* **1**. Dramatization; a reworking, as of a novel or biography into dramatic form or a reworking of an old dramatic entertainment into a new one, as from a drama to a musical, or from a stage play to a movie. **2** Non-literal translation of a dramatic entertainment into another language.

adaptation *iMedia* Change or changes depending on various conditions; often due to actions or inactions taken by a user in an interactive environment or an application, or due to the interaction of elements within an application <objects in an application simulating cells in an organism>.

adaptive *iMedia* Capable of adapting; able to be adapted.

add-on *InfoMgt* Program written to add functionality in another program or a system.

add-on contributions *Fnding* <Ticket buyers and contributors add 25% of the cost of tickets as a contribution to the organization's **development** fund>

additional paid-in capital *Eco&Fin* **1** Investments contributed by stockholders. **2** AMount over the **par** or **stated value**.

additional paid in capital *EntreP* Equity contributions to a corporation in excess of the par value of common stock as shown on a corporate balance sheet.

additions to property *E&F-Acc* Any expansion of **long-term asset** capitalized and thus depreciated over its **useful life**. <a room addition to an existing building>

additive color *iMedia* Mixing two or more colors of light; commonly a combination of red, green, and blue. In contrast: **subtractive color**.

address *InfoMgt* Number used in information storage or retrieval assigned to a specific memory location. <location of a **cell** in a spreadsheet>

adhesive tape, clear *Perf-MkUp* Used to draw the skin in order to change the shape of the eyes or mouth.

ADI *Mktg, Rdio/TV* **Area of Dominant Influence. Arbitron** market classification indicating which market area local stations have partial or complete signal dominance over stations from other market areas. *Also see* **Nielsen Media Research**.

adjacency *Mktg, Rdio/TV* Broadcast program or time period immediately preceding or following a specific commercial.

adjudicator *HR&LR* Judge of an arts-related competition.

adjunct *Genl* **1** Something attached to another in a dependent or subordinate position. **2** Person associated with another in a subordinate capacity.

adjusted entries *E&F-Acc* Used to identify **accrual accounting** transactions that span more than one accounting period. They have at least one **balance sheet** account entry and one **income statement** account entry.

adjusted trail balance *E&F-Acc* Prepared by listing all accounts and their balances after the adjusting entries have been recorded and posted. This column follows the **adjustments** in the **worksheet**.

adjustment *Flm&Vid* Special payment for a difficult stunt, rather than **SAG scale**.

admin. *Mgt* **administration**.

administration *IntelProp, MusArts* Supervision for a fee (usu. a percentage of income) by a major music publisher of a songwriter's or smaller music publisher's financial and copyright matters re-garding one or more songs or an entire **catalog**. The administrator does not necessarily own a share of the copyright, although a **co-publisher** may administer another co-publisher's share.

administration (admin.) *Mgt* Management of a public or private institution or organization; still used by some academics to describe **arts management** of **nonprofits**.

administrator *Mgt* One who administers business or public affairs. EXECUTIVE. *Also see* **Managers**.

adorn *Aes&Creat* Lend beauty to. DECORATE.

ADR *Flm&Vid* **Automatic Dialogue Replacement** (looping) Process that replaces production audio with audio from a sound studio. This **post-production** technique is accomplished by replaying the scene over and over in the sound studio while the performer **lip-syncs** to the picture. Some reasons for replacing production audio might include uncontrollable set sound sources. <planes, weather, cars, or other loud noises>

adrenaline *ArtPerf* Hormone released into the bloodstream in response to the fear of **rejection**.

ADTI *Dnce* **American Dance Theater Institute** Ω

adulation *Crit&Eval* Excessive flattery or admiration.

adult contemporary *MusArts* Soft rock popular with grown-up **baby boomers**, emphasizing romantic songs and lush **orchestrations**. *Also see* **Rock Music Styles**.

adult entertainment *PA-Variety* Entertainment offered by media or venues containing or dealing with explicitly sexual material. <adult bookstores, adult movies, strip clubs> *Also see* **ecdysiast, lap dancer, table dancer**.

advance *Eco&Fin, Mgt* Negotiated sum of money given to an artist by an employer before the **engagement**, against future royalties, or other compensation. Advances are usu. considered nonreturnable if royalties or sales do not equal or exceed the amount advanced. CASH ADVANCE

advance *Flm&Vid* Monies paid by an exhibitor to a distributor prior to the opening of a film against film rentals due. Advance is refundable if the film does not generate enough **box-office** revenue to justify the advance film rental; i.e., the portion not earned by the distributor in film rental will be returned to the exhibitor.

advance *LitArts,TheatArts* Money paid to an author by a **producer** before a **production** opens, and deducted from the author's royalties as earned.

advance notice *Mktg* Preliminary publicity announcing the time and place of a new event.

advance person *Mktg* One who travels ahead to arrange scheduling, publicity, security, and other matters connected with a public appearance or theatrical production. *Origin* Traveling circuses who needed someone to scout suitable tent locations and water supply for the elephants. ADVANCE MAN

advance sale *Mgt* Total of ticket sales, either before the opening performance or for any single future performance.

advance story *Journ* Write, and hold, a story before the event; revise after the event. Saves time and allows for more **background**.

Advanced Certified Fund Raising Executive *Fnding* » **ACFRE**

Advanced Network Services *InfoMgt* **Online** information service owned by **America Online** (AOL) *Also see* **Online Information Services**

advancing the show *Mgt,PerfA&C* Preproduction confirmation of **venue** and equipment, usu. done by the **road manager**.

advert (Brit.) *Mktg* **advertisement**.

advertisement (ad, advert, advt.) *Mktg* **1** Notice of information about a product or service run in advertising, designed to attract public attention or **patronage**. **2** Any paid form of nonpersonal presentation and promotion of a product or organization by an identified sponsor.

advertising *EntreP* Presentation of a business idea through mass media for promotional purposes.

advertising *Mktg* Any paid (or **pro bono**) form of nonpersonal presentation and promotion of a product or organization by an identified sponsor.

advertising agency *Mgt, Mktg* **1** **Entity** responsible for creating and distributing advertising for its clients. **2** On behalf of their clients, ad agencies hire entertainment personalities for **endorsements**, cast performers and musicians for radio/television commercials and dramatic shows, and commission **writers-for-hire** to write commercials and dramatic scripts. *Also see* **commissioned work**. *Also see* **Agents and Agencies**.

Advertising Media *ColEntry, Mktg»* **direct mail, electronic media (cable, internet, online services, radio, television), out-of-home (outdoor) media, print media (newspapers, magazines**, etc.), **sky writing**.

advertising plan *EntreP* Portion of the overall marketing plan that includes the mix of advertising media, the relative allocation of resources to each medium, the message to be communicated, and the scheduling of the advertising.

Advertising Research Association (ARA) *Mktg»* **ARA**

advisory council *EntreP* Group that functions like a board of directors but acts only in an advisory capacity and has no voting rights.

advocacy *Law&Pol* Act of pleading or arguing in favor of something, such as a cause, an idea, or a policy. ACTIVE SUPPORT

advt. *Mktg* **advertisement**.

AE *Mgt, Mktg* **account executive**. Person who deals with a particular client of an advertising or a public relations agency. *Also see* **Agents and Agencies**.

AEA *ArtPerf, HR&LR,TheatArts* **Actors' Equity Association**. » **Equity**

AEMM *Genl* arts, entertainment, and media management.

aerialist *ArtPerf, PA-Variety* Acrobat who performs in the air, as on a trapeze or tightrope. *Also see* **high wire**.

AES *RecA&S, Sci&Tech* **Audio Engineering Society**. Advances the interests of engineers, technicians, administrators, educators, and the technology from the fields of broadcasting, film, and recording.

aesthete *also* **esthete** (Brit.) *Aes&Creat* **1** One skilled in judging the arts or works of art. **2 Aficionado** of art or works of art. **3** One whose pursuit and admiration of beauty is considered affected and excessive. **4 Effete snob** about the arts.

aesthetic *iMedia* Principles or rules with which to critique or develop in a medium.

aesthetic arrest *Aes&Creat* Feeling of sudden, overwhelming pleasure occasioned by some expression of beauty; manifested by. <goosebumps, chills-up-and-down-the-spine, **frisson**> *Also see* **empathic response**.

aesthetic distance *Aes&Creat, TheatArts* In the theatre, the maintaining of artistic illusion by sufficient physical separation. *Also see* **empathic response**.

aestheticism *Aes&Creat* **1** Devotion to and pursuit of the beautiful; sensitivity to artistic beauty and refined taste. **2** Doctrine that beauty is the basic principle from which all other principles, esp. moral ones, are derived. **3** Belief that art and artists have no obligation other than to strive for beauty. *Also see* **art for arts sake**.

Aesthetics *Aes&Creat* one of the three **Inner Forces** of **The Arts Dynamic**

aesthetics *also* **esthetics** (Brit.) *Aes&Creat* **1** Part of philosophy concerned with discovering the principles of art or works of art, and the means for judging art as art, *Origin* Term for the experience of the senses. **2** Theories and descriptions of the psychological response to beauty and artistic experiences. "As everyone knows, there are no aesthetic values 'a priori,' but there are values which will appear in due course in the coherence of the picture, in the relation between the will to create and the finished work." — **Jean Paul Sartre** *Also see* **existentialism, Inner Forces**.

AF *Rdio/TV, RecA&S* **audio frequency**

AFA *VisArts* **American Federation of Arts**

AFAIK *InfoMgt* As Far As I Know

affectation *Crit&Eval* **1** Artificial behavior. **2** Particular habit that gives a false impression. *Also see* **camp, prim**.

affective memory *Crit&Eval,TheatArts* In the **Stanislavski method**, the recollection of feelings that an actor himself has experienced and can use on the stage. *Also see* **Group Theater**.

affetuoso (Ital.) *MusArts* Play affectionately, with warmth. *Also see* **Music Directions**.

affidavit *Journ* Notarized statement made by a newsstand distributor to book and magazine publishers verifying the sale of a certain number of copies; substitute for actually returning unsold copies. *Also see* **full returns**.

affidavit *LegAsp* Written statement sworn to before an officer who has authority to administer an oath.

affidavit *Mktg, Rdio/TV* **Notarized** statement made by a radio or television station to **co-op advertisers** verifying the time that a commercial or commercial schedule was **aired**.

affiliate *Rdio/TV* Independently-owned broadcast station that contracts with a **network** to show the network's programming in certain periods.

affinity *Crit&Eval* **1** Natural attraction or feeling of kinship. **2 Inherent** similarity between persons or things.

affinity group *Mktg* Group of individuals who share a common interest, background, or goal. <alumni, club or association members, war veterans>

affirmative action *Cult&Soc, HR&LR* Policy or a program that seeks to redress past racial and gender discrimination through active measures to ensure equal opportunity in education and employment. *Also see* **backlash**.

affordance *iMedia* Perceivable possibilities for action *Also see* **affordance theory**.

affordance theory *iMedia* Elements in an environment are perceived as possibilities for action (ways in which they can be used or interacted with) Humans have evolved to view an environment in a manner that reveals how they can operate or survive within it. Theory developed by J.J. Gibson, 1979.

AFI *Flm&Vid* **American Film Institute**. Independent, **nonprofit** est. 1967 by the **NEA** to advance the art of film and television. The institute preserves films, operates an advanced conservatory for filmmakers, makes grants to new filmmakers, publishes film books, periodicals, and reference works, supports basic research, and operates a national film **repertory** exhibition program.

aficionado *Crit&Eval* Enthusiastic admirer, a **devotee**, a fan.

AFIM *Mktg, RecA&S* **Association for Independent Music**. "Dedicated to stimulating growth and generally promoting the independent recording industry." Est. 1972 as **National Association of Independent Record Distributors** (NAIRD); name changed 1997.

AFK *InfoMgt* Away From Keyboard

AFL-CIO *HR&LR* **American Federation of Labor and Congress of Industrial Organizations** (AFL-CIO) Federation of more than 100 national and international unions in the U.S., representing more than 60,000 local unions, which conduct day-to-day relationships with their members' employers. *Also see* **Guilds & Unions**.

AFM, AFofM *ArtPerf, HR&LR, MusArts* **American Federation of Musicians**. Labor union, affiliated with the **AFL-CIO**, that represents – approx. 130, 000 members in the U.S. and Canada – instrumentalists and orchestras, **leaders** and **contractors**; **arrangers** and **orchestrators, copyists** and orchestra librarians in the following fields of work. <**club dates, lounge** dates, and other **casual engagements**, recordings, radio, television, motion pictures, theatre, and symphonic and concert presentations> *Also see* **Guilds & Unions**.

AFM Phonograph Record Labor Agreement/Special Payments Fund Agreement *ArtPerf,HR&LR, RecA&S* Basic agreement with record companies that contains the basic contractual terms under which **AFM** members make **master recordings**.

African-American (adj), **African American** (n) *Cult&Soc* Relating to Americans of African ancestry or to their history or culture. AFRO-AMERICAN *Also see* **African-American, Black**. *Also see* **Racial Designations**.

Afro *Fashn* African-inspired hairstyles, clothes, and accessories introduced in the 1960s.

Afro-American *Cult&Soc* » **African-American**

Afro-Cuban jazz *MusArts* » **Latin jazz** *Also see* **Jazz Styles**.

after hours club *PA-Variety* Night club or bar, often patronized by entertainers after their gig, that remains open after legal closing time; possible source of income for local law enforcers.

afterimage *Crit&Eval* Visual image that persists after the visual stimulus causing it has ceased to act. PHOTOGENE

aftermarket *Flm&Vid, Mktg* Income source available for exploitation following first exposure of a tape or film.

aftermarket *Mktg* One of replacement parts <toner cartridges for printers>

afterpiece *PA-Variety, TheatArts* Short play – usu. a **pantomime**

or **farce**—that followed the main play on the evening's **bill**; common in England and America in the 18th and 19th centuries.

AFTN *Journ, Rdio/TV* **Associated Press Television News.**

AFTRA *ArtPerf, HR&LR,. Rdio/TV, RecA&S* **American Federation of Radio & Television Artists.** Labor union chartered by the **Four A's**, representing – approx. 78, 000 members in the U.S. – all performers. <actors, singers, announcers, narrators, sportscasters, and sound effect artists, except **exclusive musicians**, who work in radio, videotaped television, and recording> *Also see* **Guilds & Unions.**

AFTRA National Code of Fair Practice for Phonograph Recordings *HR&LR, RecA&S* Basic agreement with record companies that contains contractual terms under which **AFTRA** members make **master recordings.**

AGAC *ArtPerf, MusArts* **American Guild of Authors and Composers.** Name changed in 1986 to **Songwriters Guild of America.** » **SGA**

against type *Crit&Eval,TheatArts* Opposite of **typecast.**

agate line *Mktg, VA-Prntng* Unit of vertical measurement, 1/14 of an inch in depth by one column wide. Thus, 14 agate lines equal one **column inch.** <Classified ads are often set in agate type>

agcy. *Mgt, Mktg* **agency.**

age *Mktg, MusArts* "The bottom line in the **music business** is that it's always better to be young." — Shawn Colvin (1956-, folk sngr., sngwri.)

age stipple *Perf-MkUp* Liquid **latex** for wrinkling the skin.

agency (agcy.) *Mktg»* **advertising agency** *Also see* **Agents and Agencies.**

agency, agent *Mgt* » **talent agency, talent agent.**

agency clause *LegAsp, LitArts* Provides for the literary **agency** – for the complete life of the contract between author and agency – to receive payments from the publisher that are due the author. *Also see* **commission**, **Contracts.**

agency power *EntreP* Ability of any one partner to legally bind the other partners.

agent (agt.) *Genl* **1** An entity or person who acts or has the power or authority to act on behalf of a **principal. 2** Means by which something is done or caused:<an instrument> **3** Force or substance that causes a change. *Also see* **Agents and Agencies.**

agent (agt.) *HR&LR* Person acting for an arts organization or the artists' union regarding an alleged **unfair labor practice** subject to a court action. *Also see* **Agents and Agencies.**

agent *iMedia* **1** Self-contained unit that operates under a set of rules or instructions. **2 Networking**: In the client-server model, the part of the system that performs information preparation and exchange on behalf of a client or server. **3.** Automatic process which can communicate with other agents to perform a collective task.

agent (agt.) *LglAsp, Mgt* **1** Party who agrees to act on behalf of another. <an artist's agent> **2** Agent has authority to enter into contracts on behalf of her or his **principal.** *Also see* **Agents and Agencies, power of attorney.**

agent's duty of accountability *LegAsp* Agent must maintain an accurate accounting of all transactions undertaken on the **principal's** behalf.

agent's duty of loyalty *LegAsp* Agent owes the **principal** a duty not to act adversely to the interests of the principal. <Undisclosed **dual agency** or an undisclosed instance of **self-dealing** violates the agent's **duty of loyalty**>

agent's duty of notification *LegAsp* Agent's duty to notify the **principal** of information learned from a third party or other source important to the **principal.**

agent's duty of obedience *LegAsp* Duty that agents have to obey the lawful instructions of their **principal** during the performance of the agency.

agent's duty of performance *LegAsp* Agent's duty to a **principal** that includes (1) performing the lawful duties expressed in the contract and (2) meeting the standards of reasonable care, skill, and diligence implicit in all contracts.

agents/brokers *EntreP* Intermediaries that do not take title to the goods they distribute but process them.

Agents and Agencies *ColEntry, LegAsp,Mgt* » **account executive, advertising agency, agency, agent, apparent agency, artist representative, attorney-in-fact, exclusive agency con-**

tract, **express agency, fiduciary, fully disclosed agency, house agency, implied agency, power of attorney, professional agent, representative, special power of attorney, undisclosed agency.** *Also see* **News Agencies, Talent Agencies.**

aggrandize *Crit&Eval* **1** Make greater in power, influence, stature, or reputation. **2** Make appear greater. EXAGGERATE.

aggregate demand *EntreP* Relationship between the level of prices and the quantity of real GDP demanded.

aggregate supply *EntreP* Relationship between the level of prices and the quantity of output supplied.

aggressive pricing *Mktg* Push hard for the highest price. *Also see* **Pricing Strategies.**

AGI *ArtPerf, HR&LR, LitArts* **Authors Guild, Inc**. Organization that represents U.S. authors in their dealings with publishers. *Also see* **Anti-Censorship Organizations, Copyright-Related Organizations, Guilds & Unions.**

aging of accounts *E&F-Acc* Way to estimate bad debts by analyzing individual **accounts receivable** according to the length of time they have been due.

aging schedule *EntreP* Categorization of accounts receivable based on the length of time they have been outstanding.

agitato (Ital.) *MusArts* Play in an agitated, restless, and hurried manner. *Also see* **Music Directions.**

agitprop, agit prop *Crit&Eval* Political propaganda via drama, literature, music, or visual art.

agitprop *TheatArts* Term incorporating "agitation" and "**propaganda**" referring to a form of **political theater** that seeks to change the social order using performance to inform and to incite. Associated with workers' rights movements ca. 1930s.

agitprop *TheatArts* Term incorporating "agitation" and "**propaganda**" referring to a form of **political theater** that seeks to change the social order using performance to inform and to incite. Associated with workers' rights movements ca. 1930s.

AGMA *ArtPerf, HR&LR, MusArts* **American Guild of Musical Artists.** Labor union chartered by the **Four A's** that represents – approx 5, 000 members in the U.S. – concert and operatic vocal soloists, choristers, dancers, dance groups, actors, narrators, stage directors, and stage managers in professional grand opera, ballet, dance, concert, recital, and **oratorio**. *Also see* **Guilds & Unions.**

agt. *Mgt* **agent.**

AGVA *ArtPerf, HR&LR, PA-Variety* Labor union chartered by the **Four A's** that represents, in the U.S., singers, dancers, comedians, skaters, acrobats, jugglers, magicians, and other variety performers who work in night clubs, **cabarets**, **music halls**, stadiums, tents, (non-Broadway) theaters at: carnivals, circuses, fairs, private clubs, resorts, banquets, business meetings and conventions, cruise ships, and in similar **venues** where there is live entertainment. *Also see* **Guilds & Unions.**

AICPA *E&F-Acc* **American Institute of Certified Public Accountants**. Professional association of **CPAs** who are licensed by individual states and ensure the quality of the profession by not compromising ties with the companies they audit.

AIDA *Mktg* Acronym for a promotional sequence: attract *attention*, hold *interest*, arouse *desire*, generate buyer *action*.

aided recall interview *Flm&Vid, Mktg* Audience survey technique in which interviewees are given hints about a particular movie in an attempt to measure moviegoers' awareness levels of a movie currently in release or one soon to be released.

AIIP *InfoMgt* **Association of Independent Information Professionals**. Membership includes independent information professionals – and information brokers – involved in computer and manual organization, retrieval, and dissemination of information.

AIM *Mgt* **American Institute for Management** Research and education organization of executives interested in management efficiency and methods of appraising management performance. Conducts professional development, correspondence courses for members, and management audits.

air *MusArts* **1** Tune or melody **2** Soprano or **treble** part in a harmonized composition. **3** Solo with or without **accompaniment**.

air *Rdio/TV* Electronic broadcast media.

air brush *VisArts* Atomizer using compressed air to spray paint.

air check *Rdio/TV, RecA&S* Recording made of a live broadcast, usu. for **archival** purposes, although a number of air checks have been made into commercially released recordings. AIR SHOT *Also see* **remote broadcast**.

Air Mosaic *InfoMgt* **Online** information service owned by Spry, Inc. *Also see* **Online Information Services**.

air shot *Rdio/TV, RecA&S* » **air check**

airplay *Rdio/TV, RecA&S* Broadcasting of recordings by a radio station for which the recording musicians receive no compensation unless, as authors, they hold copyright to the music.

AL *SportsEnt* American League (baseball) Created in 1900 to compete against the **National League**. The two leagues sued for peace in 1903 and combined to create the **Major League of Baseball**.

ALA *LegAsp, LitArts* **American Library Association**. "Oldest [1876], largest and most influential library association in the world.... It has been a leader in defending intellectual freedom [Office for Intellectual Freedom] and promoting the highest quality library and information services." — >http://www.ala.org< *Also see* **Anti-Censorship Organizations**.

ALAI *ArtPerf, HR&LR, LitArts* **Authors League of America, Inc.** *Also see* **Copyright-Related Organizations**.

Alan Smithee *Flm&Vid* Fictitious director's name used by movie studios when the real director insists her/his name be removed.

alarm clock *InfoMgt* Accessory program that displays the current time and date, and can be set to function as an alarm.

alb *Fashn* Full length, long-sleeved **liturgical** robe with drawstring neckline or cowl hood worn by priests at Mass.

album *LitArts, MusArts, VisArts* Packaged collection of literary selections, musical compositions, or photographs.

album *RecA&S* 1 One or more 12-inch, 33-1/3 **rpm** records, or the equivalent, sold in a single package. 2 Recording of different musical pieces.

Album-Oriented Rock (AOR) *MusArts,. Rdio/TV, RecA&S* » **AOR**

aleatory techniques *Flm&Vid* Techniques of filmmaking that depend on the element of chance. Images are not planned out in advance, but are composed on the spot by the camera operator. Usually employed in documentaries.

alençon lace (alon-sahn, Fr.) *Fashn* Fine homemade or machine-made needlepoint lace with solid designs on sheer net ground outline. *Origin* Alençon, France, ca. 1665.

alert box *iMedia, InfoMgt* Box that appears on the screen to give a warning or error message.

Alexa *iMedia* Software developed in 1996 Categorizes and relates online documents based on access and actions of Web users. Created by Brewster Kahle.

algorithm *iMedia* Formula or detailed series of actions that will accomplish a task. Named for an Iranian mathematician, Mohammed Ibn-Musa Al-Khowarizmi.

alias *iMedia* 1 Text string (usu. short and easy to remember) translated into another name or string (usu. long and/or difficult to remember or type) 2 Network: One of several alternative hostnames with the same Internet address.

alias *InfoMgt* Representative of the original of a document, program, or disk that can be used as the original. <Alias of a "Bibliography" document might be a list of all the references pertaining to a particular topic>

aliasing *iMedia* 1 Graphics: jagged appearance of angled lines in an image or text; often an unintended effect of compression. 2 Video: unintended effect such as pulsing, flickering, etc., as a result of sampling frequencies of an image too low. 3 Audio: Unwanted frequencies resulting from the sampling of a signal a frequency higher than half the sampling rate.

aliasing effects *iMedia* Artifacts resulting from aliasing. » **aliasing**

Algonguin Round Table *Crit&Eval* Table in the dining room of the Algonguin Hotel (NYC) where assorted wits would gather in the 1930s and 40s to dine, drink, and exchange **barbs** and **badinage**. <Robert Benchley (1889-1945, humorist, act., critic), **Dorothy Parker**, Edna Ferber (» *Showboat*), Robert Sherwood (1896-1955, **Pulitzer**-plywri.), Alexander Woolcott (1887-1943, drama critic, journ.)>

alienation effect *TheatArts* Refers to a stage technique developed by **Bertolt Brecht** in the 1920s and '30s for **estranging** the action of the play. By making the characters and their actions seem remarkable, alien or unusual, Brecht encouraged the audi-

ence to question the social realities that produced such events, the political and ideological background of the drama and of its stage production. *Origin* "Verfremdugseffekt" in German meaning "distancing effect."

alignment *iMedia, Journ* 1 As a metric, alignment measures the degree to which each part or component supports the goals and objectives of an interactive media product. 2 In team work, alignment is "that which provides the basis for organizing elements in optimal positions relative to achieving goals." — Jim and Michele McCarthy

alignment *Journ, VA-Prntng* Process of lining up visual elements on a page to create eye-pleasing composition. *Also see* **registration**.

alla breve *MusArts* Play twice as fast as the notation signifies. <2/2 instead of 4/4> *Also see* **Music Directions**.

allegory *LitArts* Literary device in which characters and events stand for abstract ideas, principles, or forces, so that the literal sense suggests a parallel, deeper symbolic sense. <John Bunyan's (1628-88, Eng. preacher, fictwri.) *Pilgrim's Progress* and Herman Melville's (1819-91, fictwri.) *Moby Dick* are allegories>

allegory *TheatArts* Dramatic technique that uses actual characters, places, and actions to represent more abstract political, moral, or religious ideas.

allegory *VisArts* Pictorial device in which characters and events stand for abstract ideas, principles, or forces, so that the literal sense has or suggests a parallel, deeper symbolic sense. <Marcel Duchamp's (Marsel Dooshammp, 1887-1968, Fr. pntr.) *Also see* **Jasper John's** works>

allegretto (Ital.) *MusArts* Play in a moderately quick tempo, slightly slower than **allegro** but faster than **andante**. *Also see* **Music Directions**.

allegro *Dnce* Sequence of ballet steps in fast tempo, performed in **class** to develop speed and clarity of execution.

allegro (allo) (Ital. for "lively") *MusArts* Play in a quick, lively tempo, faster than **allegretto** but slower than **presto**. *Also see* **Music Directions**.

allemande (alley-mond, Fr. for "German female") *Dnce* Moderately slow dance of Ger. origin. *Also see* **Dances**.

Allen, Woody (1935-, film/stage dir.-prod., scrnwrtr., act., auth., cl) *ArtPerf, Flm&Vid, Journ, LitArts, Mgt, MusArts* Unique comic actor and prolific filmmaker. <*Annie Hall* (1977, two **Oscars**)> *Also see* **immortality**.

Alliance for Public Technology (APT) *InfoMgt, Sci&Tech* » **APT**

Alliance of Artists and Recording Companies (AARC) *RecA&S* » **AARC**

Alliance of Motion Picture and Television Producers *Flm&Vid, HR&LR* Bargaining group representing film and TV studios.

Alliance of Resident Theatres/New York (ART/NY) *Mgt, TheatArts* » **ART/NY**.

alliteration *LitArts* Repetition of the same **consonant** sounds or of different vowel sounds at the beginning of words or in stressed syllables.

allo *MusArts* **allegro**

allowance *E&F-Acc, Mktg* 1 Price reduction granted in exchange for used merchandise. <The dealer offered an allowance on any old computer> 2 Consideration for unusual circumstances. <an allowance for breakage, bad weather, armed conflict> 3 Money, given at regular intervals or for a specific purpose. <a travel allowance> 4 Amount allowed or granted. *Also see* **returns**.

allowance for doubtful accounts *E&F-Acc* **Contra** account, related to **accounts receivable** that holds the estimated amount of collection losses. UNCOLLECTIBLE ACCOUNTS

allusion *LitArts* Reference to a familiar person or event, often from literature.

alpha channel *iMedia* One of four channels in 32-bit RGB images; allows fading and other types of visual effects by describing how pixels should be blended if they overlap each other.

alpha value *iMedia* Opacity amount of a **pixel** or object.

alphanumeric interface *iMedia* » **command line interface**

Alta Vista *InfoMgt* Web site providing access to Internet. *Also see* **search engine, portals**.

altering of songs *MusArts* Author of a song may grant the publisher the right to make changes in a song if, in its good-faith judgment, such changes are justified for the successful promotion of the song.

alternate (alt.)*TheatArts* One of two actors who alternate in a specific role. *Also see* **understudy**.

alternating cast *TheatArts* Cast whose members interchange parts with one another or alternates with other casts.

alternative culture *Cult&Soc* One that espouses or reflects values different from those of the **mainstream** culture.

alternative media *Crit&Eval, InfoMgt, Journ* Any medium, any place, any time outside of the networks and the **mainstream** press. <talk radio and TV **talk shows**, online bulletin boards and forums. Town meetings and church socials, parades and celebrations, jamborees and golf outings. Banquets and Dinners, Breakfasts and Luncheons, Coffees and Teas, Barbecues, Clam Bakes, and Fish Fries. American Legion, DAR, Elks, Lions, Moose, Odd Fellows, Rotary, and VFW. Chambers of commerce, conferences, conventions, seminars, and trade shows. And straight-out Fund Raisers> *Also see* **demagogue**.

alternative music *MusArts, RecA&S* 1 Music with style and **mode** different from that of the current hits. 2 Recordings played on college radio stations and other relatively **hype**-free **broadcast media**. Some of these recordings **crossover** and become hits on commercial radio and lose their alternative value.

alternative newspaper *Journ* Newspaper that espouses or reflects values different from those of the established press.

alternative title *IntelProp, LitArts* Title of a particular work other than the original copyrighted title. PREVIOUS TITLE

altissimo playing *MusArts* Dramatic effect of playing valve and slide instruments in extremely high **register**.

alto (a) *MusArts* 1 Woman's vocal range below soprano. 2 Vocal or instrumental part written for a voice or an instrument in the range between soprano and tenor. 3 **countertenor**.

alto (a.) *MusInstr* Instrument that sounds in the range between soprano and tenor. <alto saxophone, alto flute, alto recorder> *Also see* **Musical Instrument Families**.

alto clef *MusArts* » **C clef**

AM *Rdio/TV* **amplitude modulation**. AM radio broadcast 535-1,605 **kilohertz**. Signal **reception** occurs either via **ground waves** that follow the curvature of the earth or via sky waves reflected off the **ionosphere** back to earth. *Also see* **FM**.

AMA *Mgt* **American Management Association** Provides educational forums worldwide to teach members and their colleagues about superior, practical business skills and explores best practices of world-class organizations through interaction with each other and expert faculty practitioners.

amalgamation *Mgt* Consolidation or merger, as of several corporations.

amateur *Crit&Eval* Non-professional, typically, therefore, unpaid participant in an activity commonly served by those who earn their living by engaging in it. *Origin* From the Latin word for "love," i.e., an amateur is one who engages in an activity from love of the activity. *Also see* **dabbler, dilettante, non-professional, tyro**.

amateur *Flm&Vid, PerfA&C* Performer or crew member who is not paid and/or is not union affiliated.

ambiance *also* **ambience** *RecA&S* 1 Room acoustics or natural **reverberation**. 2 Recording session sound environment.

ambient *MusArts, RecA&S* Heavy European drum-and-bass beat. *Also see* **techno**. TRANS

ambient sound *BcstJourn* Recorded sound not part of an interview. *Also:* NAT sound (for natural sound), wild sound, background, or BG sound.

ambient sound *Flm&Vid* Natural background audio heard on location or in a studio without dialogue or other production-created sound. Film editor uses **ambient** sound to fill spaces between dialogue or effects with sound from that same area, thus creating a seamless audio track.

ambition *ArtPerf* Ruthless ambition is one of the three basic characteristics of a successful Artist/Performer. *Also see* **EAT+D²**.

ambivalence *Crit&Eval* 1 Coexistence of opposing attitudes or feelings, such as love and hate, toward a person, an object, or an idea. 2 Uncertainty or indecisiveness as to which course to follow.

AMC *MusArts* » **American Music Center**

AMC *MusArts, MusInstr* **American Music Conference**, public

relations wing of **NAMM**, "dedicated to promoting the value of music, music making, and music education to the general public." — >http://www.amc-music.com<

America Online (AOL) *InfoMgt* » **AOL** *Also see* **Online Information Services, portals**.

America's Sweetheart *Flm&Vid* Mary Pickford (1893-1979, Canadian-born act., prod.; co-founded **United Artists** in 1919)

American Academy of Arts and Letters (AAAL) *Genl* » **AAAL**

American Academy of Dramatic Art (AADA) *TheatArts* Est. 1884, NYC, as first conservatory for actors in the English-speaking world, "to provide a broad and practical education to those desiring to make acting their profession."

American Arbitration Association (AAA) *HR&LR, Mgt* Members are businesses, labor unions, trade and educational associations, law firms, arbitrators, and interested individuals dedicated to the resolution of disputes of all kinds through the use of **arbitration, mediation**, democratic elections, and other voluntary methods. Provides administrative services for arbitrating, mediating, or negotiating disputes and impartial administration of elections.

American art *Cult&Soc, VisArts* » **Armory Show**

American Arts Alliance *Dnce, MusArts, TheatArts, Mgt, VisArts* Principal advocate for nonprofit, professional arts organizations.

American Basketball League (ABL) *SportsEnt* » **ABL**

American Association of Advertising Agencies *Mktg* » **AAAA**

American Association of Fund Raising Counsel (AAFRC) *Fnding* » **AAFRC**

American Association of Museum Directors (AAMD) *VisArts* » **AAMD**

American Ballet Theatre (ABT) *Dnce* » **ABT**

American Bar Association (ABA) *LegAsp* » **ABA**

American Booksellers Association (ABA) *LitArts* » **ABA**

American Broadcasting Cos. (ABC) *Rdio/TV* » **ABC**

American Business Press (ABP) *Journ* » **ABP**

American Choral Directors Association (ACDA) *MusArts* » **ACDA**

American Civil Liberties Union (ACLU) *Law&Pol, LegAsp* » **ACLU**

American Composers Alliance *MusArts* Membership organization for 300+ American composers of **concert music**.

American Conservatory Theatre (ACT) *TheatArts* » **ACT**

American Council of the Arts (ACA) *Mgt* » **ACA**

American Craft Council (ACC) *Genl* » **ACC**

American Dance Theater Institute (ADTI) *Dnce* » **ADTI**

American Federation of Arts (AFA) *VisArts* Museum service association founded in 1909 to funnel art to "the **hinterlands**."

American Federation of Labor and Congress of Industrial Organizations (AFL-CIO) *HR&LR* » **AFL-CIO**

American Federation of Musicians (AFM *also* AFofM) *ArtPerf, HR&LR, MusArts* » **AFM**

American Federation of Television & Radio Artists (AFTRA) *ArtPerf, HR&LR,. Rdio/TV* » **AFTRA**

American Film Institute (AFI) *Flm&Vid* » **AFI**

American Guild of Musical Artists (AGMA) *ArtPerf, HR&LR, MusArts* » **AGMA**

American Guild of Variety Artists (AGVA) *ArtPerf, HR&LR, PA-Variety* » **AGVA** *Also see* **Four A's.**

American Institute for Management (AIM) *Mgt* » **AIM**

American Institute of Certified Public Accountants (AICPA) *Eco&Fin-Acc* » **AICPA**

American Library Association (ALA) *LegAsp, LitArts* » **ALA**

American Management Association (AMA) *Mgt* » **AMA**

American Music Center *MusArts* NYC nonprofit provides its approx. 2, 500 musician members with access to classical and jazz composer scores; provides music organizations with a data base of classical and jazz composers and their works.

American Music Conference *MusArts, MusInstr* » **AMC**

American National Theatre and Academy (ANTA) *TheatArts* » **ANTA**

American Option *EntreP* Is a right, to buy or sell some asset over some defined period of time in the future for a price that is agreed upon now.

American Research Bureau (ARB) *Mktg, Rdio/TV* » **ARB**

American Retail Federation (ARF) *Mktg* » **ARF**

American Society for Information Science (ASIS) *InfoMgt* Somewhat similar membership to **SLA's**, but its members tend to be concerned more with the theory and science of information and are somewhat more technically oriented.

American Society of Association Executives (ASAE) *Mgt* » **ASAE**

American Society of Cinematographers (ASC) *Flm&Vid* » **ASC**

American Society of Composers, Authors, and Publishers (ASCAP) *IntelProp, MusArts* » **ASCAP**

American Society of Journalists and Authors (ASJA) *Journ, Lit* » **ASJA**

American Society of Magazine Editors (ASME) *Journ* » **ASME**

American Society of Music Arrangers and Composers (AS-MAC) *MusArts* » **ASMAC**

American Standard Association (ASA) *Flm&Vid* » **ASA**

American Standard Code for Information Interchange (ASCII) *InfoMgt* » **ASCII**

American Stock Exchange (AMEX *also* ASE) *Eco&Fin* » **AMEX**

American Symphony Orchestra League (ASOL) *MusArts* » **ASOL**

American Television and Radio Commercials Festival *Mktg, Rdio/TV* » **Clio Award**

American Women in Radio and Television (AWRT) *Rdio/TV* » **AWRT**

American-Type paintings *VisArts* » **action painting**

AMEX *also* **ASE** *Eco&Fin* **American Stock Exchange** (AMEX *also* ASE) Located in the Wall Street area of Manhattan, this stock exchange is second in volume only to the **NYSE**. Mostly small-to medium companies, as well as many oil and gas companies are traded on the AMEX. Sometimes referred to as the **Curb Exchange** although the name was changed in 1921 *Also see* **NASDAQ**.

AMG *ArtPerf, Mgt* **Artists Management Group** Formed in late 1998 by Michael Ovitz (1946-, talent agent, arts mgr.), former head of **CAA**.

AMOA *MusArts, RecA&S* **Amusement and Music Operators Association** Trade organization that represents fairs, and the coin-operated music and amusement industry.

amoral *Ethcs&Phil* Apart from moral concerns; particularly applicable in cases where moral judgment is warranted, but none is made, sought out, or regarded as relevant if encountered. "[The artist] is completely amoral in that he will rob, borrow, beg, or steal from anybody and everybody to get the work done." — **William Faulkner**

amorphous *Crit&Eval* Lacking definite form. SHAPELESS

amortization *EntreP* Reduction of the loan balance by applying each month principal payment is amortization.

amortization of negative costs *E&F-Acc, Flm&Vid* Accounting procedure by which the cost of making the **negative** is charged against film revenue.

Amos and Andy *Cult&Soc, Rdio/TV* Half-hour situational comedy on prime time network radio in the 1930s and TV in the 1950s about two ordinary Negro (so then called) men. The performers who portrayed them on radio were white, black on TV. Its large and faithful radio audience reflected the need for free, easy-to-relate-to entertainment in the midst of the **Great Depression**. The TV series ran into accusations of racial **stereotyping**.

amp, amp. *MusInstr, RecA&S* » **amplifier**

AMPAS *Flm&Vid* » **Academy of Motion Pictures Arts & Sciences**. *Also see* **Academy Awards**.

amphitheater *PerfA&C* Auditorium, outdoors or indoors, circular, semicircular or **elliptical** in shape, in which a central arena is more or less surrounded by rising banks of seats. *Also see* **Stages**.

amplification *Crit&Eval* 1 Act or result of amplifying, enlarging, or extending. 2 Addition to or an expansion of a statement or idea.

amplification *Rdio/TV, RecA&S, Sci&Tech* Process of increasing the magnitude of **voltage**, power, or current, without altering any other quality. *Also see* **gain**.

amplifier (amp *also* amp.) *MusInstr, RecA&S* **Analog** or **digital** device, that produces **amplification** of an electrical signal. <Guitar amplifier>

amplitude *Sci&Tech* Maximum absolute value reached by a **volt**-age or current **waveform**.

amplitude modulation (AM) *Rdio/TV, Sci&Tech* » **AM** *Also see* **FM**.

Amusement and Music Operators Association (AMOA) *MusArts, PA-Variety, RecA&S* » **AMOA**

amusement park *PA-Variety* Commercially operated enterprise that offers rides, games, and other forms of entertainment. *Also see* **theme park**.

ANA *Mktg* Association of National Advertisers Ω

anachronism *Crit&Eval* One as existing or something as happening in other than the chronological, proper, or historical order.

anal. *Crit&Eval* **analysis, analytic**

analog *Rdio/TV, RecA&S* Electronic audio or video signals that are sent, received, and stored in the form of varying **voltage**s. Analog signals, unlike **digital** signals, **degrade** with each copy or **generation**.

analog *Flm&Vid* Any record whereby what is recorded is analogous to the source but in a different form. Analog signals in some way resemble the nature of what caused them; **digital** signals, which encode all information in a number code, need bear no such relationship. Most film equipment is **analog**, but digital audio and video devices are now used in film production and **postproduction**.

analog computer *also* **analogue computer** *iMedia, InfoMgt* Computer in which numerical data are represented by measurable physical variables. <electrical signals> *Also see* **digital**.

analog transmission *InfoMgt* Voice or data transmitted in the form of a continuous electrical signal.

analogous colors *iMedia* Colors similar and next to each other on a color wheel.

analogy *Crit&Eval* Comparison of two dissimilar things by means of two other dissimilar things. Thus the establishment of a similar relationship. <Evening is to day as old age is to life>

analysis (anal.) *Crit&Eval* Separation of an intellectual or substantial whole into its constituent parts for individual study.

analysis of tragedy *Crit&Eval* Central terms used by **Aristotle** in his treatise *The Poetics*, and by extension used by later critics and commentators in the analysis of other forms of drama, poetry, stories, and novels. <**plot**, the line of action; **character**, the moral disposition of each of the persons in the story; **thought**, the reasoning employed by the characters; **diction**, the specific characteristics of the language of any character; **melody**, the music which accompanies the songs of the drama; and **spectacle**, the staging and costuming of the drama.

analytic (anal.) *Crit&Eval* Reasoning or acting from a perception of the parts and interrelations of a subject. <Some musicians prefer a more analytic performance focused on the form and ideas of music>

anamorphic lens *Flm&Vid* Camera lens able to produce, or designate different optical magnification along mutually perpendicular radii. <CinemaScope> Invented by Henri Chretien (1879-1956, Fr. optical sci.) for which he received a 1954 **Oscar**.

anathema *Ethcs&Phil* 1 Formal ecclesiastical ban, curse, or excommunication. CURSE.

ancillary *Crit&Eval* Subordinate. <For **Picasso**, sculpture was never more than ancillary to his painting> AUXILIARY

and *MusArts* » **andante**

andante (and) (Ital.) *MusArts* Play in a moderately slow tempo ("walking" speed) slower than **allegretto** but faster than **adagio**. *Also see* **Music Directions**.

Anderson, Marian (1899-1993, contralto) *ArtPerf, MusArts* Began her concert career in 1924 mainly in Europe, American classical music careers were not then open to Negro performers. In 1939, she was banned by Daughters of the American Revolution (DAR) from singing in Constitution Hall in Wash., DC. The First Lady, Eleanor Roosevelt, resigned from the DAR in protest and arranged for Ms. Anderson to sing at the Lincoln Memorial instead. In 1955, she belatedly debuted at the **Met**. "If the planet Earth could speak, I think it would sound like **Marian Anderson**." — Jessye Norman (1945-, dramatic soprano) *Also see* **endow**.

androgynous (an-drahdg-ee-nuss) *Cult&Soc, Fashn* Being neither distinguishably masculine nor feminine, as in dress, appearance, or behavior. *Also see* **cross dressing, transvestite, unisex**.

angels *Eco&Fin, EntreP, Mgt* Informal investors in high risk ventures such as a theatrical production. "They're called 'angels' because they're in heaven until the reviews come out." — **Barbra Streisand** *Also see* **backer**.

angle of view *iMedia* Area of a scene that a lens covers or sees. It is determined by the focal length of the lens.

angst *Crit&Eval* Feeling of anxiety.

anim *MusArts* animato

anim. *Flm&Vid* animation, animator.

animal handler *Flm&Vid* One who is responsible for the care and handling of animals in a movie production.

animation *BcstJourn* Series or graphic screen pages played in succession to give the impression of sequential movement.

animato (anim) (Ital.) *MusArts* Play with animation, in a lively manner.

animator (anim.) *ArtPerf, Flm&Vid, VisArts* Artist or a technician, who designs, develops, or produces an animated **cartoon**.

animé (animay) *Rdio/TV, VisArts* **Risqué** and warlike Japanese animation.

annals *LitArts* Periodical journal in which the records and reports of a **learned** field are compiled.

Annie Oakley *Mktg, PA-Variety* Complimentary ticket. *Origin* Hole-punched free passes were thought to resemble cards used as targets by the female sharpshooter featured with Buffalo Bill's (William Frederick Cody, 1846-1917, frontier scout and showman) *Wild West Show*. COMP

annotate *LitArts* Provide a literary work with critical commentary or explanatory notes. *Also see* **gloss**.

announcer *Rdio/TV* **Voice-over** or **on camera** person who introduces and closes a radio or TV program, and gives informational and transitional announcements during the broadcast.

annual billing *Mktg* Amount invoiced buyers of advertising for a calendar year by media companies.

annual fund *Fnding* Any organized effort by a **nonprofit** institution or program to secure gifts on an annual basis.

annual improvement factor *HR&LR* Annual wage increase, fixed in advance as to the amount, and granted on the basis that the employees are entitled to share in the long-term increase in the profits of the business or organization.

annual report *Fnding* "Voluntary" report by a foundation or corporation that provides financial data and descriptions of grant-making activities. Annual reports vary in format from simple typewritten documents listing the year's grants to detailed publications that provide substantial information about the grantmaking program.

annuity *EntreP* Stream of payments paid or received usually over a period of 12 months.

annuity due *EntreP* Payments which are made or received at the beginning of each time period.

anomaly *Crit&Eval* **1** Deviation from the normal form or rule. **2** Something peculiar, irregular, abnormal, or difficult to classify.

anonymous (anon.) *Genl* Having an unknown or unacknowledged name.

anonymous work *IntelProp* Work on the copies or **phonorecords** of which no natural person is identified as author. *Also see* **Copyright Act of 1976** PSEUDONYMOUS WORK

ANTA *TheatArts* **American National Theatre and Academy**, a privately supported, Congressionally chartered organization founded in 1935 for the encouragement of "the best in the theatre, both professional and nonprofessional."

antagonist *LitArts* **Principal** character in opposition to the **protagonist** or hero of a narrative or drama.

antagonist *TheatArts* Character of force in opposition to the **protagonist** or **hero**.

antebellum *Cult&Soc* Relating to the period before a war, esp. the U.S. Civil War. *Also see* **postbellum**.

antecedent factor *EntreP* Combination of variables in an individual's background that influences the decision to start a venture.

anthem *MusArts* **1** Modern rock-style ballad **2** Hymn of praise or loyalty. **3** Sacred composition set to words from the Bible.

anthology *LitArts* Collection of literary pieces <**excerpts**, poems, short stories, plays>

anthropomorphic conflict token *iMedia* Recognizable human form as a game piece. Using anthropomorphic tokens "adds an emotional and humanizing symbolic context to the game experi-

ence"— David Gerding

anthropomorphism *LitArts* **Attribution** of human motivation, characteristics, or behavior to inanimate objects, animals, or natural **phenomena**.

anti-aliasin *iMedia* **1** Graphics: Smoothing the edges of images that have been **pixel**ized; diagonal edges may appear choppy and anti-aliasing smoothes their appearance. **2** Audio: filter used to avoid undersampling.

anti-apography *InfoMgt, Sci&Tech* Technology of utilizing papers and inks to render documents uncopyable.

anti-art *VisArts* Art, specifically **Dada**, that rejects traditional art forms and theories. <**Marcel Duchamp's** *The Fountain* at the **Indépendent** exhibition in Paris (1916)>

Anti-Censorship Organizations *ColEntry, Law&Pol, LegAsp* <**ABA** (Booksellers), **ACLU, AGI, ALA** (Office for Intellectual Freedom), **ALAI, ASJA, Media Coalition, MPAA, NCAC, VS-DA**>

anti-intellectual *Crit&Eval* Opposed or hostile to intellectuals or intellectual views.

anticlimax *LitArts* Sudden descent in speaking or writing from the impressive or significant to the ludicrous or inconsequential, or an instance of it.

anticlimax *TheatArts* Action which lowers the **tension**, usu. by not living up to the expectations it is intended to satisfy. When applied to the play as a whole, it usu. indicates a **climax** that fails to satisfy an audience: when applied to smaller segments of the play, it often indicates a basic method of encouraging humor.

antihero *LitArts* One lacking in the heroic qualities. <courage, idealism, and honesty>

antiquities *Genl* Object or a **relic** dating from ancient times.

antistrophe (Greek) *Genl* Following, responsive movement(s) of a work of art. *Also see* **strophe** .

antistrophe (Greek) *LitArts* Second stanza, and those like it, in a poem consisting of alternating stanzas in contrasting metric form. *Also see* **strophe** .

antistrophe (Greek) *TheatArts* Choral movement in classical Greek drama following and in the same meter as the **strophe**, sung while the chorus moves in the opposite direction from that of the **strophe**.

antithesis *Crit&Eval* **1** Proposition that opposes another proposition (an "anti-thesis"); important term in **Hegel's** delineation of the **dialectic** of history, in which a thesis is said to call into existence its opposing **thesis** (or, its antithesis), and the resulting conflict leads to a resolving **synthesis**. **2** Direct or exact opposite.

antithesis *LitArts* Rhetorical figure in which sharply opposing ideas are expressed within a balanced grammatical structure.

antitrust laws *Law&Pol* Federal and state laws designed to protect trade and commerce from monopolistic practices. *Also see* **Clayton Act, Robinson-Patman Act, Sherman Antitrust Act.**

AOL *InfoMgt* America Online Major online information service. *Also see* **Online Information Services.**

AOP *InfoMgt* Association of Online Professionals

AOR *Rdio/TV, RecA&S* **Album-Oriented Rock** formatted radio stations.

AP Associated Press *Journ* **Nonprofit** cooperative news agency founded 1948, serves 1,400 newspapers and 6,000 broadcast members in U.S.; printed and broadcast abroad by 8,500 subscribers in 112 countries (as of 1987) *Also see* **News Agencies.**

APAP *Mgt, PerfA&C* Association of Performing Arts Presenters (formerly **ACUCAA**) National arts service organization whose members are mainly comprised of individuals and institutional presenters, publishes *Inside Performance* and *The Bulletin,* both quarterly.

APATE *ArtPerf, HR&LR* **Asociación Puertorriqueña de Artistas e Tecnicos del Espectaculo**. Labor union chartered by the **Four A's**, represents Puerto Rican actors in Puerto Rico. *Also see* **Guilds & Unions.**

ape *Crit&Eval* **mimic**, imitator.

ape *TheatArts* To steal **lines** or **business** belonging to another actor.

APL *InfoMgt* **A Programming Language**

apocryphal *Crit&Eval* Of questionable authorship or **authenticity**. ERRONEOUS, FICTITIOUS

Apollo Theater *PA-Variety* Harlem's first-line vaudeville house and **showcase** for new talent in the 1930s and 1940s. <James Brown (1928-, r&b bndldr., sngr., sngwri), Ella Fitzgerald (a.k.a Ella, 1918-96, pop-jazz sngr.) Billie Holiday (*aka* "Lady Day," Eleanora McKay Holiday, 1915-59, jazz sngr.), **Sarah Vaughan**> Reorganized in the 1980s as a **nonprofit**.

apotheosis *Crit&Eval* 1 Exaltation to divine rank or stature; deification. 2 Exalted or glorified example.

app. *HR&LR* apprentice

Appalachia *Cult&Soc* Region of the eastern U.S. inc. the Appalachian Mountains. <Kentucky, Tennessee, West Virginia> Fertile area for Anglo-American **folk music**.

apparel *Fashn* Clothing, esp. outer garments. *Also see* **attire**.

apparent agency *LegAsp* Agency that arises when a **principal** creates the appearance of an agency that does not actually exist. *Also see* **Agents and Agencies**.

apparent authority *Mgt* Impression that a person may have the authority to make a commitment for her or his company, when, actually, the person must receive approval from a higher authority in the company.

appearance of impropriety *Ethcs&Phil* Standard of judging actions, or of maintaining rules that prohibit certain actions, not on the basis of whether these actions are truly ethically wrong (improper), but solely on the basis that others (e.g. "the public") may perceive as them improper. <"The most formal Appearance of Virtue, when it is only an Appearance, may perhaps, in very abstracted Considerations, seem to be rather less commendable than Virtue itself without this Formality; but it will, however, be always more commended." — Henry Fielding (1707-1754; author, *Tom Jones*)>

applause *ArtPerf, Crit&Eval* Approval expressed by the clapping of hands. Mother's milk for performers. *Also see* **EAT+D**[2], **love**, **rejection**.

apple boxes *Flm&Vid* Wooden boxes in three basic sizes – full, half, and quarter – used to elevate actors, furniture, lights, etc.

applets *InfoMgt* Mall program that performs a simple task.

application *InfoMgt* Task to be performed by a **computer program** or system. <**database**, graphic design, spreadsheet, word processing>

application software *EntreP* Programs that allow users to perform specific tasks on a computer.

appliqué (app-lee-kay, Fr. for "apply") *Fashn* Decoration or ornament, in needlework, made by cutting pieces of one material and applying them to the surface of another.

appoggiatura (Ital.) *MusArts* **Embellishing** note, usu. one step above or below the note it precedes, indicated by a small note or special sign. *Also see* **grace note**.

appointment viewing *BcstMedia, Mktg* Television program that viewers make a point of seeing.

appreciation *Eco&Fin, EntreP* Increase in the value of assets or currencies.

apprentice *HR&LR* 1 One bound by legal agreement to work for another for a specific amount of time in return for instruction in a trade, an art, or a business. 2 One who is learning a trade or occupation, esp. as a member of a labor union, BEGINNER, LEARNER *Also see* **membership candidate**.

approach *TheatArts* Movement towards another actor

appropriation *LegAsp* 1 Use of a person's name or **likeness** for commercial purposes without consent. 2 Invasion of privacy.

appropriationist art *VisArts* Redo of an original painting with some of the new artist's concepts added and signed.

Approved Production Contract for Musical Plays *HR&LR, LegAsp, MusArts* Contract for the production of a Broadway **musical** signed by the producer, **bookwriter**, composer, and lyricist, and certified by a representative of the **Dramatists Guild, Inc.** (DGI)

après-ski (appray-skee) *Fashn* Fashionable attire for after skiing.

apron *PerfA&C* Flat extension of the stage floor in front of the front curtain or the **front curtain line**.

APT *InfoMgt, Sci&Tech* **Alliance for Public Technology**. Washington, DC-based **nonprofit** coalition of public interest groups and individuals whose goal is to foster access to affordable, usable information and communication services and technology.

aptitude *Crit&Eval* An **inherent** ability to learn or do something. GIFT, SKILL, TALENT

ARA *Mktg* **Advertising Research Association** Helps to set standards for measuring **print media** and **broadcast media**.

arabesque *Crit&Eval* Intricate or elaborate pattern or design.

arabesque *Dnce* Ballet position in which the dancer raises one leg, with the knee straight, directly behind the body.

arabesque *MusArts* 1 Extended vocal solo in an opera or **oratorio**. 2 Short, whimsical composition for the piano featuring **embellished** passages.

arabesque *VisArts* Complex, **ornate** design of intertwined floral, foliate, and geometric figures.

ARB *Rdio/TV, Mktg,* **American Research Bureau**, owner of the **Arbitron** reports.

arbitrary symbol *iMedia* Representation that must be learned, having no perceptual basis.

arbitration *HR&LR* Process by which disputing parties submit their differences to the judgment of an impartial person or group selected by mutual consent or statutory provision. <Agreements of **AFTRA** and **SAG** stipulate that controversies arising out of their contracts are to be submitted to arbitration under the prevailing rules of the **American Arbitration Association**> *Also see* **mediation**.

arbitration clause *HR&LR, LegAsp* Contract provision that calls for the parties in conflict to submit their differences to an impartial arbiter for a binding determination. *Also see* **arbitration**, **Contracts**.

Arbitron *Mktg, Rdio/TV* 1 Arbitron Company, one of the two largest suppliers of radio and television ratings research. 2 Electronic device attached to a home television set to inform researcher what stations are turned on at a particular time. *Also see* **Birch/Scarborough**, **Nielsen Media Research**.

arbor *PerfA&C* Rectangular steel carriage that holds the **counterweights** that counterbalance the weight of **flown** scenery and equipment.

arc *TheatArts* Point at which the actor develops the character conforming to the author's intent.

arc, arc lamp, arc-lamp, arc spotlight *PerfA&C* Carbon arc spotlight. *Also see* **Stage Lighting**.

arcane *Crit&Eval* Known or understood by only a few.

archaeology, archeology *Cult&Soc* Systematic recovery and study of material evidence. <such as graves, buildings, tools, and pottery> remaining from past human life and culture.

archaic (ar-kay-ick, Greek "arkhaikos" for "old-fashioned.") *Crit&Eval* 1 Related to words and language that were once common but are now used chiefly to suggest an earlier style or period. 2 No longer current or applicable. <archaic laws> OUT OF STYLE, PASSÉ

archetype, archetypal, archetypic, archetypical *Crit&Eval* Original model or type after which other similar things are patterned. *Also see* **prototype**.

architect (archt.) *ArtPerf, VisArts* One who works at the art and profession of **architecture**.

architecture (archt.) *VisArts* Style and method of design and construction. "Shape of architecture is the shape of the earth as it is modified by the structures of mankind." — **Vincent Scully**

archival footage *Flm&Vid* » stock footage

archive *InfoMgt* 1 To copy programs and data onto an auxiliary storage medium such as a disk or tape for long-term retention. 2 To store data for long-term use.

Archive of Contemporary Music *MusArts* Collects, preserves, and provides information about popular music of all cultures from 1950 to present.

archives *InfoMgt* 1 Place or collection containing records, documents, or other materials of historical interest. 2 Repository for stored memories or information.

archt. *VisArts* **architect, architecture**.

arco *MusArts* Use the bow with string instruments of the violin family. *Also see* **Music Directions**.

area composition *Journ, VA-Prntng* Set and arrange type in several columns within a rectangular area.

area developers *EntreP* Individuals or companies that obtain the legal right to open several franchised outlets in a given area.

area of dominant influence *Rdio/TV* » **ADI**

arena *PerfA&C* Large modern building for the presentation of sports, spectacles, and superconcerts. *Origin* Area in the center of an ancient Roman amphitheater where contests and other spectacles were held.

arena stage *TheatArts* Stage completely surrounded by audience. *Also see* **Stages**.

arena stage *PerfA&C* Stage completely surrounded by audience. *Also see* **Stages**.

ARF *Mktg* **American Retail Federation** Ω

argot *Genl* Specialized vocabulary or set of idioms used by a particular group. *Also see* **jargon, slang, vernacular**.

arguably *Crit&Eval* That can be argued plausibly; defensible in argument. <Orson Welles' *Citizen Kane* is, arguably, one of the best motion pictures ever made>

argument *iMedia, InfoMgt* Value used to evaluate a procedure or subroutine.

argument *LitArts,TheatArts* **1** Compendious statement of the plot, or a section, of a play, poem, story, or novel. <Milton's (John Milton, 1608-74, Eng. poet, scholar) brief statements of what happens therein at the beginning of each of the books of *Paradise Lost*> **2** Topic, subject.

aria *MusArts,TheatArts* **1** Solo vocal piece with instrumental accompaniment, as in an opera. **2** Air, melody. *Also see* **Songs**.

Aristotelian *Crit&Eval* Person whose thinking and methods tend to be **empirical**, scientific, or commonsensical. *Also see* **Aristotle**.

Aristotle (-384 to -322 BC) *Ethcs&Phil* Greek philosopher profoundly influenced **Western** thought. In his philosophical system, theory follows **empirical** observation and **logic**, based on the **syllogism**, is the essential method of rational inquiry. Pupil of **Plato** and the author of works on **logic, metaphysics, ethics,** natural sciences, politics, and **poetics**. <*The Poetics*> *Also see* **catharsis, imitation**.

armature *VisArts* Framework core to support clay sculpture.

Armory Show *Cult&Soc, VisArts* First large-scale comprehensive showing of late 19th century and early 20th century European paintings, held in 1913 in the 69th Regiment Armory, NYC. It had a profound influence on American art, but drew criticism from leading American artists "We were all in revolt against the unhappy effects which the Armory Show… had had on American painting. We objected to the new Parisian aesthetics which was more and more turning away from the living world of active men and women into an academic world of empty pattern. We wanted an American Art which was not empty, and we believed that only by turning the formative process of art back again to meaningful subject matter, could we expect to get one…" — Thomas Hart Benton (1889-1975, pntr., art critic) *Also see* **Ashcan School, Marcel Duchamp, The Eight**.

arms length *Ethcs&Phil, LegAsp* Figurative measure of keeping one's distance from a potential **conflict of interest**. <Arts manager must keep an arm's length distance between **fiduciary** responsibility and personal involvement with the artist>

armscye *also* **arm's eye** (arm's eye) *Fashn* armhole of apparel.

Armstrong, Louis *ArtPerf, Flm&Vid MusArts* (aka "Pops," "Satchmo," 1900-71, jazz tp, sngr., comp.) "The first great jazz soloist and one of jazz's most creative innovators." — **Eileen Southern**: Recordings. <*Louis Armstrong Vol. 1 1925-1932, Vol 2 1932-40* (Classics): *Louis Armstrong, The Ultimate Collection* (1932-70, RCA Bluebird)> *Also see* **Battlefield, Chicago jazz, dig, Down Beat Jazz Hall of Fame, Joe Glaser, levee camp music, on the road, organized jazz solo, phrasing, race, scat singing**.

arpeggio *MusArts* Technique of playing the notes of a chord in rapid succession rather than simultaneously.

arr. *MusArts* arrangement, arranger.

arrangement (arr.) *MusArts* **1** Music that has been arranged for specific instruments or voices. **2** Music reset to achieve a different style. *Also see* **chart, orchestration, score**. *Also see* **Print Music**.

arranger (arr.) *ArtPerf, MusArts* One who resets a composition (writes an **arrangement**) for other instruments or voices or for another style of performance. **1** "Ms. [Rosemary] Clooney (1928-, jazz-influenced sngr.) is one singer who doesn't underestimate the importance of the arranger's role. By knowing where to support you, a good arranger can carry you through the rough places and literally make you sing with a wider range, I think Nelson (Riddle (1921-85, film/TV/record arr., cond.) gave **Frank Sinatra** back his singing career." — **Linda Ronstadt 2** "Because of the way records are made today, the role of the pop arranger has been in

eclipse for a number of years. The way it used to be, the arranger was really who shaped the record. But when pop records began to be made with **multi-track** technique… the arranger diminished in importance." — Johnny Mandel (1935-, film/TV arr.-comp., cond.), arranger of several **cuts** on Natalie Cole's (1950-, pop sngr.) album *Unforgettable*. *Also see* **orchestrator**.

arrears *Eco&Fin* Unpaid, overdue debt or an unfulfilled

art *Aes&Creat* **1** Human effort to imitate, supplement, alter, or counteract the work of **nature**. **2** High quality of conception or execution, as found in works of beauty. AESTHETIC VALUE. **3** Field or category of art. <architecture, ballet, literature, music, painting, sculpture> "Art is easy for those who can do it and impossible for those who can't." — Hanif Kureismi (wri.) *Also see* **fine art**.

art *Crit&Eval* **1** Non-scientific branch of learning, one of the liberal arts. **2** Trade or craft that applies such a system of principles and methods. **3** Skill attained by study, practice, or observation. "Art and life are subjective. Not everybody's gonna dig what I dig, but I reserve the right to dig it." — Whoopi Goldberg (1949-; actor, comic, civil rights activist.)

art *PerfA&C* "Art, esp. a performing art, is a balanced equation of art and audience." — Peter Zeisler (art critic)

art *VA-Prntng* Illustrative material *Also see* **artwork**.

art *VisArts* **1** Conscious production or arrangement of sounds, colors, forms, movements, or other elements in a manner that affects the sense of beauty, specifically the production of the beautiful in a graphic or plastic medium. **2** Product of these activities; human works of beauty considered as a group. *Also see* **fine art**.

art brut (brute) *VisArts* Raw art as developed by Jean Dubuffet (Jhahn Doo-boo-fay, 1901-85, Fr. pntr.) to express the vitality and immediacy absent from some academic art. *Also see* **impasto**.

Art Dealers Association of America (ADAA) *Mgt, VisArts* Trade organization of art dealers.

art deco *VisArts* Decorative and architectural style (ca. 1925-40), characterized by geometric designs, bold colors, and the use of plastic and glass. **Art Movements and Periods**.

art director *Flm&Vid* One responsible for designing and overseeing the construction of sets for a movie, and sometimes its interior decoration and overall visual style. *Also see* **Directors**.

art director *RecA&S* Responsible for the design and graphics of the packaging of recorded music.

art film *Flm&Vid* Motion picture meant to be a serious work of art, not intended for mass appeal.

art for art's sake *Aes&Creat* Popularized by Theophile Gautier (1811-72, Fr. critic, fictwri., poet) in 1832 in the doctrine 'l'art pour l'art, taken up in mid-19th century France by the **Symbolist** poets and painters.

art house *Flm&Vid* Movie theater featuring **art films**.

art moderne, Art Moderne *Fashn, VisArts* Striving to be modern in appearance or style but lacking taste or refinement. *Also see* **pretentious**.

Art Movements and Periods *Aes&Creat ColEntry, VisArts* » **abstract expressionism, art deco, art nouveau** *or* **Art Nouveau, ashcan school, baroque, Brotherhood, Byzantine art, classicism, color-field painting, conceptualism, constructivism, cubism, dadaism, Decadence, expressionism, fauvism, folk art, futurism, Gothic, hyperrealism, imagism, impressionism** *or* **Impressionism, luminism, Mannerism, minimalism, modernism, neoclassicism, neorealism, neosurrealism, nonobjective, op art** *or* **Op Art, photorealism, pointillism, pop art, postimpressionism, post-modernism, Pre-Raphaelite, primitivism, realism, Renaissance, rococo, Romanesque, romanticism** *or* **Romanticism, superrealism, suprematism, symbolism, visionary art**.

art music *MusArts* Usually [and tactlessly] refers to "**classical**" or "**serious**" music. [Reader should not infer that any other music is **artless**.] *Also see* **elitist**.

art nouveau *also* **Art Nouveau** *Fashn, VisArts* Style of decoration and architecture of the late 19th and early 20th centuries, characterized particularly by the depiction of leaves and flowers in flowing, sinuous lines. Its radical accomplishment was its rejection of the academic revivalism that dominated 19th century art and design by avoiding imitation or the transformation of traditional styles by creating a new style. *Also see* **Art Movements and Periods**.

art of negotiation *HR&LR* In its most simplistic style: Ask for everything. *Also see* **negotiation**.

art runner *Mktg , VisArts* Private art dealer who functions as a broker in sales transactions by linking prospective buyers and sellers of works of art. After an exhibition or an auction, the art runner moves unsold works from one gallery to another to stimulate sales.

art song *MusArts* Lyric song intended to be sung in recital, usu. accompanied by a piano.

art theatre *Flm&Vid,TheatArts* Type of non-commercial film or theatre emphasizing certain artistic purposes, such as **theatricalism** rather than **naturalism**, freedom for experimentation in design, presentation, and script. *Also see* **little theatre**, **Theaters & Theatres**.

art therapy *VisArts* Treatment of disability by means of creating or viewing visual art.

art to wear *Fashn* Craftsmanship in fabric artistry to design clothes with originality and individuality. Resulting designs are regarded as "art," reliability is secondary.

art-as-expression *Crit&Eval* » **impressionism** This theory has largely superseded **art-as-imitation**.

art-as-imitation *Crit&Eval* » **imitation** *Also see* **art-as-expression**.

art. *ArtPerf* artist.

ART/NY *Mgt,TheatArts* **Alliance of Resident Theatres/New York** (ART/NY) Provides programs to member organizations in NYC to increase managerial strengths, offers research and consulting on real estate matters, publishes several guides and *Theatre Times,* a bimonthly magazine.

artefact *Cult&Soc* » **artifact**

articles of partnership *EntreP* Document that states explicitly the rights and duties of partners.

articulate *Crit&Eval* Characterized by the use of clear, expressive language.

articulation *Crit&Eval* Relating to the production of a speech sound.

articulation *MusArts* Instrumental musician's manner of execution. <**Attack** and **decay** of a note as affected by **tonguing** on horns, finger or bowing action on stringed instruments, and the striking of percussion instrument in definite **pitch**.>

articulation *TheatArts* Accurate formation and production of sounds in a specific language or dialect. Three conditions which fulfill clear articulation are: **1** Accurate formation of the sound. **2** Sufficient support of the sound on breath. **3** Completion of the sound.

artifact *also* **artefact** *Cult&Soc* Object produced or shaped by human craft. <a tool, a weapon, or an ornament of archaeological or historical interest>

artifact *iMedia* **1** resulting effect of distortion or compression. *Also see* **aliasing**. **2** Objects that provide information about a process. *Also see* **artifact model**.

artifact model *iMedia* Reproduction of an artifact (obtained during contextual inquiry), which is annotated to provide more information. "Model extends the information on the artifact to show structure, strategy, and intent." — Hugh Beyer and Karen Holtzblatt

artifice *Crit&Eval* **1** Artful or crafty expedient. STRATAGEM. **2** Cleverness or skill. INGENUITY . **3** Subtle deception.

artificer *ArtPerf, Crit&Eval* Skilled worker; a craftsperson.

artificial blood *Perf-MkUp* Contained in **gelatin** capsules held in the mouth or hand and crushed on **cue**.

artificial intelligence *InfoMgt* Movement associated with the **fifth generation** of computers that seeks to build computers that emulate human functionalities. <vision, voice recognition, **robotics**, and expert systems> *Also see* **CRCC, Ken Thompson, UNIX**.

artificial language *InfoMgt* Language designed for use in a specific field.

artificial snow *PerfA&C* Sprayed from an aerosol can, it can be easily applied to costumes, **props**, and beards to simulate real snow.

artisan entrepreneur *EntreP* Person who starts a business with primarily technical skills and little business knowledge such as an artist.

artist (art.) *ArtPerf* **1** One whose work shows exceptional creative ability or skill. **2** One who is able by virtue of imagination and talent to create works of aesthetic value. **3** One who expressively works in the visual arts. <painter, sculptor, scenic designer, et a> **4** One who expressively works in the performing arts. <actor, dancer, singer, et al> "To be an artist means never to avert one's eyes." — **Akira Kurosawa** *Also see* **visual artist**.

Artist *ArtPerf, Law&Pol* » **Artists' Response to Illegal State Tactics**.

Artist Certification Committee *ArtPerf, Genl* Division of the New York City of Cultural Affairs responsible for certifying artists to qualify for living in commercial loft buildings.

artist development *ArtPerf, Mgt* Process of aiding and abetting the artist's image, career, and aesthetic range.

artist royalty *RecA&S* Negotiated percentage of the **list price** of the recording multiplied by the number of copies sold, MINUS the cost of recording the **master**, and cash advances made to the artist. Royalty percentage remains the same regardless of the cost of recording, but is not paid until **recoupment**. RECORD ROYALTY. *Also see* **Royalties**.

artist tie-ins *Flm&Vid, Mktg, RecA&S* Merchandise manufactured and distributed to coincide with an artist's concert tour, movie, or record release.

artist's representative *Mgt* Talent agent or agency. *Also see* **Agents and Agencies**.

artist's representative *VisArts* Agent for visual artists, sometimes a gallery owner. *Also see* **Agents and Agencies**.

artist's video *ArtPerf, Flm&Vid* Videotape that concentrates on an artist's life, method, and works, VIDEO ART

artist-in-residence *Mgt* One from the professional world employed by a school or school system to train students in an art form or in arts and entertainment management.

artist-producer *Mgt, RecA&S* Artists may choose to be the producer of their own recording when they have heavy star clout. <Ray Charles (1930-, blues/r&b/gospel/jazz pno, sngr., arr.-comp., arts mgr.) produces his own recordings on his **Tangerine** label, then leases the master to **Atlantic Records** for manufacturing and distribution> *Also see* **Producers**.

Artist/Performer *ArtPerf* a creator, the **egocentric** original, from whom all blessings flow. <art, culture, entertainment, and money>; one of the four **Principal Players** of **The Arts Dynamic**

artiste *ArtPerf, Crit&Eval* **1** Entertainer, usu. a singer or dancer, sometimes a **stripper**. **2** One with artistic pretensions.

artistic control *Crit&Eval* Power to make a final decision relating to the artistic production of a film, TV show, or recording.

artistic director *MusArts* Supervisor of all artists and performances, usu. in an opera company. *Also see* **Directors**.

artistic director *PerfA&C* Person responsible for the major artistic decisions of a theatrical production company — hiring of production personnel, selection of season, and so on. *Also see* **Directors**.

artist's print *VisArts* Part of **first printing** before the artist detects mistakes.

artistic freedom *Ethcs&Phil* Freedom to create without regulation, restraint, or censorship.

artistic temperament *ArtPerf* Condition marked occasionally by excessive irritability or sensitiveness, usu. brought on by latent feelings of insecurity and **rejection**. "[Playwright] had lived so long with flamboyant personalities, had been obliged to cope so long with what was called artistic temperament, and had been compelled to deal so long and charmingly and patiently with actors' and actresses' stupidities, that of course his own character had changed." — **John P Marquand**.

Artists & Repertoire, Artists & Repertory (A&R) *RecA&S* » **A&R**.

Artists Management Group *ArtPerf, Mgt* » **AMG**

Artists' Response to Illegal State Tactics (Artist) *Law&Pol* New York City group organized to protest limitation of sidewalk artists in front of the Metropolitan Museum of Art.

artist's video *ArtPerf, Flm&Vid* Videotape that concentrates on an artist's life, method, and works, with the main goals being rejection of the commercial qualities of network television and a deep exploration into the subject matter through the use of new techniques in imagery and sound. VIDEO ART

artless *Crit&Eval* **1** Lacking art, knowledge, or skill; uncultured and ignorant. **2** Poorly made or done; crude. **3** Free of artificiality;

natural. **4 naive.** *Also see* **ingenuous.**

artphilohistcritisophery *VisArts* "It is a historical moment in which art makers, art historians, teachers, philosophers, and critics of art are so interlocked in one another's activities that the making of any artwork whatever – even if it looks absolutely traditional – demands a complex philosophical justification." — **Arthur C. Danto**

Arts & Lectures Conference *Mgt* Annual conference sponsored by **NACA.**

.arts *InfoMgt* **Domain name** ending for cultural groups. *Also see* **Domain Name.**

Arts Alliance *Mgt* Umbrella lobbying group for many U.S. arts organizations.

Arts Dynamic, The (TAD) *Genl* »pages vi-ix.

Arts International *Cult&Soc, Law&Pol* Department within the **USIA** that deals with the arts.

arts management *Mgt* Administration, direction, and facilitation that enables an effective exchange between art or artist and audience.

Arts Manager *Mgt* **1** The essential philistine who makes the deal between artist and audience — and is ofttimes resented by either. **2** One of the four **Principal Players** of The **Arts Dynamic:** "The attitude of the artist towards these fellow [management] professionals can have a considerable impact on the nature of the professional relationship that develops. Hiring management services in a particular area can be a means of abdicating responsibility in that area or it can be a way to multiple the artist's own control and effectiveness." — Ivan Sygoda (dance co. mgr) *Also see* **Managers.**

arts medicine *Sci&Tech* Branch of medicine dealing with the special health needs of performers. <injuries and disorders suffered by musicians that result from playing a musical instrument>

arts policy *Law&Pol, Mgt* Plan or course of action by a government, political party, or business, designed to influence and determine decisions, actions, and other matters in the arts field.

arts therapy *Genl* Use of an art form as a therapeutic tool to treat mental or physical trauma. <**Dance Movement Therapy**>

artsy-craftsy *Crit&Eval* Pretentiously or self-consciously artistic.

artwork *VA-Prntng* Illustrative and decorative elements of printed materials. <borders, charts, maps, photographs, line drawings, etc>

artwork *VisArts* Work in the graphic or plastic arts. <small, hand-made decorative or artistic objects>

as is *Mktg, RecA&S* Just the way it is, with no changes or modifications. <Used records, like used cars, are sold "as is," regardless of scratches, warping, etc> *Also see* **disclaimer, guarantee, warranty.**

ASAE *Mgt* **American Society of Association Executives.** Professional society of paid executives of national, state and local trade, professional and philanthropic associations. Seeks to educate association executives on effective management. Maintains ASAE Foundation to do future-oriented research and make grants.

asbestos curtain *PerfA&C* Fireproof curtain lowered in front of the **front curtain** between performances. *Also see* **Stage Curtains.**

ASC *Flm&Vid* **American Society of Cinematographers.** Honorary society of professional **cinematographers.**

ASCAP *also* **Ascap** *IntelProp, MusArts* **American Society of Composers, Authors, and Publishers. Performance rights organization** (est. 1914) that licenses on a non-exclusive basis to users of music the non-dramatic public performance rights of its approx. 65, 000 members and affiliated foreign rights societies. *Also see* **Copyright-Related Organizations.**

ascender *iMedia, VA-Prntng* Part of the tall lowercase letters that extends above the other lowercase letters. <b, d, h> *Also see* **descender.**

ascending *MusArts* Moving upward on a musical scale. *Also see* **descending.**

ascetic *Ethcs&Phil* One who renounces material comforts and leads a life of austere self-discipline, esp. as an act of religious devotion.

asceticism *Ethcs&Phil, MusArts* Principles and practices of an ascetic, extreme self-denial and austerity. "Asceticism is one of the abiding ills of modern music. Asceticism and music do not go together. Music is a spontaneous, uninhibited expression of feel-

ing. Without feeling there can be no music. Asceticism is opposed to the expression of feeling and the indulgence of the senses. This is why ascetic faiths and philosophies have no music and why, in certain austere faiths, music is associated with evil." — **Henry Pleasants**

ASCII (ASSkey) *iMedia, InfoMgt* **American Standard Code for Information Interchange,** a standard for relating numbers to alphanumeric characters and symbols. Most **email** is ASCII text (*also* **plain text**) and thus compatible with most computers.

ASE *Eco&Fin* » **AMEX** (American Stock Exchange)

asgmt. *IntelProp, LegAsp* **assignment.**

ashcan school, Ash Can school *VisArts* Group of U.S. painters of the early 20th century who painted realistic scenes of everyday urban life. *Also see* **Armory Show, Art Movements and Periods, modern art,** The **Eight.**

Asian *Cult&Soc* "Asian" is currently preferred to describe persons of South and East Asian ancestry – Chinese, Filipinos, Indians, Indonesians, Japanese, Koreans, Pakistani, Southeast Asians, and others – rather than Oriental, Oriental has been objected to on two grounds: because it suggests racial, rather than cultural identity, and because it identifies the place of origin in terms of its location relative to the **West** (i.e., "from the **East**"), rather than in absolute terms. *Also see* **Racial Designations.**

Asian American *Cult&Soc* U.S. citizen or resident of Asian descent. *Also see* **Racial Designations.**

Asian Pacific Economic Cooperation (EPIC) **organization** *EntreP* Organization of 18 Asian nations that attempts to reduce trade barriers between their nations.

aside *TheatArts* Comment spoken by a character directly to the audience while other characters are also present on stage. Convention accepts that the other characters do not hear the aside. *Also see* **Stage Directions.**

ASJA *Journ, Lit* American Society of Journalists and Authors. "A primary voice in representing freelancers' interests, serving as spokesman for their right to control and profit from uses of their work in the new media and otherwise." — >http://www.asja.org< *Also see* **Anti-Censorship Organizations.**

ASMAC *MusArts* **American Society of Music Arrangers and Composers.** Musicians who specialize in **arranging** and **orchestrating** music. Organizes regularly scheduled workshop sessions to present experimental readings of orchestral and vocal writings by members that demonstrate new techniques in creative music. Works with the **American Federation of Musicians** (AFM) to insure fair competition and welfare for those persons engaged in music preparation in the U.S. and Canada.

ASME *Journ* **American Society of Magazine Editors** Issues guidelines for a proper and ethical relationship between editorial and advertising departments. <Advertising supplements must not masquerade as editorial articles, ads may not emulate the magazine's typefaces or design, etc> Sponsor of the annual **National Magazine Award For General Excellence.**

Asociación Puertorriqueña de Artistas e Tecnicos del Espectaculo (APATE) *ArtPerf, HR&LR* » **APATE**

ASOL *MusArts* **American Symphony Orchestra League Nonprofit** educational organization that serves to assist (1, 600 American) symphony orchestras artistically and administratively.

aspect ratio *Flm&Vid, Rdio/TV.* Ratio between the horizontal and vertical dimensions of the movie or television screen.

assemblage *Genl* Collection of people or things. GATHERING.

assemblage *VisArts* Sculptural composition consisting of an arrangement of miscellaneous objects. <pieces of metal, cloth, and string> Three dimensional counterpart of **collage** comprising an arrangement of waste articles or miscellaneous objects. <pieces of metal or glass, clothing, string, etc> Jean Dubuffet (» **art brut**) first used this technique but its origins can be traced to **Georges Braque, Pablo Picasso,** Francis Picabia (1878-1953, Fr. pntr.), and **Marcel Duchamp.** Assemblage involves the transformation of nonart objects and materials into sculpture by techniques, such as of gluing and welding. This radically new way of making sculpture rejected traditional techniques of carving stone or modeling a shape to be cast in bronze.

assemble *Dnce* Jumping ballet step in which the ballet dancer thrusts one leg up and out, at the same time springing off the other, and brings the legs together in the air before landing.

assembly *Flm&Vid* First stage of **film editing**, when all the shots are arranged in script order.

assembly *InfoMgt* Automatic translation of symbolic code into machine code.

asset *Crit&Eval* Useful or valuable quality, person, or thing.

asset *Eco&Fin* Valuable item that is owned.

asset *iMedia* **1** component content piece. Assets are often managed with a **CMS** (Content Management System) <audio> **2** resource (object, concept, process, or person) <a programmer>

asset turnover *E&F-Acc* Measures how efficiently assets are used to produce sales. Asset turnover = **net sales** ÷ average total sales.

asset-based loan *EntreP* Line of credit secured by the assets of a company.

asset-based valuation approach *EntreP* Determination of the value of a business by estimating only the value of its assets.

Assets *ColEntry,E&F-Acc* » **current —, expendable —, Intangible—, liquid —, long-term, net —, other —, quick —, tangible —**

assets *E&F-Acc* **1** Entries on a **balance sheet** showing all properties, tangible and **intangible**, and claims against others that may be applied, directly or indirectly, to cover the **liabilities** of a person or business, such as cash, stock, and **goodwill**. **2** Entire property owned by a person, esp. a bankrupt, that can be used to settle debts.

assets *EntreP* Uses of the funds of a bank, including loans and reserves.

assets *Fnding* Amount of capital or principal-money, stocks, bonds, real estate, or other resources-controlled by the foundation or corporate giving program. Generally, assets are invested and the income is used to make grants.

assign *LegAsp* Sign a document transferring ownership from one party to another.

assignee *LegAsp* **1** Party to which a transfer of property, rights, or interest is made. **2** One appointed to act for another. <a deputy, an agent>

assignment (asgmt.) *IntelProp* Transfer of a **copyright, trademark**, or **patent** to another person's control or ownership, which must be in writing to be effective.

assimilation *Cult&Soc* Process whereby a minority group gradually adopts the customs and attitudes of the prevailing culture.

associate producer *Flm&Vid* One who supplies independent money to a production but has no power.

Associated Actors and Artistes of America (Four A's) *ArtPerf, HR&LR,PerfA&C* » **Four A's**

Associated Press (AP) *Journ* » **AP**

Association for Independent Music (AFIM) *Mktg, RecA&S* » **AFIM**

Association of American Editorial Cartoonists (AAEC) *Journ, VisArts* » **AAEC**

Association of Artist and Artistes (AAAA) *HR&LR* » **AAAA (HR&LR)**

Association of Authors Representatives (AAR) *HR&LR, LitArts* Literary and dramatic agents who market books, plays, and other literary and dramatic material.

Association of College & University Arts Administrators (AC-UAA) *Mgt,PerfA&C* Name change: **Association of Performing Arts Presenters** (APAP) » **APAP**

Association of Computer Programmers and Analysts (ACPA) *InfoMgt* » **ACPA**

Association of Independent Information Professionals (AIIP) *InfoMgt* » **AIIP**

Association of National Advertisers (ANA) *Mktg* » **ANA**

Association of Online Professionals (AOP) *InfoMgt* Successor to several organizations inc. the National Association of Sysops (NAS)

Association of Performing Arts Presenters (APAP) *Mgt,PerfA&C* » **APAP**

Association of Theatrical Press Agents and Managers (AT-PAM) *HR&LR,TheatArts* » **ATPAM**

associational advertising *Mktg* Advertising run by or on behalf of an **attraction** in which the sponsor receives identification.

associative logic *iMedia* Ideas, memories or thoughts connected in a seemingly disparate or incongruous way.

asymmetric information *EntreP* One side of the market— either buyers or sellers—has better information about the good than the other.

asymmetry *Aes&Creat* Lack of balance or **symmetry**. *Also see* **Ballet Russe**.

asymmetry *iMedia* Compositionally unbalanced; emphasis not distributed evenly.

asynchronous *iMedia* Not simultaneous; not synched in time.

at liberty *ArtPerf, HR&LR* unemployed, available.

at rise *TheatArts* Moment when the rising curtain discloses a scene and the relative positions of the actors.

at risk *Eco&Fin* Exposed to the danger of loss.

at source agreement *IntelProp, LegAsp, MusArts* Provides that a songwriter's share of foreign income will be computed at the source of the income rather than after the foreign **subpublisher** has deducted its fees.

AT&T *InfoMgt* American Telephone & Telegraph Corporation (AT&T) The largest telecommunications company in the world. *Also see* **AT&T Labs, Baby Bells, Bell Labs**.

AT&T Labs *InfoMgt, Sci&Tech* Formerly, **Bell Labs**, division of American Telephone & Telegraph Company (AT&T) » **Bell Labs**

atelier (atill-ee-ay) *VisArts* Workshop or studio for an architect, artist, craftsman, designer, photographer, or sculptor.

athenaeum *LitArts* Place where printed materials are available for reading. <library>

Atlantic Records *RecA&S* Founded in the 1950s by **Jerry Wexler** and the **Ertegun** brothers, it became the foremost independent label in **gospel, jazz**, and **r&b** before becoming part of the **Warner-Elektra-Asylum** (WEA) **conglomerate**. **Tangerine Record Co.**

atmos. *Flm&Vid,TheatArts* **atmosphere**.

atmosphere (atmos.) *Flm&Vid,TheatArts* Mood, the general emotional quality, of all or part of a dramatic production. *Also see* **aura, background, empathic response**.

atonality *MusArts* Absence of a **tonal** center, has no **key**, lack of **tonality**.

ATPAM *HR&LR* Union that represents **company** managers, affiliated with **IATSE**.

attachment *LegAsp* Preliminary legal seizure of property to force compliance with a decision which may be obtained in a preceding suit.

attack *Genl* Decisiveness and clarity in artistic expression.

attack *MusArts* Beginning or manner of beginning a piece, **passage**, or sound on a musical instrument.

attack *RecA&S* Manner in which a **sound wave** begins and increases in volume. *Also see* **decay, internal dynamics, sustain**.

attire *Fashn* To dress or clothe, esp. in elaborate or splendid garments. *Also see* **apparel**.

attitude *Dnce* (Ballet) Position similar to an **arabesque** in which the dancer stands on one leg with the other raised either in front or in back and bent at the knee.

attitude *EntreP* Enduring opinion based on knowledge, feeling, and behavioral tendency.

attitudes *Mktg* Enduring systems of positive or negative evaluations of, or emotional feelings toward, an object, a concept, a product, a service.

attorney-in-fact *LegAsp* Agent in a **power of attorney** situation. *Also see* **Agents and Agencies**.

attraction *Flm&Vid* Any production, esp. a successful one. *Also see* **coming attraction**.

attraction *PA-Variety* Person, place, thing, or event intended to attract. <Cher (Cherilyn Sarkisian, 1946-, film/TV act., sngr.) and **Madonna** in matching **Mother Hubbards**.

attribute *iMedia* Programming: Something that modifies an element or object, and which takes a value (implicit or explicit)

attribute inspection *EntreP* Determination of product acceptability based on whether it will or will not work.

attribution *BcstJourn* Phrase or sentence that reveals the source of information for a news story. Helps establish credibility.

attribution *Crit&Eval* **1** Act of establishing a particular person, place, or time as the creator, **provenance**, or era of a work of art. **2** Something, such as a quality or characteristic, related to a particular possessor. *Also see* **authenticity**.

aubade *MusArts* Song or instrumental composition relating to daybreak.

auction *Mktg* Public sale in which art works, property or items of merchandise are sold to the highest bidder.

auction *Rdio/TV* "The **Federal Communication Commission** (FCC) auction of **frequencies** to non-broadcasting communication companies underscores the value of the airwaves." — Alvin H. Permutter (comm. journ.)

audience *Crit&Eval* **1** Final arbiter of the artist's fame, success, and immortality. **2** Final arbiter of what is art, classic, standard, etc. **1** "He who gives life to an audience receives life back." — **Norman Mailer 2** "If people don't want to come, nothing can stop them." — **Sol Hurok 3** "The only verdict that counts is the public's." — **Henry Pleasants** *Also see* **empathic response**.

Audience *Genl* One of the four **Principal Players** of **The Arts Dynamic**.

audience *Journ, LitArts* Readership for printed matter. <books, periodicals, etc>

audience *MusArts* Listeners assembled at a concert or individually listening to a recording or viewing a music video. *Also see* **empathic response**.

audience *Rdio/TV* Spectators or listeners attracted by a television or radio program.

audience *TheatArts* Spectators assembled at a performance *Also see* **empathic response**. "The audience is another character." — Bernadette Peters (1948-; **Tony Award**-winning singing actress.)

audience development *Mktg* Audience **marketing**, a prime responsibility of arts management.

audience enrichment *Mgt, Mktg* Enlarge the artistic menu. <multi-media, **ethnic** arts, **pop** presentations, **sing-alongs**. <Beethoven's *Ninth Symphony*>

audience expansion *Mktg* Enlarge **target markets** <students, seniors, **ethnic** groups, civic and fraternal organizations, etc>

audience proof *TheatArts* Said of a production thought to be certain of success.

audience share *Rdio/TV, Mktg* Comparative popularity of a broadcast program, determined by dividing the program rating by the number of sets in use at a particular time.

audio billboard *BcstJourn* Verbal identifier placed at the head of each take of each track that is recorded. *Also:* slate, it includes the story **slug**, the track number, the take number, and a countdown. *Ex.* "Bus crash...Track One...Take One...Coming in three...two...one..."

Audio Engineering Society (AES) *RecA&S, Sci&Tech* » **AES**

audio frequency (AF) *RecA&S* Range of **frequencies**, usu. from 15 **hertz** to 20,000 **hertz**, characteristic of signals audible to the normal human ear.

Audio Home Recording Act of 1992 *LegAsp, RecA&S* This legislation requires "the equipment, tape, and disc manufacturers of digital audio recording devices and media (recordings and blank tape) to pay royalties to creators for the loss of revenue that occurs from home taping. Royalty to be paid by the manufacturers to the **Register of Copyrights** is 2% of the transfer price, with a minimal royalty of $1 per device and a maximum royalty of $12 for certain types of devices." The royalty on blank tape and other media is 3% of the transfer price. Royalties are paid into two funds: 2/3 to the **Sound Recording Fund**, 1/3 to the **Musical Works Fund**. Money paid to the **Sound Recording Fund** is divided: 4% to nonfeatured instrumentalists (**sidemen**) and **background singers** who have performed on records distributed in the U.S. Of the remaining 96%, 40% goes to **contract artists** and 60% to record companies. The 1/3 of the total royalties paid to the **Musical Works Fund** is divided equally between the **writers** and the music publishers. — Brabec and Brabec (Music Business writers) *Also see* **Alliance of Artists and Recording Companies**.

audio output *InfoMgt* Computer output generated through voice **synthesizers** that create audible signals resembling a human voice. *Also see* **voice synthesis**.

audio output jack *InfoMgt* Connector on the back panel of the computer to attach headphones or speakers.

audio/visual work *Flm&Vid, Rdio/TV*. Industry term for film, television, or any other visual production.

audiophile *RecA&S* Ardent fan of high fidelity sound reproduction.

audiotape *RecA&S* **1** Magnetic tape used to record sound. **2** Tape recording of sound.

audiovisual *also* **audio-visual** *Flm&Vid, RecA&S* **1** Both audible and visible. **2** Relating to materials, e.g., films and tape recordings, that present information in audible and pictorial form. **3** Aids, other than printed matter, that use sight or sound to present information.

audiovisual recordings *RecA&S* Every form of recording embodying performances wherein are fixed visual images together with sound.

audit *E&F-Acc* Examined and verified account.

Audit Bureau of Circulations (ABC) *Journ, Mktg, Rdio/TV, VA-Prntng* Auditing service owned by several large advertising agencies that authenticates a publication's **paid circulation**. *Also see* **Publisher's Statement**.

audit clause *LegAsp* Portion of an agreement between an artist and an employer which allows the artist access to the employer's books and records in order to determine their accuracy.

audit stub *Mktg* Portion of admission ticket detached and kept as a record of ticket sales and compared to **window income**.

audit trail *InfoMgt* Allows data to be traced from a source document to a specific output, and from the output to the original source.

audition *MusArts, PerfA&C* Trial performance, usu. competitive, by a performer to demonstrate suitability or skill. *Also see* **casting, tryout**.

audition *TheatArts* Reading aloud of a script to prospective investors. *Also see* **casting, principal interview**.

auditorium *InfoMgt* Electronic conference halls used for large gatherings and guest speakers.

auditorium *PerfA&C* **1** Seating area from which the audience observes the action of the play **2** Large room or building to accommodate an audience for public meetings or performances.

augmentation *MusArts* Repetition of a theme in notes of usu. double time value.

augmented product *Mktg* **Core product** plus any additional services and benefits that may be supplied.

augmented reality *iMedia* Computer generated elements supplement vision; both the real world and the imposed content are seen simultaneously, and the imposed content changes depending on context. <looking at a restaurant's sign pulls up a menu and price list>. Often used with a HMD device.

aura *Crit&Eval* Distinctive but intangible quality that seems to surround a person or thing. *Also see* **atmosphere, empathic response**.

Austin High Gang *MusArts* Group of white musicians, most of whom attended Austin High School (Chicago) who were among the creators of **Chicago jazz**.

auteur theory *Flm&Vid* Theory of film popularized in the 1950s by the critics writing in the French journal, *Cahiers du Cinema*, that emphasized the director as the main creator of a film and whose personal vision, style, and thematic obsessions defined it. "It sure as shit isn't true in Hollywood. I have never met another fellow technician, not a single **cinematographer** or producer or editor, who believes it. **Godard** (Jean Luc Godard, 1930-, Fr. flmkr.) said that the whole thing was patent bullshit from the beginning, an idea devised by the then young scufflers to draw some attention to themselves." — **William Goldman** *Also see* **Producers**.

auth. *ArtPerf, LitArts, MusArts* **author**.

authentic *Genl* Conforming to fact and therefore worthy of trust, reliance, or belief. <an authentic account by an eyewitness>

authentic *Law&Pol* Executed with **due process**. <authentic document>

authentic *MusArts* Accurate and genuine representation of an **ethnic** music. "Ears trained on Western music can have trouble deciding what's 'authentic' and what's simply unusual." — **Jon Pareles**

authentic *VisArts* Having a claimed and verifiable origin or authorship; not counterfeit or copied. <authentic signed painting>

authenticity *Crit&Eval* The quality or condition of being **authentic**, trustworthy, or genuine.

author (auth.) *ArtPerf, LitArts, MusArts* **1** Creator of **intellectual property**, such as literary, musical and dramatic works, choreography; pictorial, graphic, and sculptural works; **audio/visual works**, and sound recordings. **2** Can denote **composer, lyricist, record producer, choreographer,** artist, photographer, **songwriter,** or other creator. *Also see* **Work for Hire.**

author *TheatArts* Call by the audience, at the end of a successful opening night, to summon the playwright(s) to the stage for applause. *Also see* **claque.**

authoring tool *InfoMgt* Program that allows the user to format and lay out computer-originated text as in desktop publishing. <Pagemaker software> *Also see* **DTP.**

authorization card *HR&LR* Card signed by workers indicating interest in a union representing them as their **collective bargaining** representative.

authorized stock *Eco&Fin* Number of shares of stock that a corporation is allowed to sell by its by-laws. Typically a corporation has more authorized stock that stock actually sold to investors (**outstanding stock**) Difference is called **treasury stock.**

Authors Guild, Inc. (AGI) *ArtPerf, HR&LR, LitArts* » **Copyright-Related Organizations**

Authors League of America, Inc. (ALAI) *HR&LR, IntelProp, LitArts* Parent organization of the **Authors Guild, Inc.** (AGI) and the **Dramatists Guild, Inc.** (DGI), handles matters that relate to both authors and dramatists, such as censorship, copyright, taxation, and contract terms and **subsidiary rights,** that fall within the jurisdiction of the respective guilds. *Also see* **Anti-Censorship Organizations, Copyright-Related Organizations.**

auto-answer *InfoMgt* **Modem** configured to answer a phone.

autobiography *LitArts* History of one's own life, often with philosophical significance as an art work, and involving the discovery and presentation of an art work.

autograph *LitArts* Manuscript in the author's handwriting.

automat news *Journ, Rdio/TV* **a la carte news** *Origin* Automat was a popular restaurant chain in NYC in the 1930s where food was dispensed from vending machines.

automated radio *Rdio/TV* Radio station where the programming is mostly on prerecorded tapes controlled for broadcast by a transport system that requires minimum operator attention.

Automatic Dialogue Replacement (ADR) *Flm&Vid* » **ADR**

automatic stabilizers *EntreP* Taxes and transfer payments that stabilize GDP without requiring policy-makers to take explicit action.

autonomous consumption spending *EntreP* Part of consumption that does not depend on income.

autonomy *Ethcs&Phil, Law&Pol* Ability to govern oneself. The principle that persons are by their very nature uniquely qualified to determine what is in their own best interest, that thinking individuals should be permitted to be self-determining: no one can be told what to do, except by herself or himself. <"Free will does not mean one will, but many wills conflicting in one man." — Flannery O'Connor (1925-1964, author)> It is generally distinguished from **heteronomy** — governance by another, and this, in the U.S., is one reason we recoil against censorship. *Also see* **censorship, free will.**

autoresponder *InfoMgt, Mktg* » **mailbot**

auxiliary equipment *InfoMgt* Equipment not under direct control of the **central processing unit.** *Also see* **offline.**

auxiliary storage *InfoMgt* Supplements the main storage of a computer, such as magnetic disks, **floppy disks,** and magnetic tapes. *Also see* **main storage.** EXTERNAL STORAGE

availability *Flm&Vid* Dates when a film can be shown in particular markets offered by distributors to exhibitors.

availability *Rdio/TV* Broadcast time periods available for purchase. *Also see* **drive time, housewife time.**

available lighting *Flm&Vid* Use of only the light that actually exists **on location,** either natural (the sun) or artificial (house lamps)

avant-garde (Fr. for "in the front ranks") *Aes&Creat Crit&Eval* **1** Group active in the invention and application of new techniques in the arts. **2 Minority** of artists whose works are characterized by unconventional daring and obscure, controversial, or highly personal ideas. "The problem with being avant-garde is knowing who's putting on who. — Bill Watterson (1958-, cartoonist), via his cartoon characters: *Calvin and Hobbes*> **3** "I've heard it said

that one of the earmarks of the downfall of a society is freakishness in the arts masquerading as **ingenuity** and **creativity.**" — Michael Moore (19??-, jazz bass) *Also see* **underground.**

average collection period *EntreP* Average time it takes a company to collect its accounts receivables.

average cost method *E&F-Acc* Inventory costing method that determines the average cost of a line of goods held for resale by dividing the total cost by the number of items.

average pricing *EntreP* Approach in which total cost for a given period is divided by quantity sold in that period to set a price.

average-cost pricing policy *EntreP* Regulatory policy under which the government picks the point on the demand curve at which price equals average cost.

avuncular *Crit&Eval* Similar to an uncle's benevolence.

award shows *Rdio/TV* Popular type of television network programming. <**Emmy, Grammy, Oscar, Tony**> *Also see* **Television Shows.**

awardee *Genl* Recipient of an award

Awards & Prizes *ColEntry*
» **Abe Olman Award** *MusArts*
» **Academy of American Poets Awards** *LitArts*
» **Clio Awards** *Mktg, Radio & TV*
» **Coty Awards** *Fashn*
» **Country Music Association** *Music, Re RecA&S*
» **Director's Guild Awards for Theatrical Direction** *TheatArts*
» **Dove Awards** *MusArts*
» **Drama Desk Awards** *TheatArts*
» **Drama League Awards** *TheatArts*
» **Emmy Awards** *Rdio&TV*
» **Golden Laurel Awards** *Flm&Vid*
» **Golden Score Award** *Music*
» **Grammy Awards** *LitArts, Mktg, Music, RecA&S, VisArts*
» **Joseph Jefferson Awards** *TheatArts*
» **National Book Awards** *LitArts*
» **Nobel Prize** *Eco&Fin, LitArts, Sci&Tech*
» **OBIE Awards** *TheatArts*
» **Olivier Award** *TheatArts*
» **Oscar Awards** *ArtPerf, Flm&Vid, LitArts, Fashn, Music, RecA&S, VisArts*
» **Paul Revere Award** *MusArts*
» **Perry Ellis Award** *Fashn*
» **Pulitzer Prize** *, LitArts, Music, TheatArts, VisArts-Cartooning*
» **Tony Awards** *ArtPerf, LitArts, Fashn, Music, TheatArts, VisArts.*

awe *Crit&Eval* Mixed emotion of reverence, respect, dread, and wonder inspired by authority, **genius,** great beauty, **sublimity,** or might.

AWRT *Rdio/TV* **American Women in Radio and Television** Professionals in administrative, creative, or executive positions in broadcasting and related industries as well as advertising, government, and charitable agencies, corporations, and service organizations whose work is substantially devoted to radio and television. *Also see* **Gracie Allen Awards.**

ax *MusArts* Musical instrument <guitar, sax, etc> *Also see* **Musical Instrument Families.**

- B -

b *MusArts* bass voice

B movie *Flm&Vid* » **B-film**

B picture *Flm&Vid* » **B-film**

B side *RecA&S* Other side of side A of a record *Also see* **flip side.**

B-film *Flm&Vid* **Low-budget** movie usu. shown as the second feature during the big studio era. B-films took the form of popular **genres,** like thrillers, westerns, horror films, etc., and were used as testing grounds for raw talent under contract.

B-girl *Crit&Eval* Woman employed by a bar to encourage customers to spend money freely. <In some **joints,** dancers double as B-girls>

B-roll *BcstJourn* Term for additional pictures, used for illustration and explanation, which are not on the same tape as the principal audio narration or interview.

B-team *Flm&Vid* » **second unit**

b *MusInstr* bass viol *Also see* **double bass.**

b.o. *PerfA&C* box office

B.S. *Crit&Eval* bullshit

B/E *Eco&Fin, LegAsp* » **bill of exchange**

B/P *Eco&Fin* » **bills payable**

B3 organ *MusInstr* » **Hammond B3 organ**

ba-dump-bump *MusArts, PA-Variety* Rhythmic pattern produced by a drummer pedaling the bass drum to accent a comic's **punch line, pratfall,** or **double take.** *Also see* **rimshot**

Babbage, Charles (1792-1871, Eng. math.)*iMedia, InfoMgt, Sci&Tech* Inventor of the **Difference Engine No. 1,** an early 19th century mechanical calculator, a forerunner of the modern computer. *Also see* **Ada.**

babble *Crit&Eval* **1** Meaningless talk or sounds **2** Continuous low, murmuring sound. <akin to a **babbling** brook> PRATTLE

Baby Bells *InfoMgt* Seven regional telephone companies split off from **AT&T**: Emeritae, Bell Atlantic, Bell South, NYNEX, Pacific Telesis, SPG (Southwestern Bell), and U.S. West.

baby boomers *Mktg* Large consumer market of approx. 76 million Americans born between 1946 and 1965 avidly courted by entertainment media and advertisers because of their relatively large **discretionary incomes** and **material wants.** *Also see* **war babies.**

baby grand piano *MusInstr* Small grand piano, approx. five feet long *Also see* **concert grand, Musical Instrument Families.**

baby spot *Flm&Vid,PerfA&C* Small spotlight (500-750 watts) used at a short distance to give sharp illumination to an actor's face or a limited portion of the acting area. *Also see* **Stage Lighting.**

bacchanalia *Crit&Eval* Riotous, boisterous, or drunken festivity; a **revel.** *Also see* **Bacchus, Dionysus.**

Bacchus *LitArts* » **Dionysus** *Also see* **bacchanalia.**

back cover ad *Mktg* Because of its additional exposure, magazine publishers charge a premium (usu. 50% above regular rates) for back cover advertising. *Also see* **backward reader**

back matter *LitArts* Material, such as an index or appendix, that follows the main body of a book. END MATTER

back pay *Eco&Fin, HR&LR* Wages paid to employees that have been discharged in violation of a statute or as called for in a **collective bargaining** agreement.

back story *Rdio/TV, Flm&Vid, LitArts* » **prequel**

back up *InfoMgt* To make a copy of a disk or of a file or folder on a disk. Important safety measure against loss of information.

back-to-back *BcstJourn* Audio bites from separate sources edited together and used without any narration between them

back-announce *Rdio/TV* Accumulation of a group of announcements following several uninterrupted playings of recorded music.

back-lot *Flm&Vid* Scenic areas with buildings and streets in the rear area of a motion picture studio property. <tenement street, western street, waterfront> *Also see* **lot.**

back-to-work movement *HR&LR* Collaborative effort by all parties to end a **work stoppage.**

backbeat *MusArts* Steady rhythmic beat, characteristic of jazz and later, rock, that emphasizes the second and fourth beats of a four-beat measure. In jazz the accent is on the fourth beat. TWO- AND- FOUR *Also see* **big beat.**

backbone *Journ, VA-Prntng* Binding edge of a magazine *Also see* **spine.**

backcloth *PerfA&C, VisArts* » **backdrop**

backdrop *Crit&Eval* Setting of an historical event *Also see* **background.**

backdrop *PerfA&C, VisArts* Painted curtain or scenery hung at the back of a stage set. BACKCLOTH *Also see* **Stage Curtains.**

backer *Mgt* One who backs artistic enterprises, i.e., gives financial aid to artists, performers, and producers. *Also see* **angel.**

background *BcstJourn* » **ambient sound**

background (bkgd.) *Crit&Eval* Position or an area of relative inconspicuousness or unimportance. BACKDROP

background (bkgd.) *Flm&Vid* (animation) Setting against which action takes place.

background (bkgd.) *Journ* Circumstances and events surrounding or leading up to an event or occurrence. *Also see* **on deep background.**

background (bkgd.) *MusArts* In jazz: sustained chords behind a **melodic** line.

background (bkgd.) *VisArts* **1** Ground or scenery located behind something. **2** Part of a pictorial representation that appears as if in the distance and that provides relief for the principal objects in the **foreground.** **3** General scene or surface against which designs, patterns, or figures are represented or viewed.

background *iMedia* Graphics: part of a scene that appears behind the principal subject within an image or **frame.**

background music *Flm&Vid, MusArts* **1** Music that is usu. **post-production-scored, timed,** and **cued** to action. Such music can be written for the film, or selected from a music library and edited to fit the picture. **2** Music, other than feature or theme music, that creates mood and supports the spoken dialogue of a radio program or visual action of an **audio/visual work.**

background noises *Flm&Vid* Additional sounds mixed with the **foreground** track to give a more realistic sound texture to the scene.

background printing *InfoMgt* Ability to continue working with the computer while printing a document on the printer.

background singers *MusArts* Singers who accompany a featured singer or support the presentation of audio or **audiovisual** material. <singing **backup** in **jingles** and **commercial** recordings>

backgrounder *BcstJourn* Story used to expand history and perspective on a current news event or situation.

backing *PerfA&C* Flats, drops, or draperies placed on the offstage side of doors and similar openings to prevent the audience from seeing backstage.

backing *VA-Prntng* Part of a book where the pages are stitched or glued together into the binding. *Also see* **backbone, spine.**

backing tape *MusArts* Recorded music used to accompany **hip-hop** performances.

backlash *Crit&Eval* Antagonistic reaction to an earlier action.

backlash *Cult&Soc* Antagonistic reaction to an earlier action. <White backlash threatens **affirmative action**>

backlash *Flm&Vid* Slack in **take-up** and rewind **reels**

backlighting *Flm&Vid* When the lights for a shot derive from the rear of the set and throw the foreground figures into semidarkness or silhouette.

backlighting *iMedia* Light coming from behind the subject, toward the camera lens, so that the subject stands out vividly against the background. Sometimes produces a silhouette effect.

backlist *LitArts, Mktg* List of books published in previous years and still in print.

backlog *Mktg* **1** Accumulation of unfinished work or unfilled orders. **2** Reserve supply

backstage *PerfA&C* In or toward the area behind the performing space in a theater, the dressing rooms area. *Also see* **Stage Directions.**

backtime *BcstJourn* Start time for a newscast story, if the newscast is to end at the scheduled time. This process is usu. handled by the computer formats; however, in smaller stations it is still done by hand. Backtime is most efficient when expressed in real clock time, rather than the elapsed time of the newscast.

backup *InfoMgt* To make a copy of a disk or of a file or folder on a disk. Important safety measure against loss of information.

backup *MusArts* Background accompaniment for a performer

backup copies *InfoMgt* Second copies of original data files

backup schedule *Flm&Vid* Schedule of alternative shots should the original schedule be postponed.

backup shots *Flm&Vid* Alternative film shots made in the event that the originally planned shooting cannot be done.

backward integration *Mktg* Obtaining ownership or increased control of an organization's supply systems. *Also see* **forward integration, vertical integration.**

backward reader *Journ, Mktg* One who reads a newspaper or magazine from back to front. *Also see* **back cover.**

bad actor *Crit&Eval* One who consistently misbehaves.

bad sector *InfoMgt* Area of a **floppy** or **hard disk** that won't reliably record data because of manufacturing defects. The **operating system** locks these sectors out so the disk may be used as though the bad sectors don't exist. *Also see* **sectors.**

bad-debt ratio *EntreP* Number obtained by dividing the amount of bad debts by the total amount of credit sales.

badinage (badin-ahzr, Fr.) *Crit&Eval* Light, playful **banter.** *Also see* **Algonquin Round Table.**

baffle *RecA&S* **1** Moveable, acoustically designed partition designed to prevent sound **spill** and reduce **reverberation** in a recording session. **2** Partition that prevents interference between **sound**

waves in a loudspeaker. *Also see* **gobo**.

bait advertising *EntreP* Insincere offer to sell a product or service at a very low price, used to lure customers in so that they can be switched later to a more expensive product or service.

bait and switch *Ethcs&Phil, Mktg* Unethical sales tactic in which a bargain-priced item is used to attract customers who are then pressured to buy a similar but more expensive similar item. *Also see* **rain check**.

Baker, Russell *Crit&Eval, Journ,. Rdio/TV* (1925-) Syn. columnist, *NY Times,* memorialist; **host**, *Masterpiece Theater* (TV) *Also see* **photo op, ruthlessness**.

balance *Dnce* A movement in dance: to move towards something or someone, and then back.

balance *iMedia* Graphics: harmonious or satisfying arrangement or proportion of parts or elements.

balance *Journ, VisArts* Harmonious arrangement of elements in a design or layout.

balance *MusArts* Optimum acoustical blending of the musical instruments – and the **sections** of the band or orchestra – in a live or recorded performance.

Balance of Trade *Eco&Fin* This **economic indicator** compares the plus or minus of exports to imports. As the U.S. balance of trade has been negative – more imports than exports – for so long, the indicator has been given reduced weight in economic projections. *Also see* **Economic Indicators**.

balance *RecA&S* Fine tuning of the **frequency** response in an audio circuit to adjust for any shift in the signal's **frequency** response

balance sheet (BS) *E&F-Acc* 1 **Financial statement** that shows the assets, liabilities, and the **equity** at a specific time. 2 Reflects the overall financial health of the company. STATEMENT OF FINANCIAL CONDITION

balance sheet *EntreP* Financial statement that lists all assets, liabilities, and equity of a company or individual at a given point in time. Balance sheet uses the basic accounting equation which is *Assets = Liabilities + Owner's Equity* or net assets in NFP's.

balanced mutual funds *EntreP* Mutual funds that invest in both stocks and bonds. They provide both capital growth and fixed income.

balcony *PerfA&C* One or more galleries that project over the main floor in a theater or an auditorium.

balcony booms *PerfA&C* Permanent vertical pipes, mounted with lighting instruments to the **balcony**. *Also see* **Stage Lighting**.

balcony rail *PerfA&C* Bar or pipe attached to the front of a **balcony** to which spotlights may be attached. *Also see* **Stage Lighting**.

ballabile (balla-beel, Fr.) *Dnce* Group ballet, usu. for the **corps de ballet**

ballad *LitArts* Narrative poem, often of folk origin and intended to be sung, consisting of simple stanzas and a recurrent refrain.

ballad *MusArts* Popular song, "performed at a slow tempo, usu. having lyrics (whether or not they are performed) that tell a story." — Lyons & Perlo (jazz critics) [Better instrumentalists "sing" the lyrics through their instruments to capture the theme and meaning of the lyrics.].

ballerina *Dnce* **Principal** female ballet dancer; one who dances leading roles. *Also see* **premier danseur, prima ballerina**.

ballet *Dnce* 1 Classical dance form characterized by grace and precision of movement and elaborate formal technique, usu. performed **on point** by the women dancers. 2 Theatrical presentation of group or solo dancing to a musical accompaniment, usu. with costume and scenic effects, conveying a story or theme. 3 Company or group that performs ballet. *Also see* **Dances**.

ballet *MusArts* Musical composition written or used for the ballet dance form.

ballet blanc (baa-lay blahc, Fr. for "white ballet") *Dnce* One in which the dancing is purely classical.

ballet master, ballet mistress *Dnce* Man or woman, who rehearses the dancers, casts minor roles, and performs certain administrative duties. MAÎTRE DE BALLET, MAÎTRESSE DE BALLET

Ballets Russes *Dnce* World-famous ballet company founded in 1909 in Paris by **impresario Serge Diaghilev**, Michel Fokine (1880-1942, Russ.-born choreog.), and Leonid Massine (1896-1979, Russ.-born choreog., dncr.) It revolutionized ballet with lavish productions, incorporating **asymmetry** and perpetual **motion**,

with dancers of the first rank, such as Nijinsky (Vaslav Nijinsky, 1890-1950, Russ.-born dncr., choreog.), Anna Pavlova (1882-1931, Russ. ballerina), composers Maurice Ravel (1875-1937, Fr. comp.), Igor Stravinsky (1882-1971, Russ.-born comp.), artists Fernand Léger (1881-1955, Fr. pntr.), **Pablo Picasso**.

ballon (baa-lon, Fr.) *Dnce* (Ballet) Quality of smooth, springing ascent and descent in jumping steps.

balloon *VisArts* Rounded or irregularly shaped outline containing the words that a character in a **cartoon** is saying or thinking.

ballroom dancing *Dnce* Any of various social dances, such as the **fox trot, tango,** or **waltz**, in which couples follow a conventional pattern of steps. *Also see* **big band, Dances**.

balls, ballsy *Crit&Eval* 1 Perform with gusto and strength. 2 Great presumptuousness, reckless courage. CAJONES

ballyhoo, *Ballyhoo*. *Journ, Mktg* Highly exaggerated publicity; 1920s word for hype and the title of a **girlie magazine**.

BAM *MusArts, PerfA&C* Brooklyn Academy of Music. **Prestigious** entertainment **venue** in Brooklyn, NY.

banal, banality *Crit&Eval* Lacking originality or freshness. *Also see* **platitude, trite**.

band *Fashn* Narrow strip of fabric used to trim, finish, or reinforce articles of clothing.

band *InfoMgt* Circular tracks on a computer disk

band (bnd.) *MusArts* Group of musicians who create music as an ensemble; usu., no strings. *Also see* **combo, orchestra.** BANDLEADER

band *RecA&S* Any of the distinct grooves on a long-playing phonograph record that contains an individual selection or a separate section of a whole. *Also see* **groove, land**.

band director *ArtPerf, MusArts* Music faculty member who trains and conducts a school band.

band shell *MusInstr* Bandstand with a concave, almost hemispheric wall at the rear that serves as a sounding board.

Banded Books Week *Law&Pol, LitArts* » **American Booksellers Association**

bandleader (bndldr.) *ArtPerf, MusArts* One who conducts or fronts a band or **combo**, usu. a country, dance, jazz, or rock band.

bandstand *MusInstr* Sometimes roofed platform for a band or other musical ensembles.

bandwidth *iMedia, InfoMgt* Amount of data that can travel through a **channel** in a given period of time. Usually measured in cycles per second (**hertz**) or in bits per second (**bps**) The larger the bandwidth, the more information the **network** can handle.

bang *Crit&Eval* Sense of excitement. THRILL. *Also see* **kick**.

banjo (bjo) *MusInstr* **Fretted** stringed instrument with a narrow neck and a hollow circular body with a stretched diaphragm of **vellum** or plastic upon which the bridge rests. BANJO PLAYER, BANJOIST *Also see* **Musical Instrument Families**.

bank discount *EntreP* Amount deducted by a bank from the amount borrowed. Usually a percentage rate based on the amount borrowed.

bank *Flm&Vid, PerfA&C* Cluster or strip of lights

bank *InfoMgt* Place to secure data <a computer's memory bank>

bank reconciliation *E&F-Acc* Process of explaining the reasons for the difference between a depositor's records and the bank's records about the depositor's bank account

bank statement *E&F-Acc* Document for a particular bank account in beginning and endings balances and listing the month's transactions that affected the account. *Also see* **Statements**.

bankable star *Flm&Vid* An actor whose popularity can (usu.) guarantee a film's profitability.

banked story *BcstJourn* » **HFR**

bankruptcy *EntreP* Is a state of insolvency where the liabilities of a company or individual exceed the assets and the company or individual does not have sufficient cash flow to make payment to creditors.

banks of seats *PerfA&C* Seats placed on a slope for better audience visibility. *Also see* **sightline, tiers**.

banter *Crit&Eval* Good-humored, playful conversation. *Also see* **badinage, end man**.

bar *MusArts* Vertical line dividing a **staff** into equal **measures**; a **measure**. <12-bar blues, 12-bar composition, 16-bar composition>

bar code *InfoMgt, Mktg* Used on labels, envelopes, and products to be read by a **scanner**. Series of vertical bars of varying widths printed on letters, packages, and product items for computerized inventory control. UNIVERSAL PRODUCT CODE *Also see* **UPC**.

bar code reader *InfoMgt* Device used to read a **bar code** by means of reflected light.

bar graph *Eco&Fin, Journ* Explanatory graph of vertical or horizontal bars of varying length or width to illustrate statistical differences.

barb *Crit&Eval* Cutting remark. *Also see* **Algonguin Round Table**, **badinage**.

barbarian *Cult&Soc* **1** Member of a people considered by those of another nation or group to have a **primitive** civilization. **2** Insensitive, uncultured person. BOOR. **3** One not belonging to a Greek fraternity or sorority. [Myths do linger on.].

barbed *Crit&Eval* Cutting; stinging. <barbed criticism>

barbershop quartet *MusArts* An **a capella** group performing sentimental songs in four-part harmony. *Also see* **S.P.E.B.S.Q.S.A.**

Barbizon School *VisArts* Group of French modern landscape painters (ca. 1840-70) who lived in the village of Barbizon and who painted directly from nature. <Jean-Baptiste Camille Corot (1796-1875 Fr. pntr.), Jean-François Millet (1814-75, Fr. pntr.), Théodore Rousseau (1812-67, Fr. pntr.)>

barcarole *also* **barcarolle** *MusArts* Composition imitating a Venetian gondolier's song.

bargain *HR&LR* To engage in **collective bargaining**

bargain basement *Mktg* Basement in a department store where items are sold at reduced prices.

bargaining chip *HR&LR* **Leverage**, typically in the form of an inducement or a concession, useful in successful negotiations.

bargaining in good faith *HR&LR* Duty of the parties to meet and negotiate at reasonable times with willingness to reach agreement on matters within the scope of representation; however, neither party is required to make a concession or agree to any proposal. Failure to meet and confer in good faith is an unlawful practice.

bari *MusInstr, MusArts* » **baritone sax**, **baritone** voice

baritone (bari) *MusArts* Male voice **register** between tenor and bass

baritone horn *MusInstr* » **euphonium** *Also see* **Musical Instrument Families**.

baritone sax *MusInstr* Instrument with a range between tenor and bass saxophones. BARI PLAYER, BARITONE PLAYER, BARITONE SAXIST *Also see* **Musical Instrument Families**.

barker *ArtPerf, PA-Variety* One who stands on a small platform or stage before the entrance to a **sideshow** as at a **carnival**, and solicits customers with a loud, colorful sales **spiel**. <"Step right up folks..."> TALKER

barn dance *Dnce, MusArts* Social gathering, sometimes held in a barn, with music and **square dancing**.

barn door *Flm&Vid,PerfA&C* Accessory for a **Fresnel** spotlight that has movable blades that allow the beam of light to be shaped slightly and kept off the background or audience. *Also see* **Stage Lighting**.

barnburner *Crit&Eval* Extremely impressive event

barnstorm *PA-Variety* To travel about, usu. in small towns and rural areas, making political speeches, giving lectures, performing airplane stunts, or presenting plays. *Also see* **medicine show**.

Barnum, P.T (b. Phineas Taylor Barnum, 1810-1891; impresario, "The Prince of Humbugs") *Mgt, PA-Variety* **Impresario**, circus and museum **entrepreneur**. *Also see* **grandstanding, Let's get the show on the road, Charles Ringling, Ringling Brothers and Barnum & Bailey Circus.**

baroque *MusArts* Relating to a style of composition in Europe ca. 1600-1750, marked by **chromaticism**, strict forms, and elaborate ornamentation.

baroque *VisArts* **1** Artistic style in art and architecture developed in Europe, ca. 1550-1750, "emphasizing dramatic, often strained effect and typified by bold, curving forms, elaborate ornamentation, and overall balance of disparate parts..." **2** Sometimes marked **bizarre** or incongruous ornamentation. *Also see* **Art Movements and Periods**.

barre (bar, Fr.) *Dnce* **1** Horizontal wooden pole fixed waist high to a wall of a ballet studio, and that the dancer holds on to during

the first part of **class** exercise. **2** Name of this part of ballet **class**.

barrel organ *MusInstr* » **hurdy-gurdy**

barrelhouse *MusArts* Rough, uninhibited piano style characterized by a hard touch to compensate for missing keys. *Origin* Music suited to the beer barrelhouses in New Orleans, where a patron could be bounced if he nursed his nickel beer too long.

barrelman *PA-Variety* **Clown** in a barrel who diverts rampaging horse or bull in a rodeo performance. *Also see* **Rodeo Clowns & Bullfighters Association**.

barter *EntreP, Mktg* Trading goods or services directly for other goods or services.

base 2 *iMedia* Standard digital counting system; 0 and 1. Each column equals the number two to some power. <101 in base 2 equals 11 in base 10>

base 10 *iMedia* Standard system for counting, uses numeric characters 0 to 9.

base *Perf-MkUp* **1** Skin pre-conditioner over which theatrical make-up is applied. **2** In theatrical cosmetics, the color used to cover most of the face.

bash *Crit&Eval* celebration, a party

BASIC *InfoMgt* **Beginners All Purpose Symbolic Code**, a high level language used primarily to teach concepts of programming. Developed at Dartmouth U. in the mid-60s. *Also see* **Programming Languages**.

basic network *Rdio/TV* Group of affiliated stations regarded as a unit for distribution or for placing ads.

Basic Rate Interface (BRI) *InfoMgt* » **BRI**

basic service *Rdio/TV* Cable service offering 12-20 channels available off-the-air and satellite channels supported by advertising.

basic structure *EntreP* Simplest structure of a venture, consisting of only the entrepreneur as a key manager.

bass (b) *MusArts* Having a deep tone, low in **pitch**. *Also see* **basso**.

bass (b) *MusInstr* » **bass viol**

bass clef *MusArts* Designates F below **middle C** as being on the fourth line above the bottom of the **staff**. *Also see* **treble clef**.

bass drum *MusInstr* Large drum having a cylindrical body and one or two heads and producing a low, resonant sound. *Also see* **Musical Instrument Families**. BASS DRUM PLAYER, BASS DRUMMER

bass line *MusArts* "Accompaniment played by the bassist for the purpose of keeping time and outlining the **chord changes** of a piece." — Lyons & Perlo (jazz critics) — FIGURED BASS *Also see* **continuo**, **walking bass line**.

bass reflex *RecA&S* Ported arrangement in a loudspeaker in which sound energy at the rear of the speaker is permitted to exit from the front in phase with the sound produced by the front of the speaker.

bass trumpet *MusInstr* Elongated trumpet with a range similar to a tenor trombone. *Also see* **Musical Instrument Families**.

bass viol (b) *MusInstr* » **double bass** BASS, BASSIST, BASS PLAYER *Also see* **Musical Instrument Families**.

basso *ArtPerf, MusArts* Operatic **bass** singer

bassoon (bssn) *MusInstr* Low-pitched **woodwind** instrument with a **double reed**, having a long wooden body attached to a U-shaped lateral tube that leads to the mouthpiece. Its range is typically two **octaves** lower than that of the **oboe**. BASSOONIST

bassy (base-ee) *MusArts, RecA&S* bass-like sound

baste *PerfA&C* To temporarily stitch pieces of cloth together with long, easily removable stitches.

batch file *InfoMgt* File containing data transactions for later processing.

batch manufacturing *EntreP* Type of manufacturing operation that is intermediate (between job shops and repetitive manufacturing) in volume and variety of products.

batch processing *E&F-Acc, InfoMgt* Part of the software performs each major task of the **computerized accounting system**.

bathos *Crit&Eval* **1** Abrupt, unintended **transition** in style from the exalted to the commonplace, producing a ludicrous effect. **2** **Anticlimax**. **3** Insincere or grossly sentimental. **4** **Banality**, triteness. *Also see* **pathos**.

batik *Fashn* Design or fabric created by a method of dying by which the parts of the fabric not intended to be dyed are covered with removable wax.

baton *MusInstr* **1** Slender wooden stick or rod used by a **conductor** to direct an orchestra or band. **2** Hollow metal rod with a heavy rubber tip or tips wielded, twirled, and dropped by a **drum major(ette)**

battement (bat-tuh-mont, Fr.) *Dnce* Generic ballet term describing various movements in which the leg makes a beating motion.

batten *PerfA&C* Horizontal wood or steel pipe attached to the cables of the rigging or fly system to which are clamped scenery and lighting equipment. Batten should be 20 feet longer than the width of the **proscenium**. *Also see* **electric batten, lift lines**.

Battenberg lace (*aka* Renaissance lace) *Fashn* Heavy lace with patterns formed by very open lace joined by bars that form patterns. First made in 17th century.

batter percussion *MusInstr* Drums that are battered (beaten) by a drum stick. *Also see* **Musical Instrument Families**.

battery *MusInstr* Percussion **section** of an orchestra. *Also see* **Musical Instrument Families**.

battle of the speeds *RecA&S* Marketing struggle in the 1950s between **RCA** with its **45 rpm** record disks and **Columbia Records** with its 33-1/3 **rpm LPs**.

Battlefield *Cult&Soc* New Orleans **red-light** district where **Louis Armstrong** was born. *Also see* **Storyville**.

bauble *Crit&Eval* Small, showy ornament of little value. GEWGAW, TRINKET

baud *InfoMgt* Unit of speed in data transmission usu. equal to one **bit** per second, used as a method of measuring **modem** speed. Slow baud rate would be 2400-baud, average would be 9600-baud; very fast would be 14,400-baud and beyond.

Bauhaus *Aes&Creat VisArts* **1** Characteristic of the design of architecture, furniture, typography, and weaving, the aesthetic of which was influenced by and derived from techniques and materials employed esp. in industrial fabrication and manufacturing. **2** Founded by Walter Gropius (1883-1969, German-born archt.) in Weimar, Germany in 1919, it moved in 1925 to Dessau, to Berlin in 1932 where, in 1933, it was closed by the Nazis. Eventually reborn at the Chicago Institute of Design.

bawd *Crit&Eval* **Bawdy** woman. *Origin* Woman who kept a brothel; a madam.

bawdy *Crit&Eval* Humorously coarse; **risqué**

BBB *Eco&Fin* **Better Business Bureau**

BBC *Rdio/TV* **British Broadcasting Company**. Much admired, seldom rivaled international radio and television service of the British government. *Also see* **Broadcast Stations & Networks**.

BBS *InfoMgt* **Bulletin Board System** Any system accessed by phone or **modem** where messages and data are posted for its users.

BCA *Mgt* **Business Committee for the Arts**. Organization based in NYC that raises money for the arts from corporate membership fees and advocates corporate sponsorship.

BCC *InfoMgt* Blind Carbon Copy. Used in email to send a copy of a message to one or more people without other recipients knowing about it.

bcst. *Rdio/TV* **broadcast**

bean counter *Eco&Fin* One who counts the money. <a financial executive or an accountant>

bear *Eco&Fin* One who thinks that a commodity or financial market will fall. *Also see* **bull**.

bear market *Eco&Fin* Prolonged period of falling prices for stocks and bonds. *Origin* Perhaps from a proverb about the risk of selling a bearskin before the bear is caught. *Also see* **bull market**.

bearish spread *EntreP* Portfolio of calls or puts on which the holder makes money mainly when the price of the underlying security falls.

beat *Crit&Eval* worn-out. fatigued

beat *Cult&Soc* Relating to a **beatnik**.

beat *Journ* **1** Area regularly covered by a reporter. **2** Reporting of a news item ahead of the competition.

beat *LitArts* Measured, rhythmical sound of verse. METER

beat *MusArts* **1** Regular, rhythmical unit of time. **2** Gesture used by a conductor to indicate a rhythmical unit of time. **3** To strike so as to produce music. <beat a drum>

beat *TheatArts* Unit of action in a play text

beat generation *Cult&Soc* Group of unconventional young people

of the 1950s. *Also see* **beatnik**.

beat mash *MusArts* Clean mix of rhythms of two records in **sync**, characteristic of **rave** music. *Also see* **techno music, train wreck**.

beat the band *Crit&Eval* To do something in a fast and furious manner.

beat the drum *Mktg* Energetic, enthusiastic promotion

beatnik *Cult&Soc* One who acts and dresses with exaggerated disregard for what is considered conventional and who tends to radical and social criticism or self-expression.

Beatty, Warren (1937, film act., dir., prod., wri.) *ArtPerf, Flm&Vid* Films include. <*Bonnie and Clyde* (1967), *Shampoo* (1975), *Reds* (1981 Oscar, "Best Dir.")>

beautiful people, Beautiful People (bp, BP) *Cult&Soc* Wealthy, prominent people, esp. those in international society

beaux-arts (bohz-arts, Fr.) *Aes&Creat* Arts of the beautiful. *Also see* **fine arts**.

bebop *MusArts* » **bop**

bebop songs *MusArts* Usually based on blues or **standards**

bed *Rdio/TV* Musical background for a commercial

beefcake *Crit&Eval* Minimally attired men with muscular physiques. *Also see* **cheesecake**.

beehive *Fashn* Conical tower of hair and filler resembling a beehive.

Beginners All Purpose Symbolic Code (BASIC) *InfoMgt* » **BASIC**

behavioral finance *Eco&Fin* Studies the irrational choices most investors make.

behind the scenes *Crit&Eval* Private, hidden from public view.

behind the scenes *TheatArts* » **backstage**

bel *iMedia* Ratio of differences in audio level between two sounds.

bel canto (Ital. for "beautiful song") *MusArts* Style of operatic singing characterized by rich tonal lyricism and brilliant display of vocal technique.

belaying pin *PerfA&C* Short, removable wooden or metal pin used to secure lines that hoist stage **battens**. *Also see* **pin rail**.

believability *Crit&Eval* Capable of eliciting belief or trust, the actor's prime virtue to elicit sympathetic response from an audience. *Also see* **empathic response**.

bell *MusInstr* **1** Hollow metal instrument, usu. cup-shaped with a flared opening. **2** Round, flared mouth of a **wind instrument**.

Bell Labs (Name changed in 1996 to **AT&T Labs**) *InfoMgt, RecA&S, Sci&Tech* Founded in the 1870s, this research facility has been the **R&D** component of AT&T (formerly, American Telephone & Telegraph Company, the telecommunications global giant) *Also see* **C plus plus, computer music, Computer Professionals for Social Responsibility** (CPSR), **facsimile system, hill-and-dale recording, music compression, single-groove stereo recording, UNIX**.

belles-lettres (Fr. for "beautiful letters") *LitArts* **1** Literature regarded for its aesthetic value rather than its **didactic** or informative content. **2** Light, stylish writings, usu. on literary or intellectual subjects.

bells *MusInstr* **Percussion** instrument consisting of metal tubes or bars that emit tones when struck. *Also see* **chimes, xylophone**.

bells and whistles *InfoMgt* Hardware or software with a number of added, but not really important, features.

belly laugh *Crit&Eval* deep laugh. *Also see* **farce**.

below-the-line costs *E&F-Acc, Flm&Vid* All costs, charges, and expenses not applied above-the-line, inc.: non-featured performers (extras), art and set costs, camera, utilities, wardrobe, transportation, raw-film stock, etc. *Also see* **above-the-line costs**.

belt *MusArts* Sing **show tunes** in an aggressive, brassy, and loud style. BELTER

bench-marking *EntreP* Process of studying the products, services, and practices of other companies and using the insights gained to improve quality internally.

benchmark *Eco&Fin, Mktg* **1** Known quantity or point from which something can be measured. **2** To measure a competitor's product according to specified standards in order to compare it with and improve one's own product.

bend *MusArts* Deliberate **flatting** of a note with a return to the original **pitch**.

benday, Benday *VisArts, VA-Prntng* **1** Method of adding a tone to a printed image by imposing a transparent sheet of dots or other patterns on the image at some stage of a photographic reproduction process. **2** Adds shading to a line illustration.

beneficiary *Fnding* In **philanthropic** terms, the **donee** or **grantee** receiving funds from a foundation or corporate giving program is the **beneficiary**, although society benefits as well.

benefit *Fnding* Form of fund-raising that involves the organization and staging of a special event with all proceeds above expenses designated as a contribution to a charitable institution.

benefit segmentation *Mktg* Dividing the population into different groups according to the benefits they want or require and the costs they wish to avoid.

benefit variables *EntreP* Specific characteristics that distinguish market segments according to the benefits sought by customers.

benign *Crit&Eval* Showing gentleness and mildness.

Bentham, Jeremy (1748-1832) *Ethcs&Phil, Law&Pol* Brit. n-fictwri., reformer, philos. who systematically analyzed law and legislation, thereby laying the foundations of **utilitarianism**. *Also see* **David Hume, John Stuart Mill.**

berceuse (burr-soose, Fr.) *MusArts* Lullaby, a soothing composition

Berliner, Émile (1851-1929, German-born inventor) *RecA&S, Sci&Tech* He greatly improved the telephone and invented the **Gramophone** (1887), the first machine to play discs, rather than **Edison's wax cylinders.**

Berne Convention for the Protection of Literary and Artistic Works (1989) *IntelProp* Extended copyright protection for U.S. authors in all member nations of the **Berne Union** with which the U.S. formerly had either no copyright relations or had bilateral treaty arrangements.

Berne Union *IntelProp* Treaty est. 1886 – and amended by subsequent agreements in 1908, 1928, 1948, 1967, and 1971 – by a multinational convention in Berne, Switzerland that permits citizens of countries that are signatories to the treaty to enjoy reciprocal copyright protection in all other member countries. The U.S. became a member of the Berne Union in 1989 by agreeing with the terms of the **Berne Convention for the Protection of Literary and Artistic Works.**

Bernstein, Carl *Journ* » **Bob Woodward**

best boy *Flm&Vid* Chief assistant to the **gaffer** (electrician in charge of lighting) on a movie or television set. Oversees hiring of **grips** and renting their equipment.

best time available (BTA) *Rdio/TV* » **BTA**

bestseller *LitArts, Mktg* Book among those sold in the greatest numbers. *Also see* **break-out book.**

BET *Rdio/TV* **Black Entertainment Television** est. 1979.

Beta *Flm&Vid* » **Betamax**

beta *Genl* **1** Second item in a series or system of classification. **2** Second letter of the Greek alphabet.

beta site *InfoMgt* The company, school, or individual authorized to **beta test** software.

beta test *InfoMgt* Pre-market test of software by developer's staff, media reviewers, and preferred customers.

beta version *iMedia, InfoMgt* Testing version of a software program or publication.

Betamax (Beta) *Flm&Vid* Discontinued type of videocassette recorder made by Sony.

better a line *LitArts,.Rdio/TV* Improve a line of dialog, improve a joke.

Better Business Bureau (BBB) *Eco&Fin* Consumer complaint **nonprofit** located in most every local or regional market.

betterment *E&F-Acc* An improvement that doesn't add to the physical layout of an asset. <installation of an air-conditioning system will offer benefits over a period of years>, so its cost should be charged to an asset account.

BG sound *BcstJourn* » **ambient sound**

bgo *MusInstr* **bongo drum**

bi- *Genl* Occurring at intervals of two. <bicentennial, bimonthly, biweekly>

bias *Crit&Eval* Preference or an inclination that inhibits impartial judgment.

bias *Ethcs&Phil* Unfair act or policy stemming from prejudice.

bias *InfoMgt* Statistical sampling or testing error caused by systematically favoring some outcomes over others.

bias *RecA&S* **1** Possible flaw in the manufacture of magnetic recording tape. <Recording engineer usu. tests blank recording tape for bias error> **2** High **frequency** alternating current reduces electronic distortion when directed through magnetic recording heads.

bias cut *Fashn* Cut diagonally across the grain of fabric.

bibliog. *LitArts* **bibliography**

bibliography (bibliog.) *LitArts* **1** List of the works of a specific author or publisher. **2** List of writings relating to a given subject. **3** List of writings used or considered by an author in preparing a particular work.

bicycling *Flm&Vid* **1** Transporting tapes for broadcast, storage, or review from station to station, or between studios and stations. **2** Use of one print in two theaters for staggered showings thus saving additional cost of rental. *Origin* Bicycle was used in moving a print from one **nickelodeon** to another.

bid *Flm&Vid* Written notification from an exhibitor in response to a bid request from a distributor, competing for the right to show a movie in a particular market on or about a given date. Notification usu. includes playing time, **clearances**, guarantees, advance, terms of rental and advertising, etc.

bid request *Flm&Vid* Written notification from a movie distributor to all exhibitors in a market area inviting them to submit bids.

bidirectional microphone *Rdio/TV, RecA&S* One able to pick up voice or music from its front and back sides. Useful for duets and interviews. *Also see* **Microphones.**

Big Apple *Genl* New York City

big band, Big Band *MusArts* Large dance or jazz-styled band of ten or more instrumentalists usu. featuring improvised solos by lead players. *Also see* **swing.**

big band era *MusArts* About 15 years: mid-1930s to early 1950s. *Also see* **ballroom dancing.**

big beat *MusArts* Popular music having a strong backbeat. <rock 'n' roll>

Big Board *Eco&Fin* New York Stock Exchange (NYSE)

Big Briar *MusInstr* » **Bob Moog, theremin**

Big Brother *Ethcs&Phil* **George Orwell's** chilling overlord of **conformity** in the classic *1984 Also see* **Orwellian.**

big ears *MusArts* **1** Ability to recognize slight differences in sound, esp. in the **pitch**, rhythm, etc. of musical tones. **2** Ability to recognize and remember melody and melodic changes., rhythms and rhythmic changes.

Big Easy *Cult&Soc, MusArts* New Orleans, Louisiana

big screen *Flm&Vid* movie-size **screen** *Also see* **silver screen, small screen.**

big top *PA-Variety* **1** Main circus tent that exhibits under canvas. **2** The circus itself.

big voice *Genl, MusArts* Loud and firm.

Big Willy *ArtPerf* Someone who has a long, successful career in the arts and entertainment world.

bigwig *Crit&Eval* Very important person.

bilateral contract *LegAsp* Both parties agree to do something for each other, a premise for a promise. *Also see* **unilateral contract, Contracts.**

bill *Mktg* Public notice <advertising poster>

bill *TheatArts* **1** theater program **2** Entertainment offered by a theater.

bill of exchange *Eco&Fin, LegAsp* Written order directing that a specified sum of money be paid to a specified person.

bill of lading (B/L) *Eco&Fin* Document issued by a carrier to a shipper, listing and acknowledging receipt of goods for transport and specifying terms of delivery.

Bill of Rights *Law&Pol* First ten amendments to the U.S. Constitution, added in 1791 to protect certain rights of citizens. *Also see* **ACLU.**

Billboard *Flm&Vid, Rdio/TV, MusArts, PA-Variety.* International newsweekly for the video, music, and home entertainment industry.

billboard *Mktg* Structure displaying advertising in public places or alongside a highway. *Also see* **Advertising Media, out-of-home.**

billing *Ethcs&Phil, Flm&Vid* Charging personal travel and **other expenses** to the production budget.

billing *Mgt* Relative recognition of performers and crew indicated by position and type size in which their names appear on marquees, programs, and advertisements. **1** <100% billing — type size must as large as any type used; 75% billing — type size must be no less than 75% of the largest type used> **2** <Star's agent agreed to 100% billing, above the title> *Also see* **credits, top billing**.

bills payable (B/P)*E&F-Acc* Bills required to be paid. *Also see* **accounts payable**.

bills receivable (B/R)*E&F-Acc* Bills waiting to be received. *Also see* **accounts receivable**.

bin *Mktg* Display container, usu. for discounted merchandise. <**cut-out** bin for discounted records>

binary *iMedia, InfoMgt* Condition with only two possibilities. <on or off, 1 or 0, true or false> *Also see* **bit, digital**.

binary conflict *Cult&Soc* Theory of dramatic conflict that emphasizes the conflict between culture and nature. BINARY OPERATIONS, BINARY OPPOSITION

binary file *InfoMgt* File containing data or program instructions in a computer-readable format.

binary graphic *iMedia, InfoMgt* Pure black, no gray, no color.

binary number *iMedia, InfoMgt* Numerical representation used in **digital** computers to store data in which only the digits "0" and "1" are used.

binaural *Rdio/TV, RecA&S* **1** Perception of sound with both ears. **2** Sound transmission from two sources that may vary in tone or **pitch**, to give a **stereophonic** effect.

bind *Fashn* To furnish with an edge or border for protection, reinforcement, or ornamentation.

bind *LegAsp* **1** To place under legal obligation by contract or oath. **2** To make certain or irrevocable. <Down payment can bind the deal>

bind-in card *Mktg, VA-Prntng* Card, usu. 3-in.x 5-in. size, bound in a magazine. <subscription card, reader's service card> BLOW-IN CARD

bindery *VA-Prntng* Place where books and magazines are bound.

Binomial Probability Distribution *EntreP* Binomial probability distribution assigns probability to a random variable that has two possible outcomes. It is described by two parameters N (sample size) and *p* (the probability assigned to one of the possible outcomes)

bio *LitArts* **biography**

bio, bio sheet *Mktg* Brief biography used for promotion and publicity. CREDIT SHEET

bio-bibliography *Crit&Eval, LitArts* An account of a person's life combined with an account of works written by or about that person.

biog. *Crit&Eval, LitArts* biographer.

biography (bio.) *Crit&Eval, LitArts* Critical account of a person's life written, composed, or produced by another author. *Also see* **autobiography**. BIOGRAPHER

biomechanics *TheatArts* Experimental technique for actor training and performance devised by the Russian director, Vsevolod Meyerhold, after the Russian Revolution (1917) Technique emphasized the actor's physical training, stressing acrobatic and choreographic elements in production.

biopic (bio-pic) *Flm&Vid* biographical film.

Birch/Scarborough. *Mktg, Rdio/TV* One of the two largest suppliers of radio ratings research. *Also see* **Arbitron, Nielsen Media Research**.

bird *InfoMgt* Communications satellite

Birth of a Nation, The (1915) *Cult&Soc, Flm&Vid* The first great silent film – albeit blatantly **Jim Crow** – about the Civil War, directed by D.W. Griffith, that transformed "movies" to an art form.

bit *iMedia, InfoMgt* Contraction of **BI**nary digi**T**, the smallest measure of computer information. The value of a bit (1 or 0) represents a simple two-way choice, e.g., on or off, true or false, black or white, etc. *Also see* **binary, byte, word**.

bit depth *iMedia* Number of bits used to store information about each pixel; often used to describe both monitor and image resolutions.

bit part *ArtPerf, Flm&Vid, Dnce* Insignificant role having a few spoken lines. BIT PLAYER

bit player *Flm&Vid* Actor playing a small part.

bite *BcstJourn* Portion of a recorded interview that is scheduled for use in a broadcast news story. *Also:* cut.

bites *BcstJourn* portions of **actualities**

bitmap *iMedia, InfoMgt* Set of bits that represents the graphic image of a document or font in computer memory. *Also see* **pixel**. BITMAPPED FONT

bittersweet *Crit&Eval* Engendering both pain and pleasure. <blues lyrics, nostalgic memories>

bizarre *Crit&Eval* Strikingly unconventional and far-fetched in style or appearance.

bjo *MusInstr* **banjo**

bk., bks. *LitArts, VA-Prntng* **book, books**.

bkgd. *Crit&Eval, Flm&Vid, Journ, VisArts* **background**.

Black *also* **black** *Cult&Soc* Relating to an American **ethnic** or racial group descended from African peoples having dark skin. *Origin* The Black population of South Africa. *Also see* **African-American, Racial Designations**.

black and white *VisArts* Visual medium, as in movies, photography, or printmaking, employing only black and white or black, white, and values of gray.

black book *Ethcs&Phil* Book containing names of people and organizations to **blacklist**.

Black Bottom *Dnce* Jazz dance, ca. 1920s. *Also see* **Dances**.

black box *iMedia* **1** element or component where the internal workings are not accessible or the access is discouraged. **2** device or theoretical construct with known or specified performance characteristics but unknown or unspecified constituents and means of operation. **3** Something mysterious, especially as to function.

black box theater *TheatArts* Relatively small room usu. painted black with movable stage and seating, enabling a variety of theatrical configurations.

Black Caucus *MusArts* Organization of black music educators within the **Music Educators National Conference** (MENC) that sponsors national events such as college and high school gospel choir festivals.

black classical music *MusArts* » **Duke Ellington**

Black Creoles *Cult&Soc* Black persons living in Southwest Louisiana "whose contemporary identity reflects strong French and African roots as well as other ethnic and cultural influences. Their music is widely known as **zydeco music**." — Mark Mattern (political scientist, Chapman U.) *Also see* **Cajun**.

Black Entertainment Television *Rdio/TV* » **BET**

black gospel music *MusArts* **1** African American based music similar to the blues and rhythm and blues but with religious lyrics. **2** "In this style, vocalists radically **embellish** simple melodies, and in full and falsetto voice, they shout, hum, growl, moan, whisper, scream, cry. By adding florid **melismas** and tricky **syncopations**, altering given **pitches** with **blue notes** and **glissandos**, and interpolating formulaic phrases ('Lord have mercy,' 'well, well, well'), they freely extend or repeat any fragment of the text. Spontaneous or choreographed dancing, clapping, and stomping may accompany the singing." — *New Harvard Dictionary of Music Origin* "Basic performance style of 20th century black gospel music originated in Memphis about 1907, when the founders of the sanctified Pentecostal Church of God in Christ, inspired by a revival that had attended in Los Angeles, instituted their own highly emotional service, characterized by singing or speaking or in tongues (glossolalia), shouting, trances and visions, and suitably emotional music, often improvised, and sung in a highly charged style (singing in tongues)" — Horace Boyer (gospel mus. critic) *Also see* **Gospel Music**.

black humor *LitArts* Morbid and absurd humor, esp. in its development in a literary **genre**. BLACK HUMORIST

black letter *VA-Prntng, VisArts* Heavy typeface with **counters** and thick, ornamental **serifs**.

black magic *Cult&Soc* Magic (not racially related) practiced for evil purposes or in league with supposed evil spirits. WITCHCRAFT. *Also see* **conjure, voodoo**.

black music *Cult&Soc, MusArts* Any music based on the black experience regardless of who plays it or who writes it. "Blacks invented jazz, but nobody owns it." —**Wynton Marsalis** "Sometimes the black-white thing... drives me up the wall. Jazz is where you find it." — Oliver Nelson (1932-75, jazz sop./alto/tenor sax, arr.-comp., cond. of film/TV scores, big band **charts**, author/clinician/tchr.) "The most important thing that **Quincy [Jones]** taught me was that black music was not just for black people. It's not about changing art, it's about positioning art." — Russell Simmons (founder Def Jam, **hip-hop** record label)

black musicians *Cult&Soc*, *MusArts* **1** "To say that only black musicians can be innovative is so utterly ridiculous I can hardly consider the question." — Bill Evans (1929-80, jazz pno., comp.) **2** "Social issues didn't have anything to do with hiring white musicians who were qualified: it was that simple." — **Sonny Rollins**

black road shows *PA-Variety* "From 1890 through World War I, black road shows provided the primary proving ground for the **host** of comedians who surfaced in black theaters and in films during the 1920s. These road shows, playing before primarily black audiences, were like a rich underground spring that nurtured a form of black stage comedy more closely aligned to the authentic humor of black folks. Removed from the expectations of white audiences, black comedians working in traveling shows before black patrons could and gradually did alter the image of depravity, venality and ignorance that characterized **minstrel** humor, as well as much of the humor seen in **mainstream** arenas such as **vaudeville** and Broadway **musicals**." — Lawrence W. Levine (lit. critic)

Black Rock *Rdio/TV* Color-coded **sobriquet** for the CBS headquarters building in NYC.

black sacred music *MusArts* **Spirituals**, **refrain** songs, and **gospel** music.

Black Sox scandal *SportsEnt* Most notorious scandal in baseball history. During the 1919 baseball World Series, eight players from the Chicago White Sox (later nicknamed the Black Sox) were accused of throwing the series against the Cincinnati Reds. Despite being acquitted of criminal charges, the players were banned from professional baseball for life. This scandal had major effects on the **Major League of Baseball** organization. (Scandal referred to in several films. Ex.: *Fields of Dreams, The Natural*.)

black studies *Cult&Soc* Educational programs dealing with African American culture and history.

black telegraph *Cult&Soc*, *InfoMgt* Informal word-of-mouth network used U.S. slaves. Said to be revived in **cyberspace**.

black theaters *TheatArts* Theaters in predominantly black neighborhoods that book black performers and are patronized mainly by black audiences. DARK HOUSES

black wax *Perf-MkUp* Used to black out teeth or parts of teeth.

blackface *Cult&Soc*, *Perf-MkUp*, *PA-Variety* **1** Makeup for a conventionalized comic travesty of blacks. <**minstrel show**> **2** Actor in a **minstrel show**. *Also see* **burnt cork**, **Al Jolson**, **minstrely**.

blackface *VA-Prntng* **Boldface** printing type or style.

blacklist *Ethcs&Phil* List of organizations or persons that are disapproved, boycotted, or suspected of disloyalty. <The **Hollywood Ten** were blacklisted by all movie studios and broadcast networks> *Also see* **black book**.

blackout *PA-Variety* Short comic burlesque or **vaudeville** skit ending with the stage lights suddenly turned off.

blackout *Rdio/TV*, *Law&Pol* **1** Ban on broadcasting a TV program because of commercial or political reasons. <Local or regional ban on live broadcasting of a major sporting event, some TV programs about acid rain and antiadministration views on the Vietnam war, the Contras, etc> **2** Solar flare interruption of radio communications.

blackout *TheatArts* Abrupt extinguishing of all stage lights to mark the passage of time or change of scene. *Also see* **iris**, **Stage Directions**.

blacksploitation film *Flm&Vid* Films of the mid-'70s to early 1980s that featured a black person as a hero/superhero in a **melodramatic** and sensational plot marketed with a strong emphasis on sex and violence. BLAXPLOITATION

bland *Crit&Eval* Neutral, colorless, undistinguished.

blank endorsement *E&F-Acc*, *LegAsp* Endorsement by which the endorser of a check or any negotiable instrument does not restrict or limit the condition under which the **payee** may obtain funds.

blank tape *RecA&S* Tape on which no audio signal or visual image has been recorded. *Also see* **virgin stock**.

blank verse *LitArts* Unrhymed poetry, esp. poetry written in **iambic pentameter**. *Also see* **verse**.

blanket agreement *LegAsp* Applying to or covering all conditions or instances.

blanket license *IntelProp*, *MusArts* Form of unlimited performance licensing for which radio and television stations, public broadcasters, cable stations, universities, restaurants, subscription music services, etc. pay an annual fee to a **performing rights** organization. This license grants the right to unlimitedly perform every piece of music contained in the respective repertoire during the term of the license. *Also see* **ASCAP**, **BMI**, **per-program license**, **SESAC**.

blasé (blah-zay, Fr.) *Crit&Eval* **1** Uninterested because of frequent exposure or indulgence. **2** Unconcerned; nonchalant. <The French have a blasé attitude about bathing> **3** Very sophisticated.

blasphemous *Crit&Eval* Impiously irreverent.

blasphemy *Crit&Eval* Irreverent or impious act, attitude, or utterance. *Also see* **public policy**.

blast *Crit&Eval* Exciting or very pleasurable experience or event. <a big party> *Also see* **shindig**.

blasting *RecA&S* Gross distortion of loud sounds caused by overloading an amplifier or loudspeaker.

bleak books *Crit&Eval*, *LitArts* Novels offering older adolescents stories that focus on the realities of their lives.

bleed ad *Mktg*, *VA-Prntng* Ad printed so as to go off the edge or edges of a page after trimming, for which publishers usu. charge an additional 10%. *Also see* **bleed allowance**, **full page ad**.

bleed allowance *Journ*, *VA-Prntng* Extra **pica** allowance on the outside edges of a page that will be trimmed off for binding. *Also see* **bleed**.

bleep *Rdio/TV* Delete spoken material from a broadcast or recording by replacing the unspeakable with an electronic sound.

blemish-cover sticks *Perf-MkUp* Small makeup sticks in lipstick cases used to cover skin blemishes or minimize wrinkles.

blimp *Flm&Vid* Soundproof camera housing that muffles the noise of the camera's motor.

blind audition *MusArts* One in which a screen hides the auditioning musician from the auditors.

blind bidding *Flm&Vid* Same as a bid request except that the film has not been previously screened. *Also see* **bid**, **bid request**.

Blind Carbon Copy *InfoMgt* » **BCC**

blind spot *Rdio/TV* Area where radio reception and other electronic communication is weak or nonexistent.

blip *Sci&Tech* High-**pitched** electronic sound; a **bleep**.

blister pack *Mktg* Form of displaying and packaging merchandise sealed into a transparent plastic blister backed by foil or cardboard. BUBBLE PACK.

bln. *Eco&Fin* billion.

block *TheatArts* Number of theater seats, taken together.

block *VA-Prntng* Large amount of text

block *VisArts* Substance, such as wood or **stone**, that has been prepared for engraving.

block booking *Flm&Vid*, *PerfA&C* Sometime illegal practice of making a movie exhibitor or talent buyer book several grade B-C-D films or **attractions** in order to get a grade A film or **attraction**.

block chord *MusArts* Piano style in which **chords** are played with both hands LOCKED HANDS

block out *Flm&Vid*, *TheatArts* » **blocking**

block pattern *Fashn* » **sloper**

block-level element *iMedia* Element with an inherent carriage return; anything following the element will start on a new line.

blockbuster *Flm&Vid*, *LitArts*, *Mktg* Film or book, that sustains widespread popularity and achieves enormous sales.

blocking *Flm&Vid*, *TheatArts* During rehearsals, the director's plan for the principal **business**, positions, and movements of the actors.

blocking *TheatArts* Director's organization of the stage movements of her/his cast.

block programming *Rdio/TV* Program scheduling by TV networks to hold audiences from program to program, designed to get and maintain high ratings.

bloggers *InfoMgt*, Allow users to create instant public online diaries.

bloodletting *HR&LR* The laying off of personnel or the elimination of resources. *Also see* **downsizing**.

Bloom, Alan (1930-92, cult. critic, educ., U. Chicago) *ArtPerf*,

Crit&Eval, LitArts Noted for his best-selling *The Closing of the American Mind* (1957). *Also see* **deconstruction, snob**.

bloomers *Fashn* Wide, loose trousers gathered at the knee, formerly worn by women and girls as an athletic costume; girls' underpants of similar design.

blow (one's) top, blow (one's) stack *Crit&Eval* To lose one's temper. "Do you **dig** me when I say I have a right to blow my top over injustice?" — **Louis Armstrong**

blow *MusArts* **1** To cause a wind instrument to sound a tone. **2** To improvise in a jazz ensemble.

blow the whistle *Ethcs&Phil* To expose a wrongdoing in the hope of bringing it to a halt — or to receive a reward. *Also see* **whistle-blower**.

blow up *VisArts* Enlarge a photographic image or print.

blow-in card *Mktg, VA-Prntng* Unbound subscription card inserted at random in a magazine.

blue chip *Eco&Fin* **1** Stock that sells at a high price because of public confidence in its long record of steady earnings. **2** Extremely valuable asset or property.

blue chip *PA-Variety* (Gaming) Blue poker chip of high value.

blue collar *Eco&Fin, HR&LR* Relating to wage earners as a class, whose jobs are performed in work clothes and often involve manual labor. *Also see* **wages, working class**.

blue law *Law&Pol* **1** Law aimed at regulating commercial and entertainment activities on a Sunday. <Sunday theatrical performances were not allowed in Philadelphia until the 1950s> **2** One of a body of laws in colonial New England designed to enforce strict moral standards.

blue material *Crit&Eval* Indecent, risqué. <blue joke, blue movie>

Blue Network *Rdio/TV* Former fraternal twin of the **Red Network** of the **National Broadcasting Company** (NBC) that evolved into the **American Broadcasting Cos.** (ABC) *Also see* **Broadcast Stations & Networks**.

blue nose *Ethcs&Phil* One who is offensively disposed to forbid activities or production on trivial moral grounds.

blue note *MusArts* **Flatted** note, esp. the third and seventh note of a **chord**, in place of an expected **interval**. *Also see* **Blues**.

blue notes *MusArts* "Blue notes... are exactly those off-**pitch** notes... that are derived directly from Africa. It must be clearly understood that they are neither major (E) nor (minor (E flat) but lie somewhere in between." — James Lincoln Collier (jazz critic) Used for emphasis and mood, often together with the natural notes, creating a **dissonance** and **tension**.

blue screen *iMedia* **1** Surface (painted wall, screen, dropcloth, etc.) a specific shade of blue easily replaced in an image or video sequence in post-production. **2** act of replacing part of an image or video with another image or video. Related terms: keying, chroma key, green screen.

blue-pencil *Journ, LitArts* To edit, correct, and revise as if with a blue pencil.

blue-pencil *Law&Pol* To censor.

blue-sky law *Eco&Fin, LegAsp* Law designed to protect the public from buying fraudulent securities.

bluebeat *MusArts* In the 1960s, British name for **ska**.

bluegrass *MusArts* Form of **country music** in which the singers play autoharps, fiddles, banjos, and guitars; harmonizing over lost love, and the life styles of mountain folk, *aka* **hillbillies**. Its style is characterized by fast tempos and jazzlike **improvisation**. Developed in mid-1940s in **Appalachia** by songwriters and musicians. <The Carter Family (singers, sngwri.; ca. 1930-50), Bill Monroe (1911-96; sngwri.), Lester Flatt (1914-79; gtr., sngwri.) & Earl Scruggs (1924-, sngwri., bjo.), and their Foggy Mountain Boys> *Also see* **Country Music Styles**.

blueline *VA-Prntng* **Offset** paper proof sheets that show printed areas in blue. BLUELINE

blueprint *VA-Prntng* » **blueline**

Blues *ColEntry, MusArts* » **blue note, blues, blues-rock, city —, classic —, country —, rhythm and —. Rhythm and Blues Foundation, rural —, 12-bar —, soul music, urban —, white —.**

blues *Crit&Eval* State of depression or melancholy.

blues *MusArts* Style of vocal and instrumental music usu. distinguished by slow tempo, **flatted** thirds and sevenths, and **12-bar** phrases (although there are a few 16-**bar** blues) Evolved from African **call and response** and **harmonics**, rural and urban African American **secular** songs, **antebellum** back-breaking **work songs, field hollers**, poverty, oppression, and unrequited love. <Bessie Smith (*aka* "Empress of the Blues," 1894-1937; sngr.)> *Also see* **Blues, Devil's music, Songs**.

blues harp *MusInstr* » **harmonica**

blues-rock *MusArts* Style of music that combines blues and rock. *Also see* **Blues**.

bluestocking *LitArts* Woman with strong scholarly or literary interests.

bluesy *Crit&Eval* "Referring to the earthy, soulful feeling evoked by expressive use of **blue notes** or by speech-inflected singing or playing." — Lyons & Perlo (jazz critics)

blurb *Mktg* Brief hype, like on an album cover or book **jacket**.

BMI *IntelProp, MusArts* **Broadcast Music, Inc. Performance rights** organization – est. 1940 by a group of broadcasters – that licenses on a non-exclusive basis to users of musical compositions the non-dramatic public performance rights of its members and affiliated foreign rights societies. *Also see* **Copyright-Related Organizations**.

bndldr. *MusArts* **bandleader**.

board *InfoMgt* Short for printed circuit board. Flat, thin rectangular component of a computer or **peripheral** that includes one or more layers of printed circuitry and to which chips and other electronic parts are attached. *Also see* **card**.

board *PerfA&C* » **call board**

board *Rdio/TV, RecA&S* Recording or broadcasting **console**.

board development *Mgt* Activities that serve to improve the efficiency of the board of directors or trustees.

board of directors *EntreP, Mgt* Group of individuals elected, usu. at an annual meeting, by the shareholders of a corporation and empowered to carry out certain tasks spelled out in the corporation's charter. *Also see* **inside directors, outside directors**.

Board of Governors of the Federal Reserve *EntreP* Seven-person governing body of the Federal Reserve system in Washington, DC.

board of trustees *Mgt* Group of individuals elected or appointed to direct the funds and policy of an institution, usu. a **nonprofit**.

boards *TheatArts* Stage. <**Olivier** trod the boards of the **Old Vic**>

bob *Fashn* **1** Woman's or child's short haircut. **2** Surgical reshaping of the nose.

bobbin *Fashn* **1** Spool or reel that holds thread or yarn for spinning, weaving, knitting, sewing, or making lace. **2** Narrow braid formerly used as trimming.

Bobo *Cult&Soc* Bourgeois **Bohemian**.

bodice *Fashn* **1** Fitted part of a dress that extends from the waist to the shoulder. **2** Woman's laced outer garment, worn like a vest over a blouse.

body *InfoMgt* Content of an email message, preceded by the **header**.

body *LitArts, VA-Prntng* Content of a book exclusive of prefatory matter, indexes, or appendices.

body english *Crit&Eval* Deliberate or instinctive movements of a person to try to influence the movement of a propelled object. <contortions used by a pinball player to "move" the ball to a desired goal> *Also see* **body language**.

body language *Crit&Eval* Bodily gestures, postures, and facial expressions by which a person communicates **nonverbally** with others. <The trained actor communicates attitudes and thoughts by facial expression and body language, such as: raising of an eyebrow, or a shrug of the shoulders> *Also see* **body English**.

body makeup *Perf-MkUp* Available as an opaque or transparent liquid, or as a powder.

body politic *Cult&Soc, Law&Pol* People of a politically organized nation or state considered as a group.

body popping *Dnce* Type of dancing characterized by convulsive body movements and mimed robotic gestures. *Also see* **Dances**.

body scanner *Fashn, Sci&Tech* Computerized device that registers customer's three-dimensional measurements on a **smart card**, thus making possible garment customization.

body shirt *Fashn* **1** Woman's garment for the torso made with a sewn-in or snapped crotch. **2** Tight-fitting shirt or blouse.

body shop *HR&LR, Mgt* Agency for temporary workers. *Also see* **temp**.

body snatcher *HR&LR* corporate recruiter.

body suit *Fashn* Tight-fitting one-piece garment for the torso.

body type *Journ, LitArts, VA-Prntng* Smaller typefaces (12 point or smaller) used in the **body** of a book, magazine or newspaper. <DAPM body type is 9-point New Century Schoolbook> *Also see* **display type.**

boff *Crit&Eval,PerfA&C* **1** Bit of dialogue or stage business that gets a sudden, big laugh. **2** Conspicuous success. BOFFO, BOF-FOLA *Origin* **box office.**

boggle *Crit&Eval* Be overcome with astonishment. <His convoluted reasoning boggles one's mind>

bogus *Ethcs&Phil* counterfeit or fake.

bohemia, Bohemia *Cult&Soc* **1** Community of persons with artistic or literary tastes who adopt manners and mores conspicuously different from those approved by the majority of society. **2** Where Bohemians live (in what is now Czechoslovakia.)

bohemian *Crit&Eval* **1** One who is unconventional, a non-conformist, carefree and unorthodox, usu. an offbeat Individual. **2** A gypsy. **3** Native or inhabitant of **Bohemia.**

boilerplate *Journ* Journalistic material in plate or mat form. <syndicated features or press releases>

boilerplate *LegAsp* **1** Standard pre-prepared documents or sections of documents. **2** Standard minimum contracts. "In the last 10 years, we have seen contract boilerplates get tougher and tougher, relationships between authors and editors get weaker and weaker, a few celebrity business tycoons, television actresses and celebrity authors get millions of dollars for their work, while the majority of authors get lower royalties, lower advances and in many cases cannot be published at all." — Erica Jong (1942-, wri., poet, scrnwrtr.)

boîte *PerfA&C* (bwhat, Fr.) Small restaurant or nightclub.

boldface *iMedia,* **VA-Prntng** Type with thick, heavy lines. <**bold-face**> *Also see* **lightface.**

bolero *Fashn* Very short jacket worn open in the front.

bolero *Dnce, MusArts* **1** Spanish dance and music. **2** Music and slow dance developed in Cuba and Mexico in the 1930s and 1940s. Boleros lyrics are always about romance and fickle love. *Also see* **Dances.**

bomb *InfoMgt,PerfA&C* Denotes a spectacular failure in a program or live performance. *Also see* **crash.**

bombast *Crit&Eval* **Grandiloquent, pompous** speech or writing.

bombs *InfoMgt* » **mail bombs.**

bombs *MusArts* To drop or throw bombs refers to the insertion of hard bass drum accents at irregular intervals. Style of **bop** drumming introduced by Kenny Clarke (» **bop**) and Max Roach (» **bop**)

bon mot (bonn-moh, Fr.) *Crit&Eval* Clever saying. WITTICISM.

bona fide (bona fyde, Latin) *Crit&Eval* authentic, genuine.

bona fide occupational qualifier *HR&LR* Special circumstance which justifies the use of gender, religion, or race as a specific quality needed by a job applicant <female attendant in a women's dressing room.>

bona fide union *HR&LR* One chosen freely by its employees without undue influence by the employer.

bond *EntreP* An I.O.V between a borrower (government or corporation) and a lender (individual, pension fund, mutual fund, insurance company)

bond *Mgt* Sum of money paid to secure against loss, damage, or **default.** <The Jazz Pzazzers were required to post bond against damage to the auditorium> [Talent agencies in some states have to post bond with the state against the agent's possible violations of employment agency regulations.] *Also see* **completion bond.**

bones *Crit&Eval* Fundamental plan or design. <**plot** of a book>

bones *MusInstr* Flat clappers made of bone or wood originally used in **country blues** bands and by the **end man** in a **minstrel show.** *Also see* **Musical Instrument Families, spoons.**

bongo(s) (bgo) *MusInstr* One of a pair of connected tuned drums that are played by beating with the hands. *Also see* **Musical Instrument Families.**

bonus *Eco&Fin, HR&LR* **1** Payment of money or goods given to an entertainer for signing or renewing a contract. <new car, jewelry, luxury vacation, etc> **2** Payment of money or the equivalent given to an employee in addition to the employee's usual compensation. **3** Payment of money in addition to salary given to a professional athlete for signing with a team. **4** Premium (stock)

given by one corporation to another, such as a purchaser of its securities. **5** Payment of money paid by a corporation in excess of interest or royalties charged for the granting of a privilege or a loan to that corporation **6** Reward or a subsidy from a government to an industry for exceptional performance or in the "interests of national security."

bonus *Genl* Something given or paid in addition to what is usual or expected.

bonus records *RecA&S* Records distributed free to members of record clubs as a bonus for joining or for buying a given number of records. No royalty is paid to artists on bonus records. Not applicable to **gold** or **platinum record** recognition. FREE RECORDS

boogie *Dnce, MusArts,* **1** Strongly rhythmic rock music. **2** To dance to the sound of rock music. *Also see* **Dances, Rock Music Styles.**

boogie-woogie *MusArts* Style of piano blues characterized by a steady **ostinato** bass line in the left-hand with eight beats to the **measure** and by a series of **riffs** in the right-hand. Flourished in the 1920s and 1930s.

Book *Ethcs&Phil* The Bible.

book (Passé) *Journ* Several sheets of copy paper interlarded with carbons on which reporters – before computers – typed their stories.

book (bk.) *LitArts* **1** Printed or written literary work. **2** Main division of a larger printed or written work. <a book of the Old Testament> **3** libretto. **4** Script of a play. **5** Trade name for a magazine. **6** Writing read on a screen.

book *Mgt* **1** To hire or engage. <The Aesthetic Punks are booked for New Year's Eve> **2** To allocate time for. <The Cow Palace is booked at noon for the Aesthetic Punks' **sound check**>

book club *LitArts, Mktg* Company that sells books at a discount to its members on a regular basis. <Quality Paperback Book Club> *Also see* **record club.**

book packager *LitArts* Independent book producer

book value *EntreP* Value of a fixed asset on a company's books after depreciation has been accounted for.

book value (B/V)*E&F-Acc* Carrying value of a **long-term asset** (fixed asset) representing the difference between recorded cost and accumulated **depreciation.**

book value (B/V) *Eco&Fin* **1** Monetary amount by which an asset is valued in business records, a figure not necessarily identical to the amount the asset could bring on the open market. **2** Calculated by subtracting total liabilities from total assets. OWNERS EQUITY, STOCKHOLDERS EQUITY *Also see* **equity.**

book value of a plant asset*E&F-Acc* Asset's cost less **accumulated depreciation.**

book value method of valuation *EntreP* Method of determining the value of a company by determining the actual net value of the venture's assets.

book value per share of common stock *Eco&Fin* Common stockholder's **equity** divided by the number of shares of common stock outstanding.

book-to-bill *Eco&Fin* **Economic indicator** in an industry such as the semi-conductor industry. Refers to the percentage of orders originally booked against the orders actually billed.

booker *Flm&Vid* One employed by the distributor to be responsible for all aspects of monitoring and trafficking the movie prints within the branch office's jurisdiction.

booker *Journ, Rdio/TV* One who books guests for a news program.

booker *Mgt* Person or company employed by an entertainment **venue** to **book** (engage) talent for the **venue.** HOUSE BOOKER

booking *Mgt* **Engagement** for a performance

bookmark *InfoMgt* Online procedure enabling one to return to a particular **Web site.**

bookmobile *InfoMgt, LitArt, Mktg* Truck, trailer, or van equipped to serve as a mobile lending library. *Also see* **jazzmobile.**

books *Eco&Fin* **1** Volumes in which financial or business transactions are recorded. **2** Financial or business records considered as a group.

bookstall *LitArts, Mktg* Stall where books are sold, as on a street or in a mall.

bookwriter *ArtPerf, LitArts, MusArts* Writer of a **libretto.** *Also see* **book.**

Boolean logic *iMedia* Method of solving equations that results in either TRUE or FALSE.

Boolean search *InfoMgt* Use of "and," "or," and "not" functions to combine search terms for selecting information during an online search.

Boolean value *iMedia* » **Boolean logic**

boom *Flm&Vid, Rdio&TV, RecA&S* Long, movable arm to maneuver and support a microphone, permitting the synchronous recording of sound without restricting the movements of the actors or musicians. BOOM MIC

boom *PerfA&C* Vertical pipe used for mounting lighting instruments.

boom box *RecA&S* Portable audio system, usu. consisting of a cassette player and radio, with speakers capable of producing loud sound. [Illegal to play on some public transportation systems.] *Also see* **Music Playback Devices**.

boomie *Eco&Fin* Relating to a flourishing economy.

boomie *RecA&S* Excessive accentuation on lower-pitched tones in reproduced sound, likely to distort true musical **pitch**.

boondoggle *Crit&Eval* Unnecessary, wasteful, and often counterproductive work. Term applied by critics of the **Public Works Administration** (PWA) and the **Works Progress Administration** (WPA) for providing employment to artists and performers and other unemployed workers in the mid-1930s.

boot *iMedia, InfoMgt* To start or restart a computer system. *Origin* bootstrap. *Also see* **reboot**.

booth *Mktg* Small stall or stand for display and sale of goods.

booth theater *TheatArts* Erected at fairs in the **Middle Ages** and in the **Renaissance**. *Also see* **Theatres & Theaters**.

Booth, Wayne C. (19??-, art crit., hist., philo.) *Crit&Eval, VisArts* » **ethics, ethical criticism, feminist critics, moral majority**.

bootlegging *RecA&S* To produce, distribute, or sell without permission or illegally. <Several countries bootleg record albums and tapes in order to reduce prices and gain competitive advantage>

bootlegging *Rdio/TV* To attach a transmitter to a **dish antenna**, creating an uplink by which a signal is sent to a satellite without the knowledge of the satellite's owner.

bootlegs *MusArts RecA&S* » **mash-ups**

bop *or* **bebop** *MusArts* Style of jazz meant to be listened to rather than be danced to, characterized by rhythmic and harmonic complexity, improvised solo performances, and a brilliant style of execution. Introduced in New York in the early 1940s by the likes of Kenny Clarke (1924-85, jazz drm), **Dizzy Gillespie**, Thelonious Monk (1917-82, jazz pno., comp.), **Charlie Parker**, Bud Powell (Earl Powell, 1924-66, jazz pno., comp.), and Max Roach (1924-, jazz drm, comp., educ.) **2** To dance or move to the beat of this music. *Also see* **Jazz Styles, New York Jazz.**

border *PerfA&C* Horizontal masking drape that hides items in the **fly loft** from view of the audience. *Also see* **Stage Curtains**.

border light *PerfA&C* » **striplight**

border radio *Rdio/TV* Refers to the 250,000 watt radio stations just across the border into Mexico that broadcast a signal five times stronger than the strongest U.S. station. Also *see* **pirate**.

borders *PerfA&C* Wide, short, framed, or unframed cloth drops suspended over the stage to prevent the audience from seeing above the stage.

borscht circuit *PA-Variety* Predominantly Jewish resorts in the Catskill Mountains (NY) that feature entertainment. *Also see* **tumler**.

boss *Crit&Eval* First-rate, topnotch. <**Sonny Rollins** plays boss tenor sax>

bossa nova *Dnce, MusArts* 1960s Brazilian blend of jazz and **samba**. *Also see* **Dances, Latin Dance Music**.

Boston version *Crit&Eval, TheatArts* (Passé) Show purged of indecencies. *Origin* For many years, Boston had the strictest censorship in the U.S.

bottleneck guitar *MusArts* Style of guitar playing in which an object, such as a piece of glass or metal, is passed across the strings to achieve a gliding sound.

bottom-up planning *Mgt, Mktg* Programs are developed and implemented by middle-level and lower-level managers and other employees or volunteers who work out the details and the follow through. *Also see* **Goals and Plans**.

bottomless *PA-Variety* Relating to a person without a garment below the waist. <bottomless dancer> *Also see* **topless**.

bouclé *or* **boucle** (boo-clay, Fr.) *Fashn* Three-ply yarn has one thread looser than the others that produces a rough-textured cloth.

bouffant *Fashn* puffed-out hairstyle

bouffe *MusArts* » **comic opera**

bounce *Dnce, MusArts* Rap influenced call-and-response booty-shaking dance music. *Also see* **Dances**.

bounce message *InfoMgt* Report that an email message was not properly delivered.

bounceback *Mktg* Promotional device designed to motivate the consumer to go to or return to a retail outlet in order to take advantage of the promotion. <contest, coupon, premium, sweepstakes entry>

bouncer *Mgt* One employed to expel disorderly persons from a public place, esp. a bar. *Also see* **barrelhouse, bum's rush**.

bourgeoisie (boor-schwa-zee, Fr.) *Cult&Soc* **1** middle class. **2** In **Marxist** theory, the social group opposed to the **proletariat** in the class struggle.

bourrée (boo-ray, Fr.) *Dnce* (Ballet) Weight is transferred from one foot to the other in three small steps.

boutique *Fashn* **1** Small retail shop specializing in fashionable clothes and accessories. **2** Small shop located within a large department store.

boutique *Mgt* Small talent agency offering one or more specialized services or varieties of talent. <Talent agency specializing in percussion ensembles, strippers, and cross-dressers>

boutique *Mktg* Small advertising agency offering one or more specialized services.

bow *MusInstr* **1** Rod with horsehair drawn tightly between its two raised ends, used in playing instruments of the violin family. **2** Stroke made by a bow. BOWING

bowdlerize *Ethcs&Phil, Flm&Vid, LitArts* To **expurgate** a book or film **prudishly** before publication. *Origin* After Thomas Bowdler (1754-1825), who published an **expurgated** edition of **Shakespeare** in 1818.

box *BcstJourn* » **tag**

box *also* **box seat** *PerfA&C* Seat in a box at a theater, concert hall, or stadium. *Also see* **loge, stall**.

PerfA&C Permanent vertical pipes – mounted with lighting instruments – mounted in or on a **box seat**.

box *iMedia* workstation or computer

box *Journ* Featured editorial matter enclosed by hairlines, a border, or white space and placed within or between text columns.

box *also* **box seat** *PerfA&C* Seat in a box at a theater, concert hall, or stadium. *Also see* **loge, stall**.

box booms *PerfA&C* Permanent vertical pipes – mounted with lighting instruments – mounted in or on a **box seat**.

box office *Flm&Vid, Mktg, PerfA&C* **1** Booth in a theater or stadium where tickets are sold. **2** Drawing power of a theatrical entertainment or of a performer; popular appeal. POPULAR APPEAL **3** Total attendance for an entertainment.

box step *Dnce* Dance step in which the feet are moved in a pattern approximating a square. *Also see* **Dances**.

box-office order *Eco&Fin* Financial instrument that instructs and authorizes the employer of an artist to deduct a specified amount of money due the artist and forward same to the artist's creditor. <The Pzazzers' manager signed $5,000 worth of box-office orders to repay an advanced by the talent agency for transportation>

box-office receipts *Eco&Fin, Flm&Vid* Money paid by the public to see a certain movie. Considered gross revenue.

boycott *HR&LR* To abstain from or unite with others in abstaining from using, buying, or dealing with. <The union urged a boycott of the company's products because of the company's **unfair labor practices**>

bp, BP *Cult&Soc* » **beautiful people, Beautiful People**.

bpi *InfoMgt* Bits per inch, a measure of storage density.

bps *InfoMgt* Bits per second. Measure of teleprocessing speed.

Bradlee, Ben (1921-) *Journ* Editor of the *Washington Post* during the **Watergate** scandal (1972) Portrayed by Jason Robards (1922-, stage/film/TV act.) in the movie, *All The President's Men. Also see* **editor, kerosene journalism**.

braggadocio (brag-ga-do-see-o) *Crit&Eval* **1** Empty or pretentious bragging. **2** Swaggering, cocky manner.

Brahmin *Cult&Soc* Member of a cultural and social elite, esp. descendants of old New England families. *Origin* First of the four Hindu classes.

brainstorm *iMedia* Method of idea generation or problem-solving.

branch *InfoMgt* Type of programming statement that alters the sequential processing of instructions.

branching structure *iMedia* Hierarchical navigational structure allowing the participant (user) to choose content to explore.

brand *EntreP* Verbal and/or symbolic means of identifying a product.

brand *Mktg* Distinctive name, term, sign, symbol, design, or combination of these that seeks to identify the product of an organization and differentiate it from those of competitors. *Also see* **trademark**.

brand name *Mktg»* **trade name**

brand/corporate image *Mktg* How a product or corporation is perceived by the public. <good guy/bad guy, conservative, modern, cool, high-quality, durable, reliable>

branding *Mktg* Process of creating, assigning, and publicizing a brand to one or more products.

brandmark *IntelProp* Part of the **brand** that appears in the form of a. <symbol, design, distinctive color or lettering>

Braque, Georges *ArtPerf, VisArts* (1882-1963, Fr. pntr.) Leading exponent and theorist of the cubist movement. *Also see* **collage, cubism, les fauves, papier-collé, postimpressionism**.

brass *Crit&Eval* Bold self-assurance. EFFRONTERY.

brass *MusInstr* **Section** of a band or an orchestra composed of brass instruments. <trumpets, trombones, French **horns**, tubas, and others such as **euphoniums, flügelhorns**, etc> *Also see* **Musical Instrument Families**.

brass band *MusArts* **1** Instrumental ensemble (ca. 1850-1910) usu. consisting of eight brass instruments, two clarinets, bass and snare drums; forerunner of the early jazz bands. **2** Military band. *Also see* **brass-hop**.

brass-hop *MusArts* A 1997 attempt to marry the New Orleans **brass band** sound of jazz funerals and **second-lines** to hip-hop.

brassmen *MusArts* **Brass** players in the New Orleans-style **brass bands**.

Brave New World (1932) *Cult&Soc, LitArts* Bitter satire of an inhumane society controlled by technology, written by Aldous Huxley (1894-1963, Brit. novelist, essayist, critic) *Also see* **1984, Fahrenheit 451**.

bravura *MusArts* Brilliant technique or style in performance.

BRB *InfoMgt* Be Right Back

breach *LegAsp* Breaking or violating of a law, right, or duty, either by commission or omission.

breach of contract *LegAsp* Failure, without legal excuse, to perform any promise which forms the whole or part of a contract. *Also see* **Contracts**.

bread *Eco&Fin* money. *Origin* Jazz musicians, of whom many were Jewish, began to use 'bread' – from the Yiddish "broyt" – to mean money or a living.

break *Flm&Vid* Each stage of movie release within a certain market. <first-run break, second-run break, etc>

break *HR&LR, Mgt* rest period.

break *Journ, VA-Prntng* **1** Space between two paragraphs. **2** Place where a word is or should be divided at the end of a line. **3** Make known. <Break a news story> *Also see* **ellipse**.

break *MusArts* **1** Jazz improvisation: the pause between the regular **phrases** or choruses of a **melody**. **2** Short section – one-to-four-**measures** – played as an **interlude** by a soloist (usu. the **lead** instrument) without accompaniment. **3** Where one **register** or a **tonal** quality changes to another.

break *MusArts* Short section – one-to-four-**measures** – played as an interlude by a soloist (usu. the lead instrument) without accompaniment.

break *Rdio/TV* Commercial time available for sale within a particular program or between two programs.

break a leg *PerfA&C* Phrase used by superstitious theater people to avoid bad luck by wishing good luck. <Go out there, kid, and break a leg!> *Origin* In Elizabethan theater, the bending (breaking) of a leg in a bow or curtsy to the audience in response to acclamation.

break dancing *also* **breakdancing** *Dnce* Style of dancing in which agility, and often spectacular gymnastic skills, are combined with pantomime and performed to the rhythms of **rap** music. *Also see* **Dances**.

break even *Eco&Fin* To gain an amount equal to that invested.

break even *Mktg* Volume of sales necessary, at a specific price, for a seller to recover all relevant financial costs of a product.

break-even analysis *EntreP* Process of determining how many units of production must be sold, or how much revenue must be obtained, before a business begins to earn a profit.

break-even quantity (BEQ) *EntreP* Number of units that must be produced and sold in order to cover the total costs of production. Formula is fixed costs divided by sales price minus variable costs.

break up *PerfA&C* Burst into laughter; lose composure while performing

break-of-the-book *Journ* Process of deciding what goes on each page of a magazine.

break-out book *LitArts, Mktg* Book that enjoys a quick, sudden surge of sales. *Also see* **best seller**.

breakdown *Dnce* Noisy, energetic American country dance. *Also see* **Dances**.

breakdown *Genl* Analysis, an outline, or a summary consisting of itemized data or essentials.

breakdown process (chain-ratio method) *EntreP* Forecasting method that begins with a macro-level variable and works down to the sales forecast.

breaking news *BcstJourn* Unexpected event of enough importance to be considered for coverage or inclusion in the newscast.

breakout *Eco&Fin* Classified summary of statistical data.

breakout *Journ* New article or news story derived from an existing article or news story.

breeches *Fashn* Trousers extending to or just below the knee.

Brennan, William (1906-97) *Ethcs&Phil, Law&Pol* Associate justice of the U.S. Supreme Court (1956-90) One of the great Justices of the 20th century devoted to the spirit and protection of the **Bill of Rights** *Also see* **obscenity**.

BRI *InfoMgt* **Basic Rate Interface. ISDN** connection offered by a phone company.

bric-a-brac (Fr., bric-à-brac, "expressive of confusion") *PerfA&C* Small, usually ornamental objects valued for their antiquity, rarity, originality, or sentimental associations.

bricks and mortar *Fnding* Informal term for grants for buildings or construction projects.

bridge *BcstJourn* Very short (usu. under: 10) transition used in television news packages. It can be a tracked portion or an on-camera **standup**.

bridge *Fashn* Fashion in between cheap and expensive. <The current (Dec. 1996) Evita fashion is a bridge line>

bridge *MusArts* **1** Transitional passage connecting two subjects or movements. **2** "The theme linking and contrasting the opening and closing sections of a standard song. In a thirty-two bar song structured thematically A-A-B-A, the bridge corresponds to the B section." — Lyons & Perlo (jazz critics) CHANNEL, RELEASE

bridge *MusInstr* Thin, upright piece of wood in some stringed instruments that supports the strings above the soundboard.

bridgeware *InfoMgt* **Computer programs** used to translate instructions written for one type of computer into a format that another type of computer understands.

brightness *iMedia* Perceived amount of light coming from a source.

Brill Building *MusArts* Located 1619 Broadway in the heart of New York's music district, it is a name synonymous with songwriting since it was built in 1931 By 1962 the building contained 165 music businesses. *Also see* **songplugger, Tin Pan Alley**.

bring down the house *TheatArts* Tumultuous audience reaction to a performer or performance. *Also see* **showstopper**.

brio (breeo, It.) *Crit&Eval* Spirited force or energy.

British Broadcasting Company (BBC) *Rdio/TV »* **BBC**

brittle *Crit&Eval* Difficult to deal with, snappish, lacking warmth of feeling, cold.

bro *Cult&Soc* **brother**, kinsman. "Every brother ain't a brother." — Public Enemy via **Spike Lee** *Also see* **soul brother**.

broad *Crit&Eval, TheatArts* To act without subtlety. OBVIOUS *Also see* **overact**.

broad navigation *iMedia* Navigational system with many choices (usu. with only light coverage of each topic) In contrast: **deep navigation**.

broad-reach marketing *Mktg* Opposite of **target marketing**.

broadband *Rdio/TV, InfoMgt, Sci&Tech* **1** Wide band of electromagnetic frequencies as related to electronic media. **2** Communication channel capable of transmitting at the rate of millions of bits per second.

broadcast *Rdio/TV* Transmission of a radio or television program or signal for public use. *Also see* **cablecast, narrowcast, telecast**.

Broadcast Designers Association (BDA) *Rdio/TV* Represents broadcast graphic designers.

Broadcast Music, Inc. (BMI) *IntelProp, MusArts* » **BMI**

Broadcast Stations & Networks *ColEntry,. Rdio/TV* » **ABC, Blue Network, CBS, MBS, NBC, NET, PBS, QVC, Red Network, WEAF, Westinghouse, WJZ, WNAC. WSM.**

broadsheet *Journ* » **broadside**

broadside *Crit&Eval* Strong verbal attack delivered in a speech or editorial.

broadside *Journ, VA-Prntng* Large sheet of paper, usu. printed on one side, used for an advertisement or public notice. BROADSHEET

Broadway (Bway) *TheatArts* **1** Symbolizes all commercial theatre in NYC. **2** Principal theater and amusement district of NYC, on the West Side of midtown Manhattan centered on Broadway. **3** Thoroughfare of New York state, the longest street in the world. It begins at the southern tip of Manhattan and extends about 150 miles north to Albany.

Broadway musicians *HR&LR, MusArts* **Pit** musicians playing for **Broadway** musicals. *Also see* **instrument maintenance payment**.

brocade *Fashn* Heavy fabric interwoven with a rich, raised design.

Bronx cheer *Crit&Eval* » **razz** Loud sound expressing disapproval. *Origin* After the Bronx, a NYC borough not known for genteel criticism. *Also see* **raspberry**.

Brooklyn Academy of Music *PerfA&C* » **BAM**

Brother Can You Spare a Dime? *Cult&Soc, MusArts* Song written by **Yip Harburg** in 1932 that incarnated the unemployment misery of the **Great Depression.** Some Republicans tried to ban its radio play during the 1932 Presidential campaign which was won by Franklin Delano Roosevelt.

brouhaha (brewhaha) *Crit&Eval* An uproar.

Brown vs. Board of Education *Cult&Soc, HR&LR* Supreme Court decision (1954) legally terminated racial segregation in U.S. schools. *Also see* **white flight**.

brownline *VA-Prntng* **Offset** paper proof sheets that show printed image in brown. BLUELINE

browse *Genl* **1** To read something superficially by selecting passages at random. **2** To inspect something in a leisurely and casual way.

browser *iMedia, InfoMgt* Program that interprets **HTML** code, the **Web's** standard programming language, to display a **Web** document (**page**) on your screen. Some browsers act as a complete interface to the **Internet**, others just offer graphical access to **Web** sites. » **user agent**

browsing *InfoMgt* Refers to exploring a **database** or online area.

Bruce, Lenny (b. Leonard Alfred Schneider, 1926-1966, comic) *ArtPerf, PA-Variety* Controversial 1960s **standup** comedian prosecuted and persecuted for his irreverent and uninhibited observations of contemporary **mores**. Remains a strong influence on today's comedy. *Also see* **schpritz**.

brushes *MusInstr* Wires enclosed in a metal rod that can be spread wide or together to create various swishing sounds when played by a jazz drummer on the snare drum or on cymbals. *Also see* **percussion, tap dance**.

brushwork *VisArts* Manner in which a painter applies paint with a brush.

Brussells lace *Fashn* Net lace with an **appliqué** design.

BSE&F-Acc » **balance sheet**

BSOD *iMedia* » **blue screen**

bssn. *MusInstr* **bassoon**.

BTA *Rdio/TV* **best time available**. Best time for a station to schedule commercials. <**drive time**>

BTW *InfoMgt* By The Way

bubble memory *InfoMgt* Type of memory utilizing a thin film of **semiconductor** material on which magnetic spots are used to represent binary data.

bubble pack *Mktg* » **blister pack**

bubble-gum *also* **bubblegum** *Crit&Eval* Adolescent immaturity in style or taste.

bubee (Yinglish) *Crit&Eval* Showbiz term of endearment accompanied by extravagant hugs and kisses regardless of the ethnic background of hugger or huggee.

buck *Eco&Fin, Flm&Vid* **Tinseltown** rate of exchange for $100,000; ten bucks = $1,000,000.

bucking contest *MusArts* » **cutting contest**.

budget *Eco&Fin* **1** Itemized summary of estimated or intended expenditures for a given period, with proposals for needed financing. **2** Systematic plan for the expenditure of a fixed resource, <money or time>, during a given period. **3** Total sum of money allocated for a particular purpose or period of time. **4** Budgets can also be expressed in quantities of material <manufacturing and processing> and time <intellectual service organizations like law firms and software development companies>

budget *EntreP* Plan that lays out expected revenues and expenditures and is used as a control for the operation of the venture.

budget *Journ* Budgets for periodicals are expressed in pages as well as dollars. Budgets for individual issues vary as to the total number of printed pages vs. revenue from advertising and circulation.

budget deficit *EntreP* Difference between a government's spending and its revenues from taxation.

budget records *RecA&S* Albums sold at 75% off retail **list price**.

Buenos Aires Copyright Convention of 1914 *IntelProp* Established copyright protection for U.S. authors in certain Latin American countries.

buff *Crit&Eval* Someone enthusiastic and knowledgeable about a subject. <movie buff>

buffer *iMedia, InfoMgt* Holding area in memory where information can be stored by one program or device and then read at a different rate by another. *Also see* **print buffer**.

buffoon *ArtPerf* **clown, jester, fool**.

bug *InfoMgt* Defect in the code or routine of a program.

bugalú *Dnce, MusArts* Mid-1960s combination of Latin and black music. *Also see* **Dances, Latin Dance Music**.

build *TheatArts* To increase the tempo or volume or both in order to reach a climax.

buildup *also* **build-up** *Mktg* Favorable publicity built by a systematic campaign; extravagant praise.

bulk discount *Mktg* Discount offered by **print media** to an advertiser that runs more than a given number of pages or column inches in a contract year. *Also see* **Discounts**.

bull *Eco&Fin* One who thinks that a commodity or financial market will rise. *Also see* **bear**.

bull market *Eco&Fin* Prolonged period of rising prices for stock and bonds. *Also see* **bear market**.

bullet *iMedia, VA-Prntng* Heavy dot (•) used to highlight a particular line or paragraph.

bulletin *BcstJourn* Fast-breaking news story of overwhelming importance inserted into a program other than news.

bulletin board system (BBS) *InfoMgt* » **BBS**

bullish spread *EntreP* Portfolio of calls or puts on which the holder makes money mainly when the price of the underlying security rises.

bullshit (B.S.) *Crit&Eval* Foolish, insolent talk; nonsense.

bully pulpit *Law&Pol* Advantageous position such as the U.S. Presidency for making one's views known or rallying support. *Origin* Used to describe President Theodore Roosevelt's political skill.

bum's rush *Mgt* Forcible ejection *Also see* **bouncer**.

bummer *Crit&Eval* **1** Failure. <The play is a bummer> **2** Disagreeable person, event, or situation.

bummer *Genl* Adverse reaction to a drug such as **LSD**.

bump *Dnce* Forward thrust of the pelvis, as in a **burlesque** striptease. *Also see* **grind**.

bumped *Flm&Vid* » **dubbing**

bumper *Flm&Vid* In a TV drama, a line of dialogue or piece of action used to create suspense or tension just before the commercial break to get viewers to stay tuned in for the rest of the program.

bumper *Rdio/TV* Brief additional comment or commercial announcement after the longer original has been said or done.

bumpers *Rdio/TV* Television station promos inserted as a break between news segments and paid ad spots.

bun *Fashn* Tight roll of hair worn at the back of the head.

bundle *Eco&Fin* Large sum of money

bundled software *InfoMgt* **1** Software included in the purchase price of a computer. **2** Several programs sold together as a package; **software suite**.

bunk *LegAsp* Illegitimate contract

burlesque *PA-Variety* **Slapstick** comedy + Girls! Girls! Girls!

burlesque *TheatArts* Speech, scene, or play ridiculing other drama or fiction.

burly *PA-Variety* burlesque

burn out *Crit&Eval* To be consumed with strong emotion.

burn out *VisArts* To harden or impart a finish to by subjecting to intense heat; fire: burn clay pots in a kiln.

burned-out, burnt-out *Crit&Eval* Worn out or exhausted.

burnt cork *Perf-MkUp* Mixed with glycerine to blacken the faces of white minstrelers. *Also see* **blackface**, **minstrely**.

burn-out *Crit&Eval* **1** Physical or emotional exhaustion, especially as a result of long-term stress or dissipation. **2** One who is worn out physically or emotionally, as from long-term stress.

bus *InfoMgt* **1** Internal electrical pathway along which signals are sent from one part of the computer to another. **2** In a network, a line of cable with connectors that link devices together.

bus-and-truck company *TheatArts* **Road company** of a theatrical production that travels by bus and truck and is scaled down to play smaller markets than do the national companies.

Bush, George (1924-, 41st U.S. Pres.,1988-92, Vice Pres., 1981-89 under **Ronald Reagan**.) *Law&Pol. Also see* **voodoo economics**.

Bush, Vannevar 1890-1974. *iMedia* Proposed the development of an analogue computer, and was a pivotal figure in hypertext research. His 1945 paper, "As We May Think," speculated on a machine, "memex," which in various ways anticipated hypermedia and the **World Wide Web** by nearly half a century.

bushes *PA-Variety* Plants in the audience who are paid "volunteers" to be magician's on-stage victims. *Also see* **shill**.

business *TheatArts* Incidental action performed by an actor on the stage to fill a pause between lines or to provide interesting detail. *Ex.* taking a drink, smoking a pipe, writing a letter

business agent *HR&LR* Employee of a local union who deals with the worker's **grievances** with the employer, assists in recruiting new members, and other union matters. BUSINESS REPRESENTATIVE WORKING DELEGATE

Business Committee for the Arts (BCA) *Mgt* » **BCA**

Business Dynamic, The *Genl* » Page ix

business ethics *Ethcs&Phil* "Study of how personal moral norms apply to the activities and goals of commercial enterprise. It is not a separate moral standard, but the study of how the business context poses its own unique problems for the moral person who acts as an **agent** in this system." — Laura Nash (19??-; ethicist, tchr.) "Ethics in business is, at bottom, caring thoroughly how one does business." — Richard Eastman (1916-1999; ethicist, tchr.▷

business incubator *EntreP* Facility that provides shared space, services, and management assistance to new businesses.

business interruption insurance *EntreP* Coverage of lost income and certain other expenses while the business is being rebuilt.

business magazine *Journ* » **business publication**

business manager *Mgt* Person responsible for handling business matters – finances, payroll, staff, taxes, etc. – for an artist/performer, company, or organization. *Also see* **Managers**.

business paper *Journ* » **business publication**

business plan *EntreP* **1** Overall plan for the venture. **2** Written document designed to guide the strategy of the venture or to gain financing for the venture.

business policies *EntreP* Basic statements that provide guidance for managerial decision making.

business publication *Journ* One published for readers in their business, industry, profession, or vocation. BUSINESS MAG-

Business Representative *HR&LR* » **business agent**

Business Software Alliance *InfoMgt*, Industry group known for its vigorous pursuit of digital pirates.

business symbols *Eco&Fin, Mktg*» symbols

Business Volunteers for the Arts *Mgt* » **BVA**

busker (Brit.) *PA-Variety* Street singer or player who solicits money during a performance.

bustle *Fashn* **1** Frame or pad to support and expand the fullness of the back of a woman's skirt. **2** Bow, **peplum**, or gathering of material at the back of a woman's skirt below the waist.

busy *VisArts* Cluttered with detail to the point of being distracting.

busy design *Crit&Eval, VisArts* Cluttered with detail to the point of being distracting.

butt *Crit&Eval* One who serves as an object of ridicule or contempt. LAUGHINGSTOCK.

butterflies (in the stomach) *Crit&Eval* Feeling of unease or mild nausea caused by fearful anticipation of performing. *Also see* **stage fright**, **rejection**.

butterfly *Flm&Vid* Net stretched over an outdoor scene to soften the sunlight.

button *iMedia, InfoMgt* Image on the **monitor**, sometimes resembling a pushbutton, that you click to designate, confirm, or cancel an action. MOUSE BUTTON, RADIO BUTTON *Also see* **check boxes**, **option button**.

buy and hold *EntreP* Method of investing where once purchased the investment is held for a number of years.

buy-one-get-one-free *Mktg* Sales promotion that entitles a buyer of a product to receive another of the same product at no additional cost. *Also see* **two-fers**.

buy-out *Eco&Fin* Purchase of rights in a property, as opposed to taking a percentage.

buyout *EntreP* Purchase of an existing venture as a method of launching a new venture.

buyer's market *also* **buyers' market** *Mktg* Market condition characterized by low prices and supply exceeding demand. *Also see* **seller's market**.

buzz *Crit&Eval, Mktg* **1** To talk excitingly about a book, movie, record, show, or showing prior to its release. <The higher the artist's advance for a book or a record, the more urgent the buzz> **2** Widely held perception. "Even at its bitterest and bleakest, New York has a buzz that emerges from our having more museums, more galleries, more dance groups and more concerts than any other city in the country." — Editorial, *NY Times. Also see* **heat**, **word of mouth**.

BVA *Mgt* **Business Volunteers for the Arts**. **Nonprofit** organization based in Chicago that recruits, trains, and matches business volunteers with **nonprofit** arts organizations.

Bway (abbrev. via *Variety*) *TheatArts* **Broadway**.

by-line, byline *Journ* Line at the head or end of a newspaper or magazine article with the author's name.

by-play *TheatArts* Secondary action or speech taking place while the main action proceeds during a theatrical performance.

bylaws *LegAsp, Mgt* Laws or rules governing the internal affairs of an organization.

BYOB *Genl* Bring your own booze, bring your own bottle. *Also see* **rent party**.

Byron, Ada Augusta (1815-1851) *InfoMgt* Legitimate daughter of poet, Lord Byron. Skilled mathematician and a challenger to the theories of **Charles Babbage** and his **Difference Engine No. 1**, an early 19th century mechanical calculator, a forerunner of the modern computer. *Also see* **Ada**.

Byronic hero *Crit&Eval, LitArts* Lonely, rebellious, and brooding. *Origin* Related to Lord Byron (1788-1824, Brit. poet, leading figure of **romanticism**) *Also see* **Ada**.

byte *iMedia, InfoMgt* Amount of storage required to store one keystroke of information. One byte usu. consists of a series of eight bits, and represents one character, e.g., a letter, numeral, or punctuation mark. *Also see* **gigabyte**, **kilobyte**, **megabyte**.

bytes per inch (BPI) *InfoMgt* Number of bytes that can be contained on one inch of magnetic tape. » **BPI**

byzantine *Crit&Eval* **1** Relating to or characterized by intrigue, scheming or devious. <Recent instances of intrigue in media mergers have been notoriously byzantine> **2** Highly complicated; intricate, and involved.

Byzantine art *VisArts* Characterized by rigid, monumental, stylized forms with gold backgrounds. <religious mosaics, manuscript illuminations, panel paintings> *Origin* Christian art developed ca. 330 A.D. when Constantinople became the capital of the Easter Roman Empire to 1453 when it was succeeded by the Turkish Ottoman Empire.

- C -

© *Eco&Fin*, *IntelProp* » **copyright**

C # (c sharp) *iMedia* Object-oriented programming language, extended from **C++.**

C clef *MusArts* Symbol indicating which line of a staff represents the **pitch** of **middle C**. Only movable **clef**: On the bottom line it becomes the **soprano clef**, on the middle line the **alto clef**, and on the third line above the bottom the **tenor clef**.

C corporation *EntreP* Ordinary, or regular, corporation, taxed by the federal government as a separate legal entity.

C *iMedia*, *InfoMgt* **Programming** language developed in the 1970s, it is a terse, elegant deceptively simple language that allows programmers almost unlimited flexibility. *Also see* **Programming Languages.**

C *TheatArts* **center stage**

C&W, c&w *MusArts* **Country and Western** music

C++ *iMedia*, *InfoMgt* Extension of the **C programming language** developed in the **Bell Labs** in the early 1980s. *Also see* **Programming Languages.**

C of C. *Eco&Fin* **Chamber of Commerce**

c., C. *Journ*, *VA-Prntng* **copy**

CAE&F-Acc **capital account, credit account, current account**

CAA *Mgt* **Creative Artists Agency** International talent agency based in Beverly Hills, CA. *Also see* **Talent Agencies.**

cabaret card *Law&Pol*, *PA-Variety* A "license" issued – and easily revoked – to nite-club musicians and entertainers by the NYC police in the 19404 and '50s

cable modem *InfoMgt* Using the local cable television network instead of the local phone network, it carries data at very high speeds: 500,000 bits per second. *Also see* **fat pipe.**

Cable News Network (CNN) *Rdio/TV* » **Ted Turner**

cable television, cable TV *Rdio/TV* Television distribution system in which station signals, picked up by elevated antennas, are delivered by cable to the receivers of subscribers. CABLEVISION, COMMUNITY ANTENNA TELEVISION

cablecast *Rdio/TV* **Telecast** transmitted via **cable television**

cablevision *Rdio/TV* » **cable television**

cabriole (cab-ri-ol, Fr.) *Dnce* (Ballet) Jumping step in which the dancer beats straight legs together in the air.

cache *iMedia. InfoMgt* Storage area for frequently accessed information. Retrieval of the information is faster from the cache than from the originating source. *Also see* **disk cache, memory cache.**

cacophonous *Crit&Eval* Harsh, unpleasant sound; **discordant**

cacophony *Crit&Eval* Harsh or inharmonious sounds

CAD/CAM *InfoMgt* **Computer Aided Design/Computer Aided Manufacturing.** Software used to design parts and analyze their production process.

cadence *Dnce* **Measure** or beat of movement, as in dancing or marching.

cadence *LitArts* Balanced, rhythmic flow in poetry or oratory.

cadence *MusArts* **Progression** of **chords** moving to a **harmonic** close or point of rest.

cadenza *MusArts* 1 Elaborate ornamental melodic flourish **interpolated** in a vocal piece, as an **aria**. 2 Extended **virtuosic** section for a soloist near the end of a movement of a concerto. *Also see* **improvisation.**

CAE *InfoMgt* **Computer Aided Engineering** Software that allows engineers to test the physical characteristics of a part prior to producing it.

caesura *LitArts* Pause in a line of verse dictated by sense or natural speech rhythm rather than by metrics. *Also see* **rest.**

caesura *MusArts* Pause or breathing at a point of rhythmic division in a melody. RAILROAD TRACKS

cafeteria news *Journ,*. *Rdio/TV* » **a la carte news**

caftan *Fashn* 1 Full-length garment with elbow-length or long sleeves, worn chiefly in eastern Mediterranean countries. 2 Westernized version: a loose, usu. brightly colored waist-length or ankle-length tunic.

CAI *InfoMgt* **Computer Aided Instruction** Use of a computer as a teaching aid.

cajones (ko-ho'-nes, Span.) *Crit&Eval* » **balls, ballsy**

Cajun *Cult&Soc* Person in southern Louisiana descended from French colonists deported by the British from Acadia, a former French colony of eastern Canada, during the French and Indian War (1755-1763)

Cajun Lapland *Cult&Soc* Where Cajun culture laps over into Texas from Louisiana

Cajun music *MusArts* "Blend of German, Spanish, Scottish, Irish, Anglo-American, Afro-Caribbean, and American Indian influences with a base of western French and French Acadian folk tradition." — Barry Jean Ancelet (19??-, ethnomusicologist, U. of Southwestern La) *Also see* **zydeco music.**

cake makeup *Perf-MkUp* Greaseless, water-soluble foundation applied with a dampened sponge.

cakewalk *Dnce* High-kicking **walk around dance** performed by slaves in the mid-1800s to mimic the manners of white slave owners. *Also see* **Dances.**

calamitous *Crit&Eval* Causing or involving calamity. DISASTROUS

calendar Spread *EntreP* Investment portfolio of puts and calls with fixed strike prices but varying expiration dates.

calico *Fashn* Coarse, brightly-printed cloth

call *Dnce* Shout directions in rhythm for a square dance.

call *Eco&Fin* 1 Demand to repay a **secured** bank loan usu. made when the borrower fails to meet a contractual obligation. <miss an interest payment> When a loan is called, the entire principal amount is due immediately. 2 Re bonds. Right to **redeem** outstanding bonds before their scheduled **maturity**. 3 Re options. Right to buy a specific number of shares at a specified price by a fixed date. 4 Re stocks. Demand for payment due on stock bought on margin when the value is reduced. CALLABLE

call *MusArts* Selection by the leader of the next tune to be played by an ensemble.

call and response *Cult&Soc*, *MusArts* "One of the critical features of African music that has been incorporated into [gospel music], jazz, and other forms is the call and response. Instruments, mimicking the human voice, calling out to one another, and the response comes back in creative ways. The drum has always been a key in the process. The drummer will send out something, and a horn player will pick it up and put a different twist on it. But look what's happening with pop music and **rap**. There's not even a drummer. The (electronically produced) drum rhythm is on a continuous loop, always the same. How can anybody play off of that and come up with any new ideas? No wonder they can't play." — **Wynton Marsalis**

call board *PerfA&C* Bulletin board backstage in a theater for posting instructions and notices. *Also see* **call sheet.**

call letters *Rdio/TV* Identifying code letters or numbers of a radio or television transmitting station, assigned by a regulatory body. CALL SIGN

call Option *EntreP* Option to buy some security a some pre-specified time and price.

call *PerfA&C* Notice of rehearsal times posted in a theater.

call sheet *Flm&Vid* Daily schedule showing production details and schedules, inc. where and when, and who is to be where at what time. *Also see* **call board.**

call sign *Rdio/TV* » **call letters**

call the tune *Crit&Eval* Exercise authority, be in charge.

call to action *Mktg*, *Rdio/TV* Phrase used to describe the type of advertising not allowed on most public radio or television stations. *Also see* **exhortation**, **NPR.**

call-back *TheatArts* Request to someone who has auditioned to come back for another **audition** or interview. *Also see* **rejection.**

call-in *Rdio/TV* Format that encourages listeners or viewers to have their telephone conversations with the **host** or guests on a show broadcast to other listeners.

Callable Personal Librarian (CPL) *InfoMgt* » **CPL**

calling a function *iMedia* Programming: Executing a function.

Also see **running a function** or **invoking a function**.

callboy *PerfA&C* (Passé) One who tells performers when it is time for them to go on stage. [Replaced by backstage PA.].

caller ID *InfoMgt* Telephone service that allows viewing the number of the caller before answering.

calligraphy *VisArts* Art of fine handwriting CALLIGRAPHER

calling *HR&LR* Occupation, profession, or career

calling tones *InfoMgt* » **CNG**

calliope *MusInstr* Keyboard instrument, fitted with various sized steam whistles, used in a parade down main street hyping a circus, a showboat, or a hanging. *Also see* **Musical Instrument Families.**

Calliope *LitArts* Muse of **lyric** poetry *Also see* **Muses.**

calypso *MusArts* Music from Trinidad and Tobago characterized by improvised lyrics on topical subjects. *Also see* **Latin Dance Music.**

camcorder *Flm&Vid* Self-contained unit made up of a lightweight, hand-held television camera and a videocassette recorder.

camera *Rdio/TV* Part of a television transmitting apparatus that receives the primary image on a light-sensitive **cathode ray tube** and transforms it into electrical impulses. *Also see* **off camera, on camera.**

camera-ready *VisArts, VA-Prntng* **Artwork** prepared ready for photographing prior to being made into a printing plate.

CAMI *Mgt* Columbia Arts Management, Inc. World's leading music booking and talent agency, NYC-based. *Also see* **Community Concerts, Talent Agencies.**

camisole *Fashn* 1 Woman's sleeveless undergarment, now usu. worn under a sheer blouse. 2 Short **negligee**

camp *Crit&Eval* **Affectation** or appreciation of manners and tastes commonly thought to be artificial, vulgar, or **banal.** <**Michael Jackson**>

campaign *Fndng* Organized effort to raise funds for a **nonprofit.**

Canadian Broadcasting Corporation (CBC) *Rdio/TV* » **CBC**

canary *ArtPerf, MusArts* (Passé) female singer

canned *Rdio/TV* Prerecorded rather than **live.**

canned interview *Mktg* One in which the interviewee has recorded all the right **hype** with suitable pauses for the interviewer, the deejay, to ask the scripted questions of his **main man.**

canned release *Mktg* » **press release**

canned spot *Rdio/TV* Prerecorded commercial

canned track *RecA&S* Prerecorded segment of a recording.

canon *Crit&Eval* 1 Established principle. 2 Basis for judgment. STANDARD. *Also see* **criterion.**

canon *Cult&Soc* Books of the Bible officially accepted as Holy Scripture.

canon *Dnce* Composition in which the dancers begin one after another, at regular intervals, successively dancing the same steps.

canon *Law&Pol* 1 **Secular** law, rule, or code of law. 2 Ecclesiastical law or code of laws established by a church council.

canon *MusArts* **Contrapuntal** composition in which the same melody is imitated by one or more voices overlapping in time in the same or related key.

canonical view *iMedia* Angle or view from which an image or object is most easily identified.

cant *Crit&Eval* 1 Monotonous talk filled with **platitudes.** 2 Hypocritically pious language. <Politicking is high cant> 3 Special terminology understood among the members of a profession, discipline, or class. JARGON, LINGO

cantankerous *Crit&Eval* Ill-tempered and quarrelsome. DISAGREEABLE. *Also see* **curmudgeon.**

cantata *MusArts* Vocal and instrumental piece composed of **choruses**, solos, and **recitatives.**

canticle *MusArts* 1 Song or chant 2 **Nonmetrical** hymn with words taken from a biblical text.

cape *Fashn* Sleeveless outer garment fastened at the throat and worn hanging over the shoulders.

Capezio *Dnce, Fashn* Well-known brand of ballet slippers and dance shoes.

capital account (CA)*E&F-Acc* 1 Account stating the amount of funds and assets invested in a business by the owners or stockholders, inc. retained earnings. 2 Statement of the **net worth** of a business at a given time.

capital asset*E&F-Acc* » **long-term asset**

Capital Asset Pricing Model *EntreP* Model that describes the relationship between risk and expected return for securities in the capital markets.

capital budgeting *EntreP* Method used by a business to justify the acquisition of those items that have a useful life of one year or more. Capital budgeting aids the decision maker by comparing the costs and benefits of a project.

capital budgeting analysis *EntreP* Analytical method that helps managers make decisions about long-term investments.

capital campaign *Fndng* Campaign by a **nonprofit** to raise substantial funds to finance major building projects, to supplement **endowment** funds, and to meet other demands for capital spending.

Capital Cities, Inc. *RecA&S* Media **conglomerate** and parent company of **American Broadcasting Company** (ABC) before **Disney** buyout.

capital *Eco&Fin* 1 Long-term funds of the organization. 2 Remaining assets of a business after all liabilities have been deducted, net worth. 3 Relating to financial assets, esp. those financial assets that add to the **net worth** of a business.

capital expenditure*E&F-Acc* 1 Expenditure that increases the capacity or efficiency of an asset or extends its useful life. Debited to an **asset account.** 2 Funds spent for the acquisition of a **long-term asset.**

capital expenditures budget*E&F-Acc* Organization's plan for purchases of property, plant, equipment, and other long-term assets.

capital flight *Eco&Fin* Large-scale removal of individual and corporate investment capital and income from a country because of unsettled economic conditions, or social unrest and uncertainty.

capital funds *Eco&Fin, Fndng* Funds such as **endowments** whose principal must be held intact and not expended. *Also see* **Funds.**

capital gain *Eco&Fin* Amount by which proceeds from the sale of a **capital asset** exceed the original cost.

capital gain *EntreP* Positive change in the value of an asset over two points in time.

capital gains and losses *EntreP* Gains and losses incurred from sales of property that are not a part of the company's regular business operations.

capital goods *Eco&Fin* Goods, such as machinery, used in the production of commodities. PRODUCER GOODS

capital market *EntreP* Market where suppliers of capital (such as savers and investors) enter into contracts with the users of capital (such as corporations and government)

capital resources *EntreP* Capital resources consist of economic capital and financial capital.

capital stock (CS) *Eco&Fin* 1 Total amount of stock authorized for issue by a corporation, inc. common and preferred stock. 2 Total stated or **par value** of the permanently invested capital of a corporation.

capital support *Fnding* Funds provided for **endowment** purposes, buildings, construction, or equipment, and including, for example, grants for **bricks and mortar.**

capital-intensive *Eco&Fin* Requiring a large expenditure of capital in comparison to labor.

capitalism *Eco&Fin* Economic system in which the means of production and distribution are privately or corporately owned and development is proportionate to the accumulation and reinvestment of profits gained in a free market. "Capitalism is a wonderful system, adaptable, full of vitality, and, quite literally, creative. But capitalism is not synonymous with democracy and, unchecked, it can threaten democracy." — Benjamin Barber (econ. journ) "Capitalism is the worst of possible economic systems except for the alternatives." — Anon

capitalization *Eco&Fin* Amounts and types of long-term financing used by a firm, inc. common stock, preferred stock, retained earnings, and long-term debt.

capitalization rate *EntreP* Figure, determined by the level of risk involved in the business and the expected growth rate of future earnings.

capitalize *Eco&Fin* 1 To use as or convert into capital. 2 To supply with capital or investment funds. <capitalize a new business> 3 To authorize the issue of a certain amount of **capital stock**

Capitol (EMI) *RecA&S* Hollywood-based record company owned by **EMI Music** of England. *Also see* **major labels.**

capo *MusInstr* Small movable bar placed across the **fingerboard** of a guitar to raise the **pitch** of all the strings uniformly.

captive supplier *EntreP* Venture that produces a product or provides a service for a single customer.

carbon graphite *MusInstr, Sci&Tech* Carbon compound lighter and stronger than wood – but reflects sound better than wood – used in some guitars and pianos.

carbon microphone *RecA&S* Poor quality **mic**, too often used on bus and train **public-address systems**. <Next stop: "Squawka-keegee.">*Also see* **Microphones.**

card *InfoMgt* » **board**

card in *Mgt* To sign in at a place of business by use of a magnetic card.

card out *Mgt* To sign out from a place of business by use of a magnetic card.

carders *InfoMgt* **Phishers** who seek to acquire credit card numbers.

cardioid microphone *RecA&S* Professional quality **mic** – with a heart-shaped response pattern – that picks up sound better from front than back. *Also see* **Microphones.**

careerism *Mgt* Pursuit of professional advancement as one's chief or sole aim.

caret (^) *VA-Prntng* Proofreading symbol used to indicate where something is to be inserted in a line of printed or written matter. *Also see* **Symbols.**

caricature *LitArts, VisArts* Pictorial or literary representation in which the subject's distinctive features or peculiarities are deliberately exaggerated to produce a comic or grotesque effect.

carillon *MusInstr* Set of **chromatically**- tuned bells in a tower, usu. played from a keyboard. CARILLONNEUR. *Also see* **Musical Instrument Families.**

carnival *PA-Variety* Traveling amusement show usu. inc. rides, games, and **sideshows**. *Also see* **barker, festival, Mardi Gras.**

carny *also* **carney** *PA-Variety* **1** Carnival. **2** One who works in or with a carnival.

carol *MusArts* Song of praise or joy, esp. for Christmas. *Also see* **Songs.**

CARP *IntelProp, RecA&S* **Copyright Arbitration Royalty Panel.** Successor to the Copyright Royalty Tribunal. Consists of private citizens appointed by the **Register of Copyrights** to act as arbitrators in matters of setting periodic changes in the royalty rate for the **compulsory mechanical license**, as well as for compulsory licenses for distant signal cable television transmissions and public broadcasting.

carrier *Genl* Person or an entity that transports passengers or goods.

carrier *InfoMgt* telecommunications company

cart *BcstJourn* Plastic case with enclosed tape that is used to play back **bites, voicers,** and other **actualities** for radio newscasts. Carts come in many lengths, are easy to load and cue. Sometimes, "cart" is loosely applied to any recorded element to be used in a newscast.

cartage *RecA&S* Charge against the **cost of recording** for transporting special equipment to and from place of rental. <**calliope,** organ, **timpani**>

carte blanche *LegAsp* Unlimited authority – granted by one person to another – to impose conditions which will be binding upon the person granting such authority.

cartel *EntreP* Group of companies that coordinate their pricing decisions, often by charging the same price.

cartel *Law&Pol, Mktg* Combination of independent business organizations formed to regulate production, pricing, and marketing of goods by the members. *Also see* **monopoly, oligopoly.**

Carter, Jimmy (James Earl Carter Jr., 1924-, 39th U.S. Pres., 1977-81, farmer, humanitarian, preacher)*Law&Pol* He is credited with establishing energy-conservation measures, concluding the Panama Canal treaties (1978), and negotiating the Camp David accords between Egypt and Israel (1979) *Also see* **public interest.**

cartoon *VisArts* Humorous or satirical drawing

Cartoonists Association *ArtPerf, HR&LR, LitArts, VisA&C* Nonprofit affiliate of **NWU** "that acts as facilitator between the cartoon buyer and the artist." — >http://www.nwu.org/nwu/toon>

Casablanca *InfoMgt* New version (4.0) of **AOL** software due sometime in 1997.

cascading style sheets (CSS) *iMedia* Language that describes how content should be presented; specifies details such as colors, font selection, spacing, alignment, etc.

case *Fndng* Combination of reasons advanced by a **nonprofit** to justify its appeals for support with emphasis on its services, past, present, and potential. One of the three basics of fund-raising, along with leadership and **fields of support.**

CASE *Fndng* **Council for the Advancement and Support of Education.** Organization that provides training, support, and information for its member educational institutions.

case statement *Fndng* Carefully prepared document that sets forth in detail the reasons why an institution or agency merits support, in the context of the "case bigger than the institution," with substantial documentation of its services, its **human resources**, its potential for greater service, its needs and its future plans.

case study *iMedia* Detailed account giving information about a person, group or thing, usu. as a reference for the development or redesign of a product.

cash budget *E&F-Acc* Details how the business expects to go from the beginning cash balance to the desired ending balance.

cash budget *EntreP* Planning document strictly concerned with the receipt and payment of dollars.

cash conversion period *EntreP* Time required to convert paid-for inventories and accounts receivable into cash.

cash cow *Eco&Fin* Term applied to a **strategic business unit** that has a steady share of a stable or mature market. *Also see* **dog.**

cash disbursement journal *E&F-Acc* Special **journal** used to record cash payments by check. *Also see* **Journals.**

cash discount *Eco&Fin, Mktg* Reduction in the price of an item for sale allowed if payment is made within a stipulated period. <The magazine **rate card** allows a 2% cash discount if invoice is paid within 10 days from date of invoice> *Also see* **Discounts.**

cash discounts *EntreP* Discount which is offered to credit customers as an incentive to get them to pay promptly. *Ex.* 2/10, net 30.

cash equivalents *E&F-Acc* Highly **liquid short-term investments** that can be converted into cash with little delay.

cash flow *E&F-Acc* Cash receipts and cash payments

cash flow *Eco&Fin* **1** Pattern of income and expenditures and the resulting availability of cash. <The company improved its cash flow by borrowing against **receivables**> **2 Cash receipts** or net income for a given period, reckoned after taxes and other disbursements — often used as a measure of corporate worth.

cash flow *EntreP* Movement of cash into and out of a business. For new ventures this is more important than net income.

cash flow budget *EntreP* Plan that guides and controls a company's sources and usage of cash. **Cash flow statement** Financial statement that delineates the movement of cash into and out of the company.

cash flows from financing activities *EntreP* Section of a statement of cash flow that includes cash received from stocks or bonds, the actual cash paid to owners in the form of dividends, and the repayment of long term debt.

cash in *Eco&Fin* **1** To withdraw from a venture. **2** To obtain a profit or other advantage by timely exploitation. [Like, take the money and run.].

cash method of accounting (cash-basis accounting) *EntreP* Method of accounting that reports transactions only when cash is received or a payment is made.

Cash or Deferred Arrangement plan (CODA) *Eco&Fin, HR&LR* Effective 1987, the plan permits an employee to elect, as an alternative to receive taxable cash in the form of compensation or a bonus, to contribute pretax dollars to a qualified tax-deferred retirement plan. — 401(K) Plan. **Carter, Jimmy** (James Earl Carter Jr., 1924-, 39th U.S. Pres., 1977-81, farmer, humanitarian, preacher) *Law&Pol* SALARY REDUCTION PLAN

cash out *Eco&Fin* To dispose of a long-held asset for profit.

cash over/short *E&F-Acc* Account used to record discrepancies that arise when daily cash **drawers** do not match cash receipts. Such an account can be over or under, neither situation is acceptable. Cash **drawers** should balance out.

cash payments journal *E&F-Acc* Specialized **journal** used to record all cash payments.

cash receipts journal *E&F-Acc* Special **journal** to record cash receipts. *Also see* **Journals**.

cash-basis accounting*E&F-Acc* Accounting that records only transactions in which cash is received or paid.

CASIE*Mktg* **Coalition for Advertising Supported Information and Entertainment**. Advertising research organization formed in 1994 by the **Association of National Advertisers** (ANA) and the **American Association of Advertising Agencies** (AAAA) to accelerate efforts to understand and use **interactive media**.

casino*PerfA&C* **Venue** for gambling and live entertainment.

cassette *Flm&Vid, RecA&S* Small, flat case containing two reels and a length of magnetic tape that winds between them, used in audio or video tape recorders or players.

cast *Flm&Vid, Rdio/TV, TheatArts* **1** Actors in a play, movie, or other theatrical presentation. **2** To choose actors for the parts in a play, movie, or other theatrical presentation. *Also see* **cast album**.

cast *VisArts* **1** Act of pouring molten material into a mold. **2**AMount of molten material poured into a mold at a single operation. **2** Something formed by a cast. <The sculpture was a bronze cast>

cast album *MusArts, RecA&S* Recording of the musical numbers in a musical play by the original or continuing cast. ORIGINAL CAST SHOW ALBUM

cast shadow *iMedia* Shadow from an object that falls either on itself or other objects, and which provides information about **3D** space and depth.

castanet *MusInstr* Latin rhythm instrument consisting of a pair of slightly concave shells of ivory or hardwood, held in the palm of the hand by a connecting cord over the thumb and clapped together with the fingers. *Also see* **Musical Instrument Families**.

caste *Cult&Soc* Social class separated from others by distinctions of hereditary rank, profession, or wealth. *Also see* **Brahmin**.

casting *Flm&Vid, Rdio/TV, TheatArts* Selection of actors or performers for the parts of a presentation or production. *Also see* **audition**.

casting couch *Ethcs&Phil,PerfA&C* Whereupon the villainous, lecherous agent-director-producer **auditions** ambitious innocents. *Also see* **payola, plugola**.

castrati *MusArts* Plural of **castrato**

castrato *MusArts* Male singer castrated before puberty so as to retain a soprano or alto voice. CASTRATI. *Also see* **countertenor**.

casual engagement *MusArts* **Engagement** of one or two days or nights in the same **venue**. — **American Federation of Musicians** (AFM) *Also see* **one-niter, steady engagement**.

casuistry *Ethcs&Phil* **1** Specious or excessively subtle reasoning intended to rationalize or mislead. **2** Determination of right and wrong in questions of conduct or conscience by the application of general principles of ethics.

catalog *Crit&Eval* **1** To classify. <a book or publication> according to a categorical system.

catalog*IntelProp, MusArts* Collection of songs owned by a publisher or songwriter.

catalogue raisonné (cat-ah-log ray-zon-ay, Fr.) *InfoMgt, LitArts* Publication listing titles of articles or literary works, esp. the contents of an exhibition, inc. related descriptive or critical material.

catalyst *Crit&Eval* Some one or some thing that precipitates a process or event without being involved in or changed by the consequences.

catastrophe *TheatArts* Turning point in the **plot** of a classical tragedy.

catbird seat *Crit&Eval* Position of power or prominence

catcall *Crit&Eval* Harsh or shrill call or whistle expressing derision or disapproval of a performance. *Also see* **claque**.

catch action *Flm&Vid, RecA&S* Compose a musical cue to **synchronize** with specific action on the screen.

catcher*ArtPerf, PA-Variety* » **flyer**

catchment area *Mktg* Geographic area from where most of the organization's customers are drawn.

catchy *Crit&Eval* **1** Attractive or appealing. <a catchy idea for a

new arts show> **2** Easily remembered. <a song with a catchy melody> **3** Tricky; deceptive. <a catchy exam question>

categorical colors *iMedia* Colors closer to an ideal, and which have been found to be easier to remember when used for coding or labeling data.

categorical imperative *Ethcs&Phil* In the ethical system of **Immanuel Kant**, an unconditional moral law that applies to all rational beings and is independent of any personal motive or desire.

category killer *Fashn, Mktg* Large retail store or chain specializing in a single kind of merchandise stocked in large quantity and wide variety and sold at discount prices.

catharsis *Crit&Eval* Purifying or figurative cleansing of the emotions by art, esp. **pity** and **fear** aroused by **tragedy**, described by **Aristotle** in *The Poetics* as an effect of tragic drama on its audience. *Also see* **plot**.

catharsis *TheatArts* Act of purging, cleansing, or purifying. Aristotle uses it to describe the effect of tragedy on the audience.

Cathode Ray Tube (CRT) *InfoMgt* Type of computer **monitor**. » **CRT**

cathode-ray tube (CRT) *Rdio/TV* Basic TV tube

cattle call *TheatArts* » **open auditions**

CATV *Rdio/TV* **Community Antenna Television**. » **cable television**

catwalk *PerfA&C* Narrow, elevated walkway, in the **flies** above a theater stage.

cause célèbre (sel-leb-ruh, Fr.) *Crit&Eval* **1** Issue arousing widespread controversy or heated public debate. **2** Celebrated legal case.

cause-related marketing *Fndng, Mktg* Collaborative arrangements between a company and a **nonprofit** organization in which the former promotes both its own product and the **nonprofit** cause; often ties corporate donations to sales of its product.

cave paintings *Cult&Soc, VisArts* » **Paleolithic art**

caveat *Crit&Eval* **1** Warning or caution. **2** Qualification or explanation

caveat *LegAsp* Formal notice filed by an interested party with a court requesting postponement of a proceeding until the filer is heard.

caveat emptor (Latin for "Let the buyer beware.") *Mktg* Principle in commerce that the buyer alone is responsible for assessing the quality of a purchase before buying. *Also see* **caveat venditor**.

caveat venditor (Latin for "Let the seller beware.") *Mktg* Principle in commerce that marketers consider consumer interests as most important. *Also see* **caveat emptor**.

CB *Rdio/TV* Radio-frequency band officially allocated for private radio communications. CITIZENS BAND

CBC *Rdio/TV* **Canadian Broadcasting Corporation**. Canadian government owned radio and television network operating separate English and French stations and sub-networks. *Also see* **Broadcast Stations & Networks**.

CBS*Rdio/TV* **CBS, Inc**. Major radio and television network founded in 1927 as **United Independent Broadcasters, Inc**. Sold to **William S. Paley** in 1928 who changed the name to **Columbia Broadcasting System, Inc**. Officially became CBS, Inc. in 1974 Sold to **Westinghouse** in 1996 *Also see* **Broadcast Stations & Networks**.

CC *Eco&Fin* **Chamber of Commerce**

CCC *Genl* Columbia College Chicago

CCL *InfoMgt* **Communication Control Language** initializes a **modem** and negotiates the connection between the **modem** and the selected online service.

CD *InfoMgt, RecA&S* Compact disk. 4.75-inch, read-only **optical disk** on which data or music is **encoded** as a storage medium for microcomputers. *Also see* **DVD**.

CD, C/D *Eco&Fin* **Certificate of Deposit**. Certificate from a bank stating that the named party has a specified sum on deposit for a given period of time at a fixed rate of interest.

CD-R *InfoMgt, RecA&S* Compact disk-recordable. a type of optical disk storage medium that can create **CD-ROM**s and audio CDs. Write once recordable media.

CD-ROM *InfoMgt, RecA&S* **Compact Disc w/Read-only Memory**. *Also see* **DVD, Music Playback Devices**.

CD-ROM changer *InfoMgt* Machine that will robotically load as many as 100 CD-ROMs into a CD-ROM disk drive. Synonymous with **jukebox**, a CD-ROM changer usu. requires about five seconds to locate and load a requested disk.

CDKIT *RecA&S* An online service – hosted in France by SJT – that makes **CDs** to one's order from the thousands of popular music titles in stock.

cease-and-desist order *LegAsp* Court order forbidding an action being continued. <Epic Records obtained a cease-and-desist order preventing radio stations from continuing to play **Michael Jackson's** new single, *Scream*, before the official **release date**> *Also see* **leak**.

cel *iMedia* 1 Piece of transparent paper (often celluloid acetate) used to create frame-by-frame animations. 2 Single frame in a frame-based authoring application.

cel animation *iMedia* 1 Animation method where parts of characters, objects, or scenes are drawn on transparent papers, saving time and effort for the animator(s) 2 Digital method of animation using a frame-based authoring program.

celeb *Crit&Eval* **celebrity**

celebrity (celeb) *Crit&Eval* 1 Widely known person. 2 Fame more often conferred by the media than earned by achievement; person famous for being famous. "It's like the Aristotelian rules of drama: the higher the place from which someone falls, the more dramatic it is. It's kind of an American pastime to build up **heroes** and then tear them down." — **Barbra Streisand**

celebrity authors *LitArts* Temporarily (in)famous who are signed to extravagant advances and assigned ghost writers and **cynical** editors by publishers who assert that the "best-seller" reward money is used to publish unknown but real authors. [It's a bottom-line trend common to publicly- owned publishing companies.].

celebrity profile producer *Journ, Rdio/TV* Producer of a television news program who specializes in producing biographical essays of celebrities.

celebrity service *Fashn, Mktg* One that matches fashion designers with highly visible movie and TV personalities. Another version of **endorsement** advertising.

celestial jukebox *RecA&S* Recorded music delivered by digital transmission.

cell *EntreP, InfoMgt* Intersection of a row and a column on a spreadsheet.

cello (clo.) *MusInstr* Four-stringed instrument of the **violin** family, **pitched** lower than the **viola** but higher than the **double bass**. CELLIST, VIOLONCELLO. *Also see* **Musical Instrument Families**.

CEMA *Sci&Tech* **Consumer Electronics Manufacturers Association.** Represents hundreds of manufacturers of audio, video, and home information products; sponsors international consumer electronic shows.

censor *Ethcs&Phil, Law&Pol* 1 One authorized to examine books, films, recordings, etc. and to remove or suppress what is considered morally, politically, or otherwise objectionable. 2 Agent in the unconscious responsible for (self) censorship. *Origin* Roman official who determined who was on the citizenship rolls, on the basis of the morals and conduct of citizens and candidates. *Also see* **obscene**.

censorship *Ethcs&Phil, Law&Pol* Review – by the government or some official agency – of publications, movies, plays, and other art or cultural products for the purpose of prohibiting publication or distribution, because to the reviewing body, the material is obscene, immoral, or otherwise objectionable. Censorship goes contrary to the principle of **autonomy**, and is of questionable effectiveness anyway. <"Books won't stay banned. They won't burn. Ideas won't go to jail....the censor and the inquisitor have always lost. The only sure weapon against bad ideas is better ideas." — Alfred Whitney Griswold (19??-; hist., tchr.> [Is there such a thing as **self-censorship**? [Is it censorship if one edits oneself, or is that simply using **judgment**?] *Also see* **autonomy**, **Anthony Comstock**, *Index of Forbidden Books*.**censure** *Crit&Eval* Expression of strong disapproval or harsh criticism; condemn.

censure *Law&Pol* Official rebuke, as by a legislature of one of its members. <The U.S. Senate ultimately censured Senator Joe McCarthy for his reckless charges of "communist infiltration.">

census-based measurements *InfoMgt, Mktg* Complete audience counts rather than measurements based on samples of computer

users.

center *also* **Center** *Cult&Soc, Law&Pol* 1 That which, according to **Yeats**' poem, "cannot hold," in this use, an image of the unifying principle of things. 2 Political group or a set of policies representing a moderate view between those of the right and the left. "Who says it's good? Where is the center?" — Barry Gaither (19??-, cult. critic, musm. dir.) *Also see* **mainstream**.

center *Dnce* Second part of dance class, follows **barre** work.

Center for Media Education (CME) *InfoMgt, Journ»* **CME**

Center for Research on Concepts and Cognition (CRCC) *InfoMgt »* **CRCC**

center spread *Journ, VA-Prntng* Two facing pages in the center of a magazine or newspaper.

center stage *Genl* Place of importance, in the center of attention.

center stage (C) *TheatArts* Stage location and direction. *Also see* **Stage Directions**

Center Stage *InfoMgt* Area of **AOL** that features live conferences with guest stars.

centerfold *Journ, VA-Prntng* 1 Magazine center spread. <a foldout of an oversize photograph or feature> 2 Special feature used as a centerfold. <a nude photograph, an advertisement, or calendar.

central bank *EntreP* Banker's bank; an official bank that controls the supply of money in a country.

central processing unit (cpu) *InfoMgt »* **cpu**

centralized management *Mgt* Decision-making concentrated among a small number of managers at the main office.

CEO *Mgt* Chief Executive Officer

ceramic microphone *RecA&S* Bit better than a **crystal mic** but has a very erratic **frequency response**. *Also see* **Microphones**.

ceremony *Cult&Soc* Formal act or set of acts performed as prescribed by ritual or custom.

certificate of deposit (CD, C/D) *Eco&Fin »* **CD, C/D**

Certificate of deposit (CD) *EntreP* Promissory notes issued primarily by banks where the promissor (bank) agrees to pay the purchaser (promissee) the principal amount plus interest after a stipulated period of time.

certificate of recordation *InfoMgt, IntelProp »* **Judicial Improvement Act of 1990**

certification mark *IntelProp* **Trademark** that certifies that goods or services are of a certain quality or are from a certain area.

Certified Fund Raising Executive *Fndng »* **CFRE**

certified public accountant *E&F-Acc »* **CPA**

Cézanne, Paul (Say-zan, 1839-1906, Fr. pntr, theorist) *ArtPerf, VisArts* A leading figure in the revolution toward **abstraction**. <*House of the Hanged Man* (1873-74), *The Card Players* (1890-92)> *Also see* **postimpressionism**.

CFDA *Fashn* **Council of Fashion Designers of America.** Sponsors of annual awards in the fashion industry. *Also see* **Perry Ellis award**.

CFI *Eco&Fin* Cost, Freight, and Insurance

CFRE *Fndng* **Certified Fund Raising Executive** Title awarded to those who have worked ten years in the field and pass a test by **NSFRE**.

CG or **font** *BcstJourn* Refers to computer-generated letters and numbers that either are superimposed over a picture or that make up the entire screen over a colored background. *Also:* title, key, lower-third key, or super.

cha-cha-cha *Dnce, MusArts* 1950s **Latin Dance Music**. *Also see* **Dances**.

chachka (chotch-ka, Yinglish) *Crit&Eval* Cheap, showy trinket. KNICKKNACK, TCHOTCHKE, TSATSKE.

chain *Mktg* Number of establishments under common ownership or management:<hotels/motels, restaurants, stores, or theaters> *Also see* **franchise**.

chain of command *EntreP* Official, vertical channel of communication in an organization.

chain-ratio method (breakdown process) *EntreP* Forecasting method that begins with a macro-level variable and works down to the sales forecast.

chair *MusArts* Position of a player in a **section** of an orchestra. <**first chair**, clarinet, or first clarinet, etc> *Also see* **principal player**.

challenge gift *Fndng »* **challenge grant**

challenge grant *Fnding* Grant awarded that will be paid only if the **donee** organization is able to raise additional funds from another source(s) Challenge grants are often used to stimulate giving from other donors. *Also see* **matching grant**

chamber music *MusArts* Compositions traditionally intended for performance in a private room or small concert hall and written for an instrumental ensemble, such as a trio or quartet, with one player for each part.

Chamber Music America *MusArts* National arts service organization whose members include professional chamber ensembles, presenters, organizations and individuals involved in chamber music.

Chamber of Commerce (C. of C.) *Eco&Fin* Association of business persons and merchants for the promotion of commercial interests in the community.

Chambre Syndicale de la Couture Parisienne (CSCP) *Fashn* » **CSCP**

change *MusArts* **1** To undergo transformation or **transition**. **2** Pattern or order in which bells are rung.

changeover *Mgt* Conversion to a different purpose or from one system to another, as in equipment or production techniques.

changeover *TheatArts* Time required to change from one theatrical production to the next.

changes *MusArts* Key changes and chord progressions. [Legend has it that **Charlie Parker** locked himself in a hotel room for two days. When he emerged he knew, really knew, all the changes.].

channel *Flm&Vid, PerfA&C* Term that has replaced "**dimmer**" when describing a dimmable group of lighting instruments. *Also see* **Stage Lighting**.

channel *InfoMgt* **1** Term used to describe a type of transmission media. <**microwave, coaxial cable**> **2** Major area of **AOL**, represented as a button on the main screen.

channel *Mktg* Route of access to a market. <distributors and **retailers**> *Also see* **distribution**.

channel *MusArts* » **bridge**

channel *Rdio/TV* Specified **frequency** band for transmitting and receiving electromagnetic signals. <television>

channel of distribution *EntreP* System of relationships established to guide the movement of a product.

Channel One *InfoMgt, Journ, Rdio&TV* Controversial 12-minute (2-minutes of commercials, 10 minutes of news) television program seen daily by an estimated eight million students in the U.S.

channel surfing *Rdio/TV* Couch potato's favorite board sport: skimming the broadcast waves in search of something Out There. Just think of the Olympian challenge of 500 channels! *Also see* **lurking, surf**.

channels of distribution *Mktg* » **delivery system, distribution**

chanson (Fr.) *MusArts* **Cabaret** song. *Also see* **Songs**.

chant *MusArts* **1** Short, simple melody in which a number of syllables or words are sung on or **intoned** to the same note. **2 Canticle** or prayer sung or intoned in this manner.

chanteuse (Shan-tooz) *MusArts* female nightclub singer

chantey *MusArts* (Passé) Song sung by sailors to the rhythm of their movements while working. *Also see* **Songs**.

Chantilly lace *Fashn* Delicate lace from Chantilly, a village of northern France north of Paris.

chap *LitArts* **chapter**

chapeau (shapoh, Fr.) *Fashn* hat

chapter (chap.) *LitArts* One of the main divisions of a relatively lengthy piece of writing, such as a book, usu. numbered or titled.

Chapter 7 bankruptcy *EntreP* Bankruptcy filing in which the entrepreneur liquidates the assets of the venture in an effort to pay off the liabilities owed by the company.

Chapter 11 bankruptcy *EntreP* Bankruptcy filing in which the entrepreneur is provided protection from creditors while reorganizing the company.

char. *InfoMgt, LitArts, VA-Prntng, TheatArts* **character**

character *EntreP* Term used in credit evaluation to determine if a customer has paid his or her bills on time in the past and has favorable credit references.

character (char.) *Ethcs&Phil* Complex result of one's moral development leading to a fixed disposition to conduct oneself in certain ways; one has a character, called by **Aristotle** a "second **nature**." *Also see* **analysis of tragedy, virtue**.

character (char.) *InfoMgt* Any symbol widely understood and thus conveys information. <letters, numerals, and punctuation marks> shown on a typewriter or computer keyboard.

character (char.) *LitArts, TheatArts,. Rdio/TV* One portrayed in the theater, radio/television, or a novel.

character (char.) *TheatArts* Distinctive qualities, traits, and personality of a person, place, or thing. Also the emotional quality (e.g. soft, hard, harsh, sensuous) of a **line**.

character actor *Flm&Vid, TheatArts* Male or female actor who has the ability to act in roles with traits different from those of the actor.

character arc *TheatArts* Overall action of a character during a play, and the way that character changes and develops during the course of that play.

character assassination *Ethcs&Phil* Vicious personal verbal attack intended to destroy or damage a public figure's reputation.

character entity *iMedia* Codes used to display certain characters and symbols <the alphanumeric code in **XHTML** that produces a copyright symbol>. Similarly, numeric character references (decimal or hexadecimal) also display characters and symbols, but are written in numeric form.

character-based metaphor *iMedia* Interface where content is accessed through interaction with a character(s)

character's point of view (or "internal point of view") *LitArts* Access in a third person story to a character's feelings, thoughts, memories, and history, as known by that character. — Story Workshop term by John Schultz (CCC/Fiction Writing dept.)

charge (chg.) *E&F-Acc* Debt or an entry in an account recording a debt.

charge (chg.) *Eco&Fin* **1** Expense, cost. **2** Asking price. **3** Financial burden. <tax or **lien**>

charge *Crit&Eval* Feeling of pleasant excitement; a thrill. <The audience got a real charge out of the program>

charge *LegAsp* Instruction given by a judge to a jury about its responsibility to the law, its application, and the weighing of evidence.

charge *Mgt* Supervision; management. <The general manager had overall charge of the project>

charge-back *Eco&Fin, RecA&S* Expense assessed by a record company against an artist's royalties.

charisma *Crit&Eval* Rare personal quality attributed to leaders and performers who arouse fervent popular devotion and enthusiasm. **2** Personal magnetism or charm.

charitable contribution deduction *Fndng* Tax deduction based on a donation to a charitable organization.

charitable gift annuity *Fndng* Fixed sum paid regularly by a **nonprofit** to its **donor** or other designated **beneficiary** in exchange for a cash or property contribution. This is a form of giving.

charitable institution *Fndng* Any private organization that operates on a **nonprofit** basis for the public good, and therefore is exempt from taxation, except for its commercial operations.

charitable lead trust *Fndng* Payment made to charity for a predetermined number of years, then reverting to the grantor or other **designee**.

charitable remainder unitrust *Fndng* Life income plan created by the donor permanently transferring assets to a trust from which the donor receives a fixed dollar amount.

charity *Fndng* **1** Organization existing for charitable purposes. **Nonprofits** may have charitable status, but may not be directly charitable in mission. <museums, zoos, etc> **2** Voluntary giving of funds to those in need.

charivari *Cult&Soc, MusArts* » **shivaree**

Charleston *Dnce* Jazz dance, ca. 1920s. *Also see* **Dances**.

charmeuse (shar-meuse, Fr. from "charmer," to charm) *Fashn* Satin-finished silk fabric.

chart *Mktg, RecA&S* Numerical ranking of the best selling musical recordings in a particular category in a given time period as published in a trade magazine. <*Billboard's* **Top 40** chart>

chart *MusArts* Musical **arrangement** for a jazz or pop music ensemble. *Also see* **orchestration, score**.

chart of accounts *E&F-Acc* List of all the accounts and their account numbers in the **ledger**.

chartjunk *iMedia* Decorative additions to graphics that do not convey information, or convey redundant data. *Also see* **non-data-ink.**

chase *VA-Prntng* Rectangular steel or iron frame into which pages or columns of type are locked for printing or plate making. *Also see* **letterpress.**

chase chorus *MusArts* "Solo chorus shared by two [jazz] improvisers who take turns playing short (usu. four- or eight-bar) solos, often at a fast tempo. Solos are meant to imitate, extend, or outdo one another." — Lyons & Perlo (jazz critics) *Also see* **cutting contest.**

chat *InfoMgt* Occurs when several people are simultaneously connected to an online service and are typing messages to one another in **real time.** Some online services incur a several-second **delay** in order to delete obscenities. "[The Sc-Fi Channel] is letting computer users 'chat' about a television program in progress and watch their comments scroll along the bottom of the TV screen almost simultaneously as the program unfolds." — Laurie Mifflin (info. sci. journ.)

chat room *InfoMgt* Area online where a number of people are simultaneously connected to an online service and are typing messages to one another in **real time.** Some online services incur a several-second delay in order to delete obscenities.

chattel *LegAsp* Personal property, movable or immovable. <a book, a coat, a pencil, garden, a lease>

chattel mortgage *EntreP* Loan for which items of inventory or other moveable property serve as collateral.

Chautauqua movement *Cult&Soc, PA-Variety* Adult education, offering a range of cultural, religious, and recreational activities founded in 1874 at the resort village of Chautauqua in extreme southwest New York state.

chauvinist *Crit&Eval, Law&Pol* **1** Militant devotion to the glorification of one's country; fanatical patriot. **2** Prejudiced belief in the superiority of one's own gender, group, or kind. <male **chauvinist**> *Also see* **ideologue, jingo.**

cheap songs *MusArts* "I wanted to write about the way that cheap songs are inheritors of something else.... Popular music stirred profound associations and memories for the average person. Cheap songs have something of the **Psalms** of David about them. They do illuminate."— Dennis Potter (Brit. scrnwrtr.) *Also see* **popular music, Songs.**

cheating *TheatArts* Term used without any derogatory meaning when an actor plays in a position more openly visible to the audience, or performs an action more openly than complete realism would permit.

checkbox *InfoMgt* On the computer's screen: **interactive** square-shaped control box that allows a user to choose several options from a list of options. *Also see* **option (radio) buttons.**

checked in *iMedia* "Behavior characterized by high levels of engagement, substantial presence, disclosure of self, and receptivity to others." — Jim and Michele McCarthy

checked out *iMedia* "Absence due to awareness of low productivity or unresolved conflicting commitments."— Jim and Michele McCarthy

checker *Mgt* Usually the **road manager** for the performer who checks the audience traffic in each auditorium entrance against the promoter's statement of gate receipts. *Also see* **go into percentage.**

CheckIn protocol *iMedia* Method of committing to participate fully in a team environment. "CheckIn protocol provides two major components for establishing and developing high-performance collaboration: an enlistment procedure and an interpersonal connectivity process." — Jim and Michele McCarthy

checking copy *Journ* Copies of a periodical used to check quality control, billing data, and other internal and **archival** uses.

cheerleader *Crit&Eval* **1** One who expresses or promotes thoughtless praise. **2** One who leads the cheering of spectators.

cheesecake *Crit&Eval, VisArts* **1** Photographs of minimally attired women. **2** (Passé) Photograph of a woman showing her legs above the knee. *Also see* **beefcake.**

Chekhovian *Crit&Eval, LitArt, TheatArts* Style of writing concerning the inability of human beings to comunicate with one another. Relates to the work of Anton Chekhov (1860-1904, Russ. fictwri., dram.)

chemise *Fashn* **1** Woman's loose, shirtlike undergarment. **2** Loosely-fitting dress that hangs straight, sometimes worn with a belt; a shift.

chernoff faces *iMedia* Graphical display of information that uses a human face to convey multi-dimensional data - more useful for showing trends rather than exact details.

Chevreul illusion *iMedia* Areas of solid color next to each other, moving in a uniform progression from dark to light, where gradiations seem to appear within each color area (gradiations are illusions)

chew up the scenery *Crit&Eval, TheatArts* May be said of a **ham's** acting efforts. *Also see* **overact.**

chg. *Eco&Fin* **charge.**

chiaroscuro *VisArts* Technique used to represent light and shade independently of the use of color. First used by **Leonardo da Vinci** in the 15th century.

chiaroscuro lighting *Flm&Vid* Lighting for light-dark contrast (fast **falloff**) used to emphasize volume and specific areas.

chic *Fashn* Sophistication in dress and manner; elegance, stylish; fashionable.

Chicago jazz *MusArts* **New Orleans jazz** as interpreted and played by white Chicago musicians; recognizable by its driving **staccato** improvisation. "Offshoot of the New Orleans style played in the 1920s but featuring less collective improvisational, more soloing, and more formal arrangements."... "Two distinct styles of Chicago jazz existed, one performed by blacks and the other by whites." — Lyons & Perlo (jazz critics) Black players included. <**Louis Armstrong**, King Oliver (Joseph Porter, 1885-1938, cornet, bndldr.), and Jelly Roll Morton (Ferdinand Joseph La Menthe, 1885-1941, jazz comp., orches.)> White players included native mid-Westerners. <Bix Beiderbecke (1903-31, jazz cornet, comp.) and members of the **Austin High Gang**> *Also see* **Jazz Styles.**

Chicago Symphony Orchestra (CSO) *MusArts* **Chicago Symphony Orchestra.** » **CSO**

chick *Crit&Eval* (Hiptalk) Girl or young woman.

Chief Executive Officer (CEO) *Mgt* Highest ranking officer of a company beholden only to the board of directors, i.e., the stockholders. This person may carry the title of Chairman, Chairperson, Chairwoman, President, or Managing Director (European)

chief operating officer (COO) *Mgt* In large organizations, the number two executive who reports directly to the **CEO.** The COO is responsible for the day-to-day, month-to-month, quarter-to-quarter operations of the entire company. Titles include. <president, executive vice president, corporate vice president>

chiffon *Fashn* Fabric of sheer silk or rayon.

chiffon *Perf-MkUp* Used to cover the eyebrows when blocking them out.

chignon *Fashn* Roll or knot of hair worn at the back of the head or esp. at the nape of the neck.

children's shows *Rdio/TV* Popular type of television network programming. <*Captain Kangaroo, Mickey Mouse Club, Sesame Street*> *Also see* **Television Shows.**

chimes *MusInstr* **1** Set of bells tuned to scale, used as an orchestral instrument. **2** Sound produced. *Also see* **percussion.**

chip *InfoMgt* Small component that contains a large amount of electronic circuitry. Thin **silicon** wafer on which electronic components are deposited in the form of **integrated circuits.**

chips *InfoMgt* Building blocks of a computer.

choices *TheatArts* Selection of actions accumulated during the rehearsal process which illuminate the character and play, and move the character to her/his goals/intentions/wants.

choir *MusArts* **1** Organized company of singers who perform church music or who sing in a church. **2** Part of a church used by such a company of singers. **3** Group of similar instruments. <a **woodwind** choir>

choir loft *MusArts* Gallery for a group of church singers.

choirboy, choirgirl *MusArts* Boy or girl member of a choir.

choirmaster *MusArts* Director of a group of church singers.

chops *MusArts* Technical skill with which a jazz or rock musician performs. *Origin* Lips, cheeks, jowls of an animal or a human. IRON CHOPS.

chor. *MusArts* **choral, chorister, chorus.**

choral (chor.) *MusArts* Relating to a **chorus** or **choir.**

chorale *MusArts* **1** Protestant hymn melody **2** Harmonized hymn for organ.

chord *MusArts* Combination of three or more usu. concordant tones sounded simultaneously. *Also see* **progression**.

chord changes *MusArts* » **changes**

chord organ *MusInstr* Electronic or reed organ equipped with buttons for producing **chords**. *Also see* **Musical Instrument Families, Organs**.

choreo. *Dnce* **choreography**.

choreog. *ArtPerf, Dnce* **choreographer**.

choreographer (choreog.) *ArtPerf, Dnce* One who creates and arranges dances or ballets. *Also see* **Dance Theater Workshop**.

choreography (choreo.) *Dnce* Art of creating and arranging ballets, dances, and dramatically integrated choreographic movements.

choric (korick) *MusArts, TheatArts* relating to a chorus

chorister *MusArts* **choirboy** or **choirgirl**

chorus *Dnce, TheatArts* **1** Group of persons who speak or sing in **unison** a given part or composition in drama or poetry recitation. **2** Portion of a classical Greek drama consisting of **choric** dance and song. **3** Group or performer in a modern drama serving a purpose similar to the **Greek chorus**.

chorus *MusArts* **1** Composition in four or more parts written for a large number of singers. **2** Refrain in which an audience joins a soloist in a song. **3** Repeat of the opening statement of a popular song played by the whole group. **4** Solo section based on the main melody of a popular song and played by a member of the group. **5** Body of singers who perform choral compositions. **6** Body of vocalists and dancers who support the soloists and leading performers in operas, musical comedies, and revues. *Also see* **SATB**.

chorus *TheatArts* Group of young men who sang and danced as a group in Greek tragedy and comedy: larger choruses also performed **dithyrambs**. In later drama, including Shakespeare's, the term denoted a character or characters who acted as narrator and or commented on the action. In musicals, it denotes the group of singers or dancers who support the principal actors.

Chorus America *MusArts* Est. 1977, National nonprofit "to promote the highest artistic quality, development, and growth of vocal ensembles."

chorus boy, girl *ArtPerf, Dnce* Young man or woman who dances in a theatrical **chorus**.

Christian art *VisArts* » **Byzantine art**

Christian Interactive Network *InfoMgt, Rdio/TV* » **CIN**

chroma key *iMedia* Act of replacing a particular area of color in an image or video with another image or video. *Also see* **blue screen, green screen, keying**.

chromatic aberration *iMedia* When two colors that are very different in wavelength hit the eye at the same time, one is focused before the other; one color seems in focus while the other seems blurry.

chromatic scale *MusArts* **Scale** consisting of 12 **semitones**.

chromatics *Sci&Tech* Scientific study of color.

CHRP *InfoMgt* **Common Hardware Reference Platform** New operating system able to run all major systems except Windows 95 Supposed to become operational in late 1996 Jointly developed by **Apple, IBM**, and Motorola. *Also see* **Operating Systems**.

church *Genl* Ecclesiastical power as distinguished from the **secular**. <separation of church and state>

church *Journ* Editorial content vs. business considerations. <separation of church (editorial) and **state** (business)>

churn *Eco&Fin* Questionable practice of a stock broker frequently buying and selling a client's securities in order to generate commissions.

churn *InfoMgt, Mktg* "As with all online service companies, **America Online** has suffered heavy defections among its new subscribers, a phenomenon known as churn." — *NY Times*

chutzpah (yutz-pah, Yinglish) *Crit&Eval* Astonishing, self-serving boldness; often used to suggest going to ridiculous and implausible lengths to secure an end or an advantage — a quality not lacking in ambitious artists and performers and arts managers. The **golden oldie** example. <Person who murders both parents and then pleads for mercy because of being an orphan>

CIM *InfoMgt* **Computer Integrated Manufacturing** Use of a central data base to tie together all related departments within a company.

CIN *Rdio/TV* **Christian Interactive Network**.

cine. *Flm&Vid* **cinematographer, cinematography**.

cineaste (sin-eh-ast, Fr.) *Flm&Vid* » **cinephile**

cinema verité (vehr-it-ay) *Flm&Vid* Method of **documentary** filming using **aleatory** methods that don't interfere with the way events take place in reality. Such movies are made with a minimum of equipment, usu. a handheld camera and portable sound equipment. DIRECT CINEMA.

CinemaScope *Flm&Vid* **Trade name** for a wide-screen process that employs **anamorphic** camera lenses to squeeze the image in production and then unsqueeze it during projection. Compression/expansion ratio is 2:1.

cinematheque (sin-eh-ma-tek) *Flm&Vid* Small movie theater showing classic or avant-garde films.

cinematic film *Flm&Vid* Moving pictures; **movies**. First shown in public in 1895 by Auguste Lumière (1862-1954, Fr. chemist, inventor) and his brother Louis Lumière (1864-1948) *Also see* **cinema**.

cinematize (sin-eh-mah-teyz) *Flm&Vid, LitArts* To adapt a novel or a play for film or movies.

cinematographer *Flm&Vid* Artist/technician who consults with the director (and vice versa) on lighting strategies, selection of film stock, camera angles, and all other elements that contribute to "the look" of a film. DIRECTOR OF PHOTOGRAPHY (D.P.)

cinematography (cine.) *Flm&Vid* Art or technique of film or movie photography.

cinematology *Crit&Eval, Flm&Vid* Study of film as an art form. *Also see* **filmology**.

cinephile (sin-eh-file, Fr.) *Flm&Vid* Film or movie enthusiast. CINEASTE

Cinerama (Sin-er-ahma) *Flm&Vid* **Trademark** for a motion-picture process which produces wide-screen, realistic images.

circuit *Mgt, PA-Variety, TheatArts* **1** Association of theaters in which plays, **vaudeville** acts, or films move from theater to theater for presentation. <Keith-Orpheum vaudeville circuit> **2** Group of nightclubs, show lounges, or resorts at which entertainers appear in turn.

circuitry *Sci&Tech* Detailed plan for an electric circuit.

circulation *Journ, Mktg* Number of copies of a publication sold or distributed. *Also see* **Media Circulation**.

circus *PA-Variety* **1** Entertainment, often in a tent, includes acrobats, clowns, and trained animals. **2** Roofless, oval enclosure, surrounded by tiers of seats, used in ancient times for public spectacles. <Circus Maximus in Rome> *Also see* **P.T. Barnum, Ringling Brothers and Barnum & Bailey Circus; thumbs-up, thumbs-down**.

ciré *also* **cire** (seeray, Fr.) *Fashn* Fabric or garment with a highly glazed or wax finish. <a ciré shirt>

CIS *InfoMgt* **Computer Information System** Coordinated collection of hardware, software, data, people, and support resources to perform an integrated series of functions that can include processing, storage, input, and output.

CISAC *MusArts* **International Confederation of Societies of Authors and Composers**. International association of performing rights organizations that serves to establish principles for the collection and distribution of performance royalties by societies throughout the world, strengthen copyright protection on an International level, and protect the rights of composers, songwriters, and lyricists. **ASCAP, BMI**, and **SESAC** are members; **NMPA** is an associate member. *Also see* **Copyright-Related Organizations; Copyright Service Organizations**.

cit. *Crit&Eval, Genl* **citation**

citation (cit.) *Crit&Eval, Genl* Quoting of an authoritative source for substantiation. *Also see* **quotation**.

citation (cit.) *LegAsp* Reference to previous court decisions or authoritative writings.

cite *Crit&Eval, Genl* To quote as an authority or example.

cite *LegAsp* To summon before a court of law.

citizens band (CB) *Rdio/TV* » **CB**

city blues *MusArts* Sung by women in the 1920s and 1930s accompanied by piano or band. <Ma Rainey (Gertrude Pridgett Malissa Nix Rainey, 1886-1939, link between **rural blues** and city blues)> *Also see* **Blues**. CLASSIC BLUES:

civil disobedience *Ethcs&Phil* Refusal to obey civil laws in an effort to induce change in governmental policy or legislation, characterized by the use of passive resistance or other nonviolent means. <**Mahatma Gandhi, Martin Luther King Jr.**>

Civil Rights Act (1991) *EntreP* Legislation prohibiting discrimination based on race, color, religion, sex, or national origin.

civilian *Crit&Eval* Someone outside of the world of the arts. <It's difficult for an artist/performer to have a lasting relationship with a civilian>

cl *MusArts* clarinet

claim *IntelProp* To assert one's right or ownership.

clam *MusArts* Poorly played note <flat, sharp>

clapper, clapper board, clapsticks *Flm&Vid* Two short boards hinged together which, when sharply clapped together, provide audible and visible cues used during the **synchronization** process. Slate with relevant information, such as scene and take number, is usu. attached to the clapper board. Modern cameras are usu. equipped with an electronic slate.

clappers *MusInstr* Two flat pieces of wood held between the fingers and struck together rhythmically, with a clacking, percussive sound. *Also see* **bones, Musical Instrument Families**.

claque *PerfA&C* Group of persons – paid or otherwise strongly motivated – to applaud a client's performance. [A well motivated claque also has been known to forcefully demonstrate against a client's rival.] *Also see* **curtain call; encore**.

clarinet (cl) *MusInstr* **Woodwind** instrument (usu. B-flat) having a straight, cylindrical tube with a flaring bell and a single-reed mouthpiece, played by means of finger holes and keys. CLARINETIST, CLARINETTIST. *Also see* **Musical Instrument Families**.

clarion *Crit&Eval* Loud and clear. <a clarion call to resistance or honesty>

Claris Corporation *InfoMgt* Large software developer and distributor owned by **Apple**. *Also see* **warranty**.

clarity *Crit&Eval, LitArts* Clearness of thought or style; **lucidity**.

class *Crit&Eval* Elegance of style, taste, and manner.

class *Cult&Soc* **1** Set, collection, group, or configuration containing members regarded as having certain attributes or traits in common; a kind or category. **2** Social stratum whose members share certain economic, social, or cultural characteristics. <lower-income classes> **3** Social rank or **caste**, esp. high rank.

class *Dnce* Ballet practice session <Taking class is a daily-for-ever ritual for dedicated dancers>

class act *Crit&Eval* One of distinctive and superior quality. <In this world of less than tasteful entertainment, Meryl Streep (1949-, versatile film act.) is a class act>

class act dancing *Dnce* Style of tap dancing known for its elegance, spaciousness, and musicality. *Also see* **Dances**.

class action *ArtPerf* Lawsuit brought by one or more plaintiffs on behalf of a large group of others who have a common interest.

class-conscious *Cult&Soc* **1** Aware of belonging to a particular socioeconomic class. **2** Supportive of class solidarity.

class. *Crit&Eval* **classic**

classic (class.) *Crit&Eval* **1** That which is the enduring exemplar of the highest or best accomplishment in a given field of human endeavor. <The *David* sculpture by Michelangelo (Michaelangelo Buonarroti, 1475-1564, Ital. sculp., pntr., archt., poet), symphonies by Brahms's (Johannes Brahms, (1833-97, Ger. comp.), plays of **Shakespeare**. **2** Adhering or conforming to established standards and principles. <a classic piece of research>

classic (class.) *Fashn* **1** Formal, refined, and restrained in style. **2** Simple and harmonious; elegant. <the classic cut of a suit>

classic (class.) *LitArts* "Classic is a book that doesn't have to be written again." — Carl Van Doren (1985-1950, lit-crit, ed., n-fictwri.)

classic (class.) *VisArts* » **Classical**

Classic Arts Showcase *Flm&Vid* Five-minute video clips of jazz, musical theater, ballet, animation, and ten other forms to all of North and South America 24 hours a day. No advertising Free by satellite, excerpts broadcast on 350 **PBS** stations. Est. 1994 by **Lloyd Rigler**.

classic blues *MusArts* » **city blues**

classic jazz *MusArts* "Pure," traditional jazz sound: predominantly instrumental, rarely vocal, largely improvised rather than arranged, performed primarily on acoustic instruments; genuine **New Orleans jazz**. *Also see* **Jazz Styles**.

classic rock *MusArts* Rock and roll nostalgia for the **icons** of the 1950s and 1960s. <**Elvis Presley**, The Beatles (1962-70, Brit. seminal pop group); Rolling Stones. (Brit. rock group) led by Mick Jagger (1943-)> *Also see* **Rock Music Styles**.

classical (class.) *Crit&Eval* Relating to the ancient Greek and Roman art, architecture, and literature.

classical aggregate supply curve *EntreP* Vertical aggregate supply curve. It reflects the idea that in the long run, output is determined solely by the factors of production.

classical economics *EntreP* School of thought that provides insights into the economy when it operates at or near full employment.

classical cutting *Flm&Vid* » **continuity**

classical music *MusArts* Music in the educated European tradition. "I don't think the word classical is something we ought to be too concerned about. Music, when it gets older and accepted, becomes classical music. It's not something you can look forward to. Classical is a term you apply to the past. You decide that something is classical after it's been around long enough that enough people will want to listen to it." — **Donal Henahan** *Also see* **serious music**.

classical music concerts *Mgt, MusArts* "Difficulties... confronting American orchestras were first documented in a 1992 report by the [ASOL]. Report found that virtually all the costs associated with staging classical concerts had risen faster than the rate of inflation, from musician salaries to administration to promotion, while audiences, for the first time in history, were declining. A second report the following year went to so far as to suggest that orchestras woo audiences with jazz and pop music, recruit more black and Hispanic musicians by dropping traditional **blind auditions**, and try incorporating videoscreens and special lighting in concerts." — Diana Jean Schemo (mus. critic)

Classical School of Management *Mgt* Based on the theories of **Frederick Winslow Taylor**. Every job is made as simple as possible by being analyzed, described, and exactly defined. Employees and workers allowed little or no deviation from their job description. Company so organized (**tall organization**) depends on many levels of specialized middle management and is quite bureaucratic in nature. The Classical School was the predominant influence on American company organization into the 1970s, and is still an important factor. *Also see* **Theory X**.

Classical Style, The *MusArts* Period in musical history when the emphasis was on great expression. <Beethoven (Ludwig van Beethoven, 1770-1827: Ger. comp.), Haydn (Franz Joseph Haydn, 1732-1809, Aus. comp.), Mozart (Wolfgang Amadeus Mozart, 1756-1791, Austrian comp.)

classical theater *TheatArts* Conforming to the models of ancient Greece and Rome.

classicism also **classicalism** *Aes&Creat* Aesthetic attitudes and principles manifested in the art, architecture, and literature of ancient Greece and Rome and characterized by emphasis on form, simplicity, proportion, and restraint. CLASSICIST.

classification scheme *iMedia* Classification of content according to attribute.

classified advertising *Eco&Fin* Total monthly amount of "help wanted" classified advertising in U.S. newspapers is used as an **economic indicator**: more ads means more hiring, better economy ahead.

classified advertising *Mktg, VA-Prntng* Usually small, all-type ads categorized by subject in a magazine or newspaper. <help wanted ads> *Also see* **display advertising**.

classified display advertising *Mktg* Display advertisement is classified by subject, and consequently costs less. *Also see* **ROP**.

classified financial statements *E&F-Acc* General purpose external financial statements that are divided into useful subcategories.

classism *Ethcs&Phil* Bias based on social or economic class.

classless society *Cult&Soc* Lacking social or economic distinctions of class.

classy *Crit&Eval* Highly stylish; elegant.

clave, claves *MusInstr* Creole Cuban instrument (and rhythm pattern) derived from diverse versions of rhythm sticks found throughout the musical world

Clayton Act (1914, substantially amended in 1950) *Law&Pol, Mktg* Important amendment to the **Sherman Anti-Trust Act** (1890), dealing with local price discrimination, interlocking directorates, and **restraint of trade**. *Also see* **Federal Agencies and Stat-**

utes, trust.

clean ups *Flm&Vid* (*animation*) Detailed drawings made from rough sketches.

clearance *IntelProp* Permission to use copyrighted material.

clearance *Mktg* Sale, generally at reduced prices, to dispose of old merchandise.

clearance exclusivity *Flm&Vid* **Exhibitor** may specify an **exclusive run** within an entire market or only over those theaters in the exhibitor's geographic proximity.

clearances manager *IntelProp, Mgt* One responsible for securing or granting permission to use copyrighted material. *Also see* **Managers**.

clef *MusArts* Symbol on a **staff** showing the **pitch** of the notes. *Also see* **bass clef, treble clef**.

cliché lead (cleeshay leed) *BcstJourn, Journ* Type of lead sentence built around an overused phrase.

click *InfoMgt* To press and quickly release the mouse button so as to activate a command. DOUBLE-CLICK.

click streams *InfoMgt, Mktg* Usage information derived from the button pushes made on **PC** keyboards and remote control changers.

click track *Flm&Vid, RecA&S* Large clock with audible clicks used by musicians to **synchronize** a musical **score** with film or tape.

client sign off *iMedia, Mgt* Documented approval (in writing) that a client has approved a plan of action, progress, or a finished product. Each stage in the development of a commercial interactive product should have a client sign off; an explicit description of expectations, timeline, costs, etc., with both client and developer signatures and dates.

client-side code *iMedia* Code that runs on a user agent or browser (termed "client") In contrast: **server-side code**.

client/server model *EntreP* System whereby the user's personal computer (the client) obtains data from a central computer (the server), but processing is done at the client level.

clientele *Genl* Clients of a professional person or practice considered as a group.

cliffhanger *Flm&Vid, LitArts* **Melodramatic serial** in which each episode ends in suspense. *<Perils of Pauline>*

climax *LitArts, MusArts, TheatArts* Moment of great or culminating intensity in a narrative, drama, or musical performance, esp. the conclusion of a crisis. *Also see* **tension and release**.

climax *TheatArts* Strongest point of emotional tension. Most plays have a series of climaxes culminating in a major climax.

Clinton, Bill (William Clinton, 1946-, 42nd U.S. Pres., 1992-, lawyer, tenor sax) *Law&Pol* » **cultural awareness**.

Clio *Crit&Eval* The Muse of history. *Also see* **Muses**.

Clio Award *Mktg, Rdio/TV* Award for the best TV commercials in various categories, presented annually at the **American Television and Radio Commercials Festival**. *Also see* **Awards & Prizes**.

clip *Flm&Vid* Short extract from a film or videotape. *Also see* **coming attractions**.

clip art *InfoMgt, Journ, VisArts* Stock drawings of common subjects available for all computers.

Clipboard *InfoMgt* Portion of some computer's memory set aside to store data being transferred from one file or application to another.

clipper chip *InfoMgt* Chip used as a signal filter to "clip" off noise and preserve signal integrity.

clique *Crit&Eval* Small, exclusive group or circle of friends or associates. *Also see* **in-group**.

clm *VA-Prntng* » **column**

clo *MusInstr* **cello**

cloche *Fashn* Close-fitting woman's hat with a bell-like shape; popular in the 1920s.

clock speed *InfoMgt* Number of electronic pulses produced by a computer per unit of time.

cloque (cloke, Fr.) *Fashn* Cotton, silk, or rayon fabric with a raised woven pattern and a puckered or quilted look.

close *Mgt* To complete final details or negotiations. <close a deal>

Close Distance *LitArts* Events, scenes of action and interaction, of the story tend to be dramatized in detail of dialogue, description,

and action with the sense of experiencing the story in real time. — John Schultz *Also see* **Mid and Greater Distance., vantage point**.

close shot *Flm&Vid* One where the action is filmed very tightly, but not as close as a **close-up**.

closed book *Crit&Eval* Someone or something unfathomable or puzzling.

closed circuit *Rdio/TV* Television transmission with no broadcast facilities.

closed shop *HR&LR* Made illegal by the **Taft-Hartley Act**: the employer is prohibited from hiring anyone who is not a member of the union. » **union shop**

closeout *Mktg* Sale in which all remaining inventory is disposed of at greatly reduced prices.

closet drama *TheatArts* Play to be read rather than performed.

closeup, close-up (CU) *BcstJourn* Intimate camera shot, it usu. encloses the face with some room between the image and the frame's border. An extreme closeup (ECU) will cut off the hairline and the chin and it used for emotional moments; however, it is an uncomfortable shot and should be used sparingly, if at all.

closeup, close-up (CU) *Flm&Vid* Head-and-shoulder shot of a performer. Tight close-up would be the head only. Extreme close-up could be one eye.

closing act *PA-Variety* The last act on a **vaudeville bill**. *Also see* **next to closing, opening act**.

closing credit *Flm&Vid, Rdio/TV* » **credits**

closing entries *E&F-Acc* Entries that transfer the revenue, expense, and dividends balances from these respective accounts to the **Retained Balances** account.

closing notice *TheatArts* Notice posted backstage formally advising the show closing date.

closure *iMedia* One of the **Gestalt Laws** of pattern perception. Contours that have gaps are often perceived as closed, and a closed contour tends to be perceived as an object.

clothier *Fashn* One who makes or sells clothing or cloth.

cloudscape *VisArts* Work of art representing a view of clouds.

clout *Crit&Eval* influence, pull

clown *PA-Variety* **Buffoon, mime**, or **jester** who entertains by jokes, antics, and tricks in a circus, play, or other presentation. *Also see* **fool**.

clown alley *PA-Variety* Portion of a tent or dressing room reserved for clowns.

Clown Artists in Residence (COAI) *PA-Variety* "Dedicated to the art of Clowning and to bringing Joy and Happiness to Everyone." — >http://www.clown.org<

clown white *Th-MakeUp* White make-up base used by circus clowns.

club *MusArts, PA-Variety* » **night club**.

club date *Mgt* One day or night **engagement** for a musician or performer at a convention, civic function, fraternal club (Odd Fellows, Hadassah, et al), private party, sales meeting, etc.

Cluny lace *Fashn* **Bobbin** lace usu. made from heavy linen thread. Made in Le Puy, France, with many examples displayed in the Cluny Museum in Paris.

cluster programming *Rdio/TV* Radio broadcast of several records uninterrupted by announcements.

clustering *BcstJourn* Stories of a similar nature in a newscast that are presented together – or clustered – to help the audience focus on the issues and allow a producer easy **seques** between news stories.

clutter *Mktg* Conflicting or unrelated communications that distract from an advertiser's message to members of a target audience.

clutter *Rdio/TV* Airing in rapid succession of many short spots during a television commercial break. NOISE.

CMA *MusArts* **Country Music Association**, est. 1958, is a non-profit trade organization whose purpose is to promote country music in the U.S. and overseas. It produces the CMA Awards show and the International Country Music Fan Fair. Membership is open to individuals and companies who are directly or substantially involved in the country music business. *Also see* **Awards & Prizes**.

CME *InfoMgt, Journ* **Center for Media Education**. Advocacy organization, provides journalists with information on the effect of the **electronic media** on children.

CMF *MusArts* **Country Music Foundation** Oversees the Country

Music Hall of Fame and Museum; houses a full resource center.

CMS *iMedia* See content management system

CMYK *iMedia* **1** Four colors (cyan, magenta, yellow, and black) used in offset printing. **2** Standard color model used in offset printing (also referred to as "four-color printing") as opposed to the standard color model for screen presentation (**RGB — red, green, and blue**)

CNG *InfoMgt* Calli**NG** tones <loud, long fax-calling beeps>

CNN *Rdio/TV* **Cable News Network** » Ted Turner.

co-branding *Mktg* Process by which one company pays a fee or royalties to license a well-known **trademark** belonging to another company.

co-op advertising *Mktg* Advertising costs shared by supplier and wholesaler and/or retailer. <Cost of a local newspaper ad for a concert might be shared by the promoter, the artist, the local distributor, and retailers of the artist's records and videos>

co-opt *Cult&Soc* To neutralize or win over (an independent minority, for example) through assimilation into an established group or culture.

co-publisher *IntelProp, MusArts* One who shares song publishing rights with another publisher.

co-variance *EntreP* Measure of the degree to which two random variables vary together.

coach *MusArts,PerfA&C* One who gives instruction in singing or acting.

COAI *PA-Variety* Clown Artists in Residence

coalition bargaining *HR&LR* Collaborative effort by a group of unions in negotiating contracts with one or more employers. *Also see* **collective bargaining.**

Coalition for Advertising Supported Information and Entertainment (CASIE) *Mktg*» **CASIE**

coanchor *Rdio/TV* Either of two news commentators jointly narrating or coordinating a newscast.

coaching *BcstJourn* Assisting a writer in the completion of a news story.

coauthor, co-author *LitArts* Collaborating or joint author.

coax *Rdio/TV, Sci&Tech* » **coaxial cable.**

coaxial cable (coax) *Rdio/TV, Sci&Tech* Cable consisting of a conducting outer metal tube enclosing and insulated from a central conducting core, used for **high frequency** transmission of telephone, telegraph, and television signals. COAXIAL LINE.

coaxial microphone *RecA&S* Double-element **dynamic mic** uses a **tweeter** coaxially mounted over a **woofer**. *Also see* **Microphones.**

Cobol *InfoMgt* **Common Business Oriented Language** Developed in 1961, it remains the most popular language for corporate mainframe **programming.** *Also see* **Programming Languages.**

cockamamie (cock-a-may-me, Yinglish) *Crit&Eval* Virtually valueless; ludicrous, far-fetched.

coda *Dnce* (Ballet) Fast third and final part of a **pas de deux**. *Also see* **adagio, entrée.**

CODA *Eco&Fin, HR&LR* **Cash or Deferred Arrangement plan.**

coda *MusArts* **Passage** at the end of a movement or composition that brings it to a formal close.

code of ethics *EntreP* Official standards of employee behavior formulated by a company.

CODEC *iMedia* Compression/decompression algorithm; used to compress and decompress data (encode and decode) Often used for graphics, video, and audio.

cognitariat *InfoMgt* Techno-intellectual elite of information management.

cognition *Crit&Eval, iMedia* **1** Mental process of knowing, inc. aspects such as awareness, perception, reasoning, and judgment. **2** That which comes to be known, as through perception, reasoning, or intuition; knowledge.

cognitive *Crit&Eval* Relating to the mental processing of knowing, inc. awareness, perception, reasoning, and judgment. *Also see* **empirical.**

cognitive dissonance *Crit&Eval, Mktg* Perceived inconsistency within an individual's own beliefs or attitudes or between these and one's behavior. Person will attempt to reduce the **dissonance** through changes in either behavior or cognition.

cognitive dissonance *EntreP* Anxiety that occurs when a customer

has second thoughts immediately following a purchase.

cognitive scientists *InfoMgt* Those studying the nature of various mental tasks and the processes that enable them to be performed. COGNITIVE SCIENCE. *Also see* **artificial intelligence, CRCC, prologue.**

cognoscente, cognoscenti (cog-no-skentee) *Crit&Eval* Person, or persons, with superior, usu. specialized knowledge or highly refined taste; **connoisseur**(s)

Cohan, George M. (1878-1942, sngr., dncr., sngwri., plywri., prod.) *ArtPerf, MusArts, TheatArts* Known for his flashy, patriotic **Broadway** productions. <Songs: *Over There, I'm a Yankee Doodle Dandy*> *Also see* **flag-waving.**

coif (kwawf) *Fashn* Arrange or dress the hair.

coiffure (kwawf-yoor) *Fashn* hairstyle.

coinsurance *EntreP* Clause part of an insurance policy that requires the insured to maintain a specific level of coverage or to assume a portion of any loss.

coin-operated phonograph *RecA&S* » **juke box.**

COINS *InfoMgt* **Computer and Information Sciences** Ω

col *Journ, VA-Prntng* **column.**

col (Ital. for "with") *MusArts* **Music direction** used in jazz. <If the trumpet part is to play the same **line** as the alto sax, the indication in the score on the trumpet part would be "col alto.">

COLA *Eco&Fin* Cost-of-living adjustment. Adjustment made in pensions and wages that corresponds with a change in the cost of living. *Also see* **Consumer Price Index** (CPI)

COLA *HR&LR* Cost of Living Adjustment Pay raise based on the **CPI** instead of merit; given to all employees at an establishment.

cold *Mktg, Rdio/TV* Advertising copy read on the air without musical introduction or background.

cold *MusArts,PerfA&C* Perform without preparation, without warming up.

cold *VisArts* Designating a tone or color, such as pale gray, that suggests little warmth.

cold cream *Perf-MkUp* Emulsion used to remove stage makeup. CLEANSING CREAM.

cold reading *PerfA&C* Read a part or read for a part not having seen the script beforehand.

cold type *VA-Prntng* Typesetting, such as **photocomposition**, done without the casting of metal. *Also see* **hot metal.**

collab. *Crit&Eval, TheatArts* **collaboration, collaborator.**

collaboration (collab.) *Crit&Eval* To work together in a joint artistic or intellectual effort.

collaboration (collab.) *TheatArts* "There is no successful play or musical that isn't successful because of collaboration. There is no such thing as a show being created by one person."— **Oliver Smith.**

collage (co-lodge, Fr. for "pasting") *VisArts* Artistic **composition** of materials and objects pasted over a surface, often with unifying lines and color. <**Georges Braque, Pablo Picasso**>

collate *VA-Prntng* Arrange printed sheets in proper sequence before binding.

collateral *Eco&Fin* Security in the form of assets that a company or individual pledges to a bank, to another lending institution, or individual in return for a loan. If the loan is not repaid the lender can take title to the pledged assets.

collateral *EntreP* Term used in credit evaluation to determine the ability of a customer to satisfy a debt or pay a creditor by selling assets for cash. In finance and banking collateral is the asset which is actually used to secure a loan.

collectibles *Genl* Objects prized by fanciers and hobbyists. <baseball cards, period glass, domestic utensils, etc>

collective bargaining *HR&LR* Negotiation between the union representatives of organized workers and their employer to determine wages, hours, rules, and working conditions. *Also see* **coalition bargaining, unfair labor practices.**

collective mark *IntelProp* **Trademark** used by associations, cooperatives, and fraternal organizations. <Odd Fellows>

collodion *Perf-MkUp* Clear, viscous solution of cellulose nitrates used to make a skin-like covering over real skin. It can be removed with **acetone.**

colloquial (coll., colloq.) *Genl* Characteristic of the spoken language or to writing that seeks the effect of speech; informal.

---

colophon *LitArts* **1** Publisher's emblem or trademark usu. on the title page of a book. **2** Inscription placed usu. at the end of a book, giving facts about its publication.

color frame *PerfA&C* Lightweight metal holder for color media that fits in a holder at the front of a lighting instrument.

color monitor, RBG *InfoMgt* Uses separate video signals for red, blue, and green, the three primary video colors. These signals can display almost any number of shades, depending on the software and display circuitry used. This type of monitor usu. produces clearer, sharper colors and images than **composite** monitors that use one signal that combines the three primary colors. *Also see* **monochrome monitor**.

color space *iMedia* Way to describe and alter colors; often a three-dimensional model of color including hue, saturation and value.

color wheel *iMedia* Circular diagram in which primary and usu. intermediate colors are arranged sequentially so that related colors are next to each other and complementary colors are opposite.

color wheel *InfoMgt* If the computer is colorable, this **dialog box** allows adjustments for hue, saturation, brightness, and shades of gray. *Also see* **gray scale**.

coloration *Fashn* Arrangement of colors

colorfield painting *VisArts* Technique in abstract painting developed in the 1950s, which focuses on the lyrical effects of large areas of color, often poured or stained onto the canvas. <Barnett Newman (» **abstract expressionism**), Mark Rothko (» **abstract expressionism**), Helen Frankenthaler (1928-, pntr.)>

colorization of movies *Ethcs&Phil, Flm&Vid* The legal but controversial processing of black and white movies to color – instigated by **Ted Turner** – without the permission of the director, the **cinematographer**, or the star performers.

Coltrane, John (aka "Trane," 1926-67, jazz sop/tenor/alto sax, comp.) *ArtPerf, MusArts* Leading exponent of the **modal** school of improvisation, he had a tremendous influence on many contemporary musicians. <Albums: *Giant Steps* (1959-60, Atlantic), *Impressions* (1961, MCA)> *Also see* **polytonality, soprano saxophone, sheets of sound**.

Columbia Arts Management, Inc. (CAMI) *Mgt* » **CAMI**

Columbia Broadcasting Company (CBS) *Rdio/TV* » **CBS**

Columbia Record Club *Mktg, RecA&S* » **Columbia Record Company**.

Columbia Record Company *RecA&S* Before being sold by **CBS, Inc.** to the **Sony Corp.** – in order to stave off a **Ted Turner** takeover – its marketing was the most innovative of the major record companies. <**Columbia Record Club** and the introduction of the (then) revolutionary longplaying (33-1/3 **rpm**) record> *Also see* **major labels**.

column *Journ* **By-lined** feature article that appears regularly in a newspaper, magazine, or television news program. COLUMNIST.

column *VA-Prntng* One of two or more vertical sections of typed lines lying side by side on a page and separated by a rule or a blank space.

column inch *Mktg, VA-Prntng* Smallest unit measure for display advertising in a magazine.

columnist (colum.) *Journ* Writer of a column in a newspaper or magazine.

.com *InfoMgt* Suffix of an Internet **domain name** assigned to commercial businesses. *Also see* **Domain Names, Network Solutions Inc.**

com., comm. *Eco&Fin* **commerce**.

combinations *EntreP* Portfolios of both puts and calls. Straddles, strangles, strips, and straps are examples. Used when one has no convictions about the direction of price movements.

combo *Dnce* Combination of **tap dance** steps.

combo *MusArts* Usually refers to a combination of three to six instruments.

combo ads *Flm&Vid, Mktg* Print ad advertising two or more movies, informing the readers that they can see all the features for the one admission price.

combo engagement *Flm&Vid, Mktg* Two or more movies offered to the public for consecutive viewing at the regular admission price for just one movie. Distribution costs and disbursements are negotiated.

come down *ArtPerf* Feeling of depression and disappointment that many performers have after the excitement and **empathic response** of a performance. *Also see* **down, get up**.

come down *Crit&Eval* **1** Enter a quiescent or subdued state. **2** To or at a lower intensity. *Also see* **high**.

come into (one's) own *Crit&Eval* To gain rightful recognition or prosperity. <The struggling artist has finally come into her own>

comedian *LitArts* Writer of comedy

comedian *PA-Variety* **1** Professional entertainer who tells amusing stories or performs other comic acts. **2** Actor in comedy. *Also see* **clown, comic, slapstick, stand-up**. COMEDIENNE.

Comédie-Française, Théâtre Française *TheatArts* State theater of France (in Paris) est. 1680. *Also see* **Theaters & Theatres**.

comedy *Flm&Vid, LitArts, TheatArts* Dramatic or literary portrayal of the ridiculous, endeavoring to incite the audience-reader-viewer to laughter. **2** Dramatic work that has a humorous theme and characters and a happy ending. **3** Branch of **drama** and literature comprising such works. *Also see* **tragedy**. "Dying is easy, comedy is hard." — Edmund Gwenn (1875-1959, Brit. act.)

comedy of errors *Crit&Eval* Ludicrous event or sequence of events.

comedy of humours *TheatArts* Comedy of character based on a dominant trait, such as greed or jealousy. Popularized by the Elizabethan playwright, Ben Jonson (1572-1637)

comedy of manners *LitArts* Comedy satirizing the attitudes and behavior of "fashionable" society.

comedy of manners *TheatArts* Social comedy wittily satirizing characters in terms of their shortcomings as measured against a specific code of conduct. *Ex.* Sheridan's *School for Scandal*.

comedy-variety shows *Rdio/TV* Popular type of television network programming. *Also see* **Television Shows**.

comes in *Eco&Fin* Finishes, completed. <Picture comes in under budget, picture B comes in over budget.

comic opera *MusArts* **Opera** or **operetta** with a humorous plot, spoken dialogue, and usu. a happy ending. BOUFFE, OPÉRA COMIQUE.

comic *PA-Variety* **comedian** "To me, the comic is the guy who says 'Wait a minute' as the consensus forms. He's the antithesis of the mob mentality. The comic is a flame — like Shiva the Destroyer, toppling idols no matter what they are." — Bill Hicks (1962-94, TV/vaude comic, social critic) *Also see* **humorist**.

comic relief *Crit&Eval, LitArts* Humorous break or interlude in a literary work intended to relieve the dramatic **tension** or heighten by contrast the emotional impact on the reader.

comic strip *Journ, VisArts* Narrative series of cartoons. FUNNIES, FUNNY PAPER

coming and going rule *LegAsp* Rule that a **principal** is not liable for injuries caused by its agents and employees traveling to or from work.

coming attractions *Flm&Vid* Promo clips of films "coming to this theater!" *Also see* "**Next Week,** *East Lynne*."

Coming Up Taller Awards *Cult&Soc* Created in 1998 by the President's Committee on the Arts and the Humanities "to honor exemplary arts and humanities programs for young people."

command *InfoMgt* Instruction that causes the computer to do something.

command line interface *iMedia* Interface of alphanumeric commands followed by alphanumeric responses.

command performance *MusArts, PerfA&C* Special performance requested by a head of state. *Origin* Invitation from a reigning monarch.

comme il faut (come eel foe, Fr. for "proper") *Crit&Eval, Fashn* In accord with convention or certain standards; proper.

commedia dell 'arte *PA-Variety, TheatArts* Improvised comic plays performed by itinerant companies; it originated in Italy in the 16th century and then spread through Europe. Actors each played a stock character type and improvised the action according to a shared outline **plot**.

comment *iMedia* **1** To put in information not meant for display, but which will instruct or note something about the code. <what type of a value a particular variable should store>. **2** To temporarily disable code by surrounding it with comment delimiters, usu. for debugging. <comment out a function call>

comment out *iMedia* Act of commenting code. <comment out that code and see if it will run then> » **comment**

commentator *Journ,. Rdio/TV* Broadcaster or writer who reports and analyzes events in the news.

commerce (com., comm.) *Eco&Fin* Buying and selling of goods on a large scale, as between cities or nations.

Commerce Net *InfoMgt* Consortium of businesses interested in promoting **electronic commerce**.

Commerce Net/Nielsen *InfoMgt, Cult&Soc, InfoMgt, Mktg* Periodic study of the **Internet's** impact on social and commercial systems. *Also see* **Commerce Net, Nielsen**.

Commerce, U.S. Department of (DOC) *Eco&Fin, Law&Pol* U.S. government department (est. 1903) headed by a Cabinet Secretary. *Also see* **Federal Agencies and Statutes**.

commercial *Eco&Fin* Having profit as a primary aim. <Too far out to be commercial>

commercial *MusArts* "Usually used in derogatory sense to refer to a watered-down form of jazz that is created mainly for profit rather than artistic expression. Commercial jazz (considered an **oxymoron** by some) generally involves little improvisation, stresses harmonic and rhythmic simplicity, and frequently includes string accompaniment or vocals. Term refers esp. to a bland version of jazz/rock."— Lyons & Perlo (jazz critics) *Also see* **mickey**.

commercial *Rdio/TV* Advertisement on cable, radio, or television for which the cable or the station receives some sort of compensation. *Also see* **barter, jingle, spot announcement**.

commercial *VisArts* "Throughout history, art has been commercial, with a creator and a buyer. The social circumstances have just changed." — Malcolm Rogers (musm. dir.)

commercial artist *VisArts* Artist involved in work designed or planned for a **mass market**.

commercial license *IntelProp, MusArts* Permits use of a musical composition as part of an advertisement. *Also see* **Music Licenses**.

commercial paper *Eco&Fin* Short-term, unsecured, discounted, and negotiable notes sold by one company to another in order to satisfy immediate cash needs.

commercial property insurance *EntreP* Coverage that protects against losses associated with damage to or loss of property.

commercial radio broadcast *Rdio/TV* Began in 1920 in Pittsburgh (KDKA) and Detroit (WWJ) *Also see* **Radio**.

commercial real estate *EntreP* Land and improved property that is used by the owner to generate income.

commercial uses *IntelProp Mktg* Sources of income derived from **subsidiary rights** in a **Broadway musical**. <dolls, games, souvenir programs, T-shirts, toys, etc>

commercialization of the art market *VisArts* "Too many of our generation's painters and sculptors suffer from a sense of emptiness, as though their work were about nothing. Although talented and highly skilled, they feel guilty of pretending that they have something to say, because actually they are not aware of any such substance. I believe that this deplorable situation is due to many artists' surrender to the commercialization of the art market. Too many neglect their own impulses and standards and struggle instead to adopt the latest fashion, the model that sells." — Rudolf Arnheim (art critic)

commission *Law&Pol* Group of people officially authorized to perform certain duties or functions. <**Federal Communication Commission** (FCC)>

commission, advertising agency *Mktg* Percentage, usu. 15%, of the cost of an advertisement, paid by the medium to the advertising agency who placed the **insertion order** on behalf of the advertiser.

commission, talent agency *Mgt* Talent or literary agency commission runs between 10% and 20% of the artist's or author's fee. Percentage of commission is negotiable within limits set by the labor union to which the artist or author is affiliated. *Also see* **author's clause, talent agent**.

commissioned work *IntelProp* Work of art ordered by an individual or group to mark a special occasion or to honor someone or some event. SPECIALLY ORDERED WORK *Also see* **residuals, writer-for-hire**.

commodity *Eco&Fin* **1** Something useful that can be turned to commercial or other advantage. **2** Article of trade or commerce. <an agricultural or mining product>

Common Business Oriented Language (COBOL) *InfoMgt* » **COBOL**

common carriers *EntreP* Transportation intermediaries available for hire to the general public.

common f-numbers *iMedia* Are f/1 4, f/2, f/28, f/4, f/5.6, f/8, f/11, f/16, and f/22 larger the f-number, the smaller the lens opening. In this series, f/1 4 is the largest lens opening, f/22 the smallest.

Common Hardware Reference Platform *InfoMgt* » **CHRP**

common law *LegAsp* System of laws originated and developed in England and based on court decisions, on the **doctrines** implicit in those decisions, and on customs and usages rather than on codified written laws or a constitution.

common market, Common Market (CM) *Eco&Fin* Economic unit, typically formed of nations, intended to eliminate or markedly reduce trade barriers among its members.

common measure *MusArts* » **common time**.

common stock *Eco&Fin* Ownership class of corporate capital stock.

common stock *EntreP* Stock which is issued by public or private corporations to raised financial capital. Stock is issued in shares and each share represents ownership of the corporation.

common time *MusArts* 4/4 time, i.e., four quarter notes to a measure. COMMON MEASURE.

communication *Aes&Creat Crit&Eval, InfoMgt* **1** Critical basis of human community, centering on what is common to its members, and involving the exchange of ideas, opinions, passions, rituals, or any other symbolic activity or product. **2** Exchange of thoughts, messages, or information, by speech, signals, writing, or behavior. "Certainly one of the great functions of any art is communication; certainly it has a moral function but its real reason for being is that it preserves unbroken the line of continuous human feeling and satisfies the esthetic instinct from age to age on the human level: so that a work of beauty and nobility remains forever new and never loses its preciousness as work of art, when the creed and forms of government and the very race and the language of a period have disappeared."—Katherine Anne Porter (1890-1980, fictwri., lit. critic)

Communication Control Language (CCL) *InfoMgt* » **CCL**

communication medium *Mktg* Personal or impersonal channel through which a message is transmitted to an audience or individual. *Also see* **mass media**.

communication mix *Mktg* Combination of communication elements. <personal selling, media advertising, signage, public relations, publicity, and on-site display> Used by a marketer to communicate its messages to a target market.

communications *InfoMgt, Sci&Tech* **1** Means of communicating via a system, such as mail, email, telephone, or television, for sending and receiving messages. **2** Technology employed in transmitting messages.

Communications Act of 1934 *InfoMgt,. Rdio/TV* Established the **Federal Communications Commission** (FCC) and had as its major objective: "to make available, so far as possible, to all the people of the U.S., a rapid, efficient, nation-wide and worldwide wire and radio communication service." Since its passage, it has been an ideological and technological battleground for those who seek control of the flow of information, i.e., power. *Also see* **Federal Agencies and Statutes**.

communications satellite *InfoMgt,. Rdio/TV, Sci&Tech* Artificial satellite used to aid telecommunications, as by reflecting or relaying a radio signal.

communiqué *Genl* Official announcement

communism *Eco&Fin* Economic system based on the theories of **Karl Marx**. All forms of **market economics** are completely owned and controlled by the central government in the "name of the people." Traditionally communist governments have practiced a **planned economy** though in recent years most surviving communist governments are attempting to adapt to a **market economy**. *Also see* **dialectic**.

community (com.) *Cult&Soc* Whole of what is common to a group of people living together, as in a neighborhood, a town, a city of modest size; sometimes, by extension, what is common to a group of people working together.

Community Antenna Television (CATV) *Rdio/TV* » **cable television**.

community-based financial institution *EntreP* Lender that provides financing to small businesses in low-income communities for the purpose of encouraging economic development.

Community Concerts *MusArts* Booking agency affiliated with the giant **Columbia Artists Management, Inc.** (CAMI), that organizes local audiences in the U.S. and Canada for lucrative pre-paid bookings featuring the agency's own **contract artists**.

community foundation *Fnding* A 501(c)(3) Organization that makes grants for charitable purposes in a specific community or region. Funds are usually derived from many donors and held in an **endowment** independently administered; income earned by the endowment is then used to make grants. Although a few community foundations may be classified by the IRS as private foundations, most are classified as public charities eligible for maximum income tax-deductible contributions from the general public. *Also see* **501(c)(3)**; **public charity**.

community fund *Fnding* Organized community program which makes annual appeals to the general public for funds that are usually not retained in an **endowment** but are used for the ongoing operational support of local social and health service agencies. *Also see* **Federated Giving Program**.

community performance *TheatArts* Term used for theater that seeks to build and develop community using the collaborative and empathic aspects of theater.

community-based financial institution *EntreP* Lender that provides financing to small businesses in low-income communities for the purpose of encouraging economic development.

comp *MusArts* **1** (*Jazz*) To **accompany**, usu. on piano. **2** To play chords of a song.

comp *PerfA&C* Complimentary admission to a performance or an event. *Also see* **Annie Oakley**, **hard ticket**.

comp *VisArts* comprehensive **layout**

compact disk-recordable *InfoMgt* » **CD-R**

company (co.) *Eco&Fin*, *Mgt* business enterprise; a firm.

company magazine *InfoMgt*, *Journ* » **house organ**.

company manager *TheatArts* Business manager of a theatrical touring company. *Also see* **Managers**.

company newsletter *InfoMgt*, *Journ* » **house organ**.

company *TheatArts* Group of performers and managers. *Also see* **troupe**.

company union *HR&LR* So-called labor union organized and controlled by the company. *Also see* **Guilds & Unions**.

company-sponsored foundation (also **corporate foundation**) *Fnding* **Private foundation** whose grant funds are derived primarily from the contributions of a profit-making business organization. The company-sponsored foundation may maintain close ties with the donor company, but it is an independent organization with its own **endowment** and is subject to the same rules and regulations as other private foundations.

comparable companies approach to valuation *EntreP* Method of valuation in which the selling prices of similar companies become the basis for the valuation of a venture.

compassion *Crit&Eval*, *HR&LR* Deep awareness of the suffering of another coupled with the wish to relieve it.

compensation *Eco&Fin*, *Rdio&TV* Fee paid by a network to affiliated stations for their broadcasting a network program. [High cost of programs such as NFL football and *E.R.* are causing (Feb '98) networks to ask affiliates to share the cost, that could lead to higher advertising rates and higher consumer prices.].

compere (Brit.) *PA-Variety*,. *Rdio/TV* Master of ceremonies of a television entertainment program or a variety show. *Also see* **master of ceremonies**.

competent *LglAsp* Legally qualified or fit to perform an act.

competition *Mktg* Rivalry between two or more businesses or organizations striving for the same customer or market.

competition *MusArts* "I tell each student he only has one musician to compete with the rest of his days — himself. And I try to make him understand the ethical responsibility of being a **professional musician**." — Harvey Phillips (tubist) *Also see* **professional, professionalism**.

competitive advantage *EntreP* Benefit that exists when a company has a product or service that is seen by its target market as better than those of competitors.

compilation album *RecA&S* Inclusion of previously released songs in a new record album or CD.

compilation score *Flm&Vid*, *MusArts*, *TheatArts* Inclusion of previously released songs in a movie sound track or musical show. *Also see* **interpolated songs**.

compile *Crit&Eval*, *LitArts* To select, evaluate, and put together materials gathered from several sources. <compile a dictionary such as **DAPM**>

compiler *iMedia*, InfoMgt **Operating system** program used to translate high level language programs into computer readable form.

complaint *LglAsp* **1** Presentation by the **plaintiff** in a civil action, setting forth the claim on which **relief** is sought. **2** Formal charge, made under oath, of the commission of a crime or other such offense.

compleat *Crit&Eval* **1** Characterized by a highly developed or wide-ranging skill or proficiency. **2** Being an outstanding example of a kind; **quintessential**. <Judy Garland (1922-69, film/TV/vaude act., sngr.) was a compleat entertainer>

complement *Crit&Eval* **1** Something that completes, makes up a whole, or brings to perfection. **2** Either of two parts that complete the whole or mutually complete each other. [Do not confuse with **compliment**.].

complement *MusArts* Interval that completes an octave when added to a given interval.

complementary *Crit&Eval* Supplying mutual needs or offsetting mutual lacks.

complementary colors *iMedia* Colors located across from each other on a color wheel. *Ex.* red and green, orange and blue, yellow and purple.

complements *EntreP* Two goods for which an increase in the price of one good decreases the demand for the other good.

completion bond *Flm&Vid* Insurance policy assuring movie distributors and financiers against loss because a movie is not completed.

complex *iMedia* Second period in the history of a medium that signifies the creation of an aesthetic unique to that medium.

complex adaptive system *iMedia* System where existence and persistence depend on the interactions of individual agents and the adaptation of agent behavior resulting from those interactions. resulting complex behavior is often unpredictable. *Also see* **emergent behavior, swarm intelligence**.

complication *TheatArts* Development in the action of a drama that presents an obstacle to the **protagonist**.

compliment *Crit&Eval* **1** Expression of praise, admiration, or congratulation. **2** Formal act of civility, courtesy, or respect.

complimentary ticket (comp) *Mktg* Free ticket of admission.

component media *iMedia* Elements that comprise an interactive media piece. <text, graphics, audio, animation, video, etc.>

composite element *iMedia* Output elements combined with input elements that relate information regarding the interaction between a participant and an interactive product.

compound interest *EntreP* Interest that is earned or charged on both the principal amount and on the accrued interest that has been previously earned. Formula is FV = PV (1 + *l*)

compound value of a dollar *EntreP* Increased value of a dollar over time resulting from interest earned both on the original dollar and on the interest received in prior periods.

compression *iMedia* **1** Using an algorithm to reduce (compress) data into a format that requires less storage space than the original. *Also see* **lossy, lossless**.

computer-aided design (CAD) *EntreP* Use of sophisticated computer systems to design new products.

computer-aided manufacturing (CAM) *EntreP* Use of computer-controlled machines to manufacture products.

concatenation *iMedia* » **concatenate**

concentration ratio *EntreP* Measure of the degree of concentration in a market; the four-company concentration ratio is the percentage of output produced by the four largest companies.

concentration *TheatArts* Giving complete attention to something: staying "in the moment." Ability to concentrate is a key part of effective acting.

concept map *iMedia* Graphical representation of a set of ideas, and how those ideas are related.

conceptual model *iMedia* »**mental model**

confidant(E) *TheatArts* Minor character paired with a major one. Who shares the latter's confidences, usu. for expository purposes.

conflict *TheatArts* Tension that results from a character's attempt to adjust to or circumvent an obstacle.

conflict token *iMedia* Symbol or representation of a character or entity engaged in a process of change or drama. Often represents a persona in a game (such as a pawn in chess) *Also see* **anthropomorphic conflict token**.

consistency *EntreP* Statistical requirement that a sample statistic converges in probability to the population statistic.

construction crew *PerfA&C* Those who build the set, move it into the theater, and set it up on stage.

constructivist theater *TheatArts* Movement in the Soviet theater after World War I and the Russian Revolution often associated with Vsevolod Meyerhold. Adapted from the visual arts, the style resisted the use of representational sets, using more abstract 'constructions' onstage.

consumer credit *EntreP* Financing granted by retailers to individuals who purchase for personal or family use.

consumer price index (CPI) *EntreP* Measure of inflation which represents a market basket of goods that the average American purchase each month.

consumerism *EntreP* Movement that stresses the needs of consumers and the importance of serving them honestly and well.

content *iMedia* Message or information to be conveyed in an interactive media product. Tied with form the structure that conveys the content.

content management system *iMedia* Process or application that organizes and standardizes the collection, management, and publishing of content.

contextual inquiry *iMedia* Interviews with target audiences and research on site (in context) to develop customer-centered systems more successfully. Developed by Karen Holtzblatt, 1995.

continuity *BcstJourn* Orderly flow of images for any location, action, or time period in a videotape sequence.

continuity *iMedia* One of the **Gestalt Laws** of pattern perception: elements that are continuous (as opposed to those that break or that drastically change direction) are more likely to be perceived as objects.

continuous quality improvement *EntreP* Constant and dedicated effort to improve quality.

contour *iMedia* Continuous boundary defining a space or shape.

contract carriers *EntreP* Transportation intermediaries that contract with individual shippers.

contractionary policies *EntreP* Government policy actions that lead to decreases in output.

contribution margin *EntreP* Amount of profit that will be made by a company on each unit, which is sold above the break even quantity.

control chart *EntreP* Graphic illustration of the limits used in statistical process control.

convention *TheatArts* Common (unspoken) agreement between theater worker and spectator concerning the manner of production. *Ex.* the physical separation of actor and spectator.

convertible preferred stock *EntreP* Preferred stock of a corporation that may be exchanged for shares of common stock.

cooperative venture *Fnding* Joint effort between or among two or more grantmakers including: foundations, corporations, and government agencies. Partners may share in funding responsibilities or contribute information and technical resources.

corporate foundation *Fnding* » **company-sponsored foundation**.

corporate giving program *Fnding* Grantmaking program established and administered within a profit-making company. Corporate giving programs do not have a separate **endowment** and their annual grant totals are generally more directly related to current profits. They are not subject to the same reporting requirements as **private foundations**. Some companies make charitable contributions through both a corporate giving program and a **company-sponsored foundation**.

compose *Aes&Creat* To arrange aesthetically or artistically.

compose *LitArts, MusArts* To create a literary or a musical piece.

compose *VA-Prntng* To set type or arrange matter to be printed.

composer (comp.) *ArtPerf, MusArts* Creator of a musical composition. *Also see* **lyricist**, **songwriter**, **writer**.

composing room *VA-Prntng* Room where **typesetting** is done.

composing stick *VA-Prntng* Small, shallow tray, usu. metal and with an adjustable end, in which type is set by hand. JOB STICK.

composite *Flm&Vid* **Synchronized** sound and picture on one piece of film.

composition *Dnce* 1 Piece of **choreography** 2 Dance **class** in which students examine various components of choreography.

composition *iMedia* 1 Combining of distinct parts or elements to form a whole. 2 Arrangement of artistic parts so as to form a unified whole.

composition *LitArts, MusArts, VisArts* 1 Art or act of composing a musical or literary work. 2 Work of music, literature, or art, or its structure or organization. 3 Short essay, esp. one written as an academic exercise.

composition *VA-Prntng* Typesetting

compound journal entry *E&F-Acc* Where the line entries of debits/credits are unequal, but total dollar amount of debits and credits are the same.

compression *Flm&Vid, Sci&Tech* Use of digital technology to compress information on new formats. <**Digital Versatile Disc (DVD)**>

compression *InfoMgt* » **data compression**.

compressor *RecA&S* Electronic sound device that limits the dynamic response to create a more constant, even dynamic level.

Compulsory Mechanical License *IntelProp, RecA&S* » Permits anyone to record a cover version of a song that has previously been distributed to the public (published) commercially recorded with authorization, if they follow the statutory terms and pay royalties set by a **CARP**. *Also see* **Music Licenses**.

CompuServe *InfoMgt* Taken over by **AOL** in 1997. *Also see* **Online Information Services**.

computer (comp.) *InfoMgt* Programmable electronic machine that performs high-speed mathematical or logical operations or that assembles, stores, correlates, or otherwise processes information.

Computer Aided Design/Computer Aided Manufacturing (CAD/CAM) *InfoMgt* » **CAD/CAM**.

Computer Aided Engineering (CAE) *InfoMgt* » **CAE**

Computer Aided Instruction (CAI) *InfoMgt* » **CAI**

Computer and Information Sciences (COINS) *InfoMgt* » **COINS**

computer anxiety *InfoMgt* Fear of computers and their subsequent effects on people's lives.

computer crime *InfoMgt* Criminal activity directly relating to the use of computers, specifically illegal trespass into the computer system or **database** of another, manipulation or theft of stored or online data, or sabotage of equipment and data.

computer ethics *Ethcs&Phil, InfoMgt* Term used to refer to the standard of moral conduct in computer use.

Computer Information System (CIS) *InfoMgt* » **CIS**

Computer Integrated Manufacturing (CIM) *InfoMgt* » **CIM**

computer literacy *InfoMgt* Ability to operate a computer and to understand the language used in working with a specific system or systems.

computer music *InfoMgt, MusArts* Early composition was the *Illiac Suite* for string quartet composed on the high-speed **digital** computer in 1957. First direct **synthesis** of sound by a computer was first described at the **Bell Labs** in 1963 *Also see* **synthesizer**.

Computer Professionals for Social Responsibility (CPSR) *InfoMgt, Cult&Soc* » **CPSR**

computer program *InfoMgt* Set of instructions for solving a problem or processing data. *Also see* **Intangible Assets**.

Computer Software Copyright Act (1980) *InfoMgt, IntelProp* Amendment of the **Copyright Act of 1976** that includes **computer programs** in the list of **tangible** items protected by copyright.

computer technology *InfoMgt* "Computer technology affords us many options and opportunities, but it is only a tool, not the end product." — Tess Durham (greeting card artist)

Computer Telephone Integration (CTI) *InfoMgt* » **CTI**

computer virus *InfoMgt* **Computer program** designed to replicate itself by copying itself into the other programs stored in a computer. It may be **benign** or have a negative effect, such as causing a program to operate incorrectly or filling a computer's memory with unwanted codes.

Computer-Oriented Reference System For Automatic Information Retrieval (CORSAIR) *InfoMgt* » **CORSAIR**

computerized accounting systems *E&F-Acc* Commercial accounting systems programmed to perform accounting functions.

Also see **batch processing, manual accounting systems**.

computerized mail *InfoMgt* Technique of transmitting (delivering) mail via **modems**. *Also see* **email**.

Comstock, Anthony (1844-1915, "Reformer") *Cult&Soc* Notorious moral crusader against art and literature that he considered **obscene**. Organizer of the New York Society for the Suppression of Vice. *Also see* **censorship, obscenity**.

con amore (Ital. for "with love") *MusArts* Play lovingly; tenderly; with devotion or zeal. *Also see* **Music Directions**.

con brio (Ital. for "with vigor") *MusArts* Play with great energy; vigorously. *Also see* **Music Directions**.

con legno (Ital. for "with wood") *MusArts* Play a stringed instrument with the back of the bow.

con spirito (Ital. for "with spirit") *MusArts* Play in a lively manner. *Also see* **Music Directions**.

concatenate *InfoMgt* To arrange strings of characters into a chained list. *Also see* **decatenate**.

conceit *LitArts* Fanciful poetic image, esp. an elaborate or exaggerated comparison.

concentrated marketing strategy *Mktg* In a segmented market, the marketer concentrates its efforts on one target group and designs its marketing strategy specifically to reach that group, rather than trying to be all things to all people.

concentrator *InfoMgt* Telecommunications device that combines a number of low speed lines into one high speed line.

concept *Crit&Eval, Mktg* **1** General idea derived or inferred from specific instances or occurrences. **2** Something formed in the mind; a thought or notion. *Usage:* In the fields of entertainment and advertising concept is often means a scheme or a plan as in "The Studio liked the concept for the new game show and decided to put it into development."

conceptual art *VisArts* Art intended to convey an idea or a concept to the perceiver and need not involve the creation or appreciation of a traditional art object such as a painting or a sculpture.

conceptual journalist *Journ* One more interested in figuring things out than in finding things out.

conceptualism *Ethcs&Phil* **Doctrine**, intermediate between **nominalism** and **realism**, that universals exist only within the mind and have no external or substantial reality.

conceptualism *VisArts* School of **abstract art** or an artistic **doctrine** concerned with the intellectual engagement of the viewer through conveyance of an idea and negation of the importance of the art object itself. *Also see* **Art Movements and Periods**.

concert *MusArts* Musical performance given by one or more artists.

concert edition *MusArts* Collection of compositions arranged for performance for a group of voices or instruments, commonly available in choral, orchestra, and/or band arrangements. *Also see* **Print Music**.

concert grand *MusInstr* The largest grand piano, approx., 9-11 feet long. *Also see* **Musical Instrument Families**.

concert music *MusArts* Music written to be performed in a concert.hall.

concert pitch *MusArts* **Pitch** to which orchestral instruments are tuned. *Also see* **A above middle C; international pitch**.

concertmaster, concert mistress *MusArts* First violinist and assistant **conductor** of a symphony orchestra. Responsible for making sure that all **phrasing**, **bowings**, and **articulations** are done the same way by the violinists. *Also see* **first chair, principal player**.

concerto *MusArts* Orchestral composition for one or more solo instruments, usu. in three movements.

concertogrosso (Ital.) *MusArts* Composition for a small group of solo instruments and a full orchestra.

concession *Mktg* **1** Privilege of maintaining a subsidiary business within certain premises. **2** Space allotted for such a business. **3** Business itself. <the beer **concession** at a ball park, the cloakroom **concession** at the opera, the souvenir program **concession** at the concert or play> Income from a **concession** is usu. not shared with the performers unless specifically called for in the **engagement contract**.

concessionaire *Mktg* Holder or operator of a **concession**.

conciliation *HR&LR* Efforts by a third party to accommodate the opposing viewpoints in a labor dispute.

concryption *InfoMgt* Process of **encrypting** and **compressing** data simultaneously.

concurrency *InfoMgt* » **concurrent users**.

concurrent *InfoMgt* Usually refers to a multi-programming system in which control alternates among several programs.

concurrent users *InfoMgt* Number of program users at any given time. Knowing this by means of a **software meter** would allow the company to control the number of licenses for that program. <Company with 100 Word Perfect users evenly split in day and night shifts need only 50 licenses to comply with Federal law> CONCURRENCY.

cond. *MusArts, Sci&Tech* **conductor**.

condenser microphone *RecA&S* Professional quality **mic** with faster response to rapid changes in sound pressure, flatter **frequency** response in the high end, and much higher output levels due to its built-in amplifier. However, more subject to changes in humidity and temperature than **dynamic** and **ribbon** mics. *Also see* **Microphones**.

conditional theatre *TheatArts* Early Soviet version of nonrealistic theatre.

conductor (cond.) *MusArts* One who directs an orchestra or other such group, and attempts to forge a connection between the listener and the music. *Also see* **empathic response**.

conductor (cond.) *Sci&Tech* Substance or medium that conducts heat, light, sound, or esp. an electric charge.

conference room *InfoMgt* **AOL chat room** that can hold more than the standard 23 people.

confessional rock *MusArts* <The music of David Byrne> *Also see* **Rock Music Styles**.

config. *InfoMgt* **configuration**.

configuration (config.) *InfoMgt* **1** Way the user has set up the computer. **2** Combined hardware components – computer, **monitor**, keyboard, and **peripheral** devices – that make up a computer system. **3** Software settings that allow computer hardware components to communicate with each other.

confiscation *LegAsp* Appropriation of private property for public use without compensation.

conflict *Crit&Eval, LitArts* Opposition between characters or forces in a work of drama or **fiction** that motivates or shapes the **plot**. *Also see* **tension**.

conflict *Genl* Disharmony or disagreement between persons, ideas, or interests; a clash. *Also see* **tension**.

conflict of interest *Ethcs&Phil, Law&Pol* Government and business officials must behave a certain way owing to their positions: they must act in the interest of those others who have "hired them." But the conflict is that their private – usually monetary – interests could tempt them to behave in a way that promotes their personal interests instead of their official ones. Other conflicts may arise if an agent represents two clients with competing goals, or one that compensates the agent significantly more than another. Laws and ethics codes deal with the problem by: (1) preventing officials from having certain monetary interests; or (2) forcing them to disclose their personal interests to others before acting; or 3) simply excusing them from acting in these situations at all. <"There are conflicts of interest every day. As a friend once said to me, 'the day I signed my second client there was a conflict of interest.'" — Brad Grey (Brillstein-Grey Entertainment)

confrontational *Crit&Eval* Discord or a clash of opinions and ideas.

congestion pricing *Eco&Fin,Mktg* Pricing structure for smoothing the peaks and troughs of use by linking prices to demand. <Higher admission for evening performance; lower admission for **matinee** or midnite show> *Also see* **Pricing Strategies**.

conglomerate *Mgt* Corporation that has diversified its operations, usu. by acquiring enterprises in widely varied industries.

Congressional hearings *Rdio/TV* Popular type of television network programming. <Clarence Thomas nomination show starring Anita Hill, **McCarthy** hearings, **Watergate** hearings> *Also see* **Television Shows**.

congruity *HR&LR* Condition of being in agreement; harmony; corresponding to "right" or "proper" or "reasonable." [Bit of wisdom for a the arts manager who seeks to bridge the space between artist and audience.].

conjunto bands *MusArts* Perform **rancheros**: cowboy songs with a polka beat from northern Mexico. Instrumentation: guitars, drums, vocalists, button accordions or keyboard. Favored by Mexicans and Mexican Americans from the Texas-Mexican border area. NORTENO

conjure *Cult&Soc* **1** To summon a devil by magic or supernatural power. **2** To practice **black magic**. *Also see* **voodoo**.

conjure woman *Cult&Soc* Black woman who practices **voodoo**.

conjurer *ArtPerf, PA-Variety* One who performs magic tricks; a **magician**.

conscience (In business and society) *Ethcs&Phil* **1** Faculty of recognizing the difference between right and wrong with regard to one's conduct coupled with a sense that one should act accordingly. **2** Conformity to one's own sense of proper conduct.

conscience (In personal life) *Ethcs&Phil* Psychic location of moral controls, or the psychic function that regulates conduct on moral lines; an idea associated with the rise of Christianity. "There is only one way to achieve happiness on this terrestrial ball, And that is to have either a clear conscience, or none at all." — Ogden Nash (1902-1971, poet, lyr., libret.)

consensus *Mgt* **1** Desired goal of any group decision-making session, where all parties can come to an agreement and reach a mutually satisfying conclusion. **2** General agreement or accord.

consent decree of 1948 *Flm&Vid, Law&Pol* Supreme Court order for movie studios to divest themselves of all theater holdings, thus beginning the era of independent movie exhibitors, and ending vertical integration in the movie industry. "Today, because of waivers granted during the **Reagan** Administration, [movie] studios can own movie theaters, and nothing prevents them from owning interests in cable television and videocassette distributors." — David Londoner (movie exec.) [Waivers particularly helped **MCA**, Reagan's former talent agency.] *Also see* **distribution**; **vertical integration**.

conservatism *Law&Pol* Political philosophy or attitude emphasizing respect for traditional institutions, distrust of government activism, and opposition to sudden change in the established order. *Also see* **liberalism, neoconservatism, reactionary, ultraconservative**.

conservative *Crit&Eval, Law&Pol* **1** Favoring traditional views and values; tending to oppose change. **2** Restrained in style. **3** Moderate; cautious. *Also see* **Political Philosophies**.

conservator *VisArts* One who restores valuable, damaged objects to their original state. <art works, film, manuscripts, musical instruments> *Also see* **restorer**.

consideration *LegAsp* Inducement to a contract, the impelling influence that induces a party to enter into a contract; the reason or material cause of a contract. *Also see* **Contracts**.

consignment *Mktg, RecA&S, VisArts* Product, such as records or visual art, sent to a retailer or gallery operator who is expected to pay the sale price less commission of 40-50 per cent.

console *MusInstr* Desklike part of an organ that contains the keyboard, stops, and pedals.

console *Rdio/TV, RecA&S* **1** Central control panel for a mechanical, electrical, or electronic system; instrument panel. **2** Cabinet for a radio, television set, or phonograph, designed to stand on the floor.

console *InfoMgt* Part of a computer system that enables human operators to communicate with the system.

consonance *MusArts* Simultaneous combination of sounds conventionally regarded as pleasing and final in effect. *Also see* **dissonance**.

consonant *MusArts* Harmonious in sound or tone.

consortium *Mgt* Association or a combination of businesses, financial institutions, or investors, for the purpose of engaging in a **joint venture**.

conspicuous consumption *Cult&Soc, Eco&Fin* **1** Signal of status. **2** Selection and purchase of goods for their social rather than **inherent** value. <Reboks, designer jeans, sky boxes, and such> Term made famous by **Thorstein Veblen** in his book *Theory of the Leisure Class* (1889)

constituency *Ethcs&Phil, Law&Pol* People served by an elected official; the relation between official and constituency is problematic. <Is one a Representative in Congress, or a representative of Chicago?>

constituency *Fndng* Category of current and prospective donors such as individuals, businesses, and foundations.

construction kits *RecA&S* » **digital sampler**, **sampler**.

constructivism *VisArts* Russian abstract movement founded ca. 1915 and characterized by the use of industrial materials such as glass, sheet metal, and plastic to create **nonrepresentational**, often geometric objects. <Vladimir Tatlin (1890-1977, Russ.-born sculp., dsngr.), Antoine Pevsner (1886-1962, Russ.-born sculp., dsgnr.)> *Also see* **Art Movements and Periods, modern art**.

consumer *Mktg* Individual who buys and uses products and services.

Consumer Confidence Index/Consumer Confidence Survey *Eco&Fin* This complex **economic indicator** is based on a monthly survey by the University of Michigan that measures the confidence that the average consumer has in the economy. It is used to predict whether consumer buying will go up or down. While this index is controversial among some economists, many businesses give it considerable weight. *Also see* **Economic Indicators**.

consumer distribution *Mktg* Methods or channels by which products are distributed to **consumers**. *Also see* **Distribution Methods**.

Consumer Price Index (CPI) *Eco&Fin* This **economic indicator** reported by the U.S. Dept. of Commerce is derived from a weighted average of the prices for consumer goods and services. <housing, food, transportation, entertainment, etc> It is the most common measure of the **inflation rate**. Wage and pension **Cost of Living Adjustments** (COLAS) are based on the CPI.

consumer products *Mktg* Products designed for and distributed to **consumers** (individuals or groups of individuals) as the ultimate users.

consumer services *Mktg* Services designed for the use of **consumers**, i.e., individuals or groups of individuals. <credit cards, telephone, travel, etc>

consumerism *Eco&Fin, Mktg* **1** Movement that seeks to protect consumers by requiring honest packaging and advertising, product guarantees, and improved safety standards. **2** Theory that more consumption of goods is economically beneficial. *Also see* **materialism**.

consummate *Crit&Eval* Supremely accomplished or skilled. <**Charlie Parker**, the consummate master of improvisation>

consumption *Eco&Fin, Mktg* using up of goods and services by consumer purchasing or in the production of other goods.

contact *Genl* One who might be of use; a connection. *Also see* **networking**.

contact improvisation *Dnce* Dance technique invented in 1972 by dance teacher **Steve Paxton** (choreog., dncr.)

contact improvisation *Dnce* Dance technique that involves dancers moving in and out of contact with one another. Invented in 1972 by **Steve Paxton**.

contact print *VisArts* Print made by exposing a photosensitive surface in direct contact with a photographic negative.

contact proof *VisArts* Print made by placing a film negative directly upon sensitized paper and exposing to light; used for preliminary viewing, planning and selection of negatives to print as photographs.

contact sheet *Mktg, VisArts* Sheet of several contact proofs or film rolls of negatives from which promotion and publicity prints are chosen.

contemporary (contemp.) *Crit&Eval* **1** Belonging to the same period of time. <a fact documented by two contemporary sources> **2** Of about the same age. **3** Current; modern.

contemporary art *VisArts* "For contemporary art, esp. that which positions itself in the vanguard of cultural life, is always on the edge of social acceptability and thus always vulnerable." — Andy Grundberg (art critic)

contemporary Christian music *MusArts* Genre of **white gospel music** emerged in the 1980s combining a pop or rock sound with religious lyrics. *Also see* **Gospel Music**.

contemporary gospel *MusArts* New style of black gospel music evolved in the 1970s, moving away from the sanctified-church style of **call and response**, choral refrain, and "spirit possession" towards more elaborate harmony, cultivated vocalism, and **timbres** inspired by pop music. *Also see* **Gospel Music**.

contemporary style (1945-56) *VisArts* Characterized by the brightness and minuteness seen in the applied arts.

contempt of court *LegAsp* Any willful disobedience to, or disregard of, a **court order** or any misconduct in the presence of a court;

content *Flm&Vid, LitArts, MusArts* **1** Meaning or significance of a literary or artistic work. **2** Entertainment programming. **3** Subject matter of the art form or discipline. "Our business is pretty simple. We generate content that can work on any or many platforms. Instead of generating records or a TV show or a movie, we come up with concepts that can work with all of them." — David Salzman (a business partner of **Quincy Jones**)

content analysis *Crit&Eval* Systematic analysis of the content rather than the structure of a communication, such as a written work, speech, or film, inc. the study of thematic and symbolic elements to determine the objective or meaning of the communication.

content factory *Flm&Vid, InfoMgt,. Rdio/TV, RecA&S* An arts, entertainment, and media **conglomerate** committed to adapting, creating, producing, and distributing **product**.

contents *LitArts* Subject matter of a book or magazine.

contingency *Genl* Possibility that must be prepared for; a future emergency.

contingency budget *Eco&Fin* Funds set aside in advance to finance contingency plans and response to emergencies.

contingency plans *Mgt* Plans outlining a course of action, prepared in advance to deal with situations that may arise.

contingent compensation agreement *Eco&Fin, LegalAsp* Amount of payment from employer to employee – whether **fixed fee** or percentage – depends on conditions or occurences not yet established. <If the net or gross profits of the project comes in below budget, if the artist remains scandal free during life of agreement, if the employee controls weight under x pounds; if the employee bats over. 300 and drives in 100+ runs> *Also see* **contingent scale payment**, **gross profit participant**, **net profit participant; profit participation**.

contingent scale payment *RecA&S* Royalties on record sales paid to certain **AFTRA** members.

continuity *Flm&Vid* Kind of **logic** implied between edited shots and their principle of coherence. **Cutting to continuity** emphasizes smooth transitions between shots in which time and space are unobtrusively condensed. More complex, **classical cutting** is the linking of shots according to an event's psychological as well as logical breakdown. In **thematic montage**, the continuity is determined by the symbolic association of ideas between shots rather than any literal connections in time and space.

continuo (Ital.) *MusArts* Bass accompaniment played on a keyboard; numerals written underneath the notes indicate the kinds of harmony to be played. FIGURED BASS, THOROUGHBASS.

continuous music *HR&LR, MusArts* Performance of music without break or intermission; requires additional scale payment to the musicians.

continuum *Crit&Eval* Continuous extent, succession, or whole, no part of which can be distinguished from neighboring parts except by arbitrary division. *Also see* **balance, theory**.

contr *MusArts* » **contralto**

contra account *E&F-Acc* Account that always has a companion account and whose normal balance is opposite that of the companion account.

contra asset account *E&F-Acc* » **accumulated depreciation**.

contra- *MusInstr* Lower in pitch. <contrabassoon>

contrabassoon *MusInstr* The largest and lowest-**pitched** of the **double-reed** wind musical instruments, sounding an **octave** below the **bassoon**. *Also see* **Musical Instrument Families**.

contract (contr.) *LegAsp* Agreement between two or more competent persons to do or not to do some lawful act for a **consideration**. *Also see* **Contracts**.

contract artist *ArtPerf, LegAsp* Artist or performer who is empowered to sign an engagement or management contract for her or his individual services and the services of any group or ensemble led or owned by her or him. *Also see* **sideman, studio musician**.

contract elements *LegAsp* To be enforceable, a contract must meet four basic requirements: (1) Agreement — there must be mutual assent (offer and acceptance) by the parties, (2) **Consideration** legally sufficient, (3) Contractual capacity — the parties must have the capacity to carry out the terms of the contract, and (4) Lawful Object — the contract's objective must be legal and not violate public policy. *Also see* **Contracts**.

contract player *ArtPerf,. Rdio/TV* Television performer (usu. in **soaps**) contracted to a 13-week commitment. *Also see* **day player, under five player**.

contraction and release *Dnce* "[**Martha**] Graham's 'contraction and release' was the foundation of a percussive dance technique that found drama in the body's mechanism of breathing." — Anna Kisselgoff (dance critic) *Also see* **fall and recovery, tension and relaxation**.

contractor *HR&LR* » **music contractor**.

Contracts *ColEntry, LegAsp* »... **actual —, agency clause, bilateral —, breach of —, contract, contract elements, contracts under seal, covenant, development deal, distribution deal, engagement —, exclusive agency —, Exclusive Songwriter Agreement, executed —, executory —, expressed —, franchise, implied-in-fact —, implied-in-law —, label deal, labor —, lease, letters of credit, licensing deal, management contract, negotiable instruments, objective theory of —, performance —, pink —, Popular Songwriters —, power of attorney, production deal, quasi-—, recognizances, software license, space contract, songwriter/music publisher —, special power of attorney, unilateral —, unenforceable —, valid —, void —, voidable —, white —.**

contracts under seal *LegAsp* Contract to which a seal (usu. wax) is affixed thus allowing that no **consideration** is necessary. *Also see* **Contracts**.

contralto (contr) *MusArts* The lowest female voice or voice part, intermediate in range between soprano and tenor.

contrapuntal *MusArts* Relating to, or incorporating **counterpoint**.

contrast *Crit&Eval* Juxtaposition of opposites for dramatic effect.

contrast *Flm&Vid* Difference in brightness between the light and dark areas of a picture, such as a photograph or video image.

contrast *VisArts* Use of opposing elements, such as colors, forms, or lines, in proximity to produce an intensified effect.

contrib. *Fndng* **contribution, contributor**.

contributed income *Eco&Fin, Fndng* Accounting designation for monies donated to **nonprofit** arts organizations.

contributing editor *Journ* Usually a **free-lance** writer for a magazine or a name on the masthead to lend credibility and prestige to the publication.

contribution (contrib.) *Fndng* act of contributing.

contributor (contrib.) *Fndng* One who makes a **contribution**.

contributor (contrib.) *Journ, LitArts* One who submits material for publication in a periodical.

control *ArtPerf, MusArts* "I always wanted to have control, of course, over what I did, for one thing because I wanted to make sure that what came out was the best representation of Sonny Rollins, and I thought I knew what that is." — **Sonny Rollins**

Control Processor Unit (cpu) *InfoMgt* » **cpu**

controlled circulation *Journ, Mktg* Relating to a periodical circulated only to qualified readers free or at a reduced rate. Selling point to an advertiser who wants an **homogeneous** readership. *Also see* **Media Circulation**.

controlled composition *IntelProp, RecA&S* Song written <u>or owned</u> or co-written by the recording artist – and sometimes the producer per the artist contract – under an exclusive recording agreement.

controller *PerfA&C* » **light board**.

controller *also* **comptroller** *Eco&Fin* One who audits accounts and supervises the financial affairs of a corporation or of a governmental body. <treasurer, chief accountant, auditor>

controversy *Crit&Eval* Public dispute between sides holding opposing views. "Little controversy stimulates discussion, which makes the museum relevant." — Malcolm Rogers (musm. dir.)

convenience products *Mktg* Products the consumer buys frequently, immediately, and with a minimum of comparison shopping. *Also see* **impulse buy, shopping products, speciality products**.

convention (conv.) *Crit&Eval* **1** Agreement on or acceptance of certain practices or attitudes. **2** Custom.

convention (conv.) *Genl* Formal meeting of members, representatives, or delegates, as of a political party, fraternal society, profession, or industry.

convention *LitArts, TheatArts, VisArts* Widely used and accepted device or technique in drama, literature, or painting.

convergence *InfoMgt, Sci&Tech* Melding of technologies. <televi-

sion and computers>

converter *Fashn* One employed in converting raw products into finished products.

converter *InfoMgt* **1** Device that converts data recorded on one medium to another medium. <a unit that accepts data from printed pages and records it on **floppy disks**> **2** Device that converts data in one form into data in another form. <**analog** to **digital**> *Also see* **modem, transducer.**

convoluted *Crit&Eval* Intricate. COMPLICATED. <convoluted legal language; convoluted reasoning>

convulse *Crit&Eval* To cause to shake with laughter or strong emotion. <The clown's antics convulsed the audience with laughter>

COO *Mgt* » **chief operating officer.**

Coogan's Law *HR&LR, LglAsp* Protects minor-age performers from financially irresponsible guardians or parents. *Origin* Jackie Coogan (1914-1984), child movie star in the 1920s, involved in a celebrated court battle over custody of his film earnings. Under court-approved contracts, at least 15% of gross earnings must be set aside in trust for the child.

cookies *iMedia, InfoMgt* Computer files that record information such as where one has been on the **Web.**

cool *Crit&Eval* **1** Marked by calm self-control. <No matter the provocation, she kept her cool> **2** Marked by indifference, disdain, or dislike. UNFRIENDLY, UNRESPONSIVE. **3** Excellent, first-rate. <So-and-so has a cool **pad**> "It is one of the curses of what has been called **postmodernism**: 'Tis better to be cool than to be real." — Stephen Holden (music critic)

cool *MusArts* Subdued *Also see* **cool jazz, hot.**

cool *VisArts* Relating to certain colors that produce the impression of coolness. <blue, green>

cool art *VisArts* Style of abstract and geometric art characterized by sharp images or forms and repetitive structures and units.

cool jazz *MusArts* Relaxed, laid-back style of jazz (ca. 1949-55) without the tenseness of bop. <**Miles Davis**, Gerry Mulligan (1927-96 bari. sax, arr.-comp., bndldr)> *Also see* **Jazz Styles.**

cool media *iMedia* Description of a type of media that provides less stimulation, coined by **Marshall McCluhan.**

cooperative (co-op) *Mgt* Enterprise or organization owned or managed jointly by those who use its facilities or services. <Several artists and artisans may form an artists' cooperative to reduce overhead and improve marketing>

cop out *Crit&Eval* To avoid fulfilling a commitment or responsibility.

copacetic, copasetic *Crit&Eval* (Passé) Excellent, first-rate.

coppin' *MusArts, RecA&S* Use by **hip-hop** artists and rappers of word phrases or music bits for an "original" recording. *Origin* Cop: To take unlawfully or without permission. STEAL.

Copr. *IntelProp* **copyright.**

coprocessor *InfoMgt* Auxiliary processor that performs time consuming tasks to free the **central processing unit**, thus resulting in faster execution time for the overall system.

Copy *InfoMgt* Computer command that copies selected material and places it on the **Clipboard.**

copy *Journ, VA-Prntng* **1** Suitable source material. **2** Material to be set in type. <manuscript>

copy *IntelProp* Physical manifestation of a copyrighted work. <**phonorecord, lead sheet** of a song, **score** of a composition, a book, a software disk, video of a choreographed dance, etc>

copy *Mktg* Words to be printed or spoken in an advertisement.

copy *MusArts* To make a written copy of a music manuscript. *Also see* **copyist.**

copy *VisArts* **Reproduction** or **imitation** of an **original.**

copy block *BcstJourn* In a television news script, the right half of the page that contains the words to be read by the newscaster. Quite often, this copy block is very narrow and exists between two lines on the page that show the limits of the **teleprompter** pickup.

copy boy, copy girl *Journ* Young person employed by a newspaper or broadcast news office to carry copy and run errands.

copy protection *InfoMgt* **1** Means of preventing the illegal or unauthorized copying of a software product. **2** Preventive routine incorporated into a copyrighted program.

copy story *BcstJourn* » **reader**

copy-protect *InfoMgt* Make a disk uncopyable to prevent it from being illegally duplicated.

copyediting *Journ* Reading and correcting **copy**

copyholder *Journ, VA-Prntng* **1** Assistant who reads manuscript aloud to a **proofreader. 2** Device that holds **copy** in place, esp. for a typesetter.

copyist *MusArts* One who makes manuscript copies of instrumental or vocal parts from the composer's **score.** "Small and dedicated band of professional **copyists** is still hanging in there, acting as interpreters, editors and scribes, sorting through the composer's disorganized or hastily **scribbled** pages of music to decipher what the instruments in the performance will be doing and when and then transcribing every instrument's part by hand, **measure** by **measure**, note by note." — Julia Collins (journ.)

copyright (©, Copyright, Copr.) *Eco&Fin, EntreP, LegalAsp, iMedia, IntelProp* Form of protection provided by federal law to authors of **published** and **unpublished** "original works of authorship," inc. literary, dramatic, musical, and artistic works, which gives the copyright owner the exclusive right to – and to authorize others to – reproduce the work, to prepare derivative works based upon the copyrighted work, to distribute copies of the work, to perform the copyrighted work publicly, and to display the copyrighted work publicly and with certain limitations reproduce the work. *Also see* **Intangible Assets.**

Copyright Act of 1976 *IntelProp* Current copyright law of the U.S. effective Jan. 1, 1978.

copyright deposit registration *IntelProp* Applicant must mail to the U.S. Copyright Office (USCO), Register of Copyrights, **Library of Congress**, Washington, DC 20559, (1) Properly completed application form (provided free from the **USCO**), (2) Fee of $20 per application, (3) Deposit (copy) of the original work (two copies if already published) Application forms and instructions available free from the **USCO.** *Also see* **Federal Agencies and Statutes.**

copyright form CA *IntelProp* File information about previous registration.

copyright form GR/CP *IntelProp, LitArts* **Adjunct** application for contributors to periodicals.

copyright form PA *IntelProp, PerfA&C* For published and unpublished works of the performing arts with the **Copyright Office.**

copyright form RE *IntelProp* To renew copyrights in works copyrighted before 1976.

copyright form SE *IntelProp, Journ, LitArts* For periodicals and **serials.**

copyright form SR *IntelProp, RecA&S* Appropriate for registering published and unpublished sound recording works in two situations: (1) where the copyright claim is limited to the sound recording itself, or (2) where the claimant is seeking to register the sound recording *and* the musical (or literary or dramatic) work on the sound recording.

copyright form TX *IntelProp, LitArts* For published and unpublished non-dramatic literary (textual) works, inc. **fiction, non-fiction**, poetry, textbooks, reference works, directories, catalogs, advertising copy, compilations of information, and computer programs but excluding periodicals or serial issues. For periodicals and **serials**, use **copyright form SE, work made for hire.**

copyright form VX *IntelProp, VisArts* For published and unpublished works of visual arts (2- and 3- dimensional pictorial, graphic, and sculptural works of art.)

copyright laws *Eco&Fin, IntelProp* Grant the author(s) exclusive ownership of original works – both published and unpublished – and the right to collect money for their use. *Also see* **intellectual property.**

copyright notice *IntelProp* U.S. copyright notice has three elements that must appear on the copyrighted work. (1) Word "Copyright," the abbreviation "Copr." or the symbol, ©, (2) Year of first publication, and (3) Name(s) of the author(s)

copyright registration date *IntelProp* Effective date is the day **USCO** receives a properly filled out application.

Copyright Royalty Tribunal (CRT) *IntelProp* Special review board, empowered to set and distribute royalties, established by Congress in the **Copyright Act of 1976** *Also see* **Copyright-Related Organizations.**

copyright term *IntelProp* Length of time which your work is protected under Copyright Law, after which your work falls into the

public Domain. The term is calculated based on when the work was created and who is the author of the work. Copyright is good for 50 years after the death of the last surviving author. Some copyrights issued before 1976 may be good for a total of 75 years from the date of registration.

Copyright-Related Organizations *ColEntry, IntelProp* » AGI, ALAI, ASCAP, BMI, CISAC, CRT, DGI, HFA, IIPA, NWU, SESAC, SGA, SOCAN, SODRAC, SPA, USCO, WIPO.

copywriter *Mktg* One who writes copy for advertising.

cor *MusInstr* **cornet**

core competencies *EntreP* Value-creating organizational capabilities that are unique to a company.

core product *Mktg* Principal product produced or distributed by the marketer.

core, core memory *InfoMgt* Memory made of a series of tiny doughnut-shaped masses of magnetic material.

cornerblocks *PerfA&C* Triangular shaped piece of quarter-inch plywood used to reinforce the joint between a **stile** and a **rail** of a **flat**.

cornet (cor.) *MusInstr* Wind instrument of the trumpet family, having three valves operated by pistons. Now used mostly in brass bands. *Also see* **Musical Instrument Families.** CORNET-IST.

cornrows *Fashn* To arrange or style hair by dividing it into sections and braiding close to the scalp in rows.

corny *Crit&Eval* **Trite**, melodramatic, or oversentimental.

corporate bond *EntreP* Bond issued by a public corporation that wants to borrow money to invest in assets that will help it earn revenue.

corporate charter *EntreP* Document that establishes a corporation's existence.

corporate entrepreneurship *EntreP* Entrepreneurship within an established business, usually a large corporation.

corporate foundation *Fndng* **Foundation** established by a corporation for the purpose of distributing a certain percentage of profits to charitable causes, keeping in mind certain tax considerations.

corporate raider *Mgt* » **leveraged buy out** (LBO)

corporate refugee *EntreP* Person who leaves big business to go into business for himself or herself.

corporate sponsor *Fndng, Mktg* Business enterprise willing to assist in the funding and/or marketing of an art collection, concert, or theatrical production. <Kool Jazz Festival, Merrill Lynch Series of Dance Recitals> *Also see* **artist tie-ins, merchandising tie-ins, sponsor, sponsors.**

corporate theater *Mktg, PA-Variety* Entertainment produced and performed for client's. >private function, gala dinners, incentive package, etc. < *Also see* **industrial show.**

corporation (corp.) *Eco&Fin, EntreP, Mgt.* **1** Business owned by stockholders that begins when the state approves its articles of incorporation. Ownership is based on shares of stock or percentage of ownership. **2** Legal **entity**; an artificial "person" with its own rights, privileges, and liabilities distinct from those of its members. *Also see* **Sub chapter S corporation**

Corporation for Public Broadcasting (CPB) *Rdio/TV* » **CPB**

corps de ballet (core duh baa-lay, Fr.) *Dnce* Ensemble of dancers who perform only in the group numbers.

corr. *Journ,. Rdio/TV* **correspondent**

correction *Eco&Fin* Decline of at least 10 percent in a **stock market index**. If a correction lasts long enough it eventually becomes a **bear market.**

corrective maintenance *EntreP* Repairs necessary to restore equipment or a facility to good condition.

corrective make-up *Th-MakeUp* Make-up designed to create the most pleasing appearance possible.

correlation *EntreP* Measure of how two random variables co-vary together. Scaling is such that it lies between 1 and 1. A 1 indicates that the two vary in exactly the same direction, while *a* 1 indicates a perfect negative relationship. Zero implies the variables have no correlation.

correspondence quality *InfoMgt* High-quality printing obtained by laser, daisy-wheel, and certain dot-matrix printers. *Also see* **high resolution, near-letter quality.** *Also see* **DPI**

correspondent (corr.) *Journ,. Rdio/TV* One employed by print or broadcast media to supply news stories or articles. <a foreign correspondent>

corridos *MusArts* Mexican narrative songs…

corruption *InfoMgt* bad data

CORSAIR *InfoMgt* **Computer-Oriented Reference System For Automatic Information Retrieval.** Ω

corset *Fashn* **1** Close-fitting undergarment, often reinforced by stays, worn to support and shape the waistline, hips, and breasts. **2 Medieval** outer garment, esp. a laced jacket or bodice.

CORST *TheatArts* **Council of Resident Stock Theatres.** Ω

coryphée (cory-fay, Fr.) *Dnce* (Ballet) Female or male dancer who has moved out of the **corps de ballet** into minor solo roles.

cos. *Fashn* **costume**

cost of goods available for sale *E&F-Acc* Cost of beginning inventory plus net purchases plus **freight-in** (same as transportation-in) which is a subset at the **cost of goods sold** calculation.

cost of goods sold *E&F-Acc* Cost of inventory that the business has sold to customers, the largest single expense of most merchandising businesses. COST OF SALES

cost of goods sold *EntreP* Cost of producing or acquiring goods or services to be sold by a company.

Cost of Living Adjustment *Eco&Fin, HR&LR* » **COLA, CPI**

cost of living adjustments *EntreP* Automatic increases in wages or other payments that are tied to a price index.

Cost of Living Indexes *Eco&Fin* This **economic indicator** is largely based on the **CPI**. While it is reported as a national statistic, the most useful and popular data are the regional indexes which provide a convenient comparison of regions to each other, or one city vs. another.

cost of sales *E&F-Acc* » **cost of goods sold**

cost per rating point (CPRP) *Rdio/TV* » **CPRP**

cost principle of accounting *E&F-Acc* Assets are recorded at cost, with the exception of current assets which are recorded at the **lower at cost or market**.

cost-of-living adjustment (COLA) *Eco&Fin* » **COLA**

cost-of-living index (CPI) *Eco&Fin* » **CPI**

cost-per-thousand (CPM, C.P.M.) *Mktg* Unit of measure by which advertisers evaluate the effectiveness of their programs. Ad campaign that cost $1 million to develop and execute that reached approx. 100,000 people will have a **CPM** of $10. <**CPMs** are what a magazine charges for every 1,000 copies sold that is guaranteed to its advertisers>

cost-plus *Eco&Fin* Cost of production plus a fixed rate of profit.

costar *also* **co-star** *ArtPerf* Starring actor or actress given equal status with another or others in a play or film.

costs *E&F-Acc* Sacrifice, measured by the price paid or required to be paid, to acquire goods or services. When a "cost" refers to the valuation of a good or service acquired, the "cost" is an **asset**. When the benefits of the acquisition of the goods and serviced expire, the "cost" becomes an **expense** or a **loss**. Some accountants use cost and expense as synonyms.

costume (cos.) *Fashn* **1** Prevalent fashion of dress, inc. garments, accessories, and hairstyle. **2** Style of dress characteristic of a particular country, period, or people, often worn in a play or at a masquerade. **3** Outfit or a disguise worn on Mardi Gras, Halloween, or similar occasions.

costume (cos.) *Flm&Vid, PerfA&C* Anything designed and fabricated for a performer. *Also see* **costumer, wardrobe**.

costume design *Fashn, VisArts* Art of designing original costumes.

costume designer *PerfA&C* Person responsible for the design, visual appearance, and function of the costumes, accessories, and makeup.

costume running crew *PerfA&C* Those crew members such as **dressers** and wardrobe-repair personnel who work during the dress rehearsals and performances.

costumer *Fashn, VisArts* One that makes or supplies costumes.

costumer *PerfA&C* Person responsible for the construction of the costumes and supervision of the costume shop.

Coty awards *Fashn* Annual awards sponsored by Coty, Inc., international cosmetic and perfume company, given for outstanding fashion design. Judges include newspaper and magazine fashion editors, broadcasters, and fashion retailers. *Also see* **Awards & Prizes**.

---

couch potato *Cult&Soc, Rdio/TV* Person who spends much time watching television while sitting or lying down. *Also see* **channel surfing**.

Council for the Advancement and Support of Education (CASE) *Fndng* » **CASE**

Council of Fashion Designers of America (CFDA) *Fashn* » **CFDA**

Council of Resident Stock Theatres (CORST) *TheatArts* » **CORST**

count the box *PerfA&C* Count the ticket stubs in the collection box.

count the house *TheatArts* Stare at the audience while acting. [Tsk, tsk. Very unprofessional.].

count up *PerfA&C* Prepare a box-office statement for a performance.

counter *VA-Prntng* Depression between the raised lines of a **typeface**.

counterculture *Cult&Soc* Culture, esp. of young people, with values or **lifestyles** in opposition to those of the established culture. [The counterculture of the past can become the mass culture of the present.].

counterfeit *Ethcs&Phil* Made in imitation of what is genuine with the intent to defraud. *Also see* **fake**.

counterfeiting *Flm&Vid, IntelProp, RecA&S* Illegal practice of duplicating the images and/or sounds from a legitimate recording or video without authorization and selling the counterfeits as legitimate.

counterpoint *Crit&Eval* Contrasting but parallel element, item, or theme.

counterpoint *MusArts* Technique of combining two or more melodic lines in such a way that they establish a harmonic relationship while retaining their **linear** individuality.

counterprogramming *Rdio/TV* Scheduling of television programs so as to attract viewers away from programs broadcast simultaneously on another network.

countertenor *MusArts* Adult male voice with a range above that of tenor. *Also see* **castrato**.

counterweight *PerfA&C* Sandbag or iron or steel weight used to counterbalance the weight of scenery and equipment to be flown. *Also see* **counterweight system**.

counterweight system *PerfA&C* Most common rigging system consisting of **battens** supported by metal aircraft cable counterbalanced by sandbags or steel or iron **counterweights**. *Also see* **arbor**.

country *MusArts* » **country and western, country music**

country and western (C&W, c&w) *MusArts* Originally **folk music** from the rural South and West U.S. but since its 1960s pop orientation, the more accurate title is simply: **country music**. *Also see* **Southern white soul music**

country blues *MusArts* Earliest type of blues, the singing of one man to the accompaniment of his guitar. Later these men were accompanied by **string bands** and **jug bands**. *Also see* **Blues**.

country music *MusArts* Popular music based on the folk style of the southern rural United States. *Also see* **country and western**.

Country Music Association (CMA) *MusArts* » **CMA**

Country Music Foundation (CMF) *MusArts* » **CMF**

Country Music Hall of Fame and Museum *MusArts* » **CMF**

Country Music Styles *ColEntry, MusArts* » **bluegrass, countrypolitan, country-pop, country-rock, country swing, cowpunk, folk music, hillbilly, mountain music, Nashville Sound, new traditionalist —, pop-rock, rockabilly, Southern white soul music, Tex-Mex, Western swing**.

country rock *MusArts* Pioneered by The Grateful Dead (» Bill Graham) *Also see* **Rock Music Styles**.

country swing *MusArts* » **Western swing**. *Also see* **Country Music Styles**.

country-dance *Dnce* Folk dance of English origin in which two lines of dancers face each other. *Also see* **Dances**.

country-pop *MusArts* <Kenny Rogers (1937-, country sngr., gtr., sngwri.), **Dolly Parton, Linda Ronstadt**> *Also see* **Country Music Styles**.

country-rock *MusArts* <Garth Brooks (1962-, cross-over sngr. — country/pop/rock)> *Also see* **Country Music Styles**.

countrypolitan *MusArts* » **Nashville Sound**. *Also see* **Country Music Styles**.

coup de théâtre (coo duh tee-ottruh, Fr.) *TheatArts* Sudden, dramatic turn of events in a play.

couplet *LitArts* Unit of verse consisting of two successive lines, usu. rhyming and having the same **meter** and often forming a complete thought.

coupon (cp.) *Eco&Fin* Negotiable certificate attached to a bond that represents a sum of interest due.

coupon (cp.) *Mktg* 1 Detachable part, as of a ticket or advertisement, that entitles the bearer to certain benefits, such as a cash refund or a gift. 2 Certificate accompanying a product that may be redeemed for a cash discount. 3 Printed form, as in an advertisement, to be used as an order blank or for requesting information or obtaining a discount on merchandise.

couponing *Mktg* Sending out or redemption of a manufacturer's coupon for cash.

court order *LegAsp* Order issued by a court that requires a person to do or refrain from doing something.

Court, The *Law&Pol* Supreme Court of the U.S.

courtroom drama *Rdio/TV* Popular type of television network programming. <*Law and Order, Perry Mason, The Defenders*> *Also see* **Television Shows**.

couture (koo-toor, Fr.) *Fashn* 1 Business of designing, making, and selling highly fashionable, usu. custom-made clothing for women. 2 Dressmakers and fashion designers considered as a group.

couturier (koo-toor-ee-ay, Fr.) *Fashn* 1 Establishment engaged in couture. 2 One who designs for or owns such an establishment.

couturiere (koo-toor-ee-air, Fr.) *Fashn* Woman who designs for or owns an establishment engaged in couture.

covenant *Fndng* » **tax incentive**

covenant *LegAsp* 1 Formal sealed agreement or contract. 2 Suit to recover damages for violation of such a contract. *Also see* **Contracts**.

cover (in picture stories) *BcstJourn* Collection of video that supports a certain amount of narration in a story. As a noun: "Do we have enough cover?" or as verb: "Cover that part of the narration…"

cover (in the introduction to a **SOT**) *BcstJourn* Routine production shots of an interviewee doing non-specific daily tasks such as answering phones, walking down hallways, etc

cover *Crit&Eval* One who substitutes for another.

cover band *MusArts* Band that plays mostly the original music of other bands.

cover charge *PA-Variety* Fixed amount added to the check at a nightclub or restaurant for entertainment. *Also see* **play for the door**.

cover date *Journ* Date printed on the front cover or the **spine** of a periodical usu. two-four weeks ahead of the **on-sale date**.

cover *Eco&Fin* Funds sufficient to meet an obligation or secure against loss.

cover *Journ* Report the details of an event or situation. <Reporters from local and national media covered the candidate's press conference>

cover *VA-Prntng* Binding or enclosure for a book or magazine.

cover price *Mktg, VA-Prntng* Price for a single copy of a magazine, usu. printed in the upper right-hand corner of the front cover.

cover record *RecA&S* Instrumental or vocal music recorded by other artists after the first recording by the artist who introduced it.

cover shots, covering shots *Flm&Vid* » **coverage**

cover story *Ethcs&Phil* False story intended to deceive or mislead.

cover story *Journ* Featured story in a magazine that concerns the illustration on the cover.

cover version *IntelProp, RecA&S* Refers to the right of anyone to make and sell a recording of a song – after its **first use** – without special permission of the copyright owner. The remake of the other's work must be without changing the basic melody or fundamental character of the work. *Also see* **mechanical** royalty.

coverage *Flm&Vid* Extra **shots** of a scene that can be used to bridge **transitions** in case the footage fails to edit as planned.

coverage ratios *E&F-Acc* Indicate the extent to which the company generates operating income to cover an expense. The most common coverage is times-interest-earned. *Also see* **ratios**.

covered position *EntreP* Trading of both the underlying stock and an option. Also called a hedge position.

cow-punk *MusArts* Boisterous rock steeped in country music. *Also see* **Country Music Styles, Rock Styles.**

cowbell *MusInstr* Cowbell with the clapper removed, struck with a drumstick to produce percussive effects. *Also see* **Little Instruments.**

cp. *Eco&Fin, Mktg* **coupon**

CPA *E&F-Acc* Public accountant who has been certified by a state examining board as having met the state's legal requirements.

CPB *Rdio/TV* **Corporation for Public Broadcasting.** Washington, DC, based agency in charge of distributing federal funds to public radio and TV stations. Also funds some programming in accordance to the **Public Broadcasting Act of 1967** to create and disseminate noncommercial programming. *Also see* **Federal Agencies and Statutes.**

CPI *Eco&Fin* **Consumer Price Index**

CPL *InfoMgt* **Callable Personal Librarian. Search engine** developed by **Personal Library Software, Inc.** *Also see* **portals.**

CPM *also* **C.P.M.** *Mktg* **Cost Per Thousand**

cpm *VA-Prntng* **copies per minute**

CPOD *InfoMgt* Collection, preservation, organization, and dissemination of records — a unique function of a library. *Also see* **Information Management.**

CPRP *Rdio/TV* **Cost Per Rating Point**

cps *RecA&S* **cycles per second.** » **frequency**

CPSR *InfoMgt, Cult&Soc* **Computer Professionals for Social Responsibility.** Concentrates on the interaction of computers and society from the point of view of both technical experts and concerned **Netizens.** *Also see* **Bell Labs.**

cpu *InfoMgt* **Central Processing Unit** Brain of the computer, the microprocessor that performs the actual computations. *Also see* **coprocessor, processor, RISC.**

cr. *E&F-Acc* **credit, creditor**

crack *InfoMgt* Technique of wrongfully acquiring passwords by collecting user.

cracker *InfoMgt* Someone who cracks into systems. *Also see* **hacker.**

craft union *HR&LR* Union in which all workers ply the same **craft,** frequently requiring special training often with **apprenticeships.** *Also see* **horizontal union.**

Craig, David (19??-, musical theatre tchr.) *ArtPerf, Crit&Eval, MusArts, TheatArts* "Even though I may never be a singer, my work with David helped me to be a better actor. And what's more important, he taught me how to get the job." — Sally Field (1946-, act) *Also see* **reality, style, Tin Pan Alley, tired businessman.**

crape *Fashn* **crepe**

crash *iMedia, InfoMgt* **1** Sudden, usu. drastic failure. term "system crash" usu., though not always, implies that the operating system or other software was at fault. **2** To fail suddenly. "Has the system just crashed?"

crash book *LitArts, Mktg* » **instant book**

crasher *Journ, Rdio/TV* Producer of a television news program who may spend 72 hours straight on a late-breaking story. *Also see* **Producers.**

cravat (kra-vat) *Fashn* Scarf or band of fabric worn around the neck as a tie.

Crawford, Cheryl (1902-86, stage prod., tchr.) *Crit&Eval, TheatArts* A founder of the **Group Theater** and the **Actors Studio;** also actively involved with the **Theatre Guild,** and the **American National Theater and Academy.** <Indy prod., *Porgy and Bess* (1942), *Sweet Bird of Youth* (1959)>

crawl *Flm&Vid* Words or graphics that move across, up, or down a movie or television screen, usu. giving program **credits,** news flashes, or weather alerts. *Also see* **title, titles.**

crayons *Perf-MkUp* Creme makeup in crayon form used for quickly modeling the face with highlights and shadows.

CRCC *InfoMgt* **Center for Research on Concepts and Cognition** is the new name for Fluid Analogies Research Group (FARG), Group of **cognitive scientists** at Indiana University who are pioneering an innovative approach to modeling human creativity on a computer. *Also see* **artificial intelligence, prologue.**

created *IntelProp* At the time the work of art is **fixed,** it is considered to be "created," and as of that moment is entitled to protection under the **Copyright Act of 1976**

creation and presentation *Fndng* Grants for actual artistic work — one of four categories of grants by the **National Endowment for the Arts** (NEA): *Also see* **NEA grants.**

creative accounting *E&F-Acc* Methods of accounting and financial bookkeeping that shade the intent of normal practice. *Also see* **net profit participant.**

Creative Artists Agency (CAA) *Mgt* Los Angeles based international talent agency operating in all media. *Also see* **Talent Agencies.**

creative brief *iMedia* Summary of the conceptual plans for a product. usu. a creative brief includes details on the style and "look and feel" of the product, as well as providing strategies for achieving objectives outlined in the product's proposal.

creative destruction *EntreP* Process by which competition for monopoly profits leads to technological progress.

creative director *Mktg* In an advertising agency, the individual in charge of creative advertising concepts, supervising writers, graphic artists, and audio-video producers. *Also see* **Directors.**

creative director *RecA&S* Person in charge of creative services for a **production company** or record label. *Also see* **Directors.**

creative fee *Mktg* Money paid a composer or **copywriter** by an advertising agency, producer, or **production company.**

creative process *Aes&Creat ArtPerf* "As I see it, there are three parts to the creative process: first, the extra vision with which the artist perceives a truth and conveys it by suggestion. Second, medium of expression: language for writers, paint for painters, clay or stone for sculptors, sound expressed as musical notes for composers. Third, design or structure." — **Barbara Tuchman**

creative producer *Flm&Vid* **1** One who maximizes the creative potential of a film within the available logistical parameters — now less likely to be studio heads. **2** One who supervises the making of a movie in such detail that he is virtually its main creator. During the studio era, the most famous creative producers were **David O. Selznick** and **Walt Disney.**

Creative Talent Agency (CTA) *Mgt* » **CTA**

creativity *Aes&Creat ArtPerf* Creative ability characterized by originality and expressiveness. "Creativity a type of learning process where the teacher and the pupil are located in the same individual." (1964) — Arthur Koestler (1905-83, Hung.-born fictwri.) *Also see* **magic.**

creativity *EntreP* Ability to develop new ideas, which may result in new products or services.

creativity *Journ, LitArts* "First learn the rules, the devices and the conventions associated with good writing, then go creative." — William Raspberry (19??-; syn. colum) *Also see* **avant-garde.**

credit (cr.) *E&F-Acc* **1** Right side of an account. **2** Deduction of a payment made by a debtor from an amount due. **3** Positive balance or amount remaining in a person's account. **4** Credit line.

credit (cr.) *EntreP* Agreement between a buyer and a seller that provides for delayed payment for a product or service.

credit accounts (CA) *E&F-Acc* Ones representing the extension of credit by the lender to the borrower. <accounts receivable>

credit bureaus *EntreP* Privately owned organizations that summarize a number of companies' credit experiences with particular individuals.

credit insurance *EntreP* Coverage that protects against bad-debt losses with preset limits.

credit line *Eco&Fin* Maximum amount of credit to be extended to a customer. LINE OF CREDIT.

credit line *IntelProp, Journ* Line of copy acknowledging the source or origin of a news dispatch, photograph, published article, or other work.

credit list *TheatArts* List in a theatre program with the names of individuals or companies who have provided costumes, equipment. *Also see* **dress the stage.**

credit sheet *Mktg* » **bio, bio sheet**

creditor (cr.) *Eco&Fin* One to whom money or its equivalent is owed.

creditor *EntreP* Individual, business company, institution, or government that has money which is due presently or in the future.

creditor squeeze *Eco&Fin* Occurs when suppliers demand harsher payment terms or even halt shipments.

credits *Eco&Fin* **1** Deduction of a payment made by a debtor from an amount due. **2** Right-hand side of an account on which such amounts are entered. **3** Entry or the sum of the entries on this side. **4** Positive balance or amount remaining in a person's account. **5** Credit line. *Also see* **crawl**.

credits *Flm&Vid, Rdio/TV* Acknowledgment, in-print or on-screen, at opening or closing of the film or program, of work done or contributions made – by performers, artisans, technicians, editors, producers, business and marketing staff – in the production of a movie, television program, play, or publication.

credits *TheatArts* Note in a theatre program with information about an actor's previous roles. CLOSING CREDIT, OPENING CREDIT. *Also see* **billing**.

creme makeup *Perf-MkUp* Velvety, non-greasy makeup foundation applied with fingers or brush.

CTO *Mgt* Chief Technical Officer

Creole-Zydeco *MusArts* » **zydeco**

crepe (krape) *Fashn* Light, soft, thin fabric of silk, cotton, wool, or another fiber, with a crinkled surface. CRAPE

crepe hair *Perf-MkUp* Used for making beards, eyebrows, and moustaches. <crepe-wool hair, human crepe hair> *Also see* **spirit gum**.

cres *MusArts* **crescendo**

crescendo (cres) *MusArts* Gradual increase in the volume or intensity of sound in a **passage**.

crew cut, crewcut *Fashn* Closely cropped haircut. So called because it was worn by rowers to reduce wind resistance.

crinoline *Fashn* **1** Coarse, stiff fabric of cotton or horsehair used esp. to line and stiffen hats and garments. **2** Petticoat made of this fabric.

crisis *TheatArts* Turning point in the structure of the play.

crisis management *Mgt* Situation created by an unexpected event for which management is not prepared and that requires immediate attention.

critic (critic) *Crit&Eval* One who judges, in the best case, according to sound standards. **1** "Critics apply aesthetics systems to specific art works and arrive at judgments of their worth and explanations of what gives them that worth. Those judgments produce reputations for works and artists. **Distributors** and audience members take reputations into account when they decide what to support emotionally and financially, and that affects the resources available to artists to continue their work." — Howard Becker (art critic) **2** "Almost by definition critics are people who should not need to be loved." — Alan Riding (art critic) *Also see* **critique, music critic, reviewer**.

Critic/Evaluator *Crit&Eval* One of the four **Principal Players** of **The Arts Dynamic**.

critical *Crit&Eval* **1** Inclined to judge severely and find fault. **2** Characterized by careful, exact evaluation and judgment. **3** Characteristic of critics or criticism. <critical acclaim; critical analysis>

critical *Genl* **1** Turning point; crucial decision, a decisive victory. **2** Indispensable, essential. <a critical element of the marketing plan>

critical judgment *Crit/Eval* Careful, exact evaluation coupled with a well-reasoned resolution

criticaster *Crit&Eval* (Passé) Third-rate, mean-spirited, contemptible critic.

criticism (critic) *Crit&Eval* Product of a critic's judgment; application of standards to the arts or works of art. "There is no neutrality. There is only greater or less awareness of one's bias." — Phyllis Rose (lit. critic) *Also see* **critique, evaluate, review**.

Criticism *Crit&Eval* one of the three **Inner Forces** of **The Arts Dynamic**

critique (cree-teek, Fr. for art of criticism) *Crit&Eval* To **review** or discuss critically. *Also see* **critic, criticism**. *Usage* Critique is usu. more positive than a criticism.

Croce, Benedetto (1866-195, Ital philos., hist., poet, critic) *ArtPerf, Crit&Eval, LitArts* Noted for a major work of modern idealism, *Philosophy of the Spirit* (1902-17), and as a staunch opponent of **fascism**.

crochet (crow-shay) *Fashn* To make a piece of needlework by looping thread with a hooked needle.

crock *InfoMgt* Awkward computer feature or programming technique.

croon *MusArts* **1** To sing in a low, smooth voice into a closely held microphone. **2** To hum or sing softly, as in a lullaby.

crooner *MusArts* One who sang popular songs in the 1930s in a soft, sentimental manner. <Bing Crosby (Harry Lillis Crosby, 1904-77, pop sngr., film act.)>

crop *iMedia, Journ, VA-Prntng* To trim an illustration to fit into an allotted space.

croquis (aka flat) *Fashn* Sketch of apparel design that shows construction parts of the garment; used by pattern makers and buyers so details are evident.

cross (X) *TheatArts* Direction for a performer to go/cross from one side of the stage to the other. *Also see* **Stage Directions**.

cross counter cross *TheatArts* Cross is the movement from one area to another, the **countercross** is a movement in the opposite direction in adjustment to the cross of another character,

cross cutting *Flm&Vid* Alternating of shots from two sequences, often in different locales, suggesting that they are taking place at the same time.

cross-collateralization *RecA&S* Clause in both the artist's record contract and the songwriter's publishing contract that allows the record company/publishing company to deduct from any royalties due the artist/songwriter to apply against any monies owed to the record company/publishing company by the artist/songwriter.

cross-cultural naming *iMedia* Theory that primary colors are fairly consistent across cultures, and that certain colors (black, white, red, yellow green and blue) are more useful in labeling data than others.

cross-cultural validity *iMedia* Sensory representation comprehended beyond one region or culture; borders or limits do not

cross-dressing *ArtPerf, Cult&Soc* Male performer costumed as a female and vice versa: "Numerous black performers – from Mr. T (Lawrence Tero, 1952- Film/TV act.) to **Michael Jackson** to Prince (n?a?m?e, 1958-, pop sngr., sngwri, prod., act.) – have used elements of cross-dressing to enhance their own images and careers. In this respect, they are **crossover artists** in terms of both racial appeal and gender politics." — Marjorie Garber (cult. critic) *Also see* **drag queen**.

cross-pollinate *Crit&Eval* To influence or inspire another in a reciprocal manner.

cross-promotion *Mktg* Use of secondary promotional partners to extend the effectiveness of a sponsorship program beyond simple identification; the use of a variety of promotional extensions. <sweepstakes, coupons, merchandising, etc>

cross-sectional data *Mktg* Study research information gathered from a whole population – or a representative sample of that population – at a given time.

crossover *RecA&S* Artist, recording, or song, strongly identified with a particular style of music in one market, achieves acceptance in another market. "The **cynical** appropriation of pop material by classical performers in the service of crass commercialism." — Matthew Gurewitsch (mus. critic)

crossover space *PerfA&C* Corridor-like space behind the scenery where one can cross from one side of the stage to the other out of sight of the audience.

Crow Jim *Cult&Soc* Black against white. *Also see* **Jim Crow**.

crowd surfers *Genl* Live bodies lifted aloft and waved toward the stage by a fun-loving audience.

CRT *InfoMgt* **Cathode Ray Tube** Picture tube of a video display terminal

CRT *IntelProp* **Copyright Royalty Tribunal**

crudware *InfoMgt* Pejorative term for low-quality **freeware** available from some **user's groups** and **BBS** systems.

crunch *Eco&Fin* Period of financial difficulty characterized by tight money and unavailability of credit.

crunch *InfoMgt* Manipulate or process numerical or mathematical data.

crystal microphone *RecA&S* Not suitable for professional use, usu. supplied with inexpensive tape recorders. *Also see* **Microphones**.

CS *Eco&Fin* **capital stock**

CS *TheatArts* **center stage**

CSS *iMedia* » **Cascading Style Sheets**

CSCP *Fashn* **Chambre Syndicale de la Couture Parisienne**. Agency of the French government that regulates the fashion industry.

CSO *MusArts* **Chicago Symphony Orchestra** Est. 1891, the third oldest symphony orchestra in the U.S.

CTA *Mgt* **Creative Talent Agency** *Also see* **Talent Agencies**.

CTI *InfoMgt* **Computer Telephone Integration** Allows placing and receiving calls by a computer eliminating a desktop telephone.

CTO *Mgt* Chief Technical Officer

ctr. *Crit&Eval* **center**

CU *BcstJourn* » **closeup**

CU *Flm&Vid* **closeup**

CU *InfoMgt* See you.

cubism *VisArts* School of painting and sculpture begun by **Pablo Picasso** and **George Braque** in Paris in 1907, largely as a result of a statement by **Cézanne**, "You must see in nature the cylinder, the sphere, and the cone." Characterized by the reduction and fragmentation of natural forms into abstract, often geometric structures usu. rendered as a set of discrete planes. <**George Braque, Pablo Picasso**> *Also see* **Art Movements and Periods, modern art**.

cuckoo's eggs *MusArts, RecA&S* Unusable song files imposed on the hard drives of Napster users thereby making Napster less reliable.

cue *BcstJourn* Agreed upon action, word, or phrase that is the alert to an upcoming step in whatever production is in progress.

cue *MusArts* Gesture by a conductor signaling the entrance of a performer or part.

cue *PerfA&C, TheatArts* 1 Directive for action. *Ex.* Change in the lighting. **2** Last words of a speech, or the end of an action, indicating (he time for another actor to speak or act. Actors should memorize their cues as carefully as their lines.

cue *TheatArts* Bit of stage business or dialog or signal from the **stage manager** or musical director used to prompt another event in a performance, such as an actor's speech or entrance, a change in lighting, or a sound effect.

cue light *Flm&Vid* Small indicator light to **cue** performer to start or stop in **voiceover** or **on camera** narration.

cue mark *Flm&Vid* Scratch, editor's crayon mark, or a punched hole on a piece of film or tape to **cue** a start/stop of **looping** or **editing**, or cuing the projectionist to change reels.

cuesheet *Flm&Vid, MusArts,. Rdio/TV* Listing of the music used in a TV program or motion picture by title, composer, publisher, timing and type of usage (background, feature, theme) usu. prepared by the producer of the program or film.

cue sheet *RecA&S* Logged or listed cues for audio **mixing** or **sweetening**.

cult *Cult&Soc* Exclusive group of persons sharing an esoteric, usu. artistic or intellectual interest. *Also see* **sect**.

cult. *Cult&Soc* **culture**

cultivation *Fndng* Process of developing the interest of an important prospective contributor by exposure to the organization's activities, people, needs, and plans to the point where he or she may consider a major gift.

culture *EntreP* Behavioral patterns and values that characterize a group such as consumers in a target market or members of a company.

cultural anthropology *Cult&Soc* Scientific study of the development of human cultures based on **archaeological**, **ethnologic**, **ethnographic**, **linguistic**, social, and psychological data and methods of analysis.

cultural awareness *Cult&Soc* "You know that the moral fabric of our nation depends on the arts to enrich our cultural awareness and to further our appreciation for the diversity of experiences that unite us Americans.... I don't view the arts as an isolated cause. Arts are fundamental to our history and our culture. And in this administration, support of the arts is part of a Marjorie Garber, broader social agenda that speaks to our very essence as Americans." — **Bill Clinton**

cultural diversity *Cult&Soc* "We are moving swiftly toward fragmentation and diversity not only in material production, but in art, education, and mass culture as well." — Alvin Toffler (1928-, cult. critic, futurist)

cultural relativism *Cult&Soc, Ethcs&Phil* » **relativism**

culturati *Cult&Soc* People interested in culture and cultural activities.

culture (cult.) *Cult&Soc* **1** Totality of socially transmitted behavior patterns, arts, beliefs, institutions, and all other products of human work and thought. **2** These patterns, traits, and products considered as the expression of a particular period, class, community, or population. <**Victorian** culture, Indian culture, the culture of poverty> **3** These patterns, traits, and products considered with respect to a particular category, such as a field, subject, or mode of expression. <musical culture, oral culture> **5** Intellectual and artistic activity, and the works produced by it. **6** Development of the intellect through training or education; enlightenment resulting from such training or education. **7** High degree of taste and refinement formed by aesthetic and intellectual training. *Origin* Derived from the preparation and tendance of the earth for the purpose of growing food or other useful plants; consequently, the preparation and tendance of the soul for life; as a further consequence, all that surrounds and addressed us which shapes or otherwise affects the soul. *Also see* **counterculture**, **monoculturalism**, **multicultural**, **multiculturalism**.

Culture & Society *Cult&Soc* One of the four **Outer Forces** of **The Arts Dynamic**

culture shock *Cult&Soc* Condition of confusion and anxiety affecting a person suddenly exposed to an alien culture or foreign **milieu**.

culture war *Cult&Soc* "There is in fact a culture war under way in American society — a conflict far more consequential than most politicians and, I daresay, journalist and academics have supposed."— James Davison Hunter (cult. critic)

CUME *Mktg, Rdio/TV* **Cumulative Audiences Measurement**

cummerbund *Fashn* Broad sash pleated lengthwise, worn with a **tuxedo**.

Cumulative Audiences Measurement (CUME) *Mktg, Rdio/TV* » **CUME**

cur. *Eco&Fin* **currency**

cur. *Genl* current

cura *VisArts* **curator**

curator (cura.) *InfoMgt, Mgt, VisArts* One that manages or oversees, as the administrative director of a museum collection or a library.

Curb Exchange *Eco&Fin* » **AMEX**

curmudgeon *Crit&Eval* Seemingly ill-tempered person full of resentment and stubborn notions but sometimes hiding a kinder nature under a crusty need of privacy. The real hard case is **cantankerous**.

currency (cur.) *Eco&Fin* Money in any form when in actual use as a medium of exchange, esp. circulating paper money.

current accounts (CA) *Eco&Fin* Short-term accounts of assets and liabilities, expected to be converted into cash within one year or less.

current assets *E&F-Acc* Cash or other assets that are expected to be realized in cash, or sold, or used up during a normal operating cycle of the business or within one year whichever is longer. *Also see* **Assets**.

current assets *EntreP* Liquid assets that can be converted into cash with ease.

current debt *EntreP* Borrowed money that must be repaid within 12 months or less.

current exercise value *EntreP* Cash you would receive if you exercised an option immediately.

current liabilities *E&F-Acc* Obligations due to be paid within the normal operating cycle of the business or within one year whichever is longer. *Also see* **long-term liabilities**.

current liabilities *EntreP* All of those obligations that a company expects to pay off during the accounting year. *Ex.* **accounts payable, notes payable**, **taxes payable**. *Also see* **long-term liabilities**.

current ratio *E&F-Acc* Ratio of current assets to current liabilities; measure of **liquidity** (current ratio = current assets/current liabilities)

current ratio *EntreP* Measure of a company's ability to pay dept., which is determined by dividing the company's current assets by its current liabilities.

current start-up disk *InfoMgt* Disk containing the system that the computer is currently using.

curse calendar *Dnce* Record of female dancers' menstrual cycles to indicate possible incapacity and therefore the need for a substitute dancer. *Also see* **swing dancer**.

cursive *VA-Prntng* Type style that imitates handwriting.

cursor *InfoMgt* Blinking or pulsating symbol on the computer screen that indicates: where the next character will appear, which character is to be corrected, a position in which data or graphics are to be entered.

curtain *PerfA&C* Movable screen or drape in a theater or hall that separates the stage from the auditorium or that serves as a backdrop. *Also see* **Stage Curtains**.

curtain *TheatArts* 1 Rising or opening of a theater curtain at the beginning of a performance or an act. 2 Concluding line, speech, or scene of a play or an act. *Also see* **Curtains, Stage Directions**.

curtain call *TheatArts* Appearance of performer(s) at the end of an act (opera) or performance in response to applause. **Stage manager** usu. determines the number of curtain calls. *Also see* **claque, encore, milk**.

curtain line *PerfA&C* Line where the front curtain would be when closed. *Also see* **plaster line**.

curtain raiser *TheatArts* Short play or skit presented before the principal dramatic production.

curtain speech *TheatArts* Talk given in front of the curtain at the conclusion of a theatrical performance.

curtain time *TheatArts* Time at which a theatrical performance begins or is scheduled to begin.

Curtains *ColEntry,PerfA&C* » act —, asbestos —, backdrop, border, cyclorama, draw —, fire —, front —, grand drape, house —, teaser, traveler —, traverse rod

custom label *RecA&S* Small record company that enters into an agreement with a **major record label** (manufacturer/distributor) which will pay some or all of the custom label's **recording costs** and operating expenses in exchange for the right to manufacture and distribute the custom label's product. Monies given to the custom label are considered **advances** against royalties. AFFILIATED LABEL, ASSOCIATED LABEL. *Also see* **major labels**.

customer *Mktg* One who buys goods or services.

customer list *Mktg* List of active or recently active list of customers. Valuable asset that can be leased, rented, or sold. *Also see* **mailing list**.

customer profile *EntreP* Description of potential customers in a target market.

customer satisfaction *Mktg* » customer service

customer service *Mktg* 1 Sum of the various services provided by a marketer to satisfy its customer. <technical aid, information, order taking, complaint handling, refunds, substitutions, credit terms, prompt delivery, etc> 2 Attitude of serving customer well. PATRON SERVICE

customized news *InfoMgt, Journ* News items of topics chosen by the customer selected, collated, and distributed by an Internet service company. — David Barboza (journ.) *Also see* **off-line delivery**.

customs *Eco&Fin* 1 Duty or tax imposed, usu. on imported goods. 2 Governmental agency authorized to collect duties.

customs union *Eco&Fin, Law&Pol* International association organized to eliminate customs restrictions on goods exchanged between member nations and to establish a uniform tariff policy toward nonmember nations.

cut *BcstJourn* » bite

cut *Fashn* Style in which a garment is shaped.

cut *Flm&Vid* 1 To edit film or videotape. 2 To terminate a scene in a movie. 3 Sharp **transition** between scenes, or shots, in a movie.

Cut *InfoMgt* Command in the Edit menu of some computers that removes selected material and places on the **Clipboard**.

cut *RecA&S* Single selection of a **phonorecord**

cut *VisArts* Print made from an engraved block or printing plate.

cutaways *BcstJourn* Short (:01 to: 03) shots inserted into an interview sequence to draw the point of view away from the single close-up shot. These shots are usu. reverse-angle or medium shots and allow a videotape editor to compress an interview during the editing process.

cut and paste *InfoMgt* Computer command to move something from one place to another place in the same or different document.

cut from the bottom *Journ* Editing process whereby the (copy) editor cuts the article to required length from the bottom, i.e., the least important paragraphs.

cut in *Dnce* To interrupt a dancing couple in order to dance with one of them.

cut time *MusArts* **Duple** or quadruple **meter** with the half note being the unit of time. <2/2 meter>

cut to the chase *Crit&Eval, Flm&Vid* Get to the point. *Origin* From silent movie days, a wish to get to the exciting part: good guys chasing bad guys or vice-versa.

cutoff *also* **cut-off** *MusArts* **Conductor's** signal indicating a stop or break in playing or singing.

cutoffs *Fashn* Pants, usu. blue jeans, made into shorts by cutting off part of the legs (of the pants)

cutout *Mktg, RecA&S* Recording no longer current and whose remaining stock is sold at a discounted price. *Origin* Item cut out of catalog.

cutter *Fashn* Person, device, or machine that cuts, esp. in tailoring.

cutter *Flm&Vid* 1 Editor. 2 Individual who is responsible for the mechanical rather than the creative elements of editing.

cutter *RecA&S* Editor of music recorded for film or tape **synchronization**.

cutting contest *MusArts* 1 Two or more jazz musicians trying to out-improvise the other; pushing one another to excel. 2 Competition between two or more New Orleans **brass bands** trying "to literally play another off the streets by playing louder or more brilliantly or with sweeter tones." — Eileen Southern BUCKING CONTEST *Also see* **chase chorus, trading fours**.

cutting to continuity *Flm&Vid* » **continuity**

cutting edge *Crit&Eval* Position of greatest advancement or importance. FOREFRONT

CX *BcstJourn* Script abbreviation for a commercial in a newscast.

cya (see ya) *InfoMgt* See You Later.

cybercierge *InfoMgt* One who supervises a building's telecommunications facilities on behalf of the residents. *Also see* **T1 line**.

cybernetics *InfoMgt, Sci&Tech* Theoretical study of control processes in electronic, mechanical, and biological systems, esp. mathematical analysis of the flow of data in such systems.

cyberspace *InfoMgt* 1 Where you go when you use your computer and modem to communicate with others. When you are online, you are in **cyberspace**. 2 Clean and private new world where those who can afford it live online with other fascinatingly anonymous people, and never have to smell the roses. ELECTRONIC COMMERCE

cycle *Flm&Vid* (animation) Series of animated drawings or cels that can be photographed over and over to create the illusion of continuing, repeated action.

cycles per second (cps) *Rdio/TV, RecA&S* » cps

cyclorama, cyc *PerfA&C* 1 Very large **drop** rigged at the back of the stage, with curved arms enclosing the stage. Usually designed to create sky effects and a feeling of depth and open space. *Also see* **Stage Curtains**.

cyclorama *VisArts* Large composite picture placed on the interior walls of a cylindrical room so as to appear in natural perspective to a spectator standing in the center of the room. May represent a dramatic, historic event. <*The Burning of Atlanta*>

cylinder *InfoMgt* In a **disk pack**, the tracks on all disk surfaces that may be read without re-positioning the read/write head.

cynic *Crit&Eval* disbeliever. *Also see* **skeptic**.

cynical *Ethcs&Phil* 1 Assuming a negative view of human nature, forecasting the worst outcome from any human endeavor. 2 Scornful of the virtue or motives of another. 3 Contentiously and bitterly mocking. *Origin* Name of an ancient Greek philosophical sect holding virtue to be the only good and noted for its sharp rejection of worldly pursuits and possessions. "No matter how cynical you get, it is impossible to keep up." — Lily Tomlin (1939-, stage/film/TV act., standup comic, social critic) *Also see* **skeptical**.

- D -

D&B *Eco&Fin, Mgt, Mktg* **Dun & Bradstreet. Company** that – as one of its financial information services – combines credit information obtained from commercial firms with data collected from their **creditors**, then makes it available to subscribers.

D.A.T.E. *TheatArts* **Deaf Audience Theatre Experience**

D.C. *MusArts* **da capo**

D.P. *Flm&Vid* **Director of Photography**

D/L *InfoMgt* » **download**

DA *InfoMgt* **desk accessory**

da capo (D.C.) *MusArts* **Repeat a passage.** *Also see* **Music Directions.**

dabbler *Crit&Eval* One who engaged in an activity superficially or without serious intent. *Also see* **dilettante.**

Dada, Dadaism *LitArts, VisArts* Western European literary and artistic movement (ca. 1916-23, in reaction to the madness of WWI) that sought authentic reality through the abolition of traditional cultural and aesthetic forms by comic derision in which irrationality, chance, and intuition were the guiding principles. *Also see* **anti-art, Art Movements and Periods.**

dada, dadaism *TheatArts* Nihilistic movement in art and literature founded by Tristan Tzara during World War L which protested against logic, restraint social convention and literature itself. It influenced **surrealism** which followed in the 1920s. The "happenings" of the 1960s and '70s are also direct descendants.

dailies *Flm&Vid* Selected footage from the previous day's shoot evaluated by the director and **cinematographer** before more filming takes place. RUSHES

dailies *Journ* Newspapers published every day or every weekday.

Daily News Record (DNR) *Fashn, Journ* » **DNR**

dais *PerfA&C* Raised platform for speakers or honored guests. *Also see* **lectern, rostrum.**

daisy chain *InfoMgt* Chain of **peripheral** devices that connect to the computer through a single port.

daisy-wheel printer *InfoMgt* Impact printer that uses a plastic or metal disk with printed characters along its edge. Disk rotates until the required character is brought before a hammer that strikes it against a ribbon.

damage suit *HR&LR* Lawsuit instituted by an employee or employer seeking to recover damages from the other for an alleged breach of a **collective bargaining** contract.

dance *Crit&Eval, Journ* Skillfully avoid answering the question. <He danced around the root question: "Did he inhale?">

dance *Dnce* **1** Series of rhythmical motions and steps, usu. to music. **2** Art of dancing. **3** Gathering of people for dancing. **4** One round or turn of dancing.

dance captain *Dnce* Rehearses the **chorus** line for the **choreographer.**

dance company *Dnce* **troupe** of dancers

dance hall, dancehall *Dnce* Building or part of a building with facilities for dancing.

dance marathon *Cult&Soc, Dnce* **Great Depression**-time dehumanizing entertainment where couples would dance virtually nonstop for days and nights while audiences would cheer and jeer and throw loose change at the contestants. Last surviving couple would win a cash prize, like $1,000. [See the movie, *They Shoot Horses, Don't They* (1981)].

Dance Masters of America (DMA) *Dnce* International Organization of Certified [Dance] Teachers

dance music *MusArts* Musical or rhythmical accompaniment composed or played for dancing. *Also see* **hip hop, house music.**

dance notation *Dnce* Method, originating in 16th century, of recording dances.

Dance Theater Workshop (DTW) *Dnce* "Founded in 1965... as a **choreographers'** collective devoted to the sponsorship and practical support of colleagues and early career artists." >www.dtw.org< *Also see* **NPN.**

Dance/USA *Dnce* "As a national service organization, [it] works with its membership of professional dance companies, artists, presenters, service organizations and individuals supportive of the field."

Dances *ColEntry, Dnce* » **allemand, ballet, ballroom —, body popping, Black Bottom, bolero, boogie, bossa nova, bounce, box step, break —, breakdown, buck —, cakewalk, bugalú, cha-cha-cha, Charleston, class act, country —, disco, drambalet, flamenco, folk —, galop, habanera, jazz —, jazz tap, jig, jitterbug, Juba, jungle, Lindy, lundu, mambo, maxixe, merengue, moshing, one-step, polka, ragtime, ring —, rumba, salsa, shadow —, shag, shimmy, skanking, slam dancing, slow drag, soft-shoe, tango, tap —, tea —, trance dancing, turkey trot, twist; two-step, walk around —, waltz.**

dancewear *Dnce, Fashn* Clothing such as leotards and warmup suits that are worn for dance practice and exercising.

dandy *Fashn* Man who affects extreme elegance in clothes and manners; a fop.

danseur *ArtPerf, Dnce* Male ballet dancer. *Also see* **danseuse, premier danseur.**

danseuse (dahn-sirs, Fr.) *Dnce* female dancer *Also see* **danseur.**

Danto, Arthur C. (1924-, philos., tchr., art crit/hist.) *Crit&Eval Also see* **artphilohistcritisophery, asceticism, photographists.**

DAPME *Genl Dictionary for Artists, Performers, Managers.& Entrepreneurs*

DAR *Cult&Soc* Daughters of the American Revolution » **Anderson, Marian**

daredevil *Crit&Eval* One who is recklessly bold.

Dark Ages *Cult&Soc* Period from the sacking of Rome in 476 and ending about the 10th century, characterized by intellectual stagnation, widespread ignorance and poverty. *Also see* **Middle Ages.**

dark houses *Cult&Soc, TheatArts* » **black theaters**

dark theater *PerfA&C* Not giving performances.

dark tone *MusArts* Melancholy instrumental or vocal tone

DASD *InfoMgt* **Direct Access Storage Device; peripheral** storage device where data may be stored either randomly or sequentially. This device enables the computer to retrieve information directly without having to scan a series of records.

DAT *iMedia* **1** Digital audio tape. **2** Digital audio-recording-and-playback system developed by Sony.

DAT *RecA&S* **Digital Audio Tape** » **digital**

data *iMedia, InfoMgt* Raw facts from which information is created. "Data is to information as information is to knowledge. Computers do not know anything, we do." — Anon

Data Base Administrator (DBA) *InfoMgt* » **DBA**

data base *InfoMgt* Collection of related files

Data Base Management System (DBMS) *InfoMgt* » **DBMS**

data communications *EntreP* Exchange of data among remote computers.

data compression *InfoMgt* Saves computer storage space by eliminating unnecessary data and space to reduce file size.

data density *iMedia* Amount of information contained within a graphic relative to its dimensions.

data design *iMedia* **1** process of organizing and optimizing the storage and retrieval of large quantities of data. **2** System that stores and retrieves data.

data diddling *InfoMgt* Computer crime involving the illegal manipulation of data before or during input.

data graphic *iMedia* **1** Graphic designed to convey information, and which does not distract from that purpose. **2** Visual representations of data that aid understanding.

data landscape *iMedia* Visualizing data as an environment.

data map *iMedia* Image that represents multiple forms of information

data mining *iMedia* Discovering new or unusual patterns.

data processing (DP) *InfoMgt* Steps involved in collecting, manipulating, and distributing data.

data rate *iMedia* Amount of data that can be moved or copied from one source to another during a specific amount of time (i.e., per second)

data set *InfoMgt* Collection of related computer records

data-ink *iMedia* Graphic elements which are indispensable; they provide integral visual information. Non-redundant ink arranged in response to variation in the numbers represented. *Also see* **data-ink ratio.**

data-ink ratio *iMedia* Formula dividing the amount of data-ink (integral ink needed to convey a concept) by the total ink used to print a graphic. *Also see* **data-ink.**

database *InfoMgt* Collection of data arranged for ease and speed of retrieval by a computer.

database *iMedia* One or more large structured sets of persistent data, usually associated with software to update and query the data. A simple database might be a single file containing many records, each of which contains the same set of fields where each field is a certain fixed width. *Also see* **datatype,field, record, table.**

database management program *EntreP* Application software used to manage files of related data.

datacom handler *InfoMgt* » **concentrator, multiplexer**

datastream *iMedia* Information or data streaming from one source to another.

datatype *iMedia* Programming: the category assigned to a piece of a data. Common categories include: **Boolean, number, string**.

date *MusArts* 1 Engagement for a performance. 2 Recording session.

dateline *Journ* Phrase at the beginning of a newspaper article that gives the date and place of its origin.

dating bar *Cult&Soc* » **singles bar**

Daughters of the American Revolution (DAR) *Cult&Soc* » **Anderson, Marian**

David O. Selznick Lifetime Achievement Award for Motion Pictures *Flm&Vid* Highest honor bestowed by the **PGA**.

Davis, Miles (aka "Miles," 1926-91, jazz tp., bndldr., arr.-comp.) *ArtPerf, MusArts* "Unique figure in jazz because his creativity and his influence as both player and conceptualist were sustained for more than four decades, an example which introduced the idea of permanent conceptual development into the jazz life." — Ian Carr (jazz tp., critic) <Albums: *Birth of the Cool* (1949-50, Capitol), *Milestones* (1958, Columbia), *In a Silent Way* (1969, Columbia), *Bitches Brew* (1969, Columbia)> *Also see* **cool jazz, Harmon mute, silence.**

day and date release *Flm&Vid* Same day, same date opening of a movie in two or more theaters in a given market.

day player *ArtPerf, Flm&Vid, Rdio/TV* 1 Re movies: Cast member contracted by the day rather than a more extended period of time. 2 Television performer (usu. in **soaps**) with five or more lines. One level below a **contract player**, one level above an **under five player**. 3 Re certain TV shows: cast member performing in a single episode of a series.

day-for-night shooting *Flm&Vid* Scenes filmed during day time with special filters to suggest nighttime settings.

day-of-performance ads *Mktg* Ads that run in media on the same day of the advertised performance.

day-time radio-television *Rdio/TV* Programming from nine in the morning to four in the afternoon dominated by soaps, game shows, and **talk shows**.

daybook (DB, D.B.) *Eco&Fin, Genl* Book in which daily transactions are recorded; a diary. *Also see* **journal.**

dazzle *Crit&Eval* To amaze, overwhelm, or bewilder with spectacular display. <**Charlie Parker's** improvisations>

dB *iMedia* » **decibels**

dB *RecA&S* **decibel**

DB *Rdio/TV* delayed broadcast

DBA *InfoMgt* **Data Base Administrator**; the person who has charge of maintaining the data base.

dbl. *MusArts, TheatArts, RecA&S* **double**

DBMS *InfoMgt* **Data Base Management System**; software used to maintain data base files.

DBS *Rdio/TV* **direct broadcast satellite**

DDE *InfoMgt* **dynamic data exchange** Communications link used in **Windows** NT and **OS/2** that allows two or more programs to exchange information and commands.

DDP *InfoMgt* **Distributed Data Processing**; a hardware **configuration** wherein computing power is resident throughout the **hierarchy** of a company.

de facto *LegAsp* Denotes a thing done in fact but without strict legal authority as contrasted with **de jure**, which denotes a thing done according to law.

De Forest, Lee (1873-1961) *Rdio/TV* Electrical engineer who invented the **triode electron tube** (1906, patented 1907) that made possible the amplification and detection of radio waves. He also developed first practical radio telephone (1906), and originated radio news broadcasts (1916.)

de jure *LegAsp* Denotes a thing done according to law. *Also see* **de facto.**

de luxe, deluxe *Crit&Eval* Elegant and luxurious

de rigueur (de rig-oor, Fr.) *Cult&Soc* Required by current fashion or custom; socially obligatory.

deaccession *VisArts* Formal process to discard and derecord an item as a collection object. *Also see* **accession.**

dead air *Rdio/TV* Unintended interruption in a broadcast during which there is no sound.

dead mike *RecA&S* Microphone turned off or not working.

dead *RecA&S* minimal **reverb**

dead seats *PerfA&C* Seats outside of the **sight line** or behind a pillar or post.

dead side *RecA&S* Side of the microphone not picking up sound.

dead spot *RecA&S* Geographic area where cellular phone, radio, and TV reception is poor.

dead-hung *PerfA&C* System of non-movable pipes – instead of a **grid** and fly system – from which equipment and scenery is hung.

deaden *Crit&Eval* To render less intense, sensitive, or vigorous.

deaden *RecA&S* To make soundproof by wall or ceiling tiles that deaden sound.

deadpan *ArtPerf, PA-Variety* Comedian who shows no facial expression. <Buster Keaton (Joseph Francis Keaton, 1895-1966, screen act., dir.) Wrote, directed, and starred in silent film classics. <*The Navigator* (1924), *The General* (1926)>

Deaf Audience Theatre Experience (D.A.T.E.) *TheatArts* » **D.A.T.E.**

deal *EntreP* 1 The agreement between a seller and buyer of a venture that outlines non compete agreements, methods of payment, or consulting arrangements. 2 Arrangement between an entrepreneur and venture capitalist to finance ventures.

deal *LegAsp* Contract or an agreement, esp. one mutually beneficial; a business transaction. *Also see* **Contracts.**

deal breaker *LegAsp* Issue in negotiation that cannot be settled, thus terminating the deal.

dealer (dlr.) *Mktg* One engaged in buying and selling, at retail; **retailer.**

debenture *EntreP* Corporate bond that is not backed by the collateral of the company.

debit *E&F-Acc* 1 The left side of an account. 2 Item of debt as recorded in an account.

debits *E&F-Acc* Side of the **balance sheet** that reflects the amount of money the company owes plus the **owners equity**.

debonair *Crit&Eval* 1 **suave; urbane.** 2 carefree; jaunty

Debt financing *EntreP* Financing in exchange for interest payments, usually granted by banks.

debt ratio *E&F-Acc* Total debt divided by total assets, proportion of assets financed by debt (debt ratio = debt/total assets) *Also see* **leverage ratios.**

debt ratio *EntreP* Percentage of assets financed with debt, measured by dividing total liabilities by total assets.

debt to equity ratio *E&F-Acc* Shows the proportion of the company financed by **creditors** in comparison to that financed by the owner. Debt to equity = total liabilities ÷ **owner's equity**.

debt-to-equity ratio *EntreP* Ratio that indicates what percentage of the owner's equity is debt. Formula is total liabilities divided by owner's equity.

debt-to-total-assets ratio *EntreP* Ratio that indicates what percentage of a business' assets is owned by creditors. Formula is total liabilities divided by total assets.

debt/net worth ratio *E&F-Acc* Ratio of debt to equity, debt divided by equity (debt/net worth ratio = debt/equity) *Also see* **leverage ratios.**

debugging *iMedia, InfoMgt* Process of removing **syntax** and **logic** errors from a **computer program**.

dec *MusArts* **decrescendo**

decadence *Crit&Eval, Ethcs&Phil* 1 Relating to a deterioration or decline in morals or art. 2 decay

Decadence (Fr.) *LitArts* Literary movement of late 19th century France and England characterized by refined aestheticism, **artifice**, and the quest for new sensations. *Also see* **Art Movements and Periods.**

decadents *LitArts, VisArts* Name loosely applied to the late 19th century British artists and writers who emphasized the **morbid** and **macabre** elements of human emotion. They believed that art should exist for its own sake.

decatenate *InfoMgt* Separate combined terms into two or more independent parts. *Also see* **concatenate.**

decay *RecA&S* Manner in which a **sound wave** stops. *Also see* **attack, internal dynamic, sustain.**

decibel (dB) *RecA&S* Number used to measure the level of air pressure caused by **sound waves**.

decibel *iMedia* one tenth of a **bel**

decision support system *InfoMgt* Integrated system of computer models that are used to perform "what if" types of analyses.

deck *PerfA&C* » **stage**

deco *Fashn* » **art deco**

decode *InfoMgt* 1 To convert from code into **plain text**. 2 To convert machine language into a character, routine, or program.

décolleté *Fashn* low neck line

deconstruction *Crit&Eval, iMedia* 1 View and method arising from the work of **Jacques Derrida** in the 1960s, which originates in dissatisfaction with our inability to grapple with things directly, since we always reach things through language. Thus, we are "trapped" in language, and though we can manipulate things physically, our understanding of them is always conditioned and limited by language. This view leads to a method for the investigation of texts by painstakingly searching out every possible meaning, sense, or **nuance** borne by the words which make them up, and every use in which those words participate, which in turn serves to "deconstruct" the texts, since every attempt at stating an overall meaning for any text is readily demolished by the unprincipled collections of confused meanings which comprise it. Neither principles nor the author's intentions can rescue the text, since they too are inevitably conceived and stated in language, and are equally subject to deconstruction. 2 Philosophical movement and theory of literary criticism that questions traditional assumptions about certainty, identity, and truth. "Deconstructionism is the last, predictable, stage in the suppression of reason and the denial of the possibility of truth in the name of philosophy" — **Allan Bloom**

deconstructionism *TheatArts* Movement in philosophy, and subsequently, in literary studies, associated with the work of French philosopher, Jacques Derrida (1930-) In deconstructive philosophy, the "presence" of metaphysical categories is questioned through a process that interrogates, suspends, or "de-constructs" the way in which those categories have been produced.

decor *Crit&Eval* Decoration. Decorative style or scheme, as of a room.

decor *PerfA&C* stage setting; scenery

decorate *VisArts* To furnish, provide, or adorn with something ornamental; **embellish**.

decoration *VisArts* Act, process, technique, or art of decorating. *Also see* **style**.

decorum *TheatArts* Notion associated with neoclassicism that the action and the subject matter (idealized) Language (heightened), and moral propriety (elevated), should be stylistically integrated and unified.

decree *LegAsp* Authoritative order having the force of law. *Also see* **consent decree**.

decrescendo (dec) *MusArts* » **diminuendo** *Also see* **Music Directions**.

deductions *Eco&Fin* Amounts that are or may be deducted, usu. from a pay check to pay or repay advances, payroll taxes, pension benefits, etc.

deed *LegAsp* Written document for the transfer of land or other real property from one person to another. *Also see* **title**.

deejay (DJ) *MusArts,. Rdio/TV, RecA&S* » **disc jockey**. DJ

deep navigation *iMedia* Navigation allowing in-depth exploration of content in depth; usu. only a few options, but each option has extensive coverage. In contrast: broad navigation.

deep sell *Mktg* Advertising beyond traditional media. <design, corporate identity, annual reports, entertainment marketing, etc>

defamation *LegAsp* Damage to the reputation, character, or good name by **slander** or **libel**.

default *Eco&Fin, LegAsp* Failure to fulfill a legal obligation. <meet repayment terms, make a required court appearance.

default *InfoMgt* Particular value for a variable that is assigned automatically by an operating system and remains in effect unless canceled or overridden by the operator.

default setting *InfoMgt* Value used by a computer system when no other value is specified.

defendant *LegAsp* Party against which an action is brought. *Also see* **plaintiff**.

deferred expenses *E&F-Acc* Any prepaid expenses recorded as a

prepaid asset. <prepaid advertising, prepaid rent>

deferred gift *Fndng* Creation of a vested interest in property for the benefit of a **nonprofit**. Property's current value is determined by actuarial tables.

deferred giving *Fndng* Bequests and gifts realized after a donor's death.

deferred income taxes *E&F-Acc* Difference between the Income Taxes Expense and the Current Income Taxes Payable.

deferred payment *Eco&Fin* No payment until product or project is successfully marketed.

deferred payment gift annuity *Fndng* Donor makes a substantial gift before retirement, and in return receives a guaranteed lifetime income.

deficit financing *Flm&Vid* Networks pay 70 to 80 percent of the cost of making a **pilot**, the studio covers the remainder.

deficit spending *Eco&Fin, Law&Pol* Spending of public funds obtained by borrowing rather than by taxation. *Also see* **voodoo economics**.

degradation *InfoMgt* State in which a computer operates when some of its memory or **peripherals** are not available.

degrade *RecA&S* Loss of fidelity. <**analog** signal>

deictic gesture *iMedia* » **deixis**

deixis *iMedia* Gesture that links the subject of a spoken sentence with a visual reference (aka **deictic gesture**)

déja vu *Crit&Eval* Illusion of having already experienced something actually being experienced for the first time.

delayed broadcast (DB) *Rdio/TV* Program taped by a network affiliated station for broadcast at some future time.

delegate *Mgt* One authorized to act as representative for another; a deputy or an agent. *Also see* **deputy**.

delegation of authority *EntreP* Granting to subordinates the right to act or make decisions.

delimiter *iMedia* Programming: separates one thing from another. Ex: less-than and greater-than symbols are used to indicate when **XHTML** tags begin and end - separating tags from content.

deliverable *iMedia* Any task that produces a result for an interactive product's development, usu. due at a specific time.

delivery *PerfA&C* Act or manner of speaking or singing.

delivery *RecA&S* Actual delivery of a full **mixed**, edited, and leadered master tape to the record company.

delivery system *Mktg* Means or procedure for providing a product or service to the public. *Also see* **distribution**, **JIT**.

Delphi Internet Services *InfoMgt* Online information service. *Also see* **Online Information Services**.

delphi method *EntreP* Qualitative forecasting method which uses a panel of experts to obtain a consensus of opinion.

demagogue *Crit&Eval* Wannabe leader who seeks power by means of impassioned appeals to the emotions and prejudices of the populace. *Also see* **racism**.

demand *InfoMgt* Coding technique in which a command to read or write is initiated as the need for a new block of data occurs, thus eliminating the need to store data.

demand *Mktg* Amount of goods and services that consumers are willing to buy at a given price.

demand curve *EntreP* Curve that is obtained by horizontally summing the quantity demanded at various prices in the marketplace.

demands *Mktg* Demands are **wants** for specific products backed up by an ability to pay and willingness to buy them. <One **needs** food, one **wants** a hamburger, one demands a double-decker whopper with cheese, onion, tomato, and mayo>

demeanor *Crit&Eval* Way in which a person behaves; **deportment**.

demi-plié (demi-plee-ay, Fr.) *Dnce* (Ballet) Half-bending of the knees without raising the heels off the ground at any time. *Also see* **plié**.

demi-soloist *Dnce* Possibility a step above the **corps de ballet** and a step below the soloists.

demo love *Mktg* Occurs when a client prefers the **demo** to the finished commercial.

demo *Mktg* Demonstration of a product or service meant to motivate a transaction.

demo *MusArts, PerfA&C, RecA&S* Brief audio or video recording used to illustrate the qualities of a musician, arranger-composer, performer, or recording engineer. *Also see* **audition**.

démodé *Fashn* No longer in fashion; outmoded.

demodulation *InfoMgt* Process of changing a continuous (**analog**) signal to a discrete (**digital**) signal.

demographic edition *Journ* Version of an issue of a magazine distributed only to a portion of its total circulation according to demographic characteristics. Usually only the advertising content is changed to focus on a particular market.

demographic variables *EntreP* Specific characteristics that describe customers and their purchasing power.

demographics *iMedia, Mktg* Characteristics of human populations and population segments, esp. when used to identify consumer markets. <age, sex, race, income level, education, marital status, geographical location> *Also see* **psychographics**.

demotic *Crit&Eval* Of or relating to the common people; popular. >demotic entertainments.<

denouement *TheatArts* Part of the play between the climax and the conclusion of the script and the performance, the resolution or unraveling of a **plot** so that an equilibrium is usu. restored.

denouement, dénouement *LitArts* Literally, the "unknotting," the final unraveling of the plot following the climax.

dense *Crit&Eval* **1** Difficult to understand because of complexity or obscurity. <a dense novel> **2** Slow to catch on; stupid, thickheaded.

density *InfoMgt* Number of units of useful information contained within a **linear** dimension.

deotonic *Ethcs&Phil* Approach to ethics associated with **Immanuel Kant**, based on the categorical imperative, and involving a firm system of duties.

department (dept.) *Mgt* **1** Distinct, usu. specialized division of a large organization. **2** Division of a business specializing in a particular product or service. **3** Division of a school or college dealing with a particular field of knowledge. <Management Dept>

department (dept.) *Mktg* Section of a department store offering a particular product line or service. <cosmetics, auto repair, eye examination>

deportment *Crit&Eval* Manner of personal conduct; behavior.

deposit *LegAsp, Mgt* Usually 50% of the **guarantee** called for in the **engagement contract** is paid by the employer to the artist, or the artist's agent, to seal the deal.

deposit of copyrighted works *IntelProp* » **copyright registration**

deposition *LegAsp* Testimony under oath <a statement by a witness written down or recorded for use in court at a later date>

Depository *InfoMgt* » **Library of Congress**. *Also see* **copyright registration**.

depreciation *EntreP* Dollar value assigned to the wearing out of a business asset during its useful life.

depreciation *E&F-Acc* **1** Expense associated with spreading or allocating the cost of a **plant asset** over its useful life. **2 Allowance** made for a loss in value of property. <age, wear, or market conditions>

depreciation expense *EntreP* Costs related to a fixed asset, such as a building or equipment, distributed over a period of time.

depression *Eco&Fin* Period of drastic decline in a national or international economy, characterized by decreasing business activity, falling prices, severe unemployment and increased human misery. *Also see* **Great Depression**.

depth *Crit&Eval* **1** Most profound or intense part or stage. <the depth of despair> **2** Intellectual complexity or penetration; profundity. <a novel of great depth>

depth cues *iMedia* Sources of information about **three dimensional** space or shapes.

depth *MusArts* lowness in **pitch**

depth of field *iMedia* Zone of acceptable sharpness in front of and behind the subject on which the lens is focused; dependent on three factors: aperture, focal length, and focused distance.

depth of field *Flm&Vid* Depth of a shot as measured from the nearest point from the camera at which an object is acceptably in **focus** to the furthest point.

depth *VisArts* **1** Measurement or sense of distance from an observation point, such as **linear** perspective in painting. **2** Degree of richness or intensity. <depth of color>

deputy *Mgt* One appointed or empowered to act for another. *Also see* **delegate**.

derivative *Crit&Eval* Copied or adapted from others.

derivative work *IntelProp* A new version <u>of</u> a copyrighted work derived from another copyrighted work. <a movie from a novel, a movie from a play>

dernier cri (dern-yeah cree, Fr. for "latest cry") *Fashn* The latest thing; the newest fashion.

Derrida, Jacques (1930-, Fr. philos.) *Ethcs&Phil* Concerned with the **deconstruction** of Western rationalist thought.

dervish *Crit&Eval* One that possesses frenzied energy, sometimes expressed in whirling dances. <whirling dervish>

descant *MusArts* **1** Highest part sung in part music. **2** Ornamental melody or **counterpoint** sung or played above a theme.

descender *iMedia, VA-Prntng* Part of the lowercase letters that extends below the other lowercase letters. <g, p, q> *Also see* **ascender**.

descending *MusArts* Moving downward on a musical scale. *Also see* **ascending**.

descriptive title *Journ* Should easily answer the question: "What is this article about?"

design brief *Mktg* Distills marketing strategy to its simplest form.

design guide *iMedia* » **style guide**

design *LitArts* "I found out afterward that not only each book had to have a design, but the whole output or sum of a writer's work had to have a design." — Malcolm Cowley (1898-1989, lit. critic, ed.)

design *Mktg* To form a plan <design a marketing plan>

design *VisArts* **1** Decorative or artistic work. **2** sketch or drawing. **3** Visual composition. "It doesn't cost any more to produce a good design than it does to produce lousy design.... Market research perpetuates bad design." — John Loring (Tiffany mktg. exec.) *Also see* **graphic artist**.

design patent *EntreP* Registered protection of a product and its inseparable parts.

designated market area (DMA) *Mktg, Rdio/TV* » **DMA**

designee *Fndng* One who has been designated. <The spouse was designated to receive the income from the **charitable lead trust**>

designer (dsgnr.) *Fashn* Bearing the name, signature, or identifying pattern of a specific designer.

desk accessory (DA) *InfoMgt* Small application program useful to a computer system. <alarm clock, calendar, calculator>

desk checking *InfoMgt* Method used to check program **logic** manually, prior to entering in a computer.

desk *Journ* Specific department of a newspaper. <city desk>

desk *MusInstr* music stand in an orchestra

desktop *InfoMgt* Working environment on the computer — the menu bar and the background area on the screen. Several documents and programs can be open on the desktop at the same time. *Also see* **window**. FIRST SCREEN

desktop publishing (DTP) *InfoMgt* Design and production of publications. <newsletters, trade journals, or brochures, using computers with graphics capability>

destination *also* **destination disk** *InfoMgt* Disk or folder that receives a copied or translated file.

detail *Fashn, VisArts* Small elaborated element of a work of art, craft, or design.

detection shows *Rdio/TV* Popular type of television network programming. <Magnum, P.I.; Murder, She Wrote> *Also see* **Television Shows**.

deus ex machina *Crit&Eval, PerfA&C* In the Greek theater, a "god from a machine." mechanical device used for the intervention of some outside agent to resolve the **plot**. As a general term. It refers to the intervention of any outside force to bring about a desired end.

devaluation *EntreP* Decrease in the exchange rate to which a currency is pegged in a fixed rate system.

develop *Crit&Eval* To cause gradually to acquire a specific role, function, or form. <develop a theme, develop a plot>

development *Flm&Vid. TV* Process of assembling the elements of a film, video, radio, or TV show, such as: funding, scripting, casting, distribution, etc.

development *Fndng* Total process of institutional fund-raising, inc. public relations. *Also see* **DOD**.

development *MusArts* Elaboration of a theme with rhythmic and harmonic variations.

development board *Fndng* Committee of trustees or directors charged with overseeing development operations.

development committee *Fndng* » **development board**

development deal *Flm&Vid* Usually a pre-production agreement between producer and screenwriter or script owner to develop a plot and characterizations that will meet the producer's concept and marketing strategy. If the deal works out the production phase is covered in separate contracts. [Writers describe this often agonizing and frustrating experience as **development hell**.] *Also see* **Contracts**.

development hell *Flm&Vid* » **development deal**

development site *iMedia* Development team's collection of information about a product's progress.

device *InfoMgt* Any **peripheral** connected to a **PC**. <mouse, printer, buffers/spoolers, expanded memory boards, etc>

Devil's music *Cult&Soc, MusArts* What some black churchgoers used to call the **blues**.

devotee *Crit&Eval* One who is strongly devoted to something. *Also see* **aficionado**, **fan**.

Dewey, John (1859-1952, philos., educ.) *Crit&Eval, Ethcs&Phil* Leading exponent of philosophical **pragmatism** and rejected traditional methods of teaching by **rote** in favor of a broad-based system of practical experience. <*Democracy and Education* (1916), *Logic* (1938)>

DGA *Flm&Vid* **Director's Guild of America**. *Also see* **Directors, Guilds & Unions**. Represents 10,000+ members in U.S. and abroad in theatrical, industrial, educational, and documentary films, as well as television live, filmed and taped radio, videos, and commercials.

DGI *ArtPerf, HR&LR, LitArts* The **Dramatists Guild, Inc.**, founded in 1920, has a membership of about 7,500 playwrights, composers, and lyricists whose works are performed on the live stage. Its members enjoy the protection of the Guild's various production contracts, verification of box office royalty procedures, and other services. *Also see* **Copyright-Related Organizations**, **Guilds & Unions**.

Diaghilev, Serge Pavlovich (1872-1929, Russ. ballet **impresario**) *Mgt, Dnce* Founded the **Ballets Russes**.

Dial *Flm&Vid, Sci&Tech* Device used in film and TV market research. Like a paddle with a small dial at the top and an **L.E.D.** Used to get instantaneous feedback on how screeners are responding to the show, moment by moment. Doesn't exactly tell what works, only what doesn't.

dialect *TheatArts* Geographic, socioeconomic, or ethnocultural variety of a spoken language.

dialectic (dial.) *Crit&Eval* **1** Process involving the interplay of two elements such that a new element emerges. This new element, in turn, comes into comparable relation with a fourth element, leading to a fifth element, and so on. **2** Process of change whereby a thesis is transformed into an antithesis, and the two resolved into a synthesis. — **Georg Wilhelm Friedrich Hegel 3** Process of change through the conflict of opposing forces: "force A vs. force B = force C." — **Karl Marx**

dialog box *InfoMgt* Interactive window allowing a user to respond to a program. Dialog box typically contains controls such as check boxes or option (radio) buttons.

dialogue (dial.), **dialog** (dial.) *LitArts* Literary work written in the form of a conversation. <**Plato's** dialogues>

dialogue (dial.), **dialog** (dial.) *MusArts* Composition or **passage** for two or more parts, suggestive of conversational interplay.

dialogue (dial.), **dialog** (dial.) *TheatArts* **1** Conversation between characters in a drama or narrative. **2** The lines or passages in a script that are intended to be spoken.

dialogue *iMedia* human communication via an interface or interactive media

dialogue coach *Flm&Vid* One who helps actors with their **dialogue** before the scene is filmed or taped.

dialogue replacement *Flm&Vid* Replacement of poor quality sound with studio quality by the actors **lip syncing** dialogue.

dialogue *TheatArts* **Lines** spoken by the characters in a play.

diaspora *Cult&Soc* Dispersion of an originally **homogeneous** people or entity, such as a language or a culture. <Jews and black Africans>

Diaspora *Cult&Soc* Dispersion of Jews outside of Israel from the sixth century B.C., when they were exiled to Babylonia.

diatonic accordion *MusInstr* » **zydeco music**

diatonic *MusArts* Using only the eight tones of a standard major or minor scale without **chromatic** deviations.

diatonic scale *MusArts* » **do, re, me, fa, sol, la, ti, do**. *Also see* **keynote**.

diatribe *Crit&Eval* Bitter, abusive denunciation

dichotomy *Crit&Eval* Division into two contradictory parts or opinions. *Also see* **duality**.

diction *LitArts, MusArts* Degree of **clarity** and distinctness of pronunciation in speech or singing; enunciation. *Also see* **analysis of tragedy**.

didactic *Crit&Eval* Inclined to teach or moralize excessively.

didactically *Crit&Eval* Inclined to teach or moralize excessively. *Also see* **naturalism** (*Flm&Vid*)

diesis (dye-ee-sis) *LitArts, VA-Prntng* » **double dagger** (‡)

Difference Engine No 1 *iMedia, InfoMgt, Sci&Tech* Early 19th century mechanical calculator, a forerunner of the modern computer invented by **Charles Babbage**. *Also see* **Ada**, **Ada Augusta Byron**.

differential microphone *RecA&S* Noise-cancelling **mic** that works on the principle that sound pressure on the front of the mic produces electrical output while equal pressures on both sides of the mic cancels output. *Also see* **Microphones**.

differentiated marketing *Mktg* Strategy developing different products and/or marketing programs for each market segment that the organization plans to serve.

differentiation *Mktg* Advertisement that stresses the differences between product A or B. UNIQUENESS

diffusers *Flm&Vid* **1** Fine nets, muslin or granulated or grooved glass positioned in front of the lens; **2** Cellular diffusing materials, such as spun glass, placed in front of the lamp. Both decrease the intensity of the lights.

dig *Crit&Eval* To like, enjoy, or appreciate. <"They really dig our music and, daddy, I dig swinging for them." — **Louis Armstrong**

dig *Genl* To learn by careful investigation. <dig up evidence, dug out the truth>

digger *Mgt, Mktg* One who employs people to buy tickets directly from the box office for resale at a considerable **markup**. *Also see* **ice**, **scalper**.

Digital Audio Tape *RecA&S* » **DAT**

digital computer *InfoMgt* Computer that performs calculations and logical operations with quantities represented as digits in the **binary** number system.

digital *Flm&Vid* Manipulation or storage of information using ones and zeros. D1, D2 and D3 are **digital** video formats, and **digital** audiotape (DAT), compact disks (CDs) and **digital** audio workstations (**DAWs**) use **digital** encoding. **Digital** signals, unlike **analog** signals, degrade very little with each generation.

digital *InfoMgt* Basic technology of computers and data communications wherein all information is **encoded** as bits of 1s or Øs that represent on or off states. *Also see* **analog**, **chip**, **chips**.

digital *MusInstr* Key played with the finger, as on an accordion, organ, piano, etc.

Digital Performance Right in Sound Recordings Act *LegAsp, RecA&S* Pending legislation that would grant record companies the ability to license their works to the new digital music services and to be compensated for such use. *Also see* **celestial jukebox**, **Send-A-Song**.

digital recording *RecA&S* Method of recording (introduced in 1978) in which portions of **sound waves** are converted into numbers and stored for later reproduction. Pioneered by Dr. Thomas G. Stockham Jr. (1933-, Technical **Grammy**, 1994) "Anything else is gaslight." — Herbert von Karajan (1908-1989, Austrian cond.)

digital sampler *InfoMgt, RecA&S* Essentially a **digital** recorder, this device turns sounds into strings of numbers; then play back these sounds at the touch of a key or the blip of an electronic impulse. Then manipulate the strings of numbers to imitate anything or anyone and insert the new sound into a new, original composition. *Also see* **sampling**, **techno**.

digital transmission *InfoMgt* Transmission of data as distinct "on/off."

digital video disc *InfoMgt* » **DVD**

digitize *iMedia* To convert or import analog media into a digital form. <scan an image>

dilemma *Crit&Eval* Situation that requires a choice between two unattractive alternatives.

dilettante *Crit&Eval* **1 Dabbler** in an art or a field of knowledge. **2** Lover of the **fine arts**; a connoisseur. *Also see* **amateur.**

dilution *Mktg* Lessen a sponsor's impact because of too many sponsors and consequently each sponsor gains less attention and fewer rewards.

diminishing returns *Eco&Fin* Yield rate that after a certain point fails to increase proportionately to additional outlays of capital or investments of time and labor.

diminuendo (dim) *MusArts* Decrease the volume. DECRESCENDO. *Also see* **Music Directions.**

DIMM *InfoMgt* double in-line memory module *Also see* **SIMM.**

dimmed *InfoMgt* Description of a word or icon that appears grayed. <menu commands appear dimmed when they are not available>

dimmer *PerfA&C* Electrical device that controls the intensity of a light source connected to it.

dimmers *Flm&Vid,PerfA&C* Electrical device that controls the light intensity of each lighting instrument. <footlights, floodlights, spotlights> **1 Electronic dimmers** can be remotely controlled by a single operator at a **light board. 2 Manual dimmers** require several operators and cannot follow complex, sophisticated cues, but they are virtually indestructible. *Also see* **channel.** *Also see* **Stage Lighting.**

dingbat *VA-Prntng* Typographical ornament or symbol <§ * s>

dinner jacket *Fashn* » **tuxedo**

dinner theater *TheatArts* Restaurant that presents a play during or after dinner.

dinosaur *Crit&Eval* **1** One hopelessly outmoded or unwieldy. **2** Relic of the past.

diode *Sci&Tech* **1** Electronic device that restricts current flow chiefly to one direction. **2** Two-terminal **semiconductor** device used chiefly as a **rectifier.**

Dionysus (aka **Bacchus.**) *LitArts* God of wine and of an orgiastic religion celebrating the power and fertility of **nature.** *Also see* **bacchanalia.**

diorama *VisArts* **1 Three-dimensional** miniature or life-size scene in which figures, stuffed wildlife, or other objects are arranged in a naturalistic setting against a painted background. **2** Scene reproduced on cloth transparencies with various lights shining through the cloths to produce changes in effect, intended for viewing at a distance through an aperture.

dir. *Flm&Vid , Mgt, TheatArts, MusArts,. Rdio/TV* **director**

direct access storage device *InfoMgt* » **DASD**

direct broadcast satellite *Rdio/TV* » **DBS**

direct channel *EntreP* Distribution system without intermediaries.

direct charge-off method *E&F-Acc* Method in which a loss is recognized by the company when the loss from an uncollectible account receivable by the time it is determined to be uncollectible.

direct cinema *Flm&Vid* » **cinema verité**

direct competitor *Mktg* Marketer offering goods or services that meet similar consumer's needs and is broadly similar in substance or concept to the marketer's own offerings. *Also see* **generic competitor.**

direct distribution *Mktg* Simplest channel of distribution in which the product goes directly from manufacturer to user. <consumer products such as book and record clubs; industrial products such as heavy machinery> *Also see* **direct marketing.**

direct license *IntelProp, MusArts* One obtained by a music user directly from composer and publisher allowing user to publicly perform the licensed work.

direct mail *Mktg* Advertising circulars or other printed matter sent directly through the mail to prospective customers or contributors. *Also see* **Advertising Media.**

direct marketing *EntreP* Selling via direct contact with the customer without the use of intermediaries, usually by using mail.

direct marketing *Mktg* System of sales and distribution whereby a product or service is distributed by a manufacturer or an originator directly to the end-user. <via fax, Internet, mail, telephone> *Also see* **Distribution Methods.** DIRECT MAIL, DIRECT RESPONSE

direct print *Flm&Vid* **Print** made directly from a **master.**

direct response *Mktg* » **direct marketing**

direct video *Flm&Vid, Journ,. Rdio/TV* » **small-format video.**

direct view television *Rdio/TV* Digital TV set with a picture tube.

direct-distribution expense *Flm&Vid* Incurred in the distribution of a movie. Largest two items are the cost of prints, advertising, and publicity. Other direct expenses include: checking costs, freight, guild payments, trade association fees, market research, certain taxes, etc.

direct-to-board *RecA&S* Recording process where some electric/electronic instruments, e.g., electric piano, keyboard **synthesizer,** may feed directly into the recording **console** rather than through a **mic.**

direct-to-disc recording *RecA&S* High quality recording process in which the original performance is **cut** directly onto the master **lacquer.** Tape is not used.

direction *MusArts* Word or phrase in a **score** indicating how a **passage** is to be played or sung. <p, pizz, t, etc> *Also see* **Music Directions.**

director (dir.) *Flm&Vid, TheatArts* One responsible for the supervision and guidance of the actors in a dramatic production; responsible for realizing the intentions of the scripted concept.

director (dir.) *Mgt* Member of a board of persons who control or govern the affairs of an institution or corporation *Also see* **trustee.**

director (dir.) *MusArts* conductor of an orchestra or chorus.

director (dir.) *Rdio/TV* One responsible for the supervision of a broadcast program.

Director of Development (DOD) *Fndng* Director of the total process of institutional fund-raising.

Director of Photography (D.P.) *Flm&Vid* » **cinematographer**

director *PerfA&C* Person responsible for interpreting the script, creating a viable production concept, and directing the actors.

director's chair *Flm&Vid* Collapsible armchair having a back and seat usu. made of canvas.

director's desk *PerfA&C* Desk set up in the orchestra seats for the director's use during rehearsals.

Director's Guild Awards for Theatrical Direction *TheatArts* Annual award. *Also see* **Awards & Prizes.**

Director's Guild of America *Flm&Vid* » **DGA** *Also see* **Directors, Guilds & Unions.**

Directors *ColEntry, Mgt* » **art —, artistic —, board of — creative —, DGA, director** (chorus, dance, film, radio, TV), **managing —, music —, New Wave, — of photography, producer/—, professional —, program —, régisseurs, RTDG, social —, SSDC, stage —.**

directory *InfoMgt* Index or list of the contents of a folder or a disk.

dirge *MusArts* **1** Funeral hymn or lament. **2** Slow, mournful musical composition. *Also see* **Songs.**

dirty *MusArts* Rough, hard, harsh, or earthy style of playing jazz. <The trumpet sound was down and dirty> *Also see* **sweet.**

disability insurance *EntreP* Coverage that protects against *the* disability of a company's partner or other key employee.

disaster *Crit&Eval* total failure

disc *InfoMgt* magnetic disk

disc *RecA&S* **1** phonograph record **2** Optical or compact disk. *Also see* **disk, platter.**

disc jockey (DJ, deejay), **disk jockey** *MusArts,. Rdio/TV* Radio or dance club **personality** who presents and comments on recordings.

discipline *Crit&Eval* **1** An essential factor necessary to achieve and maintain success in the arts. **2** Branch of knowledge or teaching. <art, drama, music> **3** Controlled behavior resulting from self-control. » **Arts Dynamic, EATxD²**

disclaimer *Mktg* Repudiation or denial of responsibility or connection. <The Phonee Software Company shall have no responsibility to replace or to refund the purchase price of a diskette damaged by accident, abuse, or misapplication> *Also see* **as is, guarantee, warranty.**

disclosure document *EntreP* Detailed statement that includes information about a franchisor's finances, experience, and size and informs potential franchisees of restrictions, costs, and provisions for renewal or cancellation of the franchise.

disco *Dnce* Style of dance music – popular ca. 1974-80 – "characterized by a relentless beat, throbbing rhythms, and gliding strings, it is a **hybrid** of **r&b**, Latin, Afro-Cuban, and rock. The melody and lyrics… are not as essential as danceability." — Harvey Rachlin (mus. biz wri.). *Also see* **Dances**.

disco *MusArts* Dance music marked by strong repetitive bass rhythms.

disco *PA-Variety* Nightclub with showy [even **garish**] decor and special lighting effects and featuring electronically amplified live or recorded music for dancing.

discography *InfoMgt* Study and cataloging of recordings.

discography *RecA&S* Comprehensive list of the recordings made by a particular conductor, performer, or ensemble; or of the music by a particular composer or lyricist.

discordant *Crit&Eval* 1 Not being in accord; conflicting. 2 Disagreeable in sound; harsh or **dissonant**. *Also see* **cacophonous**.

discotheque *MusArts* » **disco**

discount *Crit&Eval* 1 To leave out of account as being untrustworthy or exaggerated; disregard. <discount a rumor> 2 To underestimate the significance or effectiveness of; minimize.

discount *Eco&Fin* 1 To purchase or sell a bill, note, or other **commercial paper** at a reduction equal to the amount of interest that will accumulate before it matures. 2 To lend money on **commercial paper** not immediately payable after deducting the interest.

discount *Mktg* 1 To deduct or subtract from a cost or price. 2 To sell or offer for sale at a reduced price; to reduce in quantity or value.

discount advertising *Mktg* Practice – widespread in depressed or highly competitive media markets – in which ad pages are sold at less than the published rates.

discount rate *EntreP* Rate of interest that the Federal Reserve charges banks to borrow money from the FED.

discount rate *E&F-Acc* Management's minimum desired rate of return on an investment. COST OF CAPITAL, CUTOFF RATE, HURDLE RATE, REQUIRED RATE, TARGET RATE

Discounts *ColEntry, Eco&Fin* » **bulk** —, **cash** —, **discount coupons**, **trade** —, **frequency** —, **volume** —.

discouraged workers *EntreP* Workers who left the labor force because they could not find jobs.

discovery *LegAsp* Data or documents that a party to a legal action is compelled to disclose to another party either before or during a proceeding. *Also see* **trade secret**.

discovery *LitArts, TheatArts* Acquisition of important knowledge by or about a character, esp. the main character, of a drama or story. Thus, it is **discovery**, in **Sophocles's** *Oedipus the King*, when **Oedipus** and the other characters and the audience learn his true identity and deeds. *Also see* **plots**.

discovery *TheatArts* Revelation of important information about the characters, their motivations, feelings, and relationships. Discovery is often accompanied by recognition, when a character learns the truth about himself.

discretionary income *EntreP* Income that one has after paying taxes and fixed expenses such as rent and insurance.

discretionary income *Eco&Fin, Mktg* Amount of a consumer's income spent after essentials, such as food, housing, utilities, and prior commitments have been covered. The total amount of discretionary income can be a key **economic indicator** because spending this money spurs the economy.

discretionary spending *Eco&Fin* Measure developed by the **National Conference Board** that reflects the extent of consumer spending as the result of a decision relatively free of prior commitment, pressure of necessity, or force of habit. Good or bad times in the arts and entertainment industry largely depend on the amount – or the perception of the amount – of discretionary spending by the consumer.

diseconomies of scale *EntreP* Situation in which an increase in the quantity produced increases the long-run average cost of production.

dish antenna *Rdio/TV* **Microwave** transmitter or receiver consisting of a concave parabolic reflector.

Dish Night *Mktg, Flm&Vid* Movie box-office promotion of the **Great Depression** years, 1930-35 One dish of a set was given free to each paying adult attending neighborhood movie theaters on a mid-week evening (scheduled not to compete with **Amos and Andy** on radio) The come-on was to accumulate a complete set of "these beautiful dishes." It was never reported if anyone ever got the coveted gravy bowl or the large serving platter. Besides the dish, for 25¢ the moviegoer enjoyed a four hour escape via two full length movies featuring well-favored, well-off white people, worldwide news-of-the world, a travelogue in bilious color, a sing-along with the bouncing ball and a mighty Wurlitzer, an animated cartoon, lots of coming attractions, and an in-house commercial hyping the lobby candy counter featuring crackerjack with a prize in each-and-every package, and five-cent candy bars.

dishabille (dis-a-beel), **deshabille** *Fashn* 1 Partially or very casually dressed. 2 Casual attire.

dishonesty insurance *EntreP* Coverage that protects against employees' crimes.

disk address *InfoMgt* Method used to locate a data record on a disk is determined by surface number, track number, and record number.

disk cache *InfoMgt* Portion of a computer's main memory set aside for programs to store frequently used instructions. *Also see* **memory cache**, **RAM**.

disk capacity *InfoMgt* Maximum amount of data a disk can hold, usu. measured in **megabytes** (MB) or **kilobytes** (K)

disk drive *InfoMgt* Device that holds a disk, retrieves information from it, and saves information on it. FLOPPY DISK DRIVE, HARD DISK DRIVE

disk *InfoMgt* Thin, flat plate on which computer data can be stored. *Also see* **disc**, **floppy disk**, **hard disk**.

disk operating system (DOS) *InfoMgt* » **DOS**

disk pack *InfoMgt* stack of magnetic disk platters

diskette *InfoMgt* » **floppy disk**

Disklavier *MusInstr* Brand name of a computer-controlled **player piano** made by Yamaha. *Also see* **Musical Instrument Families**.

Disney, Walt (Walter Elias Disney, 1901-66, animator, **showman**, film prod.) *Flm&Vid* (*animation*) Animator, Produced first animated film with sound (1928), first full-length animated feature (1938) » **creative producer**

disparagement *LegAsp* False statement about a competitor's products, services, property, or business reputation.

display advertising *Mktg* Advertisement designed to catch the eye by artistic means and is not classified by subject. *Also see* **classified advertising, classified display advertising**.

display *InfoMgt* 1 To show information or graphics on a screen. 2 Device that gives information in a visual form. <a computer screen>

display *Mktg* Objects or merchandise set out for viewing.

display type *Journ, VA-Prntng* Larger sizes of type. <14 points up> used for headlines and advertising **copy**. *Also see* **body type**.

disposable income *EntreP* Income that one has after paying federal, state, and city taxes. This income can either be spent (consumed) or saved.

diss *Crit&Eval* Disrespect; put down, embarrass, humiliate.

dissemination *Fndng* Process by which project results are announced. <publish a report, present the results in a workshop>

dissolute *Crit&Eval* One who indulges in sensual pleasures or vices. » **libertine**

dissolve *Flm&Vid* Slow fading out of one shot and the gradual fading in of its sucessor, with a **superimposition** of images, usu. at midpoint.

dissonance *MusArts* Combination of tones that are unresolved, jarring. *Also see* **consonance, prepare**.

dissonant *MusArts* Harsh and inharmonious in sound; discordant.

distr. *Mktg* **distribution**, **distributor**

Distributed Data Processing (DDP) *InfoMgt* » **DDP**

distribution (distr.) *Flm&Vid* Marketing strategies employed in the release of a movie, such as where, when and how to release it, e.g. exclusive **engagement**, **wide release**, etc. Includes all interrelated activities of advertising and publicity strategy, collection of monies and disbursement of funds to participants. Major distribution companies usu. have separate departments for production, accounting, sales, advertising, publicity, and promotion.

distribution (distr.) *Mktg* Combination of internal organizational resources and external intermediaries to move goods and provide services from creation or production to the end user. Goods move through physical distribution channels, involving transportation, storage, and display. Services are delivered to the customer directly at the production site, or delivered by **audiovisual** or **electronic media**. "The wave of mergers sweeping through the entertainment industry reflects a growing belief among media executives that production and distribution must be under one roof.... What entertainment companies want today is to have maximum domination over their end markets.... If they produce films, they want to own the television stations, theaters and pay TV services that carry them." — David Londoner (econ. journ.) *Also see* **consent decree, Distribution Methods, vertical integration.**

distribution *EntreP* Physically moving products and establishing intermediary relationships to support such movement.

Distribution Committee *Fnding* The board responsible for making grant decisions. For **community foundations**, it is intended to be broadly representative of the community served by the foundation.

distribution deal *Mktg, RecA&S* Agreement between a record manufacturer/distributor and a label that calls for the distributor to manufacture and distribute recordings and remit a fixed price or royalty for each unit sold, retaining the balance for its costs and profit. The label does the marketing for its releases. Distributor has no copyright ownership and the label receives no financing from the distributor. *Also see* **Contracts.**

Distribution Methods *ColEntry, Mktg* **consumer —, direct —, direct response, industrial —, one-step —, two-step —, three-step —, telemarketing**

distributive bargaining *HR&LR* Approach to **collective bargaining** by which one or both parties view it as a win-lose situation with fixed and limited resources where each party wants to maximize its share.

distributor (distr.) *Mktg* Company or person that markets or sells merchandise to retail outlets; a wholesaler. *Also see* **Distributors.**

Distributors *ColEntry, Mktg* » **film —, independent (indie, indy) —, jobber, one-stop, movie —, MPPDA, rack jobber, wholesaler**

District, The *Cult&Soc, MusArts* » **Storyville**

dither *Crit&Eval* State of indecisive agitation.

dither *iMedia* **1** Audio: Noise added to an audio signal that greatly reduces distortion when reducing the number of bits used to represent a signal, but in exchange usu. adds a low-level hiss. **2** Graphics: combination of colors to simulate colors not available in a specific palette.

dithyramb *Dnce, TheatArts* A frenzied, impassioned **choric** hymn and dance of ancient Greece in honor of Dionysus.

dithyramb *LitArts* Wildly enthusiastic speech or piece of writing. *Origin* Ancient Greek choric hymn and dance in honor of **Dionysus** (aka **Bacchus**)

ditty *MusArts* simple song *Also see* **Songs.**

div. *Eco&Fin* **dividend**

diva *MusArts* » **prima donna**

dive *Crit&Eval* disreputable or run-down bar or nightclub

diversification *Eco&Fin* To distribute investments among different companies or securities in order to limit losses in the event of a fall in a particular market or industry.

diversification *Mktg* Process of entering new markets with one or more products that are new to the organization.

diversity *Cult&Soc* **1** Fact or quality of being diverse; difference: "Diversity is a cinnamon raisin bagel." — J. Dennis Rich (chair, CCC/Mgt. Dept.) **2** Point or respect in which things differ. **3** variety or multiformity

divertissement (die-vert-is-mont, Fr.) *Dnce* Short ballet performance presented as an interlude in an opera or a play. It usu. has little to do with the **plot.**

divertissement (die-vert-is-mont, Fr.) *MusArts* **Fantasia** on well-known tunes.

divest *Eco&Fin* To sell off or otherwise dispose of a subsidiary company or an investment.

divestiture *Law&Pol* Sale, liquidation, or **spinoff** of a corporate division or subsidiary.

dividend *EntreP* After tax payment that may be made by a corporation to a stockholder. These are usually declared by the board of directors of the company.

dividends *Eco&Fin* Periodic distribution of a corporation's assets to individuals who own shares of stock in the firm.

Dixieland jazz *MusArts* Essentially a version of the original **New Orleans** style of jazz as performed by white musicians. *Also see* **Chicago jazz, Jazz Styles.**

Dixieland jazz *MusArts* Style of written and arranged – as well as improvised – instrumental jazz adapted by white musicians from the original **New Orleans jazz** form characterized by a relatively fast two-beat rhythm and by group and solo improvisations. *Also see* **Chicago jazz, Jazz Age, Jazz Styles.**

DJ *Eco&Fin* **Dow Jones**

DJ *Rdio / TV, RecA&S* **disk jockey, deejay**

DJIA *Eco&Fin* **Dow Jones Industrial Average**

dlr. *Mktg* **dealer**

DMA *Dnce* » **Dance Masters of America**

DMA *Mktg, Rdio / TV* Designated Market Area. A **Nielsen** audience market classification designating a certain market area in which local stations have partial or complete signal dominance. Similar to **Arbitron's ADI**

dncr. *ArtPerf, Dnce* **dancer**

DNR *Fashn, Journ* Acronym for *Daily News Record*, a daily newspaper reporting menswear apparel news, published by Fairchild Publications.

DNS *InfoMgt* Domain Name Service. Behind-the-scenes Internet service which translates Internet **domain names** (such as aol.com) to their corresponding **IP** addresses (such as 128.143.7.186), and vice versa, allowing Internet users to use familiar names rather than IP addresses.

do (dough) *MusArts* First tone of a **diatonic scale.**

do *TheatArts* Play a part <Do the **ingenue**>

DOC *Eco&Fin, Law&Pol* » **Commerce, U.S. Department of.**

doc. *InfoMgt, LitArts* **document.**

dock *PerfA&C* » **scene dock.**

doctor *TheatArts* » **play doctor.**

Doctorow, E.L. (Edgar Lawrence Doctorow, 1931-, fictwri., critic) *ArtPerf, Crit&Eval, LitArts* Noted for his artful blend of history and **fiction** in novels. <*The Book of Daniel* (1971) *Also see* **simple.**

doctrinaire (Fr.) *Crit&Eval* Relating to a person inflexibly attached to a practice or theory.

doctrine *Crit&Eval* Principle or body of principles presented for acceptance or belief, as by a religious, political, scientific, or philosophic group; **dogma.**

doctrine *Law&Pol* **1** Rule or principle of law when established by precedent. **2** Statement of official government policy, esp. in foreign affairs and military strategy.

document (doc.) *InfoMgt* **1** Data file entered by a user in reference to a word processing file. **2** Whatever is created with an application program.

document object model *iMedia* Interface allowing dynamic access and updates to content, structure and style of documents.

document type declaration *LegalAsp, iMedia* **Tag** within a markup document which points to the source (a **document type definition**) that defines the legal structure the document can use.

document type definition *LegalAsp, iMedia* Collection of declarations that define the legal structure a document can use.

documentary *Flm&Vid* Film or television program, presenting political, social, or historical subject matter in a factual and informative manner and often consisting of actual news films or interviews accompanied by narration. <**Edward R. Murrow's** *Harvest of Shame* (??)>

documentation *iMedia* Information that defines and records the development of an interactive product, usu. created in two forms: "user documentation" (information to help someone use the product) and "developer documentation" (information to help those who build the product or who will maintain it)

DOD *Fndng* » **Director of Development.**

DOE *Cult&Soc, HR&LR, Law&Pol* **U.S. Department of Education** (est. 1980) when it absorbed several federal agencies inc. some from **HEW.**

dog *Crit&Eval* Person regarded as unattractive or uninteresting.

dog *Eco&Fin* **Strategic business unit** that shows a declining share of a mature or declining market. *Also see* **cash cow**.

dog *Mktg* Hopelessly inferior product or creation.

dog-and-pony show *Mktg* Elaborate presentation *Origin* Razzle-dazzle of trained animal acts at circuses. — American Historical Dictionary *Also see* **show-and-tell**.

dogfight *PA-Variety* Illegal, spectator entertainment featuring betting on an organized fight between dogs.

doggerel *LitArts* Crudely or irregularly fashioned verse, often of a humorous or burlesque nature.

dogma *Crit&Eval* Authoritative principle, belief, or statement of ideas or opinion considered – by the speaker or writer – to be absolutely true. *Also see* **doctrine**.

DOJ *Law&Pol* [U.S.] Department of Justice.

DOL *Eco&Fin, HR&LR, Law&Pol* **Labor, U.S. Department of**

dol *MusArts* » **dolce**

Dolby sound system *Flm&Vid, RecA&S* Noise-reduction system invented and developed by Ray Dolby (1933-, recording engineer, Technical **Grammy**, 1995) that pushes the audio levels higher during recording and then lowers them during playback. Side effect is the slight loss of **high frequency** response in playback.

dolce (dol) *MusArts* Play softly, sweetly. *Also see* **Music Directions**.

dolly *Flm&Vid* **1** Wheeled platform, sometimes mounted on tracks, that allows smooth movement of the camera. **2** Shot that involves a dolly move. **3** Actual movement of the camera during a dolly move. *Also see* **grip**.

dolman sleeve *Fashn* Full sleeve, very wide at the armhole and narrow at the wrist.

DOM *iMedia* » **document object model**

dom *MusArts* » **dominant**

domain *InfoMgt* Term used in expert systems to describe the area of knowledge contained in the expert system.

domain name *InfoMgt* Key component of an **Internet** address. As of 14 Sep. 1995, the cost of registering a domain name is $50 — previously there was no charge because of a **NSF** subsidy. However, a member of an online service, such as **America On-Line** (AOL), is not charged, as **AOL** is the registrant on behalf of its members. STREET NAME. *Also see* **Domain Names, Network Solutions Inc., edu., com., organization, gov., net**.

Domain Name Service *InfoMgt* » **DNS**

Domain Names *ColEntry, InfoMgt* Names proposed by the International Ad Hoc Committee, a group of 11 representatives of Internet, legal, and other international standards groups. ». **arts,. com,. edu,. firm,. gov,. info,. net,. nom,. org.,. rec,. store,. web**.

domain-name speculation *InfoMgt* Practice of a person registering a popular **Internet** address like mcdonald.com before McDonald's realized the address's value.

dominant (dom) *MusArts* Fifth tone of a **diatonic scale**.

domination *HR&LR* Control by an employer over its employees or their union; decidedly not a good and fair labor practice. *Also see* **company union**.

domino *Fashn,PerfA&C* **1** Eye mask. **2** Masquerade costume: a hooded robe worn with an eye mask.

donee *Fnding* Recipient of a grant *Also see* **beneficiary, grantee**.

Donegal tweed *Fashn* Medium to heavyweight tweed originally made in Donegal, Ireland; made in plain or twill weave, usu. of coarse yarns in various colors.

donnée *Genl, LitArts* Set of literary or artistic principles or assumptions on which a creative work is based. **2** Set of notions, facts, or conditions that governs and shapes an act or a way of life.

donor *Fnding* Individual or organization that makes a grant or contribution. *Also see* **grantor**.

donor *Fndng* One who donates to a charitable cause.

donor pyramid *Fndng* Visual device demonstrating the **hierarchy** of giving; mostest on top.

donor recognition *Fndng* Policy and practice of recognizing gifts, inc.: immediate written acknowledgment, personal expressions of appreciation, inclusion in a published list of contributors, and in other appropriate ways.

Donors Forum *Fndng* Chicago organization linked to the **Foundation Center** in New York that serves as a philanthropic library for the community.

donut *BcstJourn* Slang term for video used in a live shot. This can be either tracked or in the VO/SOT/VO format. *Also:* "insert."

doo wop *MusArts* Pop sound of the 1950s from the likes of **Sha Na Na**. Certainly not to be confused with **bebop**.

doozy, doozie *Crit&Eval* Something extraordinary or bizarre. <**Madonna's** costume was a doozy>

doppelganger (DOPP-ul-gang-er, Ger., "double walker") *ArtPerf* Shadow-self that accompanies every human, certainly inc. artists/performers. Providing sympathetic company, a doppelganger is prepared to listen and give advice, either implanting ideas in their heads, or by a sort of **osmosis**.

Doris Duke Charitable Foundation *Dnce, MusArts* New York-based foundation (est. 1997 by multimillionaire Doris Duke, 1913-1993) to provide support for a range of causes inc. dance and jazz. *Also see* **Jazznet**.

DOS *InfoMgt* **disk operating system** Usually refers to system used by **IBM**-type computers. *Also see* **Operating Systems**.

dot *MusArts* Mark after a note indicating an increase in time value by half.

dot syntax *iMedia* Programming syntax that uses a period to separate the name of an object from its properties and methods.

dot-matrix printer *InfoMgt* Creates text characters and graphics with Series of closely spaced dots by using tiny hammers to strike a needle mechanism against the paper at the precise moments the print head moves across the page.

dots per inch (DPI) *VA-Prntng* » **DPI**

double *MusArts* **1** Instrumentalist who plays two or more instruments in a performance or in a recording session and is paid extra for each additional instrument beyond her or his **primary instrument**. **2** To duplicate (another part or voice) an **octave** higher or lower or in unison.

double *RecA&S* **1** During the mix of a recording master, the process of doubling, for example, the four-player **string section** to sound like eight players. **2** Duplicate copy. *Also see* **dub**.

double bar *MusArts* Double vertical or heavy black line drawn through a **staff** to indicate the end of any of the main sections of a musical **composition**.

double bass (b) *MusInstr* The largest **bowed** stringed instrument in the modern orchestra, also used frequently in jazz ensembles, played **pizzicato**. The instrument – considered a member of the violin family – is tuned in fourths and has the sloping shoulders and flat back characteristic of the **viols**. It has a deep range beginning about three **octaves** below **middle C**. BASS FIDDLE, BASS VIOL, BULL FIDDLE, CONTRABASS, STRING BASS. *Also see* **Musical Instrument Families**.

double bassoon *MusInstr* » **contrabassoon** *Also see* **Musical Instrument Families**.

double bill *TheatArts* Theatre program with two separate dramatic productions.

double consciousness *Cult&Soc* Refers to the existence in a single individual of two different sets of psychological and cultural beliefs or orientations, or to two different ways of psychologically viewing herself or himself relative to gender, race, sexual preference, or whatever.<Two souls – one American, one Negro – warring in one earthbound body. (paraphrased) — W.E.B. Du Bois (1868-1963, scholar, black civil rights leader)>

double dagger *LitArts, VA-Prntng* Reference mark (‡) used in printing and writing. DIESIS.

double entry booking *E&F-Acc* Method of bookkeeping in which a transaction is entered both as a debit to one account and a credit to another account, so that the totals of debits and credits are equal. *Also see* **accounting equation**.

double entry system *EntreP* Self-balancing accounting system that uses journals and ledgers.

double feature *Flm&Vid* Two full-length movies in a theater for the price of one admission. *Also see* **B picture**.

double *Flm&Vid* Anonymous substitute who performs physically difficult scenes for an actor.

double knit, **double-knit** *Fashn* Jerseylike fabric knitted on a machine equipped with two sets of needles so that a double thickness of fabric is produced in which the two sides of the fabric are interlocked.

double take, **double-take** *PerfA&C* Delayed reaction to an unusual remark or circumstance, often used as a comic device.

double *TheatArts* One actor playing two or more roles in one production.

double-click *InfoMgt* Execute a command by pressing the mouse button twice in rapid succession. *Also see* mouse.

double-entendre *Crit&Eval* Word or phrase that has a double meaning, esp. when the second meaning is **risqué**.

double-reed *MusInstr* Wind instrument that has a mouthpiece formed of two joined reeds that vibrate against each other. <**English horn, oboe, bassoon**> *Also see* **Musical Instrument Families.**

double-reeds *MusArts* Section of a band or an orchestra composed of **double-reed** instruments. DOUBLE-REED PLAYER.

double-sided records *RecA&S* Recording on both sides of a disk; introduced in 1904 by Columbia Records.

double-system sound *Flm&Vid, RecA&S* Technique of synchronizing the film camera and the sound tape recorder. *Also see* **synchronous soundtrack**

double-time *MusArts* » **duple**

Dove Awards *MusArts* Awarded by the **Gospel Music Association** (GMA) *Also see* **Awards & Prizes.**

Dow *Eco&Fin* » **Dow Jones Industrial Average.**

Dow Jones Averages (DJ) *Eco&Fin* **Trademarked** index of the relative price of selected industrial, transportation, and utility stocks based on a formula developed and periodically revised by Dow Jones & Company, Inc.

Dow Jones Industrial Average (DJIA, Dow) *Eco&Fin* Price-weighted average of 30 actively traded blue chip stocks.

Dow Jones Industrials Index *EntreP* This index was created in 1884 in a newsletter by Charles Dow and Edward Jones. Today, it consists of thirty stocks, and is an adjusted simple average of the prices of these stocks.

Down Beat Jazz Hall of Fame (formerly, *Down Beat* Hall of Fame) *ArtPerf, MusArts* Established by *Down Beat* magazine in its annual Readers Poll in 1952 and in its annual Critics Poll in 1961 First inductee was **Louis Armstrong.**

Down Beat, down beat *Journ, MusArts* Jazz magazine, est. 1934 in Chicago.

down *Crit&Eval* 1 Malfunctioning or not operating temporarily. 2 Low in spirits; depressed, discouraged, sad; dejected. *Also see* **come down, up**.

down-bow, downbow *MusArts* Stroke made by drawing a bow from handle to tip across the strings of a violin or other bowed instrument.

down-home *Crit&Eval* Relating to a simple, wholesome, unpretentious **lifestyle**, associated with the rural southern U.S. *Also see* **old-timey.**

down-market, downmarket *Mktg* » **downscale**

down-to-earth *Crit&Eval* Realistic; sensible.

downbeat *MusArts* Downward stroke made by a conductor to indicate the first beat of a **measure**. [The magazine *Down Beat* is **trademarked** as two words.].

downlink *InfoMgt,. Rdio/TV* Transmission antenna contained in a satellite that conveys amplified video and audio signals back to earth for reception by any tuned earth station or **dish antenna.**

download (D/L) *InfoMgt* To transfer information from one computer to another. <from an online service> A laser printer downloads fonts automatically if they are stored in the user's computer. *Also see* **upload**.

downscale *Mktg* To redesign or market for **low-income** consumers. *Also see* **upscale.**

downsize *Eco&Fin, HR&LR* Reduce the size of a workforce *Also see* **bloodletting.**

downstage (DS) *PerfA&C* 1 In a **proscenium** theater, the area of the stage closest to the audience. 2 Front half of a stage. *Also see* **Stage Directions.**

downtime *InfoMgt* Period of time when the computer is inactive.

DP *InfoMgt* **Data processing**

DPI *InfoMgt* **Dots Per Inch** More dots, better printing. <The newest laser printers for small offices now print at 600 DPI rather than 300 DPI> QUALITY PRINTING.

drab *Crit&Eval* 1 Faded and dull in appearance. 2 Dull or commonplace in character; dreary.

drab *VisArts* 1 Of a dull light brown. 2 Of a light olive brown or khaki color.

drafting *Fashn* Pattern making technique that uses paper and measurement tools to create the pattern.

drag *Fashn, PerfA&C* Clothing characteristic of one sex when worn by a member of the opposite sex. <an actor in drag>

drag queen *Cult&Soc, PA-Variety* Man, usu. a performer, who exaggeratedly dresses as a woman. *Also see* **cross-dressing.**

dragging *InfoMgt* Technique of making displayed graphics or text follow the cursor by moving the mouse while holding down the mouse button.

DRAM chip *InfoMgt* **Dynamic Random Access Memory** chip; the type of memory chip used in most personal computers, it must be continually **refreshed.**

dram. *LitArts, TheatArts* **dramatist, playwright.**

Drama Desk Awards *TheatArts* Annual awards by New York drama critics writing for non-New York publications. *Also see* **Awards & Prizes.**

Drama League Awards *TheatArts* Oldest theatrical honors in America, est. 1935, distinguished productions and performances both on Broadway and off, as well as career achievements in theatre, musical theatre, and directing. *Also see* **Awards & Prizes.**

drama *TheatArts* 1 Play in verse or prose, usu. recounting a serious story. 2 Dramatic art of a particular kind or period. <**Shakespearean** drama> 3 Art or practice of writing or producing plays. 4 Real-life situation or succession of events having the dramatic progression or emotional content of a play. *Also see* **comedy**.

dramatic (dram.) *Crit&Eval, TheatArts* 1 Characterized by or expressive of the action or emotion associated with drama or the theatre. 2 Arresting or forceful in appearance or effect.

dramatic irony *TheatArts* The most common kind of **irony** in drama: when the audience knows something that one or more of the characters do not.

dramatic *MusArts* Having a powerful, expressive singing voice. <dramatic soprano>

dramatic productions *Rdio/TV* Popular type of television network programming. <*Hallmark Hall of Fame, Lou Grant, Playhouse 90*> *Also see* **Television Shows.**

dramatico-musical composition *IntelProp, MusArts, TheatArts* Musical work whose performance relates a story both visually and audibly, is accompanied by dramatic action, costume, and scenery, and is written for presentation in the **legitimate** theater. <ballet, musical, opera, operetta> *Also see* **grand right license.**

dramatis personae *LitArts* Characters in a play or story.

dramatist (dram.) *ArtPerf, LitArts, TheatArts* One who writes plays. *Also see* **playwright.**

Dramatists Guild, Inc. (DGI) *ArtPerf, HR&LR, LitArts* » **DGI** *Also see* **Guilds & Unions.**

dramatize *Crit&Eval* 1 To present or view in a dramatic or **melodramatic** way. 2 To indulge in self-dramatization.

dramatize *LitArts* To adapt a literary work for dramatic presentation.

dramaturge *ArtPerf, LitArts, TheatArts* Writer or adapter of plays; a playwright.

dramaturgy *LitArts, TheatArts* Art of the theater, esp. the writing of plays.

drambalet *Dnce* "Stalinist genre… in which dance was basically a vehicle for political narrative." — Joan Acocella (19??-, dance critic) *Also see* **Dances.**

draping *Fashn* To cover, dress, or hang as if with cloth in loose folds.

draw curtain *PerfA&C* Curtain that divides in the middle so that it can be pulled open to the sides of the stage. *Also see* **Stage Curtains**

drawee *E&F-Acc, LegAsp* Party against whom funds are drawn. *Also see* **drawer.**

drawer *E&F-Acc, LegAsp* Party who initiates a transaction. *Also see* **drawee.**

Dream Works SKG *Flm&Vid* An entertainment **conglomerate** and **content factory** co-owned by **Steven Spielberg**, Jeffrey Katzenberg (1950-, film exec., formerly v.p. Disney), and David Geffen (1943-, Record company exec.-prod.)

dreck (Yinglish) *Crit&Eval* Cheap, worthless, trash. <Scene: Art Gallery. Kibitzer #1: Is that a painting? It says "Night Scene." Kibitzer #2: It should say "Dreck by Moonlight." Kibitzer #1: Why do they hang stuff like that? Kibitzer #2: Because they

couldn't find the artist>

dress circle *PerfA&C* Section of seats in a theater or opera house, usu. the first tier above the orchestra level.

dress extra *ArtPerf, Flm&Vid* **Extra** actor wearing **formal** clothes. *Also see* **spear-carrier**.

dress rehearsal *PerfA&C* Run-through with all technical elements, including costumes and makeup.

dress rehearsal *TheatArts* Final rehearsal with costumes, scenery, lights, and **props**.

dresser *TheatArts* **Wardrobe** assistant

dressers *PerfA&C* Costume-crew personnel who assist actors in putting on their costumes.

dressing room *PerfA&C* Room or cubicle for changing costumes and applying makeup.

dressing the house *TheatArts* **1** To assign seats to an audience with artful spacing so that the theatre appears to be more crowded than it really is. **2** Filling a house with pass-holders likely to applaud when necessary. *Also see* **paper the house**.

dressing the stage *TheatArts* Arranging the actors the stage, furniture, and wall hangings provide the audience with a pleasing effect of balance.

dressmaking *Fashn* Making of women's clothing, esp. dresses.

dressy *Fashn* **1** Showy or elegant in dress or appearance. **2** Smart; stylish.

drive time *Rdio/TV* Times of day during which commuters drive to and from work is considered **prime time** for radio advertising, therefore higher rates prevail.

driver *InfoMgt* Devices that handle input and output between **peripherals** such as printers or mice and the **cpu** of a computer.

drm *MusInstr* **drum, drum set**.

droit (drrott, Fr.) *LegAsp* legal right.

droit de suite (drrott duh sweet, Fr.) *LegAsp, VisA&C* "As conceived in France, [it] gives the artist a **pecuniary** right parallel to that afforded the author through copyright by allowing the artist to collect three percent of the total sales price of his work each time it is sold at public auction or through a merchant (inc. dealers and agents) The French law requires registration of a work by the artist before he can claim the right, and a central organization, the Union of Artistic Property, collects and pays the fees to the artist." — Leonard D. DuBoff (law prof.) *Also see* **fine art**, **Resale Royalties Act**.

droit moral *LegAsp* **1** A personal right, protecting an artist's expression. **2** Artist's right to maintain the integrity of a work even after the work has been sold.

drop *PerfA&C* Large expanse of cloth, usu. muslin or scenic canvas, on which something (a landscape, sky street, room) is usu. painted.

drop, drop curtain *PerfA&C* **1** Unframed curtain lowered to a stage from the flies, often serving as background scenery. **2** Theater curtain lowered or raised vertically rather than drawn to the side.

drop-dead *Crit&Eval* Very impressive; spectacular. <the fashion model made a drop-dead entrance wearing a red, white, and blue **fishnet** body stocking>

dross *Crit&Eval* Worthless, commonplace, or trivial matter. <The art fair was a success but the dross outweighed the gold>

drug testing *SportsEnt* Medical examination performed on athletes at request of sports leagues or public authorities, to detect the presence of illegal substances. Goal is to protect the health of the athletes (particularly that of minors) and the establishment and maintenance of the natural competitive qualities of the performers. Due to the intrusive nature of the tests, their legality is frequently challenged as invasion of privacy. *Also see* **Fourth Amendment**.

drum (drm) *MusInstr* Percussion instrument consisting of a hollow cylinder or hemisphere with a calfskin or plastic membrane stretched tightly over one or both ends or sides, played by beating with the hands or sticks. *Also see* **Musical Instrument Families**.

drum machine *MusInstr* Synthesizer-like device that can reproduce electronically various percussion sounds in any tempo. [All boring.].

drum major, drum majorette *MusArts, PA-Variety* One who **struts** in front of – and thus leads – a marching band or drum corps, wielding or twirling a **baton**.

drum printer *InfoMgt* Output device that prints characters that are engraved on the surface.

drum set *MusInstr* Includes snare and bass drums, tom-toms, cymbals, and other percussion instruments and accessories. DRUMMER, TRAP DRUMMER. *Also see* **Musical Instrument Families; traps**.

drum-and-bass *MusArts, RecA&S* Offshoot of **techno** club music.

drummer *MusArts* One who plays drums *Also see* **trap drummer**, **percussionist**.

DS *TheatArts* **downstage**

dsgn. *Fashn, PerfA&C, VisArts* **design**

dsgnr. *Fashn* **designer**.

DTD *iMedia* » **Document Type Definition**

DTP *InfoMgt* **desk top publishing**

DTW *Dnce* **Dance Theater Workshop**

du-wah *MusArts* Special brass sound effect produced by a **plunger mute**.

dual agency *LegAsp* Situation that occurs when an agent acts for two or more different **principals** in the same transaction.

dub *Flm&Vid* To insert a new soundtrack, often a synchronized translation of the original dialogue, into a film.

dub *RecA&S* **1** To transfer recorded material onto a new recording medium. **2** To copy a record or tape. **3** To add sound into a film or tape: dub in horns behind the **rhythm section**. **4** New sounds added by **dubbing**. **5** Dubbed copy of a tape or record. *Also see* **overdub**.

dubbing *Flm&Vid* **1** Any transfer of sound. **2** Process of making a dub (copy) of a **videotape**. When a tape is copied from one format to another the image is said to have been **bumped** up or down.

dubiety *Crit&Eval* **1** Feeling of doubt that often results in wavering. **2** Matter of doubt. *Also see* **skepticism**.

Duchamp, Marcel (1887-1968, Fr.-born pntr., theorist) *ArtPerf, VisArts* One of the most influential figures of avant-garde 20th century art. <*Nude Descending a Staircase* (1912, exhibited at the **Armory Show** in 1913)> *Also see* **allegory**, **anti-art**, **kinetic art**, **ready-made art**.

ducktail *Fashn* Hairstyle in which the hair is swept back at the sides to meet in an upturned point in back.

duds *Fashn* clothing

due diligence *EntreP* Careful and objective analysis of a business situation for the purposes of funding or obtaining a loan.

due process *LegAsp* Established course for judicial proceedings or other governmental activities designed to safeguard the legal rights of the individual. *Also see* **erotic music law**, **free speech**.

duet *MusArts* **1** Composition for two players or two voices. **2** Two performers of such a composition.

dumb act *PA-Variety* One in which there are no spoken words.

dumb down *Crit&Eval, LitArts* To rewrite for a less intelligent audience.

dummy *Fashn* » **mannequin**

dummy *InfoMgt* Character or other piece of information entered into a computer only to meet prescribed conditions, such as word length, and having no effect on operations.

dummy *PA-Variety* Figure of a person or an animal manipulated by a **ventriloquist**.

dummy contract *LegAsp* Informal contract between two parties to amend conditions of a union contract.

dummy corporation *Eco&Fin* Shell of corporation existing only on paper; designed to shield the names or purposes of the real owners.

dummy, dummy page *VA-Prntng* One of a set of model pages with text and illustrations pasted into place to direct the printer.

dummy lyric *MusArts* Temporary set of words put together to help the **lyricist** work out a song's **metric** form and rhyme scheme.

dump *InfoMgt* Transfer data in a computer from one place to another without processing. <from memory to printout> *Also see* **screen dump**.

dump *Journ, VA-Prntng* To clear material from a computer into a typewriter.

dump *LitArts, Mktg* Front-of-the-**chain**-bookstore floor space for a cardboard display, available for a fee paid by a book publisher. *Also see* **endcaps**, **new arrival wall**.

dumping *Eco&Fin, Mktg* Selling goods abroad below cost in order to eliminate a surplus or to gain an edge on foreign competition. *Also see* **predatory pricing**.

dumps *LitArts, Mktg* Portable stand-up display (holding 12-15 books) provided by publishers to bookstores. Publishers pay rent to the stores for this preferred display space.

Dun & Bradstreet (D&B) *Eco&Fin, Mktg»* **D&B**.

duopoly *Rdio/TV* One company owning as many as four radio stations (two AM, two FM) in a particular market. *Also see* **monopoly, oligopoly**.

duotone *Journ, VA-Prntng* Reproduction of a halftone in two colors from two plates.

dup. *Crit&Eval* **duplicate**.

dupe *Mktg,PerfA&C* duplicate ticket.

duple meter *MusArts* Two or a multiple of two beats to the **measure**.

duplex *InfoMgt* Ability of a communication system to transmit information in both directions. *Also see* **full duplex, simplex**.

duplicate *Crit&Eval* Identically copied from an original.

durable goods *EntreP* Goods that last for a long period of time, such as household appliances.

Durable Goods Orders *Eco&Fin* This **economic indicator** is based on U.S. Dept. of Commerce data that reports on the number and value of orders for both industrial and consumer durable (tangible) goods. This statistic is subject to month to month variances, but watching it over a three-month plus period can be a valuable indicator.

duration *MusArts* The length of a tone.

dust jacket *LitArts, VA-Prntng* Removable paper cover used to protect the binding of a book. DUST COVER. *Also see* **graphic artist**.

dust jacket *RecA&S »* **sleeve**

duty *Ethcs&Phil* Central term in some approaches to ethics. That which one must do, and which others can reasonably expect will be done.

duty of fair representation *HR&LR* Requires that the Union represent the interests of all employees fairly and impartially.

DVD *InfoMgt* digital video disc, a new type **CD-ROM** that holds a minimum of **4.7GB**, enough for a full-length movie. Uses **MPEG-2** to compress video data.

DVD *InfoMgt* **Digital Video Discs** Advanced **CD** with greatly expanded capacity. About five inches in diameter, stores both audio and video binary data in microscopic pits on the surface of both sides, two layers on each side thus providing more than 25 times more data storage than a **CD** or **CD-ROM**.

DVD-Audio *RecA&S* Most disks feature two different soundtracks: a **Dolby Surround**-encoded stereo version playable through any audio system, and a six-channel **Dolby** Digital version which requires its own audio-video receiver.

DVD-Video *Flm&Vid* A single layer on one side of a DVD can store two hours of video; therefore, two versions of the same film: **widescreen** and **pan & scan** can be provided on one DVD. Video **resolution** is twice that of VHS tapes and exceeds that of **laser disks** or Digital Satellite Systems.

Dynabook *iMedia* Basis for early personal computer work conducted by **Alan Kay**. Was envisioned as a portable interactive personal computer precursor of the modern notebook computer. In 1993, Kay's vision of Dynabook finally transformed itself into reality in the form of the Apple Newton

dynamic *iMedia* Associated with time, change, activity, or progress.

dynamic headroom *RecA&S* Capacity of an amplifier or sound system to reproduce unusually strong signals without distortion.

dynamic markings *MusArts* Arranger's/composer's directions for the level of loudness-softness required for a particular piece of music.

dynamic microphone *RecA&S* Professional quality **mic** noted for its rugged construction and relatively low cost. *Also see* **Microphones**.

Dynamic Random Access Memory (DRAM) *InfoMgt »* **DRAM chip**.

Dynamic Stock Price Process *EntreP* Expression that describes how a stock price moves through time under certainty.

dynamics *Cult&Soc, iMedia* Social, intellectual, or moral forces that produce activity and change.

dynamics *MusArts, RecA&S* Variations of intensity in musical sound; loud/soft.

- E -

E Ink *InfoMgt, Sci&Tech* brand name for **electronic ink**

email [no longer "e-mail"] *InfoMgt* Electronic mail. Private mail sent from one computer to another via a central computer system or electronic mailbox. *Also see* **online, snail mail**.

E.A.T. *Aes&Creat, Sci&Tech* Experiments in Art and Technology founded in 1947 by Billy Klüver and Robert Rauschenberg.

ea. *Eco&Fin* each

ear training *MusArts* Ability to distinguish and identify musical notes, chords, and chord progressions. *Also see* **solfege**.

earned income *Eco&Fin* Income generated from salaries and wages, annuities and pensions.

earned media *Journ, Law&Pol »* **unpaid media**

earned rate *Mktg* Frequency discount earned by an advertiser based on the number of insertions actually used during a contract year.

earning out *LitArts* Earning enough in royalties to cover the publisher's advance.

earnings before taxes *EntreP* Amount of income that a corporation has before paying corporate taxes to the government. Shown on corporate income statements.

earnings per share *EntreP* How much a corporation has earned for each share of common stock outstanding. Formula is net profit minus preferred dividends divided by the number of shares of common stock.

East *Cult&Soc* 1 Eastern part of the earth, esp. eastern Asia. 2 Former Communist bloc of countries in Asia and Eastern Europe. *Also see* **West**.

Easter eggs *InfoMgt* Names of programmers hidden in the software they authored, retrieved only by **arcane** key commands.

Eastern *Cult&Soc* Political and social orientation to the eastern part of the earth, esp. eastern Asia and the former Communist bloc of countries in Asia and Eastern Europe. *Also see* **Western**.

Eastwood, Clint (1930-, Film dir-prod., act.) *ArtPerf, Flm&Vid, Mgt* <*Play Misty for Me* (1971), *Bird* (1988), *Unforgiven* (1992, **Oscars** for best dir., best pic)> *Also see* **laconic**.

Easy Access *InfoMgt* Software that assists people who have difficulty typing on the keyboard or manipulating the mouse.

easy listening *MusArts* Ballads to uptempo tunes, characterized by simple, easily hummed melodies — easy to listen to, easy to dance to, [and so easy to forget.] Aptly referred to as **middle-of-road** (MOR) or **mainstream** pop.

EAT+D² *ArtPerf* Formula expresses the three basic characteristics of a successful performer: ego, ambition, talent & technique, plus the stabilizing effect of mental and physical discipline. *Also see* **Arts Dynamic**.

Eaves-Brooks Costume Company *PerfA&C* North America's most famous theatrical costume co., est. 1863. Acquired July 2002 by Dodger Endemol Theatrical Productions (NYC)

EBCDIC *InfoMgt* **Extended Binary Coded Decimal Interchange Code**. 8-bit code used for data representation.

ebullient *Crit&Eval* zestfully enthusiastic

eccentric *Crit&Eval* Departing from conventional norm; strange.

ecdysiast *PA-Variety* **stripper** *Origin* Word coined by **H.L. Mencken**.

echo *MusArts* Soft repetition of a note or phrase.

echo *Sci&Tech* 1 Reflected wave received by a radio or radar. 2 Sound produced in this manner.

echo verse *LitArts* Verse in which the final words or syllables of a line or stanza are repeated as a response, often with an ironic effect.

éclat (ee-kla, Fr.) *Crit&Eval* 1 Great brilliance of performance or achievement. 2 Conspicuous success. 3 Great acclamation or applause.

eclectic *Crit&Eval* Selecting or employing individual elements from a variety of sources, systems, or styles: an eclectic taste in music; an eclectic approach to managing the economy. ECLECTICISM

eclipse *Crit&Eval* Become obscure. <Artist often goes into eclipse after her or his death>

ECMA-262 specification *iMedia* Standardized language similar to **JavaScript**.

ECMAscript *iMedia »* **ECMA**-262 specification

E

ECOM *InfoMgt* Electronic computer oriented mail *Also see* **email**.

econ. *Eco&Fin* economics, economist, economy

economic capital *EntreP* Those items that man manufactures by combining natural and human resources. Includes buildings, machinery, and equipment used by business and government. Economic Capital, Physical Capital, or Fixed Assets are often used synonymously.

economic freedom *LitArts* "The writer doesn't need economic freedom. All he needs is a pencil and some paper. I've never known anything good in writing to come from having accepted any free gift of money. The good writer never applies to a foundation. He's too busy writing something." — **William Faulkner**

economic growth *EntreP* Sustained increases in the real production of an economy over a period of time.

economic indicators *ColEntry, Eco&Fin* Key data used to predict how an economy will perform from the near to long range. These are important considerations for large and small companies – and **nonprofits** – for planning budgets, expenditures, investments, marketing, inventory levels, sales projections, etc. Economic indicators are a useful tool but it must be kept in mind that they are indications, not absolute guarantees, and should be tempered with good non-emotional judgment. *Also see* **Balance of Trade, book-to-bill, Consumer Confidence Index/Consumer Confidence Survey, Cost of Living Indexes, CPI, Durable Goods Orders, Employment Cost Index, Existing Home Sales, Federal Reserve Discount Rate, GDP, GNP, Inflation Rate, Inventory Levels, Long Range Weather Forecasts, Machine Tool Orders, Natural Disasters, New & Used Car Sales, New Home Construction, real GNP, regional economic indicators, specific industry economic indicators, Stock Market Indexes and Averages, Tourism and Vacation Destinations, Unemployment Rate, "Weak" and "Strong" Dollar, WPI.**

economic order quantity (EOQ) *EntreP* Quantity of items for a business to order which balances the ordering costs against the storage costs of inventory. The most economic quantity to order to minimize overall inventory costs.

economic profit *EntreP* Total revenue minus the total economic cost.

economic strike *HR&LR* Strike not caused by unfair actions of the employer but by the negative effect of economic forces.

Economics & Finance *Eco&Fin* one of the four **Outer Forces** of **The Arts Dynamic**

economics (econ.) *Eco&Fin* Social science that deals with the production, distribution, and consumption of goods and services and with the theory and management of economies or economic systems.

economics *EntreP* Study of the choices made by people who are faced with scarcity.

economies of scale *EntreP* Situation in which an increase in the quantity produced decreases the long-run average cost of production.

economies of scale *Eco&Fin* Reduction of fixed costs by increasing production, leaning on suppliers for bulk and volume discounts, and achieving dominant market share.

economist (econ.) *Eco&Fin* Specialist in economics.

economy *Crit&Eval* **1** Orderly, functional arrangement of parts; an organized system. **2** Efficient, sparing, or conservative use.

economy *Eco&Fin* **1** Careful, thrifty management of resources, such as money, materials, or labor; a saving. **2** System or range of economic activity in a country, region, or community.

ecstasy *Cult&Soc* Illegal and dangerous drug often part of a **rave** scene, *aka* methylenedioxymethamphetamine (MDMA)

ECU *BcstJourn* extreme closeup » **closeup**

ed. *Crit&Eval* education

ed. *LitArts, MusArts, VA-Prntng* Edited by, **edition, editor**

edge numbers *Flm&Vid* Numbers and key letters printed at regular intervals along the edge of film stock. as an aid to editing.

EDI *InfoMgt, Fashn* **Electronic Data Interchange,** the electronic transfer of data from one party to another via computer technology. EDI networks enable retailers to respond quickly to fashion trends and opportunities through automated inventory control and reorder capability.

Edison, Thomas Alva (1847-1931, inventor) *RecA&S, Sci&Tech*

Patented more than a thousand inventions: **microphone** (1877), **phonograph** (1878), incandescent lamp (1879) In NYC. he installed the world's first central electric power plant (1881-1882) *Also see* **Émile Berliner**.

edit *Flm&Vid, RecA&S* To assemble the components of a film or soundtrack.

edit *Journ, LitArts* **1** To prepare written material for publication or presentation by correcting, revising, or adapting. **2** To prepare an edition of for publication. **3** To modify or adapt so as to make suitable or acceptable. <edited his remarks for a school audience> **4** To supervise the publication of a. <newspaper, magazine, journal, newsletter>

edit checks *InfoMgt* Processing statements designed to identify potential errors in input data.

edit line *InfoMgt* Status report displayed on the screen when certain programs are in use. It tells the user the present location of the cursor, amount of memory left, name of the file in use; in spreadsheets. It shows the contents or formula of the cell at the cursor location.

edit menu *InfoMgt* Lists editing commands <**Copy, Clear, Cut, Paste**>

edition (ed.) *InfoMgt* File that has been designated as a publisher in a document. Material in the edition can be inserted into other documents ("subscribers") and updated automatically in all subscribing documents when the publisher in the original document is changed. *Also see* **publisher, subscriber**.

edition (ed.) *Journ* All the copies of a single press run of a newspaper. <suburban edition>

edition (ed.) *LitArts* **1** All copies of a publication issued at one time or from a single set of type; a single copy from this group. **2** Form in which a publication is issued. <paperback edition; **annotated** edition> **3** Version of an earlier publication with substantial alterations. <this revised edition of DAPM Beta version 2.0>

edition (ed.) *VA-Prntng* **1** All the copies of a publication printed from the same method of reproduction. <a single **typesetting**, set of printing plates> Single copy. <a first edition> **3** Facsimile of an earlier publication with substantial alterations.

editor (ed.) *Flm&Vid* Person or a device that edits film. "Actually the editor is a storyteller. The editor restructures and rewrites and rebalances the story by **juxtaposing** images." — Allen Heim (19??-, Oscar-winning film editor.) "Editors sit quietly in the dark and do their work. You have to like having no ego." — Michael Kahn (19??-, Oscar winner, **Steven Spielberg's** favorite editor.)

editor (ed.) *Journ, LitArts* **1** One who supervises one or more phases of the publishing process. <edit manuscripts line by line, help writers conceptualize their books and shape them into coherence. — Martin Arnold (lit-crit.)> **2** One who writes editorials. **3** One who edits copy for accuracy and style. "Editors choose." — **Ben Bradlee.** *Also see* **copy editor**.

editor (ed.) *MusArts* One who edits music manuscript for publication.

editor in chief *Journ* Editor bearing final responsibility for the editorial policies and operations of a group of publications.

editorial *Journ,. Rdio/TV* **1** Short essay in a publication expressing the opinion of its editors or publisher. **2** Commentary on television or radio expressing the opinion of the station management.

editorial calendar *Journ, Mktg* Primarily a guide for magazine advertisers, the calendar lists cover dates with corresponding special coverage. <June: Our "Annual Swim Suit Issue.">

editorial objective *Journ* Editorial staff's specific goals and evaluation criteria.

editorialize *Journ,. Rdio/TV* **1** To express an opinion in or as if in an editorial. **2** To present an opinion in the guise of an objective report. *Also see* **fair comment**.

.edu *InfoMgt* Suffix of an Internet **domain name** assigned to educational organizations. *Also see* **Domain Names, Network Solutions Inc**.

educ. *Crit&Eval* educator

education (ed.) *Crit&Eval* Knowledge or skill obtained or developed by a learning process.

education and access *Fndng* Grants for instruction and outreach — one of four categories of grants by the **National Endowment for the Arts**. *Also see* **NEA grants**.

E

Education, U.S. Department of *Cult&Soc, HR&LR, Law&Pol* » **DOE**

educational television (ETV) *Rdio/TV* » **ETV**

Educational Television Act (1962) *Law&Pol, Rdio&TV* Authorized grants to educational institutions and nonprofits to build educational television stations. *Also see* **Federal Agencies and Statutes.**

Educational Theatre Association (ETA) *TheatArts* » **ETA**

educator (educ.) *Crit&Eval* **1** teacher. **2** Specialist in the theory and practice of education. **3** Administrator of an educational institution.

EE *InfoMgt,. Rdio/TV* **Electronic Editing.** Editing of audio/visual materials by electronic means without mechanical splices, lifts, or reprints.

EEC *Eco&Fin* **European Economic Community.** Economic alliance formed in 1957 by Belgium, France, Italy, Luxembourg, The Netherlands, and West Germany to foster trade and cooperation among its members. Newer members include: Great Britain and Spain.

EEOC *Eco&Fin, HR&LR, Law&Pol* **Equal Employment Opportunity Commission.** U.S. agency created (1954) to end discrimination in hiring based on race, color, religion, sex, national origin, age, or disability, and to promote equal employment opportunities. If persuasion doesn't work, it is empowered to bring suit against offenders in federal court. [Not yet empowered to try and end discrimination based on sexual orientation.] *Also see* **Federal Agencies and Statutes.**

EFF *InfoMgt, Ethcs&Phil* » **Electronic Frontier Foundation 1** Its mission is to civilize **cyberspace** and make it useful and beneficial to everyone, not just the electronic elite. **2** Civil liberties advocacy group.

effective rate *EntreP* Rate of interest that is actually earned or charged when compounding is taken into consideration.

effects (fx) *Flm&Vid, Rdio/TV* » **sound effects, special effects**

effete (ef-feet) *Crit&Eval* **1** Overrefined; effeminate. **2** Marked by self-indulgence, triviality, or decadence. <an effete group of so-called **artistes**> **3** Depleted of vitality or effectiveness; exhausted. <the final, effete period of the **baroque** style>

efficacy *Crit&Eval* Power or capacity to produce a desired effect; effectiveness.

Efficient Markets Hypothesis *EntreP* Hypothesis that prices in the capital markets fully reflect information available to their participants.

EFTS *InfoMgt, Eco&Fin* **Electronic Fund Transfer System.** Telecommunication system designed to handle banking transactions.

egalitarian *Law&Pol* Affirming, promoting, or characterized by belief in equal political, economic, social, and civil rights for all people.

ego *ArtPerf, Mgt* **1** Some creative urge within the Artist/Performer that must be expressed at whatever the cost. **2** Self-love, self-confidence, self-esteem. **3** Self, esp. as distinct from the world and other selves. **4** One of the three basic characteristics of a successful Artist/Performer. "The workings of all major industries involve a mixture of ego, image, and economic muscle, but nowhere is this truer than in the entertainment industry." — Geraldine Fabricant and Bernard Weinraub (ent. critics) *Also see* **EAT+D².**

ego trip *ArtPerf* Something that gratifies the ego. "Love the art in yourself, and not yourself in the art." — [Konstatine] **Stanislavski**

egocentric *ArtPerf* **1** Having the view that the ego is the **center**, object, and norm of all experience. **2** Self-centered, selfish. "The Katharine Hepburn (» **censorship**) that emerges here is unsaintly, an **archetypical** American actor: **narcissistic**, ambitious, sometimes ruthless and rarely concerned about people other than herself or ideas other than those of practical use in her advancement." — **Frank Rich**

egoism *Ethcs&Phil* **1** Ethical stance involving judgment proceeding from standards that serve one's own desires, wishes, or interests. **2** Ethical **doctrine** that morality is based on self-interest. <One of George Orwell's four reasons for writing: "Sheer Egoism. Desire to seem clever, to be talked about, to be revenged after death, to get your own back on grown-ups who snubbed you in childhood, etc."— **George Orwell**>

egoist *Crit&Eval* One devoted to one's own interests and advancement.

egotism *Crit&Eval* **1** Tendency to refer to oneself in a boastful and excessive way. **2** Extreme sense of self-importance.

egotist *Crit&Eval* Conceited, boastful, self-absorbed person, selfish person.

egregious (ee-greej-us) *Crit&Eval* Conspicuously bad or offensive.

EHF *Rdio/TV, RecA&S* **extra high frequency**; very short **wavelength**

eight by ten (8 inch x 10 inch) *Mktg* » **glossy**

Eight, The *VisArts* Group of American painters who united in opposition to academic standards. They organized the **Armory Show** of 1913 which introduced modern European art to America. In 1917, they organized the Society of Independent Artists, *aka* **Ashcan School.** <Arthur Davies, William J. Glackens, Robert Henri, Ernest Lawson, George Luke, Maurice Prendergast, Everett Shinn, and John Sloan>

eighth note *MusArts* Note whose value is one-eighth of a **whole note** and double that of a **sixteenth** note. *Also see* **Musical Notes.**

Eisenstein, Sergei Mikhailovich (1898-1948, Soviet flmkr) *ArtPerf, Flm&Vid* Soviet Considered among the most influential directors in the history of motion pictures. <*Potemkin* (1925), *Alexander Nevsky* (1938, his first film with sound)>

eject *InfoMgt* Remove a disk from a **disk drive.**

elastic demand *EntreP* Demand that changes significantly when *there is* a change in the price of the product.

elasticity of demand *EntreP* Degree to which a change in price affects the quantity demanded.

elasticity of demand *Mktg* Rate of responsiveness of sales volume to a change in price. Demand is **price inelastic** when changing prices up or down has little effect on sales volume. Demand is **price elastic** when price changes materially effect sales volume.

electret microphone *RecA&S* **Condenser** mic that incorporates a self-polarized or electret capacitor element. *Also see* **Microphones.**

electric batten *Flm&Vid,PerfA&C* On-stage **batten** with cable and connectors specifically used for hanging lighting instruments. *Also see* **Stage Lighting.**

electric piano *MusInstr* Keyboard instrument that uses electronic amplification to produce sound rather than the acoustic sound produced by a piano. *Also see* **Musical Instrument Families.**

electrical recording *RecA&S* First recording and reproducing system using electricity (via microphones) developed by **Bell Labs** in 1924 Led to industry-wide electric recording in 1925 Popularized by Victor records under the name **Orthophonic.** *Also see* **acoustical recording, transducer.**

electrical transcription *RecA&S* Originally a recording specifically made for radio broadcast; a 15-minute program on each side of s 16-inch 33-1/3 rpm disk. Most commonly used in the 1930s and 1940s before the advent of taped recordings. Technically, a taped recording; cannot be considered an electrical transcription. — Harvey Rachlin (mus. biz wri.)

electricians *PerfA&C* Those who work on stage lighting for a production.

electron *Sci&Tech* stable subatomic particle

electronic commerce *InfoMgt* less glitzy name for **cyberspace**

electronic computer oriented mail (ECOM) *InfoMgt* » **ECOM**

Electronic Data Interchange (EDI) *InfoMgt, Fashn* » **EDI**

electronic editing (EE) *InfoMgt,. Rdio/TV* » **EE**

electronic feedback *RecA&S* This condition can occur when sound from a speaker is fed back at a high enough level to a **mic**, the result can be ringing or howling.

Electronic Frontier Foundation (EFF) *InfoMgt, Ethcs&Phil* » **EFF**

Electronic Fund Transfer System (EFTS) *InfoMgt, Eco&Fin* » **EFTS**

electronic funds transfer *EntreP* Electronic funds transfer is a process used to immediately transfer funds from one bank account to another via computer.

electronic ink *InfoMgt, Sci&Tech* Electrically charged ink that can change the image on a sign or printed page. *Also see* **E Ink.**

electronic instruments *MusInstr* Musical instruments that use electronic amplification to produce sound. <via vibrations, e.g., electric guitar, electric piano; via impulses, e.g., synthesizer> *Also see* **acoustic instruments, Musical Instrument Families.**

electronic mail *InfoMgt* » **email**

electronic mailbox *InfoMgt* » **email**

electronic media *Rdio/TV* Radio and television and their derivatives. *Also see* **Advertising Media**.

electronic music *MusArts* Music produced or altered by electronic means, as by a tape recorder or synthesizer. "Many of us turned to computers and electronic music because it's a way to realize some of the things we hear in our head, the different sounds — with the pragmatic consideration that at least we can hear them performed." — Howard Sandroff (comp., pno., educ.) *Also see* **MIDI**.

Electronic Numerical Integrator & Calculator *InfoMgt* » **ENIAC**

electronic organ *MusInstr* Keyboard instrument capable of producing indefinitely **sustained** sounds. <Hammond (1935) used rotating electromagnetic generators; Electrone (1938) used electrostatic generators> *Also see* **Musical Instrument Families, Organs**.

electronic publishing *InfoMgt* <**CD-ROMs**, educational software, online data bases, **email videotex**, teletext, **videotape** cassettes, videodisks> *Also see* **publishing**.

electronic spreadsheet *InfoMgt* Type of software designed to handle rows and columns of numbers similar to an accounting ledger.

electronic stylus *InfoMgt* » **light pen**

electronics *Sci&Tech* **1** Science and technology of electronic phenomena. **2** Electronic devices and systems.

electrotype *VA-Prntng* Metal plate used in **letterpress** printing.

eleemosynary *Crit&Eval* Dependent on charity.

elegy *LitArts, MusArts* **1** Poem or song composed esp. as a lament for a deceased person. **2** Composition melancholy or pensive in tone. *Also see* **Songs**.

elevation *Dnce* (Ballet) **1** Ability to jump high in the air and give the impression of remaining suspended there for an instant. <Michael Jordan> **2** Degree of height reached.

eleven o'clock number *MusArts, TheatArts* Climactic song in a musical, sung near the **finale**.

ELF *Rdio/TV, RecA&S* » **extra low frequency**; very long **wavelength**

elite *Cult&Soc* **1** Group or class of persons or a member of such a group or class, enjoying superior intellectual, social, or economic status. **2** Best or most skilled members of a group. INTELLIGENTSIA, SMART SET

elitism, élitism *Cult&Soc, Ethcs&Phil* Belief that certain persons or members of certain classes or groups deserve favored treatment by virtue of their perceived superiority, as in intellect, social status, or financial resources.

Elizabethan *Crit&Eval* Relating to Queen Elizabeth I of England (1558-1603)

Ella Award *ArtPerf, MusArts* Lifetime achievement award in honor of Ella Fitzgerald sponsored by the **Society of Singers** (SOS)

Ellington, Duke (Edward Kennedy Ellington, 1899-1974, bndldr, arr.-comp., pno.) *ArtPerf, MusArts* One of the most prolific composers in the history of music, Ellington composed more than 2,000 compositions. <popular songs — *Mood Indigo, Solitude, Sophisticated Lady, In a Sentimental Mood;* concert works — *Black, Brown and Beige, Creole Rhapsody, Far East Suite, Diminuendo and Crescendo in Blue;* and more, much more> "*Jazz is black* **classical music**" One of the leading figures in the history of American music, he was awarded the Presidential Medal of Freedom in 1969. *Also see* **good music, Pulitzer Prize, serious music**.

ellipsis (...) *VA-Prntng* Mark used in writing or printing to indicate an omission of letters or words. *Also see* "Explanatory Notes."

ellipsoidal reflector spotlight *PerfA&C* Lighting instrument characterized by hard-edged light with little diffusion. Designed for long throws, it is manufactured with fixed and variable focal-length lenses; the light beam is shaped with internally mounted shutters. *Also see* **Stage Lighting**.

elliptical *LitArts* **1** Relating to extreme economy of oral or written expression. **2** Marked by deliberate obscurity of style or expression.

elliptical sentences *BcstJourn* Sentence fragment designed to mimic speech patterns and that usu. is missing either the subject or verb.

em dash (—) *Journ, VA-Prntng* Width of an "m." Usually used before an author's name at the end of a quotation or statement. *Also see* **en**.

embellish *MusArts, VisArts* Add fanciful or ornamental details.

embellishment *Fashn* decoration, ornamentation.

Embooees *Cult&Soc, MusArts* African tribe. *Also see* **praise shouter, praise song, rap**.

embroidery *Fashn* Ornamentation by needlework

emcee *PerfA&C* » **master of ceremonies**

emergency powers *LegAsp* Implied power an agent has should an emergency arise and the agent is unable to contact the **principal**.

emergent behavior *iMedia* Behavior (usu. unpredictable) resulting from interaction between elements in an environment; complex systems can arise from the interplay of simple individual elements. *Also see* **complex adaptive system**, **swarm intelligence**.

emerging artist *ArtPerf, VisArts* One coming forth from obscurity; on the road to be an **established artist**.

emerging *Cult&Soc, Eco&Fin, Mktg* Newly formed or just coming into prominence. <emerging markets; the emerging African and Asiatic countries.

EMI *MusArts* Experiments in Musical Intelligence

EMI Music *RecA&S* One of the six **major** [record] **labels**. *Also see* **Capitol**.

Emmy Awards *Rdio/TV* Annual awards for television programs by members of the **National Academy of Television Arts & Sciences**. *Also see* **Awards & Prizes**.

emoticon *InfoMgt* Online means of facial expressions and gestures. <Smiley, :)> [Tip your head to the left and return the smile].

emotion *Crit&Eval* Part of the consciousness that involves feeling; sensibility: "The very essence of literature is the war between emotion and intellect" — Isaac Bashevis Singer (1904-91, Polish-born American Yiddish fictwri.)

emotionalism *Crit&Eval* **1** Inclination to rely on or place too much value on emotion. **2** Undue display of emotion.

empathic response *Crit&Eval* Relationship between artist and audience. "You can write a book and people will read it, but you don't hear them laugh. There's nothing like it except drug addiction." — **John P. Marquand** "You know when they start breathing with you that it's working." — Jason Robards (» **Ben Bradlee**) "Audiences will forgive anything that gives them joy." — **John Lahr** (critic) HOOK, LEAVE A TIP.

Empire styles (Ahm-peer, Fr.) *Fashn, VisArts* Neoclassic style in clothing or the decorative arts, prevalent in France during the first part of the 19th century.

empirical *Crit&Eval* **1** Verifiable or provable by means of observation or experiment. **2** Guided by practical experience and not theory. Opposite of "unproved" or "unsubstantiated." *Also see* **Aristotle, cognitive, John Stuart Mill** (1806-73, Brit. philos., econ.), **utilitarianism**.

employee *HR&LR* Person who works for another in return for some sort of compensation. *Also see* **worker**.

employee earnings *E&F-Acc* Total wages/salaries earned by employees.

employee matching gift *Fnding* Contribution to a charitable organization by a company employee that is matched by a similar contribution from the employer.

employee representation plan *HR&LR* System whereby employees elect representatives to a committee comprised of both management and labor to discuss **grievances** of either party.

employee stock option plan (ESOP) *EntreP* Harvesting plan in which employees of the company purchase shares of the company.

Employee Stock Ownership Plan (ESOP) *Eco&Fin, HR&LR* » **ESOP**

employee turnover *Eco&Fin, HR&LR* Percentage figure calculated by dividing the total average number of employees of a company into the new hires for the year. Employees hired for new jobs during the year should not be calculated into the percentage.

employee withholdings *E&F-Acc* Amount paid to employees less any deductions paid to government agencies. <**Social Security, Medicare,** federal and state income taxes> Also includes deductions requested by employees for pensions, health and life insurance premiums, union dues, and charitable contributions.

employer's liability insurance *EntreP* Coverage that protects against lawsuits brought by employees who suffer injury.

employment agency license *HR&LR, Mgt* Some states <California, Illinois, and New York> require talent agencies to be licensed and regulated as employment agencies. *Also see* **Talent Agencies**.

Employment Cost Index *Eco&Fin* **Economic indicator** that measures growth in wages. Has been singled out by the **Federal Reserve** chairman, Alan Greenspan, as a key barometer of **inflationary** pressures. *Also see* **employment costs**.

employment costs *E&F-Acc* Total costs of employment includes wages/salaries paid to employees plus payroll taxes. <**Employment Cost Index, FUTA, SUTA**>

emulate *Crit&Eval* Try to equal or excel by imitation. <**Bix Beiderbecke** was probably the first white musician to be emulated by Black musicians>

emulate *InfoMgt* To imitate the function of another program or system by modifications to hardware or software that allow the imitating program or system to achieve the same results as the imitated program or system.

emulsion *Flm&Vid* Chemically active portion of film that preserves the photographic image. Emulsion side of the film is dull; the celluloid backing is shiny.

en dash (–) *Journ, VA-Prntng* Width of an "n." Used mainly to denote an abrupt change in thought in a sentence. *Also see* **em**.

En Garde Arts *TheatArts* » **site-specific theater**

enables *LegAsp* To give legal power, capacity, or sanction to.

enabling factor *EntreP* Set of variables that makes the launch of a venture possible, including sufficient resources and a viable opportunity.

encap *LitArts, Mktg* End-of-aisle display in a (**chain**) book store, available for a fee paid by a book publisher. *Also see* **dump, new arrival wall**.

encode *InfoMgt* To convert a character, routine, or program into machine language.

encore *MusArts* Demand by an audience for an additional performance, usu. expressed by perceived or real applause. *Also see* **claque, curtain call**.

encrypt *InfoMgt* To **scramble** access codes to computerized information so as to prevent unauthorized access.

encrypted data *InfoMgt* Method of transforming data into a secret code.

encryption *InfoMgt* Scrambled access codes to prevent unauthorized access to computerized information.

end man *PA-Variety* Man in a **minstrel show** who sits at one end of the company and engages in **banter** with the **interlocutor**.

end matter *LitArts* » **back matter**

end rate *Mktg* Lowest unit rate on a medium's advertising **rate card**.

end-user *InfoMgt* Anyone who uses a computer system or its output.

(end/end) or **(# # #)** *BcstJourn* In some newsrooms, marks that are placed at the end of the story to indicate there are no additional pages. (Akin to —30—" in newspaper journalism.)

endnote *InfoMgt, LitArts* Note placed at the end of an article, a chapter, or a book that comments on or cites a reference for a designated part of the text. *Also see* **footnote**.

endorsement *Eco&Fin, LegAsp* Act of transferring title to a written negotiable instrument by having the temporary owner write his name on the back of the document.

endorsement *Mktg* Approval or support of a product or service, usu. by a celebrity. *Also see* **advertising agency, celebrity service**.

endow *Crit&Eval* To equip one with a talent or quality. <Nature endowed **Marian Anderson** with a magnificent singing voice>

endow *Fndng* To provide with property, income, or a source of income.

endowment *Crit&Eval* Natural **gift**, ability, or quality.

endowment *Fnding* Funds intended to be kept permanently and invested to provide income for continued support of an organization.

endowment funds *Eco&Fin* » **endowment** *Also see* **Funds**

endpin *MusInstr* Thin, usu. adjustable leg of a cello or double bass.

energy *ArtPerf,PerfA&C* "Energy is the actor's greatest asset." —

Harold Clurman

enfranchised *Law&Pol* Endowed with the rights of citizenship, esp. the right to vote.

Eng-h *MusInstr* **English horn**

engage *iMedia* To involve, hold the attention of, and/or entice participation; engaging media involves a participant.

engage *Mgt* Hire for a performance

engagement *iMedia* Level of involvement; high engagement level draws in a participant. *Also see* **engage**.

engagement *Mgt* Entertainment job, performance. *Also see* **casual —, steady —**.

engagement contract *LegAsp, Mgt* Legal agreement between the performer and the employer. <**Engagements** for union musicians must be contracted for on an **AFM** Engagement Contract (Form C) and a fully signed copy be filed with the **AFM** local union of jurisdiction> PERFORMANCE CONTRACT *Also see* **Contracts, deposit, guarantee, power of attorney**.

Engelbart, Douglas (1925-) *iMedia* Invented the computer mouse, experimented with adding elements from different technologies together (*Ex.* he helped create word processing by adding a keyboard to a computer

engineer (engr.) *Flm&Vid, Rdio/TV* Person who is responsible for the technical operation of a film or broadcast studio as well as **CATV** or satellite transmission and reception. *Also see* **recording engineer**.

engineer (engr.) *Rdio/TV, RecA&S* » **recording engineer; sound engineer**

engineer-producer *RecA&S* Recording engineer may also be the producer of a recording if he or she has the funding and a **distribution deal**. *Also see* **Producers**.

English horn (Eng-h.) *MusInstr* **Double-reed woodwind** instrument similar to but larger than the **oboe** and **pitched** lower by a fifth. ENGLISH HORN PLAYER, ENGLISH HORNIST (RARE) *Also see* **Musical Instrument Families**.

engr. *Rdio/TV, RecA&S* engineer.

enhanced CDs *RecA&S* Compact disks designed to play in a **CD-ROM** drive of a personal computer, in which the music is supplemented with video **excerpts**, spoken narrative, or other flourishes. It has been predicted that enhanced CDs will replace standard CDs in two or three years. "They provide so much value for the customer, and open up new forms of expression." — Charles Bermant (*RecA&S* wri.)

enhanced underwriting *Mktg, Rdio/TV* Policy of liberalizing the amount and kind of advertising on public radio or television. *Also see* **NPR, underwrite, value-added**.

enhancement money *Eco&Fin, Mgt* **1** Bonus from management to artist for extra value received. **2** Additional funding. <Enhancement money in the amount of $100,000 was needed to mount the production of *East Lynne* to a larger theater>

enharmonic *MusArts* Relating to **tones** that are identical in **pitch** but are written differently according to the key in which they occur.

ENIAC *InfoMgt* **Electronic Numerical Integrator & Calculator**, the first all-electronic **digital** computer.

enigma *Crit&Eval* **1** One that is puzzling, **ambiguous**, or inexplicable. **2** Perplexing speech or text; a riddle.

Enlightenment, The *Ethcs&Phil* Philosophical movement of the 18th century that emphasized the use of reason to scrutinize previously accepted **doctrines** and traditions and that brought about many humanitarian reforms.

Enliven *InfoMgt,* Software permits the distribution and viewing of feature-length **interactive multimedia** over the Internet using ordinary phone lines.

ensemble *Fashn* Unit or group of complementary parts that contribute to a single effect. <coordinated **outfit** or costume>

ensemble *MusArts,PerfA&C, Dnce* **1** Group of supporting musicians, singers, dancers, or actors who perform together. **2** Work for two or more vocalists or instrumentalists. **3** Vocalists or instrumentalists who perform such a work.

ensemble acting *TheatArts* Theatrical presentation in which the stress is on the performance of the group rather than the individual.

enshrine *Crit&Eval* To cherish as sacred.

enter *TheatArts* Entrance of a performer on to the stage. <enter

left, enter right, enter up, etc> *Also see* **Stage Directions**.

enter. *PerfA&C* **entertainer, entertainment**

enter key *InfoMgt* Special key on some keyboards that means "execute a command." *Also see* **return key**.

entertainer (enter.) *ArtPerf* One who entertains for money.

entertainment (enter.) *Crit&Eval* Something that amuses, pleases, or diverts. <a performance or show, amusement> "From a technical point of view, both entertainment and art require craftsmanship, but since style is one of the chief devices for liberating truth, it should be obvious that the richer the language, the worse the entertainment. Or to put the thing neutrally, entertainment requires cleverness, art richness. Needless to say, neither art nor entertainment very often get what they require." — John Gardner (1912-, psychologist, U.S. Secy., HEW, 1965-68) *Also see* **mass entertainment**.

entertainment marketing *Mktg* Process of developing and exchanging ideas, goods, and services that satisfy the entertainment needs and wants of consumers.

enthrall *Crit&Eval* To hold spellbound; captivate. <The beauty of the ballet enthralled the audience>

entitlement program *Eco&Fin, Law&Pol* Government program that guarantees and provides benefits to a particular group. <**Social security**, **Medicare**, **Medicaid**, **Social Security**> *Also see* **FICA**.

entity *E&F-Acc* Most basic concept in accounting. Organization or a section of an organization that for accounting purposes, stands apart from other organizations and individuals as a separate economic unit.

entity *iMedia* **1** Object **2** Element defined in a document type definition. *Also see* **character entity**.

entity *LegAsp* Something that exists as a particular and discrete unit. <Persons and corporations are equivalent entities under the law>

entourage (on-tour-ahge, Fr.) *Genl* Group of attendants or associates.

entr'acte (ontray-act, Fr.) *MusArts, TheatArts* **1** Interval between two acts of a theatrical performance. **2** Another performance of music or dance provided between two acts of a theatrical performance. **3** Interval similar to one occurring between two acts of a drama.

entrechat (ontray-shat, Fr.) *Dnce* (Ballet) Jump in **fifth position** during which the dancer crosses the legs a number of times, alternately back and forth.

entrée *Dnce* Make an entrance (Ballet) First part of the classical **pas de deux**. *Also see* **adagio, coda**.

entrepreneur (Entrepreneurial resources) *EntreP* Individual who assumes risk and begins business enterprises. Entrepreneur combines land, labor, and capital resources to produce a good or service that society values more highly than the sum of the individual parts.

entrepreneur *Mgt* One who organizes, operates, and assumes the risk in a business venture in expectation of gaining a profit.

entrepreneurial equation *EntreP* Conceptual equation that involves combining antecedent, precipitating, and enabling variables in order to assess the likelihood that an individual will launch a venture.

entrepreneurial personality *EntreP* Set of personality characteristics shared by most entrepreneurs. These include an internal locus of control, a need for autonomy, a need for achievement, a moderate risk-taking propensity and a willingness to make sacrifices.

entrepreneurial profit *EntreP* Amount that is earned above and beyond what the entrepreneur would have earned if he or she had chosen to invest time and money in some other enterprise. It is most closely related to the economic concept of opportunity cost.

entrepreneurial society *EntreP* Society characterized by a high number of energetic and innovative individuals willing to start or grow their own ventures.

entrepreneurial stress *EntreP* Pressures encountered by an entrepreneur either because of the direct demands of the venture or because the time required to grow the venture takes away from family needs.

entrepreneurial team *EntreP* Management of an entrepreneurial company, especially at the time of launch. Team may include a lead entrepreneur and others with specialty skills.

entrepreneurial window *EntreP* Mange of ages at which individuals are most likely to start their first venture.

entrepreneurship *EntreP* Process an individual goes through in starting and growing a business.

entry-level *Mgt* Related to one inexperienced in a field. <an entry-level job in management>

entry-level *Mktg* Related to one new to a market. <an entry-level computer>

entry-word *InfoMgt* » **headword**

environmentalism *EntreP* Effort to protect and preserve the environment.

EP record *RecA&S* **extended play record**: a 7-inch, 33-1/3 **rpm** or 45 **rpm** double-sided long-play disc phonograph record containing two selections or one longer-than-standard selections on each side.

epaulet *Fashn* Shoulder ornament, a fringed strap as worn on military uniforms.

ephemera *LitArts* Printed matter of passing interest.

ephemeral (ee-femeral) *Crit&Eval* Only lasting for a brief time. <Some thoughts are too ephemeral to be captured on the written page>

epic *LitArts* Extended narrative poem or dramatic composition in celebrating the feats of a legendary or traditional hero.

epic *TheatArts* **1** Said of acting, a drama, a setting, a style of theatre, using an anti-naturalistic technique, concerned with social documentation for purposes of propaganda. **2** "Drama with a vast historical sweep." — Bowman and Ball (biz ethicists)

epic drama *TheatArts* » **epic theatre**

Epic Records *RecA&S* » **cease-and-desist order**

epic theater *TheatArts* Term associated with the Overman director Erwin Piscator, and theorized by **Bertolt Brecht** in the late 1920s and '30s. Epic theater uses episodic dramatic action, non-representational staging, and alienation effects to demonstrate the political, economic, and social factors governing the lives of the dramatic characters. On stage, these effects are produced by visible lighting, placards to announce the action, film screens, and songs, among other devices. *Also see* **Theatres & Theaters**.

epicurean *Ethcs&Phil* **1** Ethical school associated with ancient Greece and Rome, based on the idea that pleasure is the good; in its origins the pleasure is a certain subtle and refined pleasure, but not gross sensual pleasure. **2** Commonly atheistic.

epigone *ArtPerf* Imitator, a second-rate follower of an artist or philosopher.

episode *TheatArts* In Greek tragedy, the sections of character dialog between choral odes.

epithet *Crit&Eval* Abusive or contemptuous word or phrase.

EPROM *InfoMgt* **Erasable Programmable Read Only Memory**; a form of **read-only memory** that can be erased and re-programmed by using ultra-violet light.

Equal Employment Opportunity Commission (EEOC) *Eco&Fin, HR&LR, Law&Pol* Independent federal agency created by Congress in 1964 to enforce Title VII of the **Civil Rights Act**; provides oversight, coordination, and enforcement of all federal laws dealing with discrimination.

equal time *Law&Pol, Rdio/TV* Refers to the **FCC** regulation that requires a radio or TV station to provide a candidate for political office with air time equal to any time that an opponent receives beyond the coverage of news events. *Also see* **fairness doctrine**.

equilibrium *EntreP* Point where a supply curve and demand curve for a market intersect.

equip. *Crit&Eval* **equipment**

equipment *Crit&Eval* The qualities or traits that make up the mental and emotional resources of an individual.

Equity *ArtPerf, HR&LR, TheatArts* **Actors' Equity Association**. Labor union, chartered by the **Four A's** that represents, in the U.S., all performers – actors, singers, dancers, chorus members, and **stage managers**> except **exclusive musicians** – who work in the **legitimate** and musical theater. *Also see* **Guilds & Unions**.

equity *Crit&Eval* State, quality, or ideal of being just, impartial, and fair.

equity *Eco&Fin* **1** Remaining interest from the assets of an organization after deducting its liabilities. **2** Market value of securities less any debt incurred. **3** Common stock and preferred stock. **4** Funds provided to a business by the sale of stock. *Also see* **book value**.

equity *Ethcs&Phil*, *LegAsp* **1 Doctrine** that permits judges to make decisions based on fairness, equality, moral rights, and natural law. **2** System of jurisprudence supplementing and serving to modify the rigor of common law. **3** Equitable right or claim.

equity *VisArts* "If the [art] auction houses are at the center of the art world's secondary market as the stock exchanges are at the center of the **equity** markets, then dealers in the work of living artists can be reasonably likened to underwriters of new **equity** issues. Initial sale of the work of living artists has many of the characteristics of IPOs; for instance, the prices are speculative, the products are on **consignment** to the dealers and the dealer's commissions are built into the process." — Susan Lee (econ. journ.)

equity financing *EntreP* Funding for a venture that includes at least partial ownership in the venture. Equity financing may come from individuals, informal investors, venture capitalists, or public offerings.

Erasable Programmable Read Only Memory (EPROM) *InfoMgt* » **EPROM**

Erato *LitArts*, *PA-Variety* The Muse of **lyric** poetry and mime. *Also see* **Muses**.

ergonomics *Sci&Tech* Science of studying the work environment to enhance workers productivity.

erotic *Crit&Eval* Concerning sexual love and desire.

erotic music law *Law&Pol*, *MusArts* "[The Washington state **ACLU**] affiliate, representing musicians of the Seattle-based Washington Music Industry Coalition, scored one for artistic freedom with the overturning of [the state's] 'erotic music' law — the first in the nation to target the sale of sound recordings to minors.... State Supreme Court declared the law an **infringement** of customers' and retailers' **free speech** rights, and of retailers' due process rights."— Lynn Decker (civil libertarian)

erotica *LitArts*, *VisArts* Literature or art intended to arouse sexual desire.

errata *VA-Prntng* Errors in printing or writing, esp. those noted in a list of corrections and bound into a book. (SING.) ERRATUM

error *InfoMgt* **1** Report of a malfunction of hardware or software. **2** Deviation of a computed or a measured quantity from the theoretically correct or true value.

error message *InfoMgt* Displayed on the screen reporting an error or problem in a program or the computer system.

error-correcting *InfoMgt* Modem **protocol** that check data to make sure that data being sent and data being received are the same.

Ertegun Brothers, Ahmed and **Nesuhi** *RecA&S* Turkish-Americans who, with **Jerry Wexler**, founded and managed **Atlantic Records**.

ES *BcstJourn* » **establishing shot**

escalator clause *HR&LR* Provision in a contract stipulating an increase or a decrease, as in wages, benefits, or prices, under certain conditions, such as changes in the cost of living [see **Consumer Price Index**] or increases or decreases in the employee's productivity.

escalator clause *RecA&S* Provisions in a **record contract** stipulating an increase. <amount of advance, percentage of royalty, number of releases, length of contract, etc>

escrow *Eco&Fin*, *LegAsp* Money, property, a deed, or a bond put into the custody of a third party for delivery to a **grantee** only after the fulfillment of the conditions specified.

ESOP *Eco&Fin*, *HR&LR* **Employees Stock Ownership Plan**. Program to encourage employees to purchase stock in their company. *Also see* **profit sharing**.

esoteric *Crit&Eval* **1** Intended for or understood by only a particular group. <an esoteric sect> **2** Not publicly disclosed; confidential.

essay *LitArts* Short written work of **non-fiction**, usu. on one topic.

essence *Crit&Eval* **Intrinsic** or indispensable properties that help characterize or identify something. *Also see* **existentialism**.

established artist *ArtPerf*, *VisArts* One whose talents and reputation are recognized and accepted by art critics and the art market. *Also see* **emerging artist**.

establishing shot (ES) *BcstJourn* First visual in a sequence. It orients the viewers to a new location or theme. In the past, it was usu. only a wide shot (WS), but now any shot – wide shot, medium shot (MS), or close-up (CU) – will do if it offers immediate identification for the upcoming sequence.

establishing shot *Flm&Vid* Usually a **long shot** used at the beginning of a scene that provides the audience with the context of the subsequent **tighter shots**.

establishment *Crit&Eval* Group that controls a certain field of activity. <the religious establishment>

establishment *Genl* **1** Place of residence or business with its possessions and staff. **2** Public or private institution, such as a hospital or school.

Establishment, The *Cult&Soc* Established social order: (1) Group of people holding most of the power and influence in a government or society. (2) Controlling group in a given field of activity.

estate planning *EntreP* Method of planning for use, conservation, and transfer of wealth as efficiently as possible. It is financial planning with the anticipation of eventual death.

esthete (Brit.) *Aes&Creat* » **aesthete**

esthetic bliss *Aes&Creat Crit&Eval* Phrase attributed to **Vladimir Nabokov** in describing the pleasures of art.

esthetics *or* **aesthetics** (Brit.) *Aes&Creat* "Esthetics and the modification of social behavior that come from a love of beauty and from the disciplines of accomplishment are terribly important to our civilization,... esp. in a society where both religion and political organizations have abdicated their responsibilities.... Everything, everything, quality of tone, quality of rhythm, quality of enunciation finally become spirit." — Robert Shaw (1916-, orch./choral arr., cond.)

estimated useful life *E&F-Acc* Estimate useful life of a **long-term asset** is the total number of service units expected from it. Service units may be measured in terms of years the asset is expected to be used, units expected to be produced, or similar measures.

estop *LegAsp* To impede or prohibit by **estoppel**. <When an **apparent agency** is established, the principal is **estopped** from denying the agency relationship>

estoppel *LegAsp* Bar preventing one from making an allegation or a denial that contradicts what one has previously stated as the truth.

estrange *Crit&Eval,TheatArts* To remove or change from an accustomed place or set of associations. *Also see* **alienation effect**.

ETA *TheatArts* "**Educational Theatre Association** is a professional organization for teachers of theatre and theatre professionals at all levels." — Internet

eternal *Crit&Eval* Being without beginning or end; existing outside of time. *Also see* **immortal**.

ethic *Ethcs&Phil* Principle of right or good conduct, or body of such principles.

ethical *Ethcs&Phil* **1** Pertaining to ethics. <an ethical dilemma>, commensurate with ethical concerns, sound ethical judgments. **2** Approaches behavior from a philosophical standpoint; it stresses more objective, but essentially idealistic, standards of right and wrong, such as those applicable to the practice of lawyers, doctors, and business persons. "To put it another way ethics is like the guilty conscience of aesthetics. Without an ethical frame, it might be impossible to tell a tragedy from a comedy." — **Wayne C. Booth**

ethical criticism *Crit&Eval*, *Ethcs&Phil* "All criticism is really ethical criticism, since our judgments about the things we read include appraisals about whether the values of these stories accord with our own." — **Wayne C. Booth**. *Also see* **criticism**.

ethical issues *EntreP* Questions of right and wrong.

ethics *BcstJourn* Study of moral decision making in personal or social situations. Codes of ethics are frameworks and references for making decisions in news work.

ethics *Ethcs&Phil* **1** Study of the general nature of morals and of the specific moral choices to be made by individuals in their relationship with others; the philosophy of morals. MORAL PHILOSOPHY **2** Rules or standard of governing the conduct of the members of a profession. <All citizens share in blame for lax municipal ethics. **3** Any set of moral principles or values. **4** Moral quality of a course of action; fitness; **propriety**. <I question the ethics of his decision> *Also see* **survival**.

Ethics *Ethcs&Phil* one of the three **Inner Forces** of **The Arts**

Dynamic

ethics strategy *EntreP* Development of venture strategies and day-to-day actions based on some ethical creed, model, or philosophy.

Ethiopian songs *Cult&Soc, MusArts* **Negro songs** sung in white **minstrel shows**

ethnic *Cult&Soc* **1** Relating to sizable groups of people sharing a common and distinctive racial, national, religious, **linguistic** or cultural heritage. **2** Member of a particular ethnic group, esp. one who maintains the language or customs of the group. **3** Relating to a people not Christian or Jewish.

ethnic pride *Cult&Soc* Pride in one's heritage. *Also see* **nose job**.

ethnicity *Cult&Soc* Pride in one's cultural origins.

ethnocentricity *Cult&Soc* **1** Belief in the superiority of one's own **ethnic** group. **2** Overriding concern with race. "[Also confusing are the] ethnic considerations of **black music**. On one hand, young [black] players want to reject anything not African or African American — disdaining both European forms and European techniques as white and therefore unworthy of emulation. That cultural arrogance constricts musical development."... "On the other hand, the combination of laziness and ethnocentricity is killing the essence of black music." — **Wynton Marsalis**

ethnography *Cult&Soc* Branch of anthropology that deals with the scientific description of specific human cultures.

ethnol. *Cult&Soc* **ethnology**

ethnology (ethnol.) *Cult&Soc* Science that analyzes and compares human cultures, as in social structure, language, religion, and technology; **cultural anthropology**.

ethos *Crit&Eval* Disposition, character, or fundamental values peculiar to a specific person, people, culture, or movement: "

ethos (*Greek* for "character") *Cult&Soc, Ethcs&Phil* Character or basic values of a specific culture. *Origin* Root word from which **ethics** is formed.

etude *MusArts* **1** Piece composed for the development of a specific point of technique. **2** Composition featuring a point of technique but performed because of its artistic merit.

ETV *Rdio/TV* **Educational television**. "The original name for **Public Broadcasting Service** (PBS) Original name was changed by a general consensus that the word 'educational' alienated a substantial portion of the viewing audience." — Edmund F. Penney (elec. media journ.)

eudemian *Ethcs&Phil* Approach to ethics associated with **Plato** and **Aristotle**, based on the idea that the ethical life is the path to happiness. *Origin* In the idea of one's having a good demon or guiding divinity. *Also see* **genius**.

euph *MusInstr* **euphonium**

euphemism *LitArts* Act or an example of substituting a mild, indirect, or vague term for one considered harsh, blunt, or offensive. <"School **stage band**" is a euphemism for a school jazz band>

euphonium (euph.) *MusInstr* Brass wind instrument similar to the tuba but having a somewhat higher **pitch** and a mellower sound. *Also see* **Musical Instrument Families**.

euphony *LitArts* Harmonious sounds, often used in poetry for effect.

euphoria *Crit&Eval* Feeling of great happiness or well-being. *Also see* **high**.

euro *EntreP* Common currency in Europe

Eurocentric *Cult&Soc* Centered or focused on Europe and the Europeans.

European Computer Manufacturers Association (ECMA) *iMedia* » **ECMA**

European Economic Community (EEC) *Eco&Fin* » **EEC**

European Union (EU) *EntreP* Organization of European nations that has reduced trade barriers within Europe.

Euterpe *LitArts, MusArts* The Muse of **lyric** poetry and music. *Also see* **Muses**.

evaluate *Crit&Eval* **1** To examine and judge carefully; appraise. **2** To ascertain or fix the value or worth of. *Also see* **critic**, **criticism**.

evaluation *Fndng* Grant proposals should include criteria by which the success of the project may be measured.

evangelical music *MusArts* Style of religious music characterized by ardent and crusading enthusiasm on behalf of a Christian church believing in the sole authority and inerrancy of the Bible, in salvation only through **regeneration**, and in a spiritually

transformed personal life. *Also see* **Gospel Music**.

even parity *InfoMgt* Error detection technique wherein the sum of the 1 bits is always an even number.

evening dress *Fashn* Clothing worn for evening social events: evening gown, **tails**, tuxedo. EVENING CLOTHES

event handler *iMedia* Programming: Event-based execution model authoring environments use event handlers to designate code that should be run when a certain event happens (such as a key press or mouse click)

event-based execution model *iMedia* **Asynchronous** code execution dependent on events (i.e., key press) *Also see* **event handler.**

event-based metaphor *iMedia* Content is accessed by interacting with elements influenced or determined by time.

evergreen *BcstJourn* » **HFR**

evergreen *MusArts* Music that remains perennially fresh, interesting, or well liked. *Also see* **standards**. (*MusArts*)

evergreen subscriptions *LitArts, Mktg* **Periodical** subscriptions, Internet generated, renewed automatically on credit cards unless subscribers specifically ask for them to be stopped. Also *see* **sticky subscriptions**.

evolution of media *iMedia* Media has evolved through three stages: static, dynamic, and interactive. "arrival of the interactive medium, like the arrival of dynamic media before it, represents a paradigm shift" — **Dave Gerding** *Also see* **dynamic media**, **interactive media**, **static media.**

ex officio *LegAsp* By virtue of office or position.

ex parte *LegAsp* From or on one side only, with the other side absent or unrepresented.

ex post facto *LegAsp* Designates an action taken to change the effect given to a set of circumstances This action relates back to a prior time and places this new effect upon the same set of circumstances existing at that time.

excerpt *Flm&Vid*, *LitArts, MusArts*, Segment from a longer work. <literary or musical composition, a document, or a film>

excess mechanicals *IntelProp, RecA&S* Charge made by a record company to the recording artist for **mechanical royalty** payments beyond the amount the record company agrees to pay.

excess of revenue over expenses *E&F-Acc* » **net income**

exchange *Eco&Fin* **1** Place where things are exchanged, esp. a center where securities or commodities are bought and sold. <**American Stock Exchange, Curb Exchange, New York Stock Exchange, stock exchange**> *Also see* **bill of exchange**, **rate of exchange**. **2** System of payments negotiable drafts, instead of money. **3** Fee or percentage charged for such a system of payment. **4** AMount of difference in the actual value of two or more currencies or between values of the same currency at two or more places.

exchange rate *EntreP* Rate at which currencies trade for one another in the market.

Excite *InfoMgt* Web site providing access to Internet. *Also see* **search engine**, **portals**.

exclusive *Journ* News item initially released to or obtained by only one publication or broadcaster.

exclusive *Mktg* Exclusive right or privilege to market a product.

exclusive agency contract *LegAsp* Contract between a **principal** and an **agent** that does not allow the **principal** to employ any **agent** other than the exclusive agent. *Also see* **Agents and Agencies**, **Contracts.**

exclusive musicians *ArtPerf, HR&LR, MusArts* Musicians who perform only on their instruments or sing only within an instrumental ensemble, and thus are represented exclusively by the **American Federation of Musicians** (AFM)

exclusive rights *IntelProp* Those of a copyright owner to exclusively authorize recording, performance, dramatization or other uses of her/his works. *Also see* **non-exclusive rights**.

exclusive run *Flm&Vid* Exhibition of a movie in a single theater – possibly on two screens within a theater complex – in the greater metropolitan area of a city, usu. at a **first run** theater. *Also see* **wide release**.

Exclusive Songwriter Agreement *IntelProp, MusArts* Contract between publisher and songwriter where songwriter assigns all songs written during the term of the contract to the publisher in return for a **royalty** on which an **advance** is usu. paid. *Also see*

Contracts.

exclusivity *Mktg* Right to be the single, overall sponsor of an event or attraction.

exclusivity within product category *Mktg* Event or an attraction may have multiple sponsors, but only one within each product category. <one soft drink, one airline, one bank, etc>

EXE files *InfoMgt* **1** Executable files or applications. Most programs end with this extension. **2** Used for self-extracting archives. <programs, when run, expand into several smaller programs>

exec., exec *Mgt* executive.

executed contract *LegAsp* Completed contract *Also see* **Contracts.**

executive *InfoMgt* Set of coded instructions designed to process and control other coded instructions.

executive producer *Flm&Vid* Producer responsible for the collection and disbursement of production funds. At the major film studios, this title may be given to a staff producer who tracks schedules, budgets, and other production areas. *Also see* **Producers.**

executive producer *Journ,. Rdio/TV* Editor in chief of a television news program. *Also see* **Producers.**

executive summary *EntreP* Section of the business plan that conveys a clear and concise overall picture of the proposed venture.

executory contract *LegAsp* One that has not been fully performed by either or both parties. *Also see* **Contracts.**

exegesis *Crit&Eval* Critical explanation or analysis.

exempt personnel *E&F-Acc* Those salaried employees who are exempt from the privilege of earning **overtime** pay — the opposite of **non-exempt personnel.**

exeunt (ekseeunt, Latin for "to go out") *TheatArts* Stage direction to indicate that two or more performers leave the stage. *Also see* **exit, Stage Directions.**

exhibitor *Flm&Vid* Owner or manager of a motion picture theater who supervises: accountancy, advertising, bookings, and showings.

exhibitor *or* **exhibiter** *Mktg* One who puts something on public display.

Exhibitor Relations Company *Flm&Vid, Mktg* Monitors box office sales for the movie industry.

exhortation *Crit&Eval* Speech or discourse that encourages, incites, or earnestly advises. *Also see* **call to action.**

existentialism *Crit&Eval* Philosophical view that human beings exist before they have an **essence**, and that their essence is created by human beings for themselves; consequently each of us is wholly responsible for all that we are. — **Jean Paul Sartre**

Existing Home Sales *Eco&Fin* This **economic indicator** reported nationally and regionally by the U.S. Dept. of Commerce is derived from title transfers. They show the percentage of increase or decrease of existing home re-sales compared to the previous month and to the same month in the previous year. *Also see* **New Home Construction.**

exit *InfoMgt* Computer programming technique for ending a repeated cycle of operations.

exit *TheatArts* Performer leaves the stage *Also see* **exeunt, Stage Directions.**

exp. *Eco&Fin, InfoMgt* **expenses, export**

expected return *EntreP* **S**um of possible returns weighted by their assessed chance of occurrence.

expected value *EntreP* **S**um of possible outcomes for a random variable weighted by their assessed chance of occurrence.

expendable assets *E&F-Acc* All assets reported on the **balance sheet** omitting **endowment funds** and those already expended on **fixed assets** such as land, buildings, and equipment at the end of the fiscal year. *Also see* **Assets, Funds.**

expendable funds *E&F-Acc* Expenditures not strictly necessary for the viability of the enterprise. *Also see* **Funds.**

expenditure responsibility *Fnding* In general, when a private foundation makes a grant to an organization that is not classified by the **IRS** as a **public charity**, the foundation is required by law to provide some assurance that the funds will be used for the intended charitable purposes. Special reports on such grants must be filed with the IRS. Most **grantee** organizations are public charities and many foundations do not make "expenditure responsibility" grants.

expense *Eco&Fin* **1** Decrease in retained earnings that results from operations. **2** Cost of doing business; opposite of **revenue**. **3** Expenditure of money.

expensed *E&F-Acc* **1** To charge with expenses. **2** To write off as an expense.

expenses (exp.) *Eco&Fin* **1** Charges incurred by an employee in the performance of work. <She was reimbursed for her travel expenses> **2** Money allotted for payment of such charges.

experiment *Crit&Eval* Test under controlled conditions to demonstrate a known truth, examine the validity of a **hypothesis**, or determine the **efficacy** of something previously untried.

experimental *Crit&Eval, LitArts* Attempt at innovation. "When you fail at something you call it an 'experiment,' an elite word for **flop**. Just because lines are uneven or capitals missing doesn't mean experiment. Literary magazines devoted to experimental writing are usu. filled with works by middle-aged or old people." — **Robert Penn Warren**

Experimental Music Studios *MusArts, MusInstr* Renowned leader in electro-acoustic music; founded 1958 at U. of Illinois (Urbana-Champaign)

experimental theatre *TheatArts* Ω

Experiments in Art and Technology *Aes&Creat, Sci&Tech* » **E.A.T.**

expert system *InfoMgt* Set of **computer programs** that emulate the cognitive processes of a human expert.

expire *LegAsp* To come to an end; terminate. <The term of the contract has expired>

explanatory notes *E&F-Acc* Notes that explain some of the items in the **financial statements.**

exploit *Ethcs&Phil* To make use of selfishly or unethically.

exploit *IntelProp* To encourage licensing and commercial use of a particular copyright.

exploit *Mgt* To employ to the greatest possible advantage. <exploit one's talents>

exploit *Mktg* To advertise; promote.

export (exp.) *Eco&Fin* To send abroad goods and services for sale or trade. "Entertainment is America's largest export — after weaponry." — Todd Gitlin (ent. journ.) *Also see* **import.**

export (exp.) *EntreP* **1** Product produced in one country for sale in another. **2** Strategy of selling products in other countries through direct or indirect contact with foreign buyers.

export (exp.) *InfoMgt* Command to write out the contents of a file in a form that other programs can use. *Also see* **import.**

exposition *Genl* Public exhibition or show of artistic or industrial developments.

exposition *InfoMgt, iMedia* Process of relating information from one person or source to another (one-way distribution of content) As opposed to "interaction" which is a dialogue between two people or sources (two-way distribution of content)

exposition *LegAsp, TheatArts* Play dialogue that provides the background information needed to understand the characters and the action.

exposition *MusArts* **1** First part of a composition in **sonata** form that introduces the themes. **2** Opening section of a **fugue**.

exposition *TheatArts* Part of the script devoted to information about the past or off-stage events.

exposure *Mktg* **1** Appearance in public or in the **mass media**. **2** Visibility of a sponsor's name and/or logo in a live setting or through advertising and editorial support from **media**.

express agency *LegAsp* Most common form of agency that occurs when a **principal** and an **agent** expressly agree to enter into an agency agreement with each other. *Also see* **Agents and Agencies.**

express contract *LegAsp* Agreement expressed orally or in writing. *Also see* **Contracts.**

expression marks *MusArts* Marks used to help the interpretation of a musical work concerned with dynamics, tempo, and mood to indicate **forte**, **allegro**, **con spirito**, etc.

expression of an idea *IntelProp* Something copyrightable. The idea itself is not.

expressionism *Flm&Vid* Style of filmmaking that emphasizes extreme distortion and artistic self-expression. *Also see* **Art Movements and Periods.**

expressionism *TheatArts* Style of drama from the first three decades of the 20th century which attempts to present "inner reality,"

F

the man beneath the skin. It often distorts the normal to present symbolic action in dreamlike sequences, and uses abstract characterization, episodic structure, and both rhapsodic and staccato language patterns. The style is strongly associated with German/Austrian playwrights.

expressionism *VisArts* Arts movement in the early 1900s that emphasized subjective expression of the artist's feelings, emotions, and states of mind. <Vincent Van Gogh (Van Go, 1853-90, Dutch pntr.), Paul Gauguin (Gow-gan, 1848-1903, Fr. pntr)> *Also see* **Art Movements and Periods, modern art**.

expunge *Crit&Eval* To erase or strike out errors from a manuscript.

expurgate *Ethcs&Phil, LitArts* To remove vulgar, **obscene**, or otherwise objectionable material from a book, for example, before publication. *Also see* **bowdlerize**.

EXT *Flm&Vid* **exterior**. *Also see* **location**.

extemporaneous *Crit&Eval* **1** Performed with little or no preparation, <an extemporaneous piano recital> **2** Prepared in advance but delivered without notes or text. <an extemporaneous speech> IMPROMPTU

extemporize *Crit&Eval* To perform spontaneously.

Extended Binary Coded Decimal Interchange Code (EBCDIC) *InfoMgt* » **EBCDIC**

extended play record (EP) *RecA&S* » **EP record**

Extensible Markup Language (XML) *iMedia* **Protocol** for containing and managing information, also commonly used as a set of rules for creating markup languages; allows authors to develop markup elements. Subset of **SGML.**

exterior (EXT.) *Flm&Vid* Scene out-of-doors. *Also see* **interior**.

external acting *TheatArts* » **representational actor** *Also see* **internal acting**

external circulation *Journ, Mktg* Circulation of a periodical outside the sponsoring organization. *Also see* **Media Circulation**.

external equity *EntreP* Funds that derive initially from the owners' investment in a company.

external locus of control *EntreP* Belief that one's life is controlled more by luck or fate than by one's own efforts.

external modem *InfoMgt* **Modem** housed in its case located outside the computer.

extra *ArtPerf, Flm&Vid, TheatArts* Actor who speaks no lines except as part of a crowd. *Also see* **dress extra, spear carrier, supernumerary**.

extra *Journ* Special edition of a newspaper, supplanted these days by the radio or television "bulletin."

extra high frequency (EHF) *Rdio/TV, RecA&S* » **EHF**

extra low frequency (ELF) *Rdio/TV, RecA&S* » **ELF**

extralegal *LegAsp* Not permitted or governed by law.

extramusical *Crit&Eval* Not relating to music.

extraordinary repairs *E&F-Acc* Repairs of a more significant nature that affect the estimated residual value of an asset. The amount of these types of repairs are recorded by debiting the accumulated depreciation account, under the assumption that some of the depreciation previously recorded has not been eliminated. The effect of this reduction increases the carrying value of the asset.

extrapolate *Crit&Eval* To infer or estimate by extending or projecting known information.

extreme close-up *Flm&Vid* » **close-up**

exurb *Mktg* Region lying beyond the suburbs of a city, esp. one inhabited principally by people of high income.

eye web *Rdio/TV* CBS-TV. So called because of its "eye" **on-screen** logo.

- F -

F clef *MusArts* » **bass clef**

f, F *MusArts* **forte** (loud)

f., F. *E&F-Acc, LitArts, VA-Prntng* **folio**

f.o.b., F.O.B., FOB *Eco&Fin* free on board. Without charge to the purchaser for delivery on board or into a carrier at a specified point or location. *Also see* **FOB shipping point**.

F.O.H. *PerfA&C* **front of house**. Any mounting position of lighting instruments.

f.v. *LitArts, VA-Prntng* **folio verso** (on the back of the page)

fa (fah) *MusArts* fourth note of a **diatonic scale**

Fabian Society *Law&Pol* Economic-political group, esp. in En-gland, committed to gradual rather than revolutionary means for spreading socialist principles. *Also see* **George Bernard Shaw**.

fable *Cult&Soc, LitArts* **1** Prose or poetic story that illustrates a moral. **2** Story about legendary persons and exploits.

fabric *Fashn* Cloth produced esp. by knitting, weaving, or felting fibers.

fabrication *Fashn* Construction by combining or assembling diverse fabrics.

face *Fashn* **1** To furnish a cover of a different material: bronze. **2** To line or trim the edge of, esp. with contrasting material: face.

face powder *Th-MakeUp* Used over creme or grease makeup to reduce color distortion.

face-to-face solicitation *Fndng* Personal appeal to prospective contributors at their home, office, or other suitable location.

facilitator *HR&LR* Person who leads a meeting without being its focus, reconciles conflicts, and challenges all participants to contribute to the dialog.

facing *Fashn* **1** Piece of material sewn to the edge of a garment as lining or decoration. **2** Material used for such a lining or decoration.

facsimile (fax also FAX) *Sci&Tech* **1** Exact copy of a document. **2** Image transmitted electronically. XEROX.

facsimile system *InfoMgt* Method of teleprocessing a page by **scanning** it and transmitting a bit-by-bit image. Invented at **Bell Labs** in 1925.

fact-finding board *HR&LR* Body appointed by a court or legislature to determine the facts of a labor dispute and make recommendations for **resolution**.

factoid *Crit&Eval* An imagined or simulated fact.

factoring *EntreP* Selling accounts receivable at a discount to a financing company in order to receive funds immediately and not have to deal with collecting the accounts.

factors of production *EntreP* Labor and capital used to produce goods and services.

fad *Fashn* Fashion taken up with great enthusiasm for a brief period of time; a craze. *Also see* **planned obsolescence**.

fade-in, fadein *Flm&Vid, Rdio/TV* Gradual increase in the visibility of an image or the audibility of a sound, as in cinema, television, or radio.

fade-out, fadeout *Flm&Vid, Rdio/TV* **1** Gradual disappearance of an image or a sound, as in cinema, television, or radio. **2** Gradual and temporary loss in reception of a radio or television signal, often generated by interference in transmission.

fagoting *Fashn* **1** Method of decorating cloth by pulling out horizontal threads and tying the remaining vertical threads into hourglass-shaped bunches. **2** Method of joining hemmed edges by crisscrossing thread over an open seam.

Fahrenheit 451 *Ethcs&Phil, LitArts* Novel written in 1953 by Ray Bradbury (1920-, novelist, soc. critic) that envisions a future in which books are burned and readers who must memorize the texts to preserve them, becoming walking libraries. *Also see* **Brave New World, censorship**, 1984.

fair *Mktg, PA-Variety* **1** Exhibition, as of farm products or manufactured goods, usu. accompanied by various competitions and entertainments. **2** Exhibition intended to inform people about a product or business opportunity. **3** Event, usu. for the benefit of a charity or public institution, inc. entertainment and the sale of goods; a **bazaar**.

fair comment *Crit&Eval, Rdio/TV* Critical comment about the arts and arts managers are not usu. subject to broadcast restriction as long as the comments are understood to be the opinions of the critics and the facts are reasonably accurate. *Also see* **editorialize**.

Fair Packaging and Labeling Act (FPLA) (1966) *Law&Pol, Mktg* Prevents unfair or deceptive packaging or labeling of certain consumer items. *Also see* **Federal Agencies and Statutes**.

fair use *IntelProp* May be regarded as the reasonable use of a copyrighted work, without permission from or payment to the owner of the copyright: reproduction for comment or criticism, news reporting, teaching, research. **Downloadings** from online information services complicate the interpretation of fair use.

Fairness and Accuracy in Reporting *Journ, Law&Pol* Liberal **electronic media** and **print media** watchdog group based in NYC.

fairness doctrine *Rdio/TV* **FCC** rule that forced all radio and

F

TV stations, as a condition of maintaining their broadcast licenses, to air all sides of issues important to local communities. This rule and some other public interest rules were reformed out during the **Reagan** years. *Also see* **equal time**.

fake *MusArts* » **improvise**

fake *VisArts* not authentic; possibly **counterfeit**

fakebook *MusArts* Contains hundreds of songs, in melody-line-only **arrangements**, with **chords** and lyrics, which provide quick reference to songs the musician does not know. With the melody known, an experienced musician can play (**fake**) the song. [These books used to be illegal because the repros were printed and sold without permission of the copyright owners. But they were easily available for about $30 in cash from a street **vender** clad in a raincoat and a dark slouch hat.] *Also see* **Print Music**.

fall and recovery *Dnce* Dance technique pioneered by Doris Humphrey (1895-1958, modern choreog., dncr.), which involves the use of breath visualized in a strong shift of weight. *Also see* **contraction and release, tension and relaxation**.

fall-off *MusArts* Downward **glissando** which may be either long or short.

fallacious *Crit&Eval* **1** Based on a **fallacy**. **2** Tending to mislead; deceptive.

fallacy *Crit&Eval* False notion.

falling action *TheatArts* Events occurring after the major climax. When this climax occurs late in the play, the falling action and the **denouement** occur together. In plays with a more centrally located climax, the falling action covers the events leading to a final resolution, i.e., the denouement.

falloff *Flm&Vid* "Speed" with which the brightest part of an object runs into the deepest shadow.

False Claims Law *LegAsp* » **whistle-blower**

false fingering *MusArts* Alternate fingering on a clarinet or saxophone to change the sound quality.

false pretense *LegAsp* False representation of fact or circumstance, calculated to mislead.

falsetto *MusArts* Male (usu. black) singing voice marked by artificially produced **tones** in an upper **register** beyond the normal range of a tenor.

falsies *Fashn* Padding or pads worn inside a brassiere to make the breasts appear larger. GAY DECEIVERS

fame *Crit&Eval* Estimation bestowed or withheld by the audience. "Fame consumes you, exhausts you and finally depletes you." — **Madonna**

Family and Medical Leave Act *EntreP* Legislation that assures employees of unpaid leave for childbirth or other family needs.

family business *EntreP* Company in which family members are directly involved in the ownership and/or operation.

family foundation *Fnding* Independent private foundation whose funds are derived from members of a single family. Family members often serve as officers or board members of the foundation and have a significant role in grantmaking decisions. *Also see* **operating foundation, private foundation, public charity**.

family situation comedies *Rdio/TV* Popular type of television network programming. <*All in the Family, I Love Lucy, The Cosby Show*> *Also see* **Television Shows**.

family *VA-Prntng* Variety of typefaces with similar characteristics. <gothic> *Also see* **font, typeface**.

fan *Crit&Eval* Ardent **devotee**; at times, a violent worshipper. *Origin* fanatic.

fan club *Mktg* Group of **devotees**, often organized and even subsidized by the artist's manager. *Also see* **claque**.

fan mail *Mktg* Mail sent to an entertainment **personality** by admirers, possibly motivated by a publicity initiative.

fancy dress *Fashn* Masquerade costume

fanfare *MusArts* Loud flourish of brass instruments.

fantasia, fantasy *MusArts* **1** Free composition structured according to the composer's fancy. **2** Medley of familiar themes, with variations and interludes.

fantastic *Crit&Eval* **1** Quaint or strange in form, conception, or appearance. **2** Unrestrainedly fanciful; extravagant, **bizarre**. **3** Based on or existing only in fantasy; unreal. **4** Wonderful or superb; remarkable.

fantasy *Crit&Eval* Imagined event or sequence of mental images, such as a daydream, usu. fulfilling a wish or psychological need.

fantasy *LitArts, TheatArts* **Fiction** characterized by highly fanciful or **supernatural** elements.

fanzine *Journ, Mktg* Amateur-produced fan magazine. *Also see* **zine**.

FAQs *InfoMgt* Frequently Asked Questions

far-out *Crit&Eval* Extremely unconventional.

farce *TheatArts* Comedy exaggerated and played exclusively for simple laughs, esp. **belly laughs**. Characterizations usu. resemble **caricatures**. *Also see* **low comedy**.

farcical *Crit&Eval* **1** Resembling a **farce**. LUDICROUS. **2** ridiculously clumsy; **absurd**

farewell *TheatArts* Said of an event to mark an actor's retirement from the stage. <farewell appearance>

FARG *InfoMgt* Fluid Analogies Research Group » CRCC

FASB *E&F-Acc* **Financial Accounting Standard Board**. Body that has primary responsibility for developing and issuing financial accounting standards and rules on accounting practices.

fascism, Fascism *Law&Pol* System of government marked by centralization of authority under a dictator, stringent socioeconomic controls, suppression of the opposition through terror and censorship, and typically a policy of belligerent nationalism and racism. <Italy and Germany before and during World War II>

fascist *Crit&Eval* reactionary or dictatorial person. <Adolph Hitler (*aka* "Der Führer," 1889-1945, Aus.-born founder Ger. Nazi Party, chancellor Third Reich, 1933-45), Benito Mussolini (*aka* Il Duce, 1883-1945, Ital. dictator, prime minister, 1922-43) who formalized an alliance with Germany (1939), and brought Italy into World War II (1940)>

fashion *Cult&Soc* **1** Prevailing style or custom, as in dress or behavior. <out of fashion> **2** Style characteristic of the social elite. <a man or woman of fashion> **3** Manner or mode; way. <Set the table in this fashion>

fashion *Fashn* **1** Prevailing style of dress. **2** Something, such as a garment, that is in the current mode: Her dress is the latest fashion.

fashion *PerfA&C* **1** Personal, often **idiosyncratic** manner. <He played the role in his own peculiar style> **2** Style characteristic of the social elite.

Fashion Centers *Fashn* Major fashion centers offer showrooms and fashion shows to sell apparel to retail buyers. <Paris, Milan, London, New York, Dallas, Los Angeles, Chicago, Atlanta, and San Francisco>

fashion cycle *Fashn* Fashion change: introduction, acceptance, and decline of a fashion.

Fashion Group International (FGI) *Fashn* Est. 1930, as a "global nonprofit association of over 6,000 professionals… from all areas of fashion and related industries inc. apparel, accessories, beauty, publishing, retailing, and interior design." — >http://www.fgi.org<

fashion plate *Fashn* **1** Person who consistently wears the latest fashions. **2** Illustration of current styles in dress.

fast *PerfA&C* Actor's ability to quickly learn cues, lines, and stage directions rather than waiting for **motivation** to occur. "You know when you enter certain shows that you are being paid for 'fast.'" — Colleen Dewhurst (1924-91; stage, film, TV actor) *Also see* **Method**.

fast track *Mgt* The quickest and most direct route to achievement of a goal. <competing for professional advancement>

fast-forward *Rdio/TV* Function on an video or audio tape player for rapid advancement of the tape.

FAT *InfoMgt* **file allocation table** Hidden table of every cluster on a floppy or hard disk. The FAT records how files are stored in distinct – and not necessarily contiguous – clusters.

fat cat *Crit&Eval, Law&Pol* **1** Wealthy and highly privileged person. **2** Wealthy person who is a heavy contributor to a political campaign.

Fat City, fat city *Eco&Fin* Condition or set of circumstances characterized by great prosperity.

fat lady sings *Crit/Eval* The event or the show is not over until this lady says it's over.

fat part *ArtPerf, TheatArts* One that give the performer a good chance to display her/his talents.

fat pipe *InfoMgt* Likened to a **cable modem**, i.e., information is like water and comes into one's computer in a rush or a trickle.

fatalism *Crit&Eval* Acceptance of the belief that all events are predetermined and inevitable.

Faulkner, William (1897-1962, fict., scrnwrtr., plywri.) Many of his 19 novels and 80+ short stories are set in the imaginary Yoknapatawpha County, a microcosm of the **postbellum** South, in which he explored the decay of traditional Southern values. *<The Sound and the Fury* (1929), *Absalom, Absalom!* (1936)> His acceptance speech for the 1949 **Nobel Prize** for literature reflected his **humanist** convictions: "The poet's voice need not merely be the record of man, it can be one of the props, the pillars to help him endure and prevail." *Also see* **amoral**, **economic freedom**, **hot**, **ruthless ambition**, **silence**.

fauvism *VisArts* Early 20th century movement in painting begun by a group of French artists and marked by the use of bold, often distorted forms and vivid colors. **<Henri Matisse>** *Also see* **Art Movements and Periods, modern art**.

faux (foe, Fr.) *Fashn* artificial, fake

faux parentage *Mgt*, *Mktg* Supposedly independent company actually organized and owned by a large corporation or conglomerate; a form of managed competition. <General Motor's promotion of Saturn autos as "a different kind of car" built by "a different kind of company." STEALTH PARENTAGE

faux pas (foe pah, Fr.) *Crit&Eval* social blunder; **gaffe**

faux-naif (foe nigh'-eef, Fr.) *Crit&Eval* False show of innocent simplicity.

favored nations clause *LegAsp* Used to protect one's established salary or royalty rate. <No one can be paid more than the contracting party for talent or material similarly used, and if someone is, the contracting party will receive the same treatment>

fax modem *InfoMgt* **Modem** equipped to send and receive fax messages as well as standard telecommunication.

fax, FAX *InfoMgt* facsimile. Method for sending images over telephone lines.

fax-on-demand *InfoMgt* » **FOD**

FCC *InfoMgt,. Rdio/TV* **Federal Communications Commission**. Established by the **Communications Act of 1934** to regulate broadcasting. *Also see* **Federal Agencies and Statutes**.

FDDI *InfoMgt* **Fiber Distributed Data Interface** Local area communication system.

FDIC *Eco&Fin* » **Federal Deposit Insurance Corporation**

fear *Crit&Eval* » **catharsis**

fear of the void *Crit&Eval*, *VisArts* Unwillingness to leave any part of the canvas undecorated.

feasibility study *Fndng*, *Mktg* **1** Development planning study in which the feasibility of a fundraising campaign is gauged and in which leadership, staffing, plan of action, timetable, etc. are planned. **2** Study of a proposed project or production intended to evaluate the possibility of success.

featherbedding *HR&LR* Practice of requiring an employer to hire more workers than are needed or to limit their production in keeping with a safety regulation or union rule. *Also see* **make work, walkers**.

feature *also* **soft lead** *BcstJourn* Lead sentence often used when the story angle does not involve timely or deadline information. This type of lead is usu. long, and is usu. constructed of information not found in the story.

feature *Flm&Vid* **1** Main film presentation at a theater. *2* A longer film of at least 60 minutes as opposed to a **short subject.**

feature *iMedia* **1** Component of an interactive media product that provides the means for the participant (user) to accomplish a task or a set of related tasks. **2** Aspect of a product that has marketing appeal, or will encourage users to use the product.

feature *Journ* Prominent or special article, story, or department in a newspaper, magazine, or television news program.

feature *PerfA&C* **1** Special attraction at an entertainment. **2** To have or include as a prominent part, not as the star or leading role. <The musical featured the producer's new find: a statuesque bell ringer from the typing pool>

feature creep *iMedia* Feature of a product becomes bloated with unplanned options or additions. *Also see* **featuritis**.

feature work **1** On radio, a performance that is the sole sound broadcast at the time of the performance. **2** On television, a performance that constitutes the main focus of audience attention at the time of the performance. Vocalists and/or instrumentalists, respectively, must be on camera except where the music is used

as part of a choreographic routine.

featured act *ArtPerf* » **headliner, star**.

featurette *Rdio/TV* TV promo that gives a behind-the-scenes look at the making of a movie about to be released. *Also see* **trailer**.

featuritis *iMedia* Adding components late in product development that were not initially planned, and without adjusting time, resources, or budget; often a result of client pressure or the appearance of a new technology.

Fed, (the) *Eco&Fin* » **Federal Reserve System**

FEDAPT *TheatArts* **Foundation for the Extension and Development of the American Professional Theatre**. This organization is defunct.

Federal Agencies and Statutes *ColEntry, Law&Pol* » **Clayton Act** (1914), **Communications Act** (1934), **Fair Packaging and Labeling Act** (FPLA, 1966), **Federal Communications Commission** (FCC, 1934), **Corporation for Public Broadcasting** (CPB), **Educational Television Act** (1962), **Equal Employment Opportunity Commission** (EEOC, 1954), **Federal Reserve System** (1913), **Federal Communications Commission** (FCC, 1934), **Federal Insurance Contributions Act** (FICA, 1935), **Federal Trade Commission Act** (FTC, 1914), **Freedom of Information Act** (FOIA, 1967), **GI "Bill of Rights"** (1944), **Lanham Trade-Mark Act** (1946), **Lea Act** (1952), **National Conference Board, National Endowment for the Arts** (NEA, 1965), **National Endowment for the Humanities** (NEH, 1965), **National Labor Relations Board** (NLRB, 1935), **Occupational Safety and Health Administration** (OSHA, 1970), **Public Broadcasting Act** (1967), **Public Works Administration** (PWA, 1933), **Robinson-Patman Act** (1936), **Sherman Antitrust Act** (1890), **Small Business Administration** (SBA, 1953), **U.S. Bureau of Labor Statistics, U.S. Dept. of Commerce** (DOC, 1903), **U.S. Copyright Office** (USCO), **U.S. Department of Education** (DOE, 1980), **U.S. Department of Health and Human Services** (HHS, 1980), **U.S. Dept. of Labor** (DOL, 1913), **Visual Artists' Rights Act** (1990), **Works Progress Administration** (WPA, 1935)

Federal Communications Commission (FCC) *InfoMgt,. Rdio/TV* » **FCC**

Federal Deposit Insurance Corporation (FDIC) *Eco&Fin* Independent government corporation created in 1933 (after the disastrous collapse of the banking system) with the duty to insure bank deposits in eligible banks against loss in the event of a bank failure and to regulate certain banking practices. The corporation insures bank deposits in eligible banks, and some savings and loan institutions, up to the statutory limit ($100,000) *Also see* **Great Depression**.

federal funds rate *EntreP* Interest rate that banks charge each other for overnight loans. The minimum amount of these loans is $1 million.

Federal Insurance Contribution Act (FICA) *E&F-Acc*, *EntreP*, *Law&Pol* Taxes paid by a wage earner and a business to the Federal government for Social Security and Medicare. » **FICA**

Federal Open Market Committee (FOMC) *EntreP* Group that decides on monetary policy; it consists of the 7 members of the Board of Governors plus 5 of 12 regional bank presidents on a rotating basis.

Federal Reserve Bank *Eco&Fin. EntreP* Central bank of the United States, often called the **FED**. It is the banker's bank. The United States is divided into twelve districts with each district having a Federal Reserve Bank. *Also see* **Federal Reserve Board**.

Federal Reserve Board *E&F-Acc* Uses aggregated accounting information to set economic policies and evaluate economic programs. *Also see* **Federal Agencies and Statutes, Federal Reserve Bank, Federal Reserve System**.

Federal Reserve Discount Rate *Eco&Fin* This **economic indicator** is the interest rate that the **Federal Reserve Bank** charges when it makes loans to member banks. The Fed's discount rate acts as an interest floor or base for loans made by banks to its borrowers. Virtually all bank loans are calculated from the Fed's discount rate. Thus, if the discount rate goes up so do bank interest rates, and the economy tends to slow down. Conversely, if the discount rate drops so do bank interest rates, and the economy tends to expand. Discount rate is the Fed's primary anti-inflation weapon. *Also see* **Federal Reserve System**.

Federal Reserve System (the Fed, est 1913) *Eco&Fin* Its main functions are to regulate the national money supply, set reserve requirements for member banks, supervise printing of money, act as clearinghouse for transfer of funds throughout the banking system, and examine member banks to ensure compliance with Federal Reserve regulations. *Also see* **Federal Agencies and Statutes, Federal Reserve Discount Rate.**

Federal Theatre (1935-39) *TheatArts* Branch of the **WPA** which spurred the growth of American experimental theatre. <**Group Theater, Orson Welles' Mercury Theater**> *Also see* **Theaters & Theatres.**

Federal Trade Commission (FTC) *Law&Pol, Mktg* » **FTC**

Federal Treasury Bills *EntreP* U.S. Government bonds of 3 month, 6 month and one year duration that are issued at a discount.

Federal Unemployment Insurance Act (FUTA) *E&F-Acc, HR&LR, Law&Pol* » **FUTA**

federated giving program *Fnding* Joint fundraising effort usually administered by a nonprofit **umbrella** organization which in turn distributes contributed funds to several nonprofit agencies. United Way and community chests or funds, the United Jewish Appeal and other religious appeals, the United Negro College Fund, and united arts funds are examples of federated giving programs. *Also see* Community Fund)

fee *Eco&Fin* 1 Charge for professional services. 2 Fixed sum charged, as by an institution or by law, for a privilege. <license fee; tuition fee>

feed *Rdio/TV* To distribute a local radio or television broadcast to a larger audience or group of receivers by way of a network or satellite.

feedback *InfoMgt* 1 Return of a portion of the output of a process or system to the input, esp. when used to maintain performance or to control a system or process. 2 Return of information about the result of a process or activity; an evaluative response. *Also see* **electronic feedback.**

feel the audience *MusArts, PerfA&C* To feel the emotional stimulus that comes from performing before an audience. *Also see* **empathy, empathic response.**

feel the part *ArtPerf, PerfA&C* In acting, to immerse oneself creatively in the development of a role.

Fellini, Federico (1920-97, Ital. flmkr.) *ArtPerf, Flm&Vid* Films combine social satire with fantasy. <*La Strada* (1954), *La Dolce Vita* (1960>) *Also see* **paparazzi.**

female actor *ArtPerf, Flm&Vid, TheatArts,. Rdio/TV* » **actor**

female writers *Crit&Eval, Cult&Soc, LitArts* 1 "A woman must have money and a room of her own if she is to write **fiction.**"— **Virginia Woolf.** 2 "Dear God, please make me stop writing like a woman. For Jesus Christ's sake, amen." — **Dorothy Parker**

feminism *Cult&Soc* 1 Belief in the social, political, and economic equality of the sexes. 2 Movement organized around this belief.

feminist *Cult&Soc* "Long before **Madonna**, Ms. [Barbra] **Streisand** was her own **mogul** and packager, a feminist with dignity." — **Jon Pareles**

feminist critics *Crit&Eval* "Other critics teach us things that we've missed in our own readings, points of view we've overlooked. Most striking example of that for me has been the way feminist critics have startled me into recognizing perspectives of books that never would have occurred to me on my own." — **Wayne C. Booth**

femme fatale (famm fey-tal, Fr.) *Crit&Eval, Flm&Vid* Woman of great seductive charm who leads men into compromising or dangerous situations.

FEN *LegAsp* **Free Expression Network** Est. 1991 National coalition of record producers, musicians, record and video retailers, artists, publishers, interest groups, and individuals; "supports free expression and free access to the artistic expression of others." — >http://www.freeexpression.org<

Fender, Leo (1907-91, inventor) *MusInstr* Developed guitar amplifier and pickup (1940s), first production-line solid-body electric guitar (1950) and electric bass guitar (1951) *Also see* **Musical Instrument Families, Les Paul.**

FEP *InfoMgt* » **Front-end processor**

festival *PA-Variety* 1 Usually a regularly recurring program of cultural performances, exhibitions, or competitions. <a film festival; a high-school jazz festival> 2 Occasion for feasting or celebration, esp. a day or time of religious significance that recurs at regular intervals. <**Mardi Gras**> *Also see* **carnival.**

fetish *Cult&Soc* 1 Abnormally obsessive preoccupation or attachment; a fixation. 2 Object believed to have magical or spiritual powers. *Also see* **idol.**

ff *MusArts* » **fortissimo** (very loud)

fff *MusArts* » **fortississimo**, triple forte (very, very loud)

FGI *Fashn* **Fashion Group International**

fiber *Fashn* 1 Natural or synthetic filament, as of cotton or nylon, capable of being spun into yarn. 2 Material made of such filaments.

fiber *Journ, VA-Prntng* Newsprint, paper stock, **hard copy**: "All the major publications have tried to do electronic stuff. They got it right intellectually but in their hearts they love fiber too much." — Paul Saffo (pub. ind. consultant)

Fiber Distributed Data Interface (FDDI) *InfoMgt* » **FDDI**

fiber optics *InfoMgt* Method of data transmission utilizing pulses of light (laser) to transmit data through very fine, flexible glass or plastic fibers.

FICA *E&F-Acc, EntreP, Law&Pol* **Federal Insurance Contributions Act** (1935) Money withheld each pay period by employers from each employee's earnings used by the federal government to pay **Medicaid**, **Medicare**, and **Social Security** benefits.

fict. *LitArt* **fiction.**

fiction (fict.) *LitArts* Literary work whose content is produced by the imagination and is not necessarily based on fact. <novels and short stories> *Also see* **non-fiction.**

fictwri. *LitArts* **fiction** writer.

fiddle *MusInstr* violin *Also see* **Musical Instrument Families.**

fidelity *Rdio/TV* Degree to which an audio or video system accurately reproduces the inputted sound or image.

fiduciary *ArtPerf, Mgt* Someone like a **personal manager**, who occupies a special relation of trust, confidence, or responsibility to an Artist/Performer. *Also see* **Agents and Agencies.**

fiduciary duty *LegAsp, Law&Pol* High degree of trust and confidence owed by a person who is acting primarily for another's benefit in the area of the first person's business or professional expertise. Relationship applies to **agents**, financial trustees, physicians, and attorneys in relation to their clients and patients. In the arts businesses, it usu. applies to artists' agents/managers, but has not been applied to production professionals — yet. *Also see* **fiduciary.**

field *InfoMgt* 1 Element of a database record in which one piece of information is stored. 2 Defined area of a storage medium, such as a set of bit locations or a set of adjacent columns on a punch card, used to record a type of information consistently.

field *also* **field of view** *VisArts* Usually circular area in which the image is rendered by the lens system of an optical instrument.

field holler *iMedia, MusArts* Kind of work song and communication shouted by field hands in their labors. *Also see* **Songs.**

fields of support *Fndng* Sources of prospective gifts. *Also see* **constituency.**

fife *MusInstr* Small, highest-**pitched** flute used primarily to accompany drums in a military or marching band. *Also see* **Musical Instrument Families.**

FIFO *E&F-Acc, Mktg* **First-in, First-out.** Inventory costing method by which the first costs into inventory are the first costs out to **cost of goods sold.** *Also see* **Inventory Methods.**

fifth generation *InfoMgt* » **artificial intelligence, CRCC.**

fifth *MusArts* Interval between the **tonic** and the fifth tone above it.

fifth position *Dnce* (Ballet) One foot in front of the other; heel against the joint of the big toe. *Also see* **Positions.**

fifty-second street *MusArts* One block between fifth and sixth avenues in NYC alive with **speakeasies** in the 1920s and jazz clubs in the 1930s and 1940s.

figuration *MusArts* Ornamental treatment of a passage.

figure *iMedia* Object perceived to be in the foreground; what lies behind the object is termed **ground.**

figured bass *MusArts* » **continuo**

file allocation table (FAT) *InfoMgt* » **FAT**

file *InfoMgt* Any named collection of information stored on a disk.

file menu *InfoMgt* Menu that lists commands that affect whole documents and other files. <Save, Print, Quit>

file server *InfoMgt* Computer with special software that allows a large number of network users to store and retrieve files on the hard disks or other storage devices attached it. *Also see* **shared disk**.

File Transfer Protocol (FTP) *iMedia, InfoMgt* » **FTP**

fill *MusArts* Crisp and effective bit of improvisation by the drummer to fill in the silences between the soloist's phrases.

fill light *Flm&Vid* Light used to eliminate shadows caused by the **key light**. *Also see* **Stage Lighting**.

fill the house *Crit&Eval* To draw an audience large enough to fill the **venue**. *Also see* **SRO**.

filler *Journ,. Rdio/TV* **1** Short item used to fill space in a publication. **2** Something, such as a news item, public-service message, or music, used to fill time in a radio or television presentation.

filler *MusArts, TheatArts* Music added as background for some action by a stage performer.

filling *Fashn* Horizontal threads that cross the warp in weaving.

film *Flm&Vid* Movie, movies as a whole.

film *InfoMgt, RecA&S* Coating of magnetic alloys on glass used in making storage devices.

film distributor *Flm&Vid* » **distributor** *Also see* **Distributors**

film noir (feelm no-wha, Fr. for "black cinema") *Flm&Vid* Refers to an urban American **genre** that appeared after World War II and emphasized a fatalistic, despairing universe where there is no escape from mean streets, loneliness and death. Stylistically, noir uses low key and high contrast lighting, complex compositions and a strong atmosphere of dread and **paranoia**.

film printer *Flm&Vid* Machine that copies (prints) from original, exposed film.

film rental *Flm&Vid* Rental fees paid by exhibitor- distributor for the right to license a film for public showing. Fees may be determined by: **sliding scale**, fixed percentage, minimums (floors), or a **flat-fee** charge.

filmcard *InfoMgt* » **microfiche**

filmmaker (flmkr.) *ArtPerf, Flm&Vid* One who directs or produces movies.

filmology *Crit&Eval, Flm&Vid* Study of the technological, social, economic, political, and historical nature of film as a phenomenon of cause and effect. *Also see* **cinematology**.

filmstrip *Flm&Vid* Length of film containing graphic images prepared for still projection. *Also see* **stills**. STRIPFILM

filter *iMedia* **1** Process of selection based on specific criteria. **2** Script or application that filters.

filtering *iMedia* » **filter**

filters *Flm&Vid* Glass or plastic placed in front of the camera lens that distorts the quality of light entering the camera, thereby affecting the image.

fin-de-siècle (phan-duh-see-eck-la, (Fr. for "end of century") *Crit&Eval* Characteristic of the last part of the 19th century re its artistic climate of **effete** sophistication.

final cut *Flm&Vid* Hard-to-get right for a director, performer, or screenwriter to approve the final version of a film or video.

finale (fehnalee) *MusArts* Concluding part of a musical composition or performance.

Financial Accounting Standard Board (FASB) *E&F-Acc* » **FASB**

financial acquisition *EntreP* Purchase in which the value of the business is based on the stand-alone cash-generating potential of the company being acquired.

financial asset *EntreP* Assets such as stocks, bonds, or savings that may be used to increase revenue and acquire capital assets.

financial intermediaries *EntreP* Organizations that receive funds from savers and channel them to investors.

financial leverage *E&F-Acc* Use of debt financing (borrowed funds) Sometimes referred to as "trading on the equity."

financial leverage *EntreP* Financing a company with other peoples' money.

financial planning *EntreP* Financial planning consists of establishing monetary goals and developing method and processes for achieving these goals.

financial ratios *EntreP* Restatements of selected income statement and balance sheet data in relative terms.

Financial Statement (personal form) *EntreP* Form required by a bank when one applies for a loan. Consists of two segments, a statement of financial position and a personal cash flow statement.

financial statements (accounting statements) *E&F-Acc. EntreP*

Reports of a company's financial performance and resources, including an income statement, a balance sheet, and a statement of cash flows. *Also see* **Statements**.

financing costs *EntreP* Amount of interest owed to lenders on borrowed money.

fine art, fine arts *Aes&Creat VisArts* **1** Art produced or intended primarily for beauty rather than utility. **2** Art forms such as painting and sculpture. BEAUX-ARTS "Original painting sculpture, or drawing, or an original work of art in glass."— **Resale Royalties Act** (1984) *Also see* **droit de suite**.

fine cut *Flm&Vid* Movie at its most advanced stage of editing.

finery *Fashn* Fine clothing and accessories *Also see* **tawdry**.

finger painting *VisArts* Painting by applying color to moistened paper with the fingers.

finger piano *MusInstr* » **kalimba**

finger pick *MusInstr* Pointed, slightly curved **plectrum** worn on the fingertip, used to play a guitar or banjo.

fingerboard *MusInstr* Strip of wood on the neck of a stringed instrument against which the strings are pressed in playing.

fingerpick *MusArts* To play a stringed instrument by plucking individual strings with the fingers.

finished goods *EntreP* Inventories that a company has which are actually sold by the business. Finished goods also include spare parts and repair parts.

finished goods inventory *Eco&Fin, Mktg* Finished product that the company has in storage ready to ship. *Also see* **Inventory Methods**.

fipple *MusInstr* Mouthpiece of a **recorder**

fire curtain *PerfA&C* » **asbestos** curtain *Also see* **Stage Curtains**

firewall *InfoMgt* Network hardware barriers

firewire *InfoMgt,* Fast external **bus** standard that supports data transfer rates up to 400 **Mbps** (400 million bits per second)

.firm *InfoMgt* **Domain name** ending for business or firms. *Also see* **Domain Names**.

firm *Mgt* Business partnership

firmware *InfoMgt* Programming instructions that are stored in a read-only memory (ROM) unit rather than being implemented through software.

first chair *MusArts* » **principal player**

first edition *Journ* Day's first **pressrun** of a newspaper.

first edition *LitArts, VA-Prntng* First published copies of a literary work printed from the same type and distributed at the first time; a single copy from a first edition.

first line managers *Mgt* First or lowest tier of management <foreman, forewoman, supervisor> who are directly in charge of the employees producing the company's product. *Also see* **middle managers, upper managers**.

first *MusArts* » **first chair** <first clarinet, violin, etc>

first night *TheatArts* Opening performance, excepting **previews**, of a theatrical production.

first position *Dnce* (Ballet) Heels touching, feet in a straight line. *Also see* **Positions**.

first run *Flm&Vid* First release of a movie in a given market area.

first sample *Fashn* First garment made from an original pattern; it is checked for fit and any corrections are transferred to the patter.

first screen *InfoMgt* » **desktop**

first state *LitArts* Part of the **first printing** before the publisher detects mistakes. *Also see* **artist's print**.

first use *IntelProp, RecA&S* Refers to the right of a copyright owner of a song to control the first recording of that song. *Also see* **cover version, mechanical royalty**.

First-in, First-out (FIFO) *E&F-Acc, Mktg* » **FIFO**

first-rate *Crit&Eval* Foremost in quality, rank, or importance. *Also see* **second rate, third-rate**.

first-run programming *Rdio/TV* Business of making shows directly for individual stations rather than for a network.

first-string *Flm&Vid* » **A-team**

fish or cut bait *Crit&Eval* Either proceed with an activity or abandon it altogether.

fish-eye lens *Flm&Vid* Extremely wide-angle camera lens.

fishnet *Fashn* Mesh fabric resembling such netting.

fit model *Fashn* Live model used to check the accuracy of construction and fit of a garment before it is sent to production.

fitness industry *SportsEnt* » **sports management**

FITS *InfoMgt* **functional interpolating transformational system.** Technology that enables the user to load and edit very large images quickly and apply changes at once.

fitting *Fashn,PerfA&C* Act of trying on a costume whose fit is being adjusted.

fixed *IntelProp* » **fixed work**

fixed asset *E&F-Acc* » Property, plant, and equipment.

fixed asset turnover *E&F-Acc, EntreP* Ratio that indicates how efficiently fixed assets are being used to generate revenue for the company. Formula is net sales divided by fixed assets. *Also see* **activity ratios.**

fixed assets (use assets) *EntreP* Assets that have a useful life of one year or more. Also see capital asset.

fixed costs *E&F-Acc, EntreP* Cost that remains unchanged in total for a given time period despite wide fluctuations in property taxes, executive salaries, rent, insurance, and **depreciation.**

fixed exchange rates *EntreP* System in which governments peg exchange rates.

fixed expenses *EntreP* Expenses over which we have little or no control, such as mortgage payments, automobile loan or lease payment, property taxes, insurance, and income taxes.

fixed position *Mktg, Rdio/TV* TV commercial specifically ordered to be run within a particular program or a commercial break.

fixed work *IntelProp* Re copyright: Work of art is considered to be **fixed** when it is put in a **tangible** medium of expression. <on paper, on tape, on film, on disk>

fl *MusInstr* **flute**

flack *Crit&Eval* excessive or abusive criticism

flack, flak *Mktg* » **press agent, publicist**

flag *Flm&Vid* Plywood or cloth stretched on a metal frame, used to direct or block light when filming.

flag-waving *Crit&Eval* Excessive or fanatical patriotism. CHAUVINISM "Many a bum show has been saved by the flag." — **George M. Cohan**

flair *Crit&Eval* **1** Conspicuous talent or **aptitude**. <a flair for fashion design> **2** Distinctive elegance or style. *Also see* **pizzazz.**

flaky *Crit&Eval* Said of computers and humans. If they're erratic, they're flaky.

flamboyant *Crit&Eval* **1** Highly elaborate; **ornate**. **2** Richly colored; resplendent. **3** Marked by striking audacity or **verve.**

flame *Crit&Eval* **1** Violent or intense passion. **2** To burn brightly; blaze.

flame *InfoMgt* **1** Insult someone online **2** Talk endlessly and boringly about something not that important. *Also see* **mail bombs.**

flamenco *Dnce* Andalusian Gypsy dance or dance style characterized by forceful, often improvised rhythms. *Also see* **Dances.**

flamenco *MusInstr, MusArts* Guitar or guitar music that accompanies a flamenco dance.

flameout *Crit&Eval* Failure of a artist's career, while enjoying public acclaim, caused by the extinction of her/his artistic **flame.** *Also see* **EAT+D** **Origin** Failure of a jet aircraft engine in flight, caused by the extinction of the flame in the combustion chamber.

flapper *Cult&Soc, Fashn* Young 1920s woman who disdained conventional dress and behavior. <short skirts, bobbed hair, smoked in public, danced the **Charleston**>

flare *Fashn* To open outward in shape. <a skirt that flares from the waist>

flash-in-the-pan *Crit&Eval* Something or someone that enjoys sudden success that quickly disappears.

flashback *Flm&Vid, LitArts* Device in which an earlier event is inserted into the normal chronological order of a narrative; the episode or scene depicted by means of this device. *Also see* **lift.**

flashback *TheatArts* Scene inserted into the play showing events which happened at an earlier time.

flat dead-tree cartooning *Journ, VisArts* **Two-dimensional** newspaper art. *Also see* **Golden Spike Award.**

flat *Fashn* Having a smooth, even, level surface. *Also see* **croquis.**

flat *MusArts* **1** Being below the correct **pitch. 2** Being one half step lower than the corresponding natural key. <the **key** of B **flat**>

flat *PerfA&C* Scenic piece, usu. a rectangular wooden frame covered with painted canvas, which is used as an element (e.g., a wall) in stage scenery.

flat *VA-Prntng* » **mask**

flat lighting *Flm&Vid* Omnidirectional illumination from no particular source.

flat organization *Mgt* Organization or structure with relatively few tiers of management.

flat top *Fashn* Short haircut in which the hair is brushed straight up and cropped flat across the top.

flat-bed press *VA-Prntng* Press in which the type, locked into a **chase**, is supported by a flat surface or bed and the paper is applied to the type either by a flat platen or by a cylinder against which the bed moves. *Also see* **rotary press.**

flat-fee *Eco&Fin* Payment that makes no **allowance** for volume, frequency, or other factors.

flatbed *Flm&Vid* Motorized tabletop machine designed for viewing and editing film (picture and sound)

flatted fifth *MusArts* "Most common chord alteration in **modern jazz**, achieved by lowering the dominant tone, or fifth degree of the scale, a half-step." — Lyons & Perlo (jazz critics)

flea market *Mktg* Market, usu. held outdoors, where antiques, used household goods, collectibles, and curios – *aka* junk – are sold.

flex pass *Mktg,PerfA&C* Box office term for a coupon booklet allowing a patron/customer to select any performance event offered by the producing organization. *Also see* **subscribe by design.**

flexible pricing strategy *EntreP* Marketing approach that offers different prices to reflect differences in customer demand.

flextime *HR&LR* Arrangement by which employees may set their own work schedules, esp. their starting and finishing hours. FLEXIBLE TIME, FLEXITIME

flick *Flm&Vid* movie

flies *PerfA&C* Area directly over the theater stage that houses overhead lights and scenery. *Also see* **fly, fly gallery.**

flimflam *Crit&Eval* **1** deception; a swindle. **2** nonsense; **humbug**

flip *MusArts* Jazz horn sound derived from the classical **turn** in which the player leaves one note by going up and then **glissing** to the second note.

flip it *Flm&Vid, TheatArts* Turn an emotion or an action some way other than what is expected.

flip side *RecA&S* Reverse side of a phonograph disk. *Also see* **A side, B side.**

flmkr *ArtPerf, Flm&Vid* **filmmaker**

floater *ArtPerf, HR&LR, Dnce* Dancer who is neither an apprentice nor an **AGMA** union member.

floating-point number *iMedia* Includes a fractional value (such as 3.14)

flocking *Fashn* Fabric is treated with adhesive, then pieces of fiber are applied in a pattern. Used to make a raised, velvety design.

floodlight *PerfA&C* Stage lighting instrument that disperses a soft light over a wide area; used primarily to fill in shadows caused by **spotlights**. Also *see* **Stage Lighting.**

Floor Supervisor *Mgt* Assistant to Director of Sales and Customer Relations and Ticketing Managers. >Chicago Symphony Orchestra<

floorshow *PA-Variety* nightclub entertainment

flop *Crit&Eval* utter failure. BOMB

flop sweat *Crit&Eval* What you get when you think you have a **flop**. —**Bob Fosse**

floppy disk, floppies *InfoMgt* Thin, round, flexible disk in a 5-1/4-inch flat plastic housing or the sturdier, almost square 3-1/2-inch disks.

florid *Crit&Eval* Very **ornate**; flowery. <florid prose style>

flounce *Crit&Eval* Move with exaggerated or affected motions.

flounce *Fashn* Strip of decorative, usu. gathered or pleated material attached by one edge on a garment or curtain.

flourish *Crit&Eval* **1** To be in a period of highest productivity, excellence, or influence. <a composer who flourished in the 18th century; painted when **neorealism** was flourishing> **2** Dramatic or stylish movement. <waving or brandishing> **3 Embellishment** or ornamentation. <a long speech with many rhetorical flourishes>

4 Ostentatious act or gesture.

flourish *MusArts* Showy or ceremonious **passage** <fanfare>

flow control *InfoMgt* Method used to synchronize communications between two computers.

flowchart *iMedia* **1** Graphical representation of the relationship(s) between pieces of content. usu. visualized with squares or rectangles representing content, and lines connecting the squares that represent relationships. **2** Diagram that shows step-by-step progression through a procedure or system especially using connecting lines and a set of conventional symbols

flower child *Cult&Soc* One advocating universal peace and love as antidotes to social or political problems. Symbol of the youth counterculture of the 1960s and 1970s. *Origin* From the custom of carrying or wearing flowers to symbolize peace and love. *Also see* **hippie**.

flub *Crit&Eval* To botch or bungle

flug *MusInstr* **flugelhorn** FLUGELHORN PLAYER

flügelhorn (flug) *MusInstr* Similar to a trumpet but with a lower **register**, wider bore, and darker tone. FLUGELHORNIST, FLUGELHORN PLAYER *Also see* **Musical Instrument Families.**

Fluid Analogies Research Group (FARG) *InfoMgt* » **CRCC**

flush *VA-Prntng* Align evenly with a margin, as along the left or right edge of a typeset page; not indented. <flush left, flush right> *Also see* **ragged**.

flute (fl) *MusInstr* **1** High-**pitched woodwind** instrument consisting of a slender tube closed at one end with keys and finger holes on the side and an opening near the closed end across which the player blows. <C Melody —, alto —, bass —> TRANSVERSE FLUTE. **2** Any of various similar reedless **woodwind** instruments, such as the recorder. **3** Organ stop whose flue pipe produces a flutelike tone. FLUTIST [Not flautist!] *Also see* **Musical Instrument Families.**

flute *VisArts* Long, usu. rounded groove incised as a decorative **motif** on the shaft of a column, for example; similar groove or furrow, as in a pleated **ruffle** of cloth or on a piece of furniture.

flutter *MusArts, RecA&S* **1** Extra **oscillation** in the **treble** range. **2** Rapid fluctuation in **pitch** of resulting from variations in the speed of the sound reproduction equipment. *Also see* **trill, wow**.

fly *PerfA&C* **1** Hoist a curtain or scenery into the flies. **2** Raise an object or person above the stage floor with ropes or cables. *Ex.* "Peter Pan."

fly gallery *PerfA&C* Platform at the side of the backstage area of a theater where a stage hand works the ropes/cables controlling equipment in the flies. *Also see* **grid**.

fly loft *PerfA&C* Open space above the stage where the scenery and equipment are flown. *Also see* **fly gallery**.

fly systems *PerfA&C* Rigging or fly system is a series of cables, pulleys, and **counterweights** that enable scenery, drapes, or lighting equipment to fly in and out. » **counterweight system**

fly-by-night *Crit&Eval* Unreliable or unscrupulous with regard to business dealings.

flyer *ArtPerf, PA-Variety* Principal in a flying trapeze act; her or his partner is the **catcher**.

flyer *Crit&Eval* daring venture

flyer *Mktg* Pamphlet or circular for mass distribution. HERALD

flying buttress *VisArts* Masonry support consisting usu. of a pier or buttress standing apart from the main structure and connected to it by an arch along which the thrust, as from the vaulting, is borne. *Also see* **Gothic**.

flyman *PerfA&C* One who operates a fly system. FLYPERSON

FM *Rdio/TV* **frequency modulation**. Developed in 1934 by Edwin Armstrong. This high fidelity radio signal transmits 88-108 **megahertz**, unaffected by atmosphere interference. It is a line-of-sight beam impeded by topographic or physical obstructions. <The station's FM signal was obstructed by nearby mountains and high-rise buildings> *Also see* **AM**.

fn. *LitArts* **footnote**.

FOB destination *E&F-Acc* Terms of a transaction that govern when the title of the inventory passes from the seller to the buyer: when the goods arrive at the buyer's location.

FOB shipping point *E&F-Acc* Terms of a transaction that govern when the title of the inventory passes from the seller to the buyer: when the goods leave the seller's place of business.

focus *Crit&Eval* **1** Center of interest or activity. **2** Close or narrow attention; concentration.

focus *iMedia* Portion of a program, or operating system that currently has prominence or which is activated <the text field has focus>.

focus group *iMedia, Mktg* Small-discussion group of 8-12 consumers from whom the market researcher obtains qualitative information about – or emotional response to – a particular product or idea from individuals who are representative of the target market.

FOD *InfoMgt* Fax-on-demand Fax message automatically sent to a dialed phone inquiry.

FOIA *Journ, Law&Pol* » **Freedom of Information Act**

foible *Crit&Eval* Minor weakness or failing of character.

foil *Crit&Eval* One that by contrast underscores or enhances the distinctive characteristics of another.

fol. *LitArts, VA-Prntng* **folio**

folder *InfoMgt* Holder for documents, programs, and other folders that can be organized in any way by the user.

folderol (foll-duh-role) *Crit&Eval* **1** Foolishness; nonsense. **2** Trifle; a **gewgaw**. *Origin* From a nonsense **refrain** in some old songs.

Foley *Flm&Vid* To add **post-production** sound effects.

folio (f., F., fol.) *Eco&Fin* Page in a ledger or two facing pages that are assigned a single number.

folio (f., F., fol.) *LegAsp* Specific number of words used as a unit for measuring the length of the text of a document.

folio (f., F., fol.) *LitArts, VA-Prntng* **1** To number consecutively the pages or leaves of a book. **2** Large sheet of paper folded once in the middle, making two leaves or four pages of a book or manuscript. **3** Book or manuscript of the largest common size, usu. about 38 centimeters (15 inches) in height, consisting of such folded sheets.

folio *MusArts* Collection of music written by various artists, having a common link or theme. <love songs, top hits of an era, selections from a **Broadway** show, etc> *Also see* **Print Music**.

folio verso *LitArts, VA-Prntng* » **f.v.**

folk art, folk-art *Cult&Soc, VisArts* Art originating among the common people of a nation or region and usu. reflecting their traditional culture, esp. everyday or festive items produced or decorated by unschooled artists. *Also see* **folk music, vernacular art, visionary art**.

folk dance, folk-dance, folkdance *Cult&Soc, Dnce* **1** Traditional dance originating among the common people of a nation or region. **2** Social gathering at which folk dances are performed. *Also see* **Dances**.

folk music *MusArts* **1** Music originating among the common people of a country or region and communicated orally, with variations. **2** Contemporary music in the style of traditional folk music. "Folk music is quite different from concert or commercial music. Part of the life of a community, it evolves un-self-consciously and is preserved by oral transmission and apprenticeship rather than orthodox schooling or marketing. Surest sign that a folk music tradition is endangered is an attempt to preserve it in writing." — Edward Rothstein (1952-, chief mus. critic, *NY Times*) *Also see* **Country Music Styles, folk art, hootenanny**.

folk-rock, folk rock *MusArts* Variety of pop music combining elements of rock and folk music. *Also see* **Rock Music Styles**.

folkie, folky *MusArts* folk singer or musician

folklore *Cult&Soc* **1** Traditional beliefs, **myths**, tales, and practices of a people, transmitted orally. **2** Body of widely accepted but usu. specious notions about a place, a group, or an institution. <Rumors of their antics became part of the folklore of Hollywood>

folksong, folk-song, folk song *MusArts* Song belonging to the **folk music** of a people or area, often existing in several versions or regional variations. *Also see* **Songs**.

folkways *Cult&Soc* Practices, customs, or beliefs shared by the members of a group as part of their common culture.

follow focus *Flm&Vid* Technique involving the continuous refocusing of a lens during a shot in which the distance between the camera and the subject is greater than the depth of field.

follow spot *PerfA&C* **Spotlight**, manned by a stagehand or electrician, used to illuminate and follow a performer's movements, esp. dancers. *Also see* **Stage Lighting**.

follow-the-leader pricing strategy *EntreP* Marketing approach that uses a particular competitor as a model in setting prices.

follow-up, followup *Journ* Article or report giving further information on a previously reported item of news.

followspot *PerfA&C* Lighting instrument with a high-intensity, narrow beam, mounted in a stand that allows the operator to tilt and swivel it so that the beam can follow an actor or moving object.

folo lead (for follow up *leed*) *BcstJourn* Lead sentence that advances the information of a new or breaking story. *Also:* update or second-day lead.

font *BcstJourn* » **CG**

font *iMedia, InfoMgt* Individual typeface in a particular style and of a particular size. <This text is set in 9 point New Century Schoolbook (plain, **bold**, and *italic*)> *Also see* **leading**; **point**, **scalable outline**.

fool *Crit&Eval, PA-Variety* In **medieval** times, a member of a royal or noble household who provided entertainment, as with jokes or antics. <play the fool> *Also see* **buffoon, clown, jester**.

foot candle *Flm&Vid* International unit of illumination defined as the intensity of light falling on a sphere placed one foot away from a point source of light of one candlepower.

foot *LitArts* Unit of **poetic meter** consisting of stressed and unstressed syllables in any of various set combinations. <Iambic foot has an unstressed followed by a stressed syllable>

footer *InfoMgt* Information <a title, page number, or date> positioned in the bottom margin of a page usu. repeated throughout a document created on a word-processing system. *Also see* **header**.

footing *E&F-Acc* sum of a column of figures

footlights *PerfA&C* **1** Lights placed in a row along the front of a stage floor used for scenic toning, opaquing downstage **scrims**, and as curtain warmers. Should not be used to light actors as they create unnatural shadows. **2** Theater as a profession. *Also see* **Stage Lighting**.

footnote (fn.) *Crit&Eval* Something relating to but of lesser importance than a larger work or occurrence.

footnote (fn.) *LitArts* Note placed at the bottom of a page of a book or manuscript that comments on or cites a reference for a designated part of the text. *Also see* **endnote**.

footprint *InfoMgt* Designated area affected or covered by a device. <The small business or home office benefits from the smaller footprint of the new desktop computers and printers>

footprint *Mktg, Rdio/TV* Size of market: "This deal [for more cable outlets] gives the Fox news channel a 10-million subscriber footprint." — *NY Times*

for the birds *Crit&Eval* objectionable; worthless

forced perspective *Flm&Vid* Illusion, usu. created by wide-angle lenses, in which parallel lines converge more drastically than in normal vision.

forecasting *EntreP* Process and procedures used to develop a forecast. In business it is normally the process of estimating future demand for a business' products and services.

foreground *Flm&Vid* Action area nearest the camera. *Also see* **background**.

foreign entertainer law *Law&Pol, PerfA&C* » **P-1**.

foreign royalty *IntelProp, MusArts, RecA&S* Royalties paid from exploitation of copyright in other than domestic territories. except, in some cases, the royalties are shared with a foreign counterpart and one society may represent both **mechanical** and **performance** rights. *Also see* **Royalties**.

forensic *LegAsp* Relating to courts of law or for public discussion or argumentation.

foreshadowing *TheatArts* Dramatic device by which the playwright raises expectations in the audience of possible coming events in the play. *Ex.* In *The Wild Duck*, Fledwig is admonished by her father never to play with a prominently displayed gun and the audience immediately expects a possible future accident.

foreword *LitArts* Preface or introduction at the beginning of a book.

Form 990-PF *Fnding* Annual information return that all private foundations must submit to the **IRS** each year, and also filed with appropriate state officials. Form requires information on the foundation's **assets**, income, **operating expenses**, contributions and grants, paid staff and salaries, program funding areas, grantmaking guidelines and restrictions, and grant application procedures. (**Foundation Center** libraries maintain files of 990-PFs for public inspection.)

form *Crit&Eval* **1** Performance considered with regard to acknowledged criteria. **2** Proven ability to perform. <a soloist at the top of her or his form>

form *iMedia* **1** Structure that conveys content in an interactive media product. Tied with content; form exists to convey content. **2** Shape and structure of an object. **3** Markup element allowing data to be submitted to a server.

form *LitArts, MusArts* Method of arrangement or manner of coordinating elements in literary or musical composition. <Essay is a literary form; symphony is a musical form>

form cut *Flm&Vid* Framing in a successive shot an object that has a shape or contour similar to an image in the immediately preceding shot.

formal *Crit&Eval, Fashn* Something, such as a gown or tuxedo, or ball or dance, that is formal in nature.

formal contract *LegAsp* Contract that requires a special form or method for its creation. <**contracts under seal, recognizances, negotiable instruments, letters of credit**> *Also see* **Contracts**.

formal elements *iMedia* Outward organization of visual structure arranged in a composition; includes line, shape, tone (light vs. dark), color, space, and texture.

format *BcstJourn* » **rundown**

format *InfoMgt* To produce in a specified form. *Also see* **initialize**.

format *Journ, VA-Prntng* **1** Form or layout of a publication. <dimensions, binding, color> **2** In typesetting, the instructions that are fed into an automated typesetter. <leading, size, typeface, etc>

formula *InfoMgt* Statement describes a mathematical calculation. Formulas in spreadsheets are linked to individual cells as well as to data and formulas in other cells, allowing a user to perform what-if calculations.

Formula Translator *InfoMgt* » **FORTRAN**

forte (for-tay) *Genl* Something in which a person excels. <composing was her forte>

forte (for-tay, Ital. for "strong,") (f, F) *MusArts* Play in a loud, forceful manner. <Note, passage, or chord played forte> *Also see* **Music Directions**.

forte-piano (for-tay-pee-ahno) *MusArts* Play loud, then suddenly soft. *Also see* **Music Directions**.

fortissimo (ff) (for-tis-sim-oh) *MusArts* Direction: play very loudly.

fortississimo (fff) *MusArts* Direction: play in the loudest manner possible; raise the roof.

fortnightly *Genl* Occurring once every two weeks.

FORTRAN *InfoMgt* **FOR**mula **TRAN**slator; the first high level language designed for scientific applications.

forty by sixty, 40 x 60 *Flm&Vid, Mktg* A 40-inch by 60-inch poster created primarily for use in theater display cases.

forty-fives, 45s *RecA&S* Seven-inch record disks played at 45 **rpm**; introduced by RCA in 1949. *Also see* **battle of the speeds**.

forum *InfoMgt* "place" in an online service where people with similar interests can exchange ideas and comments.

forward integration *Mgt* Term describing a marketer that seeks ownership or increased control of its distribution channels. *Also see* **backward integration, vertical integration**.

forza *MusArts* Play with force *Also see* **Music Directions**.

Fosse, Bob (1927-1987, dncr., choreog., film/stage dir.) *ArtPerf, Flm&Vid, MusArts, PerfA&C* A kingpin of the American **musical**. Awards (1973) <Oscar for *Cabaret*., Tony for *Pippin*, Emmy for *Liza*.> *Also see* **flop sweat**.

fouetté (foo-et-tay, Fr.) *Dnce* (Ballet) Turn in which the dancer, standing on one foot, uses the other leg in a circular whiplike motion to pull the body.

found theater spaces *PerfA&C* Structures originally designed for some other purpose that have been converted into performing spaces.

foundation *Mgt* Institution founded and supported by an **endowment**.

Foundation Center *Fnding* Mission is to support and improve institutional philanthropy by promoting public understanding of the field and helping grantseekers succeed. >http://fdncenter.org< *Also see* **Donors Forum**.

Foundation for the Extension and Development of the Amer-

ican Professional Theatre (FEDAPT) *TheatArts* » **FEDAPT** [Defunct].

foundation pattern *Fashn* » **sloper**

Four A's *ArtPerf, HR&LR* **American Actors and Artistes of America (Four A's)** Umbrella organization affiliated with the **AFL-CIO** authorized to issue jurisdictional charters to various performer unions, inc.: **AEA, AFTRA, AGMA, AGVA, APATE, HAU, IAU, SAG, SEG.** *Also see* **Guilds & Unions**.

Four A's *Mktg* **American Association of Advertising Agencies (Four A's)**

four-channel, 4-channel sound *RecA&S* » **quadraphonic sound**

four-color printing *VA-Prntng* Color printing or photographic process in which three primary colors and black are transferred by four different plates or filters to a surface, thereby reproducing the colors of the subject matter. *Also see* **two-color printing**.

four-part harmony *MusArts* four voices of a vocal quartet: soprano, alto, tenor, bass

four-wall *Flm&Vid, Mktg* Rental plan whereby film distributors, concert promoters, and show producers may offer **venue** operators a guaranteed flat weekly or nightly fee regardless of the box-office receipts.

four-wall *PerfA&C* Theater rental plan whereby a flat fee covers only the use of the **venue** without any front-of house or backstage services, personnel, or equipment.

four-wall studio *RecA&S* Practice more common in Los Angeles where the renter of the studio gets the **venue** without an engineer and equipment necessary for the recording session.

fours *MusArts* » **trading fours**

Fourth Amendment (of the U.S. Constitution) *SportsEnt* "It is the right of the people to be secure in their persons, house, papers, and effects, against unreasonable searches and seizures, shall not be violated, and no warrants shall issue, but upon probable cause, supported by oath or affirmation, and particularly describing the place or be searched, and the person or things to be seized." *Also see* **drug testing**.

fourth dimension *Sci&Tech* Time regarded as a coordinate dimension and required by **relativity** theory, along with three **spatial** dimensions, to specify completely the location of any event.

fourth estate *Journ* journalists as a group; the public press

fourth *MusArts* Interval between the **tonic** and the fourth **diatonic** tone above it.

fourth position *Dnce* (Ballet) Feet apart, one in front of the other; opposite of **fifth position**. *Also see* **Positions**.

fourth wall *Flm&Vid, TheatArts* The audience. *Also see* **empathic response**.

fourth-class mail *Mktg* Class of mail consisting of merchandise and some printed matter weighing over eight ounces and not sealed against inspection.

fourth-wall *TheatArts* Refers to the style of realistic theater since the late 19th century in which the stage is treated as a room with one wall missing. The audience is not acknowledged or addressed by the actors, but overlooks the scene as a silent, invisible observer.

fox trot *Dnce, MusArts* Ballroom dance or music in 2/4 or 4/4 time, featuring a variety of slow and fast steps.

FPLA *Law&Pol, Mktg* » **Fair Packaging and Label Act**

fps, f.p.s. *iMedia, Flm&Vid* frames per second

Fr-h *MusInstr* **French horn**

fractal *iMedia* Set of mathematical equations that express a pattern in which any suitably chosen sample is similar to a magnified or reduced part. Pattern is apparent no matter what the scale.

frame *Flm&Vid, iMedia* **1** Visual space within boundaries. **2** Specific point within an equal distribution of time, and which in an animation or frame-based application can contain content. **3** one individual picture on a roll of film *Also see* **frame rate**.

frame *Rdio/TV* Total area of a complete picture in television broadcasting.

frame rate *iMedia* Number of **frames** that will play per second. **Animation** delivered via web usu. has 15 frames per second.

frame story *LitArts* Narrative structure containing or connecting a series of otherwise unrelated tales.

frame-by-frame animation *iMedia* Series of images when viewed sequentially, aligned in the same physical space (flip book, film

screen, monitor, etc.), an animation occurs; each image acts as a **keyframe** and is slightly different from the preceding or following image.

frames *BcstJourn* » **topic box**

frames per second (fps, f.p.s.) *Flm&Vid* **1** Rate of speed at which film or video is shot, projected or replayed. Film is 24 frames per second; video is 30 frames per second. **2** Video rate is dependent on power frequency and is 30 frames per second in the USA where the power frequency is 60 Hz. Countries with 50 Hz power use 25 frames per second for video.

franchise *Eco&Fin, Mktg* **1** Authorization granted to someone to sell or distribute a company's goods or services in a certain area. **2** Business or group of businesses established or operated under such authorization. *Also see* **chain, Contracts, Intangible Assets**.

franchise *EntreP* Business system in which replicated units of a business are owned by individuals who pay a franchise fee and royalty in exchange for the benefits of the known name and standard operation plan.

franchise *Rdio/TV* Agreement between a cable operator and local government body that defines the rights and responsibilities of each party in the operation of a cable system within a specified geographic area. *Also see* **Contracts**.

freak *Crit&Eval* enthusiast. <rock music freak>

freak *Cult&Soc* **1** Member of a **counterculture**; **eccentric** or nonconformist. **2** Drug user or addict. <speed freak>

freak *MusArts* Perform vocal or instrumental music.

freak show *PA-Variety* A circus **sideshow** or a carnival attraction featuring such wonders as. <a two-headed calf, JoJo the Dog-Faced Boy, Lydia, the Tattooed Lady, et al> *Also see* **barker, geek**.

freaking out *Cult&Soc* "A process whereby an individual casts off outmoded and restricting standards of thinking, dress, and social etiquette in order to express creatively his relationship to his immediate environment." — **Frank Zappa**

free agents *SportsEnt* Athletes who act as **independent contractors** with their teams. They partially subtract themselves from the **Standard Player Contract** and negotiate individual contracts suited to their athletic performance and star status.

free cash flow *EntreP* Operating profits plus depreciation less cash taxes and less the investments required to grow the company.

free enterprise system *Eco&Fin, Law&Pol* Freedom of private businesses to operate competitively for profit with minimal government regulation. [And ample government subsidy.] *Also see* **laissez-faire**.

Free Expression Network *LegAsp* » **FEN**

free goods *Mktg, RecA&S* Recordings distributed for promotion purposes are considered exempt from royalty payments. [It is not unknown that recipients of free goods, i.e., deejays, reviewers, resell their free goods to a retailer who sells them via the **cutout** bin. Once upon a time there was a reviewer who sold his free goods collection to pay for a new car.].

free jazz, free-jazz *MusArts* "Soloists could play by free associating the melody without reference to the bar lines. Maybe stick with the first three notes or something. One guy would take the lead. If he stayed on the first bar for five minutes everybody would go with him. You could put the chords in any sequence you wanted." — Roswell Rudd (1935-, jazz tb., arr-comp.)

free on board *Eco&Fin* » **f.o.b**.

free records *RecA&S* » **bonus records**

Free Software Foundation *iMedia* Organization devoted to the creation and dissemination of free software, i.e., software free from licensing fees or restrictions on use.

free speech *Law&Pol* Right to express any opinion in public without censorship or restraint by the government. *Also see* **due process**; **erotic music law, second-class mail**.

free spirit *Crit&Eval* One who is not restrained by convention or obligation.

free trade *Eco&Fin* Trade between nations without protective customs tariffs. *Also see* **protectionism**.

free verse *LitArts* **Verse** composed of variable, usu. unrhymed lines having no fixed **metrical** pattern. *Also see* **blank verse**.

free will *Ethcs&Phil* The feeling that one is making decisions or choices not compelled by any external or internal forces; the belief that humans can choose to do otherwise than they do.

<"Free will does not mean one will, but many wills conflicting in one man." — Flannery O'Connor> *Also see* **autonomy**.

free-flow pattern *EntreP* Flexible retail store layout that is visually appealing and gives customers freedom of movement.

freebie *Genl* free article or service

Freed, Alan (1922-65) *Ethcs&Phil, Rdio/TV* Cleveland pioneer rock deejay who was well paid both under and over the table for his efforts. » **payola** [Mainly because of his "stature" the Rock & Roll Hall of Fame is located in Cleveland.].

freedom *Crit&Eval, Ethcs&Phil* **1** Absence of external impediments to action. **2** Capacity to exercise choice. **3** Free will. "For most people: success = prison, and an artist should never be a *prisoner*. Prisoner? Artist should never be: prisoner of himself, prisoner of a style, prisoner of a reputation, prisoner of success, etc." — **Henri Matisse**

freedom *Law&Pol* **1** Political independence. **2** Possession of civil rights; immunity from the arbitrary exercise of authority.

Freedom of Information Act (FOIA, 1966) Requires U.S. government agencies release their records to the public on request, with some exceptions re national security and individual's right of privacy. [Some government agencies continue (1998) to delay and even refuse disclosure.] *Also see* **Federal Agencies and Statutes**.

freedom of the press *Journ, Law&Pol* "Freedom of the press is guaranteed only to those who own one." — A.J. Liebling (1904-1963, journ. critic) *Also see* **Bill of Rights**.

freeform *VisArts* **1** Having a flowing asymmetrical shape or outline. <freeform sculpture> **2** Characterized by an unconventional or variable form.

freelance *ArtPerf* Writer, or other artist, who sells (or leases) or otherwise provides artistic services to an employer while operating as an independent entity. *Also see* **independent contractor**.

freeware *InfoMgt* Free software offered usu. on computer **bulletin boards**.

freeze-frame *Flm&Vid* Optical effect of stopping the film action by printing one frame over several times.

freight-in *E&F-Acc* Transportation charges on merchandise purchases for resale. TRANSPORTATION-IN

freight-out *E&F-Acc* Transportation charges acquired as a result of sales. FREIGHT, TRANSPORTATION

French cuff *Fashn* Wide cuff for a shirt sleeve folded back and fastened with a cuff link.

French heel *Fashn* Curved, moderately high heel used on women's shoes.

French horn (Fr-h) *MusInstr* Valved brass wind instrument that produces a mellow tone from a long, narrow tube coiled in a circle before ending in a flaring bell. HORN PLAYER *Also see* **Musical Instrument Families**

French knot *Fashn* Decorative embroidery stitch made by looping the thread two or more times around the needle, which is then inserted into the fabric.

french scene *TheatArts* Section of the script that begins with a character's entrance and ends when either another character enters or a character on stage exits.

French twist *Fashn* Woman's hairstyle where the hair is swept back from the temples to the back of the head where one twist of hair is pinned over the other.

frenetic *Crit&Eval* Wildly excited or active; frantic; frenzied.

frenzy *Crit&Eval* Wild excitement. *Also see* **black church music**.

freq. *Rdio/TV, RecA&S* **frequency**

frequency (freq.) *Mktg* Number of times that a consumer sees or hears a marketing message: radio/television, print advertising, etc.

frequency (freq.) *Sci&Tech* Measure of the number of times the cycle of a **wave form** is repeated in a second, expressed in **cycles** per second, or **hertz**. Short **wavelength** is equivalent to a **high frequency**.

frequency discount *Eco&Fin, Mktg* Discount offered by an advertising medium that allows an advertiser a lower rate for advertising more frequently during a contract period. *Also see* **Discounts**.

frequency modulation (FM) *Rdio/TV* » **FM** *Also see* **amplitude modulation**

fresh pilot *Flm&Vid* **Pilot** with at least a saleable idea.

Fresnel *Flm&Vid,PerfA&C* Spotlight that produces a soft, diffused light. Fresnel spotlights come in several sizes measured by the diameter of the lens — three inches to 30 inches although six and eight-inch lenses are the most common. *Also see* **Stage Lighting**.

fret *MusInstr* One of several ridges set across the **fingerboard** of a stringed instrument.

fretted instrument *MusInstr* Acoustic or electric musical instrument with frets on its **fingerboard** and played usu. by plucking the strings. <banjo, guitar, mandolin>

Freud, Sigmund (1856-1939, Aus. physician) *Crit&Eval, Ethcs&Phil* Founder of psychoanalysis who theorized that the symptoms of hysterical patients represent forgotten and unresolved infantile psychosexual conflicts. His psychoanalytic theories, which initially met with hostility, profoundly influenced 20th century thought.

Freudian *Crit&Eval* Relating to the psychoanalytic theories of **Sigmund Freud**.

frieze *VisArts* Decorative horizontal band, as along the upper part of a wall in a room.

frill *Mktg* Something desirable but not a necessity; a luxury.

fringe benefit *Eco&Fin* Employment benefit given in addition to one's wages or salary. <child day care, club dues, company car, health, **CODA** or 401(K) plan, life insurance, maternal/paternal leave, pension, sick time, vacation time.

fringe benefits *EntreP* Supplements to compensation, designed to be attractive and beneficial to employees.

fringe benefits *HR&LR* Items provided to an employee under the terms of an employment agreement or contract. <health care, paid holidays and vacations, insurance, pensions, etc>

frisson *Crit&Eval* Moment of intense excitement; a shudder. *Also see* **aesthetic arrest, empathic response, Art Movements and Periods**.

frock *Fashn* **1** woman's dress **2** Long, loose outer garment worn by artists and craftspeople; a smock. **3** Robe worn by monks, friars, and other clerics; a habit.

frolic and detour *LegAsp* When an agent does something during the course of his or her employment to further his or her own interest rather than the interests of the **principal**.

front curtain *PerfA&C* Any curtain hanging across the front of the stage. *Also see* **Stage Curtains**.

front matter *InfoMgt, LitArts, VA-Prntng* Front-of-the-book pages. <title page, table of contents, preface, introduction, etc>

front of house staff *PerfA&C* Personnel of the business staff, inc. box office, ticket takers, and ushers.

front of house, front-of-house, front of the house (F.O.H.) *PerfA&C* Parts of the theatre in front of the **proscenium**: audience, lobby and business offices.

front-end processor (FEP) *InfoMgt* Computer used to process data before it is sent to a mainframe computer for analysis or further processing.

frou frou *Fashn* **1** Fussy or showy dress or ornamentation. **2** Rustling sound, as of silk.

FTC *Law&Pol, Mktg* **Federal Trade Commission**. Est. 1914 to prevent unfair or deceptive acts or practices in commerce. *Also see* **Federal Agencies and Statutes**.

FTP *iMedia, InfoMgt* **File Transfer Protocol**. Standard **protocol** for transferring files from one computer to another over the **Internet**. *Also see* **Protocols**.

fugue *MusArts* Composition in which three or more voices enter at different times and imitate the main melody in different ways according to a set pattern.

fulfillment, fulfilment *Journ, Mktg* Process of servicing a subscription to a periodical. <billing and collection, start date and expiration date, file maintenance and renewal mailings, packaging and delivery systems>

full duplex *InfoMgt* Ability of a communication system to transmit information in both directions simultaneously. *Also see* **duplex, simplex**.

full page ad *Journ, Mktg* Ad printed on and within a full page of a magazine or newspaper. *Also see* **island page, bleed ad**.

full returns *Journ* Magazine newsstand distributors return complete copies, rather than the front covers or an **affidavit** of unsold copies.

full-fashioned *Fashn* Knitted in a shape that conforms closely to

G

body lines.

fully disclosed agency *LegAsp* One that results if the third party entering into the contract knows (1) that the agent is acting for a **principal** and (2) the actual identity of the **principal**. *Also see* **Agents and Agencies**.

function *iMedia* **1** Programming: block of reusable lines of code (statements) defined once and that can be invoked (called) repeatably. Functions may be modified with arguments. **2** Working or able to be used (metric for critique) » **functionality**

function call *iMedia* » **calling a function**

functional interpolating transformational system *InfoMgt* » **FITS**

functional prototype *iMedia* Rough draft of an interactive product created in a technology similar to, or which is a possible candidate for, the final product.

functionality *iMedia* Metric that measures the degree to which a product's components function. Low functionality describes a product where few components work.

fund *Fndng* **1** Vehicle for securing annual contributions. <alumni fund> **2** To give value to a trust, as to fund with securities, property, or cash.

fund accounting *Eco&Fin* Procedure by which, for accounting and reporting purposes, resources are classified into fund accounts that are associated with activities or objectives specific to that task.

fund balances *Eco&Fin* Since there are no direct owners in **non-profits** (in the sense of a business enterprise) who have the right to buy and sell ownership shares, the Owners' Equity section of the **balance sheet** is replaced by this account. This account reports the excess of assets over liabilities and any restrictions on the excess.

fundamental Analysis *EntreP* Analysis of the future cash flows from some asset.

fundamental *MusArts* Also called the **tonic**; the lowest tone of a chord when the chord is founded on that tone; also, the lowest note in the harmonic series.

Fundamentalism *Ethcs&Phil* **1** Organized, militant Evangelical movement originating in the U.S. (ca. 1920) in opposition to **Liberalism** and **secularism**. **2** Movement or point of view characterized by rigid adherence to fundamental or basic principles.

fundraising, fund-raising *Fndng* Organized activity or an instance of soliciting money or pledges for charitable organizations.

Funds *ColEntry, Fndng* » **capital** —, **endowment** —, **expendable** —, **nonexpendable** —, **operating** —, **restricted** —.

funk *Dnce* "'Funk is real *under*,' he says, snapping his fingers. 'Against the beat. Just *ridin'*. It's the bass line. It's like a pulse.'" — Savion Glover (1973-, tap dncr., choreog.) *Also see* **tap dance**.

funk *MusArts* Type of popular music combining elements of jazz, blues, and soul; characterized by syncopated rhythm and a heavy, repetitive bass line. *Also see* **funky**.

funky *Crit&Eval* **1** Earthy and uncomplicated; natural. **2** Outlandishly vulgar or eccentric in a humorous or tongue-in-cheek manner; campy.

funky *Fashn* Unconventional clothes characterized by self-expression, originality, and modishness.

funky *MusArts* **1** Music that has an earthy quality reminiscent of the blues. <funky jazz> **2** "[Re] the blue notes or blue mood created in jazz, blues, and soul music generally, **down-to-earth** soulfully expressed sounds; by extension [related to] the real **nitty-gritty** or fundamental essence of life, soul to the max." — Geneva Smitherman, (cult. critic).

funnies *Journ, VisArts* Comic strips. FUNNY PAPER

funny bone *Crit&Eval* Sense of humor.

funny hat band *MusArts, VisArts* Small pop ensemble not above wearing funny hats and costumes to achieve **empathic response**.

funny paper *Journ, VisArts* Newspaper section with **comic strips**. FUNNIES

funnyman *VisArts* Professional comedian

furlough *HR&LR* Temporary layoff from work.

furnishings *Fashn* Wearing apparel and accessories

fusion *MusArts* **Dialectical** term that refers to the blending elements of two or more musical styles to form a different musical composition or musical **genre**. <country music and rock, jazz and rock, Latin and soul, folk and rock, country and pop, etc>

FUTA *E&F-Acc, HR&LR, Law&Pol* **Federal Unemployment Insurance Act.** Calls for a tax to pay for programs to help unemployed workers.

futures contract *EntreP* Financial contract that requires two parties to exchange one asset for another at a price that resets daily.

futures price *EntreP* Price at which a futures contract will be executed; it resets daily as the contract is marked to market.

futurism *PerfA&C* Avant-garde movement popular in Italy and Russia in the 1910s and '20s in which the attributes of the machine were glorified: speed, regularity, brilliance

futurism *VisArts* Artistic movement originating in Italy (1911-15) whose aim was to express the energetic, dynamic, and violent quality of contemporary life, esp. as embodied in the motion and force of modern machinery. *Also see* **Art Movements and Periods, modern art**.

fuzz box *MusInstr* Electronic **sound modifier** that makes a bad rock guitarist sound at least mediocre.

fuzzy logic *iMedia* Superset of conventional (**Boolean**) logic - handles the concept of partial truth (values between "completely true" and "completely false")

fuzzy logic *InfoMgt* Form of **logic** developed by **Lofti Zadeh** that permits the use of imprecise predicates such as "sometimes," "likely," etc.

FWIW *InfoMgt* For What It Is Worth.

fx *Flm&Vid, Rdio/TV* Effects such as **sound effects** or **special effects**.

FYI *InfoMgt, For* Your Information.

- G -

G clef *MusArts* » **treble clef**

G-rated *Flm&Vid* "Suited for general viewing" regardless of age. — MPAA

G-string *Fashn, PA-Variety* Narrow loincloth supported by a waistband, usu. worn – and sometimes tossed to a patron – by strip-teasers.

G.T.C. *Eco&Fin* **Good 'til canceled.**

GA *InfoMgt* Go ahead (your turn)

GAAP *E&F-Acc* **Generally Accepted Accounting Practices.** Conventions, rules, and practices that define accepted accounting practices under certain conditions.

gadfly *Crit&Eval* Persistent, irritating critic; a nuisance.

gaffe *also* **gaff** (Fr.) *Crit&Eval* Blatant mistake. *Also see* **faux pas**.

gaffer *Flm&Vid* Electrician in charge of lighting on a movie or television set. *Also see* **best boy**, **head gaffer**.

gag *Flm&Vid* Stunt. <Stunt man **nailed** the gag in one **take**>

gag *Law&Pol* To censor free speech.

gag *PA-Variety* Comic effect or remark; joke

gag law *Law&Pol* Law intended to limit freedom of the press by censorship or restricting access to information. *Also see* **gag rule**.

gag man *PA-Variety* **1** Someone hired to write jokes or comedy routines. *Also see* **standup**. GAGSTER.

gag rule *Law&Pol* Rule imposed by a legislative body, limiting discussion or debate on an issue. *Also see* **gag law**.

gain *Rdio/TV, RecA&S, Sci&Tech* Increase in signal power, **voltage**, or current by an **amplifier**, expressed as the ratio of output to input. *Also see* **amplification**.

gaiter *Fashn* Ankle-high shoe with elastic sides.

gala *MusArts* Festive celebration often used as a special fund-raiser.

gallery *Crit&Eval* General public, inferring a lack of discrimination or sophistication.

gallery *Journ* » **press gallery**

gallery *TheatArts* **1** Upper section, often with a sloping floor, projecting from the rear or side walls of a theater or an auditorium to provide additional seating. **2** Seats in such a section, usu. cheaper than those on the main floor. **3** Cheapest seats in a theater, generally those of the uppermost gallery. **4** Audience occupying a gallery or cheap section of a theater. **5** Large audience or group of spectators. *Also see* **balcony**.

gallery *VisArts* **1** Building, an institution, or a room for the exhibition of artistic work. **2** photographer's studio.

galley *VA-Prntng* Long tray used for holding composed type. *Also see* **letterpress printing**.

galley proof *VA-Prntng* **Proof** taken from composed type before page composition to allow for the detection and correction of errors.

galop *MusArts* Quick dance in 2/4 time popular in the 19ᵗʰ century. *Also see* **Dances**.

game music *IntelProp MusArts* Money paid to the copyright owner derived from the use of music or lyrics in computer games or board games.

game show *Rdio/TV* Television show in which contestants compete for prizes by playing games of knowledge or chance. <*Jeopardy*>

game theory *Eco&Fin, Mgt* Mathematical method of decision-making in which a competitive situation is analyzed to determine the optimal course of action. THEORY OF GAMES

gaming *PA-Variety* 1 Politically correct marketing term for gambling. 2 An industry that uses entertainment as bait. *Also see* **shill**.

gamma *iMedia* Measure of brightness or darkness of a computer monitor, as determined by its hardware. Numerical parameter that describes the nonlinear relationship between **pixel** value and luminance.

gams *Crit&Eval* (Passé) Legs. <The **chick** has gorgeous gams>

gamut *iMedia* Scope of a value or set of values; such as the range of colors a monitor can display or the range of voltages allowed for a video signal (or for a video signal component)

Gandhi, Mahatma (Mohandas Karamchand Gandhi, 1869-1948, Indian nationalist, spiritual leader) *Cult&Soc, Law&Pol* Developed the practice of nonviolent, **civil disobedience** that forced Great Britain to grant independence to India (1947) He asserted the unity of mankind under one God and preached Christian and Muslim ethics along with the Hindu. He was assassinated by a Hindu fanatic who objected to Gandhi's tolerance for the Muslims. *Also see* **Martin Luther King Jr.**

gangsta rap *MusArts* » **rap music** <Ice-T, Ice Cube>

Gantt chart, GANTT Chart *EntreP, iMedia, Mgt* Used for extensively for business scheduling and planning. Shows time on its horizontal axis and tasks to be performed on its vertical axis. Gantt charts are often generated by project management software programs. Developed by Henry Gantt (1824-1867).

garage band *MusArts* Amateur band, usu. rock, that rehearses in a garage or in a similar nonprofessional **venue**.

Garbage In, Garbage Out (GIGO) *InfoMgt* Input incorrect data, retrieve incorrect data; sow what you shall reap.

garish *Crit&Eval* Marred by excessive color or ornamentation. *Also see* **quiet**.

garnishee *LegAsp* Third party who has been notified that money or property in her or his hands but belonging to a defendant has been attached. <The record company, as garnishee, was notified that the artist's **creditor** had obtained a **garnishment** of the artist's royalties>

garnishment *LegAsp* 1 Legal proceeding whereby money or property due a debtor but in the possession of another is applied to the payment of the debt owed to the plaintiff. 2 Court order directing a third party who holds money or property belonging to a defendant to withhold it and appear in court to answer inquiries. <Artist's refusal to pay the debt resulted in the **creditor** garnishing the artist's royalty payments> *Also see* **garnishee**.

gate, gate receipts *Eco&Fin,PerfA&C* Total paid attendance at a public event or performance.

gatefold *Mktg, VA-Prntng* Foldout usu. one that opens to double or triple the page size.

Gates, Henry Louis Jr. (1950-, cult. critic, educ.) *Crit&Eval, Cult&Soc* Chair, Dept. of Afro-American Studies, Harvard U. (1991-) Books include. <*The Signifying Monkey: A Theory of African-American Literary Criticism* (1988), w/Cornel West, *The Future of the Race* (1994) *Also see* **Jerry Lewis Syndrome**.

gateway *InfoMgt* Link between two online services or two different computer systems.

GATT *Eco&Fin, EntreP,Law&Pol* **General Agreement on Tariffs and Trade**. International agreement lowering tariffs and freeing trade restrictions between the signatory countries.

GATT *IntelProp* **U.S. Copyright Office** form for **restoration of copyright**.

gaudy *Crit&Eval* Tasteless or vulgar.

gauge *Flm&Vid* Width of the film, expressed in millimeters (mm)

The wider the gauge, the higher the quality of the image. Standard theatrical gauge is 35 mm.

gay deceivers *Fashn* » **falsies**

gazillion *Crit&Eval* Hyped **zillion**. *Origin* Perhaps from *ga*lactic.

GB *InfoMgt* gigabyte Loosely, one billion **bytes**, one million **kilobytes**, or one thousand **megabytes**.

GDP *Eco&Fin* **Gross Domestic Product**. This **economic indicator** is the total value if all goods and services produced by a nation's economy, *excluding* income from foreign income and investment. Like the **GNP**, an increase in GDP indicates a growing economy. GDP figures, reported by U.S. Dept. of Commerce, are adjusted for inflation. *Also see* **Economic Indicators**.

GE *Rdio/TV* **General Electric Company**.

gederim (guh-dare-im, Yinglish) *Crit&Eval* "In a lot of songs I write, I cry. I write with what they call in Yiddish *gederim* — it means the very vitals of your being. I feel everything." — Yip Harburg (Edgar Yip Harburg, b. Isidor Hochberg, 1896-1981, lyr., libret.) *Also see* **imagination**, **musical theatre**.

geek *InfoMgt* Budding **nerd**

geek *PA-Variety* Carnival performer whose show consists of **bizarre** acts, such as biting the head off a live chicken. *Also see* **sideshow**.

gel *Flm&Vid,PerfA&C* Gelatin used in theatrical lighting in a **frame** in front of a **spotlight** or **floodlight**. JELLIES *Also see* **Stage Lighting**.

gelatin *Th-MakeUp* Used for certain types of quick three-dimensional makeup.

Gelbart, Larry (1928-, film/radio/TV wrtr-prod.) *ArtPerf, Flm&Vid, Rdio&TV* Best known for the TV series *Mash* and the film *Tootsie* (1982) *Also see* **plot holes**.

gelled *Flm&Vid,PerfA&C* To choose a color **gel**.

gelt (Yinglish) *Eco&Fin* money.

General Agreement on Tariffs and Trade (GATT) *Eco&Fin, EntreP, Law&Pol* International agreement that has lowered trade barriers between the United States and other nations.

General Counsel *HR&LR* Officer of the National Labor Relations Board who has the responsibility to prosecute cases of unfair labor practices brought before the Board.

General Electric Company (GE) » *Rdio/TV* » **RCA**

general journal *E&F-Acc* **Journal** used to record all transactions that do not fit one of the special journals. *Also see* **Journals**.

general ledger *E&F-Acc* **Ledger** of accounts that are reported in the **financial statements**.

general liability insurance *EntreP* Coverage that protects against lawsuits brought by customers.

general lighting *PerfA&C* Lighting designed to illuminate large areas of the stage, usu. done by **floodlights**. *Also see* **specific lighting**, **Stage Lighting**.

general manager *EntreP* Entrepreneur who functions as an administrator of a business.

general partner *EntreP* Is in charge of day-to-day operations and is personally liable for the partnership.

general partnership *LegAsp, Mgt* General partners are responsible for the day-to-day management of the partnership's activities, whose individual acts are binding on the other partners, and who are personally liable for the partnership's total liabilities. *Also see* **limited partnership**, **partnership**.

General Principle of Valuation *EntreP* Principle that the value of an asset is the discounted present value of all future cash flows from the asset.

general public license *InfoMgt, iMedia* License intended to guarantee the freedom to share, distribute, and change free software.

general purpose foundation *Fnding* Independent **private foundation** that awards grants in many different fields of interest. *Also see* **Special Purpose Foundation**.

general purpose grant *Fnding* Grant made to further the general purpose or work of an organization, rather than for a specific purpose or project. *Also see* Operating Support Grant.

general store *Mktg* Retail store, usu. located in a rural community, that sells a wide variety of merchandise but is not divided into departments.

general/administrative expenses *Eco&Fin* General expenses incurred during the operation of a business.

Generally Accepted Accounting Practices (GAAP) *E&F-Acc* » **GAAP**

Generally Accepted Accounting Principles (GAAP) *EntreP* Rules, procedures and guidelines that accounting follows as acceptable accounting practices.

generation *Cult&Soc* Group of generally contemporaneous individuals regarded as having common cultural or social characteristics and attitudes. <computer generation, X-generation, television generation> *Also see* **music generation**.

generation *Flm&Vid, RecA&S* Term used to describe how many printing stages separate a given film or video from the original, or how many recording stages separate a given recording from the original.

generation gap *Cult&Soc* Broad difference in values and attitudes between one generation and another, esp. between adolescent children and their parents.

generic *Mktg* Not having a **trademark** or **brand name**.

generic competitor *Mktg* Marketer offering goods or services that, while possibly different in substance or concept, is capable of satisfying the same general needs as its own offerings. *Also see* **direct competitor**.

generic name *IntelProp* **Trademark** that has become a common term for a product line or type of service and therefore has lost its **trademark** protection. <frigidaire> *Also see* **public domain**.

generic visuals *BcstJourn* More specific to a particular story text than **wallpaper video** and less specific to the text than **B-roll**, these illustrate the story but are not necessarily tied to the specific current event. *Ex.* shots of aspirin bottles for a story on dangers of aspirin. "File tape" also can be an example of generic visuals. Although valuable at times, generic visuals are often overused.

genesis *Genl* Coming into being of something; the origin.

genetic algorithm *iMedia* Ways in which to evolve solutions to a problem (i.e., the strongest and fittest survive)

genetic programming *iMedia* Computer program that uses evolution and genetic algorithms to create or modify itself or another computer program. » **genetic algorithm 2** Using genetic algorithms and evolution to arrive at a solution

Genie *InfoMgt* Online information service *Also see* **Online Information Services**.

genius *ArtPerf, Crit&Eval* 1 Extraordinary intellectual and creative power. 2 Strong natural talent, **aptitude**, or inclination. "Since talent, as the innate productive faculty of the artist belongs itself to nature, we may express the matter thus: Genius is the innate mental disposition through which Nature gives the rule to art." **—Immanuel Kant**. "Endless invention." **— Stephen Sondheim**

genre *Flm&Vid* Recognizable type of movie, characterized by certain preestablished conventions. American genres. <musicals, sci-fi movies, thrillers, and westerns>

genre *LitArts, MusArts* Category of artistic composition, as in music or literature, marked by a distinctive style, form, or content.

genre *TheatArts* Group or class of works that share distinguishing features.

genre *VisArts* Realistic style of painting that depicts scenes from everyday life. <Pieter Bruegel ("the Elder," 1525-1569, Flemish pntr.), Jan Vermeer (*aka* Jan van der Meer, 1632-75, Dutch pntr)> *Also see* **Art Movements and Periods**.

geographical carve-out *LegAsp* Relating to the problem of conflicting jurisdictions of local and regional **trademarks** on the Internet.

geometric style *VisArts* Style of ancient Greek art (ca. 900BC), primarily of vase painting.

geon theory *iMedia* Proposes a hierarchical set of processing stages leading to structure-based object recognition. human visual system interprets **3D** objects by identifying 3D components called geons. Biederman, **1992**

George Carlin software *Ethcs&Phil, InfoMgt* Program used by **Prodigy** to screen about 75,000 daily messages and to delete objectionable words from its members' private mail. Based on Carlin's famous list of "forbidden words" inc. the seven most **tabued** words. <five 4-letter, one 10-letter, one 12-letter> (George Carlin, 1937-, TV/club comic, social commentator, 1960s to present.)

Gershwin, George (1898-1937, comp., sngwri, pno.) *ArtPerf, MusArts* Perhaps America's most popular composer, his works include **Broadway** musicals, **concert music**, and opera. <*Rhapsody in Blue* (1924), *Of Thee I Sing* (**Pulitzer**: musical, 1931),

Porgy and Bess (opera, 1935)> *Also see* **key, klezmer, m.**, *Porgy and Bess*, **silence, standards**.

Gershwin, Ira (1896-1983, lyr.) *ArtPerf, LitArts, MusArts* Wrote the inspired words to much of brother George's music. *Also see* **lyricist**, *Porgy and Bess*, **silence, standards, w.**

gestalt *iMedia* German word for pattern » **Gestalt Laws**

Gestalt Laws *iMedia* Rules of pattern recognition developed by the Gestalt School of Psychology (est. 1912) These rules provide guidelines for designing information displays.

gesture *Crit&Eval* Body motion or remark made to help express thought, to emphasize speech, or as a sign of intention or attitude.

gesture painting *VisArts* » **action painting**

get *Journ* To get an interview with the currently hot, popular interviewee so as to get **one-up** on the competitive **talk show** or **tabloid**.

get (one's) teeth into *Crit&Eval* To get a firm grasp. <It was a **fat part**, one that an actor could get his teeth into.

get the hook *Crit&Eval* To be unceremoniously dismissed or terminated by means of a loud bell or siren drowning out the performer or a real hook on a long stick wielded by the emcee or the house manager. Usually the hook is used as a safety valve when the audience starts to **catcall** or throw unpleasant objects at the performer. <The original Amateur Nite at the Apollo Theater in Harlem owed much of its popularity to its artfully raucous use of the hook>.

get up *ArtPerf* Be ready, ready to go on, ready to perform. *Also see* **come down**.

gewgaw *Crit&Eval* Decorative trinket. BAUBLE

ghost light *PerfA&C* "Tradition of always leaving a light burning onstage in an otherwise dark theater, to keep the ghosts at bay." — James Shapiro (19??-; teacher, critic)

ghostwriter *Journ, LitArts* One who writes for and gives credit of authorship to another.

GI "Bill of Rights" *Cult&Soc, HR&LR, Law&Pol* Established by the Servicemen's Readjustment Act of 1944 to provide educational and home ownership subsidies to U.S. war veterans. *Also see* **Federal Agencies and Statutes**.

Gibbs, Wolcott (1902-58, drama critic, n-fict., plywri., **parodist**) *Crit&Eval, LitArts, TheatArts* *New Yorker* drama critic and essayist. Play: *Season in the Sun* (19??) *Also see* **rewrite**.

Gibson girl *Cult&Soc, Fashn, VisArts* American young woman of the 1890s as idealized in sketches by illustrator Charles Dana Gibson (1867-1944) 2 Female clothing style marked by a high neck, **puffed** sleeves, and a tightly fitted waistline.

Gibson, J. J. (1904-1979) *iMedia* Perception theorist who proposed that the human visual processing system was evolved for the use of acting upon the environment. *Also see* **affordance, affordance theory, ecological optics**.

giclée (jeeclay, Fr. for "spray of ink") *VisArts, VA-Prntng* Revolutionary printing process used to create excellent reproductions of original artwork, capable of creating over 7 million colors.

GIF *iMedia, InfoMgt* **Graphic Interchange Format**, a common graphic format on the **Web**.

gift *Crit&Eval* **aptitude, bent, endowment, talent**.

gift acknowledgment process *Fndng* System, usu. computerized, within a development office by which gifts are recorded, receipted, and acknowledged-with-thanks.

gift range table *Fndng* Projection by dollar amounts and total numbers for each category of gifts believed necessary to achieve a campaign goal, and emphasizing the importance of "big" gifts.

gig *MusArts* job, **engagement**

gig piece *MusArts* "The [musical] work was a 'gig piece' written on **commission** for **CBS**." — Jeffrey Magee (cult. critic)

gigabyte (GB) *iMedia, InfoMgt* » **GB**

GIGO *InfoMgt* » **garbage in, garbage out**.

Gillespie, Dizzy (b. John Birks Gillespie, *aka* "Diz," 1917-93, jazz tp., arr-comp., bndldr.) *ArtPerf, MusArts* He rivals **Louis Armstrong** as one of the most important figures in the history of jazz. "The dizziness of Dizzy helped him to survive, and he did so without breaking through to a wider audience: his was always the cult following of the jazz world." — Ian Carr (jazz critic) *Also see* **bop, Norman Granz, quote**.

girlie magazine *Journ (Passé)* Naughty periodical featuring minimally clothed and provocatively posed women. [Big thing in barber shops when men were men and women were girlies.] *Also see* **Ballyhoo.**

given circumstance *TheatArts* Any unchangeable fact that affects the playing of the scene.

glam-rock *MusArts* Glamorously costumed rock suitable for kings and queens.

Glaser, Joe (b.??, d. 1969, talent agt., mgr.) *Mgt* **Louis Armstrong's personal manager** and booking agent. [Not the most savory of characters, Glaser permitted Armstrong to play before segregated audiences and used him as a lure for the other attractions booked by Glaser's talent agency.] *Also see* **Norman Granz, race.**

glass harmonica *MusInstr* Instrument consisting of tuned strips of metal or glass fixed to a frame and struck with a hammer. *Also see* **Musical Instrument Families.**

glee *MusArts* Simple part song, generally for male voices.

glee club *MusArts* Group of singers who perform short pieces of choral music.

gliss *MusArts* » (jazz talk for) **glissando.**

glissade (gliss-odd, Fr. for "sliding") *Dnce* (Ballet) Dancer moves to the side, front, or back from **fifth position** to **fourth** or fifth position.

glissando (gliss) *MusArts* Rapid slide through a series of consecutive **tones** in a **scalelike passage.**

glitch *Flm&Vid* Short interruption of a video signal. Glitch could be caused by bad tape stock, a poor edit, or a broadcast transmission problem.

glitter *Fashn, PerfA&C* Small pieces of light-reflecting decorative material.

glitter gel *Th-MakeUp* Transparent **gel** for applying glitter on the skin or over makeup.

glitter rock *MusArts* Characterized by **bizarre** makeup, costumes, and stage antics. *Also see* **Rock Music Styles.**

glitterati *Crit&Eval, Cult&Soc* Highly fashionable celebrities. SMART SET

glitz *Crit&Eval* **Ostentatious** showiness; flashiness. <Las Vegas>

Global Regular Expression Parsing (GREP) *InfoMgt* » **GREP**

global variable *iMedia* Variable accessible from anywhere in a program. In contrast: a local variable can be accessed only from a particular portion of a program.

global village *iMedia* Concept made popular by **Marshall McLuhan** stating that electronic media has transformed the world into a modern condition not unlike a village. This is characterized by features such as: simultaneous communication, centralized power, decentralized resources, a lack of individuality, and a return to an oral storytelling tradition rich in the use of symbols and mythology.

glockenspiel *MusInstr* Percussion instrument mounted on a pole with a series of metal bars tuned to the chromatic scale and played with a mallet. Carried upright in a marching band, it sways in the half-time wind and gets heavier every minute.

gloss *Crit&Eval* Deliberate misleading interpretation or explanation. <The witness glossed over what really happened>

gloss *InfoMgt, LitArts* 1 Brief explanatory note or translation of a difficult or technical expression inserted in the margin or between lines of a text. 2 Extensive commentary accompanying a text. *Also see* **annotate, glossary.**

glossary *InfoMgt, LitArts* List of words with their definitions.

glossolalia *Genl, MusArts* Fabricated and nonmeaningful speech; singing or speaking in **tongues.**

glossy *Mktg* Photographic publicity print on smooth, shiny paper, usu. **8 x 10** or **5 x 7** inches, suitable for good offset reproduction. *Also see* **matte.**

glycerine *Th-MakeUp* Used to make skin shine with perspiration or as a base for metallic powders.

glyph *iMedia* 1 Visual object that conveys multiple data values. 2 icon

GMA *MusArts* **Gospel Music Association** Est. 1964 in Nashville for providing [principally white] gospel music industry participants with a common ground to discuss problems, ideas, and goals of gospel music. GMA organizes Gospel Music Week and produces the **Dove Awards.**

GMTA *InfoMgt* Great Minds Think Alike

GMWA *MusArts* **Gospel Music Workshop of America.** Organized in 1968 by James Cleveland (1931-91, gospel comp., sngr., choir dir.) and other gospel choir leaders, "to set (and improve) standards of gospel choir performance."

GNP *Eco&Fin* **Gross National Product.** This **economic indicator** is the total value of all goods and services produced by a nation's economy in a given year. Rising GNP is a strong indicator of a growing economy. GNP statistics are issued quarterly by U.S. Dept. of Commerce. Inflation-adjusted version is called the **real GNP.** *Also see* **GDP.**

GNU *iMedia* Unix-workalike development effort of the **Free Software Foundation** headed by Richard Stallman. GNU EMACS and the GNU C compiler, two tools designed for this project, have become very popular in hackerdom and elsewhere.

go dead *Rdio/TV* Stop transmitting. *Also see* **go live.**

go into percentage *Mgt* Gross receipts of a performance that earn a percentage of the gross receipts rather than the guaranteed fee. <The **engagement contract** called for a $5,000 **guarantee** or 60% of the **gross receipts.** The **gross receipts** are $8,500, the **contract artist** earns $5,100. *Also see* **overage**>

go live *Rdio/TV* Start or resume transmitting. *Also see* **go dead.**

go on record *Journ* Embrace a certain position publicly.

go-through *PerfA&C* Perform. *Also see* **run-through.**

goal *EntreP* Measurable objective that can be reached in a specific time frame. All goals must be measurable, achievable, and have a time frame.

goal *Fndng* Overall financial objective of any campaign or **development** program.

Goals and Plans *ColEntry, Mgt* bottom-up —, operational —, planning, single purpose —, standing plans, strategic —, tactical —, top down —.

gobo *PerfA&C* Thin metal template inserted into an **ellipsodial reflector spotlight** to create a shadow pattern of light.

gobo *RecA&S* Short for "go-between." *Also see* **baffle.**

Godey's Lady's Book *Fashn* First American women's magazine founded in 1830 by **Louis Antoine Godey** (1804-1878)

goes up *PerfA&C* Forgets the next line (in a play)

gofer *Genl* One who goes for this and goes for that.

going public *EntreP* Selling substantial shares of a company on the open market for the first time. » **Initial public offering**

gold *RecA&S* » **Gold Record award**

Gold Record award *RecA&S* Award certified and presented by the **RIAA** for a minimum sale of one million copies of a single and 500,000 copies of an album.

Golden Laurel Awards *Flm&Vid* » **PGA** *Also see* **Awards & Prizes**

golden oldie *MusArts, RecA&S* An old recording that supposedly once won a **Golden Record award.**

golden parachute *Mgt* 1 Applied to separation compensation for top executive in case of a sale or takeover of the company. Used by boards of directors as an anti-hostile takeover strategy by making the buyout too expensive. 2 Term may also apply to the healthy compensation paid to a top executive when he or she involuntarily resigns for reasons other than illegal activity, and as such would be part of the employment contract.

Golden Rule *Ethcs&Phil* The biblical teaching that one should behave toward others as one would have others behave toward oneself.

Golden Score Award *MusArts* Presented by **American Society of Music Authors and Composers** (ASMAC) *Also see* **Awards & Prizes.**

Golden Spike Award *Journ, VisArts* Given by the **Association of American Editorial Cartoonists** (AAEC) to those editorial cartoons that never make it to press because of a frown from the publisher on behalf of an advertiser or a politically correct golfing companion.

golden time *Flm&Vid, HR&LR* Period of time after regular **overtime** and on holidays and Sundays when working calls pay as much as four-times the regular hourly pay.

Goldman, William (1931-, scrnwrtr., fict., non-fict., plywri.) *ArtPerf, Flm&Vid, LitArts* Films include. <*Butch Cassidy and the Sundance Kid* (1969), *All the President's Men* (1976) *Also see* **auteur theory, show business.**

Goldmark, Peter (engr.) *RecA&S* » **LP**

Goldwyn, Samuel (1882-1974) *Flm&Vid Mgt* Polish-born film producer who founded his own film company (1917) and merged with **Louis B. Mayer** to form Metro-Goldwyn-Mayer (MGM, 1924) *Also see* **mogul**.

Goldwynism *Crit&Eval* » **malapropism**

Gone With The Wind *Flm&Vid, LitArts* » **GWTW**

gonef (gone'-if, Yinglish) *Crit&Eval* Thief; dishonest, tricky character.

gonzo *Crit&Eval, Journ* Highly subjective style of journalism tending toward bizarre or unconventional subjects.

good 'till canceled order (GTC) *Eco&Fin, EntreP* Buy or sell order that remains valid until withdrawn by the investor.

good faith bargaining *HR&LR* Wherein both negotiators (employer and union) have the authority and the will, i.e., reasonable intent to successfully reach agreement.

good faith *Ethcs&Phil* Compliance with standards of decency and honesty.

good-faith bargaining *HR&LR* Type of bargaining that must prevail between employer and union to satisfy the bargaining obligations under the **Taft-Hartley Act**.

good music *MusArts* "Good music is music that sounds good." — **Duke Ellington**

good theatre *Crit&Eval, TheatArts* Effective on the stage but perhaps lacking in artistic plausibility.

goodwill *E&F-Acc* Excess of the cost of an acquired company over the sum of the **market values** of its **net assets** (assets minus liabilities) *Also see* **Intangible Assets**.

goodwill *Eco&Fin* Good relationship, as of a business enterprise with its customers. *Also see* **Intangible Assets**.

Google *InfoMgt,* Largest search engine source engine on the World Wide Web — offering access to an index of more than 2 billion URLs. Est. Sep 1998 by Larry Page and Sergey Brin.

GOP, G.O.P. *Law&Pol* **Grand Old Party**, i.e., the Republican Party.

Gopher *InfoMgt* Online information service *Also see* **Online Information Services**.

Gospel Music Association (GMA) *MusArts* » **GMA**

Gospel Music *ColEntry, MusArts* black —, contemporary Christian music, contemporary —, evangelical music, soul —, southern —, sweet —, white —. *Also see* **Songs**.

Gospel Music Workshop of America *MusArts* » **GMWA**

Goth. *VisArts* **Gothic**.

Gothic (Goth.) *Cult&Soc* Relating to the **Middle Ages**. MEDIEVAL

Gothic (Goth.) *VisArts* **1** Relating to architecture, painting, sculpture, or other art forms prevalent in northern Europe from the 12th through the 15th century. **2** Architectural style characterized by pointed arches, rib vaulting, and **flying buttresses**. *Origin* First used by Italian art critics of the **Renaissance** to denote a style they thought had been introduced by the Goths, who destroyed the Roman Empire. *Also see* **Art Movements and Periods**.

gothic *Crit&Eval* Barbarous; crude.

gothic *LitArts* Style of **fiction** that emphasizes the grotesque, mysterious, and desolate.

Gothic *VA-Prntng* typeface without **serifs** *Also see* **type, sans-serif**.

.gov *InfoMgt* Suffix of an Internet **domain name** assigned to government agencies. *Also see* **Domain Names, Network Solutions Inc.**

gown *Fashn* **1** Long, usu. formal dress for a woman. **2** Long, loose, flowing garment, such as a robe or nightgown.

GPL *iMedia* » **general public license**

grace note *MusArts* Note added as an **embellishment**. *Also see* **appoggiatura**

Graceland *Cult&Soc* Elvis Presley's (» **classic rock**) temporal home, now the holy land of Presliana. *Also see* **kitsch**.

grade *InfoMgt* » **bandwith transmission**

gradient *iMedia* Graphic element that rises or descends by regular degrees of hue, value, or **saturation**.

gradient microphone *RecA&S* Mic where output increases and decreases directly with the sound pressure. *Also see* **Microphones**.

graff *Cult&Soc, VisArts* **graffiti**.

graffiti *Cult&Soc, VisArts* "Graffiti art, the styles and culture associate with it, were created by young street kids from NYC.... Just like **rap**, graffiti is all about the kids and the neighborhoods

who created it. Once popularized it becomes watered down. It loses everything that made it so great." — "Graffiti in Their Own Words." *Also see* **hip-hop**.

Graham, Bill (Wolfgang Wolodia Grajonca, 1931-91, German-born prod.) *Mgt, MusArts* Famous rock impresario (1960s-1980s) <Fillmore West (San Francisco), Fillmore East (NYC), concert tours> Manager. <Bob Dylan (1941-, folk/rock sngr., sngwri., gtr.), Grateful Dead (**acid rock/country rock** group est. 1966), Jefferson Airplane (rock group est. 1965), Santana (rock/Latin music group est. 1966), Van Morrison (1945-, rock sngr., sngwri)

grain *Fashn* Direction or texture of fibers in a woven fabric.

grain *Flm&Vid* Small globules of silver halide suspended in film emulsion which, when exposed to light, creates the image on film.

grain *VisArts* Painted, stamped, or printed design that imitates the natural pattern found in wood, leather, or stone.

graininess *iMedia* Sand-like or granular appearance of a negative, print, or slide. Graininess becomes more pronounced with faster film and the degree of enlargement.

Grammy Awards *LitArts, Mktg, MusArts, RecA&S, VisArts* Annual awards in 88 categories made by the 8,000+ voting members of the **National Academy of Recording Arts & Sciences** (NARAS) *Also see* **Awards & Prizes**.

Gramophone *RecA&S* First machine to play record discs, rather than **Edison's wax cylinders**. Invented by **Émile Berliner**. *Also see* **Record Playback Equipment**.

grand drape *PerfA&C* **1** First downstage **border** that determines the height of the **proscenium** opening, called the trim height. **2** Curtain that covers the opening of the proscenium arch... *Also see* **Stage Curtains, teaser**.

Grand Guignol (Grand Gwee-nole, Fr.) *TheatArts* Drama that emphasizes the horrifying or the **macabre**. *Origin* After Le Grand Guignol, a theater in Paris.

grand jeté (grahnd je-tay, Fr.) *Dnce* (Ballet) Great jump. *Also see* **jeté**.

Grand Old Party *Law&Pol* » **GOP, G.O.P.**

Grand Ole Opry *MusArts,. Rdio/TV* Organized (1925) as the *WSM Barn Dance*. Variety show featuring **country music** entertainers on **WSM**, Nashville, Tenn. *Also see* **Broadcast Stations & Networks**.

grand piano *MusInstr* Piano with strings in a horizontal harp-shaped frame supported on three legs, approx. 5-11 feet long. *Also see* **baby grand, concert grand**.

grand rights *IntelProp, MusArts, TheatArts* Covers dramatic performances of musical comedies (**Broadway** and **off-Broadway**), operas, operettas, ballets, as well as renditions of independent musical compositions in a dramatic setting where there is narration, a plot and/or costumes, and scenery. For use of a musical work in a non-dramatic public performance see **small performing rights**. *Also see* **Music Licenses**.

grandiloquent *Crit&Eval* » **bombast**

grandstand *TheatArts* **1** Roofed stand for spectators at a stadium or racetrack. **2** Spectators or audience at an event...

grandstanding *Crit&Eval* To perform ostentatiously so as to impress an audience. *Origin* Prominent people who would sit in the best stands at the circus to be noticed.

Grantee Financial Report *Fnding* Report detailing how grant funds were used by an organization. Many corporations require this kind of report from grantees. A financial report generally includes a listing of all expenditures from grant funds as well as an overall organizational financial report covering revenue and expenses, assets and liabilities.

granularity *iMedia* Relative size, scale, level of detail, or depth of penetration that characterizes an object or activity.

Granz, Norman (1918-2001) *Mgt, PerfA&C, RecA&S* Jazz **impresario** who started the worldwide **Jazz at the Philharmonic** (JATP) concerts in Los Angeles in 1944 Musicians respected him: he paid well and on time, and encouraged racially mixed groups. He would not book a segregated **house**, and gave the likes of **Charlie Parker** and **Dizzy Gillespie** the space and time they wanted. He also recorded – and later filmed/taped – many of the concerts that sold very well on his **JATP** and **Verve** labels and gave jazz a big post-WWII market. As Ella Fitzgerald's (» **Apollo theater**) manager, he suggested and recorded her famous songbook albums.

graph *Journ* paragraph

grapheme *iMedia* Primitive visual element; meaningful perceptual objects are constructed from graphemes.

graphic artist *ArtPerf, VisArts* "I would never call myself an artist. **Fine artist** sits down at a blank canvas and just kind of does whatever he feels like doing. With a graphic designer, it's the opposite — somebody is giving you an assignment to fulfill. **Design** is about problem solving." — Chip Kidd (**dust jacket** dsngr.)

graphic arts *VisArts* Fine or applied visual arts and associated techniques in which images are produced from blocks, plates, or type, as in **engraving** and **lithography**, which enable mass prints and reproductions.

graphic design *iMedia* Practice or profession of designing print or electronic forms of visual information.

graphic designer *iMedia* One who practices the profession of designing print or electronic forms of visual information, as for an advertisement, publication, or website.

Graphic Interchange Format (GIF) *InfoMgt*

graphical user interface (GUI) *iMedia, InfoMgt* Interface based on graphics instead of text. usu. embodies a visual metaphor (i.e., a desktop) and requires the use of a mouse and keyboard.

graphics *InfoMgt* Any computer-generated picture

grass-roots *Cult&Soc* **1** People or society at a local level. **2** Groundwork or source of something.

grassroots *Mktg* Promotion that utilizes smaller-scale, community-level activities or small venues, or appeals directly to individuals rather than the large-scale approach that uses **mass media**.

grassroots fundraising *Fnding* Efforts to raise money from individuals or groups from the local community on a broad basis. Usually an organization's own constituents-people who live in the neighborhood served or clients of the agency's services-are the sources of these funds. Grassroots fundraising activities include membership drives, raffles, auctions, benefits, and a range of other activities.

gratuitous *Crit&Eval* Unnecessary or unwarranted; unjustified. <gratuitous criticism>

grave (grah-vay) *MusArts* Play in a slow and solemn manner. *Also see* **Music Directions**.

gravel box *Flm&Vid, Rdio/TV, RecA&S* Wooden box with pebbles and small rocks used to simulate walking on gravel.

graven image *Cult&Soc, VisArts* **Idol** or a **fetish** carved in wood or stone.

graveyard shift *HR&LR* Work shift that runs during the early morning hours. <midnight to 8AM>

gray-scale *InfoMgt* Series of graded grays that substitute for color. *Also see* **color wheel**.

grayscale *iMedia* **1** Range of accurately known shades of gray printed out for use in calibrating those shades on a display or printer. **2** visual document rendered only in black, white, and shades of gray.

greasepaint, grease paint *Th-MakeUp* Theatrical makeup; a preparation of grease mixed with colorings.

Great Craftsman *Cult&Soc* Title sometimes given to high priests of ancient Egypt because of their creation of monumental sculptures and **reliefs**.

Great Depression (1930-35) *Cult&Soc, Eco&Fin* Arguably the most severe **depression** in U.S. history brought on by lingering effects of WWI, protectionist and isolationist foreign policy, rampant financial speculation — exacerbated by an inept, insensitive political establishment — Finally overcome with the advent of F.D.R.'s **New Deal** and **WWII**. *Also see* ***Brother Can You Spare a Dime?***

Greatest Show on Earth, The *PA-Variety* Large circus, i.e., **Ringling Brothers and Barnum & Bailey Circus**. *Also see* **P.T. Barnum, Charles Ringling**.

Greek chorus *MusArts, TheatArts* Group in a classical Greek drama whose songs and dances present an exposition of or a disengaged commentary on the action.

green room *PerfA&C* Waiting room or lounge in a theater or concert hall for performers to use when off stage. [Does anyone know why "green?"].

green-lighted *Crit&Eval* Project permitted to proceed.

green-man *Flm&Vid* Person responsible for dressing the set with greenery. <fake or real branches, flowers, shrubs, trees>

greenlight *Flm&Vid* Agree to fund production. *Also see* **term deal**.

Greenwich Village Theatre (NYC) *TheatArts* » **Provincetown Players** *Also see* **Theaters & Theatres**.

Greeolies *Cult&Soc, MusArts* African tribe. *Also see* **praise shouter, praise song, rap**.

greeting card music *IntelProp, MusArts* Money paid to the copyright owner derived from the use of music or lyrics on a greeting card.

Gregorian chant *MusArts* **Liturgical** chant that is monodic, rhythmically unstructured, and sung without accompaniment.

Gregory, Lady (Isabella Augusta Persse, 1852-1932, Irish dram.) *ArtPerf, LitArts, Mgt, TheatArts* She was a founder (1899) and director (1904-32) of the **Abbey Theatre**, for which she wrote a number of short plays.

greige goods *Fashn* Textiles not bleached or dyed; unfinished.

gremlins *InfoMgt, VA-Prntng* Printing characters whose ASCII code ranges are 0-8, 10-12, 14-31, 127-255.

GREP *InfoMgt* **Global Regular Expression Parsing**. **Protocol** by **UNIX**. Ω

Gresham's law *Eco&Fin, Genl* Bad money drives out good money. Theory holding that if two kinds of money in circulation have the same denominational value but different **intrinsic** values, the money with higher intrinsic value will be hoarded and eventually driven out of circulation by the money with lesser **intrinsic** value. [And some would say that bad art, bad music, bad writing drives out the good.]

grid *iMedia, Journ, VA-Prntng* **1** Pattern for page layout. **2** Device in a photocomposition machine on which the characters used in composition are etched.

grid *InfoMgt* Network of uniformly spaced points or crosshatched lines displayed on a visual display screen and used for: exactly locating a position, inputting components to assist in the creation of a design layout, or constructing precise diagrams.

grid *PerfA&C* Metal structure just below the stage roof from which ropes or cables are strung to scenery and lights. The ceiling of the **fly gallery** (loft)

grid *VisArts* Structure or tool used by many abstract painters and sculptors in the early 1960s. <**Jasper Johns**>

gridiron *PerfA&C* » **grid**

grievance *HR&LR* Complaint or allegation by an employee, union, or employer that a collective bargaining contract has been violated.

grievance committee *HR&LR* Committee of union members that meets periodically with management to discuss accumulated grievances.

grimace *Crit&Eval* Severe facial expression of pain, contempt, or disgust.

grind *Dnce* To rotate the pelvis erotically, as in the manner of a stripteaser or **Elvis Presley**. *Also see* **bump**.

griot *Cult&Soc* Storyteller in western Africa who perpetuates the oral tradition and history of a village or family.

grip *Flm&Vid* Member of the production crew responsible for laying camera tracks, erecting scaffolds, helping with set construction, and sometimes assists the camera operator.

grip *PerfA&C* Stagehand who helps in shifting scenery.

gritty *Crit&Eval* **1** *showing* resolution and fortitude. **2** cheap.

groove *Crit&Eval, MusArts* To take great pleasure in music.

groove *RecA&S* Furrowed portion of the grooved surface of a record disk. *Also see* **land**.

grosgrain *Fashn* **1** Closely woven silk or rayon fabric with narrow horizontal ribs. **2** Ribbon made of this fabric.

gross *or* **gross receipts** *Eco&Fin, Flm&Vid* Total box office receipts, calculated before disbursement of funds, that a movie has generated to date for a specific engagement.

gross domestic product (GDP) *EntreP* **T**otal market value of all the final goods and services produced within an economy in a given year.

Gross Domestic Product (GDP) *Eco&Fin* » **GDP**

gross income *EntreP* All of the money received from all sources during a year. This would include wages, tips, interest earned on savings and bonds, income from rental property, and profits to entrepreneurs.

gross margin *E&F-Acc* Excess of sales revenue over **cost of capital** sold. GROSS PROFIT *Also see* **list price**, **margin of profit**, **net margin**.

H

gross national product (GNP) *Eco&Fin, EntreP* **GDP** plus net income earned abroad.

gross pay *E&F-Acc* Employee's total earnings before any deductions are made.

gross profit *E&F-Acc, EntreP* Determined by subtracting cost of goods sold (COGS) from net sales. *Also see* **gross margin**.

gross profit margin *E&F-Acc, EntreP* Ratio of revenues minus cost of goods sold to sales; percentage of earnings on sales before considering operating expenses, interest and taxes (gross profit margin = revenues - cost of goods sold/sales)*Also see* **profitability ratios**.

gross profit participant *Flm&Vid* Those individuals, usu. the producer, director and star, who have **contingent compensation agreements** – either percentage or fixed sums – based on a movie's gross receipts. <*Scene*. Two Hollywood deal makers seated at a lounge table. *Dialog*. "There are two ways we can go here — one per cent of the gross or ninety-nine per cent of the net." — Mick Stevens (cartoonist)> *Also see* **net profit participant**.

gross rating point (GRP) *Rdio/TV* » **GRP**

gross sheets *Eco&Fin, Flm&Vid* Breakout of gross box office receipts for a particular feature film by market and by theater, updated daily. Used for comparative performance analysis with previous film.

gross, gross receipts *Eco&Fin, Flm&Vid* Total box office receipts, calculated before disbursement of funds, that a movie has generated to date for a specific engagement.

grotesque *Crit&Eval, VisArts* **1** Style of painting, sculpture, and ornamentation in which natural forms and monstrous figures are intertwined in bizarre or fanciful combinations. **2** Outlandish or bizarre, as in character or appearance.

grotesquerie *Crit&Eval, VisArts* something **grotesque**

ground *iMedia* What is perceived to be behind an object or objects in an image or visual frame.

ground plan *PerfA&C* Aerial view of the stage drawn to **scale** showing all the pertinent elements of the stage — a prime tool of theatre technicians for planning productions and communicating stage information to each other.

ground plan *PerfA&C* Drawing in scale of the set viewed from above. *Also see* **plot**.

ground waves *Rdio/TV* Radio wave that travels along the surface of the earth.

group depreciation *E&F-Acc* For convenience, large companies group similar items such as trucks, power lines, office equipment, or transformers to calculate depreciation.

group sales *Fndng, PerfA&C* Sales of tickets or **subscriptions** to any group of persons who attend theatrical productions together. <Garden Club of Winnetka, Hadassah, Knights of Pythias, et al>

Group Theater *TheatArts* Breakaway group from the **Theatre Guild** (NYC), cofounded in 1931 (disbanded in 1940) by **Lee Strasberg** and Stella Adler (1902-92, act., dir., tchr.), influential exponents of the **Stanislavsky** method of acting. *Also see* **Method**, **Theaters & Theatres**.

groupie *ArtPerf, Crit&Eval* **1** Hyper emotional **fan** who wants to get real close to and with the object of their fixation. **2** Enthusiastic supporter or follower. *Also see* **junkie**.

groupthink *Ethcs&Phil* Conformity to the values or ethical standards of a group.

growth entrepreneur *EntreP* Entrepreneur who launches a venture with the intention of continually growing it.

growth rate *EntreP* Percentage rate of change of a variable.

growth trap *EntreP* Cash shortage resulting from rapid growth.

GRP *Mktg, Rdio/TV* **Gross Rating Point**. Rating basis for determining estimated percentage of households or target audience exposed to a broadcast commercial or magazine ad.

grunge rock *MusArts* » **grungy** *Also see* **Rock Music Styles**.

grungy *Cult&Soc* Old folks: Unsavory, thoroughly unpleasant clothes, music, and other evidences of youth culture. IN!

GTG (got to go) *InfoMgt* Got To Go.

gtr *MusInstr* **guitar**

guar. *Genl, HR&LR, LegAsp* **guarantee**

guarantee (guar.) *HR&LR, LegAsp* Legal obligation of an employer to pay a certain sum of money to the artist for services rendered. *Also see* **deposit**, **engagement contract**, **percentage**, **play**

for the door.

guarantee (guar.) *Mktg* **1** Promise or an assurance, esp. one given in writing, that attests to the quality or durability of a product or service. **2** Pledge that something will be performed in a specified manner. *Also see* **as is**, **disclaimer**, **warranty**.

guaranty loan *EntreP* Money provided by a private lender, with the Small Business Administration guaranteeing repayment.

guerrilla theater *TheatArts* » **street theater** *Also see* **Theatres & Theaters**.

guerrilla-style *Flm&Vid* Production using a smaller crew and less equipment to reduce costs.

Guggenheim fellowships *Fnding* The John Simon Guggenheim Memorial Foundation provides fellowships for advanced professionals in all fields (natural sciences, social sciences, humanities, creative arts) except the performing arts. Fellowships are not available for students. >www.gf.org<

GUI *InfoMgt* **Graphical User Interface**; the use of menus and pictures to allow users to more easily interact with the operating system. *Also see* **Operating Systems**.

guild *HR&LR* Association of persons of the same trade. *Also see* **Guilds & Unions**.

Guilds & Unions *ColEntry, HR&LR* **1 Performer Guilds & Unions**. <American Federation of Musicians (AFM), **Four A's** Affiliates: Artist's Equity Association (**AEA**), American Federation of Television and Radio Artists (AFTRA), Asociación Puertorriqueña de Artistas e Tecnicos del Espectaculo (APATE), American Guild of Musical Artists (AGMA), American Guild of Variety Artists (AGVA), Hebrew Actors Union (HAU), Ital. Actors Union (IAU), Screen Actors Guild (SAG)> **2 Non-Performer Guilds & Unions**. <Association of Theatrical Press Agents and Managers (ATPAM), Authors Guild, Inc. (AGI), Dramatists Guild, Inc. (DGI), International Alliance of Theatrical Stage Employees and Motion Picture Operators of the US and Canada (IATSE), International Brotherhood of Electrical Workers (IBEW), International Ladies Garment Workers Union (ILGWU), Legitimate Theatre Employees (LTE), **Newspaper Guild**. Radio and Television Directors Guild (RTDG), Theatrical Wardrobe Attendants Union (TWAU), Union of Needletrades, Industrial and Textile Employees (UNITE), Writers Guild of America (WGA)> *Also see* **horizontal union**, **industrial vertical union**.

guiro *MusInstr* Untuned Latin American percussion instrument made from a gourd (or plastic, metal, and wood) carved or notched to create a ridged surface. Played by scraping the surface with a stick…

guitar (gtr) *MusInstr* Instrument with a large, flat-backed sound box similar in shape to a violin, a long fretted neck, and usu. six strings, played by strumming or plucking. GUITARIST. *Also see* **Leo Fender**, **Musical Instrument Families**, **Les Paul**.

guitarrón *MusInstr* Large Mexican bass guitar *Also see* **mariachi**.

Gullah *Cult&Soc* **1** Person of African ancestry inhabiting the Sea Islands and coastal areas of South Carolina, Georgia, and northern Florida. **2** Creolized language of the Gullahs, based on English but inc. elements from several African languages.

guts *Crit&Eval* Innermost emotional or visceral response.

GWTW *Flm&Vid, LitArts* Book and film: *Gone With The Wind*. *Also see* **one way option**, **David O. Selznick**.

- H -

h *MusInstr* **horn**

habanera *Dnce, MusArts* Slow Cuban music and dance. *Also see* **Dances**, **Latin Dance Music**.

haberdashery *Fashn* Shop that sells men's furnishings.

hack *LitArts* One who does routine writing.

hacker *InfoMgt* **1** One who writes code and creates new software; not a **cracker**. **2** One who gains unauthorized access to a computer system. PIRATE **3** Originally a computer enthusiast who pushed a system to its highest performance through clever programming.

hacking *Fashn* Horse-back riding for pleasure, as opposed to riding to hounds, for which a specific type of clothing is worn. <hacking jacket, scarf, and pocket **detail**>

hacking *InfoMgt* Term associated with a type of computer crime whereby unauthorized users access computer systems.

hackneyed *Crit&Eval* Overfamiliar through overuse; **trite**.

hagiography *LitArts* idealizing biography

haiku *LitArts* Japanese **lyric** verse form having three unrhymed lines of five, seven, and five syllables, traditionally invoking an aspect of nature or the seasons.

hair-raising *Crit&Eval* Causing excitement, terror, or thrills.

hairlace *Th-MakeUp* Net foundation used to make wigs, toupees, beards, and moustaches.

half binding *VA-Prntng* Bookbinding in which the back and often the corners of the volume are bound in a material differing from the rest of the cover.

half note *MusArts* Note having half the time value of a whole note and twice that of a quarter note. *Also see* **Musical Notes**.

half step *MusArts* » **semitone**

half tone *MusArts* » **semitone**

half-assed *Crit&Eval* **1** Poorly planned or executed. **2** incompetent

half-baked *Crit&Eval* **1** Poorly thought out; ill-conceived. <a half-baked scheme> **2** Lack of good judgment or common sense.

half-hour *PerfA&C* Announcement on backstage **PA** a half-hour before **curtain**. *Also see* **5 minutes, 15 minutes, places**.

half-light *VisArts* Soft, subdued light seen at dusk or dawn or in dimly lit interiors.

halftone *VisArts* **1** Tone or value halfway between a highlight and a dark shadow. **2** Image in which gradations of light are obtained by the relative darkness and density of tiny dots produced by photographing the subject through a fine screen. **3** Picture made by such a process. *Also see* **stochastic screening**.

hall *PerfA&C* **1** Building for public gatherings or entertainments. **2** The large room in which such events are held. <dance hall>

hallelujah *MusArts* Composition expressing praise and based on the word "hallelujah." *Origin* Hebrew hallĕlûyăh, praise the Lord.

hallmark *Crit&Eval* Conspicuous feature or characteristic.

ham *TheatArts, PerfA&C* Actor who overacts or a performer who exaggerates. *Also see* **chew the scenery**.

hambone *Crit&Eval* (Passé) untalented actor

Hammond B3 organ *MusInstr, Sci&Tech* Only manufactured from 1955-1974, this instrument is still widely preferred by blues, gospel, jazz, and rock musicians because of its unique strong, percussive sound and its rotating Leslie speaker. *Also see* **electronic organ**.

hand *Aes&Creat Fashn* Aesthetic feel or tactile quality a fabric or textile, that indicates its fineness, texture, and durability.

hand *Crit&Eval, PerfA&C* **1** Round of applause. <C'mon folks, let's give them a great big hand> **2** Manner of doing or performing something. <a light hand with makeup>

HAND *InfoMgt* Have A Nice Day!

hand props *PerfA&C* **Property** handled by an actor onstage, esp. something the actor carries on and off stage. <a tray, a tennis racquet>

Hand-Lac *Th-MakeUp* Clear liquid that can be applied over hand makeup. It dries quickly, forming a protective film which helps to prevent makeup from rubbing off on costumes.

handbill *Mktg* Printed sheet or pamphlet distributed by hand. *Also see* **bill**.

handicraft, handcraft *ArtPerf* Craft, occupation, or work requiring skilled use of the hands.

hang *InfoMgt* Condition that occurs when a computer's operating system jams or freezes.

hang *VisArts* To display a painting or picture to a wall or ceiling.

hang it up *Crit&Eval* To give up; quit.

hang in there *Crit&Eval* To persevere despite difficulties; persist.

hang loose *Crit&Eval* To stay calm or relaxed.

hang out *Crit&Eval* **1** To spend one's free time in a certain place; to pass time idly; loiter. **2** To keep company; date.

hang tough *Crit&Eval* To remain firmly resolved.

hanger log, hanger sheet, hanging schedule *PerfA&C* Document prepared by the presenter to the **touring company** describing the location of each line and what is hung from it.

hangtag *Mktg* Tag attached to a piece of merchandise giving information about its place of origin, composition and proper care and use.

Hanz-N-Nek *Th-MakeUp* Liquid makeup for hands and neck that does not rub off on costumes but is easily removed with soap and water.

happening *Genl* Improvised, often spontaneous spectacle or performance, esp. one involving audience participation. *Also see* ac-tion.

happenings *TheatArts* Term coined by Allan Kaprowin the late 1950s, it refers to a non-structured, highly improvised and usu. mixed media artistic event which often occurred only once. This form's evolution in the 1960s influenced the Environmental Theater of the 1970s and the Performance Art of the late 1980s & '90s.

haptic feedback *iMedia* Output from a computer relating to the sense of touch.

harangue *Crit&Eval* Long, pompous speech; a **tirade**. DIATRIBE

Harburg, Yip (b. Isadore Hochberg, 1898-1981; lyricist) *ArtPerf, MusArts* » *Brother Can You Spare a Dime?*

hard bop *MusArts* Development of **modern jazz** in the early 1950s… combining bop improvisation with the funkiness derived from black gospel music… a reaction to **cool jazz**. <Horace Silver (1928-, jazz pno., arr.-comp,) Quintet, Art Blakey (1919-94, jazz bndldr., drm) Jazz Messengers> — Lyons & Perlo (jazz critics)

hard copy *InfoMgt* Printed copy of the output of a computer or word processor.

hard core *Cult&Soc* **1** Most dedicated, unfailingly loyal faction of a group or an organization. **2** Intractable core or nucleus of a society, esp. one stubbornly resistant to improvement or change.

hard disk *InfoMgt* Disk made of metal and permanently sealed into a drive or cartridge, capable of storing very large amounts of information.

hard edge *Th-MakeUp* In theatrical cosmetics, putting a highlight directly against a shadow to create the illusion of an abrupt change of direction.

hard gospel music *MusArts* This style, popular with vocal quartets about 1960-70, was characterized by: "cultivated growls, loud and high screams, and thigh-slapping for rhythmic accentuation; Five Blind Boys of Mississippi, led by Archie Brownlee." — Horace Boyer (gospel mus. critic)

hard news *Journ* News that deals with serious topics and events. *Also see* **soft news**.

hard rock *MusArts* Rock music characterized by a harsh, amplified sound and frequently employing distortion, feedback, and other electronic modulations. *Also see* **Rock Music Styles**.

hard sell *Mktg* **1** Aggressive, high-pressure selling or promotion. **2** Person or an organization that resists pressure from salespeople; a difficult sales prospect.

hard ticket *PerfA&C* Full price admission. *Also see* **Annie Oakley, comp.**

hard-core *MusArts* Variation of **punk rock** *Also see* **Rock Music Styles**.

hard-core, hardcore *Crit&Eval* **1** Intensely loyal; die-hard. **2** Stubbornly resistant to improvement or change. <hard-core poverty> **3** Extremely graphic or explicit. <hard-core pornography>

hard-wired *InfoMgt* **Logic** circuitry permanently connected within a computer or calculator and therefore not subject to change by programming.

hardback *VA-Prntng* Book bound in cloth, cardboard, or leather rather than paper. *Also see* **paperback**.

hardball *Crit&Eval* Use of any means, however, ruthless, to attain an objective.

hardcover *VA-Prntng* » **hardback**

hardware *Genl* Mechanical or electronic device that plays or activates information or entertainment **media**, i.e., **software**.

hardware *InfoMgt* Computer and its related equipment directly involved in the performance of data-processing or communications functions. *Also see* **software**.

Harlem *Genl* Section of NYC in northern Manhattan bordering on the Harlem and East rivers where the Dutch settlement of Nieuw Haarlem was est. 1658. Rapid influx of Black people beginning ca. 1910 made it one of the largest Black communities in the U.S. After World War II many Hispanics settled in East (or Spanish) Harlem.

Harlem Renaissance *Cult&Soc* African American cultural movement of the 1920s and 1930s, centered in **Harlem**, that celebrated black traditions, life styles, and the arts.

Harlequin *PA-Variety* Conventional buffoon of the **commedia dell'arte**, traditionally presented in a mask and parti-colored tights.

harlequinade *TheatArts* **Comedy** or **pantomime** in which **Har-**

lequin is the main attraction.

harmolodic *MusArts* Relating to a style of modern improvisational music in which different, contrasting instruments are played in different **keys** or **tempos**.

Harmon mute *MusInstr* Placed in the bell of a trumpet it produces a thin, ethereal sound. <**Miles Davis's** ballads of the mid-1950s>

harmonic *MusArts* 1 Relating to **harmony** 2 Pleasing to the ear. <harmonic orchestral effects> 3 Tone in the harmonic series of overtones produced by a **fundamental** tone. 4 Tone produced on a stringed instrument by lightly touching an open or stopped vibrating string at a given fraction of its length so that both segments vibrate. *Also see* **overtone, partial, partial tone.**

harmonica (hca) *MusInstr* Small, rectangular instrument consisting of a row of free reeds set back in air holes, played by exhaling or inhaling. BLUES HARP, HARMONICA PLAYER, MOUTH ORGAN *Also see* **Musical Instrument Families.**

harmonics *InfoMgt, Sci&Tech* Distortion of electrical transmissions that can be hazardous to computer systems.

harmonics *MusArts* Theory or study of the physical properties and characteristics of musical sound.

harmonist *MusArts* One skilled in **harmony**

harmonium *MusInstr* Organlike keyboard instrument that produces **tones** with free metal reeds actuated by air forced from a bellows. *Also see* **Musical Instrument Families.**

harmony *iMedia, VisArts* Pleasing combination of elements in a whole. <color harmony>

harmony *MusArts* 1 Study of the structure, **progression**, and relation of **chords**. 2 Simultaneous combination of notes in a **chord**. 3 Structure of a work or **passage** as considered from the point of view of its chordal characteristics and relationships. 4 Combination of sounds considered pleasing to the ear.

harp *MusInstr* Instrument consisting of an upright, open triangular frame with usu. 46 strings of graded lengths played by plucking with the fingers. *Also see* **Musical Instrument Families.**

harpsichord *MusInstr* Keyboard instrument whose strings are plucked by means of quills or **plectrums**. HARPSICHORDIST *Also see* **Musical Instrument Families.**

harrumph *Crit&Eval* To offer usu. brief critical comments.

Harry Fox Agency, Inc. (HFA) *IntelProp, MusArts, RecA&S* Collection and licensing agency for **mechanical** and **synchronization** rights owned by **NMPA**. *Also see* **Copyright-Related Organizations.**

harvest *EntreP* Ending the original venture. Harvesting may take the form of selling, merging, liquidating, or passing the venture on to family members.

harvest strategy *EntreP* Plan developed by the entrepreneur to guide the ending of the venture. Strategy may include a valuation of the company, as well as other actions that prepare the venture for the harvest.

harvesting *EntreP* Exit process used by entrepreneurs and investors to unlock the value of a business.

has-been *Crit&Eval* One no longer famous, popular, successful, or useful. *Also see* **old timer, over-the-hill.**

hatchet job *Crit&Eval, Mgt* Rude or ruthless effort usu. ending in destruction. <The tabloid tried a hatchet job on the politician's reputation>

hatchet man *HR&LR, Mgt* Person hired or assigned to carry out a disagreeable task or an unscrupulous order.

hatecore music *Ethcs&Phil, MusArts* » **white noise** (*Ethcs&Phil, MusArts*)

HAU *ArtPerf, HR&LR* » **Hebrew Actors Union** Labor union chartered by the **Four A's**, represents Hebrew actors in the U.S. *Also see* **Guilds & Unions.**

haughty (hawtee, Fr. for "high") *Crit&Eval* Scornfully and condescendingly proud.

haute couture (hawt koh-ture, Fr.) *Fashn* The leading establishments or designers for the creation of exclusive fashions for women. 2 Exclusive fashions for women.

hauteur (hawtour, Fr. for "high") *Crit&Eval* Condescending in bearing and attitude; arrogance.

Hayes compatible modem *InfoMgt* **Modem** that implements the Hayes Command Set: a series of **modem** commands introduced in the early 1980s.

HB Playhouse *TheatArts* An acting studio and (very) little theater

in **Greenwich Village** owned and operated by Henry Berghof and his wife Uta Hagen (1919-, Ger.-born act., tchr. <*The Country Girl* (**Tony**, 1950) *Who's Afraid of Virginia Woolf?* (**Tony**, 1962) *Also see* **Theatres & Theaters**.

HBO *Rdio/TV* **Home Box Office**. Cable movie program service owned by **Time-Warner**.

hca *MusInstr* **harmonica**

HCI (Human-Computer Interaction) *iMedia* Study of how people interact with computers, and to what extent computers are (or are not) developed for successful interactions with human beings.

head arrangement *MusArts* Impromptu (usu. big band) arrangement worked out there and then.

head crash *InfoMgt* Collision of the read-write head with the recording surface of a hard disk, resulting in loss of data. Usually caused by contamination of the disk, such as from a tiny particle of dust or smoke. DISK CRASH. *Also see* **bomb.**

head *Cult&Soc, MusArts* rap fan.

head *Flm&Vid, RecA&S* Front end of a reel of film or tape.

head *InfoMgt* Distinct topic or category <Look in the encyclopedia under the head "civility, what ever happened to."> *Also see* **headline.**

head *MusInstr* Either end of a drum, made of animal hide or plastic.

head *VA-Prntng* Top of a book or of a page.

head end *Rdio/TV* Cable system's origination center; site of signal processing equipment.

head gaffer *Flm&Vid* First electrician, works directly with the camera crew. *Also see* **gaffer.**

Head Mounted Display *iMedia* » **HMD**

head register *MusArts* One of the higher **ranges** of the voice in singing, inc. the **falsetto.**

head-trip *Crit&Eval* 1 Mentally stimulating experience. 2 Act or a pattern of behavior undertaken primarily for self-gratification.

header *InfoMgt* 1 Title, date, or page number positioned in the top margin of a page that can be repeated throughout a document. *Also see* **footer.** 2 In email, the beginning of a message containing sender's address, subject of the message, and other information.

headhunter *HR&LR* One who recruits executive personnel in or for a corporation

headline *Journ* 1 Title or caption of a newspaper article, usu. set in large type. 2 Often headlines. Important or sensational piece of news. 3 Line at the head of a page with title, author, and page number. *Also see* **screamer.**

headliner *ArtPerf* Performer who receives prominent billing. FEATURED ACT, STAR

headphone *RecA&S* Receiver held to the ear by a headband for a. <telephone, radio, computer, record or tape player>

headroom *RecA&S* » **dynamic headroom**

headword *InfoMgt* Word, phrase, or name, usu. set in **boldface** or other distinctive type, that serves as the heading for an entry in a reference work, such as a dictionary or an encyclopedia. ENTRY WORD

Health and Human Services, U.S. Department of (HHS, 1980) *HR&LR, Law&Pol* Promotes health and social and economic security, national health, and child welfare. Formerly the Federal Security Agency, then Department of Health, Education, and Welfare (HEW) *Also see* **Federal Agencies and Statutes.**

hearsay *Genl, LegAsp* 1 Information heard from another. 2 Evidence which is not entirely within the personal knowledge of the witness but is partly within the personal knowledge of another person.

heart and soul *Crit&Eval* Completely; entirely.

heartland *Cult&Soc* Central region, esp. one that is politically, economically, or militarily vital to a nation. *Also see* **Middle America.**

heartthrob *Crit&Eval* object of one's **infatuation**

heat *Journ, Mktg* Positive **word-of-mouth** about a medium that advertisers pay attention to. <*Wired* magazine continues to generate heat> *Also see* **buzz.**

heavy *LitArts, TheatArts* Serious or tragic role in a drama; an actor playing such a role; a villain.

heavy metal rock *MusArts* Very loud, greatly amplified, brash rock music often with shouted, violent lyrics. "[Heavy] metal remains in its own way the purest sort of rock and roll.... It is all about **Sturm und Drang** and **braggadocio**, drinking lots of

Jack Daniel's, having a gigantic penis, and taking so many drugs your head explodes." — Jane and Michael Stern (rock critics) *Also see* **Rock Music Styles**.

Hebrew Actors Union (HAU) *ArtPerf, HR&LR* » **HAU**

hedonism *Ethcs&Phil* Ethical **doctrine** holding that only what is pleasant or has pleasant consequences is **intrinsically** good.

heehaw *Crit&Eval* (Country talk) Noisy laugh; a guffaw. *Origin* Bray of an ass.

Hegel, Georg Wilhelm Friedrich (1770-1831, Ger. philos.) *Ethcs&Phil* Proposed that truth is reached by a continuing **dialectic**. <*Encyclopedia of the Philosophical Sciences* (1817), *The Philosophy of Right* (1821)>

height of one line of type *VA-Prntng* It is measured by the number of lines per vertical inch. <This text is set 9/9 New Century Schoolbook, i.e., New Century Schoolbook type face set in 9 point type, 9 lines per vertical inch>

Helms, Jesse (1921-) *Law&Pol* Far right-winger senior senator from North Carolina, current chair, Senate Foreign Relations Committee. *Also see* **obscenity**.

hemidemisemiquaver (Brit.) *MusArts* sixty-fourth note.

Henahan, Donal (1921-, mus. critic) *Crit&Eval, MusArts* Former chief music critic, *NY Times*. *Also see* **classical music**.

herald *Genl* Bearer or announcer of supposedly important news; a messenger.

herald *Mktg* » **flyer**

heresy *Cult&Soc, Ethcs&Phil* Opinion or doctrine at variance with established religious beliefs. HERETIC.

heretic *Cult&Soc, Ethcs&Phil* **1** One who holds controversial opinions. **2** One who publicly dissents from the official **dogma** of the Roman Catholic Church. *Also see* **heresy**.

heritage *Cult&Soc* Something passed down from preceding generations; a tradition.

heritage and preservation *Fndng* Grants for art forms reflecting the United States's diverse cultural traditions — one of four categories of grants by the **National Endowment for the Arts**. *Also see* **NEA grants**.

Hermes *InfoMgt* Academic research group that conducts survey of the **Web** in conjunction with the Georgia Institute of Technology.

hero *Flm&Vid, LitArts, TheatArts* Principal male character in literature or dramatic presentation who exhibits qualities such as courage, idealism, and honesty. *Also see* **anti-hero, heroine, villain**.

hero, heroine *Crit&Eval* Person noted for special achievement in a particular field. *Also see* **celebrity**.

heroic drama *LitArts, TheatArts* **Restoration** tragedy or **tragicomedy** composed in **heroic couplets** and generally characterized by exotic settings, **bombastic rhetoric**, and exaggerated characterization.

heroic verse *LitArts* One of several verse forms traditionally used in epic and dramatic poetry.

heroine *Flm&Vid, LitArts, TheatArts* Principal female character in literature or dramatic presentation who exhibits qualities such as courage, idealism, and honesty. *Also see* **hero**.

heroin-chic *Ethcs&Phil, Fashn, VisArts* Style of drugged-look fashion photography in vogue beginning ca. 1994 that reportedly represents a new idea of beauty and a rebellion against phony airbrushed images. [In descending order of culpability: the models, the photographers, the fashion editors, their publishers, and mindless slaves-to-fashion.]

hertz (Hz) *Rdio/TV* Unit of **frequency** equal to one **cycle** per second.

Hertz, Heinrich Rudolf (1857-94, Ger. physicist) *Sci&Tech* First person to produce radio waves artificially. *Also see* **hertz, Hz**.

heterodyning *Sci&Tech* To combine a radio-frequency wave with a locally generated wave of different frequency in order to produce a new frequency equal to the sum or difference of the two. *Also see* **theremin**.

heterogeneous *Crit&Eval* **1** Consisting of dissimilar elements or parts. **2** Completely different; incongruous.

heteronomy *Ethcs&Phil, Law&Pol* Governance by another; subject to the will or commands of another. *Also see* **autonomy**.

heterophonic [performance] *MusArts* Relating to the simultaneous playing or singing of a single melody by two or more different instruments or singers. <black gospel music> *Also see* **New Or-**

leans Jazz.

heuriste *iMedia* **1** Of, or relating to, exploratory problem-solving techniques that utilize self-educating techniques (as the evaluation of feedback) to improve performance. **2** Common sense rules drawn from experience.

heuristics *InfoMgt* "Rules of thumb" designed to solve problems under very specific circumstances.

hexadecimal system *iMedia, InfoMgt* Base sixteen number system using the symbols 0-9 and A-F.

heyday *Crit&Eval* Period of greatest popularity, power, or success.

hf *Rdio/TV, RecA&S* » **high frequency**

HFA *IntelProp, RecA&S* » **Harry Fox Agency, Inc**.

HFR *BcstJourn* hold for release; story that is finished but is being saved for a later program or date. *Also:* evergreen or a banked story.

HHS *HR&LR, Law&Pol* U.S. **Department of Health and Human Services**

hi-fi *Rdio/TV, RecA&S* » **high fidelity**

hiatus *Rdio/TV* Planned interruption in broadcast advertising or production schedule usu. for the purpose of stretching a **media** budget or providing vacation time.

hidden permission *LegAsp* Copyright clearance for a selection or artwork that has separate attribution(s)

hierarchical navigation *iMedia* Type of navigational system that allows a participant/user to choose from several options. Each option usu. allows in-depth exploration of content and implies movement from general to specific.

hierarchy *Crit&Eval* **1** Body of persons having authority. **2** Categorization of a group of people according to ability or status. **3** Series in which each element is graded or ranked.

Hierarchy plus Input-Process-Output (HIPO) *InfoMgt* » **HIPO**

hieroglyphic writing *LitArts* Relating to a system of writing, such as that of ancient Egypt, in which pictorial symbols are used to represent meaning or sounds or a combination of meaning and sound.

high *Crit&Eval* excitement or **euphoria**

high *MusArts* Having a **pitch** corresponding to a relatively large number of **soundwave cycles** per second. <high tones of a violin> *Also see* **hertz, low**.

high comedy *LitArts, TheatArts* **1** General term referring to comedy that evokes thoughtful laughter through its concern with character, ideas, and witty dialogue. **2** Comedy of a sophisticated and witty nature, often satirizing genteel society. <The plays of **Oscar Wilde, Noel Coward**> *Also see* **low comedy**.

high density disk *InfoMgt* Floppy disk that can store 1.4 **megabytes** (MB) of information.

high fall *Flm&Vid* Stunt requiring a fall or jump from high.

high fashion *Fashn* The latest in trend-setting fashion or design.

high fidelity (hi-fi) *Rdio/TV, RecA&S* Electronic reproduction of sound from broadcast or recorded sources, with minimal distortion.

high frequency (hf) *Rdio/TV, RecA&S* short **wavelength**

high hat cymbals *MusInstr* Pair of (usu. 14 inch) cymbals positioned to be worked by a foot pedal. *Also see* **Musical Instrument Families**.

high hat *Fashn* » **top hat TOPPER**

high horse *Crit&Eval* Mood or an attitude of stubborn arrogance or contempt.

high jinks, hijinks *Crit&Eval* Playful, often noisy and rowdy activity, usu. involving mischievous pranks.

high key *Flm&Vid* Style of lighting that emphasizes bright, even illumination, with few conspicuous shadows. Used mostly in comedies, musicals, and light entertainment films.

high resolution *InfoMgt* High level of quality and accuracy of detail in computer printouts. *Also see* **correspondence quality, near-letter quality**.

high tech *Sci&Tech* » **high technology**

high tech *VisArts* Style of interior decoration marked by the use of industrial materials, equipment, or design. *Also see* **high technology**.

high technology (high tech) *Sci&Tech* Technology that involves highly advanced or specialized systems or devices.

high wire *PA-Variety* Tightrope for **aerialists** stretched very high above the ground.

high-definition television (HDTV) *Flm&Vid* Wide-screen, high-resolution digital television system that is the next generation of television broadcasting. In the early years of film, the **Academy [of Motion Picture Arts & Sciences] aspect ratio** was an acceptable standard of 1.33:1, the same ratio as television today. **HDTV** will increase the horizontal ratio, to about 1.78:1, and the vertical **resolution** will be increased to at least 720 **lines** of **resolution**.

high-draped pants *Fashn* (Passé) Fashion note in the swing era, prominent on the male **jitterbug**. *Also see* **zoot suiters**.

high-end *Mktg* Appealing to sophisticated and discerning customers. <The album sold better as a high-end gift> *Also see* **audiophile**.

high-five *Crit&Eval* Gesture of greeting, elation, or victory in which one person slaps another person's upraised palm.

high-growth venture *EntreP* Venture that will likely sustain quite rapid growth over a period of time.

high-level programming *iMedia* Programming languages closer to human languages (i.e., further from machine languages), and which are easier to read, write, and maintain. Ultimately, programs written in a high-level language must be translated into machine language by a compiler or interpreter.

high-pitched *MusArts* High in **pitch**, as a voice or musical tone.

high-potential venture (gazelle) *EntreP* Small company that has great prospects for growth.

high-quality printing *InfoMgt* » **DPI**

high-wire act *Crit&Eval* Risky job or operation. *Also see* **high wire**.

highbrow *Crit&Eval* One who possesses or affects a high degree of culture or learning.

higher criticism *Crit&Eval* Critical study of biblical texts to ascertain their literary origins and history and the meaning and intention of the authors.

higher law *Ethcs&Phil* Moral or religious principle that takes precedence over the constitutions or statutes of society. *Also see* **civil disobedience**.

highest possible frequency (HPF) *Rdio/TV* shortest possible **wavelength**

highfaluting *Crit&Eval* (Passé) Pompous or pretentious.

highflier, high-flier *Crit&Eval* One who is extravagant or extreme in manner or opinions.

highflier, high-flier *Eco&Fin* Stock selling well above its original value.

highhanded *Crit&Eval* Arrogant; overbearing.

highhat, high-hat *Crit&Eval* 1 To treat in a condescending or supercilious manner. 2 Snobbish; haughty.

highlight *Crit&Eval* Especially significant or interesting detail or event.

highlight *InfoMgt* To drag the mouse over text. Hold down the left mouse button, and drag the mouse over the text. When it changes color, it's highlighted and ready to be changed.

highlight *Th-MakeUp* In make-up, an area that is lighter than the base which makes things appear larger or more prominent.

highlight *VisArts* Area or a spot in a drawing, painting, or photograph that is strongly illuminated.

hill-and-dale recording *RecA&S* Vertical cutting of vibrations into wax discs, which resulted in better **stylus** tracking, lower **harmonic distortion**, and wider **frequency response**. Developed by **Bell Labs** in 1931.

hillbilly music *MusArts* Folk music originating in the back woods and mountains of the rural South, comprised of simple, unsophisticated melodies and subjects dealing with everyday existence. First recordings on the Okeh label, ca. 1925 "You have to have smelled a lot of mule manure to sing like a hillbilly." — Hank Williams (1923-53, country sngwri., sngr.) *Also see* **Country Music Styles**.

hinterlands *Cult&Soc* Region situated beyond metropolitan centers of culture. *Also see* **sticks**.

hip *Cult&Soc* In. Got it. With it.

hip-hop *Cult&Soc, MusArts* 1 Black urban art form from the late 1970s. 2 Style of music derived from **funk**. 3 Shorter version of **house music** with more emphasis on lyric *Also see* **backing tape, break dancing, graffiti, rap, scratch, techno**.

hip-hop *Cult&Soc, MusArts* 1 Black urban art form from the late 1970s. 2 Style of music derived from **funk**. 3 Shorter version of **house music** with more emphasis on lyric *Also see* **backing tape, break dancing, graffiti, rap, scratch, techno**.

HIPO *InfoMgt*, Hierarchy plus Input-Process-Output; a logical method of diagramming a computer system.

hippie, hippy *Crit&Eval, Cult&Soc* 1 One who rejects many conventional standards and customs of society. 2 One who advocates extreme liberalism in sociopolitical attitudes and **lifestyles**. *Also see* **flower-child**.

hippodrome *PA-Variety* In the circus arena, the oval area between the **rings** and the audience.

hiring hall *HR&LR* Union-operated placement center where jobs from various employers are allotted to registered applicants according to rotation or seniority.

Hispanic *Cult&Soc* 1 Relating to Spain or Spanish-speaking Latin America. 2 Relating to a Spanish-speaking people or culture. *Also see* **Latino**.

Hispanic American *Cult&Soc* U.S. citizen or resident of Latin-American or Spanish descent. *Also see* **Racial Designations**.

hist. *Crit&Eval* **historian, history**

historian (hist.) *Crit&Eval* Writer, student, or scholar of history, i.e., a critic of the story of humankind.

historical novel *LitArts* Narrative with fictional characters or events set in historically accurate surroundings.

historicism *Crit&Eval* 1 Critical method that seeks to situate a work of art to its historical context. 2 Theory that stresses the significant influence of history as a criterion of value. 3 Theory that events are determined or influenced by conditions and **inherent** processes beyond the control of human beings.

historiography *Crit&Eval* Writing of history based on a critical analysis, evaluation, and selection of authentic source materials and composition of these materials into a narrative subject to scholarly methods of criticism.

history (hist.) *Crit&Eval* 1 Story of time past, or, in some uses, that which is past whether recounted in story or not; written from the perspective of a whole age, or of the causes that move and shape events, or of the human beings who move and shape events, or of the disciplines that constitute knowledge or artful capacities in human use. 2 Branch of knowledge that records and analyzes past events.

history (hist.) *LitArts* Narrative of events; a story; a drama based on historical events.

histrionic *PerfA&C* Excessively dramatic or emotional.

hit *Crit&Eval* Successful or popular venture.

hit *InfoMgt* Click of the mouse to request a file from a **site**.

Hitchcock, Alfred (Sir Alfred Joseph Hitchcock; 1899-1980) *Art-Perf, Flm&Vid* British director-producer known for his suspense films. <*The 39 Steps* (1935), *Strangers on a Train* (1951), *Psycho* (1960)> *Also see* **MacGuffin, suspense programs**.

HitClips *MusArts, Sci&Tech* Three-quarter inch square of plastic with a microchip inside — plays a minute of music.

hits *Mktg* 1 Measure of the gross number of requests for information or files from a specific **Web** site, i.e., the least desirable level at which to measure **cyberspace** media. 2 Flops re interactive advertising.

HMD device *iMedia* Fastened to the head, and used to display a computer-generated scene. Head Mounted Display typically provides a stereo-optic (**3D**) view through the use of two **LCD** or small **CRT** displays.

ho. *Mgt,PerfA&C* **house**

hoax (hoaks) *Crit&Eval* 1 Something done by fraudulent means. 2 Act intended to deceive or trick. *Also see* **humbug**.

Hobbes, Thomas (1588-1679, Eng. pol. philos.) *Ethcs&Phil* He wrote *Leviathan* (1651), which outlined his philosophy: human beings are fundamentally selfish. *Also see* **humor**.

hoedown *Dnce, MusArts* 1 square dance. 2 Music for a square dance. 3 Party at which square dancing takes place. *Also see* **Dances, shindig**.

hokum *Crit&Eval* Seemingly impressive, but actually false and insincere.

hokum *TheatArts* Stock technique for getting an audience response.

hold *ArtPerf, TheatArts* 1 Pause by an actor for the audience's laughter or applause. 2 Command by a director at a rehearsal to stop acting so a comment made be made. **3** When an actor or a scene captures and retains the audience's attention.

hold *Mgt* Reservation held until cancelled or confirmed. <The promoter put a hold on the Civic Auditorium for Friday and Saturday, Feb 31>

hold *MusArts* To **sustain** a note longer than its indicated time value.

hold out *HR&LR* To refuse to reach or satisfy an agreement.

hold the book *PerfA&C* Serve as the prompter.

hold the stage *TheatArts* Play or playwright that continues to be produced.

holder *Eco&Fin, LegAsp* One that legally possesses and is entitled to the payment of a check, bill, or **promissory note**.

holding *LegAsp* Term of art in law, indicating the actual decision by a court in a particular case; the part of the written opinion that affects the legal result.

holding company *Eco&Fin, EntreP* Company that serves no other purpose except to own the stock of other companies.

holdover *TheatArts* Show continuing after the announced closing date.

holdover figure *Flm&Vid* Minimum box office receipts – agreed to by distributor and exhibitor – for a movie to be held over for another week.

Hollywood (Holly.) *Ethcs&Phil* "Hollywood is rife with corruption, all right, but the occasional embezzlement, fraud, cheating, and chiseling – as serious as they are – constitute symptoms of a more pervasive and subtle corruption, a corruption that is more difficult to combat than outright theft." — David McClintic (film critic) TINSELTOWN *Also see* **lotus land**.

Hollywood (Holly.) *Flm&Vid, Mgt* Part of Los Angeles east of Beverly Hills that signifies the image of a place more than a specific locale. [Said from her elegant new offices at **Paramount Pictures**:] "There's an interesting psychological profile of people who come to Hollywood. They're insecure and unstable. And they'd be insecure and unstable anywhere. And what do they do? They choose the most insecure and unstable place to work, a place where the average executive stays in a studio job for 18 months, where you're only as good as your last movie." — Gale Anne Hurd (Paramount Pictures exec) *Also see* **lotus land**.

Hollywood Support *Cult&Soc, Flm&Vid* Hollywood-based nonprofit founded in 1991 to combat sexual discrimination and persons found to be **HIV positive**.

hologram *Sci&Tech* Three dimensional image produced in thin air by lasers interacting with one another. HOLOGRAPH., HOLOGRAPHY

Home Box Office (HBO) *Flm&Vid, Rdio/TV* » **HBO**

home page *InfoMgt* Page (file) on the Internet composed by an individual, company, or organization. Its prose and graphic content may include personal matters, business offers, political philosophy, or whatever. <Film studio **home page** featuring new releases complete with **interactive multimedia**>

home theater market *Mktg, Rdio/TV, RecA&S* Includes six product categories: compact disk transports, amplifiers, speakers, tuners, turntables, and **high-end** recordings.

home video *Flm&Vid* Videotapes for viewing in the home.

homeboy *Cult&Soc* **1** Male friend or acquaintance from one's hometown, neighborhood, or turf. *Also see* **hood**.

homes using radio (HUR) *Mktg, Rdio/TV* » **HUR**

homes using television (HUT) *Mktg, Rdio/TV* » **HUT**

homogeneous *Cult&Soc* Of the same or similar nature or kind.

homophonic *MusArts* Having a single melodic line. *Also see* **polyphonic.**

homunculus *iMedia* Human with sense organs drawn proportional to the cortical stimulation they generate.

honest broker *HR&LR, Mgt* Neutral agent, as in mediation.

honeywagon *Flm&Vid* Trailer providing portable bathrooms and dressing rooms on sets and locations.

honeywagon driver *Flm&Vid* Screen credit reference to the person who drives the trailer carrying the portable toilets.

honkytonk *MusArts* Type of ragtime characteristically played on a tinny-sounding piano.

honkytonk *PerfA&C* Cheap, noisy bar or dance hall.

honor system *Ethcs&Phil* Set of procedures under which students are trusted to act without direct supervision in situations that might allow for dishonest behavior. <cheating on exams>

honorarium *Genl* Payment given to a professional person for services for which fees are not legally or traditionally required. <The star performer was paid an honorarium for judging the college competition> HONORARIA

honoree *Crit&Eval* One who is honored by an award.

hoo-hah (Yinglish) *Crit&Eval* Fuss; a disturbance; a chortle or laugh.

hood *Cult&Soc* neighborhood. *Also see* **homeboy**.

hoofer *Dnce* Non-classical dancer adept in tap.

hook *MusArts* One or more repetitive phrases in a song or recording that hooks the listener's attention. It may occur in the form of a **lyric, chord progression**, instrumental line, **riff**, rhythmic idea, groove, or beat. **2** Catchy **motif** or refrain.

hoopla *Crit&Eval* **1** extravagant publicity **2** boisterous excitement

hootenanny *MusArts* Informal public gathering of folk singers and musicians who perform in a festival-like atmosphere. *Also see* **folkfest; sing along**.

horizontal analysis *EntreP* Process of determining the percentage increase or decrease in an account on a financial statement from a base time period to successive time periods.

horizontal integration *Mgt* Process of gaining ownership or increased control of one's competitors. *Also see* **backward integration, vertical integration**.

horizontal market *Mktg* **Mass market**, or a market catering to the general public.

horizontal union *HR&LR* Craft union. <**AFM, IATSE**, etc> *Also see* **Guilds & Unions**.

horn (h.) *MusInstr* **1** *Classical-talk*: French horn. **2** *Jazz-talk*: Any wind instrument. HORN PLAYER, HORNIST *(RARE)*

horn player *MusArts* **1** *Classical talk* One who plays **French horn. 2** *Jazz talk* One who plays a **wind instrument**.

horn section *MusArts* **1** *Classical-talk*: **French horn section** of an ensemble. *Jazz-talk:* all the **wind instruments** in an ensemble

horse opera *Flm&Vid* Film or other theatrical work about the American West.

hospital shows *Rdio/TV* Popular type of television network programming. <*Dr. Kildare, MASH, St. Elsewhere*> *Also see* **Television Shows**.

hospitality *Mktg* Reception or other post-event designed to entertain sponsors, VIPs, special guests, contest winners, etc.… Usually includes food, beverages, entertainment, photo/autograph opportunities, and an appearance by the sponsored artist(s)

host *InfoMgt* Service provider that maintains email and/or Web pages on her or his servers.

host *Rdio/TV* **Emcee** or interviewer on a radio or television program.

host, hostess *Genl* One who receives or entertains guests in a social or official capacity.

hostname *InfoMgt* Unique name by which a computer is known on a network. SITENAME

hot *ArtPerf* Currently very popular or successful. "There's a time in [the writer's life], one matchless time, when they are matched completely. The speed, and the power and the talent, they're all there and then he is… 'hot." — **William Faulkner**

hot *Crit/Eval* **1** Very popular. **2** Very passionate. *Also see* **cool, in.**

hot *MusArts* Emotionally charged style of performance marked by strong rhythms and improvisation.

hot media *iMedia* Description of media that provide a high amount of stimulation, resulting in low participation (coined by **Marshall McCluhan)**

hot metal *VA-Prntng* Type cast from molten metal. *Also see* **cold type.**

hot stage *PA-Variety* **Vaudeville** term describing enthusiastic audience response to each succeeding act.

hot *VisArts* Bold and bright color <fire red>

hot-tix *Mktg, PerfA&C* Tickets very much in demand.

HotBot *InfoMgt* Web site providing access to Internet. *Also see* **search engine, portals**.

Hotwired *InfoMgt, Mktg* Commercial **media** service – in cooperation with **Nielsen Media Research** – that measures audience size of **Internet** media.

house (ho.) *Mgt, PerfA&C* Audience and its domain. **<count the house, house lights,** noisy house> *Also see* **publishing house.**

house *PerfA&C* synonym for auditorium

house agency *Mktg* Advertising agency owned or controlled by the advertiser. *Also see* **Agents and Agencies.**

house booker *Mgt* Entertainment **booker** employed by the **venue** management.

house booms *PerfA&C* Vertical pipes – mounted with lighting instruments – mounted to an auditorium wall.

House Committee on Un-American Activities (HUAC) *Ethcs&Phil, Law&Pol* » **HUAC**

house curtain *PerfA&C* » **act curtain** *Also see* **Stage Curtains**.

house left *PerfA&C* Term used by box office and house staffs to designate the left side of the theater facing the stage.

house lights *PerfA&C* Ceiling and side lights to illuminate the audience area in a theater. <The house lights dimmed>

house manager *Mgt, PerfA&C* One in charge of the theatre building and its staff. *Also see* **Managers.**

house music *MusArts* Black dance music native to Chicago. Strong 1 and 3 beat; lyrics not important.

house of design *Fashn* Couture designer's establishment of business.

house organ *InfoMgt, Journ* Periodical published for and circulated within a business or organization. <company magazine, company news.

house physician *PerfA&C* Physician on call to give emergency treatment to a member of the cast or audience. [Not qualified to treat a sick play.].

house right *PerfA&C* Term used by box office and house staffs to designate the right side of the theater facing the stage.

house seats *PerfA&C* Tickets to a play reserved and paid for by members of the cast and production staff. Only press seats are free.

housewife time *Rdio/TV* Broadcast time periods – morning and afternoon – available for advertising purchase. *Also see* **drive time.**

HPF *Rdio/TV* » **highest possible frequency**

HR *HR&LR, Mgt* » **human resources**

HTH *InfoMgt* Hope This Helps

HTM files *InfoMgt* File designation given when you save a **Web** page to your hard drive or **floppy disk.**

HTML *InfoMgt* **HyperText Markup Language** Scripting language of the World Wide Web. *Also see* **hypertext.**

HTML Validator *iMedia* Service or application that validates HTML and **XHTML** documents against **W3C Recommendations** and other standards. Errors and warnings are displayed, and often suggestions for fixing errors are given.

HTTP *iMedia* » **Hypertext Transfer Protocol**

HTTP *InfoMgt* **Hypertext Transfer Protocol** Information retrieval mechanism for HTML documents.

HUAC *Ethcs&Phil, Law&Pol* **House Committee on Un-American Activities**. (ca. late 1940s.) "For a while, every time the Russians threw an American in jail, the [House] Un-American Activities Committee [HUAC] would retaliate by throwing an American in jail too." — Mort Sahl (1927-, Can.-born standup comic., social critic)>

hubris (hew'-bris; Greek) *Ethcs&Phil* Overweening pride. Term and idea that suggests one has stepped beyond and above what is fitting for humans to do. *Origin* Suggestive of trenching on conduct or speech appropriate only for the gods. Consequently it brought divine retribution by the goddess Ate who instilled madness leading to the destruction of one guilty of hubris.

hubris (hew'-bris; Greek) *TheatArts* Exaggerated pride or self-confidence which in Greek tragedy leads to the hero's downfall.

huckster *Mktg, Rdio/TV* 1 One who uses aggressive, showy, and sometimes devious methods to promote or sell a product. 2 One who writes advertising copy, esp. for radio or television. *Also see* **hype.**

Hudson River School *VisArts* Group of American artists of the early 19th century who painted romantic American landscapes, esp. the Hudson River valley in New York.

hue *iMedia, InfoMgt VisArts* 1 Property of colors by which they can be perceived as ranging from red through yellow, green, and blue, as determined by the dominant wavelength of the light. 2 Particular gradation of color; a shade or tint. 3 Color.

human capital *EntreP* Knowledge and skills acquired by a worker through education and experience and used to produce goods and services.

human interest story *Journ* Treating people and their problems, concerns, or achievements in such a way as to arouse the interest or sympathy of the reader or viewer.

human resources (HR) *HR&LR, Mgt* 1 Human assets of an organization, i.e., employees. 2 "The design of formal systems in an organization to ensure the effective and efficient use of human talent to accomplish the organizational goals." — *Human Resource Management. Also see* **human relations.**

Human-Computer Interaction (HCI) *iMedia* » **HCI**

humanism *Crit&Eval* 1 System of thought and concern that centers on human beings and their values, capacities, and worth. 2 Study of the **humanities**; learning in the liberal arts.

Humanism *Crit&Eval* Cultural and intellectual movement of the **Renaissance** that emphasized **secular** concerns as a result of the rediscovery and study of the literature, art, and civilization of ancient Greece and Rome.

humanist, Humanist *Crit&Eval* 1 Believer in the principles of humanism. 2 One who is concerned with the interests and welfare of human beings. 3 Classical scholar; student of the liberal arts. 4 Renaissance scholar devoted to Humanism.

humanities *Cult&Soc* Subject concerned with human beings and their culture rather than from the sciences. <**fine arts**, history, literature, philosophy>

humanity *Crit&Eval* 1 Human beings considered as a group; the human race. 2 Condition or quality of being human; humanness.

humanize *Journ* In writing, to use human references and anecdotes rather than statistics.

humankind *Cult&Soc* human race

humbug *Crit&Eval* 1 Something intended to deceive; a **hoax** or fraud. 2 Person who claims to be other than what he or she is; an impostor. 3 Nonsense; rubbish. *Also see* **flimflam.**

Hume, David (1711-76, Brit. philos., hist.) *Ethcs&Phil, Law&Pol* He argued that human knowledge arises only from sense experience. <*A Treatise of Human Nature* (1739-1740) and *Political Discourses* (1752)> *Also see* **Jeremy Bentham, John Stuart Mill, utilitarian, utilitarianism.**

hummer *MusArts* "Composer" who hums a melody, then has an arranger orchestrate and develop it for a flat fee, usu. without credit or royalty.

humor *Crit&Eval* 1 The quality that makes something amusing or funny. 2 Ability to perceive, enjoy, or express what is amusing, comical, incongruous, or absurd. "Humor is the affectionate communication of insight... I do hope you are not foolish enough to think humor a category of trivia. The humor of a people is as illuminating as its patterns of pride, guilt and ambivalence. Humor is an isotope that locates the insights of a people. It was gloomy [Thomas] Hobbes who cried, 'Laughter is sudden glory.'" — Leo Rosten (1908-1997, humorist, Yiddish lexicographer) HUMOUR

humorist *LitArts* "I'm sure there isn't a humorist alive but can recall the day, in the early stages of his career, when someone he loved and respected took him anxiously into a corner and asked him when he was 'going to write something serious.' That day is memorable, for it gives a man pause to realize that the bright star he is following is held to be not of the first magnitude." — **E.B. White.**

humorist *PA-Variety* Performer who specializes in humor. <George Carlin>

humour (Brit.) *Crit&Eval* » **humor**

HUR *Mktg, Rdio/TV* Estimated percentage of "homes using radio" at any given time.

hurdle rate *E&F-Acc* » **discount rate**

hurdy-gurdy *MusInstr* Any instrument, such as a **barrel organ**, played by turning a crank. Usually played by a street musician accompanied by a costumed monkey who solicits donations from passersby.

Hurok, Sol (1888-1974, Russ.-born **impresario**) *Mgt* He very successfully imported and presented many famous performers in recitals and concert series in NYC and elsewhere.

hustle *Crit&Eval* 1 To obtain something by deceitful or illicit means.

2 To act aggressively in business dealings or personal relationships. *Also see* **hype**. HUSTLER

hustle *Ethcs&Phil* **1** Illicit or unethical way of doing business or obtaining money; a fraud or deceit **2** To solicit customers. *Also see* **B-girl**. HUSTLER

hustle *Genl* **1** To work or move energetically and rapidly. <You better hustle or you'll miss your plane> **2** Energetic activity; drive. HUSTLER

HUT *Mktg*, *Rdio/TV* Estimated percentage of "homes using television" at any given time.

hyberbolic browser *iMedia* Hierarchical visualization of data where subsets appear in a detailed view still in context with the entire structure.

hybrid *Crit&Eval* Something of mixed origin or composition.

hydras *InfoMgt* Machine which combines several common office functions. <answering machine, copier, fax machine, printer, scanner, speakerphone, telephone>

hymn *MusArts* **1** Song of praise or thanksgiving to God or a deity. **2** Song of praise or joy. *Also see* **Songs**.

hymnody *MusArts* **1** Singing of hymns **2** Composing or writing of hymns.

hype *Ethcs&Phil*, *Mktg* **1** Something deliberately misleading. **2** Exaggerated or extravagant claims. *Also see* **huckster**, **hustle**, **hyperbole**.

hyperbole *Crit&Eval* Exaggeration or extravagant statement; a deliberate overstatement. <**Madonna** is the greatest performer in the world> *Also see* **hype**.

hypercardioid microphone *RecA&S* Cardioid-type **mic** but with a 90 degree off-axis response. *Also see* **Microphones**.

hypercello *MusInstr* Elaborated electronic version of the cello introduced in 1993 by **Yo-Yo Ma** (1955-, Fr.-born clo.), created by composer Tod Machover. *Also see* **Musical Instrument Families**.

hypergraphic *InfoMgt* Graphic image link to other Internet documents containing more information on the same or related topic. To retrieve the related document, click on the hypergraphic. *Also see* **hypertext**.

hyperlink *iMedia* Link in an **HTML** document that leads to another World Wide Web site, or another place within the same document. synonym for both **link** and **hypertext link**.

hyperrealism *VisArts* Artistic style characterized by highly realistic graphic representation. *Also see* **photorealism**, **superrealism**.

hypertext *InfoMgt* **1** Text link to other Internet documents containing more information on the same or related topic. To retrieve the related document, click on the hypertext. **2** Term coined by computer buff Ted Nelson to define the narrative made possible by computers by which the reader can enter and **browse** at will. HTML *Also see* **hypergraphic**, **HyperText Markup Language** (HTML) *InfoMgt* » **HTML** and **hypertext**

Hypertext Preprocessor *iMedia* » **PHP**

Hypertext Transfer Protocol *iMedia* **Protocol** used to transfer information to and from **World Wide Web** servers to browsers.

hypertext transfer protocol *iMedia* HyperText Transfer **protocol** used to transfer information to and from World Wide Web servers to browsers.

Hypertext Transfer Protocol *InfoMgt* » **HTTP**

hyphenate *Flm&Vid* When a screen writer and a director are one and the same, thus: writer-director.

hypothesis *Crit&Eval* **1** Tentative explanation that accounts for a set of facts and can be tested by further investigation; a theory. **2** Something taken to be true for the purpose of argument or investigation; an assumption.

Hz *Rdio/TV*, *RecA&S* » **Hertz**

- I -

IAE *InfoMgt*, In Any Event.

IAJE *MusArts* **International Association of Jazz Educators** Professional organization of school jazz educators, clinicians, and professional jazz musicians, arrangers, and composers. Formerly **National Association of Jazz Educators** (NAJE)

I.C. *BcstJourn* » **incue**

I.M. *MusArts* **industrial music**.

I.T. *Sci&Tech* **Information Technology.**

iamb *LitArts* **Metrical** foot consisting of an unstressed syllable

followed by a stressed syllable or a short syllable followed by a long syllable.

iambic pentameter *LitArts* Poetry consisting of five parts per line, each part having one short or unstressed syllable and one long or stressed syllable.

IAML *InfoMgt*, *MusArts* **International Association of Music Libraries**. Encourages and promotes activities of libraries, **archives**, and documentation centers. Fosters cooperation among members and seeks to increase the social importance of music institutions.

IASC *E&F-Acc* » **International Accounting Standards Committee**

IATSE *HR&LR*, *PerfA&C* » **International Alliance of Theatrical Stage Employees and Motion Picture Operators of the US and Canada** Labor union, affiliated with the **AFL-CIO**, represents stagehands, ushers, ticket sellers, box office treasurers, movie projectionists, and property persons in virtually all public venues where theatrical productions are staged. *Also see* **Guilds & Unions**.

IAU *ArtPerf*, *HR&LR*, *PerfA&C* » **Italian Actors Union** Labor union chartered by the **Four A's** that represents Italian actors in the U.S. *Also see* **Guilds & Unions**.

IBEW *HR&LR*, *Rdio/TV* International Brotherhood of Electrical Workers represents electricians in broadcasting, film, and recording studios, as well as stage venues. *Also see* **Guilds & Unions**.

IBM *InfoMgt* **International Business Machines** World's largest computer related company who has had difficulty in recent years with the market's move from **mainframes** to **microcomputers** and **server** networks.

IBMA *MusArts* **International Bluegrass Music Association**. **Nonprofit** located in Nashville, TN, dedicated to the development and promotion of bluegrass music.

IC *InfoMgt* I see.

IC *InfoMgt* **integrated circuit**

ice *Mgt* Bribes paid by ticket **scalpers** for prime tickets at the box office. *Origin* **Incidental campaign expenses**. *Also see* **digger**.

ICM *Mgt* **International Concert Management** Large NYC-based music booking and talent agency. *Also see* **Talent Agencies**.

icon *InfoMgt* Picture on a screen that represents a specific command. It is activated by moving the cursor onto the icon and clicking the mouse button. <On a **Macintosh** computer, a wastebasket icon represents the command to delete a file>

iconoclastic *Crit&Eval* Attack popular and traditional ideas of institutions.

ICSOM *ArtPerf*, *MusArts* **International Conference of Symphony and Opera Musicians**. Members are professional symphony, opera, and ballet musicians. Its purposes are to promote the welfare of and make more rewarding the livelihood of the orchestral performer; and disseminate orchestration information. Affiliated with **AFM**.

id *Crit&Eval* In **Freudian** theory, the division of the psyche totally unconscious and serves as the source of instinctual impulses and demands for immediate satisfaction of primitive needs.

ID *BcstJourn* » **writeup**

IDE *iMedia* » **integrated development environment**

idea *MusArts* **1** **theme** or **motif** **2** Something that can not be copyrighted unless it is expressed in **tangible** form.

ideal *Ethcs&Phil* Existing as an archetype or pattern, esp. as a **Platonic** idea or perception.

idealism *Ethcs&Phil* Theory that the object of external perception, in itself or as perceived, consists of ideas.

identifier *InfoMgt* Symbol that identifies a group of data.

identifiers *Mktg* Printed words, symbols, or designs that communicate a message.

identity *Crit&Eval* **1** Distinct personality of an individual; individuality. **2** Behavioral or structural characteristics by which an organization is recognizable as a member of a group.

ideologue *Crit&Eval*, *Law&Pol* Advocate – usu. an official exponent – of a particular ideology. *Also see* **chauvinist**, **jingo**.

ideology *Cult&Soc* Body of ideas reflecting the social needs and aspirations of an individual, group, class, and culture. "High culture, like high religion, like ideologies of all kinds, always tries to monopolize the high ground so that it can look down with contempt on the smoky shacks of the lower orders." — Ferdinand Mount

I

(cult. crits.)

IDHEC *Flm&Vid* **Institute des Hautes Etude Cinematographiques.** Ω

idiom *Crit&Eval* Style of artistic expression characteristic of a particular individual, school, period, or medium: the **idiom** of the **Ashcan school**; the hard rock **idiom**.

idiosyncrasy (idio-sin-crah-see) *Crit&Eval* Some characteristic peculiar to an individual or a group.

idiosyncratic *Crit&Eval, Cult&Soc* Structural or behavioral characteristic peculiar to an individual or a group.

idiot box *Rdio/TV* television set.

idiot savant *Crit&Eval* Mentally retarded person who exhibits genius in a highly specialized area, such as music.

idol *Crit&Eval* One that is adored, often blindly or excessively. *Also see* **matinee idol**.

idol *Cult&Soc* Image used as an object of worship; false god. *Also see* **fetish**.

idyllic *Crit&Eval* Simple and carefree.

IEEE *Sci&Tech* **Institute of Electrical and Electronics Engineers.** Information exchange, publishing, and standards-setting organization, responsible for many of the standards used in local area computer networks.

IFAR *VisArts* **International Foundation for Art Research.** NYC-based organization that maintains a data base of stolen art.

IFAS *Law&Pol* » **Institute for First Amendment Studies** *Ex*-members of fundamentalist churches and others dedicated to the principle of separation of church and state as provided for the first amendment. Monitors and reports on the activities of fundamentalist right wing groups.

IFPI *RecA&S* » **International Federation of Phonographic Industries** Est. 1933 Represents producers and distributors of sound and music video recordings; 1,200+ members from 90 countries.

IIA *InfoMgt* » **Information Industry Association** Trade association of companies interested and involved in the business opportunities associated with the generation, distribution, and use of information products, services, and technologies. Works to keep members informed about latest technologies and marketing trends, facilitates formation of partnerships, and business alliances; serves as a channel to customers, acquisitions, and venture capital. Conducts new technology, business operations, and information user workshops and seminars; sponsors senior management symposium and roundtables. <**AT&T**, McGraw-Hill, Dun's Marketing>

IIPA *IntelProp* » **International Intellectual Property Alliance** Coalition of U.S. motion picture, computer software, book publishing, and recording industries united to: encourage adherence to, and recognition and enforcement of copyright laws on national and international levels; represent the interests and views of industries engaged in the production and marketing of intellectual properties. *Also see* **Copyright-Related Organizations**.

IJS *MusArts* » **Institute of Jazz Studies**

ikat *Fashn* Resist form of decoration. Designs appear as reflections in water, therefore a blurry effect. *Origin* From the Malayan word "mengikat," meaning to tie, knot, bind, or wind around.

ILAA *HR&LR, LitArts* **Independent Literary Agents Association.** Literary and dramatic agents who market books, plays, and other literary and dramatic material. Formed by merger of **Society of Authors Representatives** (SAR) and **Independent Literary Agents Association** (ILAA)

ILGWU *Fashn, HR&LR* **International Ladies Garment Workers Union** has had close ties to the **Broadway** and **off-Broadway theatre**. Union replaced by **UNITE** in 1995.

Illiac computer *InfoMgt* » **computer music**

illuminated panel *Mktg* Lighted poster panel or billboard.

illus. *VisArts* **illustration, illustrator.**

illusion *Crit&Eval* **1** Erroneous perception of reality. **2** Erroneous concept or belief.

illusionist *ArtPerf, PA-Variety* Magician or ventriloquist.

illusory contour *iMedia* Outline or contour perceived or implied by shapes or objects but which is not explicitly rendered or physically present. *Also see* **implied line**.

illustration (illus.) *VisArts* Visual matter used to clarify or decorate a text in advertisements and **print media**.

illustrator (illus.) *VisArts* One who provides explanatory or decorative features in **print media**.

IM *InfoMgt,* Instant Message.

image consultant *Mgt* » **image-maker**

image *Crit&Eval* **1** Specific representation in art, literature, or music evocative of something else. <budding flowers as an image of new life> **2** Character projected to the public by a person or an institution as interpreted by the **mass media**. **3** Mental picture of something not real or present. *Also see* **image-maker, likeness, PR.**

image *InfoMgt* Exact copy of data in a file transferred to another medium.

image *VisArts* Reproduction of the form of a person or an object. LIKENESS.

image enhancement *Mktg* Improvement of the public's perception of a sponsor, product or service.

image-maker *Mktg* One who uses skillful techniques in publicity and advertising, esp. by way of the **mass media**, to create a favorable public view, as of a person or an institution. *Also see* **press agent, public relations**.

imagery *LitArts* Figurative language used to evoke particular mental pictures.

imagery *TheatArts* Broad term generally used to apply to all figurative uses of language (i.e., metaphor, simile, etc.) In production, it refers as well to the physicalization of ideas or concepts from the script usu. in scenery or staging.

imagination *Crit&Eval* **1** Formation of a mental image of something neither perceived as real nor present to the senses. **2** Ability to confront and deal with reality by using the creative power of the mind; resourcefulness: "The great artists have at least one thing in common: imagination." — Anon. "Man's imagination is what takes him out of his misery." — Yip Harburg (» **gederim**)

imagism *also* **Imagism** *LitArts* Literary movement by British and American poets early in the 20th century in reaction against **Victorian** sentimentalism that advocated the use of free verse, common speech patterns, and clear concrete images. *Also see* **Art Movements and Periods**.

IMG Artists *Mgt* Spinoff of IMG; an international booking and talent agency. *Also see* **Talent Agencies**.

IMG *Mgt* **International Management Group** NYC-based billion-dollar-a-year sports management agency. *Also see* **Talent Agencies**.

IMHO *InfoMgt* In My Humble Opinion

imit. *Crit&Eval, MusArts* **imitation.**

imitation (imit.) *Crit&Eval* **1** "Imitation is natural to man from childhood, one of the advantages over the lower animals being this, that he is the most imitative creature in the world, and learns first by imitation. And it is also natural for all to delight in works of imitation [works of art]." — **Aristotle**. **2** Something derived or copied from an original. **3** Made to resemble another, usu. superior material. [The trend away from art as imitation was begun by the 19th century **impressionists**.].

imitation (imit.) *MusArts* Repetition of a phrase or sequence often with variations in key, rhythm, and voice.

immediacy cue *BcstJourn* Word or phrase that adds a heightened sense of time to a story. *Ex.* "This just in" or" At this moment…"

immersion *iMedia* State of being deeply engaged in an interactive media product.

immersion level *iMedia* Level describing the amount of engagement. high immersion level is completely engaged, a low immersion level is partially engaged and easily distracted.

immortal *Crit&Eval* That which cannot or does not die, sometimes treated as a synonym for "eternal," but that which is immortal can, by some accounts, come into existence at one time, and persist forevermore; whereas that which is eternal is, and always will be. *Also see* **eternal**.

immortality *Crit&Eval* Enduring fame. **1** "What is immortality, afterall, but vanity?" — Erica Jong (» **boilerplate**) **2** "I don't want to achieve immortality through my work. I want to achieve it through not dying." — **Woody Allen**.

IMNSHO *InfoMgt* In My Not So Humble Opinion.

IMO *InfoMgt* In My Opinion

IMPA *MusArts* » **International Music Products Association**

impact printer *InfoMgt* Type of printer that forms images on the paper by physically encountering the ribbon.

impartial umpire *HR&LR* Person designated by union and management to arbitrate **grievances** or disagreements arising under a collective bargaining contract.

impasto *VisArts* **1** Application of thick layers of pigment to a canvas or other surface. **2** Paint so applied. *Also see* **art brut.**

impersonator *ArtPerf* Entertainer who impersonates celebrities; **mimic.**

implementation model *iMedia* Actual method of how a design works. *Also see* **manifest model, mental model.**

implied agency *LegAsp* Agency that occurs when a **principal** and an agent do not expressly create an agency, but it is inferred by the conduct of the parties. *Also see* **Agents and Agencies.**

implied line *iMedia* Line or contour perceived or implied by shapes or objects but which is not explicitly rendered or physically present. *Also see* **illusory contour.**

implied warranty of authority *LegAsp* Agent that enters into a contract on behalf of another party implicitly warrants that he or she has the authority to do so.

implied-in-fact contract *LegAsp* Agreement inferred by the conduct of the parties. *Also see* **Contracts.**

implied-in-law contract *LegAsp* » **quasi-contract** *Also see* **Contracts.**

import *Eco&Fin,Cult&Soc* To bring from abroad goods and services for sale or trade.

import *InfoMgt* To read a file created by another program into another program. *Also see* **export.**

imposition *VA-Prntng* Arrangement of pages on a printed sheet to form a correct sequence of pages when properly folded.

impresario *PerfA&C* Larger-than-life **showman.** <**Serge Diaghilev, Sol Hurok**> *Also see* **mogul, tycoon.**

impression *Mktg* One person's seeing or hearing a marketing message or a sponsor's name or logo.

impressionism *or* **Impressionism** *Crit&Eval* Practice of expressing or developing one's subjective response to a work of art or to actual experience. *Also see* **Art Movements and Periods.**

impressionism *or* **Impressionism** *LitArts* Literary style characterized by the use of details and mental associations to evoke subjective and sensory impressions rather than the re-creation of objective reality.

impressionism *or* **Impressionism** *MusArts* Style of the late 19th and early 20th centuries, using lush and somewhat vague harmony and rhythm to evoke suggestions of mood, place, and natural **phenomena.**

impressionism *or* **Impressionism** *VisArts* Theory or style of painting originating and developed in France during the 1870s, characterized by concentration on the immediate visual impression produced by a scene and by the use of unmixed primary colors and small strokes to simulate actual reflected light. *Also see* **Art Movements and Periods, modern art.**

impressionist *PerfA&C* Entertainer who does impressions, usu. of people.

imprint *VA-Prntng* Book publisher's name, date, address, and edition, printed at the bottom of the title page.

impromptu *Crit&Eval* Spoken, performed, done, or composed with little or no preparation. EXTEMPORANEOUS

impropriety *Cult&Soc* Improper usage in speech or writing. Also *see* **propriety.** IMPROPRIETIES

improvisation *MusArts* **1** Developing of an original melodic passage using the chord changes of a popular tune, blues, or original **progression. 2** Admitting of varying degrees of freedom from the written melody and constitutes the essence of jazz. **3** Composing on your feet: Art of performing an original **arrangement** or composition in the midst of a live performance, and never repeating it quite the same way; "[**Sonny**] **Rollins** played a medium-tempo *Long Ago and Far Away*: two bars of melody, dropped into a quick inside **run**, a double-time lunge, and a **sotto-voce turn-around,** stated the melody for two or three more bars, improvised again, offered more melody, and so forth. This kind of now-you-see it, now-you-don't melodic improvisation makes the listener, constantly teased, work twice as hard." — Whitney Balliett (jazz critic) "Improvisation is instant composing." — Hank Jones (1918-; jazz pianist) *Also see* **ad-lib, jazz characteristics.**

improvise *Crit&Eval* To invent, compose, or recite without preparation — except years of learning, listening, and performing with and against the best available. *Also see* **according to the ink, ad-lib.**

impulse buy *Mktg* Sudden wish or urge that prompts an unpremeditated purchase, usu. motivated by attractive packaging or bargain pricing. <Cover art and prose on the cover of a record album, a paperback book, a tabloid magazine> *Also see* **convenience products.**

imputed knowledge *LegAsp* Information learned by the agent attributed to the **principal.**

IMS *VisArts* **Institute of Museum Services** Federal agency that provides support to a variety of museums. <botanical gardens, zoos>

in *Cult&Soc* Aware of the latest fashion or trend. *Also see* **hip, out.**

in one *PA-Variety* Perform in front of the front curtain (where most comedians and monologists used to perform in vaudeville) [Act performing in front of the front curtain allows time to set up an act requiring a **stage set.**] *Also see* **stand-up.**

in one, in 1, in 2, in 3, etc. *TheatArts* Direction for a performer to enter to from **wing number** 1 (or 2, etc.) *Also see* **Stage Directions.**

in stock *Mktg* Available for sale or use; on hand. *Also see* **inventory, stock, out of stock.**

in the can *Flm&Vid* Film that has been shot or "wrapped," but not yet edited or **scored.**

in the can *RecA&S* Finished recording that has not yet put on the market.

in the chair *PerfA&C* Sitting in the **makeup** chair.

in the moment *Crit&Eval, TheatArts* 'When you are playing a scene, you don't bring a predetermined attitude on stage. You don't pretend to be listening, you listen. You stay in the moment." — Alan Alda (1936, act., dir.)

in the wild *InfoMgt* rampant viruses

in the works *Crit&Eval* In preparation; under development. <a play, a novel, a movie in the works>

in time *MusArts* In the proper tempo.

in-and-out *Eco&Fin* Involving the purchase and sale of a single security within a short period of time.

in-group *Crit&Eval* Group of people united by common interests; excluding outsiders. *Also see* **clique.**

in-house *Genl* Within a company or organization.

in-house advertising *Mktg* » **house agency**

in-house producer *RecA&S* » **staff producer** *Also see* **Producers.**

in-joke *Crit&Eval* Joke originated or appreciated by the members of a particular group.

in-kind contributions *Fnding* Contributions of equipment, supplies, or other property as distinguished from monetary grants. Some organizations may also donate space or staff time as an in-kind contribution.

in-process inventory *Eco&Fin* Raw materials currently manufactured and/or processed, but are not yet completed. *Also see* **Inventory Methods.**

in-transit inventory *Eco&Fin, Mktg* Form of **finished goods inventory** in which the goods are being shipped (in-transit) to the customer but that have not yet been billed, i.e., title is still being held by the selling company. *Also see* **Inventory Methods.**

inappropriately directed laughter *Crit&Eval* Unfortunate bit of **political correctness** contained in **speech codes** adapted by some American universities.

inc. *E&F-Acc* income.

incentive funding *Fnding* Plan by government to encourage philanthropy by offering some benefit to the donor. <matching funds>

inches per second (ips) *RecA&S* Measure of speed of audio tape played or recorded. <3-3/4 ips, 7-1/2 ips, etc>

incidental authority *LegAsp* Implied power an agent has where the terms of the **express agency** agreement do not cover the contingency in question.

incidental campaign expenses *Ethcs&Phil* Cash that's not accountable. *Also see* **ice.**

incidental music *MusArts, TheatArts* Music composed to accompany the action or dialogue of a drama or to fill intervals between scenes or acts.

income (inc.) *Eco&Fin* Amount of money or its equivalent received during a period of time in exchange for labor or services, from the sale of goods or property, or as profit from financial investments.

income elasticity of demand *EntreP* Measure of the responsiveness of the quantity demanded to changes in consumer income; computed by dividing the percentage change in the quantity demanded by the percentage change in income.

income gap *Eco&Fin* Difference between budgeted income and actual income.

income statement (profit and loss statement) *Eco&Fin, EntreP* **Financial statement** that measures the amount of revenue earned and expenses incurred by an organization within a specific period of time. *Also see* **Statements**.

income summary *E&F-Acc* Temporary "holding tank" account into which the revenues and expenses are transferred before their final transfer to the **capital** account.

incongruous *Crit&Eval* **1** Lacking in harmony; incompatible. <the music seemed incongruous with what was on the screen> **2** Not in agreement with principles. **3** Not in keeping with what is correct, proper, or logical; inappropriate.

increment operator *iMedia* Programming: operator that adds 1 to the current value of a variable.

incubator *EntreP* Organization or building that houses a number of new or small businesses and provides common services to its tenants.

incue or **I.C.** *BcstJourn* Refers to a phrase sometimes written on scripts news scripts that use **actualities** or soundbites. The incue usu. includes the first four words of the bite. This helps identify the right **cart** and whether or not it is cued correctly.

inculturation *Cult&Soc* Incorporation of native dance and language into an established religious service.

indemnity *LegAsp* Agreement whereby one party agrees to secure another against an anticipated loss or damage. *Also see* **Contracts**.

independent contractor *LegAsp* Person or business who is not an employee who is employed by a **principal** to perform a certain task on her or his behalf. *Also see* **freelance.**

independent distributor *Mktg* Independent company, not affiliated or owned by another **entity**, engaged in the distribution of goods and services.

independent film *Flm&Vid* Typically used to differentiate films made with an artistic imperative from those made for purely commercial reasons. (The distinction is rather arbitrary and often abused for self-promotion) The term is being reclaimed to describe films where the director/producer/writer triumvirate is the principal determiner of content and style and working in a context where the production stands alone in commercial terms. In that sense, the concept opposes the idea of a studio production roster where individual films are commercial components rather independent entities.

independent foundation *Fnding* Grantmaking organization usually classified by the **IRS** as a **private foundation**. Independent foundations may also be known as **family foundations, general purpose foundations, special purpose foundations**, or **private non-operating foundations**. The Foundation Center defines independent foundations and company-sponsored foundations separately; however, federal law normally classifies both as private, non-operating foundations subject to the same rules and requirements.

independent label (indie) *RecA&S* » **independent record company**

Independent Literary Agents Association (ILAA) *LitArts, Mgt* » **ILAA**

independent producer *RecA&S* One who produces record masters on a non-exclusive basis so that her or his services may be engaged by any label. *Also see* **Producers**.

independent promotion *RecA&S* Record promotion done by a person or a company not affiliated with the record company. *Also see* **airplay, promo person.**

independent record company (indie) *RecA&S* One that does not operate its own distribution system or manufacturing facilities. INDEPENDENT LABEL

Independent Sector *Fndng* Organization that conducts research into and advocates for the third (charitable) sector in American society.

independent station *Rdio/TV* Radio or TV station not network-affiliated or a network station that programs less than twelve hours of network programming.

Independent Television News (ITN) *Journ,. Rdio/TV* U.S.-based international news agency. *Also see* **News Agencies**.

index *EntreP* Statistic that is computed to measure the performance of some portfolio of financial securities, generally stocks.

index *InfoMgt* **Key** used to facilitate file access or sorting.

Index of Forbidden Books *Ethcs&Phil, LitArts* Published 1536-1966 by the Sacred Congregation of the Roman **Inquisition**. Last revision, 1948. *Also see* **censorship**.

Indian *Cult&Soc* » **Asian, Native American**.

Indians of Mardi Gras *Cult&Soc* Black men, elaborately costumed as native Americans, who parade in the New Orleans Mardi Gras.

indicating *TheatArts* **1** Performing an action without an intention. **2** Derogatory term in psychologically motivated acting.

indie *also* **indy** *Flm&Vid, RecA&S* Independent company, not affiliated or owned by another **entity**. <independent film company, independent record company> *Also see* **Distributors**.

indie cred *RecA&S* "Used in rock since 1985 or so, it refers to an unhyped credibility based on unpredictability, on the thrill of new music that is not formulaic." — Ben Ratliff (19??-, music critic)

indigenous *Cult&Soc* **1** Originating and growing or living in a particular area or environment. **2** **Intrinsic**; innate. *Also see* **native**.

indigo *Fashn* Dark blue to grayish purple blue.

indirect forecasting *EntreP* Forecasting method in which variables are related to sales to project future sales.

indirect taxes *EntreP* Sales and excise taxes.

individual contract *HR&LR* Agreement concerning terms of employment between an individual employee and management.

individual retirement accounts (IRA's) *EntreP* Retirement plans that allow one to contribute current annual income that have favorable tax treatment. They allow accumulation of tax deferred benefits until withdrawal.

individual supply curve *EntreP* Curve that shows the relationship between price and quantity supplied by an individual company, ceteris paribus (everything else held fixed)

individualism *Cult&Soc* Belief in the primary importance of the individual and in the virtues of self-reliance and personal independence; acts based on this belief.

individualism *Law&Pol* **Doctrine** advocating freedom from government regulation in the pursuit of a person's economic or social goals.

indorsement *E&F-Acc, LegAsp* » **endorsement**

industrial arts *Sci&Tech* Relating to the manual and technical skills required to work with tools and machinery.

industrial distribution *Mktg* Distribution methods for **industrial products**. *Also see* **Distribution Methods.**

iindustrial film *also* **industrial** *Flm&Vid* Film made for use internally within a company, or as a company's business-to-business or as a business-to-consumer communication.

industrial magazine *Journ* » **trade magazine**

industrial music (I.M.) *MusArts* An American **indigeneous** art form: "**anthems** and mini-musical productions that corporations commission to impress clients and bludgeon sales forces into action." — Harry Shearer (19??-; host of radio show, *Le Show*.)

industrial products *Eco&Fin, Mktg* Those designed for and distributed to other companies to be used for the production of the user company's products.

industrial rock *MusArts* Rooted in computer generated music.

industrial show *Mktg, PA-Variety* Entertainment or industry promotion staged to promote a new product or product line. *Also see* **corporate theater**.

industrial union *EntreP, HR&LR* Labor organization that includes all types of workers from a single industry. *Ex.* steelworkers, auto workers. *Also see* **Guilds & Unions**.

industry *Eco&Fin, Mktg* **1** Commercial production and sale of goods. **2** Specific branch of manufacture and trade. <music industry> **3** Ongoing work or study associated with a specified subject or figure. <**Elvis Presley** industry>

industry environment *EntreP* Combined forces that directly affect a given company and all of its relevant competitors.

inedited *LitArts* Not edited, not published.

inequity *Crit&Eval, HR&LR* Instance of injustice or unfairness. <The difference in compensation between top management and low-level employees in many U.S. companies. — Ed>

infatuation *Crit&Eval* Extravagant passion or attraction

inference engine *InfoMgt* **Computer programs** in an **expert system** that processes the rules contained in the knowledge base and draws logical conclusions.

inflation *EntreP* Increase in the average price of goods. Most often measured by the Consumer Price Index (CPI)

inflation rate *EntreP* Percentage rate of change of the price level in the economy.

Inflation Rate *Eco&Fin* This **economic indicator** is based on the percentage statistic that represents how much a national currency has "inflated," i.e., gone down in buying power in a given year or quarter. <If the inflation rate for 1996 is 3%, it means that it would take $1^{03} to buy the same amount of goods and services at the end of 1996 compared to the end of 1995> *Also see* **CPI**, **Fed**.

inflection *MusArts* Alteration in **pitch** or tone of the voice.

.info *InfoMgt* **Domain name** ending for information services. *Also see* **Domain Names**.

info., info *InfoMgt* **information**.

InfoBahn *InfoMgt* Informal and possibly impertinent reference to the **Information Super Highway**.

infomercial *Mktg, Rdio/TV* Commercial TV program or relatively long commercial segment offering consumer information, such as educational or instructional material, relating to the sponsor's product or service. Infomercials reportedly grossed $1 billion in 1994 *Also see* **NIMA**.

informal analysis *EntreP* Fairly quick, unscientific analysis of an opportunity to see if it merits a more in-depth, formal analysis.

informal contract *LegAsp* Contract that does not require a special form or method for its creation. *Also see* **Contracts**.

information appliance *iMedia* Device developed for performing a single task or related set of tasks. In contrast: a modern desktop computer.

information architecture *iMedia* Various methods for structuring information in order to be stored, retrieved, searched, and published.

information design *iMedia* **1** Various methods of presenting visual information. **2** Detailed planning of specific information targeted to a specific audience. **3** Visualizing information or data to aid **cognition**.

Information Highway *InfoMgt* Means of accessing a vast quantity of information via a computer and **modem**. INFOBAHN, IN-FORMATION SUPER HIGHWAY *Also see* **Internet**

information *InfoMgt* **1** Data that has been organized and processed. **2** Non-accidental signal or character used as an input to a computer or communications system. **3** Knowledge derived from study, experience, or instruction. **4** Knowledge of a specific event or situation; intelligence. *Also see* **information management, information science, information theory**.

Information Management *InfoMgt* Study and practice of managing information. Nine aspects: (1) *Identify* the information, (2) *Acquire* the information, (3) *Organize* the information, (4) *Analyze/Evaluate* the information, (5) *Store* the information, (6) *Secure* the information, (7) *Retrieve* the information, and (8) *Communicate/Disseminate* the information. "New information resides nowhere until it has been identified, objectified, assembled, and communicated." — **William Shawn**. *Also see* **information science**.

information plumbing *InfoMgt* » **bandwith**

information retrieval (IR) *InfoMgt* Process of accessing information from memory or other storage devices.

information science *InfoMgt* Science (esp. computer science) concerned with the gathering, manipulation, classification, storage, and retrieval of recorded knowledge. *Also see* **Information Management**.

Information Super Highway *InfoMgt* Hyperbolic version of **Information Highway**.

information technology manager *InfoMgt* *Also see* **Managers**, **network administrator**. Ω

information theory *InfoMgt, Sci&Tech* **1** Mathematical theory that explains aspects and problems of information and communications. In this theory, **information** is a measure of the freedom of choice with which a message is selected from the set of all possible messages. **2** Theory of the probability of transmission of messages with specified accuracy when the bits of information constituting the messages are subject, with certain probabilities, to transmission failure, distortion, and accidental additions. *Also see* **bits**, **binary**.

information visualization *iMedia* **1** Visual means of solving logical problems. **2** Using vision to think. **3** Visual aids that enhance cognitive abilities.

informational picketing *HR&LR* Picketing by a union for the purpose of informing other workers and the public about an employer that does not have a collective bargaining contract with its members.

informel *VisArts* Style of lyrical **abstraction** that appeared in Europe after WWII. Similar to **action painting** in the U.S., it rejected the geometric abstraction and is characterized as **non-representational**, passionate, and subjective. In a large sense, it may be included in **abstract expressionism**. Informal emphasized **matière** (texture) unlike **action painting** which emphasized the action or gesture of the artistic expression.

InfoSeek *InfoMgt* Web site providing access to Internet. *Also see* **search engine**, **portals**.

infotainment *Crit&Eva, Journl* Blend of hard news and opinion, gossip and gags. *Also see* **new news**.

infringement *IntelProp, LegAsp* **1** Violation of a law or agreement. **2** Encroachment of a privilege or a right. <infringement of **copyright**, a **patent**, a **trademark**>

ingénue (on-jay-nu, Fr. for "guileness") *ArtPerf* Role of an **artless**, innocent girl or young woman in a dramatic production; an actress playing such a role. *Also see* **juvenile**.

ingenuity *Crit&Eval* Inventive skill or imagination; cleverness.

ingenuous *Crit&Eval* **1** Lacking in sophistication or worldliness. **2** Openly straightforward or frank. *Also see* **artless**, **naive**.

inherent *Crit&Eval* Essential characteristic. INTRINSIC

inheritance *iMedia* **1** In object-oriented programming, the ability to derive new classes from existing classes. **2** The passing of properties or parameters from one entity to another that is related.

INIT *InfoMgt* » **system extension**

initial public offering (IPO) *Eco&Fin, EntreP* First offering of a venture's stock to the general public. An IPO is an expensive, time-consuming process that can yield several million dollars of equity capital.

initialization string *InfoMgt* Sequence of characters sent to a **modem** to set it up for communicating.

initialize *InfoMgt* **1** To prepare a disk to receive information. **2** To set to a starting position or value.

initiation fees *HR&LR* Fees required to become a member of a union or a fraternal organization.

injunction *LegAsp* Court order prohibiting a party from a specific course of action or mandating the performance of a specific course of action.

ink *Genl Variety* Talk for sign <Agency inks big **flick** contract>

ink *LegAsp* To sign <The Pzazzers were inked to a new recording contract>

ink *LitArts, TheatArts* Relates to the words of the **script**. <The director admonished the cast to act according to the ink, i.e., don't change the author's words>

inline element *iMedia* In-line elements in a markup language do not have a carriage return; the element does not "break" the line. In contrast: block-level elements.

inner above *PerfA&C* Elevated area located directly above the **inner below** in the Elizabethan theater.

inner below *PerfA&C* Curtained area at the upstage edge of the playing area in the Elizabethan theater. *Also see* **inner above**.

Inner Forces *Aes&Creat Crit&Eval, Ethcs&Phil.* Major element of **The Arts Dynamic**. *Also see* **Outer Forces**, **Principal Players**.

innocent misrepresentation *LegAsp* Occurs when an agent makes an untrue statement that he or she honestly and reasonably believes to be true. *Also see* **intentional misrepresentation**.

innocuous *Criticism* Not likely to offend or provoke to strong emotion; insipid.

innovation *EntreP* Development of new products, processes, services, or strategies that have not previously existed. Also, the transfer of creativity into marketable products.

innovation *Genl* Something newly introduced

innovator *Genl* Do, begin, or introduce something new.

innuendo *Crit&Eval* Indirect or subtle, usu. derogatory implication in expression; an insinuation.

inoculation *Mktg* Preemptive advertising tactic in which one party attempts to foresee and neutralize potentially damaging criticism from another party by being the first to confront troublesome issues.

inoculation theory *Crit&Eval* Say something often enough and it will perceived to be truth.

input *InfoMgt* Information transferred into a computer from an external source. <keyboard, mouse, **disk drive**, **modem**> *Also see* **output.**

input element *iMedia* Device or means by which a participant interacts with an interface or project.

Inquisition *Cult&Soc, Ethcs&Phil* **1** Roman Catholic Church court directed at the suppression of **heresy** (and blasphemy, sexual aberration, witchcraft, etc.) Instituted 1231, reorganized 1908 as the Congregation of the Holy Office; redefined 1965 as the Congregation for the Doctrine of the Faith with the positive task of furthering correct doctrine rather than censuring **heresy.** **2** Investigation that violates the privacy or rights of individuals. *Also see* **censorship, *Index of Forbidden Books.***

inquisition *Law&Pol* **1** An inquest. **2** Verdict of a judicial inquiry.

insert *Flm&Vid* Camera shot inserted to explain the action. <**close-up** of a letter, newspaper headline, road sign>

insert *Mktg, VA-Prntng* Usually a pre-printed advertisement or editorial supplement bound in a magazine or book, or placed loose in a newspaper. FREE-STANDING INSERT.

insertion order *Mktg, VA-Prntng* Written purchase order from an advertiser, or its ad agency, to a periodical to reserve space for one or more ads in one or more issues. *Also see* **space contract, space buyer.**

insertion point *InfoMgt* Flashing vertical bar representing the cursor for use in editing text or inserting graphics.

inside director *Mgt* Top corporate executive of a company who is a member of the company's board of directors.

inspection *EntreP* Examination of a product to determine whether it meets quality standards.

inspiration *ArtPerf* **1** Work of art that moves the intellect or emotions or prompts action or invention. **2** Sudden creative act or idea, that is inspired. "It is evident that inspiration is a most vital component of art." — Harold Shapero (mus. critic)

inspire *Crit&Eval* To fill with enlivening or exalting emotion. <young actor inspired by **Olivier's** Hamlet>

installer *InfoMgt* Program that installs or updates the computer system software.

installment account *EntreP* Line of credit that requires a down payment, with the balance paid over a specified period of time.

instant book *LitArts, Mktg* Books written and sold in less than four seeks after an event, such as: sensational scandals, government crises, death of a national figure, etc. Such books "have the **shelf life** of a head of lettuce." — Doreen Carvajal (journ.) CRASH BOOK, QUICKIE BOOK *Also see* **one-sheeter.**

Instantaneous Rate of Return *EntreP* Rate of return from a security over an infinitesimal period of time.

Institute des Hautes Etude Cinematographiques (IDHEC) *Flm&Vid* » **IDHEC**

Institute for First Amendment Studies (IFAS) *Law&Pol* » **IFAS**

Institute of Electrical and Electronics Engineers (IEEE) *InfoMgt, Sci&Tech* » **IEEE**

Institute of Jazz Studies (IJS) *MusArts* Internationally renowned research center at Rutgers U. (Newark, NJ), Dan Morgenstern, Director.

Institute of Museum Services (IMS) *VisArts* » **IMS**

Institute of Outdoor Drama (IOD) *TheatArts* » **IOD**

Institutional advancement *Fndng* Sophisticated approach to funding whereby development and marketing activities both support an organization's mission.

instruction set *InfoMgt* Basic functions of a computer such as

add, store, and retrieve data.

instrument (instr.) *Genl* **1** Means by which something is done; an agency. **2** One used by another to accomplish a purpose; a dupe. **3** Implement used to facilitate work. See Synonyms at tool.

instrument (instr.) *LegAsp* Legal document.

instrument (instr.) *MusInstr* Device for playing or producing music: a wind instrument; a keyboard instrument.

instrument (instr.) *Sci&Tech* Device for recording, measuring, or controlling, esp. such a device functioning as part of a control system.

instrument maintenance payment *HR&LR, MusInstr* Addition to **scale** for **Broadway musicians.** June 1998 contract calls for weekly scale $1,300 (from $1,100), weekly maintenance payment $50 (from $10)

instrumental *MusInstr, MusArts* Performed on or written for an instrument.

insurance *Eco&Fin, Mgt* **Risk management** technique to help protect assets of an individual or an organization from loss due to fire, flood, wind, etc. This **pure risk** is "transferred" in either whole or part to an insurance company who "bets" that the loss will not occur. Theory of insurance is that the premiums (insurance policy payments) of the many will cover the losses of the few. *Also see* **self-insurance.**

insurance, liability *EntreP* Transfer of risk to an insurance company to alleviate the cost of property damage and personal injury to others as a result of your action.

insurance, life (whole life, universal life, term, variable) *EntreP* Transfer of risk to an insurance company for a premium by one who has an insurable interest in the life of an individual. Life insurance can be purchased by a company, spouse, child, etc.

insurance, property *EntreP* Transfer of risk to an insurance company for a premium by one who has an insurable interest in the property.

INT *Flm&Vid* **interior location.** *Also see* **location.**

intaglio *VisArts* **1** Figure or design carved into or beneath the surface of hard metal or stone. **2** Art or process of carving a design in this manner.

Intangible Assets *ColEntry, Eco&Fin* Nonphysical resources that are presumed to represent an advantage to the firm's position in the marketplace. <capitalized advertising costs, **computer programs,** exploration permits, **copyrights, franchises, goodwill,** import-export permits, **leases, licenses, patents, trademarks**> *Also see* **Assets.**

intangible *Crit&Eval* **1** Something incapable of being realized or defined. **2** Something incapable of being perceived by the senses.

intangible resources *EntreP* Organizational resources that are invisible and difficult to quantify.

integer *iMedia* Whole number (positive or negative, such as 3, -3, or 0)

integrated circuit (IC) *InfoMgt* Slice of **silicon** containing the equivalent of electronic circuitry etched into the surface. *Also see* **chip.**

integrated development environment *iMedia* Application that not only compiles code, but also provides additional tools (such as a debugger)

Intel *InfoMgt* Manufacturer of the **Pentium,** brand name of a leading computer chip.

intellection *Crit&Eval* **1** Act or process of using the intellect; thinking or reasoning. **2** thought or an idea.

intellectual *Crit&Eval* **1** Rational rather than emotional. **2** Given to exercise of the intellect; inclined toward abstract thinking about aesthetic or philosophical subjects. *Also see* **egghead, highbrow.**

intellectual property *IntelProp* Ideas translated to **tangible** creations. <choreography, literature and plays, music and songs, visual art works, recordings> "Our country is the pre-eminent source of the world's music because American creativity has been nurtured through strong copyright protection. As a result, intellectual property today (1993) makes up 5.6 percent of the U.S. **gross national product** and is one of the only growing segments of our export market." — Edward P. Murphy (info. sci. wri.) *Also see* **Copyright-Related Organizations, property** (*LegAsp-Intel*)

intelligent lights *PerfA&C* Computer regulated units that swivel and generate hundreds of colors. *Also see* **floodlights, spotlights**.

intelligentsia *Crit&Eval, Cult&Soc* intellectual **elite** of a society

intensity *Crit&Eval* Exceptionally great concentration, power, or force.

intensity *Sci&Tech* Amount or degree of strength of electricity, light, heat, or sound per unit area or volume.

intensity *VisArts* Strength of a color, esp. the degree to which it lacks its complementary color.

intention *iMedia* Goal that drives the development of an interactive product (*aka* goal, intent, objective) **2** In team work the intended motivation for, or result of, an action.

intention *TheatArts* A result a character seeks from a given action in order to attain a larger goal. *Also:* action, objective, want, need.

intentional misrepresentation *LegAsp* **1** Intentionally defrauding another person out of something of value. **2** Occurs when an agent makes an untrue statement knowing that it is not true. *Also see* **innocent misrepresentation**.

interactive *iMedia* Interactive Media. Media that requires the participation of a person and responds to the actions or inaction of the participant.

interactive *InfoMgt* Re two-way communications between a computer system and its operators.

interactive media *iMedia* Interactive media are participant-centered, dynamic, responsive, adaptive, and engaging. Human communication through an interface that provides a co-authored experience between developer and participant/user. "Interactive Media represent a **paradigm** shift in terms of authorship and audience... where once there were observers or an audience, this new form requires participants." — David Gerding

interactive media *Rdio/TV* Form of television entertainment in which the signal activates electronic apparatus in the viewer's home or the viewer uses the apparatus to affect events on the screen, or both.

Interactive Services Association (ISA) *InfoMgt* Trade group for online service companies.

interactive terminal *InfoMgt* Computer or data-processing terminal capable of providing a two-way communication with the system to which it is connected.

Interchange *InfoMgt* Online information service owned by **AT&T**. *Also see* **Online Information Services**.

interest *E&F-Acc* Revenue to the **payee** for loaning out the **principal**, and the expense to the **payer** for borrowing the principal.

interest *Eco&Fin* Charge for a loan, usu. a percentage of the amount loaned. *Also see* **compound interest**.

interest *LegAsp* Right, claim, or legal share. <The XYZ record company bought an interest in the ZYX music publishing company>

interest rate *EntreP* Rate for which present consumption is sacrificed for future consumption. In the capital markets it permits claims to future cash flows to be traded now.

Interest Rate Cap *EntreP* Sequence of European call options defined on interest rates that gives the buyer the maximum of some excess over a specified floating-point rate over a specified time.

Interest Rate Floor *EntreP* Sequence of European put options defined on interest rates that gives the buyer the maximum of some negative below some specified floating-point rate over a specified time.

interface *iMedia* "Facilitates a dialog between a piece and a participant. interface is the combination of the input elements, output elements, composite elements, and the participant's reactions and actions." — David Gerding

interface *InfoMgt* **1** Way a computer communicates with the user. **2** The layout of a magazine published in **CD-ROM** format. HUMAN INTERFACE, USER INTERFACE

interior (INT.) *Flm&Vid* Setting for an indoor scene. *Also see* **exterior**.

interior setting *Flm&Vid* » **interior**

interlocutor *PA-Variety* Performer in a **minstrel show** placed midway between the **end men** and engages in banter with them.

interlude *TheatArts* Short play, usu. comic, performed during courtly feasts at the English court in the 16th century.

intermediary *Mktg* Organization or individual that serves as an agent or **facilitator** between producer, marketer, and/or customer. <wholesaler, jobber, retailer, etc>

intermediate colors *iMedia* Created by mixing two primaries in a ratio 2:1.

intermezzo (Ital.) *MusArts, TheatArts* **1** Play with music performed between the acts of an opera or drama; an **entr'acte**. **2** Short movement separating the major sections of a lengthy composition.

internal acting *TheatArts* » **presentatial actor** *Also see* **external acting**.

internal circulation *Journ* Distribution of a periodical within the sponsoring organization. *Also see* **Media Circulation**.

internal dynamics *RecA&S* Describes the volume of a **sound wave's** increases, decreases, and **sustains**. *Also see* **attack**; **decay**; **sustain**.

internal equity *EntreP* Funds that come from retaining profits within a company.

internal locus of control *EntreP* Belief that one's success depends on one's own efforts.

internal point of view *LitArts* » **character's point of view**

Internal Revenue Service (IRS) *Eco&Fin, Law&Pol* » **IRS**

International Accounting Standards Committee (IASC) *E&F-Acc* Organization that promotes the international harmonization of accounting standards.

International Alliance of Theatrical Stage Employees and Motion Picture Operators of the U.S. and Canada (IATSE) *Flm&Vid, HR&LR, PerfA&C* » **IATSE**

International Association of Assembly Managers (IAAM) *Mgt, PerfA&C* Founded in 1924, "its members are professional public assembly facility managers committed to promoting and developing the use fullback assembly facilities by the public and to standardize practices and ethics of management and relationship to the public." >www.iamm.org<

International Association of Jazz Educators (IAJE) *MusArts* » **IAJE**

International Association of Music Libraries (IAML) *InfoMgt, MusArts* » **IAML**

International Bluegrass Music Association (IBMA) *MusArts* » **IBMA**

International Brotherhood of Electrical Workers (IBEW) *HR&LR, Rdio/TV* » **IBEW** *Also see* **Guilds & Unions**.

International Business Machines (IBM) *InfoMgt* » **IBM**

International Clown Hall of Fame and Research Center, Inc. *PA-Variety* "Dedicated to the preservation and advancement of **clown** art." >www.webdom.com/chof/<

International Concert Management (ICM) *Mgt* » **ICM**

International Confederation of Societies of Authors and Composers (CISAC) *MusArts* » **CISAC**

International Conference of Symphony and Opera Musicians (ICSOM) *ArtPerf, MusArts* » **ICSOM**

International Country Music Fan Fair *Mktg, MusArts* » **CMA**

International Federation of Phonographic Industries (IFPI) *RecA&S* » **IFPI**

International Foundation for Art Research (IFAR) *VisArts* » **IFAR**

International Intellectual Property Alliance (IIPA) *IntelProp* » **IIPA** *Also see* **Copyright-Related Organizations**.

International Ladies Garment Workers Union (ILGWU) *Fashn, HR&LR,* » **ILGWU**

International Management Group (IMG) *Mgt* » **IMG, IMG Artists**

International Master Recording Licensing Agreement *RecA&S* Contractual agreement between an independent record company and one or more foreign distributors on a territory-by-territory basis. *Also see* **Copyright-Related Organizations**.

International Monetary Fund *EntreP* Organization that works closely with national governments to promote financial policies that facilitate world trade.

International Music Products Association *MusArts* Organization coordinates and supports the music retail business with two shows a year, one in Anaheim, Ca. and one in Nashville, Tenn. *Also see* **NAMM**.

International Olympic Committee *SportsEnt* » **IOC**

International Organization for Standardization (ISO) *MusArts, RecA&S* » **MP3**

international pitch *MusArts* **Sound wave frequency** of 440 **cycles** per second, assigned to the **A above middle C**. CONCERT PITCH

International Public Relations Association (IPRA) *Mktg*» **IPRA** *Also see* **PRSA**.

International Society of Performing Arts Administrators (IS-PAA) *Mgt,PerfA&C* » **ISPA** (Name changed 12/14/94.)

International Standards Organization (ISO) *iMedia* Develops documented agreements (rules or guidelines) regarding intellectual and physical properties and processes.

International Theatre Institute (ITI) *TheatArts* International non-governmental organization, with national centers in 90 countries, founded in Prague in 1948 by **UNESCO** and the international theatre community.

International Trademark Association (ITA) *IntelProp* Center for registering **trademarks** and monitoring their correct use.

Internet (net) *iMedia* Global communications network consisting of thousands of smaller networks. *Also see* **Online Information Services**.

internet bandit *Flm&Vid* Screen credit reference to the communication operator who handles traffic between the filming location and the home base.

Internet Protocol (IP) *InfoMgt* » **IP**

internet relay chat (IRC) *iMedia* Communication with others in real time over a network, usu. the Internet, using a client program that connects, sends, and receives information. Often channels are set up dedicated to specific topics or groups, and conversations can be public or private.

Internet Service Provider (ISP) *InfoMgt* » **ISP**

Internet Society, The *InfoMgt* Non-governmental organization that seeks the global cooperation and coordination of the Internet and its technologies and applications.

Internet2 *InfoMgt,* Network for universities to work together to develop advanced Internet technologies, such as: telemedicine, digital libraries and virtual laboratories.

interpolate *Genl* Insert material into a text.

interpolated song *MusArts, TheatArts* Previously published song written by someone other than the author of the **score** of the musical play in which the song is inserted, i.e., interpolated, if agreed to in a **Dramatist's Guild** contract. *Also see* **compilation score**.

interpolation *EntreP* Process of using mathematics to find an unknown value that lies between two known values.

interpretation *ArtPerf* Performer's distinctive personal version of a song, dance, piece of music, or role.

interpretation *Crit&Eval* 1 Private judgment of the critic that is beyond objective description. 2 Explanation or a conceptualization by a critic of a work of literature, painting, music, or other art form.

interpreter *iMedia* Converts the program code into **CPU**-specific instructions every time the program is run and must be 'present' in memory every time an interpreted program is run. — David Gerding

interval *MusArts* Difference in **pitch** between two tones.

intonation *MusArts* 1 Act of **intoning** or chanting. 2 Manner of producing or uttering tones with regard to accuracy of **pitch**.

intone *MusArts* To speak with a singing tone or with a particular **intonation**.

Intranet *iMedia* Networked systems not open to the public.

intranet *InfoMgt* Corporate computer networks

intrapreneurial culture *EntreP* Corporate culture that makes full use of the entrepreneurial spirit within an established organization.

intrapreneurship *EntreP* Entrepreneurship within a large corporation. » **corporate entrepreneurship**

intrinsic *Crit&Eval* Essential nature of a thing. INHERENT

intro *BcstJourn* » **writeup**

intro. *or* **intro** *Fndng, Genl, MusArts* **introduction**.

introduction (intro. *or* intro) *Fndng* Portion of a grant proposal that establishes the identity and credibility of the organization seeking funding.

introduction (intro. *or* intro) *LitArts* Something spoken, written, or otherwise presented in beginning or introducing something. <preface of a book>

introduction (intro. *or* intro) *MusArts* Short preliminary movement in a larger work.

intrusion *Journ, LegAsp* 1 Invasion of privacy by acquiring information from or about a person by physical trespass or deception. 2 Illegal entry upon or appropriation of the property of another.

intuition *Crit&Eval* 1 Act or faculty of knowing or sensing without the use of rational processes. 2 Knowledge gained by the use of this faculty; a perceptive insight. 2 Sense of something not evident or deducible; an impression.

intuitionism *Ethcs&Phil* Name for the approach to ethics that suggests we simply know "in our bones" what is right to do.

inv. *Eco&Fin* **invoice**

invective *Crit&Eval* Abusive language. OBLOQUY, VITUPERATION

invention *EntreP* Creation of an entirely new product that did not previously exist.

invention *MusArts* Short composition developing a single theme contrapuntally.

inventory *EntreP* Company's raw materials and products held in anticipation of eventual sale.

inventory *Eco&Fin* Materials and goods owned by the company that may or may not be stored on its premises. *Also see* **Inventory Methods**.

Inventory Levels *Eco&Fin* This **economic indicator** reveals that high inventory levels can indicate lower production until excess inventory is liquidated. Conversely, low inventory level may indicate increased production to meet demand. *Also see* **FIFO, LIFO**.

Inventory Methods *ColEntry, Eco&Fin, Mktg* **FIFO, finished goods** —, **in-process** —, **in-transit** —, **JIT, LIFO, merchandise** —, **periodic inventory system, perpetual inventory system, physical** —, **raw material** —, **retail method of** —.

inventory turnover *E&F-Acc* Speed with which inventory is sold. It is the annual sales divided by average inventory (inventory turnover = sales/average inventory) *Also see* **activity ratios**.

inventory turnover ratio *EntreP* Measure of the quantity of inventory on hand compared with the amount of inventory sold, measured by dividing the cost of goods sold by the average inventory.

inversion *MusArts* Transposition of the lower and upper notes of an interval.

invested assets *EntreP* Those assets found on a statement of financial position which are marketable securities such as stocks, bonds, and life insurance cash values. These items are normally listed on a business balance sheet under current assets.

Investigative journalism *Journ* Specializing in uncovering and reporting misconduct in public life. *Also see* **muckraker, Watergate**.

investigative producer *Journ,. Rdio/TV* Producer of a TV news program who may spend months on an assignment. *Also see* **Producers**.

Investigative Reporters & Editors (IRE) *Journ*» **IRE**

investment *Eco&Fin* **Long-term asset** not used in the normal operation of the organization and that management does not intend to convert to cash within one year.

investment banker *EntreP* Representative of a large bank that focuses on providing substantial capital to high-growth ventures, often as a prelude to taking the company public.

investment vehicle *EntreP* Any item which allows one to attain an investment goal. *Ex.* stocks, bonds, savings, accounts, real estate, etc.

Invisible Man (1952) *Cult&Soc, LitArts* Novel by Ralph Waldo Ellison (1914-1994) of an unnamed African American whose life encompasses much of 20th century life by Considered by many critics to be one of the most important works of this century. — *Dictionary of Global Culture*.

invoice (inv.) *Eco&Fin* Detailed list of goods shipped or services rendered; an itemized bill.

invoking a function *iMedia* » **calling a function**

IOC *SportsEnt* **International Olympic Committee**, the governing body of the **Olympic games**. Based in Lausanne, Switzerland.

IOD *TheatArts* **Institute of Outdoor Drama** Ω

ionosphere *Rdio/TV, Sci&Tech* Electrically conducting set of layers of the earth's atmosphere off which **AM** radio signals are reflected back to earth. It extends from a height of 30 -250 miles above the surface.

IOW *InfoMgt* In Other Words

IP *InfoMgt* **Internet Protocol** Provides an address which lets other machines on the Internet locate and connect to. *Also see* **Protocols.**

IPO *Eco&Fin* **initial public offering**

IPRA *Mktg* **International Public Relations Association** *Also see* **PRSA.** Senior public relations practitioners from 61 countries. Provides for exchange of professional information and standards, and education.

ips *RecA&S* inches per second.

ipso facto *LegAsp* By the fact itself or by the very nature of the case.

IR *InfoMgt* **information retrieval**

IRC *iMedia* » **internet relay chat**

IRE *Journ* **Investigative Reporters & Editors.** This premier investigative reporter's (**nonprofit**) organization was founded in 1975 by a "platoon of **muckrakers**, teachers, and publishers" located at – and partially supported by – the School of Journalism, U. of Missouri (Columbia)

iris *Flm&Vid,PerfA&C* Metallic diaphragm adjustable to vary the diameter of a central **aperture**, used on spotlights to create **pin spot** or **blackout.** *Also see* **Stage Lighting.**

iris in, iris out *Flm&Vid* Iris closed, **iris** open.

Irish National Theatre *TheatArts* » **Abbey Theater** *Also see* **Theaters & Theatres.**

IRL *InfoMgt* In Real Life

irony *Crit&Eval* Expression or utterance marked by a deliberate contrast between apparent and intended meaning.

irony *LitArts* Literary style employing contrasts between apparent and intended meaning for humorous or rhetorical effect.

irony *TheatArts* Device by which the playwright expresses a meaning contradictory to the stated or ostensible one. The most common kind of irony in drama is **dramatic irony** which occurs when the audience knows something that one or more of the characters do not. *Origin* In the Greek theatre one who dissembles, esp. through understatement and the deliberate guise of ignorance, and who typically triumphs over a boastful, self-deceiving braggart. *Also see* **Socratic irony.**

irrevocable trusts *EntreP* Trust that cannot be changed by the grantor or trustees once it is established.

IRS *Eco&Fin, Law&Pol* **Internal Revenue Service.** Bureau of the U.S. Treasury Dept., responsible for the collection of federal income taxes.

ISA *InfoMgt* » **Interactive Services Association**

ISDN *InfoMgt* **Integrated Services Data Network 1** Offers access to a digital network and connections to the **Internet. 2** Can send/receive information in **digital** format without have to translate to and from an **analog** format.

island page *Mktg*, Ad measuring 7'x10' inches on a 8-1/2' x 11' inch page. *Also see* **full page ad, bleed ad.**

ISO *iMedia* » **International Standards Organization**

ISO *MusArts, RecA&S* International Organization for Standardization. » **MP3**

ISO 9000 *EntreP* Standards governing international certification of a company's quality management procedures.

isolation booth *Rdio/TV* Closed-off space where a quiz show or game show participant is kept out of sound and sight as The Question is asked: "For 64 million dollars, who was the first president of the United States? You have 15 seconds!" [And the Big Clock goes ticky-tacky, ticky-tacky.].

isolation *RecA&S* Area in a recording studio where a performer, e.g., a drummer, is isolated to avoid sound **spill.**

ISP *InfoMgt* **Internet Service Provider** An ISP is an organization that provides access to the Internet via dial-up telephone lines. *Also see* **Online Information Services.**

ISPA *Mgt,PerfA&C* **International Society for the Performing Arts.** Formerly, **ISPAA.** International membership organization of individuals and organizations involved in the professional performing arts.

IT *InfoMgt* information technology

It's a wrap *Flm&Vid* Thus ends a shooting day.

ITA *IntelProp* » **International Trademark Association**

Italian Actors Union (IAU) *ArtPerf, HR&LR* Also see **Four A's.**

iteration *iMedia* Repetition or process of repeating. **2** Programming: an iteration (in a loop) is one complete run with the test expression and statements having been executed.

iterative theory *iMedia* Using procedures in which the repetition of a sequence of operations yields results successfully closer to a desired result.

itinerant *Crit&Eval* One who travels from place to place to perform work. ‹itinerant musician›

ITN *Journ,. Rdio/TV* » **Independent Television News**

Ivy League look *Fashn* Style worn originally in the 1940s and 1950s by college men at Eastern universities; pants and jackets were slim cut.

- J -

J/K *InfoMgt* Just Kidding.

jabot *Fashn* Ornamental cascade of **ruffles** or **frills** down the front of a shirt, blouse, or dress.

jack *PerfA&C* triangular brace

jacket *InfoMgt* Plastic or cardboard container that holds a **floppy disk**

jacket *LitArts* » **dust jacket** of a book

jacket *RecA&S* Paper or thin cardboard envelope for a phonograph record.

jackpot *Flm&Vid* » **88th episode**

Jackson, Michael (1958-, pop comp., dncr., sngr., prod.) *ArtPerf, MusArts* Controversial, pop **icon.** *Also see* **camp, cease-and-desist order, cross-dressing, leak**

jacquard *Fashn* Fabric with an intricately- woven pattern.

jaded *Crit&Eval* **1** Worn out; wearied. **2** Dulled by surfeit; sated. **3 Cynically** or pretentiously callous.

jam *MusArts* Informal performance of solo and group improvisation with or without an audience.

jam *Rdio/TV* To interfere with reception of broadcast signals by electronic means.

jamboree *PA-Variety* noisy celebration

jammed lead (leed) *BcstJourn* Lead sentence that attempts to include all story facts. Should be avoided.

jargon *Genl* Specialized or technical language of a trade, profession, or similar group. *Also see* **argot, slang, vernacular.**

jass *MusArts* Early 1900s spelling of **jazz.** *Origin* One theory has it that "jass" may have been preferred by some because of the sexual connotation of "jazz,: as in "Jazz me, baby!" *Also see* **jazz, Jazz Styles, ODJB.**

JATP *MusArts, RecA&S* » **Jazz at the Philharmonic**

jaunty *Crit&Eval* **1** Having a buoyant or self-confident air; brisk. **2** Crisp and dapper in appearance; **natty.**

Java *InfoMgt* **A programming language** developed by Sun Microsystems in the early 1990s, it is the current favorite of the computer industry. *Also see* **Programming Languages.**

JavaScript *iMedia* (Formerly LiveScript) Netscape's simple, cross-platform, **World-Wide Web** scripting language, only very vaguely related to Java.

jaz, jazz *Cult&Soc, MusArts* **1** First appeared in print as early as 1913 – the words meant "vigorous," "energetic" – but the term "jass band" would not be used until 1915-17 when New Orleans bands in Chicago identified themselves as such. — "The Original Dixieland Jass Band (ODJB)" by Tim Gracyk (www.garlic.com/~tgracyk/odjb.htm) **2** Not appearing in print was the definition meaning sexual intercourse as in a popular song lyric: "Jazz me, baby, eight to the bar!" (c. 1915)

Jazz at the Philharmonic (JATP) *MusArts, RecA&S* Since the mid-1940s, umbrella title for jazz concerts, festivals, recordings, and videos — all produced by **Norman Granz.**

jazz characteristics *MusArts* Three basic characteristics of jazz: 1 Improvisation i.e, composing on your feet; 2 Moving time, i.e, swing; 3 Individual voice, i.e., a unique sound like no one else, felt from the inside out [When and if jazz can be simply defined it will have ceased to be a continuously creative music.].

jazz dance *Dnce* **1** In the 1950s and 1960s, as a stage dance, a style emerged combining elements of **ballet, modern dance,**

J

and **tap dance. 2** As a social dance, it partially originated with 19th century black social dances. **<cakewalk, turkey trot>** *Also see* **Dances**.

Jazz Foundation of America, Inc. (JFA) *MusArts* **Nonprofit** organization formed "to stimulate and promote jazz music and jazz history by aiding in the collection and preservation of jazz **archives**, and in assisting educational programs regarding jazz. In addition, it is committed to assisting professional jazz musicians in coping with their social, medical and career development needs through its **Jazz Musicians' Emergency Fund**."

jazz narrative aesthetic *Aes&Creat LitArts* Created by Ralph Ellison in his masterpiece, *Invisible Man*, it involves "rhythm and **riff** repetition reminiscent of jazz structure." — *Dictionary of Global Culture*.

jazz origins *Cult&Soc, MusArts* "The fusion of blues and ragtime with brass-band and syncopated dance music resulted in the music called jazz."… "Ironically, the first groups to formally introduce jazz to the public were white orchestras from New Orleans, which had developed there under the influence of Negro groups. In 1915 the **Lamb's Club** of Chicago hired a white band, under the direction of **Tom Brown**, that was billed as "**Brown's Dixieland Jass Band**, Direct from New Orleans, Best Dance Music in Chicago." — **Eileen Southern**. *Also see* **Jazz Styles**.

jazz recording *MusArts, RecA&S* First jazz recording made in 1917 by a white band: **Nick LaRocca** (1889-1961, jazz bndldr.) and his **Original Dixieland Jazz Band** "The **Victor Recording Company** [forerunner of **RCA Victor**] had offered a recording contract earlier to **Freddie Keppard** (1889-1933, New Orleans-born jazz cornet, bndldr.), and **That Creole Band** but it was refused — Keppard was fearful that other trumpet players would 'steal his stuff.' — **Eileen Southern**

Jazz Singer, The *Flm&Vid, Sci&Tech* First popular **talkie**, starring **Al Jolson** (1927) *Also see* **Harry Warner**.

Jazz Styles *ColEntry, MusArts* » **Afro-Cuban** —, bebop, classic —, cool —, dixieland —, Dixieland —, hard bop, jass, Latin —, loft —, mainstream —, modal —, modern —, New Orleans —, New York Jazz, swing, trad, West Coast —, Western swing.

jazz tap *Dnce* "Jazz tap is a venerable American dance form that combines the soul of the jazz musician with the body of the dancer." — Sally Sommer (dance critic) *Also see* **Dances**, **tap dance**.

Jazzmobile, Inc. (JMI) *Crit&Eval, MusArts* **Nonprofit** enterprise in **Harlem** (NYC) founded in the 1960s by **Dr. Billy Taylor** that provides jazz instrumental training and live concerts for young musicians.

Jazznet *ArtPerf, MusArts* National network of 12 regional jazz presenters organized in cooperation with the **National Endowment for the Arts**, funded by Nonprofit Facilities Fund of New York by a 1999 grant from **Doris Duke Charitable Foundation**. The presenters commission new jazz works, finance artists' residencies, and sponsor educational and community-based jazz programs.

jazzy *Crit&Eval* **1** Resembling jazz in some form or style. **2** Showy; flashy. <a jazzy tie>

JCL *InfoMgt* **Job Control Language**; computer language used to allocate computer resources prior to processing.

Jefferson, Thomas (1743-1826, pol. philos., educ., archt. 3rd U.S. Pres. 1801-1809) *ArtPerf, Crit&Eval, Law&Pol* He drafted the Declaration of Independence (1776), designed his own estate, Monticello, and U. of Virginia buildings. *Also see* **Thomas**.

jenny *Flm&Vid* portable electric generator

Jerry Lewis Syndrome *Crit&Eval* Condition exemplified by "public figures who feel that they have been badly used by the local papers often find that solace awaits them in admiring throngs overseas." — **Henry Louis Gates Jr**. *Origin* Propensity of **Jerry Lewis** (1925-, act., comic, dir-prod.) to bask in the remarkable adulation by the French critics and public.

jester *PA-Variety* **Fool** or **buffoon** at **medieval** courts. COURT JESTER*Also see* **clown**.

jeté (je-tay, Fr. for "thrown") *Dnce* (Ballet) Jump from one leg to the other. *Also see* **grand jeté**.

jewel box *RecA&S* The plastic case enclosing a CD disk recording.

JFA *MusArts* » **Jazz Foundation of America, Inc.**

jig *Music, Dnce* Any of various lively dances in triple time; the

music for such a dance. GIGUE

jiggy *Crit&Eval, MusArts* Ambiguous in meaning but generally used by rappers as a positive feeling or a good thing to do.

Jim Crow *Cult&Soc* Practice of discriminating against African Americans. *Also see* **Crow Jim**. *Origin* A character impersonating a plantation slave as performed in **blackface minstrelsy**. *Also see* **Zip Coon**.

jingle*Rdio/TV* Catchy, often musical advertising slogan or message. *Also see* **commercial**.

jingo *Crit&Eval, Law&Pol* One who vociferously supports one's country, esp. one who supports a belligerent foreign policy; **a chauvinistic** patriot. *Also see* **ideologue**.

JIT *Eco&Fin, Mgt, Mktg* **Just in Time**. **Inventory** control system (pioneered by the Japanese government) in which raw material or parts for a company's products are delivered to that company "just in time" for production or processing thereby savings in warehouse requirements as well as cash tied up in raw material purchases. Goal of JIT is zero inventory with 100% quality. *Also see* **Inventory Methods**.

JIT *HR&LR* Just in Time training.

jitterbug *Dnce* **1** Quick-tempo swing or jazz music and consisting of various **two-step** patterns **embellished** with twirls and sometimes acrobatic maneuvers. **2** One who performs this dance. *Also see* **Dances**.

jive *Crit&Eval* Deceptive, nonsensical, or glib talk.

jive *Cult&Soc* Generally, black slang. *Origin* Code word of those in the know. Possibly coined by Louis Armstrong in mid-1920s. "Jive is a language in motion. It supplies the answer to the hunger for the unusual, the exotic, the picturesque in speech. It is a medium of escape, a safety valve of people pressed against the wall for centuries, deprived of the advantages of complete social, economic, moral and intellectual freedom." (1944) — Dan Burley. *Also see* **hip-hop**, **soul**.

jive *MusArts* **1** Jazz or swing music. **2** Jargon of jazz musicians.

jnt. *LegAsp* joint

JOA *Journ, Mgt* **Joint Operating Agreement** permits two rival newspapers in the same city to use the same presses, distribution system, and advertising staff but maintain separate editorial departments.

Joan Shorenstein Center for Press, Politics, and Public Policy *InfoMgt, Journ* Harvard U. **think tank**.

job action *HR&LR* Worker's strike or slowdown to protest a company decision.

Job Control Language (JCL) *InfoMgt* » **JCL**

job *InfoMgt* **1** Program application that may consist of several steps but is performed as a single logical unit. **2** Task for a computer.

job lot *Mktg* Collection of cheap items.

job specification *EntreP* List of skills and abilities needed to perform a specific job.

job-sharing *HR&LR* Practice whereby the responsibility for one job is shared between two or more alternating part-time workers.

jobber *Mktg* One who buys merchandise from manufacturers and sells it to retailers. *Also see* **Distributors**.

jodhpurs *Fashn* Wide-hipped riding pants of heavy cloth, fitting tightly from knee to ankle.

jog*Flm&Vid* To move a picture slowly frame by frame.

John F. Kennedy Center for the Performing Arts *Cult&Soc, Mgt, MusArts,TheatArts* **1** Designated by Congress as the **National Cultural Center** and the official memorial in Washington, DC, to President John F. Kennedy (1917-63, 35th U.S. Pres., 1961-63, U.S. Rep, 1947-53, Sen. 1953-60. Assassinated in Dallas, Texas, on November 22, 1963.) **2** Designed by Edward Durrell Stone, the center includes an opera house, a concert hall, several theaters, and a library. *Also see* **Kennedy Center Honors**.

joint (jnt.) *Crit&Eval* Cheap or disreputable gathering place.

joint *Genl* marijuana cigarette

joint (jnt.) *LegAsp* Regarded as one legal body; united in identity of interest or liability.

joint council *HR&LR* Committee of representatives from both unions and management to settle jurisdictional and contractual disputes.

joint venture *EntreP* Partnership between two companies for the purpose of developing or marketing a single product.

J

Joint Operating Agreement *Journ, Mgt* » **JOA**

Joint Photographic Experts Group *iMedia* » **JPEG**

joint venture *Mgt* Partnership or **conglomerate**, formed often to share risk or expertise. *Also see* **consortium.**

joint work *IntelProp* "Work prepared by two or more authors with the intention that their contributions be merged into inseparable or interdependent parts of a unitary whole." — Section 101, 1976 Copyright Act. <song written by a separate composer and lyricist, a recording produced by an artist and a record producer under a **coauthorship** agreement> Ownership of copyright belongs to the coauthors unless transferred.

joke *Crit&Eval* "A joke is an art form, a very swift, very short story. It is a structured narrative, designed to make a point with force. That force is intensified by the comic ingredient of surprise." — Leo Rosten, (» **humor**) *Also see* **humor.**

Jolson, **Al** (1886-1960; singer) *ArtPerf, Flm&Vid, MusArts, PA-Variety* Superstar pop film/stage/radio/vaude singer and sometime actor (in)famous for his **blackface** makeup. *Also see* ***Jazz Singer*, talkie, Harry Warner.**

Jones, **Quincy** (1933-, Film/recording arr-cond., prod., **broadcast media** and **print media** entrepreneur) *ArtPerf, MusArts, Flm&Vid, Mgt, Rdio/TV, RecA&S* Awards: **Oscar** for score of *Pawnbroker*, many **Grammys**. *Also see* **black music, content, multimedia, praise shouter, rap.**

jongleur *PerfA&C* Wandering **minstrel**, poet, or entertainer in **medieval** England and France.

Joseph Jefferson Awards *TheatArts* Founded in 1968, the Awards honor excellence in the Chicago theater. *Also see* **Awards & Prizes.**

jour. *HR&LR, Journ* **journal, journalist, journeyman**

journal *E&F-Acc* **1** Chronological accounting record of an **entity's** transactions. **2** Book of original entry in a double-entry system, listing all transactions and indicating the accounts to which they belong. **3 Daybook.**

journal *Genl* **diary**

journal *Journ* newspaper

journal *LitArts* Periodical containing articles of interest to a particular group or profession. <*Black Music Research Journal*>

journalese *Journ* Style of writing often held to be characteristic of newspapers and magazines, distinguished by clichés, sensationalism, and triteness of thought.

journalism *Journ* Collecting, writing, editing, and presentation of news or news articles in newspapers and magazines and in radio and TV broadcasts.

journalist (journ.) *Journ* **1** One whose occupation is journalism. **2** One who keeps a **journal**.

Journals *ColEntry,E&F-Acc* » **cash disbursement journal, cash receipts journal, general journal, purchase journal, purchase journal, sales journal.**

journeyman (jour.) *HR&LR* **1** One who has fully served an apprenticeship in a trade or craft and is a qualified worker in another's employ. **2** Experienced and competent but undistinguished worker.

joystick *iMedia* Control device, often attached to a fixed base, for controlling computers or machines by moving in 2 dimensions (forward/back, right/left) on its base.

JPEG *iMedia* Joint Photographic Experts Group. Lossy type of data compression for still pictures; it offers data compression of between two and 100 times and is often used to compress photographs or images with a lot of detail.

JPG *iMedia* » **JPEG**

juba *Dnce* Group dance of West African origin, characterized by complex rhythmic clapping and body movements and practiced on plantations by slaves in the southern U.S. (18th and 19th centuries) *Also see* **Dances.**

jubilant *Crit&Eval* Exultingly joyful.

judgment (Am.) *also* **judgement** (Brit.) *Crit&Eval* **1** Psychic faculty or function permitting one to decide about the worth of something according to appropriate standards; a decision or proposition that is the outcome of exercising this faculty or function. **2** Formation of an opinion after consideration or deliberation. "Nor is it possible to exclude judgment from entering into **esthetic** perception." — **John Dewey**

judgmental models *EntreP* Forecasting models which are qualitative and essentially use estimates based on expert opinion.

jump cut *BcstJourn* Sudden visual jerk in the image at the edit point of two shots that have very similar but not identical pictures. *Ex.* joining of two close-ups of the same person when each has the face in different portions of the frame. A jump cut could also occur if the person was wearing glasses in one shot but not the other. Two medium shots of the same subject might jump if taken from the same spot.

junk bonds *EntreP* Bond issued by a corporation or municipal government which is rated B or less and sold at a deep discount from the face amount ($1,000)

judgment *LegAsp* Determination of a court of law; a judicial decision.

Judicial Improvement Act of 1990 *IntelProp* Authorizes the **Register of Copyright** to accept and record any document pertaining to computer software and to issue a **certificate of recordation** to the recorder.

jug *MusInstr* Ceramic or glass jar or jug that produces a tuba-like sound when the player blows across the top soda bottle. *Also see* **Little Instruments.**

jug band *MusArts* **Country blues** or comedic music group that uses unconventional or improvised instruments. <crockery jugs, banjos, harmonicas, mandolins, **washboards**, **bones** or **spoons**, and **kazoos**>

juggler *ArtPerf, PA-Variety* One who can keep two or more objects in the air at one time by alternately tossing and catching them, or perform other tricks of manual dexterity.

juggler *Eco&Fin* Person, group, or organization that uses tricks, deception, or fraud. <The books were juggled to hide the true amount of loss>

juice *Crit&Eval* Power.

juice *MusArts* **1** Quality that imparts identity and vitality; essence. <Sing it again, this time with juice>

juice *PerfA&C Sci&Tech* Electric power.

juke joint *also* **juke** (**Gullah**, "juke" or "joog," i.e., disorderly, wicked) *Cult&Soc* **1** Bar or roadhouse offering cheap drinks, food, and music for dancing often to a **jukebox**. **2** To dance in a style befitting the ambiance of the **venue**.

jukebox *or* **juke box** *RecA&S* Coin-operated phonograph, became popular in bars when **Prohibition** was repealed in 1933 *Also see* **juke, Repeal.**

jukebox *InfoMgt* » **CD-ROM changer**

jump cut *Flm&Vid* Cut to slightly later action, creating an effect of discontinuity or acceleration.

jungle *Dnce, MusArts* "Frenzied, heavily percussive dance sound, it has been described as Britain's answer to **gangsta rap**." — Anita M. Samuels (dance critic)

junior agent *Mgt* Young, aspiring talent agent. *Also see* **Talent Agencies.**

junket *Flm&Vid* Publicity-generating, expense-paid promotional trip often "on location" for the press during which the key cast and crew of an upcoming movie give interviews.

junket *Mktg, RecA&S* Promotion tour by a recording artist or group.

junkie *also* **junky** *Crit&Eval* One who has an insatiable interest or devotion. <sports junkie> *Also see* **groupie.**

Jupiter (Roman Mythology) *Cult&Soc* Supreme god, patron of the Roman state and brother and husband of Juno. JOVE *Also see* **Muses. Zeus.**

jurisdiction *LegAsp* Right and power to interpret and apply the law. <Federal courts have jurisdiction in disputes between states; **AFTRA** has jurisdiction over all performers, except instrumental musicians, in radio, taped TV, and recordings>

jury texts *MusArts* Many verses sung to one tune, usu. with some new words appearing with each subsequent recording.

Just in Time (JIT) *Eco&Fin, Mgt, Mktg* » **JIT**

just-in-time inventory system *EntreP* Method of reducing inventory levels to an absolute minimum.

justice *Ethcs&Phil, Law&Pol* All laws and social philosophy are about what justice is, and how to administer it — how to preserve and promote human welfare. Distributive justice concerns itself with how to figure out the "proper" distribution of scarce but valuable resources. Justice also usu. means giving people what they "deserve" which means figuring out what they "deserve." "Injustice is relatively easy to bear; what stings is justice." —

K

H. L. Mencken

Justice *Law&Pol* Member, U.S. Supreme Court.

justify *Crit&Eval* To properly align data relating to a specific reference.

justify *iMedia, VA-Prntng* Set or arrange type to be flush left and right to the margins thus having the margins aligned with no indentations. JUSTIFICATION

juvenile *ArtPerf* Young male in a dramatic work. *Also see* **ingénue**.

juxtapose *Crit&Eval* To place side by side for comparison or contrast.

- K -

k *InfoMgt* kilobyte Specifically, 1024 bytes of data, used to describe memory size. <24K means a (24 x 1024 =) 24,576 byte memory system> *Also see* **byte, gigabyte, megabyte**.

Kay, Alan (1940-) *iMedia* Pioneer in the development of a graphical user interface, developed the **Dynabook** in the 1970's (regarded as the first personal computer) and worked at the Palo Alto Research Center.

Keogh plan *EntreP* Retirement plan for self-employed individuals in sole proprietorships and partnerships. Under the laws governing Keogh a retirement plan can be established based on profit sharing, money purchase or paired. Percentage and total contribution may differ depending on the type of Keogh plan selected.

key *BcstJourn* » **CG**

key light *PerfA&C* brightest light on a particular scene

key-person insurance *EntreP* Coverage that protects against the death of a company's key personnel.

keyframe *iMedia* Any **frame** in which a particular aspect of an item (its size, location, color, etc.) is specifically defined. non-keyframe frames will then contain interpolated values.

keying *iMedia* Act of replacing a particular area of color in an image or video with another image or video. *Also see* **blue screen, chroma key.**

Keynesian economics *EntreP* School of economic thought that provides insights into the economy when it operates away from full employment.

Keynesian fiscal policy *EntreP* Use of taxes and government spending to affect the level of GDP in the short run.

keywords *BcstJourn* Items in a story that trigger interest in themes, perspective, events, or details.

kabuki *also* **Kabuki** *TheatArts* Type of popular Japanese drama, evolved from the older **No** theater, in which elaborately costumed performers, nowadays men only, use stylized movements, dances, and songs in order to enact tragedies and comedies. *Also see* **Theaters & Theatres.**

kalimba *MusInstr* African instrument in the shape of a wooden box set with metal bars that are plucked with the fingers. FINGER PIANO, HAND PIANO

Kanin, Garson (1912-??, Stage/film dir.-prod., dram., act., scrnwrtr. fictwri., biog) *ArtPerf, Flm&Vid, LitArts,TheatArts* <*Born Yesterday* (Film and play), *Funny Girl* (play)> *Also see* **schizophrenia**

Kant, Immanuel (1724-1804, Ger. philos.) *Ethcs&Phil* He argued that reason is the means by which the **phenomena** of experience are translated into understanding. <*Critique of Pure Reason* (1781), *Critique of Practical Reason* (1788)> His system of ethics is based on the **categorical imperative.** *Also see* **genius.**

karaoke *RecA&S* Big thing in Japan and U.S. motel lounges: a device which combines taped pop songs and a microphone that, when connected to a PA system, allows a bar or club patron to sing live, just like the stars. Fun for the whole family and a sure-fire money maker for the bar owner. *Also see* **KISA**.

Karaoke International Sing-Along Association (KISA) *RecA&S* » **KISA**

Kaufman, George S. (1889-1961, dram., play doctor, critic, wit) *Crit&Eval, LitArts,TheatArts* Noted for his many collaborations. <*Dinner at Eight* (1932) with **Edna Ferber**, *You Can't Take It with You* (1936) with **Moss Hart**> *Also see* **satire.**

Kazan, Elia (1909-, Turkish-born stage/film dir.) *ArtPerf, Flm&Vid, TheatArts* An early member of the **Group Theater** and a founder of the **Actors Studio**. Controversial witness in the **HUAC witchhunt**. <stage dir., *A Streetcar Named Desire* (1947); film dir., *On the Waterfront* (1954)>

kazoo *MusInstr* Toy instrument with a membrane that produces a sound when a player hums or sings into the mouthpiece. Played

in early **country blues** bands. *Also see* **jug bands, Little Instruments.**

kc. *Rdio/TV* » **kilocycle**

Keith-Orpheum *PA-Variety* **vaudeville** theater circuit

Kennedy Center *Cult&Soc* » **John F. Kennedy Center for the Performing Arts**

Kennedy Center Honors *ArtPerf, Cult&Soc* Annual awards to outstanding performers in dance, film, music, and theatre under the auspices of the **John F. Kennedy Center for the Performing Arts** at the **National Cultural Center** in Washington, DC. Two-hour annual honors program is televised each December via Public Television Network.

Kennedy, John F.(itzgerald) (1917-63, 35th U.S. Pres., 1961-63) *Law&Pol* Youngest president established the Peace Corps (1961) and advocated civil rights reform. President Kennedy was assassinated in Dallas, Texas, on November 22, 1963 *Also see* **John F. Kennedy Center for the Performing Arts, Kennedy Center Honors.**

kern *VA-Prntng* Portion of a typeface that projects beyond the body or shank of a character.

kerning *iMedia, VA-Prntng* Control of the spacing between letters, ofen used to alter the spacing of letters in a headline or masthead.

kerosene journalism *Journ* "Reporters pour kerosene on whatever smoke they can find, before they determine what's smoking and why. The flames that result can come from arson, not journalism." — **Ben Bradlee**

kettle drummer *MusArts* » **timpanist**

kettledrum *MusInstr* Large copper or brass hemispheric drum, with a parchment or plastic head, tuned by adjusting the tension. *Also see* **Musical Instrument Families.**

key *Mktg* To identify by one or more letters or numerals. <The mail order coupon was keyed 040196NK to indicate it appeared in the April 1996 issue of the *New Yorker*>

key *MusArts* **1** Main **pitch** or tonal center to which all of the composition's pitches are related. <George Gershwin's *Concerto in F*> **2 Pitch** of a voice. <sing in a low key> **3** Certain tone or level of intensity of a musical performance. <The whole performance was low-key>

key *MusInstr* Button or lever on a musical instrument that can modulate the sound called Gothic. <Avant-Garde, Geneva, Franklin Gothic, Futura, Helvetica, Univers>

key *TheatArts* Characteristic tone or level of intensity of a speech or performance. <The cast gave a particularly low-keyed performance>

Key Caps *InfoMgt* **Desk accessory that** displays the standard and optional characters available in each font in the computer system.

key club *PA-Variety* Sometimes private club featuring liquor, entertainment, and the illusion of being elite. [Disappearing refuge for males excited by mini-dressed, female servers.].

key date *Mgt* When booking a tour, the date that has the best potential around which other dates can be booked.

key grip *Flm&Vid* Head of the **grip** crew.

key light *Flm&Vid* Main source of illumination to light the subject. Its direction and intensity in relation to **fill light** establishes the mood of the scene. *Also see* **Stage Lighting, subsidiary lighting.**

key man clause *LegAsp* Management contract provision that allows the artist to cancel the contract without prejudice if a particular person leaves the management company.

key numbers *Flm&Vid* » **edge numbers**

key signature *MusArts* Sharps or flats placed at the beginning of a composition to indicate its key.

key station *Rdio/TV* Prime originating station for a radio or TV broadcast.

key words *InfoMgt* Important words in a phrase, sentence, or quotation that may used as a reference point for finding other words or information.

key-escrow *InfoMgt* Unique field to identify a record in a computer field.

key. *MusInstr* **keyboard**

keyboard (key.) *InfoMgt, MusInstr* Set of keys used to activate a computer or a musical instrument. KEYBOARD PLAYER

keyboard shortcut *InfoMgt* Combination of keys that you can press to give a command or perform a task without using a

K

mouse. COMMAND-KEY EQUIVALENT, KEYBOARD EQUIV-ALENT, SHORTCUT

keyboards *MusInstr* Musical instruments activated by a keyboard. <accordion, harpsichord, organ, piano, **synthesizer**, and the like>

keynote *Crit&Eval* Prime underlying theme. <keynote address>

keynote *InfoMgt* Word used as a reference point for finding other words or information.

keynote *MusArts* **1** First note of a musical key. **2** Prime underlying musical theme.

keynote address *Law&Pol* Opening address at a political convention that outlines the issues to be considered. **keynote speech.**

keyword *InfoMgt* Word used as a shortcut to a specific destination within a **database** or online service.

khoonei *MusArts* Throat-singing (Southern Siberia, Russia)

kHz *Rdio/TV* » **kilohertz**

kibitz (Yinglish) *Crit&Eval* To look on and offer unwanted, meddlesome advice.

kibitzer (Yinglish) *Crit&Eval* One who offers unwanted, meddlesome advice.

kick *Crit&Eval* Feeling of pleasurable stimulation. <*I Get a Kick Out of You* by **Cole Porter**> *Also see* **bang.**

kicker *Crit&Eval* **1** Informal. Sudden, surprising turn of events or ending; a twist. **2** Tricky or concealed condition; a pitfall.

kicker *Journ, Rdio/TV* Light news story with strong human interest used to lead into a **commercial.**

kicks *Crit&Eval* Fun, enjoyment. <Let's do (whatever) for kicks>

kill *Crit&Eval* Overwhelm with hilarity, pleasure, or admiration:

kill *Flm&Vid,PerfA&C* Turn off a certain light or lights.

kill *Journ* Mark for deletion; rule out:

kill *Law&Pol* Prevent passage of a bill; veto **LaRoca, Nick** *MusArts* Trombonist and leader, **Original Dixieland Jazz Band.**

kill fee *Journ* Payment to a free-lance writer when a previously accepted article is not published.

kilobyte (K) *iMedia, InfoMgt* » **K**

kilocycle (kc) *InfoMgt* » **kilohertz**

kilohertz (kHz) *Sci&Tech* One thousand **hertz.**

kimono *Fashn* **1** Long, wide-sleeved Japanese robelike dress worn with an **obi** and often elaborately decorated. **2** Loose robe worn chiefly by women.

kinderslut *Fashn* Trendy look for young women (ca. 1995) "combines mock-Midwestern schoolgirl sweet with trashy makeup and an ironic, knowing attitude. All the accessories are here: bright-plastic barrettes, red 'Hello Kitty' pencil cases, plastic charms, tiny backpacks — and plenty of pink. Central to the look is the baby T-shirt." — Gareth Cook (cult. critic)

kinescope *Flm&Vid, Rdio/TV* Film of a transmitted TV program. *Also see* **picture tube.**

kinetic *Crit&Eval* Relating to, or produced by motion.

kinetic art *VisArts* Art form <an assemblage or a sculpture>, influenced by **futurism** and **dadaism**, made up of parts designed to be set in motion by an internal mechanism or an external stimulus, such as light or air. <**Marcel Duchamp's** *The Mobile* (The first kinetic art work)>

kineticism *VisArts* Theory or practice of kinetic art.

kinetoscope *Flm&Vid* Moving picture **peep-show** for a single viewer invented by **Thomas Edison.**

King, The *ArtPerf, MusArts* » **Elvis Presley**

King, Martin Luther Jr. (1929-68) *Ethcs&Phil* Alabama minister whose eloquence and commitment to nonviolent tactics formed the foundation of the U.S. civil rights movement of the 1950s and 1960s. Among the many peaceful demonstrations he led was the 1963 March on Washington, at which he delivered his "I have a dream" speech. He won the 1964 **Nobel** Peace Prize, four years before he was assassinated in Memphis. *Also see* **civil disobedience, Mahatma Gandhi.**

kingpin *Mgt* Most important person or element in an enterprise or a system.

kinky *Crit&Eval* Showing or appealing to **bizarre** or deviant tastes, esp. of a sexual or **erotic** nature.

kiosk *Mktg* **1** Small structure, often open on one or more sides, used as a newsstand or booth or an **ATM. 2** Cylindrical structure on which advertisements are posted. <an opera kiosk> *Also see* **kiosk ticketing.**

kiosk ticketing *Mktg* To use an **ATM** to buy and obtain tickets to an event by choosing seats from the **ATM** screen.

KISA *RecA&S* **Nonprofit** organized to promote trade, interest, commerce, and cooperation to and for the karaoke/sing-a-long industry.

kiss and tell *Crit&Eval* Article, a book, an interview, or a film containing confidential or embarrassing information based on firsthand knowledge.

kitsch *VisArts* **Pretentious** bad taste "The epitome of all that is **spurious** in the life of our times." — Clement Greenberg

kleig light *Flm&Vid* Powerful carbon-arc lamp producing an intense light and used esp. in making movies before lasers and other modern technologies. *Origin* **John H. Kleigl** (1869-1959) and his brother **Anton T. Kleigl** (1872-1927), German-born lighting experts. *Also see* **Stage Lighting.**

Kleigl, Anton T. and **John H.** *Flm&Vid* » **kleig light**

klezmer (Hebrew for "instruments of song") *MusArts* **1** In its modern style, klezmer is Jewish folk-jazz featuring wailing clarinet and swinging, **schmaltzy** fiddle. <The solo clarinet beginning **George Gershwin's** *Rhapsody in Blue*> **2** Jewish folk music played by small, traditionally **itinerant** bands.

kludge (var. **kluge**) *InfoMgt* **1** Something that works for the wrong reason. **2** A **crock** that works.

kludgy *InfoMgt* Said of a computer system made up of poorly matched elements.

klutz (kluts, Yinglish) *Crit&Eval* Blockhead, graceless bungler, heavy-handed, all-thumbed.

knack *Crit&Eval* **1** Clever way of doing something. **2** Specific talent for something. <A good instructor has the knack of simplifying a complex subject>

knit *Fashn* Fabric or garment made by knitting.

knock-off *Fashn* Unauthorized copy or imitation of designer clothing.

knowledge base *InfoMgt* That part of an expert system containing the base logical steps a human expert performs in analyzing a particular situation.

knowledge engineer *InfoMgt* expert programmer

knowledge of falsity *Journ, Law&Pol* » **actual malice**

Knox gelatin *Dnce* Recommended to reduce fatigue for dancers and athletes.

krewe *PA-Variety* Any of several groups – some with hereditary membership – whose members organize and participate as costumed paraders in the annual **Mardi Gras** carnival. <The Mystick Krewe of Comus founded in New Orleans in 1857, cancelled its parade in 1993 rather than integrate its membership> *Also see* **throws.**

knowledge engineer *InfoMgt* expert programmer

knowledge of falsity *Journ, Law&Pol* » **actual malice**

Knox gelatin *Dnce* Recommended to reduce fatigue for dancers and athletes.

krewe *PA-Variety* Any of several groups – some with hereditary membership – whose members organize and participate as costumed paraders in the annual **Mardi Gras** carnival. <The Mystick Krewe of Comus founded in New Orleans in 1857, cancelled its parade in 1993 rather than integrate its membership> *Also see* **throws.**

kudos (Greek for "magical glory") *Crit&Eval* Acclaim or praise for exceptional achievement. <Kudos is [*not* "are"] due her for her brilliant choreography>

Kurosawa, Akira (1910-1998, film dir-prod., pntr.) *ArtPerf, Flm&Vid* Blended Japanese folklore with Western acting styles and storytelling techniques. <*Rashomon* (1950), *Seven Samurai* (1954), *Ran* (1985) *Also see* **artist.**

kvetch (Yinglish) *Crit&Eval* Fuss, fret, complain, gripe.

- **L** -

L-85 *Fashn* Law enforced during WWII by the U.S. War Production Board restricting the use of fabric and limiting yardage: less than three yards for a dress, jackets no longer than 25 inches, limiting sweep of hem, and other restrictions.

L.E.D. *Sci&Tech* Light Emitting Diodes, common **semiconductor** light source.

L.C. *InfoMgt* **Library of Congress.**

L8R *InfoMgt* Later

L

la (lah) *MusArts* sixth tone of a **diatonic scale**

La Presse France *Journ* French-based international news agency. *Also see* **News Agencies**.

lab, labs *Sci&Tech* laboratory, laboratories

label *Fashn, RecA&S* Distinctive name or **trademark** identifying a product or manufacturer, esp. a recording company.

label *InfoMgt* Symbol or set of symbols identifying the contents of a file, memory, tape, or record.

label deal *RecA&S* Agreement between a record manufacturer/distributor and a label, i.e., a smaller record company, by which the label's operations – recording coats and operating expenses – may be partially or entirely financed by the mfgr. The label decides which artists to sign and record and decides which product shall be released and when. Agreement calls for label to receive an all-inclusive royalty on each unit sold. *Also see* **Contracts**.

labor contract *LegAsp, HR&LR* Agreement between an employer and a union of employees covering wages, hours, and conditions of employment. *Also see* **Contracts**.

labor dispute *HR&LR* Controversy involving persons in the same occupations who work for the same employer or who are affiliated with the same union.

labor intensive *EntreP* Business concern that has relatively low investment in machinery and equipment and relatively high labor costs as a percentage of its production costs.

Labor Management Relations Act *HR&LR* » **Taft-Hartley Act**

labor relations *HR&LR* Special department in major film studios and television networks to handle negotiations, press releases, and the general dissemination of partisan information.

labor union *EntreP* Organized group of workers; the objectives of the organization are to increase job security, improve working conditions, and increase wages and benefits.

Labor-management Reporting and Disclosure Act *HR&LR* » **Landrum-Griffin Act**

Labor, U.S. Department of (DOL)*HR&LR, Law&Pol* U.S. government department (est. 1913) headed by a Cabinet Secretary. *Also see* **Federal Agencies and Statutes**.

laconic (la-konick) *Crit&Eval* Use of few words; terse or concise. <**Clint Eastwood** is classically laconic> *Origin* Spartan, from the reputation of the Spartans for brevity of speech.

lacquer disc *RecA&S* Aluminum disc, used In the manufacturing of LPs, is coated on both sides with cellulose nitrate on which flat surface the heated cutting stylus produces clean and smooth grooves.

Lahr, John (1941-, drama critic, biog.) *Crit&Eval,TheatArts* Drama critic for the *Village Voice* and the *New Yorker*; his books include: *Notes on a Cowardly Lion* (1969), *Life Show* (1973) with Jonathan Price. *Also see* **empathic response, musical, musical theatre, nostalgia, personality, schlepper, youth culture**.

laid-back *Crit&Eval* Having a relaxed or casual atmosphere or character; easygoing.

laissez-faire (lay-say-fare, Fr. *for* "allow to do") *Crit&Eval* Noninterference in the affairs of others.

laissez-faire (lay-say-fare, Fr. for "allow to do")*Eco&Fin* Economic **doctrine** that opposes governmental regulation of or interference in commerce beyond the minimum necessary for a **free enterprise system** to operate according to its own economic laws.

Laliberté, Guy *ArtPerf, PA-Variety* founder president of **Cirque du Soleil**

LAM *InfoMgt* » **Library Administration & Management**

LAMDA *MusArts,TheatArts* **London Academy of Musical and Dramatic Art**. Est. 1861, in London, offering "classical teaching for the modern acting profession" and courses for Stage Managers and Technicians.

lamé *Fashn* Brocaded fabric woven with metallic threads, often of gold or silver.

lamp *Flm&Vid,PerfA&C* Device that generates light in a spotlight or floodlight; a special kind of light bulb.

LAN *iMedia, InfoMgt* **Local Area Network**. Service that allows users to access and find information through a single access point. *Also see* **Online Information Services**.

land *Crit&Eval,TheatArts* Create an **empathic response**. <Actor-singer in a musical has to simultaneously act and perform to make the song land with the audience. — **Stephen Sondheim**>

land *RecA&S* Raised portion of the grooved surface of a record disk. *Also see* **groove**.

Landrum-Griffin Act (Labor-management Reporting and Disclosure Act, 1959) *HR&LR* This act was passed to protect union members from corruption within a union: unions must have written by-laws, a bill of rights, regular financial reports — all supervised by the Secretary of Labor. *Also see* **National Labor Code**.

landscape *VisArts* **1** Scenery that can be seen in a single view: a field of wheat. **2** Style of visual art dealing with the representation of natural scenery. **3** Aspect of the land characteristic of a particular region. <The plains of Kansas>

language *InfoMgt* System of symbols and rules used for communication with or between computers.

languor *Crit&Eval* Dreamy, lazy mood.

Lanham Trade-Mark Act (1946) *IntelProp, Law&Pol* Provides for federal registration and use of **trademarks**. *Also see* **Federal Agencies and Statutes**.

lap dancer *PA-Variety* One who performs pelvic gyrations astride a seated nite club patron in return for cash payment. [Kind of a one-on-one striptease, so to speak.] *Also see* **ecdysiast**, **table dancer**.

lapel *Fashn* Part of a garment, such as a coat or jacket, that is an extension of the collar and folds back against the breast.

lapel microphone *RecA&S* Miniature **mic** with a clip that can be attached to clothing close to the performer's mouth. *Also see* **Microphones**.

laptop computer *InfoMgt* Portable computer (5-10 lbs.) operated from batteries or AC power, that offers most of the functionality of a desktop computer.

Large Scale Integration (LSI) *InfoMgt* » **LSI**

largo *MusArts* Play broadly and with dignity, more slowly than **adagio** but not as slowly as **grave**. *Also see* **Music Directions**.

laser *InfoMgt* **Light Amplification through Stimulated Emissions of Radiation**. Very dense, concentrated light beam capable of crossing great distances with little degradation of power. Lasers are basic to most computer technology.

laser disk *InfoMgt* » **optical disk**

laser printer *InfoMgt* Non-impact, low power printing device that places images on a rotating drum by a laser beam. Drum picks up a toner powder on the laser exposed areas. These areas are pressed and fused into the paper forming the characters. TYPE-WRITER

Last In, First Out *E&F-Acc* » **LIFO**

late-night entertainment *Rdio/TV* Popular type of television network programming. <*Johnny Carson, David Letterman, Tonight Show* (1954-)> *Also see* **Television Shows**.

latex *Th-MakeUp* In liquid form it is used to buildup flexible **prosthetic** pieces, attaching **crepe hair**, or creating wrinkles and texture for age. In solid form, it comes as a cap for a bald-head effect, or as pieces. <noses, chins, pouches, wrinkled foreheads, scars, burns, etc.

Latin Dance Music *Dnce, MusArts* Dance music from the Caribbean Islands, Central and South America that has influenced American pop music. <**bossa nova, bugalú, calypso, cha-cha-cha, habanera, mambo, merengue, rumba, salsa**, ska, **samba, soca, tango** plus Cuban big-band dance melodies. *Also see* **Latin music**.

Latin music *MusArts* Characterized by melodic and rhythmic influences from Brazil, Cuba, Dominican Republic, Mexico, Puerto Rico, and other Caribbean and South American cultures. *Also see* **Latin Dance Music**.

Latin percussion *MusInstr* General term for the various **percussion** instruments and accessories used in Spanish and Portuguese cultures in Africa, Europe, and the Americas. *Also see* **Musical Instrument Families**.

L

Latino *Cult&Soc* Person of **Hispanic**, esp. Latin-American, descent. *Also see* **Racial Designations**.

latitude *Flm&Vid* Film stock's ability to accommodate a certain range of lighting extremes and still produce satisfactory images.

LATPTheatArts **League of American Theatres and Producers**. Members include producers, theatre owners, and operators in the **legitimate** theatre. Principal activity is the negotiation of labor contracts and government relations. Also compiles statistics; conducts audience development, research, marketing, and educational programs.

laud *Crit&Eval* To praise.

laugh track Rdio/TV, RecA&S Recorded laughter added to a soundtrack for a radio or television show.

launch *iMedia* **1** Debut or premiere of a product. **2** To debut or premiere a product.

lavaliere microphone *RecA&S* Small **mic** designed to be worn around the neck. *Also see* **Microphones**.

lavish *Crit&Eval* Unstinting in bestowing. <The critics were lavish with their praise>

Law & Politics *Law&Pol* one of the four **Outer Forces** of **The Arts Dynamic**

law of demand *EntreP* As the price of an item decreases people will demand a larger quantity of that item, *ceteris paribus*...

law of supply *EntreP* As the payment for or price of an item increases, the quantity of the item supplied to the market will increase, *ceteris paribus*...

laws of motion economy *EntreP* Guidelines for increasing *the* efficiency of human movement and tool design.

Lawyers for the Creative Arts (LCA) *IntelProp* Illinois **nonprofit**, headquartered in Chicago, of more than 1,100 lawyers who specialize in the protection of **intellectual property**. [For information about similar groups in the U.S., contact the local bar association or the city, county, or state arts council.].

lay an egg *Crit&Eval* Total failure, a flop. <"Wall Street Lays an Egg," *Variety*, re the stock market crash that foretold the Great Depression>

lay down *RecA&S* Copying tracks onto a multitrack tape plus possible sweetening and SMPTE **time code**.

lay-down date *LitArts, Mktg* When a book first appears on bookstores' shelves.

layoff *HR&LR* Dropping a worker temporarily from the payroll because of a lack of work, the intention is to re-hire when needed.

layout *InfoMgt* Schematic arrangement of circuitry

layout *VA-Prntng* **1** Art or process of arranging printed or graphic matter on a page. **2** Overall design of a page, spread, or book, inc.: page and type size, typeface, and the arrangement of titles and page numbers. **3** Page or set of pages marked to indicate this design.

LBO *Eco&Fin, Mgt* » **leveraged buy out**

lc *VA-Prntng* » **lowercase**

LCA *IntelProp* » **Lawyers for the Creative Arts** (Chicago)

LCD *InfoMgt* **Liquid Crystal Display** Type of computer display that sandwiches a liquid compound between two transparent electrodes. LCD screens used in laptop computers because they consume less power than a standard **monitor**.

LCM *E&F-Acc* **Lower of cost or market**. Requires that an asset be reported in the **financial statements** at the lower of its historical cost or its **market value**.

Lea Act (1952) *HR&LR, Law&Pol, Rdio/TV, RecA&S* This statute, lobbied by the broadcast networks (who then owned the two major record companies) effectively prohibits anyone, particularly members of the **American Federation of Musicians** (AFM), from interfering in any way with the (free) broadcasting of records, thus effectively prevents recording artists from collecting airplay royalties from Radio/TV stations. [The **intellectual property** of the authors and composers are protected but not the creativity and labor of the musicians.] *Also see* **Federal Agencies and Statutes, royalties**.

lead (leed) *Dnce* **1** Guide a partner. **2** Start a dance step on a specified foot.

lead (leed) *Flm&Vid,TheatArts* Principal role in a film or theatrical production.

lead (leed) *Journ* **1** Introductory portion of a news story. <The news program led with the election results> **2** Important, prominently displayed news story. <The page one election **roundup** led with the local race for mayor> *Also see* **above-the-fold**.

lead (leed) *MusArts* Direct a musical performance. <lead an orchestra> *Also see* **leader**.

lead (leed) *Sci&Tech* Conductor by which one circuit element is electrically connected to another.

lead (led) *VA-Prntng* In letterpress printing: a thin strip of metal used to separate lines of type.

lead gift (leed gift) *Fndng* Any significant gift made at the beginning of a campaign that encourages others to make gifts of a similar size.

lead sheet (leed sheet) *Flm&Vid* Musical **synchronization** sheet for either *animation* or live action.

lead sheet (leed sheet) *MusArts* Usually a hand-made reproduction on paper of a newly-written song.

lead time (leed time) *Crit&Eval* Time between the initial stage of a project or policy and the appearance of results.

lead trumpet (leed trumpet) *MusArts* "The lead trumpeter's job is to keep the trumpet **section** in order, so opportunities for improvisation are rare." — Peter Watrous (1958-, pop/jazz critic)

lead-in *BcstJourn* » **writeup**

lead-in *MusArts,PerfA&C* Introduction or **transition** by an **announcer** or **master of ceremonies** to a musical number or speciality.

lead-in *Rdio/TV* Program that precedes another program.

lead-out (leed-out)*Rdio/TV* Program that immediately follows another program.

leader (ldr.) *ArtPerf, MusArts* **1** Conductor of a musical ensemble. **2** Principal performer in an orchestral **section**.

leader*Eco&Fin* **Economic indicator** that tends to foretell a change in the economy.

leader *Flm&Vid, RecA&S* Blank section at the start of a reel of film or recording tape.

leader *Mgt* Individual who takes the risk of motivating people into new and unknown areas of business and/or markets.

leader *Mktg* Article offered by a retail store at cost or less than cost to attract customers. LOSS LEADER

leader *VA-Prntng* Dots or dashes in a row leading the eye across the page. <index entry, p. 17>

leadership *Fndng* Most important element of any campaign organization, together with the case and **fields of support**. Campaign leaders provide the drive and enthusiasm essential to motivate the volunteers.

leadership *Mgt* **1** Position or office of a leader. **2** Capacity or ability to lead; the willingness to go where nobody has gone before.

leading (ledd-ing) *iMedia, VA-Prntng* Space between lines of printed type. <There are nine points of leading between the lines in this paragraph; 11 pts between paragraphs>

leading lady *Flm&Vid,TheatArts* Female star of a production.

leading man *Flm&Vid,TheatArts* Male star of a production.

leading tone *MusArts* Seventh degree or tone of the scale; a **semitone** below the **tonic**.

leaf *VA-Prntng* Any of the sheets of paper bound in a book, each side of which constitutes a page. LEAVES

League of New York Theatres and Producers (LATP)*PerfA&C* » **LATP** *Also see* **Producers**.

League of Off-Broadway Theatres and Producers (LOBL)*PerfA&C* » **LOBL**

League of Resident Theaters*PerfA&C* **Nonprofit** of 66 major theater companies in the U.S.

leak *Ethcs&Phil* To disclose without authorization or official sanction. <**Michael Jackson's** *Scream* was played on the air 13 days before its **release date**>

leakage *RecA&S* Pickup of a musical instrument by a mike intended to pick up another instrument. *Also see* **spill**.

learned (learn-ed) *Crit&Eval* Have or demonstrate profound knowledge. ERUDITE

learning by doing *EntreP* Knowledge gained during production that increases productivity.

lease *Eco&Fin* Rental agreement in which the tenant (**lessee**) agrees to make rent payments to the property owner (**lessor**) in exchange for the use of the asset. *Also see* **Intangible Assets**.

lease *LegAsp* **1** Contract granting use or occupation of property during a specified period in exchange for a specified rent. **2** Term or duration of such a contract. **3** Property used or occupied under the terms of such a contract. *Also see* **Contracts**.

leather boy *Cult&Soc* Fan or player of something akin to **punk rock**.

leave a tip *PerfA&C* A performer, particularly a comic, should leave the audience with something of herself/himself to remember. — Billy Crystal (1947, film/TV comic, act., dir., wri.) <*Saturday Night Live* comic, Academy Awards host, *When Harry Met Sally* (1989, act.)> *Also see* **empathic response**, **hook**.

leave out the last line *TheatArts* Theatrical tradition to omit the last line of the script in the cast's first reading.

leaves *VA-Prntng* » **leaf**

leaving money on the table *Fndng* Situation where the fund raiser asks a prospective donor for less money than the donor is prepared to give.

lecherous *Crit&Eval* Relating to excessive sexual activity; lewdness.

lectern *Genl* Stand that serves as a support for the notes or books of a speaker. *Also see* **dais**, **pulpit**, **rostrum**.

LED *InfoMgt* light-emitting diode **Semiconductor** diode that converts applied **voltage** to light and is used in **digital** displays.

ledger *E&F-Acc* **1** Intermediate accounting report in which all transactions over a given time are registered by the type of transaction. <advertising, payroll, sales expense, etc> **2** Book or computer file to which the record of accounts is transferred as final entry from original **postings**.

Lee, Spike (Shelton Jackson Lee, 1957-, flmkr., scrnwrtr., act., dir.-prod.) *ArtPerf, Flm&Vid, LitArts* First black filmmaker widely acclaimed both in the U.S. and abroad. <*Do the Right Thing* (1989), *Malcolm X* (1992)> *Also see* **bro**.

left wing *Crit&Eval* **Liberal** or **radical** faction of a group. *Also see* **right wing**.

left/right signal *RecA&S* Sound coming from the listener's left side, or right side if it is a right signal.

leftist *Crit&Eval, Law&Pol* Usually applies to someone who is merely liberal or believes in a form of democratic socialism. *Also see* **ultra-leftist**.

leg *MusArts* **legato**

leg *PerfA&C* Vertical masking piece hung at the side of the stage to hide the wing spaces from view of the audience. Series of legs and borders is the most common form of masking for dance. *Also see* **Stage Curtains**.

legal entity *EntreP* Business organization that is recognized by the law as having a separate legal existence.

legal monopoly *Eco&Fin, IntelProp* Exclusive ownership allowed by granting **copyright**, **patent**, **trademark**. *Also see* **monopoly**, **oligopoly**, **technopoly**.

legato (leg) (leh-got-o) *MusArts* Play evenly, smoothly, and continuously. *Also see* **Music Directions**.

legend *Cult&Soc* **1** Unverified story handed down from earlier times, esp. one popularly believed to be historical. **2 Romanticized** or popularized **myth** of modern times. **3** *Also see* **legendary**.

legend *LitArts* Explanatory caption accompanying an illustration. *Also see* **legendary**.

legendary *Cult&Soc* **1** Of, constituting, based on, or of the nature

of a legend; celebrated in legend. **2** Extremely well known; famous or renowned. *Usage:* Media have redefined the term to mean any celebrity whose fame may possibly endure.

leggings *Fashn* Close-fitting usu. knit trousers, often worn under a skirt for warmth; warm outerwear trousers for children.

legibility *iMedia* Metric to critique the degree to which it is possible to decipher text, though not necessarily how easy it is to read.

legitimate theatre *TheatArts* Refers to plays of high professional quality. <comedy, drama, and musicals; excludes burlesque, **vaudeville**, and some forms of musical comedy> *Also see* **Theaters & Theatres**.

Legitimate Theatre Employees (LTE) *HR&LR, PerfA&C* » **LTE**

legs *Flm&Vid* Said of a film that attracts strong audience interest and will therefore run for a long time.

legs *PerfA&C* Narrow, vertical stage drapes used for masking. *Also see* **mask**.

leisure time *Genl* Freedom from time-consuming duties, responsibilities, or activities.

leitmotif *also* **leitmotiv** *LitArts* Dominant and recurring theme, as in a novel, epic poem, or play. *Also see* **motif**.

leitmotif *also* **leitmotiv** *MusArts* Melodic passage or phrase, esp. in Wagnerianopera, associated with a specific character, situation, or element. (Richard Wagner, 1813-83, Ger. opera comp.) *Also see* **motif**, **theme and variation**.

Leko *PerfA&C* Acronym of the names of a Mr. Levy and a Mr. Cook who invented the **Ellipsoidal Reflector Spotlight**, the most commonly used theatre spotlight. Lekos cannot be substituted for effectively. Dance designers use them extensively. *Also see* **Stage Lighting**.

lento *MusArts* Play slowly, but not as slowly as **largo**. *Also see* **Music Directions**.

leotard *Fashn* Snugly fitting, stretchable one-piece garment with or without sleeves that covers the torso, worn esp. by dancers, gymnasts, acrobats, and exercisers.

les fauves (lay fawf, Fr. for "the wild beasts") *ArtPerf, VisArts* Group of early French **expressionist** painters who revolted against academic art and **impressionism** from about 1896 to 1908. Works characterized by pure, brilliant color and simplified drawing. Members included **Henri Matisse**, George Rouault (1871-1958, Fr. pntr.), André Derain (1880-1954, Fr. pntr.), Raoul Dufy (1877-1953, Fr. pntr.), Maurice de Vlaminck (1876-1958, Fr. pntr.), and **George Braque**.

less is more *Crit&Eval* "Less is more. You let the audience do the work." — Anthony Hopkins (1937-, film/play act.) *Also see* **silence**, **white space**.

lessee *E&F-Acc* Tenant in a **lease** agreement.

lessor *E&F-Acc* Property owner in a **lease** agreement.

let it all hang out *Crit&Eval* To be completely relaxed or candid.

Let's get the show on the road *PA-Variety* **P.T. Barnum**'s declaration when it was time to load the circus animals on the train.

letter of credit *EntreP* Agreement to honor demands for payment under certain conditions.

letter of inquiry *Fndng* Brief letter outlining a proposed funding project sent to the foundation in advance of the actual proposal to ascertain if the proposal is wanted.

letter of intent *LegAsp* Written statement expressing the intention of the undersigned to enter into a formal agreement if and when certain conditions are met. Used as a temporary agreement while awaiting verification of such items as appraisal of real property, inventory audit, assets and liabilities, copyright clearances, etc.

letter proposals *Fndng* Brief grant proposals in letter format.

letterbox mode *Flm&Vid* Film reproduced on video with bands across top and bottom of the TV screen to preserve the width-to-height they had on the movie screen.

letterpress printing *VA-Prntng*, Printing from a raised inked surface. *Also see* **hot lead**, **offset printing**.

letters *Flm&Vid, LitArts* Common plot device. <John O'Hara's (1905-70, fictwri.) short story, *Pal Joey*; the films. *Letter to Three Wives* and *Dear Ruth*, etc>

letters of credit *LegAsp* Agreement (**contract**) by the issuer of the letter to pay a sum of money upon the receipt of an **invoice** and **bill of lading**. *Also see* **Contracts**.

levee camp music *MusArts* Another name for (early) jazz. "Every time they changed the name they got a bigger check." — **Louis Armstrong**

leverage (debt) **ratios** *E&F-Acc*, *EntreP* Ratios which indicate what percentage of the assets of a business actually belong to the owners and what percentage is subject to creditors claims. » **debt/net worth ratio, debt ratio**

leverage *Eco&Fin, Mgt* Term applied when the assets, resources, and economic power of a company are used as **collateral** to finance acquisitions, expansion of facilities, and to meet common goals. <The company combined its manufacturing facilities, worker and management personnel, and financial assets as a "lever" to move the company into higher efficiency and market share>

leverage *Mktg* Use of additional promotional elements, such as sweepstakes, **bouncebacks**, and other tie-ins to extend the reach and maximize the impact of a sponsorship.

leveraged buyout (LBO) *EntreP* Purchase heavily financed with debt, where the potential cash flow of the target company is expected to be sufficient to meet debt repayments.

leverage ratios *E&F-Acc* Concerned with the company's assets. *Also see* **ratios**.

leveraged buy out (LBO) *Eco&Fin, Mgt* Method of financing the purchase of a company in which the assets of the company are used as **collateral** for purchase loans. [Method whereby an unscrupulous corporate raider can force a hostile takeover and make enormous profits by selling off assets.].

lexicographer *Crit&Eval, LitArts* One who compiles a dictionary.

lf *Rdio/TV, RecA&S* » **low frequency**

liability *E&F-Acc* Economic obligation (a debt) payable to an individual or an organization outside the business.

liable *Ethcs&Phil, LegAsp* Legally obligated; responsible. *Also see* **warranty**.

liaison *Mgt* Instance or a means of communication between different groups or units of an organization. <The **A&R** person serves as a liaison between the artist and the record company>

lib *Law&Pol* liberation. <women's lib>

lib. *InfoMgt* **librarian, library**

libel *LegAsp* 1 False publication in writing, printing, or typewriting or in signs or pictures that maliciously damages a person's reputation. 2 Act or an instance of presenting such a statement to the public. *Also see* **defamation, slander**.

liberal (lib.) *Crit&Eval, Cult&Soc, Law&Pol* 1 Not limited to or by established, traditional, orthodox, or authoritarian attitudes, views, or dogmas; free from bigotry. 2 Favoring proposals for reform, open to new ideas for progress, and tolerant of the ideas and behavior of others; broad-minded. 3 Relating to the traditional arts and sciences of a college or university curriculum. <a liberal education> *Also see* **Political Philosophies**.

liberalism *or* **Liberalism** (lib.) *Eco&Fin* Economic theory in favor of **laissez-faire**, the free market, and the gold standard.

liberalism *or* **Liberalism** (lib.) *Ethcs&Phil, Law&Pol* 1 Political theory based on the natural goodness of human beings, the autonomy of the individual, and favoring civil and political liberties, government by law with the consent of the governed, and protection from arbitrary authority. 2 19th century Protestant movement that favored free intellectual inquiry, stressed the ethical and humanitarian content of Christianity, and de-emphasized dogmatic theology. 3 19th century Roman Catholic movement that favored political democracy and ecclesiastical reform but was theologically orthodox. *Also see* **neoconservatism**.

libertarian *Crit&Eval, Law&Pol* One who believes in freedom of action and thought. *Also see* **Political Philosophies**.

libertine *Crit&Eval* One who acts without moral restraint; a **dissolute** person.

librarian (lib) *InfoMgt* **Computer program** that originates, stores, and distributes the programs that make up an operating system.

library (lib.) *InfoMgt* Collection of recorded data organized for easy use.

library *MusArts* Collection of compositions licensed for use as background, theme, or score music, on radio, broadcast and cable television, films, or video productions.

Library Administration & Management *InfoMgt* » **LAM**

Library of Congress (L.C.) *InfoMgt* Largest library in the world, est. 1800 urged on by **Thomas Jefferson**. It is the **Depository** that, under U.S. copyright laws, receives and stores all printed works. *Also see* **copyright registration**.

library science *InfoMgt* Principles, practice, or study of library administration and care.

library tape *InfoMgt* 1 Magnetic tape stored separately from the computer from which it was generated. 2 Tape containing a list of library tapes.

libret. *LitArts, MusArts* **librettist, libretto**

librettist (libret.) *LitArts, MusArts* author of a **libretto**

libretto (libret.) *LitArts, MusArts, TheatArts* 1 Text of an opera or other dramatic musical work. 2 Book containing a libretto.

lic. *LegAsp* **license**

license (lic.) *Eco&Fin, LegAsp* 1 Official or legal permission to do or own a specified thing. 2 Proof of permission granted, usu. in the form of a document, card, plate, or tag. *Also see* **Intangible Assets, music licensing**. *Also see* **Intangible Assets, Music Licenses, music licensing**.

license *IntelProp* Permit use of one or more rights of a copyright.

licensee *Eco&Fin, LegAsp* One to whom or to which a license is granted.

licensing *EntreP* Authorizing another company to produce and/or market a venture's product. The licensee pays the licensor a royalty for the right to produce and sell the product.

licensing deal *RecA&S* Record manufacturer may license its masters to different users, such as: record and tape clubs, record merchandising companies, mail order merchandisers, and program suppliers and syndicators. These licensed users manufacture and distribute recordings paying a fixed fee per unit, a flat licensing fee, or a royalty on all units sold. *Also see* **Contracts**.

licks *MusArts* Musical ornaments, brief spurts of improvisation. HOT LICKS *Also see* **improvise**.

lien *LegAsp* Right to take and hold or sell the property of a debtor as security or payment for a debt.

lifestyle *also* **life-style** *Cult&Soc* Way of life or style of living that reflects the attitudes and values of a person or group.

lifestyle marketing *Mktg* Use of events and image campaigns that appeal to or provide identification with how consumers perceive their **lifestyle**. <active, upscale, casual, sophisticated, etc>

LIFO *E&F-Acc* **Last In, First Out**. **FIFO** in reverse.

LIFO reserve *E&F-Acc* Difference between the **LIFO** cost of an inventory and what it would be under **FIFO**.

lift *Ethcs&Phil* To copy from something already published; plagiarize. <The student had lifted whole paragraphs from the encyclopedia>

lift *Flm&Vid* To incorporate a segment of one TV program or movie into another. *Also see* **flashback**.

lift lines *PerfA&C* Cables that support the batten to which scenery and lighting equipment is clamped.

ligature *MusArts* 1 Group of notes intended to be played or sung as one phrase. 2 Curved line indicating such a phrase; a slur.

ligature *VA-Prntng* Character, letter, or type, such as æ, combining two or more letters.

light *Ethcs&Phil* Lacking in ethical discrimination.

light *LitArts, MusArts, PerfA&C* Intended primarily as entertainment; not serious or profound. <light opera>

light *PerfA&C* Intended primarily as entertainment; not serious or profound.

light *VisArts* Representation of light in art.

Light Amplification through Stimulated Emissions of Radiation (laser) *InfoMgt* » **laser**

light batten *PerfA&C* » **electric batten**

light board *PerfA&C* Electronic or manually-operated mechanism for stage lighting with on-off switches and **dimmers** for the **house lights** and each stage lighting instrument. *Also see* **Stage Lighting**.

light music *MusArts* » **light**

light opera *MusArts* » **operetta**

light pen *InfoMgt* Small, photosensitive device connected to a computer and moved by hand over an output display in order to manipulate information in the computer. ELECTRONIC STYLUS.

light plot *PerfA&C* Plan of the stage with the lighting instruments superimposed showing where each is hung, the type of light, which **dimmer** it is patched into, which circuit it is plugged into, and what color it is **gelled**. *Also see* **Stage Lighting**.

light reading *LitArts* Intended primarily as entertainment; not serious or profound.

light stylus *InfoMgt* » **light pen**

Light Emitting Diodes *Sci&Tech* » **L.E.D**

lightface *VA-Prntng* Typeface or **font** of characters having relatively thin, light lines. *Also see* **boldface**.

lighting designer *PerfA&C* Person responsible for the appearance of the lighting during a production.

lighting grid *PerfA&C* Network of pipes, usu. connected on a grid pattern, from which lighting instruments, scenery, and other equipment can be hung.

lighting instrument *PerfA&C* Any dimmable stage lighting fixture. Lighting instruments are clamped to pipes — called an electric mounting position. There are two general types of lighting instruments: **spotlights** and **floodlights**.

lightness *iMedia* **1** Dimension of the color of an object by which the object appears to reflect or transmit more or less of the incident light, varying from black to white for surface colors and from black to colorless for transparent volume colors. **2** Perceived reflectance of an object or surface. Related terms: **luminance**, brightness, and **saturation**.

lightweight *Crit&Eval* One of little ability, intelligence, influence, or importance.

like *Crit&Eval* For a performer, it's akin to **love**. <Sally Field (1946-, film/TV act.) almost choking with emotion, accepting her second **Oscar**: "I've wanted more than anything to have your respect. And I can't deny the fact that you like me right now. You like me!"> *Also see* **rejection**.

likeness *Mktg, VisArts* Pictorial, graphic, or sculptured representation of something. *Also see* **image**.

lilywhite *Cult&Soc, Ethcs&Phil* Excluding or seeking to exclude Black people.

limbo *Crit&Eval* Region or condition of oblivion or neglect. <The fate of major league baseball was in limbo for many months>

limbo set *Flm&Vid* Set suggesting open space reaching to infinity. *Also see* **cyclorama**.

limelight *Crit&Eval,PerfA&C* **1** Focus of public attention; prominence. **2** Early type of stage light in which lime was heated to incandescence producing brilliant illumination. CALCIUM LIGHT.

limerick *LitArts* Light humorous, nonsensical, or bawdy verse of five anapestic lines – a metrical foot composed of two short syllables followed by one long one – usu. with the rhyme scheme AABBA.

limitation *LegAsp* Specified period during which, by statute, an action may be brought.

Limited Liability Company (LLC) *EntreP* Hybrid business entity having features of both partnerships and corporations. If formed properly it will be taxed as a partnership and its members will enjoy limited liability like corporate shareholders.

limited liability company *EntreP* Corporation in which stockholders have limited liability but pay personal income taxes on business profits.

limited partner *EntreP* Investor in a partnership who is not involved in day to day operations and whose liability is limited to the amount of his or her investment in the partnership.

limited partnership *EntreP* Partnership having one or more general partners and several limited partners.

limited partnership *Mgt* Limited partner is only liable for a sum equal to the amount invested. Theatrical productions are often funded by a number of limited partners and managed by the general partners who have general liability. *Also see* **angel**, **general partnership**.

limited release *Flm&Vid* Release of a movie with less than fifty engagements nationwide.

Lincoln Center (**for the Performing Arts**) *MusArts,PerfA&C* NYC complex built 1959-1972 includes the **Met**, Avery Fisher Hall, **Juilliard School** (and Alice Tully Hall), and the **Vivian Beaumont Theater**.

Lindy also **Lindy Hop** *Dnce* Jazz or swing dance named for **Charles Lindbergh's** solo flight to Paris in 1927. *Also see* **Dances**.

line *Flm&Vid,TheatArts* Single sentence or remark uttered by an actor. *Also see* **lines**.

line *Genl* One's trade, occupation, or field of interest.

line *iMedia* **1** Thin continuous mark **2** Contour or an outline: **3** Mark used to define a shape or represent a contour. **4** Any of the marks that make up the formal design of a picture.

line *LitArts* Unit of verse

line *Mktg* » **product line**

line *MusArts* One of the five (horizontal) parallel marks making up a **staff**.

line *VisArts* Any marks that make up the formal design of a picture.

line noise *InfoMgt* Extraneous noise on a telephone line.

line of credit *Eco&Fin, EntreP* Credit limit extended to a business which may be drawn upon when required by the business. There are no payments due on the line of credit unless the business actually borrows the money. » **credit line**

line printer *VA-Prntng* High-speed printing device, primarily used in data processing, that prints an entire line of type as a unit instead of printing each character individually.

line rehearsal *TheatArts* Special rehearsal for the actors to go over new dialog.

line set *PerfA&C* Single working group of elements that enables scenery or lighting to move up or down, i.e., to **fly**. Pipe is attached by cables and pulleys to a counterweight arbor placed against the stage wall. When the arbor is pulled up toward the grid, the pipe (or **batten**) moves toward the stage floor or "flies in." Group of line sets creates a fly system. Fifty to sixty line sets is common for a moderately large theater, while some stages have a range of 100-120 line sets.

lineage *Mktg* Number of **agate lines** representing one ad or a total advertising campaign.

linear *Crit&Eval* **1** Relating to, or resembling a straight line. **2** Having only one dimension.

linear *VisArts* Characterized by drawn lines rather than painterly effects.

linear editing *Flm&Vid* Normal method of video editing that involves recording each edit, one after another, onto a **videotape**. Since linear editing is an actual, physical recording, any change in an edit's length would require each subsequent edit to be rerecorded to reflect this change.

linear navigation *iMedia* Type of navigational system that progresses through information allowing the participant/user the choice of forward or back.

linear perspective *iMedia* Form of perspective in which parallel lines are represented as converging so as to give the illusion of depth and distance.

liner notes *RecA&S* Annotations and background information – about the recording artists, the music/lyrics, and the individual tracks – printed on the back of a disk album cover or printed separately as a brochure, pamphlet, or book and enclosed in the album or CD boxed package. *Also see* **enhanced CDs**.

liner *RecA&S* Jacket for a phonograph record.

lines *Flm&Vid,TheatArts* Speeches and dialogue of a dramatic production. RUN LINES

lines *Rdio/TV* Parts of a TV picture covered in one full horizontal sweep of the electron beam, moving from left to right on the screen. Current U.S. standard is 480-525 lines per picture. *Also see* **high-definition television**.

lineup *BcstJourn* » **rundown**

lingo *Crit&Eval* **1** Specialized **vocabulary** of a particular field or profession. **2** Language that is unintelligible or unfamiliar. CANT, JARGON, VERNACULAR

linguistic *Cult&Soc* Relating to language.

link *InfoMgt* Connection between databases or spreadsheets, with data in one affecting data in another.

LinkWorks *InfoMgt* Operating system **trademarked** by **Digital**.

Linotype *VA-Prntng* **Trademark** for a machine that sets type on a metal slug, operated by a keyboard. *Also see* **letterpress printing**.

lip microphone *RecA&S* **Mic** sensitive to lip proximity or contact, useful in live rock concerts. *Also see* **Microphones**.

lip service *Crit&Eval* Verbal expression of agreement or allegiance, unsupported by real conviction or action; hypocritical respect. <Lip service continues to be paid to improving public school education but little progress is made>

lip-synch *also* **lip-sync** *RecA&S* To move the lips in **synchronization** with recorded speech or song.

liquid asset *Eco&Fin* Cash, or something easily convertible to cash. *Also see* **Assets**.

Liquid Crystal Display (LCD) *InfoMgt* » **LCD**

liquidity *E&F-Acc* **1** Measure of how quickly an item may be converted to cash. <Blue-chip stocks have high liquidity> **2** Available cash or the capacity to obtain it on demand.

liquidity demand for money *EntreP* Demand for money that represents the needs and desires individuals or companies can fill on short notice without incurring excessive costs.

liquidity ratios *Eco&Fin, EntreP* **1** Ratio which determines how much of a companies current assets are available to meet **short term** creditor's claims... **2** Represent the ease in which assets may be converted into cash. *Also see* **current ratio**, **quick ratio**, **ratios**.

list price *Mktg* Basic published or advertised price, from which discounts are based. <Publishers usu. set a book's list price at five times the cost of production, printing and royalties. **Margins of profit** are usu. between 5 percent and 15 percent> *Also see* **margin of profit**, **retail list price**.

list song *MusArts* Song cleverly listing in rhyme a number of people, things, or events of interest or annoyance relating to the singer's role. <*I've Got A Little List*, from the *Mikado*>

listen *ArtPerf* Arguably the most important attribute of any performer: the ability to listen and react to another performer or to an audience creates genuine dialog and exceptionable ensemble performance. *Also see* **empathic response**, **listening**.

listener *Rdio/TV* Object of radio station policy and programming, regarded as the basic unit in most **demographic** and **psychographic** surveys. *Also see* **viewer**.

listening *Flm&Vid, TheatArts* **1** "Listening is everything; it's where you learn everything!" — Meryl Streep (» **class act**) **2** "Listening is essential!" — Robert DiNiro (1943-; actor, dir.)

LISTSERV *InfoMgt* Internet mailing list manager

listservs *InfoMgt, Mktg* System that sends electronic mail among members of special interest groups. They take the name of the software that automatically runs them or the NEWSGROUPS

lit., lit *LitArts* literature

litany *MusArts* repetitive or incantatory recital

literalism *Crit&Eval* **1** Adherence to the explicit sense of a given text or **doctrine**. **2** Literal portrayal; realism.

literati *LitArts* literary **intelligentsia**

literature (lit.) *LitArts* **1** Body of writings in prose or verse. **2** Imaginative or creative writing, esp. of recognized artistic value. **3** Art or occupation of a literary writer.

lith., litho. *VA-Prntng* **lithograph, lithography**

lithog. *VA-Prntng* lithographer.

lithograph (lith., litho.) *VA-Prntng* Print produced by lithography.

lithography *VA-Prntng* (lith., litho.) Printing process in which the image to be printed is rendered on a flat surface (**stone**), as on sheet zinc or aluminum, and treated to retain ink while the non-image areas are treated to repel ink.

Little Instruments *ColEntry, MusInstr* "Primitive" percussion and wind instruments used very effectively by Chicago avant-garde musicians in the mid-to-late 1960s. » **cowbell, jew's-harp, jug, kazoo, pennywhistle, slide whistle, spoons, washboard, woodblock**

little theatre *TheatArts* Any small theatre, but esp. one for amateur or school productions which are often experimental. *Also see* **Theaters & Theatres**.

liturgy *Cult&Soc* Prescribed form or set of forms for public Christian ceremonies; **ritual**. LITURGICAL

live announcer *Rdio/TV* Station announcer who does live intros, **segues**, and other **voiceovers**.

live *BcstJourn* » **reader**

live *RecA&S* High degree of reverb.

live tag *Mktg, Rdio/TV* Live portion of a commercial left open for local or regional announcements made live by a **staff announcer**.

live-er (lyve'-er) *BcstJourn* » **reader**

lively *Crit&Eval* Full of spirit; bright and animated. <a lively tune>

living newspaper *TheatArts* Play in which social and political events are realistically dramatized; based on the news of the day, rather than a traditional plot; not concerned with personal experience. *Also see* **Theaters & Theatres**.

Living Theater *TheatArts* Founded 1947, based at various times in New York, Europe, and Brazil. It featured innovative productions, often using improvisation and audience participation. *Also see* **Theaters & Theatres**.

living trust *EntreP* Trust that is set up during the life of the trustor.

LMA *InfoMgt* last minute addition

load in *PerfA&C* Scheduled period of time necessary for a stage crew to move and set up a theatrical production. <scenery, costumes, lighting, etc>

load mutual funds *EntreP* Mutual funds that charge a commission on the initial investment.

load out *PerfA&C* Scheduled period of time necessary for a stage crew to take down a theatrical production and move it out of the theater. <scenery, costumes, lighting, etc>

loading platform *PerfA&C* Platform or catwalk built near the **grid** from which the arbors are loaded with counterweights.

lobby *PerfA&C* Foyer or hall between the entrance to the theater and the entrance to the theater auditorium.

LOBL *TheatArts* **League of Off-Broadway Theatres and Producers**. Works to further the viability of **off-Broadway** theatre productions in NYC. Represents members' interests in collective bargaining negotiations and labor relations.

local *HR&LR* Local or regional union affiliated with a national parent union. <**AFM** Local 802 has jurisdiction in NYC, Local 10 in Chicago, Local 47 in L.A., etc>

local area network (LAN) *iMedia* Local network for inter-computer communication; especially a network connecting computers and word processors and other electronic office equipment to create an inter-office system.

local option Power granted to a local political subdivision to decide whether to apply a law, such as a ban on liquor sales, within its jurisdiction.

Local Or Regional Theater *TheatArts* » **LORT**

location *Flm&Vid* Any film or **videotape** interior or exterior setting located outside of the studio or **production company**.

location fee *Flm&Vid* Permit fee paid to use a locale for filming or videotaping.

location lighting *Flm&Vid* Usually lightweight lighting equipment used for location interiors and exteriors.

location manager *Flm&Vid* Production staffer in charge of scouting and/or logistics of a location shoot. *Also see* **Managers**.

location scout *Flm&Vid* One who works weeks or months ahead of the production unit to: shoot stills of possible locations, check out contacts, accommodations, permits, and assembles charts, production sheets, names, and statistics relating to the location shoot.

location scouting *Ethcs&Phil, Flm&Vid* **1** Location scouting is a legitimate job where specific production needs are matched to potential shooting locales. **2** Sometimes abused as a cover for charging travel expenses to the cost of production.

lock *InfoMgt* To prevent files or disks from being changed or deleted. **Floppy disk** can be physically locked by sliding up the small tab on the back of the plastic case.

lockbox *EntreP* Post office box that is opened by an agent of the bank and checks received there are immediately deposited in a company account.

lock-out *HR&LR* Withholding work from employees and shutdown of a plant by an employer during a labor dispute.

lock-out *InfoMgt* Prevents use of a program if the legal number of licenses is exceeded. *Also see* **licensing deal**.

locked hands *MusArts* » **block chords**

lockers *MusArts* Websites containing music collections

Loew's *PA-Variety* **vaudeville** theater **circuit**

loft jazz *MusArts* Avant-garde jazz of the 1970s played in converted warehouses or apartments in New York's Lower East Side by musicians who couldn't make it elsewhere. *Also see* **Jazz Styles**.

log *Flm&Vid* Detailed report of film shoots, sound, schedules, and logistics.

log *Rdio/TV* **1** Schedule prepared by stations for **BMI** indicating by title, writer and artist all music performed during a particular time period. Used as a basis for payment of **performance right** royalties to writers and publishers. **2** Government or privately published roster, organized by call letters, of all radio and TV stations and their **frequencies**, power, location, and call letters.

logarithm *iMedia* Exponent/power to which a stated number (the base) is raised to produce a specific number.

log in *InfoMgt* » **log on**

log on *InfoMgt* Action by which a user begins a computer session. LOG IN

loge *PerfA&C* Theater box or the front rows of a theater's **mezzanine**. *Also see* **box**.

logic *Crit&Eval* **1** Valid reasoning. **2** Relationship between elements and between an element and the whole.

logic *Ethcs&Phil* Study of the principles of reasoning. *Also see* **Aristotle**.

logic *InfoMgt* **1** Nonarithmetic operations performed by a computer, such as sorting, comparing, and matching, that involve yes-no decisions. **2** Computer circuitry.

logistics (physical distribution) *EntreP* Activities of distribution involved in the physical relocation of products.

logo *InfoMgt* Computer language used for primary school applications.

logo *Mktg* Name, symbol, or **trademark** designed for easy and definite recognition, esp. one borne on a single printing plate or piece of type. LOGOGRAM, LOGOTYPE

logogen *iMedia* "Mental representation of language information." Paivo, 1987. *Also see* **imagens**.

LOL *InfoMgt* Laughing Out Loud. Used during chat sessions. *Also see* **chat**.

London Academy of Musical and Dramatic Art (LAMDA) *MusArts,TheatArts* » **LAMDA**

London Stock Exchange *EntreP* Origins of this stock exchange in England can be traced back to the Muscovy Company, formed in 1553, for financing merchant vessels.

long-range plan (strategic plan) *EntreP* Company's overall plan for the future.

long-term debt *EntreP* It is the debt that a company owes that it does not expect to pay during the current accounting year. Used synonymously with long-term liabilities. Found on the company's balance sheet.

Long Range Weather Forecasts *Eco&Fin* This **economic indicator** is watched carefully by **commodity** markets such as the Chicago Board of Trade and the Chicago Mercantile Exchange. Forecasts affect futures trading which in turn affects food prices which affect the **WPI** and the **CPI**. *Also see* **Natural Disasters**.

long shot (LS) *Flm&Vid* Includes the subject and surroundings, or the subject in the distance. EXTREME LONG SHOT

long-play single *RecA&S* 12-inch. 33-1/3 **rpm** double-sided long-play disc phonograph record embodying not more than three **sides**.

long-playing record *RecA&S* » **LP**

long-term asset *E&F-Acc* Asset other than a **current asset**. *Also see* **Assets**.

long-term debt *E&F-Acc* Liability not due for a comparatively long time; more that one year.

long-term liability *E&F-Acc* » **long-term debt**

longitudinal data *Mktg* Research information gathered usu. at periodic intervals from the same population or demographic sample, thus allowing the market researcher to monitor individual changes among members of the study.

look *Crit&Eval, Fashn* Distinctive, unified manner of dress or fashion. <Is **grunge** look **in** or **out**?> *Also see* **style**.

loop *iMedia, InfoMgt* Sequence of instructions that repeats either a specified number of times or until a particular condition prevails.

looping *Flm&Vid* » **ADR**

lore *Cult&Soc* **1** Accumulated facts, traditions, or beliefs about a particular subject. **2** Knowledge acquired through education or experience.

Loretta Young silks *Flm&Vid* Layers of silky gauze laid over the camera lens to hide the effects of aging reminiscent of the ageless movie and TV star. <Loretta Young (Gretchen Young, 1913-)> "They should photograph me through linoleum." — Tallulah Bankhead (1903-68, whiskey baritoned film/stage act.) *Also see* **diffusers, soft focus**.

LORT *TheatArts* **Local Or Regional Theater** (LORT) About 60 first class nonprofit theatres in major American cities.

loss *RecA&S* Reduction of signal energy as transmitted from one point to another, measured in decibels.

lossless compression *iMedia* A term describing a data compression **algorithm** which retains all the information in the data, allowing it to be recovered perfectly by decompression. In contrast: **lossy compression**.

lossy *iMedia* A term describing a data compression **algorithm** which actually reduces the amount of information in the data, rather than just the number of bits used to represent that information. The lost information is usually removed because it is subjectively less important to the quality of the data (usually an image or sound) or because it can be recovered reasonably by interpolation from the remaining data. In contrast: lossless compression.

loss leader *Mktg* » **leader**

losses on exchange of plant assets *E&F-Acc* A loss is recognized for financial accounting purposes on all exchanges in which a **material loss** occurs.

lot *Flm&Vid* Movie studio.

lotus land *Crit&Eval* **Awesome** place or condition of irresponsibility and luxury. <**Hollywood**, the place and the condition>

lounge *PA-Variety* Establishment or a room in a hotel or restaurant, where liquor is served with live or recorded entertainment.

lounge lizard *Crit&Eval, PA-Variety* **1** Performer of limited scope or talent often found in cocktail lounges. **2** social parasite.

love *Crit&Eval* Principal need – or, arguably, *the* principal need – of artists and performers. "Like Peter Pan's fairy pal, Tinkerbell, [Liza Minnelli (1946-, stage/film/TV sngr., act., dncr.)] seems to require **applause** to be brought into full existence. But the sentiments behind those words underlie Ms. Minnelli's every gesture as a performer. She asks for love so nakedly and earnestly, it seems downright vicious not to respond." — Ben Brantley (drama critic) "Love me! What drives you to perform is the need for that primal connection." — Robin Williams (1952-, act., comic) *Also see* **EAT+D²**; immortality; rejection.

Lovelace, Augusta Ada (1815-1852) *iMedia, InfoMgt* Developed a program for the Analytical Engine, and is widely considered the first computer programmer. programming language, **ADA**, was named in her honor (circa 1979)

low *MusArts* Having a **pitch** corresponding to a relatively small number of sound-wave cycles per second. <**Contralto** is the lowest female voice> *Also see* **hertz, high**.

low comedy *TheatArts* General term referring to comedy which emphasizes physical action; **slapstick**. <burlesque, farce, The Three Stooges> *Also see* **high comedy**.

lower-third key *BcstJourn* » **CG**

low frequency (lf)*Rdio/TV* Long **wavelength**.

low key *Flm&Vid* Style of lighting that emphasizes diffused shadows and atmospheric pools of light. Often used in mysteries and thrillers.

low profile *Crit&Eval* Restrained or modest behavior designed not to attract attention.

low-budget movie *Flm&Vid* Movie with a not-so-bright stars, few special effects, and shot at a free or low-cost **location**. Usually made by an independent production company, major studios can't afford low-budget anything. *Also see* **B-film**.

low-end *Mktg* **1** Cheapest in a line of merchandise. <low-end TV sets> **2** Appealing to **low-income** or undiscerning customers. <a low-end department store>

low-income *Eco&Fin* Relating to individuals or households with an average or slightly below average income. *Also see* **poverty level**.

lower of cost or market (LCM) *E&F-Acc* » **LCM**

lowercase *or* **lower-case** (lc) *VA-Prntng* Relating to the printing of lowercase letters. *Also see* **uppercase**.

lowest common denominator *Crit&Eval* **1** That which is understood, believed, or accepted by a majority of people. **2 Rationale** for the tabloid press, **talk radio**, and most TV programming. [Who presumes to know who the majority is or what it really wants.?].

loyalty oath *Ethcs&Phil, Law&Pol* Oath demanded of just about everyone who thinks differently by those who wrap themselves in the flag; paranoiac superpatriots. "Even if I did submit to the signing of what amounts to a loyalty oath, how am I to decide what others consider **obscene**?" — **Joseph Papp** *Also see* **HUAC, McCarthyism**.

LP *RecA&S* Long-playing record (33-1/3 **rpm**) *Origin* **Peter Goldmark**, of **CBS** Labs, invented the lathe that made the long-playing record feasible. **LP** is a **trademark** owned by Columbia Records.

lp. *MusInstr* Latin percussion

LS *Flm&Vid* long shot.

LSD *Cult&Soc* **lysaergic acid diethylamide**. Dangerous escape trip drug. HALLUCINOGEN

LSI *InfoMgt* **Large Scale Integration**; term used to describe chips synonymous with 4ᵗʰ generation computers and containing the equivalent of millions of **transistors**.

LTE *HR&LR,TheatArts* **Legitimate Theatre Employees**. Ω

LTNS *InfoMgt* Long Time No See

lucid *Crit&Eval* Easily understood; intelligible.

Luddite *Eco&Fin, HR&LR* One who opposes technical or technological change. *Origin* Between 1811 and 1816, Ned Ludd and other British workers rioted and destroyed laborsaving textile machinery in the belief that such machinery would diminish employment. *Also see* **technophobe**.

lullaby *MusArts* Soothing song with which to lull a child to sleep.

lulu *Crit&Eval* Remarkable person, object, or idea.

luminaire *Flm&Vid ,PerfA&C* Full lighting unit: housing, lamp,

cord, and stand.

luminance *iMedia* Measured amount of light coming from a source.

luminary *Crit&Eval* **1** Person who is an inspiration to others. **2** Person who has achieved eminence in a specific field.

luminescence *Sci&Tech* Emission of light caused by chemical, biochemical, or crystallographic changes, the motions of subatomic particles, or radiation-induced excitation of an atomic system.

luminism *VisArts* Style of 19ᵗʰ century American painting concerned esp. with the precise, realistic rendering of atmospheric light and the perceived effects of that light on depicted objects. *Also see* **Art Movements and Periods**.

luminous paint *PerfA&C* For a makeup that must glow in the dark.

lump in (one's) throat *Crit&Eval* Feeling of constriction in the throat caused by emotion. *Also see* **touched**.

lunchtime theatre *TheatArts* Like it says, theatre served from noon to two; usu. located in or near the city's business district. *Also see* **Theaters & Theatres**.

lundu *Dnce* Brazilian "sensual dance where the invitation to dance was the joining of navels." — Joyce Carlson-Leavitt (**CBMR** visiting scholar) *Also see* **Dances, Latin Dance Music**.

lurid *Crit&Eval* **1** Marked by sensationalism. <a lurid account of the massacre> **2** Causing shock or horror.

lurker *InfoMgt* One who sits in a chat room, yet does not participate.

lush *Crit&Eval* **1** Luxurious; opulent. <Lush sound of an orchestra, lush foliage, lush painting> **2** drunkard. *Also see* **piano bar**.

luxury *Mktg* **1** Something inessential but conducive to pleasure and comfort. **2** Something expensive or hard to obtain. **3** Sumptuous living or surroundings.

LYBUNT *Fndng* [Contributor gave] *Last year but not this year*. *Also see* **SYBUNT**.

lyceum *PerfA&C* **1 Venue** in which public lectures, concerts, and similar programs are presented. *Origin* (Greek) School outside Athens where Aristotle taught (335-323 B.C.)

Lycos *InfoMgt* Web site providing access to Internet. *Also see* **search engine, portals**.

lyr. *MusArts* **lyric, lyricist**

lyric (lyr.) *LitArts* Relating to a category of poetry that expresses subjective thoughts and feelings, often in a songlike style or form.

lyric (lyr.) *MusArts* Singing voice of light volume and modest range.

lyricist (lyr.) *LitArts, MusArts* Writer of song lyrics. "Good lyric should be a rhymed conversation." — **Ira Gershwin** *Also see* **author, composer, songwriter, writer**.

lyrics *LitArts, MusArts* **Words** of a song. "In *Merrily We Roll Along*, **Stephen Sondheim** posed the question: 'Which comes first generally — the words or the music?' Answer: 'Generally the contract.' When we asked him the same question he was less cynical: 'Words first, always the words.'" — **Stephen Sondheim** *Also see* **w**.

lysaergic acid diethylamide *Cult&Soc* » **LSD**

- M -

m *Sci&Tech* » **meter**

m. *MusArts* **music**. Used to indicate the composer of a song with lyrics. <*A Foggy Day* (m. **George Gershwin**, w. **Ira Gershwin**)> *Also see* **w**.

m.e. *Journ* **managing editor**.

ma-and-pa dealer *Mktg, RecA&S* Small, independent record retailer.

Mac *InfoMgt* » **Macintosh**

macabre (ma-kobrre) *Crit&Eval* Suggesting the horror of death and decay; gruesome.

Macbeth *PerfA&C* Blue spotlight on stage, used to depict the ghost of Banquo.

Macbeth trap *PerfA&C* **Trap** with an elevator, used to deliver a ghost on stage.

Macguffin, McGuffin, Maguffin *Flm&Vid, Rdio/TV* **1** Coined by **Alfred Hitchcock** to describe "an object that the audience doesn't have to care about (or even understand) but the characters

M

care plenty about — enough, at least, to keep them running from one dangerous situation to another..." — *New Yorker* **2** Really an excuse to create a good deal of action and dramatic effect *Also see* **suspense programs**.

macher (mocka, Yinglish) *Crit&Eval* One who makes it big; a big shot.

machine language *InfoMgt* Very low level language directly executable by the computer.

machine-oriented interface *iMedia* Interface from the 1940s where computer operators used switches to set the machine's memory; entering data using binary values (one bit at a time)

Machine Tool Orders *Eco&Fin* This **economic indicator** measures the number and value of machine tools – tools that make machinery – ordered by industry. But technical changes in industrial production has reduced the indicator's value, and has been largely replaced by **Durable Goods Orders**.

Macintosh (Mac) *InfoMgt* Tradename for a line of computers manufactured by Apple, Inc.

macramé *Fashn* Coarse lace work made by weaving and knotting cords into a pattern.

macro *iMedia, InfoMgt* Set of computer instructions that can be named and treated as a single instruction.

macro-environment *EntreP* Broad environment, with its multiple factors, that affects most businesses in a society.

macrocode *InfoMgt* Coding system in which single codes generate several sets of instructions.

macroeconomics *Eco&Fin, EntreP* Study of the overall aspects and workings of a national economy, such as income, output, and the interrelationship among diverse economic sectors. *Also see* **microeconomics**.

MACRS *E&F-Acc* **Modified Accumulated Cost Recovery System.** » **Tax Reform Act of 1986**

made-up *Th-MakeUp* Changed by the application of makeup. <a made-up actor>

made-up *VA-Prntng* Finished; put together. <a made-up page of type>

Madison Avenue *Mktg* American advertising industry *Also see* **marketer**.

Madonna (b. Madonna Ciccone; 1958-, Film/stage act., sngr., dncr., prod., n-fictwri.) *ArtPerf, Flm&Vid, LitArts, MusArts, PA-Variety, Rdio/TV* Famous, ofttimes notorious, for her public and private **lifestyles**. *Also see* **attraction**, **fame**, **feminist**, **hyperbole**.

madras *Fashn* **1** Cotton cloth of fine texture, usu. with a plaid, striped, or checked pattern. **2** Silk, generally striped, cloth. **3** Light cotton cloth used for drapery; a similar cloth of rayon. **4** Large handkerchief of brightly colored silk or cotton, often worn as a turban.

madrigal *MusArts* Unaccompanied song for three or more voices using **counterpoint** and **imitation**.

maestro *MusArts* Master in an art, esp. as a composer or conductor.

mag. *LitArts* **magazine**

magapaper *Journ* Periodical that combines magazine content with newspaper design.

magazine (mag.) *LitArts, VA-Prntng* Periodical containing a collection of articles, stories, pictures, and other features. BUSINESS MAGAZINES, CONSUMER MAGAZINES, GENERAL INTEREST MAGAZINES, SPECIAL INTEREST MAGAZINES, TRADE MAGAZINES

Magazine Publishers of America (MPA) *Journ* Trade association representing principally the large magazine publishers. *Also see* **American Business Press**.

magazine theatre *TheatArts* In which several events and personalities of the current or past years are presented.

magic *Crit&Eval* Mysterious quality of enchantment: "There is something bedazzling about the creative act; always a surprise, it shocks with its unimaginable perfection, its strange eloquence, its balance between the fresh and the familiar. Perhaps it's because we want to make such magic ourselves that we are so intrigued by how others do it." — Daniel Goleman (psychologist) *Also see* **creativity**.

magic *PA-Variety* **Sleight-of-hand** or conjuring for entertainment. *Also see* **conjurer**, **magician**, **prestidigitator**.

magic lantern *Flm&Vid* Optical device formerly used to project an enlarged image of a picture. *Also see* **stereopticon**.

magician *ArtPerf, PA-Variety* **1** One who performs magic for entertainment. **2** One whose formidable skill or art seems to be magical. *Also see* **conjurer**, **prestidigitator**. ILLUSIONIST

magnetic disk *InfoMgt* Disk made of rigid material, i.e., **hard disk**; or heavy mylar, i.e, **floppy disk**. Disk surface holds magnetized data written on and retrieved from the disk by a **disk drive**.

Magnetic Ink Character Recognition (MICR) *InfoMgt* » **MICR**

magnetic soundtrack *Flm&Vid* One with an iron oxide coating on the edge of the film. *Also see* **optical soundtrack**.

magnificat (Latin) *MusArts* Hymn or song of praise.

mail bombs *InfoMgt* Nasty messages via electronic mail on the Internet. *Also see* **flame**.

mail campaign *Fndng* Broadly based campaign conducted by several mailings over a specified period.

mail reflector *InfoMgt* » **mailbot**

mailbot *InfoMgt, Mktg* Kind of electronic message robot that automatically responds to email inquiries. <The XYZ software company will automatically send a catalog or catalog items in response to the customer's email message> AUTORESPONDER, MAIL REFLECTOR

mailer *Mktg* **1** Advertising piece included with a letter or a bill. **2** Container used to hold material to be mailed. <cardboard book mailer, cardboard tube for rolled items> **3** One who prepares mail. <large commercial mailer>

Mailer, Norman (1923-, fictwri., n-fictwri., social critic) *ArtPerf, Crit&Eval, LitArts* Acclaimed for his WWII novel *The Naked and the Dead* (1948), *The Deer Park* (1955), *The Executioner's Song* (1979) *Also see* **Audience**.

mailing list *Mktg* List of active or prospective customers. *Also see* **customer list**.

main drape *PerfA&C* synonym for the grand drape

main logic board *InfoMgt* Large circuit board that holds **RAM**, **ROM**, the **microprocessor**, **custom integrated circuits**, and other components that make the computer work.

main man *Crit&Eval* Refers to a man admired for what he does and what he stands for. *Also see* **bro**.

main memory *InfoMgt* » **RAM**

Main Stem *PerfA&C* » **Broadway**

main storage *InfoMgt* Storage of programs being executed and data being processed. INTERNAL STORAGE, PRIMARY STORAGE *Also see* **auxiliary storage**.

mainframe *InfoMgt* **1** Large, powerful computer, often serving several connected terminals. **2 Central processing unit** (CPU) of a computer exclusive of **peripheral** and remote devices.

mainstream *Cult&Soc* Prevailing current or direction of a movement or influence; influenced by, or in agreement, with the prevailing attitudes and values of a society or group: "I'm not sympathetic to the notion that there is a mainstream. I think that everybody ought to take the position that any stream they're in is the main one because that's the only one in which they can drown. From that basis, a mainstream is not a meaningful concept because the intention of it is to set up categories of who is the real standard, and who are the standardless. And if you accept the premise that a culture can generate its own standard; it is **a priori** its own mainstream."— Barry Gaither (cult. critic, musm. dir.)

mainstream jazz *MusArts* Style of soloing in the big band era.

mainstream pop *MusArts* » **easy listening**

mainstreaming *Journ* "Positive inclusion [of minorities] in stories that are not necessarily about race — inc. minorities in stories about the weather, banking, or government." — Gannett newspaper chain

maître de ballet (metre duh baa-lay, Fr for "master of the dance") *Dnce* » **ballet master**

major *MusArts* Major scale, key, interval, or mode. *Also see* **minor**.

major category methods *E&F-Acc* Total cost and total market values for each category of items are compared. Each category is then valued at its lower amount.

major gift *Fndng* Any gift deemed of significant size by a charitable organization; usu. the top third tier of gifts in a gift range table.

major labels *RecA&S* Record companies that own their own manufacturing and distribution facilities in the U.S. and abroad, and offer many styles of music (classical, country, pop, etc.) on subsid-

M

iary labels. The big six and their parent companies — all global entertainment and media conglomerates: **Capitol** (EMI, England), **Columbia** (Sony, Japan), **MCA** (Seagram, Canada), **Polygram** (Phillips Electronics, Netherlands), **RCA**. (Bertlesman, Germany), **Warner-Elektra-Asylum** (WEA, Time-Warner, U.S. – distribute more than 90% of all the records in the U.S) *Also see* **oligopoly**.

Major League of Baseball *SportsEnt* Created in 1903 from the combination of the **National League** and the **American League**. A national commission was then established with the president of each league and members agreed upon by both. After the **Black Sox** gambling scandal at the 1919 World Series, the commission was viewed as ineffective: only an outsider of impeccable integrity could restore baseball's good name. Thus, Judge Kennesaw Mountain Landis became the first commissioner of **organized baseball**; he held the position for 24 years. Bud Selig **[??]** is the eighth and current commissioner.

major leagues *SportsEnt* » **Major League of Baseball**

major scale *MusArts* **Diatonic scale** in which the half steps occur between the third and fourth and the seventh and eighth tones.

major studios *Flm&Vid* Five major studios of **Hollywood's Golden Age** (ca. 1920s to the 1940s): **MGM, Paramount Pictures, RKO, Twentieth Century Fox**, and **Warner Brothers**.

make good *Mktg* Offer by a medium to rerun, at no additional charge, an ad or commercial that appeared incorrectly because of some error by the medium. Rerun is of equal or greater value than the original placement.

make it land *PerfA&C* Effort by the composer, the director, the actors, et al to make the idea or the theme of the performance land, i.e., connect with the audience. *Also see* **empathic response**.

make up *VA-Prntng* Arrangement or composition, as of type or illustrations, on a page or in a book.

make-believe *Crit&Eval* Fanciful or playful nonsense.

make-or-buy decision analysis *E&F-Acc, Mgt* Managerial decision about whether the company should produce a product internally or purchase it from others.

make-work *Eco&Fin, HR&LR* Work of little value. *Also see* **featherbedding, walkers**.

maker of promissory note *E&F-Acc* The person or entity who signs the note and thereby promises to pay a definite sum of money on demand or a future date, according to the note agreement. DEBTOR

makeup *or* **make-up** *Th-MakeUp* **1** Change the appearances of one's face and other body areas by means of cosmetics, false hair, nose putty, etc. in order to emphasize characteristics appropriate to one's role or public image or to compensate for, or enhance, the effects of lighting and distance. **2** Materials that an act. uses in portraying a role. <cosmetics, wigs>

makeup *or* **make-up** *VA-Prntng* Arrangement or composition of printing type and illustrations in a book or on a page.

makeup designer *Th-MakeUp* Craftsperson responsible for creating makeup for one or actors after consultation with the director, costume designer, lighting designer, and the actor(s) "The relationship between the make-up man and the film actor is that of accomplices in crime." — Marlin Dietrich (1901-92, film act., sngr.)

makeup kit *Th-MakeUp* Container that holds a variety of stage cosmetics, brushes, etc.

making rounds *TheatArts* While not waiting tables, acts make the rounds of the booking and casting agencies looking for work and hope. *Also see* **rejection**.

maladaptive *Crit&Eval* Inadequate adaptation. *Also see* **reconstruct**.

malapropism *LitArts* Ludicrous misuse of a word, esp. by confusion with one of similar sound. "A verbal contract isn't worth the paper it's written on." — Said by, or written for, **Samuel Goldwyn**.

malfeasance *Law&Pol* Misconduct or wrongdoing by a public official. *Also see* **malpractice, Watergate**.

mallet percussion *MusInstr* **Percussion** instruments played by mallets. <chimes, glockenspiel, marimba, vibes, xylophone.

malpractice *Crit&Eval* Improper or unethical conduct by someone in a professional or official position. *Also see* **malfeasance**.

mambo *Dnce, MusArts* Mid-1940s and 1950s Latin Cuban Dance and Music style with heavy influence from American Swing.

Also see **Dances**.

MAN (Metropolitan Area Network) *iMedia* Data network intended to serve an area the size of a large city. Such networks are being implemented by innovative techniques, such as running optical fibre through subway tunnels.

management *EntreP* Process of working with or through others to achieve an individual or business goal by efficiently and effectively using resources.

management contract *LegAsp* Legal agreement between the artist and the **personal manager** or between the artist and the talent agency. Some performer unions, e.g., **AFM, AFTRA, SAG**, provide their own management or talent agency contract forms. *Also see* **Contracts, Talent Agencies**.

management functions *EntreP* Activities of planning, leading, organizing, and controlling.

Management Information System (MIS) *InfoMgt* » **MIS**

management *Mgt* **1** Act, manner, or practice of managing; handling, supervision, or control of an enterprise, or an artist, or group of artists. **2** Person or persons who control or direct a business or enterprise.

management team *EntreP* Managers and other key persons who give a company its general direction.

manager *Mgt* One who handles, controls, or directs a business or other enterprise to pre-defined, specific goals. *Also see* **Managers**.

Managers *ColEntry, Mgt* » **actor** —, **administrator, Arts** —, **ATPAM, business** —, **clearances** —, **company** —, **house** —, **information** —, **information technology** —, **location** —, **manager, managing director, network administrator, personal** —, **presenter, production** —, **production stage manager** —, **radio station** —, **road** —, **stage** —, **tour** —, **unit** —.

managing director *Mgt, PerfA&C* **1** Person responsible for the business functions of a theatrical production company: fund raising, ticket sales, box office management. **2** Basically, a not-for-profit theatrical producer. *Also see* **Directors, Managers**.

mandolin *MusInstr* Instrument with a usu. pear-shaped body and a fretted neck over which several pairs of strings are stretched. *Also see* **Musical Instrument Families**.

manifest model *iMedia* Describes the way in which the application (interface) presents itself to its users.

mannequin *Fashn* **1** Life-size full or partial representation of the human body, used for the fitting or displaying of clothes; a dummy. **2** Jointed model of the human body used by artists, esp. to demonstrate the arrangement of drapery. LAY FIGURE **3** One who models clothes; a model. *Also see* **merchandising**.

manner-means-object *Crit&Eval* **A priori** analytical terms by which any form of imitative art can be distinguished from any other form. Roughly, the **means** refers to the material from which the form of art is composed (bronze, paint, music, rhythmic motions, language), the **object** to that which is imitated, and the **manner** to the choice of the artist to be present in the work or not, e.g., narrative vs. dramatic presentation.

mannerism *Crit&Eval* **1** Affected style or habit in dress or speech. **2** Distinctive behavioral trait; an **idiosyncrasy**.

Mannerism *VisArts* Artistic style of the late 16th century characterized by distortion of elements such as scale and perspective. *Also see* **Art Movements and Periods**.

mano a mano (Span. for "hand to hand") *Crit&Eval* Face-to-face encounter or contest.

manqué (man-kay, Fr. for "to fail") *Crit&Eval* Frustrated in the realization of one's aspirations. <an artist manqué; a writer manqué>

mantle *Fashn* Loose, sleeveless coat worn over outer garments; a cloak.

manual accounting systems *E&F-Acc* Data are fed into the system manually by entering each transaction from a source document to the **general journal**. Then, each debit and credit is posted to the correct **ledger account**. A **worksheet** is used as a tool to prepare the financial statement. Usually used by small companies. Larger companies use a more efficient and economical way of recording transactions. <computerized accounting systems>

manuals *MusInstr* Keyboards of an organ

manuscript *LitArts, MusArts* **1** Book, document, or other composition written by hand. **2** Computer-written, typewritten or handwritten version of a book, an article, a document, or other work,

---

esp. the author's own copy, prepared and submitted for publication in print.

manuscript receipt record *Journ* Form used to log the receipt and processing of free-lance manuscripts.

MAP *ArtPerf, MusArts* **Musicians' Assistance Program/Project Straight Life, Inc.** Free service – supported Local 802, **AFM** – "committed to the goal of helping musicians, a largely uninsured population, get appropriate free or low cost treatment for drug and alcohol problems as well as personal, relational, and work-related problems."

MAR *Journ* **Mythical Average Reader**

Mardi Gras *or* **Mardi gras** *PA-Variety* **1** Carnival period coming to a climax on the day before Ash Wednesday. **2** Celebrated as a holiday in many places – particularly in New Orleans – with carnivals, masquerade balls, and parades of costumed merry-makers. *Also see* **festival, krewe, throws.**

margin *Eco&Fin* **1** Minimum return that an enterprise may earn and still pay for itself. **2** Difference between the cost and the selling price of products and services or securities or commodities. **3** Difference between the **market value** of collateral and the face value of a loan. **4**Amount in money, or represented by securities, deposited by a customer with a broker as a provision against loss on transactions made on account. *Also see* **gross profit, margin of profit.**

margin *iMedia* **1** Blank space bordering the written or printed area on a page. **2**. Area between the edge of a screen and content, or between pieces of content.

margin of profit *Eco&Fin* Relationship of **gross profits** to **net sales.** *Also see* **list price. net margin.**

marginal *Crit&Eval* **1** Barely within a lower standard or limit of quality. **2** Written or printed in the margin of a book.

marginal *Eco&Fin* Having to do with enterprises that produce goods or provide services at a rate that barely covers production costs.

marginal cost *EntreP* Cost of hiring one more unit of labor or the cost of producing one more unit of output.

mariachi *MusArts* **1** Mexican street band, consisting of violins, guitars, **guitarrón** (large bass guitar), and trumpets that play music from the state of Jalisco. **2** Music performed by such a band.

Marian Anderson Award *ArtPerf, MusArts* Annual award made to an artist "whose leadership benefits humanity." *Also see* **Marian Anderson.**

marimba *MusInstr* Large **mallet percussion** instrument played on hard wooden bars, with **resonators**, resembling a **vibraphone** and **xylophone.** MARIMBA PLAYER, MARIMBAIST (RARE) *Also see* **Musical Instrument Families.**

marionette *PA-Variety* Jointed **puppet** moved by strings or **wires** by operators working from above the miniature stage.

mark *InfoMgt* Character or feature in a file or record used to locate a specific point or condition.

mark *MusArts* To sing in half-voice, leaving out high notes altogether so as to save voice during rehearsals.

mark down *Mktg* To mark for sale at a lower price. *Also see* **markdown.**

mark up *Mktg* To mark for sale at a higher price. *Also see* **markup.**

markdown *Mktg* Amount by which a price is reduced below the original selling price. *Also see* **mark down.**

marker *Fashn* Cutting guide or pattern layout made on a sheet of lightweight paper the same width as the fabric thus avoid waste of fabric and accommodate the cutting order.

market *EntreP, Mktg* **1** All current and potential consumers of particular goods or services. **2** Any place or environment in which ideas and concepts, and goods and services are exchanged for money or bartered for other goods and services. <Open area public market, commodity or stock market, catalog sales, electronic shopping, domestic or world market, etc>

market aggregation *Mktg* Sum differentiated marketing strategy.

market analysis *EntreP* Evaluation process that encompasses market segmentation, marketing research, and sales forecasting.

market definition *Mktg* Attempt by the marketer to determine which segment of the market its operations are or should be serving.

market demand curve *EntreP* Curve showing the relationship between price and quantity demanded by all consumers together, ceteris paribus (other things being equal)

market development *Mktg* Marketer marketing its current goods or services.

market economy *Eco&Fin* One controlled by market forces based on the **Law of Supply and Demand**.

market equilibrium *EntreP* Situation in which the quantity of a product demanded equals the quantity supplied, so there is no pressure to change the price.

market forces *Mktg* External factors that affect or change the marketing environment; these factors over which marketers have limited control, if any, include. <economics, nature, politics, regulations, technology, society, and competition> *Also see* **Outside Forces.**

market maker *EntreP* Member of an exchange who posts bid/ask spreads.

market making *EntreP* Activity of posting a bid and an ask.

market niche *Mktg* Segment of the market where there is a demand for a product or a service with specific attributes different from competing offerings.

market order *EntreP* Order to buy or sell at the best possible current price.

market penetration pricing *Mktg* Strategy whereby the initial price of a product or service is set low in relation to the target market's price range.

market potential *Mktg* Calculation of maximum possible sales or usage opportunities in a defined territorial area for all marketers of a product or service during a given period of time.

market price *Eco&Fin, Mktg* Prevailing price at which merchandise, securities, or commodities are sold.

market ratios *EntreP* Ratios which are used by investors to determine if they should invest capital in a company in exchange for ownership.

market research *EntreP* Qualitative method of forecasting which uses surveys, tests, and observations to project sales.

market risk *EntreP* Uncertainty associated with an investment decision.

market segment *Mktg* Smaller portion of the overall market for a product, usu. defined by very specific demographic criteria.

market segmentation *EntreP, Mktg* Dividing the total market into specific segments in order to market a product more effectively to its primary customers. Each segment has specific characteristics unique to that group.

market share *Mktg* Ratio of an organization's sales volume for a particular product category total market volume on either an actual or a potential basis.

market supply curve *EntreP* Curve showing the relationship between price and quantity supplied by all producers together, ceteris paribus (other things being equal)

market supply curve for labor *EntreP, HR&LR* Curve showing the relationship between the wage and the quantity of labor supplied.

market value *Eco&Fin, E&F-Acc, EntreP, Mktg* **1** Current replacement cost for inventory. **2**Amount that a seller may expect for merchandise, services, or securities in the open market. **3** Value of a share of common stock that the investor is willing to pay in the market place. Also the value of any asset that an investor is willing to pay in the marketplace.

marketable securities *E&F-Acc* Investments that have a maturity of more than ninety days but are intended to be held only until cash is needed for current operations. SHORT-TERM investments. *Also see* **short-term.**

marketer *also* **marketeer** *Mktg* One who sells goods or services in or to a market, "Frequently, artists will be suspicious and antagonistic toward the marketing director and his efforts because they have a negative attitude about the whole idea of selling their work. There are artists who believe that it is vulgar, cheap, insulting, or even destructive to the art. This opinion is, of course, based upon experiences with the stereotypical 'Madison Avenue' type of marketing person, or a basic misunderstanding of the marketing process." — Patricia Cox (arts marketer)

marketing *Mktg* Commercial functions involved in transferring goods and services from producer to user.

marketing audit *Mktg* Unbiased and comprehensive review and appraisal of a marketer's policies, objectives, strategies, and results.

marketing mix *Mktg* Combination of media, strategies, and operational technique that make up a total marketing plan. Such a combination may include: (1) Market research, (2) Develop the product or service, (3) Develop sales strategies, (4) Advertising and Promotion, (5) Physical distribution, (6) Customer satisfaction, evaluation.

marketing planning *Mktg* Establishing objectives for marketing activity and to determine and schedule the procedure to achieve such objectives.

marketing research *Mktg* Systematic gathering, recording, and analyzing of data to provide information for marketing decision making.

marketoid jargon *Mktg* Internet entry that smacks of market oversell.

marketplace *also* **market-place** *Mktg* » **market**

markup *iMedia* **1** Refers to the sequence of characters or other symbols inserted at certain places in a document to indicate the document's logical structure. *Ex.* **XHTML**, (<element attribute = "value">) Markup indicators are often called tags. *Also see* **HTML, XML.**

markup *Mktg* Amount added to a cost price in calculating a selling price, esp. an amount that takes into account **overhead** and profit. *Also see* **markon, markdown.**

markup *VA-Prntng* Detailed stylistic instructions to the typesetter marked on a manuscript to be typeset.

Marley floor *Dnce* Thin, vinyl floor covering rolled out and taped down whenever dance is performed on a stage, thus covering floor splinters, irregularities and giving a consistent surface for the dancer.

Marquand, John P (1893-1960, fictwri.) *ArtPerf, LitArts* Novelist who wrote, and satirized, the mannered traditions of the Boston upper class. <*The Late George Apley* (1937, **Pulitzer**) *Point of No Return* (1949) » *Also see* **artistic temperament, empathic response, presence, talent.**

marquee *PerfA&C* **1** Rooflike structure, often bearing a signboard, projecting over an entrance to a theater. **2** Large tent with open sides, used chiefly for outdoor entertainment.

Marsalis, Wynton (1961-, jazz and classical tp., arr.-comp., arts mgr., prod., educ.) *Also see* **black music, call and response, ethnocentricity, quote.**

mart *Mktg* Trading center; a market.

Marx, Karl (1818-1883, Ger. philos., econ., revolutionary) *Eco&Fin, Law&Pol* <*The Communist Manifesto* (1848) with Friedrich Engels (1820-1895, Ger. socialist theorist.)

Marxism *Crit&Eval, Eco&Fin* Relating to the political and economic ideas of **Karl Marx** and Friedrich Engels (» Karl Marx) *Also see* **communism.**

Mary Tyler Moore (MTM) *Flm&Vid, Rdio/TV* » **MTM**

mash-ups *MusArts, RecA&S* Mixing two or three quite different recordings by established stars, often in contravention of copyright law. BOOTLEGS

mask (n) *PerfA&C* **1** Facial covering worn for ritual. **2** Figure of a head worn by actors in Greek and Roman drama to identify a character or trait and to amplify the voice. Occasionally used by modern playwrights. <**Eugene O'Neill's** *Great God Brown* (1926)>

mask (v) *PerfA&C* To block the audience's view, generally, of backstage equipment and space.

mask *Rdio/TV* **Translucent** border framing a TV picture tube and screen.

mask *iMedia, InfoMgt* Pattern of characters, bits, or bytes used to control the elimination or retention of another pattern of characters, bits, or bytes.

mask *VA-Prntng* Sheet of opaque paper or plastic that holds negatives in position as offset plates are exposed.

masking *PerfA&C* Any drapery or scenic piece used to define the stage or block the view of the audience. *Also see* **border, leg.**

masque *TheatArts* Brief, usu. symbolic, mythological or allegorical play with elaborate scenic effects, performed at the English court in the 16th and 11th centuries: performed both by actors and courtiers. Ben Jonson (1572-1637), playwright, and Indigo Jones (1573-1652), scenic artist, are famously associated with the form.

masquerade *Crit&Eval* **1** To go about in disguise. **2** Deceptive appearance.

mass *Crit&Eval* **1** Relating to a large number of people. <mass education; mass communication> **2** Done or carried out on a large scale. <mass production>

mass *MusArts* Musical setting of certain parts of the Mass. <Kyrie, Gloria, Credo, Sanctus, Benedictus, and Agnus Dei>

mass *VisArts* Area of unified light, shade, or color in a painting.

mass appeal *Mktg* Something that appeals to a large number of people; **mass market.**

mass entertainment *Crit&Eval* Forms and styles of entertainment available via **mass media.** MASS AUDIENCE

mass market *Mktg* Relating to the consumption of goods and services by large numbers of people. <**tabloid** press, paperback books, network TV>

mass media *Journ ,Mktg* **1** Means of public communication reaching a large audience. **2** Informational and opinionated outlets – newspapers, magazines, radio and TV, billboards, direct mail – that contain news, features, and advertising that convey marketing messages to large numbers of people.

Massachusetts Institute of Technology *InfoMgt* » **MIT**

masscult *Cult&Soc* Culture at the level of the masses. *Also see* **elitism.**

master *ArtPerf* **1** Artist or a performer of great and exemplary skill. **2** Worker qualified to teach apprentices and carry on the craft independently.

master *Flm&Vid* Original **negative** ready for printing in composite form; vaulted for later runs of additional submasters or direct prints.

master *Genl* Original from which copies are made.

master *RecA&S* » **master recording**

master class *MusArts* Teaching and demonstration session by a virtuosa or virtuoso to a select group of aspiring professional instrumentalists or singers.

master of ceremonies *PerfA&C* Performer who conducts a program of varied entertainment by introducing other performers or speakers to the audience. EMCEE *Also see* **compere.**

master pattern *Fashn* » **sloper**

master recording *RecA&S* Any recording of sound, whether or not coupled with a visual image, by any method and on any substance or material intended for reproduction in the form of phonograph records or otherwise. *Also see* **lacquer disc, plating, pressing, safety master.**

master recording license royalty *IntelProp, RecA&S* Royalties on the sale of records and tapes containing a licensed master track (on **record club** editions, compilation albums and CDs) are paid by the **licensee** (**record club**, merchandising company, mail order company) to the record company, recording artist, and record producer. *Also see* **Royalties.**

master shot *Flm&Vid* Uninterrupted shot that contains an entire scene. **Tighter shots** are photographed later, and an edited sequence, composed of a variety of shots, is constructed in **post-production.**

masterpiece *Genl* **1** Greatest work of an artist. **2** Outstanding work of art or craft. MASTERWORK

mat *VA-Prntng* *Also see* **plate**

mat *VisArts* Decorative border around a picture as a frame or to provide contrast between the picture and the frame.

mat *PerfA&C* matinee

matching action *Flm&Vid* Movement repeated in several camera angles and then edited so that the action seems to be in one continuous flow.

matching grant *Fnding* Grant made to match funds provided by another donor. *Also see* **challenge grant, employee matching gift**

material *Crit&Eval* Concept, idea, or information that may be reshaped and made or incorporated into a finished effort: material for a comedy. **2** Substance from which an idea or an object or product is made.

material *MusArts, PerfA&C* Something, such as an idea or a sketch, to be refined and made or incorporated into a finished effort. <material for a comic routine>

material wants *Mktg* » **wants**

materialism *Cult&Soc* Theory that worldly possessions constitute the greatest good and highest value in life. *Also see* **consumerism (2)**

materiality *E&F-Acc* Refers to the relative important of an items or an event. If an item or event is material, it is probably relevant to the users of financial statements.

matière *VisArts* **Texture** of the image on the artwork or the work itself made by pigments, brush touches or strokes, canvas, and other **mixed media**. *Also see* **informal**.

matinee *or* **matinée** (mat.) *MusArts,PerfA&C* Entertainment, such as a dramatic or musical performance, given in the daytime, usu. in the afternoon.

matinee idol *Crit&Eval* (Passé) Male film or stage star in the 1920s and 1930s — handsome, **debonair**, and sexy. *Also see* **idol**.

Matisse, Henri (1869-1954, Fr. pntr., sculp., lithog.) *ArtPerf, VisArts* One of the greatest painters of the 20th century whose "supreme accomplishment, which may be seen in all his work, was to liberate color from its traditionally realistic function and to make it the foundation of a decorative art of the highest order." — Carter Ratcliff (art critic) <*Woman with a Hat* (1905), *Piano lesson* (1917) *Also see* **fauvism freedom**, **les fauves**, **postimpressionism**.

matrix *InfoMgt* Network of intersections between input and output leads in a computer, functioning as an **encoder** or a **decoder**.

matrix *RecA&S* Electroplated impression of a phonograph record used to make duplicate records.

matrix *VA-Prntng* Mold used in stereotyping and designed to receive positive impressions of type or illustrations from which metal plates can be cast. MAT

matte *VisArts* dull finish, unlike **glossy**

matte shot *Flm&Vid* Process of combining two separate shots on one print, resulting in an image that looks as though it had been photographed normally. Used mostly for **special effects**, such as combining a human figure with giant dinosaurs.

mature *Mktg* Said of an industry, a market, or a product no longer subject to great expansion or development.

maturity *Crit&Eval* State or quality of being fully grown or developed.

maturity date *E&F-Acc* Time at which the final payment of the note is due.

maturity value *E&F-Acc* Sum of the **principal** and interest due at the maturity date of a **note**.

maudlin *Crit&Eval* Effusively or tearfully sentimental.

maven (may'-ven, Yinglish*) Crit&Eval* Person who has special knowledge or experience; an expert.

maw *Flm&Vid* "What they call in Hollywood a model, actress, and whatever." — James Lipton (drama tchr., plywri)

mawkish *Crit&Eval* Excessively and objectionably sentimental; sickening or insipid in taste.

maxixe *Dnce* Brazilian **tango** derived from the polka and the **lundu**; evolved into the **samba**.

Mayer, Louis B.(urt) (1885-1957, Russ.-born motion-picture prod.) *Flm&Vid, Mgt* He formed a film company (1918) that merged with **Samuel Goldwyn** to form **Metro-Goldwyn-Mayer** (MGM, 1924) *Also see* **mogul**.

mazel (mahzel, Yinglish) *Genl* Luck.

mazel tov (mahzel'-tuff, Yinglish) *Genl* Good luck, congratulations, Thank God!, at last.

MB *InfoMgt* **megabyte**

MBG *Mktg* money-back guarantee

mbira *MusInstr* Bantu (African) instrument consisting of a hollow gourd or wooden resonator and a number of usu. metal strips that vibrate when plucked by the player's thumb. THUMB PIANO

MBS*Rdio/TV* » **Mutual Broadcasting System**

MCA *Flm&Vid, Mgt, PA-Variety, Rdio/TV, RecA&S* Founded by **Jules Stein** in 1924 in Chicago as **Music Corporation of America**, a talent agency and booking office. It became **MCA** after a federal **divestiture** order in the 1950s. In 1993, sold to **Matsushita** (Japan) in 1995, sold to **Seagram** (Canada) Now a global entertainment **conglomerate**. <MCA Records and affiliated labels, Universal film studio, TV syndication, **theme parks**, music publishing, cinemas> *Also see* **Talent Agencies**.

MCA Records *RecA&S* Division of the **MCA** entertainment conglomerate. *Also see* **major labels**.

MCANA *Crit&Eval* » **Music Critics Association of North America**

McCarthy, Joseph Raymond (1908-57, U.S. Sen., Wis, 1947-57) *Law&Pol* He presided over the permanent subcommittee on investigations and held public hearings in which he accused army officials, members of the media, and public figures of being Communists. His charges were never proved, and he was censured by the Senate in 1954 *Also see* **Edward R. Murrow**.

McCarthyism *Ethcs&Phil, Law&Pol* **1** Political wake of former Senator **Joseph McCarthy**. **2** Practice of publicizing accusations of political disloyalty or subversion with insufficient regard to evidence. **3** Use of unfair investigatory or accusatory methods in order to suppress opposition. *Also see* **loyalty oath**.

McCluhan, Marshall (1911-1980) *iMedia* Philosopher, writer, and director, Center for Culture and Technology, U. of Toronto. McLuhan saw electronic media as a return to collective ways of perceiving the world. His "global village" theory posited the ability of electronic media to unify and retribalize the human race. Master of the aphorism, McLuhan is the originator of the phrases "medium is the message," and "hot" and "cool" media.

m.e. *Journ* managing editor.

MCI *InfoMgt* **Microwave Communications, Inc**. Second largest (to **AT&T**) long distance phone carrier in the U.S.

MDMA *Cult&Soc* » **ecstasy**

mdse. *Mktg* merchandise

me (mee) *MusArts* third tone of a **diatonic scale**

me generation *Cult&Soc* Younger people of the 1970s, viewed as self-centered and self-indulgent.

means *Crit&Eval* » **manner-means-object**

measure *Law&Pol* Legislative bill or enactment.

measure *LitArts* Poetic **meter**

measure *MusArts* Metric unit between two bars on the **staff**; a **bar**.

mechanical *VA-Prntng* Layout of type proofs, artwork, or both, exactly positioned and prepared for making a printing plate.

mechanical age modeling *iMedia* Showing or resembling a process from a physical machine as a metaphor within an explicitly non-mechanical medium. example is the "play" or "fast forward" button of common media player interfaces.

mechanical license *IntelProp, RecA&S* Granted by a publisher to a record company, allowing the right to record and release a specific composition at an agreed-upon fee per unit manufactured and sold. *Also see* **music licenses**.

mechanical right *IntelProp, RecA&S* » **Compulsory Mechanical License, Music Licenses**

mechanical rights agency *IntelProp, RecA&S* Special representative of music publishers who is engaged to license their music for use by record companies, film producers, and others who reproduce copyrighted musical works in mechanical and **audio-visual** devices. *Also see* **Harry Fox Agency, Inc**. (HFA) and **Copyright-Related Organizations**.

mechanical royalty *IntelProp, RecA&S* Record company periodically pays to the authors and publishers of recorded music, the total sum of six-plus cents – the rate is adjusted every two (2) years, based upon the **Consumer Price Index** – per tune per copy sold. <Album with ten tunes sells 40,000 copies. Mechanical royalty = $24,000 (10 x 6¢ x 40,000) usu. divided equally between the publisher and the authors. Authors divide their share without formula. If it so happens, and it often does, that the record company is also the publisher, that share of the **mechanical** royalty merely shifts from one pocket to another. [By various means, record companies try hard, and succeed often, to arbitrarily reduce the amount of mechanical royalties due the author and publisher.] *Also see* **cross-collateralization, excess mechanicals, Royalties**.

Media *ColEntry, InfoMgt, Journ, Rdio/TV* <**Advertising Media, alternative —, broadcast, cablecast, electronic —, interactive —, narrowcast, mass —, mixed —, multimedia, narrowcast, new —, print —, telecast., unpaid —>**

media *iMedia* **1** More than one medium. **2** Form of communication, information, or entertainment; technologies that convey human experiences.

media *InfoMgt, Journ, Rdio/TV* Means of mass communication. <television, local and network; Cable, local and network; Radio,

local and network; Magazines, inc. inserts; Newspapers inc. Sunday Supplements and other inserts; **out-of-home** advertising, and **direct marketing**> DIRECT MAIL, DIRECT RESPONSE, OUTDOOR ADVERTISING.

media buy *Mktg* Purchase of advertising in one or more media. <newspapers, magazines, radio, TV, etc>

Media Circulation *ColEntry, Journ* >**circulation, controlled —, external —, internal —. nonpaid —, paid —>**

Media Coalition, The *LegAsp* Association of booksellers, book and periodical publishers, wholesalers, and distributors that defends the First Amendment right to produce and sell books, magazines, recordings, and videotapes; and defends the public's right to have access to the broadest possible range of opinion and entertainment. goodworks, jobs, 584<

media conversion *Mktg* **Media** exposure of an advertiser evaluated in terms of media dollars, i.e, determine the cost of purchasing an equivalent amount of advertising.

media event *Journ* Staged event designed to attract press coverage and public interest. PSEUDO-EVENT

mediation *HR&LR* Attempt to bring about a peaceful settlement or compromise between disputants through the objective intervention of a neutral party.

Medicaid *also* **medicaid** (MEDICal + AID) *Eco&Fin, Law&Pol* Program in the U.S., jointly funded by the states and the federal government, that reimburses hospitals and physicians for providing care to qualifying people who cannot finance their own medical expenses. [MEDIC(AL) + AID.] Also *see* **FICA, Medicare, Social Security.**

Medicare *also* **medicare** *Eco&Fin, Law&Pol* Program under the U.S. Social Security Administration that reimburses hospitals and physicians for medical care provided to qualifying people over 65 years old. Also *see* **FICA, Medicaid, Social Security.**

medicine show *PA-Variety* Traveling show, popular esp. in the 19th century, that offered varied entertainment, between the acts of which medicines of dubious quality but high alcohol content were peddled. <Lydia Pinkham's Vegetable Compound, and Hadacol, an all-purpose nostrum distilled "from an ole Cajun recipe," that was hyped in big pop name travelling shows in the late 1940s> Also *see* **barnstorm.**

medieval *also* **mediaeval** *Crit&Eval, Cult&Soc* Old-fashioned; unenlightened. <those men and women who believe that women belong at home. 2 Relating to the **Middle Ages.** Also *see* **romance.**

medievalist *Cult&Soc* Connoisseur of **medieval** culture.

mediocre *Crit&Eval* Moderate to inferior in quality; ordinary.

mediocrity *Crit&Eval* 1 Mediocre ability, achievement, or performance. 2 One that displays mediocre qualities.

medium frequency (mf.) *Rdio/TV* Radio frequency or radio-frequency band in the range 300 to 3,000 **kilohertz.**

medium *iMedia* Technology that conveys human experience.

medium *InfoMgt, Journ, Rdio/TV* singular of **media**

medium *VA-Prntng* Size of paper: 18 x 23 inches or 171/2 x 22 inches.

medium *VisArts* Specific artistic technique or means of expression determined by the materials or the creative methods used. <the technique of etching; watercolor as a medium>

medley *MusArts* Musical arrangement comprising various songs.

Meet the Composer *MusArts* National program which provides money to communities or organizations to **host** composers in conjunction with the performance of their works.

mega *InfoMgt* One million <megabucks, **megahertz**>

megabyte (MG) *InfoMgt* One thousand **kilobytes.** Also *see* **byte; gigabyte.**

megacycle *Rdio/TV* » **megahertz**

megahertz (MHz) *InfoMgt, Rdio/TV* » **MHz**

megalomania *Crit&Eval* 1 Psychopathological condition in which delusional fantasies of wealth, power, or omnipotence predominate. 2 Obsession with grandiose or extravagant things or actions.

megaphone *RecA&S* Funnel-shaped device used to direct and acoustically amplify the voice. Also *see* **acoustic recording.**

megapixel *InfoMgt* One million **pixels**, used in reference to the **resolution** of a graphics device.

megillah (m'gill'-a, Yinglish) *Crit&Eval* Very long, boring or verbose rigmarole; same old familiar story or excuse.

MEIEA *Mgt, MusArts* **Music & Entertainment Industry Ed-**

ucators **Association.** National professional organization whose members are teachers and administrators in music and entertainment undergraduate and graduate programs.

Meistersinger *MusArts* Member of one of the guilds organized in the principal cities of Germany in the 14th, 15th, and 16th centuries to establish competitive standards for the composition and performance of music and poetry.

Melancholy Baby (© 1911) *MusArts* "We've all heard this song so many times I think we may have forgotten a few salient facts about it. First, its title is most unusual, the seldom-used and dignified adjective 'melancholy' qualifying the **colloquial** term of endearment 'baby.' Second, the melody is not only good, containing highly unexpected phrases for that era, but it also just might be the first **torch song**. Third, its melody writer, listed as Ernie Burnett, may have been a **'one-shot'** writer. For as far as I can determine, this was his only big song." — **Alec Wilder** *Also see* **piano bar.**

melee (maylay) *Crit&Eval* Violent free-for-all. <**mosh pit**>

melisma *MusArts* Decorative passage of several notes sung to one syllable of text. <black gospel music, **Gregorian chant**>

mellifluous *Crit&Eval* 1 Smooth and sweet. <The commentator had a mellifluous, well-educated voice> 2 Flowing with sweetness or honey.

mellow *Crit&Eval* 1 Having the gentleness, wisdom, or tolerance often characteristic of **maturity**. 2 Relaxed and unhurried; easygoing. 3 Slightly and pleasantly intoxicated; pleasantly high from smoking [inhaling] marijuana.

mellow *MusArts* Sound rich and soft

melodeon *MusInstr* small reed organ Also *see* **Musical Instrument Families.**

melodious *Crit&Eval* Relating to a pleasing succession of sounds; tuneful; agreeable to hear. Also *see* **musical.**

melodrama *Flm&Vid* Drama, such as a film, or television program, involving exaggerated violence, emotion, or malevolent intrigue, usu. with flat stereotypical characters. *Origin* Any musical play, inc. opera. In modern usage, melodrama bears roughly the same relation to tragedy that farce bears to comedy.

melodrama *TheatArts* Serious dramatic form employing exciting action with the emphasis on situation rather than character, and utilizing a schematic opposition between good and evil in which good usu. prevails. In its 18th century origins, it referred to popular plays which used music to support their clear- cut moral action. Its simplest examples are 19th century "tied-to-the-railroads" plays. Now, the form is found in mystery and suspense dramas.

melodramatic *Crit&Eval* 1 Exaggeratedly emotional or sentimental; histrionic: 2 Characterized by false **pathos** and sentiment.

melody *MusArts* 1 Pleasing succession or arrangement of sounds. 2 Musical quality: the melody of verse. 3 Rhythmically organized sequence of single tones so related to one another as to make up a particular phrase or idea. 4 Poem suitable for setting to music or singing. Also *see* **analysis of tragedy.**

Melpomene *TheatArts* The Muse of **tragedy** Also *see* **Muses.**

members *Fndng, Mktg* Individuals who join an organization and pay dues and support it periodically with funds and/or services.

membership candidate *HR&LR* **Apprentice**-type program within **Actors Equity Association** (AEA)

memento *Genl* reminder of the past Also *see* **relic.**

memes *iMedia* Unit of cultural information, such as a cultural practice or idea, transmitted verbally or by repeated action from one mind to another.

memex *iMedia* Theoretical device thought of by **Vannevar Bush** which would store various types of information (including text and graphics) on microfilm. Access to the information would be through associative logic.

memoir, memoirs *LitArts* 1 Account of the personal experiences of an author. 2 Autobiography. 3 Biography or biographical sketch. 4 Report on a scientific or scholarly topic. Also *see* **memorialist.**

memorabilia *Crit&Eval* 1 Objects valued for their connection with historical events, culture, or entertainment. <coins, posters, photographs, plates, etc> 2 Events or experiences worthy of remembrance.

memorialist *LitArts* One who writes **memoirs**

memory *InfoMgt* Portion of the **central processing unit** that holds data and instructions; also known as primary storage or main memory.

memory cache *InfoMgt* Memory dedicated to increasing the efficiency and operating speed of the computer.

MENC *MusArts* **Music Educators National Conference** Professional organization – headquartered in Reston, VA – whose members are music teachers, or music department administrators in all grades through university level. *Also see* **National Coalition for Music Education.**

Mencken, HL (Henry Louis Mencken, 1880-1956, critic, ed., n-fictwri, philologist) *Crit&Eval, Journ* His essays were models of literary form and profound **acerbity.** <*Prejudices* (6 vols., 1919-27), *The American Language* (1919, 4th ed., 1936 plus supplements)> *Also see* **ecdysiast, justice, puritanism.**

mental model *iMedia* **1** Abstract, simplified version of a complex system or procedure held in one's mind. **2** way in which the user thinks of the task that the application is automating.

mention *Mktg* Verbal or printed identification of a sponsor in association with an event or an attraction.

mento *MusArts* Early rural music of Jamaica that emphasized the drum beat and **kalimba.** *Also see* **ska.**

mentor *Crit&Eval* Wise and trusted counselor or teacher.

mentsh (mench, Yinglish) *Crit&Eval* Upright, honorable decent person; someone of consequence; someone to emulate.

menu *InfoMgt* On-screen series of program options that allows you to select the course of action you wish to take.

merchandise (mdse.) *Fndng* Articles, marked with sponsor identification, for sale or give-away that have an association with the sponsored artist(s) or events.

merchandise (mdse.) *Mktg* Goods bought and sold in business.

merchandise inventory (beginning and ending) *E&F-Acc* Those goods held for resale. Distinguished beginning or ending inventory amounts are used in calculations of **cost of goods sold.** *Also see* **Inventory Methods.**

merchandising *Mktg* Promotion of merchandise sales by developing advertising and display strategies.

merchandising aids *Mktg* Audio or visual announcement or displays at the **point-of sale** (**point-of purchase**) <videos, counter cards, **hangtags, mannequins**>

merchandising right(s) *Mktg* Permission to merchandise a product is allowed by a license issued by rights owner to the merchandiser for a fee and/or royalties.

merchandising tie-ins *Mgt, Mktg* Royalties derived from the licensing of merchandising rights associated with an artist is an important source of income for copyright and **trademark** owners. <artists, authors, publishers, record companies> *Also see* **artist tie-ins, corporate tie-ins.**

Mercury Theater *TheatArts* Founded in New York in the late 1930s by **Orson Welles.** It featured contemporary drama, modern dress classics, and the new **genre** spawned by the **Federal Theatre.** *Also see* **Theaters & Theatres.**

merengue *Dnce, MusArts* 1950s dance music of Dominican/Haitian folk origin. *Also see* **Dances; Latin Dance Music.**

merger *LegAsp* **1** Union of two or more commercial interests or corporations. **2** Absorption of a lesser estate, liability, right, action, or offense into a greater one.

merits *LegAsp* Party's strict legal rights, excluding jurisdictional, personal, or technical aspects. **2** Factual content of a matter, apart from emotional, contextual, or formal considerations.

meshugaas *or* **mishegaas** *or* **mishegoss** (Yinglish) *Crit&Eval* Crazy or senseless activity or behavior; craziness.

meshugge (m'-shu'-geh, Yinglish) *Crit&Eval* Crazy, obsessed; maddened by a phobia; bizarre.

mesmeric *Crit&Eval* Strong or spellbinding appeal; fascination.

mesmerize *Crit&Eval* To spellbind; **enthrall.** <Richard Burton (Richard Jenkins, 1925-84, Welsh-born film/stage act.) could mesmerize an audience by the force of his presence and voice>

message *Ethcs&Phil* Basic thesis or lesson; a moral. <a stage play with a message>

message board *InfoMgt* "Places" where online users engage in informal discussion.

Met *MusArts* Metropolitan Opera (NYC) First performance, 1883 In 1966, it moved to the **Lincoln Center for the Performing Arts.**

metadata *iMedia* **1** Information about data **2** Self-referential information about information.

metamorphoses *Crit&Eval* Marked change in appearance, character, condition, or function.

metaphor *iMedia* Definition of something by comparing it to something else. Interactive media products often employ or reference **spatial**, event, or character-based metaphors (or a combination of the three)

metaphor *LitArts* Figure of speech in which a word or phrase that ordinarily designates one thing is used to designate another, thus making an implicit comparison. <a sea of troubles>

metaphysics *Ethcs&Phil* Branch of philosophy that examines the nature of reality, inc. the relationship between mind and matter, substance and attribute, fact and value.

metatheater *TheatArts* Term used to describe plays that self-consciously comment on the process of "theatre" and so treat the relationship between theater and life. Such plays sometimes use the play-within-the- play device.

meter *LitArts* **1** Measured arrangement of words in poetry, as by accentual **rhythm**, syllabic quantity, or the number of syllables in a line. **2 Rhythmic** pattern of a stanza, determined by the kind and number of lines.

meter *MusArts* Division into **measures** or bars.

method *iMedia* Programming: function associated with a specific object. <dog character wags tail — wag would be a method of tail (such as "dog.tail.wag()") Syntax varies by language.

Method, The *TheatArts* » **method acting**

method acting *TheatArts* Technique of acting adapted by **Lee Strasburg** from the work of **[Konstantin] Stanislavski** which teaches actors to use an inner psychological response as a basis for physical action. *Also see* **Aristotle, affective memory, Group Theater, psychodrama.**

method book *MusArts* Containing instructions and exercises for developing and improving techniques categorized to their level of difficulty. *Also see* **Print Music.**

methods *Fndng* Means by which goals and objectives of a fundraising campaign are achieved.

methods *Genl* Means or manner of procedure, esp. a regular and systematic way of accomplishing something.

metrical *Genl* Relating to measurement; measure.

metrical *LitArts* Relating to or composed in **poetic meter**.

metrical verse *LitArts* Five metrical units in a line.

metro edition *Journ* Edition distributed to the newspaper's metropolitan area. <the city and its suburbs, **exurbs**, and satellite towns; not downstate, upstate, or out-of-state>

Metro-Goldwyn-Mayer (MGM) *Flm&Vid* » **MGM**

Metropolitan Opera (Met) *MusArts* » **Met**

mezzanine *PerfA&C* Lowest balcony in a theater or the first few rows of that balcony.

mezzo forte (mf) (metzo for-tay, Ital. for "half loud") *MusArts* Play moderately loud. *Also see* **Music Directions.**

mezzo-soprano *ArtPerf, MusArts* Voice having a range between soprano and contralto.

mezzotint *VA-Prntng, VisArts* Method of engraving a copper or steel plate by scraping and burnishing areas to produce effects of light and shadow.

MF *ArtPerf, HR&LR, MusArts* **Musicians Foundation.** Represents the interests and advances the condition and social welfare of professional musicians and their families.

mf *MusArts* **mezzo forte**

mf *Rdio/TV* **medium frequency**

MFN *Eco&Fin, Law&Pol* **Most Favored Nation** trading status vis-à-vis U.S. and other countries.

MGM *Flm&Vid* **Metro-Goldwyn-Mayer.** Now with its library and its **backlot** sold, it's a faint shadow of its former glory as the largest, and most **prestigious** movie studio in Hollywood's golden age, ca. 1920s to the 1940s. **Samuel Goldwyn, Louis B. Mayer, major studios.**

mgr. *Mgt* **manager**

mgt. *Mgt* **management**

MHz *iMedia, InfoMgt, Rdio/TV* **megahertz. 1** One million **cycles** per second memory the portion of the **cpu** that holds data and instructions; also known as primary storage or main memory. **2**

radio-frequency unit.

mic or **mike** *Rdio / TV, RecA&S* microphone.

mickey *MusArts* Very **commercial** music; rickey-tick.

Mickey Finn *Genl* Off-menu alcoholic drink "fixed" to incapacitate the person who drinks it, usu. a prelude to robbery or worse. *Also see* **B-girl**, **dive**, **bouncer**.

mickeymousing *Flm&Vid* Type of film music purely descriptive and attempts to **mimic** the visual action with musical equivalents. Often used in cartoons.

MICR *InfoMgt* Magnetic Ink Character Recognition; a form of source data entry wherein the data is scanned directly into the computer.

micro *Fashn* Fashion term from the late 1960s as a synonym for tiny or very short skirts.

microcomputer *InfoMgt* Very small computer, such as a laptop or personal computer, built around a **microprocessor** and designed to be used by one person at a time or on a related network. *Also see* **mainframe, personal computer**.

microeconomics *Eco&Fin, EntreP* Study of the choices made by consumers, companies, and government, and how these decisions affect the market for a particular good or service. *Also see* **macroeconomics**.

microfiche *InfoMgt* Card of **microfilm** capable of accommodating and preserving a considerable number of printed pages in reduced form. FILMCARD *Also see* **microfilm**.

microfilm *InfoMgt* Film on which printed materials are photographed at greatly reduced size for ease of storage. *Also see* **microfiche**.

microphone (mic or mike) *Rdio / TV, RecA&S* Transducer that converts acoustical waves into an electric current which is usu. fed into an amplifier, recorder, or broadcast transmitter.

Microphones *ColEntry, RecA&S* » **bidirectional** —, **carbon** —, **cardioid** —, **ceramic** —, **coaxial** —, **condenser** —, **crystal** —, **differential** —, **dynamic** —, **electret** —, **gradient** —, **hypercardioid** —, **lapel** —, **lavaliere** —, **lip** —, **omnidirectional** —, **ribbon** —, **unidirectional** —, **shotgun** —, **stereo condenser** —, **wireless** —. *Also see* **transducer**.

microprocessor *InfoMgt* Programmable device resident on a chip that contains an **Arithmetic Logic Unit** (ALU), primary storage, and control section. *Also see* **microcomputer**.

Microsoft *InfoMgt* Largest software company in the world and looking for more. » **vaporware, Windows**

Microsoft Disk Operating System (MS-DOS) *InfoMgt* » **MS-DOS**

Microsoft Network *InfoMgt* Online information service *Also see* **Online Information Services**.

microwave *InfoMgt, Sci&Tech* High-frequency electromagnetic wave, one millimeter to one meter in wavelength, intermediate between infrared and short-wave radio wavelengths.

Microwave Communications, Inc. (MCI) *InfoMgt* » **MCI**

Mid and Greater Distance *LitArts* The greater the storyteller's distance from the events, the more the techniques of compression and summary are used to deal with time and content. At Mid and Greater Distance, telling and dramatization may combine summary with vivid, up close dramatic images. — John Schultz *Also see* **Close Distance**.

MID files *InfoMgt* » **MIDI**

Middle Ages *Cult&Soc* Period (5th to 15th centuries) in European history between antiquity and the **Renaissance**. *Also see* **Dark Ages**.

Middle America *Cult&Soc* **1** That part of the U.S. middle class thought of as being average in income and education and moderately conservative in values and attitudes. **2** The American heartland thought of as being made up of small towns, small cities, and suburbs. *Also see* **heartland**.

middle C *MusArts* Tone represented by a note on the first ledger line below a **treble clef** or the first ledger line above a **bass clef**. It is the first C below **international pitch**.

Middle East *also* **Mideast** *Cult&Soc* **1** Area comprising the countries of southwest Asia and northeast Africa. **2** Region of continuing political, religious, and economic turmoil.

middle managers *Mgt* Tier of management personnel directly below **upper managers** and above **first line managers**. Titles include. <vice-president, assistant vice-president, general manager, manager, director, associate director, deputy director>

middle-of-the-road *Law&Pol* Pursuing a course of action midway

between political extremes; neither liberal nor conservative.

middle-of-the road (MOR) *MusArts, RecA&S* » **easy listening**

middleman *Mktg* Trader who buys from producers and sells to retailers or consumers.

MIDI *iMedia, InfoMgt, MusInstr* Musical Instrument **Digital** Interface: "Electronic keyboard linked to a computer, a versatile compositional tool. MIDI gives you the luxury of hearing your own works performed." — Howard Sandroff (» **electronic music**)

mike or **mic** *RecA&S* microphone

mike boom *Flm&Vid* » **boom**

milestone *iMedia* Target state for a product to be in, and the time at which that state will be achieved. Most interactive media projects have between 4 and 7 major milestones depending on scope.

milk *PerfA&C* To draw out or extract approval from an audience as if by milking. <Veteran performers are adept in milking the audience for more laughs, more tears, more applause, more encores, and more curtain calls> *Also see* **claque**.

Mill, John Stuart (1806-73, Brit. econ., philos.) *Crit&Eval, Ethcs&Phil* Known esp. for his interpretations of **empiricism** and **utilitarianism**. <*A System of Logic* (1843), *Principles of Political Economy* (1848), and *The Subjection of Women* (1869)> *Also see* **Jeremy Bentham, David Hume**.

miller's bran *Th-MakeUp* Used with **latex** to create rough skin texture.

millimeter (mm) *Genl* Unit of length equal to one thousandth (10^{-3}) of a meter, or 0.0394 inch.

milliner *Fashn,PerfA&C* **1** One who designs, makes, or sells hats for women. **2** One who supervises hat costumes within a theater costume shop. MILLINERY.

millinery *Fashn* **1** Profession or business of a **milliner**. **2** Articles sold by a **milliner**.

MIME *InfoMgt* Multi-purpose Internet Mail Extensions, a method of encoding a file for delivery over the Internet.

mime *TheatArts* **1** Modern performer who specializes in comic **mimicry**. **2** Art of portraying characters and acting out situations or a narrative by gestures and body movement without the use of words; **pantomime**. **3** Performance of **pantomime**; an actor skilled in **pantomime**.

mimesis *LitArts* **Imitation** or representation of nature in art and literature. *Origin* Root of **imitate**.

mimic *ArtPerf,TheatArts* One who imitates, esp. an actor in a **mime**.

mimic *Crit&Eval* **1** Imitate closely. APE **2** Imitate so as to ridicule. MOCK

mimicry *PerfA&C* Act, practice, or art of mimicking.

mind map *iMedia* » **concept map**

mind's eye *Crit&Eval* **1** Inherent mental ability to imagine or remember scenes. **2** imagination.

mind-blowing *Crit&Eval* **1** Intensely affecting the mind or emotions. **2** Producing hallucinatory effects: mind-blowing drugs.

mind-boggling *Crit&Eval* Intellectually or emotionally overwhelming.

mind-control *Ethcs&Phil* Regulation of the thoughts of another, often by deception, fraud, threat of force or actual force.

mindset or **mind-set** *Crit&Eval* Fixed mental attitude or disposition that predetermines a person's responses to and interpretations of situations; an inclination or a habit.

mini-doc *BcstJourn* Stands for mini-documentary. A longer (2:30-7:00) package that runs during a regular newscast but usu. covers a timeless topic or angle and is prepared in advance. mini doc may run in segments over the course of several days. Also called a segment report or two-, three-, four-, or five-parter, or a series.

minimalism *Crit&Eval* Use of the fewest and barest essentials or elements, as in the arts, literature, or design.

minimalism *LitArts* Spare, straightforward writing form, "with a flat, laid-back, unemotional tone, in an appropriately bare, unadorned style." — X.J. Kennedy and Dana Gioia. Popularized most notably by author Raymond Carver in the 1970s and 1980s.

minimalism *MusArts* School or mode of contemporary music marked by extreme simplification of rhythms and patterns, prolonged chordal or melodic repetitions, and often the achievement of a throbbing, trancelike effect.

minimalism *VisArts* Primarily American movement that originated in NYC in the 1960s and attempted to explore essential elements of an art form. **MINIMAL ART, REDUCTIVISM, REJECTIVE ART** *Also see* **Art Movements and Periods, modern art**.

minimalist design *Fashn* Simple design

minor *MusArts* Minor key, scale, or interval. *Also see* **major**.

minor scale *MusArts* **Diatonic scale** having an interval of a minor third between the first and third tones and several forms with different intervals above the fifth.

Minsky, Marvin (1911-1980) *iMedia* Important contributor to the fields of artificial intelligence, emergent behavior, mathematics, and psychology, among others. Author of several books, e.g., *Society of Mind*, and *Perceptrons*.

minstrel *PA-Variety* **1** Medieval entertainer who traveled from place to place, esp. to sing and recite poetry. **2 Lyric** poet; a musician. **3** One of a **troupe** of entertainers made up in **blackface** and presenting a comic variety show. *Also see* **minstrelsy, Mr. Bones, rap, troubadour**.

minstrel show *Cult&Soc, PA-Variety* » **minstrelsy**

minstrelsy *Cult&Soc, MusArts, PA-Variety* Art or profession of a **minstrel**. **1** "Minstrelsy swept the country in the 19th century just as ragtime, jazz and rock would in the 20th." — Margo Jefferson (cul. critic) **2** "By the 1840's, a systematized form of blackface [on white skins] stage entertainment – minstrelsy – would emerge as the rage of American popular culture, the first concerted appropriation and commercial exploitation of a black expressive form. African-American humor (along with elements of song and dance) was lifted from its original context, transformed and **parodied**, then spotlighted for the entertainment and amusement of non-black audiences." — Lawrence W. Levine (cult. critic) *Also see* **Mr. Bones**.

MIPS *InfoMgt* Millions of (computer) Instructions Per Second.

miracle play *TheatArts* Medieval cycle play based on the life of a saint.

mirrors *InfoMgt* FTP sites that duplicate the contents of the popular **servers**. <AOL, CompuServe> *Also see* **black road shows**.

MIS *InfoMgt, Mgt* **Management Information System**. **1** Design concept that emphasizes the transformation of raw data into meaningful information. **2** Computer system designed to help managers plan and direct business and organizational operations.

misappropriation of the right to publicity *LegAsp, Mktg* Violation of an individual's exclusive legal right to control and profit from the commercial use of her or his name and **personality** during her or his lifetime.

miscellaneous royalties *IntelProp, MusArts, RecA&S* Royalties paid on the sales of products using the copyright, such as lyrics used in posters, greeting cards or based on the copyright, such as games, drinks, etc. paid by the copyright user to the authors and the music publisher. *Also see* **Royalties**.

mise en scène (meeze awn sen, Fr.) *Flm&Vid* Arrangement of visual weights and movements within a given space. In theater, the space is usu. defined by the **proscenium** arch; in movies, it is defined by the frame that encloses the images. Cinematic mise en scène encompasses both the staging of the action and the way that it's photographed.

mise-en-scene, mise en scène ((meeze awn sen, Fr.)) *TheatArts* French phrase for the "putting on stage" of a play. It refers to the total environment of a play including the blocking, props, visual effects, scenery, and costumes. Thus, the "look" of a play.

misrepresentation *LegAsp* Assertion not in accord with the facts.

mission statement *EntreP, Mktg* **1** Concise written description of a company's philosophy. **2** Necessary, self-defining statement by a business or arts organization that must answer these basic questions: "What is our business?" or "What is it we want to accomplish?"

misuse of confidential information *LegAsp* Agent cannot disclose or misuse confidential information about the **principal's** affairs obtained during an agency.

MIT *Crit&Eval, InfoMgt* **Massachusetts Institute of Technology** (Cambridge, Mass.) **World-class** research university, founded in 1861.

mit out sound *Flm&Vid* » **MOS**

mitzve (mitz'-veh, Yinglish) *Crit&Eval* Meritorious act, one that expresses God's will; a kind, considerate, worthy deed.

mix *Flm&Vid, RecA&S* Process of combining separately recorded soundtracks onto a master track. **MIXER**

mixed economy *Eco&Fin* One that has elements of socialism and capitalism, or **planned economy** and **market economy**. To widely varying degrees, most national economies can be loosely described as mixed.

mixed media *Genl* » **multimedia**

mixer *RecA&S* Experienced recording engineer who has the exacting job of mixing the separately recorded soundtracks into a coherent, exciting **master recording** from which individual copies will be manufactured.

mkt., mktg. *Mktg* **market, marketing**

MLB *SportsEnt* » **Major League of Baseball**

MLIA *InfoMgt, MusArts* **Music Library International Association** (MLIA) Ω

mnemonics *InfoMgt* Symbolic name normally associated with the instructions of low level languages.

Mnemosyne (Greek *Mythology*) *Cult&Soc* Goddess of memory, mother of the **Muses**

Moby Dick (or *The Whale*) *LitArts* Written by **Herman Melville** in 1851, *Moby Dick* is regarded as one of the world's greatest novels. On one level it is an exciting sea story, on a deeper level it is an **allegory** of good vs. evil.

mock-up *iMedia* **1** Full-scale working model of something built for study or testing or display **2** Construct a model.

mockery *Crit&Eval* Scornfully contemptuous ridicule; derision.

MOD files *InfoMgt, MusArts* **1** Music Modules Amiga [computer brand] files adopted by the PC community. **2** Music files that include the instruments as well as the score, and play through a sound card, not **MIDI**.

modal *MusArts* Relating to any of the modes typical of medieval church music.

mode *Crit&Eval* Manner, way, or method of doing or acting.

mode *Fashn* Current or customary fashion or style.

mode *MusArts* Any of certain fixed arrangements of the **diatonic tones** of an **octave**, as the major and minor **scales** of Western music.

model *Fashn* Person employed to display clothing or cosmetics.

modeling clay *Th-MakeUp* Oil-based clay that will not dry out used to model heads for studying facial structure and to model features for **prosthesis**.

modem *InfoMgt* **Module/Modulator Device** translates **digital** pulses from a computer into **analog** signals for telephone transmission, and **analog** signals from the telephone into **digital** pulses the computer can understand. Modems provide communication capabilities between computer equipment over common telephone facilities. *Also see* **external —, fax —, converter, transducer**.

Modern Art *ColEntry, VisArts* Closely related to the European art movements from ca. 1910-38. [Like many references to "ages," "eras," and "periods" of transitions in art, the ultimate judgment is in the eye and ear of the beholder, albeit aided and abetted by responsible critics. One might examine the following "isms" and come to one's own definitive judgment.] "Modern art often seems to be an attempt to bridge the gap between fact and miracle." — Wallace Stevens (art critic) *Also see* **Art Movements and Periods**.

modern dance *Dnce* Style of theatrical dance that rejects the limitations of classical ballet and favors movement deriving from the expression of inner feeling. <Martha Graham (1894-1991, choreog., modern dncr.), Doris Humphrey (» **fall and recovery**)>

modern jazz *MusArts* » **bop** *Also see* **Jazz Styles**.

moderne (mah-dearn, Fr. for "modern") *Crit&Eval* Striving to be modern in appearance or style but lacking taste or refinement; pretentious.

Modernism *Ethcs&Phil* Roman Catholic movement, officially condemned in 1907, that attempted to examine traditional belief according to contemporary philosophy, criticism, and **historiography**.

modernism *Crit&Eval* Sympathy with or **conformity** to modern ideas, practices, or standards.

Modernism *Cult&Soc, LitArts, VisArts* Deliberate departure from tradition and the use of innovative forms of expression that distinguish many styles in the arts and literature of the 20th century. *Also see* **Art Movements and Periods**.

modernism *TheatArts* Term denoting a direction in the arts in the 20th century characterized by a break with traditional forms and techniques of expression, by a greater concern for the individual per se rather than as a social being, by an increased emphasis on the unconscious, and by embracing the concept of an imagination that is self-referential.

modernity *Crit&Eval* State or quality of being modern.

modest *Crit&Eval* **1** Moderate estimate of one's own talents, abilities, and value. **2** Disinclination to call attention to oneself; diffident. **3** Observing conventional proprieties in speech, behavior, or dress. **4** Unpretentious. **5** Moderate or limited in size, quantity, or range; not extreme. <the record had a modest success>

Modified Accumulated Cost Recovery System (MACRS) *E&F-Acc* » **MACRS, Tax Reform Act of 1986**.

modular chunking *iMedia* Process of breaking content up into logical units or components.

modulation *InfoMgt* Procedure used by **modems** to convert **digital** computer signals to a form acceptable by communications equipment.

modulation *LitArts* Harmonious use of language, as in poetry or prose.

modulation *MusArts* **1** Passing from one key or **tonality** to another by means of a regular melodic or **chord progression**. **2** Change in stress, **pitch**, loudness, or tone of the voice; an **inflection** of the voice.

Module/Modulator Device *InfoMgt* » **modem**

mogul *Flm&Vid* Very rich and powerful movie producer. <**Louis B. Mayer, Samuel Goldwyn, Harry Warner**> *Also see* **impresario; Producers; sachem; tycoon.**

Mohawk *Fashn* Hairstyle in which the scalp is shaved except for an upright strip of hair that runs across the crown of the head from the forehead to the nape of the neck.

moiré *iMedia* Graphics: patterned effect that forms when screens of differing angles or frequency are overlaid, or when scanning a half-toned image.

mojo *Cult&Soc* Usually made in the form of a charm-bag that may contain many different things. <herbs, coins, magnets, beads, feathers, hair, etc> It is carried on the person or hung in the home, car, or workplace for good luck, protection, harmony, health, attracting love or money, etc.

mom and pop *Mktg* Independent family-size (usu. retail) business.

monaural *RecA&S* **1** Sound reception by one ear. **2** System of transmitting, recording, or reproducing sound in which one or more sources are connected to a single channel; monophonic.

monetary policy *EntreP* Range of actions taken by the Federal Reserve to influence the level of GDP or the rate of inflation.

monetary symbols *Eco&Fin* » **Symbols**

money *EntreP* Anything that is regularly used in exchange.

money illusion *EntreP* Confusion of real and nominal magnitudes.

money market mutual funds *EntreP* Mutual funds that invest primarily in short term highly liquid investments such as CDs, short term government treasuries, commercial paper, repurchase agreements, and banker's acceptances. These funds are the mutual fund equivalent of a checking account.

money supply (Ml) *EntreP* Money in circulation plus the money in checking accounts.

money supply (M2) *EntreP* Ml + money in passbook savings accounts + money market accounts + small time deposits (CDs)

monitor *Crit&Eval* One that admonishes, cautions, or reminds, with respect to matters of conduct.

monitor *InfoMgt* » **color monitor, monochrome monitor, video monitor**

monochrome monitor *InfoMgt* Computer display screen that displays a black characters or graphics on a white background, or white, amber, or green on a black background. *Also see* **color monitor**.

monoculturalism *Cult&Soc* Single, homogeneous culture without diversity or dissension. *Also see* **multiculturalism**.

monody *LitArts* **1** Ode for one voice or actor, as in Greek drama. **2** Poem in which the poet or speaker mourns another's death.

monody *MusArts* Style of composition having or dominated by a single melodic line.

monolith *Crit&Eval* Something suggestive of a large block of stone, as in immovability, massiveness, or uniformity.

monologue *also* **monolog** *Crit&Eval* Long speech made by one person, often monopolizing a conversation.

monologue *also* **monolog** *LitArts* Literary composition in the form of a **soliloquy**. MONOLOGIST

monologue *also* **monolog** *PA-Variety* Continuous series of jokes or comic stories delivered by one comedian. MONOLOGIST

monologue *also* **monolog** *TheatArts* Talking aloud when alone. Otherwise it's a **dialogue**. MONOLOGIST *Also see* **aside.**

monophonic *MusArts* Relating to music with a single melodic line.

monopoly *Eco&Fin* **1** Exclusive control by one group of the means of producing or selling a commodity or service. **2** Market in which a single company serves the entire market. *Also see* **legal monopoly, oligopoly, technopoly.**

montage *Flm&Vid* Transitional sequences of rapidly edited images, often employing dissolves which are used to suggest the lapse of time or the passing of events.

montage *Genl* In Europe, montage means the art of editing in general.

montage *RecA&S* Composite of closely juxtaposed elements of sound; a montage of voices on an audiotape.

montage *VisArts* Single pictorial composition made by juxtaposing or superimposing many pictures or designs.

Moog synthesizer (Mohg) *MusInstr* First synthesizer to suit the creative needs of the working musician developed by **Robert Moog** in 1965 The Moog III had two five-octave keyboards that controlled voltage changes and thus **pitch, timbre, attack, decay,** and other aspects of sound.

Moog, Bob (Mohg, b. Robert Moog, 1934-, phyicist and electronic engineer) *ArtPerf, MusInstr* Inventor of the **Moog synthesizers** and other instruments. *Also see* **Big Briar, theremin.**

mooks *Cult&Soc* "Knuckleheads or young white guys.... We've all seen them at the mall: kids who ostentatiously say "whuzzup" to one another; the frat brothers who wear stop-and-frisk fashions;... the legion who wish they, too, could vote for Jesse Ventura, if not Howard Stern." — R.J. Smith (pop-music critic) *Also see* **rap-metal.**

Moore's law *iMedia, InfoMgt, Sci&Tech* Observation made in 1965 by Gordon Moore (1929-), co-founder of Intel, that the number of transistors per square inch on integrated circuits had doubled every year since the integrated circuit was invented. Although this is no longer technically true, the law still applies to data density. current model holds that data density doubles approximately every 18 months. This law is often used to predict computing power up to 20 years into the future.

MOR *Rdio/TV, RecA&S* **Middle-of-the Road** music programming. *Also see* **easy listening**.

moral *Ethcs&Phil* **1** Being or acting in accordance with standards and precepts of goodness or with established codes of behavior, esp. with regard to sexual conduct. **2** Arising from conscience or the sense of right and wrong. <a moral obligation>

moral clarity *Ethcs&Phil* Seeing things for what they are really are.

moral majority *Ethcs&Phil* 1970s term for the majority of **enfranchised** Americans who remained silent in political affairs, associated with the Reverend Jerry Falwell (1933-, Baptist min., TV evangelist, religious/political conservative) "The word 'ethical' makes some of us nervous. It now has a negative connotation, like 'moral' in 'the moral majority.' We think of ethics as a surgical mask tied over the mouth of literature. We are more afraid of censorship than we are of evil." —**Wayne C. Booth**

moral philosophy *Ethcs&Phil* » **ethics**

moral rights *IntelProp, LegAsp* French system of copyright protection requires the legal sympathy rest with the artist who is always accorded absolute protection against commercial exploitation of original work.

morality *Aes&Creat* **1** Evaluation of, or means of understanding human content, as a set of ideas of right and wrong. <Christian morality> **2** Set of customs of a given society, class, or social group that regulates relationships and prescribe modes of behavior to enhance the group's survival. <middle class morality> "Writers have to concern themselves with the moral consequences of their art." — Jack Beatty (author) **3** "It is on the basis of quality, not morality, that posterity judges art. While awaiting that verdict, arts organizations must not give in to political intimidation for fear of losing grants." — Robert Brustein (art critic)

morality play *Ethcs&Phil*, *TheatArts* Late medieval dramatic form using allegorical characters to dramatize moral and ethical problems involved in leading a Christian life. *Ex. Everyman.*

morality police *Ethcs&Phil* Term applied to officials who ban the works of famous authors based on an 1873 law prohibiting the mailing, shipping, or importation of **obscene** and **immoral** matter.

morals *Aes&Creat* Similar to "morality," but taken piecemeal rather than as a body of standards, or as manifest in a particular person's statements or conduct; thus, often, a term for reference to particular moral standards. *"So* far about morals, I know only that what is moral is what you feel good after and what is immoral is what you feel bad after." — Ernest Hemingway (1899-1961, fict-wri., adventurer, journ) "Food comes first, then morals." — Bertolt Brecht (» **epic drama**)

morals clause *Ethcs&Phil*, *LegAsp* "[If an artist/performer] should, prior to or during the term hereof or thereafter, fail, refuse or neglect to govern [artist/performer's] conduct with due regard to social conventions and public morals and decency, or commit any act which brings [artist/performer] into public disrepute, scandal, contempt or ridicule or which shocks, insults or offends a substantial portion or group of the community or reflects unfavorably on [artist/performer] or [employer], then [employer] may, in addition to and without prejudice to any other remedy of any kind or nature set forth herein, terminate this Agreement at any time after the occurrence of such an event..." — April Smith (author)

morbid *Crit&Eval* **1** Psychologically unhealthy or unwholesome. **2** Preoccupied with unwholesome thoughts or feelings.

more bang for the buck *Genl* Greater or higher return for the time, money, or energy expended.

(more/more) *BcstJourn* In some newsrooms, a mark that is placed at the bottom of a script page to indicate the story continues on the next page. Its use is a matter of individual newsroom style.

morning dress *Fashn* Man's outfit of striped trousers, swallowtail jacket, grey waistcoat suitable for a formal occasion before five o'clock in the afternoon, such as a wedding.

morphing *InfoMgt* One picture **metamorphoses** into another.

mortgage *EntreP* Long-term loan from a creditor for which real estate is pledged as collateral.

MOS *Flm&Vid* Silent filming. Expression from the early days of cinema when immigrant German technicians spoke of shooting "mit out sound."

Moscow Art Theater *TheatArts* Russian **repertory** company, established by **Konstantin Stanislavsky** and others. Its emphasis on the illusion of reality marked the beginning of modern theatre. *Also see* **Theaters & Theatres**.

mosh, moshing *Dnce* Dance to rock music in large groups, ricocheting off each other, and passing one another around on raised hands. *Also see* **Dances, mosh pit**.

mosh pit *PA-Variety* Area in front of a stage where **mosh** "dancers" frolic amid the **melee**.

Most Favored Nation *Eco&Fin*, *Law&Pol* » **MFN**

mot juste (moh joost, Fr. for "right word") *Crit&Eval* Exactly the right word or expression.

mother *RecA&S* Nickel-plated clone of the **lacquer disc**, used to make as many stampers as required for the number of finished LPs.

Mother Hubbard *Fashn* Woman's loose, unbelted dress. *Origin* Probably from illustrations of Mother Hubbard, character in a nursery rhyme by British writer Sarah Catherine Martin (1768-1826)

mother lode *Flm&Vid* » **88ᵗʰ episode**

mother ship *RecA&S* Venue with high tech recording equipment where artists can comfortably perform and record.

motherboard *InfoMgt* Main board of a computer containing the circuitry for the **central processing unit** (CPU), keyboard, and monitor and often having slots for accepting additional circuitry.

motif *Flm&Vid* Any unobtrusive technique, object or thematic idea that's systematically repeated throughout a film.

motif *LitArts* Recurrent thematic element in a literary work; a dominant theme or central idea. *Also see* **leitmotif**.

motif *MusArts* Short significant phrase in a composition. **leitmotif, motto, theme and variation**.

motif *VisArts* **1** Repeated figure or design in architecture or decoration. **2** Motive, object, or theme of an art work.

motility *Crit&Eval* Relating to mental imagery that arises primarily from sensations of bodily movement and position rather than from visual or auditory sensations.

motion *Dnce* Meaningful or expressive change in the position of the body or a part of the body; a gesture.

motion *iMedia* **1** Act or process of changing position or place. **2** meaningful or expressive change in a position or part. **3** ability or power to move. 4. manner in which something moves.

motion *LegAsp* Application made to a court for an order or a ruling.

motion graphics *iMedia* Graphics that are dynamic and which have motion as an integral part of their presentation. Motion graphics often employ animation and animation techniques.

motion *MusArts* Melodic ascent and descent of **pitch**.

Motion Picture and Television Fund *Flm&Vid* **Nonprofit** organization offering "a variety of medical, social, and educational services to industry employees, dependents and retirees."

Motion Picture Association of America (MPAA) *Flm&Vid* » **MPAA**

Motion Picture Producers and Distributors Association (MP-PDA) *Flm&Vid* » **MPPDA** *Also see* **Distributors, Producers**.

Motion Pictures Experts Group *Flm&Vid*, *InfoMgt* » **MPG files**

motion pictures *Rdio/TV* Popular type of television programming. <reruns of Hollywood and foreign films, and made-for-TV movies> *Also see* **Television Shows**.

motivate *ArtPerf*, *Mgt* To provide with an incentive; move to action; impel: "If your motivation is money, you'll never make it [as an artist]." — Norman Jewison (1926-, Canadian-born film dir.-prod) *Also see* **professional musicians**.

motivation to start a venture *EntreP* Effect of influences on a person to launch a venture; includes the impact of antecedent variables and triggering variables.

motivational research *Mktg* Systematic analysis of the motives behind consumer decisions. MOTIVATION RESEARCH.

motley *Fashn* Having many colors; variegated; parti-colored. <Court **jester** wore a motley tunic.

motto *MusArts* Musical phrase used to identify an emotion or a character in an opera. *Also see* **leitmotif, motif, theme and variation**.

moulage *Th-MakeUp* Gelatinous material used to make plaster or stone casts for **prosthesis**.

mountain music *MusArts* Principally the folk music from **Appalachia** and the **Ozarks**. *Also see* **Country Music Styles**.

mountebank *PerfA&C* **1** Hawker of who attracts customers with stories, jokes, or tricks. **2** Flamboyant charlatan.

mourning clothes *Fashn* Black clothes to show grief for a death.

mouse *Crit&Eval*, *TheatArts* Young, attractive female.

mouse *InfoMgt* Device for moving a cursor or selected objects around on the display screen.

mouse potato *InfoMgt* Cyberspeak equivalent of a **couch potato**.

mouth organ *MusInstr* » **harmonica** *Also see* **Musical Instrument Families, reed instruments**.

movie *Flm&Vid* **1** Sequence of photographs projected onto a screen with sufficient rapidity as to create the illusion of motion and continuity. **2** Connected cinematic narrative represented in this form. **3** Theater that shows movies. *Also see* **cinematic film**.

movie mud *Th-MakeUp* Makeup that simulates real dirt or mud.

Movie of the Week (MOW) *Flm&Vid*, *Rdio/TV* » **MOW**

movie producer *Flm&Vid* One who finances and supervises the making and public presentation of a movie. *Also see* **Producers**.

moviegoer *TheatArts* One who frequently attends the movies. *Also see* **playgoer**.

movies *Flm&Vid* movie industry.

Moving Picture Experts Group (MPEG) *MusArts*, *RecA&S* » **MPEG** *Also see* **MP3**.

MOW *Flm&Vid* **Movie of the Week**. Film made for cable.

MP3 *MusArts, RecA&S, Sci&Tech* Digital compression algorithm that realizes a compression factor of about twelve, maintaining excellence in sound quality, under official sponsorship of the **Moving Picture Experts Group** (MPEG) recognized by the International Organization for Standardization (ISO) Advantages of portable MP3 players over **CD** players: no skipping, smaller size (about the size and weight of a pack of playing cards), ability to customize music sets, and that music can be downloaded from the Internet or other media.

MPA *Journ»* **Magazine Publishers of America**

MPA *MusArts* **Music Publishers' Association** Trade association representing music publishers. Resources. <Copyright Resource Center, Sales Agency List, Calendar of Events, **Paul Revere Awards.**

MPAA *Flm&Vid* Est. 1922 Motion Picture Association of America. "The voice and advocate of the American motion picture, home video, and television industries." *Also see* **Anti-Censorship Organizations.**

MPEG *Flm&Vid, Multimedia, MusArts, RecA&S* **Moving Picture Experts Group**, a working group of International Organization for Standardization (ISO) MPEG is comprised of 300+ experts employed by 200+ companies from 20+ countries, from all-industry domains, with a substantial investment in digital audio, video, and multimedia technology. *Also see* **MP3, MPEG-1, MPEG-2, MPEG-4, MPEG-7.**

MPEG *iMedia »* **MPG files**

MPEG-1 *Flm&Vid, Multimedia, MusArts, RecA&S* Standard on which products employing Video CD and **MP3** are based.

MPEG-2 *Flm&Vid, Multimedia, MusArts, RecA&S* Standard on which products inc. Digital TV **set-top boxes** and DVD are based

MPEG-4 *Flm&Vid, Multimedia, MusArts, RecA&S* Standard in multimedia for fixed and mobile web compression.

MPEG-7 *Flm&Vid, Multimedia, MusArts, RecA&S* Standard for description and search of audio and visual content.

MPG *iMedia* Filename extension for a file in **MPEG** format. » **MPG files**

MPG files *Flm&Vid, InfoMgt* Format for the digitization and compression of video images created by the Motion Picture Experts Group.

MPPDA *Flm&Vid* **Motion Picture Producers and Distributors Association** organized in 1922 to oversee movie morality. *Also see* **Distributors, Producers.**

MPTF *MusArts »* **Music Performance Trust Fund**

Mr. Abbott Award *TheatArts* Given annually to a stage director by the **Stage Directors and Choreographers Foundation** in honor of director **George Abbott.**

Mr. Bones *PA-Variety* **end man** in a **minstrel show**

MS *BcstJourn* **medium show »** **establishing shot**

MS-DOS *InfoMgt* **Microsoft Disk Operating System**, a computer operating system. *Also see* **Operating Systems.**

MSG *InfoMgt* Message

musm. *VisArts* **museum**

MTM *Flm&Vid, Rdio/TV* **Mary Tyler Moore** (1937-, film/TV act., sngr., dncr.) Major producing organization for TV series and movies-of-the-week named for its leading star.

MTV *Flm&Vid, MusArts* Cable TV network that plays various styles of pop and rock music videos – and other programs aimed at the youth and single markets.

muckraker *Crit&Eval, Journ* One who searches for and exposes misconduct in public life. *Origin* From the man with the muckrake, who cannot look up to heaven because he is so obsessed with the muck of worldly profit. — John Bunyan (» **allegory**), *Pilgrim's Progress. Also see* **investigative journalism.**

mud colors *Fashn, VisArts* "The costumes in The Dead have no crimson, no blue, no green, no violet. I used mud colors – olive, nutmeg, clove, persimmon, faded red – the colors of real life, to get the kind of oppressive quality of Dublin social live. They conveyed lamplight and the dour color of a Dublin house." — **Dorothy Jeakins** (1914-95, cos. dsgnr.)

mud shows *PA-Variety* (Passé) Small circuses. *Origin* From the days when circuses travelled in wagons over muddy roads.

muggles *Cult&Soc* Pre-WWII musicians' name for marijuana cigarettes. [No way related to Harry Potter.]

multi-participant interface *iMedia* Interface that allows several participants to interact with each other and their environment simultaneously.

Multi-purpose Internet Mail Extensions *InfoMgt »* **MIME**

multi-track *RecA&S* Relating to multiple recording tracks. *Also see* **Les Paul.**

multicultural, multiculturalism *Cult&Soc* 1 Relating to several cultures. 2 In the arts it promotes diversity and tolerance for subjects of ethnicity and opens the discourse to new voices previously disenfranchised. *Also see* **monoculturalism.**

multifunctioning graphical elements *iMedia* Images where the ink used serves several purposes.

multihoming *InfoMgt* multiple addresses for the same **port**

multimedia *Crit&Eval* 1 Combination of text, graphics, full-motion video, audio, and **animation.** 2 Use of several **mass media**, such as print, radio, and TV for advertising or promotion. MIXED MEDIA "I have a passion for all... forms of media. We can have a financial contribution to make, and the whole idea is to **cross-pollinate** disciplines." — **Quincy Jones**

multimedia *InfoMgt* Interactive computer applications having voice and audio components.

multimedia sound *InfoMgt, MusArts* Music for games mostly composed by The Fat Man (George Sanger, comp.)

multinational alliance *InfoMgt* Group of companies that pool their communication networks, marketing, and sales forces to offer one set of services to consumers across several geographic markets.

multiplex *Flm&Vid* Movie theater or with multiple separate units.

multiplexer *InfoMgt* Telecommunications device that permits more than one device to share a signal communications line.

multiprocessing *InfoMgt* Two or more computers running under the control of one operating system.

multiprocessor *iMedia* Computer using more than one CPU to share computing work.

multiprogramming *InfoMgt* Process of executing more than one program simultaneously.

Multitasking *iMedia* 1 Working through several tasks during the same time period, seemingly simultaneously. 2 Method of performing several processes on one CPU by sequentially switching between them.

mummer *ArtPerf, TheatArts* 1 Masked or costumed merrymaker at a festival. 2 One who acts or plays in a pantomime; an actor.

mummery *Crit&Eval* **Pretentious** or hypocritical show or ceremony.

mummery *PerfA&C* performance by **mummers**

munge *InfoMgt* Spoil a file or transmission.

municipal Bond *EntreP* Bond that is issued by a government agency other than the federal government. Usually state and local governments issue these bonds to finance projects.

Murphy's Law *Mgt* If anything can go wrong, it will.

Murrow, Edward R. (Roscoe) (1908-65) *Journ, Rdio/TV* American broadcast journalist noted for his dramatic factual reports from London during World War II and superb investigative journalism. <Senator **Joe McCarthy**, Migrant Workers> *Also see* **documentary.**

mus. *MusArts* **music, musical, musician**

muse *LitArts* poet *Also see* **Muses.**

Muse *LitArts, MusArts, PerfA&C* Represented by the nine daughters of **Mnemosyne** and **Zeus**, each of whom presided over a different art or science. Guiding spirit, a source of inspiration "Art is about taking risks. Danger and chaos — these are the real **muses** an artist must court." — **Robert Rauschenberg** *Also see* **Muses.**

Muses *Aes&Creat ColEntry* **Calliope, Clio, Erato, Euterpe, Melpomene, Polyhymania, Terpsichore**, and **Thalia**. [Urania, the ninth Muse, belongs in a dictionary of astronomy.].

museum *VisArts* Building, place, or institution devoted to the acquisition, conservation, study, exhibition, and educational interpretation of objects having scientific, historical, or artistic value.

museum loan network *VisArts* Its mission is to compile a vast database of artworks available for loans of several years to fill gaps in significant collections. Created in October 1995 by the John S. and James L. **Knight Foundation** and the **Pew Charitable Trusts**, administered by **M.I.T.**

Music & Entertainment Industry Educators Association

music (mus.) *Aes&Creat* All that is ruled by the **Muses**, inc. all that we customarily call "music," but also history, dance, all forms of creative poetry, and other pursuits; consequently, roughly, the "arts," or the **belles-lettres** and the **beaux arts**. *Also see* **Muses**.

music (mus.) *MusArts* **1** Art of arranging sounds in time so as to produce a continuous, unified, and evocative composition, as through melody, harmony, rhythm, and **timbre**. **2** Vocal or instrumental sounds possessing a degree of melody, harmony, or rhythm. **3** Musical composition; the **score** for such a composition.

music box *MusInstr* Music-making device with a sounding mechanism, usu. one in which a row of tuned steel teeth are plucked by pins set in a revolving cylinder to produce a delicate-sounding melody.

music business *Mgt, MusArts* **Amalgamation** of several large businesses related to the performance and production of music. <music performers (instrumentalists, singers, composers, arranger-orchestrators), musical instrument industry, music publishing business, live music business, recorded music business. "Music business isn't all glamorous; it's more like a 35-year bus ride." — Merle Haggard (1937-, country comp., sngr., gtr.)

music business publicist *Mktg, RecA&S* Does publicity for the record company: distribution, management, manufacturing, publishing company, studio operation; corporate profit statements, company spin on legal matters. *Also see* **music publicist**.

music clearance *IntelProp, MusArts* Establishing the right to use copyrighted music. *Also see* **music licensing**.

music compression *InfoMgt, MusArts* Electronic system that can squish a piece of music to one-tenth of its length, without any audible loss of quality developed by **Ken Thompson**, the father of **Unix**, at **Bell Labs**.

music contractor *Flm&Vid, HR&LR, MusArts, Rdio&TV, RecA&S* One who is hired by a producer to contract musicians and performers for a live or recorded performance. Contractor hires from a pool of the best available **free lances**. Only AFM members may contract union musicians.

Music Corporation of America *Mgt* » **MCA**

music critic *Crit&Eval, Journ, MusArts* "Colleagues. We are involved in a strange trade. Some of us know what we are doing; some of us don't. My first advice is this: Don't let the title 'music critic' go to your head. You have taken no bar exam, fulfilled no residency, acquired no license to practice. The day I put 'music critic' after my name, people started asking me about music; before that, no one asked my opinion about anything."— Bernard Holland (mus. critic) *Also see* **critic**.

Music Critics Association of North America (MCANA) *Crit&Eval* Ω

Music Directions *ColEntry, MusArts* » **a tempo, accelerando** (acc), **adagio, affettuoso, agitato, alla breve, allegro** (allo), **allegretto, andante** (and.), **arco, col, con amore, con brio, con spirito, da capo, decrescendo, diminuendo, dolce, forte** (f), **fortissimo** (ff), **fortississimo** (fff), **forza, grave, largo, legato** (leg), **lento, mezzo forte** (mf), **piano** (p), **pianissimo** (pp), **pizzicato** (pizz), **poco, prestissimo, presto, subito, tacet, tutti**.

music director *MusArts, Rdio/TV* One who has the responsibility of seeing that music is composed or selected for a film, and is orchestrated and copied. He or she supervises or conducts the scoring sessions, and may even compose the score.

music drama *MusArts* Opera in which the continuity is not interrupted by **arias, recitatives**, or **ensembles**, and in which the music relates to the action of the drama.

Music Educators National Conference (MENC) *MusArts* » **MENC**

music generation *Cult&Soc, Mktg, MusArts* Period of time in which the marketing name given to the latest new style of pop music remains saleable. New technologies and recycled marketing techniques seem to create instant golden oldies. *Also see* **generation, popular music**.

music hall *MusArts, PA-Variety* **1** Auditorium for musical performances. **2** (Brit.) **vaudeville** theater

music library *InfoMgt, MusArts* Company or organization that hires its own composers, producers, singers, musicians, and technical staff to produce songs in all idioms. This music is often used in commercials, advertisements, sales meetings, industrial shows, etc.

Music Library International Association (MLIA) *InfoMgt, MusArts* » **MLIA**

Music Licenses *ColEntry, IntelProp, MusArts* <commercial —, grand rights, mechanical —, non-dramatic performance —, per-program —, print —, single song agreement, small performance rights, source license, synchronization right>

music licensing *IntelProp, MusArts* Granting by the music copyright owner the right to publicly perform the owner's copyrighted music. In return, the recipient of the right – the **licensee** – pays the owner, or her or his representative, (**ASCAP, BMI, SESAC**) a royalty fee. *Also see* **public domain**.

Music Licensing Task Force *IntelProp, MusArts* **American Society of Association Executives** (ASAE) and a group of meeting-industry associations negotiated music licensing agreements and fee schedules with both **ASCAP** and **BMI. BMI's** music licensing agreement became effective 1 Oct. 1990, **ASCAP's** agreement 1 Jan. 1991 "We have an ethical responsibility to comply with this law. When we have a meeting, we don't try to avoid any of the other laws, rules, and regulations. Avoiding this law is stealing, because copyrighted pieces of music belong to the composers, not to us." — **ASAE** *Association Report*

Music Modules *InfoMgt MusArts* » **MOD files**

music of the spheres *MusArts* Perfectly harmonious music, inaudible on Earth, thought by **Pythagoras** and later classical and medieval philosophers to be produced by the movement of celestial bodies.

Music Performance Trust Fund (MPTF) *HR&LR, RecA&S* Recording companies make semiannual payments to this fund, based on their record sales. Proceeds are used exclusively for admission-free public concerts in the U.S. and Canada. *Also see* **AFM**.

Music Playback Devices *ColEntry, RecA&S* **boom box, CD-ROM, compact disk, gramophone, nickelodeon, phonograph, player piano, record player, synthesizers, tape player, tape recorder, turntable, wax cylinders, wire recorders**.

music police *IntelProp, MusArts* Employees of **ASCAP** or **BMI** who look for commercial establishments playing music without performing rights licenses.

music publicist *Mktg, RecA&S* Does publicity for the label's record artists and their albums, **junkets, and** tours. *Also see* **music business publicist**.

Music Publishers' Association *MusArts* » **MPA**

music video *Flm&Vid, MusArts* Filmed or videotaped **rendition** of a recorded song, either portraying musicians performing the song or inc. visual images interpreting the lyrics and the mood of the music.

musical *Crit&Eval* **1** Devoted to or skilled in music. **2** Resembling music; **melodious**. <The actor had a musical speaking voice>

musical *Flm&Vid, MusArts, TheatArts* Play or movie in which the **plot** is interspersed with songs and sometimes dances. "As America's Dream becomes increasingly threadbare, so has the art form that best promoted it. In this, at least, the musical remains the perfect metaphor for the time." — **John Lahr** MUSICALE *Also see* **musical comedy, musical theatre**.

musical *MusArts* Relating to the production of music. <a musical instrument>

musical chairs *Crit&Eval* Rearrangement, as of the elements of a problem, having little practical influence or significance.

musical chairs *MusArts* Game in which players walk to music around a group of chairs containing one chair fewer than the number of players and rush to sit down when the music stops. Player left standing in each round is eliminated.

musical comedy *MusArts, TheatArts* In recent years, the "comedy" is seriocomic or even tragic, resembling opera more than the English musical stage and the Spanish zarzuela from which musical comedy is derived. More accurate term is simply, "musical."

musical director *MusArts* Conductor of an orchestra or a chorus. *Also see* **Directors**.

musical glasses *MusInstr* Glasses tuned and arranged to produce musical notes when struck or rubbed.

Musical Instrument Digital Interface (MIDI) *InfoMgt, MusInstr* » **MIDI**

Musical Instrument Families (Used in contemporary music.)

ColEntry, MusInstr **High Brass** (hi-to-lo range): piccolo (D) trumpet, trumpet (B flat), cornet, flugelhorn, French horn. **Low Brass** (hi-to-lo range): bass trumpet, tenor trombone, bass trombone, euphonium or baritone horn, tubas. **Single Reeds — Saxophones** (hi-to-lo range): sopranino, soprano, alto, tenor, baritone, bass. **Clarinets** (hi-to-lo range): clarinet (usu. B-flat), bass clarinet, contrabass clarinet. **Flutes** (hi-to-lo range): fife, piccolo, flute, alto flute, bass flute. **Double Reeds** (hi-to-lo range): oboe, English horn, bassoon, contrabass bassoon. **Strings** *or* **Violin Family** (hi-to-lo range): violin, viola, cello, piccolo bass, double bass. **Keyboards**: accordion, pianos (upright, baby grand, grand, concert grand), electric and electronic pianos, harpsichord; **Organs, Synthesizers**: drum machine, guitar, keyboard. **Guitars**: classical —, Spanish —, flamenco —, folk —; electric — and electric bass —; mandolin, ukulele; **Batter percussion**: snare drum, bass drum, timpani, tom-toms. **Mallet Percussion**: xylophone or orchestra bells, vibraphone or vibes, marimba, chimes. **African/Latin percussion**: conga drum, bongo drum, maracas, **Other Instruments**: banjo, calliope, carillon, harmonica (blues harp, mouth organ), recorders (sop, a, ten, bari, b), harps (Concert, Irish) *Also see* **Little Instruments**.

musical notation *MusArts* Symbols used to make a written record of musical sounds. <expression, key signatures, notes, **pitch**, rhythm, and tempo>

Musical Notes *ColEntry, MusArts* Whole —, half —, quarter —, eighth —, sixteenth —, thirty-second —, sixty-fourth —.

musical saw *MusInstr* Flexible handsaw on which varying musical **tones** are produced by flexing the blade and stroking it with a violin bow or striking it with a hammer.

musical theatre *MusArts, TheatArts* American musical theatre generally refers to a production characterized by a strong **libretto** – based on a social theme or a well-known book or drama – advanced by a superior **score** and choreography. <*Carousel, Guys & Dolls, My Fair Lady, Oklahoma!, Showboat, West Side Story*> "The musical is – and always has been – America's most persuasive political theatre." — **John Lahr** *Also see* **Theaters & Theatres**.

Musical Works Fund *Eco&Fin, RecA&S* » **Audio Home Recording Act of 1992**

musicale *MusArts* (Passé) Program of music performed at a party or social gathering.

musicality *Crit&Eval* **1** Quality or condition of being musical. **2** Musical sensitivity or talent.

musicalize *MusArts, TheatArts* To adapt for performance with singing and musical accompaniment; set to music. <to musicalize a novel or a **Shakespeare** play>

musician (mus.) *MusArts* One who arranges, composes, conducts, orchestrates, or performs music. Usually refers to an instrumental musician.

Musicians Foundation (MF) *ArtPerf, HR&LR, MusArts* » **MF**

Musicians' Assistance Program/Project Straight Life, Inc. *ArtPerf, MusArts* » **MAP**

musicology *MusArts* Historical and scientific study of music and musicians.

musique concrète (muse-eek konkret, Fr. *for* "music" + "concrete") *MusArts* Compositional technique developed ca. 1948 by Pierre Schaeffer (1910-??, Fr. comp., acoustician, electronics engr.) and associates at the Studio d'Essai of the French radio system. Assemblage of various natural sounds recorded on tape or disks to produce a **montage** of sound. Precursor to electronically generated sound.

muslin *Fashn, PerfA&C* flat-surfaced, woven cotton fabric *Also see* **ruche**.

mute *LegAsp* Refusing to plead when under arraignment.

Mutual Broadcasting System (MBS) *Rdio/TV* Est. 1934 Major radio network headquartered in New York and Chicago. *Also see* **Broadcast Stations & Networks**.

mutual fund *EntreP* Pool of money which is invested by a manager in specific investment vehicles with a defined goal and risk objective.

MYOB *InfoMgt* Mind Your Own Business

myopic *Crit&Eval* Lack of long-range perspective in thinking or planning:

mystery *Crit&Eval* Something not fully understood or that baffles or eludes the understanding; an **enigma**: "Ability to convey a sense of mystery is one of the most powerful assets possessed by

the theatre." — Ralph Richardson (1902-83, Brit. film/play act) *Also see* **magic**.

mystery play *TheatArts* Play, usu. part of a cycle of plays, dramatizing Christian history from the Creation to the Last Judgment, devised and performed in the Middle Ages by craft-guilds.

myth *Cult&Soc* Legend, usu. made up in part of historical events, that helps define the beliefs of a people and that often has evolved as an explanation of rituals and natural **phenomena**.

myth. *LitArts* mythology

mythology (myth.) *Cult&Soc* **1** Body or collection of **myths** belonging to a people and addressing their origin, history, deities, ancestors, and heroes. **2** Body of **myths** concerning an individual, event, or institution.

- N -

n-fict. *LitArts* non-fiction

N.E.S.C. *Mgt* **National Executives Service Corps**. Volunteer retired senior executives provide **pro bono** consulting services to **nonprofits** in the arts and other fields.

n.s.f. *or* **N.S.F.** *Eco&Fin* Not sufficient funds in one's checking account to cover a check drawn on the account.

NAA *Journ, Mgt* Newspaper Association of America, a nonprofit organization representing the $55 billion newspaper industry.

NAACP *or* **N.A.A.C.P.** *Cult&Soc* **National Association for the Advancement of Colored People**. Honored civil rights and civil justice organization currently undergoing a wrenching adjustment to a widening generation gap, internal dysfunction, and the implacable far right.

NAAO *VisArts* **National Association of Artists Organizations**. National membership organization that provides support and communication between artists and organizations working in contemporary art.

NAB *Rdio/TV* **National Association of Broadcasters**. Est. 1923, representing radio and television industries before Congress, federal agencies, and the courts

NABET *HR&LR, Rdio/TV* **National Association of Broadcast Employees and Technicians**. Technical union that began in the TV industry to oversee filming assignments of TV crews. *Also see* **Guilds & Unions**.

NACA *Genl* **National Association for Campus Activities** National organization whose members are events presenters on university and college campuses. It sponsors an annual convention in February in rotating cities. Formerly **NECAA**

NACAA *Genl* **National Assembly of Community Arts Agencies**. Ω

NAFTA *Eco&Fin* **North American Free Trade Agreement**. Controversial free trade agreement signed by Canada, Mexico, and the U.S. in 1994.

nail *Crit&Eval, PA-Variety* To master an action. <The stunt man nailed the **gag** in one **take**>

NAIRD *Mktg, RecA&S* » **AFIM**

naive *Crit&Eval* **1** Lacking critical ability or analytical insight. **2** Lacking worldliness and sophistication. *Also see* **artless, ingenuous**.

naive art *Cult&Soc, VisArts* Artists with limited or no formal artistic training but usu. exhibiting a freshness of vision. *Also see* **folk, primitive**.

NAJE *MusArts* **National Association of Jazz Educators**. Name changed to **International Association of Jazz Educators** (IAJE)

NALAA *Genl* **National Assembly of Local Arts Agencies**. Members are local and community arts agencies, state art associations, universities and others. Service organization for local arts agencies and councils. Seeks to enhance and strengthen management and development of local arts agencies.

name-drop *Crit&Eval* To mention casually the names of famous people as a transparent means of self-promotion. <I saw Meryl and Demi at the deli this morning>

naming opportunities *Fndng* Programs or places that can be named in honor of a donor.

NAMM *Mktg, MusInstr* **National Association of Music Merchants**. Trade association of musical instrument retailers, wholesalers, and manufacturers. *Also see* **National Coalition for Music Education**.

NAPM *MusArts* **National Academy of Popular Music**. Sponsors the annual **Songwriters Hall of Fame Awards**, songwriter showcases, and workshops.

NARAS *RecA&S* **National Academy of Recording Arts & Sciences**. Professional organization that represents creative people in the recording field. It serves to recognize, encourage, and reward artistic achievement (**Grammy Awards**) within the recording field and to advance its standards. *Also see* **National Coalition for Music Education**.

NARAS chapter cities *RecA&S* Atlanta, Chicago, Florida (Miami Beach), Los Angeles, Memphis, Mid-Atlantic (Phila.), Nashville, New York, Pacific Northwest (Seattle), San Francisco, Texas (Austin), Washington, DC (organization in progress — Fall '97) *Also see* **Grammy Awards**.

narcissism *Crit&Eval* Excessive admiration or love of oneself. *Also see* **ego**, **egocentric**, **egoism**, **egotism**.

NARM *RecA&S* **National Association of Recording Merchandisers**. Trade association that represents (approx. 1,200) merchandisers of recorded entertainment, audio and video. ⊲retailers, distributors, one-stops, rack jobbers.

narrative *Crit&Eval* Art, technique, or process of telling a story.

narrative *InfoMgt* Comment

narrator *Flm&Vid* Voiceover commentator who relates the story or explains points of information.

narrow bandwidth *InfoMgt* Slow communications channel capable of transmitting between 30-90 bits per second.

narrowcast *Rdio/TV* To transmit by cable, programs confined to the interests of a specific group of viewers, subscribers, or listeners, such as physicians, business people, or teenagers. *Also see* **broadcast**.

NAS *ArtPerf, MusArts* **National Academy of Songwriters**. Est. 1973 as a nonprofit membership organization "dedicated to the protection, education, and promotion of songwriters and their craft." Publishes *Songtalk* newspaper.

NAS *InfoMgt* **National Association of Sysops** » **Association of Online Professionals**

NASAA *Genl* **National Assembly of State Arts Agencies**. National organization that provides information about state arts councils, federal or state partnership programs.

NASDAQ (est. 1971) *Eco&Fin, EntreP* **National Association of Securities Dealers Automated Quotation** (computerized) system that provides brokers and dealers with price quotations for securities traded **over the counter** and for many **NYSE** listed securities. *Also see* **AMEX**.

NASDAQ Composite *EntreP* This index includes all over-the-counter stocks.

Nashville Sound *MusArts* Seemingly improbable mix of country, honkytonk, jazz, and **r&b**. COUNTRYPOLITAN. *Also see* **Country Music Styles**.

nasolabial fold *Th-MakeUp* Aging line that runs from the nostril to the corner of the mouth.

NAT *BcstJourn* natural sound » **ambient sound**

NATAS *Rdio/TV* **National Academy of Television Arts & Sciences**. *Also see* **Awards & Prizes**.

National Academy of Popular Music (NAPM) *MusArts* » **NAPM**

National Academy of Recording Arts & Sciences (NARAS, Recording Academy) *RecA&S* » **NARAS** *Also see* **Awards & Prizes**.

National Academy of Songwriters (NAS) *MusArts* » **NAS**

National Academy of Television Arts & Sciences (NATAS) *Rdio/TV* » **NATAS**

National Assembly of Community Arts Agencies (NACAA) *Genl* » **NACAA**

National Assembly of Local Arts Agencies (NALAA) *Genl* » **NACAA**

National Assembly of State Arts Agencies (NASAA) *Genl* » **NALAA**

National Association for Campus Activities (NACA) *Genl* » **NACA**

National Association of Artists Organizations (NAAO) *ArtPerf* » **NAAO**

National Association of Broadcast Employees and Technicians (NABET) *HR&LR, Rdio/TV* » **NABET**

National Association of Broadcasters (NAB) *Rdio/TV* » **NAB**

National Association of Independent Record Distributors (NAIRD) *Mktg, RecA&S* » **AFIM**

National Association of Music Merchants (NAMM) *Mktg, MusInstr* » **NAMM**

National Association of Recording Merchandisers (NARM) *RecA&S* » **NARM**

National Association of Securities Dealers Automated Quotation (system) *Eco&Fin* » **NASDAQ**

National Association of Sysops (NAS) *InfoMgt. InfoMgt* » **Association of Online Professionals**

National Basketball Association (NBA.) *SportsEnt* » **NBA**

National Book Awards *Crit&Eval, LitArts* » **Awards & Prizes**, **National Book Critics Circle**. *Also see* **Awards & Prizes**.

National Book Critics Circle (NBCC) *Crit&Eval, LitArts* Founded in 1974, membership consists of nearly 700 active book reviewers. Presents annual National Book Awards in five categories: **fiction**, **non-fiction**, biography, poetry, and criticism. *Also see* **Awards & Prizes**.

National Broadcasting Company (NBC) *Rdio/TV* » **NBC**

National Campaign for Freedom of Expression (NCFE) *Law&Pol, LegAsp* » **NCFE**

National Coalition Against Censorship (NCAC) *Law&Pol, LegAsp* » **NCAC**

National Coalition for Music Education (NCME) *MusArts* » **NCME**

National Collegiate Athletic Association » **NCAA**

national company *TheatArts* Touring version of the original company production. ROAD COMPANY

National Conference Board (NCB) *Eco&Fin* Periodically measures **discretionary spending** of U.S. consumers. *Also see* **Federal Agencies and Statutes**.

National Convention of Gospel Choirs and Choruses *MusArts* Organized (ca.??) by Thomas A. Dorsey (*aka* Georgia Tom, 1899-1993, gospel comp., choir dir., blues pno., accomp., arr.)

National Council for the Arts *Mgt* Created by Congress in 1964 to oversee the **NEA** and the **NEH**.

National Cultural Center *Cult&Soc* » **John F Kennedy Center for the Performing Arts**

National Education Network *Rdio/TV* » **Public Broadcasting Act of 1967**

National Empowerment Television (NET) *Rdio/TV* » **NET**

National Endowment for the Arts (NEA) *Fndng* » **NEA**

National Endowment for the Humanities (NEH) *Cult&Soc* » **NEH**

National Executives Service Corps (N.E.S.C.) *Mgt* » **N.E.S.C**

National Football League *SportsEnt* » **NFL**

national game *SportsEnt* In the U.S. it's baseball.

National Guild of Community Schools of the Arts (NGCSA) *Genl* » **NGCSA**

National Hockey League *SportsEnt* » **NHL**

National Infomercial Marketing Association (NIMA) » **NIMA** *Mktg, Rdio/TV Also see* **infomercial**.

National Information Infrastructure (NII) *InfoMgt* » **Internet**, **NII**

National Information Infrastructure Copyright Act (NIICA) *IntelProp, LegAsp* » **NIICA**

National Jazz Service Organization (NJSO) *MusArts* » **NJSO**

National Labor Code *HR&LR* Comprises a set of three laws which have had a profound continuing impact on American employers, unions and their members: **Wagner** Act (Labor Relations Act of 1935), **Taft-Hartley Act** (Labor-Management relations Act of 1947), and the **Landrum-Griffin** Act (Labor Reporting and Disclosure Act of 1959)

National Labor Relations Act *HR&LR* » **Wagner Act**

National Labor Relations Board (NLRB) *Mgt, HR&LR* » **NLRB**

National League (baseball) *SportsEnt* » **NL**

National League of Professional Baseball (NL) *» SportsEnt* **NL**

National Magazine Award For General Excellence *Journ* Awarded by **American Society of Magazine Editors** (ASME) *Also see* **Awards & Prizes**, **Wired**.

National Medal of Arts *Crit&Eval* Annual awards presented by the White House, for "outstanding contributions to cultural life in the U.S...." *Also see* **Awards & Prizes**.

natural monopoly *EntreP* Market in which the entry of a second company would make price less than average cost, so a single company serves the entire market.

National Music Publishers Association (NMPA) *MusArts* » **NM-PA**

National Performance Network *Mgt,PerfA&C* » **NPN**

National Public Radio (NPR)*Rdio/TV* » **NPR**

National Religious Broadcasters (NRB) *IntelProp, Rdio/TV* Organization – in alliance with restaurant owners – seeking to reduce **performance licensing** fees to **ASCAP** and **BMI**. *Also see* **blanket license, per-program license.**

National Science Foundation (NSF) *Sci&Tech* » **NSF**

National Small Press Publishing Institute (NSPPI) *Mktg, VA-Prntng* » **NSPPI**

National Society of Fund Raising Executives (NSFRE) *Mgt, Fndng* » **NSFRE**

National Speakers Forum (NSF) *Mgt* Large, national agency for lecturers and speakers inc. many prominent journalists. *Also see* **Talent Agencies.**

National Television Standards Committee (NTSC) *Flm&Vid, Rdio/TV* » **NTSC**

National Theatre of Great Britain*TheatArts* Established in 1963 in London's Old Vic theater with **Laurence Olivier** as its first director. Government funded, it moved (1976) to its own complex on the Thames South bank. *Also see* **Theaters & Theatres.**

National Video Resources (NVR) *Flm&Vid* » **NVR**

National Writers Union (NWU) *ArtPerf, HR&LR, Journ, Lit* » **NWU**

native *Cult&Soc* Characteristic of the original inhabitants of a particular place. *Also see* **indigenous.**

Native American *Cult&Soc* Earliest inhabitants of the Americas rather than the culturally offensive 'Indian' as in 'cowboys and Indians.'. *Also see* **Racial Designations.**

natty *Crit&Eval, Fashn* Neat, trim, and smart.

Natural Disasters *Eco&Fin* As a rule, natural disasters. <floods, earthquakes, hurricanes, forest fires> do not materially affect the over-all U.S. economy, though they can have a very serious effect on the local or regional level and this serve as a viable **economic indicator** for the stricken areas. However, exceptions like the Midwest "dust bowl" droughts of the 1930s, the southern drought of the mid-1980s, and the Mississippi floods had national consequences on the economy. *Also see* **Long Range Weather Forecasts.**

natural law *Cult&Soc, Ethcs&Phil* Codes, laws, rules, and principles obtained (arguably) using reason from an examination of nature, or the universe, in contrast to those derived by intuition, revelation, or feelings.

natural resources *EntreP* Things created by acts of nature and used to produce goods and services.

naturalism *Ethcs&Phil* System of thought holding that all **phenomena** can be explained in terms of natural causes and laws without attributing moral, spiritual, or **supernatural** significance to them.

naturalism *Flm&Vid* Style of realism showing characters in social events over which they have little or no control. Human values are implied rather than **didactically** stated.

naturalism *LitArts* Practice of describing precisely the actual circumstances of human life.

naturalism *VisArts* 1 Practice of reproducing subjects as precisely as possible. 2 Practice of reproducing natural objects as they are pursuing and idealizing the beauty of nature.

nature *Cult&Soc* 1 Primitive state of existence, untouched and uninfluenced by civilization or artificiality. *Origin* The genesis of growing things. 2 Source of primary motion and rest in things.

navigation *iMedia* Movement through an interface to interact with content (access, retrieve, submit, alter, etc.)

Navigator *InfoMgt* Leading direction finder for the **Internet.**

Nazi *Law&Pol* (Notzee) 1 Member of the National Socialist German Workers' Party, founded in Germany in 1919 and brought to power in 1933 under Adolf Hitler (» **fascist**) 2 **nazi** Advocate of Nazism.

NBA *SportsEnt* National Basketball Association. Has 30 teams. Its broadcast contract with **NBC** and **Turner Broadcasting System** is worth approx. $300

NBC*Rdio/TV* » **RCA** *Also see* **Broadcast Stations & Networks.**

NBCC *Crit&Eval, LitArts* » **National Book Critics Circle**

NC *InfoMgt* **network computer** Simpler, less costly alternative to a **personal computer**. It has no disk drive, little memory.

NCAA *SportsEnt* **National Collegiate Athletic Association** Largest and most influential governing body of intercollegiate athletics. With operating revenues of approx. $300 million per year, two-thirds come from TV rights to NCAA men's Division I basketball championship. NCAA offers championships in 16 male sports, 14 female sports and 3 coed sports, classified in 3 levels or Divisions (I, II, III) At least 35,000 student athletes compete in those championships every year. A few of the best athletes will be selected for professional careers.

NCAC *Law&Pol, LegAsp* **National Coalition Against Censorship.** Est. 1974, NYC. "Alliance of over 40 national nonprofit organizations, inc. literary, artistic, religious, educational, professional, labor, and civil liberties groups. United by a conviction that freedom of thought, inquiry, and expression must be defended." — *Also see* **Anti-Censorship Organizations.**

NC-17 *Flm&Vid* **No children under 17**. Current rating for films formerly **X-rated.**

NCB *Eco&Fin* » **National Conference Board**

NCFE *Law&Pol, LegAsp* **National Campaign for Freedom of Expression.** "Educational and advocacy network of artists, arts organizations, audience members, and concerned citizens formed to protect and extend freedom of artistic expression and fight censorship throughout the United States." — >http://www.artswire.org< *Also see* **Anti-Censorship Organizations.**

NCME *MusArts* Organized to influence public policy for music education by **Music Educators National Conference** (MENC), **National Academy of Recording Arts & Sciences** (NARAS), **National Association of Music Merchants** (NAMM)

NCOA *Mktg* **National Change of Address** program operated by private businesses licensed by the U.S. Postal Service. NCOA makes available current change-of-address information throughout the U.S. — all in one place. "Provides the opportunity for faster marketing through accurate mail delivery." — U.S. Postal Service, 1990.

NDA *iMedia* » **non-disclosure agreement**

ND filters *Flm&Vid* Colorless filters in a range of densities used to cut down the amount of light if it is too intense for a given shot or a required f-stop.

ne plus ultra (nee plus ultra, Latin) *Crit&Eval* The highest point of excellence or achievement; the ultimate.

NEA *Fndng* **National Endowment for the Arts**. Founded in 1965 Artists, arts administrators and patrons appointed by the President of the United States to advise the Chairperson of the National Endowment for the Art on policy and grants. *Also see* **Federal Agencies and Statutes, Public Policy, Regional Arts Councils, States Arts Councils.**

NEA grants *Fndng* Four new (1996) categories of grants by the **National Endowment for the Arts**: **heritage and preservation, education and access, creation and presentation, planning and stabilization.**

near-letter quality *InfoMgt* Inferior to correspondence quality re computer printouts. *Also see* **correspondence quality, high resolution.**

nebech *or* **nebbish** *or* **neb** (neb'-ish, Yinglish) *Crit&Eval* Born loser, very unlucky person, nonentity. <Nebech is the dope who always picks up what a **shlemiel** knocks over>

NECAA *Mgt* » **NACA**

necessity *Mktg* Something deemed necessary for survival or to maintain a certain **lifestyle**. *Also see* **desire, need, want.**

need *TheatArts* » **intention**

need for achievement *EntreP* Desire to succeed, where success is measured against a personal standard of excellence.

need for autonomy *EntreP* Personality characteristic of having a high need for independence.

needlepoint *Fashn* 1 Decorative needlework on canvas, usu. in a diagonal stitch covering the entire surface of the material. 2 Type of lace worked on paper patterns with a needle. In this sense, also called point lace.

needs *Mktg* 1 Some condition or thing deemed necessary for basic survival. <air, food and water, clothing and shelter> 2 Additional conditions or things deemed necessary to live a civilized life. <communication, pleasure, sex, and transportation> *Also see* **desire, necessity, want**.

needs analysis *iMedia* Analysis of the needs of the target audience.

needs assessment *Mgt,PerfA&C* Promoter's first step in designing an event with a client. Method of appraising goals and objectives; analyzing feasibility of the project.

negative cost *Flm&Vid* All costs, charges, and expenses incurred in the acquisition and production of a movie. Usually separated as **above-the-line** production-period costs and **post-production**-period costs.

negative growth *E&F-Acc* A gentler, misleading term for "decline."

negative option plan *Mktg* Contractual arrangement in which the seller, e.g., record club, periodically sends its members an announcement identifying merchandise it will ship and bill unless an enclosed response (negative option) is returned by a given date. PRENOTIFICATION PLAN. *Also see* **positive option plan**.

negative space *iMedia* Background space around objects; generally intended to be ignored, or to not contain information or data. In contrast: positive space.

negligee *also* **negligée** *Fashn* Woman's loose dressing gown, often of soft, delicate fabric.

negotiable instruments *LegAsp* Special forms of contracts. <certificates of deposit, checks, drafts, notes> *Also see* **Contracts**.

negotiate *Eco&Fin* To sell or discount. <assets or securities>

negotiate *Genl* To succeed in accomplishing or managing. <negotiate the connection between a modem and an online service; negotiate a difficult musical passage.

negotiate *HR&LR. LegAsp* **1** To arrange or settle by discussion and mutual agreement. <negotiate a contract; negotiate a labor agreement> **2** To transfer title to or ownership. <a promissory note> *Also see* **art of negotiation**.

negotiation committee *HR&LR* One representing a union or management chosen to **negotiate** a **collective bargaining** contract. *Also see* **art of negotiation**.

Negro music *MusArts* "Scrutiny of American Negro music reveals something about the essential nature of this country." — LeRoi Jones (*aka* Imamu Amiri Baraka, 1934-, dram., poet, pol. activist)

Negro songs *Cult&Soc, MusArts* Mid-eighteenth century antecedent of 19th century if black and white **minstrel** songs.

NEH *Cult&Soc, Fndng* **National Endowment for the Humanities**. Created in 1965 by the U.S. Congress to foster the **humanities**. *Also see* **Federal Agencies and Statutes, National Council for the Arts. NEA, Public Policy**.

neo-Nazi *Cult&Soc* Member of a fringe group inspired by Adolf Hitler's **Nazis**. *Also see* **skinhead**.

neoclassicism *Aes&Creat LitArts* Revival of classical aesthetics and forms, esp. revival in literature in the late 17th and 18th centuries, characterized by a regard for the classical ideals of reason, form, and restraint.

neoclassicism *MusArts* Movement in music in the late 19th and early 20th centuries that sought to avoid subjective emotionalism and to return to the style of the pre-Romantic composers. *Also see* **Art Movements and Periods**.

neoclassicism *TheatArts* Attempt in the 16th, 17th, and 18th, centuries to "regularize" dramatic techniques by following scrupulously what were thought to be the practices of the ancients, including adherence to the "unities." Use of a chorus, preservation of **decorum** in language and action, avoiding acts of violence on stage, and use of only royal or noble characters in tragedy.

neoclassicism *VisArts* Revival in the 18th and 19th centuries in architecture and art, esp. in the decorative arts, characterized by order, **symmetry**, and simplicity of style. Heroic events and mythological characters were favorite subjects. *Also see* **Art Movements and Periods**.

neoconservatism *also* **neo-conservatism** *Law&Pol* Intellectual and political movement (1980s) in favor of political, economic, and social conservatism that arose in opposition to the perceived **liberalism** of the 1960s. *Also see* **conservatism**.

neoexpressionism *VisArts* Art movement based on **expressionism** that developed in the early 1980s in Germany, Italy, and the United States and is characterized by crudely drawn, **garishly** colored canvases depicting violent or erotic subject matter. *Also see* **Art Movements and Periods**.

neoimpressionism *VisArts* Movement in late 19th century painting led by Georges Seurat (1859-91, Fr. pntr.) that was stricter and more formal than **impressionism** in composition and employed **pointillism** as a technique. *Also see* **Art Movements and Periods**.

neophyte *Crit&Eval* beginner or **novice**

neorealism *Flm&Vid* Italian film movement that produced its best works between 1945 and 1955 Strongly realistic in its techniques, neorealism emphasized **documentary** aspects of film art, stressing loose episodic plots, unextraordinary events and characters, natural lighting, actual location settings, nonprofessional actors, a preoccupation with poverty and social problems, and an emphasis on humanistic and democratic ideals. *Also see* **Art Movements and Periods**.

neosurrealism *VisArts* Revival of **surrealism** mixed with **pop art** in the late 1970s and the 1980s, marked by an attempt to illustrate the **bizarre** imagery of dreams or the subconscious mind in painting and photography. *Also see* **Art Movements and Periods, modern art**.

nepotism *Ethcs&Phil* Favoritism shown to relatives.

nerd *also* **nurd** *Crit&Eval* One regarded as stupid, inept, or unattractive.

nerd *also* **nurd** *InfoMgt* One who is single-minded or accomplished in scientific pursuits (usu. in the computer sciences) but is felt to be socially inept. "[Many young people] – and they seem to be more common in Japan – resemble the stereotype of the computer nerd: brilliant, driven but utterly lost when in human company." — Sheryl WuDunn (info sci. journ.) Also *see* **suits, techie**.

nest *iMedia* Set of data contained sequentially within another.

nest *InfoMgt* Subset of data contained sequentially within another.

nested phrases *BcstJourn* Midsentence phrases that break up the continuity of the sentence elementsÑusually the subject and verb.

nested series *Mktg,PerfA&C* Box office term for a smaller subscription package within a larger package.

nesting *iMedia* » **nest**

net *InfoMgt* **Internet**

.net *InfoMgt* Suffix of an Internet **domain name** assigned to network service providers. *Also see* **Domain Names, Network Solutions Inc**.

NET *Rdio/TV* **National Empowerment Television**, a politically conservative cable network. *Also see* **Broadcast Stations & Networks**.

net assets *E&F-Acc* » **net worth** *Also see* **Assets**.

net income *Eco&Fin, EntreP* **1** Excess of total revenues over total expenses. Profit after provision for income taxes and interest expenses for the corporation, and the profit after interest expense for the sole proprietorship, partnership, **LLC**, or **Subchapter S corporation**. **2** All-inclusive "**bottom line**" that reflects all economic activity by the organization for the period being reported. NET EARNINGS, NET PROFIT

net investment *EntreP* Gross investment minus depreciation.

net loss *E&F-Acc* Excess of total expenses over total revenue.

net margin *E&F-Acc* Obtained by deducting operating expenses in addition to cost of goods sold and dividing the result by **net sales**. *Also see* **gross margin, list price, margin of profit**.

net national product (NNP) *EntreP* GNP less depreciation.

net pay *Eco&Fin* Amount paid to an employee from their gross earnings after any deductions are made.

net present value (NPV) *EntreP* In capital budgeting, it is a technique which uses the time value of money by discounting future benefits and costs back to the present. The NPV is the difference between the present value of the benefits and the present value of the costs.

net profit *E&F-Acc ,Flm&Vid* Usually, the amount of gross receipts remaining after deducting costs of manufacturing, distribution, certain deferments, and gross participations.

net profit margin *Eco&Fin, EntreP* **1** Ratio of earnings after interest and taxes divided by sales (net profit margin = earnings after interest and taxes/sales) Determines how much a company earned on each dollar of **net sales** after paying its obligations of tax and interest. *Also see* **profitability ratios**.

net profit participant *Flm&Vid* Those individuals – usu. the producer, director and star – who have **contingent compensa-**

tion agreements (either percentage or fixed sums) based on a movie's net profits: "Mr. [Art] Buchwald (1925-, humorist, columnist, scrnwrtr.) (and [his co-author] who share 19 percent of the net profits of *Coming to America* must prove that there are profits to share. **Paramount** contends that the movie, which has sold more than $300 million worth of tickets, has no net profits. In the **arcane** world of studio bookkeeping every time a **gross profit** participant like Mr. [Eddie] Murphy (1961-, Film/TV act., dir.) gets his profit, it puts the movie a little more in debt." — Aljean Harmetz (movie journ.) *Also see* **gross profit participant.**

net sales *Eco&Fin, EntreP* Revenue that a business has after accounting for returns and allowances. Net sales equals gross sales minus returns and allowances.

net worth *Eco&Fin* Assets of an individual or company minus its liabilities. For a corporation this is also known as **net assets** or "shareholders' equity." For an individual, net worth is the total value of all possessions minus all outstanding debts.

Netcom Inc. *InfoMgt* Online information service *Also see* **Online Information Services.**

netiquette *InfoMgt* etiquette on the **Net**

netizens *InfoMgt* Citizens of the brave new network world.

Netscape *InfoMgt* Web site providing access to Internet. *Also see* **search engine, portals.**

NetWare Loadable Module (NLM) *InfoMgt* » **NLM**

network *HR&LR* To make connections among people or groups of a like kind, object: jobs, knowledge, and skills. *Also see* **networking, support system.**

network *iMedia, InfoMgt* 1 Hardware and software data communication systems interconnected by telephone wires or other means in order to share information. 2 Networks are often also classified according to their geographical extent: local area 3 Means of communication that allows information exchange, storage, and retrieval and the sharing of printers.

network *Rdio/TV* Chain of interconnected broadcasting stations that share a large proportion of their programs. <local or national radio or TV network> *Also see* **Broadcast Stations & Networks.**

network administrator *InfoMgt* One who supervises a computer network. <user-licenses, security, traffic flow> INFORMATION TECHNOLOGY MANAGER

network computer (NC) *InfoMgt* » **NC**

Network News Transfer Protocol (NNTP) *InfoMgt* » **NNTP**

network radio *Rdio/TV* First attempt made on 4 Jan. 1923, when **WEAF**-NYC and **WNAC**-Boston fed programs to each other by telephone lines for simultaneous broadcast. *Also see* **Broadcast Stations & Networks.**

Network Solutions Inc. *InfoMgt* Handles Internet registrations under contract to the **National Science Foundation** (NSF) *Also see* **domain name.**

networking *HR&LR* Informal system whereby persons having common interests or concerns assist each other in the exchange of information or the development of professional contacts. *Also see* **support system.**

networking *iMedia, InfoMgt* Process of connecting two or more computers so that they can communicate with each other... *Also see* **network.**

neural network *InfoMgt* Method of constructing a computer memory using an architecture based on the human brain.

neutral density filters *Flm&Vid* » **ND filters**

never-never land *Crit&Eval* Imaginary and wonderful place; a fantasy land. *Origin* Never-Never Land from the play *Peter Pan.*

New & Used Car Sales *Eco&Fin* This **economic indicator** is based on car license registrations in the 50 states. Increase in new car sales projects a growing economy; the reverse indicates a slowing economy and a possible **recession**. Same theory holds that a rise in used car sales also points to a sinking economy. Problem with this indicator is that reports from some states are not accurate or timely.

New Age *Crit&Eval, Cult&Soc* Relating to a complex of spiritual and consciousness-raising movements of the 1980s.

New Age *MusArts* In the 1980s, music characterized by quiet improvisation marked by a dreamy texture and touches of **ethnic** (acoustic) instrumentation.

New Age music *MusArts* Works of various composers and musicians who strive to create soothing audio environments rather than follow song structures. Born of an interest in spirituality and healing in the late 1970s, it is often used as an aid to meditation. Characterized by harmonic resonance, contemplative melodies, nonlinear song forms, and uplifting themes. <Brian Eno (1948-, Eng. comp., key., sngr.), George Winston (1949-, comp., pno)> — Patti Jean Birosik (music critic)

new arrival wall *LitArts, Mktg* Face-out display in a (chain) book store, available for a fee paid by a book publisher. *Also see* **dumps, endcap.**

new boy *Flm&Vid* New **stuntperson**, usu. with less than five years of experience. *Also see* **okay guy.**

New Criticism *Crit&Eval* Method of literary evaluation and interpretation (mid-20th century) that emphasizes close examination of a text with minimum regard for the biographical or historical circumstances in which it was produced. *Also see* **professional critic., John Crowe Ransom, Robert Penn Warren.**

New Deal *Cult&Soc, Law&Pol* Domestic reform program of **President Franklin D. Roosevelt** (F.D.R.) intended to help the U.S. recover from the **Great Depression** of the 1930s. <**Social Security**, banking reform, conservation and reforestation, labor reform (collective bargaining, minimum wage), and much more> "On the day of my husband's first inauguration, I asked him what was his greatest concern. He answered: 'To save capitalism from itself.'" — **Eleanor Roosevelt**

New Home Construction *Eco&Fin* This **economic indicator** is based on building permits issued by local governments, as reported by U.S. Dept. of Commerce in two ways: one shows the number of new single family home starts for the month, the second shows the number of "living units" (apartments) construction starts. Data is compared to the previous month and to the same month in the previous year. *Also see* **Existing Home Sales.**

New Left *Cult&Soc, Law&Pol* A 1960s political movement among college students who advocated radical changes in government and society. *Also see* **Political Philosophies.**

new media *InfoMgt* 1 Includes new configurations of audio and visual recordings. <**optical disks, CDs, laser disks, Digital Audio Tape, DVDs**> Also includes **online services, interactive TV, satellite TV**, and more coming (or promised) every day. 2 Regarded by media managers as an opportunity to generate additional revenue from existing properties. <Time Warner's CD-ROM version of the *Sports Illustrated* "Swimsuit Issue." *Also see* **multimedia.** [Term eludes precise definition as it rapidly converges and evolves as fast as the technology that spawns and supports it.]

new news *InfoMgt, Journ* Characterized by Marvin Kalb (1930-, former CBS Chief Diplomatic Correspondent and Harvard journalism scholar) as news coverage marred by: inadequate **sourcing**, rush to judgment, blurred lines between fact and opinion, editorializing within news stories, and **infotainment.**

New Orleans jazz *Cult&Soc, MusArts* Anecdotal and factual evidence make it clear: jazz – the word and music began in the **Big Easy**, in the late 1890s. Some of it came from instrumental (citified) blues. By 1900 blues bands were playing for **slow drag** (very close) dancing in the **honkytonks**. The horns did whatever it took to wail like vocal blues. <note bending, throat tones, lip **vibrato**, and mutes of any kind> Influences on early jazz also included ragtime and the marches relating to the 1905 Spanish-American War. "New Orleans... was different from other American cities... It was tolerant of pleasure, it was rich with music – undoubtedly it was the most musical American city – and it afforded the black man a little more room for expression than was generally true of the South." — **Eileen Southern** *Also see* **jazz origins, Jazz Styles, Storyville.**

new story lead *BcstJourn* Lead sentence used for stories being heard for the first time.

new traditionalist country music *MusArts* Style (mid-1980s) of **country music** that retains the electric guitars of **country-rock** but emphasizes an older instrumentation: steel guitar, fiddle, mandolin. <Ricky Skaggs (1954-), George Strait (1952-), Randy Travis (1959-)> *Also see* **Country Music Styles.**

new use *Genl* Art work of one medium used in another medium. <a painting or a recorded song used on stage or screen>

New Wave *Flm&Vid* 1 Filmmaking movement marked by unconventional techniques, such as **abstraction** and subjective **symbolism**, and often by experimental photography. 2 Group of young

French directors who came to prominence during the late 1950s. Most widely known are **François Truffaut**, Jean-Luc Godard (» **auteur**), and **Alain Resnais**. *Also see* **Directors**.

new wave *Genl* New movement in a particular area of the arts.

new wave, New Wave *MusArts* Rock music characterized by ensemble playing rather than lengthy solo passages and by lyrics that express anger or social alienation. *Also see* **Rock Music Styles**.

New York Jazz *MusArts* "Be-bop was the electrifying first-time translation of post-**Depression** into musical language, and its creators found in New York their capital." — Ann Douglas (19??-, jazz critic) *Also see* **bop**.

New York Stock Exchange (**NYSE**) *Eco&Fin, EntreP* Largest stock exchange in the world, trading about 70% of US equity. Origins can be traced back to the Buttonwood Agreement, a document drawn up by 24 brokers under a buttonwood tree on Wall Street in 1792. BIG BOARD

New York Times v. Sullivan Journ, LegAsp "[This case] made a highly important contribution to the development of First Amendment law by holding, for the first time, that state libel laws are subject to Constitutional limitations." — Renata Adler (» **actual malice**) *Also see* **reckless disregard**.

New York Women in Film and Television *ArtPerf, Flm&Vid* "Founded in 1978, self-support network of more than 1,000 members presents year-round calendar of seminars, workshops, and programs designed to give women the chance to wheel and deal like the 'old boys.' Members must have five experiences above entry level." — Lena Williams (reporter)

New York World Journ NYC newspaper noted for sensationalism. *Also see* **yellow journalism**.

newbie *InfoMgt* Anyone new to a **cyberspace** area.

News Agencies *ColEntry, Journ*» **Associated Press** (AP), **Independent TV News** (ITN), **La Presse France, Reuters, United Press International** (UPI), **Video News International** (VNI)

news agency *Journ* Organization that provides news coverage to subscribers. <newspapers or periodicals> PRESS AGENCY, PRESS ASSOCIATION *Also see* **News Agencies**.

news boxes *Journ, Mktg* » **news racks**

news conference *Journ* » **press conference**

news flash *Journ, Rdio/TV* » **newsbreak**

news racks *Journ, Mktg* Newspaper vending machines. usu. placed on street corners. NEWS BOXES

news. *Journ* newspaper.

newsbreak *Journ, Rdio/TV* **1** Urgent or immediate item of news. **2** Act or an instance of interrupting previously scheduled radio or television programming in order to report a newsworthy event or story. NEWS FLASH

newscast *Journ, Rdio/TV* **1** Radio or television broadcast of the news. **2** Popular type of television network programming. <*ABC World News Tonight, 60 Minutes, Newshour, Meet the Press*> *Also see* **Television Shows**.

newsgroups *InfoMgt, Mktg* » **listservs, Usenet**

newshole *Journ* Amount of space in a newspaper supposedly reserved for **hard news**. *Also see* **ad stacks**.

newsletter *VA-Prntng* Printed report giving news or information of interest to a special group.

newsmagazine *Journ* Magazine, usu. published weekly, that contains reports and analyses of current events. <*Newsweek, Time*>

newsmagazine *Rdio/TV* TV news program featuring several different stories (segments) <*60 Minutes; 20/20*>

newsmonger *Crit&Eval* One who spreads news. <a gossip>

newspaper (news.) *Journ, VA-Prntng* » **newsprint**

Newspaper Association of America *Journ, Mgt* » **NAA**

Newspaper Guild, The *HR&LR, Journ* Washington-based union for newspaper and news service employees, generally those in the news and business departments. *Also see* **Guilds & Unions**.

newspeak *Ethcs&Phil* Deliberately **ambiguous** and contradictory language used to mislead and manipulate the public. *Origin* "Newspeak," a language invented by **George Orwell** in his novel *1984*.

newspeople *Journ* Newspersons considered as a group.

newsperson *Journ* Newsman or a newswoman

newsprint *Journ, VA-Prntng* Paper, usu. off-white, made from wood **pulp** and used chiefly for printing newspapers. NEWSPA-

PER

newsreel *Flm&Vid, Journ* Short film dealing with recent or current events shown in movie theaters, from the 1920s until supplanted by TV news in the 1950s.

newsroom *Journ, Rdio/TV* Room in a newspaper office or radio or television station, where news stories are written and edited.

newsstand vehicle *Journ, Mktg* Magazine or newspaper that depends on the income from newsstand sales.

newsworthy *Journ* Of sufficient interest or importance to the public to warrant reporting in the **media**. *Also see* **press conference**.

newsy *Crit&Eval, Journ* Full of news; informative.

Next Century Media *InfoMgt, Mktg* Research company in New Paltz, NY, developing measurement systems for **interactive media**.

next to closing *PA-Variety* Most favored time spot on a **vaudeville** program or variety show. *Also see* **opening act, closing act**.

Next Week, *East Lynne* *TheatArts* Classic **coming attraction** notice in the **heyday** of English provincial repertory.

nexus *Crit&Eval* **1** Link or tie. **2** Connected series or group. **3** Core or center.

NFL *SportsEnt* National Football League. Has 32 teams with an approximate average value of $280 million per team

NGCSA *Genl* **National Guild of Community Schools of the Arts**. Nationwide service and education organization that fosters the growth and development of **nonprofit**, nondegree-granting community schools offering instruction in the performing and visual arts to students of all ages and backgrounds. Programs include: communications, research, advocacy and professional development for trustees, administrators and faculty; assistance for starting schools; technical assistance, consultancy, referral services, and replication of model arts education programs.

NGO *Fndng* Nongovernmental org. This term is most commonly used outside the USA to refer to **nonprofits**. NGO may represent a partnership between government and a **nonprofit**.

NGO *Mgt* Nongovernmental organization <foundations, councils, centers for policy studies, think tanks>

NHL *SportsEnt* National Hockey League. Has 26 teams that generate an average per team of $25 million a year from attendance.

niche marketing *EntreP, Mktg* **1** Appeal to a specifically defined or tightly focused segment of a **target market** in conjunction with strategic image positioning of a brand or product. **2** Choosing market segments not adequately served by competitors.

niche strategy *EntreP* Strategy in which the company targets a small segment of the total market. This is a common strategy for entrepreneurial companies, but it can be risky.

nickel-and-dime *Crit&Eval* minor; small-time <nickel-and-dime operation> *Also see* **shoestring**.

nickelodeon *Flm&Vid* Early movie theater, ca. 1905, charging an admission price of five cents. *Also see* **bicycling**.

nickelodeon *MusInstr* **Player piano** activated by the insertion of a coin. *Also see* **Music Playack Device**.

nickelodeon *RecA&S* **jukebox**

Nielsen, Jacob (1958-) *iMedia* Founded the "discount usability engineering" movement for fast and cheap improvements of user interfaces and has invented several usability methods, including heuristic evaluation. He holds 66 U.S. patents, mainly on ways of making the Internet easier to use.

Nielsen Media Research *Mktg* **Media** research unit of **Dun & Bradstreet** (D&B) that evaluates audience measurement systems. *Also see* **Commerce Net/Nielsen**.

Nielsen Station Index (NSI) *LitArts, Rdio/TV* » **NSI**

night club *PA-Variety* Establishment that stays open late at night and provides food, drink, entertainment, and music for dancing.

nightscape *VisArts* View or representation of a night scene.

nihilism *Ethcs&Phil* **1** Extreme form of **skepticism** that denies all existence. **2** **Doctrine** holding that all values are baseless and that nothing can be known or communicated.

NII *Crit&Eval, InfoMgt* » **National Information Infrastructure**

NIICA *IntelProp, LegAsp* **National Information Infrastructure Copyright Act**. Proposed extension of the current copyright law.

Nikkei 225 *EntreP* This index is the arithmetic average of 225 major Japanese stocks.

NIMA *Mktg, Rdio/TV* **National Infomercial Marketing Associ-**

ation. Members include: information producers, marketers, advertisers, telemarketers, duplication video services, home shopping networks, and cable television networks. Promotes the electronic retailing industry in the best interests of the public and the association's membership. Works to maintain and further the development of a commercial environment in which the consumer can make an informed choice based on the information offered throughout the industry's programming.

NIMBY *InfoMgt* Not In My Back Yard.

ninas *TheatArts, VisArts* Al Hirshfield (1903-, artist) has done, for more than 50 years, wonderful line drawings of theatrical people – mostly for the *NY Times*. Next to his signature, he'll have a number: 3 or 4 or 2, indicating the number of times he has incorporated in his drawing, the name of his daughter, Nina, hidden in curls, **flounces, ruffles**, etc.

nite spot *PA-Variety* » **night club**

nitty-gritty *Crit&Eval* Specific or practical details; the heart of a matter.

nix *Crit&Eval* Forbid, refuse, or veto.

Nixon, Richard Milhous (1913-94) *Law&Pol* The 37th President of the United States (1969-74) Vice President (1953-61) When Congress recommended three articles of impeachment for Nixon's involvement in the Watergate scandal, he resigned from office (8/9/74) [And never apologized to the citizens of the United States for violating his oath of office.].

NJSO *MusArts* **National Jazz Service Organization** "Nonprofit benefit arts service agency that was founded in 1985 to nurture the growth and enhancement of jazz as an American musical art form." — NJSO

NL *SportsEnt* National League of baseball. Oldest professional sports league in the U.S. (est. 1876) Set a precedent for all professional sports leagues that would follow: team owners control the league, players are "employees." Many of the governing practices set forth by the National League are still in effect in all professional sport leagues today, inc. **salary caps**. *Also see* **AL.**

NLM *InfoMgt* **NetWare Loadable Module** Program that monitors the number of copies of a software application in use in each file **server** across a network.

NLRB *Mgt, HR&LR* **National Labor Relations Board** est. 1935 by the **National Labor Relations Act** which affirmed labor's right to organize and engage in collective bargaining, or to refrain from such activities. *Also see* **Federal Agencies and Statutes**.

NMPA *MusArts* **National Music Publishers Association** Est. 1917 as a trade association representing the U.S. music publishing industry. NMPA owns the **Harry Fox Agency, Inc.** which licenses **mechanical rights** on behalf of music publishers and their authors.

NNTP *InfoMgt* **Network News Transfer Protocol** *Also see* **Protocols.** Ω

No children under 17 (NC-17) *Flm&Vid* » **NC-17**

no-frills *Mktg* Marked by the absence of extra or special features; basic.

no-show *Mktg,PerfA&C* Person who buys a ticket for an event but does not attend.

Nobel Prize (Nobel Memorial Prize) *Eco&Fin, LitArts, Sci&Tech* Annual international awards est. 1901, economics prize, 1969, by Alfred B. Nobel (1833-96, Swed. inventor of dynamite, philanthropist) *Also see* **Awards & Prizes**.

node *InfoMgt* **1** Collection of modems that provide local **access** to a system. **2** Terminal in a computer network.

Noh drama *TheatArts* Japanese classical theater dating from the 14th century; the plays are highly poetic dramas given extremely formal production outage. Noh dramas influenced such 20th century playwrights as W.B. Yeats (1865-1939) *Also see* **Theaters & Theatres.**

noise *Flm&Vid* Unwanted sound or signal generated in a sound or video system or transferred by these systems from other sources such as the power supply.

noise *iMedia* Distortion or interference that alters or obscures the intended signal or content.

noise *Mktg* » » **clutter**

.nom *InfoMgt* **Domain name** ending for individuals who want personal sites. *Also see* **Domain Names.**

nom de plume (nahm dee ploom) *LitArts* » **pen name**

nominal account *E&F-Acc* » **temporary account**

nominal GDP *EntreP* Value of GDP in current dollars.

non sequitur *Crit&Eval* Inference or conclusion that does not follow from the premises or evidence.

non-accelerated depreciation methods *E&F-Acc* Opposite of **accelerated depreciation methods**. <straight-line **depreciation**>

non-data-ink *iMedia* Graphic elements which are dispensable; they do not provide integral visual information. Literally ink that does not represent data or information. *Also see* **chartjunk**.

non-disclosure agreement (NDA) *LegalAsp, iMedia* Legal document, signed by two or more parties, in which it is agreed that confidential information will not be shared (outside of the parties entering into the agreement) within a specific amount of time.

non-dramatic performance license *IntelProp, MusArts* Permits use of public performance of a song: over radio, TV; at clubs, hotels, and concerts. *Also see* **Music Licenses**.

non-exclusive rights *IntelProp, MusArts* Performing rights held by American performing rights organizations are non-exclusive, because at the same time that the organizations have the right to license performances, writers and publishers have the right to license directly to music users. Other rights may also be granted on a non-exclusive basis. *Also see* **exclusive rights**.

non-family situation comedies *Rdio/TV* Popular type of television network programming. <*Cheers, The Mary Tyler Moore Show, Taxi*> *Also see* **Television Shows**.

non-fiction (n-fict.) *LitArts* prose other than **fiction**

non-impact printer *InfoMgt* Uses electricity, heat, laser technology, or photographic techniques to print images.

non-performer unions *HR&LR* » **Guilds & Unions**

non-returnable advance *LegAsp, Mgt* Advance against royalties considered non-returnable if royalties fail to **accrue** to the equivalent of the advance.

non-trivial *InfoMgt* Delicate way of describing a program or online service as not user-friendly.

nondurable goods *EntreP* Goods that last for short periods of time, such as food.

nonet *MusArts* **1** Composition of nine instruments or voices. **2** Nine singers or instrumentalists.

nonexpendable funds *E&F-Acc, Fndng* Monies allocated or reserved for a particular purpose, and thus cannot be considered **expendable**. *Also see* **Funds**.

Nongovernmental organization *Mgt* » **NGO**

nonlinear *Flm&Vid* In **post-production**, a system's ability to allow users to change any edit and not have to specifically alter other edits to accommodate the change. In video, nonlinear editing is accomplished through the use of sophisticated, computer-controlled editing machines. Film editing is, by nature, nonlinear since shots are physically spliced together and can be altered without affecting other shots.

nonmetrical *LitArts* opposite of **metrical**

nonobjective *VisArts* Style of art in which natural objects are not represented realistically; abstract. *Also see* **Art Movements and Periods, modern art, nonrepresentational**.

nonpaid circulation *Journ, Mktg* In a **controlled circulation** periodical, circulation that meets the requirements of qualified circulation but is sent free to people and organizations in a particular field covered by the periodical. *Also see* **Media Circulation**.

nonpaid distribution *Journ, Mktg* Terms used by the **Audit Bureau of Circulations** (ABC) for copies of a periodical distributed free at trade shows, **checking copies**, promotional copies to advertisers and their agencies, in-house staff copies — not included in reported total circulation on which ad rates are based.

nonprofit *also* **not-for-profit** *Eco&Fin, Fndng, Mgt* Organization not seeking or producing a profit. While organizations can make a profit, it's called a **surplus** which is reinvested in the organization and its mission rather than distributed to shareholders.

Nonprofit Facilities Fund of New York *ArtPerf, MusArts* » **Jazznet**

nonprofit theater *TheatArts* "Most plays each year came from **nonprofit** theaters, which are protected by taxbreaks and charity." — Donald G. McNeil Jr.

nonrepresentational *VisArts* Relating to a style of art in which natural objects are not represented realistically; **nonobjective**. *Also see* **Art Movements and Periods**.

nonsense verse *LitArts* Verse characterized by humor or **whimsy** and often featuring nonce (invented just for the occasion) words.

nonunion *HR&LR* **1** Not belonging to a labor union. <Most beginning rockers are nonunion musicians> **2** Not employing union members. <nonunion shop>

noodle *MusArts* » **improvise**

normal account balances *E&F-Acc* All assets and expense accounts should have debit balances. All liability, capital, and revenue accounts should have credit balances.

normal good *EntreP* Good for which an increase in income increases demand.

normalization *iMedia* Process of structuring data in information systems such that redundant data is removed and all implicit relationships in the data are expressed in the data structure.

norteño *MusArts* **1** Pop groups with a strong following in central and northern Mexico. ranchera. **2** Musical style from Northern Mexico for singing **corridos**. The accordion and the guitar are its principal instruments. Called **Tex-Mex** in the U.S. *Also see* **conjunto bands**.

North American Free Trade Agreement (NAFTA) *Eco&Fin, EntreP* An international agreement that lowers barriers to trade between the United States, Mexico, and Canada (signed in 1994)

Northern Light *InfoMgt* Web site providing access to Internet. *Also see* **search engine**, **portals**.

nose job *Cult&Soc* Cosmetic surgery: "And long before the latest surge of identity politics and **ethnic** pride, she... refused assimilation by nose job and went on to emphasize her Jewishness in projects like *Funny Girl* and *Yentl*." — **Jon Pareles** *Also see* **ethnic pride**

nose putty *Th-MakeUp* Used to build up the nose and other bony parts of the face.

nosebleed country *MusArts* Metaphor for playing an instrument or singing at a range so high as to cause bleeding from the nose.

nostalgia *Crit&Eval* **Bittersweet** longing for persons, things, or situations of the past. "Most of the smash hits of the past twenty years have been nostalgic for the elegance, innocence, lavishness, and values of earlier times." — **John Lahr**

nostalgic suspense *Flm&Vid* Affection for the memory of the fresh thrill [**thriller**] movies delivered the first time around.

not-for-profit *Mgt* » **nonprofit**

not-for-profit bulk rate *Mgt* Special low postage rate for certain **nonprofits**

not-for-profit exemption *Law&Pol* Tax or fee reduction for **nonprofits**

not-for-profit organization *EntreP* Organization that provides products or services but does not have profit as a goal; also known as nonprofit organizations. *Ex.* include churches, United Way, American Red Cross.

notarize *LegAsp* To certify or attest to the validity of a signature on a document, as a **notary public**.

notary public *LegAsp* Person legally empowered to witness and certify the validity of documents and to take affidavits and depositions.

notation *Genl* System of figures or symbols used in a specialized field to represent numbers, quantities, tones, or values: **musical notation**.

note (n.) *Eco&Fin* **1** Piece of paper currency. **2** Certificate issued by a government or a bank and sometimes negotiable as money. *Also see* **promissory note**.

note (n.) *Genl* **1** Brief informal letter. **2** Brief record, written to aid the memory. <lecture notes>

note (n.) *Law&Pol* Formal written diplomatic or official communication.

note (n.) *LitArts* Comment or an explanation: as on a passage in a text.

note (n.) *MusArts* **1** Tone of definite **pitch**. **2** Symbol for such a tone, indicating **pitch** by its position on the **staff** and duration by its shape. **3** Key of a musical instrument. **4** Characteristic vocal sound made by a songbird or other animal.

notebook computer *InfoMgt* Small (less than 10 lbs.) portable computer about the size of a large notebook. *Also see* **laptop computer**.

notes payable *EntreP* Businesses promise to pay a creditor or lender an amount owed plus interest for a specified period of time, normally one year or less.

notice *Journ* review

notice *TheatArts* » **closing notice**

notice of copyright *IntelProp* When a work is published (publicly distributed), notice of copyright should be placed on all copies. Since March 1, 1989, use of notice has been optional. If a notice is used, it should contain three elements: (**c**), or the word "Copyright," or the abbreviation "**Copr.**" year of first publication, name of copyright owner.

nouveau swing *MusArts* fusion of jazz and **funk**

nouvelle vague *Flm&Vid* » **New Wave**

novel *LitArts* Long work of fictional prose.

novella *LitArts* Short novel

novice *Crit&Eval* Person new to a field or activity; a beginner.

NPN *Genl* **National Performance Network** Nationwide consortium of progressive alternative cultural organizers, initiated and directed by New York's **Dance Theater Workshop** to support the work and creative processes of contemporary, culturally diverse performing artists based in all regions of the U.S. who work in dance, theater, music **performance art** and puppetry. *Also see* **Broadcast Stations & Networks**.

NRB *IntelProp, Rdio/TV* » **National Religious Broadcasters**

nsf *Eco&Fin* Not sufficient funds.

NSF *Mgt* » **National Speakers Forum**

NSF *Sci&Tech* **National Science Foundation**. Independent Agency in the Executive Branch of the U.S. government concerned primarily with the support of basic and applied research and education in the sciences and engineering. Founded **Internet**

NSFRE *Fndng* **National Society of Fund Raising Executives**. Authorizes the title of **Certified Fund Raising Executive** (CFRE)

NSI *LitArts, Rdio/TV* **Nielsen Station Index**. A.C. **Nielsen** Company TV rating service for viewing habits and audience profiles within a given broadcast market. *Also see* **Arbitron**, **Birch/Scarborough**.

NSPPI *Mktg, VA-Prntng* **National Small Press Publishing Institute**. Ω

NTSC *Flm&Vid, Rdio/TV* **National Television Standards Committee**. Technical method (standard in the U.S.) of recording and playing back video; named for the group originally responsible for determining the U.S. system of color broadcasting.

nuance *Crit&Eval* Expression or appreciation of subtle shades of meaning, feeling, or tone. <a rich artistic performance, full of nuance>

nudnik *also* **nudnick** (Yinglish) *Crit&Eval* Obtuse, boring, or bothersome person; pest.

null *LegAsp* Having no legal force; invalid. <render a contract null and void> *Also see* **Contracts**.

nullity *LegAsp* Something that is **null**, esp. an act having no legal validity. *Also see* **Contracts**.

number *MusArts, PerfA&C* One of the separate offerings in a program of music or other entertainment.

numbered rack *LitArts, Mktg* Paperback book rack numbered from 1 to 10, supposedly representing placement on a bestseller list. [Position #1 has been known to have been bought rather than earned.].

numbers *Journ, Mktg* Circulation figures: "Our decisions about where to advertise are rarely based on numbers and rarely based on **buzz**, because we rarely pay attention to anyone's **buzz** except our own." — Leonard A. Lauder (pres., CEO, Estée Lauder)

numeric character reference *iMedia* Numeric character references (decimal or hexadecimal) are used to display certain characters and symbols (in **XHTML** the copyright symbol is ©) *Also see* **character entity**.

nurd *Crit&Eval, InfoMgt* » **nerd**

nut *Eco&Fin, PerfA&C* Cost of launching a business venture. **2** Operating expenses of a theater, theatrical production, or similar enterprise.

nut *MusInstr* **1** Ridge of wood at the top of the **fingerboard** or neck of a stringed instrument, over which the strings pass. **2** Device at the lower end of the bow for a stringed instrument, used for tightening the hairs.

NVR *Flm&Vid* **National Video Resources. Nonprofit** established by the **Rockefeller Foundation** in 1990 to help independent video makers to produce and sell their videotapes.

NWU *ArtPerf, HR&LR, Journ, LitArts* **National Writers Union.** "Trade union (AFL-CIO) for freelance writers of all **genres** publishing in U.S. Markets." — >http://www.nwu.org<. *Also see* **Cartoonists Association.**

NYC *Genl* New York City

NYP *LitArts* Not Yet Published

nyquist theorem *iMedia* States that the highest frequency that should be recorded is one half of the sampling rate.

NYSE *Eco&Fin* » **New York Stock Exchange** Oldest (1792) and largest stock exchange in the U.S. » **Big Board** THE EXCHANGE *Also see* **AMEX, NASDAQ.**

- O -

O&O *InfoMgt* Over & Out.

O&O *Mgt* Owned and operated.

O&O station *Rdio/TV* Broadcasting station owned and operated by a commercial network.

O'Neill, Eugene (1888-1953, dram.) *ArtPerf, LitArts,TheatArts* Arguably America's preeminent playwright, he was the first American playwright (1936) to win the **Nobel Prize** for literature. <*Mourning Becomes Electra* (1931), *The Iceman Cometh* (1946), *Long Day's Journey into Night* (1956)> *Also see* » **mask, Provincetown Players.**

O.J. (**Simpson**) **story** *Journ* » **Woodstock Nation.**

o.t., O.T. *HR&LR* **overtime.**

O/C *BcstJourn* Television script abbreviation for on-camera. This indicates to the director that the picture and sound come from the newscaster reading in the studio. Live is also used.

o/c *Eco&Fin* Overcharge.

O/S *Mktg* Out of stock.

ob. *MusInstr* oboe.

obbligato *MusArts* **1** Indispensable part of the music. **2** (Jazz) "Prominent, **embellished** countermelody." — Lyons & Perlo (jazz critics)

obfuscate *Crit&Eval* **1** To make so confused or opaque as to be difficult to perceive or understand. **2** To render indistinct or dim; darken.

obi *Fashn* Wide sash fastened in the back with a large flat bow, worn by women in Japan as a part of the traditional kimono.

Obie, OBIE Awards *TheatArts* Est. 1956 by the *Village Voice* to acknowledge and encourage **Off Broadway** theater. *Also see* **Awards & Prizes.**

object *Crit&Eval* Something intelligible or perceptible by the mind. » **manner- means-object.**

object *iMedia* **1** Discrete item that can be selected and maneuvered, such as an onscreen graphic. **2** In object-oriented programming, objects include data and the procedures necessary to operate on that data.

object program *InfoMgt* Translated version of a high level program into computer executable form.

object recognition *iMedia* visual perception of familiar objects

object-oriented programming (OOP) *iMedia, InfoMgt* Programming made up of objects that interact with each other. Each object can contain one or more program routines and data structures.

objective *TheatArts* » **intention**

objective correlative *Crit&Eval* Situation or a sequence of events or objects that evokes a particular emotion in a reader or an audience.

objective theory of contracts *LegAsp* Premise that the intent to contract is judged by the **reasonable person standard** and not by the subjective intent of the parties. *Also see* **Contracts.**

objectives *Fndng* Smaller steps that must be taken to achieve a goal. But unlike goals, objectives are **quantifiable** and time-specific.

objectives *Mktg* Results a sponsor wants for a particular sponsorship: visibility, brand awareness, favorable publicity, image enhancement, trade hospitality, etc.

objet d'art (ob-jay-dart, Fr.) *Crit&Eval* Object of artistic merit. *Also see* **virtu.**

obligatory cut *iMedia* Information that a participant or user must see; data that cannot be skipped or by-passed. *Ex.* a screen to fill out billing information for an online bookstore.

obligatory scene *TheatArts* In French: *scene a fairs.* An episode, usu. highly emotional, in which the **protagonist** must confront the central conflict of her/his dramatic existence. It may also refer to a scene so strongly anticipated by the audience that the author is obliged to write it.

obloquy (ob'-la-kwee) *Crit&Eval* Abusively detractive language. INVECTIVE, VITUPERATION

oboe (ob) *MusInstr* **1** Slender **woodwind** instrument with a conical bore and a double reed mouthpiece, having a range of three **octaves** and a penetrating, poignant sound. **2** Reed stop in an organ that produces a sound similar to that of the oboe. OBOIST, OBOE PLAYER *Also see* **Musical Instrument Families.**

obscene *Ethcs&Phil* **1** Offensive or repulsive to the senses; loathsome. **2** All that is held to be morally offensive to see or hear. *Origin* That which cannot be or ought not to be shown on stage in the drama. <woundings, maimings, killings, dead bodies>

obscenity *Law&Pol* Something, such as a word, an act, or an expression, considered by some to be indecent or lewd. "If you can't define it, you can't prosecute people for it." — **Justice William Brennan** [To **Jesse Helms** it's a gay **lifestyle**; to others, it's Jesse Helms.— Ed.] *Also see* **censorship.**

obsolescent *Crit&Eval* In the process of becoming useless; becoming obsolete.

obsolete (obs.) *Crit&Eval* **1** No longer in use, an obsolete expression. <23-skidoo> **2** Outmoded in design, style, or construction.

obstacle *TheatArts* Event, activity, or force that prevents the character from direct satisfaction of a goal or objective.

occasional poem *LitArts* One written for a particular occasion. <eulogy, Presidential inauguration, monument dedication>

occlusion *iMedia* Overlapping of objects, creating a sense of depth or perspective.

Occupational Safety and Health Administration (OSHA) *Eco&Fin, EntreP, HR&LR, Law&Pol* Established by legislation (1970) that regulates the safety of workplaces and work practices.

OCR *InfoMgt* **1** **Optical Character Recognition** System whereby the computer attempts to read human writing. **2** **Optical Communications Receiver.** Transmission of data, pictures, speech, or other information by light. Information-carrying light wave signal originates in a transmitter, passes through an optical channel, and enters a receiver, which reconstructs the original information. Optical fibers and lasers make up a technology that offers the maximum transmitting capacity using devices that occupy little physical space. *Also see* **scanner.**

octave *MusArts* **1** Tone eight full tones above or below another given tone. **2** Distance between two pitches having the same name and located 12 half steps apart.

octet *MusArts* **1** Composition written for eight voices or eight instruments. **2** Group of eight singers or eight instrumentalists.

octoroon *Cult&Soc* Person having one-eighth Black ancestry. *Also see* **quadroon, Storyville.**

odd parity *InfoMgt* Error detection technique wherein the sum of the 1 bits is always an odd number.

ode *LitArts* **Lyric** poem marked by strong feelings and an involved style.

ODJB *MusArts* **Original Dixieland Jazz Band,** *originally* **Original Dixieland Jass Band** (ODJB) *MusArts* Organized in New Orleans (c. 1917) by **Nick LaRoca.** Recorded first successful jazz recording in 1917 for Victor Talking Machine Company.

OEM *InfoMgt, Mktg* » **Original Equipment Manufacturer** Company that purchases computers or other complex components from manufacturers, adds other hardware or software, and sells the systems, often for specific applications.

oeuvre (oo-vra, Fr.) *Genl* **1** Work of art. **2** Sum of the lifework of an artist, a writer, or a composer.

ofay *Crit&Eval* Disparaging term for a white person.

off *Crit&Eval* Not up to the usual standard. <The cast knew early on that the songs were off>

off camera *Flm&Vid, Rdio/TV* Outside the **field of view** of a TV or movie camera.

off the book *PerfA&C* In play rehearsal, when actors speak their lines from memory rather than read from script. *Also see* **on your feet.**

off the record *Journ* Not for publication or **attribution** if so requested by the newsmaker to the journalist. *Also see* **on record**. "It means that I can't use [the story or quote] unless I can get it elsewhere." — Edward Pound (journ.) *Also see* **background**.

off-beat *MusArts* Unaccented beat in a musical **measure**.

off-Broadway theatre *TheatArts* **1 Experimental** and lower-cost theatrical activity presented outside the **Broadway** entertainment district in NYC. **2** Distinctions made by union contracts, not to location of theater. *Also see* **OBIE Awards, Theaters & Theatres**.

off-color *Ethcs&Phil* In poor taste. <off-color remark>

off-line *Flm&Vid* Video editing process that produces a rough **cut** from which most final editing decisions are made.

off-line delivery *InfoMgt* Technology that periodically logs onto the Internet and retrieves only the information that users have selected and stores it on a **channel** viewer, which also acts as a screen saver program. *Also see* **customized news**. — David Barboza (info sci. journ.)

off-off-Broadway theatre *TheatArts* **1** Theatrical movement in NYC emphasizing **experimental**, **avant-garde** techniques and productions. **2** Distinctions made by union contracts, not to location of theater. *Also see* **Theaters & Theatres**.

off-print *VA-Prntng* Reproduction of a printed article reprinted from a larger publication.

off-screen *Flm&Vid, Rdio/TV* Out of sight of the TV or movie viewer.

off-stage or **offstage** *Genl* **1** Relating to one's private life. **2** Behind the scenes; not visible to the public.

off-stage or **offstage** *PerfA&C* Area of a stage invisible to the audience. *Also see* **on-stage, Stage Directions, wings**.

off-the-air *Rdio/TV* No radio-TV transmission.

offer *Mgt, Mktg* **1** To present for sale. **2** To put forward for consideration. <offer a deal>

office automation *InfoMgt* Integrated use of communications and computer equipment to increase productivity.

Office for Intellectual Freedom *Law&Pol, LegAsp* » **ALA**

official product, official service *Mktg* Type of sponsorship whereby one brand or **vender** within a product category is designated the "official" product or service. <Official Soft Drink, Official Hot Dog, Official Airline> So designated, the brand or vender is permitted to use the "official" designation in all of its advertising. It is usual that the brand or vender is granted **exclusivity** as well and is also given first right of refusal to provide the product or service for and at the event.

offset, offset printing *VA-Prntng* Printing from a smooth surface by indirect image transfer. *Also see* **letterpress printing, photocomposition**.

OIC *InfoMgt* Oh, I See.

OJT *HR&LR* On the job training.

okay guy *Flm&Vid* Experienced and responsible **stuntperson**. *Also see* **new boy**.

old hat *Crit&Eval* **1** Behind the times; old-fashioned. **2** Overused; **trite**.

old master *ArtPerf, VisArts* **1** Great European painter ca. 1500-1700s. <Pieter Bruegel (» **genre**); Rembrandt van Rijn (1606-69, Dutch pntr., etcher, draftsman); Diego Velazquez (1599-1660, Span. pntr.); Jan Vermeer (» **genre**) **2** Work created by one of these artists.

old school *Crit&Eval* Group committed to traditional ideas or practices.

Old Vic *TheatArts* London theater (1914-81) famous for its Shakespearean **repertoire** and classic revivals featuring the finest English actors. Temporary home of the National Theatre of Great Britain (1963-76)

old-boy network *Cult&Soc* Informal, exclusive system of mutual assistance and friendship through which men belonging to a particular group exchange favors and connections. <fraternity, school alumni, social club, political party, profession> *Also see* **old-girl network**.

old-fashioned *Crit&Eval* Attached to or favoring methods, ideas, or customs of an earlier time.

old-fashioned *Fashn* Of a style or method formerly in **vogue**; outdated.

old-girl network *Cult&Soc* Informal, exclusive system of mutual assistance and friendship through which women belonging to a particular group exchange favors and connections, as in politics or business. <sorority, school alumnae, social club, political party, profession> *Also see* **old-boy network**.

old-line *Crit&Eval, Cult&Soc, Law&Pol* Adhering to conservative or reactionary principles.

old-timey music *MusArts* Relating to a simple, wholesome, unpretentious music usu. associated with the U.S. *Also see* **down-home**.

oldie *MusArts* Song that was once popular. *Also see* **golden oldie**.

oldie, oldies *Rdio/TV, RecA&S* **1** Refers to a use by a radio station of records that have dropped from the charts **2** Oldie is generally regarded as a single that has been off the charts for at least six months. GOLDEN OLDIE

oligopoly *EntreP, Mktg* Market condition in which sellers are so few that the actions of any one of them can affect price and hence the costs that competitors must pay. *Also see* **legal monopoly, major labels, monopoly, technopoly**.

olio *PA-Variety* **1** Vaudeville or musical entertainment presented between the acts of a burlesque or minstrel show. **2** Collection of various artistic or literary works or musical pieces; a miscellany.

Olivier Award *TheatArts* The **Laurence Olivier** Awards, est. 1987, to honor excellence in the British theater. *Also see* **Awards & Prizes**.

Olivier, Sir Laurence (*aka* Baron Olivier of Brighton, 1907-89, Brit stage/film act., dir., prod.) *ArtPerf, Flm&Vid, Mgt, TheatArts* He was knighted in 1947 for his contributions to the theater and directed the **National Theatre of Great Britain** (1962 to 1973) *Also see* **actor, actor-manager, boards, inspire, stage manager**.

Olympian *Crit&Eval* **1** Majestic in manner. **2** Surpassing all others. *Origin* Greek Mythology: One of the 12 major gods and goddesses inhabiting Mount Olympus.

Olympic Games *SportsEnt* Single largest international sport event. *Origin* Sports competition among opposing free cities of ancient Greece. It was the greatest religious festival dedicated to Zeus, the supreme Greek god... The sanctuary of Olympia imposed its authority throughout the Greek world, whereas the Olympic games became the symbol of Panhellenic unity. A Frenchman Pierre de Coubertin, inspired by the Greek tradition, created an international athletic competition at regular periodical intervals at which representatives of all countries and all sports would be invited under the aegis of a universal authority, which would impact to them "a halo of grandeur and glory, that is the patronage of classical antiquity." In 1896, to purify the notion of rivalry and to transform it in noble contest representatives of all the nations created the First International Olympic Games in Athens, Greece, the first Olympic city.

omnidirectional mic *RecA&S* Capable of responding to sound from all directions. *Also see* **Microphones**.

OMS *InfoMgt* **Optical Mark Sense** Method of scanning that reads pencil marks on paper.

on *Crit&Eval, PerfA&C* **1** Perform. <Get ready, you're on next> **2** Performing at a high degree of competence. <Last night, the whole cast was really on>

on *PerfA&C* Perform.

on camera *Flm&Vid, Rdio/TV* Any person or thing in the shot being made.

on camera musicians *Flm&Vid, MusArts* Musicians who play their instruments while being filmed or taped for movie or TV screens are paid more than **off-screen** musicians. <The *Tonight Show* musicians are paid on a different scale when on- or off-camera>

on deep background *Journ* "It means that I'm not going to identify the source [of a story] but I'm going to use it all." — **Bob Woodward** *Also see* **off the record**.

on its ear *Crit&Eval* In a state of amazement, excitement, or uproar. <Success of the movie set the entertainment world on its ear>

on point *Dnce* On toes, a ballet position.

on record *Journ* Known to have been stated or to have taken a certain position. *Also see* **off the record**.

on the board *Journ* Wall or board display of the pages of an article or an issue of a publication for editorial evaluation.

on the come *Eco&Fin* Future income will pay for future expense.

<Royalty payments are made on the come, i.e., the artist doesn't get paid until the company gets paid>

on the cutting edge *Crit&Eval* One or something in the vanguard of a movement.

on the house *Genl* Free; at the expense of the establishment.

on the job training (OJT) *HR&LR* Learn a skill or craft while actually working the job.

on the road *MusArts,PerfA&C* On tour: "This life I got is very rough and few can do it. Now I'll come off five months on the road, have maybe a week off, then right back out. We don't have no days off — feel like I spent nine thousand hours on buses, get off a bus, hop a plane, Get in town just in time to play a gig, **chops** are cold, Come off that stage too tired to raise an eyelash. Sometimes up at 5:30 the next morning to get to that next gig — just a whole lot of ringing and twisting and jumping and bumping and things." — **Louis Armstrong** *Also see* **road dog, tour**.

on the take *Crit&Eval* Taking or seeking to take bribes or illegal income. *Also see* **Alan Freed, payola, plugola**.

on your feet *PerfA&C* In play rehearsal, when actors move about, rather than sit and read from script. *Also see* **off the book.**

on-air *Rdio/TV* Spoken, occurring, or used during broadcasting or while being recorded for broadcasting.

on-demand printing *LitArts, VA-Prntng* Thanks to digital printing technologies, books and journals can be produced cost effectively and quickly in short **print runs** (300 copies or less) comparable in quality to those printed by conventional **lithography**.

ondes martinot (ohnd martinoh, Fr.) *MusInstr* Early French keyboard **synthesizer** developed from the **Theremin**. Invented by (??) Martinot (??)

onion skinning *iMedia* Displaying multiple frames as if they were each depicted on transparent papers. This method allows animators to see the placement of parts across multiple frames.

online *Flm&Vid* Video editing process that incorporates all final picture, sound and effects decisions.

online *Genl, Journ* In progress; ongoing. <online editorial projects>

online *InfoMgt* 1 Description of equipment, devices, and persons who are in direct communication with the **central processing unit** of a computer. 2 Equipment physically connected to the computer. 3 Connected to a computer network. <an **online database**> *Also see* **offline, Online Information Services**.

online access *InfoMgt* Relating to the ways and means of gaining entrance to an **online information service**.

online data base *InfoMgt* Data base that can be directly accessed by a user from a terminal, usu. a visual display device.

Online Information Services *ColEntry, InfoMgt* 1 Companies and organizations that – for a monthly and/or hourly fee – provide access to their **databases** and other resources. 2 Programs that facilitate access to online services. » **Advanced Network Services, Air Mosaic, America Online** (AOL), **CompuServe, Delphi Internet Services, Genie, Gopher, Interchange, Internet, LAN, Microsoft Network, Netcom Inc., PBS Online, Performance Systems International, Prodigy, SprintNet, Spry Inc., Thomas, Usenet, WAIS, World Wide Web** *Also see* **Broadcast Stations & Networks, portals**.

on-sale date *VA-Prntng* Date on which a magazine actually goes on sale at retail outlets, usu. two-four weeks before the magazine's **cover date**.

on-screen *or* **onscreen** *Flm&Vid* Within sight of the viewer of a movie or television.

on-site sales *Mktg* Sales of a sponsor's product or service at or during the event.

on-stage *or* **onstage** *TheatArts* Area of a stage visible to the audience. *Also see* **Stage Directions**.

on-stage booms *PerfA&C* Portable vertical pipes mounted with lighting instruments.

on-stream *Crit&Eval* In or into operation or production.

one-acter *TheatArts* Play consisting of only one act.

one-and-three *MusArts* Indicates that the rhythmic accent in a four-beat measure is on the first and third beat. <most classical music> TWO-AND-FOUR

one-dimensional *iMedia, Crit&Eval* 1 Lacking depth; superficial. 2 Having or existing in one dimension only. *Also see* **two-dimensional, three-dimensional**.

one-liner *Crit&Eval* Short joke or witticism expressed in a single phrase or sentence.

one-man show *PerfA&C* Exhibition or a performance featuring the artistic work of one man. *Also see* **one-woman show**.

one-night stand *also* **one-nite stand** *MusArts,TheatArts* 1 Musical or dramatic performance in one place on one night only. 2 **Venue** where such a performance is given. *Also see* **casual engagement, steady engagement, one-niter**.

one-niter *also* **one-nighter** *MusArts* » **casual engagement**

one-off contract *IntelProp, MusArts* » **single song agreement**

one-person play *TheatArts* Solo dramatic performance

one-sheet *Mktg* Minor billing *Origin* Name of the smallest theatrical advertising poster used on billboards.

one-sheeter *LitArts, Mktg* **Prepublication** cover of an **instant book** distributed by the publisher's **sales reps** so as to lock up advance sales.

one-shot *Crit&Eval* Only one, not likely to be repeated. <Tour was a one-shot effort>

one-shot magazine *Journ* Magazine published for a special event, unlikely to be repeated.

one-step *Dnce, MusArts* 1 Ballroom dance consisting of a series of unbroken rapid steps in 2/4 **time**. 2 Piece of music for this dance. *Also see* **Dances**.

one-step distribution *Mktg* System whereby a product or service is distributed by a manufacturer or an originator directly to retailers. *Also see* **Distribution Methods**.

one-stop *Mktg, RecA&S* Subdistricts that buys recordings from a variety of distributors and resells them to **ma-and-pa** record stores and jukebox operators. *Also see* **Distributors**.

one-up *Crit&Eval* To keep one step ahead of a competitor or an opponent.

one-way option *LegAsp, Mgt* Contract provision whereby only the employer may extend or renew the contract: "David [Selznick] took every advantage possible in Vivien's [Vivien Leigh (1913-67, Brit. act.)] contractual negotiations, insisting on a one-way option contract for seven years — seven years is the most legally allowed in any American contract on account of an old anti-slavery law." — **Laurence Olivier** *Also see* **option**.

one-woman show *PerfA&C* Exhibition or a performance featuring the artistic work of one woman. *Also see* **one-man show**.

onomatopoeia *LitArts* Formation or use of words that imitate the sounds associated with the objects or actions. <buzz, cackle, etc>

OOP *InfoMgt* Object-oriented programming

op art *also* **Op Art** *VisArts* School of abstract art characterized by the use of geometric shapes and brilliant colors to create dynamic optical illusions of motion, and free the art of all but visual associations. *Also see* **Art Movements and Periods**.

op, Op *MusArts* opus.

op, ops *Mgt* operation(s)

op-ed *or* **Op-Ed** *Journ* Newspaper page, usu. opposite the editorial page, that features **syndicated** columnists and articles expressing personal viewpoints.

op., o. p. *LitArts, VA-Prntng* out of print.

OPACT *ArtPerf,TheatArts* **Organization of Professional Acting Coaches and Teachers. Ω**

open *MusArts* 1 Produced by an unstopped string or hole or without the use of slides, valves, or keys. <an open note on a trumpet> 2 Wind instrument played without a **mute**.

open *VA-Prntng* Type or printed matter widely spaced or leaded.

open audition *TheatArts* Audition open to all aspirants. CATTLE CALL

open letter *Journ* Published letter on a subject of general interest, addressed to a person but intended for general readership.

open loop *InfoMgt* Control system not self-correcting.

open market operations *EntreP* Purchase and sale of U.S. securities by the Federal Reserve.

open season *Crit&Eval, Ethcs&Phil* Time of unrestrained harassment, criticism, or attack.

open shop *HR&LR* Situation where a workers union status is not recognized even when there is a union contract in place. *Also see* **closed shop, right-to-work law, union shop**.

Open Software Foundation (OSF) *InfoMgt* » **OSF**

open stock *Mktg* Merchandise kept in stock so as to enable customers to replace or supplement previously purchased items.

open-ended run *TheatArts* Theatrical production in an unlimited number of performances.

opening *LitArts* First part a book

opening act *MusArts, PA-Variety* First music group or act to perform in a rock concert or **vaudeville** program.

opening credit *Mgt* » **credits**

opera *MusArts, TheatArts* 1 Dramatic work in which the words are wholly or partly sung to an instrumental accompaniment almost always assigned to an orchestra. 2 "Opera is whatever you put on in an opera house." — Bernard Holland (music critic) BOUFFE, GRAND OPERA, OPÉRA COMIQUE *Also see* **operetta**.

OPERA America *MusArts* National arts service organization established to support professional opera companies in North, Central and South America.

opéra comique *MusArts* » **comic opera**

operating budget *Eco&Fin* Over-all budget that covers an organization's operating costs over a given time period usu. expressed in quarterly, semi-annual, and one year time periods.

operating cash flow *Rdio/TV* In the cable industry, earnings before **depreciation**, interest, other income, and taxes.

operating expenses (fixed costs) *Eco&Fin, EntreP* Those payments for expenses of a business that are not directly related to revenues or cost of goods sold. <selling expenses, general and administrative expenses>

Operating Foundation *Fnding* 501(c)(3) organization classified by the **IRS** as a private foundation whose primary purpose is to conduct research, social welfare, or other programs determined by its governing body or establishment charter. Some grants may be made, but the sum is generally small relative to the funds used for the foundation's own programs.

operating funds *Eco&Fin, Fnding* 1 Current funds. 2 Funds sought by an organization to be used for general operating costs. <rent, salaries, etc> *Also see* **project funds**, **restricted funds**, **unrestricted funds**.

operating income *EntreP* Result of subtracting operating expenses from gross profit on an income statement.

operating plan *EntreP* Section of the business plan that offers information on how a product will be produced or a service provided, including descriptions of the new company's facilities, labor, raw materials, and processing requirements.

operating profit margin *Eco&Fin, EntreP* Ratio which is used to determine how much each dollar of sales generates in operating income. Formula is operating income divided by net sales. *Also see* **profitability ratios**.

operating return on assets *EntreP* Ratio which determines how much a company earns on each dollar of assets prior to paying interest and taxes. Formula is operating income divided by total assets.

operating statement *Eco&Fin* » **income statement** *Also see* **Statements**.

operating support grant *Fnding* Grant to cover the regular personnel, administrative, and other expenses of an existing program or project. *Also see* **general purpose grant**.

operating system (OS) *InfoMgt* Program that organizes the internal activities of the computer and its **peripheral** devices. It moves data to and from devices, manages information in and out of memory, etc.

Operating Systems *InfoMgt* » **CHRP, DOS, GUI, MS-DOS, OS/2** *Also see* **Programming Languages**.

operational goals and plans *Eco&Fin, Mgt* These are short range goals and plans, usu. with a zero to one year time frame, in two forms: single purpose plan and standing plan. When a single purpose plan is completed it is done and finished. Standing plan remains in effect continually and includes rules and regulations, employee handbooks, etc. **First line managers** are primarily responsible for the formulating and implementing short range goals and plans. *Also see* **Goals and Plans**.

operations management *EntreP* Planning and control of the operations process.

operations process (production process) *EntreP* Activities that produce a company's goods and services.

operetta *MusArts, TheatArts* Originally a short comic opera but in the 19th century it evolved into a long play with music in which the action was **farcical**, usu. inc. elements of social or political satire and music **burlesque**. American **musical theater** evolved from the American operettas of the early 20th century.

opinion leader *Mktg* Individual who influences other people's purchasing and consumption behavior.

opportunistic entrepreneur *EntreP* Person who starts a business with both sophisticated managerial skills and technical knowledge.

opportunity *EntreP* Possibility of making a profit by marketing a product or service.

Opportunity analysis The careful study of an opportunity to determine if it is feasible. This analysis includes the opportunity's marketing, technological, and financial feasibility.

opportunity cost *EntreP, Mgt* Highest value that is surrendered when a decision is made. If you give up a $30,000 a year job to attend school full time, the decision was to attend school, the opportunity cost was $30,000.

opportunity window *EntreP* Period of time during which an opportunity has the greatest possibility of success.

Optical Character Recognition (OCR) *InfoMgt* » **OCR**

Optical Communications Receiver (OCR) *InfoMgt* » **OCR**

optical disk *InfoMgt* Random access storage device that stores **digital** data, such as music or text, as tiny pits etched onto the surface and is read with a **laser** scanning the surface. LASER DISK

Optical Mark Sense *InfoMgt* » **OMS**

optical soundtrack *Flm&Vid* Consists of one or more narrow stripes at the edge of the film. *Also see* **magnetic soundtrack**.

opticals *Flm&Vid* Special visual effects.

optimization *iMedia* 1 Programming: to fine-tune or tweak an application so that it runs more efficiently or is smaller in file size. 2 Graphics: To reduce file size (often at the expense of image quality) to make a file smaller in size. 3 To defragment a hard drive or disk. 4 To change an application's configuration to improve performance.

option *Crit&Eval* Power or freedom to choose.

option *Eco&Fin* Right to buy or sell specific securities or commodities at a stated price within a specified time.

option *LegAsp* 1 Exclusive right, usu. obtained for a fee, to buy or sell something within a specified time at a set price. 2 Privilege of demanding fulfillment of a contract at a specified time. *Also see* **one-way option**.

option *Mgt* To acquire or grant an option on. <One is likely to option the story of the latest celebrity scandal for a movie or TV>

option button *InfoMgt* Interactive control that allows a user to choose an option from a list of options. Unlike square-shaped check boxes, which allow several options to be selected, circle-shaped option (radio) buttons allows only one option to be selected at a time. *Also see* **check boxes**.

opus (op., Op) *MusArts* Musical composition numbered to designate the order of a composer's works.

oratorio *MusArts* Composition for voices and orchestra, telling a sacred story without costumes, scenery, or dramatic action.

orch. *MusArts* orchestra, orchestration.

orches. *MusArts* orchestrator.

orchestra (orch.) *MusArts* 1 Large group of musicians who play together on various instruments: strings, **woodwinds**, brass and percussion instruments.

orchestra (orch.) *PerfA&C* 1 Front section of seats nearest the stage in a theater, the entire main floor of a theater. *Also see* **pit**. 2 Circular area on which the majority of the action of the play took place in Greek theater. 3 Area in a theater or concert hall where the musicians sit, immediately in front of and below the stage.

orchestra librarian *InfoMgt, MusArts* One on the staff of an orchestral organization who is responsible for the integrity of the music manuscripts and recordings. <mend or replace damaged or lost music scores or parts; catalog, file, and retrieve all items>

orchestra pit *PerfA&C* Space between the stage and auditorium, usu. below stage level, that holds the orchestra.

orchestration *MusArts* Arranging instrumental music, usu. classical or musical theatre, for an orchestra. *Also see* **arrangement**, **chart**.

orchestrator *MusArts* One who composes or arranges music for performance by an orchestra. *Also see* **arranger**, **score**.

ordinary annuity *EntreP* Payments which are made or received at the end of each time period.

ordinary income *EntreP* Income earned in the ordinary course of business, including any salary.

ordinary repairs *E&F-Acc* Repair work that creates a revenue expenditure, which is debited to an **expense account**.

.org *InfoMgt* Suffix of an Internet **domain name** assigned to **nonprofit** organizations. *Also see* **Domain Names**, **Network Solutions, Inc.**

organization (org.) *Mgt* **1** Group of persons organized for a particular purpose; an association: a benevolent organization. **2** Structure through which individuals cooperate systematically to conduct business. **3** Administrative personnel of such a structure.

Organization of Professional Acting Coaches and Teachers (OPACT) *ArtPerf,TheatArts* » **OPACT**

organizational culture *EntreP* Behaviors, beliefs, and values that characterize a particular company.

organizational map *iMedia* Organizational map is a clear concept of visual, content, and navigational structures. It is a more polished version, and an extension of, a concept map. It shows the layout and design of content, navigation, and visuals, and how all the parts will interact with each other and the participant who will be using the finished product.

Organized Baseball, organized baseball *SportsEnt* As the oldest professional sports in the US (**NL** est. 1876) Organized Baseball has set a precedent for all professional sports organizations that would follow. It is likely that any crisis or evolution affecting Organized Baseball would impact other professional sports.

organized jazz solo *MusArts* Attributed to **Louis Armstrong**.

organizing *EntreP* Structure developed by managers that will allow them to carry out a plan.

Organs *ColEntry*, *MusInstr* » **chord** —, **electronic** —, **harmonium**, **mouth** —, **pipe** —, **reed** —.

orgiastic *Crit&Eval* Relating to an **orgy**.

orgy *Crit&Eval* **1 Revel** involving unrestrained sexual activity. **2** Moderate indulgence in an activity: an orgy of eating. *Origin* Secret **rite** peculiar to the cults of ancient Greek or Roman deities, typically involving frenzied singing, dancing, drinking, and sexual activity.

Oriental *Cult&Soc* » **Asian**

origin *Cult&Soc, MusArts* Ancestry, derivation. "Any art if it is to have life must be able to trace its origin to a fundamental need. Such **needs** find prompt expression among people even in their most **primitive** and uncultivated state. To this rule music is no exception.... It has been said that if we did not know by experience of the existence of **folk-song** we should have to presuppose it theoretically to account for the art of music."— Ralph Vaughan Williams (1872-1958, English "nationalist" comp.)

original *VisArts* Authentic work of art as distinguished from an imitation or reproduction. *Also see* **reproduction**.

original cast *TheatArts* » **original company**

original cast show album *MusArts, RecA&S* » **cast album**

original company *TheatArts* Cast that first performed the dramatist's work in public. ORIGINAL CAST

Original Equipment Manufacturer (OEM) *Mktg* » **OEM**

ornament *MusArts* Note or group of notes that **embellishes** a melody. ORNAMENTATION

ornate *Crit&Eval* Elaborately, heavily, and often excessively ornamented. FLAMBOYANT

orthodox *Crit&Eval* What is commonly accepted, customary, or traditional.

Orwell, George (b. Eric Arthur Blair, 1903-50, Brit. journ., fictwri., social justice n-fictwri.) *Journ* <*Animal Farm* (1945) and *1984* (1949)> *Also see* **Big Brother**, **egoism**, **newspeak**, **Orwellian**.

Orwellian *Crit&Eval* » **George Orwell**, *1984*.

OS *InfoMgt* Operating systems (for computers)

OS/2 *InfoMgt* **IBM** operating system. *Also see* **Operating Systems**.

Oscar *ArtPerf, Fashn, Flm&Vid, LitArts, MusArts, VisArts* Golden statuette representing annual **Academy Awards**.

oscillation *Sci&Tech* **1** To swing back and forth with a steady, uninterrupted rhythm. **2** To vary between alternate extremes, usu. within a definable period of time. *Also see* **pickup**, **resonator**.

OSF *InfoMgt* "Open Software Foundation is a nonprofit research and development organization whose goal is to provide a software solution that enables computers from multiple vendors to work together in a true, open systems computing environment." —>http://www.yahoo.com/Business_and_Economy/OSF<

OSF/1 *InfoMgt* Operating system **trademarked** by **Open Software Foundation** *Also see* **Operating Systems**.

OSHA *Eco&Fin*, *HR&LR*, *Law&Pol* **Occupational Safety and Health Administration** est. 1970 "to assure so far as possible every working man and woman in the nation safe and healthful working conditions." [Enforcement subject to prevailing political winds: criticized by industry for over zealousness, and by labor for underperformance.] *Also see* **Federal Agencies and Statutes**.

osmosis *Crit&Eval* Gradual, often unconscious process of assimilation or absorption:

ostentatious *Crit&Eval* » **pretentious**

ostinato (Ital. for "to persist") *MusArts* Short melody or phrase constantly repeated, usu. the same part at the same **pitch**. *Also see* **rock beat**, **vamp**.

OT, *or* **o.t.**, *or* **O.T.** *HR&LR* **overtime**

other assets *Eco&Fin* It can be claimed that **intangible assets** fall in this category. Cash surrender value of life insurance, or prepaid expenses, inc. unexpired multi-year insurance premiums; and maybe deferred charges as organization costs or start up costs. *Also see* **Assets**, **Intangible Assets**.

other expenses and income *Eco&Fin* Non-operating revenues and expenses. <Revenues from investments (dividends and interest from savings account, stocks and bonds), interest earned on credit or notes extended to customers, interest expense, and other expenses that result from borrowing money or from credit being extended to the company>

OTOH *InfoMgt* On The Other Hand

out *BcstJourn* » **tag**

out *Crit&Eval* No longer fashionable. *Also see* **far-out**.

out of print *LitArts, VA-Prntng* **op.**, **o.p.**

Out of stock (O/S) *Mktg* Not available for sale or use. *Also see* **in stock**, **inventory**, **stock**.

out-of-home advertising *Mktg* Medium not included in direct response advertising or **electronic media** and **print media**. <billboards, transit ads, sales **pitch** displays in airports, bus terminals, and neon **spectaculars**> OUTDOOR ADVERTISING *Also see* **Advertising Media**.

out-of-pocket expense *Eco&Fin* Spending of cash.

out-sourcing *EntreP* Purchasing products or services that are outside the company's area of competitive advantage.

outcue or **endcue** *BcstJourn* Phrase that usu. includes the last four words of an actuality or soundbite. This helps the engineer, producer, or director know when to cue the newscaster to resume reading. Although the incue is often unnecessary, the outcue is vital on a news script.

outboard equipment *RecA&S* Additional recording equipment added to the sound console.

Outdoor Advertising Association of America (OAAA) *Mktg* Trade organization of companies specializing in **out-of-home** (outdoor) **advertising media**. <Billboards, transit advertising, sales pitches at airports, shopping malls, etc>

outdoor advertising *Mktg* » **out-of-home advertising** *Also see* **Advertising Media**.

Outer Forces *Mgt* Major element in **The Arts Dynamic**. *Also see* **Inner Forces**, **Principal Players**.

outfit *Fashn* Set of clothing, often with accessories.

outgo *Eco&Fin* Something that goes out. <an expenditure or a cost>

outperform *Genl* To surpass another in performance.

output *InfoMgt* Information produced by the computer.

output element *iMedia* Output element is the way in which a product interacts with, or conveys information to, a participant.

outro *BcstJourn* » **tag**

outro *MusArts* Opposite of **intro**; jazz-type chord or set of chords at the end of a song.

outside director *Mgt* Member of a company's board of directors who is not an employee of the company.

outsider *VisArts* One who creates art outside the arts community;

P

usu. an untrained, **primitive** artist. *Also see* **visionary art.**

outsourcing *Eco&Fin, HR&LR* To farm out work to an outside provider or manufacturer in order to cut costs. [Considered by some to be an anti-organized labor tactic.].

outstanding stock *Eco&Fin* Total number of shares of a company owned by the stockholders. *Also see* **authorized stock.**

outtakes *Flm&Vid* Shots or parts of shots that are not used in the final **cut** of a film.

ovation *Crit&Eval* 1 Enthusiastic, prolonged applause. 2 Show of public homage or welcome.

over the top *Crit&Eval* Surpassing a goal or quota.

over-the-air *Rdio/TV* Medium of broadcast transmission. <over-the-air programming>

over-the-hill *Crit&Eval* Past one's prime; past the peak of one's youthful vigor, freshness, and, possibly, creativity. *Also see* **washed-up.**

over-the-transom *Journ, MusArts* Unsolicited manuscripts.

overact *TheatArts* To act a dramatic role with unnecessary exaggeration. *Also see* **chew up the scenery, ham.**

overage *Mgt* Money paid to a performer in excess of the **guarantee** called for in the **engagement contract.** *Also see* **go into percentage.**

overall storyteller *LitArts* "The presence in prose fiction that combines authorial voice and sensibility with technical choices of time, distance, and points of view to tell and dramatize the story. Most obviously present in third person stories, but also functioning though unacknowledged in the choices of the first person story." — John Schultz (CCC/Fiction Writing dept. originator and developer of the Story Workshop approach to the teaching of writing.)

overcall *Eco&Fin, TheatArts* Amount of additional money, often 10 to 20 percent of the original amount invested, that can be requested from the financial backers of a theatrical production.

overcall *RecA&S* Recording requested of the artist by the record company which was not covered in the original contract.

overdub *RecA&S* Additional recorded sound blended into a musical recording. *Also see* **dub.**

overhead *Eco&Fin* Operating expenses of a business. <rent, utilities, interior decoration, and taxes, exclusive of labor and materials>

overhype *Mktg* To promote or publicize to excess.

overlay *VA-Prntng* Transparent sheet containing graphic matter, such as labels or colored areas, placed on illustrative matter to be incorporated into it.

overnights *LitArts, Rdio/TV* Ratings derived from TV sets plugged in directly to a computer. Results from the major markets – New York, Chicago, and Los Angeles – are tabulated and released the morning following the telecast.

overplay *PerfA&C, TheatArts* » **overact**

overprint *VA-Prntng* To imprint over with something more, esp. to print over with another color.

overqualified *HR&LR* Educated or skilled beyond what is necessary or desired for a particular job.

override *Mgt* Sales commission collected by a sales manager in addition to the commission received by a subordinate salesperson.

overrun *VA-Prntng* 1 To rearrange or move type or graphics from one column, line, or page to another. 2 To print more than that ordered. *Also see* **overset.**

overscale artist *HR&LR* Performer who is paid more than the minimum fee (**scale**) set by the prevailing union's agreement with the employer.

oversell *Mktg* To present with excessive or unwarranted enthusiasm; overpraise.

overset *VA-Prntng* 1 To typeset more **copy** than what is needed. 2 To set too much material for a given space. *Also see* **overrun.**

overstock *Mktg* To stock more than necessary or desirable.

overtime (OT, o.t., O.T.) *HR&LR* Payment for additional work done outside of regular working hours. *Also see* **golden time.**

overtone *MusArts* » **harmonic**

overture *MusArts* Instrumental composition intended as an introduction to an opera or a musical play.

owners equity *Eco&Fin* » **book value, equity.**

owners' equity capital *EntreP* 'Owners' financial investments in a company, including profits retained in the company.

oxymoron *LitArts* Figure of speech that uses two contradictory terms. <deafening silence>

Ozarks *Cult&Soc* Refers to the Ozark Plateau or the Ozark Mountains, an upland region of the south-central U.S. extending from southwest Missouri across northwest Arkansas into eastern Oklahoma. Home of a portion of Anglo-American **folk music** and **country music.**

Ozzie and Harriet *Rdio/TV* The 1950s television series that exemplified the happy, suburban, White American values, acted by former big band leader, Ozzie Nelson and his wife Harriet Hilliard former vocalist with his band.

-P-

p *MusArts* » **piano** *Also see* **Music Directions.**

P&D *RecA&S* Contractual relation for the pressing and distribution of recordings.

P&L *or* **P and L** *Eco&Fin* Profit and loss statement.

P-1 *LegAsp, PerfA&C* Section of U.S. immigration law which states that work visas can be issued to foreign entertainment groups if they are "internationally recognized" entertainment groups outstanding in their discipline, or that these groups are coming to the U.S. "to perform services which require an internationally recognized entertainment group."

p., pp. *LitArts, VA-Prntng* **page(s)**

P.M.R.C. *Cult&Soc, Law&Pol, MusArts* **Parents Music Resource Center.** Record-label lobbying group organized in the mid-1980s led by Tipper Gore, wife of then Senator Al Gore, and Susan Baker, wife of the then Secretary of the Treasury James Baker III. [In 1985, **Frank Zappa**, at a hearing before the Senate Commerce, Science, and Transportation Committee, referred to Mrs. Gore and Baker as "bored housewives" and read the First Amendment in protest against record-labelling.]

P.O.P. *Mktg* **point-of-purchase** (P.O.P.)

p.p. *Mktg* parcel post, post paid.

P.R., p.r. *Mktg* **public relations.**

P/A *LegAsp, Mgt* **power of attorney.**

p/c, P/C *Eco&Fin* 1 Petty cash. 2 Prices current.

P/NE&F-Acc **Promissory note.**

PA *Mktg* **press agent**

PA *RecA&S* **public-address system.**

PACA *VisArts* **Picture Agency Council of America.** Trade organization of photographic archive companies.

pace *TheatArts* Speed at which the action of the play proceeds.

pacing *BcstJourn* Flow of the newscast

package deal *Mgt* Proposition or offer consisting of several items each of which has to be accepted for the package to be complete.

packager *Mgt* One who assembles the components of the package deal. *Also see* **Producers.**

packet *iMedia, InfoMgt* Standard unit of information sent over the internet.

paean *Crit&Eval, MusArts* 1 Fervent expression of joy or praise. 2 Song of joyful praise or exultation. *Also see* **Songs.**

pagan *Crit&Eval* 1 One who has no religion. 2 Hedonist.

page *BcstJourn* Entire individual screen of a computer. Each still picture that is called up from a computer or still store with visuals, CGs, or composites is always on a separate page of memory in those machines. Each page is usu. identified by its numerical location within the machines. Also called a screen.

page *InfoMgt* 1 Quantity of memory storage equal to between 512 and 4,096 bytes. 2 Quantity of source program coding equal to between 8 and 64 lines.

page (p., pp.) *LitArts, VA-Prntng* 1 One side of a **leaf**, as of a book, letter, newspaper, or manuscript, esp. the entire **leaf.** 2 Writing or printing on one side of a **leaf.**

page *Rdio/TV* One employed by a large broadcast station to act a combination usher, floor attendant, and guest relations representative, esp. in ushering studio audiences.

page-boy *Fashn* Hairstyle, usu. shoulder-length, with the ends of the hair curled under smoothly in a loose roll.

page-turner *Crit&Eval, LitArts* Very interesting, exciting, or suspenseful book, usu. a novel.

page-turner *MusArts* One who sits **upstage** of the pianist and turns the sheet music pages for her or him.

pages per minute (PPM) *InfoMgt* » **PPM**

pagination *InfoMgt, Journ* Creation of full-page layouts on a computer screen.

pagination *VA-Prntng* System by which pages are numbered.

paging *InfoMgt* Transfer of pages of data between a computer's main memory and an auxiliary memory.

paid circulation *Journ, Mktg* Number of copies of a magazine or newspaper for which payment is received. Excludes free copies and spoilage. *Also see* **ABC, Circulation, print run.**

paid-in capital *Eco&Fin* Capital received from investors in exchange for stock, as distinguished from capital donated or generated from earnings.

painter (pntr.) *ArtPerf, Genl, VisArts* One who paints, either as an artist or a worker.

painting *Fashn* Cosmetic, such as rouge, used to give color to the face; makeup.

paisley *Fashn* Made of a soft wool fabric with a colorful, woven or printed and swirled pattern of abstract, curved shapes.

PAL *Flm&Vid* **Phase Alternation Line** A 625-line TV system of recording and playing back video; standard in the United Kingdom and other West European countries.

Paleolithic art *Cult&Soc, VisArts* Art of the most recent ice age largely confined to about 150 sites in northern Spain and southwest France from ca. 14,000 BC to ca. 9,500 BC. These sites include cave paintings, outdoor sculpture, and rock carvings.

palette *Crit&Eval* Range of qualities inherent in nongraphic art forms such as music and literature.

palette *VisArts* 1 Board, typically with a hole for the thumb, which an artist can hold while painting and on which the artist mixes colors. 2 Range of colors used in a particular painting or by a particular artist.

Paley, William S. (1901-90, media mgr.)*Rdio/TV* Broadcasting executive who founded the **Columbia Broadcasting System** (CBS) in 1929.

palming off *LegAsp* Unfair competition that occurs when a seller tries to pass its product as that of another seller.

palmtop computer (hand-held computer) *InfoMgt* Computer small enough to be held in one hand, usu. weighing less than two pounds.

palpable *Crit&Eval* 1 Capable of being handled, touched, or felt; **tangible.** 2 Easily perceived; obvious.

pan *Crit&Eval* Severe negative review.

pan *Flm&Vid* Pivotal camera movement in a horizontal plane.

pan & scan *Flm&Vid* Movie format **cropped** to fit a TV screen. *Also see* **DVD-Video, letterbox, widescreen.**

pan pot *RecA&S* Fader control on a recording console used to place a signal in a particular direction in the stereo sound **spectrum.**

panache *Crit&Eval* » **verve**

pancake *Th-MakeUp* Theatrical makeup: Applied with water or a wet sponge; removed with soap and water.

panegyric *Crit&Eval* Elaborate praise intended as a public compliment.

Pantages *PA-Variety* **Vaudeville** theater **circuit**

Pantaloon*TheatArts* 1 Character in the **commedia dell'arte**, portrayed as a foolish old man in tight trousers and slippers. 2 Butt of a clown's jokes.

pantaloons *Fashn* 1 Men's wide breeches extending from waist to ankle, worn esp. in England in the late 17th century. Often used in the plural. 2 Tight trousers extending from waist to ankle with straps passing under the instep, worn esp. in the 19th century. Often used in the plural.

pantheon *Cult&Soc* 1 Temple dedicated to all gods. 2 All the gods of a people. 3 Public building commemorating and dedicated to the heroes and heroines of a nation. 4 Group of persons most highly regarded for contributions to a field or an endeavor

panto *PA-Variety* » **pantomime**

pantomime (panto) *PA-Variety, TheatArts* 1 Telling of a story without words, by means of bodily movements, gestures, and facial expressions. 2 Play, dance, or other theatrical performance characterized by wordless storytelling. 3 Ancient Roman theatrical performance in which one actor played all the parts by means of gesture and movement, accompanied by a narrative chorus. 4 *Also see* **mime, mimicry.**

Pantone book *Fashn* Universal color chart for designers.

paparazzi (paps) *Journ* Freelance photographers who pursue celebrities to take candid pictures for sale to certain voracious print and TV **media.** *Origin* After Signor Paparazzo, a character in *La Dolce Vita,* a movie by Federico **Fellini** *Also see* **tabloid.**

paper business *MusArts* » **printed music**

paper prototype *iMedia* Rough paper draft of an interactive piece, used for testing and further design decisions.

paper the house *Mktg,PerfA&C* Issue free tickets so the entertainment will appear to be successful. *Also see* **claque, dressing the house.**

paperback *VA-Prntng* Book bound in flexible paper. *Also see* **hardback**

paperbound *VA-Prntng* » **paperback**

papers *LitArts* Collection of letters, diaries, and other writings, usu. by one person. <the Jefferson papers>

paperwork *also* **paper work** *Crit&Eval* Work involving the handling of reports, letters, and forms.

papier-collé *VisArts* Artistic composition of papers pasted on a surface, initiated by **George Braque** and **Pablo Picasso** (» **ancillary**) during the **Synthetic Cubism** period.

papier-mâché (pay-per-mashay) *VisArts* Material, made from paper pulp or shreds of paper mixed with glue or paste, that can be molded into various shapes when wet and becomes hard and suitable for painting and varnishing when dry.

Papp, Joseph (1921-91, stage dir.-prod)*TheatArts* Stage producer and director known for his productions of *Hair* (1967), *A Chorus Line* (1975), and New York Shakespeare Festival. *Also see* **loyalty oath.**

paps *Journ* **paparazzi**

par excellence *Crit&Eval* Being the best or truest of a kind; **quintessential.**

PAR lamps *PerfA&C* **Parabolic Aluminized Reflector**, similar to an automobile headlight used principally by stage technicians and designers who learned their craft doing rock and roll shows.

par value (bonds) *Eco&Fin, EntreP* Value of a bond which is printed on the bond and is the value at which the bond is redeemed for by the issuer at maturity. This is also referred to as the face value, maturity value, or principal value of a bond. For corporate bonds the face value is $1,000. NOMINAL VALUE

par value (stock) *EntreP* Arbitrary value placed on each share of stock when a corporation issues stock. This is the face value of one share of stock and does not normally change during the life of the corporation.

parable *Cult&Soc, LitArts* Simple story illustrating a moral or religious lesson.

Parabolic Aluminized Reflector *PerfA&C* » **PAR lamps**

paradigm (paradee-em) *Crit&Eval* Example that serves as pattern or model. [This term has been so overused and misused that it has become a faddish term without real meaning.].

paradigm *iMedia* Set of assumptions, concepts, values, and practices that constitutes a way of viewing reality for the community that shares them, especially in an intellectual discipline.

paradigm shift *iMedia* 1 Change of patterns on a massive scale. 2 Universal change of the assumptions that define reality. *Also see* **paradigm.**

paradox *Crit&Eval* 1 Statement that contains, implies, or relies upon a formal logical contradiction. 2 Seemingly contradictory statement that may nonetheless be true. Generally we are uneasy about – or intrigued by – statements that are simultaneously true and false in the same sense. *Origin* The "liar paradox" which involved a native of Crete claiming that all Cretans are liars. If the speaker speaks truly, his statement is a lie, and therefore *false*, but if false, it meets the criterion for being a lie and is therefore *true*.

paragon *Crit&Eval* Model of excellence or perfection of a kind; a peerless example: a paragon of virtue.

paragon *VA-Prntng* Type size of 20 **points.**

parajournalism *Journ* Subjective journalism that uses some of the techniques or license of **fiction.**

parallel port *InfoMgt* Parallel ports allow computer to connect to devices such as printers that use parallel interfacing. Usually parallel ports send information from the computer to an attached device but do not receive information. *Also see* **serial port.**

Paramount Pictures *Flm&Vid* One of the early movie studios that started as a **nickelodeon** in the early 1900s.

paranoia *Crit&Eval* **1 Psychotic** disorder characterized by delusions of persecution or grandeur, often strenuously defended with apparent **logic** and reason. **2** Extreme, irrational distrust of others.

parallel distributed processing *iMedia* Method of information processing by simultaneous independent entities networked and working together to accomplish a task. Related topics: neurobiology, **artificial intelligence**, and **cognition.**

parallel processor *iMedia* Multiprocessor computer system that breaks work into many parts which are distributed among many **CPUs.**

parallel production *iMedia* Development method where all aspects of production are produced in tandem, reducing bottlenecks. This type of production relies heavily on a solid shared vision.

paraprofessional *Crit&Eval* Trained worker who is not a member of a profession but assists a professional.

parchment *VA-Prntng* **1** Skin of a sheep or goat prepared as a material on which to write or paint. **2** Written text or drawing on a sheet of this material. **3** Paper made in imitation of this material. *Also see* **vellum.**

Pareles, Jon (1953-, *NY Times* pop/jazz critic) *Crit&Eval, MusArts* *Also see* **authentic, feminist, nose job, serious music, star power.**

parent company *Mgt* Company that owns another company or operation. <affiliate, division, satellite, **subsidiary**, etc>

parental advisory *RecA&S* Printed notice on a recording indicating strong language, sexual themes, and/or racial slurs.

parental control *InfoMgt, Rdio/TV* Device or software program that allows parents a kind of **benign** censorship that controls access to various online features. <**chat, forums, message boards**>

Parents Music Resource Center (P.M.R.C.) *Cult&Soc, Law&Pol, MusArts* » **P.M.R.C.**

parity *Eco&Fin* **1** Equality, as in amount, status, or value. **2** Equivalent in value of a sum of money expressed in terms of a different currency at a fixed, official rate of exchange. **3** Equality of prices of goods or securities in two different markets. **4** Level for farm-product prices maintained by governmental support and intended to give farmers the same purchasing power they had during a chosen base period.

parity bit *InfoMgt* Even or odd quality of the number of 1s or 0s in a **binary** code, often used to determine the integrity of data after transmission. *Also see* **even parity, odd parity.**

Parker, Charlie *ArtPerf, MusArts* (aka "Bird," "Yardbird," 1920-55, jazz alto sax, comp., tenor sax) One of the most innovative and influential musicians in the history of jazz; a leader in the development of **bop.** <Albums: *Charlie Parker Memorial* (1946-7, Savoy), *Now's the Time* (1952-3, Verve), *Jazz at Massey Hall* (1953, Debut/OJC)> "[Charlie Parker] was one of the people who really wanted jazz to be looked at as an art music rather than as an entertainment music… there was a certain dignity he had about playing the music." — **Sonny Rollins** *Also see* **changes, consummate, dazzle, Norman Granz.**

Parker, Dorothy (Dorothy Rothschild, 1893-67, fictwri. critic, wit) *ArtPerf, Crit&Eval, LitArts* Writer noted for her satirical wit, poetry, and short stories. Drama critic for *Vanity Fair* (1916-17) and book critic for *New Yorker* (1927-33) *Also see* **female writers.**

Parkinson's Law *Eco&Fin, Mgt* Work expands to fill the time available for its completion. Formulated by C. Northcote Parkinson (1909-93, Brit. hist.), noted for his humorous works ridiculing the inefficiency of bureaucracies. *Origin* From the book, *Law: The Pursuit of Progress* (1957)

parlor grand *MusInstr* **Grand piano** shorter in length than a **concert grand** yet longer than a **baby grand.** *Also see* **Musical Instrument Families.**

parody *IntelProp* Permission from the owner of the copyright is generally required before commercial exploitation of a parody.

parody *LitArts, MusArts* Literary or musical work that broadly **mimics** an author's style and holds it up to ridicule. *Also see* **send-up.** PARODIST

parody *TheatArts* Mockery of a style of writing or performing by exaggerated imitation.

parquet circle (parkay)*PerfA&C* Part of the main floor of a theater

under the **balcony.** PARTERRE.

part *Flm&Vid,TheatArts* Role in a play or film. "It's parts. Everybody who does it knows it's about parts. Nobody – even those in the business – can ever quite separate the dancer from the dance." — Mike Nichols (b. Berlin. Michael, Igor Peschkowsky, 1931-, stage/film act., dir.)

part *MusArts* Sheet music for an individual player or singer adapted from the composer's **score.**

parterre (partair, Fr.) *PerfA&C* » **parquet circle**

participating sponsor *Mktg* Level of sponsorship not as prominent as the title or presenting sponsor.

participative management *Mgt* Term applied to various methods used to improve product quality and job satisfaction by allowing employees a voice in management of the company and their jobs.

partisan *Crit&Eval* Fervent, sometimes militant supporter of a party, cause, faction, person, or idea.

partita *MusArts* Instrumental piece composed of a series of variations. <suite>

partitions *InfoMgt* Hard disks are divided logically into one or more areas called partitions.

partnership (general partnership) *Eco&Fin, EntreP, LegAsp, Mgt* **1** Business with two or more owners. **2** Legal contract entered into by two or more persons in which each agrees to furnish a part of the capital and labor for a business enterprise, and by which each shares a fixed proportion of profits and losses. *Also see* **corporation, sole proprietor.** FIRM

Parton, Dolly (1946-, pop-country sngr., act., prod., mgt., n-fict.) *ArtPerf, Flm&Vid, MusArts* Talented, versatile entertainer in virtually all **media.**

pas (pah, Fr. for "step") *Dnce* Single step or series of steps forming a dance. <**pas de deux**>

pas de deux (pah duh dieu, Fr.) *Dnce* Ballet for a man and woman. It traditionally begins with an **entrée** and **adagio**, followed by solo variations for each dancer, ending with a **coda.**

Pascal *InfoMgt* Program language invented in the late 1960s, its **syntax** practically forces programmers to write, neat, structured, well-mannered code. *Also see* **Programming Languages.**

pass *Crit&Eval* Reject, turn down.

pass *Genl* free ticket

pass *LegAsp* To pronounce an opinion, a judgment, or a sentence.

pass-along audience *Journ, Mktg* » **pass-along readership**

pass-along readership *Journ, Mktg* Persons other than the original purchaser or subscriber who read all or part of a periodical.

pass-through pages *InfoMgt, Journ* Web pages with little content. [Used by some editors to trade reader satisfaction for artificially inflated **hit** numbers.]

passage *MusArts* Segment of a **composition**, esp. one that demonstrates the **virtuosity** of the composer or performer: a **passage** of exquisite beauty, played to perfection.

passage *LitArts* Segment of a written work or speech.

passage *VisArts* Section of a painting or other piece of **artwork**; a detail.

passé (pass-ay, Fr.) *Crit&Eval* Out-of-date, old-fashioned, out-of-style.

passementerie *Fashn* Ornamental trimming for a garment, as braid, lace, or metallic beads.

passerelle *PerfA&C* » **runway**

passion *Crit&Eval* **1** That which one undergoes or suffers, in contrast to **action** which is what one does, or to **thought**, one's mental activity. Three terms: **action, passion,** and **thought** serve to divide human experience into its essential regions. **2** Powerful emotion. <love, joy, hatred, anger> **3** Ardent love; strong sexual desire, lust. **4** Boundless enthusiasm. **5** Abandoned display of emotion, esp. of anger.

passion play *TheatArts* Dramatic representation of the scenes connected with the passion and crucifixion of Christ.

passive matrix *InfoMgt* LCD-type display found on most **laptop** and **notebook** computers.

passive voice *BcstJourn* Verb form in which the thing or person responsible for the action follows the verb. This form is to be avoided by newswriters.

password *InfoMgt* Secret word or a string of letters or numbers that must be entered in order to access **electronic mail** or **confidential files.**

Pasta *HR&LR*, *VisArts* » **Professional and Administrative Staff Association**

paste-down type *Journ, VA-Prntng* Type with adhesive backing that can be pasted on **mechanicals**.

pastiche *LitArts*, *MusArts,PerfA&C* Dramatic, literary, or musical piece openly imitating the work of another artist, often with **satirical** intent.

pastoral music, pastorale *MusArts* Instrumental or vocal composition with a tender melody in a moderately slow **rhythm**, suggestive of traditional shepherds' music and **idyllic** rural life.

pat. *Eco&Fin, IntelProp* **patent**.

patch *PerfA&C* To connect a stage electrical power circuit to a dimmer circuit.

patent (pat.) *Eco&Fin, EntreP, IntelProp* **1** Government grant that confers upon the creator of an invention the sole right to make, use, and sell that invention for a set period of time (usu. 17 years) **2** Invention protected by such a grant. **3** Exclusive right or title. *Also see* **Intangible Assets, legal monopoly**.

Patent and Trademark Office *IntelProp, Law&Pol* Division of the U.S. Dept. of Commerce responsible for granting **patents** and **trademarks**. *Also see* **Federal Agencies and Statutes**.

pathos *Crit&Eval* Quality of a work of art, that arouses feelings of **pity**, sympathy, tenderness, or sorrow. *Origin* Word from which **passion** is derived. It meant very deep feelings or emotions.

patois *Crit&Eval* Regional dialect, esp. one without a literary traditional; non-standard speech.

patron *Fndng* One who supports, protects, or sponsors artists, arts events, and arts institutions because of genuine interest, or because of the social standing that can result, or because its good public relations with "the people who really count."

patron service *Mktg* » customer service

patronage *Law&Pol* Power to distribute or appoint people to governmental or political positions.

patronage *Mktg* **1** Trade given to a commercial establishment by its customers. **2** Customers or patrons considered as a group; clientele. <The ballet has a loyal but demanding patronage>

pattern language *iMedia* A practical language for building and planning based on natural considerations. By understanding recurrent design problems in our environment, interactive media creators can identify patterns in their own design projects and use these patterns to create a language of their own.

Paul Revere Award *MusArts*, *VisArts* Granted annually by the **Music Publishers' Association** to music publishers "for their efforts in creating art for the music industry." *Also see* **Awards & Prizes**.

Paul, Les (1916-, Lester William Polfus, country/pop/jazz gtr., inventor)*ArtPerf*, *MusArts*, *MusInstr* After early career in country music, he formed the Les Paul Trio in late 1930s. In 1941 he sold a prototype of his solid-body electric guitar to the Gibson company which marketed the "Les Paul guitar." In 1954 he constructed the first 8-track tape recorder in his home studio (built into the side of a New Jersey hill) where he experimented with multitrack guitar overdubs and multiple vocal lines with his partner and then wife Mary Ford. <*Chester & Lester*, w/Chet Atkins, (RCA, Grammy 1976)>

pavement *Crit&Eval* **Urban** equivalent of **down-to-earth**. <Such and such an actor is strictly pavement>

Paxton, Steve *Dnce, MusArts, TheatArts* (19??-' choreog., comp., dncr... interarts collaborator, tchr.) Specializes in interarts collaborations involving theatre, dance, poetry, and music.

pay cable*Rdio/TV* **Pay-TV** received over a cable.

pay dirt *Crit&Eval* Useful or profitable discovery or venture.

pay in kind *Fndng* » **in kind**

pay (one's) dues *Crit&Eval* Earn a position or a privilege through hard work, hands-on experience, or privation. <Most overnight sensations have long paid their dues making the breakthrough possible>

pay the piper *Crit&Eval* Bear the consequences.

Pay-per-view (PPV)*Rdio/TV* Cable service offering subscribers a movie, sporting event, or concert for a one-time fee.

pay-TV*Rdio/TV* Term for subscriber-paid-for TV. PAY CABLE

payee*E&F-Acc* One to whom money is due or is paid.

payer*E&F-Acc* One responsible for paying a bill or **note**.

payola *Ethcs&Phil*, *RecA&S* Bribe paid by a record label to a disc jockey to play a certain record: "**Jerry Wexler**, co-founder of **Atlantic records**, once begged the seminal rock disc jockey **Alan Freed** to forgo his customary bribe, but the godfather of payola politely demurred. 'I'd love to, Wex, but I can't do it... that's taking the bread out of my children's mouths.'" — **Jerry Wexler** and David Ritz (journ.) *Also see* **plugola**.

payout requirement*Fnding* Minimum amount that **private foundations** are required to expend for charitable purposes (includes grants and, within certain limits, the administrative cost of making grants) In general, a private foundation must meet or exceed an annual payout requirement of five percent of the average market value of the foundation's **assets**.

payroll register *E&F-Acc* Subsidiary ledger that records **employee earnings, withholding, and payroll taxes**.

payroll taxes *E&F-Acc* Include employer's portion of **Social Security** and **Medicare** taxes for each employee and all **FUTA** and **SUTA** taxes.

payt. *Eco&Fin* **payment**.

pd. *Eco&Fin* **paid**.

PBS*Rdio/TV* » **Public Broadcasting System** *Also see* **Broadcast Stations & Networks**.

PBS Online *InfoMgt* Nationwide **bulletin board** system offered by the **Public Broadcasting System**. *Also see* **Online Information Services**.

PBX *InfoMgt* **private branch exchange** Local switching system for the routing of telephone messages.

PC *Crit&Eval* **political correctness**.

PC *InfoMgt* **personal computer**

PCS *InfoMgt* **Personal Communication Service** re wireless **telephony**.

pct. *Eco&Fin* per cent.

pd. *Eco&Fin* paid.

PDF files *InfoMgt* Adobe's Portable Document Format is a translation format used primarily for distributing files across a network, or on a **Web site**.

peau de soie (poh duh swah, Fr.) *Fashn* Soft silk fabric of satin weave having a dull finish.

pecuniary *Eco&Fin* Relating to money.

pedal keyboard *MusInstr* Keyboard of pedals in an instrument such as a pipe organ. *Also see* **Musical Instrument Families**.

pedal point *MusArts* Note, usu. in the bass and on the **tonic** or the **dominant**, sustained through harmonic changes in the other parts.

pedal steel guitar *MusInstr* Electronically amplified guitar mounted on legs, with up to ten strings whose **pitch** can be altered by sliding a steel bar across them or by depressing pedals attached to them. *Also see* **Musical Instrument Families**.

pedestal presenter *Mgt* Now old-fashioned way of presenting artists, i.e., book them and present them well. *Also see* **presenter**.

peepshow *also* **peep show** *Flm&Vid, PA-Variety* **1** Exhibition of pictures or objects viewed through a small hole or magnifying glass. **2** Short pornographic film presentation seen usu. in a small coin-operated projection booth. RAREE SHOW

peer *Crit&Eval* One who has equal standing with others, as in age, class, or rank. "Man can't help but seek evidence of his own effectiveness, and there is no measure of effectiveness – not titles, not salaries, nor prizes – equal to that of one's peers." — **Ben Bradlee**

peg *MusArts* One of the pins of a stringed instrument that are turned to tighten or slacken the strings so as to regulate their pitch.

peignoir (penwahr, Fr.) *Fashn* Woman's loose-fitting dressing gown.

pejorative *Crit&Eval* **1** Tending to make or become worse. **2** Disparaging; belittling.

Pellegrina viola *MusInstr* Ergonomically designed **viola** with a bulging, asymmetrical body designed in 1993 by David Rivinus (1949-), a Vermont violin maker.

PEN or **P.E.N.** *LitArts* Poets, International organization of **Playwrights, Editors, Essayists, and Novelists**.

pen name *LitArts* **pseudonym** <John LeCarré (1931-, spy fictwri.) was born David Cornwell; Mark Twain (1835-1910, fictwri., humorist, journ.) was born Samuel Longhorne Clemens> NOM DE PLUME

penetration pricing strategy *EntreP* Marketing approach that sets lower than normal prices to hasten market acceptance of a

pennywhistle *also* **penny whistle** *MusInstr* Inexpensive vertical flute, with a plastic or tin mouthpiece and a tin body. *Also see* **Little Instruments.**

Pentium *InfoMgt* Brand name of a leading computer chip made by **Intel.**

peplum *Fashn* Short overskirt or **ruffle** attached at the waistline of a jacket, blouse, or dress.

per diem (per dee-em, Latin) *Eco&Fin* **Allowance** for daily expenses.

per diem (per dee-em, Latin) *TheatArts* Sum paid to a performer for housing expenses away from the performer's home city.

per se (Latin) *LegAsp* By or of itself. <slander per se>, where the words spoken are obviously **defamatory** and the injured party is not required to prove damage to her or his character.

per-program license *IntelProp, MusArts* Opposite of a **blanket license.** *Also see* **music licenses.**

per-program license *IntelProp, MusArts* Form of limited performance licensing that depends on the size of the user's operation and the popularity of a particular music title. *Also see* **blanket license.**

perc. *MusInstr* **percussion**

percentage *Eco&Fin* Amount, such as an allowance, a duty, or a commission, that varies in proportion to a larger sum, such as total sales. <talent agents earn 10% to 20% on their clients' net or gross income> *Also see* **go into percentage.**

percentage of sales method for calculating a pro forma balance sheet *E&F-Acc, EntreP* Method of calculating a pro forma balance sheet based upon the fact that assets and liabilities historically vary with sales.

perception *EntreP* Individual processes that give meaning to the stimuli confronting consumers.

percussion (perc.) *MusInstr* **Section** of a band or an orchestra composed of percussion instruments. <drums, **marimbas, vibes,** and **xylophones, bells** and **chimes, cymbals** and **gongs,** etc> PERCUSSIONIST *Also see* **Latin percussion, Musical Instrument Families.**

percussionist *MusArts* One who plays **percussion** instruments. [It has been said that a percussionist is a **drummer** who can read music.].

perf. *ArtPerf* **performer**

perfect *MusArts* **1** Designating the three basic intervals of the **octave,** fourth, and fifth. **2** Designating a cadence or **chord progression** from the **dominant** to the **tonic** at the end of a phrase or piece of music.

perfect binding *VA-Prntng* Binding process that uses flexible glue as a flexible **backbone** of a publication.

perfect pitch *MusArts* » **absolute pitch**

perfervid *Crit&Eval* Extremely or extravagantly eager or impassioned. *Also see* **zeal.**

performance *IntelProp, LegAsp* **Copyright Act of 1976** defines it "as to recite, render, play, dance, or act it, either directly or by means of any device or process." —*Art Law Forum*

performance *PerfA&C* **1** Presentation, esp. a theatrical one, before an audience. **2** Act or style of performing a work or role before an audience.

performance art *TheatArts, VisArts* Late 20th century phenomenon, performance art arose in the "happenings" of Alan Kaprow in the 1960s: it is a kind of performance which may be unscripted, is often autobiographical. In which the performer engages in a direct communication with the audience. Performance art is distinguished from drama in that there is no fictive "play" being performed: the performance itself is the work of art. *Also see* **political theater.**

performance contract *LegAsp, Mgt* » **engagement contract**

performance rights *IntelProp, RecA&S* Exclusive right granted to the owners and publishers of musical works to authorize (license) their musical works for public performance.

performance royalty *IntelProp, RecA&S* Any person or organization who uses copyrighted music for public performance must pay a license fee to a performance rights agency <**ASCAP, BMI, SESAC**> that pays a portion of the licensing fees to the authors, composers, and publishers of the copyrighted music. *Also see* **Royalties.**

Performance Systems International (PSI) *InfoMgt* **online information service**

performer (perf.) *ArtPerf* One who portrays a role or demonstrates a skill before an audience.

performer unions *ArtPerf, HR&LR* » **Guilds & Unions**

performing rights organization *IntelProp, RecA&S* Agent or agency for authors, composers, and music publishers for licensing the non-dramatic **performing rights** of their musical works to the users of music. *Also see* **Copyright-Related Organizations.**

Perils of Pauline Flm&Vid Classic silent movie **serial.**

periodic inventory system *Eco&Fin* Business does not keep a continuous record of the inventory on hand. Instead, at the end of the period the business makes a **physical count** of the on hand inventory and applies the appropriate unit costs to determine the cost of the **ending inventory.** *Also see* **Inventory Methods.**

periodical *VA-Prntng* Publication issued at regular intervals of more than one day.

peripety *Crit&Eval* Reversal of the fortunes of a **character,** esp. the main character, of a drama or story. *Origin* Change from **Oedipus** the King of Thebes to **Oedipus** the despised outcast of Thebes is central to Artistotle's treatment of tragic **plots** in *The Poetics.*

peripheral device *InfoMgt* Piece of hardware <video monitor, **disk drive,** pointer, **modem.,** etc> used with a computer and under the computer's control.

permanent account *E&F-Acc* Accounts that are not closed at the end of the period. *Also see* **temporary account.**

permissions editor *LitArts, MusArts* One who is empowered by the owner of a copyright to grant or refuse its use by someone else.

perpetual inventory system *E&F-Acc, EntreP* Business keeps a continuous record for each inventory item to show the inventory on hand at all times. *Also see* **Inventory Methods.**

Perry Ellis Award *Fashn* Annual award for New Designer, chosen by 60 fashion business insiders on behalf of the **Council of Fashion Designers of America** (CFDA) *Also see* **Awards & Prizes.**

Perry, Antoinette (1888-1946)*TheatArts* Actress and director for whom the **Tony Awards** are named.

pers. *ArtPerf, Crit&Eval* **personality**

persistence of vision *Flm&Vid* Phenomenon of the eye retaining for a short period of time the image just seen. Stream of images of short duration (such as projected frames of film) are therefore seen as a continuous picture without flicker.

persona *ArtPerf, Genl* Role that one assumes or displays in public or society; one's public image or **personality,** as distinguished from the inner self. "I had a persona. Unfortunately my persona became bigger than my acting." — Burt Remolds (1936-, film act., prod.)

persona, personae *LitArts, TheatArts* Characters in a dramatic or literary work.

personal cash flow statement *EntreP* Personal income statement consisting of all annual income before taxes and outflows of fixed expenses and variable expenses.

Personal Communication Service *InfoMgt* » **PCS**

personal computer (PC) *InfoMgt* Microcomputer for use by an individual in an office or at home or school.

Personal Digital Assistant (PDA) *InfoMgt* » **PDA**

personal information management (PIM) *InfoMgt* Computer programs such as. <address and phone books, appointment calendars, data organizers, etc>

personal manager (PM) *Mgt* One who guides the artist's career by: helping to choose material that highlight the artist's talents and play down the weaknesses, creating and maintaining the artist's public **personna,** acting as chief-of staff of the artist's **entourage,** and properly exercising the **fiduciary** relationship (and power-of-attorney) with the artist: "I believe a manager is as much a hero as his client is good. It's the clients who make the manager. We don't suffer the delusion that we can make silk purses out of sow's ears." — Charlie Joffe and Eric Lax (Managers of **Woody Allen**)> *Also see* **Managers.**

personal manager producer *RecA&S* Personal managers may produce their clients' recordings if financing and distribution can be arranged. *Also see* **Producers.**

personal selling *Mktg* Personal interaction between the representative of a marketer and one or more purchasers with the objective of making a sale or developing a favorable attitude toward the marketer and its products.

personality (pers.) *Crit&Eval* **1** Distinctive qualities of a person, esp. those distinguishing personal characteristics that make the person appealing to an audience. "We do not see ourselves as actors, but the very concept of *personality* has its roots in the Latin *persona* — a dramatic mask." — **John Lahr 2** Often used journalistically to mean "**celebrity**." Persons so described are best known simply for who they are rather than what they have done.

personas *Ethcs&Phil* Role that one assumes or displays in public or society; one's public image or personality, as distinguished from the inner self.

personification *LitArts* Figure of speech in which inanimate objects or **abstractions** are endowed with human qualities or are represented as possessing human form.

perspective *iMedia* **1** One of the indicators, or depth cues, of **3D** space. *Also see* **depth cue. 2** Rendition of apparent space in a flat photograph, i.e., how far the foreground and background appear to be separated from each other.

perspective *VisArts* Technique of representing **three-dimensional** objects and depth relationships on a **two-dimensional** surface. Relationship of aspects of a subject to each other and to a whole.

perspective lead *BcstJourn* Lead sentence that relates the current story to previous events or trends.

PERT chart *Mgt, iMedia* **1** Project management tool used to schedule, organize, and coordinate tasks within a project. **2** PERT — Program Evaluation Review Technique, a methodology developed by the U.S. Navy in the 1950s to manage the Polaris submarine missile program.

petticoat *Fashn* Woman's slip or underskirt full and trimmed with **ruffles** or lace. PETTISKIRT

petty cash (p/c, P/C) *Eco&Fin, EntreP* Small fund of money for incidental expenses. <postage due, fares (bus, cab), small gift, newspaper, parking meter, etc>

Pew Charitable Trusts *Fndng* Philadelphia-based foundation which is a significant contributor to visual and performing arts. *Also see* **museum loan network.**

PGA *Flm&Vid* **Producers Guild of America.** Est. 1952 "The only group in the world which represents, supports, guides, defends, and defines the complex leadership role of the producer." — >http://www.producers guild.com< *Also see* **David O. Selznick Lifetime Achievement Award for Motion Pictures, Golden Laurel Awards.**

pgm. *PerfA&C* **program**

phase alternation line *Flm&Vid* » **PAL**

phenomenon *Crit&Eval* **1** Occurrence, a circumstance, or a fact perceptible by the senses; a marvel. **2** Remarkable or outstanding person; a paragon.

philanthropic *Fnding* Organized to provide humanitarian or charitable assistance.

philanthropy *Fnding* **1** Effort or inclination to increase the well-being of humankind by charitable aid or donations. **2** Something, such as an activity or institution, intended to promote human welfare.

philharmonic *MusArts* Relating to a symphony orchestra.

philistine *Crit&Eval* Smug, ignorant person antagonistic or indifferent to artistic and cultural values: "For Philistines who derive no esthetic value from ownership of a work of art but who nevertheless chose to buy one purely for financial gain, the pecuniary punishment can be expected to fit the crime." — William J. Baumel (art critic)

philology *Crit&Eval* Study of language and its change over time. HISTORICAL LINGUISTICS *Also see* **H.L. Mencken.**

philos. *Ethcs&Phil* **philosopher, philosophy**

philosopher (philos.) *Ethcs&Phil* Student of or specialist in philosophy.

philosophy (philos.) *Crit&Eval, Cult&Soc* **1** Critique and analysis of fundamental beliefs as they come to be conceptualized and formulated. **2** System of motivating concepts or principles. <the philosophy of a culture>

philosophy (philos.) *Ethcs&Phil* **1** Synthesis of all learning. **2** All learning except technical precepts and practical arts. **3** System of values by which one lives. **4** Love and pursuit of wisdom by intellectual means and moral self-discipline. **5** Investigation of causes and laws underlying reality. **6** Science of philosophy. <comprising **logic, ethics, aesthetics, metaphysics,** and **epistemology**>

phish *InfoMgt* Trying to illegally obtain someone's online **password** by false representations.

phishers *InfoMgt* **Hackers** who send computer list subscribers instant messages trying to acquire passwords. *Also see* **carders, crack.**

phonathon *Fndng* » **telethon**

phone it in *TheatArts* This may be said when an actor is so well suited to her or his role that rehearsals may not be necessary.

phoneme *InfoMgt* In voice synthesis: the smallest phonetic unit in a language capable of conveying a distinction in meaning, as the "m" of mat and the "b" of bat in English.

phono *RecA&S* Phonograph, in the days of **78 rpm** records. *Also see* **Music Playback Devices.**

phonograph (phono) *RecA&S* Machine that reproduces sound by means of a stylus in contact with a grooved rotating disk. *Also see* **Music Playback Devices.**

phonograph record *RecA&S* Grooved disc that stores sound and mechanically reproduces it.

Phonograph Record Manufacturers' Special Payments Fund *HR&LR, RecA&S* Record companies make semi-annual payments into this fund, based on the number of records sold. Payments are distributed to musicians based on their **scale** wages earned in recording sessions.

phonorecords *IntelProp, RecA&S* As defined in the 1976 Copyright Act (Section 101): "material objects in which sounds, other than those accompanying a motion picture or other **audiovisual** work, are fixed by any method now known or later developed, and from which the sounds can be perceived, reproduced or otherwise communicated, either directly or indirectly or with aid of a machine or device. Term '**phonorecords**' includes the material object in which the sounds are first fixed." "Phonorecord may embody two types of authorship: (1) the sound recording, (2) the recorded musical, literary, or dramatic work." — Harvey Rachlin (mus. biz wri.) *Also see* **sound recordings.**

photo *VisArts* **photograph**

photo op *Journ* Photo opportunity. Brief period reserved for the press to photograph the participants in a newsworthy event. <"Photo ops' are contrivances by which great men get themselves photographed doing things of little or no consequence." — **Russell Baker**>

photo opportunity *Journ* » **photo op**

photo-essay *also* **photo essay** *LitArts, VisArts* Story told chiefly through photographs, usu. supplemented by a written commentary.

photo-offset *VA-Prntng* Method of **offset** printing using photomechanical plates.

photo-optic memory *InfoMgt* Memory that uses an optical medium for storage. <A laser might be used to record on photographic film>

photocomposition *VA-Prntng* Preparation of manuscript for printing by the projection of images of type characters on photographic film, which is then used to make printing plates. PHOTOTYPESETTING *Also see* **offset.**

photocopier *VA-Prntng* Machine for ally photographic reproducing written, printed, or graphic material, esp. by **xerography.**

photodrama *Flm&Vid, TheatArts* » **photoplay**

photog. *VisArts* **photography**

photogene *Crit&Eval* » **afterimage**

photogenic *Crit&Eval, VisArts* Attractive as a subject for photography.

photographic realism *VisArts* In vogue in the late 1960s. Paintings made to resemble a sharply focused photograph. SUPERREALISM

photographists *ArtPerf, VisArts* "Photographers who are artists first, with little interest in learning about exposure times, lighting, darkroom technology, and the like." — **Arthur C. Danto**

photography (photog.) *VisArts* **1** Art or process of producing images of objects on photosensitive surfaces. **2** Art, practice, or occupation of taking and printing photographs. **3** Body of photographs.

photogravure *VA-Prntng* Process of printing from an **intaglio** plate, etched according to a photographic image.

photojournalism *Journ, VisArts* Journalism in which a news story is presented primarily through photographs with supplementary written copy.

photomontage *VisArts* **1** Technique of making a picture by assembling pieces of photographs, often in combination with other types of graphic material. **2** Composite picture produced by this technique. <works of **Robert Rauschenberg**>

photomural *VisArts* Greatly enlarged photograph or series of photographs placed on a wall esp. as decoration.

photoplay *Flm&Vid,TheatArts* Play filmed or arranged for filming as a movie. PHOTODRAMA

photorealism *VisArts* International art movement of the ca. late 1960s-1970s that stressed the precise rendering of subject matter, often taken from actual photographs or painted with the aid of slides. <painters Chuck Close (Charles Thomas Close, 1940-, pntr.) and Richard Estes (1936-, pntr.)> *Also see* **superrealism**.

phototelegraphy system *InfoMgt* » **facsimile system**

phototypesetting *VA-Prntng* » **photocomposition**

PHP (PHP: Hypertext Preprocessor) *iMedia* Open source language for developing dynamic web applications, similar to Active Server Pages (ASP) The first word of the acronym is the acronym - it is recursive)

PHP Hypertext Preprocessor *iMedia* » **PHP**

phrase *Dnce* Series of dance movements forming a unit in a choreographic pattern.

phrase *MusArts* Segment of a composition, usu. consisting of four or eight **measures**.

phrasing *MusArts* Manner in which a musical or lyrical phrase is rendered or interpreted. <**Louis Armstrong**, Billie Holiday (» **Apollo Theater**) for whom **Frank Sinatra** credits for his phrasing, and **Sarah Vaughan** phrased lyrics in the manner of jazz instrumentalists>

physical distribution (logistics) *EntreP* **A**ctivities of distribution involved in the physical relocation of products.

physical inventory *E&F-Acc* Actually counting each item rather than depending on computer or written records. *Also see* **Inventory Methods**.

pianissimo (pp) (pee-on-is-si-moh, Ital. "for very softly") *MusArts* Play very softly. *Also see* **Music Directions**.

piano (p) (pee-ahno, Ital. for "softly") *MusArts* Play softly, quietly. *Also see* **Music Directions**.

piano (pno.) *MusInstr* **1** Instrument with a manual keyboard actuating hammers that strike wire strings, producing sounds that may be softened or **sustained** by means of pedals. **2** Regular piano keyboard has 88 black and white keys. Each key, when struck, produces a distinctive **tone**. Each key has a **vibration** rate that is exactly twice as great as that of the one an **octave** below it. PIANIST, PIANO PLAYER, PIANOFORTE *Also see* **electric piano, frequency, keyboards, Musical Instrument Families**.

piano bar *MusArts, PA-Variety* Cocktail lounge with live entertainment, usu. a singing pianist who knows all the standards, inc. *Melancholy Baby* for the lush in the corner.

piano board *PerfA&C* Large board with a control of each light was the standard device for controlling stage lights until the development of a small computerized board that can be programmed to play lights and sound simultaneously.

piano quartet *MusArts* Piano, violin, viola, and cello.

piano quintet *MusArts* Piano plus a string quartet.

pic (plural, **pix**) *Flm&Vid, VisArts* **movie, photograph**

pica *VA-Prntng* Unit of type size equal to 12 points or approx. 1/4 inch.

Picasso, Pablo (1881-1973, Span. pntr., sculp., scenic dsgnr.) *Art-Perf, VisArts* Most influential and successful artist of the 20th century. <*Les Demoiselles d'Avignon* (1907), *Guernica* (1937)> "To me there is no past or future in art. If a work of art cannot live always in the present it must not be considered at all. The art of the Greeks, of the Egyptians, of the great painters who lived in other times, is not an art of the past, perhaps it is more alive today than it ever was." (1923) — **Pablo Picasso** *Also see* **ancillary, assemblage, Ballets Russes, collage, cubism, Di-**

aghilev, papier-collé.

picc *MusInstr* **piccolo**

piccolo (picc) *MusInstr* **1** Small flute **pitched** an **octave** above a regular flute. **2** Relating to an instrument considerably smaller than the usual size. <piccolo trumpet, piccolo bass> PICCOLO PLAYER, PICCOLOIST (RARE) *Also see* **Musical Instrument Families**.

piccolo bass *MusInstr* Violin family instrument sized and **pitched** between a cello and a bass viol. *Also see* **Musical Instrument Families**.

piccolo trumpet *MusInstr* D trumpet, higher than the regular B flat trumpet. *Also see* **Musical Instrument Families**.

pick *MusArts* **1** Pluck the strings of a musical instrument. **2** Play a tune by plucking strings.

pick *MusInstr* Small, flat piece of plastic held between thumb and forefinger used to pluck the strings of a guitar or banjo.

picket *HR&LR* One or more persons stationed outside a place of employment, usu. during a strike, to express a **grievance** or to protest and discourage entry by nonstriking employees or customers.

pick up the cues *TheatArts* Direction for the actor to begin speaking immediately on cue without allowing any lapse of time.

pickup *E&F-Acc* Balance brought forward.

pickup *Journ* Previous journalistic copy to which succeeding copy is added.

pickup *MusArts* Unstressed note or notes introductory to a phrase or composition.

pickup *Rdio/TV* **1** Telecast originating outside a studio. **2** Apparatus for transmitting a broadcast from an outside place to the broadcasting station.

pickup *RecA&S* Tone arm of a record player that converts the **oscillations** of a phonograph **stylus** into electrical impulses for subsequent conversion into sound. *Also see* **transducer**.

pickup *Sci&Tech* Reception of light or **sound waves** for conversion to electrical impulses; the apparatus used for such reception. *Also see* **transducer**.

pickup band *MusArts* Musical group of instrumentalists assembled informally for a temporary purpose.

PICT *InfoMgt* Document format used by a number of graphics and page layout programs.

pictogram *VA-Prntng* » **pictograph**

pictograph *VA-Prntng* **1** Picture representing a word or idea; a **hieroglyph**. **2** Pictorial representation of numerical data or relationships, esp. a graph, but having each value represented by a proportional number of pictures. PICTOGRAM.

pictorial *VisArts* Relating to, characterized by, or composed of pictures.

picture *Crit&Eval* Person, an object, or a scene that typifies or embodies an emotion, a state of mind, or a mood.

picture (pic., pic, pix) *Flm&Vid* movie

picture *LitArts* Vivid or realistic verbal description; a vivid mental image.

picture *VisArts* Visual representation or image painted, drawn, photographed, or otherwise rendered on a flat, two-dimensional surface.

Picture Agency Council of America (PACA) *VisArts* » **PACA**

picture element *InfoMgt* » **pixel**

picture hat *Fashn* Elaborately decorated, broad-brimmed hat for women.

picture tube *Rdio/TV* Cathode-ray tube in a television receiver that translates received electrical signals into a visible picture on a luminescent screen. KINESCOPE

Picturephone *InfoMgt, Sci&Tech* » Trade name for **videophone**

pictures *Flm&Vid* » **movies**

pie chart *Eco&Fin* Explanatory graphic showing a circle divided into pie-shaped segments to illustrate comparative quantities.

pie-in-the-sky *Crit&Eval* Empty wish or promise.

piece *Crit&Eval* Artistic, musical, or literary work or composition.

pièce de résistance (pee-ess duh ray-sis-tance, Fr.) *Crit&Eval* outstanding accomplishment.

piece goods *Fashn* Fabrics made and sold in standard lengths. YARD GOODS

piece of work *Crit&Eval* Remarkable person, achievement, or product.

pied *VA-Prntng* Type jumbled or randomly thrown together.

pied *VisArts* Patchy in color; splotched or piebald.

Pied Piper Award *MusArts* ASCAP, s highest accolade, given for lifetime achievement.

piggyback promotion *Mktg* Combines sales promotion with another effort in order to save money and attain **economies of scale**. <enclosing a direct mail flier for an arts event in the regular mailing of a local bank statement so that additional postage is not required>

pigment *VisArts* Substance used as coloring

pilling *Fashn* To form small balls resembling pills. <a sweater that pills>

pima cotton *Fashn* Very strong, high-grade cotton of medium staple developed from selected Egyptian cottons in the southwest U.S.

pin *MusInstr* One of the pegs securing the strings and regulating their tension on a stringed instrument.

pin rail *PerfA&C* Rail on a **gallery**, or at stage level, or on a wall that holds two rows of **belaying pins** or cleats.

pin spot *PerfA&C* **Spotlight** that has been focused (by an **iris**) to a very small beam, used to illuminate just the performer's face or a small portion of the stage. *Also see* **Stage Lighting**.

pinafore *Fashn* Sleeveless garment similar to an apron, worn esp. by small girls as a dress or an overdress.

pink contract *LglAsp, PerfA&C* **Equity** or **LORT** contract between producer and chorus member. *Also see* **white contract**.

pingponging *BcstJourn* Many newscasts use a double anchor format. To keep up the pace, producers often begin switching anchors on almost every story. Too much of it becomes very disconcerting to watch.

pipe *PerfA&C* Counterweighted **batten** or fixed metal pipe that holds lighting instruments or scenery.

pipe organ *MusInstr* Keyboard instrument in which the sound is produced by pipes to which wind is supplied. *Also see* **Musical Instrument Families, Organs**.

piquant (pee-kahnt, Fr. for "stinging") *Crit&Eval* Appealingly provocative; charming, interesting, or attractive. <Audrey Hepburn (1929-93, film act., dncr., humanitarian)>

pique (peek, Fr. for "irritation") *Crit&Eval* State of vexation caused by a perceived slight or indignity; a feeling of wounded pride.

piqué (pee'-kay, Fr. for "to quilt") *Fashn* Tightly woven fabric with various raised patterns, produced by a double warp.

piracy *IntelProp* Unauthorized use or reproduction of copyrighted or patented material.

piracy *Rdio/TV* Operation of an unlicensed, illegal radio or TV station.

piracy *RecA&S* "At least 26 **pirate** compact disc factories (1994) are operating in China with a production capacity of 50 million **CD's** a year. In addition to causing American recording artists to lose more than $820 million last year in revenue, the Chinese factories are also beginning to compete with American subsidiaries in other Asian markets." — Douglas Jehl (journ.)

pirate *Ethcs&Phil* To make use of or reproduce another's work without authorization.

pirouette (peer-oo-et, Fr.) *Dnce* (Ballet) Complete turn of the body performed on the point of the toe or the ball of the foot.

pit *Eco&Fin* Section of an **exchange** where **commodity** trading takes place.

pit *MusArts, PerfA&C* 1 Section of the theater in which the musicians sit, directly in front of the stage. Some large theaters <Radio City Music Hall (NYC)> have an elevator pit that can rise from the basement to a level several feet above the stage. 2 Ground in front of the stage where lower-class audiences stood to watch the play in the Elizabethan theater: 3 In modern theaters, a commonly used abbreviation for **orchestra pit**.

pit *PA-Variety* Gambling area of a casino.

pit musicians *MusArts* Musicians who play in the orchestra pit for theatrical performances. *Also see* **rehearsal musicians**.

pitch *Mktg* Promote or sell, often in a high-pressure manner. *Also see* **hype**.

pitch *MusArts* 1 Distinctive quality of a sound, dependent primarily on the **frequency** of the **sound waves** produced by its source. 2 Relative position of a tone within a range of musical sounds, as

determined by this quality. 3 Any of various standards for this quality associating each tone with a particular **frequency**.

pits *Sci&Tech* Small indentation in a surface. <pits of information etched unto the surface of an **optical disk**>

pity *Crit&Eval* » **catharsis**

PIX *BcstJourn* Abbreviation for photographs on a news script.

pix *Flm&Vid* **pictures** (**movies**)

pixel *InfoMgt* **picture element** Visual display screen is divided into rows and columns of tiny dots, squares, or cells, each of which is a pixel. Smallest unit on the display screen grid that can be stored, displayed, or addressed. Computed picture is typically composed of a rectangular array of pixels, 300 by 450. **Resolution** of a picture is expressed by the number of pixels in the display. <Picture with 560 x 720 pixels is much sharper than a picture with 275 x 400 pixels>

pixelated *iMedia* Describes the effects of **pixelization**.

pixelization *iMedia* When individual **pixels** are made apparent (and often jagged or degraded in quality) due to compression.

pixie *Fashn* Woman's hair style

pixy, pixie *Crit&Eval* Fairylike creature, esp. one that is mischievous.

pizz *MusArts* **pizzicato**

pizzazz or **pizzaz** *Crit&Eval* 1 Dazzling style. FLAMBOYANCE 2 Vigorous spirit; energy or excitement. *Also see* **flair**.

pizzicato (**pizz**) *MusArts* Played by plucking rather than bowing the strings. <jazz string bass>

pl. *VA-Prntng, VisArts* **plate**

places *TheatArts* Announcement on backstage **PA** that performers should take their places; the performance is about to begin. *Also see* **five minutes, fifteen minutes, half-hour**.

plagiarize *IntelProp* To use and pass off as one's own the ideas or writings of another.

plain old telephone system (**pots**) *InfoMgt* » **pots**

plain text or **plaintext** *Genl* Original form of a message as opposed to the **encrypted** form.

plain text *InfoMgt* Plain style of type: not **bold**, or *italic*, or underlined, etc. <This example is in plain text>

plain vanilla *Crit&Eval* limited choice. *Also see* **vanilla**.

plainsong *MusArts* **Nonmetrical** chant in one of the church modes. <**Gregorian chant**>

plaintiff *LegAsp* Party that institutes a suit in a court. *Also see* **defendant**.

plan (n) *EntreP* Document that lays out the strategy and/or financial projections for the company.

plan (v) *EntreP* Careful study of opportunities and the venture's capabilities and the development of strategies to capture those opportunities.

planned economy *Eco&Fin* One in which the central government (usu. Communist) plans all increments of the economy in advance, usu. in five year periods. This also means that the central government controls all production forms and levels, distribution channels, and pricing. *Also see* **market economy**.

planned giving *Fndng* Planning necessary to allow donors of money or property to a charitable institution to maintain some benefits during their lifetime.

planned obsolescence *Mgt, Mktg* Marketing strategy by which a product is regarded as obsolete or out-of-fashion, in the mind of the consumer, before the end of its practical life. <Recording industry "resells" its catalog each time a new format is introduced; fashion **fads**>

planning *EntreP* Systematic process that takes us from some current state to some future desired state.

planning *Mgt* Formal process of developing and implementing plans for an organization. <**operational, strategic**, and **operational** planning> *Also see* **Goals and Plans**.

planning and stabilization *Fndng* Grants for strengthening arts institutions — one of four categories of grants by the **National Endowment for the Arts**. *Also see* **NEA grants**.

planning model *EntreP* **Schematic** that details the nine steps of the planning process.

plant asset *E&F-Acc* Long-lived assets used in the operation of the business <**property, plant, and equipment**>

plaque (plak) *Mktg.* Flat plate, slab, or disk ornamented or engraved for mounting, as on a wall for decoration or on a monument for information.

plasma display *InfoMgt* In place of crystals, this display uses tiny **pixel** cells of electrically-charged gases to produce a high-resolution image.

plaster line *PerfA&C* Line drawn across the stage at the upstage edge of the **proscenium** that determines the downstage limit of the stage separating it from the **apron.** *Also see* **curtain line.**

plaster of Paris *Th-MakeUp* Used to make both positive casts and negative molds in rubber **prosthesis.**

plastic film *Th-MakeUp* In liquid form, similar to **latex.**

plate (pl.) *VA-Prntng* 1 Sheet of metal, plastic, rubber, paperboard, or other material prepared for use as a printing surface, such as an electrotype or a stereotype. 2 Full-page book illustration, often in color and printed on paper different from that used on the text pages.

plate *VisArts* Print of a woodcut, lithograph, or other engraved material, esp. when reproduced.

platform *Crit&Eval* Place, means, or opportunity for public expression of opinion. <a **journal** that serves as a platform for an **ideology.**

platform *Fashn* Shoe with a thick layer of leather or cork between the inner and outer soles thus giving added height.

platform *Law&Pol* Formal declaration of the principles of a political party.

platform *PerfA&C* Elevated surface. <**riser,** stage>

platforming *Flm&Vid, Mktg* Strategy of opening a new movie in a few cities and building the market from there.

plating *RecA&S* Electroplating the master **lacquer disc** to produce **mothers** and then **stampers** used to press an LP.

platinum *RecA&S* » **Platinum Record award**

Platinum Record award *RecA&S* Award certified and presented by the **RIAA** for a minimum sale of two million copies of a single, one million copies of an album.

platitude *Crit&Eval* **Trite** or **banal** remark or statement expressed as if it were original or significant. CLICHÉ

Plato (427?-347? BC; Greek philos.) *Ethcs&Phil* Follower of **Socrates,** he founded the Academy (386 BC), where he taught and wrote for much of the rest of his life. Plato presented his ideas in the form of dramatic dialogues, as in *The Republic.*

platonic *Crit&Eval* Relationship based on the spiritual and the ideal rather than on physical desire. *Origin* **Plato's** philosophy.

platter *InfoMgt* That part of a hard **disk drive** that actually stores the information. It is a round, flat, metallic plate covered on both surfaces with a brown magnetic substance.

play *LitArts* Literary work written for performance on the stage; a drama.

play *MusArts* To perform on an instrument. <play piano>

play *RecA&S* To cause a record or phonograph to emit recorded sounds.

play *TheatArts* 1 To act in a dramatic performance. 2 To present a theatrical performance in a given place.

play back, playback *RecA&S* 1 Act or process of replaying a newly made recording. 2 Method or apparatus for reproducing sound recordings.

play by ear *MusArts* Ability to play – usu. piano – without having read the music; improvise. *Also see* **play it by ear.**

play doctor *PerfA&C* One skilled in rewriting and redirection hired by desperate producers to improve production before its official **Broadway** opening. <George S. Kaufman>

play for pay centers *PerfA&C* Indoor entertainment and fitness venues for adults and children. <Discovery Zone Fun Centers, Leaps & Bounds>

play games *Crit&Eval* To be evasive or deceptive.

play in Peoria *Mktg* To be acceptable to average consumers in Heartland, USA.

play it by ear *Crit&Eval* To act according to the circumstances; improvise. *Also see* **play by ear.**

play producer *PerfA&C* One who finances and supervises the making and public presentation of a theatrical production. *Also see* **Producers.**

play-act *Crit&Eval* To behave in an histrionic or artificial way.

play-act *TheatArts* To play a role

play-along records *RecA&S* Recordings with sheet music offer a musician an opportunity to play to the **accompaniment** of a professional ensemble. <Music-Minus-One records>

play-for-the-door *MusArts, PerfA&S* Arrangement whereby the performer receives no fee other than the venue's admission or **cover charges.** Management keeps everything else. *Also see* **guarantee, percentage, scale.**

playa hataz *MusArts* rap talk for "player haters"

playback head *iMedia* Element used in time-based applications to indicate the current frame, or to track which frame is being played at a given time. *Also see* **scrubbing.**

Playbill *Mktg, PerfA&C* **Trademark** for a theater program.

playbill *Mktg, PerfA&C* Poster announcing a theatrical performance.

player *Genl* active participant

player *MusArts, TheatArts* Instrumentalist or actor.

player *RecA&S* Phonograph. <record player> *Also see* **Music Playback Devices.**

player piano *MusInstr* Electrically or mechanically activated piano whose keys are actuated by a recording or a perforated paper roll. *Also see* **Music Playback Devices.**

Players' associations *SportsEnt* Labor unions organized to protect the collective and individual rights of professional athletes. Despite earlier attempts – National Brotherhood of Professional [Base] Ball players in 1885 – their effective development is recent. Players' associations are less than 30 years but they are firmly established and play a major role in **collective bargaining** agreements and the creation of the **Standard Player Contract** between players and owners.

playgoer *TheatArts* One who frequently attends the theater. *Also see* **moviegoer.**

playhouse *PerfA&C* theater.

playlet *TheatArts* short play

playlist *Rdio/TV, RecA&S* Recorded music schedule for broadcast.

playwright (plywri.) *ArtPerf, LitArts, PerfA&C* Person who develops and writes the **script.** *Also see* **dramatist, librettist, screenwriter.** SCENARIST

Playwrights, Editors, Essayists, and Novelists *LitArts* » **PEN**

Pleasants, Henry (1910-??, mus. critic) *Crit&Eval, MusArts* <*The Agony of Modern Music* (1955), *The Great American Popular Singers* (1985)> *Also see* **asceticism, Audience.**

plectrum *MusInstr* Small, thin piece of metal, plastic, bone, or similar material, used to pluck the strings of certain instruments. <banjo, guitar, ither> *Also see* **finger pick.**

pledged accounts receivable *EntreP* Accounts receivable used as collateral for a loan.

plethora *Crit&Eval* Superabundance, excess.

plié (plee-ay, Fr.) *Dnce* (Ballet) Full bending of the knees. *Also see* **demi-plié.**

plot *LitArts* Plan of events or main story in a narrative or drama. *Also see* **analysis of tragedy.**

plot *PerfA&C* diagram » **light plot**

plot *TheatArts* structure of the incidents of the "play"

plot holes *Crit&Eval, Flm&Vid, LitArts* "Individual scenes that work while the whole of the picture doesn't, all too often leaving the audience as much in the dark as the theater it's sitting in." — **Larry Gelbart**

plug *Mktg* Favorable public mention of a product, business, or performance, usu. spoken on radio or spoken and/or shown on TV. *Also see* **payola, plugola, song plugger.**

plug-in *InfoMgt* Smaller add-on computer program that works in conjunction with a larger application, such as a **browser.**

plugola *Ethcs&Phil, Journ, Mktg, Rdio/TV* Deceptive self-promotion by **broadcast media** or **print media.** *Also see* **payola.**

plugola *MusArts* 1 Before **Alan Freed** and **payola**, there were music publisher **song pluggers** who begged and bribed band leaders, **vaudeville** and radio performers, and movie producers to "play our song." Some even offered the performer a share of copyright. 2 On the other hand, there were – and are – some sleazy managers, music publishers, performers, and record company execs, who insist on a share of copyright – or some other form of **under-the-table** payment – as a price for their cooperation. *Also see* **casting couch.**

plunger mute *MusInstr* Rubber suction cup from a "plumber's helper" placed or waved in front of the bell of a trumpet or trombone. WAH-WAH MUTE. *Also see* **du-wah**, wah-wah **pedal**.

pluralism *Cult&Soc* Condition of society in which numerous distinct **ethnic**, religious, or cultural groups coexist within one nation.

PM *Mgt* **personal manager**

PMA *Mktg* **Publishers Marketing Association**, an organization of more than 2,800 small publishers who market books cooperatively.

PNG *iMedia* » **Portable Network Graphics**

pno *MusInstr* **piano**

pntr. *ArtPerf, Genl, VisArts* painter.

pocket trumpet *MusInstr* Smaller version of the regular B flat trumpet but plays in the same range. *Also see* **Musical Instrument Families**.

poco *MusArts* To a slight degree or amount. *Also see* **Music Directions**.

podium *Genl, MusArts* Elevated platform used by a public speaker or an orchestra conductor. *Also see* **lectern**.

poem *Aes&Creat* Creation, an object, or an experience having beauty suggestive of poetry. *Origin* In the ancient Greek significance, a thing made; but, also a work of art, and more narrowly, a work of verbal art, principally inc. tragedy, epic poetry, and hymns to the gods.

poem *LitArts* **1** Composition in verse rather than in prose. **2** Literary composition written with an intensity or beauty of language more characteristic of poetry than of prose.

poesy, poesies *LitArts* **1** Poetical works; poetry. **2** Art or practice of composing poems.

poet *ArtPerf, LitArts* **1** One who demonstrates great imaginative power, insight, or beauty of expression. **2** Writer of poems.

poet laureate *ArtPerf, LitArts* Poet acclaimed as the most excellent or most representative of a locality or group. *Also see* **Robert Penn Warren**.

poetester *LitArts* Writer of insignificant, meretricious, or shoddy poetry.

poetic *LitArts* **1** Having a quality or style characteristic of poetry. **2** Characterized by **romantic** imagery.

poetic justice *Crit&Eval* Outcome in which virtue is rewarded and vice punished in an appropriate or ironic manner.

poetic license *Crit&Eval* Liberty taken by an artist or a writer in deviating from conventional form or fact to achieve a desired effect.

poetic meter *LitArts* » **foot, meter, metrical verse**

poeticize *LitArts* To describe or express in poetry or in a poetic manner.

poetics *Crit&Eval, LitArts* **1** Literary criticism that deals with the nature, forms, and laws of poetry. **2** Treatise on or study of poetry or **aesthetics**. **3** Practice of writing poetry; poetic composition.

poetry *LitArts* **1** Piece of literature written in **meter**; verse. **2** Poetic works of a given author, group, nation, or kind. **3** Prose that resembles a poem in some respect, as in form or sound: "Poetry like painting, cannot be rendered in logical terms." — **Benedetto Croce**

pogrom *Cult&Soc* Organized, often officially directed massacre or persecution of Jews.

poignant *Crit&Eval* **1** Profoundly moving; touching. **2** Piercing; incisive.

point *Eco&Fin* Equal to one percentage point, used in reference to ownership. <Instead of salary, the star's agent insisted on five points to do the movie>

point *MusArts* Phrase, as a **fugue** subject, in **contrapuntal** music.

point *VA-Prntng* » **typesize**

point of attack *TheatArts* Moment in a play when a precipitating sets the mechanisms in motion and disrupts the equilibrium: the first complication: the intrusion into stasis.

point of view shots (POV) *BcstJourn* Camera angle in which the lens appears to be an eye of a person watching the action. An example would be shots out the front window of a car during a sequence picturing someone driving a car. As with the reaction shot, inserting a POV shot in a sequence allows other cuts to take place that might have been awkward.

point of view (POV) *Crit&Eval* Attitude or outlook of a narrator or character in a piece of literature, a movie, or another art form.

point of view (POV) *Flm&Vid* Looking at the scene of action with the camera serving as the "eye" of one of the characters.

point-of-purchase (**P.O.P.**) *Mktg* **Merchandising aids**. <counter cards, hang tags, banners, etc> *Also see* **point-of-sale**.

point-of-sale (POS) *Mktg* Physical place where an item or service is purchased.

point-of-sale system *InfoMgt, Mktg*» **POS system**

point-of-view *Flm&Vid* » **POV**

Point-to-Point Protocol (PPP) *InfoMgt* » **PPP**

pointe (point, Fr.) *Dnce* Ballet dancing performed on the tips of the toes.

pointer *InfoMgt* **1** Arrow or other symbol on the screen that moves as the mouse moves, used to chose commands, select and move icons and text, and draw images. **2** Word that gives the address of a core storage location. *Also see* **cursor**.

pointillism *VisArts* **Postimpressionist** school of painting exemplified by Georges Seurat (» **neoimpressionism**) and his followers in late 19th century France, characterized by the application of paint in small dots and brush strokes. *Also see* **Art Movements and Periods**.

pointing *TheatArts* Giving special emphasis to a word or phrase. An actor may also be directed to *point* a movement or a piece of business.

points-of-presence (POPs) *InfoMgt* » **POPs**

pol *Law&Pol* **politician**. Sometimes used **cynically** as a **pejorative** term for someone running for or occupying public office.

pol. *Law&Pol* **political, politics, politician**

polemic *Crit&Eval* Controversial argument refuting or attacking a specific opinion or **doctrine**.

police shows *Rdio/TV* Popular type of television network programming. <*Dragnet, Cagney and Lacey, Hill Street Blues, N.Y.P.D. Blue*> *Also see* **Television Shows**.

politic *Crit&Eval* Using or marked by prudence, expedience, and shrewdness; artful.

political correctness (PC) *Ethcs&Phil, Law&Pol* Application of noisy majority rule to "inoffensive" language and "safe" expression of ideas. [Exercise by some educators, journalists, and politicians to inhibit freedom of assembly and speech in the illusory pursuit of consensus. Putting double-speak labels on contentious issues only confuses the issue and delays real solution.].

Political Philosophies *ColEntry, Law&Pol* » **conservative, liberal, libertarian, radical, reactionary, revolutionary**

political theater *Law&Pol* **1** Theatrical posturing in politics. **2** **Polemic** theatre. <Bughouse Square> *Also see* **Theaters & Theatres**.

politically correct *Crit&Eval, Cult&Soc* Opposite of free, frank, and open discussion; an unsatisfactory compromise with honesty that brings no relief to issues that cannot be resolved without straight talk. In recent years it has been attacked by both the right and the left as an attempt to silence free speech. **1** "But are culture and the arts obliged to be socially responsible? Who, or what, should determine art — the untrammeled visions of the artist or society's political goals and strivings for social justice? And, if society's political goals prevail, isn't there a very real danger that the result will be a kind of 'politically correct' art, an art suffocated by a requirement that nobody be either offended or excluded?" — "Who Controls Art?" (*NY Times,??*) **2** "No book is genuinely free from political bias. The opinion that art should have nothing to with politics is itself a political attitude." — **George Orwell**

politics (pol.) *Law&Pol* **1** Activity of a government, politician, or political party. **2** Participation in political affairs. "The artist's obligation is to bring an artistic perspective to bear on politics, not to sell art into political servitude. It is to advocate and embody, not to evaluate and adjudicate." — Conrad L. Osborne (journ.)

polity *Law&Pol* Political community, or a community considered from the point of the view of its politics.

polka *Dnce, MusArts* **1** Lively round dance originating in Bohemia and performed by couples. **2** Music for this dance, having **duple** meter. *Also see* **Dances**.

polling *InfoMgt* Method of controlling network traffic by allowing only one device to transmit at a time.

polonaise *Fashn* Woman's dress of the 18th century, having a fitted bodice and draped cutaway skirt, worn over an elaborate underskirt.

polonaise *Dnce, MusArts* Stately, marchlike Polish dance and music, primarily a promenade by couples.

polyglot *Crit&Eval* Speaking, writing, written in, or composed of several languages.

Polygram *RecA&S* Record division of the **media** conglomerate, **Phillips Electronics** of the Netherlands. *Also see* **major labels**.

Polyhymnia, Polymnia *MusArts,TheatArts* The **Muse** of sacred song, rhetoric, and mime. *Also see* **Muses**.

polyphonic *MusArts* Having two or more independent melodic parts sounded together.

polytonality *MusArts* **1** Use of two or more keys at once a la **John Coltrane**. **2** Simultaneous use of two or more tonalities in a composition.

ponies *Dnce* Dancers in the chorus

pool *Ethcs&Phil, Mktg* Agreement between competing business concerns to establish controls over production, market, and prices for common profit.

pool *Journ* Limited group of journalists who cover an event and then by agreement share their reports with participating news **media**.

pooled-income fund gifts *Fndng* Transfer of money or securities to a pooled income fund maintained by the charity which then pays the donor a life-long income.

pop *RecA&S* Explosive breath sound when a puff of air from the mouth strikes the **mic** diaphragm. Occurs most often with "p," "t," and "b" sounds. *Also see* **wind screen**.

pop art *Aes&Creat VisArts* Form of art that depicts objects or scenes from everyday life and employs techniques of commercial art and popular illustration. <Andy Warhol (1930?-87, pntr.), Roy Lichtenstein (1923-, pntr.), Claes Oldenburg (1929-, Swed.-born sculp.)> *Also see* **Art Movements and Periods, modern art**.

pop, pop. *Genl* popular.

POPs *InfoMgt* **Points-of-presence** Local access points for Internet service providers (**ISPs**)

pops *MusArts* Orchestral concert program featuring light classical music, **show tunes**, and orchestral popular music.

popular music *Cult&Soc* "I've been tooting this horn for a long time. American popular music is based on cultural diversity." — **Linda Ronstadt**

popular music (pop) *Mktg, MusArts* Any music bought by the most number of people at a particular time. "The primary buyer of popular music is between the ages of 18 and 25, After that, consumer interest falls dramatically. People over 35 still buy music, but it's an eclectic mix of classical, jazz, and old friends, which is to say, established stars. Less established stars are particularly hard to sell to this market." — Tom Vickers (Mercury records exec.) *Also see* **cheap music**.

Popular Songwriters Contract *IntelProp, LegAsp* » **SGA** *Also see* **Contracts**.

por. *VisArts* portrait

Porgy and Bess MusArts,TheatArts "The" American opera adapted from Dubose Hayward's novel *Porgy* (1925), music by **George Gershwin**, lyrics by **Ira Gershwin**, **libretto** by Dubose Hayward (1885-1940) based on his and Dorothy Heyward's play *Porgy* (1927), adapted from Dubose Hayward's novel (1925) First presented by the **Theatre Guild** in NYC, Oct. 1935.

porkpie hat *Fashn* Man's hat having a low, flat crown and a flexible brim; popular during the **swing** era. *Also see* **high-draped pants, zoot suiters**.

porn *Crit&Eval* » **pornography**

pornography (porn) *Crit&Eval* Pictures, writing, or other material sexually explicit and sometimes equates sex with power and violence.

port *InfoMgt* Electronic circuity connection point between the **host** computer and the input/output devices.

port de bras (port duh bra, Fr.) *Dnce* (Ballet) Group of exercises designed to make the arms move gracefully.

Portable Document Format *InfoMgt* » **PDF files**

Portable Network Graphics (PNG) *iMedia* File format for lossless image compression, primarily for use on the **World Wide Web.** PNG intended to be a single-image format only.

portal *InfoMgt* Web site database or index that can be queried to help user find information on the Internet. *Also see* **portals, search engine**.

portals *ColEntry, InfoMgt* <**Alta Vista, Excite, HotBot, InfoSeek, Lycos, Netscape, Northern Light, Snap, Web Crawler, Yahoo**> For features see "Search Engine Watch"

portamento *MusArts* Smooth, uninterrupted glide in passing from one tone to another, esp. with the voice or a bowed stringed instrument. SMEAR

Porter, Cole (1892-1964, comp., lyr.) *ArtPerf, MusArts* Known for his witty and sophisticated **Broadway scores**: galley proof

portfolio *Eco&Fin* Group of investments.

portfolio *Law&Pol* Office or post of a cabinet member or minister of state.

portfolio *VisArts* **1** Representative collection of an artist's work. **2** Portable case for holding such a collection.

portrait (por.) *VisArts* Likeness of a person created by a painter or photographer. PORTRAITIST

portraiture *VisArts* Art or practice of making portraits.

portray *LitArts* To depict or describe in words.

portray *TheatArts* To represent dramatically, as on the stage.

portray *VisArts* To depict or represent pictorially; make a picture of.

POS *Mktg* point-of-sale

POS system *InfoMgt, Mktg* **Point-Of-Sale system**. Cash register used as a point-of sale computer terminal that monitors and records transactions directly in the store's data files for inventory control, credit checks, and other data handling.

poseur *Crit&Eval* (pohz-ure, Fr. from "poser," to pose) One who affects a particular attitude, character, or manner to impress others.

position *Cult&Soc* Social standing or status; rank.

position *Eco&Fin* **1** Commitment to buy or sell a given amount of securities or commodities. **2** Amount of securities or commodities held by a person, company, or institution. **3** Ownership status of a person's or an institution's investments.

position *HR&LR* job.

positioning *Flm&Vid* Concept of a movie's advertising campaign about how the movie's creative elements are able to connect the nature of the film to its potential audience.

positioning *Mktg* Process of achieving a desired spot in the minds of customer and potential customers, particularly in relation to how competing products are perceived, one can position a company, products, technologies, or any other **entity** that commands customer attention. *Also see* **repositioning**.

Positions (Ballet) *ColEntry, Dnce*» first —, second —, third —, fourth —, fifth —.

positive association *Mktg* Benefit a sponsor receives by being connected with a successful and popular event or attraction.

positive option plan *Mktg* Contractual arrangement in which the seller, e.g., **record club**, periodically sends its members an announcement identifying merchandise it will ship and bill only if the member affirmatively orders the selection(s) offered. *Also see* **negative option plan**.

positive space *iMedia* Element(s) that can be thought of as objects (text, pictures, windows, etc.) In contrast: negative space.

post *E&F-Acc* To transfer an item to a ledger in bookkeeping.

post *InfoMgt* To enter a unit of information on a record or into a section of storage.

post *Mktg* **1** Trading post **2** To display an announcement in a place of public view.

post audit *EntreP* Procedures that determine how well the outcome of a decision correlates with the proposal.

post-buy analysis *Mktg* Day of reckoning after the ad campaign has run its course. Have we met our goal? Was it cost effective?

post-closing trial balance *E&F-Acc* **1** List of the **ledger** accounts and their balances at the end of the period after the journalizing and **posting** of the **closing entries**. **2** Last step of the accounting cycle, ensures that the ledger is in balance for the start of the next accounting period.

post-production *Flm&Vid* Editing and completion stages of a movie during which **special effects**, sound, and music are added. *Also see* **foley**.

postbellum *Cult&Soc* Relating to the period after a war, esp. the U.S. Civil War. *Also see* **antebellum**.

poster color, poster paint *VisArts* » **tempera**

posthumous work *LitArts, MusArts* Literary work or a musical composition published (not necessarily performed) after the author's death.

postimpressionism *VisArts* School of painting in France in the late 19th century that rejected the objective naturalism of **impressionism** and used form and color in more personally expressive ways. <George Braques, Paul Cézanne, Henri Matisse> *Also see* **Art Movements and Periods, modern art**.

posting *E&F-Acc* Transferring amounts from the **journal** to the **ledger**.

postmodernism, post-modernism *LitArts, VisArts* Visual art, architecture, or literature that reacts against earlier **modernist** principles by reintroducing traditional or classical elements of style or by carrying **modernist** styles or practices to extremes. *Also see* **Art Movements and Periods, cool** (*Crit&Eval*)

postmodernism *TheatArts* Characterizes the complex transformation of culture in the late 20th century. Although the postmodern is not confined to the sphere of art. Postmodern works are generally characterized by stylistic "quotation," an invocation of and disengagement from history and the fragmentation of artistic surface.

pot *InfoMgt* Section of storage reserved for storing accumulated data.

potpourri (poh-poo-ree, Fr.) *LitArts* Miscellaneous anthology or collection of stories and verse.

potpourri (poh-poo-ree, Fr.) *MusArts* 1 Collection of musical miscellany. 2 Series of disconnected musical sketches.

pots *InfoMgt* plain old telephone system

potted palm music *MusArts* Solo harpist or pianist or a small string group playing politely in the lobby or **mezzanine** of a hotel, usu. partially hidden by the foliage of potted plants.

POV *Flm&Vid* Point of view. Shot taken from the vantage point of a character. SUBJECTIVE CAMERA

poverty budget *EntreP* Minimum amount the government estimates that a family needs to avoid being in poverty; equal to three times the minimum food budget.

poverty level *Eco&Fin* Minimum income level below which one is officially considered to lack adequate subsistence and to be living in poverty. POVERTY LINE *Also see* **low-income**.

power *Crit&Eval* That which makes it possible to accomplish things in action; it arises from people coming together to solve common problems.

power of attorney (P/A) *LegAsp* Legal instrument authorizing one to act as another's attorney or **agent**. *Also see* **Agents and Agencies, special power of attorney**.

power structure *Mgt* 1 Elite group constituted by people holding influential positions within a government, a society, or an organization. 2 Hierarchy of managerial authority.

pp *MusArts* pianissimo

PPM *InfoMgt* Pages Per Minute. Print speed for a computer printer.

PPP *InfoMgt* **Point-to-Point Protocol** Allows a computer to pretend it's a full Internet machine with just a **modem** and an analog phone line. Superior to **SLIP** software. *Also see* **Protocols**.

PPV *Flm&Vid, Rdio/TV* pay-per-view

pr. *Eco&Fin, Mktg* price

practical *Flm&Vid* Lamp or other **prop** on the set wrigged to be operational during the scene's action.

pragma *Crit&Eval* Practicality, reality.

pragmatism *Crit&Eval* Practical, matter-of-fact way of approaching or assessing situations or of solving problems. *Also see* **John Dewey, realism**.

praise poetry *Cult&Soc* » **praise song**

praise shouter, praise singer *Cult&Soc, MusArts* Oral historians who capture the history of the tribe inside a vocal expression, i.e., oral history. *Also see* **hip-hop, rap**.

praise song *Cult&Soc, MusArts* **Chant** – sometimes to music and/or a percussion beat – developed in almost every African traditional society. Contains praise names and **epithets,** with no connector words. In communal performance, the lines of the praise song (or **praise poetry**) would be called and the audience-participants would respond, i.e., **call and response**. *Also see* **hip-hop,**

praise-house *Cult&Soc* Pre-Civil War black house of worship. *Also see* **ring dance, shout.**

pratfall *PA-Variety* 1 Deliberate, comic fall on the behind. 2 Humiliating error, failure, or defeat. *Also see* **low comedy, slapstick...**

prayer meeting *PA-Variety* **Evangelical** service in which laypersons sing, pray, or testify.

PRC *IntelProp, Journ, Lit* **Publication Rights Clearinghouse**

pre-attentive processing *iMedia* Determines what visual objects are offered to our attention.

pre-production *iMedia* Planning, organizing and design of a project before production begins. Often includes budgeting, team building, research and contextual inquiry.

Pre-Raphaelite Brotherhood *VisArts* Society founded in England in 1848 to advance the style and spirit of Italian painting before **Raphael** (1483-1520, Ital. pntr.) *Also see* **Art Movements**.

pre-scoring *Flm&Vid* Recording of a sound to accompany the action of a scene which is then played back while filming is actually occurring. Often used when shooting singers or musicians performing in acoustically inferior locations.

precedent *Crit&Eval* 1 Act or instance that may be used as an example in dealing with subsequent similar instances. 2 Convention or custom arising from long practice.

precedent *LegAsp* Judicial decision that may be used as a standard in subsequent similar cases: a landmark decision that set a legal precedent.

précis (pray-see) *Crit&Eval* Concise summary of a book, an article, or a text; an abstract.

predatory pricing *Eco&Fin, EntreP, Mktg* Pricing scheme under which a company decreases its price to drive a rival out of business, and increases the price when the other company disappears. <Established manufacturer or service provider cuts prices to prevent new competitor from making a profit; then raises prices when the competitor has to abandon the market> *Also see* **dumping**.

preempt *Rdio/TV* To exclude existing program for one with a higher priority. <a political convention, a murder trial, **Watergate**, movie-of-the-week, late-breaking, major news>

preferred stock *Eco&Fin, EntreP* Hybrid vehicle which has features of both bonds and common stock. Owner's of preferred stock are guaranteed a percentage return on their investment but are stockholders with no voting rights.

prejudice *Crit&Eval* 1 Adverse judgment or opinion formed beforehand or without knowledge or examination of the facts; a preconceived preference or idea. 2 Irrational suspicion or hatred of a particular group, race, or religion.

prejudice *LegAsp* Detriment or injury caused to a person by the preconceived, unfavorable conviction of another or others.

preliminary planning *Journ* Early generation of ideas and planning of the contents of an issue of a publication.

preload *iMedia* Arranging for streaming content delivery to refrain from playing until a certain portion (or the entire amount) of material has downloaded. Often utilized with animation, audio or video so that playback is not skipped or choppy if streaming slows. usu. a "preloader" is in place to notify how much time remains for download, or to entertain or distract from a slow download process.

preloaded software *InfoMgt* Software already set up in a computer.

preloader *iMedia* Component of content delivery in place to notify how much time remains for content to download, or to entertain or distract from a slow download process.

prelude *MusArts* 1 Introductory movement complete in itself, as opposed to an **introduction**. 2 Short piano piece in one movement.

premier danseur *Dnce* **Principal** male ballet dancer in a **troupe**. *Also see* **ballerina**.

premier danseur *Dnce* Star male dancer *Also see* **danseur**.

premium *Eco&Fin* Payments made by an individual or a business to an insurance company for **insurance** coverage.

premium *Mktg* 1 Prize or an award. 2 Something offered free or at a reduced price as an inducement to buy something else.

premiums *Fndng* Incentives offered to members or prospective members or donors to encourage memberships and donations.

prenotification plan *Mktg* » **negative option plan**

prepackage *Mktg* To wrap or package a product before marketing.

preparation *MusArts* Anticipation of a **dissonant** tone by means of its introduction as a **consonant** tone in the preceding chord.

preparation *TheatArts* Brief but comprehensive litany of observations, actions and concentrations which centers the actor before performance.

prepare *MusArts* To lead up to and soften a **dissonance** or its impact by means of **preparation**.

prepared piano *MusArts, MusInstr* Term and a technique introduced by John Cage (1912-92, avant-garde comp.) in the early 1940s: a piano's sound is altered by placing one or miscellaneous objects on or under the piano strings. Objects include: cardboard, clothespins, paper clips, rubber wedges or whatever.

preprocess *InfoMgt* To perform conversion, formatting, or other functions on data before further processing.

preproduction *Flm&Vid* Activities that occur in preparation for the actual filming or taping of a production. <casting, contracts, location scouting, set construction>

preproduction*TheatArts* Preliminary arrangements, such as financing or casting, made before going into actual **production**.

preprofessional *ArtPerf* Preparatory to the practice of a profession or to its specialized field of study. <In his preprofessional career, the guitarist played in a neighborhood **garage band**>

prepublication *LitArts, Mktg* Relating to the time just before a publication date of a book or journal. <The publisher's marketing department was pleased by the number of prepublication orders>

prequel *Flm&Vid, LitArts, Rdio/TV* **1** Work taking place in or concerned with a time before the action of a preexisting work. <a prequel that featured the story characters before their marriage> **2** Work that precedes, introduces, or leads up to a later work. *Also see* **back story.**

prerecord*Rdio/TV* To record a radio or TV program at an earlier time for a later broadcast.

prerelease *Genl* Article, entertainment product, press release, or software program released before an official or scheduled date.

prerequisite (pree-rek-wee-zit) *Genl* Required or necessary as a prior condition.

Pres., pres. *Law&Pol* President, president.

presale *Mktg, VisArts* **1** Period before something, such as a work of art, is available for sale to the public. **2** Exclusive or private sale held before an advertised sale.

prescience (pres-sience) *Crit&Eval* Knowledge of actions or events before they occur; foresight.

prescreen *Flm&Vid* To view a movie before release for public showing.

presell *Mktg* **1** To promote a product not yet on the market by means of advertising and promotion. **2** To condition potential customers in advance for later purchase of a product. *Also see* **buzz.**

presence *ArtPerf,TheatArts* The quality of self-assurance and effectiveness that permits a performer to achieve a rapport with the audience; stage presence. "In... college it might have been called 'quality of leadership'; in the theatre, most markedly among the critics, it was usu. called 'presence'; it was something that had always made [the actor] noticed, no matter how terrible the play." —**John P. Marquand**. *Also see* **empathic response.**

presence *Flm&Vid* » **ambient sound**

present *Genl* **1** To introduce with formal ceremony. **2** To bring before the public. <present a play, a movie, a dance recital, etc>

presentatial actor*TheatArts* "The presentatial actor attempts to reveal human behavior through a use of himself, through an understanding of himself and consequently an understanding of the character he is portraying." — Uta Hagen (» **talent**) *Also see* **represential actor.**

presentation *Flm&Vid* Somewhere between a **preview** and the show itself.

presentation *iMedia* **1** Visual display of information. communication of interactive media content is usu. accomplished with separate but interconnected processes: structure, interaction, and presentation. Separating structure from presentation allows more flexibility (content can be repurposed dynamically depending on context) **2** lecture or speech, given to an audience. **3** "formal introduction." **4** "Act of presenting, or the state of being presented." **5**. "social debut"

presentation *Mktg* Process of offering for consideration or display.

presentation *PerfA&C* » **performance**

presentation house *Flm&Vid, PA-Variety* (Passé) Movie theaters with live acts.

presentational staging *TheatArts* **1** Production that is frankly theatrical, free from the illusion of reality. **2** Performer confronts the audience directly.

presenter *Genl* **1** To introduce with formal ceremony. **2** To make or give a gift or an award.

presenter *Mgt* One who brings an artist, performer, or a work of art to an audience. <"Now presenters are taking responsibility for **commissioning** new work and educating our audiences, and we're asking much more of the artists. We'd like them to stick around, do a **master class** or post-performance chat. We think it's good for business." — Kenneth Fischer (dir., Musical Society of the U. Michigan, Ann Arbor)> *Also see* **APAP, Managers, pedestal presenter.**

presenting sponsor *Mktg* Level of sponsorship where the sponsor is identified as "Presenting" the event or attraction. Similar designations include: "Brought to you by..." or "— welcomes you to —"

preside *MusArts* To be the featured instrumental performer.

Presley, Elvis (aka "The King," 1935-77, pop/rock/country sngr., act., gtr., sngwri.) *ArtPerf, MusArts* Musician most responsible for the rock musical and cultural phenomenon. *Also see* **classic rock, Graceland, grind, industry.**

press *RecA&S* To make a phonograph record or videodisk from a mold or **matrix.**

press *VA-Prntng* **1** Any equipment used for printing; a printing press. **2** Place where matter is printed. **3** Art, method, or business of printing. **4** Journalism in general. **5** Collecting and publishing or broadcasting of news. **6** All **media** and agencies that collect, publish, transmit, or broadcast the news. **7.Media** persons: broadcasters, editors, news reporters, photographers, publishers. **8** Commentary or coverage esp. in newspapers or periodicals.

press agency *Journ* » **news agency** *Also see* **News Agencies.**

press agent (PA) *Mktg* One who arranges **promotion** and **publicity** for a performer or **troupe** or **venue**. FLACK, FLAK *Also see* **image-maker, P.R., publicist.**

press association *Journ*» **news agency**

press conference *Journ* Interview held for news reporters by a **newsworthy** person or organization.

press corps *Journ* Ladies and gentlemen of the press, as a group.

press count *LitArts, VA-Prntng* Number of times a publisher goes to press for additional printings.

press gallery *Journ* Special section of the balcony in a legislative **venue** reserved for members of the working press. <Capitol Hill daily press gallery, periodical press gallery, and the radio-TV gallery>

press kit *Mktg* Packaged set of promotional materials for distribution to the press at a news conference or before the release of a new product. <8"x10" **glossies**, bios, itinerary, background info, latest CD, **collage** of press clips, **canned interviews**, and other assorted **hype**>

press release *Mktg* Announcement of an event or other news or publicity item given to the press and other **media**.

press run *or* **pressrun** *Journ, LitArts, VA-Prntng* Number of copies printed in one such continuous operation. *Also see* **press count.**

press seats *Mktg* Free tickets given to the authorized press.

press secretary *Mktg* One who manages the public affairs and press conferences of a public figure or government agency.

pressing *RecA&S* **1** Phonograph record pressed from a master. **2** Number of recordings pressed at the same time. <The album went into its third pressing>

pressmark *VA-Prntng* **Notation** or figure in the margin of a printed sheet indicating the press on which it was printed.

pressrun *Journ, VA-Prntng* Specific number of copies printed during a continuous operation of a printing press. PRINTRUN *Also see* **first edition.**

pressure group *Law&Pol* **Special interest group** that endeavors to influence public policy.

prestidigitator *ArtPerf, PA-Variety* Sleight-of-hand performer. <someone who does card tricks> *Also see* **magician.**

prestige film *Flm&Vid* Big budget film that will colorfully add character and repute to a particular film studio.

prestigious *Crit&Eval* Having prestige; esteemed.

prestissimo (Ital. for superlative of **presto**) *MusArts* Play in as fast a tempo as possible. *Also see* **Music Directions**.

presto (Ital. for "quick") *MusArts* Play in a very fast tempo, faster than **allegro** but slower than **prestissimo**. *Also see* **Music Directions**.

presumption *LegAsp* Conclusion derived from a particular set of facts based on law, rather than probable reasoning.

pretentious *Crit&Eval* **1** Claiming or demanding a position of distinction or merit, esp. when unjustified. **2** Making or marked by an extravagant outward show; **ostentatious**.

preview, prevue *Flm&Vid* **1** Advance showing, as of a movie, play, or an art exhibition, to which a selected audience is invited before public presentation begins. **2** Presentation of several scenes advertising a forthcoming movie; a **trailer**.

preview, prevue *TheatArts* **1** Preview performances give players and crew an opportunity to work under performance conditions without drawing critical attention. **2** New industry practice calls for previews to be clearly labeled for "all shows that have not been open to review." "Many producers link the growing reliance on previews to a concentration of power in the hands of ever fewer critics. 'There's an undue dependence of the **Broadway** theater on the critic. They want to run as long as possible before the death sentence.'"— Robert Brustein (artistic dir. American Repertory Theater, Cambridge, Mass.)" — Ralph Blumenthal (lit. critic)

prewriting *Cult&Soc* Creation, form, and communication of ideas preliminary to writing.

prf. *VA-Prntng* **proof**

price (pr.) *Eco&Fin, Mktg* **1** Narrow view: amount of money or goods or services, asked for or given in exchange for something else. **2** Broader view: Includes other monetary and nonmonetary costs associated with purchasing and use of the goods and services, or the adoption of a social behavior, or a political stance, such as time, physical and psychological effort.

price ceiling *EntreP* Maximum price; transactions above the maximum price are outlawed.

price earnings ratio *EntreP* Ratio that indicated what multiple of earnings per share investors are (willing to pay for the stock. Formula is market price of stock divided by earnings per share.

price elasticity *Mktg* » **elasticity of demand**

price fixing, price-fixing *Eco&Fin, Law&Pol* **1** Setting of commodity prices artificially by a government. **2** Result of an unlawful agreement between manufacturers or dealers to set and maintain specified prices on typically competing products. *Also see* **Pricing Strategies**.

price floor *EntreP* Minimum price; transactions below the minimum price are outlawed.

price inelasticity *Mktg* » **elasticity of demand**

price level *EntreP* Average of all the prices in the economy as measured by a price index.

price out of the market *Eco&Fin, Mktg* To charge so much for goods or services that people no longer buy or use them.

price point *Fashn* Price range of an apparel product or group.

price support *Eco&Fin* Maintenance of prices, as of a raw material or commodity, at a certain level through public **subsidy** or government intervention.

price tag *Mktg* **1** Label attached to a piece of merchandise indicating its price. **2** Cost of something.

price war *Mktg* Period of intense competition among businesses in which each competitor tries to cut retail prices below those of the others.

price-cutting *Mktg* Reduction of retail prices to a level low enough to eliminate competition or to **liquidate** inventory. *Also see* **Pricing Strategies**.

price-earnings multiple *EntreP* Reciprocal of the capitalization rate, equal to a company's value divided by its earnings.

price-earnings ratio (P/E) *Eco&Fin* Ratio of a common stock's market price in its earnings per share, used as an indicator of a corporation's profitability.

price-lining strategy *Mktg* Retail pricing strategy that establishes similar price levels for like products in order to attract multiple types of consumers. <Men's suits may have price points at $175, $250, and $350. There may be multiple brands under each price

point calculated to appeal to different types of consumers> *Also see* **Pricing Strategies**.

price-penetration strategy *Mktg* Pricing a product so that it gains as large a market as possible. *Also see* **Pricing Strategies**.

price-skimming strategy *Mktg* Pricing a product or service to gain the highest price possible. Initial introductory pricing of new concept products <cellular phones, computers, VCRs, etc> have been frequently priced this way until competition and waning demand forces the prices down. This strategy is also used for short product life products <cosmetics, pop CD's, etc>, and fad products <Hula Hoops, Pet Rocks, etc> *Also see* **Pricing Strategies**.

priceless *Crit&Eval* **1** Of inestimable worth; invaluable. **2** Highly amusing, absurd.

pricey, pricy *Mktg* expensive.

pricing *Mktg* To fix or establish a price for goods or services. <Book publishers usu. price their books to compete with other titles and with the cost of entertainment — two tickets for a movie, for instance, or a concert. *Also see* **market will bear**, **Pricing Strategies**.

Pricing Strategies *ColEntry, Eco&Fin, Mktg* **aggressive pricing, congestion —, price cutting, price fixing, price-lineing —, price-penetration —, price-skimming —, pricing strategy, pricing, psychological pricing, time-of-day pricing**.

pricing strategy *Mktg* Mix of monetary price level charged to the final purchaser. <terms of payment, e.g., checks, credit cards, exact change, and discounts offered to intermediaries and final purchasers> *Also see* **Pricing Strategies**.

pride *Crit&Eval* **1** Sense of one's own proper dignity or value; self-respect. **2** Pleasure or satisfaction taken in an achievement, a possession, or an association: parental pride. **3** Arrogant or disdainful conduct or treatment; haughtiness. **4** Excessively high opinion of oneself; conceit.

pride of place *VisArts* Premium position (of an art work) due to excellence.

prig *Crit&Eval* One showing an exaggerated **conformity** or **propriety** in an arrogant or smug manner. *Also see* **prude**.

prim *Crit&Eval* Precise or proper to the point of **affectation**; excessively; strait-laced. PRUDISH.

prima ballerina *ArtPerf, Dnce* Leading woman dancer in a ballet company; first dancer. *Also see* **ballerina**.

prima donna (Ital.) *Crit&Eval* Temperamental, conceited female person.

prima donna (Ital.) *MusArts* Leading woman soloist in an opera company. DIVA

prima facie (pryma faysha, *Latin*) *Ethcs&Phil, Law&Pol* At first glance; on the face of it. Something, like a law or rule, that appears to be true or apply ("thou shalt not lie"), unless and until it's outweighed by something else (except, perhaps, to the axe murderer asking you whether your mother is hiding in your basement)

primary audience *Mktg* Particular audience composition or **demographic** to whom a message is believed to have the most appeal and is, therefore, primarily directed. TARGET AUDIENCE

primary colors *iMedia* Three basic colors of the color wheel: red, green, and blue.

primary data *Mktg* Information the researcher collects through observation, experimentation, or survey research. *Also see* **secondary data**.

primary demand *Mktg* Current level of demand from all sources for the entire product classification.

primary instrument *MusArts* Principal instrument used by a musician in performance. <The bass is his primary instrument but he likes **doubling** on cello>

primary market *EntreP* First sale of newly issued financial assets. Proceeds from this sale of new securities go to the issuer of the security, and the quantity issued alters the total supply of the security.

primary reporter *Journ, Rdio/TV* One immersed in the details of investigating a story.

prime interest rate *Eco&Fin* » **prime rate**

prime orchestra seats *PerfA&C* Seats in the fifth to tenth rows in the orchestra section of a theatre.

prime rate *Eco&Fin, EntreP* Interest rate charged by a commercial bank on loans to its most creditworthy customers. *Also see* **prime interest rate**

prime time*Rdio/TV* Time period with the highest listenership or viewership; for radio, it's **drive time**, i.e., early morning and late afternoon; for TV, it's 7-9PM

priming *iMedia* People can more easily identify objects if given prior exposure.

primitive *Aes&Creat* One belonging to an early stage in the development of an artistic trend.

primitive *Cult&Soc* 1 Relating to an earliest or original stage or state. 2 Marked by simplicity or crudity. 3 Relating to early stages in the development of human culture: "The mental processes of man are the same everywhere, regardless of race and culture, and regardless of the apparent absurdity of beliefs and customs.... Some theorists assume a menial equipment of primitive man distinct from that of civilized man. I have never seen a person in primitive life to whom this theory would apply.... Behavior of everybody, no matter to what culture he may belong, is determined by the traditional material he handles, and man, the world over, handles the material transmitted to him according to the same methods." — Franz Boas (1858-1942, German-born anthropologist, cult. critic) RUDE

primitive *InfoMgt* Basic or fundamental unit of machine instruction or translation.

primitive *VisArts* Artist having or affecting a primitive style.

primitivism *Cult&Soc* 1 Belief that it is best to live simply and in a natural environment. 2 Belief that the acquisitions of civilization are evil or that the earliest period of human history was the best.

primitivism *VisArts* Style characteristic of a **primitive** artist. <Paul Gauguin (» **expressionism**)> *Also see* **Art Movements and Periods**.

princess*Fashn* Designed to hang in smooth, close-fitting, unbroken lines from shoulder to **flared** hem. <a princess dress>

principal *E&F-Acc* Sum of money owed as a debt, upon which interest is calculated.

principal *Eco&Fin* Capital or main body of an estate or a financial holding as distinguished from the interest or revenue from it.

principal *Genl* Main participant in a situation. *Also see* **agent**, **agency**.

principal *LegAsp* 1 Person who empowers another to act as her or his representative. 2 Person having prime responsibility for an obligation distinguished from one who acts as surety or as an endorser. *Also see* **agent**, **agency**.

principal *PerfA&C* Performer having a leading or starring role.

principal amount*E&F-Acc* Amount loaned out by the **payee** and borrowed by the maker of a **note**.

principal interviews/auditions *ArtPerf, HR&LR,TheatArts* "Initial interview or **audition** at a scheduled time and place at which **Equity** members will be seen without appointment for **principal** roles and all stage managerial positions..." — **Actors' Equity Association**, "Agreement and Rules Governing Employment under the Production Contract."

principal player *MusArts* **Section leader** in a concert orchestra. <the principal clarinetist, the first horn player, et al> FIRST, FIRST CHAIR

Principal Players *Mgt* Major element of **The Arts Dynamic**. *Also see* **Inner Forces**, **Outer Forces**.

principal's duties *LegAsp* **Principal** owes four basic duties to the **agent**: (1) duty of **compensation**, (2) duty of **reimbursement** and **indemnification**, (3) duty of **cooperation**, (4) duty to provide **safe working conditions**.

principal's duty of compensation *LegAsp* **Principal** must pay an agreed-upon amount of **compensation** upon the completion of the agency or some other mutually agreeable time.

principal's duty of cooperation *LegAsp* **Principal** must cooperate with and assist the agent in the performance of the agent's duties and the accomplishment of the agency.

principal's duty of indemnification *LegAsp* **Principal** must protect the agent for losses suffered during the agency because of the principal's misconduct.

principal's duty of reimbursement *LegAsp* **Principal** must reimburse the agent for any money spent by the agent on the **principal's** behalf.

principal's duty to provide safe working conditions *LegAsp* **Principal** must provide safe premises, equipment, and other working conditions; includes inspection by the **principal** to ensure safety.

principled bargaining *HR&LR* Approach to collective bargaining where both parties view it as an opportunity to participate in joint problem solving in order to reach an agreement. This approach focuses more on interests than positions.

print *Fashn* Fabric or garment with a dyed pattern that has been pressed onto it, usu. by engraved rollers; the pattern itself.

print *Flm&Vid* Copy of a film or movie for distribution made from the **master negative**. Number of prints duplicated depends on box-office receipts and marketing strategy.

print *Mktg* Advertising placed in newspapers and magazines. <The budget for print was larger than for radio-TV>

print *VisArts, VA-Prntng* 1 Printed publication, such as a magazine, newspaper or other printed matter. 2 Design or picture transferred from an engraved plate, **wood block**, lithographic stone, or other medium.

print buffer *InfoMgt* » **buffer**

print license*IntelProp, MusArts* Grants right to print **sheet music**, **folios**, songbooks, or other printed editions for a specified period of time and for a designated territory. *Also see* **Music Licenses**.

print media *Mktg* Direct mail, journals, magazines and **inserts**, newspapers and **inserts**.

print media music *IntelProp, MusArts* Money paid to the copyright owner derived from the use of music or lyrics in a book, magazine, or newspaper.

print rights*IntelProp, MusArts* Exclusive right to print copyrighted music. *Also see* **Print Music**.

print wheel *VA-Prntng* Disk-shaped mechanism in a printing device that carries the **template** of the characters.

printed circuit board *InfoMgt* » **board**

printed matter *VA-Prntng* Entitled to a special postage rate.

printed music royalty *IntelProp, MusArts, RecA&S* Royalty paid on the sale of printed music by the **licensee** (printer or distributor) to the authors and publisher. *Also see* **Royalties**.

printer's devil *VA-Prntng* printer's apprentice

printery *Fashn* Factory that prints fabrics

printery *VA-Prntng* Place that does typographic printing.

printmaking *VisArts, VA-Prntng* 1 Artistic design and production of prints. <woodcuts, silkscreens> 2 Combine with painting. <Robert Rauschenberg's *Gloria* (1956)>

printout *InfoMgt* Printed output of a computer.

printrun *Journ, VA-Prntng* » **pressrun**

privacy *Crit&Eval* 1 Personal aspects one chooses to shield from public scrutiny. 2 Free from unsanctioned intrusion. *Also see* **right of privacy**.

private branch exchange *InfoMgt* » **PBX**

private corporation *EntreP* Corporation that has been formed under state law, but does not sell its shares of stock to the public.

private facts *Journ, LegAsp* Facts about a person that are relevant to a published article of public interest and, if published, invades the person's privacy.

private foundation *Fnding* 1 Nongovernmental, nonprofit organization with funds (usually from a single source, such as an individual, family, or corporation) and program managed by its own trustees or directors established to maintain or aid social, educational, religious, or other charitable activities serving the common welfare, primarily through the making of grants... 2 Organization that is tax-exempt under code section **501**(c)(3) and is classified by the **IRS** as a private foundation as defined in the code. The code definition usually, but not always, identifies a foundation with the characteristics first described. *Also see* 501(c)(3); **public charity**.

private placement *EntreP* Sale of a company's capital stock to selected individuals.

privilege *LegAsp* Right to privileged communication in a confidential relationship, as between client and attorney, patient and physician, or communicant and priest.

privileged situations *BcstJourn* In reporting, the open and public proceedings of courts and of federal, state, and local governments.

pro *Crit&Eval* » **professional**

pro bono (Latin) *LegAsp* Done without compensation for the public good.

pro forma (Latin) *LegAsp* Provided in advance so as to prescribe form or describe items.

pro forma financial statements *EntreP* Reports that provide projections of a company's financial condition.

pro rata (Latin) *Genl, MusArts* In proportion, according to a factor that can be calculated exactly. <The **engagement contract** called for the group to be paid $1,500 for a three-hour **gig**, additional time to be pro rated, e.g., an additional hour would be $500>

proactive selling *Mktg* Actively seeking out prospective consumers. *Also see* **reactive selling**.

problem/needs statement *Fndng* Part of a grant proposal that presents the segment of the population being served and the problem or need addressed by the proposed project.

proceeds *E&F-Acc* Net amount received from bank or lender when a business discounts a note receivable. It is the difference between **maturity** value and amount discounted.

proceeds *Eco&Fin* Amount of money derived from a commercial or **fundraising** venture.

process *TheatArts* **Method** of acting taught by The **Actors Studio**.

process color *VA-Prntng* » **process printing**

process printing *VA-Prntng* Printing process done from four half-tone images, each inked with a different color, the four primary colors plus black. Composite impression reproduces the colors of the original image. PROCESS COLOR

processor *InfoMgt* 1 Computer 2 **Central processing unit (cpu)** 3 Program that translates another program into a form acceptable by the computer being used.

prod. *Flm&Vid, Rdio/TV, RecA&S* **producer**

prodigy *Crit&Eval* 1 Person with exceptional talents or powers. 2 Act or event so extraordinary or rare as to inspire wonder.

Prodigy *InfoMgt* Online information service that some consider over-priced. *Also see* **Online Information Services**.

prodn. *LitArts, Flm&Vid, TheatArts, Rdio/TV* **production**

producer (prod.) *Flm&Vid, Mgt, Rdio/TV* **Ambiguous** term referring to the individual or company that controls the financing of a film or a radio or television program, and often the way it's made. The producer may do anything, from dealing with business matters to negotiating package deals (obtaining scripts, hiring talent, etc.) to simply functioning as an expeditor who smooths over problems during production. *Also see* **Producers**.

producer *PerfA&C* Person who selects the script, finds financial backing, and hires production personnel.

producer (prod.) *RecA&S* One who has artistic and financial control of a recording session. [And may thus supersedes the competing egos of the artist, arranger-composer, and recording engineer.].

producer royalty *IntelProp, MusArts, RecA&S* Similar to an **artist royalty** except that the record producer is the recipient. *Also see* **Royalties**.

producer/director *Flm&Vid* Filmmaker who finances projects independently in order to retain maximum creative control. *Also see* **Directors, Producers**.

Producers *ColEntry, Mgt* » **artist —, auteur, celebrity —, engineer —, publisher —, personal manager —, profile —, creative —, crasher, executive —, independent —, in-house —, investigative —, League of New York Theatres and —, mogul, movie —, play —, packager, producer, producer-director, radio —, record —, staff —, supervisory —, television —**

Producers Guild of America *Flm&Vid* » **PGA**

product *EntreP* Total bundle of satisfaction—a service, a good, or both—offered to consumers in an exchange transaction.

product *Flm&Vid* Term synonymous with feature film releases that are produced, distributed and theatrically presented to an audience.

product *Mktg* What the marketer creates or sponsors and then offers to prospective customers; may include physical goods, personal and group services, social behaviors, or political and religious causes.

product class *Mktg* Group of goods or services that serve the same general function or fulfill the same need, want, or desire.

product development *Mktg* Process of developing or acquiring new or improved goods or services for a marketer's current mar-

kets.

product line *Mktg* All the products marketed by a given marketer, sometimes subdivided into sets of product lines.

product mix *EntreP* Company's total product lines.

product placement *Flm&Vid, Mktg, TheatArts* Display or use of a sponsor's product **on camera**, **on stage** or in the actual performance, a practice common in film and video. It is considered unethical to not note the sponsor's participation in the printed program or on the film/video crawl. <Scene in which the brand of cigarette or liquor is noticeable>

product strategy *EntreP* Way the product component of the marketing mix is used to achieve a company's objectives.

production *Crit&Eval* 1 Something less than meets the eye. 2 Exaggerated spectacle or display. <President **Nixon's** TV presentations of "Checkers" and the "transcribed **Watergate** tapes.">. *Also see* **chutzpah**.

production (prod.) *Eco&Fin, Mktg* 1 Creation of value or wealth by producing goods and services. 2 Something produced; a product. 3 Amount or quantity produced; output.

production (prod.) *LitArts, Flm&Vid, TheatArts, Rdio/TV* 1 Work of art or literature. 2 Work produced for the stage, screen, TV, or radio. 3 Actual processes involved with the shooting of a movie.

production company *Mgt* **Arts management** organization responsible for the production of a performance.

production coordinator *PerfA&C* Responsible for overall event management, hiring and firing all production staff. Primary decision maker on the day of the show; produces the event. *Also see* **production secretary**.

production deal *Flm&Vid* Agreement between a movie company or studio and a movie producer (or production company) whereby the producer promises to supply a stipulated number of film masters during the contract period. Producer has **artistic control** but the copyrights are usu. owned by the movie company. *Also see* **Contracts**.

production deal *RecA&S* Agreement between a record company and a record producer (or production company) whereby the producer promises to supply a stipulated number of masters during the contract period. Producer has **artistic control**; copyrights are usu. owned by the record company. *Also see* **Contracts**.

production expenses/selling expenses *Eco&Fin* Costs that are associated with the preparation of goods, making them available for sale.

production guide *iMedia* Document that has specific instructions for all aspects of an interactive media product's development.

production manager *Mgt, PerfA&C* Coordinator of production scheduling and administrative logistic details of a multi-show theatrical season.

production meeting *PerfA&C* Conference of appropriate production personnel to share information.

production method *E&F-Acc* This method of **depreciation** assumes that depreciation is solely the result of use and the passage of time plays no role in the depreciation process.

production protocol *PerfA&C* Established, formal procedures; conventional manners and consideration.

production secretary *TheatArts* Employee of the producer or the production coordinator, he or she is responsible for intracompany communication (notes, bulletins, etc.) and coordinating all the elements of a theatrical production. <book, choreography, music, staging, etc>

production stage manager *TheatArts* Represents the director during rehearsals. *Also see* **Managers**.

production unit *Flm&Vid* Self-contained group: director, camera and sound crews, technicians, assigned to shoot a picture or section of picture on a soundstage or on location.

production values *Flm&Vid* Box-office appeal, usu. proportional to its budget, of the physical mounting of a film, such as sets, costumes, **props**, etc.

production-design team *PerfA&C* Producer, director, and scenic, costume, lighting and sound designers who working together, develop the visual/aural concept for the production.

productivity *Eco&Fin, EntreP* Efficiency with which inputs are transformed into **outputs**.

prof. *ArtPerf, Crit&Eval* **professional**.

profane music *MusArts* **Secular** music *Also see* **sacred music**.

professional (prof.) *ArtPerf, Crit&Eval* **1** Engaged in a specific activity as a means of livelihood. **2** Possessing great skill or experience, and considerable ego and ambition: "Humphrey Bogart [1899-1957, film act.] measured all his fellow workers by the test of professionalism, and a professional was a man who can do his best work when he doesn't feel like it." — Alistair Cooke (1908-, Brit-born journ., broadcaster) *Also see* **amateur, competition, EAT+D².**

professional (**visual**) **artist** *ArtPerf, Mktg, VisArts* "I invest my time in art. And most of all I never give away a work. That's for amateurs. The professional thinks in terms of selling." — John McCrory (pntr.)

professional agent *LegAsp* **Independent contractor** who is considered a professional. *Also see* **Agents and Agencies.**

Professional and Administrative Staff Association (Pasta) *HR&LR, VisArts* Museum of Modern Art's (NYC) union of professional employees.

professional courtesy *Genl* Charge is discounted or free.

professional critic *Crit&Eval* One who has the job. "A professional critic is a man who in dealing with a work of art creates a little work of art in its honor." — **John Crowe Ransom**

professional dancers *Dnce* "Even the most famous of professional dancers begins the day as a student: by taking class."— Cobbett Steinberg (dance critic)

professional directors and screenwriters *Flm&Vid, LitArts, TheatArts* "Many of them are eager to earn piles of money, and do so. But their professional lives are torn between wheeling and dealing on the one hand, and viewing themselves, on the other, as serious artists surviving in a sea of sharks."— Bernard Weinraub (ent. critic) *Also see* **Directors.**

professional ethics *Ethcs&Phil* Code of conduct that applies to the practice of a profession. The ethical actions of a profession are a collection of individual actions.

professional league *SportsEnt* Regulatory body made up of several privately owned teams practicing the same sport and based in various cities. A league allocates a territorial market to an individual member team, eliminating intra league competition for the sports consumer within the territory. At the same time, the league expands to cover the major population centers in the country. Each league is a form of monopoly, sometimes operating under an exemption to the anti trust regulation (**Sherman Act**, 1890) Each member team is an independent legal entity. However, each must sign a league agreement, submit to league rules, and must remain within the league to stay in business.

professional musicians *ArtPerf, MusArts* "I don't recommend going into music to anybody…. Music is only for musicians, it's not for the average guy, it's for somebody who loves that music so much he doesn't care whether he makes a dollar, a dime, a penny, or nothing at all." — Roland Hanna (1932-, jazz pno., comp.) *Also see* **motivate.**

professional sport *SportsEnt* Implies participants are financially compensated for their talents and services. There are four major professional sports leagues in the USA: football — **NFL**; basketball — **NBA** and **ABL**; baseball — **NL** and **AL**; and hockey — **NHL** There are professional **tours** in golf, tennis, ice skating, beach volleyball, bowling, skiing, boxing, auto-racing and horse racing. Professional sport leagues also exist in indoor and outdoor soccer, women's basketball, lacrosse and roller hockey. The first all-professional sport team in America was the Cincinnati Red Stockings baseball team est. 1869. As America's oldest professional sport, baseball has provided a model of labor relations upon which the other major sports are patterned.

profile *LitArts* Biographical essay presenting the subject's most noteworthy characteristics and achievements.

profit *Eco&Fin, EntreP* **1** Absolute number (actual dollar value) that is earned on an investment. **2** Return received on a business undertaking after all operating expenses have been met. *Also see* **net profit, gross profit.**

profit and loss (**P&L**) *E&F-Acc* Account showing net profit and loss over a given period.

profit and loss statement (**P&L**) *E&F-Acc* Summary of the revenue, costs, and expenses of an organization during an accounting period. *Also see* **income statement, Statements.**

profit and loss statement (income statement) *EntreP* Financial report showing the profit or loss from a company's operations over a given period of time.

profit center *Eco&Fin, Mktg* Organizational unit whose revenues and costs are clearly identifiable and whose management is responsible for controlling both income and expenses.

profit margin *E&F-Acc* Shows the percentage of each sales dollar that produced income. Profit margin = **net income ÷ net sales.** MARGIN OF PROFIT

profit participation *Flm&Vid* **Contingent compensation** (either percentages or fixed sums) offered to talent as an incentive, or in recognition of their contribution to the quality and commerciality of the product. Participation deals may be based on anything from **gross receipts** to **net profits**, depending on individual negotiations. *Also see* **gross profit participation, net profit participation.**

profit sharing *Eco&Fin, HR&LR* System by which employees receive a share of the profits of a business enterprise. *Also see* **ESOP.**

profitability *E&F-Acc* Ability to save a satisfactory income. As a goal, profitability compares with **liquidity** for managerial attention because **liquid assets** (cash, accounts receivable), while important, are not the best profit producing resources. Most common measures are profit margin, **asset turnover**, return on assets, **debt to equity**, and return on equity.

profitability ratios *E&F-Acc* Measure of performance that indicate what the company is earning on its sales or equity. *Also see* **operating profit margin, net profit margin, gross profit margin, ratios, return on total assets, return on equity.**

profiteer *Ethcs&Phil, Mktg* One who makes excessive profits on goods in short supply.

proforma projected *EntreP* As in proforma balance sheets, income statements, or cash flow statements.

program *InfoMgt* **1** Series of instructions to a computer that causes the computer to solve a problem or perform a task. **2** Such a procedure coded for a computer.

program *PerfA&C* **1** Listing of the order of events and other pertinent information for a public presentation. **2** The presentation itself.

program *Rdio/TV* Scheduled radio or television show.

program amount *Fnding* Funds that are expended to support a particular program administered internally by the foundation or corporate giving program.

program director *Rdio/TV* Radio or TV station director responsible for selecting, planning, and scheduling programs. *Also see* **Directors.**

Program Evaluation Review Technique *iMedia* » **PERT**

program music *MusArts* Compositions intended – or are interpreted – to depict or suggest definite incidents, scenes, or images.

program officer *Fnding* Staff member of a foundation who reviews grant proposals and processes applications for the board of trustees. Only a small percentage of foundations have program officers. *Also see* **grantees.**

program-related investment (PRI) *Fnding* Loan or other investment (as distinguished from a grant) made by a foundation or corporate giving program to another organization for a project related to the grantmaker's stated charitable purpose and interests. Program-related investments are often made from a **revolving fund**; the foundation generally expects to receive its money back with interest or some other form of return at less than current market rates, and it then becomes available for further program-related investments.

Programmable Read Only Memory *InfoMgt* » **PROM**

programmer, programer *InfoMgt* One who writes **computer programs.**

programming *MusArts* Process of choosing and sequencing musical selections to be performed in concert or on a recording; program a new musical composition.

programming *Rdio/TV* Designing, scheduling, or planning of a program.

programming language *InfoMgt* » **a programming language**

Programming Languages *ColEntry, InfoMgt* » **BASIC, C, C plus plus** (C++), **Cobol, Java, Pascal, UNIX.** *Also see* **Operating Systems.**

progression *MusArts* **1** Succession of **tones** or **chords. 2** Series of repetitions of a phrase, each in a new position on the **scale.** <the

II, V, VII **progression**>

progressive margins *VA-Prntng* Page setup where the bottom margin is largest, outside margin is smaller, top margin still smaller, and the gutter is smallest.

progressive rendering *InfoMgt* **Download** method where the file begins to display itself before the download is completed.

progressive tax *E&F-Acc* One that becomes larger as the amount of taxable income increases. This represents the current income tax system.

Prohibition *Law&Pol* Period (1920-33) during which the manufacture and sale of alcoholic beverages was forbidden in the U.S. by the 18th Amendment. *Also see* **Repeal, speakeasy, Storyville.**

project *Crit&Eval* **1** Plan or proposal; a scheme. **2** Undertaking requiring concerted effort.

project funds *Fndng* Funds used to fund a specific project. *Also see* **operating funds**.

projection *Eco&Fin* Estimate of future performance.

projection booth *Flm&Vid* Booth or room in the rear of a theater from which a movie projector is operated.

projectionist *Flm&Vid* One who operates a movie projector.

projector *Flm&Vid* Machine for projecting an image onto a screen.

projst. *Flm&Vid* **projectionist**

prole-theatre *TheatArts* Workers-theatre Theatre company devoted to proletarian drama, i.e., working-class drama. <**Group Theater**>

proletariat *Cult&Soc, Eco&Fin* **1** Class of industrial wage earners who, possessing neither capital nor production means, must earn their living by selling their labor. **2** Poorest class of working people.

prolific *Crit&Eval* Producing abundant works or results. <prolific artist, prolific composer>

prolog *InfoMgt* Programming language used for writing programs that model human thinking. *Also see* **artificial intelligence; CRCC.**

prologue, prolog *LitArts* Introduction or introductory chapter, as to a novel.

prologue, prolog *TheatArts* Introductory speech or **monologue** delivered by an actor before a play, which prepares the audience for what ensues.

PROM *InfoMgt* **Programmable Read Only Memory** Form of memory programed by the manufacturer that cannot be reprogrammed.

promissory note (P/N) *E&F-Acc* Written promise to pay or repay a specified sum of money at a stated time or on demand. — note of hand.

promo *Mktg, RecA&S* **1** Promotional literature. **2** Audition recording used to promote financing and distribution.

promo kit *Mktg* » **press kit**

promo pack *Mktg* » **press kit**

promo person, promo man *RecA&S* One hired by a record company, or by an independent promotion company, to convince a radio station manager, or disco club manager, to play the label's current release. [Very competitive, stressful, unlimited-hours job requiring a constitutional immunity to **rejection**.] *Also see* **airplay, payola, plugola, song plugger.**

promoed *Mktg* Promoted as in **hyped**

promote *Mgt* To help establish or organize a new enterprise by securing financial backing. <promote a **Broadway** show>

promote *Mktg* To attempt to sell or popularize by advertising or publicity.

promoter *Mgt,PerfA&C* **1** Primary financial guarantor for an event; a backer. **2** Publicity organizer of an entertainment. *Also see* **angel.**

promotion (promo) *Mktg* Advertising; publicity.

promotional activities *Mktg* Various nonrecurrent selling efforts, usu. short-term. <contests, **discount coupons**, special displays, and introductory offers>

promotional mix *EntreP* Blend of personal and nonpersonal communication techniques aimed at a target market.

prompt *InfoMgt* Message cue provided by the computer to guide the user.

prompt *PerfA&C* To assist an actor by providing the next words of a forgotten **passage**; **cue**.

prompt book *PerfA&C* **1** Copy of the script with details about each actor's blocking as well as the location, timing, and as necessary, action, of all set, prop, light, and sound **cues**. **2** Play text containing production notes and cues for the use of the **stage manager** or the **prompter**.

prompter *PerfA&C* One who gives **cues** to actors or opera singers.

prompter's box *PerfA&C* Covered opening, facing the performers, in the floor of a stage **apron** in which the **prompter** is housed.

promulgated agreement *HR&LR* Contract that one party writes – usu. the union – which mirrors existing **collective bargaining** agreements for the use of companies new to a relationship with the union.

pronouncer *BcstJourn* Phonetic spelling of a word in a broadcast story. Usually the pronouncer is broken into syllables and placed in the copy behind the true spelling of the word. *Ex.* 'King Abu Saud (SAH-AH-UDE)' The pronouncer is the writer's responsibility.

proof (prf.), **proof sheet** *iMedia, VA-Prntng* Trial sheet of printed material checked against the original manuscript and on which corrections are made.

proof (prf.) *VisArts* Trial impression of a **plate**, **stone**, or **block** taken at any of various stages in engraving.

proof-of-purchase *Mktg* Document, such as a sales slip or a product label, that is valid evidence for claiming a refund or a premium.

proofread *Journ, LitArts, VA-Prntng* To read copy or proof for purposes of error detection and correction. *Also see* **edit.**

proofreaders' marks *VA-Prntng* Marks made on **galleys** or on **proofs** by the proofreader to the typesetter or printer.

prop, prop. *Flm&Vid,PerfA&C* » **property**

propaganda *Ethcs&Phil* **Secular** or religious beliefs spread here or abroad by advocates of a **doctrine**.

properties *PerfA&C* Such elements as furniture, lamps, pictures, table linens, **bric-a-brac** and window draperies that provide the finished set with visual character.

property *Crit&Eval* **1** Characteristic trait or peculiarity, esp. one serving to define or describe its possessor. **2** Characteristic attribute possessed by all members of a class.

property (prop, prop) *Flm&Vid,PerfA&C* **1** Article, except costumes and scenery, that appears on the stage or on screen during a dramatic performance. **2** Anything with a profit-making potential, although generally used to describe a screenplay, novel, short story, etc. *Also see* **props.**

property *Genl* Something owned <a possession>

property *IntelProp* Something tangible or intangible to which its owner – usu. the creator – has legal title. <**copyrights** and **trademarks**> *Also see* **intellectual property.**

property, plant, and equipment *Eco&Fin* **Tangible assets**, fixed or permanent, used in the continuing operation of the owner. FIXED ASSETS, PLANT ASSETS

proportion *iMedia* Agreeable relation of parts within a whole.

proportional spacing *VA-Prntng* Typeface in which narrow letters such as *i* and *j* occupy less space than wide letters such *m* and *w*.

proportional tax *E&F-Acc* One in which the rate is the same percentage regardless of income. <most sales taxes and the Illinois state income tax>

proportionate giving *Fndng* Giving commensurate with the prospective donor's age, family commitments, and overall economic resources.

proposal *Fnding* Written application, often with supporting documents, submitted to a foundation or corporate giving program i requesting a grant. Preferred procedures and formats vary. Consult published guidelines. *Also see* **presentation.**

proposal *iMedia, Mgt* Document that states the goal of an interactive media project how that goal will be accomplished. interactive media proposal usu. includes: pre-production strategies (goals and objectives, target audience, success measurement, etc.), design strategy (structure – navigational and content, technologies to be used, visual — look and feel, etc.), production strategy (types of media and technologies to be used, pseudo-code, database-structure, etc.) In addition, commercial proposals often include: an executive summary containing a brief description of development methods and costs, qualifications of developer(s) and company, delivery methods, projected timeline, quality assurance and testing strategies, and terms and conditions.

proprietary foundation *Fndng* Foundation in which the donor or donor's spouse is actively involved.

proprietary systems *InfoMgt, Journ* Special word processing systems designed for high quality publishing.

proprietary tag *iMedia* Tags created by a company which usu. do not conform to standards.

proprieties *Cult&Soc* Customs of polite society.

proprietor (prop., propr.) *LegAsp, Mgt* **1** One who has legal **title** to something; an owner. **2** One who owns or owns and manages a business or other such establishment. *Also see* **sole proprietor**.

proprietorship *LegAsp, Mgt* Business with a single owner.

propriety *Cult&Soc* **Conformity** to current customs. *Also see* **impropriety**. PROPRIETIES

props *Cult&Soc*, *MusArts* Rapper's desire: recognition and respect.

props *TheatArts* **property**, properties. Some objects other than costumes and scenery, used by the actors in a theatrical performance. <telephone, food, gun, etc> *Also see* **hand props**.

prosaic *Crit&Eval* **1** Matter-of-fact; straightforward. **2** Lacking in imagination and spirit; dull.

proscenium, proscenium arch *PerfA&C* Frames the opening through which the audience views the acting area. *Also see* **Stages**.

prose *Crit&Eval* Ordinary speech or writing, without **metrical** structure.

prose poem *LitArts* Prose work that has poetic characteristics such as vivid imagery and concentrated expression.

proselytize *Crit&Eval* To induce someone to join one's own political party, religious affiliation, or **secular doctrine**.

prosody *InfoMgt* In voice **synthesis**: a particular system of **versification**.

prosody *LitArts* Study of the metrical structure of verse.

prospect *Mktg* Potential customer, client, or purchaser.

prospect rating *Fndng* Procedure for evaluating the giving potentials of various prospects by the judgments of knowledgeable persons, functioning as a special campaign committee.

prospect research *Fndng* Continuing search by development personnel for new and pertinent information about current and prospective donors, utilizing numerous interviews and reference sources.

prospecting *EntreP* Systematic process of continually looking for new customers.

prospectus *EntreP, Mgt* Document describing the chief features of a business, an educational program, or esp. a stock offering or mutual fund, for prospective buyers, investors, or participants.

prosthesis *Th-MakeUp* Device for creating a **three-dimensional** addition to the face, neck, and hands.

prostitute (art) *Ethcs&Phil* One who sells one's abilities, judgment, talent, or reputation for an unworthy purpose.

protagonist *LitArts, TheatArts* main character in a drama or other literary work

protean *Crit&Eval* Assuming or exhibiting considerable variety or diversity of shapes, forms, or meanings.

protectionism *Law&Pol, Mktg* Advocacy, system, or theory of protecting domestic producers by impeding or limiting, by tariffs or quotas, the importation of foreign goods and services. *Also see* **free trade**.

protege *Genl* One whose training, or career is promoted by an influential person.

protocol *iMedia, InfoMgt* **1** Set of formal specifications used for transmitting telecommunications messages. **2** Technique by which an online sender and receiver can validate the integrity of transmitted data. *Also see* **line noise**. *Also see* **Protocols**.

Protocols *ColEntry, InfoMgt* **File Transfer Protocol** (FTP), **Internet Protocol** (IP), **Hypertext Transfer Protocol** (HTTP), **Network News Transfer Protocol** (NNTP), **Point-to-Point Protocol** (PPP), **Simple Mail Transfer Protocol** (SMTP), **Transfer Protocol Program** (TCP), **Serial-Line Internet Protocol** (SLIP)

prototype *Fashn* Original design or garment that serves as a model on which later designs or garments are judged.

prototype *Genl* Early, typical example

prototype *iMedia* Rough draft of an interactive piece, usu. created first on paper, used for testing and further design decisions.

Once a paper prototype is approved, a functional prototype is created in a technology similar to, or which is a possible candidate for, the final product.

provenance (prohven-ahnts, Fr.) *VisArts* Proof of authenticity or of past ownership of art works and antiques. *Also see* **attribution**.

Provincetown Players (1916-29) *TheatArts* Theatre company began at Provincetown, Mass., later associated with **Greenwich Village Theatre** (NYC) Premiered several plays of **Eugene O'Neill** and other high quality, "noncommercial" plays. *Also see* **Theaters & Theatres**.

proximity *iMedia* One of **Gestalt Laws** of pattern perception: things close together are perceptually grouped together:

PRSA *Mktg* **Public Relations Society of America**. Professional society of public relations practitioners in business and industry, counseling firms, government, associations, hospitals, schools and **nonprofit** organizations. Conducts professional development programs. Maintains job referral services, speakers bureaus and research information center. *Also see* **IPRA**.

prude *Crit&Eval* One excessively concerned with being or appearing to be proper. PRUDISH *Also see* **prig**.

prudence *Ethcs&Phil* Sometimes called "practical wisdom," the virtue which recognizes what is good and bad in human affairs, and acts to assure the good and avoid the bad.

prurient *Crit&Eval* Arousing or appealing to an inordinate interest in sex. <prurient films, literature, etc>

PSA *Mktg, Rdio/TV* Public service announcement. Message from a **nonprofit** broadcast at no charge.

psalm, Psalms *MusArts* Sacred song; a hymn. David (b.??, d. ca. 962 BC, second king of Judah and Israel) is the reputed author of many of the Psalms. *Also see* **Songs**.

pseudo *Crit&Eval* false, phony

pseudo-event *Journ* Event caused to occur or staged to engender press coverage and public interest. *Also see* **photo op**.

pseudocode *iMedia* Instructions written in human readable language, not yet converted to a programming language for computer interpreting.

pseudonym (pseud.) *Genl* Fictitious name. PEN NAME

pseudonymous work *IntelProp* Work by an artist or author using a fictitious name. *Also see* **anonymous work**.

PSI *InfoMgt* » **Performance Systems International**

psyche *Crit&Eval* spirit, soul.

psychedelic *Crit&Eval* **1** Characterized by hallucinations, distortions of perception, altered states of awareness, and occasionally states resembling **psychosis**. **2** Drug, such as **LSD** that produces such effects.

psychedelic rock *MusArts* » **acid rock** *Also see* **Rock Music Styles**.

psychic *Crit&Eval* Of, relating to, affecting, or influenced by the human mind or psyche.

psychoacoustics *Sci&Tech* Scientific study of the perception of sound. *Also see* **acoustics**.

psychobiography *LitArts* Biography that analyzes the psychological makeup, character, or motivations of its subject.

psychographics *iMedia, Mktg* Psychological and subjective profiles of an audience's **lifestyle** used by marketers to learn why their products or services are (not) purchased or used. *Also see* **demographics**.

psychological pricing strategy *Mktg* One that caters to the consumer's irrational buying psychology. <$4^{95} rather than $5^{00}. $10^{99} rather than $11^{00}> *Also see* **Pricing Strategies**.

pub. *InfoMgt, LitArts, Mktg, MusArts* publication, published, publicity

publ *InfoMgt, Journ, LitArts, MusArts, VA-Prntng* publisher

public access *Cult&Soc, Rdio/TV* Availability of television or radio broadcast facilities, as provided by law, for use by the public for presentation of programs of community interest.

Public Broadcasting Act of 1967 *Rdio/TV* "A Congressional act signed by President Johnson to create the **Public Broadcasting System** from the originally FCC-allocated stations. This network of about 80 **VHF** stations and 160 **UHF** stations was est. 1952 and became known as the **National Education Network** (NET) Act also created the **Corporation for Public Broadcasting**. This organization channels government funds to stations and also helps to secure additional funding from the private and public sectors, esp. foundation funding." — Edmund F. Penney (comm. wri.)*Also see* **Broadcast Stations & Networks, Federal Agencies and Statutes.**

Public Broadcasting System (PBS)*Rdio/TV* » **Public Broadcasting Act of 1967**

public charity *Fnding* In general, an organization that is tax-exempt under code section **501**(c)(**3**) and is classified by the *IRS* as a public charity, not a **private foundation**. Public charities generally derive their funding or support primarily from the general public in carrying out their social, educational, religious, or other charitable activities serving the common welfare. Some public charities engage in grantmaking activities, although most engage in direct service or other tax-exempt activities. Public charities are eligible for maximum income tax-deductible contributions from the public and are not subject to the same rules and restrictions as private foundations. Some are also referred to as "public foundations" or "publicly supported organizations" and may use the term "foundation" in their names.

public domain (PD) *IntelProp* Product, publication, process, or computer software unprotected by copyright or **patent**, and thus is freely available for use by anyone. Except for works eligible for restoration of copyright, once a work falls into PD, it cannot be recaptured by the owner. *Also see* **generic name, music licensing, term of copyright.**

public interest *Law&Pol* **1** Well-being of the general public. **2** Attention of the people with respect to events or occurrences.

public interest*Rdio/TV* Part of the phrase "public interest, convenience, and necessity" that was the legal obligation of broadcasters in their use of the public airwaves before deregulation was begun by **Jimmy Carter** and well-nigh completed in the **Reagan-Bush** administrations.

public offering *EntreP* Offering of stock to the general public that is usually handled by investment bankers. » **initial public offering**

public opinion *Crit&Eval* Public consensus with respect to an issue or a situation.

public policy *Cult&Soc, Law&Pol* Basic policy or set of policies forming the foundation of public laws, esp. such policy not yet formally enunciated. **1** "We... condemn the use of public funds to subsidize **obscenity** and **blasphemy** masquerading as art. No artist has the inherent right to claim taxpayer support for her or his private vision of art if that vision mocks the moral and spiritual basis on which our society is founded." — Republican Party platform (1996) **2** "It's a pleasure to come down to Washington and speak in support of the **National Endowment for the Arts,** one of the wisest and happiest pieces of legislation ever to come through Congress. I'm grateful to those who have so ably attacked the Endowment over the past year or so for making it necessary to defend it. I enjoy controversy and I recognize the adversary: they are us." — Garrison Keillor (1942-, humorist, broadcaster, essayist)*Also see* **NEA, NEH.**

public relations (P.R., p.r.)*Mktg* **1** Managing of public perceptions of individuals and organizations, and their products, by making available newstories and press releases or by interacting directly with opinion leaders. **2** "Management function of a continued and planned character through which... institutions [and individuals] seek to win and retain the understanding, sympathy, and support of those whom they are or may be concerned." — **International Public Relations Association** (IPRA) *Also see* **image, image-maker, PRSA.**

Public Relations Society of America (PRSA) *Mktg*» **PRSA** *Also see* **IPRA.**

public service advertising *Mktg* Advertising produced and distributed **pro bono** by advertising agencies and media; usu. for noncontroversial messages and issues. <Cancer Society, Red Cross>

public service announcement (PSA) *Mktg, Rdio/TV* » **PSA**

public service announcement music *IntelProp, MusArts* Permission to use music or lyrics on a **PSA** is usu. given at no charge or for minimal fee.

public television*Rdio/TV* Noncommercial television that provides programs, esp. of an educational nature, for the public. **EDUCATIONAL TELEVISION**

public use doctrine *LegAsp* Patent may not be granted if the invention was used by the public for more than one year before filing the patent application.

Public Works Administration (PWA) *Law&Pol* » **PWA**

public-address system *RecA&S* One or more microphones, amplifiers, and loudspeakers.

publication (pub.) *IntelProp* Publication is the distribution of copies of a work of art or **phonorecords** of a sound recording to the public by sale or some other means of transferring ownership, such as renting, leasing, lending, or even giving the work away. Public performance of the work – singing a song, acting a play, dancing a choreographed work – is not considered publication because there is no transfer of ownership. <The **Working Group on Intellectual Property Rights** has stated that publication may occur if a sufficient number of copies of a work were offered to an online service for **upload** onto the **NII**> However, merely performing a new song in public doesn't "publish" it.

publication (pub.) *MusArts, RecA&S* When a copy of sheet music or a **phonorecord** is sold or distributed, songs (musical works) in it are considered published.

publication date *LitArts* Usually found on the same page in a book that has the date of copyright.

Publication Rights Clearinghouse (PRC) *IntelProp, Journ, Lit* Collective-licensing agency owned by the **National Writers Union** (NWU) *Also see* **Copyright-Related Organizations.**

publicist*Mktg* One who publicizes <**press agent**> *Also see* **music publicist, music business publicist.** <"A publicist's job is to protect, defend, and inflate the client's life and career, via the media, while at the same time reducing or eliminating the person's unflattering aspects (process currently known as lying) — Lawrence Eisenberg (19??-; publicist)>

publicity*EntreP* Information about a company and its products or services that appears as a news item, free of charge. [However, it sometimes happens that advertiser's products or services receive favored treatment] *Also see* **advertising, infomercial.**

publicity (pub.) *InfoMgt, Mktg* **1** Information about a person, a group, an event, or a product disseminated through various media to attract public notice. **2** Public interest, notice, or notoriety achieved by the spreading of such information.

publish (pub.) *Genl* To bring to the public attention; announce.

publish (pub.) *InfoMgt* When a **floppy disk** is sold or distributed, the software on it is considered published.

publish (pub.) *Mktg* **1** To prepare and issue a book for public distribution or sale; to author a published work.

publish (pub.) *MusArts* To compose and issue printed or recorded music for public distribution or sale.

publish (pub.) *VA-Prntng* To prepare and issue printed material for public distribution or sale.

publisher *InfoMgt* Material in a document that you want to update automatically in other documents (**subscribers**) When you designate a publisher in a document, a special file is created. User inserts the edition into the subscribing documents.

publisher (pub.) *Journ, Mgt, MusArts, VA-Prntng* Owner or the owner's representative in charge of all phases of publishing **print media** or music, usu. acquired from the author via assignment of copyright. *Also see* **self publisher.**

publisher's editorial profile *Journ* Statement by a periodical's publisher in the **SRDS** advertising rate directory that outlines the periodical's editorial policy and its commitment to its primary and secondary target markets.

Publisher's Statement *Journ, Mktg* Newspapers and magazines that belong to the **Audit Bureau of Circulations** (ABC) issue a sworn statement twice a year detailing their **paid circulation,** inc. the number of copies sold on newsstands (**single copy sales**), and by subscription in each state and each geographical market region.

publisher-producer *RecA&S* Music publishers may produce their own recordings in order to best exploit their own copyrights. *Also see* **Producers.**

Publishers Marketing Association (PMA) *Mktg*» **PMA**

public-address system *RecA&S* Electronic apparatus with amplifiers, microphones, and loudspeakers for broadcasting in public or performing areas.

puff *Crit&Eval, Mktg* Exaggerated praise – as on the **jacket** of a book – used for promotional purposes. *Also see* **blurb, hype.**

Pulitzer *Journ, LitArts, MusArts, TheatArts, VisArts* » **Pulitzer**

Prize

Pulitzer Prize *Journ, LitArts, MusArts, TheatArts, VisArts (Cartooning)* Annual awards by the president of Columbia University on the recommendation of the Pulitzer Prize Board. Endowed by **Joseph Pulitzer** (1847-1911), publisher of the *New York World*. "In 1965 the Pulitzer Prize advisory committee voted unanimously that **[Duke Ellington]** be given an award for long-term achievements, and the Columbia University committee that controlled the award refused to accept the recommendation." — **Eileen Southern** *Also see* **Awards & Prizes.**

pulp *LitArts, VA-Prntng* Magazine or book printed on **newsprint,** usu. containing **lurid** and sensational subject matter.

pulpit *PerfA&C* Elevated platform, **lectern,** or stand used in preaching or **exhortation.** *Also see* **dais, rostrum.**

pulse *InfoMgt* Brief variation of electric current as a signal.

pulse *MusArts* "Feeling of rhythmic continuity and momentum whether or not the beat is stated explicitly." — Lyons & Perlo (jazz critics)

punch in *InfoMgt, RecA&S* To depress a key or button to activate a device or perform an operation. <punch in a note or a musical phrase in the mixing console>

punch line *PerfA&C* Climax of a joke or a funny story.

punch up *InfoMgt* Select, organize, and retrieve personalized information. "People are going to be able to turn on their computers and basically punch up their own newscasts." — Les Blatt (ABC News)

punch up *Journ* Inject more life into the article or story.

punk *Cult&Soc* Style of dress by punk rockers and their **devotees,** typified by **bizarre** make-up and outlandish, shocking clothing.

punk rock *Cult&Soc, MusArts* Hard-driving rock music marked by extremely bitter treatment of alienation and social discontent. *Also see* **leather boy, Rock Music Styles.**

punt *InfoMgt* Term for being disconnected during an online session.

punto de guajiro *MusArts* Improvisational Cuban or Venezuelan verses accompanied by guitar, flute, **guiro** and **clave.**

puppet *PA-Variety* Figure with a cloth body and a hollow head, designed to be fitted over and manipulated by hand usu. from under the miniature stage. *Also see* **marionette.**

puppeteer *PA-Variety* One who operates and entertains with **puppets** or **marionettes.**

puppetry *PA-Variety* Art of making puppets and presenting puppet shows.

purchase discounts *E&F-Acc* **General ledger** account used to record discounts against purchases from venders; *aka* **contra purchase account.**

purchase journals *E&F-Acc* Special journal used to record all purchases of inventory, supplies, and other assets on account. *Also see* **Journals.**

purchases *E&F-Acc* **General ledger** account that identifies all purchases made for retail goods in a given period. *Also see* **temporary (nominal) account.**

purchasing *EntreP* Process of obtaining materials, equipment, and services from outside suppliers.

pure risk *Eco&Fin, EntreP, Mgt* Risks of loss (related to **insurance**) that are mathematically predictable. <explosion, fire, flood, product failure, wind, etc> To be a pure risk the potential loss must be predictable, and only involves the question of loss or no loss. *Also see* **risk management.**

purge the cache *InfoMgt* To delete the files the **Web** browser has stored (**cached**) on the user's disk.

puritanism *Crit&Eval* Scrupulous moral rigor, hostility to social pleasures and indulgences. "The haunting fear that someone, somewhere may be happy." — **H.L. Mencken**

push technology *InfoMgt* "How [**content providers**] supposedly mean to deliver automatically bucketloads of information to every computer user's **desktop,** freeing the user to stop **surfing** the internet in search of stuff to pull." — Seth Schiesel (comp. journ)

push the envelope *Crit&Eval, Sci&Tech* To increase the operating capabilities of a technological system.

push/pull hypothesis *EntreP* Theory that entrepreneurs are either pulled, or enticed, into starting a venture, or pushed, or forced, into starting it. The pull is a positive reason; the push is a negative reason.

pushing film *Flm&Vid* Laboratory process in which film underex-

posed during the production process is corrected in the lab.

putz (putts, Yinglish) *Crit&Eval* fool, an idiot, a penis.

PWA *Law&Pol* **Public Works Administration.** Federal agency est. 1933-mid 1940s by the **New Deal** administration of **President Franklin Roosevelt** to promote employment and increase public purchasing power. Program provided employment for a consideration number of artisans and artists. *Also see* **boondoggle, Federal Agencies and Statutes.**

Pythagoras (ca. sixth century B.C.) *Ethcs&Phil, Sci&Tech* Greek philosopher and mathematician who founded a school that emphasized the study of musical harmony; considered the first true mathematician. *Also see* **music of the spheres.**

- Q -

Q&A *BcstJourn* Live question-and-answer session between studio anchor and reporter in the field. *Also:* "debrief."

q., Q., qto *LitArts, VA-Prntng* **quarto**

QA *iMedia* » **quality assurance**

quad *RecA&S* **quadraphonic**

quadraphonic sound (quad) *RecA&S* Relating to a **four-channel sound** system in which speakers are positioned at all four corners of the listening space, reproducing signals that are independent of each other. [Introduced in 1971 with much hype but poor sales. Not enough people believed that stereo times two should equal the cost of four speakers.].

quadroon *Cult&Soc* Person having one-quarter Black ancestry. *Also see* **octoroon.**

qualified privilege *Journ, LegAsp* **Media** cannot be sued for **libel** for stories about elected officials while speaking in their official **venues** if the stories are presented in a fair, reasonable manner and as accurately as possible.

qualifying distributions *Fnding* Expenditures of **private foundations** used to satisfy the annual payout requirement. These can include grants, reasonable administrative expenses, **set-asides,** loans and program-related investments, and amounts paid to acquire assets used directly in carrying out exempt purposes.

quality *Fashn* Degree or grade of excellence with reference to yard goods.

quality *MusArts* **Timbre,** as determined by **overtones.**

quality assurance *iMedia* Specific strategies and techniques that assure that a product is fulfilling its requirements and meeting its goals and objectives.

quality circles *Mgt* Quality control method patterned after Japanese models. Groups of employees from various related work areas meet regularly on company time to define, analyze, and solve common product and production problems. Used frequently in **participative management** programs.

Quality Value Control *Rdio/TV* » **QVC**

quantifiable *Crit&Eval* To determine or express the quantity of.

quantitative studies *Mktg* Market research conducted by mail or telephone utilizing a detailed questionnaire to determine market overviews, attitudes, product or service usage, and possible market segmentation.

quarter note *MusArts* Note having one quarter the time value of a whole note and twice that of an eighth note. *Also see* **Musical Notes.**

quartet *MusArts* **1** Composition of four parts or voices. **2** Four singers or four instrumentalists.

quarto (q., Q., qto.) *LitArts, VA-Prntng* Page size of a book obtained by folding a whole sheet into four **leaves.**

quasi-contract *LegAsp* In the absence of an **actual contract,** a contract is implied to exist if (1) one party confers a benefit on another who keeps the benefit, and (2) it would be unjust not to require that person to pay for the benefit received. *Also see* **Contracts.**

quaver *MusArts* To produce a **trill** on an instrument or with the voice. *Also see* **vibrato.**

query *iMedia* User's (or agent's) request for information, generally as a formal request to a database or search engine.

query letter *Fnding* Brief letter outlining an organization's activities and its request for funding sent to a foundation or corporation to determine whether it would be appropriate for that organization to submit a full grant **proposal.** Many grantmakers prefer to be contacted in this way before receiving a full proposal.

question lead *BcstJourn* Lead sentence that begins with a rhetorical question. Avoid!.

question mark *Eco&Fin* **Strategic business unit** not yet classified as a **cash cow, dog,** or **star.**

quick and dirty *Flm&Vid* Film print used for reference purposes only with no concern for quality and that audio and video are in **sync.**

quick assets *Eco&Fin* **Liquid assets,** inc. cash on hand and assets readily convertible to cash. *Also see* **Assets.**

quick ratio *E&F-Acc* Ratio of current assets excluding inventory, divided by current liabilities; also a measure of **liquidity** (quick ratio = current assets - inventory/current liabilities) ACID test.

quick response *Fashn* Computer strategy to reduce the waiting time in ordering and distribution among textile and apparel producers and retailers.

quick study *Flm&Vid, TheatArts* Said of a performer who learns lines and **blocking** swiftly.

quickie *Flm&Vid* **1** Derogatory term for a hastily conceived and executed production. **2** Film or videotape put together rapidly and released on a short schedule to save money or to make a release deadline.

quickie book *LitArts, Mktg*» **instant book**

quid pro quo (Latin for "what for what") *Genl* Equal exchange or substitution.

quiet *Crit&Eval, VisArts* Not showy or **garish**; restrained. <a room or scene painted in quiet colors> *Also see* **silence.**

quintessential *Crit&Eval* Most typical. <Vladimir Horowitz (1904-89, Russ.-born pno.) was the quintessential **Romantic** pianist>

quintet *MusArts* **1** Composition of five voices or instruments. **2** Five singers or five instrumentalists.

quip *Crit&Eval* Clever, witty remark often prompted by the occasion. QUIPSTER. *Also see* **ad-lib.**

quirk *Crit&Eval* **1** Peculiarity of behavior, an **idiosyncrasy. 2** Unpredictable or unaccountable act or event. <a quirk of fate> **3** Sudden sharp turn or twist. QUIBBLE

quiver *Crit&Eval* To shake with a slight, rapid, tremulous movement. *Also see* **vibrate, vibration.**

quiz and game shows *Rdio/TV* Popular type of television network programming. <*Jeopardy, The Price Is Right, Wheel of Fortune*> *Also see* **Television Shows.**

quiz show *Rdio/TV* Radio or television program in which the contestants' knowledge is tested by questioning, with some contestants winning money or prizes.

quota *Fndng* Percentage of a total fund-raising goal assigned to a division or other unit of the campaign organization.

quotation *Crit&Eval* Explicit reference or allusion in an artistic work to a passage or element from another, usu. a well-known work. *Also see* **citation.**

quote *Eco&Fin, Mktg* To state a current price for securities, goods, or services.

quote *Genl* **1** To repeat or copy the words of another, usu. with acknowledgment of the source. **2** To cite or refer to for illustration or proof.

quote *MusArts* To repeat a brief passage or play an **excerpt.** <Wynton Marsalis quoted a **Dizzy Gillespie riff** in his trumpet solo>

quote lead *BcstJourn* Lead sentence that begins with an unattributed quote. Avoid!.

quotidian *Crit&Eval* Everyday, commonplace.

QVC *Rdio/TV* **Quality Value Control.** Home shopping network; zircons unlimited. *Also see* **Broadcast Stations & Networks.**

- R -

r&b, R&B *MusArts* **rhythm and blues** *Also see* **Blues.**

R&D *Sci&Tech* Research and development.

RA *RecA&S* **return authorization**

RAB *Mktg, Rdio/TV* **Radio Advertising Bureau. Ω**

race *Cult&Soc, Law&Pol* **1** Term for the grouping of humans, most commonly with the suggestion of genetic grounds, but sometimes on national, cultural, **linguistic,** or other grounds. <the Irish race, a race of poets> **2** Louis Armstrong regarded **Joe Glaser,** his white manager and agent, as his protector. "If you didn't have a white captain to back you in the old days - to put

his hand on your shoulder - you was just a damn sad nigger.... If a Negro had the proper white man to reach the law and say, 'What the hell you mean locking up MY nigger?' then - quite naturally - the law would walk him free. Get in that jail *without* your white boss, and yonder comes the chain gang." — **Louis Armstrong** [Possibly not politically correct, but an historically accurate commentary on the "good old days."]

race records *Cult&Soc, RecA&S* Term used in the record industry prior to the end of WWII for recordings made by black performers. By the late 1940s, the changing social climate forced a change to **rhythm and blues.** *Origin* First commercial recording of a vocal blues by a Negro was in 1920 when pop singer Mamie Smith (1883-1946, sngr.) recorded *Crazy Blues* for Okeh records, substituting for the ailing, white singing star, Sophie Tucker (1884-1966, Russ.-born pseudo blues sngr.) "*Crazy Blues* broke all records selling more than 7,500 discs a week. Recording companies suddenly realized the vast potential audience among the black population for the blues of Negro singers. Within a year or two, companies were selling 'race records' to blacks [and whites] at the rate of more than five million copies annually." — **Eileen Southern** *Also see* **Jerry Wexler.**

Racial Designations *Cult&Soc* **African-American, Asian, Asian American, Black, Hispanic, Hispanic-American, Latino, Native American, white.**

racism *Cult&Soc* **1** Belief that race accounts for differences in human character or ability and that a particular race is superior to others. **2** Discrimination or prejudice based on race. *Also see* **demagogue.**

rack focusing *Flm&Vid* Blurring of focal planes in sequence that force the viewer's eyes to travel with the areas of the image that remain in sharp focus. SELECTIVE FOCUSING

rack jobber *InfoMgt, Mktg, RecA&S* Distributor of records, tapes, and computer software contracts with large, heavily trafficked retailers for the rental of space for records, tapes, and computer software display racks.

rack up *Rdio/TV* Procedure whereby a technician can preset a succession of audio or video cassettes for orderly broadcast.

RADA *TheatArts* **Royal Academy of Dramatic Art. Ω**

radical *Crit&Eval, Law&Pol* **1** Favoring or effecting fundamental or revolutionary changes in current practices, conditions, or institutions. **2** Departing markedly from the usual or customary. EXTREME.

radio *Rdio/TV* **1** Only nonvisual art form other than music, radio uses sound effects to stimulate the listener's own images of people and objects, time, place, and movement. **2** Wireless transmission through space of electromagnetic **waves** in the approximate **frequency** range from 10 **kilohertz** to 300,000 **megahertz. 2** Transmission of programs for the public by radio broadcast. *Also see* **commercial radio broadcast.**

Radio Advertising Bureau (RAB) *Mktg, Rdio/TV* » **RAB**

radio producer *Rdio/TV* One who supervises the production of a radio program. *Also see* **Producers.**

radio station manager *Rdio/TV* Usually the head of operations, reporting to the president of the station or the network. *Also see* **Managers.**

Radio-Keith-Orpheum (RKO) *Flm&Vid, PA-Variety* » **RKO**

rag *Journ* Newspaper specializing in sensationalism or gossip.

rag *MusArts* **ragtime** tune

rag trade *Fashn* Garment industry

ragged *VA-Prntng* Column of text set with a ragged right margin. *Also see* **flush.**

raglan *Fashn* Sleeve that extends in one piece to the neckline of the garment, with slanted seams from the armhole to the neck.

ragtime *Dnce, MusArts* Dance music form, ca. 1890-1920, similar to early jazz characterized by elaborately syncopated **rhythm** in the melody and a steadily accented **accompaniment.** Written chiefly for the piano, it has been successfully arranged for band and orchestra. *Also see* **Dances.**

rai *MusArts* Pop music of Algerian youth.

rail *Crit&Eval* To express objections or criticisms in bitter, harsh, or abusive language.

rail *PerfA&C* Top or bottom framing member of a **flat.**

railroad tracks *MusArts* (*Jazz*) » **caesura**

rain check *Mktg* Guarantee to a customer that a sale item not immediately available may be purchased later at the sale price. *Also see* **bait and switch**.

rainbird *Flm&Vid* Contraption that simulates rain from an overhead grid of pipes sprouting droplets onto the set.

rainmaker *Eco&Fin* In a company, one who brings in business, i.e., money.

rake *Crit&Eval* One who lives to seduce and abandon women, for any motive, but esp. for pleasure. <Don Juan, a legendary 14th century Spanish nobleman and **libertine**> RAKEHELL

raked stage *PerfA&C* Stage built on an incline that is higher upstage than downstage. *Also see* **Stages**.

RAM *iMedia, InfoMgt* **Random Access Memory**. 1 Memory into which the user can "write," i.e, enter information and instructions and from which the user can "read," i.e, recall data. 2 Computer's working memory into which application programs can be loaded and then executed. *Also see* **ROM**.

ramie *Fashn* Fabric made from the flaxlike fiber of the ramie herb.

ranchera *MusArts* 1 Mexican urban music tradition from the first half of the 20th century with lyrics of betrayal and lost love. 2 Cowboy songs with a polka beat from northern Mexico. *Also see* **norteño**.

Random Access Memory (RAM) *InfoMgt* » **RAM**

random variable *Mktg* Variable whose values are distributed according to a probability distribution.

range *MusArts* Gamut of **tones** that a voice or an instrument is capable of producing. *Also see* **head register**.

Ransom, John Crowe (1888-1974, poet, lit critic) *ArtPerf, Crit&Eval, LitArts* Founder-editor (1939-1959) of the *Kenyon Review*; leading proponent of **New Criticism**. <Chills and Fevers (1924)>

rant *Crit&Eval* To speak in a violent, loud, or vehement manner; **rave**.

rant *InfoMgt* complain

rap *Cult&Soc, MusArts* » **rap music** Origin "It started way back with the Embooees and the Greeolies in Africa with the **praise shouter**. We were at the inauguration of Nelson Mandela in South Africa. The praise shouter opened the ceremony and it's like a group of **troubadours** that rapped in rhythm.... If you think back even with the Ink Spots and the Mills Brothers, there was some form of rap even though it wasn't rhythmic beats and rhythm like rappers now are. The imagination with rappers is the same... as with **be-bop** to me. — **Quincy Jones**

rap-metal *Cult&Soc, MusArts* "Aggressive, hypermacho and extremely lucrative [Sep 2000] new pop- music genre that mixes rap with rock."... "At its best, the current fusion of rap and metal lets people who feel unblessed by the economy express some righteous anger. But more often, it tells people who feel they've been treated badly that it's O.K. to act badly in return." — R.J. Smith (19??-, pop-music critic.) *Also see* **mooks, techno**.

rap music *MusArts* Combination of rhymed lyrics spoken over **rhythm tracks** and **sampling** sounds. Developed by African-American urban disc jockeys in the mid-1970s, who manipulated the records they were playing in dance clubs to make **scratching** rhythms and other sounds, creating a musical **collage**. "Rap lyrics deal with boasting, drug dealing, killers (gangsta rap), and political issues." — Adam Sexton (rap critic) "Rap Music is the language of social protest. He who fails to listen, fails to hear at his own peril." — Warren Beatty (1937-, film act., dir., prod.)

rap session *Genl* Informal discussion among a group of people with similar interests.

rappers *MusArts* "I have been in the studio with dozens and dozens of rappers and 10 minutes before they record, they say let me hear the track. They sit down and write themselves the most amazing, structured, free styling situation you can ever imagine and they go and do it in one or two takes... some of the most creative people I have ever worked with." — **Quincy Jones**

rapt *Crit&Eval* Deeply moved or delighted; enraptured. <As the play enfolded, the audience sat in rapt attention>

rapturous *Crit&Eval* Filled with great joy or rapture; ecstatic.

rara avis (Latin for "rare bird") *Crit&Eval* Rare or unique person or thing. <The Maltese Falcon as described by Dashiel Hammett (1894-1961, detective fictwri.) in the similarly titled book and movie>

raree show *PA-Variety* Exhibition of pictures or objects viewed through a small hole or magnifying glass. *Also see* **peep-show**.

Rashomon *Flm&Vid* Best Foreign Language Film (1972 Oscar) by Japanese film maker, Akira Kurosawa (1910-1998) The story, both surprisingly simple and deceptively complex, tells of a rape of a woman and a murder of a man presented entirely in flashbacks from the perspectives of four narrators. In each of the four versions of the story, the characters and many of the details are the same but the accounts are very different. In the end, the audience is left recognizing only one thing: here is no such thing as an objective truth.

Raskin, Jef *iMedia* Creator of Apple's Macintosh, Canon Cat, and other inventions, and authored *Humane Interface: New Directions for Designing Interactive Systems* (2000)

raspberry (razz) *Crit&Eval* Derisive or contemptuous sound made by vibrating the extended tongue and the lips while exhaling.

raster *iMedia* 1 Set of horizontal lines composed of **pixels**, used to form an image on a cathode-ray tube (CRT) screen. 2 Abbreviation for "raster image." <email me the raster of the client's logo>

raster image *iMedia* Image comprised of data points or **pixels**. *Also see* **bitmap**.

rat pack *Crit&Eval* Closely knit group of people sharing interests. <**Frank Sinatra**, Dean Martin (1917-96, film/TV act., sngr.), Sammy Davis, (1925-90, dncr., pop sngr., film/TV act.), and lesser lights. <comedian Joey Bishop and actor Peter Lawford>

rate card *Mktg* Statement published by an advertising medium – magazine, newspaper, Radio/TV station – that details advertising rates, discounts, deadlines, and production requirements. *Also see* **SRDS**.

rate of return *EntreP* Change in the value of a position between two points in time (end of period beginning of period) scaled by the beginning of period value.

rate of return on common stockholder's equity *Eco&Fin* Net **income** minus preferred dividends, divided by average common stockholders' **equity**. Measure of profitability sometimes called **return on equity**.

rate of return on total assets *E&F-Acc* Sum of **net income** plus **interest expense** divided by **average total assets**. RETURN ON ASSETS

rating *Flm&Vid, RecA&S* Classification of content and treatment, e.g., sex, profanity, and violence. <R-rated movie>

rating *Rdio/TV* Popularity of a radio or TV program as estimated by an audience poll. *Also see* **Arbitron, Nielsen Media Research**.

rating point *Rdio/TV* Each rating point represents 942,000 homes tuned to a particular radio or TV program.

ratio *EntreP* Relationship between two variables expressed as a fraction.

ratio analysis *E&F-Acc* Important way to state meaningful relationships between the components of financial statements. The interpretation of ratio must include a study of the underlying data. Analysis of ratios, makes it possible to point out areas requiring further investigation.

ratio analysis *EntreP* Process used to determine the health of a business as it compares to other companies in the same industry or similar industries. Process makes use of mathematical ratios to express numbers.

rationale *Crit&Eval* Fundamental reasons; the basis.

ratios *E&F-Acc* Computed by financial analysts and used to compare results of a company over a period of time. Also used to compare different companies in the same industry at a point of time. *Also see* **activity ratios, coverage ratios, leverage ratios, liquidity ratios, profitability ratios**.

Rauschenberg, Robert (1925-, pntr.) *ArtPerf, VisArts* Noted for his **collages, photomontages**, and paintings that incorporate photographs and real objects. <*Monogram* (1959)> *Also see* **Muse, printmaking**.

rave *Crit&Eval* 1 Extravagantly enthusiastic opinion or review: 2 To speak wildly, irrationally, or incoherently. *Also see* **rant**.

rave *Cult&Soc MusArts* 1 Sound-and-light dance party often featuring drug cocktails, described by surviving ravers as "awesome." 2 An all-night global dance party bringing people together through dance and techno, house, or other electronically synthesized music based on the principles of love and unity.

raw data *iMedia* Unanalyzed data

R

raw material inventory *Eco&Fin* Raw materials that a company has in storage ready to be manufactured or processed. *Also see* **Inventory Methods**.

raw materials *Eco&Fin* Goods, materials, and packaging items that make up a company's product.

raw talent *Crit&Eval* Powerfully impressive; stark.

rawstock *Flm&Vid* » **stock**

rayon *Fashn* Synthetic textile fiber

razz *Crit&Eval* » **Bronx cheer, raspberry**

razzle-dazzle *Crit&Eval* Dazzling excitement.

razzmatazz *Crit&Eval* Flashy action or display intended to bewilder, confuse, or deceive. **2 ambiguous** or evasive language; double talk. **3 Ebullient** energy.

RCA *Rdio/TV* **Radio Corporation of America**. Founded by **General Electric** (GE) Company in 1919, with **David Sarnoff** as general manager. On 15 Nov. 1926, the **National Broadcasting Corporation** (NBC) was established as the first national radio network by RCA, **GE**, and **Westinghouse Electric Corporation**. NBC owned two semi-independent radio networks: the **Blue Network** based on **WJZ** (Newark, NJ) and the **Red Network** based on **WEAF** (NYC) About 1990 GE reacquired RCA and **NBC**.

RCA Records *RecA&S* Record division of the **Bertlesman** media conglomerate of Germany. *Also see* **major labels**.

RCBA *PA-Variety* **Rodeo Clowns & Bullfighters Association**

re (ray) *Genl* Relating to, in reference to, concerning.

re (ray) *MusArts* second tone of a **diatonic scale**

reach *Mktg* Degree to which a marketing campaign penetrates the market or makes an impact on the public.

reach and frequency *Mktg* Number of households or the target audience exposed to an ad at least one time over a period of time x average number of exposures (frequency) over a given period of time = gross rating points.

reactionary *Crit&Eval, Law&Pol* Characterized by reaction, esp. opposition to progress or liberalism; extremely conservative. *Also see* **Political Philosophies**.

reactionary *Law&Pol* Characterized by reaction, esp. opposition to progress or liberalism; extremely **conservative**. *Also see* **ultraconservative**.

reactive selling *Mktg* Wait for the customer to request or buy the product or service. *Also see* **proactive selling**.

read *BcstJourn* » **reader**

read *InfoMgt* Recall data stored in the computer memory. *Also see* **RAM**; **write**.

read *PerfA&C* Listen to an actor read **lines**.

Read-Only-Memory *InfoMgt* » **ROM**

read-out, readout *InfoMgt* Presentation of data, usu. in digital form, from calculations or storage.

readability *iMedia* Metric to critique the ease of a text's reading; type easier to read has a higher readability rating.

readability research *Journ, Mktg* Measurement of the ability of an average reader to understand.

reader *BcstJourn* Most frequently used broadcast format. It is a story — usually short and under 40 seconds — read by the newscaster without accompanying sound, actualities, or videotape. *Also:*" *read*," "live," "live-er," or "copy story."

reader *Journ* Object of editorial policy and content, regarded as the basic unit in most **demographic** and **psychographic** surveys.

reader's response card *Mktg* Return postage paid card bound in a magazine on which the reader can request further information on an advertiser's product or service.

readership *Journ* Readers of a publication considered as a group. *Also see* **audience, market**.

readership studies *Journ, Mktg* Research into the how, when, where, and to what extent readers read and use publications, and the **demographic** and **psychographic** profiles of the readers. *Also see* **market research**.

ready-made *Crit&Eval* Already made, prepared, or available. <ready-made clothes> *Also see* **store-bought**.

ready-made art *Crit&Eval VisArts* **Store-bought** object declared and displayed as "art" by the "artist," i.e., the concepualizer, the presenter. <**Marcel Duchamp's** *The Fountain* (an unadorned urinal)>

ready-to-wear (RTW) *Fashn* Clothing marketed in a finished condition in standard sizes. PRET-A-PORTER

Reagan, Ronald (Wilson) (1911-) The 40th President of the U.S. (1981-89) *ArtPerf, Flm&Vid, Law&Pol* Movie actor turned politician, early **New Deal** Democrat turned right-wing Republican, he was governor of California (1967-75) His two administrations as President were marked by economic recovery fueled by record budget deficits (see **voodoo economics**), constitutional crises and political controversy over "invasion" of Granada, arms-for-hostages in Iran, support of repressive "freedom fighters" in Central America, and more. He took important steps in U.S./Soviet nuclear disarmament negotiations. *Also see* **consent decree of 1948, fairness doctrine**.

real account *E&F-Acc* » **permanent account**

real book *MusArts* Collection of jazz standards consisting of melody line and chords. *Also see* **fake book**.

real estate *iMedia, InfoMgt* Amount of visual space available on a screen.

real exchange rate *EntreP* The market exchange rate adjusted for prices.

real GDP per capita *EntreP* **1** Gross domestic product per person adjusted for changes in prices. It is the usual measure of living standards across time and between countries. **2 GNP** adjusted for inflation. *Also see* **Economic Indicators**.

real rate of interest *EntreP* The nominal interest rate minus the inflation rate.

real time *InfoMgt* **1** Events that happen virtually at a particular moment. When chatting in a **chat room**, or sending an instant message, the user is in real time since it is immediate. **2** Re computer systems that update information at the same rate as they receive data.

realism *Crit&Eval* Inclination toward literal truth and **pragmatism**.

realism *LitArts, VisArts* French movement of the 19th century. Representation in art or literature of objects, actions, or social conditions as they actually are, without idealization or presentation in **abstract** form. *Also see* **Art Movements and Periods**.

realism *TheatArts* Style of drama that attempts to establish authenticity through the use of observed facts of daily existence.

realist *Crit&Eval* **1** One who is inclined to literal truth and **pragmatism**. **2** Practitioner of artistic or philosophic realism.

reality *Crit&Eval* The quality or state of being actual or true: "The truth is that there never was, is not now, and never will be a **scintilla** of **reality** in a performer's standing on a stage and singing what must be sung instead of spoken." — **David Craig**

reality *Ethcs&Phil* That which has necessary existence and not contingent existence.

really up *Crit&Eval* Said of a performer who is working at full creative and technical capacity. *Also see* **up**.

reasonable person standard *LegAsp* What a hypothetical reasonable person would conclude. *Also see* **Contracts**.

reax lead (reeax leed) for reaction) *BcstJourn* Lead that emphasizes the responses of persons or groups to previous stories.

reboot *InfoMgt* To stop and restart the computer's operating system because of a problem or malfunction. *Also see* **boot**.

rebop *MusArts* » **bebop**

.rec *InfoMgt* **Domain name** ending for recreational or entertainment activities. *Also see* **Domain Names**.

rec. *RecA&S* **record, recording**

recapture of rights *IntelProp* Right granted to an author and certain of her/his successors (but excluding **works made for hire**) under certain conditions and certain limitations, to recapture rights to a copyright previously granted to a publisher or other grantee.

receivable(s) *E&F-Acc* **1** Suitable for being received or accepted for payment. **2** Awaiting or requiring payment; due or collectible. **3** Business asset due to one business from another. *Also see* **accounts receivable**.

receivables turnover *E&F-Acc* Speed with which accounts receivable are collected. It is defined as annual credit sales divided by receivables (receivables turnover = annual credit sales/accounts receivable) *Also see* **activity ratios**.

recession *Eco&Fin* Extended decline in general business activity, typically three consecutive quarters of falling real **gross national product**. *Also see* **depression**, **economic indicators**.

recession *EntreP* six consecutive months of negative economic growth

recital *Dnce, MusArts* Performance by a musician or dancer, esp. by an solo dancer, instrumentalist, or singer.

recital *PerfA&C* Act of reading or reciting in a public place.

recitative *MusArts* Style used in opera and **oratorio** in which the text is declaimed in natural speech with slight melodic variation.

recitative *TheatArts* Rhythmically free vocal style that imitates the natural inflections of speech and that is used for sung dialogue and narrative in operas, oratorios, operettas, and some musicals.

reckless disregard *Journ, Law&Pol* » **actual malice**

recognition point *E&F-Acc* Underlying accounting issue that decides when a business transaction should be recorded. Accounting tradition says the transaction is recorded when **title** passes from the supplier to the purchaser creating an obligation to buy.

recognizances *LegAsp* Party acknowledges in court that he or she will pay a specified sum of money if a certain event occurs. <a bail bond> *Also see* **Contracts**.

reconcile *E&F-Acc* To become compatible or consistent. <The figures on the bank statement didn't reconcile with the checkbook>

recondation *IntelProp* Filing of certain documents with the **Copyright Office** as a prerequisite to bringing a suit for **infringement**.

record (n) *iMedia* Collection of related, often adjacent items of data, treated as a unit.

record *RecA&S* » **disc, phonorecord, platter**

record club *Mktg, RecA&S* "Membership" organization in which subscribers agree to purchase a minimum number of recordings or tapes or videos – under a **negative option plan** or a **positive option plan** – within a given period of time. TAPE CLUB

record player *RecA&S* Electric powered device that can reproduce sounds from a phonograph disk at speeds ranging from 16 **rpm** to 78 **rpm**. May have a built-in record changer by which a number of disks can be played in the order in which they are stacked. *Also see* **Music Playback Devices**.

record pool *RecA&S* Service organization distributes records from the labels to its members, disco deejays and **discotheque** operators, and in turn, provides feedback to the labels.

record producer *RecA&S* One who has complete control over all artistic and financial aspects in the making of a phonograph recording. *Also see* **Producers**.

record royalty *RecA&S* » **artist royalty, Royalties**

record session *RecA&S* Period of time, usu. three hours, in which an audio recording is done in a studio. [A **jingle** session is usu. one hour.].

recorder (rec) *MusInstr* Vertically-held flute with eight finger holes and a whistlelike mouthpiece. RECORDER PLAYER

recorder *RecA&S* Device that makes recordings or records.

recording *RecA&S* **1** Something on which sound or visual images have been recorded. **2** Recorded sound or picture. *Also see* **phonorecord**.

Recording Academy, recording academy *RecA&S* » **NARAS**

recording costs *RecA&S* All costs inc. pre- and post-production costs incurred in the production of the **master recording**.

recording engineer *RecA&S* One responsible for the technical aspects of a recording session. <mic selection and placement, check blank tape for **bias** error, test and run equipment, and most importantly, try to capture the sound that the producer thinks will go **gold**, if not **platinum**> *Also see* **engineer, mixer**.

Recording Industry Association of America (RIAA) *RecA&S* » **RIAA**

recording right *IntelProp, RecA&S* » **mechanical right**

recordist *RecA&S* One who records sound electronically for films or recordings. *Also see* **recording engineer, sound engineer**.

records, recordings *RecA&S* » **phonorecords, sound recordings**

recoup *Eco&Fin, LglAsp* To deduct or withhold (part of something due) for an equitable reason.

recoup *LitArts* <Publisher recouped its advance to the author by deducting money from royalties due>

recoup *MusArts* <The record label recouped its advance to the recording artist by deducting money from royalties due>

recto *VA-Prntng* Right-hand page of a book. *Also see* **verso**.

recurrents *RecA&S* Records recently off the charts but are still programmed because of demand and are too recent to be **oldies**.

red flag words and expressions *LegAsp* Those that may lead to a libel lawsuit if not carefully handled by writers. <addict, adulteration of products, adultery — **ACLU**>

Red Network *Rdio/TV* Former fraternal twin of the **Blue Network** of the **National Broadcasting Company** (NBC) *Also see* **Broadcast Stations & Networks**.

red tape *Mgt* Oppressively complex and time consuming forms and procedures. Guilty parties may include government agencies, big business, and **nonprofits**. *Origin* From its former use in tying British official documents.

red-light district *Cult&Soc* Neighborhood with many brothels. *Also see* **Battlefield, Storyville**.

redeem *Eco&Fin* **1** To recover ownership of by paying a specified sum. <recover something mortgaged, pawned, or pledged> **2** To pay off. <a promissory note> **3** To convert into cash. <redeem stocks> REDEMPTION

redeem *Mktg* To turn in and receive something in exchange. <coupons> REDEMPTION

Redford, Robert *ArtPerf, Flm&Vid, TheatArts* (1937-, film/stage act., dir., prod., wri.) Also active in ecology and political issues. Awards: Oscar, 1980 Best Dir., *Ordinary People*. *Also see* **silence**, **Sundance Institute**.

redress *Ethcs&Phil* To set right something considered immoral or unethical; usu. involves making reparation.

reductivism *VisArts* » **minimalism**

redundant *Crit&Eval* Exceedingly repetitive.

reed *MusInstr* **1** Flexible strip of cane or metal set into the mouthpiece or air opening of certain instruments to produce tone by vibrating in response to a stream of air. **2** Instrument, such as a clarinet, fitted with a reed. **3** Primitive wind instrument made of a hollow reed stalk. REED PLAYER *Also see* **Musical Instrument Families**.

reed organ *MusInstr* » **harmonium** *Also see* **Musical Instrument Families, Organs**.

reed section *MusInstr* **Section** of a band or an orchestra composed of reed instruments. <clarinets, saxophones> *Also see* **double-reeds, woodwinds, Musical Instrument Families**.

reedman *MusArts* Jazz player of reed instruments. <jazz saxophonist, jazz clarinetist>

reeds *MusInstr* » **reed section**

reel-to-reel *RecA&S* Sound recording equipment or sound recordings that use magnetic tape threaded through the equipment and onto an empty reel.

reflector *Flm&Vid* Board with a light-reflecting surface, used mainly to redirect sunlight for use as **fill light**. *Also see* **Stage Lighting**.

refrain *LitArts, MusArts* **1** Phrase or verse repeated at intervals throughout a song or poem, esp. at the end of each stanza. **2** Music for the refrain of a poem; a song or melody.

refresh *InfoMgt* Restore capacity or power expended in prior use.

regeneration *Crit&Eval* Spiritual or moral revival or rebirth.

reggae *MusArts* Pop music from Jamaica has elements of **Calypso**, soul, and rock 'n' roll; characterized by a strongly accentuated **offbeat**. *Also see* **Latin dance music**.

Regional Arts Councils *Law&Pol, Mgt* Twenty per cent of their programming funds come from **NEA or NEH**; remainder is raised from regional sources. *Also see* **States Arts Councils**.

regional economic indicators *Eco&Fin* Many of the **national economic indicators** are broken down as regional statistics. Region may be. <Midwest, New England, Rust Belt>; a metropolitan area. <Chicago, Los Angeles, Baltimore-Washington corridor>; or a state. *Also see* **specific industry indicators**.

regional edition *Journ* Version of a periodical's issue distributed to a defined geographical area. Some editorial and advertising content will be directed to that area's readership. <suburban edition, out-of-state edition, national edition>

régisseurs (redgee-sewers, Fr. for "to direct") *Dnce* Ballet stage director. *Also see* **Directors**.

register *InfoMgt* Form of computer memory used for holding temporary data.

register *MusArts, MusInstr* **1** Range of a musical instrument or voice. **2** Group of matched organ pipes.

register *VA-Prntng* **1** Exact alignment of the lines and margins on the opposite sides of a **leaf**. **2** Proper positioning of colors in color printing.

register mark ® *IntelProp* Symbol attesting that a **trademark** has been approved and registered by the **U.S. Patent and Trademark Office** in the U.S. Dept. of Commerce.

Register of Copyrights *IntelProp* » **copyright registration**

registration *MusArts* Combination of organ stops selected to be used in playing a piece.

registration *VA-Prntng* Correct **alignment** or positioning of the different plates or filters used in color printing.

regressive tax *E&F-Acc* One, in contrast to the **progressive tax** becomes less as one's income rises. <**Social Security** (FICA) tax based on incomes only up to a certain amount>

regulation *Crit&Eval* Principle, rule, or law designed to control or govern conduct.

rehearsal *PerfA&C* Practice in preparation for a public performance.

rehearsal marks *MusArts* Notations made on an instrumental **part** by musicians during rehearsal.

rehearsal musician *MusArts* Instrumentalist hired to accompany singers and dancers during rehearsals. <rehearsal pianist, rehearsal guitarist, rehearsal drummer, et al> Same or different player hired for the actual production is called a **pit pianist**, et al.

rehearsal studio *MusArts,PerfA&C* Indoor location where rehearsals can take place.

reinstalling *InfoMgt* Installing a program onto a computer for a second time in order to overwrite the old software and hopefully fix a problem.

reinstatement *HR&LR* Return to employment of an employee unlawfully discharged.

Reisenweber's Café *MusArts* NYC Fashionable restaurant and night-spot, Columbus Circle and 58th Street, where **Original Dixieland Jazz Band** opened in 1918. » **dixieland jazz**

reissues *Flm&Vid* TV series made available for home via videocassettes, videodiscs, or **CD-ROMs**. *Also see* **reruns**.

reject *Crit&Eval* **1** To refuse to accept, submit to, believe, or make use of. **2** To refuse to consider or grant. DENY

rejection *ArtPerf, Crit&Eval* "Try 40 years of performing before the public, I don't know anybody – anybody – who takes more rejection than an actor. From trying to get the job to then being subjected to merciless criticism in the press and constantly being subjected, if you are not onstage every night, to audience approval or disapproval." — **Jane Alexander**

rejection slip *Crit&Eval, LitArts* Printed note accompanying a manuscript rejected for publication and returned to the author.

rejective art *VisArts* » **minimalism**

relational data base *InfoMgt* Collection of inter-related files that can be easily manipulated by the user.

relative path *iMedia* Programming: Instructions to something (i.e., a directory, file, object, variable, etc.) in relation to the specific position of the object or code giving the instructions. Syntax varies by language. In contrast, absolute path. <./media/img.jpg>

relative pitch *MusArts* **1** **Pitch** of a tone as determined by its position in a **scale**. **2** Ability to recognize or produce a tone by mentally establishing a relationship between its **pitch** and that of a recently heard tone. *Also see* **absolute pitch**.

relative size *iMedia* One of **Gestalt Laws** of pattern perception: Smaller components of a pattern tend to be perceived as objects.

relativism *Cult&Soc. Ethcs&Phil* Ethical relativism is the theory that ethical principles and values are valid only for the cultures in which they are found. If we find another culture's values to be wrong, it's because we haven't been raised in that society and don't think that way. "So our virtues lie in the interpretation of the time." — Shakespeare (*Coriolanus*) Problems: 1 The statement "relativism is true" applies to all cultures, so how can one person, from one culture, make it? 2 Cultures may really differ only in their factual beliefs, not their ethical ones. This is not to be confused with cultural relativism, a theory that holds that different cultures simply have different ways of expressing certain basic human ideas, such as family, society, love, beauty, etc. The theory is important in business ethics when applied to companies doing business in many different countries.

relativity *Ethcs&Phil* **1** Existence dependent solely on relation to a thinking mind. **2** State of dependence in which the existence or significance of one entity is solely dependent on that of another. *Also see* **relativism**.

relaxation *TheatArts* Freedom from muscular tension that will permit freedom of action.

release *Flm&Vid* Complete film going into distribution and exhibition.

release *LegAsp* To relinquish a right or claim.

release *Mktg* **1** To issue for performance, sale, publication, or distribution; to make known or available. **2** **Press release**. **3** Signed agreement by a performer allowing the producer the right to reproduce the performer's **likeness** and "use it in any reasonable manner."

release *MusArts* » **bridge** (*MusArts*)

release date *Mktg* Date of issue for performance, sale, publication, or distribution. *Also see* **leak**.

release print *Flm&Vid* Final **composite** print with completed soundtrack for theatrical distribution.

relic *Cult&Soc, Genl* **1** Something that has survived the passage of time, esp. an object or a custom whose original culture has disappeared. **2** Something cherished for its age or historic interest. **3** Object kept for its association with the past. MEMENTO

relief *LegAsp* Redress awarded by a court.

religious right *Cult&Soc, Ethcs&Phil* "Since every idea the religious right [of all persuasions] does not support is **anathema** to them and since their beliefs are so narrow and **ambiguous** – unlike real life – they target many of the most important institutions in American life, inc. libraries, art museums and public schools. It is truly, as they have declared it, a culture war, and it is pervasive." — Leanne Katz (journ.) *Also see* **center**; **Fundamentalism, ideology**; **left**.

remainder *LitArts, Mktg* Book that remains with a publisher after sales have fallen off, usu. sold at a reduced price. *Also see* **returns**.

remedy *LegAsp* Legal order to prevent or redress a wrong or to enforce a right.

reminiscences *LitArts* Narration of past experiences

remote *BcstJourn* Story done by the reporter live from the field while the reporter is at the story's location.

remote broadcast *Rdio/TV* Any broadcast away from the station's studios. *Origin* **Big band** movement got a big boost in 1933 at the Chicago World's Fair when radio stations began to air remote broadcasts via telephone lines, after the 10:30PM news, from the city's many hotels and ballrooms and beamed the music throughout the Midwest. *Also see* **air check**.

remote viewing *InfoMgt* Ability to attend and interact with public or private online web community from any location employing computer, modem, video, and chat applications.

renaissance *Crit&Eval* Rebirth or revival. Revival of intellectual or artistic achievement and vigor. <The **Harlem renaissance**>

Renaissance (ca. 14th-16th centuries) *Cult&Soc, LitArts, VisArts* Humanistic revival of classical art, architecture, literature, and learning originated in Italy in the 14th century and later spread throughout Europe. *Also see* **Art Movements and Periods**.

Renaissance lace *Fashn* » **Battenberg lace**

renascence *Cult&Soc* **1** Cultural revival; a **renaissance**. **2** New birth or life; a rebirth.

rendering *Genl* **1** Depiction or an interpretation, as in painting or music. **2** Drawing in perspective of a proposed structure. **3** Translation from one language to another.

rendering *iMedia* Conversion of a high-level object-based description into a graphical image for display, or for output to a file or display source.

rendition *Crit&Eval* Interpretation or performance of a musical or dramatic work.

renewal *Journ, Mktg* Subscription to a periodical renewed within six months after expiration.

rent party *Cult&Soc, MusArts* **Harlem** fundraising affair during the hard-time 1920s and 30s. Necessaries: Rent-past due-apartment, neighbors and guests who were holding (a dollar or whatever), **BYOB** catering, a piano of sorts, and shouters and wailers and grinders and jumpers from anywhere. Performance times: Friday to Sunday, give a day or two.

rep *TheatArts* **Repertory** company or theater

Rep. *Law&Pol* Representative, member U.S. House of Representatives.

repartee *Crit&Eval* Swift, witty reply.

Repeal *Law&Pol* Applies specifically to the 21st Amendment (1933) to the U.S. Constitution which repealed **Prohibition** (18th Amendment) Repeal, part of **F.D.R.'s New Deal**, had a positive effect on the live entertainment business. *Also see* **juke box**.

repeat (rpt.) *MusArts* **Passage** or section that is to be repeated indicated by a sign usu. consisting of two vertical dots. *Also see* **da capo**.

repeat (rpt.) *Rdio/TV* Repeat of a television program. *Also see* **rerun**.

repertoire *MusArts, PerfA&C* Stock of music, songs, plays, operas, or other material that a player or company is prepared to perform. *Also see* **A&R, repertory**.

repertory (rep) *MusArts* » **repertoire**

repertory (rep) *TheatArts* 1 Company that performs several plays in rotation throughout a season. 2 Term also refers to a set of plays.

repertory company (rep) *TheatArts* Company that presents and performs a number of different plays or other works during a season, usu. in alternation.

replacement value of assets *EntreP* The valuation of assets based on the cost of replacing them with new assets at today's prices.

replica *VisArts* 1 Copy or reproduction of a work of art, esp. one made by the original artist. 2 Copy or reproduction, esp. one on a scale smaller than the original.

replication *InfoMgt* In a spreadsheet, the capability of copying a text string or numerical value from one cell to another.

replication *VisArts* Copy or reproduction

reply *LegAsp* **Plaintiff's** response to the defendant's answer or plea.

report *InfoMgt* Extraction of data from a database or spreadsheet, generated on a regular or irregular basis, listing, or summarizing a particular type of activity. <payroll, inventory control>

reporter *Journ* Writer, investigator, or presenter of news stories. *Also see* **primary reporter**.

reports *LegAsp* Published collection of authoritative accounts of court cases or of judicial decisions.

repositioning *Mktg* "How to take a high profile brand, whose product has grown tired and whose appeal has narrowed, and move it forward without leaving its well-known identity behind." — Sarah Lyall (fashion wri.) *Also see* **positioning**.

repository *VisArts* **museum**

representation *LegAsp* Statement of fact made by one party in order to induce another party to enter into a contract.

representational *iMedia* First stage in the evolution within a medium: "Representations of reality do little more than present reality with the greatest verisimilitude possible to the technological state of the art." — David Gerding

representational *VisArts* Relating to realistic graphic representation.

representational staging *TheatArts* Production that imitates experience, seeks to create the illusion of reality.

representative (rep.) *LegAsp, Mgt* One who serves as an agent for another. *Also see* **Agents and Agencies**.

represential actor *TheatArts* "The Represential actor deliberately chooses to imitate or illustrate the character's behavior." — Uta Hagen (» **talent**) *Also see* **presentatial actor**.

reprint *VA-Prntng* Something printed again, a printed **excerpt**.

reprise *LitArts, MusArts* 1 Repetition of a phrase or verse. 2 Return to an original theme.

repro *VA-Prntng, VisArts* reproduction **proof**

reproduction *Crit&Eval* Something reproduced resembling the form and elements of the **original**.

reproduction right *IntelProp* Right **inherent** in the ownership of a copyright. *Also see* **infringement**.

republish *LegAsp* To revive a libel

Request For Proposal (RFP) *Fnding* When the government issues a new contract or grant program, it sends out RFPs to agencies that might be qualified to participate. The RFP lists project specifications and application procedures. A few foundations occasionally use RFPs in specific fields, but most prefer to consider proposals that are initiated by applicants.

requiem *MusArts* Hymn for the dead

required rate *E&F-Acc* » **discount rate**

requirements analysis *iMedia* 1 Process of investigating and documenting the requirements of a project. usu. includes: user profiles, contextual inquiry and analysis, goals, and technological restrictions or requirements. 2 Document that sums up the investigation and analysis of the requirements of a product. Allows developers to identify the goal and objectives of a product; it is the foundation for development.

requirements specification *iMedia* Document that details and clearly describes the requirements of a product (before product development begins) It is the result of requirements analysis and specifies the requirements that a product must meet.

rerelease *Flm&Vid, RecA&S* To release a movie or recording again.

reruns *Flm&Vid, Rdio/TV* 1 Film put back in distribution. 2 TV series put back on the air in syndication, cable, or network release or into secondary markets. *Also see* **reissues, repeat**.

Resale Royalties Act (1983) *LegAsp, VisArts* "The California Act provides: 'Whenever a work of **fine art** is sold and the reseller resides in California or the sale takes place in California, the seller or the seller's agent shall pay to the artist of such work of fine art or to such artist's agent 5 percent of the amount of such sale.'" — Cal. Civ. Code §986 (West 1983) *Also see* **droit de suite**.

research and development (R&D) *Sci&Tech* » **R&D**.

reserve requirement *EntreP* Percentage of deposits that are placed in banks to conduct daily operations which cannot be used for loans. Reserve requirements are established by the FED. These reserves must be kept in the banks vault or kept on deposit with the FED.

reserves *EntreP* Fraction of banks' deposits set aside in either vault cash or as deposits at the Federal Reserve.

residual payment *Flm&Vid, Rdio/TV* Additional payments to **announcers, arrangers, composers, copyists, directors, performers**, and **writers** for replays of TV programs, inc. **jingles** and **commercials** after their first showing or 13-week cycle.

Resnais, Alain (1922-) *ArtPerf, Flm&Vid* One of a group of young French directors who came to prominence during the late 1950s. <w/Maguerite Duras, *Hiroshima, Mon Amour* (1959), *Stavisky* (1974, **m. Stephen Sondheim**)> *Also see* **New Wave**.

resolution *Flm&Vid* Ability to recreate detail in an electronic or film recording medium. The higher the number of **lines** of resolution, the more precise the reproduction of the actual scene.

resolution *Genl* Explanation of a problem; a solution.

resolution *iMedia, InfoMgt* 1 Sharpness and clarity of an image. 2 Amount of **dpi** (dots per inch) of an image (either displayed or printed) Generally the higher the dpi of an image, the better it will look. 3 Screen resolution. maximum number of **pixels** per square inch on a computer-generated display, expressed as (number of horizontal **pixels**) x (number of vertical **pixels**), i.e., 1024x768. greater the resolution, the better the picture.

resolution *LegAsp* court decision

resolution *LitArts* 1 Part of a literary work in which the complications of the plot are resolved or simplified. 2 Substitution of one **metrical** unit for another. <the substitution of two short syllables for one long syllable in quantitative verse>

resolution *MusArts* Progression of a **dissonant** tone or chord to a **consonant** tone or chord.

resonance *MusArts* Intensification and prolongation of a musical tone, produced by sympathetic vibration.

resonating *TheatArts* selective amplification and reinforcement of the vocal tone

resonator *MusInstr* Hollow chamber or cavity with dimensions chosen to permit internal **resonant oscillation** of electromagnetic or acoustical waves of specific frequencies.

resource(s) *Crit&Eval* 1 Ability to deal with a difficult situation effectively; initiative. 2 Means that can be used to cope with a difficult situation.

resource(s) *Eco&Fin, Mgt* Total means available to a company for increasing efficiency and profit. <capital, plant, labor, raw material> *Also see* **assets**.

resource(s) *InfoMgt* Something or somebody that can be used for support or help. <library, reference librarian, internet, etc>

resource(s) *Law&Pol* Total means available for economic and political development. <mineral wealth, labor force, armaments, etc>

resplendent *Crit&Eval* Splendid or dazzling in appearance; brilliant.

respondeat superior (res-pon-dee-at, Latin for "let the master answer") *LegAsp* Rule that states an employer is liable for the **tortious** conduct of its employees or agents while they are acting within the scope of its authority.

respondent *LegAsp* defendant *Also see* **plaintiff**.

response time *InfoMgt* Time required between a user's request at a computer terminal and the computer's reply.

responsive *Crit&Eval, iMedia* 1 Readily reacting to suggestions, influences, appeals, or efforts. 2 Media that responds to a user's actions or inactions.

rest *LitArts* Short pause in a line of poetry; a **caesura**.

rest *MusArts* 1 Interval of silence corresponding to one of the possible time values within a measure. 2 Mark or symbol indicating such a pause and its length.

Restoration *Cult&Soc, Law&Pol* Revival of drama and poetry in the Period between the crowning of Charles II of England in 1660 and the Revolution of 1688.

restoration of copyright *IntelProp* Registration of a restored work can be done by filing form **GATT** with the U.S. **Copyright Office**.

restorer *Flm&Vid, MusInstr, VA-Prntng* One who restores valuable but damaged objects to their original state. <art works, film, manuscripts, musical instruments, etc> *Also see* **conservator**.

restraint of trade *Eco&Fin, Mktg* Action or a condition that tends to prevent free competition in business, as the creation of a **monopoly** or **trust**. *Also see* **Clayton Act, Sherman Anti-Trust Act**.

restricted endorsement *E&F-Acc* When the endorser of a check or other negotiable instrument restricts or limits the conditions under which the **payee** obtains the funds.

restricted funds *E&F-Acc* Funds that are collected and allocated for a specific purpose and may be used for no other. *Also see* **operating funds, unrestricted funds**.

restricted gift *Fndng* Gift that has been made for a specific purpose and may be used for no other.

restructured *Eco&Fin, Mgt* Too often, a **euphemism** for **bankrupt**.

retail *Mktg* Sale of goods or commodities in small quantities directly to consumers.

retail list price *RecA&S* Basic retail price of a recording established by the record company, from which discounts and **royalties** are based. *Also see* **wholesale basis**.

retail method of inventory *E&F-Acc* This estimation method means the amount of the inventory at the marked seeking price of the items. *Also see* **Inventory Methods**.

retailer *Mktg* Individual, company, or organization that sells product to consumers. *Also see* **dealer**.

retained earnings *E&F-Acc* Corporation's **capital** earned through profitable operation of the business.

retire *Eco&Fin* Remove from circulation. <retired the bonds>

retro *Crit&Eval* Fashion, **decor**, design, or style reminiscent of things past.

retro *PA-Variety* Variety show reminiscent of **vaudeville**.

retrobopper *ArtPerf, MusArts* Young musician who plays 1940s **bop**.

retrograde inversion *MusArts* Playing a melody upside down and backward.

retrospective *Crit&Eval* Extensive exhibition or performance of the work of an artist or an art form over a period of years.

rets. *Mktg* **returns**

return authorization (RA) *RecA&S* Permission for a record dealer to return merchandise for credit or exchange. *Also see* **returns**.

return on assets *E&F-Acc* » **rate of return on total assets**

return on equity *E&F-Acc* This ratio uses the beginning and ending **owner's equity** to compute the average owner's equity as follows. <return on equity = net income average owner's equity>

return on total assets *E&F-Acc* *Also see* **profitability ratios**.

return privilege *LitArts, Mktg, RecA&S* Books and recordings and tapes are sold to wholesalers and retailers with the privilege of returning a certain percentage of unsold copies for credit or exchange. [When sales are sluggish, retailers may invoke a return privilege to get credits to pay their bills before reordering again.] *Also see* **remainder, returns**.

returns *Fashn, LitArts, Mktg, RecA&S* Merchandise returned to a retailer by a consumer or to a wholesaler by a retailer. <clothing, books, records, etc> [Suppliers' gloomy reality: "Gone today, here tomorrow."] *Also see* **remainder**.

Reuters *Journ* London-based international financial news and information company founded in 1851 *Also see* **News Agencies**.

Reuters New Media Inc. *InfoMgt, Journ* Develops **multimedia** information and transaction services for **emerging** corporate, consumer, and educational markets.

rev. *Crit&Eval, Journ, LitArts, VA-Prntng* **reverse, review, revise, revision**

reveal *BcstJourn* Sequence of CG pages that, when played in succession, gives the impression that lines of copy are being added one at a time.

revel *Crit&Eval* Make merry; a boisterous festivity. *Also see* **bacchanalia**.

revenue *E&F-Acc* 1 Increase in retained earnings from delivering goods or services to customers or clients. 2 Money collected when a customer pays for a good or service provided by an organization. *Also see* **expense**.

revenue expenditure *E&F-Acc* Expenditure that merely maintains an asset in its existing condition or restores the asset to good working order. Expensed (matched) against revenue.

revenues *EntreP* Money generated due to sales of a product and services for a company.

reverb *MusInstr, RecA&S* 1 Reverberative effect produced in recorded music by electronic means. 2 Device used for producing this effect.

reverberate *RecA&S* 1 To resound like a succession of echoes or reechoes. 2 Sound waves repeatedly reflected. REVERBERATION.

reversal *TheatArts* Aristotelian critical term ("peripatetic") referring to a sudden change in the fortunes of the **protagonist**.

reverse (rev.) *Journ, VA-Prntng* Normally colored type or illustration appears white against a colored or black background.

reverse angle shot *Flm&Vid* If the camera is filming from the point of view of subject Looking at subject at B, the reverse angle is filming from subject B to A.

reversing entry *E&F-Acc* One that switches the debit and the credit of a previous adjusting entry, made the first day of the period following the adjusting entry.

review (rev.) *Crit&Eval, Journ* 1 Write or give a critical report on a new work or performance. 2 Periodical devoted to reviews.

reviewer *Crit&Eval, Journ* One who writes or delivers reviews for a newspaper, magazine, radio, or TV program. *Also see* **critic**.

revise (rev.) *VA-Prntng* 1 To prepare a newly edited version. 2 **Proof** made from an earlier proof on which corrections have been made.

revision (rev.) *LitArts* Revised or new version of a book or other written material.

revisionist *Crit&Eval* Advocacy of the revision of an accepted, long-standing view, theory, or **doctrine**, esp. a revision of historical events and movements.

revival *PerfA&C* New presentation of an old play, movie, opera, ballet, or similar **vehicle**.

revivals *MusArts* Meeting or series of meetings for the purpose of reawakening religious faith, often characterized by impassioned preaching, public testimony, and featuring (black or white) gospel music.

revolution per minute (rpm, r.p.m.) *RecA&S* » **rpm**

revolutionary *Crit&Eval, Law&Pol* 1 Characterized by, or resulting in, radical change. 2 Bringing about or supporting a political or social revolution. *Also see* **Political Philosophies**.

revolutions per second (rps) *RecA&S* » **rps**

revolve (n) *PerfA&C* Large, circular platform that pivots on its central axis. *Also see* **turntable**

revolving fund *Fnding* Fund established for a certain purpose, such as making loans, with the stipulation that repayments to the fund may be used anew for the same purpose.

revue *TheatArts* **Satirical** musical show consisting of **skits**, songs, and dances. *Also see* **variety show**.

rewrite *Flm&Vid* Attempt to improve the script of a play or film.

rewrite *Journ* Newspaper practice for a rewrite editor to write a news story from someone else's notes or dictation. <Once upon a *Time* practice of its editors to rewrite all copy to **Timestyle**, e.g., "Backward ran sentences until reeled the mind." — **Woolcott Gibbs**

rewrite *LitArts* Improve the script of a play or film.

rewrite *TheatArts* Rewrite a script by the playwright or a **play doctor**.

RFP *Fnding, iMedia* » **Request For Proposal**

RGB *iMedia* Red, Green, Blue. Three colors of light that can be mixed to produce any other color. Colored images are often stored as a sequence of RGB triplets or as separate red, green and blue overlays.

rhetoric *Crit&Eval* **1** Language that is elaborate, pretentious, insincere, or intellectually **vacuous**. **2** Art or study of using language effectively and persuasively.

rhyme *LitArts* **1** Poem or **verse** having a regular correspondence of sounds, esp. at the ends of lines. **2** Word that corresponds with another in terminal sound. <behold and cuckold>

rhythm *iMedia* Movement or variation characterized by the regular recurrence or alternation of different quantities or conditions.

rhythm *LitArts* Pattern or flow of sound created by the arrangement of stressed and unstressed syllables in accentual verse or of long and short syllables in quantitative verse.

rhythm *MusArts* Regular pattern formed by a series of notes of differing duration and stress.

rhythm and blues (r&b, R&B) *MusArts* Music developed by African Americans that combines black folk music, southern **rural blues**, and various styles of jazz — characterized by a strong **backbeat** and repeated variations on **syncopated** instrumental phrases. "'Rhythm and blues' was coined by small record labels in the late 1940s as a substitute for the unsavory term 'race music,' hitherto used to describe various forms of black music." — Harvey Rachlin (mus. biz wri.) *Also see* **blues, jazz; race records**.

Rhythm and Blues Foundation, The (1989-) *ArtPerf, MusArts* "A **nonprofit** fosters wider recognition, financial support, and historic and cultural preservation of **rhythm and blues** music through various grants and programs in support of artists of the Forties, Fifties, and Sixties." — >http://www.zappa.com< Sponsors its annual awards ceremony the day after the **Grammy Awards**.

rhythm section *MusInstr* Group of instruments in a band supplying the **rhythm**. <piano or other **keyboard** instruments, bass, acoustic or electric; drums and other percussion, and guitar or other frets> *Also see* **Musical Instrument Families**.

rhythm track *RecA&S* Recording of just the **rhythm section** upon which other instrumental and vocal tracks will be **layered** and **mixed**.

RIAA *RecA&S* **Recording Industry Association of America**. Est. 1952 Trade association (348 members in 1996), based in Wash. (DC), for the major record companies. Authenticates record sales, i.e., **gold** and **platinum** recognition; vigorously prosecutes **counterfeiting**, **bootlegging**, and record **piracy**; assembles record industry marketing statistics, and lobbies Congress and the federal agencies at every opportunity.

ribbon microphone *RecA&S* Professional quality **bidirectional mic** noted for its sensitivity. *Also see* **Microphones**.

Rich, Frank (1949-, columnis, drama critic, *New York Times*) *Crit&Eval, Journ, TheatArts* Former chief drama critic for the *New York Times*, now Op-Ed columnist on national affairs. *Also see* **egocentric, Woodstock Nation**.

ricky-tick *MusArts* » **mickey**

ride cymbal *MusInstr* » **ride rhythm**

ride rhythm *MusArts* "Varied pattern of swing eighth and quarter notes played on the ride cymbal or **high hat**. Its sound is something like *chung-ching-a-ching-ching*. Ride rhythm together with the **walking bass line**, provides the basic rhythmic **pulse** (also referred to as the **beat** or the **time**) of swing and **modern jazz**. Ride rhythm first appeared in the mid-1930s, when Jo Jones of **Count Basie's** band began keeping time on the high hat instead of the snare drum." — Lyons & Perlo (jazz critics)

rider *LegAsp* Amendment to a contract. Rider to an **engagement contract** may include. <technical requirements, local transpor-

tation, meals and refreshment for performers, backstage security, extra damage insurance, personal appearance restrictions, etc> *Also see* **A above Middle C**, **road manager**, **tech rider**.

riff *MusArts* Short, simple, repeated melodic phrase of two or four bars played behind a soloist or as the basis of a theme.

right of first refusal *IntelProp, RecA&S* Copyright owner has the right to decide who shall be the first artist to record the copyrighted song.

right of first refusal *Mktg* **1** Opportunity for a current advertiser in a print medium to buy a special advertising position such as the first right-hand page or the **back cover** before it is offered to another advertiser. **2** Opportunity to accept a renewal or extension of a sponsorship before it is offered to another sponsor.

right of privacy *Journ, LegAsp* Right to restrict the use of a person's name and **likeness** in published materials; generally applies to advertisements and editorial material on subjects *not* of public interest.

right of publicity *IntelProp, LegAsp* Gives the individual the right to control the use of her/his image or voice for commercial purposes.

right wing *Crit&Eval* **Conservative** or **reactionary** faction of a group. *Also see* **left wing**.

right-on *Crit&Eval* **1** Up-to-date and sophisticated. **2** Absolutely right; perfectly true.

right to work laws *HR&LR, Law&Pol* State laws[†] that prohibit both the **union shop** and the **closed shop**. Made possible by a provision of the **Taft-Hartley Act**. [Particularly in most Southern and Southwestern states.] *Also see* **open shop**.

rights *Cult&Soc Ethcs&Phil* That group of things which one may do as one wishes; the opportunities to act or not to act which one can successfully maintain against all adversaries. Some rights are created by custom or law and can be altered or eliminated by custom or law; others – natural laws – may be **inherent** in our nature or in the nature of things, and therefore beyond the reach of custom or law, at least in some respects.

rights of copyright *IntelProp* Copyright owners have these five rights: (1) the right to reproduce the copyrighted work in either copies or **phonorecords**, (2) the right to prepare **derivative works** based on the copyrighted work, (3) the right to distribute to the public copies or **phonorecords** of the copyrighted work, (4) the right to perform publicly a copyrighted literary, musical, dramatic, or choreographic work, pantomime, motion picture, or other **audio/visual work**, (5) the right to display publicly a copyrighted literary, musical, dramatic, or choreographic work, a pantomime or pictorial, graphic, or sculptural work, inc. the individual images in a motion picture or other **audio/visual work**.

Rigler & Deutsch Index of Recorded Sound *RecA&S* Sound recording holdings (from the first Edison disk onward) of five archives, inc. the Library of Congress, on tape (now on CD Rom) Many of the current re-releases of recordings on CD owe their discovery to this project. *Also see* **Lloyd Rigler**.

Rigler, Lloyd (19??-; philanthropist, film/video producer.) *Flm&Vid Mgt* Founder of **Classic Arts Showcase** and *Rigler & Deutsch Index of Recorded Sound.*

rimshot *MusArts, PA-Variety* **1** Sudden, loud crack sound produced by the drummer striking the snare drum head and rim simultaneously. Decided accent in bop. **2** Made on a comedian's **punch line**, **pratfall**, **double take**, etc., accenting the tension, thus causing the audience to laugh or applaud. *Also see* **ba-dump-bump, empathic response**.

ring *PerfA&C* Enclosed, circular area in which performances take place. <Standard-sized **circus** ring is about 42 feet in diameter> *Also see* **ringmaster**.

ring dance *Cult&Soc, Dnce* Dance of African origin. "More than half of the population of the plantation is gathered together... either in the **praise-house** or in some cabin in which a regular religious meeting has been held... The benches are pushed back to the wall when the formal meeting is over, and old and young, men and women... all stand up in the middle of the floor, and when the **sperichil** is struck up, begin first walking and by-and-by shuffling round, one after the other, in a ring. The foot is hardly taken from the floor, and the progression is mainly due to a jerking, hitching motion, which agitates the entire shouter." — **Eileen Southern** *Also see* **Dances, shout**.

ring down the curtain *PerfA&C* End a performance, an event, or an action.

ring up the curtain *PerfA&C* Begin a performance, an event, or an action.

Ringling Brothers and Barnum & Bailey Circus *PA-Variety* Formed in 1882 as a song-and-dance **troop** by Charles Ringling (1863-1926) and his brothers; merged with Barnum & Bailey Circus in 1907. *Also see* **P.T. Barnum, Charles Ringling**.

Ringling, Charles (1863-1926) *Mgt, PA-Variety* With his brothers he formed (1882) a song-and-dance troop that evolved into the **Ringling Brothers and Barnum & Bailey Circus** (1907) *Also see* **P.T. Barnum...**

ringmaster *PA-Variety* Performer in charge of the performances in a circus **ring**. VOICE

rip and read *Journ,. Rdio/TV* To broadcast, unedited, the news from a wire service.

rip-o-matics *Ethcs&Phil, InfoMgt* Use of video data bases to **rip-off** old commercials.

rip-off *Crit&Eval* **1** Something <artwork film, story, tune, etc> that is clearly imitative of, or based on, something else. **2** Act of exploitation.

riser *PerfA&C* Portable stage platform, usu. 4-feet by 8-feet, the size of a sheet of plywood. Heights run 6 to 24 inches.

rising action *TheatArts* Events of the drama leading to the climax.

risk *EntreP* Probability that an expected outcome will occur, and the variability in that expected outcome. In financial terms the probability that the actual return on an investment will be different from the desired return.

risk assumption *EntreP* The willingness to endure the risk that exists in any venture.

risk avoidance *EntreP* Method of managing a business by distancing yourself from a hazard that may cause a loss. *Ex.* Dealing in cash only to avoid credit risk.

risk capital *EntreP* Capital that is provided to high-risk, high-potential ventures, typically by informal investors or venture capitalists.

risk exposure *EntreP* Placement of a business in a situation in which there is uncertainty of outcome. Smoking cigarettes for an individual is risk exposure, some but not all smokers will get cancer. Introducing a new product for a business is risk exposure, some but not all products will succeed.

risk financing *EntreP* Making funds available to cover losses that could not be managed by risk control.

risk loving *EntreP* Risk preference that strictly prefers an uncertain return to a sure return of the same magnitude.

risk management *EntreP, Mgt* Ways of coping with risk that are designed to preserve assets and the earning power of a company. *Also see* **insurance, self-insurance**.

risk neutral *EntreP* Risk preference that is indifferent between a sure return and any uncertain return of the same magnitude.

risk premium *EntreP* Additional compensation in expected return over the risk-free rate that is demanded for assuming some level of risk greater than zero.

risk reduction *EntreP* Program used by a business or individual to lessen the severity of an outcome due to risk. Fastening your seat belt or having air bags in a car are methods of risk reduction.

risk retention *EntreP* Choosing—whether consciously or unconsciously, voluntarily or involuntarily—to manage risk internally.

risk transfer *Eco&Fin, EntreP, Mgt* Having another party assume the risk and agree to pay you for your loss as long as you pay the fee (or premium) charged by the agency assuming the risk. *Ex.* Fire insurance policy on your house. *Also see* **insurance**.

risk version *EntreP* Preference for a sure return to any uncertain return of the same magnitude.

risk, pure *EntreP*. Pure risk involves only the chance of loss and it is therefore insurable. *Ex.* Having your house catch on fire is pure risk.

risk, speculative *EntreP*. Speculative risk is the risk in which there may be a possible gain or loss which is uninsurable. *Ex.* Buying a lottery ticket is speculative risk. You can either gain a dollar or more or lose a dollar.

risk-free rate *EntreP* Rate of interest paid by a debt security with zero default risk.

risqué (ris-kay) *Crit&Eval* Suggestive of or bordering on indelicacy or **impropriety**. *Also see* **double-entendre**.

rite *Cult&Soc* **1** Prescribed or customary form for conducting a religious or other solemn ceremony. <the rite of baptism> **2** Ceremonial act or series of acts. <fertility rites>

rites of passage *Cult&Soc* Ritual or ceremony signifying an event in a person's life indicative of a **transition** from one stage to another, as from adolescence to adulthood.

ritual *Cult&Soc* Prescribed form or order of conducting a religious or **secular** ceremony: "Religion, ritual, and art began as one, and a religious or metaphysical element is still present in all art." — **Camille Paglia** .

ritual *TheatArts* Social customs, events, and ceremonies whose repeated actions are directed toward specific goals,

RKO *Flm&Vid, PA-Variety* **Radio-Keith-Orpheum** (RKO) Known as RKO Radio Pictures, it was a joint enterprise of **Radio Corporation of America** (RCA) and the Keith-Orpheum movie and **vaudeville** theater **circuit**. *Also see* **major studios**.

road company *PerfA&C* » **national company**

road crew *Mgt* Stagehands and technicians who travel with a touring theatrical production.

road dog *ArtPerf, Crit&Eval* Performer that travels (**on the road**) a great deal and seems to enjoy it.

Rock and Roll Hall of Fame (RRHF) *ArtPerf, MusArts* Est. Sept. 1995 on the Cleveland lakefront; architect, I.M. Pei (Chinese-born, 1917-, arch.) New expanded RRHF, presented by **AT&T**, opened April 1998.

road manager *Mgt, MusArts* Represents the group's **personal manager** while **on the road**. Responsible for artists' aid and comfort, payroll, transportation, housing, collecting the money, and fulfillment of the terms of **engagement contracts**. *Also see* **Managers, riders, tour manager**.

road show *Flm&Vid* New movie shown at selected theaters usu. for higher ticket prices.

road show *PerfA&C* Show presented by a **troupe** of theatrical performers on tour.

roadhouse *PerfA&C* Restaurant or nightclub located on a road usu. on the outskirts of town. INN

roadie, roady *PerfA&C* **1** Person engaged to load, unload, and set up equipment and to perform errands of mercy for musicians on tour. **2** Travelling stagehand. *Also see* **Roadie School© Survival Tool Kit**.

Robinson-Patman Act (1936) *Law&Pol, Mktg* Amended the **Clayton Act** (1914) to prohibit price discrimination. This law requires sellers to sell goods of like grade and quality at the same price. Cost-justified discounts are permitted. <bulk discount, cash discount, frequency discount, volume discount> *Also see* **Federal Agencies and Statutes**.

robot *Crit&Eval* Person who works mechanically without original thought, and who responds automatically to the commands of others. *Also see* **robotics**.

robot *Sci&Tech* **1** Mechanical device that sometimes resembles a human being and can be programmed to do complex human tasks on command. **2** Machine or device that operates automatically or by remote control. *Also see* **robotics**.

robotics *InfoMgt* Form of **artificial intelligence** devoted to designing and constructing **robots**.

rock *Cult&Soc* "The scope and significance of rock remains without precedent in the history of popular music. Beginning as a minority expression on the fringe of American society, it developed into a distinct counterculture during the 1960s, and a decade later had become a dominant cultural force, affecting and reflecting the **mores** and moods of American youth and weaving itself into the very fabric of society." — Edward A. Berlin (rock critic)

rock *MusArts* All-encompassing term for a variety of musical styles that share one common feature: a heavy emphasis on the beat. *Also see* **Rock Music Styles**.

rock beat *MusArts* "Rhythmic **ostinato** based on eight straight-eighth notes per bar (8/8 meter), with emphasis on the third and seventh eighth notes in each measure (the backbeats) The effect is a more static type of rhythmic feeling compared with the forward motion suggested by swing." — Lyons & Perlo (jazz critics) *Also see* **Rock Music Styles**.

rock gospel *MusArts, RecA&S* **Grammy** award category without a clear definition.

Rock Music Styles *ColEntry, MusArts* » **acid —, adult contem-**

porary —, boogie, classic —, confessional —, country —, cow-punk, folk —, glitter —, grunge —, hard —, hard-core, heavy metal —, industrial —, new wave, psychedelic —, punk—, rock 'n' roll, rockabilly, soft —.

rock 'n' roll, rock-and-roll *MusArts* 1 Form of popular music developed in the U.S. by 1954 from a mix of musical styles, esp. **rhythm and blues, rockabilly**, and **pop music**. Characterized by electronically amplified instrumentation, a heavily accented beat, and simple **chord progressions**. *Also see* **Elvis Presley, Rock Music Styles.**

Rock the Vote *Law&Pol, RecA&S* Encourages 18-24-year-olds to become involved in the political process by exercising their right to vote. Founded by members of the recording industry.

rockabilly *MusArts* Pop mix of uptempo country music and rhythm and blues — the same combination from which rock 'n' roll derived. Pioneered by Carl Perkins (1933-1998, gtr., sngwri.) *Also see* **Country Music Styles, Rock Music Styles.**

Rockefeller Foundation (1913) *Fndng* Founded by John D. Rockefeller, Sr., founder of Standard Oil Company, it focuses on: cultural improvement, ecology, education, equal opportunity, hunger, and overpopulation. *Also see* **National Video Resources.**

rococo, Rococo *LitArts* Very ornate style of speech or writing.

rococo, Rococo *MusArts* Style of composition from 18th century Europe immediately following the **baroque** period characterized by a certain lightness or daintiness of form, largely because of a high degree of ornamentation.

rococo, Rococo *VisArts* Style of art, esp. architecture and decorative art, from early 18th century France, marked by elaborate ornamentation: scrolls galore, foliage, and animal forms. <*The Embarkation for Cythera* (1717) by **Jean Antoine Watteau** (1684-1721, Fr. pntr)> *Also see* **Art Movements and Periods.**

Rodeo Clowns & Bullfighters Association (RCBA) *PA-Variety, SportsEnt* "Dedicated group of professionals in the rodeo business interested in promoting professionalism in our sport." >www.prorodeoinfo.com<

ROFL, ROTFL *InfoMgt* Rolling On (the) Floor Laughing.

role *ArtPerf, Flm&Vid, Rdio&TV, TheatArts* Character or part played by a performer.

role *Cult&Soc* Characteristic and expected social behavior of an individual.

role indicator *InfoMgt* Re information retrieval: a code assigned to a **key word** to indicate the part of speech or function of the word in the text where it occurs.

role model *EntreP* Person that significantly influences another's life. Most entrepreneurs had an entrepreneurial role model.

roll *MusArts* Rapid succession of short sounds. <the roll of a drum>

roll out *Flm&Vid* Release pattern for a movie with schedule phases close together. <certain markets open a picture, followed in a week or two for additional markets>

roller coasters *Crit&Eval* People only too happy to climb aboard for another ride on the popularity train.

rolling break (even) *Eco&Fin, Flm&Vid* After all deductions are made in each accounting period, the rolling break participants – star talent, directors, et al – receive their share of profits IF the picture is in a profit position. *Also see* **gross profit participant, net profit participant.**

rolling in the mud *Rdio/TV* Condition felt by the cast and crew of a regularly scheduled live TV program that has to stand by while preempted by a special program. <Afternoon soap operas waiting for a break in the O.J. Simpson trial coverage>

Rollins, Sonny (Theodore Walter Rollins, 1929-, jazz tenor/sop. sax, comp.) *ArtPerf, MusArts* "One of the most important jazz musicians in the last 40 years." — Brian Priestly (jazz pno., critic) <*Saxophone Colossus* (1956, Prestige), *Dancing in the Dark* (1987, Milestone)> *Also see* **black musicians, boss, Charlie Parker, control, improvisation.**

rollover *Eco&Fin* 1 Refinancing of an existing loan. 2 Selling of new securities to pay off old ones coming due.

ROM *InfoMgt* **Read-Only-Memory** Amount of memory in the computer's **solid state** storage chip programmed at the time of its manufacture and cannot be reprogrammed by the user. It is not lost when power is turned off. *Also see* **RAM.**

romance *Flm&Vid, LitArts* 1 Novel, story, or film that deals with love in an idealized form. 2 Long **medieval** narrative in prose or verse that tells of the adventures and heroic exploits of knights rescuing fair damsels or killing off fire-breathing dragons. <King Arthur and the Knights of the Round Table> 3 Fictitiously **embellished** account or explanation.

romance *MusArts* Lyrical, tender, usu. sentimental song or short instrumental piece.

Romanesque (ca 11th-12th centuries) *VisArts* Relating to a style of European architecture, painting and sculpture containing both Roman and **Byzantine** elements. *Also see* **Art Movements and Periods.**

romantic *Crit&Eval* 1 Characteristic of **romanticism** in the arts. 2 Given to thoughts or feelings of romance 3 Displaying, expressive of, or conducive to love. 4 Imaginative but impractical; visionary. <romantic notions> 5 Not based on fact; imaginary or fictitious. <Their view of their life was romanticized beyond belief>

romantic, Romantic *Crit&Eval* Characteristic of **romanticism** in the arts.

romantic comedy *TheatArts* Comic form centering on the romance between two lovers, or between several sets of lovers. Romantic comedy typically begins with some unreasonable impediment to the lovers' union. When after a complicated series of events the obstacle is overcome, the play ends in the lovers coming together.

romanticism *Aes&Creat* In art and other history, a contrary to **classicism**, centering on the individuality of the artist (or doer), and indicating the authentic and distinctive expression of that artist's experience and view. If **classical** forms can be said to cause delight, **romantic** forms tend toward joy. *Origin* Romantic movement originated after **The Enlightenment**, drawing some inspiration from **Kant's** aesthetic ideas. 2 **Romantic** quality or spirit in thought, expression, or action. *Also see* **Art Movements and Periods.**

Romanticism *Crit&Eval* Artistic and intellectual movement originating in Europe in the late 18th century, characterized by a heightened interest in nature, emphasis on the individual's expression of emotion and imagination, departure from the attitudes and forms of classicism, and rebellion against established social rules and conventions. ROMANTICIST. *Also see* **Art Movements and Periods.**

romanticism *TheatArts* Style of drama that concerns itself with adventurous, emotionally loaded characters in remote and exotic circumstances in contrast to classical drama.

rondo (Ital.) *MusArts* Composition with a principal theme that occurs at least three times in its original key between contrasting subordinate themes.

Ronstadt, Linda (1946-, act., sngr.) *ArtPerf, MusArts* Gutsy and talented pop/rock singer who dares to break out — country. <*Trio, 1986*>, jazz. <*What's New, 19??*>, operetta. <*Pirates of Penzance, 1981*>; Hispanic music. <*Mas Canciones, 1991*> *Also see* **arranger, pop-country-pop, popular music.**

roof garden *PerfA&C* Roof or top floor of a building that often contains a dining or entertainment facility.

room tone *Flm&Vid, RecA&S* » **ambient sound**

Roosevelt, Eleanor (Anna Eleanor Roosevelt, 1884-1962) *Journ, Law&Pol* Diplomat, humanitarian, writer, and First Lady of the United States (1933-45) as the wife of **President Franklin D. Roosevelt**. Delegate to the United Nations (1945-52 and 1961-62), she was an outspoken advocate of human rights. Her written works include *This I Remember* (1949)

Roosevelt, Franklin Delano (1882-1945) *Law&Pol* The 32nd President of the United States (1933-45) Governor of New York (1929-32), he ran for President with the promise of a **New Deal** for the American people. Regarded by some (even today) as "an enemy to his class," his administrations were marked by relief programs, measures to increase employment and assist industrial and agricultural recovery from the **Depression**, and World War II. He was the only U.S. President to be reelected three times (1936, 1940, and 1944) He died in office.

root *MusArts* Note from which a chord is built.

ROP *Journ, Mktg* **Run Of Paper, Run Of Position.** Random ad placement; no special position in the newspaper or magazine.

ROS *Mktg, Rdio/TV* **Run Of Schedule, Run Of Station.** Commercial scheduled for no particular time but at the discretion of the station manager.

Ross Reports *PerfA&C* NYC directory of talent agents, casting agencies, and commercial agents.

rostrum *PerfA&C* Elevated platform for public speaking. *Also see* **dais**, **lectern**, **pulpit**.

rotary press *VA-Prntng* Printing press consisting of curved plates attached to a revolving cylinder that prints onto a continuous roll of paper. *Also see* **flat-bed press**.

rotary unit *PA-Variety* **Vaudeville** acts that would play a different theater each night.

rotate *MusArts* repeat

rotation *Rdio/TV, RecA&S* Number of times a record is played on a radio station in a 24 hour period; high rotation = frequent plays; light rotation = less frequent plays. *Also see* **Top 40**.

rote *Crit&Eval* Memorizing process using routine or repetition, often without full attention or comprehension.

Roth IRA *EntreP* An individual retirement account that allows you to contribute up to $2,000 of after tax dollars. Earnings on this account are tax free.

Rotoscope *Flm&Vid* Device developed by the Fleischer studios projects live-action images on a screen where they are then traced frame by frame in order to capture a move difficult to draw.

rouge *Th-MakeUp* Red or pink, dry or creme cosmetic for coloring the skin.

rough cut *Flm&Vid* Crudely edited footage of a movie before the editor starts to edit.

roulade *MusArts* **1 Embellishment** consisting of a rapid run of several notes sung to one syllable. **2** Drum **roll**.

round *MusArts* **Canon** for three or more voices; common name for a circle canon in which each singer returns from the conclusion of the melody to its beginning, repeating it.

round robin *BcstJourn* Series of reports, usu. done live, in which the studio anchor starts by tossing to one field reporter who tosses to the next, who tosses to the next, and so on.

rounds *TheatArts* » **making rounds**

roundup *Journ* summary <a news roundup>

routine *PerfA&C* Set piece of entertainment.

routing a tour *Mgt,PerfA&C* Process of arranging performances in various cities to minimize transportation costs and maximize box office income.

Royal Academy of Dramatic Art (RADA) *TheatArts* » **RADA**

Royal Shakespeare Company *TheatArts* British **repertory** theater with two London companies: Stratford and Aldwych Theatre. Productions include contemporary plays as well as **Shakespeare** and other classics. *Also see* **Theaters & Theatres**.

Royalties *ColEntry, IntelProp* » **artist** (record) —, **Copyright Royalty Tribunal, foreign —, master recording license —, mechanical —, miscellaneous —, performance —, printed music —, producer —, royalty, royalty statement**.

royalty *IntelProp* **1** Share paid to a writer or composer out of the proceeds resulting from the sale or performance of her or his work. **2** Share in the proceeds paid to an inventor or a **proprietor** for the right to use her or his invention or services. *Also see* **Royalties**

royalty statement *IntelProp* Periodic (usu. Jan. 1 and Jul. 1) accounting of accrued and paid **royalties**: "Acting after some authors said they did not trust publisher's royalty statements, the **Authors Guild** announced yesterday that it would pay for an audit of royalty statements of two books a year." — Edwin McDowell (lit. critic) *Also see* **Royalties**.

rpm, r.p.m. *RecA&S* **revolutions per minute.** Measure of the speed of a phonograph record. <16 rpm, 33-1/3 rpm, 45 rpm, 78 rpm>

rps, r.p.s. *RecA&S* **revolutions per second.** Measure of the speed of a reel of magnetic recording tape. <3-3/4 rps, 7-1/2 rps, etc>

rpt. *MusArts,. Rdio/TV* **repeat.**

RRHF *ArtPerf, MusArts* **Rock and Roll Hall of Fame.**

RSN *InfoMgt* Right Soon Now

RTDG *ArtPerf, HR&LR,. Rdio/TV* **Radio and Television Directors Guild** (RTDG) *Also see* **Directors**.

rts. *IntelProp* **rights.**

RTFM *iMedia, InfoMgt* Acronym suggesting that a person read the manual before asking a common question. Often used when the question has an easy-to-find or straightforward answer that askers should be able to quickly find on their own.

rtf file *iMedia* File saved in "rich-text format." more accessible format (most word processors support it) than some application specific formats that still provides some limited style options.

RTW *Fashn* **ready to wear**

rub board *MusInstr* » **washboard**

rubato *MusArts* Rhythmic flexibility within a phrase or **measure**. <play without meter for dramatic effect in the verse of a ballad>

ruche (roosh, Fr.) *Fashn* Ruffle or pleat of lace, **muslin**, or other fine fabric used for trimming women's garments.

ruching (rooshing, Fr.) *Fashn* Gathering look created by pleating a strip of fabric so it **ruffles** on both sides, then stitching the pleating through the center.

rude *Cult&Soc* **primitive**.

rude *InfoMgt* Badly written or functionally poor computer program.

ruffle *Fashn* Strip of frilled or closely pleated fabric used for trimming or decoration.

rule of 70 *EntreP* If an economy grows at x percent per year output will double in 70/x years.

rule of 72 *EntreP* An approximation of the amount of time that it takes for a present sum of money to double by dividing the number 72 by the annual interest rate.

rule utilitarian *Ethcs&Phil* » **utilitarianism**

rumba *Dnce, MusArts* **1** Complex Cuban dance music import, ca. 1930s. **2** Cuban dance and music developed by slaves at latter part of the 19th century. *Also see* **Dances, Latin Dance Music**.

Rumba *Dnce, MusArts* Generic term embracing a variety of names – Son, Danzon, Guagira, Guaracha, Naningo – for a type of West Indian music or dancing. The exact meaning varies from island to island. *Also see* **Dances, Latin Dance Music**.

run *LegAsp* Continue in effect <Contract has two years to run>

run *MusArts* Rapid sequence of eighth or sixteenth notes; a **roulade**. *Also see* **tickle**, **warble**.

run *PA-Variety* Distance between one town where a circus will exhibit and the next.

run *TheatArts* **1** To be presented or performed for a continuous time period. **2** Unbroken sequence of theatrical performances. <The play ran for three months, the concert ran two performances>

run lines *PerfA&C* Rehearse dialogue, informally, no acting out. *Also see* **lines**.

Run of Paper *Journ, Mktg* » **ROP**

Run of Position *Journ, Mktg* » **ROP**

Run Of Schedule *Mktg, Rdio/TV* » **ROS**

Run Of Station *Mktg, Rdio/TV* » **ROS**

run-of-the-mill *Crit&Eval* Nothing special; average.

run-through *PerfA&C* Complete but rapid review or rehearsal of a theatrical production.

runaway production *Flm&Vid* Film production funded and/or originated in the U.S. undertaken in other countries primarily to achieve lower production cost rather than meet creative needs. Most runaway production occurs in Canada where different regulations backed by government subsidies made filming less expensive for American producers than mounting the same production in the U.S. <Film a New Orleans scene in Montreal.> **running order** *TheatArts* Notice posted backstage informing cast and crew of the sequences of scenes to be rehearsed.

rundown *BcstJourn* Story order for a newscast. *Also:* "format" or "lineup."

running a function *iMedia* » **calling a function**

running crew *PerfA&C* Those responsible for operating lighting equipment and shifting scenery and props during rehearsals and performances.

running the story *Journ* "Setting the terms, setting the pace, deciding the **agenda**, determining when and where the story exists, and shaping what the story shall be." — Joan Didion (1934-; author, critic)

runtime *iMedia* Time during which a program is being executed or interpreted (in contrast: compile-time and load time)

runway *PerfA&C* Walkway from the stage into the auditorium. <Here they are! Where beauty queens parade, models slink, and strippers strip> PASSERELLE

rural blues *MusArts* » **country blues** *Also see* **Blues**.

rush *Crit&Eval* **1** Sudden, brief exhilaration. <The performance produced a sudden rush of emotion> **2** Intensely pleasurable sensation experienced immediately after use of a stimulant or a mind-altering drug. *Also see* **aesthetic rush**.

S

rushes *Flm&Vid* First, unedited print of a movie scene. *Also see* **dailies.**

ruthless *Crit&Eval* No compassion or pity; merciless.

ruthless ambition *ArtPerf* Determination not to allow anyone or anything to stand in the way of making it. "Writer's only responsibility is to his art. He will be completely ruthless if he is a good one. He has a dream. It anguishes him so much he must get rid of it. He has no peace until then. Everything goes by the board: honor, pride, decency, security." — **William Faulkner** *Also see* **EAT+D²**

ruthlessness *Eco&Fin, Ethcs&Phil* "Ruthlessness is the [business] executive's philosophical duty. His job is to **crunch** (*InfoMgt*) the numbers, increase productivity, reduce or abolish **fringe benefits** for undownsized employees, export jobs to faraway lands free of unions and child-labor laws, and keep American Number One despite intense global competition." — **Russell Baker.**

- S-

S&P 500 *Eco&Fin* » **Standard & Poor's Index.**

s. *MusArts* **solo.**

S.I.P.C. *InfoMgt* **Simply Interactive Personal Computer.** Class of low-cost computers.

S.P.E.B.S.Q.S.A. *MusArts* **Society for the Preservation and Encouragement of Barber Shop Quartet Singing in America.**

s/h *Mktg* » **shipping and handling**

S/W *InfoMgt* » **shareware**

SA *Fashn* Seventh Avenue (NYC garment district)

saccades *iMedia* Fast, jerky movements that eyes make (two to five saccades per second)

saccharine *Crit&Eval* Cloyingly sweet attitude, tone, or character; excessively sentimental.

sachem (*Native American*) *Mgt* Chief of the tribe; said irreverently of some Hollywood chiefs of studios.

sacred music *MusArts* Religious music

saddle stitch *VA-Prntng* Type of binding to which sections of a publication are inserted rather than stacked, and bound by staples driven through the fold from the outside of the middle of the center form.

safety master *RecA&S* Taped duplicate of the master mix or the original tape or disc recording stored in temperature-controlled vault for safety and backup.

SAG *ArtPerf, HR&LR, Flm&Vid, TheatArts* **Screen Actors Guild.** Labor union chartered by the **Four A's** that represents, in the U.S., actors, singers, **announcers, narrators,** specialty dancers, and specialty acts who work in theatrical, **industrial,** or educational motion pictures, filmed TV programs, and/or filmed TV commercials. *Also see* **Guilds & Unions.**

SAIL *InfoMgt* » **Stanford Artificial Intelligence Laboratory** (Stanford U.) *Also see* **artificial intelligence. Ω**

salary cap *SportsEnt* Complex system first put in place by some professional sports leagues (such as the **National League of Baseball**) to limit team payrolls, while guaranteeing the players a percentage of overall league revenues.

salaries *E&F-Acc* Payment made to employees for services rendered. *Also see* **white collar.** *Also see* **white collar.**

Salary Reduction Plan *Eco&Fin* » **Cash Or Deferred Arrangement plan** (CODA)

sales *E&F-Acc* » **sales revenue**

sales discount *E&F-Acc* Discount given to customers for early payment of sales originally made on credit; sales discount is a contra-revenue (sales) account. *Also see* **trade discount, two percent, net 30.**

sales forecast *EntreP* Prediction of how much of a product or service will be purchased within a market during a specified time period.

sales promotion *EntreP* Inclusive term for any promotional techniques that are neither personal selling nor advertising.

sales rep *Mktg* Salesperson or agent for a seller.

sales representative *Mktg* » **sales rep**

sales revenues *E&F-Acc* Amount that merchandisers earn from selling inventory before subtracting expenses. SALES

salon *VisArts* Public exhibition of works of art. <exhibition sponsored by the Academy of Fine Arts, Paris>

salsa *Dnce, MusArts* Caribbean and **Latin Dance Music** developed by Cuban and Puerto Rican immigrants in NYC in the 1960s. There are Colombian, Venezuelan, Panamanian, and Peruvian varieties. characterized by Afro-Caribbean rhythms that have been around in different forms since the early 1900s. Also *see* **Dances, Latin Dance Music.**

samba *Dnce, MusArts* 1 Brazilian ballroom carnival dance of African origin. 2 Music in 4/4 time for performing this dance. *Also see* **Dances, Latin Dance Music.**

same percentage as film rental earned (SPFRE) *Flm&Vid* » **SPFRE**

same-store sales *Mktg* Sales in stores open at least one year.

"Sammy Glick" *Flm&Vid, LitArts* Main male character, an **archetypal hustler,** in the classic Hollywood novel, *What Makes Sammy Run?* (1941) by **Budd Schulberg.**

sampler *InfoMgt* 1 Snippets of music recorded on a disk. 2 Computer that records and plays back **sound waves.** *Also see* **digital sampler, rap music.**

sampler *VisArts* Decorative piece of cloth embroidered with various designs or mottoes; an example of skill at needlework.

sampling *IntelProp, RecA&S* Sound bytes removed electronically from a master recording and through technological imitation placed within the context of another composition. The length of the bytes can be limitless and can contain lyric and music in combination or in part from any segment of the score. Depending upon the length of the bytes and how they are used, unauthorized sampling could be held to be a copyright infringement of the sound recording from which they were taken and from the musical work they first appeared in. *Also see* **digital sampler; sampler.**

sampling *Mktg* Give away free samples of a product.

sampling rate *iMedia* Number of samples per second.

sampling recorder *RecA&S* Electronic keyboard with **random access memory** (RAM), which allows the user to record sounds into it, play them back, and change them.

sanctify *Crit&Eval* To give social or moral sanction to.

Sand, George (Amandine Aurore Lucie Dupin, Baroness Dudevant, 1804-76, Fr. dram., fictwri., n-fictwri, social critic) *ArtPerf, Crit&Eval LitArts* Her writings concern the freedom and independence of women. <*Lélia* (novel, 1833), *Consuelo* (novel, 1842)> *Also see* **wisdom.**

sanguine *Crit&Eval* Cheerfully confident; optimistic.

sans serif type *iMedia, VA-Prntng* Typeface without **serifs.** Also

sales promotion *EntreP* Inclusive term for any promotional techniques that are neither personal selling nor advertising.

sales rep *Mktg* Salesperson or agent for a seller.

sales representative *Mktg* » **sales rep**

sales revenues *E&F-Acc* Amount that merchandisers earn from selling inventory before subtracting expenses. SALES

salon *VisArts* Public exhibition of works of art. <exhibition sponsored by the Academy of Fine Arts, Paris>

salsa *Dnce, MusArts* Caribbean and **Latin Dance Music** developed by Cuban and Puerto Rican immigrants in NYC in the 1960s. There are Colombian, Venezuelan, Panamanian, and Peruvian varieties. characterized by Afro-Caribbean rhythms that have been around in different forms since the early 1900s. Also *see* **Dances, Latin Dance Music.**

samba *Dnce, MusArts* 1 Brazilian ballroom carnival dance of African origin. 2 Music in 4/4 time for performing this dance. *Also see* **Dances, Latin Dance Music.**

same percentage as film rental earned (SPFRE) *Flm&Vid* » **SPFRE**

same-store sales *Mktg* Sales in stores open at least one year.

"Sammy Glick" *Flm&Vid, LitArts* Main male character, an **archetypal hustler,** in the classic Hollywood novel, *What Makes Sammy Run?* (1941) by **Budd Schulberg.**

sampler *InfoMgt* 1 Snippets of music recorded on a disk. 2 Computer that records and plays back **sound waves.** *Also see* **digital sampler, rap music.**

sampler *VisArts* Decorative piece of cloth embroidered with various designs or mottoes; an example of skill at needlework.

sampling *IntelProp, RecA&S* Sound bytes removed electronically from a master recording and through technological imitation placed within the context of another composition. The length of the bytes can be limitless and can contain lyric and music in combination or in part from any segment of the score. Depending upon the length of the bytes and how they are used, unauthorized sampling could be held to be a copyright infringement of the sound recording from which they were taken and from the musical work they first appeared in. *Also see* **digital sampler, sampler**.

sampling *Mktg* Give away free samples of a product.

sampling rate *iMedia* Number of samples per second.

sampling recorder *RecA&S* Electronic keyboard with **random access memory** (RAM), which allows the user to record sounds into it, play them back, and change them.

sanctify *Crit&Eval* To give social or moral sanction to.

Sand, George (Amandine Aurore Lucie Dupin, Baroness Dudevant, 1804-76, Fr. dram., fictwri., n-fictwri, social critic) *ArtPerf, Crit&Eval LitArts* Her writings concern the freedom and independence of women. <*Lélia* (novel, 1833), *Consuelo* (novel, 1842)> *Also see* **wisdom**.

sanguine *Crit&Eval* Cheerfully confident; optimistic.

sans serif type *iMedia, VA-Prntng* Typeface without **serifs**. Also called Gothic. <Avant-Garde, Geneva, Franklin Gothic, Futura, Helvetica, Univers>

SAR *HR&LR, LitArts* **Society of Authors Representatives.»** **ILAA**

sari *Fashn* Outer garment worn chiefly by women of India and Pakistan, consisting of a length of lightweight cloth with one end wrapped about the waist to form a skirt and the other draped over the shoulder or covering the head.

Sarnoff, David (1891-1971) *Mgt, Rdio/TV* Radio and television pioneer who proposed the first commercial radio receiver and in 1926 formed the **National Broadcasting Company** (NBC) Later bought **RCA** from **GE**.

sarong *Fashn* Skirt consisting of a length of brightly-colored cloth wrapped about the waist worn by men and women in Malaysia, Indonesia, and the Pacific islands.

Sartre, Jean Paul (1905-80, Fr. wri., philos.) *ArtPerf, LitArts* A leading **existentialist**, his works include. <autobiographical novel *Nausea* (1938), play *No Exit* (1944), and philos. vols. that include *Being* and *Nothingness* (1943)> He declined the 1957 **Nobel Prize** for literature. *Also see* **aesthetics, existentialism**.

SATB *MusArts* Soprano, alto, tenor, and bass voices — a vocal ensemble; a chorus.

satellite *Sci&Tech* Device that has been launched into orbit around the earth or other planets, which contains receiving, recording, or transmitting instruments for purposes of communication or research.

satire *LitArts, TheatArts* Writing which tries to correct manners or morals by ridicule. "Satire is what closes Saturday night." — **George S. Kaufman**.

saturation *Flm&Vid* Simultaneous release of a movie throughout a given area in an unusually large number of theaters for a limited period of time. Very heavy **media** buys are made, particularly in TV, in an attempt to build immediate public awareness for maximum box office results: "at theaters everywhere."

saturation *iMedia* vividness of hue

Saturday Nite Live (SNL) *Rdio/TV* weekly TV network satire – sometimes funny – program

satyr play *TheatArts* Brief rugged comedy performed by actors in satyr costumes (half man. half goat) after the performance of a tragic trilogy at the Athens Dionysia festival. usu. on mythological subjects.

save *InfoMgt* To store information somewhere other than in the computer's main memory, such as on a tape disk, so it can be used again. Invaluable insurance against system failure.

Save The Music *MusArts* **» VH1 Save The Music**

saving *EntreP* Total income minus consumption.

savings function *EntreP* Relationship between the level of income and the level of savings.

savvy *Crit&Eval* well informed; perceptive; shrewd

sax *MusInstr* **» saxophone**

Sax, Adolph (Antoine Joseph Sax, 1814-1894) *MusInstr* Belgian instrument maker and the inventor of the **saxophone** (patented 1846)

saxophone (sax) *MusInstr* **Woodwind** instrument with a single-reed mouthpiece and a usu. curved conical metal tube. <soprano —, alto — tenor —, baritone —, bass —> SAX PLAYER, SAXIST

(RARE), SAXOPHONIST. *Origin* Named for its inventor, **Adolph Sax**. *Also see* **Musical Instrument Families**.

SBA *Law&Pol, Mgt* **Small Business Administration**. Established as U.S. agency (1953) to aid, counsel, and protect the interests of small businesses. [Reagan administration tried to abolish the SBA in 1980-81.] *Also see* **Federal Agencies and Statutes**.

SBU *Mgt* **» strategic business unit** *Also see* **SMU, strategic management unit**.

SC *PerfA&C* Stage Center (stage direction)

sc. *Flm&Vid, LitArts, TheatArts»* **scene**

SCA *HR&LR* Self-critical analysis. Method of monitoring workplace conduct.

scab *HR&LR* Worker who refuses membership in a labor union. 2 Employee who works while others are on strike; a **strikebreaker**. 3 Person hired to replace a striking worker.

scalable outline fonts *InfoMgt* Enable an individual character to be changed almost infinitely in size from about 4 points to something in the hundreds of points, allowing variations of tenths or hundredths of points in between. *Also see* **TrueType**.

scale *HR&LR* Minimum wage fixed by contract.

Scale *iMedia* 1 System of ordered marks at fixed intervals used as a reference standard in measurement: 2 Proportion used in determining the dimensional relationship of a representation to that which it represents.

scale *MusArts* Ascending or descending series of **pitches**.

scale plus 10 *Flm&Vid* Refers to an attempt of the major studios to cut the costs of production inflated by the multimillion salaried + percentage of gross paid to box-office stars. "Scale" refers to the **Screen Actors Guild's** minimum daily wage plus 10%, for nonstarring actors or about $522 each working day. In reality the 10% goes to the actor's agent for if the wage is just scale, the agent is not entitled to a commission.

scaling the house *Mgt,PerfA&C* 1 Method of determining the various ticket prices for a particular performance in a particular **venue** at a particular time. 2 Break-even formula based on estimated attendance vs. total costs.

scalper *Mktg* ticket speculator

scan *iMedia, InfoMgt* 1 To search stored data automatically for specific data. 2 To use a scanner to **digitize** an image. <to scan a photo>

scan *LitArts* Analyze verse into **metrical** patterns.

scan *Rdio/TV* Single sweep of the beam of electrons across a TV screen. *Also see* **line**.

scan lines *Rdio/TV* Horizontal lines that compose a television screen image: 525 in the U.S., 625 in Europe.

scanner *InfoMgt* Device that moves a finely focused beam of light or electrons in a systematic pattern over a surface in order to reproduce or sense and subsequently transmit an image. *Also see* **facsimile system, OCR**.

scarcity *EntreP* Situation in which resources are limited and can be used in different ways, so we must sacrifice one thing for another.

scat singing *MusArts* Jazz vocal style in which nonsense syllables imitate the inflection and phrasing of a wind instrument. Sometimes used to cover up forgotten lyrics but most often a brilliant exercise of vocal improvisation. "Scat is the alter ego of improvisation." — Mel Tormé (1925-, stage/film/TV arr.-comp., sngr., pno., drm) <Louis Armstrong, Ella Fitzgerald (» **Apollo Theater**), **Sarah Vaughan**>

scatter market *Rdio/TV* In network TV, the remnants of unsold commercial time that remain after preseason buying has finished.

scenario *LitArts* outline of the plot of a dramatic or literary work

scenario *TheatArts* skeletal outline of the **plot**

scenarist *Flm&Vid* **» screenwriter**

scene (sc.) *Flm&Vid, LitArts,* 1 Place in which the action of a play, movie, novel, or other narrative occurs; a setting. 2 Subdivision of an act in a dramatic presentation in which the setting is fixed and the time continuous. 3 Shot or series of shots in a movie constituting a unit of continuous related action. 4 Scenery and properties for a dramatic presentation. 5 Theater stage.

scene dock, scenery dock *PerfA&C* Place in the theater where scenery is stored.

scene-stealer *ArtPerf* Actor who draws attention from or overshadows other actors in the same scene by charm, quality of performance, or assuming an out-of-character facial expression or body movement. <Babies and dogs are inveterate scene-stealers> *Also see* **upstage**.

scenery *PerfA&C, VisArts* Painted backdrops on a theatrical stage. *Also see* **sets**.

scenic artist *PerfA&C, VisArts* Designer or decorator of scenery.

scenic design *PerfA&C, TheatArts, VisArts* Decoration, the scenic setting, the artistic preparation of the stage. "The awful truth: **Broadway** depends more on inventive, original scenic design than it does on inventive, original new work." — Vincent Canby (19??-, drama critic) STAGE DESIGN *Also see* **decoration**.

scenic designer *PerfA&C* Person responsible for the design and function of the scenery and properties.

scenography *PerfA&C, VisArts* Art of representing objects in perspective, esp. as applied in the design and painting of theatrical scenery.

schadenfreude (German, sha den froyde) *Crit&Eval* Malicious enjoyment of the misfortunes of others.

scheme *iMedia* **1** Orderly combination of related parts. **2** chart, diagram, or outline of a system or object. **3** systematic plan of action.

schematic *Sci&Tech* Structural or procedural diagram, esp. of an electrical or mechanical system.

scherzo *MusArts* Playful, humorous instrumental composition in 3/4 time.

schizophrenia *Crit&Eval* Any of a group of psychotic disorders usu. characterized by withdrawal from reality, illogical patterns of thinking, delusions, and hallucinations, and accompanied in varying degrees by other emotional, behavioral, or intellectual disturbances. "To understand the art of acting, it is necessary to understand a special sort of schizophrenia. On the stage or screen, we deal with the phenomenon of the split personality. The actor and the character sharing one body, one brain. Ideally, the actor – hidden – lives inside the body of the character, controlling thoughts, feelings and actions." — **Garson Kanin**

schlep (shlep, Yinglish) *ArtPerf, Crit&Eval* **1** Bring or take one's self and one's gear or equipment to and from a **gig** site necessitating several, if not more, trips to and fro. **2** To carry clumsily or with difficulty.

schlepper (shlep-per, Yinglish) *Crit&Eval* Clumsy or stupid person: "As schlepper triumphant, **Woody Allen** is living refutation of every Jewish mother's nightmare." — **John Lahr**

schlock *also* **shlock** (Yinglish) *Crit&Eval* Shoddy, cheap, fake.

schmate (shmata, Yiddish for "rag") *Fashn, Yinglish* women's garment. "Oh, you mean this schmate" — said deprecatingly in reply to a compliment.>

schmooze (also *schmoose*, Yinglish) *Crit&Eval* Friendly, aimless talk; chitchat; heart-to-heart talk.

schnook (shuhnook, Yinglish) *Crit&Eval* Stupid or easily victimized person; dupe.

school (sch.) *Crit&Eval* Group of philosophers, artists, or writers, whose thought, work, or style demonstrates a common origin or influence or unifying belief.

school of thought *Crit&Eval* Point of view held by a particular group.

schpritz (Yinglish) *PA-Variety* Style of **standup** comedy typified by **Lenny Bruce**, i.e., a **Joycean** spray of short **riffs** on social and political topics. *Origin* Middle High German "sprützen," to spray.

Schulberg, Budd Wilson (1914-, fict., scrnwrtr.) *ArtPerf, Flm&Vid, LitArts* Best known for his novel about the corrupting power of success, *What Makes Sammy Run?* (1941) <*On the Waterfront* (screenplay, **Oscar** 1954) *Also see* **"Sammy Glick."**

sci-fi *Flm&Vid, LitArts* » **science fiction**

Science & Technology *Sci&Tech* One of the four **Outer Forces** of **The Arts Dynamic**.

science fiction (sci-fi) *Flm&Vid, LitArts* Literary or cinematic **genre** in which **fantasy**, typically based on speculative scientific discoveries or developments, environmental changes, space travel, or life on other planets, forms part of the plot or background.

scintilla *Crit&Eval* Minute amount; an iota or a trace.

SCL *ArtPerf, Flm&Vid, MusArts, Rdio/TV* **Society of Composers and Lyricists** has as its main focus the education, promotion, and support of film and television composers and songwriters.

The SCL, founded in 1983, conducts workshops for writers and filmmakers on the creative, financial, and practical benefits of music in film. Membership open to professionals and new writers as well as film and television business personnel.

scoop *Crit&Eval* Current information or details.

scoop *Flm&Vid* Semicircular-shaped light trough, powered by 500- to 1500-watt globes; a soft light. *Also see* **Stage Lighting**.

scoop *Journ* Exclusive news story acquired by luck or initiative before a competitor.

scoop neck *Fashn* Rounded, usu. low-cut neckline on a blouse or dress.

scope *Flm&Vid* **Gauge** of film. <70mm, 35mm. CinamaScope, Pianissimo, etc>

scope *iMedia* **1** Extent of a project; scope is directly affected by time, budget, resources and assets. **2** region of a program source within which it represents a certain thing. This usu. extends from the place where it is declared to the end of the smallest enclosing block (begin/end or procedure/function body) inner block may contain a re-declaration of the same identifier in which case the scope of the outer declaration does not include (is "shadowed" or "occluded" by) the scope of the inner.

scope creep *iMedia* Project's growth from what was originally planned into something larger without an appropriate adjustment in time, resources, or budget. related syndrome is "featuritis."

score *Flm&Vid* **1** To compose or to match appropriate music to a film or TV program. **2** Musical accompaniment to a film or TV program.

score *MusArts* Written form of a musical composition for orchestral or vocal parts. *Also see* **Print Music**.

scramble *InfoMgt* To transmit a signal in a garbled form so that it can be decoded only by a special receiver and not by normal reception equipment.

scrambler *InfoMgt* Electronic device that **scrambles** telecommunication signals to make them unintelligible to anyone without a special receiver.

Scrapbook *InfoMgt* Computer desk accessory in which pictures or text can be stored temporarily to be inserted in another place or another document.

scratch track *Flm&Vid* Temporary audio track often used for editing purposes.

scratchboard *VisArts* Drawing board covered with white clay and a black surface layer scraped away with a scratching tool to produce black-and-white line drawings. SCRAPERBOARD

scratchpad *InfoMgt* High-speed internal register in a computer for temporary storage of preliminary data or notes.

screamer *Journ* Sensational headline <Congress Passes Campaign Reform Bill>

screamer *PA-Variety* Comedy routine that evokes screams or laughter.

screed *Crit&Eval* Long, monotonous **harangue** or piece of writing.

screen (scrn.) *Flm&Vid* **1** White or silver surface on which a picture is projected for viewing. **2** Movie industry. SILVER SCREEN

screen *HR&LR* System for preliminary appraisal and selection of personnel as to their suitability for particular jobs.

screen *InfoMgt, Rdio/TV* **1** Phosphorescent surface on which an image is displayed on a TV or computer monitor. **2** Information or image displayed at a given time on a monitor, display, or video terminal. *Also see* **big screen, silver screen, small screen**.

screen *VA-Prntng* Glass plate or sheet of film marked off with intersecting opaque lines, placed before the lens of a camera which breaks a continuous tone image into dots as it exposes the film. Number of dots per square inch determine the tone of the exposed photograph.

Screen Actors Guild (SAG) *ArtPerf, Flm&Vid, HR&LR* » **SAG**

Screen Actors Guild Foundation *ArtPerf, Flm&Vid* **Nonprofit** that offers financial assistance and scholarships to **SAG** members or their children.

screen direction *Flm&Vid* Whichever direction, left or right, the actor is looking at or moving toward, described from the audience point of view.

screen dump *InfoMgt* Transferring on-screen data to a printer or a storage medium.

screen name *InfoMgt* Identification used to gain access to an online service.

screen test *Flm&Vid* Brief movie sequence filmed to test the ability of an aspiring performer.

screen-print *VisArts, VA-Prntng* To print using the silk-screen process.

screening *Flm&Vid* Presentation of a movie.

screenland *Flm&Vid* Movie industry; Hollywood.

screenplay (sp.) *Flm&Vid, LitArts* Script for a movie, inc. camera directions and descriptions of scenes.

screenwriter (scrnwrtr.) *Flm&Vid* One who writes screenplays. SCENARIST

screwball *Crit&Eval* Person, idea, or plot regarded as eccentric, impulsively whimsical, or simply irrational:<Lucille Ball (1911-89, film/TV/vaude comic, prod.)

scribble *Crit&Eval, LitArts* Careless, hurried writing. SCRIB-BLER.

scribe *LitArts* Professional copyist of manuscripts and documents.

scrim *PerfA&C* **Drop** made from **translucent** or transparent material.

scrimshaw *VisArts* Art of carving or incising intricate designs on whalebone or whale ivory.

script *Flm&Vid, Rdio/TV* Text of a play, broadcast, or movie.

script *InfoMgt* Feature of some computer systems that allow the user to "write" or automate a series of commands that can be activated by one or two key strokes.

script *LegAsp* original document

script *VA-Prntng* Style of type that imitates handwriting.

script clerk *Flm&Vid* One responsible for keeping complete records of the shooting of all scenes.

script supervisor *Flm&Vid* » **script clerk**

scriptorium, scriptoria (Latin for *scriptus*, "to write") *LitArts, VisArts* Room(s) in a monastery for the copying, writing, or illuminating of manuscripts.

scriptwriter *Flm&Vid, Rdio/TV* Writer of a script. SCENARIST *Also see* **dramatist, playwright, screenwriter**.

scrn. *Flm&Vid* **screen**

scrnwrtr. *ArtPerf, Flm&Vid* **screenwriter**

scroll *InfoMgt* To cause displayed text or graphics to move vertically or horizontally across the screen so that a line of text or graphics appears at one edge of the screen for each line that moves off the opposite edge.

scroll *MusInstr* **1** Curved head on an instrument of the violin family. **2** Ornament or ornamental design that resembles a partially rolled scroll of paper.

scrubbing *iMedia* Moving a playback head through a span of frames (video editing, animation software, etc.)

SCS *InfoMgt* **Society for Computer Simulation**. Worldwide technical society devoted primarily to the advancement of **simulation** and allied technologies, notably those dealing with management, social, scientific, biological, and environmental problems.

SCSI (scuzzy) *InfoMgt* **Small Computer System Interface**. Specification of mechanical, electrical and functional standards for connecting **peripheral** devices to small computers.

Scully, Vincent (1920-, critic, hist.) *Crit&Eval, VisArts* Architectural historian; professor, Yale College. <*Architecture: The Natural and the Manmade* (1991) *Also see* **architecture**

sculp. *VisArts* **sculptor, sculpture**

sculpt *VisArts* To shape, mold, or fashion with artistry or precision.

sculptor (sculp.) One who produces sculptural artwork.

sculpture (sculp.) *VisArts* Art or practice of shaping figures or designs in the round or in relief, as by chiseling marble, modeling clay, or casting in metal.

scumble *LitArts* To blur lines or areas. <a writer who scumbles the line between fact and **fiction**.

scumble *VisArts* To soften the colors or outlines of a painting or a drawing by covering with a film of opaque or semi-opaque color or by rubbing.

scummerazzi *Crit&Eval* Another name for **videorazzi**. *Also see* **paparazzi**.

scuzzy *Crit&Eval* disreputable; sleazy

scuzzy *InfoMgt* » **SCSI**

SD *InfoMgt, Flm&Vid* **Super-density disk**. Double-sided **digital** video disk the size of a CD.

SE *Eco&Fin* **stock exchange**

.sea *InfoMgt* » **self-extracting archive** *Also see* **sea change**.

sea change *Crit&Eval* marked transformation.

sea change *InfoMgt* Considerable difference in an expansion or a construction of a file.

Sea island cotton *Fashn* Tropical American species of cotton widely cultivated for its fine, long-staple fibers.

sealer *Th-MakeUp* Liquid plastic skin adhesive used to provide a protective coating for various makeup constructions.

sealer *VisArts* Undercoat of paint or varnish used to **size** a surface.

seamless *Crit&Eval* perfectly consistent.

search engine *InfoMgt* Redefined (in 1998) by many Web site companies as a **portal**. *Also see* **portals**.

seascape *VisArts* View or picture of the sea.

season ticket *PerfA&C* Ticket valid for a series of performances for a specified period of time.

seat *Eco&Fin* Membership in a stock exchange obtained by purchase.

SEC *Eco&Fin, Law&Pol* **Securities Exchange Commission**. U.S. government agency that supervises the exchange of securities so as to protect investors against **malpractice**.

sec. *LegAsp, LitArts, PerfA&C* section

second *MusArts* **1** Singing or playing a part having a lower range. **2** Interval between consecutive **tones** on the **diatonic scale**. **3** Second part, instrument, or voice in a harmonized composition. <second violin, second soprano>

Second City, The *PA-Theat* Improvisationally based theatre group est. 1959 in Chicago. "The entire recent tradition of American theatrical satire can be summed up in three works: 'The Second City.'" — Clive Barnes, *NY Times*...

second fiddle *Crit&Eval* Secondary role. <vice president, lieutenant governor>

second generation *InfoMgt* Period of computer technology distinguished by the use of **solid-state circuitry**.

second position *Dnce* (Ballet) Feet apart, in a straight line. *Also see* **Positions**.

second unit *Flm&Vid* Subunit of the production team assigned to do pickup shots, overseas location shots to establish locale, stunt shots, and backup shots in conjunction with the main crew, i.e., the A-team. *Also see* **stunt coordinator**.

second-class mail *InfoMgt, Mktg* Class of U.S. and Canadian mail consisting of newspapers and periodicals. Mailing rate based on a formula that includes unit weight, percentage of advertising, and delivery zone. Historically, the rate is low in order that **free speech** be easily disseminated.

second-day lead *BcstJourn* This is the first attempt to restructure the information from a breaking story. It could happen on the second day. *Also see* **folo, folo lead**...

second-line *MusArts* "When on parade, [**brass**] **bands** were generally accompanied by a grand marshal, his aides, and a host of non-musicians, chiefly children, who danced along in time to the music."— **Eileen Southern**. [And they all still do it real good.].

second-rate *Crit&Eval* Inferior or mediocre quality or value; less than **first-rate**, better than **third-rate**.

secondary boycott *HR&LR* Boycott against a business for making or selling goods made by nonunionized labor.

secondary colors *iMedia* Created by an equal mixture of the three primaries.

secondary data *InfoMgt, Mgt* Existing and accessible information that can provide material for management decision making or serve as inputs or leads to new primary-collection efforts. *Also see* **primary data**.

secondary market *EntreP* Subsequent to their initial sale securities are traded on a secondary markets such as stock exchanges and over the counter markets.

secondary meaning *IntelProp* When an ordinary term has become a recognizable brand name and has acquired a **trademark**. <Apple Computer>

secondary storage *InfoMgt* Computer's external storage disk or tape.

sect *Cult&Soc* **1** Group of people forming a distinct unit within a larger group by virtue of certain refinements or distinctions of belief or practice. **2** Religious body that has separated from a larger denomination. *Also see* **cult**.

section *Journ* Separate division of a newspaper. <sports section>

section *Law&Pol* Division of a statute or legal code.

section *LitArts* Subdivision of a written work.

section *MusArts* Group of similar instruments or voices in the same **ensemble**:<rhythm section, string section, etc>

section *PerfA&C* Drawing of the side view of the stage as seen through the middle of the stage to allow a designer or technician to see if the show will **mask**.

sectors *InfoMgt* Disks are divided in concentric circles called **tracks**... each track is further divided into wedges called sectors. Sectors can be identified by the side of the disk they're located on, their track number, and the sector number within the track. *Also see* **bad sector**.

secular *Crit&Eval* Worldly rather than spiritual.

secular humanism *Ethcs&Phil* Outlook or a philosophy that advocates human rather than religious values.

secularism *Cult&Soc* **1** View that religious considerations should be excluded from civil affairs or public education. **2** Religious **skepticism** or indifference. *Also see* **Fundamentalism**.

Secure Digital Music Initiative *IntelProp, LegAsp, MusArts* Agreement made in Dec. 1998 by a coalition of the five major record companies and various Internet companies to stop software piracy by the development of a universal digital copyright protective strategy.

Secure Sockets Layer *InfoMgt* » **SSL**

secured debt *EntreP* Debt of a company or individual that is backed by specific assets which are pledged to guarantee the debt.

Securities and Exchange Commission (SEC) *Eco&Fin, EntreP, Law&Pol* Agency that regulates the sale and exchange of publicly traded securities. The SEC is an independent, nonpartisan, quasi judicial regulatory agency with responsibility for administering the federal securities laws.

seed capital *Eco&Fin* Initial funds that can help develop additional capital on a fixed asset project.

seed funding *Eco&Fin, Fndng* Start-up funds used to organize a new foundation or to begin a pilot project. *Also see* **seed money**.

seed money *Eco&Fin, Fnding* **1** Venture capitalist's first contribution toward the financing or capital requirements of a start-up business. **2** Grant or contribution used to start a new project or organization. Seed grants may cover salaries and other operating expenses of a new project. *Also see* **venture capital**.

seeing-in-the-mind *LitArts* The term "mental imagery" suggests a product rather than the stream of interactions that characterizes the activity of "seeing-in-the-mind." "**Mind's eye**" is commonly used and carries with it a useful and accurate implication of a **spatial** relationship, of an "eye" seeing what passes before it. — Betty Shiflett and John Schultz

segue (seg'-way) *BcstJourn* Transition between parts of a presentation. In news, the segue is the transition into the next story.

segue (seg'-way) *Crit&Eval* To move smoothly and unhesitatingly from one state, condition, situation, or element to another.

segue (seg'-way) *Flm&Vid, MusArts* **Transition** from one element or theme of sound or music to another.

select *InfoMgt* To designate where the next action will take place.

selection *InfoMgt* Information or items that will be affected by the next command. Selected item is usu. highlighted.

selection *LitArts, MusArts* Literary text or a musical composition chosen for reading performance.

selective focusing *Flm&Vid* » **rack focusing**

self publisher *LitArts, VA-Prntng* One who assumes the responsibilities of an established book publisher, i.e., select the manuscript, typeset, edit, and manufacture the manuscript. Some self publishers attempt distribution but usu. seek an independent book distributor or a production-distribution deal with an established publisher.

self-censorship *Ethcs&Phil, Journ, Law&Pol* Voluntarily choosing, for various reasons, possibly inc. real or perceived pressure from peers, management, career advancement, or "the competition," to avoid writing, performing, or pursuing certain news stories that would otherwise be considered legitimate, or to write or perform them in specific ways in response to these real or perceived pressures. *Also see* **survival**. [I agree with Steve Berlin (19??-; Dep. Dir., City of Chicago Board of Ethics) that 'self-censorship' is simply cowardice that can't be blamed on another

or else it's real **censorship**.]

self-contained group *ArtPerf, IntelProp, MusArts* Musical ensemble that performs and writes – and copyrights – its own material. *Also see* **controlled compositions**, **singer-songwriter**.

self-cover *VA-Prntng* Cover pages of a publication that are not printed separately on different paper stock but are part of the outside **signature**.

self-dealing *LegAsp* When an agent deals with the **principal** in a **conflict of interest** manner; a violation of an agent's duty of loyalty to the principal. <selling to or buying property from the **principal**>

self-extracting archive (.sea) *InfoMgt* **Archive** that contains not only compressed data but also the means to decompress itself.

self-insurance *Eco&Fin, Mgt* Insurance of oneself or one's possessions against possible loss by regularly setting aside funds. *Also see* **risk management**.

self-management *ArtPerf* Act, manner, or practice of managing, supervising, or controlling one's own artistic work.

self-organizing system *InfoMgt, Mgt* Emerging theory of management based on a phrase biologists use to describe organisms that continually adapt to the environment without losing their basic identity. "Self-organizing systems do not simply take in information, they change their environments as well." — Margaret Wheatley (mgt. theorist)

self-production *ArtPerf* Create, promote, and produce artistic work through one's own efforts, often as an unaffiliated, independent entity.

self-referential *iMedia* Third stage in the evolution with in a medium: Begins somewhere with in the complex phase signifying a time when the audience is so aware of the aesthetic that the piece self-confidence exploits this knowledge to its own ends.

self-taught art *Cult&Soc, VisArts* "Self-taught art is many things, inc. work by academically untrained artists and by others who, through choice or necessity, live at society's margins." — Holland Cotter (art critic)

sell short *Crit&Eval* To underestimate the true value or worth.

sell short *Eco&Fin* To contract for the sale of securities or commodities one expects to own at a later date and at more advantageous terms.

sell-off rights *RecA&S* Right of a licensee to sell-off recordings that have been distributed but remain unsold at the end of the foreign licensing agreement.

seller's market, sellers' market *Mktg* Market condition with high prices and supply falling short of demand. *Also see* **buyer's market**.

selling expenses *Eco&Fin* » **production expenses/selling expenses**

Selznick, David O. (1902-65, flmkr.) *Flm&Vid* Known for his adaptation of popular novels. <*Gone With the Wind* (1939), *A Farewell to Arms* (1958)> *Also see* **creative producer**, **one way option**, **PGA**.

semiclassical *MusArts* Relating to a style or form that falls between the classical and popular **genres**.

semiconductor *Sci&Tech* Any of various solid crystalline substances having electrical conductivity greater than insulators but less than good **conductors**. <silicon> *Also see* **solid-state**.

semiconductor memory *InfoMgt* **Volatile** form of memory contained on **silicon** chips.

seminal *Crit&Eval* Highly influential in an original way; providing a basis for further development.

semiotics *iMedia* Theory and study of signs and symbols, especially as elements of language or other systems of communication, and comprising semantics, syntactics, and pragmatics.

semitone *MusArts* Interval equal to a half tone in the standard **diatonic scale**. HALF STEP, HALF TONE

Sen. *Law&Pol* Senator

Send-A-Song *IntelProp, RecA&S* Commercial service that exploits copyrighted recordings by sending audio "greeting cards" by telephone without permission from the record companies.

send-up or **sendup** *Crit&Eval* Amusing imitation or parody; a **takeoff**.

seniority *HR&LR* Length of service with an employer. <preference is usu. given to employees with seniority>

SeniorNet *InfoMgt* Nonprofit organization for older adults interested in using computers.

sensational *Crit&Eval* **1** Outstanding; spectacular. <The play was sensational — one never to be forgotten> **2** Arousing or intended to arouse strong curiosity, interest, or reaction, esp. by exaggerated or lurid details. <sensational journalism>

sense memory Recall of physical sensations.

sensitive *ArtPerf, Crit&Eval* **1** Capable of adjusting one's performance: to the demands of ensemble performance (i.e., **balance**, **blend, harmony**), to the perceived mood and temper of the audience (i.e., **empathic response**), to the special atmosphere or mood created by a particular environment (i.e., **ambiance**) **2** Quick to take offense; touchy.

sensitivity *Rdio/TV* **Signal** strength required by an FM tuner to reduce noise and distortion.

sensory symbol *iMedia* "Symbol and aspect of visualization that derives its expressive power from its ability to use the perceptual processing power of the brain without learning" — Colin Ware

sensual *Crit&Eval* **1** Relating to the senses. **2** Suggesting sexuality. **3** Physical rather than spiritual or intellectual. **4** Lacking in moral or spiritual interests.

sensualism *Ethcs&Phil* Ethical **doctrine** that the pleasures of the senses are the highest good.

separation *Mktg, Rdio/TV* Amount of time – determined by station policy – that elapses between one commercial and another, esp. advertising of competitive products.

sepia *VisArts* Color or a photograph in color that ranges from a dark grayish yellow brown to dark or moderate olive brown.

septet *MusArts* **1** Composition for seven voices or instruments. **2** Seven singers or instrumentalists.

sequel *Flm&Vid, LitArts* Film or literary work complete in itself but continuing the narrative of an earlier work.

sequence *BcstJourn* Series of videotape shots that tells the story of a single action, event, or time period. Sequence usu. intercuts different focal length shots, such as **close-ups** (**CUs**), medium shots (**MSs**), and wide shots (**WSs**), to achieve variety.

sequence *Flm&Vid* Series of single film shots edited to constitute an aesthetic or dramatic unit; an episode.

sequence *MusArts* Repetition of a short musical phrase at a different **pitch**.

sequencer *InfoMgt* Device that sorts data in a prearranged sequence. *Also see* **sort**.

sequencing *RecA&S* Arranging of the individual **tracks** in the order they will appear on the finished album. Usually the first track on side 1 is believed to have the best chance of being a commercial hit because that's the track played first by **AOR** radio stations.

sequential *Rdio/TV* Color TV system in which the primary colors red, green, and blue are transmitted as dots in sequence and displayed in the same sequence to produce a complete color image.

sequential giving *Fndng* Cardinal principle of fund-raising that gifts in a campaign should be sought "from the **top down**," i.e, that the largest gifts in a gift range table should be sought at the outset of the campaign, followed sequentially by a search for lesser gifts.

sequential processing *InfoMgt* Process of creating a new master file each time transactions are processed.

serenade *MusArts* **1** Instrumental composition written for a small **ensemble** and having characteristics of the **suite** and the **sonata**. **2** Complimentary performance given to honor or express love for someone.

serene *Crit&Eval* Unaffected by disturbance; calm and unruffled.

serial *Flm&Vid, LitArts* Literary or dramatic work published or produced in installments. *Also see* **cliffhanger**.

serial *InfoMgt* Relating to the sequential transmission of all the bits of a byte over one wire. <serial port, serial printer>

serial *MusArts* Relating to a **12-tone** row.

serial music *MusArts* Composition based on a series or row of patterns of **pitch**, rhythm, or **dynamics**; synonymous with **twelve-tone music**.

serial port *InfoMgt* Connects devices that, unlike **parallel ports**, send and receive information via a serial interface, i.e., one signal at a time is sent through the serial port; the information is reassembled on the receiving end.

serial processing *InfoMgt* Method of processing computer instruc-

tions and programs in a predetermined order.

Serial-Line Internet Protocol (SLIP) *InfoMgt* » **SLIP**

series *Journ, LitArts* Succession of continuously numbered issues or volumes of a publication, published with related authors or subjects and similar formats.

series *Rdio/TV* Succession of regularly-aired programs, each complete in itself.

serif type *iMedia, VA-Prntng* Fine line finishing off the main strokes of a letter, as at the top and bottom of "M." <Bodini, Bookman, Garamond, Century, Times, etc> *Also see* **sans-serif type**.

serious artist *ArtPerf* Any artist or performer who is serious about their work; not restricted to classical performers or **fine artists**. **1** "The world likes humor, but it treats it patronizingly. It decorates its serious artists with laurel, and its wags with Brussels spouts. It feels that if a thing is funny it can be presumed to be something less than great, because if it were truly great it would be wholly serious." — **E.B. White**. **2** "When the work of a serious artist who has become fashionable undergoes a subsequent falling off in quality, we are quick to assume that it is his fashionableness that has done him in. Maybe yes and maybe no; one too many factors enter into the production of works of art, esp. over a lifetime, for anyone to be sure what part the Grand Opposites – health, sickness wealth, poverty fame, obscurity – play in an artist's career." — Brendan Gill (1914-1997, staff writer, *New Yorker* for 61 years.)

serious literature *LitArts* "If the publishing of particular book is highly successful – in publishing terms, if the book 'really *sells*' – it is unlikely that the book will be considered literature, or at least serious literature. Conversely, if the publishing fails, the same book is much more likely to be hailed as a masterpiece long after it ceases to be available except by special order."— James Landis (lit. critic)

serious music *MusArts* Any music composed or performed by anyone who is serious about their work; not necessarily synonymic with "classical" music. "Why call it classical? Why hand it an anchor? Do we have to call it classical to certify that it's good? People know it's good. If you call it classical, are you saying it's serious music? I mean **Cole Porter** and **Duke Ellington** took themselves seriously. They also cracked jokes." — **Jon Pareles**

serious writers *LitArts* "Serious writers, I should say, are on the whole more vain and self-centered than journalists, though less interested in money." — **George Orwell**

server *InfoMgt* Processor in a **Local Area Network** (LAN) that controls the shared use of a resource such as disk storage or a printer.

server-side code *iMedia* Code that runs on a server during a client-server interaction.

service mark *IntelProp* **Trademark** that distinguishes the services of its holder from those of its competitors.

service units *E&F-Acc* » **estimated useful life**

SESAC Inc. *MusArts, IntelProp* **Performance rights organization** that represents authors and publishers for performance, mechanical, and **synchronization** rights. **SESAC** also licenses the dramatic music performing rights in its affiliates' works. *Also see* **Copyright-Related Organizations**.

sess. *RecA&S* **session**

session (sess.) *RecA&S* Period of time devoted to a specific **recording session**

session musician *MusArts, RecA&S* » **session player**

session player *MusArts, RecA&S* Instrumentalist performing in a recording session. SESSION MUSICIAN, STUDIO MUSICIAN *Also see* **contract artist**.

set *Dnce* **1** Number of couples in a square dance. **2** Movements of a square dance.

set *Flm&Vid* Entire enclosure in which a movie is filmed. *Also see* **sound stage**.

set *LitArts* Group of books or periodicals published as a unit.

set *MusArts* <Set music to a poem; set words to a piece of instrumental music> **2** Session of music, usu. dance music, played before an intermission. *Also see* **take five**.

set, sets *PerfA&C* **scenery** on a theater stage

set list *MusArts* List of tunes to be played in a musical performance. *Also see* **set**.

set piece *LitArts, VisArts* Often brilliantly executed artistic or literary work characterized by a formal pattern.

set piece *PerfA&C* Realistic piece of stage scenery constructed to stand by itself.

set *TheatArts* To specify a place for a play or a scene in a play. <The play is set in Chicago, the scene is set in a southside home>

set *VA-Prntng* Arrange type into words and sentences before printing.

set up shop *Mgt* Establish a business operation…

setting *TheatArts* scenic environment of the action

set-asides *Fnding* funds set aside by a foundation for a specific purpose or project that are counted as qualifying distributions toward the foundation's annual payout requirement. Amounts for the project must be paid within five years of the first set-aside.

set-up *PerfA&C* Establish a premise, e.g.: a joke. *Also see* **standup comedy formula.**

setup *Flm&Vid* Positioning of the camera and lights for a specific shot.

Seventh Avenue (SA) *Fashn* » **SA**

seventh *MusArts* Interval between the **tonic** and the seventh tone of a **diatonic scale.**

severe *Crit&Eval* Marked by or requiring strict adherence to rigorous standards or high principles. *Also see* **Dances.**

sex appeal *Crit&Eval* **1** General appeal; power to interest or attract. **2** Personal qualities that arouse others sexually.

sexual orientation *Cult&Soc, HR&LR* Direction of one's sexual interest toward members of the same, opposite, or both sexes. Discrimination in hiring based on sexual orientation can be considered an **unfair employment practice** in some states.

SFX *Flm&Vid, Rdio/TV, RecA&S* » **sound effects**

SGA *ArtPerf, MusArts* **Songwriters' Guild of America.** Est. 1931 as the **American Guild of Authors and Composers** (AGAC), that serves to represent, protest, and strengthen the rights of composers and lyricists in their dealings with music publishers, SGA is noted for its **Popular Songwriters Contract**, and is active in the legislative and judicial areas. *Also see* **Copyright-Related Organizations.**

SGML *iMedia* » **Standard Generalized Markup Language**

SGML *iMedia* Standard Generalized Markup Language for describing the logical structure of a computer document.

shadow *Th-MakeUp* In make-up, an area that is darker than the base which makes things appear smaller or less prominent.

shadow box *Flm&Vid, PerfA&C* Metal hood containing **spill** shields suspended from the first border to control light **spill.**

shadow box *Mktg* Shallow, framed, rectangular box usu. with a glass front used for holding and protecting items on display.

shadow dance *Dnce* One presented by casting shadows of dancers on a screen. *Also see* **Dances.**

shag *Fashn* Coarse long nap on a woolen cloth.

shag *Dnce* 1930s dance step consisting of a hop on each foot in turn. *Also see* **Dances.**

shake *MusArts* **1** Special trumpet effect that resembles a slow **trill** by which the tone is varied upward. **2** Altering **pitch** by changing the **embouchure** very rapidly and forcefully.

shake a leg *Dnce* (Passé) To dance.

Shakespeare, William (1564-1616, Eng. dram., poet, act.-mgr.) *ArtPerf, LitArts, Mgt,* His body of works is considered the greatest in English literature. *Also see* **actor-manager, classic. drama, relativism, Royal Shakespeare Company.**

shallow *Crit&Eval* Lacking depth of intellect, emotion, or knowledge.

shaman *Cult&Soc* Member of certain tribal societies who acts as a medium between the visible world and an invisible spirit world and who practices magic or sorcery for purposes of healing, divination, and control over natural events.

shape *iMedia* characteristic surface configuration of a thing; an outline or contour

share *EntreP* Contract that provide it's owner with residual rights to the earnings of a company, it's assets in the case of dissolution, and other rights may be provided such as voting.

share, shares *Eco&Fin, Mgt* Single units of **stock** (ownership) that a stockholder owns in a corporation. <If a stockholder owns 100 shares of a corporation that has 1000 outstanding shares,

then the stockholder owns 10% of the corporation>

share of audience *Rdio/TV* Percentage of total households or population in a particular market area that use radio or TV during a specific time and that are also tuned in to a particular program.

share of market *Mktg* » **market share**

shared disk *InfoMgt* Hard disk connected to a computer on a network that contains files that other computers on the network can access. *Also see* **file server.**

shared vision *iMedia* Overarching pattern that describes the application of the team's collective imagination to the problem of formulating a group intention. This intention provides an architecture of purpose that will support the realization of that intention over time.

shareholders' equity *Eco&Fin* » **net worth**

shareware (S/W) *InfoMgt* Software distributed to the general public with payment made to the author on a donation basis only; can be downloaded free or for a small fee from an online service.

Shavian *ArtPerf, Crit&Eval, LitArts,* .Pertaining to **George Bernard Shaw.** <Shavian wit>

Shaw, George Bernard (1856-1950, Ir.-born, Brit. plywri, music critic, wit) *ArtPerf, Crit&Eval, LitArts,* .A founder of the **Fabian Society,** his plays include. <*Arms and the Man* (1894), *Pygmalion* (1913), *Saint Joan* (1923)> Awarded 1925 **Nobel Prize** for literature. SHAVIAN

Shawn, William (1907-92) *Journ, LitArts* Editor, *The New Yorker* magazine. (1952-87) *Also see* **Information Management.**

sheet *Journ* Newspaper, esp. a **tabloid**

sheet feed *InfoMgt* Mechanism that uses friction to move single sheets of paper through a printer. *Also see* **tractor feed.**

sheet music *MusArts* Compositions printed on unbound sheets of paper containing the music and lyrics for both popular and classical music. *Also see* **Print Music.**

sheetfed *VA-Prntng* Type of press that prints on sheets of paper rather than rolls. *Also see* **letterpress.**

sheets of sound *MusArts* Musical sounds by and of **John Coltrane.** Ω

shelf space *Mktg* Amount of room or space on a retailer's shelf (or **rack space**) for a given product. Suppliers with the most number of best-selling brands or labels can command more shelf space than less fortunate competitors. *Also see* **market share.**

shell *InfoMgt* Software program provides a means to control the operating system. DOS shell programs are usu. add-on programs designed to make it easier to use MS-DOS.

Sherman Antitrust Act *Eco&Fin, Mktg* U.S. federal statute (1890) forbids contracts in **restraint of trade** and attempts at monopolization in order to maintain free enterprise and price competition. Enforcement by the Dept. of Justice varies with the economic philosophy and political ideology of the incumbent administration. *Also see* **Federal Agencies and Statutes, trust.**

shibboleth *Crit/Eval* Commonplace saying or idea.

shikse (shik'-sa, Yinglish) *Crit&Eval* Woman who is not Jewish.

shill *PA-Variety* One who poses as an eager or satisfied customer at a rigged auction, **carny** game, or similar minor frauds and swindles. *Also see* **bushes.**

shimmy *Dnce* Popular dance of the 1920s characterized by rapid shaking of the body. *Also see* **Dances.**

shindig *Dnce, MusArts* Festive party, often with dancing. *Also see* **Dances.**

ship *iMedia* Act of releasing a product version. <version 4.5 shipped today>

shipping point *E&F-Acc* » **FOB Shipping Point**

shirr *Fashn* To gather cloth into decorative rows by parallel stitching.

shirtwaist *Fashn* Woman's blouse or bodice styled like a tailored shirt.

shivaree *Cult&Soc, MusArts* Noisy mock **serenade** for newlyweds. CHARIVARI

shlemiel (schle-meal, Yinglish) *Crit&Eval* Simpleton, unlucky person, born loser, social misfit.

shmalz (shmall'-ts, Yinglish) *Crit&Eval* Chicken fat. Excessive sentimentality, **bathos**; corny, **mawkish**; **hackneyed**; greatly exaggerated. Staple in the technical vocabulary of show business.

shnook (Yinglish) *Crit&Eval* Timid, unassertive sap; pathetic, but not despicable.

---

shock radio *Rdio/TV* Talk radio format relies on whatever lower-than-common repartee will boost ratings. <Howard Stern>

shoestring *Crit&Eval* Barely adequate capital. <company that started on a shoestring> *Also see* **nickel-and-dime**.

shofar *Cult&Soc, MusInstr* Trumpet made of a ram's horn, used in Hebrew religious services.

shoot *Flm&Vid, VisArts* Photographic assignment or a cinematographic picture.

shooter *BcstJourn, Flm&Vid* One who records on film.

shooter *Fashn* To change the appearance of colored cloth by interweaving weft threads of a different color.

shooting ratio *Flm&Vid* Total amount of film stock photographed compared to the amount selected for use in the **fine cut**. Shooting ratio of 20:1 means that twenty feet of film where shot for every foot used in the finished product.

shooting script *Flm&Vid* Written breakdown of a script into separate shots complete with technical instructions.

shop *Mgt* Seek to **book** an **attraction**. "When we 'shop' for artists these days, we do most of our business with the giants [talent agencies] or the **boutiques**." — Peter Pastreich (exec. dir., San Francisco Sym.)

shop *Mktg, RecA&S* Offer an audition tape or a finished recording to potential lessors, buyers, or distributors.

shop steward *HR&LR* Union member elected to represent co-workers in dealings with management.

shopping mall intercepts *Mktg* This market research technique calls for an interviewer to elicit responses about a particular product or service from mall shoppers.

shopping products *Mktg* Products that the consumer, in the process of selection and purchase, characteristically compares suitability, quality, price, and style. *Also see* **convenience products**, **specialty products**.

short lens *Flm&Vid* » **wide-angle lens**

short-range plan *EntreP* Plan that governs a company's operations for one year or less.

short rate *Mktg* When an advertiser falls short of using the amount of advertising contracted for, the medium may rebill the advertiser at a higher **earned rate**.

short sale *Eco&Fin* Sale of a security that one does not own but has borrowed in anticipation of making a profit by paying for it after its price has fallen.

short story *LitArts* Short piece of prose **fiction**, having few characters and aiming at unity of effect.

short subject *Flm&Vid* Brief film often shown before a **feature**-length film.

short-term *Eco&Fin* Payable or reaching **maturity** within a relatively brief time. <short-term loan, short-term note>

shortfall *Eco&Fin* If revenues are less than costs, the shortfall is the difference between an attraction's revenues and the actual costs of production.

shortfall *Mktg* Amount by which supply falls short of expectation, need, or demand.

shot *Flm&Vid, VisArts* **1** Single cinematic view or take. **2** Photograph or one in a series of photographs.

shotgun mic *RecA&S* Highly directional **mic** used in the broadcasting of sports events, questions/answers at press conferences, and **boom** use in film and TV studios. *Also see* **Microphones**.

shout *Cult&Soc, MusArts* **1** Style of black gospel music, sung very fast and loud. <*Shout Hallelujah*> **2** Loud, spirited piece of instrumental music played in the **stride-piano** style. **3** Special religious service (18th, 19th century) of two groups, dancers and singers. *Origin* African tradition. DRAMA SHOUT, RING SHOUT

show *Fashn* Showing of the latest in fashion.

show *TheatArts* Theatrical company or **troupe**

show *PerfA&C* Public exhibition or entertainment.

show bill *Mktg* Advertising poster.

show biz *PerfA&C* » **show business**

Show Boat *LitArts, MusArts,* Landmark **musical play** originally staged in 1927, adapted from Edna Ferber's (1887-1968, fictwri.) 1926 novel, music by Jerome Kern (1885-1945, comp.), lyrics by Oscar Hammerstein II (1895-1960, lyr.) Also made into several movie versions. **Broadway** company and several touring companies were in production in 1996 *Also see* ***Oklahoma***.

show business, show-business *PerfA&C* Entertainment industry. **1** "When you come into show business early, there is one simple truth that applies to one and all 'The business takes over your life.'" — **William Goldman 2** "**Satchmo [Louis Armstrong]** chose show business over art." — James Lincoln Collier (jazz critic)

show room *Fashn* Large room in which merchandise is displayed.

show tunes *MusArts,* Music and songs from **musical comedy** or **musical theater**.

show-and-tell *or* **show and tell** *Mktg* Public presentation or display. *Also see* **dog-and-pony show**.

showboat *Crit&Eval* Show-off.

showboat *PerfA&C* Riverboat with a theater and a **troupe** of performers.

showcase *Crit&Eval* Setting in which something may be displayed advantageously.

showcase *Mktg* Display case or cabinet in a store or museum.

showcase *MusArts,PerfA&C* **Venue** where new talent can strut their stuff.

showgirl *ArtPerf,* Tall, high-heeled woman, attired in an elaborately decorated costume, or tastefully sans costumed, who performs — poses, walks slowly, seductively, poses again — in a musical or theatrical production. *Also see* **Ziegfield girl**.

showman *Crit&Eval* Man who has a **flair** for dramatic or **ostentatious** behavior.

showman *PerfA&C* theatrical **producer**

showpiece *Crit&Eval* Outstanding example of its kind.

showstopper *PerfA&C* Act or performer that evokes so much audience approval that the performance is temporarily interrupted. *Also see* **bring down the house, encore, ovation**.

showtime *or* **show time** *PerfA&C* When the entertainment is scheduled to begin.

SHRM *HR&LR, Mgt* » **Society for Human Resource Management**

shtick, schtick (Yinglish) *Crit&Eval* **1** Someone's way of doing something. **2** Entertainment routine.

shuffle *Dnce* Dance, usu. to the blues, in which the feet slide along or move close to the floor. *Also see* **Dances**.

shuffle *MusArts* Blues rhythm of which each main beat is divided into three smaller beats.

shund *Cult&Soc,* Yiddish theatre melodrama on contemporary issues. <assimilation, discrimination>

si *MusArts* Seventh tone in a **diatonic scale**. *Also see* **ti**.

Si *Sci&Tech* » **silicon**

side *Flm&Vid* Individual auditorium in a multiple theater complex usu. numbered, 1,2,3, etc.

side *RecA&S* Recording of sufficient playing time to constitute one side of a 7-inch, 45 rpm disc phonograph record, but not less than two and one-half minutes of continuous sound embodying performances of the artist.

side drum *MusInstr* » **snare drum**

side-door marketing *Mktg* Efforts by an arts organization to broaden its market base by aiding and working with local groups and businesses to improve their promotions, speeches, presentations, sales meetings, theatricals, etc.

side-stitch *VA-Prntng* Binding in which staples are driven through stacked **signatures** about 1/8 inch from the **backbone**.

side-wire *VA-Prntng* » **side-stitch**

sidebar *Journ* Short, often boxed auxiliary news story printed alongside a longer article and that typically presents additional, contrasting, or late-breaking news.

sidebar *LegAsp* Conference between the judge and the opposing attorneys outside of the jury's hearing.

sideman *MusArts* Instrumentalist in a dance or jazz band who is not the **leader** or the **contract artist**.

sideshow *Crit&Eval* Diversion or spectacle incidental to a larger set of circumstances or a bigger issue of concern.

sideshow *PA-Variety* Small show offered in addition to the main attraction, as at a **carnival** or circus. *Also see* **barker, freak show**.

sidesplitting *Crit&Eval* Causing convulsive laughter; extremely funny. <a sidesplitting comedy>

sig *Flm&Vid, Mktg* Signature of a theater used in ads.

SIG *InfoMgt* **special interest group**. Group of subscribers or participants on an electronic **bulletin board, videotex**, or other computer system who exchange information on their topic of common interest.

sight gag *PerfA&C* Comic bit or effect that depends on sight rather than words.

sight line *PerfA&C* Sighting extending from any seat in the house to any position on stage. *Also see* **dead seats**.

sight-raising *Fndng* Calculated attempts employing various strategies to induce previous donors as well as undecided prospects to raise their levels of giving.

sight-read *MusArts* To read music without preparation or prior acquaintance. *Also see* **read music**.

Sigma Delta Chi *Journ* » **SPJ**

sign off *iMedia* » **client sign off**

sign off *Rdio/TV* **1** End of a communication. **2** Stop transmission after identifying the broadcasting station.

signal *Sci&Tech* Sound, image, or message transmitted or received in telegraphy, telephony, radio, television, or radar.

signatory *LegAsp* Bound by signed agreement. <signatory parties to a contract>

signature *Genl* Distinctive mark, characteristic, or sound indicating identity.

signature *MusArts* Sign used to indicate key or tempo.

signature *VA-Prntng* **1** Large sheet printed with four or a multiple of four pages that when folded becomes a section of the publication. **2** Letter, number, or symbol placed at the bottom of the first page on each sheet as a guide to the proper sequence of the sheets in binding.

silence *Crit&Eval, LitArts* Condition or quality of being or keeping still and silent: "I prefer silence to sound, and the image produced by words occurs in silence. That is, the thunder and the music of the prose take place in silence." — **William Faulkner** "Silence is golden." — *Anon Also see* **white space**.

silence *Cult&Soc, Flm&Vid* "I'm an advocate of silence in film. Some people think music should always lead the moment. There's a pressure now to fill every frame with a barrage of music and image. It's the culture that's changing. I can see that, but I don't go along with it." — **Robert Redford**

silence *MusArts* Absence of sound, when properly used, can be very effective. **1** <Re *Porgy & Bess* recordings, ca. 1960. "You know this young trumpet player, **[Miles] Davis**? I played his record and took it right off. It disturbed me but I kept thinking about it so I listened again. **George [Gershwin]** would love it! He plays the silences." — **Ira Gershwin**> **2** "I have found a method... of conveying emotion in the arias of singers. It is silence. Silence is really the only way to properly show the meaning of a phrase." — Claude Debussy (1862-1918; French composer, early exponent of musical impressionism)

silence *TheatArts* "In the theater sound is imposed whereas silence provokes the imagination. First comes the initial mystery before there is any sound. Later, silence is the destination of dramatic dialogue, and silence is the final challenge after the last sounds have been heard and the action has ended, leaving the audience to its thoughts." — Robert J. Kornfeld (19??-; libret., plywri.)

silence *VisArts* Silence in the visual arts evolves into a question of apparently empty spaces. That the spaces are not merely empty, and the interaction between them and the perceived design, creates the visual art. *Also see* **quiet**.

silent film *Flm&Vid* One without recorded sound.

silent partner *Mgt* One that makes a financial investment in an enterprise but does not visibly participate in its management.

silhouette *Fashn* Outline image of a designed garment.

silhouette *VisArts* **1** Drawing consisting of the outline of something, esp. a human profile, filled in with a solid color. **2** Outline that appears dark against a light background.

silk-screen *also* **silkscreen** *VisArts, VA-Prntng* Stencil method of printmaking in which a design is imposed on a screen of silk or other fine mesh, with blank areas coated with an impermeable substance, and ink is forced through the mesh onto the printing surface. SCREEN-PRINTING, SILK-SCREEN PROCESS

silver screen *Flm&Vid* » **screen**

similarity *iMedia* One of **Gestalt Laws** of pattern perception: Similar elements tend to be grouped together.

simile *LitArts* Comparison of two unlike things that employs "like" or "as."

SIMM *InfoMgt* Single inline memory module. Type of compact printed circuit board that holds multiple memory chips. Additional SIMMS can add speed and storage capacity to an existing computer. *Also see* **DIMM. RAM, ROM**.

simple *MusArts* "Keep it simple. The simpler, the better." — **E.L. Doctorow**

simple interest *E&F-Acc* Interest cost for one or more periods, under the assumption that the amount on which the interest is computed stays the same from period to period.

Simple Mail Transfer Protocol (SMTP) *InfoMgt* » **SMTP**

simplex *InfoMgt* Ability of a communication system to transmit information in one direction at a time. <TV, fax machines, data transmission> *Also see* **duplex, full duplex**.

simplism *Crit&Eval* Tendency to oversimplify an issue or a problem by ignoring complexities or complications.

Simply Interactive Personal Computer *InfoMgt* » **S.I.P.C.**

simulation *InfoMgt* Representation of the operation or features of one process or system through the use of another. <computer simulation of an in-flight emergency>

simulation systems *InfoMgt* Process of using a computer model to manipulate real world parameters.

simulcast *Rdio/TV* To broadcast a program simultaneously by FM and AM radio or by a radio and television station.

Sinatra, Frank (Francis Albert Sinatra, 1915-1998-, film/TV act., sngr., prod.) *ArtPerf, Flm&Vid, MusArts* Musically sophisticated singer highly respected by songwriters for his lyric delivery, by musicians for his phrasing and musicianship, by the public for his polished **empathy**. <Films: *From Here to Eternity* (1953, Oscar), *High Society* (1956) *Also see* **arranger, phrasing, Rat Pack** THE VOICE

sine qua non (sin'-ay qua non, Latin) *Crit&Eval* Essential element or condition.

sine waves *iMedia* Waveform of a single constant frequency and amplitude that can be graphically expressed as a sine curve.

sinfonia *MusArts* Instrumental composition serving as an **overture** to an opera or a **cantata**, esp. in the 18th century.

sinfonietta *MusArts* **1** Symphonic composition shorter than usual. **2** Small symphony orchestra, esp. one with **stringed instruments** only.

sing-along *MusArts* **1** Casual gathering for group singing; a **songfest**. **2** Group singing by an audience at a performance. *Also see* **hootenanny**.

singer *LitArts Also see* **poet**

singer (sngr.) *MusArts* Usually a trained or professional vocalist.

singer-songwriter *MusArts* Individual singer who writes most, if not all of the songs that he or she performs and records. *Also see* **self-contained group**.

singing in tongues *MusArts* » **tongues**

single *RecA&S* 7-inch, 45 rpm, double-sided phonograph record.

Sometimes referred to as an "extended play single." *Also see* **long-play single**.

single inline memory module (SIMM) *InfoMgt* » **SIMM**

single purpose plan *Eco&Fin, Mgt* » **operational goals and plans** *Also see* **Goals and Plans**.

single song agreement *IntelProp, MusArts* Contract between publisher and songwriter where the songwriter assigns to the publisher the copyright in one particular song in return for a percentage of royalty income. ONE-OFF CONTRACT. *Also see* **Music Licenses**.

single ticket *Mktg,PerfA&C* One ticket of admission to one performance, not sold as part of a **subscription** or series.

single-entry system *EntreP* Checkbook system of accounting reflecting only receipts and disbursements.

single-groove stereo recording *RecA&S* Recording system introduced by **Bell Labs** in 1940. *Also see* **hill-and-dale recording**.

single-space *VA-Prntng* To type or print without leaving a blank line between lines.

single-step form *E&F-Acc* Said of an **income statement** where ordinary income and gain items are shown first and totaled. Then all ordinary expenses and losses are totaled. Their difference, plus the effect of income from discontinued operations and extraordinary items, is shown as net income. The advantage of the single-step form is its simplicity.

singles bar *Cult&Soc* Dating bar patronized by (allegedly) unmarried men and women.

sister *Cult&Soc* » **soul sister**

sit *VisArts* To pose for an artist or a photographer.

sit in *MusArts* Play in a jazz ensemble as a visitor.

sit on (one's) hands *Crit&Eval* **1** Lack of approval; lack of applause. <The **audience** expressed its disapproval by sitting on its hands through the performance> **2** Fail to act. *Also see* **tough audience**.

sit-down *HR&LR* **1** Work stoppage in which the workers refuse to leave their place of employment until their demands are considered or met. **2** Obstruction of normal activity by the act of a large group sitting down in public to express a grievance or protest. SIT-DOWN STRIKE *Also see* **sit-in**.

sit-in *Cult&Soc* Act of occupying the seats or an area of a segregated establishment to protest racial discrimination or other social grievances. *Also see* **sit-down**.

sitcom *Rdio/TV* » **situation comedy**

site kill files *InfoMgt* Computer file originated by a network administrator or user to block messages from a particular computer or certain parts of the network. Could be likened to censorship.

site license *InfoMgt, IntelProp* Allows businesses and organizations to make unlimited copies of certain software instead of buying a license for each user.

site-specific theater *TheatArts* <NYC's **En Garde Arts** site-specific theater company staged a contemporary variation of *The Brothers Karamazov* over several blocks of the meatpacking district> *Also see* **Theaters & Theatres**.

sitemap *iMedia* Visualization of site architecture, often textual and formatted as an outline.

sitename *InfoMgt* » **hostname**

sitting on (one's) hands *Crit&Eval* Said of an audience chary with applause.

situation ethics *Ethcs&Phil* System of ethics that evaluates acts in light of their situational context rather than by the application of moral absolutes.

sitzprobe *MusArts,* Rehearsal occasion when performers in a musical first sing accompanied by full orchestra.

sixteenth note *MusArts* Note whose value is one-sixteenth of a **whole note** and double that of thirty-second note. *Also see* **Musical Notes**.

sixth *MusArts* Interval between the **tonic** and the sixth tone of a **diatonic scale**.

sixty-fourth note *MusArts* Note whose value is one-sixty-fourth of a **whole note**. *Also see* **Musical Notes**.

size *Fashn, VisArts* Substance used as a glaze or filler for porous materials such as paper, cloth, or wall surfaces.

size *iMedia* Physical dimensions, proportions, magnitude, or extent of an object.

ska *MusArts* Jamaican music, with roots in the 1950s, characterized by choppy **staccato**, 4/4 time, beat emphasized at the beginning and end of each **bar**. Influenced by **calypso**, early rock, jazz, **mento**, r&b, reggae, and swing. *Also see* **Latin dance music**. BLUEBEAT

skanking *Dnce* Style of West Indian dancing to **reggae** music with hands clawing the air in time to the beat. — William Safire (1929-, critic, syn. colum.) *Also see* **Dances**.

skeptic *Crit&Eval* One who instinctively or habitually doubts, questions, or disagrees with assertions or generally accepted conclusions. *Also see* **cynic**.

skepticism, scepticism *Crit&Eval* Doubting or questioning attitude or state of mind; **dubiety**. *Also see* **cynicism**.

sketch *iMedia* **1** Visualization of an idea, in a rough draft form. Used to work out a visual idea of how composition and visual hierarchy for an interface will be developed, or to show the relationships between data in a proposed database or data store. It may also include notes and ideas about the intended interaction. **2** quick visual rendering of something, usu. with graphite.

sketch *LitArts* **1** Brief, incomplete presentation, as of a book to be completed. **2** Informal literary composition.

sketch *MusArts* Brief composition, esp. for the piano.

sketch *PA-Variety* Short, often satirical scene or play in a revue or variety show. *Also see* **skit**.

sketchbook *LitArts, VisArts* **1** Book of literary sketches. **2** Pad of paper used for sketching. SKETCHPAD

sketchpad *VisArts* » **sketchbook**

skim *Crit&Eval* To read or glance through a document quickly or superficially.

skim *Eco&Fin, Ethcs&Phil* Fail to declare part of income to avoid tax payment.

skimming *Eco&Fin* **price skimming**

skin flick *Flm&Vid* **pornographic** film.

skinhead *Cult&Soc* Member of any of various groups of white British or American youths who shave their heads, gather at rock concerts and sports events, and sometimes participate in white-supremacist and anti-immigrant activities. *Also see* **neo-Nazi**.

skinzine *Journ* Magazine for **skinheads**

skit *TheatArts* Short, usu. comic theatrical **sketch**

skivvis *Fashn* **Trademark** used for underwear.

skull session *Mgt* Meeting of managers or advisers to discuss policy or strategy.

skywriting *Mktg* Process of writing in the sky by releasing a visible vapor from an airplane. *Also see* **Advertising Media**.

SL *PerfA&C* **stage left**

SLA *InfoMgt* **Special Libraries Association**. Highly respected organization of librarians that work in corporations, technical organizations, and various institutions outside the traditional public library.

slam poetry *LitArts* Tongue-in-cheek spoken word poetry competition.

slander *Crit&Eval, LegAsp* **1** Oral communication of false statements injurious to a person's reputation. **2** False and malicious statement or report about someone. *Also see* **defamation, libel**.

slang *Genl* Language peculiar to a group. *Also see* **argot, jargon, vernacular**. [Usually each generation prefers to create its own slang rather than be thought old, i.e., over the hill.].

slant *Crit&Eval, Journ* **1** Approach taken in writing an article or editorial. **2** Personal point of view or opinion; bias.

slap bass *MusArts* "Bass technique developed in the 1930s in which the strumming hand alternately plucks a note and then is used as a hammer to dampen the strings against the **fingerboard**, producing a deep *thwack* sound." — Lyon and Perlo (jazz critics)

slap tongue *MusArts* Percussive, popping jazz saxophone sound made by tonguing the reed. <Featured in the 1930s by Coleman Hawkins (*aka* "Bean," 1904-69, jazz tenor sax, bndldr.) even as he led the **transition** to a smooth **attack**; brilliantly restored in the mid-1990s by saxophonist James Carter (1969-, all style jazz saxes)

slapstick *PA-Variety* 1 Comedy marked by chases, collisions, crude practical jokes. <pie-in-the-face>, and similar boisterous actions. 2 Hinged, two-board paddle designed to make a loud whacking sound used by **burlesque** comedians.

slate *BcstJourn* » **audio billboard**

sleazy *Crit&Eval* 1 Shabby, dirty, and vulgar. 2 Dishonest or corrupt. DISREPUTABLE.

sleazy *Fashn* 1 Made of low-quality materials. CHEAP, SHODDY 2 Thin and loosely woven. FLIMSY

sleeper *Crit&Eval* One or something that achieves unexpected recognition or success. <a movie, or a marketed product>

sleeper *VisArts* lost portrait

sleeve *RecA&S* Case into which a record disk fits.

slick *Crit&Eval* superficial, **glib**

slick *LitArts* Magazine, usu. of large popular readership, printed on high-quality glossy paper.

slicks *Mktg* Glossy repros of print advertising used in a promotion campaign.

slide *Dnce* Jazz tap dance step. "When [Jimmy] Slyde (1928-, jazz tap dncr., choreog.) taps across a stage, the audience faces a contradiction. He skims the floor like a dragonfly, all the while playing it like a drum, tapping out heavy swing beats. The king of slides, he uses everything from tiny skids to great slaloms to whisk him along. Then he brakes to a stop with a flurry of chattering taps, throwing up his hands for balance, always seeming to be surprised by the dexterity of his own feet." — Sally Sommer (dance critic)

slide *MusArts* 1 Slight **portamento** used in violin playing, passing quickly from one note to another. 2 Ornamentation consisting of two **grace notes** approaching the main note.

slide whistle *MusInstr* Vertical metal flute with – no holes – a slide to produce a range of glissandos. *Also see* **Little Instruments**.

sliding scale *Eco&Fin* Scale in which prices, taxes, or wages vary in accordance with another factor. <wages with the cost-of-living index>

sliding scale *Flm&Vid* Applicable if the rental fee paid by a distributor is determined by the number of admissions or the gross receipts, rather than by a flat-fee.

slime ball *Crit&Eval* loathsome person.

SLIP *InfoMgt* 1 **Serial-Line Internet Protocol** One of two standard methods of connecting to the Internet. Not as reliable as **PPP**. 2 **Symmetric list processor**. *Also see* **Protocols**.

slip-sheet *VA-Prntng* Blank sheet of paper slipped between newly printed sheets to prevent smudging.

slo-mo *Flm&Vid* **slow motion**.

sloper *Fashn* Basic pattern for a garment section, without style lines or seam allowances, developed from a model form, live models, specific measurements, or manufacturers's specifications. Used to develop original patterns and create new designs. STANDARD PATTERN, FOUNDATION PATTERN, BLOCK PATTERN, AND MASTER PATTERN

slotted *Crit&Eval*, » **typecast**

slow drag dancing *Dnce, MusArts* Intimate style of coupled dancing popular in the early days of instrumental blues (ca. 1900) *Also see* **Dances, New Orleans jazz**.

slow motion *Flm&Vid* Filmmaking technique in which the action as projected is slower than the original action. SLO-MO

slowdown *HR&LR* Deliberate slowing of production by workers to protest a company's decision. *Also see* **job action**.

slug *BcstJourn* Single-word identifier for a news story. Chosen when the story is assigned and should remain the same until the story is broadcast. It will also be applied to all parts of the story

and to **carts** in radio and videotape in television.

slug *Journ, VA-Prntng* Mark or instruction to identify a piece of copy.

slur *Genl* Disparaging remark; an aspersion.

slur *MusArts* Curved line over a series of notes that are to be played smoothly and continuously.

slur *VA-Prntng* smeared or blurred impression.

SM *PerfA&C* **stage manager**

SMA *HR&LR,PerfA&C* Society of Makeup Artists. Ω

Small Business Administration (SBA) *EntreP* The government agency that provides financing and management assistance to small businesses.

Small Business Administration (SBA) *Law&Pol, Mgt* » **SBA**

Small Business Development Centers (SBDCs) *EntreP* university-affiliated centers offering consulting, education, and other support to small businesses.

small business entrepreneur *EntreP* » **low-growth entrepreneur**

Small Business Investment Company (SBIC) *EntreP* Venture capital company that combines government money with private capital to provide funding for growth ventures.

small business marketing *EntreP* Business activities that identify a target market, determine that market's potential, and prepare, communicate, and deliver a bundle of satisfaction to that market.

Small Computer System Interface (SCSI) *InfoMgt* » **SCSI**

small group *MusArts* » **combo**

small performing rights *IntelProp, MusArts* Non-dramatic public performing rights that are represented by and licensed through **performing rights organizations**. <Performances of individual musical works on radio and TV, hotels, restaurants, background music services, and in concerts> *Also see* **grand rights**.

small screen *Flm&Vid* TV-size screen. *Also see* **big screen, silver screen**.

small time *PA-Variety* Vaudeville circuits on which performers were required to perform more than three times a day. *Also see* **two-a-day**.

small-format video *Flm&Vid, Journ, Rdio/TV* Personal journalism by camcorder. DIRECT VIDEO, VERNACULAR VIDEO

smart *Fashn* fashionable ELEGANT

smart *InfoMgt* Ability to perform operations independently of the computer. <computer terminal>

smart ads *InfoMgt, Mktg* "Advertising on the Internet while not full-motion video, does run up to 10 frames a second, going the ads a near-television effect."— David Barboza. (info sci. journ.)

smart card *InfoMgt* Plastic card, similar to a credit card, that contains a computer chip thus allowing storage and easy retrieval of information.

smart set *Crit&Eval, Cult&Soc* Fashionable society. GLITTERATI

smear *MusArts* » **portamento**

smiley *InfoMgt* » **emoticon**

Smith, Oliver (1918-94, dsgnr ballet, musical theater prods.) *ArtPerf*, Noted for his **collaborative** skills.

smocking *Fashn* Decorative needlework that binds gathered cloth together; stitches are made on alternating folds.

SMPTE *Flm&Vid* **Society of Motion Picture and Television Engineers**. State-of-the art arbiters of **media** technologies. *Also see* **time coding**.

SMTP *InfoMgt* **Simple Mail Transfer Protocol**. *Also see* **Protocols**. Ω

SMU *Mgt* » **strategic management unit** *Also see* **SBU, strategic business unit**.

smut *Crit&Eval* obscenity, pornography

snail mail *InfoMgt* Mail sent via U.S. Postal Service (USPS)

Snap *InfoMgt* Web site providing access to Internet. *Also see* **search engine, portals**.

snare drum *MusInstr* Double-headed drum with a set of wires stretched across the bottom head to increase **reverberation**. SIDE DRUM. *Also see* **drum set**.

sneak preview *Flm&Vid* Public showing of a movie before its general release

snert *InfoMgt* Rude or malicious user who disrupts **chat rooms** or **message boards**.

sngr. *ArtPerf, MusArts* sngr.

sngwri. *MusArts* **songwriter**

snide *Crit&Eval* Derogatory in a malicious, superior way; sarcastic.

snipe *Mktg* Area left blank in a print ad or on a poster on which the local advertiser may imprint **logo, sigs**, show times, etc.

sniping *Mktg* Frowned-on practice of stapling advertising posters on fences, telephone poles, walls of buildings, etc.

SNL*Rdio/TV* Saturday Nite Live

snob *Crit&Eval* **1** One who overtly imitates, obsequiously admires, and offensively seeks to associate only with those one regards as one's superiors and who tends to rebuff or ignore altogether those one regards as one's inferiors. **2** One who lacks humility. **3** One who affects an offensive air of self-satisfied superiority in matters of taste or intellect. "Anyone who questions the beneficence of the modern fun industry is certain to be labeled a snob, and lumped with conservative **esthetes** like **Allan Bloom**." — Jackson Lears (journ.)

snob appeal *Crit&Eval* Qualities that seem to substantiate social or intellectual pretensions.

snow job *Crit&Eval* Effort to deceive, overwhelm, or persuade with insincere talk, esp. flattery.

soap opera, soap*Rdio/TV* Drama, typically performed as a serial on daytime TV or radio, characterized by **stock characters** and situations, sentimentality, and melodrama. *<All My Children, As the World Turns, Dallas> Origin* Originally sponsored on radio by soap companies. *Also see* **Television Shows**.

soapbox *Crit&Eval* To engage in impromptu or non-official public speaking, often flamboyantly.

sob sister *Crit&Eval* **1** Woman journalist, esp. a woman, employed as a writer or an editor of sob stories. **2** Sentimental, ineffective man or woman who seeks to do good.

sob story *Crit&Eval* **1** Tale of personal hardship or misfortune intended to arouse pity. **2 Maudlin** plea given as an explanation or a rationalization.

sober-sided *Crit&Eval* Devoid of extreme qualities, such as exaggeration; sober.

SOCAN *IntelProp* Canadian performing rights society formed in early 1990s combining CAPAC (ASCAP in USA) and PROCAN (formerly BMI Canada) *Also see* **SODRAC**. *Also see* **Copyright-Related Organizations. social director** *PA-Variety* Person responsible for seeing that all the guests in the resort hotel or aboard a Love Boat are kept happy. No matter what! *Also see* **Catskills, Directors, tumler**.

social contract *Cult&Soc* Agreement between the governed and their government defining the rights and duties of each.

social engineering *Cult&Soc* Practical application of sociological principles to particular social problems.

Small Business Development Centers (SBDCs) *EntreP* university-affiliated centers offering consulting, education, and other support to small businesses.

small business entrepreneur *EntreP* » **low-growth entrepreneur**

Small Business Investment Company (SBIC) *EntreP* Venture capital company that combines government money with private capital to provide funding for growth ventures.

small business marketing *EntreP* Business activities that identify a target market, determine that market's potential, and prepare, communicate, and deliver a bundle of satisfaction to that market.

Small Computer System Interface (SCSI) *InfoMgt* » **SCSI**

social profit *Cult&Soc, Mktg* Benefit received by an organization or society from its ethical practices, community service, efforts to promote cultural diversity, and concern for the natural environment.

social realism *TheatArts* Form of modern realistic drama emphasizing social messages and themes: social realism was the official style of the Communist Party in the Soviet Union after the revolution.

Social Security tax *E&F-Acc, Law&Pol* » **FICA**

socialism *Eco&Fin, Law&Pol* **1** *Marxist.* Social system in which the means of producing and distributing goods are owned collectively and political power is exercised by the whole community. **2** *Reality* Economic and political system in which the major factors of production <major manufacturing, public utilities, transportation> are "collectively" owned by the local or central government. Smaller companies may indeed be privately owned and operated. Some formerly socialist nations <France, Mexico, and United Kingdom> are privatizing some operations owned by the central government. *Also see* **capitalism**.

socialist realism *Crit&Eval Genl* **Marxist** aesthetic **doctrine** that seeks to promote the development of social consciousness through **didactic** use of literature, art, and music.

society (soc.) *Cult&Soc* **1** Totality of social relationships among human beings. **2** Group of human beings broadly distinguished from other groups by mutual interests, participation in characteristic relationships, shared institutions, and a common **culture**. **3** Organization or association of persons engaged in a common profession, activity, or interest. <a society of arts managers> **4** Rich, privileged, and fashionable social class. **5** Socially dominant members of a community.

Society for Computer Simulation (SCS) *InfoMgt* » **SCS**

Society for Human Resource Management (SHRM) *HR&LR, Mgt* Membership organization for human resource professionals.

Society for the Preservation and Encouragement of Barber Shop Quartet Singing in America (S.P.E.B.S.Q.S.A.) *MusArts* Incorporated 1938, its international headquarters in Kenosha, Wis. includes the Heritage Hall Museum of Barbershop Harmony. *Also see* **barbershop quartet**.

Society of Authors Representatives (SAR) *HR&LR, LitArts* » **SAR** *Also see* **ILAA**.

Society of Composers and Lyricists (SCL) *ArtPerf, MusArts* » **SCL**

Society of Independent Artists *ArtPerf, VisArts* » **Ashcan School, Eight**

Society of Makeup Artists (SMA) *HR&LR, Th-MakeUp* » **SMA**

Society of Motion Picture and Television Engineers (SMPTE) *Flm&Vid* » **SMPTE**

Society of Professional Journalists (SBJ) *Journ* » **SBJ**

Society of Singers (SOS) *ArtPerf, MusArts* **Nonprofit** dedicated to providing compassionate understanding, counseling and financial assistance to persons who are, or have been, professional singers. Sponsors the Ella (Fitzgerald) Award for lifetime achievement.

Society of Stage Directors and Choreographers *Dnce, HR&LR* » **SSDC**

Socrates (470?-399 BC) *Ethcs&Phil* Greek philosopher who initiated a question-and-answer method of teaching as a means of achieving self-knowledge. His theories of virtue and justice have survived through the writings of **Plato**, his most important pupil. Socrates was tried for corrupting the minds of Athenian youth and subsequently put to death.

Socratic irony *Crit&Eval* Feigned ignorance; learning by professing ignorance while asking questions about the meaning of terms. *Also see* **dramatic irony, irony, Socrates**.

Socratic method *Crit&Eval* Employment of **Socratic irony** in a philosophical discussion resulting either in a mutual confession of ignorance with a promise of further investigation or in the elicitation of a truth assumed to be innate in all rational beings. *Also see* **Socrates**.

soda can music *IntelProp, MusArts* Money paid to the copyright owner derived from the use of music or lyrics on a soda can or other consumer product packaging.

SODRAC *IntelProp* Performing rights society in the province of Quebec, Canada, covering the Quebecois recording and publishing industry. *Also see* **SOCAN**. *Also see* **Copyright-Related Organizations**.

SOF *Flm&Vid* **Sound On Film camera**

soft edge *Th-MakeUp* In theatrical cosmetics, blending highlight and shadow with base between them to create the illusion of a rounded form.

soft focus *Flm&Vid* **1** Blurring out of focus of all actors, sets and **props** except at one desired distance. **2** Glamorizing technique that softens the sharpness of definition so that facial wrinkles can be smoothed over and even eliminated. *Also see* **Loretta Young silks**.

soft lead (leed) *BcstJourn* » **feature**

soft news *Journ, Rdio/TV* **1** News, as in a newspaper or television report, that does not deal with formal or serious topics and events. **2** Stories that are not ongoing. <human interest stories> *Also see* **hard news**.

soft pedal *Crit&Eval* To make less emphatic or obvious; play down.

soft pedal *MusArts, MusInstr* To soften or mute the tone by depressing the soft pedal, esp. on a piano or vibraphone.

soft rock *MusArts* Characterized by the predominance of melody and minimal use of electronic modulations. *Also see* **Rock Music Styles**.

soft sculpture *VisArts* Sculpture made of pliant materials. <cloth or foam rubber>

soft soap *Crit&Eval* flattery.

soft-core *Crit&Eval* moderate.

soft-shoe *Dnce* Tap dancing performed while wearing shoes without metal taps. *Also see* **Dances**.

softcover *LitArts, VA-Prntng* Not bound between hard covers. <softcover books; a softcover edition> *Also see* paperback.

software *Flm&Vid, LitArts, RecA&S* Any information or entertainment medium played or activated by a mechanical or electronic device, i.e., **hardware**. <audio/visual recordings, **computer programs**, movies, periodicals and books — software of TV and movie **media**>

software *InfoMgt* Programs, routines, and symbolic languages that control the functioning of computer **hardware** and direct its operation.

software license *InfoMgt, IntelProp* Agreement stated by software publisher and automatically agreed to by the buyer upon opening the envelope containing the program software disks that a separate license must be purchased for each end-user. Violators are subject to substantial fines and jail terms. <First paragraph of a Claris Software License: "Please read this license carefully before opening this [software] package. You agree to become bound by the terms of this license. If you do not agree to the terms of this license, do not open this package. Promptly return it unopened to the place where you obtained it for a full refund."> LICENSING AGREEMENT. *Also see* **Contracts**.

software meter *InfoMgt* Enables information manager to evaluate number of employees actually using an application. Allows companies to buy fewer licenses. *Also see* **concurrency**.

Software Publishers Association (SPA) *InfoMgt* » **SPA**

software suite *InfoMgt* » **bundled software**

SoHo *Genl* **1** Southwest Manhattan district (NYC) noted for its galleries and artists' lofts. *Origin* Area is *s*outh of *Ho*uston [Howston] Street. **2** District of central London known for its restaurants, theaters, and nightclubs.

SoHo market *Mktg* One embracing both the small-office and home-office markets.

sol (sole) *MusArts* fifth tone of a **diatonic scale**

sole proprietor *Eco&Fin, Mgt* » **proprietorship**

solfege, solfeggio (Ital.) *MusArts* Use of the sol-fa syllables to note the **tones** of the **scale**. *Also see* **ear training**.

solicitation *Fndng* Activity by which individuals and organizations are requested to make donations.

solid *VA-Prntng* No **leads** (leds) between the lines.

solid-body guitar *MusInstr* » **Leo Fender, Les Paul**. *Also see*

Musical Instrument Families

solid-state *Sci&Tech* Based on or consisting chiefly or exclusively of **semiconducting** materials, components, and related devices. *Also see* **second generation**.

soliloquy *LitArts* Dramatic or literary form of discourse in which a character reveals her or his thoughts when alone or unaware of the presence of other characters. *Also see* **monologue**.

soliloquy *TheatArts* Speech delivered by a character alone on stage, speaking to herself or himself, or to the audience.

solo *MusArts* **1** Composition or passage for an individual voice or instrument, with or without **accompaniment**. **2** Performance by or intended for a single individual. SOLOIST, SOLOISTIC

something else *Crit&Eval* One or something very special or quite remarkable. <Her new play is something else>

son et lumière (sawn ay loom-ee-air, Fr. for "sound and light") *PA-Variety* Dramatic spectacle using special light and **sound effects**.

sonata *MusArts* Instrumental musical composition for the piano or other instruments, consisting of three or four independent movements varying in key, mood, and tempo.

Sondheim, Stephen (1930-, mus. theatre comp., lyr., prod.) *ArtPerf, MusArts* Musicals include. <w., *West Side Story* (1957) **w**, *Gypsy* (1959), **m/w** *Sweeney Todd* (1979) *Also see* **genius, land, lyrics**.

song and dance *Crit&Eval* Excessively elaborate attempt to explain or justify.

song and dance team *PA-Variety* Two-person **vaudeville** act featuring popular songs and dances.

Song of Songs *LitArts* Book of the Bible.

song plugger *Mktg, MusArts* Fast talking person hired by a music publisher to persuade a performer, by any means, to sing or play the publisher's latest **Tin Pan Alley** tune. When recordings superseded **vaudeville** as hit-makers, the same type hypester evolved as a promo man or even a promo person... *Also see* **Brill Building, plug**. CONTACT MAN.

song shark *Ethcs&Phil, MusArts* Term used for agents known for – or having the reputation of – feeding on the hopes of aspiring songwriters and recording artists by promises that sound too good to be true. Check the hype with the **Better Business Bureau, SGA**, or the local equivalent of **Lawyers for the Creative Arts**.

songbook *MusArts* Book of popular song lyrics with piano or guitar accompaniment. *Also see* **Print Music**.

songfest *MusArts* Casual gathering for group singing.

Songs *MusArts* Brief compositions written or adapted for singing. <aria, blues, canticle, carol, chantey, cheap —, dirge, ditty, elegy, field holler, folk —, gospel music, hymn, paen, psalm, Psalms, spiritual, work —>

songwriter (sngwri.) *MusArts* One who writes song lyrics and/or tunes. SONGSMITH, SONGSTER, TUNESMITH

songwriter/music publisher contract *MusArts* Negotiated agreement – there is no bona fide "standard contract form – between a songwriter and a music publisher whereby the publisher acquires a potentially profitable property which is administers, promotes, and protects; and the songwriter acquires the professional marketing expertise of the publisher. *Also see* **Contracts**.

Songwriters Hall of Fame *ArtPerf, MusArts Also see* **Abe Olman Award, Awards & Prizes, NAPM**.

Songwriters' Guild of America (SGA) *ArtPerf, MusArts* » **SGA**

sonnet *LitArts* 14-line verse form usu. having one of several conventional rhyme schemes.

sonority *MusArts* Production of a full, rich sound.

SOP *Mgt* » **sound operating procedure**

sop *MusArts* **soprano** voice

sophist *Crit&Eval* **1** One skilled in elaborate and devious argumentation. **2** scholar or thinker.

sophistry *Crit&Eval* Plausible but misleading or fallacious argument.

soprano (sop) *MusArts* Highest singing voice of a woman or a young boy.

soprano clef *MusArts* » **C clef**

soprano saxophone (sop sax) *MusInstr* Popularity of this highest-range saxophone, and its ascendancy over the clarinet in jazz, is largely due to **John Coltrane**. SOPRANO PLAYER, SOPRANO SAX PLAYER, SOPRANO SAXIST. *Also see* **Musical Instrument Families.**

sort *InfoMgt* To arrange, via a computer command or program, data as to class, kind, or size; classify. *Also see* **sequencer.**

SOS *ArtPerf, MusArts* » **Society of Singers**

SOT *BcstJourn* sound on tape. This alerts anyone working on the newscast that the audio portion will come from videotape.

sotto-voce (sot-toe-vo-chay, Ital. for "under voice") *MusArts* Direction: play or sing very softly.

sotto-voce (sot-toe-vo-chay, Ital. for "under voice") *TheatArts* Speak softly, so as not to be overheard.

soubrette (Fr.) *MusArts,* Saucy, coquettish, intriguing maidservant in comedies or comic opera.

soukous *Dnce* Zaire dance music.

soul *Crit&Eval* Deeply felt emotion conveyed by an artist or performer.

soul *Cult&Soc* **1** Principle of life; that which distinguishes a living thing from one not living; in its highest form, the seat of thought, action, and passion, and therefore of all the faculties which make experience in all its forms possible. **2** Sense of **ethnic** pride among Black people and esp. African Americans, expressed in many ways. <language, social customs, religion, and music>

soul *MusArts* "Music is the soul of society." — Itzhak Perlman (1945-, Israeli-born class. vlo.)

soul brother *Cult&Soc* Fellow Black man. *Also see* **bro.**

soul gospel *MusArts Also see* **Gospel Music**

soul music *MusArts* Music developed by African Americans, combining elements of **gospel** music and **rhythm & blues**. *Also see* **Southern white soul music.**

soul sister *Cult&Soc* Fellow Black woman.

sound *MusArts* **1** Musical sound, or **tone**, results from the regular **vibration** of an object. <vocal chords, musical instrument> (Irregular vibrations produce noise.) Not until late in the 19th century, was it known that electric impulses could produce sounds from an instrument. Up to then, the human performer was indispensable. **2** Distinctive style of a singer or a musical ensemble. <Basie's band always had a distinctive sound>

sound *RecA&S* Auditory material that is recorded. <records, movies, television>

sound *Sci&Tech* **1 Vibrations** transmitted through an elastic material or a solid, liquid, or gas, with **frequencies** in the approximate range of 20 to 20,000 **hertz**, capable of being detected by humans. **2** Transmitted vibrations of any frequency.

sound chain *RecA&S* Series of interconnected audio equipment used for recording or **public-address systems.**

sound designer *PerfA&C* Person responsible for the design, recording, and playback of all music and sound effects used in a production.

sound effects (SFX) *Flm&Vid, Rdio/TV* Imitative sounds – bird calls, train whistles, thunder – produced mechanically or electronically in films, plays, or on radio and TV.

sound effects *RecA&S* All sounds recorded onto the film soundtrack that are not part of the normal synchronized dialogue or music. Usually recorded on separate "effects" tracks and later added to the main soundtrack.

sound on film (SOF) **camera** *Flm&Vid* Records a magnetic or optical track running parallel to the picture area.

sound on tape *BcstJourn* » **SOT**

Sound Recording Fund *Eco&Fin, RecA&S* » **Audio Home Recording Act of 1992**

sound recordings *IntelProp, RecA&S* **1** Total amount of "fixed" sounds produced from vocal and/or instrumental performances and is a work of authorship. **2** Work that is a series of recorded

sounds. Each song on the recording is a separate work in its own right. *Also see* **phonorecords.**

sound reinforcement *PerfA&C, RecA&S* Public address system installation necessary to project audio in live performance.

sound reinforcement equipment (SRE) *RecA&S* <amplifiers, mics, speakers> » **SRE**

sound stage *also* **soundstage** *Flm&Vid* **Soundproof** studio used for movie production. *Also see* **set, Stages.**

sound track, soundtrack *Flm&Vid, RecA&S* **1** Narrow strip at one side of a movie film that carries the sound recording. **2** Music that accompanies a movie. **3** Commercial phonograph record or tape of such music.

sound truck *RecA&S* Truck or other vehicle having one or more loudspeakers, usu. situated on top, typically used for broadcasting political, or commercial messages.

sound wave *Sci&Tech* Longitudinal pressure wave of audible or inaudible sound that travels in air approx. 1130 feet per second at 70 degrees F. *Also see* **attack, decay, internal dynamics, sustain.**

sound-on-sound recording *RecA&S* Overlay new tracks on previously recorded material.

sounding *MusArts* Emitting a full sound; resonant.

sounding board *Mktg* **1** Person or group whose reactions to an idea, opinion, or point of view will serve as a measure of its effectiveness or acceptability. **2** Device or means serving to spread or popularize an idea or a point of view.

sounding board, soundboard *MusInstr* **1** Thin board forming the upper portion of the resonant chamber in an instrument, such as a violin or piano, and serving to increase resonance. **2** Structure placed behind or over a podium or platform to reflect music or a speaker's voice to an audience.

soundproof *Genl* Not penetrable by audible sound.

soundtrack *Flm&Vid* Optical or magnetic band carrying the sound alongside the picture frame on a release print. Also, any optical or magnetic sound at the editing or **mixing** stage.

soup *Flm&Vid* Developing solutions used to process unexposed film.

source *InfoMgt* Disk or folder that holds the original of a file to be copied or translated.

source *Journ* Person or document, that supplies information. <Reporter is only as reliable as her or his sources>

sourcing *Journ* Specifying the origin of a document or a news story. *Also see* **new news.**

sourcing *Mgt* Process of obtaining parts or materials from another business, country, or locale.

Southern white soul music *Crit&Eval, MusArts* "Country-and-western" music. — Tom Piazza (author, critic)

Southern, Eileen (1920-, hist.) *Cult&Soc, LitArts* Cultural historian, specializing in Black culture. *Also see* **jazz origins, jazz recording, race records, ring dance.**

Southwest Louisiana music *MusArts* » **zydeco**

sp. *Flm&Vid, LitArts* **screenplay**

SPA *InfoMgt* Software Publishers Association. On behalf of its member companies, performs routine audits for infractions of licensing agreements. *Also see* **Copyright-Related Organizations.**

Space *iMedia* **1** Manipulation of form and design resulting in the illusion of depth. (overlapping, tone changes, and scale changes) **2** Dead space. area around an object or objects where there is limited or no visual interest. **3.** Unlimited **3D** expanse in which everything is located.

space *Mktg* Blank areas in printed material available for advertising.

space *MusArts* One of the intervals between the lines of a **staff.**

space *VA-Prntng* One of the blank pieces of type or other means used for separating words or characters.

space buyer *VA-Prntng* **Advertising media** specialist who buys ad space in **printed media** and usu. works in an ad agency.

Also see **insertion order; rate card; SRDS, time buyer.**

space contract *VA-Prntng* Written intention of an advertiser, or its ad agency, to run a certain number of ads in a particular print medium within a specified period of time. *Also see* **Contracts, insertion order, rate card.**

space holder *Journ* Row of meaningless characters or symbols indicating new **copy** to come.

spam *InfoMgt* To insult someone via online dialog. *Origin* Term derived from a TV skit on *Monty Python's Flying Circus* **sending-up** Spam, ca. **WWII,** a brand of canned, pink, something-like-meat that splatters messily when hurled.

spamming *InfoMgt* Scatter-shot advertising messages within an online service.

span of control *EntreP* Number of subordinates supervised by one manager.

Spanish tinge *MusArts* So-called by Jelly Roll Morton, it's a rumba-flavored pattern of rhythmic accenting by percussion instruments.

spare *Crit&Eval* not excessive; lean and trim

spatial *Crit&Eval* Relating to the nature of space.

spatial metaphor *iMedia* Interface built to resemble and react as though it were an actual physical space. Interacting with an environment accesses content. *Also see* **character-based metaphor, event-based metaphor.**

speaking in tongues *MusArts* » **glossolalia, tongues.**

spear-carrier *ArtPerf, TheatArts* Minor member of an operatic or dramatic cast, having no speaking part, but may be called on to shout or murmur something.

spear-carrier *Genl* One whose presence or performance has little effect on what is going on, or on a group, or an organization.

spec *PA-Variety* **spectacle**

spec. *Mktg, Rdio/TV* **special**

spec., spec *Eco&Fin* **speculate**

special (spec.) *Mktg* Featured attraction. <a reduced price, a free **premium**>

special (spec.) *Rdio/TV* Single television production that features a specific work, a given topic, or a particular performer.

special effects (fx) *Flm&Vid* **1** Trick photography. Optical special effects. <split-screens, microphotography, matting, use of models, multiple-image sequences, laser-scan techniques> **2** Mechanical special effects. <simulated motion within a moving object, building collapse, fires, floods, etc>

special event *Fndng* Public ceremony such as a dedication or a ground-breaking ceremony, or an event specially contrived, which focuses attention on the organization during a fund-raising campaign and thus aids the **cultivation** process.

special interest group *InfoMgt* » **SIG**

special interest group *Law&Pol* » **pressure group**

Special Libraries Association (SLA) *InfoMgt* » **SLA**

special power of attorney *LegAsp* One that limits the agent to those acts specifically enumerated in an agreement. *Also see* **Agents and Agencies, Contracts.**

special project *Fndng* Program or project requiring special funding but usu. not of sufficient proportions to necessitate a full campaign.

special purpose foundation *Fnding* private foundation that focuses its grantmaking activities in one or a few special areas of interest. *Ex.* A foundation may only award grants in the area of cancer research or child development. *Also see* general purpose foundation)

specially ordered work *IntelProp* » **commissioned work**

specialties *PerfA&C* Performer's inventory of skills and talents.

specialty products *Mktg* Products with unique characteristics and/or brand identification for which a significant group of buyers are habitually willing to make a special purchasing effort. *Also see* **convenience products, shopping products.**

specific industry economic indicators *Eco&Fin* In addition to the national and regional **economic indicators,** many national trade and industry associations publish statistics based on a particular industry. <**Association of Performing Arts Presenters** (APAP), **National Association of Music Merchants** (NAMM), **Record Industry Association of America** (RIAA), **National Society of Fund Raising Executives** (NSFRE)>

specific lighting *PerfA&C* Lighting designed to illuminate a specific area of the stage, done by one or more spotlights. *Also see* **general lighting, Stage Lighting.**

specific planning session *Journ* Meeting of editorial staff members to particularize general ideas into specific article and assignments.

specification *iMedia* Document describing, in exact detail, how a system should work, or how a process should be employed.

specious *Crit&Eval* Having the ring of truth or plausibility but actually fallacious.

spectacle *Crit&Eval* Something that can be seen or viewed, esp. something of a remarkable or impressive nature. *Also see* **analysis of tragedy.**

spectacle (spec) *PA-Variety* Circus's opening parade of performers and animals around the **hippodrome** track.

spectacle *PerfA&C* Public performance on a large or lavish scale. *Also see* **analysis of tragedy.**

spectacle *TheatArts* Aristotle's term for the visual element of theatrical performance in the *Poetics.*

spectacular *Mktg* Elaborate outdoor advertising display. <Display for Maxwell House coffee at NYC Times Square>

spectacular *PerfA&C* Single dramatic production of unusual length or lavishness.

specular shading *iMedia* Light reflected directly form the surface, i.e., highlights on a glossy object.

speculate (spec., spec) *Crit&Eval* To engage in a course of reasoning often based on inconclusive evidence.

speculate (spec., spec) *Eco&Fin* To engage in the buying or selling of a commodity with an element of risk on the chance of profit.

speculative risk *Eco&Fin, Mgt* One that involves the possibility of gain or loss. <Starting or buying a business or introducing a new product>

speech codes *Ethcs&Phil, Law&Pol* » **political correctness** *Also see* **inappropriately directed laughter.**

speech recognition *InfoMgt* Recognition of speech wave patterns by a computer that matches them with stored speech patterns of word. Current technique for orally entering data and inquiries into a computer.

sperichil *MusArts* » **spiritual** *Also see* **ring dance.**

SPFRE *Flm&Vid* Same percentage as film rental earned.

spiel *Crit&Eval* Lengthy, usu. extravagant speech or argument intended to persuade. *Also see* **barker.**

Spielberg, Steven *Flm&Vid, Mgt* (1947-, film dir.-prod.) <*E.T.,* 1982; *Schindler's List,* 1993; *Saving Private Ryan,* 1998> The most commercially-successful filmmaker in Hollywood history. *Also see* **editor** (*Flm&Vid*)

spiff *Mktg* To make attractive, stylish, or up-to-date. <The publisher hired a top designer to spiff up the book by using heavy paper and elegant reproductions>

spiffy *Fashn* Smart in appearance or dress; stylish.

spike heel *Fashn* Very thin high heel used on a woman's shoe.

spill *PerfA&C* Condition that may occur when the light directed at one area of the stage unintentionally spills over into another section.

spill *RecA&S* Condition that may occur in a recording session when the sound from one instrumental **section** unintentionally spills over into another section. *Also see* **leakage.**

spin *RecA&S* To play a phonograph record or records, esp. as a disc jockey.

spin control *Law&Pol, Mktg* Efforts made by politicians and marketers to ensure a favorable interpretation of their words and actions.

spin doctor *Law&Pol, Mktg* One experienced in the practice of delivering **spins.**

spine *LitArts*, *VA-Prntng* Hinged back of a book or periodical on which the title and other information may be printed. *Also see* **backbone**.

spine *TheatArts* **1 Stanislavski's** idea of "the line of through-action" of an acting role. **2** A Means of connecting motivations and objectives of all parts of a play.

spinoff or **spin-off** *Rdio/TV* Something derived from an earlier work. <a television show starring a character who had a popular minor role in another show>

spinoff, spin-off *Eco&Fin, EntreP* Occurs when a **parent company** "sells" a subsidiary or division to the parent company's stockholders. Parent company assigns shares in the subsidiary operation to its stockholders in direct proportion to the amount of stock held in the parent. Though the parent company may retain some of the stock, the "spun off" company becomes independent of the parent in every way, and its stock can be bought and sold like any other company.

spinoff, spin-off *Mktg* Something, such as a product, derived from something larger and more or less unrelated; a by-product.

spinto (Ital.) *MusArts* Relating to a lyric operatic voice with some attributes of the dramatic voice.

spirit gum *Th-MakeUp* all-purpose cosmetic adhesive

spirit possession *Crit&Eval* Emotional state characterized by vigor and animation, as if possessed by a **supernatural** being. » **contemporary gospel**

spiritual *MusArts* Religious folk song of African American origin. *Also see* **Songs, sperichil.**

spit take, spit-take *PerfA&C* Similar to a **double take**. Characterized by surprised actor spraying liquid after drinking.

SPJ *Journ* "Founded in 1909 as Sigma Delta Chi, SPJ promotes the free flow of information vital to a well-informed citizenry; works to inspire and educate the next generation of journalists; and protects First Amendment guarantees of freedom of speech and press."

split publishing *IntelProp, MusArts* When song publishing rights in a song are held by more than one publisher. Each of the several publishers are called **co-publishers**.

split screen *InfoMgt* Display technique that divides the **screen** into two or more **windows**.

sponsor *Genl* One who finances a project or an event carried out by another person or group.

sponsor *Mktg, Rdio/TV* Business enterprise that pays for radio or television **programming** in return for advertising time.

sponsors *Fndng* Prominent individuals who agree to the use of their names on letterheads and other campaign literature so as to convince prospects that the campaign has high-level **endorsements**.

sponsownership *Mktg* Event wholly owned by the sponsor, affording maximum control and potential revenue.

spontaneous *Crit&Eval* Happening or arising without apparent external cause; self-generated.

spontaneous *Crit&Eval* Happening without apparent external cause.

spontaneous invention *MusArts* » **improvisation**

spoof *Crit&Eval* Gentle satirical imitation; a light **parody**.

spool *RecA&S* Reel for magnetic tape.

spoonerism *LitArts* Transposition of sounds of two or more words, esp. a ludicrous one, such as: Let me sew you to your sheet for Let me show you to your seat.

spoons *MusInstr* Two ordinary metal spoons clicked rhythmically back to back make a sounds similar to **bones** used in **country blues, country music.** *Also see* **Little Instruments.**

sport *SportsEnt* **1** Activity involving physical exertion and skill governed by a set of rules or customs and often undertaken competitively. **2** Active pastime; recreation. **3** One known for the manner of one's acceptance of rules. *Ex.* good sport, poor sport. **4** A gambler at sporting events. *Also see* **sportsmanship**.

sports events *Rdio/TV* Popular type of television network programming. <*Monday Night Football, Super Bowl, Wide World of*

Sports> *Also see* **Television Shows**.

sports industry *SportsEnt* Collective term for all the public and private, for profit or nonprofit, professional or non professional organizations whose activities can be classified among the following: recreational and competitive sports, exercise and fitness activities, and health-related dance. It also encompasses the apparel and equipment companies dedicated to those types of activities, e.g., Nike. Although still fragmented, the sports industry is no longer represents the amateur spirit of the early Olympic games. Rather it has become an important member of the entertainment industry, next to music and film, which it largely surpasses in size and revenues. It is a major purveyor of images for the TV industry, has invaded the fashion industry, and is a major force in shaping the youth culture. It is also a factor of integration for minorities, and of understanding between groups of different ethnic origins. *Also see* **sport management**.

sports management *SportsEnt* Application of business management techniques – planning, controlling, marketing, finance, law – to sports activities, defined as the **spectator sport industry** (focusing on consumer entertainment) and the **fitness industry** (concentrating on consumer participation) Its human and organizational challenges makes it a necessary adjunct to the Arts, Entertainment & Media Management curriculum.

sports medicine *SportsEnt* Branch of the medical profession that specializes in the prevention, diagnosis, and rehabilitation of sports and exercise-related neuro-musculoskeletal [??] injuries, disorders, dysfunctions, and disease processes. A sports medicine specialist needs to understand the principles of performance enhancers, coaching techniques, training methods and sports' specific rules and regulations. *Also see* **drug testing**.

sports scholarships *SportsEnt* In return for the college athlete's services, sports scholarships generally provide room, board, tuition, and books. College athletes are not recognized as employees; they are student athletes with amateur-status subject to strict rules promulgated and enforced by the **NCAA**. As such, they are prohibited from sharing income (no salary) generated by their services. Since major college sports such as football and basketball have become significant revenue producers, the question of fairness is raised. Payment of cash, transportation, and equipment have been the most-often violated rules as athletic programs compete for the best athletes. Coaches can make scholarship renewal decisions on the basis of athletic performance. *Also see* **Title XI.**

sportsmanship *Ethcs&Phil, SportsEnt* Conduct and attitude befitting participants in sports, esp. fair play, courtesy, striving spirit, and grace in losing.

sportscast *Rdio/TV* Radio or television broadcast of a sports event or of sports news.

sportswear *Fashn* Clothes designed for comfort and casual wear.

spot *Flm&Vid PerfA&C* » **spotlight** *Also see* **Stage Lighting**.

spot, spot announcement *Rdio/TV* Local TV commercial purchased through a local salesperson within that market or through a national representative of the station. <30-second spot> *Also see* **commercial**.

spotlight *Crit&Eval* Public **notoriety** or prominence.

spotlight *Flm&Vid,PerfA&C* Stage lighting instrument that throws a beam of concentrated, intense light over a small area. *Also see* **floodlight, Stage Lighting**.

spray painting *BcstJourn* » **wallpaper video**

spread spectrum *InfoMgt* Refers to the 900 Mhz cordless telephone which spread sounds or signals over several frequencies rather than locking in on only one. These phone can continuously scan channels to find the clearest available channel.

spreadsheet *InfoMgt* » **electronic spreadsheet**

sprechstimme (shprecht-stimma) *MusArts* Form of dramatic declamation between singing and speaking, in which the speaker uses lilt and rhythm but not precise pitches.

springboard *Mktg* Something that helps to launch a career.

Sprint *InfoMgt* American telecommunications company.

SprintNet *InfoMgt* Service of U.S. Sprint offering local telephone numbers (**nodes**) for local access to a regional or national online service. *Also see* **Online Information Services**.

Spry Inc. *InfoMgt* Online information service. *Also see* **Online Information Services**.

spurious *Crit&Eval* Not genuine; false.

spy shows *Rdio/TV* Popular type of television network programming. *<I Spy, Mission Impossible, The Man from U.N.C.L.E> Also see* **Television Shows**.

SQL *iMedia* » **structured query language**

square dance *Dnce* Dance of rural origin in which sets of couples form squares.

square type *iMedia, VA-Prntng* Each character occupies the same width of space. <Courier, Monaco>

squeezebox *MusInstr* » **accordion**

squeezes *BcstJourn* » **topic box**

SR *TheatArts* **stage right**

SRDS *Journ, Mktg, Rdio/TV, VA-Prntng* **Standard Rate & Data Service**. Essential service for all **space buyers** and **time buyers**: monthly compilations of **media** information, such as advertising rates, circulation figures, mechanical specifications, and publisher's statements. *<Business Magazines, Consumer Magazines, Newspapers, Radio & TV Stations>*

SRE *RecA&S* Sound Reinforcement Equipment consists of one or more **microphones** supplying a signal to an **amplifier** operating one or more **speakers**.

SRO *Mktg* **Standing Room Only**. Sign or notice advising that all seats have been sold.

SS *BcstJourn* » **still store**

SSDC *Dnce, HR&LR* **Society of Stage Directors and Choreographers**. Performing arts union. *Also see* **Directors**, **Society of Stage Directors and Choreographers Foundation**.

SSL *InfoMgt* Secure Sockets Layer **protocol**, a standard for transmitting confidential data such as credit card numbers over the Internet.

st. *LitArts* **stanza**

sta. *Rdio/TV* **station**

stacc *MusArts* **staccato**

staccato (stacc) *MusArts* **1** Play short, crisply, and disconnected. **2** Marked by or composed of abrupt, disconnected parts or sounds.

stack *InfoMgt* Section of memory and its associated registers used for temporary storage of information in which the item most recently stored is the first to be retrieved.

stacked *Mktg, VA-Prntng* Said of a stack of magazines that are placed in a separate pile at the retail outlet so as to increase the visibility of the front cover, thereby encouraging an **impulse buy**.

stacking the newscast *BcstJourn* Procedure for ordering stories within the timed segments of the newscast. *Also:* "formatting." Normally, producer or editor stacks the newscast, but at smaller stations, newscaster may do this.

stacks *InfoMgt* **1** Extensive arrangement of bookshelves. **2** Area of a library in which most of the books are shelved.

staff producer *RecA&S* Record producer employed exclusively by record companies to produce one or more artists signed to the label. *Also see* **in-house producer**, **Producers**.

staff songwriter *ArtPerf, MusArts* One who has an exclusive agreement with a publisher.

staff, **stave** *MusArts* Set of five horizontal lines and four intermediate spaces used in **notation** to represent a sequence of **pitches**.

stage *PerfA&C* Area where the action of the play takes place.

stage band *MusArts* **1** School-related jazz band. *Origin* In the late 1940s, Music Educator Dr. Gene Hall (band dir., arr., educ.) at North Texas State Teachers College (now North Texas State U.) referred to his student **big band** as a stage band because jazz was a naughty and dangerous word in academia and in some religious minds. Hall also pioneered High School Stage Band Festivals in the 1950s. [First college (stage band) jazz festival was held at Notre Dame in 1959.] **2** Band performing on stage during an opera or theatrical production. <the military marching band in the second act of *La Boheme*>

Stage Curtains *ColEntry,PerfA&C* » act —, asbestos —, backdrop, border, cyclorama, draw —, fire —, front —, grand drape, house —, teaser, traveler —, traverse rod

stage design *PerfA&C* » **scenic design**

Stage Directions *ColEntry, PerfA&C* aside, backstage, blackout, center stage (C), cross (X), curtain, downstage (DS), enter, exeunt, exit, in 1 (2, 3, etc.), off-stage, on-stage, stage left (SL), stage right (SR), stage whisper, up stage (US)

Stage Directors and Choreographers Foundation *Dnce, HR&LR, PerfA&C* Created in 1985 by the **Society of Stage Directors and Choreographers** to provide seminars and other services to the members of SDCF. Administers the annual **Mr. Abbott Award** program. >www.ssdc1.com<

stage fright *ArtPerf* Fright or nervousness at the prospect of performing or talking in front of an audience or even facing a camera. *Also see* **butterflies**, **rejection**, **tension**.

stage hand *PerfA&C* One who works backstage in a theater. *Also see* **IATSE**.

stage house *PerfA&C* Physical structure enclosing the area above the stage and wings.

stage in-the-round *PerfA&C* » **arena stage**

stage left (SL) *PerfA&C* Area of the stage to one's left when facing the audience. *Also see* **Stage Directions**.

stage left, stage right *TheatArts* Left or right side of the stage from the actor's point of view facing the audience.

Stage Lighting *ColEntry,. PerfA&C* » accent lighting, arc spotlight, baby spot, balcony booms, balcony rail, barn door, channel, dimmers, electric batten, Ellipsoidal Reflector Spotlight, fill light, floodlight, follow spot, footlights, Fresnel, gel, general lighting, iris, key light, kleig light, Leko, light board, light plot, pin spot, reflector, scoop, specific lighting, spot, spotlight, wing spot

stage manage *PerfA&C* To direct or manipulate from behind the scenes, as to achieve a desired effect.

stage manager (SM) *Mgt, PerfA&C* Person who assists the director during rehearsals and manages all backstage activity once the play has opened. "I have always been fascinated by the theater in all its aspects. I like to know how every nut and bolt fits together. I've attempted to learn every little detail. Believe me, when you are second assistant **stage manager** at eighteen for Sybil Thorndike's company, you learn very quickly." — **Laurence Olivier** *Also see* **Managers**.

stage musicians *MusArts, PerfA&C* Musicians who play their instruments on stage as part of the performance. <Small marching band in the second act of *La Boheme*> *Also see* **on-screen musicians**, **pit musicians**.

stage plat *PerfA&C* Diagram or illustration – often attached as a rider to an engagement contract by the artist's agent – of a stage showing placement and type of microphones, power sources, standing lights, risers and platforms, etc.

stage presence *ArtPerf, TheatArts* » **presence** *Also see* **empathic response**.

stage right (SR) *PerfA&C* Area of the stage to one's right when facing the audience. *Also see* **Stage Directions**.

stage wait *TheatArts* To stop or pause. <awaiting an actor's entrance>

stage whisper *TheatArts* Uttered by an actor intended to be heard by the audience but supposedly not audible to the other performers. *Also see* **Stage Directions**.

stage-struck *ArtPerf* Entranced by the glamour of the theater or the screen or by the hope of becoming an actor. *Also see* **EAT+D**^{2}.

Stages *ColEntry, PerfA&C* » amphitheater, arena —, proscenium —, rake —, sound —, theatre-in-the-round, thrust —

stagy, stagey *Crit&Eval* Having a theatrical character or quality; artificial and affected.

staid *Crit&Eval* Characterized by sedate dignity and often a straitlaced sense of **propriety**.

stair fall *Flm&Vid* Stunt involving a fall down stairs.

stakeholder *Eco&Fin, EntreP* Originally, a stockholder, partner, or owner in an enterprise, Current usage by government and media has broadened the term to include bondholders, hourly employees, employee unions, salaried employees, suppliers, most everyone who has a stake in the well-being of the enterprise."

stakeholder *iMedia* Person(s) who have the definitive say in a project's sign off and acceptance.

stamper *RecA&S* Nickel-plated clone of the master **lacquer disc** mounted on a large hydraulic press to biscuit-cut the vinyl disc into a finished LP.

stand by *Rdio / TV* **1** To wait for a cue to go on the air. **2** To wait for a broadcast to resume.

stand-in *Flm&Vid* One who substitutes for an actor during lights and camera adjustments. *Also see* **understudy**.

Standard & Poor *Eco&Fin* Subsidiary of McGraw-Hill, Inc. that provides a broad range of investment services. <rating of bonds, stocks, etc>

Standard & Poor's Index (S&P 500) *Eco&Fin* Broad-based measurement of daily changes in stock-market conditions based on the average performance of 500 widely-held common stocks.

standard (std.) *Crit&Eval, Ethcs&Phil* **1** Acknowledged measure of comparison for quantitative or qualitative value; criterion, norm. **2** Degree or level of requirement, excellence, or attainment. **3** Requirement of moral conduct often used in the plural to indicate moral character. <Maintain standards in the face of temptation> <standard bearer>

standard pattern *Fashn* » **sloper**

Standard Generalized Markup Language *iMedia* Generic markup language for representing documents. **SGML** is an International Standard that describes the relationship between a document's content and its structure, which allows document-based information to be shared and re-used across applications and computer platforms in an open, vendor-neutral format.

standard player contract *SportsEnt* Each league's basic working agreement between players and owners. *Also see* **free agents**.

Standard Rate & Data Service (SRDS) *Journ, Mktg, Rdio / TV* » **SRDS**

standards (std.) *MusArts* Popular songs that are continually performed, recorded, and purchased for one or more decades. Includes much of the music of Irving Berlin (Israel Baline, 1888-1989, sngwri.), **George Gershwin** and **Ira Gershwin**, Jerome Kern (» *Showboat*), **Cole Porter**, Richard Rodgers (1902-79, musical theatre comp.) and Hammerstein (Oscar Hammerstein II (» **Show Boat**), **Stephen Sondheim**, et al. *Also see* **evergreen**, **Tin Pan Alley**.

standee *PerfA&C* Occupant of standing room. *Also see* **SRO**.

standing plans *Eco&Fin, Mgt* **Operational plans** that have a continuing life. <employee manuals, rules and regulations, policy statements> *Also see* **Goals and Plans**.

standing room only (SRO) *Mktg* » **SRO**

standup (SU) *BcstJourn* Reporter on camera in the field. It could be live but is principally a videotaped segment. Standups are used mostly as bridges and closers.

standup, stand-up comic *PA-Variety* Performer working without costume, **props**, or assisting persons. *Also see* **gag man**.

standup comedy formula *PerfA&C* » **set-up, punch line, segue**

Stanford Artificial Intelligence Laboratory *InfoMgt* » **SAIL**

Stanislavski, Konstantine (1863-1938, Russ. act., dir.) *ArtPerf*, Founder of the **Moscow Art Theater**, he produced many of **Chekhov's** plays and developed an innovative method of acting that emphasizes the psychological motivation of the actor. *Also see* **Group Theater**, **Method**.

Stanislavski method *ArtPerf*, » **method**

stanza (st) *LitArts* One of the divisions of a poem, composed of two or more lines usu. characterized by a common pattern of **meter**, rhyme, and number of lines.

star *ArtPerf* Performer whose leading role or superior performance is acknowledged by **billing**, money, and promotion, and by no means least, a star on her or his dressing room. *Also see* **costar**, headliner.

star *Mgt* **Strategic business unit** that shows an increasing **market share** in a growing market. *Also see* **cash cow**, **dog**.

star power *ArtPerf* "Every arena concert is an exercise of star power, whether for rockers who claim to share it with the audience or for divas, like Ms. [Barbra] **Streisand**., who revel in it. Ms. **Streisand's** long absence from the stage coupled with her various projects have given her more star power than anyone on the concert **circuit**, and that power is its own message." — **Jon Pareles**

star system *Flm&Vid* Exploitation of the charisma of popular performers to enhance the box-office appeal of films. Star system was developed in America and has been the backbone of Hollywood since the mid-1910s.

starstruck *Crit&Eval* Fascinated by or exhibiting a fascination with fame or famous people.

start-up *Eco&Fin* New business venture. This is the earliest stage at which a venture capital investor or investment pool will provide funds to an enterprise, usu. on the basis of a business plan detailing the background of the management group together with market and financial projections.

start-up or startup *Mgt* Business or an undertaking that has recently begun operation.

startup *EntreP* New venture that never existed before, as opposed to a buyout.

startup costs *EntreP* All of the dollars that a business spends to get a project under way. Startup costs normally include acquisition costs, training costs, and maintenance costs.

startup drive *InfoMgt* **Disk drive** from which you start your computer system.

stasis *Crit&Eval* Condition of balance among various forces; motionlessness. <"Language is a primary element of culture, and stasis in the arts is tantamount to death" — Charles Marsh (critic)>

stat. *Eco&Fin, Mktg* **statistics**

state *Journ* Business considerations <separation of **church** (editorial) and state (business)>

state merit-ratings *E&F-Acc* Rating system set up by individual states that determine the business's state unemployment contribution rate (SUTA) This system takes into account annual employee turnover for a business based on the number of unemployment claims filed the previous years.

state of the art *Crit&Eval* Highest level of development, as of a device, technique, or scientific field, achieved at a particular time.

State Unemployment (insurance) **Tax Act.** *E&F-Acc, Law&Pol* » **SUTA**

statement *Eco&Fin, E&F-Acc* **1** Abstract of a commercial or financial account showing an amount due; a bill. **2** Monthly report sent to a debtor or bank depositor.

statement *InfoMgt* Elementary instruction in a source language.

statement *LegAsp* Formal pleading

statement of cash flows *Eco&Fin, EntreP* Financial statement that determines what has happened to the working capital account (the amount of cash available) of a company between the beginning and end of an accounting period. *Also see* **Statements**.

statement of changes in financial position *E&F-Acc* » **statement of cash flows** *Also see* **Statements**.

statement of financial condition *E&F-Acc* » **balance sheet** *Also see* **Statements**.

statement of financial position On *EntreP* Personal balance sheet, it indicates all of the items that are owned and all of the items that are owed by an individual or family at a specific point in time.

statement of operations *E&F-Acc* » **income statement** *Also see* **Statements**.

Statements *ColEntry, E&F-Acc, EntreP* **bank —, financial —, income —, profit and loss —, statement of cash flows, statement of financial condition, operating —, statement, statement of operations.** *Also see* **Statements**.

States Arts Councils *Genl* Public bodies established in each U.S. state under the authority of the **National Endowment of the Arts** in 1965 Twenty per cent of their programming funds come from **NEA or NEH**; remainder is raised from state-wide sources. *Also see* **Regional Arts Councils.**

static *iMedia* Having no motion; fixed; stationary

station *Crit&Eval* Social position; rank. <Too often, a person is judged by her or his station in life>

station (sta.)*Rdio/TV* **Venue** equipped for radio or television transmission.

stationery *InfoMgt* Document that serves as a **template.**

statistics *Eco&Fin, Mktg* Mathematics of the collection, organization, and interpretation of numerical data, esp. the analysis of population characteristics by inference from sampling.

statute of limitation *LegAsp* » **limitation**

statutory copyright *IntelProp* » **Copyright Act of 1976**

steady engagement *MusArts* Be engaged at least three days in one week at the same **venue** — **American Federation of Musicians** (AFM) *Also see* **casual engagement.**

stealth enhancement *PerfA&C* Subtle use of performance technology. "On the way home, if the public says, 'Great lights,' then we haven't done our job." — Kenneth Feld, pres./prod., "The **Greatest Show on Earth.**"

stealth parentage *Mgt, Mktg* » **faux parentage**

steel band *MusArts* Band of Trinidadian origin, composed chiefly of tuned percussion instruments fashioned from oil drums.

steel drum *MusInstr* Metal percussion instrument of Trinidadian origin, fashioned from an oil barrel and having a concave array of flattened areas that produce different tones when struck. *Also see* **Musical Instrument Families.**

steel engraving *VisArts* Art or process of engraving on a steel plate.

steel guitar *MusInstr* Acoustic guitar with a metal resonator built into the body, often played with a slide and producing a twangy, variable tone. *Also see* **Musical Instrument Families.**

Stein, Jules (1896-1981, talent agent, arts mgr., prod.) *Mgt* Founded **Music Corporation of America** in 1924 which evolved into **MCA** after WWII.

step *Dnce* **1** To move rhythmically to music, using patterns of steps or gestures. **2** Moving in or out of rhythm. IN STEP, OUT OF STEP

stereo condenser microphone *RecA&S* Two complete and separate **mic** systems in one body. *Also see* **Microphones.**

stereo, stereophonic *RecA&S* Relating to a sound-reproduction system (introduced in 1958) that uses two or more separate channels for a more natural distribution of sound. *Also see* **binaural.**

stereopticon *Flm&Vid* **Magic lantern**, esp. one with two projectors, arranged so as to produce dissolving views.

stereotype *Crit&Eval* Conventional, oversimplified conception. <Californians are trendy>

stereotype *VA-Prntng* Metal printing plate cast from a **matrix** molded from type.

stet *VA-Prntng* Retain, do not delete; a **proofreader**'s mark.

stick *MusInstr* Bow for stringed instruments.

sticker price *Mktg* » **list price**

stickiness *iMedia* » **sticky**

sticks *Cult&Soc* City or town regarded as dull or unsophisticated. *Also see* **hinterlands.**

sticks *Rdio/TV* Relating to a number of radio stations. "The **FCC** measures a company's power in the radio industry by its raw number of stations, or 'sticks' in the parlance of the business. But these sticks can range in size anywhere from delicate twigs [small stations] to huge trunks [super-stations]." — Mark Landler (**broadcast media** journ.)

sticky *iMedia* Indicates how often a particular participant or user will return to a product. highly sticky product would be one that a person uses everyday or several times a day.

sticky subscriptions *LitArts, Mktg* Internet-generated "free trial" **periodical** subscriptions that may not be paid for. *Also see* **evergreen subscriptions.**

stile *PerfA&C* vertical side member of a **flat**

stiletto heel *Fashn* High heel on women's shoes thinner than a **spike heel.**

still life *VisArts* Painting of inanimate objects; widely used by modern artists because the subject lends itself to purely formal **composition.**

still, stills *Flm&Vid, Mktg* **1** Single or static photograph as opposed to a movie. **2** Still photographs taken from a scenes of a movie and used for promotion.

stillborn *Crit&Eval* An idea or proposal that fails before inception.

stilling *Crit&Eval* Emotional variant of **stillness.** "As the comedy of the first two acts died away and the serious themes of the play began to grip, we noticed a sudden stilling, that change in the air which comes from a theatrical feeling way beyond language." — David Hare (Eng. plywri.) *Also see* **empathic response, silence, stillness.**

stillness *Crit&Eval* State or instance of being acoustically or visually quiet or calm. *Also see* **silence, stilling.**

still store (SS) *BcstJourn* Electronic memory unit for storing single screens.

stink *Crit&Eval* To be of an extremely low or bad quality: "New talent has no place to stink." — George Burns (1896-1996, comedian, act., star of vaudeville, radio, TV, and movies.) STUNK

stippling *Th-MakeUp* Cosmetic painting technique involving tiny dots, using for creating texture.

stock *Eco&Fin, EntreP* **1** Capital (ownership) of a corporation expressed in "**shares.**" **2** Contract that provides its owner with residual rights to the earnings of a company, it's assets in the case of dissolution, and other rights may be provided, such as voting.

stock *Flm&Vid* Unexposed film. There are many types of stocks, inc. those highly sensitive to light (fast stocks) and those relatively insensitive to light (slow stocks) RAWSTOCK

stock *Mktg* **1** In retailing, stock is the inventory of goods that the retailer (dealer) has for sale. **2** In manufacturing, stock is the inventory of unsold goods that the company has in storage.

stock *TheatArts* **1** Theatrical stock company. **2** **Repertoire** of such a company. **3** Theater or theatrical activity, esp. outside of a main theatrical **center.**

stock certificate *EntreP* Document specifying the number of shares owned by a stockholder.

stock character *LitArts,* Conventional character or situation that recurs in many books, films, and TV shows.

stock company *TheatArts* Group of actors attached to a single theater and performing in **repertory.**

stock exchange (SE) **1** Place where stocks, bonds, or other securities are bought and sold. **2** Association of stockbrokers who meet to buy and sell stocks and bonds according to fixed regulations. <**AMEX, NASDAQ, NYSE**> *Also see* **stock market.**

stock footage *Flm&Vid* Film library clips of famous or typical places, situations, historical events, etc. ARCHIVAL FOOTAGE

stock market *Eco&Fin* Business transacted at a **stock exchange.** <prices offered for stocks and bonds>

Stock Market Indexes and Averages *Eco&Fin* This **economic indicator** used to measure and report value changes in representative stock groupings. Rising index tends to indicate a growing economy. <The **Dow, S&P 500**>

stock performances *IntelProp, TheatArts* Sources of income derived from **subsidiary rights** in a **musical.** <dinner theaters, summer theaters, university resident theaters.

stock-in-trade *also* **stock in trade** *Mgt* All merchandise and equipment kept on hand and used doing business.

stockholders *Eco&Fin, Mgt* Owners of stock in a company. <individuals, institutions, or another company> SHAREHOLDERS

stockholders' equity *Eco&Fin* » **book value, equity**

stoic *Crit&Eval, Ethcs&Phil* Ethical school associated with ancient Greece and Rome, based on the effort to live in accord with nature, and by maintaining one's calm in the face of adversity since we are responsible not for what is, but for how we are affected by what is.

stomp *Dnce, MusArts* **1** Lively dance involving a rhythmical, heavy step. **2** Jazz music for this dance.

stone *VA-Prntng* Table with a smooth surface on which page **forms** are composed.

stop *MusArts* **1** To press down a string on the fingerboard to produce a desired **pitch. 2** To close (a hole on a wind instrument) with the finger in sounding a desired **pitch.**

stop bit *InfoMgt* Bit that follows a byte of data to signify the end of a character.

stop time *MusArts* "Part of an arrangement in which the rhythm **section** does not keep time, but rather plays in **unison** a pattern of **attacks** followed by silence." — Lyon and Perlo (jazz critics)

StorageWorks *InfoMgt* Operating system **trademarked** by **Digital.**

.store *InfoMgt* **Domain name** ending for businesses offering goods. *Also see* **Domain Names.**

store of value *EntreP* Property of money that it preserves value until it is used in an exchange.

store-bought *Crit&Eval, Mktg* Manufactured and purchased at retail; not homemade. <store-bought clothes> *Also see* **ready-made.**

story line *LitArts* Plot of a story or dramatic work.

storyboards *Flm&Vid* Series of drawings as visual representations of the shooting script. Drawings represent the key situations (shots) in the scripted scenes, and dialogue or indication of music, effects.

story building *Flm&Vid* Creation of a **scenario.**

storyteller vantage point *LitArts* In a third person story, the sense of a presence perceiving and telling the story standing at a **Close Distance** or **Mid and Greater Distance** to the events without being identified with a character. — Story Workshop term by John Schultz (CCC/Fiction Writing dept.)

Storyville (*aka,* The District, 1897-1917) *Cult&Soc, MusArts* Brothel district of New Orleans – est. 1897 to contain prostitution, drugs, and gambling – provided employment for many jazz musicians, esp. piano players, and classical musicians in the more refined (**octoroon**) houses In 1917, as the U.S. entered WWI the use of alcohol was banned from all Navy ships and bases, and the District. Storyville passed into legend and the musicians went looking for work "up the river." Two years later **Prohibition** became the law of the land. *Also see* **New Orleans jazz.**

str. *Genl, LitArts, PerfA&C* **strophe**

straight *Crit&Eval* **1** Concerned with serious or important matters. <straight drama without comedy or music, **straight man> 2** Not being under the influence of alcohol or drugs. **3** Heterosexual. *Also see* **straight arrow, suits.**

straight arrow *Crit&Eval* **1** Morally upright person. **2** Person regarded as being extremely conventional.

straight face *Crit&Eval* Face that betrays no sign of emotion.

straight man *PA-Variety* Partner in a comedy team who feeds lines to the other comedian, who then makes witty replies. *Also see* **top banana.**

straight-ahead *Crit&Eval* Conforming to a conventional or standard style or mode straight-ahead pop concert.

straight-line *Eco&Fin* Mode of amortization by equal payments at stated intervals over a given period of time.

strait-laced, straight-laced *Crit&Eval* Excessively strict in behavior, morality, or opinions.

strait-laced, straight-laced *Fashn* Tightly laced garment. <corset>

strategic alliance *EntreP* Organizational relationship that links two or more independent business entities in a common endeavor.

strategic business unit (SBU) *Mgt* Unit within a larger organization essentially treated as a separate **entity** and established as an independent profit center, usu. with a distinct mission, objectives, competitive environment, and managerial requirements. *Also see* **profit center.**

strategic decision *EntreP* Decision regarding the direction a company will take in relating to its customers and competitors.

strategic goals and plans *Mgt* Long range goals and plans, usu. with a three to five year plus time frame. Primary responsibility lies with **upper management.** *Also see* **Goals and Plans.**

strategic management unit (SGU) *Mgt* » **strategic business unit** (SBU)

strategic plan *EntreP* Document that delineates an overall venture strategy and its supporting strategies.

strategic planning *Eco&Fin, EntreP, Mgt* Task of setting long range goals analyzing opportunities, and developing **strategies** to achieve those goals. *Also see* **Strategic Plans.**

strategy *EntreP* Combination of actions that will lead to the achievement of a venture's objectives.

straw hat circuit *PerfA&C* Summer theaters that operate in suburban or resort areas.

stream of consciousness *LitArts* Literary technique that presents the thoughts and feelings of a character as they develop. <*Ulysses* (1922) and *Finnegans Wake* (1939) by James Joyce (1882-1941, Irish fictwri.)>

streaming *iMedia, InfoMgt* Playing sound or video in **real time** as it is downloaded over the Internet.

streaming media *Rdio/TV, InfoMgt* Digital broadcasting platform that distributes audio and video media over the Internet.

street name *InfoMgt* » **domain name**

street smarts *Crit&Eval, Cult&Soc* Shrewd awareness of how to survive in an often hostile urban environment.

street theater Dramatization of social and political issues, usu. enacted on the street or in a park. <San Francisco Mime Troupe> *Also see* **Theatres & Theaters.**

Street, The *MusArts* » **fifty-second street** (NYC)

Streisand, Barbra (1942-, film/stage act., sngr., prod., sngwri.) *ArtPerf, Flm&Vid, MusArts, PA-Variety.*

stride piano *MusArts* Style of jazz piano playing in which the melody is played by the right-hand while a single note is played by the left-hand in alternation with a **chord** an **octave** or more higher. Three of the best. <Albert Ammons (1907-49, pno.), Pete Johnson (1904-67, pno.), Meade Lux Lewis (1905-64 pno.)>

strident *Crit&Eval* Loud, harsh, grating, or shrill; discordant.

strike *HR&LR* Employees refusing to work in order to bring pressure on management to accept the employees' terms.

strike *PerfA&C* Remove scenery and **props** from the stage.

strike off *Fashn* Short, test length of fabric specially printed in order to check the pattern **register** (*VA-Prntng*) and the matching of shade in the design.

strike up *MusArts* To start to play music or sing. <*Strike up the band!*>

strikebound *HR&LR* Closed, immobilized, or slowed down by a strike.

strikebreaker *HR&LR* One who works or provides an employer with workers during a strike. *Also see* **scab.**

string *InfoMgt* Set of consecutive characters treated by a computer as a single item.

string *MusInstr* Gut or wire cord stretched on an instrument and bowed, plucked, or struck to produce **tones.**

string bands (1890s, 1900s) *MusArts* Instrumentation for **country blues** bands. <fiddles, guitars, banjos, mandolins, and basses. *Also see* **Blues.**

stringer *BcstJourn* Independent reporter or shooter who covers stories with hopes of selling the results to a station.

stringer *Journ* Part-time or freelance correspondent for a newspaper or Radio/TV.

strings *MusInstr* **Section** of an orchestra composed of stringed instruments. <violins, violas, cellos, basses> *Also see* **fretted**

instruments, Musical Instrument Families.

strip *Genl* Area, as along a busy street or highway, lined with a great number and variety of commercial establishments. <The Las Vegas Strip of Glitz>

strip *PA-Variety* Remove clothing *Also see* **stripper**, **striptease**.

strip *VA-Prntng* To mount a photographic positive or negative on paper to be used in making a printing plate.

stripboards *Flm&Vid* Production manager's bible.

striplight *PerfA&C* Form of **floodlight** used to light drops and cycloramas. STRIPLIGHT *Also see* **Stage Lighting**.

stripped house *PerfA&C* **Touring company's** contract provision that requires the **host** stage to be stripped of all its hung lights and drapes.

stripper *PA-Variety* One who performs a striptease. ECDYSIAST

striptease *PA-Variety* Performance in which a person slowly removes clothing, usu. to musical accompaniment. BOTTOMLESS, BUMP, GRIND, TOPLESS

"Strong" Dollar *Eco&Fin* » **"Weak" and "Strong" Dollar** *Also see* **Economic Indicators**.

strophe (str.) (Greek) *Genl* Beginning, initiating movement(s) of a work of art. *Also see* **antistrophe**.

strophe (str.) (Greek) *LitArts* **1** First of a pair of stanzas of alternating form on which the structure of a given poem is based; a stanza containing irregular lines. *Also see* **antistrophe**.

strophe (str.) (Greek) *PerfA&C* First movement of the chorus in classical Greek drama while turning from one side of the orchestra to the other. *Also see* **antistrophe**.

structure *iMedia* **1** Way in which parts are arranged or put together to form a whole. **2** interrelation or arrangement of parts in a complex entity. **3** Something made up of a number of parts held or put together in a particular way.

structured query language *iMedia* Industry-standard language for creating, updating and, querying relational database management systems.

strut *Crit&Eval* To parade with exaggerated high steps and arched torso. *Also see* **drum major(ette)**

studio *Dnce, VisArts* Artist's workroom. Establishment where an art is taught, studied, or create.

studio *Flm&Vid, Rdio/TV, RecA&S* Room or building for film, radio, recording, video, or TV production.

studio *MusArts* Room or building where musicians practice or rehearse.

studio archives *Flm&Vid, InfoMgt* Repository of silent-film prints and **outtakes**.

studio era *Flm&Vid* » **major studios**

studio musician *MusArts, RecA&S* » **session player** *Origin* Once upon a time (1920s-1950s) radio stations and movie studios employed staff musicians 52-weeks a year.

Stuffit *InfoMgt* File compression software.

stunning *Crit&Eval* **1** Impressive. <a stunning performance> **2 Surprising**. <The show's closing came as a stunning shock>

stunning *Fashn* Of a strikingly attractive appearance. <a stunning gown>

stunt *Mktg* Something of an unusual nature done for publicity.

stunt *PA-Variety* Feat displaying unusual strength, skill, or daring. *Also see* **gag**.

stunt coordinator *Flm&Vid* Usually the **second unit** director. *Also see* **gag**.

stuntperson *Flm&Vid* Performer who substitutes for featured actors when dangerous stunts are filmed. STUNTPERSON, STUNTWOMAN *Also see* **new boy**, **okay guy**.

Sturm und Drang (Ger. for storm and stress) *Crit&Eval, LitArts* **1** turmoil; ferment. **2** Late 18th century German **Romantic** literary movement whose works typically depicted the struggles of a highly emotional individual against conventional society. *Origin* A drama, *Sturm und Drang*, by Friedrich Maximilian von Klinger (1752-1831)

STV *Rdio/TV* » **Subscription television**

style *Crit&Eval* **1** Particular mode or form of skilled construction, execution, or production; and the manner in which a work of art is executed, regarded as characteristic of the individual artist or of her or his time and place, or of a particular group, school, or era. **2** Sort; type. **3** Quality of imagination and individuality expressed in one's actions and tastes. **4** Comfortable and elegant mode of existence. "[Style] never stops changing and always stays the same. Without it the performer is unidentifiable in the crowd, and with it her or his recognition factor is unique and preeminent. For me it is number one on the list of what one must not only comprehend but come to grips with and, throughout a lifetime's career, attempt to cultivate." —**David Craig**

style *Fashn* Fashion of the moment, esp. of dress; **vogue**.

style *Flm&Vid*, "Style that shows is decoration, not style." — Sidney Lumet (1924-, flmkr, *Long Day's Journey into Night*, 1962)

style *LitArts* Customary manner of presenting printed material, inc. usage, punctuation, spelling, **typography**, and arrangement.

style *MusArts* "Style is the distinguisher. It separates the true creator from the player. You see, creators establish a style so whenever they start playing, everybody know who it is." —**Dizzy Gillespie**

style *TheatArts* Manner in which all the elements of a work are integrated into a whole.

style book *Journ* Manual with rules and examples of usage, punctuation, and **typography** used in the preparation of copy for publication.

style guide *iMedia* Document that provides clear and detailed information about a project's visual design; includes information such as exact colors (i.e., the hexadecimal code #0000CC), font faces, font sizes, etc., and usu. includes a printed sample of each aspect of the design. style guide is part of a larger document called a production guide.

stylist *Crit/Eval* **1.** A master or a model of **style**, esp. writing or speaking. **2.** A critic of **style**.

stylist *Mgt* One who helps creates a **style** for a performer. <arrangements, choreography, costumes, lighting, makeup, scenic background, special material, sound, etc.> *Also see* **empathic response.**

stylize *Crit&Eval* To restrict or make conform to a particular style.

stylus *RecA&S* **1** Phonograph needle. **2** Sharp, pointed tool used for cutting record grooves.

stylus *VisArts* Sharp, pointed instrument used for writing, marking, or engraving.

SU *BcstJourn* » **standup**

suave (swahve) *Crit&Eval* Smoothly agreeable and courteous. *Also see* **debonair**, **urbane**.

sub, sub. *Fndng, Journ, Mktg, PerfA&C* » **subscription**

sub-agent *LegAsp, Mgt* Agent authorized to operate on her or his employer's talent agency's license. *Also see*» **bond**, **employment agency license**, **Talent Agencies**.

sub-rosa *Crit&Eval* Secret, private, or confidential.

subaddress *InfoMgt* Section of a computer device for input and output accessible through an operation code.

Subchapter S corporation *Eco&Fin, EntreP, Mgt* One that is privately held, has more than one owner but not more than seventy-five, and is granted Subchapter S status by the Internal Revenue Service. A choice of legal corporation to avoid double taxation.) *Also see* **corporation**.

subhead *Journ* **1** Heading between paragraphs used for emphasis, identification, and to break up grey areas. **2** Subordinate heading or title.

subito *MusArts* Play quickly, suddenly. *Also see* **Music Directions**.

subject *MusArts* Melody or melody fragment that, because of its character, design, position, or treatment, is used in the basic musical form of a composition.

subjective camera *Flm&Vid* » **POV**

sublicense *LegAsp, Mktg* License giving rights of production or marketing of products or services to a person or company that is not the primary holder of such rights.

sublimate *Crit&Eval* To modify one's instinctual impulse (esp. a sexual one) in a socially acceptable manner.

sublime *Crit&Eval* **1** Characterized by nobility; majestic. **2** Of high spiritual, moral, or intellectual worth; not to be excelled; supreme. **3** Inspiring awe; impressive.

subliminal *Crit&Eval* Below the threshold of conscious perception.

sublimity *Crit&Eval* Of high spiritual, moral, or intellectual worth.

subliterature *Crit&Eval, LitArts* Writings like romance novels and mysteries that appeal to popular tastes and are considered inferior in style and content to more artistic literature.

submarine patent *IntelProp* Patent, usu. applied for by a lone inventor [of software, for example], that spends years hidden in prosecution. Eventually the submarine surfaces, laying claim to huge license fees from companies that suddenly discover themselves to be **infringers**.

submaster *Flm&Vid* One generation from a **master**, used to make **prints**.

subordinate file *Fndng* One of various categories of files maintained by development offices, such as foundations, corporations, organizations and the like, all of which are listed alphabetically in a master locator file.

subplot *TheatArts* Strand of dramatic action in a play in which the hero or heroine do not actively participate.

subpoena *LegAsp* Writ requiring appearance in court, or before an official government body, to give testimony or produce documents.

subpublisher *MusArts* Foreign music publisher licensed by a U.S. publisher to represent its catalogs. Subpublishers charge 5% to 25% for their services.

subscribe by design *Mktg,PerfA&C* Box office term for a subscription package of events chosen by the purchaser, rather than a pre-designated package of events offered by the producing organization. *Also see* **flex pass.**

subscriber *Flm&Vid, Rdio/TV, VA-Prntng* One who contracts to receive and pay for: periodicals, monthly cable services, monthly online services, recordings, books. <Columbia Record Club, Book-Of-The-Month Club, Dial-A-Movie>

subscriber *InfoMgt* Material that the computer user inserts into a document ("publisher") is changed. To insert a subscriber into a document, you open an edition file, which is created when material in the original document is designated as a publisher.

subscriber *Mgt* One who pledges or contributes money to an arts organization.

subscription (sub.) *Fndng* Raising of money from subscribers; the sum of money so raised.

subscription (sub, sub.) *Journ, Mktg,PerfA&C* Purchase made for a periodical for a specified period of time or for a series of performances.

Subscription TV (STV)*Rdio/TV* Cable transmission that requires a one-time or monthly fee for reception service.

subsidiary company *Eco&Fin, Mgt* Company having more than half of its stock owned by another company.

subsidiary lighting *PerfA&C* Lighting from any direction that supplements the **key light.**

subsidiary rights *IntelProp, MusArts,* Sources of possible income paid to those entitled to share revenue generated by a **Broadway musical** include: **cast album**, motion picture sale, home videos, **commercial uses**, **stock performances**, amateur performances by non-union performers, concert tour versions, and certain foreign performances.

subsidy *Eco&Fin, Law&Pol* Money given by a government to a person or group in support of an enterprise regarded as being in the public interest.

subtext *Flm&Vid* Dramatic implications beneath the language of a play or movie. Often the subtext concerns ideas and emotions that are totally independent of the language of a text.

substitutes *EntreP* Two goods related in such a way that an increase in the price of one good increases the demand for the other good.

substitution effect for price changes *EntreP* Change in consumption resulting from a change in the price of one good relative to the price of other goods.

substitution effect for wage changes *EntreP* Increase in the wage rate increases the opportunity cost of leisure and leads workers to demand less leisure and supply more labor.

subtext *TheatArts* Term first elaborated by **Konstantine Stanislavski**, "subtext" refers to the unspoken motive for a given line or speech, what the character wants to get or do by saying the line. It is sometimes now used more generally to suggest a text's undertaking sense or meaning.

subtitle *Flm&Vid* **1** Printed translation of the dialogue of a foreign-language film shown at the bottom of the screen. **2** Narration or dialogue flashed on the screen between the scenes of a silent film.

subtitle *Journ, LitArts* Secondary, usu. explanatory title.

subtle, subtlety *Crit&Eval* **1** So slight as to be difficult to detect or analyze; not immediately obvious; abstruse. **2** Able to make fine distinctions: a subtle mind. **3** Characterized by skill or ingenuity; clever.

subtonic *MusArts* Seventh tone of a **diatonic scale**.

subtractive color *iMedia* Physical elements (such as pigments or dyes) are mixed to create color. In contrast: additive color.

subway circuit *TheatArts* All the theaters within reach of the New York subways.

success *Crit&Eval* **1** Gaining of fame or prosperity or the love of audiences. **2** Achievement of something desired, planned, or attempted. *Also see* **"Sammy Glick."**

suite *MusArts* **1** Instrumental composition consisting of a series of movements or distinct compositions. **2** Cycle of dance tunes.

suits *InfoMgt* Employees dressed in corporate life uniform, i.e., business suits. *Also see* **nerd, techie.**

summer stock *TheatArts* Theatrical productions of **stock companies** presented during the summer, mainly in resort areas.

Sundance Film Festival *Flm&Vid* » **Sundance Institute**

Sundance Institute *Flm&Vid* Nonprofit organized in 1981 by **Robert Redford** and friends. "Dedicated to the support and development of emerging screenwriters and directors of vision, and to the national and international exhibition of new, independent dramatic and documentary films." Sponsors the Sundance Film Festival and the Sundance Theatre.

Sundance Theatre *TheatArts* » **Sundance Institute**

sunshine law *Law&Pol* Requiring governmental bodies to hold open meetings and sometimes to permit public access to records.

super *BcstJourn* » **CG**

super *Flm&Vid,* » **supernumerary**

Super-density disk *InfoMgt, Flm&Vid* » **SD**

supercardioid microphone *RecA&S* Mic with an elongated front lobe. *Also see* **Microphones.**

superconductivity *Sci&Tech* Flow of electric current without resistance in certain metals, alloys, and ceramics at temperatures at extremely temperatures. It will make possible highly efficient, miniaturized, or super-sensitive electrical and electronic products. <Fast computers and telecommunication equipment>

superimposition *Flm&Vid* Optical technique by which two or more shots appear in the same frame, one atop the other.

supernatural *Crit&Eval* **1** Relating to existence outside the natural world. **2** Attributed to a power that seems to violate or go beyond natural forces. **3** Relating to a deity. **4** Relating to the immediate exercise of divine power; miraculous.

supernumerary (super) *Flm&Vid,* Actor without a speaking part, who appears in a crowd scene in an opera, a play, or a spectacle. *Also see* **extra.**

superrealism *LitArts* Literary movement characterized by extreme **realism**.

superrealism *VisArts* Artistic movement characterized by extreme **realism**. *Also see* **photorealism.**

superstar *ArtPerf* **1** Widely acclaimed star who is extremely popular or prominent or who is a major attraction.

superstation *Rdio/TV* Television or radio station that broadcasts to a nationwide audience by cable, and/or satellite.

supertitle *PerfA&C* Written translation of the dialogue or lyrics of a foreign-language performance of an opera or a choral work shown on a screen at the top of the proscenium above the performers. SURTITLE

supervisory control system *iMedia* Term used for complex semi-autonomous systems that are only indirectly controlled by human operators.

supp. *Journ, LitArts* **supplement**

supplement (supp.) *Journ, LitArts* **1** Separate section devoted to a special subject inserted into a periodical, such as a newspaper or magazine. **2** Section added to a book or document to give further information or to correct errors. *Also see* **ASME**.

supply *Mktg* Amount of goods and services available for meeting demand or for purchase at a given price.

supply-side *Eco&Fin, Law&Pol* Relating to an economic theory that increased availability of money for investment, achieved through reduction of taxes esp. in the higher tax brackets, will increase productivity, economic activity, and income throughout the economic system. [Flawed feature of President **Ronald Reagan's** economic program that led to record budget deficits.] *Also see* **trickle-down theory, voodoo economics**.

support and revenue *Eco&Fin* Sources of income/revenues peculiar to each organization.

support services *Fndng* Technical aspects of a development program or fund-raising campaign concerning **prospect research**, mailings of appeal letters, gift processing, list preparation, and general clerical operations.

support system *HR&LR* **Network** of personal or professional contacts available to a person or an organization for practical or moral support when needed. *Also see* **networking**.

supporting act *ArtPerf* Performer or group of performers who backup the well-established **headliner**.

suprematism *VisArts* School and theory of geometric abstract art that originated in Russia in the early 20th century and influenced constructivism. *Also see* **Art Movements and Periods, modern art**.

surety bonds *EntreP* Coverage that protects against another's failure to fulfill a contractual obligation.

surf *InfoMgt, Rdio/TV* **1** Seek happiness and thrills as one maneuvers around vast **cyberspaces** or 500+ TV channels. **2** Skip from one peak or crest of a wave of light, heat, or other energy and the next corresponding peak or crest. *Also see* **channel surfing, lurking, wavelength**.

surplus *Eco&Fin* **1** Total assets minus the sum of all liabilities. **2** Excess of a corporation's net assets over the face value of its capital stock. **3** Excess of receipts over expenditures. **4** What a **nonprofit** calls a profit.

surreal *Crit&Eval* Oddly dreamlike quality.

surrealism *Flm&Vid, LitArts, VisArts, TheatArts* **Avant-garde** movement (between WWI and WWII) in the arts and literature that stressed **Freudian** and **Marxist** ideas, unconscious elements, irrationalism and the symbolic association of ideas. Surrealist movies were produced roughly from 1924 to 1931, primarily in France, although there are surrealistic elements in the work of many directors, esp. in today's **music videos**. *Also see* **Art Movements and Periods, modern art**, Salvador Dali (1904-89, Span. pntr.)

surtitle *PerfA&C* » **supertitle**

survival *Ethcs&Phil* "Survival – or one's perception of survival – is ethics' most persistent antagonist." *Also see* **self-censorship**.

Survival Tool Kit *MusArts, PerfA&C* » **Roadie School © Survival Tool Kit**

survivorship *LegAsp* Right of a person who survives a partner or joint owner to the entire ownership of something that was previously owned jointly.

suspense programs *Rdio/TV* Popular type of television network programming. <Alfred *Hitchcock Presents, Twilight Zone*> *Also*

see **Television Shows**.

sustain *RecA&S* Manner in which a **sound wave** is maintained. *Also see* **attack, decay, internal dynamics**.

SUTA *E&F-Acc, Law&Pol* **State Unemployment** (insurance) **Tax Act**. Payroll tax paid by employers to cover unemployment claims of their terminated employees.

swallow-tailed coat *Fashn* Man's black coat worn for formal daytime occasions and having a long rounded and split tail. *Also see* **evening dress, tails, tuxedo**.

swan song *Crit&Eval* Farewell or final appearance, action, or work. *Origin* From the belief that the swan sings as it dies.

swarm intelligence *iMedia* Collective behaviors of simple agents interacting with each other in an environment result in complex, global patterns or behaviors usu. not predicted, and which can appear premeditated or "intelligent."

sweeps *Mktg, Rdio/TV* Period each Nov., Feb., and May when the networks engage in special programming designed to help their local affiliates gain bigger audiences and therefore increased advertising rates. *Also see* **Nielsen Station Index** (NSI)

sweet *MusArts* Style of playing jazz characterized by adherence to a melodic line and to a time signature. *Also see* **dirty**.

sweet band *MusArts* White dance band of the 1920s to the 1950s that played pop songs with minimal swing or blues feeling. Very square. *Also see* **swing**.

sweet gospel music *MusArts* This style, popular with vocal quartets about 1945-60, was "characterized by close-harmony background that provided a rhythmic foil for a mellow tenor or light baritone lead singer; the songs were based on the **call and response** technique". <Golden Gate Quartet> — Horace Boyer (gospel mus. critic) *Also see* **Gospel Music**.

sweetening *RecA&S* Addition of more instruments onto an already recorded track or master, or combining two recordings into one.

sweetheart contract *Mgt* **1** Contract negotiated by on-the-take union officers that is decidedly against the best interests of the union membership. **2** Contract between a company and a vendor that secretly agrees to terms, conditions, and opportunities that effectively block competitive bidding.

swing *MusArts* **1** Type of popular dance music that evolved in the mid-1930s from 1920s Dixieland styles based on Dixieland jazz but employing a larger band and simpler **harmonic** and rhythmic patterns. Declined in popularity with the advent of U.S. involvement with WWII. **2** To play with a subtle, intuitively felt sense of rhythm; a moving beat. *Also see* **Jazz Styles**.

swing *Dnce* Ballroom dance performed to swing music. *Also see* **Dances**.

swing dancer *PerfA&C* Extra dancer who substitutes for one indisposed. *Also see* **curse calendar**.

SWOT *EntreP* Acronym that stands for strengths, weaknesses, opportunities, and threats. These pertain to both the internal workings (strengths, weaknesses) and external factors (opportunities, threats) external factors of a company.

SWOT analysis *EntreP* Framework that provides a concise overview of a company's strategic situation.

SYBUNT *Fndng* [Contributor gave] Some year but not this year. *Also see* **LYBUNT**.

sycophant *Crit&Eval* Servile self-seeker who attempts to win favor and reward by flattering powerful or wealthy people. *Origin* One who brought suit on another's behalf, usu. reaping part of the proceeds from a successful lawsuit — a practice that became predatory and socially destructive.

syllogism *Crit&Eval* **1** Form of deductive reasoning consisting of a major premise, a minor premise, and a conclusion. **2** Reasoning from the general to the specific; deduction. *Also see* **Aristotle**.

sym. *MusArts* **symphony**

symbol *Crit&Eval, LitArts* **1** Printed or written sign used to represent an operation, an element, a quantity, a quality, or a relation, as in mathematics or music. **2** Term in the analysis of texts, esp. literary texts, for the relation between an image, object, or word and a significant idea crucial to the meaning of the text. Thus in many Christian texts, the cross is a symbol of Jesus or the Christian church. *Origin* Token of a promise or agreement between two people formed by breaking a coin in two, each party to the promise or agreement taking half.

symbolic address *InfoMgt* Address expressed in symbolic form as a convenience to the programmer.

symbolism *Crit&Eval* Revelation or suggestion of intangible conditions or truths by artistic invention.

symbolism *TheatArts* Method of making a character or an action, a situation or a setting, stand for more than itself.

symbolism *VisArts* Practice of representing things by means of symbols or of attributing symbolic meanings or significance to objects, events, or relationships. *Also see* **Art Movements and Periods**.

Symbolist *LitArts* Any of a group of chiefly French writers and artists of the late 19th century who expressed their ideas and emotions indirectly through symbols. *Also see* **arts for arts sake**.

symbolist theater *TheatArts* European movement of the late 19th and early 20th centuries in reaction to realism and naturalism. Symbolist theater attempted to dramatize more poetic or metaphorical situations, often using unusual stage settings and ethereal dramatic action and language.

Symmetric list processor (SLIP) *InfoMgt»* **SLIP**

symmetry *Aes&Creat* **1** Beauty as a result of balance or harmonious arrangement. **2** Exact correspondence of form and constituent **configuration** on opposite sides of a dividing line or plane or about a center or an axis. *Also see* **asymmetry**.

symmetry *iMedia* **1 Gestalt Law** of pattern perception: mirror images are perceived as one entity **2.** balanced proportions

sympathetic vibration *MusArts* Relating to **vibrations**, esp. musical tones, produced in one body by energy from a nearby vibrating body and having the same **frequency** as the **vibration** of the nearby body.

symphonic poem *MusArts* » **tone poem**

symphonist *MusArts* One who composes symphonies.

symphony (sym.) *MusArts* **1** Extended piece in three or more movements for symphony orchestra, essentially a large-scale, complex **sonata**. **2** Instrumental **passage** in a vocal or choral composition. **3** Symphony orchestra. **4** Orchestral concert. SYMPHONIST, SYMPHONY COMPOSER

symphony orchestra *MusArts* Large orchestra composed of string, wind, and percussion **sections**.

symposium *Mgt* Meeting or conference for discussion of a topic, esp. one in which the participants form an audience and make presentations.

syn. *Journ, Rdio/TV* **syndicate, syndication**

syn. *MusInstr* **synthesizer**

sync sound *Flm&Vid* Sound recorded simultaneously with picture.

sync., sync *Flm&Vid, RecA&S* **synchronize**

synchronization right *Flm&Vid, IntelProp, MusArts* Authorizes recording, i.e., synchronizing music with screen images, of a musical work onto the soundtrack of an **audio/visual work**. *Also see* **Music Licenses**

synchronization royalties *IntelProp, MusArts* Money earned by the publisher (and, consequently, divided with the songwriter) for the use of a song for which a synchronization license has been issued.

synchronize (sync., sync) *Crit&Eval* **1** To occur at the same time; be simultaneous. **2** To operate in unison.

synchronize (sync., sync) *Flm&Vid, RecA&S* To cause soundtrack and action to match exactly in a film.

synchronous soundtrack *Flm&Vid* One in which the picture and sound are synchronized. *Also see* **synchronous soundtrack**.

syncopation *MusArts* **1** Shift of accent in a passage or composition that occurs when a normally weak beat is stressed. **2** Something, such as rhythm, that is syncopated.

syncretic *Crit&Eval* Reconciliation or fusion of differing systems of belief, as in philosophy or religion, especially when success is partial or the result is heterogeneous

syndicate (syn.) *Journ* Agency that sells articles and features. <columnists, comic strips, astrology charts, etc> for publication in a number of newspapers and periodicals.

syndication (syn.) *Journ* Process whereby certain articles and features are reprinted by (licensed to) newspapers and periodicals.

syndication (syn.) *Rdio/TV* Process whereby previously broadcast radio or TV programs are reused by (licensed to) independent radio and TV stations. *Also see* **reruns**.

synecdoche *Crit&Eval* Rhetorical figure in which a part represents or signifies the whole or a whole part. <image of a page of music representing Mozart's (» **classical style**) life work.

synergy *Crit&Eval* Interaction of two or more agents or forces so that their combined effect is greater than the sum of their individual effects.

syntax *InfoMgt* Rules governing construction of a machine language.

synth *MusInstr* » **synthesizer**

synthesis *Crit&Eval* **1** Outcome of the interplay of thesis and antithesis, esp. in the philosophy of **Hegel**; more generally the fruitful combination of opposing ideas or tendencies different from and more than the mere sum of the conflicting elements. **2** Reasoning from the general to the particular; logical deduction.

synthesizer (syn., synth.) *MusInstr* Electronic instrument, usu. played with a keyboard, that combines simple **waveforms** to produce more complex sounds, such as those of other musical instruments. *Origin* Some early instruments designed to produce new sounds, rather than simulate existing sounds included: the **theremin** (1920), the trautonium (1930), the mixtur trautonium (1954) Modern day synthesizer was introduced by **RCA** labs in 1955, refined in the 1960s by **Moog** and others. SYNTHESIZER PLAYER, SYNTHESIST ALSO SEE **computer music, Music Playback Devices, Musical Instrument Families**.

Synthetic Cubism period *VisArts* » **papier-collé** Ω

sys. *InfoMgt* **system**

SysOp *InfoMgt* System Operator, the manager of a **bulletin board** service or an online area.

system (sys.) *InfoMgt* » **operating system** (OS)

system *Rdio/TV* **network**. <ABC, CBS, NBC>

system commands *InfoMgt* Instructions to the computer to execute programs.

system design *iMedia* Process of developing a systemic design. » **systemic design**

system extension (INIT) *InfoMgt* Program that expands the capabilities of system software.

System Operator *InfoMgt* » **SysOp**

system software *InfoMgt* Supports application programs by managing memory and by communicating with input/output devices.

system, the *Cult&Soc* The **Establishment**

systemic *Crit&Eval* Relating to systems or a system.

systemic design *iMedia* Design that addresses a product as a whole. Each part of the design is integrated and developed in context of the entire product.

systems *Genl* Networks of structures and channels for communication, travel, or distribution.

systems analysis *Crit&Eval* Study of an activity or a procedure to determine the desired end and the most efficient method of obtaining this end.

systems analysts *InfoMgt* Those who design computer systems on the basis of information needs.

- T -

t *MusArts* tempo

T-Accounts *E&F-Acc* Modified versions of **general ledger** accounts, that are drawn like T's, and used for lecture and learning programs. Account name is written on the top horizontal line. Left column used for debit entries; right column used for credit entries.

T-bill *EntreP* U.S. Treasury bond that matures in less than one year, typically three and six months.

T-bond *EntreP* U.S. Treasury bond that has a maturity greater than ten years.

T-note *EntreP* U.S. Treasury bonds that mature in ten years or less.

T.O.B.A. *PA-Variety* **Theater Owners Booking Association** (*aka* Tough On Black Artists; Tough On Black Asses.) Booked black entertainers in black **vaudeville** theaters in small towns and cities of the South and Midwest (ca late 1800s-early 1900s.)

T1 line *InfoMgt* Access to the Internet installed in the basement of an office or apartment building for the use of the subscriber tenants or residents. Data enter and leave the building through **fiber-optic** cables. Users plug into a jack that is slightly larger than a telephone jack.

tab show *MusArts, PA-Variety* mini-**musical**. *Origin* Probably from "**tabloid**," i.e., something in a condensed form.

tabazine *Journ* » **magapaper**

table *iMedia, InfoMgt* Orderly arrangement of data in which the data are arranged in columns and rows in an essentially rectangular form.

table *MusInstr* Front part of the body of a stringed instrument.

table dancer *PA-Variety* One who performs erotic motions on the patron's nite club table in return for cash payment. *Also see* **ecdysiast, lap dancer.**

table reading *TheatArts* First readings of a script with actors sitting at a table.

tableau (tablow) *Crit&Eval* Vivid or graphic description.

tableau *TheatArts* Scene, or an interlude during a scene, presented on stage by costumed actors who remain silent and motionless as in a picture.

tabloid *Journ* Newspaper of small format giving the news in condensed form, usu. with illustrated, often sensational material. <*New York Daily News, New York Post, Newsday*> "*Newsday* played the news straight but parent Times-Mirror Corp. closed it down (July 1995) for not being competitive.... Big circulation numbers needed to support a successful tabloid have to come from readers held in contempt by the advertisers." — Bob Herbert (journ.) "Anyone who reads the tabloids deserves to be lied to." — Jerry Seinfeld (1954-, TV comic, act., scrnwrtr.)

tabloid journalism *Journ* Form of journalism that demonstrates a sensational view of events and occurrences, an exaggerated focus on celebrities' failings and the absence of a serious devotion to the truth. Although tabloid journalism has roots in newspaper tradition in this country and in England, the designation springs largely from the practices of the supermarket tabloids widely sold throughout the U.S. In some cases, the truth may be trivialized or distorted; in others, it does not exist at all or is drastically fictionalized. Tabloid journalism exists in all **media**, not simply in print, and is the guiding approach in many TV feature/magazine/**talk shows**. *Also see* **schlock.**

taboo, tabu *Crit&Eval, Cult&Soc* Ban or an inhibition resulting from social custom or emotional aversion. *Also see* **George Carlin software.**

tacet *MusArts* Be silent, don't play or sing. *Also see* **Musical Directions.**

tacit *LegAsp* **1** Implied by or inferred from actions or statements. <The **FCC** gave its tacit approval for broadcasting stations to disregard community service requirements. [Bequest of the Reagan administration.] **2** Arising by operation of the law rather than through direct expression.

tack *InfoMgt* Leave a message or response on a **bulletin board system.**

tag *BcstJourn* Portion of copy, usu. short, that follows an actuality or soundbite and ends the story. *Also:* "out" or "outro."

target audience *iMedia* Participants (users) for whom a product or content is intended.

Technicolor *Flm&Vid* Trademarked method of making color motion pictures in which films sensitive to different primary colors are exposed simultaneously and are later superimposed to produce the full-color print.

technol. *Sci&Tech* **technology**

technology (technol.) *Cult&Soc, Sci&Tech* Application of science to industrial or commercial uses. "Ultimately technology, like art and music, induces changes in the way we view ourselves. In this way, the most significant impact of modern technology may be cultural, not material." — Lawrence M. Krauss (chair, Physics

Dept, Case Western Reserve U.)

tacky *Crit&Eval* **1** Lacking style or good taste. <tacky clothes> **2** **tawdry. 3** distasteful or offensive. TICKY-TACKY

tactical goals and plans *Mgt* Goals and plans with an intermediate time frame, usu. a one to three years. Primary responsibility lies with **middle management.** *Also see* **Goals and Plans.**

TAD *Mgt* » **The Arts Dynamic**, pp. viii-x.

taffeta *Fashn* Crisp, smooth, plain-woven fabric with a slight sheen, made from silk, rayon, or nylon, used for women's garments.

TAFN *InfoMgt* That's All For Now.

Taft-Hartley Act (in full, the Labor Management Relations Act, 1947) *HR&LR* Republican Party sponsored bill that restored to management in unionized industries some of the bargaining power it lost in pre-WWII New Deal legislation. <Permitted states to enact **right-to-work laws**, prohibited unions from directly making contributions to candidates running for federal offices, forbade **featherbedding, secondary boycotts**, etc> *Also see* **National Labor Code.**

tag *InfoMgt* Label assigned to identify data in memory.

tag *LitArts* Refrain or last lines of a poem or song.

tag *TheatArts* Closing lines of a speech in a play.

tag *Rdio/TV* Something added to a prerecorded jingle.

tag, tagline *Crit&Eval, PA-Variety* An ending line, as in a play or joke, that makes a point.

tag, tagline *Mktg* Often repeated phrase associated with an individual, an organization, or a commercial product; a slogan.

Tagged Image File Format *InfoMgt* » **TIF files, TIFF**

tail *LitArts* Short closing line of certain stanzas of verse.

tail *VA-Prntng* Bottom of a page; bottom margin.

tailgate *MusArts* New Orleans-**style** trombone playing. *Origin* When early jazz or ragtime bands were loaded on advertising wagons or trucks, the trombonist had to stand near the tailgate so as not to stick the slide in someone's ear.

tailoring *Fashn* Making and altering of garments.

tails *Fashn* **Formal** evening costume typically worn by men. *Also see* **evening dress, swallow-tailed coat.**

take *Flm&Vid* **1** Act of recording a specific event or set of action onto film or video. **2** Name of the artifact so created.

take *RecA&S* One version of a recorded performance. <take one, eight, twenty, etc>

take class *Dnce* Participate in a dance practice session.

take five *PerfA&C* Take a short rest period.

take stock *Mktg* To take an inventory.

takeaway *HR&LR* Concession made by a labor union to a company in negotiating a new contract. <lower level of health benefits>

takeoff *Crit&Eval* Amusing imitative **caricature** or **burlesque.**

tale *Cult&Soc* Recital of real or imaginary events; a story.

talent *ArtPerf* **1** Marked innate ability for artistic accomplishment. **2** Natural endowment or ability of a superior quality. **3** Person or group of people having such ability. "Talent was a variable, merging on one side into skill and approaching **genius** on the other, changing from day to day, from year to year, in quality and content. You could not cultivate talents like hothouse lettuce or keep it sterile like a commercial orchid. Talent was one of the most indefinable things in the world, and closest in the world to God. There it was and there it wasn't and there it was again." — **John P. Marquand.** *Also see* **technique.**

talent *TheatArts* "Talent is an amalgam of high sensitivity; easy vulnerability; high sensory equipment (seeing, hearing, touching, smelling, tasting — *intensely*); a vivid imagination as well as a grip on reality; the desire to communicate one's own experience and sensations, to make one's self heard and seen."— Uta Hagen (1919-; German-born actor, teacher, author)

Talent Agencies *ColEntry, Mgt* » **CAA, CTA, CAMI, ICM, IMG, IMG Artists, WMA**

talent agency, talent agent *Mgt* Company or person who represents the artist in securing employment, and is compensated by a percentage (usu. 10%-20%) of the artist's fee. *Also see* **Agents and Agencies, Talent Agencies.**

talent scout *Mgt* One who searches for new or replacement talent on behalf of a producer. *Also see* **A&R.**

talent/technique *ArtPerf* One of the three basic characteristics of a successful Artist/Performer. *Also see* **EAT+D^2.**

talk radio *Rdio/TV* » **talk show** <Howard Stern, 1954-, broadcast pers> TALK JOCKS

talk show *Rdio/TV* Informal radio or TV interview and discussion program starring a **host**, featuring talks with **celebrities**, newsmakers, and people willing to say or do anything to be on the air or on camera. Some show are taped before a live and very involved audience with screened telephone calls accepted from the the-no-longer silent majority. [Talk show format – and its kissing cousin, **talk radio** – has become an important part of the **alternative media** so successfully used by radical politicians to "reach the common people" and avoid the **mainstream** press who ask impertinent "left-wing" questions. Even the president of the U.S., with or without his tenor sax, reach out to the **heartland** via *Larry King Live*.] *Also see* **Television Shows**.

talkathon *Crit&Eval* Lengthy session of discussions, speeches, or debates.

talkback *Rdio/TV* System of communications links in a television or radio studio that enables directions to be given while a program is being produced.

talkie *Flm&Vid* Early name (late 1920s) for a movie with a sound track. <*The Jazz Singer* starring **Al Jolson** (1886-1950, pop film/stage/radio/vaude sngr.) produced in 1927 by **Warner Bros.** as a desperate move to avoid bankruptcy.

talking book *LitArts, RecA&S* Recording of a reading of a book. *Origin* Material recorded for use by the blind.

talking drum *Cult&Soc, MusInstr* African instrument used in ritual and for communication. Its sounds reproduce tones, stresses, and rhythms of African languages.

talking head *Rdio/TV* News telecaster who talks directly to the camera and usu. on screen with only the head and shoulders visible.

tall organization *Mgt* » **Classical School of Management**

tam-tam *MusInstr* » **tom-tom**

tambourine *MusInstr* Percussion instrument consisting of a small drumhead with jingling metal disks fitted into the rim. Played by shaking it with one hand and striking it with the other. *Also see* **Musical Instrument Families**.

Tangerine Record Co. *RecA&S* Principal Ray Charles (» Artist/Producer): A&R administrator, major artist, in-house producer, and owner. *Also see* **artist-producer**. *Also see* **Atlantic Records**.

tangible *Crit&Eval* Something **palpable** or concrete.

tangible *IntelProp* In order to secure a copyright the submitted work must be in **tangible** form, i.e., on paper, on tape, on film, on disk> *Also see* **fixed work**.

tangible *LegAsp* Something that can be valued monetarily. <tangible property>

tangible asset *E&F-Acc* Any asset not meeting the definition of an **intangible asset**. *Also see* **Assets**.

tango *Dnce, MusArts* **Latin Dance Music** popularized in Argentina, pre-WWII. *Also see* **Dances**.

TANJ *InfoMgt* There Ain't No Justice.

tanks *Crit&Eval* Take a dive; business sinks.

tap dance *Dnce* **1** Dance in which the rhythm is sounded out by the clicking (metal) taps on the heels and toes of a dancer's shoes. **2** African American folk art, "Tap is like a drum solo. I believe you can get so many tones out of using your foot. Your heel is like your bass drum. The ball of your foot is the snare. Side is like a **rim shot**. A regular tap dancer knows ball and heel; he doesn't know about the side of your foot. We get sounds from the pinkie toe to all sides of the foot, back to the heel. I try to get these stupid wings." He stops, stands up, and demonstrates a **wing**, rapidly sliding his feet apart and making a graceful swishing sound. "It's like **brushes**.... Drummers carry around their sticks; we carry around our tap shoes." — Savion Glover (» funk) *Also see* **combo, Dances, funk**.

tape club *Mktg, RecA&S* » **record club**

tape drive *InfoMgt* **Peripheral** storage device that accesses data sequentially on a magnetic tape.

tape player *RecA&S* Self-contained machine for playing back recorded magnetic tapes. *Also see* **Music Playback Devices**.

tape recorder *RecA&S* Mechanical device for recording on magnetic tape; usu. capable of also playing back the recorded material. *Also see* **Music Playback Devices**.

tape transport *RecA&S* Device that carries sound from source to replay. *Also see* **tape drive, tape player, tape recorder**.

TAPI *InfoMgt* **Telephone Applications Program Interface**. Allows linkage between a telephone and computer, or to place a call directly from the computer.

target audience *Mktg* » **primary audience**

target market *Mktg* That portion of the total market the marketer chooses to serve. *Also see* **primary audience**.

target marketing *Mktg* Focuses the marketing efforts on specific segments within the total market. *Also see* **broad-reach marketing**.

target rate *E&F-Acc* » **discount rate**

task *iMedia* Action that a participant or user will accomplish.

task analysis *iMedia* Analysis of what actions the participant or user will need or want to accomplish.

taste *Aes&Creat Crit&Eval* **1** Characteristic preferences for art shown by a particular person; often, the best or most highly developed of such preferences as judged by those most concerned with the field in which choices or judgments are to be made. **2** Faculty of discerning what is aesthetically excellent or appropriate. **3** Sense of what is proper in certain circumstances. **4** Personal preference or liking. "Deciding taste is egotistical, but that's how taste is established, by somebody having the courage to say, 'I don't want to sell that." — Stanley Marcus (1905-2001-, Chairman Emeritus, Neiman Marcus)

tatting *Fashn* Handmade lace fashioned by looping and knotting a single strand of heavy-duty thread on a small hand shuttle.

tautology *Crit&Eval* Needless repetition of the same sense in different words; redundancy. <Statement of the form "A is A"; the form may not be obvious, thus, "a bachelor is an unmarried man" is tautological in a sense>

tawdry *Crit&Eval, Fashn* **Gaudy** and cheap in nature or appearance. <Cheap and gaudy **finery**> TACKY

tax incentive *Fndng* Like the **charitable contribution deduction** in the U.S. or the **covenant** in the U.K., a tax incentive is a device used by government to encourage corporations and private citizens to give to **nonprofits**.

Tax Reform Act of 1986 *E&F-Acc, Law&Pol* Most sweeping revision of federal tax laws since the inception of the Internal Revenue Code in 1913 This act established the **MACRS depreciation** system, gradually eliminated deductions for credit card interest paid by individuals, established the 10 year average for lump sum distribution, and many other changes.

Taylor, Dr. Billy (William Taylor Jr., 1921-, jazz pno., arr.-comp., arts mgr., educ., and n-fictwri.) *ArtPerf, Crit&Eval, Mgt, MusArts* Also see **Jazzmobile, Inc.**

Taylor, Frederick Winslow (1856-1915, inventor, eng., efficiency expert) *Mgt* Noted for his innovations in industrial engineering and management. *Also see* **Classical School of Management**.

tb. *MusInstr* **trombone**

TBC *Flm&Vid* Electronic device that corrects timing errors in video signals normally created by fluctuations in the speed of video recorders.

TBC *InfoMgt* To Be Continued.

TCG » **Theater Communications Group**

tchotchke (chotch-ka, Yinglish) *Crit&Eval* » **chachka**

tchr. *Crit&Eval* **teacher**

TCP-IP *iMedia* (Transmission Control Protocol/Internet Protocol) **Protocol** for communication between computers, used as a standard for transmitting data over networks and as the basis for standard Internet protocols.

TDWR *ArtPerf, MusArts* Talent Deserving of Wider Recognition, a category in the annual *Down Beat* Critics Poll.

tea dance *Dnce, MusArts* Late afternoon dance, usu. at a hotel. *Also see* **Dances, potted palm music**.

teacher (tchr) *Crit&Eval* **1** One who lets learning take place, often by arranging and presenting the circumstances in which it can take place for particular students. **2** One who attempts to impart knowledge and instruction in a particular subject or discipline. **3** One who conditions to a certain action or frame of mind. **4** One who presents analysis, criticism, and points of view.

TeachText *InfoMgt* Software that functions as a limited word-processing program, allows user to view and select PICT graphics.

tearjerker *LitArts, PerfA&C,* Grossly sentimental story, drama, or performance.

tears *Th-MakeUp* To create: Apply **glycerine** with an eyedropper just below the corner of the eye.

tearsheet *Mktg, VA-Prntng* Page removed from a publication, used as evidence of the insertion of an ad, usu. mailed with the **invoice** by the publisher to the advertiser or its agency.

tease *BcstJourn* Short item that is designed to attract listeners or viewers to a later story in the newscast. In television, videotape might be used with the tease.

teaser *Mktg* Advertisement that attracts customers by offering something extra or free.

teaser *PerfA&C* Short, horizontal drape used for masking the flies. Synonym for **border**. *Also see* **Stage Curtains**.

teaser *Rdio/TV* Attention-getting **vignette** or highlight presented before the start of a TV show.

Teatro Farnese *TheatArts* Designed by Gian-Battista Aleotti (b. late 16th century; d. mid-17th century; arch.) in 1618; regarded as the first modern theater, it used the **proscenium arch** to create a picture-frame stage and a U-shaped seating area for the audience. *Also see* **Theatres & Theaters**.

tech, techie *Mgt* Technician for a traveling **musical** or theatrical show. *Also see* **roadie**.

tech rider, technical rider *LegAsp, PerfA&C* **Rider** to an **engagement** contract that may require the **venue** operator to supply certain power outlets, lighting, sound, and stage equipment, etc. *Also see* **A above middle C**.

techie *InfoMgt* Employees who are not **suits**, esp. in computer technology companies. *Also see* **nerd**.

technic *ArtPerf* » **technique**

technical assistance *Fnding* Operational or management assistance given to nonprofit organizations. It can include fundraising assistance, budgeting and financial planning, program planning, legal advice, marketing, and other aids to management. Assistance may be offered directly by a foundation or corporate staff member, or be offered in the form of a grant to pay for the services of an outside consultant. *Also see* In-Kind Contributions)

technical director *PerfA&C* Person responsible for supervising the construction, mounting, rigging, and shifting of the scenery and properties.

technical rehearsals *PerfA&C* Run-throughs in which the sets. lights, props, and sound are integrated into the action of the play.

technical specification *iMedia* Document that clearly describes, from an engineering standpoint, how a component or product will be developed.

technique *ArtPerf* **1** Way in which the fundamentals of an artistic work or performance are handled. **2** Skill in handling such fundamentals. *Also see* **EAT+D²** *Also see* **talent, Talent/Technique**.

techno *MusArts, RecA&S* "Electronic dance music that has been around for years but is. the big thing by **MTV** and record labels eager to find a successor to alternative rock, relies on computers, synthesizers, drum machines, and **samplers** to purvey a cold, distinctly antihumanistic agenda. Many of its practitioners are key punchers, not guitar players; deejays and computer **geeks**, no musicians." — Michiko Kakutani (lit. critic *NY Times*) *Also see* **ambient**.

techno music *MusArts* » **rave**

technocracy *Cult&Soc* Government or social system controlled by scientists and technical experts. *Also see* **technopoly**.

technocrat *Cult&Soc* **1** Technical expert, esp. one in a managerial or administrative position. **2** proponent of **technocracy**

technographics *iMedia* Profile of a target audience that includes information such as: type of computer platform, software, connection speed, etc.

technology *iMedia* Mankind's ability to manipulate matter and energy to various ends.

technology *Sci&Tech* Application of science to industrial or commercial objectives.

technophile *Cult&Soc* One in favor of technology and its consequences.

technophobe *Cult&Soc* One distrustful or opposed to new technology and its consequences. *Also see* **Luddite**.

technopoly *Cult&Soc* Society in which all forms of cultural life are subordinate to technology. *Also see* **technocracy**.

technostructure *Cult&Soc* **1** Large-scale corporate system. **2** Network of skilled professionals who control such a corporate system.

teenybopper *Cult&Soc* Young teenage girl who follows the latest fad or craze in dress or music.

Tejano *MusArts* Very popular music in South Texas and the Mexican border featuring a "fast-paced mix of accordion, guitars, and lyrics in both English and Spanish." "It's got polka in it, a little bit of country, a little bit of jazz," — Selena Quintanilla (mus. critic)

telecast *Rdio/TV* television broadcast.

telecine *Flm&Vid* Machine and the process of transferring a filmed image to **videotape**.

telecommunications *InfoMgt* Science and technique of communication by electronic transmission of impulses via telegraph, cable, telephone, radio, or TV.

telecommute *InfoMgt* Communicate with one's office by telecommunication.

telefilm *Flm&Vid* Film produced for television broadcasting.

telemarketing *Mktg* Use of the telephone in marketing goods or services. [Used more and more to the increasing dismay of those who don't like their quiet time interrupted by honey-voiced pitchpersons.] *Also see* **Distribution Methods**.

Telephone Applications Program Interface (TAPI) *InfoMgt* » **TAPI**

telephone campaign *Fnding* Technique, employed esp. in alumni fund campaigns, to secure verbal commitments for gifts via telephone calls from teams of solicitors working out of a central headquarters.

teleprompter, TelePrompTer *Rdio/TV* **Trademarked** device employed in TV or in a public forum to show an actor or a speaker an enlarged line-by-line reproduction of a script.

teletext *InfoMgt* Electronic communications system in which printed information is broadcast by TV signal to sets equipped with decoders.

telethon *Fnding* Organized fundraising effort by telephone solicitation. Often used in conjunction with direct mail. PHONATHON

television broadcast *Rdio/TV* Development: 1928 — First daily experimental broadcasts by **General Electric** (Schenectady, NY); 1940 — First official network television broadcast by **NBC** (NYC); 1940 — **CBS** makes first successful color television broadcast; 1950s — **NTSC** color television standard based on RCA's black and white compatible system accepted by major manufacturers and the FCC.

television producer *Rdio/TV* One who supervises the production of a TV program. *Also see* **Producers**.

Television Shows *ColEntry, Rdio/TV* Following are some popular types of TV network shows: **award —, children's —, comedy-variety —, Congressional hearings, courtroom drama, detection —, dramatic productions, family situation comedies, hospital —, late-night entertainment, motion pictures, newscasts, non-family situation comedies, police —, quiz and game —, soap operas, special programs, spectaculars, sports events, spy —, suspense programs. talk —, variety —, Westerns**

telly (Brit.) *Flm&Vid* television set.

telnet *InfoMgt* Application that allows a connection to another computer using the connection you've already established through a local provider.

temp *Eco&Fin, HR&LR* Temporary employee or worker. *Also see* **body shop**.

tempera *VisArts* Painting medium in which pigment is mixed with water-soluble glutinous materials or egg yolk. POSTER COLOR, POSTER PAINT

temperament *ArtPerf* » **artistic temperament**

template *BcstJourn* Screen format of a news computer system. Template provides a place for information and newswriting.

template *iMedia* Document or file having a preset format, used as a starting point for a particular application so that the format does not have to be recreated each time it is used.

template *InfoMgt* **1** Set of pre-defined formulas on a spreadsheet. **2** pattern

tempo *Crit&Eval* Characteristic rate or rhythm of activity. PACE.

tempo *MusArts* Relative speed at which music is or ought to be played, often indicated on written compositions by a descriptive or **metronomic** direction to the performer. (PL) TEMPI *Also see*

beat, time.

tempo *TheatArts* Variations in pace in which a scene is acted.

temporary account *E&F-Acc* Revenue and expense accounts that relate to a particular accounting period and are closed at the end of the period. NOMINAL ACCOUNT *Also see* **permanent account.**

temporary employee (temp) *Eco&Fin, HR&LR* » **temp**

ten *MusArts* **tenor**

ten percenter *Mgt* » **talent agency, talent agent**

ten-song cap *IntelProp, RecA&S* Refers to the practice of most record companies to limit payment of **mechanical royalties** to ten songs per vinyl album and now continued on CDs, which average about twelve songs per CD. *Also see* **excess mechanicals.**

tenor *Crit&Eval* Course of thought running through something written or spoken.

tenor (ten) *MusArts* Highest natural adult male voice.

tenor *LegAsp* Exact meaning or actual wording of a document as distinct from its effect.

tenor band *MusArts* Band without alto saxes, used today in a derogatory manner.

tenor clef *MusArts* » **C clef**

tenor sax *MusInstr* Instrument in range between alto and baritone saxophones. TENOR PLAYER, TENOR SAX PLAYER, TENOR SAXIST *Also see* **Musical Instrument Families.**

tension *Crit&Eval* **1** Balanced relation between strongly opposing elements. **2** Uneasy suspense. *Also see* **conflict.**

tension *LitArts* Interplay of conflicting elements in a poem or a plot. *Also see* **conflict.**

tension and relaxation *Aes&Creat* "It is the right distribution of light and shade, or of tension and relaxation, that is formative in every art, in music as well painting, sculpture, architecture, poetry." — **Ernst Toch** *Also see* **contraction and release, fall and recovery, silence, tension and release.**

tension and release *MusArts* Term used by many musicians instead of **tension and relaxation.** *Also see* **silence.**

tenterhooks *Crit&Eval* In a state of uneasiness, suspense, or anxiety.

term *Genl* **1** Limited period of time. **2** Point in time at which something ends; a deadline.

term deal *Flm&Vid* Approval of money to finance a production. *Also see* **greenlight.** *Also see* **greenlight.**

term loan *EntreP* Money loaned for a five to ten-year term, corresponding to the length of time the investment will bring in profits.

term of copyright *IntelProp* » **copyright term**

termination by acts of the parties *LegAsp* Parties to an **agency contract** can terminate the relationship by. <mutual agreement, lapse of time, purpose achieved, occurence of a specified event>

termination by operation of law *LegAsp* **Agency contract** can be terminated by law by. <death, insanity, bankruptcy, war, changed circumstances, and impossibility (loss or destruction of the subject matter of the agency, loss of a required qualification, change in the law)>

termination clause *LegAsp* Clause in a contract that details the conditions by which the contract may be terminated.

termination for cause *HR&LR* To discharge an employee for a stated reason set forth in the company regulations or in the contract of employment.

terms *Flm&Vid* Conditions under which the distributor and exhibitor agree to show product in a given theater. Terms are based on film rental costs (flat fee or percentage of gross receipts), number of weeks, advertising, etc.

terms *LegAsp* Elements of a proposed or concluded agreement; a condition. <terms of the contract, terms of the agreement>

Terpsichore *Dnce, MusArts* **Muse** of dance and choral singing. *Also see* **Muses.**

terpsichorean *Dnce* dancer

terrace seating *PerfA&C* Audience seating on rear or side of stage.

tertiary colors *iMedia* Created by mixing the three primaries together in different percentages.

tessitura (Ital. for "texture") *MusArts* **1** Proportionate use of high or low **register** in a given vocal range. **2** Prevailing range of a vocal or instrumental part, within which most of the tones lie.

test case *LegAsp* Legal action whose outcome is likely to set a precedent or test the constitutionality of a statute.

test pattern *Rdio/TV* Geometric chart transmitted by a television station to assist viewers in adjusting reception.

Tex-Mex music *MusArts* Mix of Texas flavored country music and Mexican pop. *Also see* **Country Music Styles.**

Texaco Star Theater (1948) *Cult&Soc, Rdio&TV* First significantly popular network television program, starring Milton Berle (1908-; film/TV/vaude. comedian, actor)

TexMex *Cult&Soc* Blend of South Texas and North Mexican pop culture.

text *Crit&Eval* Passage from a written work used as the starting point of a discussion. SUBJECT, TOPIC

text *LitArts* **1** Body of a printed work as distinct from headings and illustrative matter on a page or from front and back matter in a book. **2** textbook.

text edition *LitArts, Mktg* Edition of a book adapted for the educational market.

textiles *Fashn* Fabrics manufactured by weaving or knitting.

textual criticism *Crit&Eval, LitArts* **1** Study of manuscripts or printings to determine the original or most authoritative form of a text, esp. of a piece of literature. **2** Literary criticism stressing close reading and detailed analysis of a particular text.

texture *Crit&Eval* **1** Appearance and feel of a surface. **2** Distinctive or identifying character or characteristics.

texture *Fashn* structure of interwoven fibers.

texture *iMedia* Distinctive physical composition or structure of something, especially with respect to the size, shape, and arrangement of its parts.

texture *LitArts, MusArts, VisArts* In artistic composition, the characteristic structural quality resulting from the artist's blending of elements, such as the **parts** in music, the **pigment** and brushwork in painting, or words, rhythms, etc., in poetry.

Thalia *LitArts, TheatArts* The **Muse** of comedy and pastoral poetry. *Also see* **Muses.**

The Whale *LitArts* » **Moby Dick**, Herman Melville

theat. *PerfA&C* **theater, theatre**

theater (theat.) *PerfA&C* Building, room, or outdoor structure for the presentation of dramatic and musical performances, and variety entertainment. *Also see* **theatre.** PLAYHOUSE

Theater Communications Group (TCG) Umbrella organization of **nonprofit** theaters.

theater of the absurd *TheatArts* Form of drama that emphasizes the absurdity of human existence by employing disjointed, repetitious, and meaningless **dialogue**, purposeless and confusing situations, and plots that lack realistic or logical development. *Also see* **Theaters & Theatres.**

Theater Owners Booking Association (T.O.B.A.) *Mgt* » **T.O.B.A**

theater *PerfA&C* Building, room, or outdoor structure for the presentation of dramatic and musical performances, and variety entertainment. *Also see* **theatre.**

theater-in-the-round *PerfA&C* Stage surrounded by audience. *Also see* **Stages.**

theatre *TheatArts* **1** Dramatic literature or its performance. <the theatre of **Tennessee Williams** (Thomas Lanier Williams, 1911-83, dram., poet)> **2** Milieu of actors and playwrights. **3** Quality or effectiveness of a theatrical production "Possibly no other art has so consistently taken such extravagant chances in provoking authority." — James T. Maher (1917-, mus-crit, journ, educ.) *Usage* The *-re* spelling is preferred in the professional theatre and now prevails in England. The *-er* spelling usu. refers to a specific theater, theater chain, or theater complex. *Also see* **theater.**

Théâtre Française *TheatArts* » **Comédie-Française**

Theatre Guild *TheatArts* NYC play-producing organization founded 1918. *Also see* **Group Theater.**

theatre of the absurd *TheatArts* Phrase coined by critic Martin Esslin to denote a certain strain of post-World War II drama which in both form and content seemed to demonstrate the purposelessness of man in an age of disbelief.

theatre party *Mktg, PerfA&C* **1** Special performance such as a benefit. **2** Group of persons who attend the theatre together. *Also see* **group sales.**

Theatres & Theaters *ColEntry, TheatArts* » **Abbey Theatre,**

American National Theatre and Academy (ANTA), art —, booth —, Comédie-Française, Théâtre Française, En Garde Arts Theater, Epic —, Federal Theatre, Greenwich Village Theatre, Group Theater, guerrilla —, HB Playhouse, Irish National Theatre, Kabuki, legitimate —, little —, living newspaper, Living Theater, lunchtime —, Lyceum Theatre, Mercury Theater, Moscow Art Theater, musical —, National Theatre of Great Britain, No (Noh), off-Broadway —, off-off Broadway —, Old Vic, prole-theatre, Provincetown Players, regional —, Royal Shakespeare Company, site-specific —, street —, Teatro Farmese, Theatre Guild, theatre of the absurd, Yiddish —.

Theatrical Wardrobe Attendants Union (TWAU) *HR&LR, PerfA&C* » **TWAU**

theatrical, theatric (theat.) *TheatArts* **1** Suitable for dramatic performance or the theater. **2** Marked by exaggerated self-display and unnatural behavior; affectedly dramatic.

theatricalism *Crit&Eval* Theatrical manner or style. SHOWINESS.

theatricals *TheatArts* Stage performances, usu. by amateurs.

theatrics *Crit&Eval*, **1** Exaggerated theatrical mannerisms. **2** Art of the theater. HISTRIONICS, MELODRAMATICS

Thelonious Monk Institute of Jazz (1986-) *ArtPerf, MusArts* "Its mission is to offer the world's most promising young musicians college level training by America's jazz masters and to present public school-based jazz education programs for young people around the globe." — Internet *Also see* **bop**.

thematic montage *Flm&Vid* Type of editing, propounded by **Eisenstein**, in which separate shots are linked together not by their literal continuity in reality, but by symbolic association. Most commonly used in documentaries, in which shots are connected in accordance to the filmmaker's thesis. *Also see* **continuity**.

theme *TheatArts* General idea (or real subject) behind a play. In the *Poetics* Aristotle calls it "thought," his third element of drama — the reasoning aspect or **argument** of a play.

theme and variation *MusArts* Musical form in which the theme is repeated and varied. *Also see* **leitmotif, motif, motto**.

theme park *Mktg, PA-Variety* **Amusement park** in which all the settings and attractions have a central [marketing] theme. <Disneyland, Opryland> *Also see* **MCA, Walt Disney Company**.

Theory J *Mgt* Management techniques that follow Japanese models. Decisions are based on the collective consensus of all concerned. Decisions are delayed until a strong consensus is reached. Once a decision is made, everyone follows it exactly with further input limited to improving the quality of the end result. *Also see* **quality circles, Theory X, Theory Y**.

theory of games *Eco&Fin, Mgt* » **game theory**

Theory X *Mgt* Management techniques based on **Frederick Taylor's** theories. Theory X assumes that employees are **inherently** lazy, want to have the easiest job possible, are not ambitious, and are motivated only by money. "It's a horrid life for any man to live not being able to look any workman in the face without seeing hostility there, and a feeling that every man around you is your virtual enemy." — **Frederick Winslow Taylor** *Also see* **Theory J, Theory Y**.

Theory Y *Mgt* opposite of **Theory X**

Theory Z *Mgt* **1** Good managers use both **Theory X** and **Theory Y** dependent on the situation. **2** A **Malgamation** of Japanese consensus collectivism (**Theory J**) and American individualism (**Theory Y**) Workers have more input and more responsibility. Final decisions, even on the lower levels, are more apt to be individual. PARTICIPATIVE MANAGEMENT

theremin *MusInstr* Electronic instrument played by moving the hands near its two antennas. Technical principle based on **heterodyning**. First instrument built in Russia in 1920; gained audience ca. 1928. Transistorized version available from **Bob Moog's** company, **Big Briar**.

Theremin, Leo (1896-1993, Russ.-born eng.) *MusInstr, Sci&Tech* Inventor of the **theremin**. Strong influence on **Bob Moog**.

thin *LitArts* Lacking vivid, full imagery or comprehensive thought.

thin *MusArts* Musical performance lacking **resonance**, said of **tone**; lacking richness of **texture**, said of **harmony**.

thin *VisArts* A film negative not having enough photographic density or contrast to make satisfactory prints.

thin client *iMedia* Simple client program or hardware device that relies on most of the function of the system being in the server.

think piece *Journ* Newspaper article consisting of news analysis, background material, and personal opinion.

think tank *also* **think-tank** *Mgt* Group or an institution organized for intensive research and solving of problems.

third *MusArts* Interval between the **tonic** and the third tone of a **diatonic** scale.

third position *Dnce* (Ballet) One foot in front of the other; heel against the instep. *Also see* **Positions**.

third-class *Mktg* Class of mail in the U.S. postal system inc. all printed matter, except newspapers and magazines, that weighs less than 16 ounces and is unsealed. *Also see* **second-class mail**.

third-party payers *Mktg* Persons or organizations that provide the funding for projects, products, or services that benefit the user or consumer.

third-rate *Crit&Eval* Even less quality or value than **second-rate**.

third-stream music *MusArts* Attempt to blend classical composition with jazz improvisation. *Origin* Term and concept by Gunther Schuller (1925-, comp., educ., n-fictwri.)

thirty-second note *MusArts* Note whose value is thirty-second of a **whole note** and double that of a **sixteenth** note. *Also see* **Musical Notes**.

Thomas *InfoMgt* **Library of Congress** database, named after Thomas Jefferson, will eventually hold the texts of every piece of legislation introduced in Congress and the official text of every speech made on the floor. *Also see* **Online Information Services**.

Thompson, Ken (19??-, info. sci.) *InfoMgt, Sci&Tech* Working at **Bell Labs** for thirty years, Thompson invented and developed the **UNIX** computer operating system; has also done original work on **artificial intelligence** to **music compression**. Ω

Thorndike, Dame Sybil (1882-1976, Brit. act.-mgr.) *ArtPerf, Flm&Vid, Mgt*, Created the title role in **George Bernard Shaw's** *Saint Joan* (1924), known for her great versatility and demanding management style. *Also see* **Sir Laurence Olivier stage manager**.

thoroughbass *or* **thorough bass** *MusArts* » **continuo**

thought *Crit&Eval* Intellectual activity or production of a particular time or group. *Also see* **analysis of tragedy**.

thought police *Ethcs&Phil, Law&Pol* Those who would censor or control thoughts as well as deeds.

thrashing *InfoMgt* Condition arising in a virtual storage environment whereby the same program instructions are continually swapped in and out of memory.

thread *InfoMgt* Topic of conversation, theme of dialogue.

threads *Fashn* clothes

three-act structure *iMedia* Drama starting with a problem, continuing with a confrontation, and ending with a resolution.

three-dimensional *Genl, iMedia*, **1** Having or appearing to have extension in depth. **2** Treating many aspects of a subject. LIFELIKE. **3** Relating to existing in three dimensions: *Also see* **one-dimensional, two-dimensional**.

Three-Hour Education Rule *Rdio/TV* **FTC** regulation mandates all major network and cable stations to air at least 3-hours of educational programs a week.

three-quarter time *MusArts* Waltz time: three beats to the **measure**, every quarter-note gets one beat. 3/4 TIME

three-ring circus *Crit&Eval* Situation characterized by confusing, engrossing, or amusing activity. — American Historical Dictionary

three-ring circus *PA-Variety* **Circus** with simultaneous performances in three separate **rings**.

three-sheet *Mktg,PerfA&C* Advertising poster for a billboard consisting of three sheets, each approx. 20 by 30 inches.

three-step distribution *Mktg* Channel of distribution where the product goes (1) from manufacturer to **wholesaler**, (2) to **rack jobber**, (3) to retailer. *Also see* **Distribution Methods**.

threshold of feeling *RecA&S* Level of sound that will cause discomfort to a listener 50% of the time.

threshold of hearing *RecA&S* Level of sound that will cause hearing in a listener 50% of the time: zero **decibels**, 1000-4000 **hertz**

threshold of pain *RecA&S* Level of sound that causes pain in a listener 50% of the time, 140 **decibels**, between 200 **Hz** and 10 **kHz**.

thrill capacity *Aes&Creat,Crit&Eval* Ability of a performer to suddenly connect with an audience. > "Any artist – you see it very clearly in jazz musicians – comes out there, and what differentiates the great ones from the lesser ones is that they can thrill you with the turn of a phrase, a run, or the bending of a note. This is [also] true of acting."

thriller *Flm&Vid* A suspenseful book, story, play, or movie. *Also see* **nostalgic suspense.**

Throat Cut *ArtPerf* Tea made from the bark of the slippery elm. > "That's what all actors have to take for their voice." — Rosie Perez (1964-; actor)<

throw *VisArts* To form (throw clay) on a potter's wheel: throw a bowl.

throw away line *PerfA&C* Funny line delivered by a comic in an offhand, seemingly careless way.

throw line *BcstJourn* » **writeup**

throws *PA-Variety* Trinkets thrown by **Mardi Gras** float riders to the crowds lining the parade routes. [It is alleged that comely, topless women attract an ungodly number of throws.] *Also see* **krewes.**

thrush *MusArts* Outdated slang for a female pop singer.

thrust stage *PerfA&C* Stage projecting into and surrounded on three sides by the audience. *Also see* **Stages.**

thumbnails *iMedia* Small, quick sketches.

thumb piano *MusInstr* » **mbira**

thumbs-up, thumbs-down *Crit&Eval* Approved, disapproved. *Origin* Final opinion made by a Roman emperor, the severest critic of his day, as to whether a gladiator should live or die in a Coliseum fight-to-the death game. *Also see* **circus.**

ti (tee) *MusArts* Seventh tone in a **diatonic scale.** *Also see* **si.**

TIA *InfoMgt* Thanks In Advance.

ticket agency *Mktg, PerfA&C* Business, independent of an arena or theater that sells tickets at a **markup** to the public. *Also see* **scalper.**

ticket broker *Mgt* » **ticket agency**

ticket hustling *Ethcs&Phil* Illegal speculation in ticket sales. *Also see* **scalper.**

ticket manifest *Mgt* Inventory of tickets for a particular event, broken down by seat location and price.

ticket rack *Mktg ,PerfA&C* Board with slots, in a box office, where tickets are kept until sold.

tickle *MusArts* Sing a **run.**

ticky-tacky *Crit&Eval* Mediocre uniformity of appearance or style: *Also see* **tacky.**

tie *MusArts* Curved line that combines the duration of two notes of the same **pitch.**

tie-clip microphone *RecA&S* Works well for voice recording. *Also see* **Microphones.**

tiers *PerfA&C* One of a series of rows of seats placed one above another. *Also see* **banks of seats.**

TIF files *InfoMgt* **Tagged Image File Format. Bit** mapped graphic images popular among desktop publishers.

TIFF *iMedia, InfoMgt* **Tagged Image File Format.** Process of making copies on a disk of the image on the monitor.

tight *MusArts* Relating to a well-arranged, well-rehearsed, seamless performance; nothing wasted.

tight money *Eco&Fin* Obtainable with difficulty.

tight ship *Crit&Eval, Mgt* Well-managed and efficient business or organization.

tight shot *Flm&Vid* One in which the person or object takes up the entire frame or screen. *Also see* **close-up.**

tilt *Flm&Vid* Pivotal camera movement in a vertical plane.

tim., timp *MusInstr* **timpani** KETTLEDRUMS

timbre *MusArts* Distinctive quality of sound made by a voice or musical instrument.

time *MusArts* Characteristic **beat** of musical rhythm. <**three-quarter time, five-four time**> 2 Rate of speed at which a piece of music is played. <The rhythm **section** must keep good time> *Also see* **tempo.**

time base corrector (TBC) *Flm&Vid* » **TBC**

time buy *Mktg, Rdio/TV* Written intention of an advertiser, or its ad agency, to run a certain number of spots in a particular electronic medium within a specified period of time. *Also see* **insertion order, rate card, SRDS.**

time buyer *Mktg, Rdio/TV* Specialist in choosing the right station and time slot for an advertiser's marketing plan.

time coding *Flm&Vid* **Synchronization** of sound and film **encoded** with matching frame-to-frame numbers, standardized by **SMPTE.**

time frame *Crit&Eval* Period during which something takes place or is projected to occur.

time signature *MusArts* Sign placed on a staff to indicate the meter, commonly a numerical fraction of which the numerator is the number of beats per measure and the denominator represents the kind of note getting one beat. <2/4, 3/4, 4/4, 5/4, etc>

Time Value of Money *EntreP* Claim to one dollar in the present is valued differently to a claim to one dollar in the future because the former can be reinvested at the prevailing interest rate.

time-honored *Crit&Eval* Respected or adhered to because of age or age-old observance.

time-lapse *Flm&Vid* Technique that photographs a naturally slow process, such as plant growth, on movie film at intervals, so that continuous projection of the frames gives an accelerated view of the process.

time-of-day pricing *Eco&Fin, Mktg* <Early Bird reduced prices, **drive time, matinee** admission> *Also see* **Pricing Strategies.**

time-series data *Mktg* » **longitudinal data**

time-sharing system *InfoMgt* Computer system available to many users simultaneously, normally from a remote site.

Time-Warner *Flm&Vid, Journ, LitArts, Rdio/TV, RecA&S* Worldwide **media** conglomerate includes. <**Time-Life** magazines, **Warner Brothers Pictures, Warner-Elektra-Asylum** (WEA) records, **HBO** cable, and more>

timed *Flm&Vid* Evaluation of the proper **film printer**-light setting appropriate to a particular shot.

timeline *iMedia* 1 Development: graphical representation, often frame by frame, of the temporal (and sometimes spatial) amount which elements such as video, audio, graphics, typography, and code occupy. 2 Project Management: visual representation of deadlines and milestones, with accountability and responsibility for deadlines assigned to team members.

times and policy *Flm&Vid, Mktg* Advertised feature in print ads showing times and pricing policy of a theater.

times-interest-earned *E&F-Acc* Ratio of operating income to interest expense; it is a measure of safety of a debt instrument (times-interest-earned = earnings before taxes and interest/annual interest charges)

timpani (tim., timp.) *MusInstr* Set of **kettledrums.** *Also see* **Musical Instrument Families.** KETTLE DRUMMER, TIMPANIST, TIMPANI PLAYER

Tin Pan Alley, tin pan alley *MusArts* 1 Near-fabled district – on and about W. 28th St., NYC – associated with musicians, composers, and publishers of popular music, ca. 1900-50. 2 Publishers and composers of popular music as a group. "It is now less a place than a catchall reference to all popular music, just as 'Broadway' is used to define all theater in New York City." — **David Craig** *Also see* **standards.**

tinseltown *Flm&Vid* » **Hollywood**

tip-in *VA-Prntng* Single card, object, or sheet glued onto the binding of a publication.

tirade *Crit&Eval* Long, angry or violent speech. *Also see* **harangue.** DIATRIBE

tired-businessman *Crit&Eval, PerfA&C* Member of the audience of a musical theatre production not "too deep, too meaningful, and too lacking in good tunes and good-looking girls." — **David Craig**

titillate *Crit&Eval* To excite another, esp. in a superficial, pleasurable manner.

title *BcstJourn* » **CG**

title *Crit&Eval* Identifying name given to a book, play, film, musical composition, or other work.

title *LegAsp* 1 Heading that names a document, statute, or proceeding. 2 Coincidence of all the elements that constitute the fullest legal right to control and dispose of property or a claim. 2 Aggregate evidence that gives rise to a legal right of possession or control. 3 Instrument, such as a deed, that constitutes this evidence.

Title IX *SportsEnt* Amendment to the U.S. Education Act (1972)::

"No person in the United States shall, on the basis of sex, be excluded from participation in, be denied the benefits of, or be subject to discrimination under any education program or activity receiving Federal financial assistance." Title IX was envisioned as a way of persuading young women to participate in programs and aspire to careers similar to those selected by men. Initially very controversial, it has raised women's sports programs (except for football and baseball) to near parity with men's programs.

title safe area *iMedia* Area on a television screen or monitor, measured from the center outwards, that always provides a safe area for text (or titles), no matter how out of alignment a monitor or screen may be.

title, titles *Flm&Vid* **1** Written material to be read by viewers included in a film or TV show, typically presenting credits, narration, or dialogue. **2** Written piece of translated dialogue superimposed at the bottom of the frame during a film; a subtitle.

title-producing company *Flm&Vid* One that creates design and production of **crawl** titles.

tix *PerfA&C* tickets

tkt. *PerfA&C* ticket

to top *TheatArts* To build a **line** higher than the one that preceded it.

Toch, Ernst (1887-1964, Aus.-born comp., music theorist) *ArtPerf, Crit&Eval, MusArts* Noted for his major work: *The Shaping Forces in Music, An Inquiry into the Nature of Harmony, Melody, Counterpoint, and Form* Also see **tension and relaxation, tension and release.**

Tom *Cult&Soc* » **Uncle Tom**

tom-tom, tam-tam *MusInstr* **1** Any of various small-headed drums, usu. long and narrow, that are usu. beaten with the hands. **2** Monotonous rhythmical drumbeat or similar sound. *Also see* **Musical Instrument Families.**

tome *LitArts* **1** One of the books in a work of several volumes. **2** Large or scholarly book.

tonal center *MusArts* **Tonic** pitch around which a composition or scale is centered.

tonality *MusArts* Arrangement of all the **tones** and **chords** of a musical composition in relation to a **tonic,** i.e, the first note of a **diatonic scale.** *Also see* **atonality, keynote.**

tonality *VisArts* Scheme or interrelation of the color **tones** in a painting.

tone *iMedia, LitArts* **1** Manner of expression in speech or writing. **2 Pitch** of a word used to determine its meaning or to distinguish differences in meaning.

tone *MusArts* **1** Characteristic quality or **timbre** of a particular instrument or voice. **2** Sound of distinct **pitch,** quality, and duration; a note. **2** Interval of a major second in the **diatonic scale;** a whole step.

tone *VisArts* **1** General effect in painting of light, color, and shade. **2** Color or shade of color. **3** Quality of color.

tone arm *RecA&S* Arm of a phonograph **turntable** that holds the **cartridge.**

tone cluster *MusArts* Dissonant group of close notes played at the same time.

tone control *Sci&Tech* Circuit or device in an amplifier designed to increase or decrease the **amplification** in a specific **frequency** range without affecting other **frequencies.**

tone poem *MusArts* Piece of music, most popular in the late 19th century by composers such as Richard Strauss (1864-1949, Ger. comp.) based on an extramusical theme, such as a story or nationalistic ideal, and consists of a single extended movement for a symphony orchestra. <*Sprach Zoroastrian* (1896), *Till Eulenspiegel* (1895), *Don Quixote*> SYMPHONIC POEM

tone row *MusArts* Unique, arbitrary series of notes used in the **12-tone** system of composition.

tone-deaf *MusArts* Unable to distinguish differences in musical **pitch.**

toner *Sci&Tech* Powdery ink used dry or suspended in a liquid to produce a photocopy.

tongue *MusArts* To **articulate** notes played on a brass or wind instrument by shutting off the stream of air with the tongue.

tongues *MusArts* Speech or vocal sounds produced in a state of religious ecstasy. **SINGING IN TONGUES, SPEAKING IN TONGUES**

tonic *MusArts* first note of a **diatonic scale.** *Also see* **keynote.**

tony *Crit&Eval* Luxurious or exclusive manner or quality. *Origin* From "tone."

Tony Awards *ArtPerf, Fashn, LitArts, MusArts, TheatArts, VisArts* Annual drama awards made by the **New York Drama Critics Circle** in the name of **Antoinette Perry.** *Also see* **Awards & Prizes.**

Top 40 *MusArts, Rdio/TV, RecA&S* Radio station **programming** characterized by a high rotation of the current pop hit singles, light rotation of up-and-coming hits and **recurrents,** and an occasional oldie.

top banana *Mgt* Head person of a group, company, or project.

top banana *PA-Variety* Top burlesque **comedian.** *Origin* From the presentation of a banana to the comedian who had the **punch line** in a three-man burlesque routine.

top billing *ArtPerf, Mgt* The most prestigious, ego-salving **billing.**

top down planning *Mgt* Programs implemented by top-level management; participation filters down to the lower levels.

top gun *Crit&Eval* **1** One who performs at the pinnacle of professional ability. **2** One who is the best at what one does.

top hat *Fashn* Man's hat having a narrow brim and a tall cylindrical crown, usu. made of silk. **HIGH HAT**

top managers *Mgt* » **upper managers**

top of the mountain *Crit&Eval* Peak of artistic or emotional pleasure.

top of the show *Rdio/TV* Program segment shown at the beginning or near the beginning of the program. <The **feed** from Russia was scheduled at the top of the show,>

top-heavy *Eco&Fin* overcapitalized.

top-heavy *Mgt* Having a disproportionately large number of administrators.

top-hole (Brit.) *Crit&Eval* first-rate, excellent.

topflight *Crit&Eval* first-rate, excellent.

topic box or **box** *BcstJourn* Generic identifiers usu. placed in a box format to the newscaster's left or right. These usu. remain in view throughout the story. *Also:* "squeezes" or "frames."

topical song *MusArts* Song relating to a current event.

topless *PA-Variety* Relating to a person without a garment above the waist. <topless bar, topless dancer> *Also see* **bottomless.**

topnotch *Crit&Eval* First-rate, excellent.

topper *Crit&Eval* Witticism, joke, or prank that surpasses all that have gone before.

topper *Fashn* Woman's short, lightweight coat. *Also see* **top heat.**

topstitching *Fashn* Row of stitching close to the seam or edge of a garment on the outer side of the fabric.

torch song *MusArts* Sentimental pop love song in which the singer laments a lost or abusive love while leaning against a lamp post in the mist. *Also see* ***Melancholy Baby.***

torchon lace (tore-shon, Fr.) *Fashn* Lace made of coarse linen or cotton thread twisted in simple geometric patterns.

torm *PerfA&C* » **tormentor**

tormentor *Flm&Vid* Sound-absorbent screen used on a film set to prevent echo.

tormentor *PerfA&C* Sets of curtains used at each side of a stage directly behind the **proscenium** to **mask wings** and **sidelights** from the audience. *Also see* **Stage Curtains.**

tort *LegAsp* Damage, injury, or a wrongful act done willfully, negligently, or in circumstances involving strict liability, but not involving **breach** of contract, for which a civil suit can be brought.

tortious *LegAsp* Relating to a **tort,** i.e., damage, injury, or a wrongful act done willfully, negligently, or in circumstances involving strict liability.

toss *BcstJourn* Short item designed to make the transition to another newscaster.

total asset turnover *E&F-Acc* Measure of assets required to generate sales. It is defined as sales divided by total assets (total asset turnover - sales/total assets) *Also see* **activity ratios.**

total support and revenue *Eco&Fin* Includes all operating support and revenue that represent the major sources and uses of funds.

totalitarian *Law&Pol* Form of government in which the political authority exercises absolute and centralized control over all aspects of life, the individual is subordinated to the state, and opposing political and cultural expression is suppressed.

totem *Cult&Soc* Venerated emblem or symbol.

totemism *Cult&Soc* Social system based on affiliations to totems.

touché (too-shay) *Crit&Eval* To acknowledge a successful criticism or an effective point in argument. *Origin* From the French "toucher," to hit or wound in fencing.

touched *Crit&Eval* Emotionally affected, moved. *Also see* **lump in (one's) throat.**

tough *Crit&Eval* **1** Unfortunate, too bad. <a tough break> **2** Fine, great.

tough audience *Crit&Eval* One difficult to please. *Also see* **sit on (one's) hands.**

tough it out *Ethcs&Phil* To get through despite hardship. ENDURE.

tough love *Crit&Eval* To love someone so much that you will not support her or his addiction. Ban the loved one from the house; cut off support until he or she is willing to accept treatment.

tour *Mgt, PerfA&C, SportsEnt* **1** Series of engagements in several places. *Ex.* Book tour, concert tour, golf tour, **touring company** of *Cats* **2** In a team sport context, a specific complication arises: the visiting team plays in front of the host team's natural audience whose partisanship can result in aggression behavior against the visiting athletes. Special security measures might be needed. *Also see* **junket, on the road.**

tour de force (tour duh force, Fr. for "feat of strength") *Crit&Eval* Feat requiring great **virtuosity** or strength, often deliberately undertaken for its difficulty.

tour en l'air (tour on lair, FR.) *Dnce* Complete turn of the body while jumping vertically in the air. Male dancers are expected to perform double turns, some can do triples. Rarely performed by women.

tour manager *Mgt, PerfA&C* Person, with assistants, responsible for all aspects of a traveling musical ensemble, e.g., contract fulfillment, local **public relations**, lodging, payroll, security, and transportation. ROAD MANAGER *Also see* **Managers.**

tour support *Mktg, RecA&S* Financial assistance paid by a record company to assist a group with the expense of a road tour. This practice was eliminated by most record companies in the late 1980s. *Also see* **underwrite.**

touring company *PerfA&C* » **national company, road company.**

Tourism and Vacation Destinations *Eco&Fin* When tourism drops it is an **economic indicator** of a falling economy. Similarly, when vacation travel destinations tend to become "close to home" it is a clue that consumers are tightening the purse strings.

tournant (Fr. for "turning") *Dnce* (Ballet) While executing steps, the dancer makes a revolution of the body or describes a circle on the floor.

tp *MusInstr* trumpet.

TPP *InfoMgt* **Transfer Protocol Program**, a communications format for connecting to the **Internet.** *Also see* **Protocols.**

tr. *LegAsp* **trust.**

Tr., tr. *InfoMgt, LitArts* translator.

track *InfoMgt* Method of storing data either in horizontal rows on a magnetic tape or in concentric rings on a magnetic disk.

trackball *InfoMgt* Input device used as an alternative to the mouse. When the ball is rolled, the pointer moves on the screen.

tracker *Mktg, RecA&S* Marketing analyst who tracks (follows) the progress of a record release via airplay, chart action, sales, and returns.

tracking session *RecA&S* Recording session after the basic tracks are laid down. *Also see* **overdub.**

tract *LitArts* Paper or pamphlet containing a declaration or appeal, usu. by a special interest group.

tractor feed *InfoMgt* Mechanism for automatically advancing continuous-form paper through a printer by means of two or more toothed tractors that catch the perforations along the edges of the paper. *Also see* **sheet feed.**

trad (Brit.) *MusArts* » **traditional jazz,** i.e., **New Orleans** or **Dixieland** jazz.

trade *Mktg* **1** Act or an instance of buying or selling. TRANSACTION. **2** People working in or associated with a business or an industry. *<Variety* is a publication for the entertainment trade> **3** Customers of a specified business or industry; **clientele. 4** Exchange of one thing for another. *Also see* **barter. 5** Occupation, esp. one requiring skilled labor; craft. <the scenic trades>

trade acceptance *Eco&Fin* **Bill of exchange** for the amount of a purchase drawn by the seller on the purchaser, bearing the purchaser's signature and specifying time and place of payment.

trade book *LitArts, VA-Prntng* Book published for distribution to the general public through booksellers.

trade discount *Mktg* Discount on the **list price** granted by a manufacturer or wholesaler to buyers in the same trade. Not to be confused with **sales discount.**

trade down *Mktg* To trade something for something else of lower value or price. *Also see* **trade up.**

trade edition *LitArts, Mktg* Trade version of a book. <a trade edition of a history textbook>

trade in *Mktg* To surrender or sell an old or used item, using the proceeds as partial payment on a new purchase.

trade journal *Journ* » **trade magazine**

trade magazine *VA-Prntng* Magazine devoted to news and developments pertaining to a particular trade or industry. *<Variety* is the showbiz bible> TRADE JOURNAL

trade name *LegAsp* Name used to identify a commercial product or service, which may or may not be registered as a **trademark.**

trade name *Mgt, Mktg* **1** Name by which a commodity, service, or process is known to the trade. **2** Name under which a business firm operates. BRAND NAME

trade paperback *LitArts, VA-Prntng* Paperback book that is typically of better production quality, larger size, and higher price than a **mass market** edition, intended for sale in bookstores rather than newsstands.

trade secret *InfoMgt, LegAsp* Product, formula, design, compilation of data, customer list or other business secrets. Business must properly secure such information to prevent unwanted discovery.

trade secret *IntelProp* Secret formula, method, or device that gives one an advantage over competitors.

trade show *Mktg* Convention of suppliers and distributors in a particular trade or industry where product lines are exhibited, bought and sold, and matters of mutual concern are discussed.

trade union *HR&LR* Labor union whose membership is limited to people in the same trade. <**American Federation of Musicians (AFM)**>

trade up *Mktg* To trade something in for something else of greater value or price. *Also see* **trade down.**

trade-out *Mktg* Bartering event tickets and/or visibility for services. <Sponsorship mention on print marketing materials traded for free air time for radio spots>

trademark™ *Eco&Fin, IntelProp* (™ trademark applied for; ® Registered trademark) **1** Distinctive identification of a product or service. **2** Name, symbol, or other device, identifying a product, officially registered and legally restricted to the use of the owner. TRADE NAME *Also see* **copyright, Intangible Assets, logo, Symbols.**

tradeoff, trade-off *Crit&Eval* Exchange of one thing in return for another, esp. relinquishment of one benefit or advantage for another regarded as more desirable.

trading fours *MusArts* Exchange of four-bar solos by two or more jazz instrumentalists or singers. Other trades include are two- or eight bar phrases. *Also see* **cutting contest.**

trading on the equity *E&F-Acc* » **financial leverage**

tradition *Cult&Soc* **1** Passing down of elements of a culture from generation to generation, esp. by oral communication. **2** Mode of thought or behavior followed by a people continuously from generation to generation, a custom or usage.

traditional jazz *MusArts* » **trad**

traffic department *Rdio/TV* Has the responsibility of scheduling commercials in accordance with advertising contracts.

trafficking *Flm&Vid, Mktg, Rdio/TV* Movement of commercials and other broadcast materials from point of origin or warehouse to appropriate stations, agencies, theaters, etc. <spots, one sheets, teaser trailers, prints, slicks, etc>

tragedian *ArtPerf, LitArts, TheatArts* **1** Writer of tragedies. **2** One who performs tragic roles in the theater. *Also see* **tragedienne.**

tragedienne (Fr.) *ArtPerf, TheatArts* Woman who performs tragic roles in the theater. *Also see* **tragedian.**

tragedy *Flm&Vid, LitArts, TheatArts* **1** Dramatic or literary portrayal of the noble, usu. presenting the terrifying and piteous consequences of an error of judgment, a flaw in character, or an inability to cope with unfavorable circumstances. **2** Play, film, television program, or other narrative work that portrays or depicts calamitous events and has an unhappy but meaningful ending. **3** Branch of drama comprising such works. *Also see* **analysis of tragedy, comedy, drama.**

tragic *Crit&Eval* Having the elements of tragedy, involving death, grief, or destruction.

tragic *TheatArts* **1** Relating to dramatic tragedy: tragic plays. <the tragic hero> **2** Writing or performing in tragedy.

tragic flaw *TheatArts* Frailty or error of a tragic hero that results in his downfall. In Greek, *hamartla.*

tragic irony *Crit&Eval* **Dramatic irony** in a **tragedy**.

tragicomedy *Genl, TheatArts* Drama which combines the effects of tragedy and comedy.

trailer *Flm&Vid* **1** Short filmed ad for a movie. **2** Short, blank strip of film at the end of a reel. *Also see* **featurette.**

train wreck *MusArts* Occurs when two tempos clash and create a painful **cacophony**... *Also see* **beat mash, rave, techno music.**

tramp art *VisArts* Folk art characterized by the use of ordinary household items **worked** by anonymous vagrants.

trance dancing *Dnce* West Coast people whirling on their own to **minimalist** music for six to eight hours nonstop.

trance music *MusArts* **New Age** music by electronic instruments with traditional acoustic sounds and a strong beat, creating an aid to meditation." *Origin* Shamanist tribal music played in Ethiopia.

Trane *ArtPerf, MusArts* » **John Coltrane.**

tranquil *Crit&Eval* **1** Free from commotion or disturbance. **2** Free from anxiety, tension, or restlessness. COMPOSED

transact *Mgt* Conduct business

transactions (trans.) *Mgt* Record of business conducted at a meeting. PROCEEDINGS.

transcendence *Crit&Eval* That which goes beyond ordinary things, often reaching regions of the mind or spirit held to be esp. profound, worthwhile, or enlightening.

transcendental *Crit&Eval* **1** Concerned with the **a priori** or intuitive basis of knowledge as independent of experience. **2** Asserting a fundamental irrationality or **supernatural** element in experience. **3** Surpassing all others. SUPERIOR

transducer *RecA&S* Device that converts one form of energy to another. <Microphone converts acoustic energy to electrical energy; speaker converts electrical energy to acoustic energy> *Also see* **converter, Microphones, modem.**

Transfer Protocol Program (TPP) *InfoMgt*» **TPP**

transgress *Crit&Eval* To go beyond or over a limit or boundary, exceed or overstep. "This desire to see artists as 'transgressive' figures, unfaily condemned by a **smug, bourgeois** society, naturally encourages supporters to absolve them of personal responsibility." — Michiko Kakutani (lit. critic *NY Times*)

transistor *InfoMgt* Electrical component common to **second generation** computers and used for switching signals.

transition *Crit&Eval* **Passage** from one form, state, style, or place to another.

transition *Flm&Vid* Something that joins two scenes together, taking the viewer from one to the other. <dissolve, a musical theme, a sound effect, a **segue.**

transition *MusArts* Brief **modulation**, a **passage** connecting two themes. *Also see* **segue.**

transition *TheatArts* In the structure of a scene or play, the actor must pass from one inevitable, logical beat to the next. This passing is the transition.

translucent *Crit&Eval* clear, **lucid.**

translucent *Sci&Tech* Transmitting light but causing sufficient diffusion to prevent perception of distinct images.

transmission *InfoMgt* Sending of a signal, picture, or other information.

transmission facility *InfoMgt* Communications link between remote terminals and computers. <communication lines, **microwave** transmission lines, communications satellites, lasers, telephone lines, **fiber optics**, and **waveguides**>

transparency *VisArts* Photographic slide viewed by light shining through it from behind or by projection.

transponder *InfoMgt, Sci&Tech* Receiving and retransmitting mechanism on a communications satellite. Transponders receive the signal, **refresh** it, and retransmit it to a **downlink** at a slightly higher **frequency** than the receiving **frequency** in order to prevent the incoming signal from being overwhelmed.

transpose *MusArts* To write or perform music in a different key.

transposition *MusArts* Rewriting or playing of a composition in a key other than the original one.

trap drummer *MusArts* » **traps**

trap, trap door *PerfA&C* Sliding or hinged opening in the stage floor for the passage of actors or objects.

traps *MusArts* Certain percussion instruments and accessories used in other than classical music ensembles. <bass drum and pedal, snare drum, hi-hat cymbals, tom-toms> TRAP DRUMMER. *Also see* **drum set.**

trash *Crit&Eval* **1** Worthless or offensive literary or artistic material. **2** Empty words or ideas. **3** Person or group of people regarded as worthless or contemptible. <white trash>

Trash *InfoMgt* Desktop icon for discarding files and folders.

trashy *Crit&Eval* In very poor taste, of very poor quality.

trav. *PerfA&C* traveler.

traveler *PerfA&C* Stage curtain that moves or opens horizontally. Travelers are usu. composed of two sections of stage drapes covering the full width of the **proscenium**: the sections split in the middle, and each section retracts in an off stage direction.

traveler curtain *PerfA&C* » **draw curtain** *Also see* **Stage Curtains.**

traverse rod *PerfA&C* Horizontal rod having a mechanism by which attached curtains or draperies can be drawn with a pull rope or cord. *Also see* **Stage Curtains.**

treasury stock *Eco&Fin* Difference between **authorized stock** and **outstanding stock**. It is company stock owned by the company, that cannot be voted and it cannot receive dividends.

treatment *Flm&Vid* Narrative, in the present tense, of a film or TV story.

treble clef *MusArts* Symbol indicating that the second line from the bottom of a **staff** represents the **pitch** of G above **middle C.** G CLEF

tree *iMedia* Visual structure that represents a hierarchical set of data.

tremolo *MusArts* **1 Tremulous** (quivering) effect produced by rapid repetition of a single tone. **2** Similar effect produced by rapid alternation of two tones. **3** Excessive or poorly controlled **vibrato.**

tremolo *MusInstr* Device on an organ or **vibraphone** for producing a tremulous effect.

tremulous sound *MusArts, RecA&S* Marked by trembling, quivering, or shaking. *Also see* **trill, vibrato, warble.**

trend *Crit&Eval* General direction in which something tends to move.

trendy *Crit&Eval* Of or in accord with the latest fad or fashion.

trespass *Crit&Eval* Transgression of a moral or social law, code, or duty.

trespass *LegAsp* To commit an unlawful injury to the person, property, or rights of another, with actual or implied force or violence, esp. to enter onto another's land wrongfully.

triad *MusArts* Chord composed of a fundamental tone and the third and fifth above it.

trial balance *E&F-Acc* List of all the **ledger** accounts with their balances.

trial balloon *Mktg* Idea, campaign, or plan advanced tentatively to test buyer's reaction.

tribalism *Cult&Soc* Strong feeling of identity with one's group.

trickle-down theory *Eco&Fin, Law&Pol* Theory in economics that financial benefits accorded to big business enterprises will in turn pass down to smaller businesses and consumers. [Fiscal ultraconservatives drag this one out when tax breaks for big business and the very wealthy are being discussed. "Let them eat the cake crumbs that fall to the floor."] *Also see* **supply-side, voodoo economics.**

tricot (tree-ko, Fr. from "tricoter," to knit) *Fashn* Soft, ribbed cloth of wool or a wool blend, usu. used for dresses.

trill *MusArts* **1** Rapid alternation of two **tones** either a whole or a **half tone** apart. **2 Fluttering** or **tremulous** sound, as that made by certain birds. *Also see* **vibrato, warble.**

trims *Flm&Vid* Unused pieces of film that are filed in the event that the editor decides to recut.

---

trio *MusArts* **1** Composition for three parts or voices, the second part of a minuet or march. **2** Three singers or three instrumentalists.

triode electron tube *Rdio/TV* » **Lee De Forest**

trip-hop *MusArts, RecA&S* Offshoot of **techno** club music. "A spacey, down-tempo mutant of **hip-hop** often instrumental or song-oriented rather than based on rapping. It is a music intended for headphone-listening, not parties; for reverie, not revelry." — Simon Reynolds (mus. critic)

triple time *MusArts* Three beats to a measure.

triplet *MusArts* Three notes played in the time value of two.

tripod *iMedia* Three-legged supporting stand used to hold the camera steady.

trite *Crit&Eval* Uninteresting because of overuse or repetition; **hackneyed**. *Also see* **banal**, **platitude**.

Trojan horse *InfoMgt* File containing a hidden program that can harm one's files or hard drive.

trombone (tb) *MusInstr* **1** Brass instrument consisting of a long cylindrical tube bent upon itself twice, ending in a bell-shaped mouth, and having a movable U-shaped slide for producing different **pitches**. <tenor trombone, bass trombone> **2 valve trombone** Similar to a trombone except that three valves replace the movable slide. TROMBONIST, TROMBONE PLAYER *Also see* **Musical Instrument Families**.

trompe l'oeil (tromp loy, Fr.) *VisArts* Style of painting that gives an illusion of photographic reality.

trope *TheatArts* Enlargement on Catholic liturgy, through song or dramatic performance. *Origin* Medieval liturgical drama is thought to have begun with an acting out of the *Quern quaentls* trope ("Who do you seek?") in the Easter Sunday liturgy sometime in the 10th century.

troubadour (troo-ba-dur, Fr.) *Cult&Soc, MusArts* Travelling entertainer who sings and recited poetry. *Also see* **minstrel**, **rap**.

troupe *TheatArts* **Company** or group of touring actors, singers, or dancers.

trouper *Genl* Reliable, uncomplaining, often hard-working person.

trouper *PerfA&C* **1** Member of a theatrical company. **2** Veteran actor or performer.

TRT *BcstJourn* Stands for total tape running time. This refers to a tape's time from the beginning of the tape until the end. It is used for the tape only, not for writing copy.

TrueType *InfoMgt* Font that can be displayed or printed in any size. *Also see* **scalable outline font**.

Truffaut, François (1932-84, Fr. flmkr.) *ArtPerf, Flm&Vid* **New Wave** filmmaker. <*The 400 Blows* (1959), *Jules and Jim* (1961)>

trumpet (tp) *MusInstr* **1** Soprano brass wind instrument consisting of a long metal tube looped once, equipped with three valves for producing variations in **pitch**, and ending in a flared bell. **2** Organ stop that produces a tone like that of the brass wind instrument. TRUMPET PLAYER, TRUMPETER (RARE), POCKET OR PICCOLO TRUMPET, BASS TRUMPET *Also see* **Musical Instrument Families**.

truncate *Genl* Shorten by or cut off.

trust *Eco&Fin, Law&Pol* Combination of companies in an attempt to reduce competition and control prices throughout a business or an industry. *Also see* **Federal Agencies and Statutes**.

trust *EntreP* Arrangement under which the owners of several companies transfer their decision-making powers to a small group of trustees, who then make decisions for all the companies in the trust.

trust (tr.) *LegAsp* **1** Legal title to property held by one party for the benefit of another. **2** Confidence reposed in a trustee when giving the trustee legal title to property to administer for another, together with the trustee's obligation regarding that property and the beneficiary. **3** Property so held.

trust *Mktg* Heart of the buying decision.

trustee *Fnding* Member of a governing board. Foundation's board of trustees meets to review grant proposals and make decisions. Often also referred to as a "director" or "board member."

trustee *Mgt* Member of a board elected or appointed to direct the funds and policy of an institution.

tryout *TheatArts* **1** Test to ascertain the suitability of applicants for a theatrical role. **2 Experimental** performance of a play before its official opening.

tsatske (tsats-ka, Yinglish) *Crit&Eval* » **chachka**

TST *BcstJourn* total story time. Refers to a story's running time from beginning to end, usu. including the **TRT** of the tape within the story. Not used as commonly as TRT.

tsuris, tsouris (tsur'-is, Yinglish) *Crit&Eval* Troubles, worries, problems, afflictions.

TTFN *InfoMgt* Ta-Ta For Now

TTYL non-fiction *InfoMgt* Talk To You Later

tuba *MusInstr* **1** Large, valved, brass wind instrument with a bass **pitch**. **2** Reed stop in an organ, having an eight-foot **pitch**. TUBA PLAYER, TUBIST.

Tuchman, Barbara W. (1912-89, hist.) *ArtPerf, Crit&Eval* <*The Guns of August* (**Pulitzer**, 1962), *The Proud Tower* (1966)> *Also see* **creative process**.

tumler (tum'-lerr, Yinglish) *PA-Variety* Noisy, lively creator of commotions, "the life of the party," **social director**, or **emcee** of a resort in the **Catskills**. *Also see* **Borsht Belt**.

tumult *Crit&Eval* Agitation of the mind or emotions.

tune *Crit&Eval* Agreement, harmony. <in tune with the times>

tune *MusArts* **1** Simple and easily remembered **melody**, a song. **2** Correct **pitch**. **3** Properly adjusted for **pitch**. <a tuned piano> **4** Agreement in **pitch**. <play in tune with the piano>

tune *Sci&Tech* Adjustment of a receiver or circuit for maximum response to a given signal or **frequency**.

tuneful *MusArts* » **Melodious**

tuneless *MusArts* **1** Lack **melody**, not tuneful. **2** Producing no music, silent.

tuner *MusArts* One that tunes. <a piano tuner>

tuner *Rdio/TV* Device for tuning, used to select signals at a specific radio **frequency** for **amplification** and conversion to sound. <an AM/FM tuner>

tunesmith *ArtPerf, MusArts* Composer of popular songs, **songwriter**.

tunic *Fashn* **1** Short pleated and belted dress. **2** Long, plain, sleeved or sleeveless blouse. **3** Long, plain, close-fitting military jacket, usu. with a stiff high collar. **4** Loose-fitting garment, sleeved or sleeveless, extending to the knees a — worn by men and women in ancient Greece and Rome.

tuning fork *MusInstr* Small two-pronged metal device that when struck produces a sound of fixed **pitch** used as a reference for tuning musical instruments.

turgid *Crit&Eval* **1** Excessively ornate or complex in style or language. GRANDILOQUENT. **2** clumsy, stiff.

Turing machine *iMedia* Hypothetical machine for computability theory proofs that would allow the writing to, and reading of, data from a tape (**Alan Turing**, 1935)

Turing test *iMedia* Criterion proposed by **Alan Turing** in 1950 for deciding whether a computer is intelligent.

Turing, Alan *iMedia* 1912-1954. English mathematician whose works explored the possibility of computers and raised fundamental questions about artificial intelligence.

turkey *Flm&Vid, TheatArts* Failure, esp. a failed theatrical production or movie.

turkey trot *Dnce* **Ragtime** dance characterized by a springy walk with feet well apart and a swinging up-and-down movement of the shoulders. *Also see* **Dances**.

turn *MusArts* Figure of four or more notes in rapid succession plus the note above and below the principal note.

turn *TheatArts* **1** Brief theatrical act. **2** Performer in such an act. **3** Histrionic performance.

turn of phrase *LitArts* Distinctive, graceful, or artistic arrangement of words.

turn-on *Crit&Eval* Something that causes pleasure or excitement.

turnaround *Mgt, Mktg* **1** Number of times an inventory of a product or a company is replaced in a year. <If a company has an average inventory of 200 units of a product, and sell 1000 units in a year, the the company has a turnaround of 5> **2** Term can also apply to cash by dividing the average cost for a given peiod into the sales for the year. *Also see* **turnover**.

turnaround *MusArts* Changing of the chord structure at the end of a theme so that it leads back to a repeat, similar to a first ending.

Turner Broadcasting System *SportsEnt* Part of the **AOL Time**

U

Warner media conglomerate.

Turner, Ted (1938- *Flm&Vid, Mgt, Rdio/TV*) Founder (1938), **Cable News Network** (CNN) *Also see* **colorization of movies**.

turnout *Crit&Eval* Number of people gathered for a particular event or purpose. <Her fans turned out in record numbers> ATTENDANCE

turnout *Dnce* Rotation of a dancer's legs from the hip sockets in classical ballet.

turnover *Eco&Fin* **1** AMount of business transacted during a given period of time. **2** Number of shares of stock sold on the market during a given period of time. *Also see* **turnaround**.

turnover *HR&LR* Number of workers hired to replace those who have left in a given period of time.

turnover *Mktg* Number of times a particular **stock** of goods is sold and restocked during a given period of time. *Also see* **turnaround**.

turntable *RecA&S* **1** Circular horizontal rotating platform of a phonograph on which the record disk is placed. **2** Phonograph exclusive of amplifying circuitry and speakers, used by radio stations and disco deejays. *Also see* **Music Playback Devices**.

turntable *PerfA&C* rotating platform. *Also see* **revolve**.

turntable hit *RecA&S* Single recording that gets heavy air play but whose sale is relatively poor.

turret *Flm&Vid* Revolving lens mount for two to four lenses that enables the cameraman to quickly change over from one lens to another.

tutti *MusArts* All performers are to take part. *Also see* **Music Directions.**

tutu *Dnce, Fashn* Ballet skirt, either calf length or projecting straightout at hip level, with many layers of **ruffles** underneath.

tux *Fashn* » **tuxedo**

tuxedo (tux) *Fashn* **1** Man's dress jacket, usu. black with satin or grosgrain lapels, worn for formal or semiformal occasions. DINNER JACKET **2** Complete outfit inc. jacket, trousers usu. with a silken stripe down the side, a bow tie, and often a **cummerbund**. *Origin* After a fashionable country club at Tuxedo Park, N.Y.

TV *Rdio/TV* television.

TWAU *HR&LR, PerfA&C* **Theatrical Wardrobe Attendants Union** (TWAU) Ω

tweak *iMedia, InfoMgt, Genl* adjust, fine-tune.

tween *iMedia* Series of frames that complete the transition from one keyframe to another. > **tweening**

tweening *iMedia* Filling in the space between keyframes so that the transition from one to another is complete.

tweeter *RecA&S* Loudspeaker that reproduces high frequencies. *Also see* **woofer**.

twist *Dnce* 1950s dance characterized by vigorous gyrations of the hips and arms. *Also see* **Dances**.

two percent, net 30, 2/10, n/30 *Eco&Fin, Mktg* **Sales discount**: **1** If an invoice is paid within 10 days of the invoice date, the buyer may deduct 2% from the invoiced amount; otherwise the full amount is due within 30 days of the invoice date. **2** Common incentive to get buyers to pay their credit balances sooner. [Advertising agencies with good cash flow welcome this discount offered by some print and **broadcast media**. It adds up to 36% a year.].

two sets of books *E&F-Acc, Ethcs&Phil* Two sets of financial records designed to deceive one's actual worth.

two-a-day *PA-Variety* Big time vaudeville circuits on which performers only performed **matinee** and evening shows. *Also see* **small time**.

two-and-four *MusArts* Indicates that the rhythmic accent in a four-beat measure is on the second and fourth beat. <jazz and rock> *Also see* **backbeat, one-and-three**.

two-color printing *VA-Prntng* Printing black and one other color. *Also see* **four-color printing**.

two-dimensional *Genl, iMedia,* **1** Lacking the requisite or expected range or depth. **2** Having only two dimensions, esp. length and width. *Also see* **one- dimensional, three-dimensional**.

two-fers *Mktg* Ticket sales promotion offering two tickets for the price of one.

two-hander *TheatArts* two-character play.

two-lid piano or **2-lid piano** *MusInstr* A lid (made of **carbon graphite**) similar to an acoustic piano's top lid is attached to the rear underside of the piano and rests on the floor, and serves the same purpose: to capture and project sound outward. Invented.

two-piece *Fashn* Garment consisting of two parts. <a swimsuit>

two-sided records *RecA&S* Audio recorded on both sides of a disk.

two-step *Dnce* Ballroom dance in 2/4 time, characterized by long, sliding steps. *Also see* **Dances**.

two-step distribution *Mktg* System whereby a product or service is first distributed from manufacturers or originators to wholesalers who then distribute to retailers. *Also see* **Distribution Methods.**

twofer *HR&LR* One who belongs to two minority groups and can be counted by an employer, as part of two quotas. <a black woman>

twofer *Mktg* Offering of two tickets for a play for the price of one.

TXT files *iMedia, InfoMgt* Text files; just **plain text** that can be read by most programs.

tycoon *Mgt* Wealthy, powerful businessman.

typ., typo., typog. *VA-Prntng* **typographer, typography**.

type A ideas *EntreP* Startup ideas centered around providing customers with an existing product not available in their market.

type B ideas *EntreP* Startup ideas, involving new technology, centered around providing customers with a new product.

type C ideas *EntreP* Startup ideas centered around providing customers with an improved product.

type *iMedia, InfoMgt* Printed or typewritten characters.

type font *InfoMgt, VA-Prntng* Complete set of characters in a consistent and unique typeface.

type page *Journ, VA-Prntng* Page of type without margins.

typecast *Crit&Eval, TheatArts* **1** To cast an actor in an acting role similar the actor's own personality or physical appearance. **2** To assign performer repeatedly to the same kind of acting role. SLOTTED

typeface *iMedia, VA-Prntng* **1** Size or style of a letter or character. **2** Full range of type of the same design. *Also see* **serif, sans serif**

typeset *VA-Prntng* To set written material into type. COMPOSE.

typesize *iMedia, InfoMgt, VA-Prntng* Size of type, and type fonts, which are given and measured in points that give an approximate measure of the vertical size of type. A point is about 172 of an inch. <This sentence is set in 9 point type in a New Century Schoolbook font, expressed as "9 Cent."*Also see* **font, leading**.

typestyle *iMedia, InfoMgt, VA-Prntng* <plain, **bold**, *italic* or *oblique*, underscore>

typo *VA-Prntng* » **typographical error**

typographical error (typo) *iMedia, VA-Prntng* Caused by striking an incorrect key on a keyboard.

typography (typ., typo., typog.) *iMedia, VA-Prntng* Arrangement and appearance of printed matter.

tyro *Crit&Eval* A beginner in learning something. *Also see* **amateur**.

- U -

U.K., UK *Genl* **United Kingdom**. Commonly called Great Britain or Britain, comprising England, Scotland, Wales, and Northern Ireland.

U.S., USA, U.S.A. *Genl* United States of America.

U.S. Bureau of Labor Statistics *Law&Pol* » **CPI**

U.S. Copyright Office (USCO) *Law&Pol, IntelProp* **1** Provides expert assistance to Congress on **intellectual property** matters. **2** Assists in the drafting of copyright legislation. **3** Offers advice re multilateral agreements such as the **Berne Convention**. **4** A place where claims to copyright are registered and where documents relating to copyright may be recorded when the requirements of the copyright law are met. **5** Administers various compulsory licensing provisions of the law, which include collecting royalties **6** With the **Library of Congress** administer the **Copyright Arbitration Royalty Panels**, which meet for limited times for the purpose of adjusting rates and distributing royalties/

U/L *InfoMgt* » **upload**

ubiquitous *Crit&Eval* Being or seeming to be everywhere at the same time. OMNIPRESENT.

UBIT *Eco&Fin* **Unrelated Business Income Tax**, applicable to **nonprofits.**

UC *VA-Prntng* **uppercase**

U

UCC *IntelProp* » **Universal Copyright Convention**

UCC *LegAsp* **Uniform Commercial Code**, a codification of commercial law which controls most business transactions in the U.S., except Louisiana. UCC governs "sales of goods, commercial paper, bank deposits and collections, letters of credit, bulk transfers, warehouse receipts, bills of lading, investment securities, and secured transactions." — *Black's Law Dictionary*

UFOV *iMedia* » **Useful Field of View**

UHF *Rdio/TV* Band of radio and TV **frequencies** from 300-3,000 **megacycles (hertz)** per second.

UK *Genl* United Kingdom, i.e., England.

ultra high frequency (UHF) *Rdio/TV* » **UHF**

ultra-leftist *Crit&Eval, Law&Pol* **1** One who subscribes to a communist view. **2** One who believes that liberal change cannot come within the present form of government.

ultraconservative *Law&Pol* **Conservative** to an extreme, esp. in political beliefs. *Also see* **reactionary**.

umbrella *Genl* Something that encompasses or covers many different elements or groups.

UML *iMedia* » **unified modeling language**

UN *Law&Pol* United Nations.

un-American *Ethcs&Phil, Law&Pol* Considered contrary to the institutions or principles of the U.S. Accusation made mostly by demagogues and zealots against anyone not conforming to their vision of patriotism.

un-pub. *IntelProp, LitArts* **unpublished work**.

Uncle Tom *Crit&Eval, Cult&Soc* Black person regarded as being humiliatingly subservient or deferential to white people. *Origin* After Uncle Tom, a character in *Uncle Tom's Cabin*, a novel by Harriet Beecher Stowe (1811-96, fictwri.)

uncollectible accounts *E&F-Acc* » **allowance for doubtful accounts**

under five player *ArtPerf, Rdio/TV* Television performer (usu. in **soaps**) with less than five lines. One level below a **day player**. *Also see* **contract player**.

under the table, under-the-table *Crit&Eval* Not straightforward, secret or underhand.

underemployed *EntreP* Workers who hold a part-time job but prefer to work full time or hold jobs that are far below their capabilities.

underexposure *iMedia* Condition in which too little light reaches the film, producing a thin negative, a dark slide, or a muddy-looking print.

underground *Crit&Eval, Genl* Relating to an avant-garde movement or its films, publications, and art, usu. privately produced and of special appeal and often concerned with social or artistic experiment or protest.

underground economy *Eco&Fin* One that operates out of sight of government regulators and tax collectors.

underlying work *IntelProp, RecA&S* Term related to U.S. copyright law. Individual song that is recorded is the underlying work of the overall recording. *Also see* **mechanical royalty**.

underplay *Crit&Eval* To act subtly, with restraint. *Also see* **broad**.

undersampling *iMedia* When a wave is not sampled enough in accordance to the Nyquist theorem (aliasing may occur)

underscore *Flm&Vid, MusArts, RecA&S* To record music behind a film.

understudy Performer able to replace the regular performer when required. *Also see* **stand-in**.

underwrite *Eco&Fin, Fndng* **1** Assume financial responsibility, guarantee against failure. <underwrite a theatrical production, insure against losses> *Also see* **tour support**. **2** Guarantee the purchase of a stock or bond issue.

underwrite *Mktg, Rdio/TV* **Euphemism** for paid advertising on public radio or television. *Also see* **NPR**.

undifferentiated marketing strategy *Mktg* Marketer regards the market as an aggregate and designs its goods or services and marketing program to appeal to the greatest possible number of consumers. MARKET AGGREGATION *Also see* **mass market**.

undisclosed agency *LegAsp* One that occurs when the third party is unaware of both (1) the existence of an agency and (2) the actual identity of the **principal**. *Also see* **Agents and Agencies**.

unearned income *Eco&Fin, Fndng* Contributed income not earned by subscription, sales, or other marketing activities.

Unemployment Compensation Tax *Eco&Fin, EntreP, HR&LR* U.S. government mandated tax paid by employers – based on an employee's compensation – to pay benefits to unemployed workers.

Unemployment Rate *Eco&Fin* This **economic indicator is based on** U.S. Labor Dept. data that expresses the percentage of the total employable work force currently *un*employed. Rising rate indicates a slowing national economy. Because of seasonal anomalies, the rate is best used over a three to six month period, rather than month to month. Unemployment rate tends to exclude those workers whose unemployment compensation has run out and so have fallen off the government's statistical map.

unenforceable contract *LegAsp* Everything is in order but there is some legal defense to the enforcement of the contract. *Also see* **Contracts**.

UNESCO *Law&Pol* **United Nations Educational, Scientific, and Cultural Organization** (UNESCO) Mission is to reduce social tensions by encouraging interchange of ideas, cultural achievements, improve education.

unfair employment practice *HR&LR* Discrimination based on race, color, religion, age, sex, or national origin; forbidden by federal and some state laws.

unfair labor practice *HR&LR* Behavior by an employer contrary to government regulations or labor union agreement. <Firing without cause, sexual harassment, forced overtime, etc> *Also see* **agent** (*HR&LR*), **collective bargaining, Guilds & Unions**.

unidirectional mic *RecA&S* » **cardioid mic** *Also see* **Microphones**.

unified modeling language (UML) *iMedia* Non-proprietary, third generation modeling language used to specify, visualize, construct and document the artifacts of an object-oriented software-intensive system under development. UML represents a compilation of "best engineering practices" which have proven successful in modeling large, complex systems.

unified modeling language (UML) *iMedia* Non-proprietary, third generation modeling language used to specify, visualize, construct and document the artifacts of an object-oriented software-intensive system under development.

Uniform Commercial Code (UCC) *LegAsp* » **UCC**

Uniform Resource Identifier (URI) *iMedia* Strings which point to content available via protocols such as HTTP, FTP.

Uniform Resource Locator *InfoMgt* » **URL**

unilateral contract *LegAsp* One party agrees to do something for the other party, a promise for an act. *Also see* **bilateral contract, Contracts**.

union *HR&LR* **1** Labor union. **2** Alliance or confederation of people, parties, or political entities for mutual interest or benefit. *Also see* **Guilds & Unions**.

union card *HR&LR* Proof of union membership.

Union of Artistic Property *LegAsp, VisArts* » **droit de suite**

Union of Needletrades, Industrial and Textile Employees (UNITE) *Fashn., HR&LR* » **UNITE**

union shop *HR&LR* Business or factory whose employees are required to be union members or to agree to join the union within a specified time after being hired. CLOSED SHOP, OPEN SHOP

unique *Crit&Eval* Without an equal or equivalent; unparalleled. [Unless you believe it possible to be a little pregnant, never say "more" or "very" unique; rarely say "nearly" or "almost" unique.]

unisex *Crit&Eval* Designed for or suitable to both sexes. <clothing, hairstyle>

unisex *Fashn* Designed for or suitable to both sexes. <unisex clothing, unisex hairstyles> *Also see* **androgynous**.

unison *MusArts* Combination of parts at the same **pitch** or in octaves.

unit contribution margin *Eco&Fin, Mktg* Difference between the price at which an item is sold by the marketer and the costs directly associated with producing and selling it — sometimes expressed as a percentage of the selling price received by the marketer.

unit manager *Flm&Vid* Person in control of the business aspects of a production unit on location.

unit production manager *Flm&Vid* » **unit manager**

UNITE *also* **Unite** *Fashn, HR&LR* **Union of Needletrades, Industrial and Textile Employees**. Organized in 1995 replacing the **ILGWU**.

United Artists (Est. 1919) *EntreP, Flm&Vid*, A revolutionary concept of performers running their own careers artistically and financially, founded by five film legends: Mary Pickford, Douglas Fairbanks, Charlie Chaplin, William S. Hart (left soon after the official formation), and D.W. Griffith. Known today as M-G-M/UA. *Also see* **America's Sweetheart**.

United Independent Broadcasters, Inc. *Rdio/TV* » **CBS**

United Kingdom (U.K.) *Genl* » **U.K.**

United Nations Educational, Scientific, and Cultural Organization (UNESCO) *Law&Pol* » **UNESCO**

United Press International (UPI) *Journ* » **UPI**

United Scenic Artists of America (USAA) *HR&LR,PerfA&C, VisArts* » **USAA**

United Service Organization (USO) *PerfA&C* » **USO**

United States Information Agency *Cult&Soc* » **USIA**

United Students Against Sweatshops *Fashn* Organization of students and community members at over 200 campuses. http://www.usasnet.org/

United Talent Agency *Mgt,PerfA&C* » **UTA**

unity of action *TheatArts* Action having one **plot** only.

unity of peace *TheatArts* Action supposedly in one place only.

unity of time *TheatArts* Action supposedly lasting no more than twenty-tour hours (i.e., one day)

universal *Cult&Soc* Trait or pattern of behavior characteristic of all the members of a particular culture or of all human beings.

Universal Copyright Convention (UCC) *IntelProp* Extended copyright protection to certain works of U.S. authors in various foreign countries throughout the world. *Also see* **Copyright Service Organizations.**

Universal Product Code (UPC) *InfoMgt, Mktg* » **bar code**

Universal Serial Bus (USB) *InfoMgt* » **USB**

universal turing machine *iMedia* Machine programmed to read instructions, as well as data, off a tape, giving rise to the idea of a general-purpose programmable computing device (Alan Turing)

UNIX *InfoMgt* Operating system developed by **Ken Thompson** at **Bell Labs**, licensed exclusively through **X/Open Company, Ltd.** *Also see* **Programming Languages.**

unorthodox *Crit&Eval* Breaking with convention or tradition; not orthodox.

unpacking messages *InfoMgt* Open, read and file email messages.

unpaid media *Journ, Law&Pol* Media exposure not paid for by candidates for political office. <talk shows, news interviews or broadcasts> EARNED MEDIA

unprofessional *Crit&Eval* Not conforming to the standards of a profession.

unpublished motion picture *Flm&Vid, IntelProp* Film or tape that has no copies for distribution but is nonetheless subject to copyright protection; a registration may be submitted with proper application to the **Copyright Office.**

unpublished work *IntelProp, LitArts, MusArts* Literary or music manuscript that has not been offered for distribution to the public. *Also see* **publish.**

Unrelated Business Income Tax *Eco&Fin* » **UBIT**

unrestricted funds *Eco&Fin* Current funds which have no outside restrictions for their application and can be used for the general operating activities of the organization. *Also see* **operating funds, restricted funds.**

unsecured debt *EntreP* Debt that is not backed by collateral.

unsystematic risk *EntreP* Risk that is unique to an individual, company, or industry.

up *Crit&Eval* Get up emotionally. *Also see* **really up.**

up full *MusArts* Bring the musical ensemble to full volume or intensity.

up-front buying *Rdio/TV* In network TV, the preseason purchasing of commercial time in selected program blocks.

upcut *BcstJourn* Error in transition that happens when the end of the audio currently being played conflicts with the beginning of the audio from the next source. This usu. results from an error in timing; however, it forces the director or engineer on the audio board to make a sudden choice about which audio will play. If the upcut is severe, it often results in a situation where one audio portion will not make much sense.

up-front money *Eco&Fin, Genl* Payment made in advance of performance or completion of production.

up-tempo *MusArts* Fast or lively tempo.

update *BcstJourn* » **folo lead**

upstage *TheatArts* Acting area farthest from the audience.

upstaging *TheatArts* Derogatory term for activities by an actor that steal focus usu. unwarrantedly. from another actor. Specifically, it refers to standing where another actor has to face upstage (away from the audience) to look at you.

UPC *InfoMgt, Mktg* **Universal Product Code**, a standardized method of identifying products using a series of bars of varying thicknesses. *Also see* **bar-code.**

UPI *Journ* **United Press International**. American based international news agency. *Also see* **News Agencies.**

upload (D/L) *InfoMgt* To send a file from one computer to another via modem or other telecommunication method. *Also see* **download.**

upmarket *Mktg* Appealing to or designed for high-income consumers.

upper class *Cult&Soc* Highest socioeconomic class in a society.

upper crust *Cult&Soc* Highest social class or group.

upper managers *Mgt* Highest level of management in a company. Titles include. <chief executive officer (CEO), chairperson (man or woman), president, executive vice president, senior vice president, corporate vice president> TOP MANAGERS

uppercase (UC) *iMedia, VA-Prntng* Relating to the printing of capital letters. *Also see* **lowercase.**

upscale *Mktg* To redesign or market for higher-income consumers. *Also see* **lowscale.**

unsend *InfoMgt* Command used with email.

upstage *ArtPerf* To distract attention from another performer by moving upstage, thus forcing the other performer to face away from the audience. *Also see* **scene-stealer.**

upstage *Crit&Eval* To divert attention or praise from, force out of the spotlight.

upstage (US) *PerfA&C* Rear part of a stage, away from the audience. *Also see* **Stage Directions.**

upstairs *PA-Variety* Refers to the **high wire**, usu. 40 feet from the circus floor.

upstream *Eco&Fin, Flm&Vid* Position to receive a percentage of a movie's **gross profit** rather than elusive **net profit**.

urban blues *MusArts* Came about when **country blues** moved to the cities in the 1940s to catch some of that war-time money; exchanging harmonicas, jugs, and bones for drum sets, electric guitars and basses, on the way to **rhythm & blues** (and white rock 'roll) *Also see* **Blues**.

urbane *Crit&Eval* Polite, refined, and often elegant in manner. *Also see* **debonair**, **suave.**

URI *iMedia* » **Uniform Resource Identifier**

URL *iMedia, InfoMgt* **Uniform Resource Locator**. The Internet address for documents located on the Internet.

US *TheatArts* **upstage**

USAA *HR&LR,PerfA&C, VisArts* **United Scenic Artists of America**. Labor union providing contracts and benefits for professional scenic designers, scenic artists, costume and lighting designers, diorama and display workers, mural artists, and costume painters employed by television, theatre, motion picture studios, and producers of commercials.

usability *iMedia* Effectiveness, efficiency, and satisfaction with which users can achieve tasks in a particular environment of a product. High usability means a system is: easy to learn and remember; efficient, visually pleasing and fun to use; and quick to recover from errors.

usability engineering lifecycle *iMedia* Production method with three stages: Requirements Analysis, Design/Testing/Development and Installation.

usage segmentation *Mktg* Subdividing the total consumer market on the basis of where, when, and why the product is used.

USB *InfoMgt* **Universal Serial Bus**. Interface between **PC**s and **peripheral devices.**

USCO *IntelProp, Law&Pol* **United States Copyright Office** » **copyright registration** *Also see* **Copyright-Related Organizations, Federal Agencies and Statutes.**

Useful Field of View *iMedia* Size of the region from which one can rapidly take in information.

useful life *E&F-Acc* » **Estimated useful life**

Usenet *InfoMgt* Shared network of thousands of separate **bulletin boards** that can be accessed through **Internet** or the major commercial services. *Also see* **Online Information Services.** NEWSGROUPS

user feedback *iMedia* Responses from members of a target audience to a version release, or a version in-progress.

user group *iMedia, InfoMgt* Computer club where computer users exchange tips and information and email addresses.

user interrupt *iMedia* Method of attracting a computer user's attention to events.

user profile *iMedia* Information about a typical user that helps developers design a product. Often fictional information is used to develop general profiles of the target audience (*aka* **persona**)

user-friendly *InfoMgt* Description of computer hardware or software, or online service easy and fast to learn and to use.

usher *PerfA&C* One who escorts or directs people to their seats in a performing **venue**.

USIA *Cult&Soc* **United States Information Agency.** Sponsors international cultural exchange programs and administers the **Fulbright Scholarships**.

USO *PerfA&C* **United Service Organization** (est. ca. 1941), coordinates the booking of entertainers in U.S. armed service facilities throughout the world.

USPS *Genl* United States Postal Service. SNAIL MAIL

usurp an opportunity *LegAsp* When an agent appropriates an opportunity for herself or himself by failing to let the **principal** know about it.

UTA *Mgt,PerfA&C* United Talent Agency (UTA) Large-Hollywood based talent agency. *Also see* **Talent Agencies**.

utilitarian *Ethcs&Phil* Approach to ethics associated with **Jeremy Bentham, David Hume,** and **John Stuart Mill**. Based on the idea that the principle underpinning ethics is the primacy of achieving the greatest good for the greatest number. *Also see* **utilitarianism**.

utilitarianism *Ethcs&Phil* The principle that what makes an action moral is whether it contributes to the greatest possible balance of good over evil in the world, or the least possible balance of evil over good. If you believe that each individual action you take should do this, you're an "act utilitarian;" if you instead ask what is the effect on overall good if people always did such in comparable circumstances, then you're a "rule utilitarian." Of course, a utilitarian must already have some ideas about what is good and what is evil.

utility programs *InfoMgt* Programs used to perform special operations. <installing or updating software, checking disk damage, magnifying the screen image, etc>

- V -

V format *InfoMgt* Method of presenting data processor output so that each record begins with an indication of its length.

v. *LegAsp* Versus. Against, as in law cases. *Also see* **vs**.

v. *LitArts* 1 volume (book) 2 verse.

v. *MusArts* 1 voice. 2 verse.

vacate *LegAsp* To make void or annul. COUNTERMAND.

vacation pay liability *E&F-Acc* In most companies, employees earn the right to paid vacation days or weeks, as they work during the year. For every week an employee works the business accrues a small portion of that future pay and must account for it.

vacuous *Crit&Eval* 1 Devoid of expression or matter. EMPTY VACANT. 2 Lacking intelligence; stupid. 3 Devoid of substance or meaning; inane. <a vacuous comment> 4 Lacking serious purpose or occupation; idle.

vacuum tube *iMedia* Device the first digital electronic computers used to store values; each tube held either a charge (1) or no charge (0) and many tubes together could hold information in the form of binary numbers.

vacuum tube *Rdio/TV* » **triode electron tube**

Valhalla *Flm&Vid* » **88th episode** *Origin* Mythological heaven of slain heroes.

valid contract *LegAsp* One that has all the **contract elements** and is enforceable. *Also see* **Contracts**.

valuation issue *E&F-Acc* Focuses on assigning a monetary value to a business transaction. Generally accepted accounting principles state the appropriate value to assign to all business is the original cost.

value *iMedia* 1 Property of a color by which it is distinguished as bright or dark. 2 lightness or relative darkness of a color.

value judgment *Crit&Eval* Judgment that assigns a value to an object or action, subjective evaluation.

value-added *Eco&Fin* Relating to the estimated value added to a product or material at each stage of its manufacture or distribution.

value-added *Mktg, Rdio/TV* Add to the length and depth of paid advertising on public radio or television. <Add longer credits, corporate theme music, flashy logos and graphics> *Also see* **NPR**.

value-added tax *Eco&Fin* Tax on the estimated **market value** added to a product or material at each stage of its manufacture or distribution, ultimately passed on to the consumer. [Common in Europe, it is currently thought of in some anticonsumer circles as a substitute for the U.S. income tax.].

vamp *Crit&Eval, Flm&Vid* (Passé) In the silent movies, an unscrupulous, seductive woman who used her sex appeal to entrap and exploit men, accompanied by much eye-rolling, parted lips, slinky sidling, and heaving of creamy bosoms.

vamp *MusArts* 1 Feature of **black gospel** music wherein a **chord progression** is repeated indefinitely, over which a solo singer improvises textual and musical variations while a background group reiterates a single phrase. 2 Short introductory bit of instrumental music, often repeated more than once, before a song or dance, usu. in **vaudeville** routines. 3 To improvise simple accompaniment or variation of a tune. *Also see* **ostinato**.

vamp until ready To improvise until whoever or whatever is missing is ready to go.

vanguard *Crit&Eval* Foremost or leading position in a trend or movement.

vanilla *Crit&Eval, Cult&Soc* White, as in race; colorless. *Also see* **plain vanilla**.

vanity *Fashn* Excessive pride in one's appearance.

vantage point *LitArts* Seeing things in a third person story as if over a character's shoulder or standing beside the character or nearby without necessarily entering the character's internal point of view. Usually at a **Close Distance** or **Mid and Greater Distance**. — Story Workshop term by John Schultz (CCC/Fiction Writing dept.) *Also see* **storyteller vantage point**.

vaporware *InfoMgt* Non-existent software promoted to scare rivals.

var. *Dnce, MusArts* **variation**.

varia *LitArts* Miscellany of literary works.

variable *iMedia* Container for data consisting of a datum (value) and its identifying label (name); a variable stores a value.

variable cost *Mktg* Cost that changes in direct proportion to changes in activity, such as materials and parts, sales commissions, and certain labor and supplies. *Also see* **fixed cost**.

variable costs *EntreP* Costs directly driven by the volume of product flow.

variable expenses *EntreP* Pertains to a personal cash flow statement. Expenses over which we have some control such as food, clothing and automobile expenses.

variable pricing strategy *EntreP* Marketing approach that sets more than one price for a good or service in order to offer price concessions to certain customers.

variable-size font *InfoMgt* » **scalable outline font** *Also see* **TrueType**.

variation (var.) *Dnce* Solo dance, esp. one forming part of a larger work.

variation (var.) *MusArts* Form that is an altered version of a given theme, diverging from it by melodic ornamentation and by changes in harmony, rhythm, or key.

Variety *Genl, Journ* Highly respected weekly newspaper, in tabloid format, covering all areas of showbiz.

variety show *PA-Variety* Entertainment consisting of successive, unrelated acts, as songs, dances, and comedy skits. *Also see* **revue**.

variety shows *Rdio/TV* Popular type of television network programming. <*The Ed Sullivan Show, Lawrence Welk*> *Also see* **Television Shows**.

vaude *PA-Variety* **vaudeville**

V

vaudeville (vaude) *MusArts* Popular, often satirical song.

vaudeville (vaude) *PA-Variety* **1** Stage entertainment offering a variety of short acts: acrobats, jugglers, and magicians, song-and-dance routines, **standup** comedians, newsmakers — accompanied by a **pit orchestra**; a variety show. **2** Light comic play that often includes songs, pantomime, and dances. *Also see* **circuit, headliner.**

Vaughan, Sarah (*aka* "Sassy," 1924-90, jazz sngr., pno.) *ArtPerf, MusArts* Known for her complex bebop **phrasing**, her **scat singing** virtuosity, and her amazing **tonal** range, Sassy was probably the most gifted of all jazz-associated singers. <*Gershwin Live!* (**Grammy**, 1982)> *Also see* **Apollo Theater.**

vault *Flm&Vid, RecA&S* Secure, climate-controlled room or space where reels of film or tape are stored.

VCR *Flm&Vid, Rdio/TV, RecA&S* videocassette recorder.

Veblen, Thorstein (1857-1929, econ., social critic) *Cult&Soc, Eco&Fin* Described a basic conflict between industry which tends to maximum efficiency of production and business which restricts output and manipulates prices to maximize profits. <*Theory of the Leisure Class* (1889) in which he said: "**Conspicuous consumption** of valuable goods is a means of reputability to the gentleman of leisure."

vection *iMedia* Sensation of self-movement induced even when the subject is not moving

vector *iMedia, InfoMgt* **1** Graphics: line or movement defined by its end points, or by the current position and one other point. » **vector graphics 2** Operating system: memory location containing the address of some code, often some kind of exception handler or other operating system service. **3** Programming: one-dimensional array.

vector graphics *iMedia* Graphics represented with lines and shapes instead of individual **pixels**; usu. smaller in file size than bitmaps, and can be resized without loss of resolution.

vee-jay *Rdio/TV* Video jockey, off-screen commentator.

vehicle *MusArts, TheatArts* Play, role, or piece of music used to display the special talents of one performer or company. *Also see* **revival.**

vellum *MusInstr* Fine parchment made from calfskin, lambskin, or kidskin and used as a diaphragm for a musical instrument. <banjo>

vellum *VA-Prntng* **1** Fine parchment made from calfskin, lambskin, or kidskin and used for the pages and binding of books. **2** Work written or printed on this parchment. **3** Heavy off-white fine-quality paper resembling this parchment.

velox *VA-Prntng* Screened photoprint that can be reproduced as a line illustration.

vender, vendor *E&F-Acc, Mktg* **1** One that sells or vends, a street vender, vendors of cheap merchandise. **2** Vending machine.

Venn diagram *iMedia* Diagram using circles to represent sets, with the position and overlap of the circles indicating the relationships between the sets.

ventilating needles *Th-MakeUp* Used for knotting hair into net or gauze for wigs or beards.

ventriloquist *ArtPerf, PA-Variety* **Illusionist** who can project one's voice so that it seems to come from another source. *Also see* **dummy.**

venture capital *Eco&Fin, EntreP* High-risk capital provided to growth ventures in exchange for significant ownership in the venture. RISK CAPITAL

venture capitalist *EntreP* Representative of a company providing high-risk capital to growth ventures.

venue *Crit&Eval* Scene or setting in which something takes place. LOCALE

ver. *LitArt, MusArts* **verse.**

verisimilitude *Crit&Eval* Quality of appearing to be true or real.

verisimilitude *iMedia* **1** Quality of appearing to be true or real. **2** Something that has the appearance of being true or real.

verisimilitude *TheatArts* Term that refers to the extent to which the drama or stage setting appears to copy the superficial appearance of life offstage.

verism *Crit&Eval* Realism in art and literature.

verismo (Ital. for "true") *MusArts* Artistic movement of the late 19th century, originating in Italy and influential esp. in grand opera, marked by the use of common, everyday themes often treated in a **melodramatic** manner. *Also see* **Art Movements and Periods.**

verity *Ethcs&Phil* Statement, principle, or belief, that is true, esp. an enduring truth.

vernacular *Crit&Eval* Idiom of a particular trade or profession; jargon. <showbiz vernacular> *Also see* **jargon.**

vernacular art *VisArts* Style of **folk art** common in a particular region, culture, or period.

vernacular music *Cult&Soc, MusArts* Music that "evolved mainly through aural practice... independent of **notation**." — Thomas Brothers (19??-, African American history prof., Duke U.)

vernacular video *Flm&Vid, Journ, Rdio/TV* » **small-format video**

verse (v., ver.) *LitArts* **1** Single metrical line in a poetic composition, one line of poetry. **2** Division of a metrical composition. <stanza of a poem or hymn> **3** Poem. **4** Art or work of a poet. **5** Metrical writing that lacks depth or artistic merit. **6** Particular type of metrical composition. <blank verse, free verse> **7** One of the numbered subdivisions of a chapter in the Bible.

verse (v., ver.) *MusArts* Unrepeated introduction of a standard ballad, usu. shorter than the chorus and played **rubato**.

versification *LitArts* **1** Process of changing from prose into metrical form. **2** To treat or tell in verse.

versify *LitArts* To treat or express in verse.

version *Crit&Eval* Adaptation of a work of art or literature into another medium or style.

version control *iMedia* Assuring that a version is archived and documented before work on the next version begins.

version *iMedia, InfoMgt* Number indicating the release of a particular piece of software. Usually, the higher the number, the more recent the version.

versioning *iMedia* Using an iterative development model to produce a product. » **iterative theory**

Versit *InfoMgt* Group organized by Apple, AT&T, **IBM**, and Siemens, dedicated to creating specifications for interoperability between phones and computers.

verso *VA-Prntng* left-hand page of a book *Also see* **recto.**

vertical analysis *EntreP* Process of using a single variable on a financial statement as a constant and determining how all of the other variables relate as a percentage of the single variable.

vertical file *InfoMgt* **1** Collection of resource materials, such as pamphlets, clippings from periodicals, and mounted photographs, arranged for ready reference, as in a library or an **archive**. **2** Wastebasket.

vertical integration *Mktg* Process of purchasing or acquiring control over one's suppliers and/or one's distributors. <Disney, **Time-Warner**> *Also see* **backward integration, forward integration, horizontal integration.**

vertical spread *EntreP* Describes portfolio of different call or put options that differ only by the strike prices. "Vertical" refers to the way option prices are listed in the financial press.

vertical union *HR&LR* » **industrial union** *Also see* **Guilds & Unions.**

verve *Crit&Eval* Energy and enthusiasm in the expression of emotions and ideas in artistic performance or composition. PANACHE

very high frequency (VHF) *Rdio/TV* » **VHF**

Very Large Scale Integration (VLSI) *InfoMgt* » **VLSI**

very low frequency (VLF) *Rdio/TV* » **VLF**

VH1 Save The Music program *MusArts, Rdio/TV* Nonprofit "dedicated to restoring music education to America's public elementary schools, and raising awareness of scientific research proving that music education dramatically increases early brain development and improves student's overall performance." Program created in 1996 in NYC with the cooperation of VH1 and nationwide cable systems

VHF *Rdio/TV* **very high frequency**. Band of radio and TV **frequencies** between 300-300 **megahertz**, TV channels 2-13 *Also see* **VLF**

viable *Crit&Eval* Capable of success or continuing effectiveness. PRACTICABLE.

vibes *MusArts* » **vibraphone**

vibraharp *MusInstr* » **vibraphone** VIBRAHARPIST

vibraphone (vibe, vibes) *MusInstr* Instrument similar to a **marimba** but having metal bars and rotating disks in the **resonators**

V

to produce a **vibrato**. Played with various types of mallets. VIBE PLAYER, VIBIST, VIBRAPHONIST *Also see* **Musical Instrument Families, tremolo.**

vibrate *MusArts* To produce a sound. *Also see* **resonate.**

vibration *MusArts* Single complete vibrating motion; a **quiver.** *Also see* **piano, sound. sympathetic vibration.**

vibrato *MusArts* Tremulous or pulsating effect produced in an instrumental or vocal tone by barely perceptible minute and rapid variations in **pitch.** *Also see* **tremolo, trill.**

vice *Ethcs&Phil* **1** Contrary to virtue, that which is base, vile, harmful. **2** Serious moral failing, sexual immorality, esp. prostitution. **3** Slight personal failing; a **foible.**

Vice *TheatArts* Character representing generalized or particular **vice** in English **morality plays.**

Victor Recording Company *RecA&S* Forerunner of **RCA Records.** *Also see* **dixieland jazz.**

Victorian *Crit&Eval, Ethcs&Phil* Relating to the standards or ideals of morality characteristic of the time of **Queen Victoria** (1819-1901), Queen of Great Britain and Ireland, 1837-1901, Empress of India, 1876-1901) <Victorian manners>

Victorian *VisArts* Being in the highly ornamented, massive style of architecture, **decor,** and furnishings popular in 19th century England.

victrola *RecA&S* Pre-electric phonograph run by a wind-up motor. *Also see* **Music Playback Devices.**

video art *Flm&Vid* » **artist's video**

video assist *Flm&Vid* System of recording a video image simultaneously with a film image so that a shot can be viewed immediately. The video footage can then be used as preliminary editing footage or simply as a check for performance, framing, focus, etc. Used frequently for complicated setups, esp. involving lots of extras or **special effects.**

video buyout *Flm&Vid, IntelProp, MusArts* Agreement by which the buyer (user) agrees to pay the licensor a flat fee for the use of a song, with no increase based on sales. *Also see* **video rollover.**

video monitor *InfoMgt* Display device that can receive video signals by direct connection. Sometimes called a **monitor** or **display.**

Video News International (VNI) *Journ, Rdio/TV* » **VNI**

video rollover *Flm&Vid, IntelProp, MusArts* Agreement by which the buyer (user) agrees to pay the licensor a continuing fee (either in advance or based on sales as per agreement) Every time a specific sales point has been reached, the fee is "rolled over," i.e., paid again. *Also see* **video buyout.**

Video Software Dealers Association (VSDA) *Flm&Vid* Nonprofit international trade association works to monitor and prevent legislation that limits access to constitutionally protected material. *Also see* **Anti-Censorship Organizations.**

videocassette *Flm&Vid* Cassette containing blank or prerecorded **videotape** introduced by Sony in 1969.

videocassette recorder *Flm&Vid, Rdio/TV, RecA&S* » **VCR**

videodisc, videodisk *InfoMgt* Plastic platter resembling a phonograph record uses low-intensity laser beams to store visual materials appearing on a display screen. Introduced in 1972 by Phillips Corp. (Holland)

videojournalist *Journ, Rdio/TV* Journalist in the TV medium.

videophone *InfoMgt, Sci&Tech* Telephone equipped for both audio and video transmission. PICTUREPHONE

videorazzi *Crit&Eval* Freelance video camera operators who lie on wait or stalk celebrities in the hope of filming/taping an embarrassing scene that can be peddled to a TV tabloid program, such as *Hard Copy,* for $1,500 to $3,000. — *Time Also see* **paparazzi.**

videotape *Flm&Vid* **1** Relatively wide magnetic tape used to record visual images and associated sound for subsequent playback or broadcasting. **2** Recording made on such a tape.

videotape editor *Rdio/TV* One, who with the producer, establishes the pace of the TV program or story and selects the most effective pictures and sound.

videotape recorder (VTR) *Flm&Vid* A device for making a videotape recording.

videotex *InfoMgt* System in which computer-stored information is transmitted over TV cables or telephone lines and displayed on home TV screens or computer terminals, used for various services such as electronic banking, electronic mail, and home shopping.

viewdata *InfoMgt* Interactive **videotex** system in which information can be retrieved or transmitted over television cables or telephone lines.

viewer *Rdio/TV* Object of television station policy and programming, regarded as the basic unit in most **demographic** and **psychographic** surveys. *Also see* **listener.**

vignette *Flm&Vid* Short scene in a movie.

vignette *VisArts* **1** Short, usu. descriptive literary sketch. **2** Decorative design placed at the beginning or end of a book or chapter of a book or along the border of a page. **3** Unbordered picture, often a portrait, that shades off into the surrounding color at the edges.

villain *Flm&Vid, LitArts,* Dramatic or fictional character who at odds with the **hero.** *Also see* **melodrama, serial.**

viola (vla) *MusInstr* **1** Stringed instrument of the violin family, slightly larger than a violin, tuned a fifth lower, and having a deeper, more sonorous tone. Music for viola written in **treble clef. 2** Organ stop usu. of eight-foot or four-foot **pitch** yielding stringlike **tones.** VIOLIST *Also see* **Musical Instrument Families.**

violin (vlo) *MusInstr* Stringed instrument played with a bow, having four strings tuned at intervals of a fifth, an unfrocked **fingerboard,** and a shallower body than the viola and capable of great flexibility in range, tone, and **dynamics.** VIOLINIST *Also see* **Musical Instrument Families.**

virgin stock *Flm&Vid* Film stock not yet exposed or **videotape** on which no signal has been recorded.

virtu *Crit&Eval, VisArts* **1** Knowledge of, love for, or taste for fine objects of arts. **2** Art objects, esp. fine antiques. OBJECTS D'ART

virtual *iMedia* Existing in essence or effect.

virtual memory *InfoMgt* Computer memory, distinct from a specific machine, that can be used to extend the machine's own memory.

virtual reality *iMedia, InfoMgt* **1** Computer simulation of a real or imaginary system that enables a user to perform operations on the simulated system and shows the effects in real time. **2** Hypothetical three-dimensional visual world through which movement and interaction with objects is simulated as if it were reality.

Virtual Reality Modeling Language *iMedia* Language for creation of multi-user interactive simulations.

virtue *Ethcs&Phil* **1** Ethics of virtue stresses that one should cultivate what some call "**character**" that one should constantly strive to be a person who tends to act honestly, kindly, and benevolently. However, "Few... have virtue to withstand the highest bidder." — George Washington (1732-99, 1st President of the United States (1789-1797) **2** **Aristotle** defined virtue as a matter of habit of the trained faculty of judgment.

virtuosa, virtuoso *ArtPerf, MusArts* Female or male musician with superb ability, technique, or personal style.

virtuosity *Crit&Eval* **1** Technical skill, fluency, or style exhibited by a **virtuosa/virtuoso.** **2** Appreciation for or interest in fine objects of art.

virus *InfoMgt* » **computer virus**

vis-à-vis *Crit&Eval* **1** Face to face with, opposite to. **2** Compared with. **3** In relation to.

visceral *Crit&Eval* » **guts**

visionary art *Aes&Creat VisArts* "Unlike other forms of expression, visionary art – often called **outsider** art – knows no boundary, **genre,** or style, only the defining rule of art by artists who are entirely self-taught. It differs from **folk art** in that folk artists generally follow well-known and long-practiced norms, with less **spontaneity** or **whimsy** that seems so apparent among the unschooled." — Michael Janofsky (art critic) *Also see* **Art Movements and Periods.**

visual aid *Genl* Visual instructional aid. <chart, filmstrip, picture, scale model, slide, videotape>

visual art *VisArts* Painting, sculpting, scenic design, and related endeavors.

Visual Artists' Rights Act *IntelProp, LegAsp, VisArts* Amendment to the Federal copyright law enacted in 1990, effective June 1991, which seeks to protect certain categories of visual art from distortion, mutilation, or destruction, and protect artists' moral rights. *Also see* **work for hire.** *Also see* **Federal Agencies and Statutes.**

visual stress *iMedia* When a pattern causes ill effects on people, i.e., seizures, headaches, and vomiting.

vituperation *Crit&Eval* Harshly abusive language. INVECTIVE, OBLOQUY

viva (vee-vah, Ital./Span. for "long live") *Crit&Eval* Used by an audience to express strong approval. APPLAUSE.

vivace (viv-otchay, Ital. for "lively") *MusArts* Direction: play in a lively or vivacious manner.

vivacious *Crit&Eval* Full of animation and spirit. LIVELY.

vivid *Crit&Eval* 1 Bright and distinct. BRILLIANT. 2 Having intensely bright colors. 3 Full of the vigor and freshness of immediate experience. <a vivid memory> 4 Evoking lifelike images within the mind; heard, seen, or felt as if real. <a vivid description>

VJ *Rdio/TV* vee-jay.

vla *MusInstr* viola

Victor Talking Machine Company *RecA&S* » **Original Dixieland Jazz Band**

Village Voice, The (est. 1955, NYC) *Mdia-Prnt* "The nation's first and largest alternative newsweekly."

virtue ethics *Ethcs&Phil* Stresses that people should not focus on individual action as much as cultivate what some call "character" — to constantly *strive to be* a person who tends to act honestly, kindly, and benevolently, and to avoid the pitfalls of **casuistry**. <"In moral discussions, it is to be remembered that many impediments obstruct our practice, which very easily give way to theory." — Samuel Johnson> However: < "Few... have virtue to withstand the highest bidder." — George Washington > **Aristotle** defined virtue as a matter of habit or the trained faculty of judgment.

visualization *iMedia* 1 Mental image similar to a visual perception. 2 Using visuals or graphics to aid **cognition** or to resolve logical problems. 3 Physical creation that supports decision-making; often an image or representation of data.

VLF *Rdio/TV* very low frequency. Band of radio **frequencies** falling between 3 and 30 **kilohertz**.

vlo. *MusInstr* violin.

VLSI *InfoMgt* Very Large Scale Integration, a densely compacted chip common to 4th generation computers.

VNI *Journ, Rdio/TV* **Video News International**. Global video news-gathering service for TV and cable. Majority shares owned by *The New York Times*. *Also see* **News Agencies**.

VO *Flm&Vid* » voiceover

VO or **voice over** *BcstJourn* Television news story format that uses a studio newscaster for picture and audio but inserts videotape for visuals during a portion of the story.

VO/SOT *BcstJourn* Commonly used story format in television news that combines a studio voice over segment with a soundbite. This can also be expanded to a VO/SOT/VO or even a VO/SOT/VO/SOT/VO. In some areas, this is called a VOB or **voice over** bite.

voc. *MusArts* vocal, vocalist, vocals.

vocal *MusArts* pop composition for a singer

vocal cords *MusArts* One of two pairs of bands of mucous membrane in the throat that project into the larynx. Lower pair vibrate when pulled together and when air is passed up from the lungs, thereby producing vocal sounds.

vocalise *MusArts* Setting of lyrics to improvised instrumental solos a la Lambert, Hendricks, and Ross, and the group Manhattan Transfer.

vocalist (singer) *MusArts* One who vocalizes or sings.

vogue *Crit&Eval, Fashn* Prevailing fashion, practice, or style.

voice *Law&Pol* 1 Wish, choice, or opinion openly or formally expressed <the voice of the people> 2 right of expression

voice *LitArts* 1 In prose fiction, the speaking-writing connection resolves the contradictions among such voice characterizations as your own voice, personal voice, authentic voice, untruthful voice, collective and cultural voices, persona voices, and different registers of voice. Each of these identifies a working aspect of voice. In resolving the seeming contradictions, the speaking-writing connection finds a deeply realized persona for its freest and strongest activation in the internal drama of the act of writing. No matter how silently we think we read, the connection of hearable language to written language is so inextricably necessary for our understanding of what we read or write that throat surgeons forbid patients to do any reading after throat surgery,

because of the faint movements in the larynx. All forms of writing are speakable, a visual representation of language. — Betty Shiflett and John Schultz (CCC/Fiction Writing dept.) 2 Distinctive style or manner of expression of an author or a character in a book.

voice *MusArts* Vocal or instrumental part of a composition.

Voice *PA-Variety* Circus **ringmaster**

Voice, The *ArtPerf, MusArts* » **Frank Sinatra**

voice culture *ArtPerf* Special training and development for singers and actors.

voice grade line *InfoMgt* Hardware/software system, which normally includes a head mounted display, that allows users to "immerse" themselves in an experience.

voice mail *InfoMgt* Messages spoken into a telephone, converted into **digital** form, and stored in the computer's memory until recalled, at which time they are reconverted into voice form.

voice placement *MusArts* Singer's technique of originating (placing) vocal music sounds from different locations, i.e., throat, chest, head, in order to achieve a variety of tones. *Also see* **color**.

voice synthesis, voice synthesizer *InfoMgt* » **phoneme, prosody, speech synthesizer**.

voice-over, voiceover (VO) *Flm&Vid, Rdio/TV* Voice of an unseen speaker, or of an **on-screen** character not seen speaking, in a movie or a television broadcast.

voice-over *BcstJourn* » **VO**

voicer *BcstJourn* Report, narrated by someone other than the newscaster, that does not contain a bite or other actuality. Usu. recorded and played back from a **cart**.

voiceprint *Sci&Tech* Electronically recorded graphic representation of a person's voice, in which the **configuration** for any given utterance is uniquely characteristic of the individual speaker.

voicing *MusArts* 1 Assignment of melody and accompanying lines to particular instruments. "Arranger's voicings are as unique as a fingerprint." — Lyon and Perlo (jazz critics) 2 Tonal quality of an instrument in an ensemble, esp. a jazz ensemble, or of the ensemble as a whole. *Also see* **jazz characteristics**.

void *LegAsp* » **null** *Also see* **Contracts**.

void contract *LegAsp* One that has no legal effect. *Also see* **Contracts**.

voidable contract *LegAsp* One in which either party has the option to avoid the contract's obligations. *Also see* **Contracts**.

voile *Fashn* Light, plain-weave, sheer fabric of cotton, rayon, silk, or wool used to make dresses and curtains.

vol. *InfoMgt, RecA&S, VA-Prntng* **volume**.

volatile *Crit&Eval* 1 Tending to vary often or widely. 2 Ephemeral, fleeting. 3 Tending to violence. EXPLOSIVE.

volt *PerfA&C, Sci&Tech* Unit of measurement of electrical potential.

voltage *Sci&Tech* Electromotive force or potential difference, usu. expressed in volts.

volume (vol.) *InfoMgt* General term referring to a storage device, a source of or a destination for information. Often used in reference to hard disks and file servers. Volume can be an entire disk or only part of a disk.

volume (vol.) *RecA&S* Loudness of a sound, a control for regulating loudness.

volume (vol.) *VA-Prntng* 1 Book, one of a books in a set. 2 Written material in a library that has been brought together and cataloged as an individual unit.

volume discount *Mktg* Discount off the regular price based on the quantity ordered. *Also see* **Discounts**.

voluntarism, volunteerism *Fndng* Willingness of private citizens to serve voluntarily in a great variety of programs and causes.

voluptuary *Crit&Eval* Person whose life is given over to luxury and sensual pleasures. *Also see* **sensualist**.

von Leibnitz, Gottfried Wilhelm (1646-1716) *iMedia* Invented differential and integral calculus. Inventor of the first calculating machine. Developed the binary number system in 1679.

von Neumann architecture *iMedia* Computer architecture that forms the core of nearly every computer system in use today; has random-access memory (RAM), and a central processing unit (CPU)

voodoo (Louisiana Fr., *voudou*) *Cult&Soc* 1 **Syncretic** religion developed by slaves in Haiti from Catholic and Central African beliefs. **2** To place under the influence of a spell or curse. *Also see* **bewitch**, **black magic**, **conjure**, **conjure woman**.

voodoo economics *Eco&Fin*, *Law&Pol* **Prescient** description of presidential candidate **Ronald Reagan's** economic platform as delivered by his future Vice President, **George Bush**. *Also see* **supply-side**, **trickle-down theory**.

VR *iMedia* » **virtual reality**

VRML *iMedia* » **Virtual Reality Modeling Language**

VSDA *Flm&Vid* Video Software Dealers Association.

VTR *Flm&Vid* **videotape** recorder, **videotape** recording.

vulgar *Crit&Eval* Deficient in taste, delicacy, or refinement.

- W -

w. *LitArts*, *MusArts* **words**. Used to indicate the lyricist of a song. <*A Foggy Day* **m.** George Gershwin, **w.** Ira Gershwin> *Also see* **m.**

w.b., **W.B.** *Eco&Fin* **waybill**, **Waybill**.

W3C *iMedia* » **World Wide Web Consortium**

wages *E&F-Acc* Payment to employees for services rendered, usu. at an hourly rate. *Also see* **blue collar**.

Wagner Act (National Labor Relations Act, 1935) *HR&LR* This act was an outgrowth of the **Great Depression** It declared in effect that the official policy of the U.S. government was to encourage collective bargaining. It established the principle that employees would be protected in their right to form a union and to bargain collectively. The act also prohibited employers from undertaking several unfair labor practices. *Also see* **National Labor Code**.

wah-wah, **wa-wa** *MusArts* **1** Wavering sound produced by alternately covering and uncovering the bell of a trumpet or trombone with a **mute**.

wah-wah mute *MusInstr* » **plunger mute**

wah-wah pedal *MusInstr* Electronic attachment on an electric guitar reproduces a **wah-wah** sound.

WAIS *InfoMgt* **Wide-Area Information Servers**. Service of **Internet** that allows users to access and find information through a single access point. *Also see* **Online Server**(s)

waiver *LegAsp* Intentional relinquishment of a right, claim, or privilege.

walk around dance *Dnce*» **cakewalk** *Also see* **Dances**.

walk the walk *Crit&Eval* » **pay** (one's) **dues**.

walk-on *Flm&Vid*, Performer who has no lines.

walk-through *Flm&Vid*, Marking rehearsal in which the actors speak only cue lines, or no dialogue at all, relative to on- stage or on-set positioning.

walkers *HR&LR*, *MusArts* Musicians who just walk in and get their weekly salary but who do not play. When a musical is staged in a theater where the minimum number of musicians required by musicians union rules is more than the producer wants to use. <Theater has a 14-musician minimum. **Score** calls for only ten. Four musicians become walkers> *Also see* **featherbedding**, **make work**.

walking bass line *MusArts* "Each beat of each measure receives a different tone, creating the sensation of forward motion." — Lyons & Perlo (jazz critics) *Also see* **bassline**.

walkout *HR&LR* **1** Labor strike. **2** Leaving or quitting a meeting, a company, or an organization as a sign of protest.

Walla-Walla *Flm&Vid*, *Rdio/TV* Originally a radio term meaning off-mike background, conversational **babble**.

wallpaper video *BcstJourn* Use of random, unconnected shots out of sequence – shots that have only a remote connection to the story – as cover for studio **VO** or a reporter's narration. Generally the lowest form of video, sometimes referred to as 'spray painting' to cover the story.

Walt Disney Company *Flm&Vid*, *LitArts MusArts*, *PA-Variety*, *Rdio/TV*, *VisArts* World's largest entertainment **conglomerate**, headquartered in Los Angeles. Its properties include: **ABC** Radio & TV, Disney Land, Disney World, and other **theme parks**, book and music publishers; animation, film, and television studios; retail stores, and of course, Mickey Mouse et al. *Also see* **Disney, Walt**

waltz *Dnce*, *MusArts* Dance, and music, in triple time performed by couples, which reached its peak of popularity during the nineteenth century. *Also see* **3/4 time**.

WAN (Wide Area Network) *iMedia* Communications network that uses telephone lines, satellite dishes, or radio waves to span a larger geographic area than can be covered by a **LAN**.

want *TheatArts* » **intention**

wants *Mktg* Things or conditions to satisfy a particular **need**. <One needs food, one wants a hamburger> MATERIAL WANTS *Also see* **demands**.

war babies *Cult&Soc* Children born during World War I or World War II.

warble *MusArts* To sing a note or song with **trills**, **runs**, or other melodic **embellishments**.

wardrobe *Flm&Vid*, *PerfA&C* **1** Clothes worn by a performer, either self-supplied or supplied or supplied by the producer. **2** Place in which theatrical costumes are kept. *Also see* **costume**.

wardrobe department *Flm&Vid* All costumes, street wardrobe, materials, special truck, and personnel. WARDROBE MISTRESS, WARDROBE MASTER.

warehouse *Mktg* Place in which goods or merchandise are stored.

warez *InfoMgt* Software that has been liberated from **encryption**.

Warner Brothers Pictures *Flm&Vid* » **Harry Warner**

Warner, Harry Morris (1881-1958, flmkr.) *Flm&Vid Mgt* He and his brothers Albert (1884-1967), Samuel Louis (1887-1927), and Jack (1892-1978) founded **Warner Brothers Pictures**, which produced the first talkie, *The Jazz Singer* (1927), and many film classics, inc. *Casablanca* (1942) *Also see* **mogul**.

Warner-Elektra-Asylum (WEA) *RecA&S* » **WEA** *Also see* **major labels**.

warranty *Mktg* **Guarantee** given to the purchaser by a company stating that a product is reliable and free from known defects and that the seller will, without charge, repair or replace defective parts within a given time limit and under certain conditions. "The Software is provided **'as is'** without a warranty of any kind, and Claris expressly disclaims all implied warranties..." — Claris Corp. *Also see* **disclaimer**.

Warren, Robert Penn (1905-89, critic, fictwri., poet, tchr.) *ArtPerf*, *Crit&Eval*, *LitArts* In 1985 he was appointed the first American **poet laureate**. <*King's Men* (novel, 1946), *Promises* (poetry collection)> *Also see* **experimental**, **modern art**, **New Criticism**.

wash *VisArts* Thin layer of water color or India ink spread on a drawing.

wash-and-wear *Fashn* Clothing treated so as to be easily or quickly washed or rinsed clean and to require little or no ironing. <wash-and-wear shirt>

washboard *MusInstr* Board having a corrugated surface on which clothes can be rubbed and thus laundered is also used as a percussion instrument. RUB BOARD *Also see* **Little Instruments**.

washed-up *Crit&Eval* No longer successful or needed. FINISHED. *Also see* **over the hill**.

watercolor *VisArts* Paint composed of a water-soluble pigment; a work using this paint.

Watergate *Ethcs&Phil*, *Law&Pol* Scandal involving abuse of power by President **Nixon** (ultimately forced to resign) and other public officials, violation of the public trust, bribery, contempt of Congress, and attempted obstruction of justice. *Origin* Watergate, a Washington building complex, the site of the breaking and entering crime (1972) that gave rise to this scandal. *Also see* **investigative journalism**. *Also see* **Ben Bradlee**, **Bob Woodward**.

WATS *InfoMgt* Wide-Area Telecommunications

wave length *Rdio/TV* Broadcast **frequencies**. *Also see* **wavelength**.

waveband *Rdio/TV* Range of **frequencies** assigned to communication transmissions. <radio>

waveform *Sci&Tech* Mathematical representation of a wave, esp. a graph obtained by plotting a characteristic of the wave against time.

wavelength (WL) *iMedia*, *Sci&Tech* Distance between one peak or crest of a wave of light, heat, or other energy and the next corresponding peak or crest.

wax *RecA&S* **1** phonograph record. **2** To make a phonograph record. *Also see* **Music Playback Devices**. *Origin* Wax cylinder was in the original **configuration** of the phonograph invented by **Thomas Edison**.

wax museum *PA-Variety*, *VisArts* Place where life-size wax figures

W

of famous or infamous people are exhibited.

waybill (w.b., W.B.) *Eco&Fin* Document giving details and instructions relating to a shipment of goods.

wayfinding *iMedia* How people build up an understanding of larger environments over time.

WEA *RecA&S* **Warner-Elektra-Asylum** (WEA) Record division of **Time-Warner.** *Also see* **major labels.**

WEAF *Rdio/TV* Base radio station of **NBC's red network.** *Also see* **Broadcast Stations & Networks, RCA.**

wealth therapy *Eco&Fin* Helps clients emotionally and practically with **windfall** wealth.

"Weak" and "Strong" Dollar *Eco&Fin* This **economic indicator** is based on the trading of international currency. It measures the value of the American dollar against foreign currency, esp. the German mark and the Japanese yen. "Weak" dollar means it takes fewer marks or yen to buy a dollar; a "strong" dollar takes more marks or yen to buy a dollar. Weak dollar tends to favor exports, strong dollar tends to favor imports (and foreign vacation travel)

wealth effect *EntreP* Increase in spending that occurs because the real value of money increases when the price level falls.

Web *InfoMgt* » **Internet, World Wide Web.**

.web *InfoMgt* **Domain** name ending for **entities** relating to the **World Wide Web.** *Also see* **Domain Names.**

web *Rdio/TV* radio or television network.

Web Crawler *InfoMgt* Web site providing access to Internet. *Also see* **search engine, portals.**

web fed *VA-Prntng* Press fed from a roll rather than sheets. *Also see* **sheetfed.**

web navigation *iMedia* Type of navigational system that allows a user to follow threads through content, moving from topic to topic at will. As opposed to linear and hierarchical navigation, the participant is encouraged to explore via associations between concepts instead of following through only one topic to its conclusion.

Web site *InfoMgt* A computer system set up for publishing documents on the **Web.** *Also see* **World Wide Web.**

webmaster *InfoMgt* Person in charge of a **Web site.**

wedgie *Fashn* Shoe having a wedge-shaped heel joined to a half sole so as to form a continuous undersurface.

weight *Fashn* To increase the weight or body of fabrics by treating with chemicals.

weighted average cost of capital (WACC) *EntreP* Method of determining a company's cost of capital when it takes into consideration the rate charged by the lender(s) and the opportunity cost foregone by the borrower(s) Using these rates and the proportion of total financing funded by the lender and borrower, the WACC is calculated.

weighting formula *MusArts, RecA&S* Formula for determining the amount of royalty due authors and publishers by performing rights organizations, e.g., **ASCAP, BMI, SESAC,** that takes into account such factors as the number of local, regional, or national airplays.

well-made play *TheatArts* Form of drama popularized in the 19th century, especially in France *(une piece bienfaite)* The **plot** usu. turns on the revelation of a secret and includes a character who explains and moralizes the action of the play to others: the **plot** is often relentlessly coincidental often mechanically so.

Welles, Orson (1915-85, stage/film/radio dir., prod., act.-mgr.) *ArtPerf, Flm&Vid, Mgt, Rdio/TV, TheatArts* Directed, produced, and starred in several remarkable films, plays, and radio dramas in his **Mercury Theater** productions. His *Citizen Kane* (1941) is on most lists of all-time best movies. *Also see* **actor-manager, Federal Theatre, Mercury Theater.**

West *Cult&Soc* **1** Western part of the earth, esp. Europe and the Western Hemisphere. **2** Noncommunist countries of Europe and the Americas.

West Coast jazz *MusArts* Mid-1950s white offshoot of the eastern school of the cool. *Also see* **Jazz Styles.**

Western *Cult&Soc* Political and social orientation to the western part of the earth, esp. Europe and the Western Hemisphere. *Also see* **Eastern.**

western, Western *Flm&Vid, LitArts, Rdio/TV* Novel, film, or television or radio program about frontier life in the American West.

Western swing *MusArts* Mix popular – particularly in Texas in the 1930s and early 1940s – of Texas fiddle music, traditional country music, big-band jazz, and Cajun styles performed on steel guitars, fiddles, and horns. COUNTRY SWING. <Bob Wills (1905-75, bndldr., sngwri.)> *Also see* **big band jazz, Country Music Styles, Jazz Styles.**

Westerns *Rdio/TV* Popular type of television network programming. *<Bonanza, Gunsmoke> Also see* **Television Shows.**

Westinghouse Electric Corporation *Rdio/TV* Cofounding company of **National Broadcasting Co,** and then owner of a radio and TV network. Westinghouse bought **CBS** in 1996 *Also see* **Broadcast Stations & Networks, RCA.**

wet blanket *Crit&Eval* One that discourages enjoyment or enthusiasm.

Wexler, Jerry (1917-, record co. exec.) *Mgt, RecA&S* Important record producer of **soul music** in the 1960s. In the 1950s, as a staff member of *Billboard,* he claimed to be the one who changed the name of the **race records chart** to rhythm and blues. Became a director of **Atlantic Record** in 1953 *Also see* **Ertegun Bros., Payola.**

WGA *Flm&Vid, HR&LR, Rdio/TV* **Writers Guild of America.** Labor union for writers in the fields of motion pictures, television, cable, radio and new technologies. Represents members in collective bargaining and other labor matters. Works to obtain adequate domestic and foreign copyright legislation and to promote better copyright relations between the United States and other countries. *Also see* **Guilds & Unions.**

What if? *InfoMgt* Premise on which most electronic spreadsheet programs operate. New values may be substituted to determine the resultant effect on other values.

What Makes Sammy Run? *Flm&Vid, LitArts* » **"Sammy Glick."**

What You See Is What You Get *InfoMgt* » **WYSIWYG**

wheeze *Crit&Eval* old joke.

whim *Crit&Eval* Sudden or capricious idea. FANCY

whimsy *Crit&Eval* **1** Odd or fanciful idea; a **whim. 2** Quaint or fanciful quality.

whistle-blower *Ethcs&Phil* Employee of a company, organization, or a government agency who reports, i.e, **blows the whistle,** to an outside authority about illegal activity. **False Claims Law** (aka Whistle-Blower Law) now protects the employee from employer retribution: "In the era of corporate 'downsizing,' with legions of laid-off workers, disgruntled former employees have often become whistle-blowers in cases of software piracy." — Lawrence M. Fisher (journ.) *Also see* **piracy.**

white, White *Cult&Soc* Member of a racial group of people having light skin coloration, esp. one of European origin. *Also see* **Black, Racial Designations.**

white ballet (baa-lay, Fr.) *Dnce* » **ballet blanc**

white blues *MusArts* » **Blues**

white collar *Eco&Fin, HR&LR* Relating to workers whose work usu. does not involve manual labor and who are often expected to dress with a degree of formality. *Also see* **blue collar, salaries, suits.**

white contract *LegAsp, PerfA&C* **Equity** or **LORT** contract between producer and **principal.** *Also see* **pink contract.**

white flight *Cult&Soc, HR&LR* Movement largely triggered by Supreme Court's 1954 decision to legally end racial segregation in U.S. schools. Hundreds of thousands of white families have either moved to "safer" suburbs or placed their children in private schools or academies leaving inner city schools without adequate financing or educational resources. [Has played particular havoc with school arts programs.] *Also see* ***Brown vs. Board of Education.***

white gospel music *MusArts* **1** Anglo-American religious music associated with evangelism and is based on the simple melodies of folk music. **2** "Commercial white gospel recordings have sacred texts and occasional imitations of black gospel singing. They are otherwise stylistically indistinguishable from pop, country, or rock." — *New Harvard Dictionary of Music Also see* **Gospel Music.**

white noise *Sci&Tech* Acoustical or electrical noise of which the intensity is the same at all frequencies within a given band.

white space *VA-Prntng, VisArts* Space on a page or poster not covered by print or graphic matter. *Also see* **quiet, silence.**

white trash *Cult&Soc* Disparaging term for a poor white person or poor white people. *Also see* **trash**.

White, E.B. (Elwyn Brooks White, 1899-1985, fictwri., critic, humorist, editor) *ArtPerf, Crit&Eval, LitArts* Contributed essays, editorials, and parodies to the *New Yorker*. He also wrote children's books, inc. *Charlotte's Web* (1952), and revised William Strunk Jr's 1918 writing manual, *The Elements of Style* (1959), which remains a classic of good taste and graceful writing. *Also see* **humorist, serious artist**.

whiteprint *VisArts* Photomechanical copy, usu. of a line drawing, in which black or colored lines appear on a white background.

whois *InfoMgt* Means of looking up names in a remote database. to find the "who" behind the **domain name**.

whole note *MusArts* Longest note in common use. *Also see* **Musical Notes**.

wholesale basis *RecA&S* Charge by a record company on what basis **royalties** are reckoned. *Also see* **retail list price**.

Wholesale Price Index (WPI) *Eco&Fin, EntreP* This **economic indicator** issued by the U.S. Dept. of Commerce measures prices at the wholesale level. It serves as a projection of possible inflation as an increase in wholesale prices can result in consumer price increases within 30 to 60 days.

wholesaler *Mktg* *Also see* **Distributors**.

whs. *Mktg* warehouse.

whsle *Mktg* wholesale

wide release *Flm&Vid* General release to most, if not all, markets. *Also see* **exclusive run**.

wide-angle lens *Flm&Vid* Lens that permits the camera to photograph a wider area than a normal lens. Side effect is its tendency to exaggerate perspective. SHORT LENS

Wide-Area Information Servers (WAIS) *InfoMgt»* **WAIS**

wide-area telecommunications *InfoMgt »* **WATS**

widescreen *Flm&Vid* Movie format exactly as shown in theaters but with black bars at top and bottom. *Also see* **DVD-Video, letterbox, pan & scan**.

widget *iMedia* combination of a graphic symbol and some program code to perform a specific function, e.g., a scroll-bar or button.

wigger *Cult&Soc* Derived from "nigger," which **rap** musicians have transformed from a term of derision to an all-purpose pronoun and term of endearment. Originated by white teen-agers in the San Francisco area who identify blackness with the power to generate fear. — Brent Staples (journ.)

wigmakers' gauze *Th-MakeUp* Thin, tough foundation material for wigs and beards.

wild line *Flm&Vid, RecA&S* Audio recorded without accompanying picture. When recording wild lines on the set, the camera is not rolled. Can also be recorded in a sound studio. WILD RECORDING, WILD TRACK

wild posting *Mktg* Unauthorized placement of posters advertising movies, concerts, dances, etc. on fences, walls, and other sites in high traffic areas.

wild recording *Flm&Vid, RecA&S »* **wild line**

wild sound *BcstJourn »* **ambient sound**

wild sound bite *Flm&Vid, RecA&S* Recorded sound segment, usu. recorded on-site. <factory noise, sirens, violent weather>, used in the edited film.

wild spot *Rdio/TV* **Spot** broadcast locally rather than in the body of a program.

wild track *Flm&Vid »* **wild line**

William Morris Agency (WMA) *Mgt* L.A.-based international talent and literary agency. Oldest talent agency in the U.S., founded in 1898. *Also see* **Talent Agencies**.

wind instrument *MusInstr* Musical instrument in which sound is produced by the movement of an enclosed column of air, i.e, the player's breath. <clarinet, harmonica, trumpet> *Also see* **horn**.

wind machine *Flm&Vid, PerfA&C* Powerful fan that simulates light breezes to zephyrs.

wind screen *Flm&Vid, RecA&S »* **wind sleeve**

wind sleeve *Flm&Vid, RecA&S* Light porous plastic covering for a microphone to diminish wind noise.

windfall *Eco&Fin* Sudden, unexpected piece of good fortune or personal gain.

window *InfoMgt* Portion of the computer screen dedicated to some specific purpose. Windows allow the user to treat the computer display screen like a desktop where various files can remain open simultaneously.

window income *Eco&Fin, Mktg* Money collected at the **box office**. *Also see* **audit stub**.

window-dressing *Crit&Eval* Means of improving appearances or creating a falsely favorable impression.

window-dressing *Mktg* Decorative exhibition of retail merchandise in store windows.

Windows *InfoMgt* Computer screen display using icon commands **trademarked** by **Microsoft** based on a similar system originated by **Xerox** and further developed by **Apple Computer**. *Also see* **Windoze, Wintel**.

Windoze *InfoMgt* "Windows" as referred to by Macintosh addicts.

winds *MusInstr »* **wind instruments**

wing *Dnce* tap dance step.

wing *PerfA&C* Area of stage hidden from view of the audience by masking with a flat or curtain. *Also see* **leg**.

wing it *ArtPerf,PerfA&C* **1** To act without having learned one's lines, relying on prompting or a quick glance at one's part before coming onstage. **2** To say or do something without preparation, forethought, or sufficient information or experience. **3** Improvise.

wing spot *PerfA&C* **Spotlight** located in a wing area. *Also see* **Stage Lighting**.

wings *PerfA&C* **1** Backstage area on either side of a **proscenium** stage. **2** Tall cloth-covered frames or narrow unframed drops that are placed on either side of the stage, parallel with the **proscenium arch**, to prevent the audience from seeing backstage.

Wintel *InfoMgt* Windows + Intel

wipe *Flm&Vid* Another **transition** option whereby a portion or all of one image is replaced by another. The second sequence wipes the first one from the screen.

WIPO *IntelProp, LegAsp* **World Intellectual Property Organization**, one of the 16 specialized agencies of the United Nations systems of organizations, is an intergovernmental organization in Geneva, Switz. It is responsible for the promotion of the protection of **intellectual property** throughout the world through cooperation among States (over 170 countries in Aug. 1998) and for the administration of various multilateral treaties dealing with the legal and administrative aspects of intellectual property. **wire** *InfoMgt* Pin in the print head of a computer printer.

wire capture *BcstJourn* Ability of a news computer system to record, store, and display wire service stories when needed for data.

wire recorder *RecA&S* Preceded tape recorders, ca. 1940s. *Also see* **Music Playback Devices**.

wire service *Journ* News-gathering organization that distributes syndicated copy electronically to subscribers. *Also see* **news service**.

Wired *InfoMgt, Journ* Recipient of the 1994 **National Magazine Award For General Excellence** by the **American Society of Magazine Editors** (ASME)

wireframe *iMedia* **1** Underlying structure of a **3D** object. **2** Prototype for an interactive media product.

wireless *Rdio/TV* **1** Radio telegraph or radiotelephone system. **2** (Brit.) Radio.

wireless cable *InfoMgt* Transmitting cable TV programming via microwave frequencies.

wireless mic, wireless mike *RecA&S* Combination of a minitransmitter and **mic** that can be concealed on or about the performer. *Also see* **Microphones**.

Wirephoto *InfoMgt* **Trademark** used for a photograph electrically transmitted over telephone wires.

wires *PA-Variety* System of strings employed in manipulating puppets in a show.

wirewalker *PA-Variety* Acrobat who walks on a wire tightrope.

wisdom *Crit&Eval* **1** Understanding of what is true, right, and lasting. **2** Good judgment, common sense. **3** Learning, erudition. "Art, at its greatest, is nothing but the expression of wisdom. Wisdom… teaches us to see something outside ourselves that is higher than what is within us, and gradually, through contemplation and admiration, to come to resemble it." — **George Sand**

wisdom *Ethcs&Phil* Highest of the intellectual virtues, characterized by knowledge of the whole of things, and thus reserved for the gods in its fullest sense. Human wisdom approximates to that of the gods, though in **Socrates's** view human wisdom consists in the full appreciation of our lack of knowledge. Modern ideas of wisdom sometimes recognize an ethical aspect and a "scientific" aspect as together constituting wisdom when each is fully developed.

wisecrack *Crit&Eval* Offhand, flippant remark. *Also see* **wit**.

wit *Crit&Eval* **1** Ability to perceive and express in an ingeniously humorous manner the relationship between seemingly incongruous or disparate things: "Wit has truth in it; **wisecracking** is simply calisthenics with words." —**Dorothy Parker 2** One skilled in repartee. **3** Person of exceptional intelligence.

witch-hunt *Ethcs&Phil, Law&Pol* Investigation carried out ostensibly to uncover subversive activities but actually used to harass and undermine those with differing views. <**HUAC, Hollywood Ten, McCarthy** hearings> *Also see* **blacklist, McCarthyism**.

with *Flm&Vid, Mktg,PerfA&C* This word is used in programs and advertisements immediately below the title of a production, to identify a featured actor or attraction.

withdraw *Eco&Fin* Remove money from an account.

WJZRdio / TV Base radio station of **NBC's blue network** *Also see* **Broadcast Stations & Networks**.

WL *Sci&Tech* **wavelength**. *Also see* **wave length**.

WMA *Mgt* William Morris Agency.

WNACRdio / TV » **network radio** *Also see* **Broadcast Stations & Networks**.

Women's Wear Daily *Fashn* » **WWD**

wood block *VisArts, VA-Prntng* » **woodcut**

woodblock *MusInstr* Hollow block of wood struck with a drumstick. *Also see* **Little Instruments**.

woodcut *VisArts, VA-Prntng* **1** Block of wood on whose surface a design for printing is engraved along the grain. **2** Print made from a woodcut. WOODBLOCK, WOODPRINT

woodshed *MusArts* To practice on a musical instrument.

Woodstock Nation *Cult&Soc, MusArts* "It's easy to decry the commercialism of this onslaught and contrast it with innocence of Woodstock '69. But what's also been lost in the intervening '25 years is the simple thrill of discovering cultural **phenomena** by ourselves, without being lashed into submission by hypesters. These days it's hard to go to a hit movie or attend a pop concert without feeling we've seen it before we arrived. If you're looking for another reason for the **O.J. story** is so popular, consider the fact that it's one major American drama that caught the public by surprise, with no plot twists divulged in advance and no product tie-ins to upstage the show." — **Frank Rich**

Woodward, Bob (1943-, journ., ed., n-fict.) *ArtPerf, Journ, LitArts* With Carl Bernstein, his colleague on the *Washington Post*, helped expose the **Watergate** scandal which caused President **Nixon** to resign (1974) <*All the President's Men* (1974), *Wired: The Short Life and Fast Times of John Belushi*(1984)> *Also see* **Ben Bradlee, Carl Bernstein, on deep background**.

woodwind, woodwinds *MusInstr* **1** Wind instrument in which sound is produced by the vibration of reeds in or by the passing of air across the mouthpiece. <bassoon, clarinet, flute, oboe, recorder, saxophone> **2 Section** of a band or an orchestra composed of woodwind instruments. WOODWIND PLAYER *Also see* **Musical Instrument Families, reeds**.

woofer *RecA&S* Loudspeaker that reproduces low **frequencies**. *Also see* **tweeter**.

Woolf, Virginia (Adeline Virginia Stephen, 1882-1941, Brit. critic, fictwri.) *ArtPerf, Crit&Eval, LitArts* Her works include literary criticism and **fiction** written in an **experimental** stream-of-consciousness style, novels. <*Mrs. Dalloway* (1925), *To the Lighthouse* (1927), and collections of essays, *A Room of One's Own* (1929)> *Also see* **female writers**.

word *InfoMgt* Set of **bits** constituting the smallest unit of addressable memory.

word of mouth *Crit&Eval, Mktg* Voluntary, usu. favorable, non-sponsored opinion about a product or a service. <Word of mouth kept the show open longer than the critics had forecast> *Also see* **buzz**.

word processing *InfoMgt* Creation, input, editing, and production of documents and texts by means of computer systems.

word processor *InfoMgt* Software program that provides extensive functionality for manipulating text.

word size *InfoMgt* Number of bits processed at one time.

words *LitArts, MusArts* lyrics. *Also see* **m., w**.

wordsmith *LitArts* **1** Fluent and prolific writer, usu. a **professional**. **2** Expert on words.

work *Crit&Eval* To gratify, cajole, or enchant artfully for the purpose of influencing. <The politician worked the crowd> *Also see* **working the room**.

work *VisArts* **1** To shape or forge. <work metal into a sculpture> **2** To make or decorate by needlework. <work a sampler>

work, works *Crit&Eval* **1** Artistic creation, such as a painting, sculpture, or literary or musical composition; a work of art. **2** Output of a writer, an artist, or a musician considered or collected as a whole.

work, works *IntelProp* Refers to the authors' original creations that the copyright laws protect. Seven works categories are: (1) literary works, (2) musical works (inc. accompanying words), (3) dramatic works (inc. accompanying music), (4) Pantomimes and choreographic works, (5) pictorial, graphic, and sculptural works, (6) motion pictures and other **audio/visual works**, and (7) sound recordings. *Also see* **copyright forms**.

work ethic *Ethcs&Phil, HR&LR* Set of values based on the moral virtues of hard work and diligence.

work in progress (WIP) *LitArts, MusArts, PerfA&C, VisArts* Artistic concept in the process of being created, Yet incomplete artistic, theatrical, or musical work, sometimes made available for public scrutiny.

work made for hire *HR&LR, IntelProp* **1** Work prepared by an employee within the scope of her or his employment. **2** Work specially ordered or **commissioned** from an independent contractor for use as a contribution to a collective work, as a part of a motion picture or other **audio/visual work**, as a translation, as a supplementary work, as a compilation, as an instructional text, as a test, an answer material for a test, or as an atlas, if the parties agree in a written instrument signed by them that the works shall be considered as a work for hire. — **Copyright Application Form TX 3** Employer considered the author of the work and thereby owns rights. WORK FOR HIRE.

Work Projects Administration (WPA) *Law&Pol* » **WPA**

work song *MusArts* One sung to accompany work, typically having a steady rhythm. *Also see* **Songs**.

work stoppage *HR&LR* Cessation of work by a group of employees as a means of protest.

work up *Crit&Eval* **1** To intensify gradually. <The dancers work up to a wild finish> **2** To develop or formulate by mental or physical effort. <work up a comedy routine>

work-in-process *EntreP* Inventories that a company uses while in the assembly or transformation process.

workarounds *InfoMgt* Minor **tweaking** tricks used by experienced computer operators and developers to alleviate a particular problem.

workers' compensation *HR&LR* Payments required by law to be made to an employee who is injured or disabled in connection with work.

workforce diversity *EntreP* Differences among employees in terms of such dimensions as gender, age, and race.

working capital *E&F-Acc* **Current assets** minus **current liabilities** measures business's ability to meet its short-term obligations with current assets.

working capital (current assets) *EntreP* Liquid assets that can be converted into cash within a company's operating cycle.

working class *Cult&Soc* Part of society consisting of those who work for wages. <manual or industrial laborers> *Also see* **blue collar**.

working delegate *HR&LR* » **business agent**

Working Group on Intellectual Property Rights *IntelProp* Group chaired by the Commissioner of Patents and Trademarks is examining the implications of possible changes to the current Copyright Act. According to the Group, **intellectual property** laws need to adapt to technological innovation.

working papers *E&F-Acc* Documents prepared and used by accountants to organize their work and support the information in the **financial statements**.

working sketch *Fashn* Simple, first rough sketch of a garment design.

working the room *PerfA&C* Way that a **comedian** works on an audience: challenging it, shocking it, kidding it, getting it to laugh and to feel free for a time. *Also see* **empathic response**.

working title *Flm&Vid, LitArts* Temporary title for a media project.

workload *HR&LR* Amount of work assigned to or expected from a worker in a specified time period.

Works Progress Administration (WPA) *Law&Pol* » **WPA**

worksheet *E&F-Acc* Type of **working paper** used as a preliminary step and tool in the preparation of **financial statements**.

workstation *InfoMgt* Area, as in an office, outfitted with equipment and furnishings for one worker, often inc. a computer or computer terminal.

World Intellectual Property Organization *IntelProp, LegAsp* » **WIPO**

World Trade Organization (WTO) *EntreP* Organization that oversees **GATT** and other international trade agreements.

World War I (WWI) (1914-18) *Cult&Soc* Great Britain, France, Russia, Belgium, Italy, Japan, the United States, and other allies defeated Germany, Austria-Hungary, Turkey, and Bulgaria.

World War II (WWII) (1939-45) *Cult&Soc* Great Britain, France, the Soviet Union, the United States (1941-45), China, and other allies defeated Germany, Italy, and Japan.

World Wide Web *iMedia, InfoMgt* Type of file transfer over the **Internet** that has the capability to display graphics, sound, video, and other media in addition to text. Generally credited as the concept of researcher Tim Berners-Lee who developed the first practical system in 1989 at the European Laboratory for Particle Research.

World Wide Web Consortium (W3C) *iMedia* Organization that creates and recommends standardized client and server protocols, specifications, guidelines, software, and tools that enable on-line communications on the Internet.

world-class *Crit&Eval* **1** Ranking among the foremost in the world. **2** Great, as in importance, concern, or notoriety.

wow *MusArts, RecA&S* **1** Extra **oscillation** in the lower ranges. **2** Slow variation in **pitch** resulting from variations in the speed of the sound reproduction equipment.

wowed *Crit&Eval* Have a strong, positive effect on an audience.

WPA *Law&Pol* **Works Progress Administration** (1935) name changed in 1939 to **Work Projects Administration**. One of President F.D.R.'s anti **Great Depression** projects that gave employment to millions of unemployed inc. artists and performers. » **Federal Theatre** *Also see* **Federal Agencies and Statutes**.

WPI *Eco&Fin* **Wholesale Price Index**. *Also see* **economic indicators**.

wrangler *Flm&Vid* » **animal handler**

wrap *also* **wraparound** *BcstJourn* Field story format that differs from the **voicer** in that is contains at least one, and usu. more, **actualities** Sometimes "wraparound" is used for any story in which a presenter's voice wraps around an actuality.

wrap *Flm&Vid* Term indicating the end of a production or session. <That's a wrap>

wrap *VA-Prntng* Four-page **insert** wrapped around a **signature** in the binding process.

wri. *ArtPerf, LitArts* **writer**.

writ *LegAsp* Written order issued by a court, commanding the party to whom it is addressed to perform or cease performing a specified act.

write *InfoMgt* Enter information and instructions into the computer's memory. *Also see* **RAM**, **read**.

write down *Crit&Eval* **1** To disparage in writing. **2** To write in a conspicuously simple or condescending style. <He felt he had to write down to his students>

write down *Eco&Fin* To reduce value or price.

write home about *Crit&Eval* Term used negatively about something not to brag about. <The play was okay but nothing to write home about>

write off *E&F-Acc* **1** To reduce to zero the **book value** of an asset that has become worthless. **2** To cancel from accounts as a loss.

write up *Eco&Fin* To overstate the value of assets.

write-down *E&F-Acc* Reduction of the entered value of an asset.

write-down *Journ* To disparage in writing.

write-off *Eco&Fin* **1** Cancellation of an item in account books, the amount canceled or lost. **2** Reduction or **depreciation** of the entered value of an item.

write-up *E&F-Acc* Intentional overevaluation of a corporation's assets.

write-up *Journ* Published account, review, or notice, esp. a favorable one.

writer (wri.) *ArtPerf, LitArts, MusArts* **1** Composer or lyricist of a musical composition. **2** Author of a literary composition. **3** One who writes as an occupation.

writer's block *ArtPerf, LitArts* Temporary psychological inability to begin or continue writing.

writer-for-hire *IntelProp* » **work made for hire**

writers *Cult&Soc, "VisArts"* **graffiti** artists.

writers *Flm&Vid, PA-Variety, Rdio/TV* Refers to comedy writers, radio and TV writers, and screenwriters. "Whereas most comics are privately contemptuous of their writers (because they resent being dependent on them for material), [Jackie] Gleason (Herbert John Gleason, 1916-87, film/TV/vaude act., comic, cond.) displayed his contempt openly." — Jack Winter (**broadcast media** critic)

Writers Guild of America (WGA) *Flm&Vid, HR&LR, Rdio/TV* » **WGA**

writeup *BcstJourn* Broadcast story sentence immediately preceding a bite. It is also called the **lead-in**, the **intro**, the **throw line**, or the **ID**.

WS *BcstJourn* wide shot » **establishing shot**

WSM (Nashville) *Rdio/TV* » **Grand Ole Opry**

wunderkind (voondarkind, Ger.; *plural*, wunderkinder) *ArtPerf, Crit&Eval* One of remarkable talent or ability who achieves great acclaim at an early age; child prodigy *Origin* From German "wunder" = wonder, + "kind" = child.

WWD *Fashn* **Women's Wear Daily**. Leading trade paper for the fashion industry.

WWI *Cult&Soc* World War I

WWII *Cult&Soc* World War II

WWW *iMedia* » **World Wide Web**

WYSIWYG *iMedia, InfoMgt* What You See Is What You Get. Term common to word processors and desktop publishers: what appears on the computer monitor is what will be printed.

- X -

X » **cross**

x-axis *iMedia* **1** Horizontal plane. **2** 3D and graphics: Editing an object's x-axis alters it's placement horizontally in space (left to right)

X-rated *Flm&Vid* Originally a movie rating for "adults only," it is now applied automatically to **porn**, and the rating "NC-17" (no children under 17) is applied to movie goers over 17, or 18, or 21 depending on the tolerance level of the community.

X/Open Company, Lt. *InfoMgt* » **UNIX**

xerography *VA-Prntng* Dry photographic or photocopying process in which a negative image formed by a resinous powder on an electrically charged plate is electrically transferred to and thermally fixed as positive on a paper or other copying surface. *Also see* **photocopier**, **Xerox**.

Xerox *VA-Prntng* **Trademark** used for a photocopying process or machine employing **xerography**.

XHTML *iMedia* Reformulation of HTML 4.01 in XML that can be viewed, edited, and validated with standard XML-conforming applications; maintains the simplicity of HTML yet allows access to more powerful capabilities of XML.

XML *iMedia* » **Extensible Markup Language**

xylophone *MusInstr* **Mallet percussion** instrument consisting of a mounted row of metal or wooden bars graduated in length to sound a **chromatic scale**, played with two small mallets. XYLOPHONIST *Also see* **Musical Instrument Families**.

- Y -

y-axis *iMedia* **1** Vertical plane. **2** 3D and graphics: Editing an object's y-axis alters its placement vertically in space (up or down)

Y2K *InfoMgt* Year 2000 when it was thought that some **myopic** computer programs would propel the world into Utter Chaos or back to 1900.— Chicken Little.

X
Y
Z

yada yada yada *Genl* Et cetera and so forth. <Strike the set, kill the lights, and yada yada yada>

Yahoo *InfoMgt* Most visited Web site providing access to Internet. Also *see* **search engine**, **portals**.

YAI *Mktg*» **Young Audiences, Inc.**

yak (yack, Yinglish) *Crit&Eval* Chatter away, gossip.

Yardbird *ArtPerf, MusArts* **Charlie Parker**.

yard goods *Fashn* » **piece goods**.

yare (yahr) *Crit&Eval* Agile, lively. <Katharine Hepburn (» **censorship**) as described in *The Philadelphia Story* (play and film)>

year-end-giving *Fndng* Practice among many charitable organizations for seeking gifts, usu. via mail campaigns, in the last two or three months of a calendar year on the premise that prospects will take timely advantage of opportunities to secure tax deductions.

Yeats, William Butler (1865-1939, Irish dram., poet, arts mgr.) *LitArts, TheatArts* Considered among the greatest poets of the 20th century. Founder of the **Irish National Theatre** at the **Abbey Theatre**, Dublin, he wrote many short plays. His poetry ranges from early love lyrics to the complex symbolist works of his later years. Awarded the 1923 **Nobel Prize** for literature. *Also see* **center**.

yellow card *PerfA&C* Request from a touring **company** asking a local labor union to furnish stagehands.

yellow journalism *Ethcs&Phil, Journ* Journalism that exploits, distorts, or exaggerates the news to create sensations and attract readers. *Origin* From the use of yellow ink in printing "Yellow Kid," a cartoon strip in the *New York World*.

Yiddish theatre *Cult&Soc, TheatArts* Plays featuring Yiddish culture and dialogue.

yoke *Fashn* **1** Piece of a garment that is closely fitted, either around the neck and shoulders or at the hips, and from which an unfitted or gathered part of the garment is hung. **2** Usually small flat panels of fabric at the shoulder, waist, or midriff.

yoke *RecA&S* Series of two or more magnetic recording heads fastened.

Young Audiences, Inc. (YAI) *Mgt* **Nonprofit** with branches in several American cities that promotes and provides arts education.

young room *PerfA&C* Venue suitable for young audiences.

youth culture *Cult&Soc* "Youth culture made mockery a **lifestyle**, and *Hair* brought it into show business."— **John Lahr**.

youth market *Mktg* Set of all actual or potential, under-adult age consumers of specific products.

- Z -

z-axis *iMedia* **1** depth **2 3D** and graphics: Editing an object's z-axis alters its depth (either forward or back)

Zadeh, Lofti (emeritus prof., computer sci., U. Calif-Berkeley) *InfoMgt* Father of **fuzzy logic**, he published the paper *Fuzzy Sets* in 1965 that formally developed multivalued set theory.

zaftig, zoftig (Yinglish) *Crit&Eval* full-bosomed.

Zappa, Frank (1940-1993, arr-comp, gtr, prod., social activist) *ArtPerf, Mgt, MusArts* One of the most accomplished pop/rock/fusion composers of the rock era. His talent marked by a sharp gift of satire and humor; uniquely unmarked by drugs. *Also see* **P.M.R.C.**

zarzuela *MusArts, TheatArts* Form of Spanish musical theater that preceded the American and English "musical comedy." *Origin* In the 17th century as an aristocratic entertainment with mythological or heroic themes. Revived in the mid-19th century as witty and satirical treatments of every day life and included folk music, dance, and improvisation.

zeal *Crit&Eval* Enthusiastic devotion to a cause, an ideal, or a goal. *Also see* **perfervid**.

zero population growth (ZPG) *Mktg* Limiting of population increase to the number of live births needed to replace the existing population.

zero-base *Eco&Fin* Having each expenditure or item justified as to need or cost.

Zeus (Greek Mythology) *Cult&Soc* Principal god of the Greek **pantheon**, ruler of the heavens, and father of other gods and mortal heroes. *Also see* **Jupiter, Muses**.

Ziegfeld Follies *TheatArts* Extravagant **musicals** produced annually from 1907 to 1931 (except 1926, 1928, and 1929) by Florenz Ziegfeld (1869-1932) *Also see* **revue**.

Ziegfeld girl *ArtPerf, TheatArts* **Showgirl** featured in a Ziegfeld Follies production.

zine *Cult&Soc* Magazine usu. produced at low cost, e.g., photocopies. <Skinzine is a magazine for **skinheads**>

Zip Coon *Cult&Soc* A character impersonating a city slave, the dandy dressed in the latest fashion, as performed in **blackface minstrelsy**. *Also see* **Jim Crow**.

zither *MusInstr* Instrument composed of a flat sound box with about 30 to 40 strings stretched over it and played horizontally with the fingertips or a **plectrum**.

zone of silence *Rdio/TV* Geographical area between two transmitting/receiving points where radio signals cannot be heard.

zoom *Flm&Vid* Apparent motion of the camera toward or away from its object. <zoom in, zoom out>

zoom box *InfoMgt* Small box in the top-right corner of the title bar of some **windows**. Clicking the zoom box resizes the window.

zoom shot *Flm&Vid* Lens of variable focal length that permits the **cinematographer** to change between wide angle and **telephoto** shots in one continuous movement, often rapidly moving the audience in or out of a scene.

zoot-suiters *Cult&Soc* Cool cats of the late 1930s uniformed in their tourniquet-tight cuffs, baggy, **high-draped pants**, knee-length jacket with wide lapels, wide, wide padded shoulders, and the inevitable long, looping watch chain. Credit for creating and naming the zoot suit claimed by Harold Fox (1910-96), a Chicago clothier and sometime big-band trumpeter. "The reet pleat, the reave sleeve, the ripe stripe, the stuff cuff, and the drape shape"... from the "boogie-woogie rhyme time" of the [late 1930s to mid 1940s] — Robert McG. Thomas Jr. (journ.) *Also see* **jitterbug**.

ZPG *Mktg* **zero population growth**. Condition where population increase (births plus immigration) equal population decrease (deaths plus emigration)

zydeco music *MusArts* Folk/pop music of southwest Louisiana developed on parallel and crossover tracks by **Black Creoles** and **Cajuns**. It combines French folk tunes, Afro-Caribbean rhythms and styles, and a strong dose of **rural blues**. Instrumentation varies but authenticity minimally demands **diatonic** accordion, fiddle, guitar, and percussion, e.g., drum set, **washboard**, etc. CAJUN MUSIC, FRENCH-CREOLE MUSIC, CREOLE-ZYDECO, SOUTHWEST LOUISIANA MUSIC

DAPME

X

Y

Z

Key to Index of Topics

Note. All entries in the Main Text are classified (A-Z) under one or more of these 37 topics.

TOPIC	EXPLANATION and RELATED TOPICS	SEE PAGES (column)

Aes&Creat — AESTHETICS & CREATIVITY. One of the three Inner Forces of The Arts Dynamic©. Re nature and expression of beauty. Also see *Crit&Eval, Ethcs* 229 (1)

ArtPerf — ARTIST/PERFORMER. One of the four Principal elements of The Arts Dynamic©. Re nature and deportment of the artist/performer, and supporting guilds/unions, and orgs. 229 (1)

BcstJourn — BROADCAST JOURNALISM. Entries (preceded by an asterisk* within *Journ*) re the practice of news reporting via radio and television Also see *iMedia, InfoMgt, VA-Prntng.* .... **(See "Journalism.")**

Crit&Eval — CRITICISM & EVALUATION. One of the three elements of the Inner Forces of The Arts Dynamic©. Also see *Aes&Creat,Ethcs* . Re words and terms, persons and institutions involved in criticism and evaluation. Also includes CRITIC/EVALUATOR, one of the four Principal elements of The Arts Dynamic©..231 (2)

Cult&Soc — CULTURE & SOCIETY. One of the four elements of the Outer Forces of The Arts Dynamic©. Re cultural diversity, ethnicity, gender, origins, race, religion, supporting orgs., and venues. 234 (4)

Dnce — DANCE. Re dance, choreography, performance, presentation, supporting orgs., and venues Also see *PerfA&C.*...235 (3)

Eco&Fin — ECONOMICS & FINANCE. One of the four elements of the Outer Forces of The Arts Dynamic©. Re financial management, financial markets, imports/exports, indicators, investments, regulatory and supporting orgs. Also see *Fndng, Mktg.* Includes *E&F-Acc* 236 (1)

E&F-Acc — ECONOMICS & FINANCE-Accounting. Entries (preceded by an asterisk) re accounting principles and practices. 236 (1)

EntreP — ARTS ENTREPRENEURSHIP. Entries relate to all aspects of starting an arts based for-profit or not-for-profit business, inc. planning, legal requirements, organization, organizational and sales strategies, accounting, personnel, marketing, regulatory issues, and operations. Also see *Eco&Fin, Eco&Fin-A, Mgt.* 238 (3)

Ethcs — ETHICS & PHILOSOPHY. One of three elements of the Inner Forces of The Arts Dynamic©. Re aspects of Ethcs , philosophy, and religion relevant to the understanding of the arts and arts management. Also see *Aes&Creat, Crit&Eval.* 240 (2)

Fashn — FASHION/RETAIL MANAGEMENT. Entries so related. Also see *Mktg, VisArts.* 240 (5)

Flm&Vid — FILM & VIDEO. Re movie production: arts and crafts, design and technical aspects, and supporting orgs. Also see *BcstJourn* (See *RecA&S* for film/video audio technology.) 241 (4)

Fndng — FUND RAISING. Re development, corporate sponsorship, grant proposals, and supporting orgs. Also see *Eco&Fin, Mgt.*...244 (1)

Genl — GENERAL INTEREST. Entries include words, terms, and institutions that apply to all elements of AEMM..244 (3)

HR&LR — HUMAN RESOURCES & LABOR RELATIONS. Re job-related discrimination, guilds and unions, regulatory agencies, and supporting orgs. Also see *ArtPerf, Law&Pol, Mgt.*...............................245 (1)

iMedia — INTERACTIVE MULTIMEDIA. Entries relate to the production, critique, and management of media that require dialogue between creator and audience, and which respond to the action or inaction of participant(s); media which are participant-centered, dynamic, responsive, adaptive and engaging.......................................246 (1)

InfoMgt — INFORMATION MANAGEMENT. Re those terms techniques, and systems that affect the flow and management of information, inc.: computer and information science, the Internet and on-line media, and regulatory and supporting orgs. Also see *iMedia* 247 (4)

IntelProp — INTELLECTUAL PROPERTY. Re copyrights, patents, trademarks – in all media – and regulatory and supporting orgs. Also see *Law&Pol, LegalAsp.* 251 (1)

Journ — JOURNALISM. Re gathering and dissemination of news and criticism/evaluation via various print media <newspapers, magazines, newsletters, journals> and supporting orgs. 251 (4)

Law&Pol — LAW & POLITICS. Re arts and arts mgt. as affected by laws, gov. agencies, regulatory bodies, Bill of Rights (censorship, freedom of speech, etc.), and politics and politicians. Also see *LegAsp*..........252 (5)

LegalAsp — LEGAL ASPECTS. Re arts and arts mgt. as affected by case law, contracts, procedures, terms, and regulatory and supporting orgs. Also see *IntelProp, Law&Pol.*..253 (4)

LitArts — LITERARY ARTS. Entries relate to drama, fiction and non-fiction literature, librettos, playwriting, poetry; radio-TV scripts, screenwriting, and supporting orgs. Also see *Journ.* (See *MusArts* for lyrics and songwriting.) 254 (4)

Undergraduate and graduate students who choose an **Area of Concentration** (major or minor) should pay particular attention to Topics related to their field.

AREA OF CONCENTRATION	DIRECTLY RELATED TOPICS
Arts Entrepreneurship/Small Business Mgt.	*Eco&Fin, Entrep, LegAsp, Mktg, Mgt*
Fashion/Retail Management	*Fashn, Mktg, VisArts*
Media Management	*BcstJourn, Flm&Vid, iMedia, InfoMgt, Journ, LitArts*
Music Business	*MusArts, MusInstr, RecA&S*
Performing Arts Management	*Dnce, PerfA&C, TheatArts, PA-Variety*
(Sports Entertainment)	*SportsEnt*
Visual Arts Management	*iMedia, , VisArts*

The Arts & Business Dynamic©

Undergraduate students are expected to have a general understanding of The Arts & Business Dynamic© particularly the function of the Arts Manager/Entrepreneur in relation to the Artist/Performer and the Audience/Market. Graduate students are expected to be have a working knowledge of all aspects of The Arts & Business Dynamic© and thus be able to apply its elements to the AEMM graduate curriculum.

DAPME

Index to Topics

Each DAPME entry is classified by one or more topics. (For descriptions and page references, see the two previous pages.)

Key
- Names of persons are shown second name first. except after the symbol "»." that indicates the entry in which the person's name is mentioned.
- » See entry indicated

lightweight
like
limbo
limelight
linear
lingo
lip service
literalism
lively
logic
look
lotus land
lounge lizard
love
low profile
lowest common
    denominator
lucid
lulu
luminary
lump in throat
lurid
lush
macabre
macher
magic
Maher, James T. »
    theatre
Mailer, Norman
main man
make-believe
maladaptive
malpractice
manner-means-object
mannerism
mano a mano
manq
marginal
Marsalis, Wynton
Marxism
masquerade
mass
mass entertainment
material
matinee idol
maturity
maudlin
maven
mawkish
MCANA
means
medieval, mediaeval
mediocre
mediocrity
megalomania
megillah
melee
mellifluous
mellow
melodious
melodramatic
memorabilia
Mencken, H.L.
mentor
mentsh
meshugaas
meshugge
mesmeric
mesmerize
metamorphoses
Mill, John Stuart
Milton, John » argument
mimic
mind's eye
mind-blowing
mind-boggling
mindset, mind-set
minimalism

mitzve
mockery
mode
moderne
modernism
modernity
modest
monitor
monolith
monologue, monolog
morbid
mot juste
motility
mouse
muckraker
multimedia
mummery
music critic
Music Critics Association
    of North America
musical
musical chairs
musicality
myopic
mystery
nail
naive
name-drop
narcissism
narrative
National Book Awards
National Book Critics
    Circle
National Information
    Infrastructure
National Medal of Arts
natty
NBCC
ne plus ultra
nebech, neb
neophyte
nerd, nurd
never-never land
New Age
New Criticism
newsmonger
newsy
nexus
nickel-and-dime
NII
nitty-gritty
nix
non sequitur
nostalgia
novice
nuance
nudnik, nudnick
nurd
obfuscate
object
objective correlative
objet d'art
obloquy
obsolescent
obsolete
ofay
off
old hat
old school
old-fashioned
old-line
Olympian
on
on its ear
on the cutting edge
on the take
on-stream
one-dimensional

one-liner
one-shot
one-up
open season
option
Oreo
orgiastic
orgy
ornate
orthodox
Orwellian
osmosis
ostentatious
out
over the top
over-the-hill
paean
pagan
page-turner
palette
palpable
pan
panache
panegyric
paparazzi
paperwork, paper work
par excellence
paradigm
paradox
paragon
paranoia
paraprofessional
Pareles, Jon
Parker, Dorothy
partisan
pass
passé
passion
pathos
patois
pavement
pay dirt
pay dues
pay the piper
PC
peer
pejorative
perfervid
peripety
pers.
personality
phenomena
phenomenon
philistine
philology
philos.
philosophy
photogene
photogenic
picture
pie-in-the-sky
piece
pièce de résistance
piece of work
piquant
pique
pixy, pixie
pizzazz, pizzaz
plain vanilla
platform
platitude
Platonic
platonic
play games
play it by ear
play-act
Pleasants, Henry

plethora
plot holes
poetic justice
poetic license
poetics
poignant
point of view
polemic
politic
political correctness
polyglot
porn
pornography
Porter, Katherine Anne »
    communication
poseur
power
pragma
pragmatism
precedent
précis
prejudice
prescience
prestigious
pretentious
priceless
pride
prig
prim
prima donna
prima facie
privacy
pro
prodigy
production
prof.
professional
professional critic
project
prolific
property
prosaic
prose
proselytize
protean
prude
prurient
pseudo-
psyche
psychedelic
psychic
public opinion
puff
puritanism
push the envelope
putz
quantifiable
quiet
quintessential
quip
quirk
quiver
quotation
quotidian
radical
rail
rake
Ransom, John Crowe
rant
rapt
rapturous
rara avis
raspberry
rat pack
rationale
rave
raw talent
razz

razzle-dazzle
razzmatazz
reactionary
ready-made
ready-made art
realism
realist
reality
really up
redundant
regeneration
regulation
reject
rejection
rejection slip
Renaissance
renaissance
rendition
repartee
reproduction
resource
resplendent
responsive
retro
retrospective
rev.
revel
review
reviewer
revisionist
revolutionary
rhetoric
Rich, Frank
right wing
right-on
rip-off
risqué
road dog
robot
roller coasters
romantic
romantic, Romantic
romanticism, Romanti-
    cism
rote
Rothstein, Edward » folk
    music, performance art
run-of-the-mill
rush
ruthless
saccharine
Safire, William »
    skanking
Sahl, Mort » HUAC
"Sammy Glick"
sanctify
Sand, George
sanguine
Sartre, Jean Paul
savvy
schadenfreude
schizophrenia
schlep, schlepper
Schlesinger Jr., Arthur
    M. » totalitarian
schlock, shlock
schmooze
schnook
school
school of thought
Schuller, Gunther »
    third-stream
scintilla
scoop
screed
screwball
scribble
Scully, Vincent

restructured
*retail method of
    inventory
*retained earnings
retire
*return on assets
*return on equity
*return on total assets
*revenue
*revenue expenditure
*reversing entry
risk transfer
rolling break
rollover
ruthlessness
S&P 500
*salaries
Salary Reduction Plan
*sales
*sales discount
*sales returns &
    allowances
*sales revenues
SE
seat
SEC
Securities and Exchange
    Commission
seed capital
seed funding
seed money
self-insurance
sell short
selling expenses
*service units
share, shares
shareholders' equity
Sherman Antitrust Act
*shipping point
short sale
short-term
*short-term investments
shortfall
*simple interest
single purpose plan
*single-step form
skim
skimming
sliding scale
*Social Security tax
socialism
sole proprietor
Sound Recording Fund
spec., spec
specific industry
    economic indicators
speculate
speculative risk
spinoff, spin-off
stakeholder
Standard & Poor
Standard & Poor's Index
standing plans
start-up
stat.
*state merit-ratings
*State Unemployment
State Unemployment
    Tax
*statement
*statement of cash flows
*statement of changes in
    financial position
*statement of financial
    condition
*statement of operations
*Statements
statistics

stock exchange
stock market
Stock Market Indexes
    and Averages
stockholders
stockholders equity
straight-line
strategic planning
"Strong" Dollar
Subchapter S corporation
subsidiary company
subsidy
supply-side
support and revenue
surplus
*SUTA
*systems analysts
*T-Accounts
*target rate
*Tax Reform Act of 1986
temp
*temporary account
temporary employee
theory of games
tight money
time-of-day pricing
top-heavy
*total asset turnover
total support and
    revenue
Tourism and Vacation
    Destinations
trade acceptance
trade discount
trademark™
treasury stock
*trial balance
trickle-down theory
trust
turnover
two percent, net 30
*two sets of books
UBIT
*uncollectible accounts
underground economy
underwrite
unearned income
Unemployment
    Compensation Tax
unemployment
    compensation tax
Unemployment Rate
unit contribution margin
Unrelated Business
    Income Tax
unrestricted funds
up-front money
upstream
*useful life
*vacation pay liability
*valuation issue
value-added
value-added tax
Veblen, Thorstein
*vender, vendor
venture capital
voodoo economics
w.b., W.B.
*wages
waybill
"Weak" and "Strong"
    Dollar
wealth therapy
white collar
Wholesale Price Index
windfall
window income
withdraw

*working capital
working capital
*working papers
*worksheet
WPI
*write down
*write-off
*write-up
zero-base

EntreP
**ARTS
ENTREPRENEURSHP**

401k plans
501(c)(3)
503b
504 loan program
604 loan program
ABC method
absolute deviation
accelerated Cost Recover
    System
accelerator theory
acceptance sampling
account return on
    investment technique
accounting profit
accounting rate of return
    (ARR)
accounting statements
    (financial statements)
accounts payable (trade
    credit)
accounts receivable
accounts receivable
    turnover
accrual method
    (accrual-basis
    accounting)
accrued expenses
accrued liabilities
accumulated
    depreciation
acid-test ratio (quick
    ratio)
acquisition
activity ratios
additional paid in capital
advertising
advertising plan
advisory council
agency power
agents/brokers
aggregate demand
aggregate supply
aging schedule
American Option
amortization
angel's
annuity
annuity due
antecedent factor
application software
appreciation
area developers
articles of partnership
artisan entrepreneur
Asian Pacific Economic
    Cooperation (EPIC)
    organization
asset-based loan
asset-based valuation
    approach
assets
asymmetric information
attitude
attribute inspection

automatic stabilizers
autonomous consumption
    spending
average collection period
average pricing
average-cost pricing
    policy
bad-debt ratio
balance sheet
balanced mutual funds
bank discount
bankruptcy
barter
basic structure
batch manufacturing
bearish spread
bench-marking
benefit variables
Binomial Probability
    Distribution
board of directors
Board of Governors of the
    Federal Reserve
bond
book value
book value method of
    valuation
brand
break-even analysis
break-even quantity
    (BEQ)
breakdown process
    (chain-ratio method)
budget
budget deficit
bullish spread
business incubator
business interruption
    insurance
business plan
business policies
buy and hold
buyout
C corporation
calendar Spread
call Option
Capital Asset Pricing
    Model
Capital Budgeting
capital budgeting
    analysis
capital gain
capital gains and losses
capital market
capital resources
capitalization rate
captive supplier
cartel
cash budget
cash conversion period
cash discounts
cash flow
cash flow budget
cash flows from financing
    activities
cash method of
    accounting (cash-basis
    accounting)
cell
central bank
Certificate of deposit
    (CD)
chain of command
chain-ratio method
    (breakdown process)
channel of distribution
Chapter 11 bankruptcy

Chapter 7 bankruptcy
character
chattel mortgage
Civil Rights Act
classical aggregate
    supply curve
classical economics
client/server model
co-variance
code of ethics
cognitive dissonance
coinsurance
collateral
combinations
commercial property
    insurance
commercial real estate
common carriers
common stock
community-based
    financial institution
comparable companies
    approach to valuation
competitive advantage
complements
compound interest
compound value of a
    dollar
computer-aided design
    (CAD)
computer-aided
    manufacturing (CAM)
concentration ratio
consistency
consumer credit
consumer price index
    (CPI)
consumerism
continuous quality
    improvement
contract carriers
contractionary policies
contribution margin
control chart
convertible preferred
    stock
copyright
core competencies
corporate bond
corporate charter
corporate
    entrepreneurship
corporate refugee
corporation
corporation (C
    corporation)
corrective maintenance
correlation
cost of goods sold
cost-of-living
    adjustments
covered position
creative destruction
creativity
credit
credit bureaus
credit insurance
creditor
culture
current assets
current debt
current exercise value
current liabilities
current ratio
customer profile
data communications
database management
    program

clotheshorse
clothier
Cluny lace
coif
coiffure
coloration
comme il faut
converter
cornrows
corset
cos.
costume
costume design
costumer
Coty Award
Council of Fashion
    Designers of America
couture
couturier
couturiere
crape
cravat
crepe
crew cut
crinoline
crochet
croquis
cummerbund
cut
cutoffs
cutter
Daily News Record
dancewear
dandy
deco
décolleté
démodé
dernier cri
designer
dishabille
DNR
Donegal tweed
drafting
drag
draping
dressmaking
ducktail
duds
dummy
EDI
Electronic Data
    Interchange
Ellis, Perry » Perry Ellis
    Award
embellishment
embroidery
Empire styles
ensemble
epaulet
evening dress
fabric
fabrication
face
facing
fad
fagoting
falsies
fancy dress
fashion
Fashion Centers
fashion cycle
Fashion Group
    International
fashion plate
faux
FGI
fiber
filling

finery
first sample
fishnet
fit model
fitting
flapper
flare
flat
flat top
flocking
flounce
formal
French cuff
French heel
French knot
French twist
frock
frou frou
full-fashioned
funky
furnishings
G-string
gaiter
gay deceivers
Gibson girl
glitter
Godey's Lady's Book
Godey, Louis Antoine
gown
grain
greige goods
grosgrain
haberdashery
hacking
hand
haute couture
heroin-chic
high fashion
high hat
high-draped pants
house of design
ikat
ILGWU
indigo
International Ladies
    Garment Workers
    Union
Ivy League look
jabot
jacquard
Jeakins, Dorothy » mud
    colors
jodhpurs
kimono
knit
knock-off
L-85
lab dip
label
lamé
lapel
leggings
leotard
look
macramé
madras
mannequin
mantle
marker
micro
milliner
millinery
minimalist design
mode
model
Mohawk
morning dress
Mother Hubbard

motley
mourning clothes
mud colors
muslin
natty
needlepoint
negligee, negligée
obi
old-fashioned
Oscar Awards
outfit
page-boy
painting
paisley
pantaloons
Pantone book
passementerie
peau de soie
peignoir
peplum
Perry Ellis Award
petticoat
picture hat
piece goods
pilling
pima cotton
pinafore
piqué
pixie
platform
porkpie hat
price point
princess
print
printery
prototype
quality
quick response
rag trade
raglan
ramie
rayon
ready-to-wear
returns
RTW
ruche
ruching
ruffle
SA
sari
sarong
schmate
scoop neck
Sea island cotton
Seventh Avenue
shag
shirr
shirtwaist
show
show room
silhouette
size
skivvis
sleazy
sloper
smart
smocking
spiffy
spike heel
sportswear
stiletto heel
strait-laced, straight-
    laced
strike off
stunning
style
swallow-tailed coat
taffeta

tailoring
tails
tatting
tawdry
textiles
texture
threads
top hat
topper
topstitching
torchon lace
tricot
tunic
tutu
tux
tuxedo
two-piece
Union of Needletrades,
    Industrial and Textile
    Employees
unisex
UNITE, Unite
United Students Against
    Sweatshops
vanity
vogue
voile
wedgie
weight
Women's Wear Daily
working sketch
WWD
yard goods
yoke

Flm&Vid
FILM & VIDEO

44-minute pilot
88th episode
A-team
above-the-line costs
Academy Awards
academy leader
Academy of Motion
    Picture Arts and
    Sciences
accent lighting
according to the ink
act.
action
actor
actress
adaptation
adjustment
ADR
advance
AFI
aided recall interview
Alan Smithee
aleatory techniques
Allen, Woody
Alliance of Motion
    Picture and Television
    Producers
amateur
ambient sound
America's Sweetheart
American Film Institute
American Society of
    Cinematographers
American Standard
    Association
amortization of negative
    costs
AMPAS
analog
anamorphic lens

anim.
animal handler
animator
apple boxes
archival footage
Armstrong, Louis
art director
art film
art house
art theatre
artist tie-ins
artist's video
ASA
ASC
aspect ratio
assembly
associate producer
atmos.
atmosphere
attraction
audio/visual work
audiovisual, audio-visual
auteur theory
Automatic Dialogue
    Replacement
availability
available lighting
B movie
B picture
B-film
B-team
baby spot
back story
back-lot
background
background music
background noises
backlash
backlighting
backup schedule
backup shots
Ball, Lucille » screwball
bank
bankable star
Bankhead, Tallulah »
    Loretta Young silks
barn door
Beatty, Warren
below-the-line costs
Benny, Jack » ad lib
Berle, Milton » Texaco
    Star Theater
best boy
Beta
Betamax
bicycling
bid
bid request
big screen
Billboard
billing
Birth of a Nation, The
bit part
bit player
bkgd.
blacksploitation film
blimp
blind bidding
block booking
blockbuster
blocking, block out
Bogart, Humphrey »
    professional
booker
boom
bowdlerize
box office
box-office receipts

iMedia
INTERACTIVE
MULTIMEDIA

absolute path
active program
Active Server Pages (ASP)
active window
ADA
adapt
adaptation
adaptive
additive color
aesthetic
affordance
affordance theory
agent
alert box
Alexa
algorithm
alias
aliasing
aliasing effects
alignment
alpha channel
alpha value
alphanumeric interface
amplitude
analog
analogous colors
angle of view
anthropomorphic conflict token
anti-aliasing
arbitrary symbol
argument
artifact
artifact model
ascender
ASCII
asset
associative logic
asymmetry
asynchronous
attribute
augmented reality
Babbage, Charles
background
backlighting
balance
bandwidth
base 10
base 2
bel
beta version
binary
binary number
bit
bit depth
bitmap
black box
block-level element
blue screen
boldface
boolean logic
boolean value
boot
box
brainstorm
branching structure
break
brightness
broad navigation
browser
buffer

bullet
Bush, Vannevar
button
byte
C
C # (c sharp)
c ++
cache
calling a function
canonical view
cascading style sheets
case study
cast shadow
categorical colors
cel
cel animation
character entity
character-based metaphor
chartjunk
checked in
checked out
CheckIn protocol
chernoff faces
Chevreul illusion
chroma key
chromatic aberration
classification scheme
client sign off
client-side code
closure
CMS
CMYK
CODEC
color space
color wheel
command line interface
comment
comment out
common f-numbers
compiler
complementary colors
complex
complex adaptive system
component media
composite element
composition
compression
concatenation
concept map
conceptual model
conflict token
content
content management system
contextual inquiry
continuity
contour
cookies
cool media
Copyright
crash
creative brief
crop
cross-cultural naming
cross-cultural validity
CSS
DAT
data
data density
data design
data graphic
data landscape
data map
data mining
data rate
data-ink ratio
database

datastream
datatype
dB
debugging
decibel
deconstruction
deep navigation
deictic gesture
deixis
delimiter
deliverable
demographics
depth cues
depth of field
descender
design guide
development site
dialogue
difference engine
digitize
dither
document object model
document type declaration
document type definition
documentation
DOM
dot syntax
DTD
dynamic
dynamics
ECMA-262 specification
ECMAscript
emergent behavior
engagement
Engelbart, Douglas
entity
European Computer Manufacturers Association (ECMA)
event handler
event-based execution model
event-based metaphor
evolution of a medium
evolution of media
exposition
Extensible Markup Language (XML)
feature
feature creep
featuritis
field
figure
file transfer protocol
filter
filtering
floating-point number
flowchart
focus
focus group
font
form
formal elements
fps
fractal
frame
frame rate
frame-by-frame animation
Free Software Foundation (FSF)
FTP
function
function call
functional prototype
functionality
fuzzy logic

gamma
GANTT chart
general public license
genetic algorithm
genetic programming
geon theory
gestalt
Gestalt Laws
Gibson, J. J.
GIF
gigabyte
global variable
global village
glyph
GNU
GPL
gradient
graininess
granularity
grapheme
graphic design
graphic designer
graphical user interface
grayscale
grid
ground
haptic feedback
harmony
HCI (Human-Computer Interaction)
Head Mounted Display
heuristics
hexadecimal system
hierarchical navigation
high-level programming
HMD device
homunculus
hot media
HTML Validator
HTTP
hue
Human-Computer Interaction (HCI)
hyberbolic browser
hyperlink
Hypertext Transfer Protocol
IDE
illusory contour
imagen
immersion
immersion level
implementation model
implied line
increment operator
information appliance
information architecture
information design
information visualization
inheritance
inline element
input element
integer
integrated development environment
intention
interactive
interactive media
interface
intermediate colors
International Standards Organization (ISO)
Internet
internet relay chat (IRC)
interpreter
Intranet
invoking a function
IRC

ISO
iteration
iterative theory
JavaScript
Joint Photographic Experts Group
joystick
JPEG
JPG
justify
Kay, Alan
kerning
keying
kilobyte
LAN
launch
leading
legibility
lightness
line
linear navigation
linear perspective
local area network (LAN)
logarithm
loop
lossless compression
lossy
Lovelace, Augusta Ada
luminance
machine-oriented interface
macro
MAN (Metropolitan Area Network)
manifest model
margin
markup
mask
McCluhan, Marshall
mechanical age modeling
media
medium
memes
memex
mental model
metadata
metaphor
method
MHz
MIDI
milestone
mind map
Minsky, Marvin
mock-up
modular chunking
moiré
Moore's law
motion
motion graphics
MPEG
MPG
multi-participant interface
multifunctioning graphical elements
multiprocessor
Multitasking
navigation
NDA
needs analysis
negative space
nest
nesting
network, networking
Nielsen, Jacob
node
node-link diagram
noise

non-data-ink
non-disclosure
   agreement (NDA)
normalization
numeric character
   reference
nyquist theorem
object
object oriented
   programming
object recognition
obligatory cut
occlusion
one-dimensional
onion skinning
optimization
organizational map
output element
packet
paper prototype
paradigm
paradigm shift
parallel distributed
   processing
parallel processor
parallel production
pattern language
perspective
PERT chart Mgt,
PHP (PHP: Hypertext
   Preprocessor)
pixel
pixelated
pixelization
playback head
PNG
Portable Network
   Graphics (PNG)
positive space
pre-attentive processing
pre-production
preload
preloader
presentation
primary colors
priming
production guide
Program Evaluation
   Review Technique
project manager
project plan
proof
proportion
proposal
proprietary tag
protocol
prototype
proximity
pseudocode
psychographics
QA
quality assurance
query
RAM
Raskin, Jef
raster
raster image
raw data
readability
real estate
record
relative path
relative size
rendering
representational
requirements analysis
requirements
   specification

resolution
responsive
RFP
RGB
rhythm
rtf file
RTFM
running a function
runtime
saccades
sampling rate
sans serif
saturation
Scale
scan
scheme
scope
scope creep
scrubbing
secondary colors
self-referential
semiotics
sensory symbol
serif
server-side code
SGML
shape
shared vision
ship
sign off
similarity
sine waves
sitemap
size
sketch
Space
spatial metaphor
specification
specular shading
SQL
square type
stakeholder
Standard Generalized
   Markup Language
static
stickiness
sticky
streaming
structure
structured query
   language
style guide
subtractive color
supervisory control
   system
swarm intelligence
symmetry
system design
systemic design
table
target audience
task
task analysis
TCP-IP
technical specification
technographics
technology
template
tertiary colors
texture
thin client
three-act structure
three-dimensional
thumbnails
TIFF
timeline
title safe area
Tone

tree
tripod
Turing machine
Turing test
Turing, Alan
tweak
tween
tweening
two dimensional
TXT files
type
typeface
typesize
typestyle
typographical error
typography
UFOV
UML
underexposure
undersampling
unified modeling
   language (UML)
Uniform Resource
   Identifier
universal turing machine
uppercase
URL
usability
usability engineering
usability engineering
   lifecycle
user agent
user feedback
user group
user interrupt
user profile
vacuum tube
value
variable
vection
vector
vector graphics
Venn diagram
verisimilitude
version
version control
versioning
virtual
virtual reality
Virtual Reality Modeling
   Language
visual stress
visualization
von Leibnitz, Gottfried
   Willheml
von Neumann
   architecture
VR
VRML
W3C
WAN (Wide Area
   Network)
wavelength
wayfinding
web navigation
widget
wireframe
World Wide Web
World Wide Web
   Consortium (W3C)
WWW
WYSIWYG
x-axis
XHTML
XML
y-axis
z-axis

InfoMgt
**INFORMATION
MANAGEMENT**
_____

555
a programming language
abort
access
access mechanism
access time
accessory
acoustic coupler
ACPA
active application
   program
active matrix
active program
active window
ADA
add-on
address
Advanced Network
   Services
AFAIK
AFK
AIIP
Air Mosaic
alarm clock
alert box
alias
Alliance for Public
   Technology
Alta Vista
alternative media
ALU
America
America Online
American Society for
   Information Science
American Standard Code
   for Information
   Interchange
American Telephone &
   Telegraph Corporation
analog computer
analog transmission
anti-apography
AOL
AOP
APL
Apple Computer
applets
application
APT
archivearchives
argument
Arithmetic Logic Unit
artificial intelligence
artificial language
.arts
ASCII
ASIS
assembly
Association of Computer
   Programmers and
   Analysts
Association of Indepen-
   dent Information
   Professionals
Association of Online
   Professionals
AT&T
AT&T Labs
audio output
audio output jack
audit trail
auditorium
authoring tool

auto-answer
autoresponder
auxiliary equipment
auxiliary storage
Babbage, Charles
Baby Bells
background printing
backupbackup copies
bad sector
band
bandwidth
bandwidth transmission
bank
bar codebar code reader
BASIC
Basic Rate Interface
batch file
baud
BBS
BCC
Beginners All Purpose
   Symbolic Code
Bell Labs
bells and whistles
beta site
beta test
beta version
bias
Big Three
binary
binary file
binary graphic
binary number
bird
bit
bitmap
black telegraph
Blind Carbon Copy
bloggers
board
body
bomb
bombs
Booklink Technologies
bookmark
bookmobile
Boolean search
boot
bounce message
bpi
bps
branch
BRB
bridgeware
broad band
broadband
browser
browsing
BTW
bubble memory
buffer
bug
bulletin board system
bundled software
bus
Business Software
   Alliance
button
buttons
Byron, Ada Augusta »
   ADA
byte
bytes per inch
C
C++
cable modem
cache
CAD/CAM

IntelProp
INTELLECTUAL PROPERTY

administration

Journ
JOURNALISM
and
BcstJourn
**BROADCAST
JOURNALISM**

Mktg
MARKETING

combo
comic opera
command performance
commercial
commercial license
common measure
common time
Community Concerts
comp
comp.
competition
compilation score
complement
compose
composer
composition
computer music
con amore
con brio
con legno
con spirito
concert
concert edition
concert music
concert pitch
concertmaster, concert mistress
concerto
concertogrosso
cond.
conductor
confessional rock
conjunto bands
consonance
consonant
contemporary Christian
contemporary gospel
content
continuo
continuous music
contr
contralto
contrapuntal
control
cool
cool jazz
coppin'
copy
copyist
corridos
counterpoint
countertenor
country
country and western
country blues
country music
Country Music Association
Country Music Foundation
Country Music Hall of Fame and Museum
Country Music Styles
country pop
country rock
country swing
country-rock
countrypolitan
cover band
cow-punk
Craig, David
Creole-Zydeco
cres
crescendo
croon
crooner
Crosby, Bing » crooner
CSO

cue
cuesheet
cut time
cutoff, cut-off
cutting contest
D.C.
da capo
dance music
dark tone
date
David » Psalms
Davis Jr., Sammy » rat pack
Davis, Miles
DB/HF
dbl.
decrescendo
deejay
demo
depth
descant
descending
development
Devil's music
dialogue
diatonic scale
diction
dim
diminuendo
dir.
direct license
direction
director
dirge
dirty
disc jockey, disk jockey (DJ)
disco
discotheque
Disney Corporation
dissonance
dissonant
District, The
ditty
diva
divertissement
Dixieland jazz
dixieland, Dixieland
Diz
DJ
do
dol
dolce
dom
dominant
doo wop
Doris Duke Charitable Foundation » Jazznet
Dorsey, Thomas A. » National Convention of Gospel Singers
dot
double
double bar
double-reeds
double-time
Dove Awards
Down Beat Jazz Hall of Fame
Down Beat, down beat
down-bow, downbow
downbeat
dramatic
dramatico-musical composition
drum major, drum majorette
drummer

du-wah
duet
Duke » Duke Ellington
dummy lyric
duple meter
duration
Dylan, Bob » Bill Graham
dynamic markings
dynamics
ear training
easy listening
echo
ed.
editor
eighth note
electronic music
elegy
eleven o'clock number
Ella » Ella Fitzgerald
Ella Award
Ellington, Duke
embellish
Embooees
EMI
Empress of the Blues » Bessie Smith
encore
enharmonic
Eno, Brian » New Age music
ensemble
entr'acte
erotic music law
Ethiopian songs
etude
Euterpe
evangelical music
Evans, Bill » black musicians
evergreen
excerpt
exclusive musicians
Exclusive Songwriter Agreement
Experimental Music Studios
exposition
expression marks
F clef
f, F
fa
fake
fakebook
fall-off
false fingering
falsetto
fanfare
fantasia, fantasy
Fat Man, The » multimedia sound
feel the audience
ff
fff
field holler
fifth
fifty-second street
figuration
figured bass
fill
filler
finale
fingerpick
first
first chair
Fitzgerald, Ella » Apollo Theater, scat singing
flamenco

flat
Flatt, Lester » bluegrass
flatted fifth
flip
three-quarter time
flourish
flutter
Foggy Mountain Boys » bluegrass
folio
folk music
folk-rock, folk rock
folkie, folky
Ford, Mary » Les Paul
forte
forte-piano
fortissimo
fortississimo
forza
Fosse, Bob
four-part harmony
fours
fourth
fox trot
Fox, Charlie » countrypolitan
freak
free jazz, free-jazz
French-Creole music
fugue
fundamental
funk
funky
funny hat band
fusion
G clef
gala
galop
game music
gangsta rap
garage band
Garland, Judy » compleat
genre
Georgia Tom » Dorsey, Thomas A.
Gershwin, George
Gershwin, Ira
gig
gig piece
Gillespie, Dizzy
glam-rock
glee
glee club
gliss
glissando
glitter rock
glossolalia
Glover, Savion » funk, tap dance
GMA
GMWA
golden oldie
Golden Score Award
good music
Gospel Music
Gospel Music Association
Gospel Music Workshop of America
grace note
Graham, Bill
Grammy Awards
Grand Ole Opry
grand rights
Grateful Dead » Bill Graham
grave
Greek chorus
Greeolies

greeting card music
Gregorian chant
groove
grunge rock
guiro
guitarrón
habanera
Haggard, Merle » music business
half note
half step
half tone
Hall, Gene » stage band
hallelujah
Hanna, Roland » professional musicians
Harburg, Yip
Harburg, Yip » gederim, imagination
hard bop
hard gospel music
hard rock
hard-core
harmolodic
harmonic
harmonics
harmonist
harmony
hatecore music
Hawkins, Coleman » slap tongue
Haydn, Franz Josef » Classical Style
head
head arrangement
head register
heavy metal rock
hemidemisemiquaver
Henahan, Donal
heterophonic
high
high-pitched
hillbilly music
hip-hop
HitClips
hoedown
hold
Holden, Stephen » cool
Holiday, Billie » Apollo Theater, phrasing
homophonic
honkytonk
hook
hootenanny
horn player
horn section
Horowitz, Vladimir » quintessential
hot
house music
hummer
Hurok, Sol
hymn
hymnody
I.M.
IAJE
IAML
IBMA
ICSOM
idea
IJS
imit.
imitation
IMPA
impressionism, Impressionism
improvisation
in time

ten
tenor
tenor band
tenor clef
tension and release
Terpsichore
tessitura
Tex-Mex music
texture
Thelonious Monk
    Institute of Jazz
    (1986-)
theme and variation
thin
third
third-stream music
thirty-second note
thoroughbass, thorough
    bass
thrush
ti
tickle
tie
tight
timbre
time
time signature
Tin Pan Alley
Toch, Ernst
tonal center
tonality
tone
tone cluster
tone poem
tone row
tone-deaf
tongue
tongues
tonic
Tony Awards
Top 40
topical song
torch song
Tormé, Mel » scat singing
trad
trading fours
traditional jazz
train wreck
trance music
Trane
trans
transition
transpose
transposition
trap drummer
traps
Travis, Randy » new
    traditionalist country
    music
treble clef
tremolo
tremulous sound
triad
trill
trio
trip-hop
triple time
triplet
troubadour
Tucker, Sophie » race
    records
tune
tuneful
tuneless
tuner
tunesmith
turn
turnaround

tutti
two-and-four
underscore
unison
unpublished work
up full
up-tempo
urban blues
v.
vamp
var.
variation
vaude
vaudeville
Vaughan, Sarah
vehicle
ver.
verismo
vernacular music
verse
VH1 Save The Music
    program
vibes
vibrate
vibration
vibrato
video buyout
video rollover
virtuosa, virtuoso
vivace
voc.
vocal
vocal cords
vocalise
vocalist
voice
voice placement
Voice, The
voicing
von Karajan, Herbert »
    digital recording.
w.
Wagner, Richard »
    leitmotif
wah-wah, wa-wa
walkers
walking bass
Walt Disney Company
waltz
warble
weighting formula
Weill, Kurt » epic drama
West Coast jazz
Western swing
white blues
white gospel music
whole note
Wilder, Alec
Williams, Hank » hillbilly
    music
Williams, Ralph
    Vaughan » origin
Wills, Bob » Western
    Swing
Winston, George » New
    Age music
WIP
woodshed
Woodstock Nation
words
work in progress (WIP)
work song
wow
writer
Yardbird » Charlie
    Parker
Zappa, Frank
zarzuela

zydeco

MusInstr
**MUSICAL
INSTRUMENTS**

acc.
accessory
accordion
acoustic instruments
action
alto
AMC
American Music
    Conference
amp, amp.
amplifier
b.
B3 organ
baby grand piano
band shell
bandstand
banjo
baritone horn
baritone sax
barrel organ
bass
bass drum
bass trumpet
bass viol
bassoon
baton
batter percussion
battery
bell
bells
bgo
Big Briar
bjo
blues harp
bones
bongo
bow
brass
bridge
brushes
bssn.
calliope
capo
carbon graphite
carillon
castanet
cello
chimes
chord organ
cl.
clappers
clarinet
clave, claves
clo.
concert grand
console
contra-
contrabassoon
cor.
cornet
cowbell
desk
diatonic accordion
digital
Disklavier
double bass
double bassoon
double-reed
drm
drum
drum machine
drum set

electric piano
electronic instruments
electronic organ
endpin
Eng-h
English horn
euph
euphonium
Experimental Music
    Studios
Fender, Leo
fiddle
fife
finger piano
finger pick
fingerboard
fipple
fl
flamenco
flug
flugelhorn
flute
Fr-h.
French horn
fret
fretted instrument
fuzz box
glass harmonica
glockenspiel
grand piano
gtr
guitar
h
Hammond B3 organ
Harmon mute
harmonica
harmonium
harp
harpsichord
hca
head
high hat cymbals
horn
hurdy-gurdy
hypercello
instr.
instrument
instrument maintenance
    payment
instrumental
jew's harp, jews'-harp
jug
kalimba
kazoo
kettledrum
key
keyboard
Latin percussion
Little Instruments
lp.
mallet percussion
mandolin
manuals
marimba
mbira
MIDI
Moog synthesizer
Moog, Bob
Moog, Robert » Moog
    synthesizer
mouth organ
music box
music business
musical glasses
Musical Instrument
    Digital Interface
Musical Instrument
    Families

musical saw
NAMM
National Association of
    Music Merchants
nickelodeon
nut
ob
oboe
ondes martinot Ω
oratorio
orch.
orchestra
Organs
origin
ostinato
parlor grand
Paul, Les
pedal keyboard
pedal steel guitar
peg
Pellegrina viola
pennywhistle, penny
    whistle
perc
percussion
piano
picc
piccolo
piccolo bass
piccolo trumpet
pick
pin
pipe organ
player piano
plectrum
plunger mute
pno
pocket trumpet
recorder
reed
reed organ
reed section
reeds
register
resonator
restorer
reverb
rhythm section
ride cymbal
Rivinus, David »
    Pellegrina viola
rub board
Sax, Adolph
sax, saxophone
scroll
shofar
side drum
sitar
slide whistle
snare drum
soft pedal
solid-body guitar
soprano saxophone
sounding board,
    soundboard
spoons
squeezebox
steel drum
steel guitar
stick
string
strings
syn
synth
synthesizer
talking drum
tam-tam
tambourine

PA-Variety
**PERFORMING
ARTS-Variety**

Hirshfield, Al » ninas
hot
Hudson River School
hue
hyperrealism
IFAR
illus.
illustration
illustrator
image
impasto
impost
impressionism,
    Impressionism
IMS
informel
Institute of Museum
    Services
intaglio
intensity
International Foundation
    for Art Research
kinetic art
Knight Foundation
landscape
les fauves
Lichtenstein, Roy » pop
    art
light
likeness
line
linear
luminism
Mannerism
mass
mat
matière
Matisse, Henri
matte
McCrory, John »
    professional artist
medium
mezzotint
Michaelangelo » classic
Millet, Jean-François »
    Barbizon School
minimalism
modern art
Modernism
montage
Motherwell, Robert »
    abstract expressionism
motif
mud colors
museum
museum loan network
musm.
NAAO
NAD
naive art
National Association of
    Artists Organizations
naturalism
neoclassicism
neoexpressionism
neoimpressionism
neosurrealism
Newman, Barnett »
    abstract expression-
    ism, color field
    painting
nightscape
ninas
nonobjective
nonrepresentational
old master
Oldenburg, Claes » pop
    art

op art, Op Art
original
Oscar Awards
outsider
PACA
painter
Paleolithic art
palette
papier-collé
papier-mâché
passage
Pasta
Paul Revere Award
Pei, I.M. » Rock and Roll
    Hall of Fame
performance art
perspective
Pevsner, Antoine »
    constructivism
Pew Charitable Trusts
photo
photo-essay
photog.
photogenic
photograph
photographic realism
photographists
photography
photojournalism
photomontage
photomural
photorealism
pic
Picabia, Francis »
    assemblage
Picasso, Pablo
pictorial
picture
Picture Agency Council
    of America
pied
pigment
pl.
plate
pntr.
pointillism
Pollock, Jackson »
    abstract expression-
    ism, action painting
pop art
por.
portfolio
portrait
portraiture
portray
poster color, poster paint
postimpressionism
postmodernism,
    post-modernism
Pre-Raphaelite
    Brotherhood
presale
prf
pricing criteria
pride of place
primitive
primitivism
print
printmaking
Professional and
    Administrative Staff
    Association
professional artist
proof
provenance
Pulitzer Prize
quiet
Raphael » Pre-Raphaelite

Brotherhood
Rauschenberg, Robert
ready-made art
realism
reductivism
rejective art
Rembrandt, van Rijn »
    old master
Renaissance
replica
replication
repository
representational
repro
Resale Royalties Act
rococo, Rococo
Rogers, Malcolm »
    commercial
Romanesque
Rothko, Mark » abstract
    expressionism,
    colorfield
Rouault, George » les
    fauves
Rousseau, Théodore »
    Barbizon School
salon
scenery
scenic artist
scenic design
scenography
scratchboard
screen-print
scrimshaw
scriptorium, scriptoria
Scully, Vincent
sculp.
sculpt
sculptor
sculpture
scumble
sealer
seascape
self-taught art
sepia
set piece
Seurat, Georges »
    neoimpressionism,
    pointillism
shoot
shot
silence
silhouette
silk-screen, silkscreen
sit
size
sketchbook
sketchpad
sleeper
Society of Independent
    Artists
soft sculpture
steel engraving
still life
studio
stylus
superrealism
surrealism
symbolism
Synthetic Cubism
tempera
texture
thin
throw
tonality
tone
Tony Awards
tramp art

transparency
trompe l'oeil
Union of Artistic
    Property
United Scenic Artists of
    America
USAA
Van Gogh, Vincent »
    expressionism
Velazquez, Diego » old
    master
Vermeer, Jan » genre
vernacular art
Victorian
vignette
virtu
visionary art
visual art
Visual Artists' Rights Act
Vlaminck, Maurice de »
    les fauves
Walt Disney Company
Warhol, Andy »pop art
watercolor
Watteau, Jean Antoine »
    rococo
Watterson, Bill »
    avant-garde
wax museum
white space
whiteprint
wood block
woodcut
work
work in progress (WIP)
writers

_____

VA-Prntng
**VISUAL ARTS-
Printing**

_____

ADAA
agate line
alignment
area composition
art
Art Dealers Association
    of America (ADAA)
artwork
ascender
backbone
backing
benday, Benday
bind-in card
bindery
black letter
blackface
bleed ad
bleed allowance
block
blow-in card
blueline
blueprint
body
body type
boldface
break
broadside
brownline
bullet
camera-ready
caret
center spread
centerfold
char.
chase
classified advertising
clm.

col.
cold type
collate
column
column inch
compose
composing room
composing stick
composition
copy
copyholder
counter
cover
cover price
crop
cursive
descender
diesis
dingbat
display type
dots per inch
double dagger
DPI
dummy, dummy page
dump
duotone
dust jacket
ed.
edition
electrotype
ellipsis
em dash
en dash
errata
f., F.
f.v.
family
fiber
first edition
flat
flat-bed press
flush
fol.
folio
Folio verso
format
four-color printing
galley
galley proof
gatefold
giclée
Gothic
gremlin
grid
half binding
hardback
hardcover
head
height of one line of type
hot metal
imposition
imprint
insert
insertion order
justify
kern
kerning
layout
lc
lead
leader
leading
leaf
leaves
letterpress printing
ligature
lightface
line printer

Citations

These citations refer to the direct quotations within the **entry** indicated.

?? Data unknown

————————A————————

accordion *MusInstr.* George Shearing, *South Bank Show* (Bravo Cable, New Orleans, 07/26/96).

accordion *MusInstr.* Ambrose Pierce (??).

actor *ArtPerf.* Lawrence Olivier, *Confessions of an Actor: An Autobiography.* (NY: Penguin, 1984), 20-21.

actual malice *Journ, LegalAsp.* Renata Adler, *Reckless Disregard: Westmoreland v. CBS et al.; Sharon v. Time* (NY: Vintage, 1986), 244-245.

ad lib *PerfA&C.* Jack Benny (??).

ad lib *PerfA&C.* Hamlet, *Hamlet*, Shakespeare.

aesthetics *Aes&Creat.* Jean Paul Sartre, *Existentialism, From Dostoevsky to Sartre.* (Cleveland: Meridian, 1956), 305-306.

amoral *Eth&Phil.* William Faulkner, *Paris Review: Interviews, Writers at Work* (NY: Penguin, 1958), 123-124.

angels *Eco&Fin, Mgt.* Barbra Streisand, *Playbill*, Oct. 1969.

anonymous work *IntelProp.* Copyright Act of 1976 (Sec. 101).

Armstrong, Louis *ArtPerf, Flm&Vid, MusArts.* Eileen Southern, *The Music of Black Americans* (NY: Norton, 1971), 382.

architecture *VisArts.* Vincent Scully, "America, The Sacred Mountain," *Architecture: The Natural and the Manmade* (NY: St. Martin's Press, 1991), 1.

Armory Show *Cult&Soc, VisA&C.* Thomas Hart Benton, in Daniel J. Boorstin, *The Americans, The Democratic Experience* (NY: Vintage, 1974), 511-512.

arranger *MusArts.* Linda Ronstadt and Johnny Mandel, in Stephen Holden, "Arrangers? What're They? Ask Rosemary Clooney," *NY Times*, 10/11/91, B8.

art *Crit&Eval.* Hanif Kureismi, "Intimacy," *New Yorker*, 05/11/98, 90.

art *Crit&Eval.* Whoopi Goldberg. Creative Coalition: creativecoalition.com.

art *PerfA&C.* Peter Zeisler, in Mel Gussow, "Is All the Stage a World?" *NY Times*, 06/30/94, B3.

artist *ArtPerf.* Akira Kurosawa in Rick Lyman, "Akira Kurosawa, Director of Epics, Dies at 88," *NY Times*, 09/7/98, A1, A12.

artist *ArtPerf.* Akira Kurosawa in Rick Lyman, "Akira Kurosawa, Director of Epics, Dies at 88," *NY Times*, 09/7/98, A1, A12.

artistic temperament *ArtPerf.* John P. Marquand, *Women and Thomas Harrow* (Boston: Little, Brown, 1958), 142.

audience *TheatArts* Bernadette Peters, *Actors Studio*, PBS-TV.

artphilohistcritisophery *VisArts.* Arthur C. Danto, "Introduction," *Encounters & Reflections* (NY: Farrar Straus Giroux, 1990), 7-8.

Arts Manager *Mgt.* Ivan Sygoda, "Management," *Poor Dancer's Almanac: A Survival Manual for Choreographers, Managers and Performers* (NY: DTW Publications, Dance Theater Workshop, 1983), 75.

asceticism *Eth&Phil, MusArts.* Henry Pleasants, *The Agony of Modern Music* (NY: Simon & Schuster, 1955).

auction *Rdio&TV.* Alvin H. Permutter, *NY Times*, 12/29/94.

audience *Crit&Eval.* Henry Pleasants, *The Agony of Modern Music* (NY: Simon & Schuster, 1955), 63.

audience *Crit&Eval.* Norman Mailer, *Harlot's Ghost* (NY: Ballantine, 1991), 396.

audience *Crit&Eval.* Sol Hurok, in Martin Mayer, *Making News*, rev. and updated, (Boston: Harvard Business School Press, 1993), 153.

Audio Home Recording Act of 1992 *LegalAsp, RecA&S.* Jeffrey Brabec and Todd Brabec, *Music, Money, and Success* (NY: Schirmer, 1994), 354.

auteur theory *Flm&Vid.* William Goldman, "Auteurs," *Adventures in the Screen Trade, A Personal View of Hollywood and Screenwriting* (NY: Warner Books, 1983), 101.

authentic *MusArts.* Jon Pareles, "A Critic's Quandary: What's Authentic?" *NY Times*, 03/13/88.

avant-garde *Aes&Creat.* Bill Watterson, *Calvin and Hobbes* (Universal Press Syn.), "Comics," *Times-Picayune*, 01/10/93, 1.

avant-garde *Aes&Creat.* Michael Moore, *down beat*, 05/05/77, 18.

————————B————————

ballad *MusArts.* Len Lyons and Don Perlo, *Jazz Portraits: The Lives and Music of the Jazz Masters* (NY: Quill, William Morrow, 1989), Glossary.

Broadcast Journalism *BcstJourn.* Recommended source: Hewitt, John. *Writing for Broadcast News*, 2nd ed. Mountain View, Ca: Mayfield Publishing Company, 1995 (or later).

bass line *MusArts.* Len Lyons and Don Perlo, *Jazz Portraits: The Lives and Music of the Jazz Masters* (NY: Quill, William Morrow, 1989), Glossary.

Black Creoles *Cult&Soc.* Mark Mattern, "Let the Good Times Unroll: Music and Race Relations in Southwest Louisiana," *Black Music Research Journal*, Fall 1997, 159.

black gospel music *MusArts. New Harvard Dictionary of Music*, ed. by Don Michael Randel (??: The Belknap Press of Harvard University Press, 19??), 344.

black music *Cult&Soc, MusArts.* Oliver Nelson, "The First Chorus," *down beat*, 04/25/75, 4.

black music *Cult&Soc, MusArts.* Russell Simmons, "Listen Up! Quincy Jones Has A New Gig, and It's In Multimedia," *NY Times*, 06/5/95, C4.

black music *Cult&Soc, MusArts.* Wynton Marsalis, "Jazz: Wynton Looks Back," *New Yorker*, 10/14/91, 100.

black musicians *Cult&Soc, MusArts.* Bill Evans, "The First Chorus," *down beat*, 02/11/76, 4.

black musicians *Cult&Soc, MusArts.* Sonny Rollins, "Sonny Rollins and His Friends Reassemble for a Carnegie Reunion," *NY Times*, 04/13/91, B5.

black road shows *Cult&Soc, PA-Variety.* Lawrence W. Levine, "Laughing Matters, How black Americans have used humor as A strategy for survival," *NY Times Book Review*, 02/27/94; 1,27,28; in a review of Mel Watkins, *On the Real Side* (*Laughing, Lying, and Signifying The Underground Tradition of African-American Humor That Transformed American Culture, From Slavery to Richard Pryor*) (NY: Simon & Schuster, 1993?).

blow (one's) top *or* **blow (one's) stack** *Crit&Eval.* Louis Armstrong re Little Rock school integration struggle (1957), exhibit placard, in *Louis Armstrong., A Cultural Legacy*, New Orleans Museum of Art, Dec. 1995.

blue notes *MusArts.* James Lincoln Collier, *The Making of Jazz* (NY: Delta Book/Dell, 1978), 26.

bluesy *Crit&Eval.* Len Lyons and Don Perlo, *Jazz Portraits: The Lives and Music of the Jazz Masters* (NY: Quill, William Morrow, 1989), Glossary.

boilerplate *LegalAsp*. Erica Jong, in Roger Cohen "Erica Jong is Elected President of the Authors Guild," *NY Times*, 03/06/91, B3.

bridge *MusArts.* Len Lyons and Don Perlo, *Jazz Portraits: The Lives and Music of the Jazz Masters* (NY: Quill, William Morrow, 1989), Glossary.

bro *Cult&Soc.* Spike Lee, in Henry Louis Gates Jr. "Just Whose 'Malcolm' Is It, Anyway?" *NY Times*, 05/31/92, 16.

business ethics *Eth&Phil.* Laura Nash, *Good Intentions Aside* (??, 1995).

buzz *Crit&Eval, Mktg.* "Art, Money and N.Y. (Editorial), *NY Times*, 05/29/95, 16.

————————C————————

Cajun music *MusArts.* Barry Jean Ancelet, *Cajun Music, Its Origins and Development* (Lafayette, La.: Center for Louisiana Studies, U. of Southwestern Louisiana, 1989), 1.

call and response *Cult&Soc, MusArts.* Wynton Marsalis, in William Raspberry. "The Write Stuff," *Times-Picayune*, 06/10/94, B7.

capitalism *Eco&Fin.* Benjamin Barber, *Jihad v. McWorld* (Times Books), as paraphrased by Gareth Cook, *Washington Monthly*, Nov. 1995, 57.

career *Mgt, MusArts.* Merle Haggard (source unk)

celebrity (celeb) *Crit&Eval.* Barbra Streisand, in Bernard Weinraub, "Barbra Streisand, Still Not Pretty Enough," *NY Times*, 11/13/96, B1, B4.

censorship *Eth&Phil, Law&Pol.* Andrew Miltenberg, "Battle Over Street Art in Museum's Shadow," *NY Times*, 3/22/98, 26.

censorship *Eth&Phil, Law&Pol.* Katherine Hepburn, in Anne Edwards, *A Remarkable Woman* (NY: Pocket Books, 1985), 237.

center *also* **Center** *Cult&Soc, Law&Pol.* Barry Gaither, "Whose Culture Is It Anyhow?" *Cultural Democracy*, Winter 1987.

character's point of view *LitArts.* "Story Workshop As a Method of Teaching Writing," by Betty Sheflett, College English, November 1973.

chase chorus *MusArts.* Len Lyons and Don Perlo, *Jazz Portraits: The Lives and Music of the Jazz Masters* (NY: Quill, William Morrow, 1989), Glossary.

chat *InfoMgt.* Laurie Mifflin, "Sci-Fi Channel Allows 'Chats' While a Show Is in Progress," *NY Times*, 06/19/95, C8.

cheap songs *MusArts.* Dennis Potter, in William Grimes. "Dennis Potter, Television Auteur, Dies at 59," *NY Times*, 06/08/94, C19.

checked in, checked out, CheckIn protocol *iMedia.* Jim and Michele McCarthy,. *Software For Your Head*, 2002, Addison Wesley Publishers, 96.

Chicago jazz *MusArts.* Len Lyons and Don Perlo, *Jazz Portraits: The Lives and Music of the Jazz Masters* (NY: Quill, William Morrow, 1989), Glossary.

Christian Art *VisArts.* Leo Tolstoy, "Preface" (1898), *What Is Art*, trans. by Aylmer Maude (NY: Thomas Y. Crowell, 19??).

churn *InfoMgt, Mktg. NY Times*, 11/08/96, C2.

classic *LitArts.* Carl Van Doren, "Ave Atque Vale," *Collecting Himself, James Thurber on Writing and Writers, Humor and Himself* (NY: Harper Perennial, 1989), 89.

classical music concerts *Mgt, MusArts.* Diana Jean Schemo, "Philharmonic Deficits Persist Despite Gains of New Regime," *NY Times*, 06/30/94, B1, B6.

classical music *MusArts.* Donal Henahan, "The Changing World of Classical Music: What Next?" *NY Times*, 01/31/88, 1, 28.

collaboration *TheatArts.* Oliver Smith, in Lehman Engel, *Getting the Show On* (NY: Schirmer, 1983), 79.

comedy *Flm&Vid, LitArts, TheatArts.* Edmund Gwenn quoted by James Tipton to Neil Simon, *Inside the Actors Studio* (Bravo cablecast, 1996).

comic *PA-Variety.* Bill Hicks, in John Lahr, "Annals of Comedy" "The Goat Boy Rises," *New Yorker*, 11/01/93, 113-115.

command line interface. *iMedia* David Gerding, "Aesthetics of Interactive Multimedia," 1997, online article.

commercial *MusArts.* Len Lyons and Don Perlo, *Jazz Portraits: The Lives and Music of the Jazz Masters* (NY: Quill, William Morrow, 1989), Glossary.

commercial *VisA&C.* Malcolm Rogers, Director, Museum of Fine Arts (Boston), in Susan Diesenhouse, "Banned in Boston, but Sure to Make a Show a Hit," *NY Times*, 12/12/96, B1, B4.

commercialization of the art market *VisArts.* Rudolf Arnheim, *To The Rescue of Art: Twenty-Six Essays* (Berkeley: U. California Press, 19??).

communication *Aes&Creat, Crit&Eval, InfoMgt.* Katherine Anne Porter, *Letters of Katherine Anne Porter* (NY: Atlantic Monthly Press, 1990), 358.

competition *MusArts.* Harvey Phillips, *New Yorker*, 12/15/75.

complex *iMedia.* David Gerding, *Aesthetics of Interactive Media*, 1996; 97, 98, 99.

computer technology *InfoMgt.* Tess

Durham, Creating Staffing, Hallmark Cards, Kansas City, MO.

conscience *Eth&Phil.* Ogden Nash, "Inter-Office Memorandum," *I'm a Stranger Here Myself* (Boston: Little Brown, 1938), 28.

consent decree of 1948 *Flm&Vid, Law&Pol.* David Londoner, in Geraldine Fabricant, "Let's Make a Deal: Entertainment Mergers Show Desire to Run Production and Distribution," *NY Times* (??).

contemporary art *VisArts.* Andy Grundberg, "The Cincinnati Obscenity Trial and What Makes Photos Art?" *NY Times*, 10/10/90.

content *Flm&Vid, LitArts, MusArts.* David Salzman, "Listen Up! Quincy Jones Has A New Gig, and It's In Multimedia," *NY Times*, 06/05/95, C4.

contraction and release *Dnce.* Anna Kisselgoff, "Límon Troupe in Tribute to a Mentor and Early Guide, *NY Times*, 11/16/95, B2.

control *MusArts.* Sonny Rollins, in Bob Beden, "Sonny Rollins," *Down Beat*, Aug. 1997, 25.

controversy *Crit&Eval.* Malcolm Rogers, Director, Museum of Fine Arts (Boston), in Susan Diesenhouse, "Banned in Boston, but Sure to Make a Show a Hit," *NY Times*, 12/12/96, B1, B4.

cool *Crit&Eval.* Stephen Holden, "As icon, Sinatra Image May Reflect Style Over Talent," *NY Times*, 05/17/98, 23.

copyist *MusArts.* Julia Collins, "Music Copyists: Dwindling Breed, But a Hardy One," *NY Times*, 01/28/88,

creative process *Aes&Creat, ArtPerf.* Barbara Tuchman, "The Historian as Artist," *Practicing History* (NY: Knopf, 1981), 45-46.

creativity *ArtPerf.* Arthur Koestler, in Daniel J. Boorstin, "Book Three: Creating the Self," *The Creators: A History of Heroes of the Imagination* (NY: Random House, 1992), 553.

creativity *Journ, LitArts.* William Raspberry "The Write Stuff," *Times-Picayune*, 06/10/94, B7.

critic *Crit&Eval.* Howard Becker, "Aesthetics, Aestheticians, and Critics," *Art Worlds* (Berkeley: U. California Press, 1982), 131.

critic *Crit&Eval.* Alan Riding, "R.B. Kitaj's Revenge on British Art Critics," *International Herald Tribune*, 06/11/97, 24.

criticism *Crit&Eval.* Phyllis Rose, *Writing on Women: Essays in a Renaissance* (Middleton, CT: Wesleyan U. Press, 1980), 77.

cross-dressing *ArtPerf, Cult&Soc.* Marjorie Garber, *Vested Interests Cross-Dressing and Cultural Anxiety* (??, Routledge, 19??).

crossover *RecA&S.* Matthew Gurewitsch, *Town & Country*, Sep. 1996.

cultural awareness *Cult&Soc.* Bill Clinton, in Jacques Trescott, "The First Fan: Sure, Clinton likes culture, but does he have a supportive policy?" *The Washington Post National Weekly Edition*, 05/16-22/94, 9.

cultural diversity *Cult&Soc.* Alvin Toffler, "Diversity, Computers and Classrooms,"

Future Shock (NY: Bantam, 1971), 270.

culture war *Cult&Soc.* James Davison Hunter, "Covering The Culture War: Before the Shooting Begins," *Columbia Journalism Review*, Jul./Aug. 1993, 29.

customized news *InfoMgt, Journ.* David Barboza, *NY Times*, "The Media Business," 10/01/96, C5.

cutting contest *MusArts.* Eileen Southern, *The Music of Black Americans* (NY: Norton, 1971), 343.

cynical *Eth&Phil.* Lily Tomlin, National Public Radio, 05/17/91.

<hr/>

D

Davis, Miles *ArtPerf, MusArts.* Ian Carr, *Jazz, The Rough Guide* (London: The Rough Guides, 1995), 158-161.

deconstruction *Crit&Eval.* Allan Bloom, *The Closing of the American Mind*, in Mitchell Stephens, "Deconstruction and the Get-Real Press, *Columbia Journalism Review*, Sep./Oct. 1991, 38.

design *LitArts.* Malcolm Cowley, *Paris Review: Interviews, Writers at Work* (NY: Penguin, 1958), 21.

design *VisArts.* John Loring, in Holly Brubach, "Profiles: Giving Good Value," *New Yorker*, 08/10/92, 54.

digital recording *RecA&S.* Herbert von Karajan, in Thomas Hohlhase, Annotation, Tschaikowsky's *Symphony No. 6 (Pathetique)* (Polydor).

disco *Dnce.* Harvey Rachlin, *Encyclopedia of the Music Business* (NY: Harper & Row, 1981), 140.

distribution *Mktg.* David Londoner, *NY Times*, (??).

diversity *Cult&Soc.* Dennis Rich, Columbia College Chicago, 1995.

Dorsey, Thomas A. *ArtPerf, MusArts.* Eileen Southern, *The Music of Black Americans* (NY: Norton, 1971), 403-404.

drambalet *Dnce.* Joan Acocella, "Lost and Found," *New Yorker*, 07/26/99, 88.

droit de suite *LegalAsp, VisArts.* Leonard D. DuBoff, *Art Law in a Nutshell* (1 St. Paul, Minn.: West Publishing Co., 1984), 240.

<hr/>

E

economic freedom *LitArts.* William Faulkner, *Paris Review: Interviews, Writers at Work* (NY: Penguin, 1958), 125.

editor *Flm&Vid.* Michael Kahn in Bernard Weinraub, "Hollywood's Kindest Cuts," *NY Times*, 08/20/98, B1.

editor *Journ, LegalAsp.* Ben Bradlee (??).

editor *Journ, LitArts.* Martin Arnold, "Making Books," *NY Times*, 09/17/98, B3.

ego *Mgt.* Geraldine Fabricant and Bernard Weinraub, "One Deal Off. One Deal On. Well, That's Entertainment." *NY Times*, 06/19/95, C1.

ego trip *ArtPerf.* [Konstantine] Stanislavski, in Conrad L Osborne, "Opera's Fabulous Vanishing Act," *NY Times*, 02/17/91, sect. 2, 30.

egocentric *ArtPerf.* Frank Rich, "A Wild Desire to Be Absolutely Fascinating," *NY*

Times Book Review, 09/29/91, 3.

17:2&**egoism** *Eth&Phil.* George Orwell, *George Orwell, The Orwell Reader, Fiction, Essays* (NY: Harcourt Brace Jovanovich, 1956); 271.

electronic music *MusArts.* Howard Sandroff, *Gramaphone* (NARAS-Chicago, Apr. 1993), 3.

empathic response *Crit&Eval.* Jason Robards, in John Patrick Shanley, "Two Helpings for a Stage-Hungry Actor," *NY Times,* 09/12/95, B1.

empathic response *Crit&Eval.* John P. Marquand, *Women and Thomas Harrow* (Boston: Little, Brown, 1958), 18.

enhanced CDs *RecA&S.* Charles Bermant, "Enhanced CDs Promise To Redefine 'Liner Notes," *NY Times,* 12/11/94, F9.

epic *TheatArts.* Bowman and Ball, *Theatre Language,* (??), 124.

equity *VisArts.* Susan Lee, "Greed Is Not Just for Profit," *Forbes,* 04/18/88, 66.

erotic music law *Law&Pol, MusArts.* Lynn Decker, *Civil Liberties,* Spring 1994, 16.

esthetics *Aes&Creat.* Robert Shaw, in James. E. Oestreich, "Lesson in Humanity from a Master," *NY Times,* 01/25/94, B3.

ethical *Eth&Phil* Wayne C. Booth, *The Company We Keep, An Ethics of Fiction* (Berkeley: U. California Press, 1988).

ethical criticism *Crit&Eval, Eth&Phil.* Wayne C. Booth, *The Company We Keep, An Ethics of Fiction* (Berkeley: U. California Press, 1988).

ethnocentricity *Cult&Soc.* Wynton Marsalis, in William Raspberry, "The Write Stuff," *Times-Picayune,* 06/10/94, B7.

ETV *Rdio&TV.* Edmund F. Penney, *Facts On File Dictionary of Film and Broadcast Terms* (NY: Facts on File, 1991), 79.

experimental *Crit&Eval, LitArts.* Robert Penn Warren, *Paris Review: Interviews, Writers at Work* (NY: Penguin, 1958), 200.

export *Eco&Fin.* Todd Gitlin, "World Leaders: Mickey, et al.," *NY Times,* 05/03/92, sect. 2,1.

_____ **F** _____

fame *Crit&Eval.* Madonna, "Loveless Madonna" in "People," *Times-Picayune,* 08/27/98, A22.

fast *PerfA&C.* Colleen Dewhurst, *Her Autobiography,* written and completed by Tom Viola, (NY: Scribner, 1993), 144.

female writers *Cult&Soc, LitArts.* Dorothy Parker, in Marion Meade, *Dorothy Parker: What Fresh Hell Is This?* (NY: Penguin, 1989), 205.

female writers *Cult&Soc, LitArts.* Virginia Woolf, *Concise Columbia Dictionary of Quotations* (NY: Avon Books, 1990), 292.

feminist critics *Crit&Eval.* Wayne C. Booth, *The Company We Keep, An Ethics of Fiction* (Berkeley: U. California Press, 1988).

feminist *Cult&Soc.* Jon Pareles, "In New York, Streisand is a Hometown Hero." *NY Times,* 06/22/94, B3.

fiber *Journ, VA-Prntng.* Paul Saffo, in John Markoff, "With a Debut, A Test of On-line Publishing," *NY Times,* 11/13/95.

fine art, fine arts *Aes&Creat, VisArts.* **Resale Royalties Act** (1984), in Leonard D. DuBoff, *Art Law in a Nutshell,* (St. Paul, Minn.: West Publishing Co., 1984), 240.

flag-waving *Crit&Eval.* George M. Cohan, in "Stars, Bars and Cars," *NY Times,* 06/17/97, A14.

flatted fifth *MusArts.* Len Lyons and Don Perlo, *Jazz Portraits: The Lives and Music of the Jazz Masters* (NY: Quill, William Morrow, 1989), Glossary.

folk music *MusArts.* Edward Rothstein, "Classical View" "'60's 'Folk' Is Giving Up The Ghost," *NY Times,* 05/30/93, H25.

footprint *Mktg, Rdio&TV.* *NY Times,* 06/25/96.

freaking out *Cult&Soc.* Frank Zappa, liner notes for his Mothers of Invention album, *Freak Out* (1966) in Connie Bruck, "Life of the Party," *New Yorker,* 01/25/99, 31.

free jazz *MusArts.* James Lincoln Collier, *The Making of Jazz* (NY: Delta Book/Dell, 1978), 469.

freedom *Crit&Eval, Eth&Phil.* Henri Matisse, *Jazz* (NYC: George Braziller, 1983, 1992), xxiv-xxvii.

freedom of the press *Journ, Law&Pol.* A. J. Liebling, *The Press,* 2nd rev. ed, (NY: Ballantine, 1975), 32.

funk *Dnce* Savion Glover, in John Lahr, "King Tap," *New Yorker,* 10/30/95, 90.

_____ **G** _____

Garland, Judy *ArtPerf, Flm&Vid, MusArts, PA-Variety, Rdio&TV.* Margo Jefferson, "An Unhappy Ending For the Girl Next Door," *NY Times,* 08/12/93, B4; in a review of David Shipman, *Judy Garland, The Secret Life of an American Legend* (Hyperion, 1993).

gederim *Crit&Eval.* Yip Harburg, in John Lahr, "The Lemon-Drop Kid [Yip Harburg]," *New Yorker,* 09/30/96, 71.

genius *ArtPerf, Crit&Eval.* Stephen Sondheim in Frank Rich, "Shall We Dance," *NY Times,* 8/1/98, A23.

genius *ArtPerf, Crit&Eval.* Immanuel Kant, in Arthur C. Danto, *Encounters & Reflections* (NY: Farrar Straus Giroux, 1990), 327.

ghost light *PerfA&C.* James Shapiro, "Lullaby of Broadway," *NY Times Book Review,* 10/29/2000, 6.

gig piece *MusArts.* Jeffrey Magee, "Report on the Integrative Studies Retreat," *Lenox Avenue,* vol.2/1996.

Gillespie, Dizzy *ArtPerf, MusArts.* Ian Carr, *Jazz, The Rough Guide* (London: The Rough Guides, 1995), 234-237.

good music *MusArts.* Duke Ellington, in Eileen Southern, *The Music of Black Americans* (NY: Norton, 1971), 387.

graffiti *Cult&Soc, VisA&C.* "Graffiti in Their Own Words," >http://www.dougweb.com/pgraf.html<

graphic artist *ArtPerf, VisA&C.* Chip Kidd, "Cover Boy," *NY Times Magazine,* 11/10/96, 50.

gross profit participant *Flm&Vid.* Mick Stevens's cartoon, *New Yorker,* 06/12/95, 43.

_____ **H** _____

hard bop *MusArts.* Len Lyons and Don Perlo, *Jazz Portraits: The Lives and Music of the Jazz Masters* (NY: Quill, William Morrow, 1989), Glossary.

heavy metal rock *MusArts.* Jane and Michael Stern, *The Encyclopedia of Bad Taste,* in Gareth Cook, "The Dark Side of Camp," *Washington Monthly,* Sep. 1995, 12.

Hicks, Bill *ArtPerf, PA-Variety.* John Lahr, "Annals of Comedy" — "The Goat Boy Rises," *New Yorker,* 11/01/93, 113-115.

hillbilly music *MusArts.* Hank Williams, in Douglas Green, "Hank Williams," *George Simon and Friends: The Best of the Music Makers* (NY: Doubleday, 1979), 616.

Holiday, Billie *ArtPerf, MusArts.* Len Lyons and Don Perlo, *Jazz Portraits: The Lives and Music of the Jazz Masters* (NY: Quill, William Morrow, 1989), 282.

Hollywood *Eth&Phil.* David McClintic, *Indecent Exposure: A True Story of Hollywood & Wall Street* (NY, Dell Publishing, 1983), 513.

Hollywood *Flm&Vid, Mgt.* Gale Anne Hurd, in Bernard Weinraub. "A Woman Knows What Men Like: Action Films," *NY Times,* 05/03/94, B1.

hot *ArtPerf.* William Faulkner, in Alfred Kazin, "William Faulkner: The Stillness of Light in August" (1957), *Contemporaries* (Boston: Little, Brown, 1962), 148.

HUAC *Eth&Phil, Law&Pol.* Mort Sahl, in Eric Lax, *Woody Allen: A Biography* (NY: Knopf, 1991), 137.

human resources (HR) *HR&LR, Mgt. Human Resource Management,* Mathis & Jackson, 9th ed., South-Western College Publishing Co., 2000.

humor *Crit&Eval* Leo Rosten, "Introduction, "*Hooray for Yiddish! A Book About English* (NY: Simon & Schuster, 1982), 12.

humorist *LitArts.* E.B. White, "Preface," *A Subtreasury of American Humor,* eds. E.B. White and Katharine S. White (NY: Coward • McCann, 1941), xix, xviii.

_____ **I** _____

ideology *Cult&Soc.* Ferdinand Mount, *The Subversive Family* (NY: Free Press, 19??).

imagination *Crit&Eval.* Yip Harburg, in John Lahr, "The Lemon-Drop Kid [Yip Harburg]," *New Yorker,* 09/30/96, 73.

imitation *Crit&Eval.* Aristotle, *Poetics,* 4th chap.

immortality *Crit&Eval.* Erica Jong, *Parachutes & Kisses* (NY: New American Library, 1984), 42.

immortality *Crit&Eval.* Woody Allen, in Eric Lax, *Woody Allen: A Biography* (NY: Knopf, 1991), in Molly Haskell, "Making an Art of Angst." *NY Times Book Review,* 05/12/91, 1, 30-31.

improvisation Whitney Balliett, "Jazz: Rollins Rampant," *New Yorker,* 07/29/91; 58, 59.

in the moment *Crit&Eval, TheatArts.* Alan Alda in William Safire, "In Language — Great Moments in Moments," *NY Times*

Magazine, 05/10/98, 12.

Information Management *InfoMgt.* William Shawn, in Eric Pace. "William Shawn, 85, Is Dead; *New Yorker's* Gentle Despot," *NY Times,* 09/09/92, 15.

inspiration *ArtPerf.* Harold Shapero, "The Musical Mind," *Modern Music,* Winter 1946, 49.

instant book *LitArts, Mktg.* Doreen Carvajal, "The Long Unaboma Manhunt Becomes a Paperback Sprint," *NY Times,* 05/12/96, 1.

instant gratification *Mktg.* Allan Kozinn, "Critic's Notebook:" "Promoting Classical Music as a Cool Summer Postlude," *NY Times,* 09/05/95, B1.

intellectual property *IntelProp.* Edward P. Murphy, "Songwriters See Copyrights Infringed in Rap Parody Case," *NY Times,* 12/03/93.

────────── **J** ──────────

JAVA, *InfoMgt.* John Markoff, "Making the PC Come Alive," *NY Times,* 09/25/95, C1.

jazz origins *Cult&Soc, MusArts.* Eileen Southern, *The Music of Black Americans: A History* (NY: Norton, 1971), 374-375.

jazz tap *Dnce.* Sally Sommer, *NY Times* News Service,?? /??/95.

Jazznet *ArtPerf, MusArts.* Ben Ratliff, "$6 Million in Grants Will Go to Jazz," *NY Times,* 07/28/99, B3.

Jerry Lewis Syndrome *Crit&Eval.* Henry Louis Gates, Jr., "The Charmer [Louis Farrakhan]," *New Yorker,* 04/29&05/06/96, 120.

joke *Crit&Eval.* Leo Rosten, *Hooray for Yiddish! A Book About English* (NY: Simon & Schuster, 1982), 12.

judgment *Crit&Eval.* John Dewey, "Criticism and Perception," *Art As Experience* (NY: Capricon Books, 1959).

jungle *MusArts, Dnce.* Anita M. Samuels, "Freeze-Dried Music: Just Add Artists," *NY Times,* 09/04/95, B1, B22.

justice *Eth&Phil, Law&Pol.* H.L. Mencken, (??).

────────── **K** ──────────

kerosene journalism *Journ.* Ben Bradlee, *"A Good Life,"* NYC: Simon & Schuster, 1995, 487.

kinderslut *Fashn.* Gareth Cook, "The Dark Side of Camp," *Washington Monthly,* Sep. 1995, 12.

kitsch *VisA&C.* Clement Greenberg, *Hollywood Diva (Jeanette Diva),* Edward Baron Turk, U. of California Press, 1998, 343.

────────── **L** ──────────

land *Crit&Eval, MusArts, TheatArts.* Stephen Sondheim, *Inside the Actors Studio* (Bravo cablecast, 1995).

lay an egg *Crit&Eval.* "Wall Street Lays an Egg," *Variety* headline, Oct. 1929.

lead trumpet *MusArts.* Peter Watrous, *NY Times* News Service, (??), 1995.

leave a tip *PerfA&C.* Billy Crystal, Interview on *Actors Studio,* PBS-TV, 1998.

less is more *ArtPerf, Crit&Eval.* Anthony Hopkins, *Charlie Rose,* PBS-TV, 11/25/93.

levee camp music *MusArts.* Louis Armstrong, exhibit placard, in *Louis Armstrong., A Cultural Legacy,* New Orleans Museum of Art, Dec. 1995.

licking the script *Flm&Vid* Joan Didion, *Political Fictions* (NY: Alfred A. Knopf.

listening *TheatArts.* Robert DiNiro, *Actors Studio,* PBS-TV.

lurking *InfoMgt.* AT&T *Powersource,* Spring-Summer 1996, 10.

Loretta Young silks *Flm&Vid.* Tallulah Bankhead, in Abby Adams, *An Uncommon Scold* (NY: Simon & Schuster, 1989), 173.

love *Crit&Eval.* Ben Brantley, "For Liza Minnelli, the Affection of Her Fans Is the Milk of Life," *NY Times,* 01/14/97, B1.

love *Crit&Eval.* Robin Williams in Dotson Rader, "What Really Makes Life Fun," *Parade Magazine,* 09/20/98, 4.

loyalty oath *Eth&Phil, Law&Pol.* Joseph Papp, "I'm a Producer, Not a Censor," *NY Times,* 04/24/90, Op-Ed.

lundu *Dnce.* Joyce Carlson-Leavitt, "Chiquinha Gonzaga, Mulatta Originator of Forerunners of the Samba," *Kalinda!,* CBMR, Winter 1996, 2.

lyricist *LitArts, MusArts.* Ira Gershwin, in Philip Furia, *Ira Gershwin, The Art of the Lyricist* (NY: Oxford, 1996).

lyrics *LitArts, MusArts.* Stephen Sondheim, in Annette Grant. "Line by Line by Sondheim," *NY Times Magazine,* 03/20/94, 43.

────────── **M** ──────────

MacGuffin *Flm&Vid, Rdio&TV. New Yorker,* 06/03/96.

magic *Crit&Eval.* Daniel Goleman, in Mihaly Csikzentmihalyi, *Flow: The Psychology of Optimal Experience* (NY: Harper Perennial, 1990), 266.

makeup designer *PerfA&C.* Marlene Dietrich, Abby Adams, *An Uncommon Scold* (NY: Simon & Schuster, 1989), 173.

mainstream *Cult&Soc.* Barry Gaither, *Cultural Democracy,* Winter 1987.

mainstreaming *Journ.* Wanda Lloyd, a Gannett editor, "Just Add Color," *Brill's Content,* Mar '99, 82.

marketer *also* **marketeer** *Mktg.* Patricia Cox, "Marketing the Performing Arts: A Personal View," *Market the Arts!* compiled and edited by Joseph V. Melillo (NY: FEDAPT, 1983), 43.

Matisse, Henri *ArtPerf, VisA&C.* Carter Ratcliff, "Matisse, Henri," *Grolier Multimedia Encyclopedia* (AOL 07/18/97).

maw *Flm&Vid.* James Tipton, *Inside the Actors Studio* (Bravo cablecast, 1996).

Melancholy Baby *MusArts.* Alec Wilder, *American Popular Song — The Great Innovators, 1900-1950.* Ed. and Intro. by James T. Maher. (NY: Oxford U. Press, 1972), 17.

MIDI *InfoMgt, MusInstr.* Howard Sandroff, *Gramaphone,* Apr. 1993.

minimalism *LitArts.* X.J. Kennedy and Dana Gioia, *An Introduction to Fiction,* 6th ed., HarperCollins)

minstrelsy *Cult&Soc, MusArts, PA-Variety.* Margo Jefferson, "Beautiful Dreamer," *NY Times Book Review,* 06/29/97, 5; in a book review of *Doo-Dah!: Stephen Foster and the Rise of American Popular Culture* by Ken Emerson (NY: Simon & Schuster, 1997).

minstrelsy *Cult&Soc, PA-Variety.* Lawrence W. Levine, *NY Times Book Review,* 02/27/94.

modern art *VisArts.* Wallace Stevens, "Introduction," *Robert Penn Warren: A Collection of Critical Essays* (Englewood Cliffs, NJ: Prentice-Hall, 1980).

mooks *Cult&Soc, MusArts.* R.J. Smith, "Among the Mooks,: *NY Times Magazine,* 08/06/2000, 36, 41.

moral majority *Eth&Phil* Wayne C. Booth, *The Company We Keep, An Ethics of Fiction* (Berkeley: U. California Press, 1988),

morality *Aes&Creat.* Jack Beatty, in Roger Cohen. "Book Notes: Of Chopped Up Women and a Rejected Review," *NY Times,* 07/03/91, B2.

morality *Aes&Creat.* Robert Brustein, "Don't Punish the Arts," *NY Times,* 06/23/89.

morals *Aes&Creat.* Bertolt Brecht, *Threepenny Opera,* 1928.

morals *Aes&Creat.* Ernest Hemingway, *Paris Review,* Spring 1958.

morals clause *Eth&Phil, LegalAsp.* April Smith, *North of Montana* (NY: Ballantine Books, 1994), 287.

mud colors *Fashn, VisArts.* Dorothy Jeakins, in Lawrence Van Gelder, "Dorothy Jeakins Dies at 81; Designed Costumes for Films*NY Times,* 11/30/95.

multimedia *Crit&Eval.* Quincy Jones, *NY Times,* 06/05/95, C4.

Muse *LitArts, MusArts, PerfA&C.* Robert Rauschenberg, in John Russell, *Rauschenberg: Art and Life* (??: Abrams, 19??).

music critic *Crit&Eval, Journ, MusArts* Bernard Holland, "Classical View: Colleagues, Critique Thyselves," *NY Times,* 07/21/86, 4, 25.

Music Licensing Task Force *IntelProp, MusArts.* ASAE *Association Report,* a supplement to *Association Management,* (American Society of Association Executives, Wash., DC), Nov. 1990.

musical *TheatArts.* John Lahr, *Automatic Vaudeville, Essays on Star Turns* (NY: Limelight Editions, 1985), 6.

musical theatre *MusArts, TheatArts.* John Lahr, "The Lemon-Drop Kid [Yip Harburg]," *New Yorker,* 09/30/96, 70.

mystery *Crit&Eval.* Ralph Richardson, in Kenneth Tynan, *At Three Minutes Past Eight, You Must Dream* (NY: Simon & Schuster, 1979), 15.

────────── **N** ──────────

Negro music *Cult&Soc, MusArts.* LeRoi Jones, (a.k.a. Imamu Amiri Baraka) "Introduction," *Blues People* (NY: William Morrow, 1963), ix-x.

nerd *InfoMgt.* Sheryl WuDunn, "Japanese Critics Assert Schools Led Best and Brightest Into Sect," *NY Times,* 05/22/95,1.

net profit participant *Flm&Vid.* Aljean Harmetz, "Buchwald Ruling: Film Writers vs. Star Power," *NY Times,* 01/14/91.

New Deal *Cult&Soc*, *Law&Pol*. Eleanor Roosevelt, (??).

New Orleans jazz *Cult&Soc*, *MusArts*. Eileen Southern, *The Music of Black Americans: A History* (NY: Norton, 1971), 58.

New York Jazz *MusArts*. Ann Douglas, "Feel the City's Pulse. It's Be-bop, Man!" *NY Times,* 08/28/98, B1.

New York Times v. Sullivan *Journ*, *LegalAsp*. Renata Adler, *Reckless Disregard: Westmoreland v. CBS et al.; Sharon v. Time* (NY: Vintage, 1986), 244-245.

nonprofit theater *TheatArts*. Donald G. McNeil, Jr., "On Stage, and Off," *NY Times,* 06/09/95, B2.

nose job *Cult&Soc*. Jon Pareles, *NY Times,* 06/22/94, B3.

nostalgia *Crit&Eval*. John Lahr, *Automatic Vaudeville, Essays on Star Turns* (NY: Limelight Editions, 1985), 6.

numbers *Journ* , *Mktg*. Leonard A. Lauder, in Deirdre Carmody, "Big Challenge for *Harper's Bazaar* Is Beating Back Gossip," *NY Times,* 06/19/95, C7.

—————————**O**—————————

obbligato *MusArts*. Len Lyons and Don Perlo, *Jazz Portraits: The Lives and Music of the Jazz Masters* (NY: Quill, William Morrow, 1989), Glossary.

obscenity *Law&Pol*. Justice William Brennan, in Nat Hentoff, "Profiles, The Constitutionalist," *New Yorker,* 03/12/90, 56.

off-line delivery *InfoMgt*. David Barboza, *NY Times,* "The Media Business," 10/01/96, C5.

off the record *Journ*. Edward Pound (reporter, *U.S. News & World Report*), "On Deep Background," *American Journalism Review,* Dec. 1994, 23.

on deep background *Journ*. Bob Woodward, "On Deep Background," *American Journalism Review,* Dec. 1994, 23.

on the road *MusArts*, *TheatArts*. Louis Armstrong, in Whitney Balliett, "King Louis," *New Yorker,* 08/08/94, 70, 72.

one-way option *LegalAsp*, *Mgt*. Lawrence Olivier, *Confessions of an Actor: An Autobiography.* (NY: Penguin, 1984),109.

origin *Cult&Soc*, *MusArts*. Ralph Vaughan Williams, "Folk-Song," *The Treasury of the Encyclopaedia Britannica* (NY: Viking Penguin, 1992), 663.

overall storyteller *LitArts*. *Writing from Start to Finish*, by John Schultz, 1982, 1983, 1990, Heinemann/Boynton-Cook. Teacher's Manual for *Writing from Start to Finish*, by John Schultz, 1983, Heinemann/Boynton-Cook...

—————————**P**—————————

Charlie Parker *ArtPerf*, *MusArts*. Sonny Rollins, in Bob Beden, "Sonny Rollins," *Down Beat,* Aug. 1997, 22.

part *Flm&Vid*, *TheatArts*. Mike Nichols to Robert Redford in Richard Rayner, "Essential Cowboy, *New Yorker,* 05/18/98, 64.

payola *Eth&Phil*, *RecA&S*. Jerry Wexler and David Ritz, *Rhythm and the Blues, A Life in American Music* (NY: Knopf, 1993).

pedestal presenter *Mgt*. Kenneth Fischer, director, Musical Society of the U. of Michigan, Ann Arbor, in Barbara Jepson, "A New Era in the Care and Feeding of Artists," *NY Times,* 06/16/96, H28.

peer *Crit&Eval*. Ben Bradlee, *"A Good Life,"* NYC: Simon & Schuster, 1995, 487.

performance *IntelProp*, *LglAsp*. "An Act of Fairness?" *Art Law Forum,* Sep. 1998, 1.

personal manager (PM) *Mgt*. Charlie Joffe, and Eric Lax, *Woody Allen, A Biography* (NY: Knopf, 1991), 149.

personas *Genl*. Burt Reynolds, in Lynn Hirschberg, "Deliverance," *NY Times Magazine,* 06/16/96.

philistine *Crit&Eval*. William J. Baumel in Allen R. Myerson, "What's the Worst Place to Keep Art? A Portfolio," *NY Times,* 08/28/93, Y29.

phonorecords *IntelProp*, *RecA&S*. Harvey Rachlin, *Encyclopedia of the Music Business* (NY: Harper & Row, 1981), 257.

photo op *Journ*, *VA-Photo*. Russell Baker, "Observer — Oh, What Fun It Is," *NY Times,* 05/11/96, 15.

photographists *ArtPerf*, *VisA&C*. Arthur C. Danto, "Nan Goldin's World," *The Nation,* 12/02/96, 35.

Picasso, Pablo *ArtPerf*, *VisA&C*. Pablo Picasso, in Daniel J. Boorstin, *The Creators: A History of Heroes of the Imagination* (NY: Random House, 1992), ix.

piracy *RecA&S*. Douglas Jehl, "Warning To China On Trade," *NY Times,* 04/30/94, Y17.

plot holes *Crit&Eval*, *Flm&Vid*, *LitArts*. Larry Gelbart, "A Beginning, a Muddle, and an End," *NY Times Book Review,* 03/02/97, 8.

poetry *LitArts*. Benedetto Croce, "The Condition of Criticism in Italy," *The John Hopkins U. Lectures in Criticism,* Bollingen ser. xvi (NY: Pantheon, 1949), 180-181.

politically correct *Cult&Soc*. "Who Controls Art? Artists or Social Goals?" (Unsigned editorial), *NY Times,* 01/??/91,??.

politically correct *Cult&Soc*. George Orwell, "Why I Write," *George Orwell, The Orwell Reader, Fiction, Essays* (NY: Harcourt Brace Jovanovich, 1956).

politics *Law&Pol*. [Konstantine] Stanislavski, in Conrad L. Osborne, "Opera's Fabulous Vanishing Act," *NY Times,* 02/17/91, sect. 2, 30.

popular music *Cult&Soc*. Linda Ronstadt, in Stephen Holden, "The Pop Life: Linda Ronstadt Singing More Songs In Spanish," *NY Times,* 12/07/91, 12.

popular music *Mktg*, *MusArts*. Tom Vickers, in John Milward, "Competing With the Kids is No Simple Matter," *NY Times,* ?? /??/97.

presence *ArtPerf*, *TheatArts*. John P. Marquand, *Women and Thomas Harrow* (Boston: Little, Brown, 1958), 424.

presentatial actor *TheatArts*. Uta Hagen, with Haskel Frankel, *Respect for Acting* (NY: Macmillan, 1973), 11-12.

Presley, Elvis *ArtPerf*, *Flm&Vid*, *MusArts*.

Henry Pleasants, *The Great American Popular Singers,* 1985.

preview *also* **prevue** *TheatArts*. Ralph Blumenthal, "More Previews Than Performances," *NY Times,* 08/10/96, B12.

primitive *Cult&Soc*. Franz Boas, "Preface," *Primitive Art* (NY: Dover Publications, 1955), 1.

professional (**visual**) **artist** *ArtPerf*, *Mktg*, *VisArts*. John McCrory, in Curtis W. Casewit, *Making a Living In the Fine Arts: Advice From the Pros* (NY: Collier, 1984), 18.

professional *ArtPerf*. Alistair Cooke, "Humphrey Bogart: Epitaph for a Tough Guy," *Six Men* (NY: Berkeley Book, 1978), 220-221.

professional critic *Crit&Eval*. John Crowe Ransom, (??).

professional dancers *Dnce*. Cobbett Steinberg, *The Dance Anthology,* ed. Cobbett Steinberg (NY: New American Library, 1980), 171.

professional directors and screenwriters *Flm&Vid*, *LitArts*, *TheatArts*. Bernard Weinraub, "A Consumer Warning On Movie Alterations," *NY Times,* 03/09/93, B1.

professional musicians *ArtPerf*, *MusArts*. Roland Hanna, "The First Chorus," *down beat,* 04/10/75, 4.

Public Broadcasting Act of 1967 *Rdio&TV*. Edmund F. Penney. *Facts On File Dictionary of Film and Broadcast Terms* (NY: Facts on File, 1991), 177.

public policy *Cult&Soc*, *Law&Pol*. Garrison Keillor, "Thanks for Attacking the N.E.A.," *NY Times,* 04/04/90, Op-Ed.

public policy *Cult&Soc*, *Law&Pol*. Republican Party, excerpt from its platform adopted in convention, Houston, 08/17/92.

pulse *MusArts*. Len Lyons and Don Perlo, *Jazz Portraits: The Lives and Music of the Jazz Masters* (NY: Quill, William Morrow, 1989), Glossary.

Pulitzer Prize *Journ*, *LitArts*, *MusArts*, *TheatArts*, *VisA&C*. Eileen Southern, *The Music of Black Americans,* (NY: Norton, 1971), 482.

punch up *InfoMgt* Les Blatt, ABC News. in Marc Gunther, "News You Can Choose," *American Journalism Review,* Nov. 1995, 37.

puritanism. *Crit&Eval*. H.L. Mencken, ??.

push technology *InfoMgt*. Seth Schiesel, "Technology," *NY Times,* 06/02/97, C4.

—————————**R**—————————

race *PerfA&C*. Louis Armstrong, in Whitney Balliett, "King Louis," *New Yorker,* 08/08/94, 70, 72.

race records *Cult&Soc*, *RecA&S*. Eileen Southern, *The Music of Black Americans: A History* (NY: Norton, 1971), 398.

Rainey, Ma *ArtPerf*, *MusArts*, *RecA&S*. Eileen Southern, *The Music of Black Americans: A History* (NY: Norton, 1971), 398.

rap music *MusArts*. Adam Sexton, comp., *Rap in Rap* (1995), in *Grolier Multimedia Encyclopedia* (AOL 07/24/97).

rap-metal *Cult&Soc, MusArts*. R.J. Smith, "Among the Mooks, *NY Times Magazine,* 08/06/2000, 36, 41.

reality *Crit&Eval*. David Craig, "Act One, Scene One: Style," *On Performing* (NY: McGraw-Hill, 1989), 9.

red flag words and expressions *LglAsp*. Kenneth P. Norwick, Jerry Simon Chasen, *The Rights of Authors, Artists, and Other Creative People*, 2nd ed., (Carbondale, IL: Southern Ill. U. Press, 1992).

rejection *ArtPerf, Crit&Eval*. Jane Alexander, "Jane Alexander's Next Stage," *Washington Post National Weekly Edition,* 11/22-28/93, 11.

religious right *Cult&Soc, Eth&Phil*. Leanne Katz, "How Censorship Efforts by Religious Right Disrupt Education," *NY Times,* 12/11/92, A20.

repositioning *Mktg*. Sarah Lyall, "Resuscitating a Chintz Elephant," *NY Times,* 01/25/97, Y19.

represential actor *TheatArts*. Uta Hagen, with Haskel Frankel, *Respect for Acting* (NY: Macmillan, 1973), 11.

Resale Royalties Act (1983) *LegalAsp, VisArts*. Cal.Civ.Code §986 (West 1983), in Leonard D. Duboff, *Art Law in a Nutshell* (St. Paul, Minn.: West Pub., 1984), 240.

rewrite *Journ*. Woolcott Gibbs, *New Yorker,* (??).

rhythm and blues *MusArts*. Harvey Rachlin, *Encyclopedia of the Music Business* (NY: Harper & Row, 1981), 381.

ride rhythm *MusArts*. Len Lyons and Don Perlo, *Jazz Portraits: The Lives and Music of the Jazz Masters* (NY: Quill, William Morrow, 1989), Glossary.

ring dance *Cult&Soc, Dnce*. Eileen Southern, *The Music of Black Americans* (NY: Norton, 1971) 160-161.

ritual *Cult&Soc*. Camille Paglia , *Sexual Personae: Art and Decadence From Nefertiti to Emily Dickinson* (NY: Vintage, 1990).

rock beat *MusArts*. Len Lyons and Don Perlo, *Jazz Portraits: The Lives and Music of the Jazz Masters* (NY: Quill, William Morrow, 1989), Glossary.

Rollins, Sonny *ArtPerf, MusArts*. Brian Priestly, "Sonny Rollins, *Jazz, The Rough Guide* (London: The Rough Guides, 1995), 547.

royalty statement *IntelProp*. Edwin McDowell, "The Media Business: Authors Guild to Audit Some Royalty Statements," *NY Times,* 02/22/90.

ruthless ambition *ArtPerf*. William Faulkner, *Paris Review: Interviews, Writers at Work* (NY: Penguin, 1958), 123-124.

ruthlessness *Eco&Fin, Eth&Phil*. Russell Baker, "Lean, Mean, Love Ya," *NY Times.* OP-ED, 05/13/97, A15.

_____ S _____

satire *LitArts*. George S. Kaufman, in Sylvia Fine Kaye, *Musical Theatre* (PBS telecast, 1984).

scat singing *MusArts*. Mel Tormé, in Jonathan Schwartz, "The Divine Plea-

sures of an 'Absent Genius' [Ella Fitzgerald], *NY Times,* 06/23/96, H34.

scenic design *TheatArts, VisArts*. Vincent Canby, "Ready for Another Unflattering Closeup," *NY Times,* 06/04/95, 5.

schizophrenia *Crit&Eval*. Garson Kanin, *Hollywood* (NY: Bantam, 1976), 57.

schlepper *Crit&Eval*. John Lahr, *Automatic Vaudeville, Essays on Star Turns* (NY: Limelight Editions, 1985), 89.

second-line *MusArts*. Eileen Southern, *The Music of Black Americans* (NY: Norton, 1971), 343.

self-organizing system *InfoMgt, Mgt*. Margaret Wheatley, in Thomas Petzinger Jr., "This Company Uses Sound Business Rules From Mother Nature," *Wall Street Journal,* 07/12/96, B1.

self-taught art *Cult&Soc, VisA&C*. Holland Carter, "When Outsiders Make it Inside," *NY Times,* 04/10/98, B33.

sensory symbol *iMedia*. Colin Ware, *Information Visualization.,* San Diego: Academic Press, 2000.

serious artist *ArtPerf*. Brendan Gill, "The Sky Line: World Wide Plaza," *New Yorker,* 12/24/90, 86.

serious artist *ArtPerf*. E.B. White, "Preface," *A Subtreasury of American Humor,* eds. E.B. White and Katharine S. White (NY: Coward • McCann, 1941), xix, xviii.

serious literature *LitArts*. James Landis, "The Editor As Undertaker Or This Way To Temporary Immortality," *The Art of Literary Publishing: Editors On Their Craft* (Wainscott, NY: Pushcart Press, 1980), 137.

serious music *MusArts*. Jon Pareles, *NY Times,* 01/31/88, 28.

serious writers *LitArts*. George Orwell, *George Orwell, The Orwell Reader, Fiction, Essays* (NY: Harcourt Brace Jovanovich, 1956), 271.

shop *Mgt*. Peter Pastreich (executive director, San Francisco Symphony), in Barbara Jepson, "A New Era in the Care and Feeding of Artists," *NY Times,* 06/16/96, H28.

show biz *TheatArts* James Surowiecki, "TV On the Cheap," *New Yorker,* 03/04/02, 33.

show business *PerfA&C*. James Lincoln Collier, *Duke Ellington* (Oxford U. Press, 1987).

show business *PerfA&C*. William Goldman, *Adventures in the Screen Trade (A Personal View of Hollywood and Screenwriting)* (NY Warner Books, 1984), 29.

silence *Crit&Eval*. William Faulkner, *Paris Review: Interviews, Writers at Work* (NY: Penguin, 1958), 133.

silence *Flm&Vid*. Robert Redford in Richard Rayner, "Essential Cowboy, *New Yorker,* 05/18/98, 64.

silence *MusArts*. Claude Debussy in a letter to Ernest Chausson quoted in the Metropolitan Opera Broadcast of *Pelleas and Melisande,* April 2000.

silence *MusArts*. Ira Gershwin, recalled by Charles Suber from a 1960 interview for *down beat*, with West Coast editor John Tynan, in Ira Gershwin's home.

silence *TheatArts*. Robert J. Kornfeld, personal letter to Charles Suber (May, 1997).

simple *MusArts*. E.L. Doctorow, "Standards: How Great Songs Name Us," *Harper's,* Nov. 1991, 64-65.

skanking *Dnce*. William Safire, William Safire, "In Language — Great Moments in Moments," *NY Times Magazine,* 05/10/98, 14.

slap bass *MusArts*. Len Lyons and Don Perlo, *Jazz Portraits: The Lives and Music of the Jazz Masters* (NY: Quill, William Morrow, 1989), Glossary.

slide *Dnce* Sally Sommer, *NY Times* News Service,?? /??/95.

Smith, Bessie *ArtPerf, MusArts*. Len Lyons and Don Perlo, *Jazz Portraits: The Lives and Music of the Jazz Masters* (NY: Quill, William Morrow, 1989), 473.

snob *Crit&Eval*. Jackson Lears, "Don't Get Around Much Anymore, (How did our republic of pleasure seekers become so theme-parked and shopping-malled.?)," *NY Times Book Review,* 01/09/94, 29, in a review of David Nasow, *The Rise and Fall of Public Amusements* (NY: Basic Books, 1993?).

soul *MusArts*. Itzhak Perlman, *Great Performances,Itzhak Perlman in the Fiddler's House* (PBS telecast, 1996).

stage band *MusArts*. Charles Suber, "Jazz Education," *Encyclopedia of Jazz in the Seventies* (NY: Horizon Press, 1976), 366 ff.

stage manager *Mgt, TheatArts*. Lawrence Olivier, *On Acting* (NY: Simon & Schuster, 1986), 352.

star power *ArtPerf*. Jon Pareles, *NY Times,* 06/22/94, B3.

stealth enhancement *PerfA&C*. "Technology Gives Circus a Mighty Roar," *NY Times,* 03/19/98, D5.

sticks *Rdio&TV*. Mark Landler, "Merging Voices That Roar: Is a Radio Deal Too Big?" *NY Times* 06/21/96, C-1,5.

stilling *Crit&Eval*. David Hare, "Command Performance," *New Yorker,* 05/19/97, 40.

stink *Crit&Eval*. George Burns, in Abel Green, *Celebrity Register* (NY: Harper & Row, 1963), 256.

stop time *MusArts*. Len Lyons and Don Perlo, *Jazz Portraits: The Lives and Music of the Jazz Masters* (NY: Quill, William Morrow, 1989), Glossary.

style *Flm&Vid, TheatArts*. Sidney Lumet, *Inside the Actors Studio* (Bravo cablecast, 1996).

style *Crit&Eval, LitArts*. On Writers and Writing (Reading, Mass.: Addison-Wesley Publishing, 19??).

style *Crit&Eval, PerfA&C*. David Craig, *On Performing: A Handbook for Actors, Dancers, Singers on the Musical Stage* (NY: McGraw-Hill, 1987), i-xii.

style *MusArts*, "Diz on Bird," *Bird: The Complete Charlie Parker on Verve* (album booklet), 4-5.

sumptuous *Crit&Eval*. David Craig, *On Performing: A Handbook for Actors, Dancers, Singers on the Musical Stage* (NY:

McGraw-Hill, 1987), 7.

_____T_____

tabloid *Journ*. Bob Herbert, "In America: Tabloid Trouble," *NY Times*, 07/19/95, A11.

talent *ArtPerf*. John P. Marquand, *Women and Thomas Harrow* (Boston: Little, Brown, 1958), 195.

talent *TheatArts*. Uta Hagen, with Haskel Frankel, *Respect for Acting* (NY: Macmillan, 1973), 13.

tap dance *Dnce*. Savion Glover, in John Lahr, "King Tap," *New Yorker*, 10/30/95, 92.

taste *Aes&Creat*. Stanley Marcus, "So, What does a 90 Year Old Retailing Legend Buy?" *NY Times*, 05/25/95, B4.

techno *MusArts, RecA&S*. Michiko Kakutani, "Escape Artists," *NY Times Magazine*, 07/06/97, 14.

technology *Sci&Tech* Lawrence M. Krauss, *NY Times*,??.

Tejano *MusArts*. Selena Quintanilla, (1972-95). *San Jose Mercury News*, 1994, in *NY Times*, 04/01/95, 1,7.

tension and relaxation *Aes&Creat, Genl*. Ernst Toch "The Bases of Form," *The Shaping Forces in Music, An Inquiry into the Nature of Harmony, Melody, Counterpoint, and Form* (NY: Dover, 1977), 157.

Theory X *Mgt*. Frederick Taylor, in John Dos Passos, *USA, III. The Big Money* (NY, The Modern Library,1939), 22.

theatre *TheatArts*. James T. Maher, in Alec Wilder, *American Popular Song: The Great Innovators 1900-50* (NY: Oxford U. Press, 1972), xxii.

Throat Cut *ArtPerf*. *New Yorker*, 04/16/01. 28.

Tin Pan Alley *MusArts*. David Craig, *On Performing: A Handbook for Actors, Dancers, Singers on the Musical Stage* (NY: McGraw-Hill, 1987), 3.

tired-businessman *Crit&Eval, TheatArts*. David Craig, *On Performing: A Handbook for Actors, Dancers, Singers on the Musical Stage* (NY: McGraw-Hill, 1987), 11.

transgress *Crit&Eval*. Michiko Kakutani, "Bigotry in Motion," [re T.S. Eliot], *NY Times Magazine*, 03/16/97, 24.

trip-hop *MusArts*. Simon Reynolds, *NY Times*, 05/28/95, 26.

_____U_____

UCC *LegalAsp*. *Black's Law Dictionary*, Fifth Edition.

_____V_____

vantage point *LitArts*. "Story Workshop As a Method of Teaching Writing," by Betty Sheflett, College English, Nov. 1973.

vernacular music *Cult&Soc, MusArts*. Thomas Brothers, "Ideology and Aurality in the Vernacular Traditions of African-American Music (ca. 1890-1950), *Black Music Research Journal*, Fall 1997, 170.

videorazzi *Crit&Eval*. "Light, Camera, Reaction," *Time*, 11/13/95, 102.

visionary art *Aes&Creat, VisArts*. Michael Janofsky, "A National Museum, for Self-Taught Artists Opens in Baltimore," *NY Times*, 11/25/95, 11.

voice *LitArts*. *Writing from Start to Finish*, by John Schultz, 1982, 1983, 1990, Heinemann/Boynton-Cook.

voicing *MusArts*. Len Lyons and Don Perlo, *Jazz Portraits: The Lives and Music of the Jazz Masters* (NY: Quill, William Morrow, 1989), Glossary.

_____W_____

walking bass line *MusArts*. Len Lyons and Don Perlo, *Jazz Portraits: The Lives and Music of the Jazz Masters* (NY: Quill, William Morrow, 1989), Glossary.

warranty *Mktg*. Claris Corporation, *FileMaker Pro Installation Guide*, 1992.

whistle-blower *Eth&Phil*. Lawrence M. Fisher, "Using Software Metering to Save Money and Stay Legal," *NY Times*, 08/21/94, F8.

wigger *Cult&Soc*. Brent Staples, "Editorial Notebook" — "Dying to be Black," *NY Times*, 12/09/96.

wisdom *Crit&Eval*. George Sand, in Francine Du Plessix Gray, "A Critic at Large: Chère Maître, *New Yorker*, 07/26/93, 88.

Woodstock Nation *Cult&Soc, MusArts*. Frank Rich, "Peace and Love, '94 Style," *NY Times*, 07/10/94.

writers *Flm&Vid, Rdio&TV*. Jack Winter, "How Sweet It Wasn't," *Atlantic Monthly*. Jun. 95, 76.

_____Y_____

youth culture *Cult&Soc*. John Lahr, *Automatic Vaudeville, Essays on Star Turns* (NY: Limelight Editions, 1985), 9.

_____Z_____

zoot-suiters *Cult&Soc*. Robert McG. Thomas Jr., "Harold Fox, Who Took Credit for the Zoot Suit, Dies at 86," *NY Times*. 08/??/96.

DAPME

AEMMPubs Catalog

Arts, Entertainment & Media Management Publications
a Project of the Arts, Entertainment & Media Management Department
of Columbia College Chicago

<u>Catalog No.</u>	<u>Title and Description</u>
*AEMM 101-Q4/**hc**	*"Quotations for Artists, Performers, Managers & Entrepreneurs,"* compiled and edited by Chuck Suber, 4th rev. ed., Sep 2002; 8-3/8" x 10-7/8", laminated paperback, printed spine, 226 pp. ISBN 0-929911-06-7 **CCC $22.50** (Other $24.95)
*AEMM 102-D3/**hc**	*Dictionary for Artists, Performers, Managers & Entrepreneurs* (**The Arts-Related Vocabulary of Columbia College Chicago**), compiled and edited by Chuck Suber, 3rd ed, Sep 2002; 8-3/8" x 10-7/8", laminated paperback, printed spine, ??? pp. ISBN 0-929911-05-9 **CCC $22.50** (Other $24.95)
AEMM 102-D3/**ol**	*Dictionary for Artists, Performers, Managers & Entrepreneurs* — **On-Line Edition, (The Arts-Related Vocabulary of Columbia College Chicago)**, compiled and edited by Chuck Suber, Expanded, unabridged on-line edition produced by CCC/Interactive MultiMedia Dept.: Fully searchable, added graphics, updated quarterly. Available Spring 2003 by **annual subscription.**
AEMM 103-G&R/**hc**	*Arts Entrepreneurship - Making Money in the Arts* [working title] by Clarke Greene and Joseph Roberts. Available Spring 2003.
AEMM 104-AR/**hc**	*ReissSource Directory of Arts Organizations* compiled by Alvin H. Reiss. Available Fall 2003.

* These titles will be available at the Columbia College Chicago Bookstore the week of 16 Sep 2002.

For mail orders and further information on all current and pending AEMMPubs
visit the Arts, Entertainment & Media Management Department website
http://aemmp.colum.edu/AEMMPubs/

Arts, Entertainment & Media Management Dept. (AEMMDept)
624 South Michigan Ave. #700 • Chicago, IL 60605
voice 312-344-7652 • fax 312-344-8063 •e-mail aemmpubs@aol.com

This book belongs to:

Name_____

Address _____

Address _____

City/St/ZIP _____

Voice (day) _____

Voice (eve.)_____

Fax_____

E-mail_____

If found, please notify me or return book to:
AEMMDept
624 South Michigan Ave. (Suite 700)
Chicago, IL 60605
or email >AEMMPubs@aol.com<

Reader's Notes
Sugested new or altered entries,
assignments, or whatever.
Email comments to
>AEMMPubs@aol.com<

Reader's Notes